Nineteenth-Century
Literature Criticism

Guide to Gale Literary Criticism Series

For criticism on	Consult these Gale series
Authors now living or who died after December 31, 1999	*CONTEMPORARY LITERARY CRITICISM (CLC)*
Authors who died between 1900 and 1999	*TWENTIETH-CENTURY LITERARY CRITICISM (TCLC)*
Authors who died between 1800 and 1899	*NINETEENTH-CENTURY LITERATURE CRITICISM (NCLC)*
Authors who died between 1400 and 1799	*LITERATURE CRITICISM FROM 1400 TO 1800 (LC)* *SHAKESPEAREAN CRITICISM (SC)*
Authors who died before 1400	*CLASSICAL AND MEDIEVAL LITERATURE CRITICISM (CMLC)*
Authors of books for children and young adults	*CHILDREN'S LITERATURE REVIEW (CLR)*
Dramatists	*DRAMA CRITICISM (DC)*
Poets	*POETRY CRITICISM (PC)*
Short story writers	*SHORT STORY CRITICISM (SSC)*
Literary topics and movements	*HARLEM RENAISSANCE: A GALE CRITICAL COMPANION (HR)* *THE BEAT GENERATION: A GALE CRITICAL COMPANION (BG)* *FEMINISM IN LITERATURE: A GALE CRITICAL COMPANION (FL)* *GOTHIC LITERATURE: A GALE CRITICAL COMPANION (GL)*
Asian American writers of the last two hundred years	*ASIAN AMERICAN LITERATURE (AAL)*
Black writers of the past two hundred years	*BLACK LITERATURE CRITICISM (BLC)* *BLACK LITERATURE CRITICISM SUPPLEMENT (BLCS)* *BLACK LITERATURE CRITICISM: CLASSIC AND EMERGING AUTHORS SINCE 1950 (BLC-2)*
Hispanic writers of the late nineteenth and twentieth centuries	*HISPANIC LITERATURE CRITICISM (HLC)* *HISPANIC LITERATURE CRITICISM SUPPLEMENT (HLCS)*
Native North American writers and orators of the eighteenth, nineteenth, and twentieth centuries	*NATIVE NORTH AMERICAN LITERATURE (NNAL)*
Major authors from the Renaissance to the present	*WORLD LITERATURE CRITICISM, 1500 TO THE PRESENT (WLC)* *WORLD LITERATURE CRITICISM SUPPLEMENT (WLCS)*

ISSN 0732-1864

Volume 207

Nineteenth-Century Literature Criticism

Criticism of the
Works of Novelists, Philosophers, and Other
Creative Writers Who Died between 1800
and 1899, from the First Published Critical
Appraisals to Current Evaluations

Kathy D. Darrow
Project Editor

GALE
CENGAGE Learning

Detroit • New York • San Francisco • New Haven, Conn • Waterville, Maine • London

Nineteenth-Century Literature Criticism, Vol. 207

Project Editor: Kathy D. Darrow

Editorial: Dana Barnes, Elizabeth Cranston, Kristen Dorsch, Jeffrey W. Hunter, Jelena O. Krstović, Michelle Lee, Thomas J. Schoenberg, Lawrence J. Trudeau

Data Capture: Frances Monroe, Gwen Tucker

Rights and Acquisitions: Jermaine Bobbitt, Scott Bragg, Jacqueline Flowers

Composition and Electronic Capture: Gary Oudersluys

Manufacturing: Cynde Bishop

Associate Product Manager: Marc Cormier

Gale
27500 Drake Rd.
Farmington Hills, MI, 48331-3535

LIBRARY OF CONGRESS CATALOG CARD NUMBER 84-643008

ISBN-13: 978-1-4144-2139-1
ISBN-10: 1-4144-2139-7

ISSN 0732-1864

Printed in the United States of America
1 2 3 4 5 6 7 13 12 11 10 09

Contents

Preface vii

Acknowledgments xi

Literary Criticism Series Advisory Board xiii

Preface

Since its inception in 1981, *Nineteenth-Century Literature Criticism* (*NCLC*) has been a valuable resource for students and librarians seeking critical commentary on writers of this transitional period in world history. Designated an "Outstanding Reference Source" by the American Library Association with the publication of is first volume, *NCLC* has since been purchased by over 6,000 school, public, and university libraries. The series has covered more than 500 authors representing 38 nationalities and over 28,000 titles. No other reference source has surveyed the critical reaction to nineteenth-century authors and literature as thoroughly as *NCLC*.

Scope of the Series

NCLC is designed to introduce students and advanced readers to the authors of the nineteenth century and to the most significant interpretations of these authors' works. The great poets, novelists, short story writers, playwrights, and philosophers of this period are frequently studied in high school and college literature courses. By organizing and reprinting commentary written on these authors, *NCLC* helps students develop valuable insight into literary history, promotes a better understanding of the texts, and sparks ideas for papers and assignments. Each entry in *NCLC* presents a comprehensive survey of an author's career or an individual work of literature and provides the user with a multiplicity of interpretations and assessments. Such variety allows students to pursue their own interests; furthermore, it fosters an awareness that literature is dynamic and responsive to many different opinions.

Every fourth volume of *NCLC* is devoted to literary topics that cannot be covered under the author approach used in the rest of the series. Such topics include literary movements, prominent themes in nineteenth-century literature, literary reaction to political and historical events, significant eras in literary history, prominent literary anniversaries, and the literatures of cultures that are often overlooked by English-speaking readers.

NCLC continues the survey of criticism of world literature begun by Gale's *Contemporary Literary Criticism* (*CLC*) and *Twentieth-Century Literary Criticism* (*TCLC*).

Organization of the Book

An *NCLC* entry consists of the following elements:

■ The **Author Heading** cites the name under which the author most commonly wrote, followed by birth and death dates. Also located here are any name variations under which an author wrote, including transliterated forms for authors whose native languages use nonroman alphabets. If the author wrote consistently under a pseudonym, the pseudonym will be listed in the author heading and the author's actual name given in parenthesis on the first line of the biographical and critical information. Uncertain birth or death dates are indicated by question marks. Single-work entries are preceded by a heading that consists of the most common form of the title in English translation (if applicable) and the original date of composition.

■ The **Introduction** contains background information that introduces the reader to the author, work, or topic that is the subject of the entry.

■ The list of **Principal Works** is ordered chronologically by date of first publication and lists the most important works by the author. The genre and publication date of each work is given. In the case of foreign authors whose works have been translated into English, the list will focus primarily on twentieth-century translations, selecting those works most commonly considered the best by critics. Unless otherwise indicated, dramas are dated by first performance, not first publication. Lists of **Representative Works** by different authors appear with topic entries.

- Reprinted **Criticism** is arranged chronologically in each entry to provide a useful perspective on changes in critical evaluation over time. The critic's name and the date of composition or publication of the critical work are given at the beginning of each piece of criticism. Unsigned criticism is preceded by the title of the source in which it appeared. All titles by the author featured in the text are printed in boldface type. Footnotes are reprinted at the end of each essay or excerpt. In the case of excerpted criticism, only those footnotes that pertain to the excerpted texts are included. Criticism in topic entries is arranged chronologically under a variety of subheadings to facilitate the study of different aspects of the topic.

- A complete **Bibliographical Citation** of the original essay or book precedes each piece of criticism.

- Critical essays are prefaced by brief **Annotations** explicating each piece.

- An annotated bibliography of **Further Reading** appears at the end of each entry and suggests resources for additional study. In some cases, significant essays for which the editors could not obtain reprint rights are included here. Boxed material following the further reading list provides references to other biographical and critical sources on the author in series published by Gale.

Indexes

Each volume of *NCLC* contains a **Cumulative Author Index** listing all authors who have appeared in a wide variety of reference sources published by Gale, including *NCLC*. A complete list of these sources is found facing the first page of the Author Index. The index also includes birth and death dates and cross references between pseudonyms and actual names.

A **Cumulative Nationality Index** lists all authors featured in *NCLC* by nationality, followed by the number of the *NCLC* volume in which their entry appears.

A **Cumulative Topic Index** lists the literary themes and topics treated in the series as well as in *Classical and Medieval Literature Criticism, Literature Criticism from 1400 to 1800, Twentieth-Century Literary Criticism,* and the *Contemporary Literary Criticism* Yearbook, which was discontinued in 1998.

An alphabetical **Title Index** accompanies each volume of *NCLC*, with the exception of the Topics volumes. Listings of titles by authors covered in the given volume are followed by the author's name and the corresponding page numbers where the titles are discussed. English translations of foreign titles and variations of titles are cross-referenced to the title under which a work was originally published. Titles of novels, dramas, nonfiction books, and poetry, short story, or essay collections are printed in italics, while individual poems, short stories, and essays are printed in roman type within quotation marks.

In response to numerous suggestions from librarians, Gale also produces an annual paperbound edition of the *NCLC* cumulative title index. This annual cumulation, which alphabetically lists all titles reviewed in the series, is available to all customers. Additional copies of this index are available upon request. Librarians and patrons will welcome this separate index; it saves shelf space, is easy to use, and is recyclable upon receipt of the next edition.

Citing *Nineteenth-Century Literature Criticism*

When citing criticism reprinted in the Literary Criticism Series, students should provide complete bibliographic information so that the cited essay can be located in the original print or electronic source. Students who quote directly from reprinted criticism may use any accepted bibliographic format, such as University of Chicago Press style or Modern Language Association style.

The examples below follow recommendations for preparing a bibliography set forth in *The Chicago Manual of Style,* 14th ed. (Chicago: The University of Chicago Press, 1993); the first example pertains to material drawn from periodicals, the second to material reprinted from books:

Franklin, J. Jeffrey. "The Victorian Discourse of Gambling: Speculations on *Middlemarch* and *The Duke's Children*." *ELH* 61, no. 4 (winter 1994): 899-921. Reprinted in *Nineteenth-Century Literature Criticism*. Vol. 168, edited by Jessica Bomarito and Russel Whitaker, 39-51. Detroit: Thomson Gale, 2006.

Frank, Joseph. "*The Gambler*: A Study in Ethnopsychology." In *Freedom and Responsibility in Russian Literature: Essays in Honor of Robert Louis Jackson,* edited by Elizabeth Cheresh Allen and Gary Saul Morson, 69-85. Evanston, Ill.: Northwestern University Press, 1995. Reprinted in *Nineteenth-Century Literature Criticism*. Vol. 168, edited by Jessica Bomarito and Russel Whitaker, 75-84. Detroit: Thomson Gale, 2006.

The examples below follow recommendations for preparing a works cited list set forth in the *MLA Handbook for Writers of Research Papers,* 6th ed. (New York: The Modern Language Association of America, 2003); the first example pertains to material drawn from periodicals, the second to material reprinted from books:

Franklin, J. Jeffrey. "The Victorian Discourse of Gambling: Speculations on *Middlemarch* and *The Duke's Children*." *ELH* 61.4 (winter 1994): 899-921. Reprinted in *Nineteenth-Century Literature Criticism*. Eds. Jessica Bomarito and Russel Whitaker. Vol. 168. Detroit: Thomson Gale, 2006. 39-51.

Frank, Joseph. "*The Gambler*: A Study in Ethnopsychology." *Freedom and Responsibility in Russian Literature: Essays in Honor of Robert Louis Jackson*. Eds. Elizabeth Cheresh Allen and Gary Saul Morson. Evanston, Ill.: Northwestern University Press, 1995. 69-85. Reprinted in *Nineteenth-Century Literature Criticism*. Eds. Jessica Bomarito and Russel Whitaker. Vol. 168. Detroit: Thomson Gale, 2006. 75-84.

Suggestions are Welcome

Readers who wish to suggest new features, topics, or authors to appear in future volumes, or who have other suggestions or comments are cordially invited to call, write, or fax the Associate Product Manager:

Associate Product Manager, Literary Criticism Series
Gale
27500 Drake Road
Farmington Hills, MI 48331-3535
1-800-347-4253 (GALE)
Fax: 248-699-8054

Acknowledgments

The editors wish to thank the copyright holders of the criticism included in this volume and the permissions managers of many book and magazine publishing companies for assisting us in securing reproduction rights. Following is a list of the copyright holders who have granted us permission to reproduce material in this volume of *NCLC*. Every effort has been made to trace copyright, but if omissions have been made, please let us know.

COPYRIGHTED MATERIAL IN *NCLC*, VOLUME 207, WAS REPRODUCED FROM THE FOLLOWING PERIODICALS:

American Literature, v. 60, October, 1988; v. 64, June, 1992; v. 68, June, 1996. Copyright © 1988, 1992, 1996 Duke University Press. All rights reserved. All used by permission of the publishers.—*American Quarterly,* v. 24, May, 1972; v. 39, summer, 1987. Copyright © 1972, 1987 The Johns Hopkins University Press. Reproduced by permission.—*American Scholar,* v. 73, summer, 2004. Copyright © 2004 by Robert Pinsky. Reproduced by permission.—*Eighteenth-Century Studies,* v. 39, April, 2006. Copyright © 2006 The Johns Hopkins University Press. Reproduced by permission.—*ELH,* v. 33, March, 1966; v. 39, September, 1972; v. 50, winter, 1983; v. 51, winter, 1984; v. 59, fall, 1992. Copyright © 1966, 1972, 1983, 1984, 1992. The Johns Hopkins University Press. All reproduced by permission.—*ESQ: A Journal of the American Renaissance,* first quarter, 1969 for "Thoreau on Civil Resistance" by John A. Christie. Copyright © 1969 by the Board of Regents of Washington State University. Reproduced by permission of the publisher and the author.—*Genre: Forms of Discourse and Culture,* v. 35, fall/winter, 2002 for "'They Locked the Door on My Meditations': Thoreau and the Prison House of Identity" by Jason Haslam. Copyright © 2002 by the University of Oklahoma. Reproduced by permission of Genre, the University of Oklahoma, and the author.—*Journal of the History of Ideas,* v. 26, April-June, 1965. Copyright © 1965 University of Pennsylvania Press. All rights reserved. Reprinted by permission of the University of Pennsylvania Press.—*Midwest Quarterly,* v. 48, January, 2007. Copyright © 2007 by *The Midwest Quarterly,* Pittsburgh State University. Reproduced by permission.—*Modern Language Studies,* v. 25, fall, 1995 for "At the Heart of *Tom Brown's Schooldays*: Thomas Arnold and Christian Friendship" by Paul M. Puccio. Copyright © Northeast Modern Language Association 1995. Reproduced by permission of the publisher and the author.—*Nineteenth-Century Fiction,* v. 30, December, 1975 for "Plot, Character, Speech, and Place in *Pride and Prejudice*" by Walter E. Anderson. Copyright © 1975 by The Regents of the University of California. Reproduced by permission of the publisher and the author.—*Nineteenth-Century Literature,* v. 51, December, 1996 for "Thoreau's Critique of the American Pastoral in *A Week*" by Ning Yu; 57, September, 2002 for "Sighing for a Soldier: Jane Austen and Military Pride and Prejudice" by Tim Fulford. Copyright © 1996, 2002 by The Regents of the University of California. Both reproduced by permission of the publisher and authors.—*Philosophy and Literature,* v. 25, April, 2001. Copyright © 2001 The Johns Hopkins University Press. Reproduced by permission.—*Representations,* v. 82, spring, 2003 for "Rent to Own; or, What's Entailed in *Pride and Prejudice*" by Sandra Macpherson. Copyright © 2003 by The Regents of the University of California. Reproduced by permission of the publisher and the author.—*SEL: Studies in English Literature, 1500-1900,* v. 7, summer, 1967; v. 19, autumn, 1979. Copyright © William Marsh Rice University, 1967, 1979. Both reproduced by permission.—*South Atlantic Bulletin,* v. 41, May, 1976. Copyright © 1976 by the South Atlantic Modern Language Association. Reproduced by permission.—*Southern Quarterly,* v. 11, January, 1973. Copyright © 1973 by the University of Southern Mississippi. Reproduced by permission.—*Studies in the Novel,* v. 39, summer, 2007. Copyright © 2007 by the University of North Texas. Reproduced by permission.—*Victorian Newsletter,* fall, 1973 for "Childhood and the Victorian Ideal of Manliness in *Tom Brown's Schooldays*" by Henry R. Harrington. Reproduced by permission of *The Victorian Newsletter* and the author.—*Victorian Review,* v. 22, summer, 1996. Copyright © University of Toronto Press 1996. Reproduced by permission of University of Toronto Press Incorporated.—*Zeitschrift fur Anglistik und Amerikanistik,* v. 29, 1981. Copyright © 1981 Stauffenburg Verlag Brigitte Narr GmbH. Reproduced by permission.

COPYRIGHTED MATERIAL IN *NCLC*, VOLUME 207, WAS REPRODUCED FROM THE FOLLOWING BOOKS:

Kaplan, Morris B. From "Civil Disobedience, Conscience, and Community: Thoreau's 'Double Self' and the Problematic of Political Action," in *The Delegated Intellect: Emersonian Essays on Literature, Science, and Art in Honor of Don Gifford.* Edited by Donald E. Morse. Peter Lang, 1995. Copyright © 1995 Peter Lang Publishing, Inc., New York. All

Gale Literature Product Advisory Board

The members of the Gale Literature Product Advisory Board—reference librarians from public and academic library systems—represent a cross-section of our customer base and offer a variety of informed perspectives on both the presentation and content of our literature products. Advisory board members assess and define such quality issues as the relevance, currency, and usefulness of the author coverage, critical content, and literary topics included in our series; evaluate the layout, presentation, and general quality of our printed volumes; provide feedback on the criteria used for selecting authors and topics covered in our series; provide suggestions for potential enhancements to our series; identify any gaps in our coverage of authors or literary topics, recommending authors or topics for inclusion; analyze the appropriateness of our content and presentation for various user audiences, such as high school students, undergraduates, graduate students, librarians, and educators; and offer feedback on any proposed changes/enhancements to our series. We wish to thank the following advisors for their advice throughout the year.

Pride and Prejudice

Jane Austen

English novelist and letter writer.

The following entry presents criticism of Jane Austen's novel *Pride and Prejudice* (1813). For additional discussion of the novel, see *NCLC*, Volumes 13 and 150; for discussion of the novel *Emma* (1815), see *NCLC*, Volume 19; for discussion of the novel *Persuasion* (1817), see *NCLC*, Volume 33; for discussion of the novel *Northanger Abbey* (1817), see *NCLC*, Volume 51; for discussion of the novel *Sense and Sensibility* (1810), see *NCLC*, Volume 81; for discussion of the novel *Mansfield Park* (1814), see *NCLC*, Volume 95; and for information on Austen's complete career, see *NCLC*, Volumes 1 and 119.

INTRODUCTION

Many scholars regard *Pride and Prejudice* as Jane Austen's most important novel. Austen completed an early draft of the work in 1797 under the title *First Impressions,* but she put it aside after failing to find a publisher. More than a decade later, Austen revised the manuscript and renamed it *Pride and Prejudice,* publishing it anonymously in 1813. The book revolves around the character of Elizabeth Bennet, a strong-willed, intelligent young woman whose willingness to speak her mind frequently runs counter to the societal expectations of her era. As the novel progresses, Elizabeth gradually falls in love with the aristocratic Fitzwilliam Darcy; although Darcy's haughty attitude initially repels Elizabeth, his fundamental integrity soon proves an equal match to her own strength of character, and the novel ends with a celebration of their marriage. Austen tells her story primarily through the dialogue of her characters; their distinctive speaking styles reveal much about their individual personalities, while the complicated network of their social interactions are disclosed. Over the course of its history, the novel has emerged as Austen's most popular work of fiction. W. Somerset Maugham summarized the enduring legacy of *Pride and Prejudice* in his 1954 study *The Art of Fiction: An Introduction to Ten Novels and Their Authors.* Hailing Austen's novel as a "masterpiece," Maugham declared, "What makes a classic is not that it is praised by critics . . . but that large numbers of readers, generation after generation, have found pleasure and spiri-tual profit in reading it." In the twentieth century the novel inspired several theatrical productions in addition to numerous film adaptations and television miniseries.

PLOT AND MAJOR CHARACTERS

Pride and Prejudice focuses on the Bennet family, middle-class landowners living in Longbourn, a village outside of London. The story centers upon finding suitable marriages for the five Bennet daughters, a mission that Mrs. Bennet, who is a bit flighty and shallow, approaches with fierce single-mindedness. Mr. Bennet is a kindhearted but remote figure, a calm man of action behind the scenes, whose interactions with others are seemingly either sarcastic or indifferent. Jane, the oldest and most beautiful of the Bennet sisters, is a reserved, compassionate, and charming young woman who interacts gracefully with others. By contrast, the second Bennet daughter, Elizabeth, is outspoken and opinionated, frequently sparking conflict with her sharp wit. Because of her intelligence and independence, Elizabeth is her father's favorite daughter; she enjoys an intimacy with Mr. Bennet unavailable to others, including Mrs. Bennet. The younger Bennet daughters, Mary, Kitty, and Lydia, are portrayed as immature and foolish, each in her own way. As the narrative unfolds, Elizabeth quickly emerges as the work's most compelling character.

The novel begins with the Bennets receiving the news that a wealthy young gentleman, Charles Bingley, has rented Netherfield Park, a nearby estate. Mrs. Bennet, recognizing the possibility of a union between Bingley and one of her daughters, hectors her husband into paying Bingley a visit in the hopes that the girls will subsequently be invited to his house. Mr. Bennet obliges his wife without appearing to, and a short time later the Bennet daughters attend a gala event at Netherfield Park. Jane and Bingley take to each other immediately and spend most of the evening talking and dancing. Despite the evident success of this first meeting, Jane does not find favor with Bingley's sister, the haughty, condescending Caroline Bingley, who immediately disapproves of the potential match. The scene at Netherfield also introduces Bingley's close friend, Fitzwilliam Darcy, an honest but self-important, arrogant young man. Darcy regards the other guests with disdain and even insults Elizabeth, declaring her "not handsome enough" to tempt him. Elizabeth overhears and laughs off Darcy's rudeness, dismissing it jokingly to her family and friends.

As time passes, however, Darcy begins to recognize Elizabeth's intellect and strength of character, and his attitude toward her changes. Darcy's overtures fail to impress Elizabeth, however, who remains disenchanted with his snobbish attitude toward other people in the village. Darcy's attraction to Elizabeth also provokes the ire of Caroline Bingley, who has long been in love with him and who acts contemptuously toward Elizabeth and her sisters throughout the novel. Her antipathy for the Bennets becomes particularly pronounced after Jane becomes ill during a visit to Netherfield Park, which compels Jane and Elizabeth to stay there for several days.

After Jane recovers, the sisters return home to find their cousin, the Reverend William Collins, paying a visit to the family. Collins is Mr. Bennet's legal heir; British law decrees that a man's inheritance must go to the closest male relative, so the Bennet sisters have no claim to their father's property. A foolish, condescending man, Collins magnanimously suggests that he might marry one of the Bennet girls so that they might retain some ownership of their father's estate. He proposes marriage to Elizabeth, but she promptly refuses him, much to her mother's dismay. During Collins's visit, the sisters meet a group of militia soldiers stationed in a nearby town. One of the officers, George Wickham, befriends Elizabeth. When Wickham confides to her that Darcy, with whom he was raised, has cheated him out of an inheritance, Elizabeth becomes indignant and vows to stay away from Netherfield Park.

As winter approaches, Bingley, Darcy, and Caroline abruptly leave the mansion and return to London, causing much speculation in the neighborhood about the sincerity of Bingley's regard for Jane. Jane visits the city with her aunt in hopes of seeing him, but Bingley neglects to visit her. Meanwhile, Collins proposes to Elizabeth's friend, Charlotte Lucas, who immediately accepts him in order to ensure her future security; after their marriage they move into a house near the estate of Darcy's aunt, Lady Catherine de Bourgh, a very wealthy, imposing woman. When Elizabeth visits Charlotte and Collins the following spring, she unexpectedly encounters Darcy, who is traveling with his cousin. Elizabeth discovers through the cousin that Darcy has purposely separated Bingley and Jane. Unaware of this conversation, Darcy proposes to Elizabeth, and she turns him down, berating him sharply for his mistreatment of both Jane and Wickham. Stunned, Darcy departs abruptly. Elizabeth immediately receives a letter of explanation from him in which he confesses to urging Bingley to stay away from Jane, although with only

good intentions (he believed Jane did not love his friend); he also decries Wickham as a liar and an opportunist who once tried to cajole Darcy's young sister into eloping with him. As she considers Darcy's letter, Elizabeth must confront her assumptions and biases against him, and she begins to reassess his character.

A short time later, to the great distress of the youngest two Bennet sisters, Kitty and Lydia, the militia departs from the neighborhood of Longbourn. Lydia, who has enjoyed a lively social life with the regiment, is particularly upset; she persuades her parents to allow her to spend the summer months with an acquaintance in Brighton, near the regiment's new garrison. Mr. Bennet ignores Elizabeth's strong representations against the plan; the only harm that can come to Lydia, he assures Elizabeth, is that of discovering her own insignificance. At the same time, Elizabeth goes on a trip with her aunt and uncle, the Gardiners. They take a tour of the countryside north of London, eventually stopping at Pemberley, Darcy's estate. Elizabeth, who only agrees to tour the estate once she is assured that its owner is absent, is immediately impressed by the natural beauty of Darcy's home; she is also touched by the testimonies of Darcy's servants, who attest to his decency and honesty. Unexpectedly, however, Darcy shows up. Elizabeth is mortified, but Darcy proves a gracious host, deftly avoiding the subject of his marriage proposal.

During her visit, Elizabeth receives a letter from her parents informing her that Lydia has eloped with Wickham. Fearing that Wickham will not marry her sister and that Lydia's ruined honor will disgrace the family, Elizabeth and the Gardiners immediately return home to do what they can to help. Eventually Mr. Gardiner discovers the lovers hidden in London, living together and unmarried. Wickham blackmails Mr. Bennet and Mr. Gardiner into paying him an enormous sum, in addition to an annual income, in exchange for marrying Lydia. The whole family is relieved at the resolution, although Mr. Bennet is unhappy about the marriage and his own negligence as a parent. Elizabeth feels it more deeply; while stunned at the cost to both her father and uncle as a result of Lydia's willful impropriety, she is convinced that she has now lost Darcy's regard forever. She soon receives a letter from her Aunt Gardiner, however, who accidentally reveals a secret: Darcy is the one who has paid Wickham off; he holds himself to blame for the pride that prevented him from making Wickham's degeneracy more widely known. Elizabeth suffers anew from the shame of both her sister's behavior and her own in so misjudging Darcy.

At around this time, Bingley and Darcy return to Netherfield Park. Bingley immediately recommences courting Jane and soon proposes to her. Darcy resumes his friendship with Elizabeth but doesn't broach the subject of marriage. At this point Lady Catherine de Bourgh visits the village for the express purpose of forbidding Elizabeth to marry her nephew. Elizabeth is amazed to learn that Darcy intends to renew his proposals; she rebuffs the old woman on principle in any case, insisting that she will do whatever she pleases. A short time later, Darcy indeed proposes, and Elizabeth accepts him. At the novel's conclusion, the Bennets celebrate two marriages: Jane and Bingley's and Elizabeth and Darcy's.

MAJOR THEMES

In a broad sense, *Pride and Prejudice* concerns the various cultural pressures inherent in genteel British society in the late-eighteenth century. Austen explored a number of crucial dualities in the work. In the abstract, these dualities are reflected in the tensions that arise between intellect and action, solitude and community, and appearance and reality. At the novel's core, however, the principal dichotomy runs along gender lines; men have power and freedom while women are inevitably dependent on men for security and happiness. Symbolically, the marriage of Mr. and Mrs. Bennet offers an extreme example of the potentially devastating imbalance caused by this schism. Mr. Bennet's independence and complacency ultimately render him emotionally vacant, unwilling or unable to participate in the lives of his own daughters, while Mrs. Bennet's single-minded obsession with her daughters' marriages and financial security leaves her incapable of comprehending the deeper, more fulfilling aspects of human happiness. Elizabeth and Darcy are also at opposite poles, particularly in the beginning of the novel. One of the divides that separates them is the discrepancy in their social and financial circumstances; Darcy's wealth and prominence elevate him a considerable distance above Elizabeth's more modest status. In the realm of appearances, the difference between their class situations is significant. As Austen reveals the true depth and complexity of their characters, however, these distinctions gradually become irrelevant. When Elizabeth and Darcy fall in love, the boundaries of their incompatibility begin to blur; what emerges in its place is a sense of the complementary nature of their personalities. In the end they are able to overcome their differences through the union of marriage, which enables them to bring together their respective strengths.

For modern feminist scholars, *Pride and Prejudice* highlights the limited roles and rights of women in eighteenth-century English society. One of the novel's key plot points revolves around the question of entailment, a legal statute that prioritized the inheritance rights of men over those of women, even in cases in which there was no immediate male heir. The inequities of this law are made evident throughout *Pride and Prejudice,* particularly in the desperation with which Mrs. Bennet and her younger daughters approach the prospect of marriage. In this respect the fundamental injustice of the entailment laws sheds new light on the relentless plotting of Mrs. Bennet, whose sense of urgency concerning her daughters' futures is arguably driven more by economic anxiety than class ambition.

CRITICAL RECEPTION

On the whole, nineteenth-century reactions to *Pride and Prejudice* were mixed. A reviewer in the March 1813 issue of the *Critical Review* lauded the novel's entertainment value, claiming that every character in the book "excites the interest" and that the work as a whole "very agreeably divides the attention of the reader"; the writer expressed particularly high praise for the novel's protagonist, Elizabeth, whose "sense and conduct are of a superior order to those of the common heroines of novels." In a diary entry dated January 12, 1819, writer Henry Crabbe Robinson hailed the "perfectly colloquial style of the dialogue." One prominent voice of dissent was that of author Mary Russell Mitford, who, in a letter dated December 20, 1814, lamented the "entire want of taste" characterizing the novel's language and characters. Austen herself wasn't entirely satisfied with the work; in a letter to her sister Cassandra dated February 14, 1813, she complained that the novel was "rather too light, & bright, & sparkling," and needed "to be stretched out here & there" with "anything that would form a contrast & bring the reader with increased delight to the playfulness & Epigrammatism of the general stile." Writing in 1848, Charlotte Brontë dismissed the novel as too artificial and contrived, comparing it to a "carefully fenced, highly cultivated garden" where she "should hardly like to live." In the March 1860 issue of *Blackwood's Magazine,* the critic George Henry Lewes remarked on the "fine artistic sense" underlying the novel's plot and structure. Author Margaret Oliphant, on the other hand, found the novel's characterizations of Elizabeth and Darcy uninteresting, a product of Austen's "strange delusion," although she commended the "varied and vivid originality" of the work's minor characters. Mark Twain was famously dismissive of the novel, proclaiming that as he tried to read the book, he felt as bewildered as a "barkeeper entering the kingdom of heaven."

In the twentieth century, scholars and critics have proven far more receptive to the book's inventiveness and humor. Sir Walter Raleigh described the novel's female characters as "marvelous and incomparable" in a letter dated October 23, 1917. In her 1929 work *A Room of One's Own,* Virginia Woolf praised the stylistic mastery of Austen's prose, as well as the "architectural quality" of the novel's structure with the brief statement, "*Pride and Prejudice* has form." Scholar Dorothy Van Ghent offered an in-depth analysis of the novel within its historical and social context in her 1953 study *The English Novel: Form and Function*. A number of modern critics have focused on the novel's characters. More recently, Kenneth L. Moler examines the fundamental contrasts between Elizabeth and Darcy's personalities, while James Sherry describes the evolution of their relationship as a form of dialectic. Some scholars, notably Tim Fulford and Sandra McPherson, focus on the novel's treatment of British military and economic power at the dawn of the nineteenth century. Other commentators address issues of female identity in the work; Michael J. Stasio and Kathryn Duncan discuss the relationship between gender and marriage in the novel in their essay "An Evolutionary Approach to Jane Austen: Prehistoric Preferences in *Pride and Prejudice*."

PRINCIPAL WORKS

Sense and Sensibility. 3 vols. (novel) 1810
Pride and Prejudice. 3 vols. (novel) 1813
Mansfield Park. 3 vols. (novel) 1814
Emma. 3 vols. (novel) 1815
Northanger Abbey and Persuasion. 4 vols. (novels) 1817
Lady Susan, and the Watsons (novella and unfinished novel) 1882
The Novels of Jane Austen. 5 vols. (novels) 1923
Jane Austen's Letters to Her Sister Cassandra and Others (letters) 1959

CRITICISM

Edd Winfield Parks (essay date June 1952)

SOURCE: Parks, Edd Winfield. "Jane Austen's Lure of the Next Chapter." *Nineteenth-Century Fiction* 7, no. 1 (June 1952): 56-60.

[*In the following essay, Parks analyzes Austen's storytelling techniques in* Pride and Prejudice. *According to Parks, Austen concludes many of the novel's chapters with character summaries as a way of sustaining the reader's interest in the plot.*]

For a novelist who rarely mentioned the technical devices of fiction and apparently gave little thought to them, Jane Austen uncannily grasped the essential ones

in a way that many conscious artists have not equaled. Some of these devices have been analyzed at length, but one that has apparently escaped comment is Miss Austen's ability to lure the reader on to the next chapter. She had to a remarkable degree the ability to keep the reader interested, to make him anxious to go on, *now,* with the story. Yet she rarely uses the obvious "what-happened-next" technique, or leaves the reader dangling in the midst of unfinished action after the manner beloved by writers who think in terms of installments rather than of a completed whole. With very few exceptions each chapter has a unified, rounded structure that leaves the reader satisfied with it as a unit. But the sense of continuity extends beyond the unit; the pattern is not complete, and the reader is aware of threads yet to be woven into the continuing whole. Miss Austen induces a strong desire to follow the development of the pattern.

This is the more remarkable because many chapters end with a brief summarizing paragraph. A summary by its nature would seem to provide a convenient stopping place, but Miss Austen's summaries do not. Since the six novels have an unusual homogeneity of method, an examination of one can be applied to the others. The quotations and references in this paper are taken entirely from **Pride and Prejudice,** but the generalizations could as easily be substantiated with references to other novels.

* * *

In the first chapter Mrs. Bennet is attempting to persuade her husband to call upon the newly arrived and eligible bachelor Bingley. Although Mr. Bennet never quite refuses, he never agrees to go, and the incident is stopped with a brief summing up by the author.

> Mr. Bennet was so odd a mixture of quick parts, sarcastic humour, reserve, and caprice, that the experience of three-and-twenty years had been insufficient to make his wife understand his character. *Her* mind was less difficult to develop. She was a woman of mean understanding, little information, and uncertain temper. When she was discontented, she fancied herself nervous. The business of her life was to get her daughters married; its solace was visiting and news.

This is Miss Austen's favorite and most effective device for enticing us on into the story. She has shifted from action to character, and only on rare occasions does she supply us with summaries of events. She is concerned rather with summations of character, with pointing up the incidents through the persons, than with the events. The interest which she engenders is in following changes and revelations of character instead of changes in plot. Mrs. Bennet is fixed, and remains so, but Mr. Bennet is an unstable element. We have been dexterously told what to look for, but the paradox of character will be resolved only by action. The art seems so artless that at first glance these final sentences do not seem to be leading anywhere; they may even appear to be closing off the action. Instead, they arouse curiosity by making us feel that only a part of the evidence is in, and that character may be confirmed, modified, or contradicted by additional evidence.

The subtle use of this method is more completely revealed when Mr. Darcy is becoming aware of Elizabeth Bennet's attractiveness and Miss Bingley is jealously aware of his feelings. Miss Austen concludes a conversation and a chapter (xi):

> "Do let us have a little music," cried Miss Bingley, tired of a conversation in which she had no share.
>
> "Louisa, you will not mind my waking Mr. Hurst?"
>
> Her sister made not the smallest objection, and the pianoforte was opened; and Darcy, after a few moments' recollection, was not sorry for it. He began to feel the danger of paying Elizabeth too much attention.

For Miss Austen's purposes the evening is over. With the next chapter the time sequence and the episodes are changed, so that there is a proper and inevitable break. But clearly more birds have been raised than have been killed. The people have been defined only as of the one night; they are not static, and Miss Austen makes us feel that they are not. The paragraph promises more than it tells, although the promise is implicit and not stated. If there are no sensational secrets to be dramatically revealed, there are reticences to be unclothed slowly and privately. This reticence becomes in itself a dramatic device, made the more alluring by the air of frankness with which the author tells us just so much of the matter that we feel certain there are more important matters yet to be told. Miss Austen's method works backward as well as forward: she makes us feel that the episode just ended will be given greater meaning by episodes yet to come.[1]

Miss Austen evidently enjoyed, also, concluding a chapter with an ironical paradox, but the paradox is in character rather than in action. Sometimes this quality depends upon a play on words, as when the Bingley sisters "solaced their wretchedness" over Jane Bennet's illness by duets after supper (x); sometimes on what the reader suspects but does not know to be a misjudgment, as when Darcy is condemned by the "society of Hertfordshire" as "the worst of men" (xxiii); sometimes simply on a misunderstanding between characters (lvii).[2] The method works best when it changes the interpretation of earlier actions without nullifying them, and reveals characters in a new light, as the concluding part of Darcy's letter (xxxv) subtly changes without distortion the actions and characters of Wickham and of Darcy, and promises implicitly that through these disclosures Elizabeth will be able to make new discoveries about herself.

Even when Miss Austen is only summarizing events for persons who have been absent (xii) or rounding out an episode (xxxi), she spices the final sentences with biting wit and occasionally with an epigram. One long paragraph sums up the conclusion of the first evening that Elizabeth Bennet and her friends spent at Rosings, with Lady Catherine de Bourgh (xxix):

> When Lady Catherine and her daughter had played as long as they chose, the tables were broken up, the carriage was offered to Mrs. Collins, gratefully accepted, and immediately ordered. The party then gathered round the fire to hear Lady Catherine determine what weather they were to have on the morrow. From these instructions they were summoned by the arrival of the coach; and with many speeches of thankfulness on Mr. Collins's side, and as many bows on Sir William's, they departed. As soon as they had driven from the door, Elizabeth was called on by her cousin to give her opinion of all that she had seen at Rosings, which, for Charlotte's sake, she made more favourable than it really was. But her commendation, though costing her some trouble, could by no means satisfy Mr. Collins, and he was very soon obliged to take her ladyship's praise into his own hands.

Thus ends the evening. There is no indication of future action; there is no likelihood that Lady Catherine or Mr. Collins will change much, for better or worse. But the apt, pointed phrasing has implications of future comic developments, and augments interest in the persons. One other element is more subtly introduced: that of a future antagonism between Darcy's aunt and the already prejudiced heroine. This is done entirely in terms of character, and unobtrusively, but it helps to whet our interest.

I do not mean to say or imply that Miss Austen always embedded in the conclusion of one chapter matter that would entice the reader immediately into the next. Whether consciously or unconsciously, she was too good an artist constantly to play variations on the same theme. Also, there were chapters that simply needed to be ended, and she ended them—usually abruptly. When Mrs. Bennet and a Lucas boy argue about how much wine a man should drink (v), the author notes dryly that "the argument ended only with the visit," and turns back, to the reader's relief as well as her own, to more important and interesting affairs.[3] Occasionally Miss Austen breaks a longish episode into parts, although she does not generally seem concerned as to the length or brevity of each chapter; but when confronted (xx) with the long-windedness of Mr. Collins, the volubility of Mrs. Bennet, and the stubbornness of Elizabeth in connection with his proposal of marriage, Miss Austen evidently felt that matters were getting out of hand, and provided for a brief summary and slight change of emphasis by a break in the narrative.[4] These endings fit naturally enough into the framework and do not impede the action, but they are part of the stock-in-trade of every competent novelist.

Miss Austen does not use them often. Her distinctive chapter endings were at the time she wrote peculiarly her own, and few later novelists have been able to imitate them consistently and successfully. The secret, I believe, is in her ability to achieve an easy, flowing transition from what her people are doing to the people themselves. This is so smoothly done that the reader is hardly aware of the change of emphasis, or that she is preparing the way for new incidents growing out of complexities in the persons, but he feels that important modifications and changes are to be made. By engendering an interest primarily in character, Miss Austen gives us a sense of living, developing continuity. Episodes may end, but her people continue to grow, and it is this growth which she entices us to follow avidly.

Notes

1. For other excellent examples of summations of character with implications of action yet to come, see the concluding parts of chapters iv, vi, x, xiii, xiv, xix, xlii, lvii.

2. This device is employed much more frequently in *Northanger Abbey* and in *Emma*.

3. See also chapters xxxi and xli.

4. Much the same purpose may have caused the break between chapters xlvi and xlvii, although here the summary appears at the end of the chapter, instead of beginning the new one; and the break between lviii and lix.

Kenneth L. Moler (essay date summer 1967)

SOURCE: Moler, Kenneth L. "*Pride and Prejudice*: Jane Austen's 'Patrician Hero.'" *SEL: Studies in English Literature, 1500-1900* 7, no. 3 (summer 1967): 491-508.

[*In the following essay, Moler traces the evolution of Darcy's character. In Moler's view, the novel hinges on the central tension between Elizabeth Bennet's individualism and Darcy's faith in an established social order.*]

It is Generally Agreed that *Pride and Prejudice* deals with a variant of the "art-nature" theme with which *Sense and Sensibility* is concerned. *Sense and Sensibility* primarily treats the opposition between the head and the heart, between feeling and reason; in *Pride and Prejudice* Elizabeth Bennet's forceful and engaging individualism is pitted against Darcy's not indefensible respect for the social order and his class pride. Most critics agree that *Pride and Prejudice* does not suffer from the appearance of one-sidedness that makes *Sense and Sensibility* unattractive. Obviously neither Eliza- beth nor Darcy embodies the novel's moral norm. Each is admirable in his way, and each must have his pride and prejudice corrected by self-knowledge and come to a fuller appreciation of the other's temperament and beliefs. Ultimately their conflicting points of view are adjusted, and each achieves a mean between "nature" and "art." Elizabeth gains some appreciation of Darcy's sound qualities and comes to see the validity of class relationships. Darcy, under Elizabeth's influence, gains in naturalness and learns to respect the innate dignity of the individual.[1]

One of the few features of *Pride and Prejudice* to which exception has been taken is Jane Austen's treatment of the character of her Mr. Darcy. It is said that the transition between the arrogant young man of the early chapters of the novel and the polite gentleman whom Elizabeth Bennet marries is too great and too abrupt to be completely credible.[2] Reuben A. Brower and Howard S. Babb have vindicated Jane Austen to some extent, showing that much of Darcy's early conversation can be interpreted in various ways, and that our reactions to him are often conditioned by the fact that we see him largely through the eyes of the prejudiced Elizabeth.[3] Still there remain grounds for objection to Jane Austen's handling of Darcy. His remark about Elizabeth at the Meryton assembly is almost unbelievably boorish, and we have no reason to believe that Elizabeth has misunderstood it. We hear with our own ears his fears lest he should be encouraging Elizabeth to fall in love with him, and the objectionable language of his first proposal. Such things remain stumbling blocks to our acceptance of Darcy's speedy reformation.

This essay is concerned with Jane Austen's rather unusual treatment of a popular eighteenth-century character-type and situation. Mr. Darcy bears a marked resemblance to what I shall call the "patrician hero," a character-type best known as represented in the novels of Richardson and Fanny Burney; and it is rewarding to investigate the relationship between Darcy and his love affair with Elizabeth Bennet and the heroes of Richardson's and Fanny Burney's novels and their relations with their heroines. Jane Austen's treatment of her patrician hero has a marked relevance to the theme of the reconciliation of opposites that plays such an important part in *Pride and Prejudice*. And a study of Darcy's possible origins helps to account for those flaws in his character for which Jane Austen has been criticized.

Authority-figures of various sorts play prominent roles in many eighteenth and nineteenth century novels. There is the patriarch or matriarch—Fielding's benevolent Allworthy, Godwin's terrifying Falkland, Dickens's Miss Havisham—whose relationship with a young dependent acts as a metaphor for the relationship between the social order and individual, "natural" man. In the novels of Richardson the relationship—prosperous, or, in the case of Lovelace and Clarissa, mutually destructive—between a young man of rank and fortune and a girl who is naturally good but socially inferior performs a similar function. This essay will be chiefly concerned with the particular type of figure that Richardson's Sir Charles Grandison represents.

Richardson's Lovelace is a lost soul; his Mr. B——has to be reformed by the virtuous Pamela.[4] In Sir Charles Grandison, however, Richardson depicted a perfect Christian aristocrat. Sir Charles is handsome and accomplished, dresses exquisitely (out of respect for his father's memory!), and has charming manners. He is immensely wealthy, an owner of splendid mansions and manors, and a powerful, important landholder. Yet he is a man of the strictest Christian virtue, a just, benevolent, and super-efficient steward of his estates, a protector of the weak, and a friend to the poor. As Richardson describes him in the preface to *Grandison* [*Sir Charles Grandison*], Sir Charles is "a man of religion and virtue; of liveliness and spirit; accomplished and agreeable; happy in himself, and a blessing to others."[5]

In the concluding note to *Grandison* Richardson admits that "it has been observed by some, that, in general [Sir Charles] approaches too near the faultless character which some critics censure as above nature" (XX.327). The reaction Richardson describes is not uncommon among readers of his novel. "Pictures of perfection," Jane Austen once wrote, "make me sick and wicked"; and most readers are wicked enough to resent a character who demands so much admiration as Sir Charles does. In addition to being annoyed by Sir Charles's incredible glamor and goodness, one tends to be revolted by the sycophantic deference with which he is treated by nearly every character in his history. Sir Charles's male friends attempt to emulate his virtues. His female acquaintance worship him as "the best of men," take his word for law, and all too frequently fall in love with him. His admirers—repeatedly, indeed *ad nauseam*—entrust their most important affairs to him when they are living, and leave their estates to his management when they die. Thus, Sir Charles, at his sister's request, frees her from an unfortunate engagement; later he arranges a suitable marriage for her. He extricates his uncle from the clutches of an unmanageable mistress and, on the uncle's insistence, provides him with a worthy wife. He sees to it that the relatives of Mr. Danby—Mr. Danby having left his estate in Sir Charles's hands—are provided with fortunes, employment, and matrimonial partners, and arranges for the distribution of the remainder of Danby's estate in charity. Indeed, it is a rare moment when Sir Charles is not dispensing advice and assistance to half a dozen of his family and friends simultaneously. At one point in the story the lovelorn Harriet Byron, after giving a list of some seven persons or families whose affairs Sir Charles is at present re-arranging, declares in despair: "O Lucy!—

What leisure has this man to be in love!" (XVII.49-50. *Grandison,* IV, Letter V).

Among the most fervent of Sir Charles's *aficionados* is the heroine of *Grandison,* Miss Byron. Sir Charles is her oracle; she treasures up his every word, and is embarrassingly grateful when he condescends to give her advice. Her relationship with him is like that of an adoring younger sister to an older brother, or that of an infatuated pupil with a favorite teacher. He is, to use her own word, her "monitor," as much as he is her lover. Harriet is in love with Sir Charles long before she knows that he cares for her; and when, after months of heart-burning, she learns that he has decided to marry her, she is overwhelmed with joy and gratitude. "O my God!" she prays shortly after their marriage, "do Thou make me thankful for such a friend, protector, director, husband! Increase with my gratitude to THEE, my merits to him" (XX. 316. *Grandison,* VII, Letter LX).

As I have said, all of this deference, added to Richardson's insistence on Sir Charles's perfection, tends to make the reader react unfavorably towards both Sir Charles and his creator. One is inclined, in spite of Richardson's insistence on his humility, to think of Sir Charles as a stuffily superior, rather supercilious character, rather than as the noble and magnanimous hero that Richardson envisioned. And one is inclined to tax Richardson, as well as some of the characters in his novel, with an unduly sycophantic attitude towards his highborn hero. That Jane Austen reacted to *Grandison* similarly will become apparent later in this essay.

All of the three novels that Fanny Burney published before 1813 deal, as *Grandison* does, with the relationships between exemplary young authority-figures who are wealthy or well-born or both and heroines who are in some respect their social inferiors. *Cecilia,* however, is the Burneyan novel most frequently cited as a source for **Pride and Prejudice.** Many critics feel that Jane Austen's novel is simply a realistic rewriting of *Cecilia.* R. Brimley Johnson, for instance, has referred to the "title and plot, the leading characters and most dramatic scenes of **Pride and Prejudice**" as "frank appropriations" from *Cecilia.*[6]

Cecilia is certainly an important source for **Pride and Prejudice.** In plot and theme it resembles Jane Austen's novel more nearly than any other single work does. It is possible—though not certain—that the title of **Pride and Prejudice** was borrowed from *Cecilia.*[7] It is often suggested that the first proposal scene in **Pride and Prejudice** was influenced by the scenes in *Cecilia* in which Mortimer Delvile states his objections to a marriage with Cecilia. And there are similarities between the scene in which Mrs. Delvile prevails on Cecilia to give Mortimer up and the scene in which Lady Catherine de Bourgh descends on Elizabeth Bennet. There are, however, a number of significant points of resemblance between *Pride and Prejudice* and novels other than *Cecilia*. In some respects the situation of Fanny Burney's Evelina is closer to that of Elizabeth Bennet than Cecilia's is. Both Elizabeth and Evelina are relatively poor in addition to being inferior in rank to their heroes, while Cecilia is rich. And both Elizabeth and Evelina are surrounded by sets of vulgar relatives by whom they are embarrassed in the presence of their lovers. Moreover, as I shall show later, some specific scenes in *Pride and Prejudice* are certainly based on similar scenes in *Evelina*. Some others, on the other hand, have their originals in *Sir Charles Grandison*. I am certain that in *Pride and Prejudice* Jane Austen is not merely rewriting *Cecilia,* but manipulating a character-type and a situation made familiar to her audience in various novels by Richardson and Fanny Burney—and in numerous works by their imitators as well. The relationship between *Evelina* and *Pride and Prejudice* has never been fully explored; and since it seems to me that it is in some respects very rewarding to compare Jane Austen's Mr. Darcy to Fanny Burney's Lord Orville, I shall use *Evelina* to illustrate Fanny Burney's treatment of the patrician hero.

While all of Fanny Burney's heroes resemble Richardson's patrician hero somewhat, Lord Orville is Sir Charles Grandison writ small. He is a picture of perfection, a paragon among men—at least in the eyes of his heroine and his author. He is handsome, well-born, rich; yet he is wise and good. A heartsick Evelina describes him as "one who seemed formed as a pattern for his fellow-creatures, as a model of perfection."[8] The relationship between Orville and Evelina is much the same as that between Sir Charles Grandison and Harriet Byron. Evelina adores Orville from their first meeting, and she is fully convinced of her own inferiority. "That he should be so much my superior in every way, quite disconcerted me," she writes after their first dance together (I, Letter XI, p. 36). She cringes when she learns that he has referred to her as "a poor weak girl" and is "grateful for his attention" even after she believes that he has insulted her with a dishonorable proposal. Orville, like Sir Charles, is regarded as an oracular "monitor" by his heroine. Evelina seeks, and is delighted to receive, his counsel. "There is no young creature, my Lord, who so greatly wants, or so earnestly wishes for, the advice and assistance of her friends, as I do," she says to him on one occasion (III, Letter V, p. 383); and Orville quickly becomes a substitute for her absent guardian. It is he who arranges an interview with Mr. Macartney for her at Bristol, who persuades the repentant Sir John Belmont to receive her—and who, later on, magnanimously disposes of half of her fortune to provide for Macartney and the one-time Miss Belmont. Like Harriet Byron, Evelina is overcome with gratitude when her hero finally proposes to her. "To be loved by Lord Orville," she writes "—to be the honoured choice

of his noble heart,—my happiness seemed too infinite to be borne, and I wept, even bitterly I wept, from the excess of joy which overpowered me." (III, Letter XV, p. 443).

The Burney-Richardson character-type and situation were imitated in the sub-literature of the period. In Thomas Hull's *The History of Sir William Harrington,* for example (1771), the exemplary Lord C——, nobly born, extremely wealthy, and "as perfect as a human being can be" in person, mind, and character, is very obviously modeled on Sir Charles Grandison. And Mr. Charlemont, the hero of a novel by Anna Maria Porter entitled *The Lake of Killarney* (1804), is "a young Apollo," "the god of his sex," and the son of a lord. Rose, a dependent in a family of Charlemont's acquaintance, loves him desperately, but is by no means unaware of his vast superiority to her. At one point in the novel, in an episode that may have been inspired by the scene in *Cecilia* in which Mrs. Delvile warns Cecilia to beware of falling in love with Delvile, Rose is cross-examined by an older woman who is a friend of Charlemont's family. "If nothing else were wanting to crush presumptuous hopes on my part," Rose replies, ". . . the difference in our rank, our birth, our fortune, would place them beyond all doubt. Mr. Charlemont is . . . a prize, for which all his equals may contend."[9] Similar heroes, often similarly difficult of attainment to admiring heroines, are to be found in numerous other works of Jane Austen's day.

Jane Austen must have been as much amused by the all-conquering heroes and too humble heroines of the day as many other readers have been, for in the juvenile sketch entitled "Jack and Alice" she reduces the patrician hero to absurdity with gusto. Charles Adams, in that sketch, is the most exaggerated "picture of perfection" conceivable. He is incredibly handsome, a man "of so dazzling a Beauty that none but Eagles could look him in the Face."[10] (The continual references in "Jack and Alice" to the brilliance of Charles's countenance are probably specific allusions to *Sir Charles Grandison*: Richardson repeatedly describes Sir Charles in similar language.[11]) But the beauties of Charles's person are nothing to those of his mind. As he tells us himself:

> I imagine my Manners & Address to be of the most polished kind; there is a certain elegance, a peculiar sweetness in them that I never saw equalled. . . . I am certainly more accomplished in every Language, every Science, every Art and every thing than any other person in Europe. My temper is even, my virtues innumerable, my self unparalleled.
>
> (VI.25)

The superciliousness and conceit that readers cannot help attributing to Sir Charles Grandison or Orville becomes the very essence of Charles Adams's being. The kind of praise that Richardson and Fanny Burney heap on their heroes is most liberally bestowed by Charles on himself. And just as Charles is a burlesque version of the too perfect Burney-Richardson hero, so he is provided with two heroines who are ten times more inferior, and twenty times more devoted to him than Evelina and Harriet Byron are to their heroes. Charles is the owner of the "principal estate" in the neighborhood in which the lovely Lucy lives, and Lucy adores him. She is the daughter of a tailor and the niece of an alehouse-keeper, and she is fearful that Charles may think her "deficient in Rank, & in being so, unworthy of his hand" (VI.21). Screwing up her courage, however, she proposes marriage to him. But to her sorrow, she receives "an angry & peremptory refusal" from the unapproachable young man (VI.21). Alice Johnson, the titular heroine of the novel, is also infatuated with Charles. Although, like the rest of her family, Alice is "a little addicted to the Bottle & the Dice," she hopes, after she has inherited a considerable estate, to be found worthy of Charles. But when Alice's father proposes the match to him, Charles declares that she is neither "sufficiently beautifull, sufficiently amiable, sufficiently witty, nor sufficiently rich for me—." "I expect," he says, "nothing more in my wife than my wife will find in me—Perfection" (VI.25-26). Fortunately, Alice is able to find consolation in her bottle. "Jack and Alice," I believe, was not Jane Austen's only attack on the patrician hero. There is a good deal of Charles Adams in her Mr. Darcy.

Darcy's actual circumstances are not an exaggeration of those of the patrician hero, as Charles Adams's are. In fact Jane Austen seems at times to be uncritically borrowing the popular Burney-Richardson character type and situation in *Pride and Prejudice*—altering them, if at all, only by toning them down a bit. Mr. Darcy is not the picture of perfection that Sir Charles Grandison is, but he shares many of the advantages of Sir Charles and Lord Orville. He has, for instance, a "fine, tall person, handsome features, noble mien . . . and ten thousand a year" (II.10). He has mental powers that command respect. He is not as powerful and important as Sir Charles Grandison, but he is the owner of a large estate and a giver, and withholder, of clerical livings. He marries a woman who, like Evelina, is embarrassed by the inferiority of some of her nearest connections, although even Mrs. Bennet can scarcely approach the supreme vulgarity of Madame Duval.

But Darcy is a Charles Adams in spirit, if not in circumstances. It is his exaggerated conception of the importance of his advantages, his supercilious determination "to think well of myself, and meanly of others" who are not so fortunate that causes him at times to sound very much like a caricature of the Burney-Richardson hero. He may not expect to have to address "an angry & peremptory refusal" to a fawning, lovelorn Elizabeth Bennet; but during Elizabeth's visit at Nether-

field he is anxious lest, by devoting so much of his conversation to her, he may have been encouraging her to hope for the honor of his hand. On the eve of her departure from Netherfield, we are told: "He wisely resolved to be particularly careful that no sign of admiration should *now* escape him, nothing that could elevate her with the hope of influencing his felicity. . . . Steady to his purpose, he scarcely spoke ten words to her through the whole of Saturday" (II.60). The idea of a proposal which is humiliating to a heroine may come from *Cecilia*. But the language of Darcy's first proposal to Elizabeth sounds like something that might have come from Charles Adams's lips, rather than the gallant, ardent language of a Delvile. During Darcy's proposal, we are told that "his sense of her inferiority" was "dwelt on with a warmth which seemed due to the consequence he was wounding, but was very unlikely to recommend his suit" (II.189). And when Elizabeth rebukes him, he declares that he is not "ashamed of the feelings I related. . . . Could you expect me to rejoice in the inferiority of your connections? To congratulate myself on the hope of relations, whose condition in life is so decidedly beneath my own?" (II.192).

On two occasions, I believe, Darcy is specifically a caricature of Fanny Burney's Lord Orville. The scene at the Meryton assembly in which Darcy makes rude remarks about Elizabeth Bennet is a burlesque of Orville's unfavorable first impression of Evelina.[12] In *Evelina,* shortly after Orville and Evelina have had their first dance together, there is a conversation between Orville and Sir Clement Willoughby on the subject of Evelina's merits. Sir Clement says to Orville:

> "Why, my Lord, what have you done with your lovely partner?"
>
> "*Nothing!*" answered Lord Orville, with a smile and a shrug.
>
> "By Jove," cried the man, "she is the most beautiful creature I ever saw in my life!"
>
> Lord Orville . . . laughed, but answered, "Yes; a pretty modest-looking girl."
>
> "O my Lord!" cried the madman, "she is an angel!"
>
> "A *silent* one," returned he.
>
> "Why ay, my Lord, how stands she as to that? She looks all intelligence and expression."
>
> "A poor weak girl!" answered Lord Orville, shaking his head.
>
> (I, Letter XII, p. 42)

In Darcy's remarks about Elizabeth at the Meryton assembly, Orville's gentle mockery becomes supercilious rudeness. Mr. Bingley sounds Darcy on the merits of the various ladies at the assembly, hoping to persuade his friend to dance. Like Sir Clement Willoughby, Bingley praises the heroine: Elizabeth, he declares, is "very pretty, and I dare say, very agreeable"; and he proposes that Darcy ask her to dance. Darcy replies that Elizabeth is "tolerable; but not handsome enough to tempt *me*; and I am in no humour at present to give consequence to young ladies who are slighted by other men" (II.12).

And another ballroom scene in *Evelina* is burlesqued in **Pride and Prejudice.** At one point in *Evelina* Sir Clement Willoughby, who is determined to punish the heroine for pretending that Lord Orville is to be her partner in a dance for which Sir Clement wished to engage her, conducts her to Lord Orville and presents him with her hand. Evelina writes:

> —he suddenly seized my hand, saying, "think, my Lord, what must be my reluctance to resign this fair hand to your Lordship!"
>
> In the same instant, Lord Orville took it of him; I coloured violently, and made an effort to recover it. "You do me too much honour, Sir," cried he, (with an air of gallantry, pressing it to his lips before he let it go) "however, I shall be happy to profit by it, if this lady," (turning to Mrs. Mirvan) "will permit me to seek for her party."
>
> To compel him thus to dance, I could not endure, and eagerly called out, "By no means,—not for the world!—I must beg—"
>
> (I. Letter XIII, p. 57)

Orville politely attempts to help Evelina recover from her confusion. Darcy, "all politeness," as Elizabeth ironically describes him, signifies his willingness to oblige Elizabeth Bennet with a dance when Elizabeth is placed in a similarly embarrassing situation at Sir William Lucas's ball.[13] Sir William and Darcy are conversing. Elizabeth approaches them and Sir William, "struck with the notion of doing a very gallant thing," declares:

> "Mr. Darcy, you must allow me to present this young lady to you as a very desirable partner.—You cannot refuse to dance, I am sure, when so much beauty is before you." And taking her hand, he would have given it to Mr. Darcy, who, though extremely surprised, was not unwilling to receive it, when she instantly drew back, and said with some discomposure to Sir William,
>
> "Indeed, Sir, I have not the least intention of dancing.—I entreat you not to suppose that I moved this way in order to beg for a partner."
>
> Mr. Darcy with grave propriety requested to be allowed the honour of her hand; but in vain. Elizabeth was determined; nor did Sir William at all shake her purpose by his attempt at persuasion.
>
> "You excel so much in the dance, Miss Eliza . . . and though this gentleman dislikes the amusement in general, he can have no objection, I am sure, to oblige us for one half hour."
>
> "Mr. Darcy is all politeness," said Elizabeth, smiling.
>
> (II.26)

Mr. Darcy is a complex human being rather than a mere vehicle for satire such as Charles Adams. Nevertheless, I think it is likely that Darcy has somewhere in his ancestry a parody-figure similar to the ones in which Jane Austen's juvenilia abound. Such a theory is consistent with current assumptions about Jane Austen's habits of composition. Her first three novels are the products of reworkings of drafts written at a period much closer to the time when her juvenile parodies of fiction were written than to that at which *Sense and Sensibility* as we have it was published. Both *Northanger Abbey* and *Sense and Sensibility* contain marked traces of satiric originals, and it seems reasonable to assume that *Pride and Prejudice,* as well as the other two novels, grew, through a process of refinement, from a criticism of literature into a criticism of life. Moreover, the theory accounts for what is perhaps the most serious flaw in *Pride and Prejudice*: the vast difference between the Darcy of the first ballroom scene and the man whom Elizabeth Bennet marries at the end of the novel. We have seen that the most exaggerated displays of conceit and rudeness on Darcy's part—his speech at the Meryton assembly, his fears lest he should be encouraging Elizabeth to fall in love with him, and the language of his first proposal—could have originated as burlesques of the patrician hero. If we postulate an origin in parody for Darcy and assume that he was later subjected to a refining process, the early, exaggerated displays of rudeness can be explained as traces of the original purely parodic figure that Jane Austen was not able to manage with complete success.

Regardless of its origins, *Pride and Prejudice,* even as it stands, is in many respects a subtly ironic reflection on Richardson and Fanny Burney and their patrician heroes. In addition to Darcy's role as an ironically treated Orville or Sir Charles Grandison, Lady Catherine de Bourgh is a reminiscence of Mrs. Delvile in *Cecilia* or Dr. Marchmont in *Camilla,* a humorous version of the kindly but mistaken friend who frowns upon the patrician hero's intended bride. And the scene in which she attempts to persuade Elizabeth not to marry Darcy is an exaggeration of what is potentially ridiculous in similar situations in *Cecilia*—not, as R. B. Johnson and others have suggested, a refined imitation. Mrs. Delvile is Mortimer's mother and exercises, according to Cecilia, an almost maternal prerogative upon Cecilia herself. Cecilia is grateful—exaggeratedly, unnecessarily grateful, many readers feel—to Mrs. Delvile for that lady's interest in her and for her kindness in providing her with a home during part of her minority. Mrs. Delvile has as much right as anyone could have to interfere in the love affair between Mortimer and Cecilia. And when she persuades Cecilia not to marry Mortimer, although what she says is prideful and humiliating to Cecilia, her language, at least, is kind and respectful.[14] Lady Catherine is Darcy's aunt, and she hardly knows Elizabeth. Her attempt to prevent Elizabeth's and Darcy's marriage, her arrogant language, and the manner in which she taxes Elizabeth with ingratitude, on the strength of having invited her to Rosings several times in the past, are a parody of the situation in *Cecilia*. Again, Darcy's relationship with Mr. Bingley is humorously reminiscent of Sir Charles Grandison and the friends who continually depend on him for advice and assistance. Richardson's super-competent hero was notable for his propensity to manage the lives and loves of his friends. Darcy, to our and Elizabeth Bennet's amusement, domineers over the spineless Bingley, arranging and rearranging Bingley's love-life, and at one point officiously separating him from the amiable and disinterested young woman whom Bingley truly loves. Darcy is provided with a mock-Evelina or Harriet Byron in Miss Bingley, who is all too obviously willing to play the role of the patrician hero's female adorer in order to become the mistress of Pemberley. The flattery Evelina and Harriet Byron unconsciously heap upon their heroes, their willingness to take their young men's pronouncements as law, become Miss Bingley's determined toadeating: when she is not praising Darcy's library or his sister, she is defending his views on feminine accomplishments or inviting his comments on the company at Sir William Lucas's ball.

Most important, while Miss Bingley is a caricature of Evelina or Harriet Byron, Elizabeth Bennet plays the role of an anti-Evelina in the novel's satiric pattern.[15] Throughout most of the novel she acts in a manner directly contrary to the way in which one would expect a Richardson or Burney heroine to behave. While the would-be Harriet Byron, Miss Bingley, courts Darcy in the traditional manner, Elizabeth makes him the butt of her wit, the prime target of her attacks on snobbery. While he worries lest he should have encouraged her to hope for the honor of his hand, she regards him as "only the man who made himself agreeable no where, and who had not thought her handsome enough to dance with" (II.23). Instead of being overwhelmed with gratitude when he proposes to her, she prefaces her refusal by saying: "if I could *feel* gratitude, I would now thank you. But I cannot—I have never desired your good opinion, and you have certainly bestowed it most unwillingly" (II.190). And she goes on to tax him with "arrogance," "conceit," and a "selfish disdain for the feelings of others" (II.193), and to accuse him of being snobbish and overbearing in his interference with Jane and Bingley and of abusing the power he holds over Wickham. Even when she and Darcy are reconciled she cannot help smiling at his casual assumption of the right to arrange and rearrange his friend Bingley's love-life, "his easy manner of directing his friend" (II.371). (We might also note that she answers Lady Catherine de Bourgh's demand that she renounce Darcy in a manner calculated to warm the hearts of readers irritated by Cecilia Beverly's deference to Mrs. Delvile's pride and prejudice.)

In the early stages of the novel's development, I believe, Lady Catherine, Mr. Bingley, and Miss Bingley were more exaggerated and distorted versions of their prototypes than they are at present. Elizabeth Bennet was merely an anti-type to the Burney-Richardson sycophantic heroine; Darcy, a caricature of the patrician hero. Later, although she retained an element of ironic imitation, Jane Austen refined her characters, transforming them from mere vehicles for satire into human beings interesting in their own right as well as because of their relationship to their literary prototypes. And, as the remainder of this essay implies, she also changed her attitude toward her patrician hero and her anti-Evelina, and accordingly altered her treatment of Darcy drastically and made Elizabeth, as well as Darcy, a target for her irony. Theories about the development of the novel aside, however, the fact remains that *Pride and Prejudice* as we have it is not simply, as critics have suggested, an imitation of the work of Jane Austen's fellow-novelists. It is, in part at least, an attack on Richardson and Fanny Burney and their patrician heroes.

Jane Austen thoroughly humbles her patrician hero. Darcy is subjected to a series of "set-downs" at the hands of the anti-Evelina, Elizabeth Bennet, and through his love for Elizabeth and the shock he receives from her behavior, he comes to see himself as he really is, and to repent of his pomposity and pride. "By you, I was properly humbled," he admits to Elizabeth towards the end of the novel (II.369).

Interestingly enough, however, Jane Austen does not allow her anti-Evelina to rout her patrician hero completely. For once Darcy has been humbled, she turns her irony on Elizabeth Bennet. She shows that Elizabeth, in her resentment of Darcy's conscious superiority, has exaggerated his faults and failed to see that there is much in him that is good. Elizabeth proves to have been blind and prejudiced in her views on the relationship between Darcy and Wickham, too willing to accept Wickham's stories because they so nicely confirm her own feelings about Darcy. When she reads the letter that follows Darcy's first proposal, she is forced to admit that her resentment has led her to be foolish and unjust. Again, until Darcy's letter shocks her into self-knowledge, Elizabeth has seen Darcy's interference in the affair between Jane and Bingley only as an instance of cold-hearted snobbery on Darcy's part. Reading Darcy's letter, and considering Jane's disposition, Elizabeth is forced to admit that Darcy's view of the affair, his belief that Jane was little more than a complacent pawn in her mother's matrimonial game, is not unjustified. Darcy's interference, Elizabeth must admit, was motivated not merely by snobbery, but by concern for his guileless friend's welfare as well. With her eyes thus opened, Elizabeth comes to see later in the novel that Darcy's position and fortune, and his pride in them, can be forces for good as well as sources of snobbery and authoritarianism. Seeing Pemberley, and hearing his housekeeper's praise of Darcy's conduct as a brother and a landlord, she learns that Darcy's position is a trust and a responsibility, and that his not unjustifiable self-respect leads to a code of conduct worthy of admiration. And in his action in the Lydia-Wickham affair she is provided with an impressive and gratifying instance of his power to do good and his sense of responsibility. At the end of the novel Jane Austen's anti-Evelina is defending her patrician hero. "I love him," Elizabeth says of Darcy to the astounded Mr. Bennet. "Indeed, he has no improper pride" (II.376).

As many critics have pointed out, a pattern of "art-nature" symbolism in *Pride and Prejudice* added depth of suggestion, for Jane Austen's early nineteenth century audience, to the novel's love plot. I suggest that Jane Austen's continual allusions, through parody, to her fellow-novelists' treatment of an eighteenth century authority-figure served a purpose similar to that which the "art-nature" symbolism served. We cannot, of course, assume that Jane Austen thought of her Mr. Darcy as an "authority-figure," in our sense of the term, any more than we can assume that she considered *Pride and Prejudice* a treatise on the eighteenth-century "art-nature" antithesis. But we can be sure that she expected the novel-reading audience for which she wrote to respond to her work on the basis of their impressions of the insufferable Sir Charles Grandisons and Lord Orvilles, the sycophantic Evelinas and Harriet Byrons, of noveldom. At the beginning of *Pride and Prejudice* Darcy is a pompous Burney-Richardson aristocrat, with many of the most disagreeable attributes of his literary progenitors as well as a representative of "art" and excessive class pride. Elizabeth is a determined anti-Evelina as well as a symbol for "nature" and aggressive individualism. The marriage at the end of the story joins a "properly humbled" patrician hero and an anti-Evelina who has also undergone a partial reformation. This element of burlesque-with-a-difference co-operates with the novel's "art-nature" symbolism in broadening and deepening the significance of Elizabeth and Darcy's love story.

In view of what has just been said, it is interesting to note that in the latter part of *Pride and Prejudice* Jane Austen ceases to laugh at the works of Richardson and Fanny Burney and even imitates them rather obviously. At Pemberley Darcy behaves toward Elizabeth with a marked tact and gallantry that is reminiscent of Sir Charles Grandison or Lord Orville. In the manner of Richardson's and Fanny Burney's heroes he takes over his heroine's affairs, rescuing Elizabeth and her family from imminent disgrace and providing for the erring Lydia. Moreover, the scenes in which Elizabeth visits Pemberley may well be specific imitations of similar scenes in *Sir Charles Grandison*. Sir Charles, we are told, "pretends not to level hills, or to force and distort

nature; but to help it, as he finds it, without letting art be seen in his works, where he can possibly avoid it" (XVI.246. *Grandison*, III, Letter XXIII). He has a

> large and convenient house, . . . situated in a spacious park; which has several fine avenues leading to it.
>
> On the north side of the park flows a winding stream, that may well be called a river, abounding with trout and other fish; the current quickened by a noble cascade, which tumbles down its foaming waters from a rock, which is continued to some extent, in a ledge of rock-work, rudely disposed.
>
> The park is remarkable for its prospects, lawns, and rich-appearing clumps of trees of large growth.
>
> (XX.30. *Grandison*, VII, Letter VI)

The Pemberley grounds are kept up with a similar regard for nature and timber, and there is even a similarly managed, artificially swelled trout stream. Pemberley House, we are told, was

> situated on the opposite side of a valley, into which the road with some abruptness wound. It was a large, handsome, stone building, standing well on rising ground, and backed by a ridge of high woody hills;—and in front, a stream of some natural importance was swelled into greater, but without any artificial appearance. Its banks were neither formal, nor falsely adorned. Elizabeth was delighted. She had never seen a place for which nature had done more, or where natural beauty had been so little counteracted by an awkward taste.
>
> (II.245)

Was Jane Austen thinking of Harriet Byron's tour of Sir Charles Grandison's property when she described Elizabeth Bennet's visit to Pemberley? Both Elizabeth and Harriet are conducted around magnificent but tastefully appointed houses and both talk to elderly, respectable housekeepers who praise their masters' kindness to servants and tenants. "Don't your ladyship see," Sir Charles's housekeeper asks Harriet Byron, "how all his servants love him as they attend him at table? . . . Indeed, madam, we all adore him; and have prayed morning, noon, and night, for his coming hither, and settling among us" (XX.52. *Grandison*, VII, Letter IX). Darcy's housekeeper, we remember, laments the fact that he is not at Pemberley "so much as I could wish" and declares him "the best landlord, and the best master . . . that ever lived. There is not one of his tenants or servants but what will give him a good name" (II.248, 249). Harriet and Elizabeth are both conducted around noble picture-galleries, and both view pictures of their lovers with admiration during their tours.

As Darcy becomes a modified but genuine Sir Charles Grandison, so does Elizabeth cease to resemble an aggressive anti-Evelina or Harriet Byron. She becomes more and more impressed with her patrician hero, more and more attracted to his many good qualities. Indeed, as she stands in the gallery at Pemberley, there is even a trace of Evelina-like gratitude in her thoughts, and she feels honored by the love of such a man as Darcy:

> As a brother, a landlord, a master, she considered how many people's happiness were in his guardianship!— How much of pleasure or pain it was in his power to bestow! . . . Every idea that had been brought forward by the housekeeper was favourable to his character. . . . Elizabeth thought of his regard with a deeper sentiment of gratitude than it had ever raised before.
>
> (II.250, 251)

Pride and Prejudice is a story about two complex, sensitive and often blindly wrong-headed "intricate characters" and their progress toward a better understanding of one another, the world, and themselves. This drama of self-knowledge is played out in the context of a symbolism based on the antithesis between "art" and "nature," in the comprehensive eighteenth-century sense of those terms. It is also referred, at many points, to the fiction of Jane Austen's day—particularly to her fellow-novelists' handling of the figure that I have called the patrician hero. Jane Austen's first response to the patrician hero, I believe, was purely satiric. Later, I think, she refined, revised, and greatly complicated her treatment of him. At any rate, *Pride and Prejudice* is something more than a much-improved imitation of the novels Jane Austen knew. It is a work in which she tumbles an eighteenth-century authority-figure from the pedestal on which Richardson and Fanny Burney had placed him—and, with a gesture that distinguishes her also from some later novelists, then stoops to retrieve him from the dust.

Notes

1. The most detailed study of *Pride and Prejudice* in terms of the "art-nature" dichotomy is Samuel Kliger's "Jane Austen's *Pride and Prejudice* in the Eighteenth-Century Mode," *UTQ* [*University of Toronto Quarterly*], XVI (1947), 357-370.

2. See, for example, the comments in Mary Lascelles's *Jane Austen and Her Art* (Oxford, 1939), pp. 22 and 162, and Marvin Mudrick's complaints about the change in Darcy in his *Jane Austen: Irony as Defense and Discovery* (Princeton, 1952), pp. 117-119.

3. See Brower's *The Fields of Light* (New York, Oxford University Press, 1951), pp. 164-181, and Babb's *Jane Austen's Novels: The Fabric of Dialogue* (Columbus, Ohio, 1962), pp. 115-118.

4. Jane Austen's Mr. Darcy is sometimes compared to Richardson's patrician "villain-hero," Mr. B——. E. E. Duncan-Jones, in "Proposals of Marriage in *Pamela* and *Pride and Prejudice*," *N & Q* [*Notes and Queries*] (N.S.), IV, 76, calls the pro-

posal scene in *Pride and Prejudice* a reminiscence of Mr. B——'s first honorable proposal to Pamela. More general resemblances between *Pamela* and Jane Austen's novel are discussed in Henrietta Ten Harmsel's "The Villain Hero in *Pamela* and *Pride and Prejudice*," *CE* [*College English*], 23 (1961), 104-108. Although I do not think that it is entirely unprofitable to compare *Pamela* and *Pride and Prejudice,* I believe, for reasons that will be apparent later, that it is more rewarding to compare Darcy to heroes modeled on Sir Charles Grandison.

5. Samuel Richardson, *Novels* (London, 1902), XIV, p. x. All references will be to this edition.

6. The quotation is from Johnson's introduction to *Sense and Sensibility* in *The Works of Jane Austen,* ed. R. Brimley Johnson (London, 1950), p. v. The relationship between *Cecilia* and *Pride and Prejudice* is more fully discussed in Johnson's *Jane Austen* (London, 1927), pp. 124-127, and in his *Jane Austen: Her Life, Her Work, Her Family, and Her Critics* (London, 1930), pp. 137-139.

7. *Cecilia* is not necessarily the source for the title of *Pride and Prejudice,* since the terms "pride" and "prejudice" were very often used in conjunction in Jane Austen's day. R. W. Chapman's notes to the Oxford edition of *Pride and Prejudice* and numerous articles in the *TLS* [*Times Literary Supplement*] and *N & Q* testify to the popularity of the expression.

8. Fanny Burney, *Evelina,* ed. Sir Frank D. MacKinnon (Oxford, 1930), II, Letter XXVII, p. 321. All references will be to this edition.

9. Anna Maria Porter, *The Lake of Killarney* (London, 1804), I, iv, 219. Jane Austen mentions this novel in a letter of 24 October 1808: see the *Letters,* ed. R. W. Chapman, 2nd ed. (London, 1959), pp. 58-59.

10. Jane Austen, *Works,* ed. R. W. Chapman (London, 1954), VI, 13. All references will be to this edition.

11. As E. E. Duncan-Jones points out in "Notes on Jane Austen," *N&Q,* 196 (1951), 114-116. Numbers of heroes in the minor fiction of the period, however, among them Lord C——in *The History of Sir William Harrington* and Mr. Charlemont in *The Lake of Killarney,* are similarly described.

12. In "A Critical Theory of Jane Austen's Writings," Part I, *Scrutiny,* 10 (1941-42), 61-87, Mrs. Leavis recognizes the similarity between the two scenes.

13. Of course, as Brower (*Fields of Light,* pp. 168-169) points out, we see this scene largely through the eyes of the prejudiced Elizabeth Bennet. Darcy

is actually eager to dance with Elizabeth, although his manner of expressing himself is not very gallant.

14. See, for example, *Cecilia,* ed. R. Brimley Johnson (London, 1893), III, Bk. VIII, Ch. iii, p. 22 and Ch. iv, p. 37.

15. Mrs. Leavis ("Critical Theory ['A Critical Theory of Jane Austen's Novels']," Part I) adopts a somewhat similar view of Elizabeth's origins. She holds that much of *Pride and Prejudice* was originally a satire of *Cecilia,* and that Elizabeth is an "anti-Cecilia." She feels, however, that Darcy is simply a refined imitation of Mortimer Delvile—"Delvile with the minimum of inside necessary to make plausible his conduct." I am primarily concerned here with Darcy's role as a mock patrician hero; and, of course, I believe that Elizabeth is an anti-type to a number of heroines, and not simply a vehicle for satire of one novel.

Joel Weinsheimer (essay date September 1972)

SOURCE: Weinsheimer, Joel. "Chance and the Hierarchy of Marriages in *Pride and Prejudice.*" *ELH* 39, no. 3 (September 1972): 404-19.

[*In the following essay, Weinsheimer examines the role of chance in Austen's novel. Weinsheimer identifies a thematic relationship between self-knowledge and "rational and deliberate choice" in the work.*]

Chance is given significance in Jane Austen's novels by her insistence on the value of its opposite—rational and deliberate choice. And it is an important aspect of her realism that she does not divide choice and chance into two mutually exclusive forces. Ideal choice made in full awareness of motives and consequences is, after all, a rare occurrence in her novels. Few characters achieve it at all, and they more often reach it as a climax rather than as the norm of their moral life. In general decision and action are determined by a variously composed mixture of choice and chance, and only as a given character increases his knowledge of self and others does choice begin to predominate.

Little critical comment has been devoted to the operation of chance in Jane Austen's works, perhaps because it has been eclipsed by the tightness of her plots and the preeminently unchaotic sanity of her ideals. But Lionel Trilling has wisely observed that "Jane Austen's first or basic irony is the recognition that the spirit is not free, that it is conditioned, that it is limited by circumstance" and that "only by reason of this anomaly does spirit have virtue and meaning."[1] Just as the spirit is morally dependent on and made meaningful by uncontrolled cir-

cumstance, so also is plot enriched by Jane Austen's consciousness of chance. W. J. Harvey, in discussing the plot of *Emma,* attributes the "solidity and openness of the novel" to the fact that "it allows for the contingent."[2] Again, Lionel Trilling finds *Mansfield Park* more unique than typical in its "need to find security, to establish, in fixity and enclosure, a refuge from the dangers of openness and chance."[3]

Paul Zietlow presents by far the most extensive analysis of chance in Jane Austen's novels in his examination of *Persuasion,* which is the novel of her canon that most overtly invites this treatment. But the presence of chance in *Pride and Prejudice* is neither so striking nor obtrusive as in *Persuasion,* where, as Zietlow has pointed out, the reunion of Anne and Wentworth seems almost Providential. The "dark, menacing quality"[4] which he and others sense in *Persuasion* is absent in the "light, and bright, and sparkling" *Pride and Prejudice.* Nor do the fortunes of Elizabeth Bennet undergo so complete a reversal as those of Anne Elliot. This comparative uniformity of happiness in *Pride and Prejudice* tends to conceal the operation of chance as a thematic motif and plot device in bringing the novel to a felicitous conclusion. But, like *Persuasion,* the fortuitous emerges in *Pride and Prejudice* as a force with which both its characters and its readers must contend.

As a working definition, we may suggest that all effects not voluntarily produced be considered, morally speaking, as the results of chance. Supplementing this definition, there are two distinct, but connected, phases of action[5] in which chance can interpose. The first occurs in the process of decision when, through self-ignorance or self-deception, a character remains unaware of the actual motivation that brings him to a specific conclusion or plan of action. The second occurs simply when a given intention fails to produce the desired effect, when the consequences of an action are unforeseen and unexpected. Chance then fills the gap left by the lapse of control either of one's self or one's circumstances.[6] Both instances are caused by a more or less avoidable (and thus morally significant) ignorance, and both are imaged in Jane Austen's novels as a variety of "blindness."

With this definition of chance in mind, we may investigate, first, Jane Austen's method of establishing chance as a credible and effective plot device, and, second, her evaluation of the balance of chance and choice in the novel's several marriages. Critics have already suggested several perspectives on the hierarchy of marriages in *Pride and Prejudice;*[7] each couple seems to be yoked because both partners achieve the same moral rank, and thus are fit mates. What has not yet been fully explored is the fact that the characters' responses to chance are significant criteria for the evaluation of their relative merits. Ranked by their reactions to the fortuitous, the characters range from partial self-determination to complete domination by chance, and each married couple illustrates a double view of one position in the novel's scale of imperfect responses to chance.[8]

To assess the operation of chance in *Pride and Prejudice,* it may first be helpful to consider Jane Austen's method of making the most fortuitous incidents seem probable and natural. Dorothy Van Ghent replies to those readers who feel that *Pride and Prejudice* is so limited that its value is minimal by reminding them that "when we begin to look upon these limitations . . . as having the positive function of defining the form and meaning of the book, we begin also to understand that kind of value that can lie in artistic mastery over a restricted range."[9] "The exclusions and limitations are deliberate,"[10] and as soon as we acknowledge them so, we also realize that the novel's restricted setting is defined by and thus implies the larger world which comprehends it. How this double awareness of part and whole can account for the credibility of chance events in *Pride and Prejudice* is best illustrated by examining the three incidents that appear most fortuitous.

The rerouting and rescheduling of the proposed trip to the Lake country, the early return of Darcy to Pemberley in time to meet Elizabeth there, and Elizabeth's failure to expose Wickham to Lydia or her parents all seem to be the result of chance. Yet the author assigns each a cause: Mr. Gardiner is "prevented by business" (283)[11] from his original plans; Darcy's "business with his steward had occasioned his coming forward a few hours before the rest of the party" (256); and Wickham is spared exposure because when Elizabeth "returned home [from the Collins parsonage], the—shire was to leave Meryton in a week or a fortnight's time" (285). Here the duties of an active businessman, the concerns of the landed nobility, and the directives of the war office each signify a sphere of causation alien to the provincial setting of the novel. Yet precisely because of its provinciality, they achieve significance and probability. Jane Austen balances the surprise and the credibility of improbable events by imposing limitations that both suspend and maintain our awareness of the larger world. Thus whether chance occurrences will imply direction by Providence becomes a matter of choice for Jane Austen, since she suggests in the novel an alternative sphere of terrestrial causation intervening between the Providential and the immediate.

By establishing chance as a realistic technique of plot development, Jane Austen enables the reader to acknowledge its presence without apology for mystery or legerdemain. Consequently, we can understand that the operation of chance minimizes the danger (which Mary Lascelles warns is inherent in its "exactness of symmetry"[12]) of imposing a benumbing order on the material of the novel. Chance has its own symbology, and is employed in a pervasive thematic pattern paralleling that of choice.

Two significant symbols of chance underlying the affairs of the Longbourn circle are the entail by which Mr. Bennet's estate will devolve on Mr. Collins ("'such things . . . are all chance in this world'" [65]) and the lottery at the Phillips home, where Lydia "soon grew too much interested in the game, too eager in making bets and exclaiming after prizes, to have attention for anyone in particular" (77). The entail typifies the financial insecurity of the middle-class woman, which participation in the marriage lottery is intended to remedy. As Mr. Collins remarks using an associated metaphor, "'When persons sit down to a card table, they must take their chance of these things'" (83). Here Jane Austen depicts the hope of chance solutions for chance ills. But the gamble of the marriage lottery also symbolizes design—even though we usually conceive of design as effort directed toward a particular end, thus limiting the operation of chance.

In *Pride and Prejudice* (as in *Emma*) design and its correlates—art, scheming, contrivance, and cunning—become associated with chance by the partial disjunction of intention and effect. In the cases of Mrs. Bennet's contrivances for Jane, Lady Catherine's frank condescension to Elizabeth at Longbourn, and Miss Bingley's arts of captivating Darcy, the existence of the design *per se* initiates its own frustration. The "quality of powerlessness"[13] which Marvin Mudrick finds characteristic of the "simple" characters in the novel derives from their inability to conceive of an event as a somewhat unpredictable intersection of diverse causes. There are, for example, at least five forces operating in Jane's estrangement from Bingley: her reserve, her parent's impropriety, Darcy's interference, Miss Bingley's cooperation with Darcy, and Bingley's malleability—any one of which would have been insufficient to separate them. Without an awareness of this multiplicity, design is ineffectual, and its bafflement will seem attributable to the perversity of ill fortune.

If Charlotte Lucas is typical of the designers engaged in the marriage lottery, it becomes clear that those who most credit chance, most employ art. Her marriage, of the three we will center on, is the most pathetic. Charlotte demonstrates her intelligence, as does Elizabeth, by acknowledging that marriage does not always bring happiness. Marriage, Charlotte implies, can be contrived successfully: "'Bingley likes your sister undoubtedly; but he may never do more than like her, if she does not help him on.' '. . . Your plan is a good one,' replied Elizabeth, 'where nothing is in question but the desire of being well married; and if I were determined to get a rich husband, or any husband, I dare say I should adopt it'" (22). Conversely, from Charlotte's perspective, "'Happiness in marriage is entirely a matter of chance. . . . And it is better to know as little as possible of the defects of the person with whom you are to pass your life'" (23).

Charlotte's plan *is* a good one if she is to catch "any husband."[14] She succeeds in the same way as Lydia, who is also too involved in the lottery "to have attention for anyone in particular" (77). But the pathos of Charlotte's marriage is that, because of her intelligence, her ignorance must be a pretense. And thus she never arrives, as does Lydia, at the "sublime and refined point of felicity, called, the possession of being well deceived."[15] Charlotte begins, as we have seen, by espousing the value of ignorance in courtship, since the knowledge of the partner's defects has no bearing on one's chance of happiness, and she follows her prescription unswervingly. After Elizabeth rejects Collins, Charlotte satisfies her curiosity by "walking toward the window and pretending not to hear" (114) Mr. Collins rationalize his disappointment. When thus informed that Collins is, for the moment, unattached, she sets the pretended ignorance of her marriage scheme into motion: "Miss Lucas perceived him from an upper window as he walked toward the house, and instantly set out to meet him accidentally in the lane" (121). And as is usual in Jane Austen's novels, the means justify the end. During Elizabeth's visit to the parsonage, she notices that "when Mr. Collins said anything of which his wife might reasonably be ashamed, . . . Charlotte wisely did not hear" (156). Whatever modicum of happiness Charlotte enjoys in her marriage results not from chance, as she had predicted, but from her persistence in the same pretended self-deception that characterized her courtship. In this way she unwittingly becomes a fit mate for Collins, who is similarly defined by the "perseverance in wilful self-deception" (109) in his deafness to Elizabeth's rejection.

Collins himself remarks the perfection of this union at Elizabeth's departure: "'My dear Charlotte and I have but one mind and one way of thinking. There is in everything a most remarkable resemblance of character and ideas between us. We seem to have been designed for each other'" (216). Here is at least a triple irony. Since their compatibility is small, only a perverse design could have joined them. Nevertheless, Collins does design Charlotte for a wife, and at the same time, she designs him for a husband—though both are merely searching for any mate available. But, most important, they are attracted to each other by a force superior to them both—their mutual identity. Here again Jane Austen posits a new sphere of causation, non-Providential, yet extrinsic to the forces of which the characters are immediately aware. In *The Family Reunion* Agatha concisely describes this sphere and the folly of ignoring it:

Thus with the most careful devotion
Thus with precise attention

To detail, interfering preparation
Of that which is already prepared
Men tighten the knot of confusion
Into perfect misunderstanding.
Reflecting a pocket-torch of observation
Upon each other's opacity. . . .[16]

Although all the characters in the novel get what they want, their designs do not affect their felicity. Contrivance is either the ignorant "preparation of that which is already prepared," or else it is simply irrelevant to the outcome. The most explicit instance of the folly of design occurs in Mrs. Bennet's self-applause for keeping Jane and Bingley together at Netherfield: "'This was a lucky idea of mine, indeed!' said Mrs. Bennet, more than once, as if the credit of making it rain were all her own" (31). Design and chance are allied in *Pride and Prejudice* because Jane's marriage and the rain are equally of Mrs. Bennet's devising.

While Jane Austen validates Darcy's claim that "whatever bears affinity to cunning is despicable" (40), she does not conclude that its opposite is more laudable. Mr. Bennet's indolent detachment from his wife and daughters increases their vulnerability, and signals his moral deficiency. And Bingley, though not at all cunning, is fit for no better than Jane. The marriage of Jane and Bingley, like that of Charlotte and Collins, also discloses a dual perspective on a single position in the hierarchy of marriages, and, as we noticed in the parson and his wife, their placement in this moral scale results in part from their similar responses to chance.

It is the chance involved in Bingley's spontaneously picking Netherfield as a home that initiates the novel's action. "Mr. Bingley had not been of age two years, when he was tempted by an accidental recommendation to look at Netherfield House. He did look at it and into it for half an hour, was pleased with what the owner said in its praise, and took it immediately" (16). But his caprice is more estimable than that of Mr. Collins, since by this method Bingley chooses a house, Collins a wife. Bingley's "needless precipitance" is further developed in his reply to Mrs. Bennet's inquiry whether he will stay long at Netherfield: "'Whatever I do is done in a hurry . . . and therefore if I should resolve to quit Netherfield, I should probably be off in five minutes'" (42). However, Darcy remains unconvinced of his friend's resoluteness; such decisiveness is mere fantasy. On the contrary, Darcy informs him, "'Your conduct would be quite as dependent on chance as that of any man I know; and if, as you were mounting your horse, a friend were to say, "Bingley, you had better stay till next week," you would probably do it, you would probably not go—and, at another word, might stay a month'" (49). What Darcy clarifies for us is that capricious choice is not the affirmation of individual power or of freedom from external restraint; rather it is the reliance on an immediate cause (the nearby friend, Darcy) whose presence is accidental. Caprice is no more than the unacknowledged determination of choice by chance.

Bingley's unconscious dependence on chance parallels that of Jane, and thereby prepares us for their marriage. Like Bingley, Jane is without design. Quite the opposite, she nearly fulfills Charlotte's prophecy that her reserve will not suffice to hold Bingley. The complement of Jane's restraint in the display of affection is her restraint in censure, and the basis of both is her response to that ignorance which produces the appearance of chance. Jane's recognition that she does not know the degree of Bingley's affection accounts for her unwillingness to entrap him. Because of the same self-acknowledged ignorance she suspends judgment when Elizabeth repeats Wickham's version of Darcy's duplicity. Nothing remained for Jane to do "but to think well of them both, to defend the conduct of each, and throw into the account of accident or mistake, what ever could not otherwise be explained" (85). Jane's *sancta simplicitas* is thus preserved by her remaining in a cocoon of ignorance. In one sense, Jane is the personification of the comic hope of *Pride and Prejudice.* Of all the characters, she most consistently expects that all will end well (287). But this prognosis is undermined as the reader comes to realize that the "account of accident or mistake" will not sustain the new data continually being unfolded. And as chance yields to pattern, we understand more clearly that the "sanguine hope of good" which makes possible Jane's favorable interpretations of the presence of evil does not result from an accurate observation of her world, but is merely the projected "benevolence of her heart" (287). Our reaction therefore is twofold: we reverence her benevolence, and deprecate her fixation in it.

Jane's "angelic" response to chance is initially adequate. She humbly presumes the possibility of ignorance and error. But her benign skepticism produces no knowledge, and thus becomes its own caricature—stultified and incapable of adapting to the flux of the sublunary world. Her control is diminished, her choice incapacitated, and in their absence Jane is governed by chance. Both Bingley and Jane are characterized by a perseverance in self-deception like that of Charlotte and Collins, but their unscheming good nature elevates them above the parson and his wife. Of Bingley's ductility and Jane's petrification, we are forced to say (as does Elizabeth describing Darcy and Wickham), "'There is but such a quantity of merit between them; just enough to make one good sort of man'" (225).

Jane's fixation is not unique within the Bennet family. In the marriage of Mr. and Mrs. Bennet the reader discovers that both "neglect and mistaken indulgence" (280), both detachment and design, are manifestations of internal necessity or fixation. Elizabeth upbraids her father's indolence by illustrating its effect on his children: if he will not bestir himself, she says, "'Lydia's character will be fixed, and she will, at sixteen, be the most determined flirt that ever made herself and her family ridiculous'" (231). Nor is even Lydia's flirtation free; it is fixed on a scarlet coat (64). That the parents' fixation will contribute to the child's fixation is probable and natural. What is surprising is that any of the Bennet daughters escape "the disadvantages of so unsuitable a marriage" (236) as that of their parents. How Elizabeth does so is the central concern of *Pride and Prejudice.* And her liberation involves a response to chance that raises the moral value of her marriage above that of the others.

A significant form of verbal irony in the first half of the novel[17] is Elizabeth's perversion of metaphors of chance: "'Mr. Bingley's defence of his friend was a very able one I *dare* say, but since he is unacquainted with several parts of the story, and has learnt the rest from that friend himself, I shall *venture* still to think of both gentlemen as I did before'" (96; my italics). Ironically, the limitations of Bingley's defence of Darcy are identical to the defects in Elizabeth's defence of Wickham. Yet Elizabeth is unaware that her evaluation of Wickham is a "venture," not a certainty. Similarly, while trying to penetrate Mr. Collins' deafness, Elizabeth assures him, "'I am not one of those young ladies (if such young ladies there are) who are so *daring* as to *risk* their happiness on the *chance* of being asked a second time'" (107; my italics). Elizabeth knows that to refuse Collins' offer does not "risk" her happiness since the chance of any is nil: "'You could not make *me* happy, and I am convinced that I am the last woman in the world who could make you so'" (107). The similarity of this rebuff of Collins to Elizabeth's rejection of Darcy is striking: "'I had not known you a month before I felt that you were the last man in the world whom I could ever be prevailed on to marry'" (193). This parallel phrasing in Elizabeth's two refusals of marriage suggests one facet of her fixation. To refuse Darcy does risk her happiness, but Elizabeth denies the gambling metaphor by presuming an omniscience of Darcy like that she possessed of Collins. In the first half of the novel Elizabeth's continual repetition of the metaphors associated with the marriage lottery indicates that while she seems unaffected by it, her attempt to deny chance proves it real and threatening.

If Collins is often impenetrably deaf to Elizabeth, the reverse is also true. "'My dear Miss Elizabeth,'" he remarks to her at the Netherfield ball, "'I have the highest opinion in the world of your excellent judgment in all matters within the scope of your understanding, but permit me to say . . .'" (97). Disguised in Mr. Collins' flatulence is Elizabeth's unawareness that the scope of her understanding is too small, that it has gathered too little data, to evaluate circumstances accurately. These limitations of self-knowledge must become conscious if she is to escape entrapment in her own illusory omniscience. What Elizabeth must learn, among other things, is that chance is predicated on ignorance, and insofar as ignorance can be under one's control, to that extent is chance capable of regulation. The paradigm of her awakening occurs in Rosings Park. "More than once did Elizabeth in her ramble within the Park, unexpectedly meet Mr. Darcy.—She felt all the perverseness of the mischance that should bring him where no one else was brought; and to prevent its ever happening again, took care to inform him at first that it was a favorite haunt of hers.—How it could occur a second time was very odd!—Yet it did, even a third" (182). At least one critic has noted that it is a "series of incidents over which Elizabeth has no control that reunites"[18] her with Darcy. And in Rosings Park only by an involuntary empiricism does Elizabeth discover a pattern emerging from what seemed to be fortuitous in his actions.

On the possibility of Darcy's knavery Jane is in a quandary: "'It is difficult indeed—it is distressing.—One does not know what to think.'" But Elizabeth retorts, "'I beg your pardon;—one knows exactly what to think'" (86). Throughout the novel Elizabeth recognizes, as Jane does not, the necessity of judgment in the presence of evil. But Elizabeth here manifests the same needless precipitancy in decision that characterizes Bingley, and is thus to a similar extent directed by chance. Her prejudice originates in the coincidence of her being near enough to overhear Darcy's snub. And only when Elizabeth comes to understand that she has persevered in willful self-deception, has "'courted prepossession and ignorance, and driven reason away'" (208), is she released from the dominion of chance. Her perspective is then broadened, and she becomes capable of "giving way to every variety of thought," of "reconsidering events," and, most significantly, of "determining probabilities" (209).

Although Reuben Brower finds it "an odd, rather legalistic process,"[19] "determining probabilities" is, nevertheless, the most appropriate of the responses to chance dramatized in *Pride and Prejudice,* and Elizabeth's capacity to determine the probabilities of possible events validates the novel's placement of her marriage above that of Jane in the moral hierarchy. If one must have a fixation, Jane's fixation in the suspension of censure is more praiseworthy than Elizabeth's in prejudice. But because Elizabeth escapes herself, she achieves the higher moral status. If Jane superficially affirms chance but ultimately denies it, the reverse is true of Elizabeth. She finally credits chance and attempts to cope with it.

For a gambler, determining probabilities is relatively easy. He knows the dice and how they are marked. But Elizabeth and Darcy must discover while blindfolded how the dice are constructed. They are forced to define

their world inductively before deciding the probability of a given outcome. The possibility of error in this process destroys the self-assurance with which Elizabeth had judged Darcy and Wickham. And had Darcy known the difficulty of determining probabilities when he first proposed, his countenance would not have "expressed real security" while "he *spoke* of apprehension and anxiety" (189). Such security only causes vexation. As Jane comments, "'His being so sure of succeeding, was wrong . . . and certainly ought not to have appeared; but consider how much it must increase his disappointment'" (224). That by the time of his second proposal Darcy has been educated in the vagaries of mischance is shown by the "more than common awkwardness and anxiety of his situation" (366). And here his humility is rewarded with success because it presumes that Elizabeth is free either to accept or reject him. Likewise, when Darcy returns at last to the Bennet home, Elizabeth acknowledges the possibility of a variety of motives and distrusts what appears to be simple cause and effect relationship. She hopes that his return means "that his affection and wishes must still be unshaken. But she would not be secure" (334).

The anxiety of Elizabeth and Darcy demonstrates that their reappraisal of the operation of chance does not make them capable of molding the world to their satisfaction. Whatever additional control the recognition of chance gives them is dwarfed by their glimpse of the far greater chaos beyond their direction. Nor does Jane Austen lead us toward the pride of Stoicism. The inner world, like the outer, is susceptible of only small (though significant) control. "Health and temper to bear inconveniencies—cheerfulness to enhance every pleasure—and affection and intelligence, which might supply it among themselves if there were disappointments abroad" (240) characterize the Gardiners as a couple high in the moral scale; but these qualities are rare and can be generated only in a naturally fertile soil of which there is very little on this earth.

It is true that for Jane Austen self-knowledge and self-control crown the moral hierarchy, and where her characters fail in these respects they fall under the lash of her wit. The art of self-manipulation to prevent the deception of others is laudable and difficult of mastery. But the qualms one has about the value of complete self-consciousness result from its persistent tendency toward knavery; or from a more Romantic perspective, self-consciousness might be imaged as the wearing of a true mask, a persona identical to the person behind it. But what the viewer of such a mask always realizes is that this duality is perilously close to the duplicity of such as Wickham.

Jane Austen circumvents the problems involved in over-rationalizing behavior by reminding us of the operation of the unconscious even in the most consequential choices. Reason is parodied in Mary's windy moralizing and in Mr. Collins' formulaic proposal to Elizabeth. But, more important, the central marriage of *Pride and Prejudice* is based not alone on reason and the growing mutual understanding between Darcy and Elizabeth, but also on a thoroughly spontaneous affection—one which flowers entirely contrary to the efforts and expectations of the characters. Bingley and Jane "considered it, we talked of it as impossible" (373). One reason why the marriage of Darcy and Elizabeth seems impossible is that "it has been most unconsciously done" (190). Elizabeth can take no credit for having knowingly elicited Darcy's addresses, yet "it was gratifying to have inspired unconsciously so strong an affection" (193). Elizabeth cannot say how long she has loved Darcy: "'It has been coming on so gradually, that I hardly know when it began'" (373). And similarly Darcy, when Elizabeth asks him to describe the origin of his love, replies, "'I cannot fix on the hour, or the spot, or the look, or the words, which laid the foundation. It is too long ago. I was in the middle before I knew that I *had* begun'" (380). Finally, there is no immediate cause—not even conscious will—for the affection of Darcy and Elizabeth, and this freedom constitutes their peculiar felicity.

Elizabeth wonders at one point "how far it would be for the happiness of both that she should employ the power, which her fancy told her she still possessed, of bringing on the renewal of [Darcy's] addresses" (266). Luckily she never has the opportunity to do so, for this would bring her to the level of Miss Bingley. As we have seen, it is superfluous or worse to arrange what is already arranged. This inefficacy of the will in matters of affection is found not only in the "simple" characters, as Mudrick contends, but in "complex" characters as well.[20] Rather than attempting to snare Darcy, Elizabeth acts toward him as she resolves to act toward Bingley. It is hard, she thought, "'that this poor man cannot come to a house, which he has legally hired, without raising all this speculation! I *will* leave him to himself'" (332). Such is Elizabeth's response to the "truth universally acknowledged" that governs the novel. What she here clarifies for us is that when left alone by the Mrs. Bennets of this world, the individual's self emerges lucidly, without being falsified by the pattern imposed by other's wishes.

The unpredictability of events in *Pride and Prejudice* results from the fact that, from the characters' point of view, all manner of improbability is discovered. Wickham's knavery teaches Elizabeth to "draw no limits in the future to the impudence of an impudent man" (317). And at the other extreme, she finds in Darcy's assistance of Lydia "an exertion of goodness too great to be probable" (326). Even determining probabilities is inadequate if we are not prepared for the unlikely.

On the other hand, when probability of action or motivation is too easily calculated, Jane Austen puts us on our guard. Just as she portrays the improbable, so also do we find the over-probable, and sometimes both simultaneously:

> Never, since reading Jane's second letter, had [Elizabeth] entertained a hope of Wickham's meaning to marry [Lydia]. No one but Jane, she thought, could flatter herself with such an expectation. *Surprise was the least of her feelings* on this developement. . . . But now *it was all too natural.* For such an attachment as this, she might have sufficient charms; and though she did not suppose Lydia to be deliberately engaging in an elopement, without the intention of marriage, *she had no difficulty in believing* that neither her virtue nor her understanding would preserve her from falling an easy prey.
>
> (279-80; my italics)

Here the over-probable becomes a source of pity or aversion because it implies an involuntary entrapment by an exterior and mechanical cause. Lydia falls an "easy prey" to Wickham because he is thoroughly self-conscious, and she is not. And she is a prey to herself by her self-will and carelessness (213). Here, as elsewhere, Wickham falls victim to his own contrivance. Nevertheless, they do surprisingly marry, contrary to Elizabeth's expectations, and at the same time fulfill her suspicion that little "permanent happiness could belong to a couple who were only brought together because their passions were stronger than their virtue" (312). Likewise, the over-probable and improbable are combined when Miss Bingley teases Darcy about his pleasure from Elizabeth's fine eyes: "'I am all astonishment. How long has she been such a favorite?—and pray when am I to wish you joy?'" To which Darcy replies, "'That is exactly the question I expected you to ask'" (27). Miss Bingley's comment is completely predictable and therefore inane; yet ultimately it is justified.

Samuel Kliger has observed that in *Pride and Prejudice* the eighteenth century's "rationalistic quest of the mean between two extremes requires that the probabilities for the heroine's behavior be set up between two alternatives, neither of which is acceptable alone. . . ."[21] Just such a quest for the mean is completed in Jane Austen's reconciliation of the over-probable and the improbable, the inevitable and the impossible. Indeed this union informs the whole of *Pride and Prejudice* since it is the basis of the "truth universally acknowledged, that a single man in possession of a good fortune, must be in want of a wife." We would assume any truth universally acknowledged in a Jane Austen novel to be either false or trite; yet, as one critic concedes, "by the end of the novel we are willing to acknowledge that both Bingley and Darcy were 'in want of a wife.'"[22]

The ignorance of this truth occasions the most significant illusion of chance in *Pride and Prejudice* and, perhaps, in all Jane Austen's novels. It is an illusion that appears in the frequent, but repressed, response that the impossibly happy conclusion of the novel is, after all, fortuitous. This response springs from the only partial awareness of a cause neither Providential nor physical, but rather moral. **Pride and Prejudice,** taken as a whole, enforces our recognition that an unmarried man or woman is incomplete. Not only is the urge to mate a physical drive, but it is a moral necessity if one is to become more than the sum of the multiple idiosyncrasies that compose the individual personality. Jane Austen sees the individual "not as a solitary being completed in himself, but only as completed in society."[23] The "complex" individual is not isolated by his freedom, as Mudrick contends,[24] quite the opposite. If anyone, only the "simple," myopic, and fixated individuals are isolated, since for them other people never become real. Darcy increases the scope of his freedom by enlarging his society to include not only Elizabeth, but her family as well. And in Wickham he creates a brother. By his freedom Darcy establishes and vindicates his position in society.

The truth universally acknowledged that *humanitas* cannot be achieved alone is sometimes lost among the welter of socio-economic interpretations of the novel's marriages, but the driving force of **Pride and Prejudice** cannot be explained by reference to the pocketbook. Rather, Jane Austen invites us to examine the possibility that an individual can merit and achieve happiness in a community that becomes valuable by his joining it. "'Without scheming to do wrong, or to make others unhappy, there may be error, and there may be misery. Thoughtlessness, and want of attention to other people's feelings, and want of resolution, will do the business'" (136). The sources of misery are various; but when informed by thoughtfulness, sympathy, and commitment, fulfillment in marriage is not a matter of chance.

Notes

1. Lionel Trilling, "*Mansfield Park,*" in *The Opposing Self* (New York, 1955), p. 207.
2. W. J. Harvey, "The Plot of *Emma,*" *Essays in Criticism,* 17 (1967), 56-57.
3. Lionel Trilling, p. 210.
4. Paul N. Zietlow, "Luck and Fortuitous Circumstance in *Persuasion*: Two Interpretations," *ELH,* 32 (1965), 179.
5. I have deliberately excluded from this discussion what may be called "circumstantial chance," for example, the coincidence that Darcy's aunt is Mr. Collins' patron. This form of chance has little moral significance—at any rate, far less than the chance involved in decision and action.
6. I am not suggesting by this definition that chance should be identified with causelessness, but rather that it is the ignorance of causes or consequences.
7. For a useful summary see Mordecai Marcus, "A Major Thematic Pattern in *Pride and Prejudice,*" *NCF* [*Nineteenth-Century Fiction*], 16 (1961), 274-79.
8. For an analogous discussion of the novel's scale of imperfection, see W. A. Craik's observation that "all of the characters are deficient in some way" in *Jane Austen: The Six Novels* (London, 1965), p. 64.
9. *The English Novel: Form and Function* (1953; rpt., New York, 1967), p. 124.
10. Van Ghent, p. 123.
11. All references to *Pride and Prejudice* are from *The Novels of Jane Austen,* ed. R. W. Chapman, 3rd ed. (London, 1932), Vol. II.
12. *Jane Austen and Her Art* (London, 1939), p. 165.
13. *Jane Austen: Irony as Defense and Discovery* (Princeton, N. J., 1952), p. 104.
14. From another perspective, Collins is not "any husband," since he is heir apparent to the Bennet estate. And it is significant that Charlotte, the spokeswoman of chance, should marry the recipient of a fortuitous sufficiency.
15. Jonathan Swift, *A Tale of a Tub,* eds. A. C. Guthkelch and D. Nichol Smith, 2nd ed. (London, 1958), p. 174.
16. T. S. Eliot, *The Complete Poems and Plays 1909-1950* (New York, 1952), pp. 230-31.
17. For a convincing argument that "irony is more totally verbal in the first half of the novel than in the second," see Joseph Wiesenfarth, *The Errand of Form* (New York, 1954), pp. 63 ff.
18. Wiesenfarth, p. 83.
19. Reuber A. Brower, "Light and Bright and Sparkling: Irony and Fiction in *Pride and Prejudice,*" in *The Fields of Light: An Experiment in Critical Reading* (New York, 1951), pp. 176-77.
20. Mudrick, p. 104. We may note that Elizabeth equates the inefficacy of Darcy with that of Miss Bingley in attempting to separate Jane and Bingley: "'And this . . . is the end of all his friend's anxious circumspection! of all his sister's falsehood and contrivance! the happiest, wisest, and most reasonable end!'" (347).
21. "Jane Austen's *Pride and Prejudice* in the Eighteenth Century Mode," *UTQ* [*University of Toronto Quarterly*], 16 (1947), 360.
22. A. Walton Litz, *Jane Austen: A Study of Her Artistic Development* (London, 1965), p. 107.

23. Richard Simpson, rev. of the *Memoir, North British Review* (April, 1870), rpt. in B. C. Southam, *Jane Austen: The Critical Heritage* (New York, 1968), p. 249.

24. Mudrick, pp. 124-25.

Walter E. Anderson (essay date December 1975)

SOURCE: Anderson, Walter E. "Plot, Character, Speech, and Place in *Pride and Prejudice*." *Nineteenth-Century Fiction* 30, no. 3 (December 1975): 367-82.

[*In the following essay, Anderson provides an in-depth analysis of the novel's plot. Anderson asserts that the novel's "luminosity" derives from "its central love story."*]

> By you, I was properly humbled. I came to you without a doubt of my reception. You shewed me how insufficient were all my pretensions to please a woman worthy of being pleased.
>
> Darcy to Elizabeth Bennet

Jane Austen has been praised for "a most perfect mastery of her weapons, a most faultless and precise adjustment of means to ends."[1] But the house of criticism has many windows, and what a critic conceives those ends to be and how he thinks Austen shapes her materials to achieve them vary according to his assumptions about the fundamental nature and appeal of her novels. The wealth of Austen studies has kept critical interest alive and alert. Yet never before has opinion varied more widely as to the precise form, meaning, and value of each of her novels. This variety reflects the diversity of current critical assumptions regarding the nature of the novel form itself and the basic terms in which it might be discussed most fruitfully.

Recent formal criticism of Austen has confined itself largely to the analysis of theme, rhetoric, and style, relegating plot to a place of least significance. In her influential essay on *Pride and Prejudice,* Dorothy Van Ghent claims that "significant form . . . is a far more complex structure of relationships than those merely of plot. An Austen novel offers a particularly luminous illustration of the function of style in determining the major form."[2] The tendency to think of plot as "merely" plot so thoroughly permeates modern critical thinking that Northrop Frye assumes the plot of *Pride and Prejudice* (one of the finest in our literature) "does not account for any of the merits of the novel."[3] And Reuben Brower's examination of this novel's structure becomes so exclusively a consideration of "the play of ambiguities" and "the displays of ironic wit" that he concludes Austen's plot—the business of getting the Bennet girls married—is "static as drama." Once Darcy changes, the

fun is over for Brower, because in changing he is no longer subject to the author's ironic treatment. The union of the lovers reduces to plot-mechanics, which Austen must go through to wind up her story once the opportunities for "single scenes of a broadly satiric sort" have been exhausted.[4]

The luminosity of *Pride and Prejudice* resides in its central love story. In it we may discover the relatively subordinate formal place of character, thought, and language to plot. The dramatic action itself, organized by Elizabeth Bennet's change in situation and fortune, determines the work's essential form, power, and interest. Getting married, in conjunction with a just distribution of happiness according to merit, is its object. Darcy's disparagement of Elizabeth at the first ball initiates the chief instability, which is further complicated when he persuades Bingley to leave Netherfield and Jane Bennet. The probability of Elizabeth rejecting Darcy's proposal is established by the end of the first volume, and that event climaxes the development midway through the novel. Darcy's letter of explanation to Elizabeth forcefully follows from the preceding action and the situation veers round to its opposite after a series of moral and emotional recognitions moving the lovers toward a more perfect knowledge of each other. At the close of volume two it is announced that to Pemberley Elizabeth would go. When Elizabeth realizes that Darcy is the man she would most like to marry, the denouement is complicated by Lydia's elopement with Wickham. Darcy, led by his love for Elizabeth and a sense of responsibility, acts to make the best of wrongs done. He does good by stealth and blushes to find it fame. The lovers finally come to know each other's disposition toward a second proposal through the interposition of the busy Lady Catherine, whose meddling now works against her efforts to separate them. The novel's conclusion emphasizes the happiness of the united lovers. We feel that the match is, as Elizabeth says of Jane and Bingley's, "the happiest, wisest, most reasonable end" to the story.

Jane Austen's handling of the two proposals in *Pride and Prejudice* especially masterful. Although Elizabeth and Darcy's union is the goal of the plot, Elizabeth harshly rejects his first proposal: "I had not known you a month before I felt that you were the last man in the world whom I could ever be prevailed on to marry."[5] In a traditional romantic comedy, an understanding between lovers may occur at the beginning and start a crisis, with some other external obstacle sustaining their separation:

> The course of true love never did run smooth;
> But either it was different in blood . . .
> Or else misgraffed in respect of years . . .
> Or else it stood upon the choice of friends . . .
> Or, if there were a sympathy in choice,
> War, death, or sickness did lay siege to it . . .

> If then true lovers have been ever crossed,
> It stands as an edict in destiny.[6]

In an Austen novel the course of true love is often disturbed partly by the crosses Shakespeare catalogues, but causes internal to the protagonists generate the principal conflict, a feature which constitutes one of Austen's major contributions to the novel.[7] In *Pride and Prejudice* she brings about the frustration of the lovers with the very act—a proposal—which ought to lead to the happy resolution. Despite this striking employment of means, Austen keeps the main line of action wholly intact: neither our desire nor expectation changes. We still ask how, not whether, the lovers will get together.[8] Though this novel is almost universally admired, perhaps William Dean Howells does most justice to its plot. From the point of Elizabeth's rejection of Darcy, he wrote, "the affair, already so daringly imagined, is one of the most daring in fiction; and less courage, less art, less truth than the author brings to its management would not have availed."[9]

Before Darcy proposes a second time, Austen richly enhances the moral scope of the novel. After his first offer of marriage he realizes how much he must change in order to deserve Elizabeth. Nor is the test made easier with time, for the original causes of his conflict are aggravated, not diminished. The vulgarity of some members of the Bennet family becomes more extreme; Mr. Bennet's irresponsibility and careless indolence increase; and Lydia's deplorable elopement compromises the whole family. In addition, Elizabeth displays intense scorn in rejecting Darcy, and he once described his temper as "resentful" (58). She cannot imagine that he will bring himself to renew his addresses. And she, ironically, thought herself not one of those young ladies "who are so daring as to risk their happiness on the chance of being asked a second time" (107). The fact that Darcy proposes again, despite such additional mortifications as having to deal with the infamous Mrs. Younge, Lydia, and Wickham, indicates his true gentility. His measure may be taken by what he overcomes. Had he not been really amiable and just, he would, as Elizabeth says to him, have hated rather than loved her (380). Possessing the wisdom to become acquainted with himself, Darcy learns to perform those offices by which, in the words of Dr. Johnson, "the concatenation of society is preserved, and mutual tenderness excited and maintained."[10]

Although Elizabeth and Darcy both undergo changes of thought and feeling in the course of the action, his affect the plot more profoundly. Necessary as each of their internal changes is structurally, both are subordinate to the chief expectation and desire—the marriage which resolves the love story. All character relationships, even one so prominent as Jane and Bingley's, have their principal justification as they contribute to the complication and interest of Elizabeth and Darcy's affair, or, more strictly, as they affect Elizabeth's career. Character development and change are prominent elements in each of Austen's novels, but their formal place differs considerably from one to another. After Elizabeth rejects Darcy's proposal, his explanatory letter causes her to recognize her own headstrong errors. Though she gives powerful expression to her mortification (208), we look primarily to the consequences Elizabeth's re-evaluation will have for stabilizing her and Darcy's relationship. This novel as a whole is not, like *Emma,* organized by a change in character. Elizabeth is mistaken about certain facts, but her character is sound, as Darcy makes clear in his confession to her near the close: "What did you say of me, that I did not deserve? For, though your accusations were ill-founded, formed on mistaken premises, my behaviour to you at the time, had merited the severest reproof. It was unpardonable. I cannot think of it without abhorrence" (367). The principal concern of the entire third volume is to demonstrate the new attitudes Darcy has learned to take toward himself and Elizabeth. Darcy's abhorrence of his former conduct, not Elizabeth's of hers, is what we most wish to discover. Austen keeps us in suspense concerning the fullness of Darcy's change by every means at her disposal. Close to Elizabeth's consciousness from the novel's beginning, we must infer as she does, from partial signs, the manner and meaning of Darcy's activities. Their love eventually flourishes, intensified by rational appreciation which takes passion into account.

Although the importance of marriage is never denied, the conditions under which it might be achieved in the interest of lasting happiness are nicely discriminated (22-23). The novel's moral and emotional effects proceed from Elizabeth and Darcy's learning to appreciate each other's merits and their taking a real interest in each other's welfare (266, 366). The question is much larger than "the desire of being well married," as Elizabeth tries to explain to Charlotte Lucas (22). Charlotte believes that "happiness in marriage is entirely a matter of chance" (23), and marries Collins on that plan. But in Austen happiness or suffering depends on moral action, not accident (140). With principles leading her in another direction from Charlotte's, Elizabeth never considers an expedient course. Refusing to be treated as a commodity in the marriage market, taken home by anyone who deems her adequate, she demands proper respect for herself as "a rational creature" (109). Mr. Collins takes a two-week business trip to procure himself a wife because Lady Catherine thought it the proper thing to be done and he always endeavored, he writes, "to demean myself with grateful respect towards her Ladyship" (63). He quickly turns from Jane to propose to Elizabeth, who gives him a direct rebuff for his trouble. Her forthrightness is lost on him, for he takes it as a charming example of "the affectation and coquetry of an elegant female" (109). To Charlotte Lucas, Collins is a "preservative from want" (123), but in accepting him she proves false to sense and casts a shadow over her and Elizabeth's friendship: "no real confidence could ever subsist between them again" (128). For Elizabeth "the meaning of principle and integrity" cannot be changed (135-36).

In the uncompromising assertion of her dignity and in her responsible concern for the fates of her sisters and friends, Elizabeth rises, first in the reader's view and later in Darcy's, above Pemberley and all that is implied by worldly advantage. Darcy's proper pride and his love for Elizabeth move him to conform with the essential qualities latent within himself and so manifest in her. The moral beauty of the novel emerges, by virtue of Elizabeth's character and Darcy's potential, from a series of revelations making apparent the best values in that common enterprise, marriage. The principles Darcy learns are made significant and crucial because Elizabeth, whose fate concerns us most, hazards her chance at marriage in affirming them. Mr. Collins warns her that she might never be asked again should she refuse his offer, yet she repulses a better man than he. Darcy's meeting her standards, nobly and generously, enhances our pleasure, since what they become to each other makes their marriage, and the joy we take in it, very uncommon affairs. The supreme moral value of Austen's novels lies in her convincing demonstration that domestic felicity is founded essentially on principles of goodness and rationality. The things we ought to believe in are few, and plain.

All parts of *Pride and Prejudice* are devoted to the intensification of the romantic plot. As it discloses Elizabeth's and Darcy's resistance to each other, it simultaneously shows the indelible impression each makes upon the other's mind and heart. Sharing in their mutual attraction, the reader takes increased pleasure in each step of the action which draws them closer together after first dividing them. The heroine finally discovers that had she been in love, she could "not have been more wretchedly blind" (208). Austen vivifies the rightness of Darcy and Elizabeth for each other even as she makes them appear most opposed, adding considerably to both the tension and charm of the drama.

Upon Darcy's introduction, nearly everyone doubts his worth. Yet Austen's ambiguous treatment of him prevents the reader from sharing even Elizabeth's initial judgment, though we know little more than she does. Positive signals equally match negative ones, and we feel sentence upon him must be suspended.[11] After a first rude encounter dislocates their acquaintance, Elizabeth and Darcy are quickly brought together at another party. Observing her more carefully, he is attracted by the expression of her dark eyes: "To this discovery succeeded some others equally mortifying. Though he had

detected with a critical eye more than one failure of perfect symmetry in her form, he was forced to acknowledge her figure to be light and pleasing; and in spite of his asserting that her manners were not those of the fashionable world, he was caught by their easy playfulness" (23). Because of his original rudeness, Elizabeth refuses his request to dance, but her pertness has a winning charm: "Her resistance had not injured her with the gentleman, and he was thinking of her with some complacency" (26-27). Despite Miss Bingley's attempts to sabotage Elizabeth's chances while promoting her own, this pattern continues as Elizabeth and Darcy's relationship gradually takes shape. After observing her eyes, figure, and manner, Darcy discovers that Elizabeth also has a mind, but he does not learn to assess her character fully until she rejects his offer to become mistress of Pemberley.

When Elizabeth walks across the wet countryside to visit Jane at Netherfield, Miss Bingley abuses her to Darcy for the dirt on her petticoat, yet he finds that the walk has brightened her eyes (36). Elizabeth's preference for books over cards next impresses him, for he possesses one of England's great private libraries at Pemberley (37-38). But Elizabeth no sooner gains a favorable footing with Darcy—despite any design on her part—than Mrs. Bennet, with Lydia and Mary in tow, visits Netherfield. They arrive as if to verify Darcy's observation that, good as Elizabeth and Jane are, those closest to them might "very materially lessen their chance of marrying men of any consideration in the world" (37). For every foot Elizabeth advances, she is set back nine inches; but through the cloud of Mrs. Bennet's vulgarity and stupidity, Elizabeth shines, and Darcy smiles his approval (45). Elizabeth is more acutely aware of her mother's vulgarity than even Darcy could be, yet she never disparages her before others or attempts to justify herself at her family's expense.[12]

Because Darcy is more attracted to Elizabeth than he could wish (59) and because she is more interested in him than she can admit, we expect to see them come to a better understanding. Precisely because we follow the narrative mainly with a sense of Elizabeth's and Darcy's changing awareness of each other, we can say that the plot complicating their romance and leading to their union defines our principal interest in the novel. In composing a plot, the novelist's earliest decisions about the action as a whole exert pressure on the creation and treatment of incident, character, thought, and language.[13] The delineation of Elizabeth's character begins in the first chapter, before her appearance. She has, her father says, "something more of quickness than her sisters" (5). With her wit and epigrammatic style, she seems equal to the narrator and is superior to all her female companions. Darcy similarly dominates the men. He is intelligent and, like Elizabeth, a great reader. After listening to Mr. Collins's letter—that delightful revelation of "servility and self-importance" which announces his intention of visiting the Bennets at Longbourn—Elizabeth says to her father, "He must be an oddity. . . . There is something very pompous in his stile. . . . Can he be a sensible man, sir?" Mary Bennet holds another opinion: "In point of composition . . . his letter does not seem defective. The idea of the olive branch perhaps is not wholly new, yet I think it is well expressed" (64). Serious thought and proper expression obviously carry a premium value in the world of *Pride and Prejudice,* but their significance is not so solemnly appraised as to exclude ease and playfulness. Elizabeth's response is not only plain and just, it is funny. Mary's pedantically dry approval ironically confirms Elizabeth's judgment, and her father concurs. In his general search for foolishness, however, Mr. Bennet does not care sufficiently about the moral and social implications of Collins's defects. He sees them simply as further provision for his fun. Yet the last thing Elizabeth wishes or needs is for Darcy to meet another family fool.

Character again functions as a touchstone for style in the discussion between Elizabeth, Mary, and Charlotte Lucas on Darcy's rudeness at the first ball. Elizabeth's combination of acuity and interested tolerance counterpoints Mary's prosy observation, telling more on the subject of pride than a treatise by Mary could. After Charlotte defends Darcy's "right to be proud," being the child of fortune that he is, Elizabeth humorously replies, "That is very true . . . and I could easily forgive *his* pride, if he had not mortified *mine*" (20). We easily assent to Elizabeth's wit and worth. The peculiar power of the plot depends upon our valuing her moral character in action vis-à-vis Darcy, for we come to wish that she gain the happiness she deserves and ultimately enjoys.

Values of ease and unaffectedness also relate to the characters' general style or deportment. Bingley, comparatively deficient in wit and intelligence (but not so deficient as to make him an inappropriate match for Jane Bennet), excels in ease. Darcy is reserved in manner—haughty, fastidious, uninviting. Elizabeth, never so serious as to lose her sense of humor, is the first to relate Darcy's depreciation of her at the ball (12). With unaffectedness we may include the values of sincerity and straightforwardness, honesty in personal relations. The use of arts and design, so evident in the manner of Miss Bingley and Mrs. Bennet, are condemned outright by Darcy: "There is meanness in *all* the arts which ladies sometimes condescend to employ for captivation. Whatever bears affinity to cunning is despicable" (40). Although he rightly sees that Miss Bingley, by practicing these arts, concedes much that is due her dignity, he mistakenly includes Jane Bennet in his suspicion. As a consequence, he temporarily obstructs the course of her and Bingley's true love by persuading his friend to leave the neighborhood. But Darcy's comment on female cunning most significantly qualifies the plot morally and dramatically as it touches his relationship with Elizabeth. She is as open as Miss Bingley is deceitful; and since we know that Darcy has the moral intelligence to mark the difference, we feel assured that he must move in Elizabeth's direction at last. She is the only one capable of meeting his high standards and adorning Pemberley. Both, however, have standards that must be met, and Darcy has yet to reckon with those which will affect him. Darcy, who first appeared so proud as to be "above being pleased" (10), ends by striving mightily "to please a woman worthy of being pleased" (369).

Elizabeth's sensitivity to Darcy matches his awareness of her. "I see what he is about," she says to Charlotte. "He has a very satirical eye, and if I do not begin by being impertinent myself, I shall soon grow afraid of him" (24). Possessing a proper notion of her true worth, Elizabeth feels compelled to oppose the imagined censure of Darcy's penetrating eyes. She is guilty of no design, yet her erring impertinence bewitches the hero's heart more than could any adultery of art. Austen imposes design on her heroine's artless grace. Darcy's initial rudeness was the very act to provoke such an intelligent, attractive, spirited girl, and for a time she entertains "no very cordial feelings towards him" (12). But having seen the comedy in the episode, she is not overly resentful. Nevertheless, she henceforth takes measures to resist him and, if possible, to vindicate herself against even his fastidiousness. When she encounters Darcy thereafter, we expect her to challenge him in order to forestall intimidation. Such a development culminates in chapter 10 with an exchange marked by Darcy's becoming gradually so impressed with Elizabeth that he ends by treating her almost as an equal, a reversal putting him in fear of his own safety: "He began to feel the danger of paying Elizabeth too much attention" (58).

After Elizabeth joins the party at Netherfield, on the evening of the second day of Jane's illness she meets the company in conversation on subjects which range from carelessness in letter writing to rash leave-taking, a topic which foreshadows Bingley's sudden departure for London. Intelligent and reflective as they are, both Elizabeth and Darcy value good conversation; each of them expects sometimes "to say something that will amaze the whole room, and be handed down to posterity with all the eclat of a proverb" (91). We are not surprised to learn that Darcy, as Bingley says, "does *not* write with ease. He studies too much for words of four syllables" (48). We expect his speech to be formal in style, less amiable in tone than Bingley's, less spontaneous and witty than Elizabeth's. And so it proves to be:

"Nothing is more deceitful," said Darcy, "than the appearance of humility. It is often only carelessness of opinion, and sometimes an indirect boast."

"And which of the two do you call *my* little recent piece of modesty?" [Bingley asks.]

"The indirect boast;—for you are really proud of your defects in writing, because you consider them as proceeding from a rapidity of thought and carelessness of execution, which if not estimable, you think at least highly interesting. The power of doing any thing with quickness is always much prized by the possessor, and often without any attention to the imperfection of the performance. When you told Mrs. Bennet this morning that if you ever resolved on quitting Netherfield you should be gone in five minutes, you meant it to be a sort of panegyric, of compliment to yourself—and yet what is there so very laudable in a precipitance which must leave very necessary business undone, and can be of no real advantage to yourself or any one else?"

(48-49)

Austen successfully mastered here the difficult problem of conveying Darcy's intelligence and stiff reserve without making him appear ridiculous. His speech has the tone and weight of Dr. Johnson: "all censure of a man's self is oblique praise. It is in order to shew how much he can spare. It has all the invidiousness of self-praise, and all the reproach of falsehood."[14] Darcy critically ruminates, to Bingley's chagrin, on "all the foolish things that were said in the morning" (49). He turns a particular observation into a *sententia* ("The power of doing any thing," etc.). When he shifts from the general to the personal, Elizabeth moves to defend Bingley, who modestly withdraws, indicating that the wit of the main actors is beyond him. Only Darcy and Elizabeth are a fit match for each other.

It is precisely Darcy's reflectiveness, so apparent in his speech, which crucially affects the plot, for later he carefully considers the drawbacks of connecting himself with Elizabeth's family, given, especially, his just disapproval of her parents. Yet he considers with equal care the merits of Elizabeth and, still later, the justice of her charges against him. As might have been predicted on the basis of previously stipulated character traits, the style of his sentences reflects his peculiar turn of mind in its balance, parallelism, and antithesis of phrase, clause, and idea. In addition there is the philosophical diction which so alarms Bingley: "panegyric," "laudable," "precipitance," "celerity," "appertain," "subsisting."[15]

Elizabeth shows herself more amiable, and perhaps more discriminating, than Darcy as she answers him on the general subject of carelessness and rashness:

You appear to me, Mr. Darcy, to allow nothing for the influence of friendship and affection. A regard for the requester would often make one readily yield to a re-

quest, without waiting for arguments to reason one into it. I am not particularly speaking of such a case as you have supposed about Mr. Bingley. We may as well wait, perhaps, till the circumstance occurs, before we discuss the discretion of his behaviour thereupon. But in general and ordinary cases between friend and friend, where one of them is desired by the other to change a resolution of no very great moment, should you think ill of that person for complying with the desire, without waiting to be argued into it?

(50)

Elizabeth and Darcy mutually exercise social restraint by ending their remarks in the civilized form of a question rather than an assertion, but at the same time the implicit challenge is clear. By reverting to general considerations touching on friendship and affection, Elizabeth graciously removes the onus from Bingley and takes up the gauntlet herself.

Elizabeth is on her mettle, as her sensitivity to style and situation proves. In her turn she shows, however, a spontaneity which results at first in some clumsiness. Unlike Darcy, she has not been in quiet meditation since morning and consequently forms her argument extemporaneously. Her speech gives the impression of thought in motion, the quick reaction of a clever mind. She states the same general argument twice: "A regard for the requester would often make one readily yield to a request, without waiting for arguments to reason one into it"; and, "but in general and ordinary cases between friend and friend, where one of them is desired by the other to change a resolution of no very great moment, should you think ill of that person for complying with the desire, without waiting to be argued into it?" Her initial attempt roughly defines the problem; the second is more formal. The redundancy of "to a request" after "requester" may be considered natural to a first articulation. And the sentence ends with a slightly awkward phrase: "without waiting for arguments to reason one into it," which she quickly reconstructs: "without waiting to be argued into it." "For arguments to reason" is telescoped into "to be argued"; and the whole phrase "without waiting. . . ." now parallels the preceding one, "for complying. . . ." In the second version she also makes an important qualification: "of no very great moment." Later, of course, an issue of moment does arise when Bingley suddenly departs and at Darcy's prompting estranges himself from Jane. Hypothesis transforms into fictional reality.

The contrasting styles within Elizabeth's speech suggest some emotional tumult, caused by her dueling with Darcy and her wish to impress him. The qualification I mention above supports the idea of her desire to please, as well as of her mind's reach and independence. In reexpressing her thought, especially in the last sentence, she tends to imitate his style, a compliment he returns by desiring to carry on the debate after first refining its terms (50). Words and tone suggest he is being called to attention by Elizabeth, but just then Bingley interferes. "'I see your design, Bingley,' said his friend.—'You dislike an argument, and want to silence this'" (51). By then, however, the episode has well served its purposes.

In challenging Darcy, Elizabeth asserts what Dr. Johnson calls a defensive pride, which makes her appear progressively more interesting to Darcy's "satirical eye." Immediately after their discussion, Elizabeth retires to another part of the room, and those "eyes were fixed on her" admiringly (51). She, however, sees them only as critical and cynical, and archly tells him to his face, "despise me if you dare." By now, he can only answer, "Indeed I do not dare" (52).

The stylistic choices of this debate are called for by schemes of plot and characterization shaped prior to the episode itself, and are justified in light of them. The general pleasure we take in the work increases noticeably when style suits the characters and action, but such elements provide nuance not principal form. In the passages just analyzed, Elizabeth's and Darcy's language expresses their different habits of mind—he is "too little yielding," she is lively and adaptable—as well as their personal sensitivity to each other. We infer the intensity of Elizabeth's and Darcy's feelings for one another when they are still a long way from recognizing their own dispositions. More importantly, we look ahead to possible future developments affecting our expectations and desires. Clearly infatuated by Elizabeth, Darcy just may propose; but would she accept him? In consequence of the first proposal and Darcy's letter, we are not surprised to see Elizabeth quickly adapt to new impressions and new feelings about him. Thereafter Darcy's enigmatic actions seem to hold their fates in suspension as we wait to see his stiffness and reserve dissolve under the influence of tender love.

Sir Walter Scott said of Elizabeth that, "the lady . . . refuses the hand which he [Darcy] ungraciously offers, and does not perceive that she had done a foolish thing until she accidentally visits a very handsome seat and ground belonging to her admirer."[16] Though the Darcy that Elizabeth rejects differs from the one she accepts, Scott's notion compels us to bring certain matters into clear view. Elizabeth's reversal in thought and feeling serves as probable cause in moving her quickly toward a recognition of her love for Darcy. As Mary Lascelles observes, "there is no time to lose; she must have revised her whole impression of him before her visit to Pemberley."[17] The visit provides a confirming basis, not the cause, for the alteration in Elizabeth's opinion. She has grown into a proper frame of mind to appreciate Darcy's change when he reveals it; and as he does so, her feelings toward him give way to gratitude, "not merely for having once loved her, but for loving her

still well enough, to forgive. . . ." (265). Position and property make Darcy desirable, but by the end of the novel more important characteristics qualify him as a guarantor of Elizabeth's happiness. Because she has proven herself superior to Pemberley before seeing it, she is allowed upon viewing it for the first time to feel that "to be mistress of Pemberley might be something!" (245). After the scene in which she first rejects Darcy, we know almost all we need to know of Elizabeth's values. In subsequent action he moves up to her; his change and her recognition of all it implies open the way to their happy union.

As Pemberley weaves itself into the moral of the love story, our discrimination of the quality of happiness accruing to the lovers improves. Pemberley is more than simply the property of ten thousand per year that so animates the mind of Mrs. Bennet. It possesses a character and a style of its own, representing freedom without excess, restraint without austerity, and generosity without ostentation. All the best characters in *Pride and Prejudice* are endowed with these qualities, and the worst, who lack them, are incapable of realizing much happiness. As its new mistress, Elizabeth brings to Pemberley humor and moral intelligence united with spirit and virtue. Pemberley is at once more than Darcy and less. The sense in which it is more is conveyed in an early reference. Darcy does not create the library at Pemberley, but maintains and adds to what "has been the work of many generations" (38). Unlike Bingley, who has yet to purchase an estate and found a family, Darcy sustains values long established. Pemberley is an "ancient pile." Its tradition, as Bingley observes, can neither be purchased nor easily imitated.

> Now, Penshurst, they that will proportion thee
> With other edifices, when they see
> Those proud, ambitious heaps, and nothing else,
> May say, their lords have built, but thy lord dwells.[18]

On her excursion to Pemberley with the Gardiners, Elizabeth ascends for half a mile through beautiful woods; the woods cease and her eyes light on the House, "a large, handsome, stone building, standing well on rising ground." Nothing is falsely adorned, nothing betrays an awkward taste. Entering, Elizabeth delightedly finds more to admire. The furnishings are "neither gaudy nor uselessly fine"; they show "less of splendor, and more real elegance" than the furniture of Rosings, Lady Catherine's home (245-46).

> Something there is more needful than Expence,
> And something previous ev'n to Taste—'tis Sense.
> 'Tis Use alone that sanctifies Expence,
> And Splendor borrows all her rays from Sense.[19]

Inside Pemberley House, Elizabeth first confronts miniatures of Wickham and Darcy hanging in what had been his father's "favourite room." Darcy's allowing a picture of Wickham to hang in his halls reveals a filial piety expressing duty over passion.[20] Nothing is lost on Elizabeth, who with increasing interest recomposes Darcy in her thoughts. Each observation raises as it modifies her emotions. She returns more than once to the full portrait of Darcy in the main gallery: perplexed but pleased she discovers "such a smile over the face, as she remembered to have sometimes seen, when he looked at her." She feels "a more gentle sensation towards the original, than she had ever felt in the height of their acquaintance" (250). Formerly she interpreted that look as supercilious disdain. Now she is sure of nothing except the truth of Darcy's warning upon their first acquaintance that any attempt to sketch his character might prove premature. As she leaves Pemberley, Elizabeth encounters the master himself not twenty paces away.

Notes

1. Reginald Farrer, "Jane Austen," *The Quarterly Review,* 228 (July 1917), 6. Farrer's outstanding essay on Austen was written in celebration of "the hundredth year of her immortality" (p. 1). He invokes George Henry Lewes's early tribute: "no novelist has approached her in what we may style the 'economy of art,' by which is meant the easy adaptation of means to ends, with no aid from extraneous or superfluous elements." "The Novels of Jane Austen," *Blackwood's Magazine* (1859); rpt. in *Literary Criticism of George Henry Lewes,* ed. Alice R. Kaminsky (Lincoln: Univ. of Nebraska Press, 1964), p. 91.

2. *The English Novel: Form and Function* (1953; rpt. New York: Harper Brothers, 1961), p. 104.

3. *Fables of Identity: Studies in Poetic Mythology* (New York: Harcourt, Brace and World, 1963), p. 34.

4. "Light and Bright and Sparkling: Irony and Fiction in *Pride and Prejudice*," in *The Fields of Light: An Experiment in Critical Reading* (New York: Oxford Univ. Press, 1951), pp. 164, 167, 180.

5. *Pride and Prejudice,* p. 193. Page references in the text are to Vol. II of *The Novels of Jane Austen,* ed. R. W. Chapman, 3rd ed. (London: Oxford Univ. Press, 1932).

6. *A Midsummer Night's Dream,* I.i.134-35, 137, 139, 141-42, 150-51.

7. See Sheldon Sacks, "Golden Birds and Dying Generations," *Comparative Literature Studies,* 6 (Sept. 1969), 285.

8. Cf. Sheldon Sacks, *Fiction and the Shape of Belief* (Berkeley: Univ. of California Press, 1964), p. 23.

9. "Jane Austen's Elizabeth Bennet," *Heroines of Fiction* (1901); rpt. in Pride and Prejudice: *Text, Backgrounds, Criticism,* ed. Bradford A. Booth (New York: Harbrace, 1963), p. 185.

10. *The Rambler,* No. 24, 9 June 1750.

11. Cf. Brower, p. 175.

12. Jane Austen evidently had Fanny Burney's *Evelina* (1778) much in mind while composing *Pride and Prejudice* (1813). Burney continually strives to make Evelina shine by having her depreciate her relatives, even for their poverty. Both author and heroine are betrayed as snobs.

13. For an elaboration of this principle of formal control and the hierarchy implied see R. S. Crane, "The Concept of Plot and the Plot of *Tom Jones,*" in *Critics and Criticism,* ed. R. S. Crane (Chicago: Univ. of Chicago Press, 1952), pp. 617-18, fn. 7.

14. *Boswell's Life of Johnson* (1791) (London: Oxford Univ. Press, 1953), p. 972 (28 April 1778).

15. The last three words are from speeches just following the one quoted, pp. 49, 50. Cf. W. K. Wimsatt, Jr., *The Prose Style of Samuel Johnson* (New Haven: Yale Univ. Press, 1963), pp. 59-61.

16. "*Emma,*" *Quarterly Review* (1815); rpt. in *Discussions of Jane Austen,* ed. William Heath (Boston: Heath, 1961), p. 8.

17. *Jane Austen and Her Art* (London: Oxford Univ. Press, 1939), p. 162.

18. Ben Jonson, "To Penshurst" (1616), ll. 99-102.

19. Alexander Pope, "Epistle IV: To Richard Boyle, Earl of Burlington" (1731), ll. 41-42, 179-80.

20. The reader may recall that Mr. Collins, whose acts throughout are the comic and moral converse of Darcy's, would not "be on good terms with any one, with whom it had always pleased [his father] to be at variance" (p. 62). Prior to Darcy's declaring that he wishes to marry Elizabeth in spite of her connections (p. 189), we have Collins assuring her that he will not mention her inadequate dowry after their marriage (p. 106). The presumptuous absurdity in the latter case serves to keep us in charity with Darcy when he appears most culpable. Similarly, Lady Catherine's being made to carry arrogance and class conceit to an extremity mitigates our reprehension of Darcy when he appears most to share her traits.

James Sherry (essay date autumn 1979)

SOURCE: Sherry, James. "*Pride and Prejudice*: The Limits of Society." *SEL: Studies in English Literature, 1500-1900* 19, no. 4 (autumn 1979): 609-22.

[*In the following essay, Sherry investigates the novel's various thematic oppositions. Sherry describes the evolving relationship between Elizabeth and Darcy, with its movement from contentiousness to conciliation, as "dialectical" in nature.*]

I think it is probably fair to say that for most people both the interest and the meaning of **Pride and Prejudice** reside in the splendid opposition and gradual reconciliation of Darcy and Elizabeth. There may be differences in the interpretation of individual episodes, or in the estimation of where or with whom the values of the novel finally lie; but there seems to be general agreement that the essential impulse of the novel is dialectical, and hence that both Darcy and Elizabeth must undergo some changes of heart and of opinion before the novel can reach its beautifully poised and profound resolution in their marriage.

But even beyond this initial agreement about the dialectical thrust of the novel, there has been a remarkable consensus about the terms which ought to be used to describe its antitheses. Again and again in discussions of **Pride and Prejudice** we come upon some variation of the terms "individual" and "society." In Dorothy Van Ghent's essay in *The English Novel: Form and Function* (1953), for instance, **Pride and Prejudice** is described as illuminating "the difficult and delicate reconciliation of the sensitively developed individual with the terms of his social existence."[1] In A. Walton Litz's *Jane Austen: A Study of Her Artistic Development* (1965), Darcy and Elizabeth are said to "dramatize the persistent conflict between social restraint and the individual will, between tradition and self-expression."[2] And in *The Improvement of the Estate* (1971) written almost twenty years after Dorothy Van Ghent's essay, we find Alistair Duckworth still working within what is clearly the same framework of description. "Only when Elizabeth recognizes that individualism must find its social limits," he says, "and Darcy concedes that tradition without individual energy is empty form, can [**Pride and Prejudice**] reach its eminently satisfactory conclusion."[3]

In the face of such a long-standing consensus of interpretation it may seem merely ingenious at this point in time to question either the essential validity or the usefulness of this description of the novel. But in at least two important respects it seems open to objection. In all the interpretations to which I have referred, the word "society" and its derivatives suggest a sociological abstraction—an institution, a set of laws, or a tradition (to use a word common to two of them). For Jane Austen, on the other hand, the word has quite a different meaning.

Here, for instance, in a passage from **Pride and Prejudice,** is how Elizabeth uses the word in a conversation with Lady Catherine.[4]

> But really, Ma'am, I think it would be very hard upon younger sisters, that they should not have their share of

society and amusement because the elder may not have the means or inclination to marry early.

(165)

And here is how one of those younger sisters uses it in the same novel while providing her own appropriate remark on the subject.

> "While I can have my mornings to myself," said [Mary], "it is enough.—I think it no sacrifice to join occasionally in evening engagements. Society has claims on us all; and I profess myself one of those who consider intervals of recreation and amusement as desirable for every body."

(87)

And finally, here is how the narrator of **Emma** uses the adjectival form of the word in her description of the background and character of Mr. Weston.

> He had received a good education, but on succeeding early in life to a small independence . . . had satisfied an active, cheerful mind and social temper by entering into the militia of his county, then embodied.

(**E** [*Emma*]: 15)

"Society" in these examples has nothing to do with conventions, laws, or traditions; perhaps its closest synonyms are "company" or "companionship." Similarly, "social" does not mean "of or pertaining to the institutions of society" but "gregarious" or, as we would now say it, "sociable." Far from being an abstraction, then, "society" always suggests for Jane Austen the presence of other individuals with whom it is either a duty or a pleasure to mix.

Of course it may be objected that criticism need not be limited to the vocabulary of its subjects. After all, Jane Austen never uses the word "irony," and yet that term has proven to be one of the most useful words for describing the quality of her vision. Indeed, it is not part of my intention to bar any word from criticism that serves its function in illuminating a text. But in this case, the "sociological" definition of "society" has had the effect of disinfecting Jane Austen's novels a little too thoroughly, of removing from them the complex sense of lived social life.

In the Austen criticism of the 40s (I am thinking now of D. W. Harding's classic "Regulated Hatred: An Aspect of the Work of Jane Austen"[5]), this strong and sometimes sardonic sense of "other people" was, of course, much emphasized—in fact, too much so, for it led to an essentially false image of Jane Austen as a silent rebel with an unspoken hatred of the people around her. But though such criticism certainly overstated its case, it had at least the salutary effect of reminding us that Jane Austen wrote as a private individual in a milieu in which publicity—Mrs. Bennet's "visiting and news"

(5)—was a matter of course. To downplay or ignore this sense of social life, of "other people," is to lose something important in any of Jane Austen's novels. But it is particularly regrettable in the case of *Pride and Prejudice,* where the aura of a small, enclosed community of talking, visiting, and company is so strong.

It is not simply that an important historical dimension to the novel is lost, however. For the abstraction of the word "society" has also led, I think, to a fundamental misconception of Jane Austen's dialectic. As we can see most explicitly in the quotation from Alistair Duckworth, there has been a tendency in such discussions of the "individual" and "society" to allegorize Elizabeth and Darcy into representatives of those respective terms. Elizabeth, then, reveals the energy, the impulsiveness, the respect for personal merit which characterizes individualism, while Darcy, with his sense of propriety and his noble family connections, stands for "society" or the established social codes.

But if society for Jane Austen is not so much opposed to individuals as composed of them, we may be justified in turning such well-established associations on their heads. After all, it is Elizabeth whose values are primarily gregarious and social and who might fittingly stand for what Jane Austen conceives of as society, while it is Darcy whose reserve, privacy, and discretion are, in fact, protective of the individual.

Putting these terms aside, however, what is important is that the issues of *Pride and Prejudice* are much less abstract and much more localized than sometimes stated. And they have to do with nothing less than the conditions of personal existence in the small town world of three or four country families which Jane Austen delighted to describe. For in such a world social participation could be a duty, a delight, or a danger. In a novel like *Emma,* for instance, it is clear that society does have claims, not simply, as Emma learns, because the repetition of "old news, and heavy jokes" (**E**: 219) may be all that is left of enjoyment to people like Miss Bates and her mother, but because the quality of that society depends upon the willingness of those with superior moral and intellectual qualifications (like Emma and Darcy) to contribute to its tone and to be responsible for its sanity and generosity.

But just as clearly, there are limits to society and sociability which are inherent in the very confinement of small-town living. These limits are explored in such characters as Sir John Middleton in *Sense and Sensibility,* Mr. Weston and Miss Bates in *Emma* and, in very specific ways, in Bingley and Jane Bennet in *Pride and Prejudice.* But it is finally in *Pride and Prejudice* as a whole that we get our clearest look at what might be called the dialectic of social participation in Jane Aus-

ten's novels. For it is only there that she fully explored the necessary tension between the impulse, indeed the responsibility, to be open, engaged and responsive members of a community, and the need for reserve, distance, and privacy lest social intercourse become vulgarized and degraded by familiarity.

I

At the beginning of *Pride and Prejudice,* in fact even before we have proceeded twenty pages, our disposition towards much that follows is formed by an initial, and seemingly simple, antithesis. At the Meryton ball, the first public event of the novel, we meet two men between whom there is "a great opposition of character" (16). Charles Bingley is everything a sociable gentleman should be—lively, open, unreserved, with a pleasant countenance and an agreeable manner. He mixes well with the rest of the company, dances every dance, and soon finds himself liking, and liked by, nearly everyone in the room. (10, 16).

"What a contrast between him and his friend"! (11). Mr. Darcy, on the other hand, is almost completely antisocial. Haughty and reserved, he declines being introduced to anyone, talks only to members of his own small party, and dances only twice. He feels not the slightest interest in any other people at the assembly, and in return is heartily disliked for it. (11, 16).

Unlike her cousin, Egerton Brydges, whom she criticized for his sloppy novelistic methods, Jane Austen never introduces characters merely to be described.[6] Nor does she ever describe a character simply because he figures in the action of the novel. Her characterizations always serve thematic as well as mimetic purposes. The extended contrast between Darcy and Bingley is no exception. For the opposition between openness, candour, and sociability on the one hand, and reserve, fastidiousness, and exclusiveness on the other is not allowed to end here. Indeed, once we have expanded our notion of Darcy's social distance to include its apparent source in his snobbish regard for wealth and great connections, we can trace the same opposition at work in the "grouping" of some of the other characters.

At almost the same time that we encounter the differences between Darcy and Bingley, we are also introduced to the characters and dispositions of Bingley's sisters. Elizabeth immediately suspects that they do not possess the same open temper and sociable good nature as their brother—"their behaviour at the assembly had not been calculated to please in general"—and the narrator soon leaves us no doubt about it. The sisters, we are told, are "proud and conceited," and though not incapable of being agreeable when they wished to please, have become so enamoured of their own beauty, wealth, and rank (the latter almost entirely mythical, of course) that they now believe themselves fully "entitled to think well of themselves, and meanly of others" (15).

If this description were not in itself sufficient to suggest the association of Bingley's sisters with Darcy's own apparent brand of pride and conceit,[7] we are certainly invited to make the connection by subsequent events. For once Elizabeth has taken the measure of Bingley's sisters' "superciliousness" (21), she finds it easy to believe them as "charmingly group'd" (53) with Darcy in their opinions as they are in their walks. In fact, much of the animosity we feel towards Darcy in the first part of the novel is created by a form of guilt by association. We are *shown* the snobbishness, the shallowness, the ill-nature of the Bingley sisters; we *extrapolate* Darcy's few remarks or actions, as Jane Austen quite intends that we should, to resemble those of the people who are so much his companions.[8]

But while we are thus building up a sense of Darcy and the two Bingley sisters as a group united by a common pride and selfishness, it is hard to resist seeing Bingley and the two Bennet sisters as an antithetical group characterized by a generous sociability. At least part of this sense of polarization is the result of our age-old interest in comic resolution. Jane and Bingley are clearly established as lovers, and we can see quite as well as Elizabeth that they are meant for one another. Darcy and Bingley's sisters, on the other hand, are cast in the role of the "blocking society," holding out for wealth and connections against true love. But though plot certainly reinforces our sense of the polarity of the two groups, the real contrasts and differences are established by the remarks and reactions of Elizabeth.

A noble tradition in Jane Austen criticism has cast Elizabeth in the role of ironic commentator and has even suggested that her irony is subversive of society.[9] But this is again to misunderstand the nature of society in the novel. For while Elizabeth is certainly fond of laughing at the follies and inconsistencies of her fellows, her wit is almost completely social in its bias. Far from being either detached from or subversive of society, her irony normally claims as its victims precisely those selfish, vain, or foolish people (like Miss Bingley, Darcy, Collins or Lady Catherine) who either cannot or will not contribute to making society as lively, open, and full of community as a good conversation. The people whom she instinctively prefers, men like Bingley, Wickham, and Colonel Fitzwilliam, are all open, agreeable, sociable people, with "a happy readiness of conversation" (72). And even Elizabeth's occasional bitternesses arise not from any real detachment from society, but from too great a dependence upon its merely superficial aspects, from a failure not dissimilar to her father's to distinguish between a pleasing face or manner and something more substantial. With Elizabeth as

the basis of our point of view, then, our sense of the contrast between the pride and exclusiveness of some of the characters and the generosity and sociability of others is strengthened by the force of her own social convictions.

II

Throughout much of the first half of *Pride and Prejudice* we have little reason to doubt the justice of these convictions or the polarization of character and judgment to which they lead. For despite our superior view of events (particularly where Darcy's interest in Elizabeth is concerned), so much of the action seems to support Elizabeth's "reading" of the other characters that we scarcely notice the inconsistencies and ambiguities that do exist. Consider the arrival of Wickham, for instance. Coming as he does almost immediately after the introduction of Mr. Collins, he seems to confirm the fact that in this novel only characters without inflated notions of wealth and rank can be rational, unprejudiced, and attractive. Like Bingley, he is open, unreserved, agreeable, and with such easy and engaging manners that he seems as clearly a member of that sociable "good" group of characters as Mr. Collins, with his eternal prating about Lady Catherine, seems to belong with the Darcys and Miss Bingleys. Indeed, Wickham's subsequent revelations make both associations even more appropriate. For not only does he admit to a dislike for Darcy (and at this point a dislike for Darcy is an almost certain passport to Elizabeth's and the reader's affections), but he also reveals the hitherto unknown link between Darcy and Collins through Collins's characteristically proud and conceited patroness.

But if Wickham's story appears to confirm the opposition between sociable and unsociable characters, it also deepens our sense of the antagonism. Up till now we have been concerned with what has seemed to be a question of manners, of courtesy, though not without larger implications. Wickham's story adds a new dimension to the action, for now we get our first glimpse of the power of wealth and rank, a power capable of ruining a young man for life. For if Wickham's story is true, his chances for economic security have been destroyed almost solely as a result of Darcy's dislike for his warmth of temper, and his envy of Wickham's more intimate relationship with Darcy's father. Moreover, it is an injustice which Wickham's own comparative poverty prevents him from redressing.

Nor is this the only instance in which lives are capriciously altered and fates menaced or determined by the power concentrated in the hands of a privileged few. Bingley's sudden disappearance and Jane's resulting suffering, Charlotte Lucas's miserable capitulation, Colonel Fitzwilliam's pathetic admission that younger sons cannot marry where they will—all of these point to the difficulty, if not the impossibility, of maintaining values like simple openness, candour, and kindness in a world dominated by their opposites. Perhaps the most striking and symptomatic example of this deepening of tone, this antagonism of viewpoints, is the confrontation between Elizabeth and Collins at the time of his proposal. For though the scene begins light-heartedly enough with the incomparable foolishness of Collins's pretended passion, it ends with the menace of poverty and loneliness for those, like Elizabeth, without money and rank. And whatever else one might wish to say about it, the threat cannot be ignored.

At Rosings, of course, we return briefly to the broader comic contrast of pride and sociability in the characters of Lady Catherine and Colonel Fitzwilliam. The "superlatively stupid" (166) conversation at dinner and cards, in fact, seems to sum up once and for all the kind of stifling parody of society to which wealth and rank seem to lead. But the hints inadvertently dropped by Colonel Fitzwilliam of Darcy's "triumph" in detaching Bingley from Jane bring us back once again to the level of antagonism. Responsible for Jane's suffering, Wickham's poverty, Bingley's inconsiderateness and, we almost feel, for Colonel Fitzwilliam's hesitation, Darcy seems now to symbolize all that inhibits real happiness and sociability. His arrogance, his conceit, his disdain for the feelings of others, these have become more than personal qualities. They have come to stand for a whole way of life. And thus, Darcy's rejection by Elizabeth at the moment when he seems to have felt an impulse stronger than pride is an irony which we as readers have been fully prepared to appreciate.

III

It is a short-lived irony, however. For with the arrival of Darcy's letter, both Elizabeth and (to a lesser extent) the reader are shown to be partly wrong. The neat polarization of characters into groups and the unambiguous judgments of events are revealed to be too simple—at least where Darcy is concerned. It is appropriate, of course, that our common disillusionment should come by way of a letter, a simple narrative. For it has been largely the result of personality, of the dramatic immediacy of the events in the first part of the narrative that we have been deceived. Like Elizabeth, we have trusted ourselves too implicitly to qualities like liveliness, openness, and apparent good nature, without really questioning their ultimate value. Darcy's letter is thus the herald of a new sobriety and detachment which can be felt even in the mode of the novel itself as we move away from dramatic presentation towards the less exciting but more mediated account of events which characterizes the last half of *Pride and Prejudice,* particularly Lydia's elopement which we do not "see" at all.

This new sense of "distance" or detachment in the novel is, of course, entirely in keeping with the devaluation of sociability which now takes place. For if Elizabeth learns to distinguish between personal agreeableness and the more important quality of moral integrity, she also learns how little one can be taken as the index of the other. Furthermore, she now realizes the part played by her own desire to be thought agreeable in her mistaken judgments of Darcy and Wickham. "Pleased with the preference of one, and offended by the neglect of the other . . . [she had] courted prepossession and ignorance" (208).

But to say that Elizabeth now sees the danger of judging people solely on the basis of qualities such as liveliness, candour, or conversability is to recognize only one part of a rather complex shift of perspective. For in admitting that she has misjudged Darcy, Elizabeth is now faced with the problem of understanding him. It is a problem she shares with the reader. With Darcy's departure from Rosings, our chance of observing him first hand is gone for another fifty pages. It is upon Darcy's letter, then, and the light it throws upon his earlier actions that we must rely in beginning to reassess his character. And if it is to be a positive revaluation, that letter must enable us to see the past action of the novel in quite a different way. If it does not allow us to excuse the *extent* of Darcy's pride, it must at least make it possible for us to accept Darcy's own estimate of his character—that his faults are rather of temper than understanding (58).

In fact, this is exactly what the letter does. By explaining that his objections to Elizabeth's family were based primarily on the grounds of their "impropriety" rather than their deficiency in great connections, Darcy's letter opens the way not only for a reassessment of his character and behaviour but to the recognition that there may be a form of pride and reserve which differs from that of mere snobbishness, and which may be both unobjectionable and necessary. But before we can get anywhere with this new look at Darcy, we must first get rid of some important misconceptions about "propriety." For most modern readers the word "propriety" has nothing but unfortunate connotations. Seen through the distorting lens of the Victorian age, the word has come to stand for a kind of rigid and even hypocritical adherence to the outward customs and usages of polite society. Indeed it is perhaps this conception of the word as much as anything which has contributed to the idea that Darcy "stands for" the "social restraints" imposed upon individual freedom.

For Jane Austen and, in fact, for most people of the 18th century, on the other hand, the word had not become so fixed or so pejorative. It was in a state of flux. For though it was just beginning to take on something like the meaning we now attribute to it, most of the eighteenth-century definitions of "propriety" still carried the impress of its Latin root, *proprius,* meaning "belonging to the individual," or, in other words, "peculiar," "characteristic." Far from suggesting a conformity to common rule, then, most senses of the word still connoted a concern for what was unique, special, or "proper" to a circumstance or person. We must keep this in mind if we are to see how Jane Austen understood the word.

As it is most frequently used in *Pride and Prejudice,* "propriety" suggests a kind of behaviour which is particularly careful not to violate the privacy, the integrity, and the right to respectability of every individual. As a concept governing social relations, then, "propriety" is intimately concerned with the discretion and reserve necessary to prevent individuals or actions from becoming "common" through excessive familiarity. Wickham's "general unreserve" about his relations with Mr. Darcy, his freedom in allowing his claims to be "openly acknowledged and publicly canvassed" (138), though another instance of his apparent sociability, is, in truth, an act of "impropriety" because it represents a breach of such discretion and privacy, a breach made all the more culpable since "respect for [Darcy's] father" ought to have stopped him from "exposing the son" (207).

Mr. Bennet's "impropriety . . . as a husband" (236) shows a similar disregard for necessary social distance. By continually "exposing his wife to the contempt of her own children" (236), Mr. Bennet is, in effect, robbing her of the respect which is due to her as both a wife and mother, no matter how silly she is.

But if "propriety" thus enjoins a certain respect for the individuality and reputation of other people, it also prescribes a concern for, indeed a pride in, one's own name and character. And it is in this sense of the word "propriety" that Darcy finds the Bennets lacking as a family. And it is for this reason that he is reluctant to see Bingley connect himself with them. "'For what do we live,'" Mr. Bennet asks Elizabeth, "'but to make sport for our neighbours, and laugh at them in our turn?'" (364). It is all too typical a question. For having lost all respect and esteem for his wife, Mr. Bennet has now lost any respect he might have had for the name and character of the man who was fool enough to marry her. Caring little or nothing for his reputation as a gentleman, he allows his wife and daughters to make spectacles of themselves (and him) at any public place, and even contributes to their exposure. In so doing, of course, he may purchase a kind of grim entertainment, but it is finally at the expense of his own respectability as well as that of his family. And given the kind of talking, gossiping world described at the beginning of *Pride and Prejudice,* it is not to be expected that the contempt that Mr. Bennet shows for himself and his kin will be slow to be communicated to the rest of the community.

With this in mind, then, I think we can now see the importance of Darcy's letter and the interval of time between its arrival and his reappearance in the novel. It is not that we give up our earlier notion of the contrast between reserve and sociability, but that our attitude towards both is radically redefined. Through Darcy's letter, we are forced to "re-see" the entire first half of the novel, to recognize not only the errors of judgment which can proceed from a prejudice for sociable people, but the limitations of sociability itself, the danger of living so much in the public eye that familiarity turns to contempt. But in thus revising our sense of the rights and wrongs of characters like Mr. and Mrs. Bennet and Wickham, we are slowly led to an appreciation of Darcy's superiority. For though we may still deplore the snobbishness and lack of consideration for others which is evident in his manner, we can now see that there is a positive need for qualities like pride and discretion that Darcy possesses.

The prominence given to Lydia in the fifty pages following Darcy's letter is only too obvious a reflection of these same issues. Lydia has been called "highly sexed" by at least one critic, and Jane Austen has been praised for her refusal to sentimentalize Lydia's strong "animal spirits."[10] But what characterizes Lydia is not so much passion as it is a mere carelessness about herself and her reputation. Brought out into society before her time and consequently without the kind of reserve or shyness which ought to characterize girls of her age[11] (contrast Georgiana Darcy at the other extreme), Lydia has always been loud and forward. But in the pages that follow Elizabeth's return to Longbourn, Lydia's indifference to publicity is stressed with such a heavy hand— "'we talked and laughed so loud, that any body might have heard us ten miles off'" (222)—that it seems surprising it has gone so long unnoticed.

That we should now see all this through Elizabeth's eyes is one of Jane Austen's usual triumphs of plotting. For not only is Darcy further justified in his characterization of the Bennets' behaviour, and Elizabeth raised in our eyes by the conscientiousness of her attempts to act upon that knowledge, but the scene is thereby prepared for Elizabeth's trip to Pemberley just a few chapters off. Though she doesn't know it yet, Elizabeth's conversation with her father, her representations of the "improprieties of Lydia's general behaviour" (230), her concern for her family's "importance, [its] respectability in the world" (231—all of these are bringing her closer in spirit to Darcy than ever before in the novel, and helping to make possible the rapprochement which begins at Pemberley.

The chapters at Pemberley, indeed, represent the second climax of the novel, and for many people its essential resolution.[12] Elizabeth has come to realize what we might call the "limits of sociability," the function of reserve, and the need for a "proper pride" in one's character. And Darcy, on his side, now reveals that he has recognized the errors of manner into which his excessive self-regard and exclusiveness have led. The result of this recognition is a new sociability. Never before has Elizabeth seen him so friendly, "so desirous to please, so free from self-consequence, or unbending reserve" (263) as he is at Pemberley. Instead of remaining detached and distant, he now makes every effort to be agreeable to Elizabeth and to the Gardiners to whom she now introduces him. The dialectic of sociability and reserve seems to have resolved itself perfectly into a new synthesis, and there seems to be little more reason to continue the novel except to complete the engagement between Darcy and Elizabeth.

IV

Why then does the novel go on? Why is Lydia's elopement necessary? Is it merely to prolong the suspense of the love plot? Is it a concession to the popular-novel-reading audience and its desire for melodrama? Is it that the elopement section of the novel is part of an earlier and insufficiently revised draft? All of these are possibilities, of course; but if we now shift attention away from the elopement as such and turn again to Darcy, I think we can at least make a case for another explanation.

The course of Darcy's progress in the novel is both consistent and revealing. Beginning in his chill refusal to participate in a dance, the entire history of his relationship with Elizabeth can be described as a struggle between the contrary impulses of pride and love—the one keeping him reserved and aloof, the other leading him increasingly towards that form of social communion which Jane Austen once likened to a dance.[13] His first proposal comes at the midway point of this struggle. For though love has by this time so far gotten the better of pride that all Darcy's efforts to remain unintrigued by Elizabeth have failed, yet pride still musters sufficient strength to make his proposal as vain and complacent as Mr. Collins's own. At Pemberley, however, Darcy takes a clear step forward and begins to get out of the closed circle of his pride by consciously and concertedly taking Elizabeth's advice and "practicing" sociability.[14] But is this really enough? Aren't we trivializing Jane Austen's own sense of society by suggesting that all Darcy owes to it is a certain refinement of manner? It is true, of course, that at Pemberley both Elizabeth and the reader become aware of the larger sphere of influence which is Darcy's by right of his position as landlord. But as Wickham has pointed out earlier, Darcy's efforts here are completely consistent with his pride. Are there no obligations to society which run against the notion of pride? Or, to put it another way, is Darcy now immune to the laughter, the foolishness, which seems to be so much a part of Jane Austen's own vision of social relations. The answer, I think, is no.

As is perhaps already obvious, the direction in which Darcy is moving in the last half of *Pride and Prejudice* is not only towards an attitude of greater candour and sociability but also towards an involvement in laughter and ridicule. Darcy is as clearly aware as Elizabeth herself that such attentions as he pays to the Gardiners "would draw down the ridicule and censure of the ladies both of Netherfield and Rosings" (263). But now he willingly exposes himself to it.

With Lydia's elopement, however, Darcy takes the last step: he risks the exposure of his own name and reputation by actively involving himself in retrieving the fallen reputation of the Bennets. Love is, of course, a major factor in Darcy's decision to open his family name to the remarks of such a scandal, but love only provides the willingness, the impulse. As Darcy realizes, and as I think Jane Austen intends the reader to realize too, the duty, the responsibility of such a risk has always been there.

Before Elizabeth's refusal, Darcy thought it beneath him "to lay his private actions open to the world" (322). With the same (in this case mistaken) pride which he had shown in his proposal to Elizabeth, he had simply assumed that his reputation would speak for itself without further effort on his part, that his character, his wealth, his position would be more than sufficient to confound any lies that Wickham might dare to spread. But as Darcy discovers more than once in the novel, people are not to be moved in this way. And it is precisely because of his refusal to be open, his inordinate fear of involving himself in ridicule that Wickham's designs are able to succeed.

But it is not simply that Darcy thereby exposed his name to greater indignities by his fear of publicity than he would have if he had been more open. He also allowed a great number of people in Hertfordshire (particularly the Bennets) to be seriously victimized through their ignorance of Wickham's past. "It was owing to him," as Darcy tells Mrs. Gardiner, "to his reserve, and want of proper consideration, that Wickham's character had been so misunderstood, and consequently that he had been received and noticed as he was" (324). Had Darcy been less proudly reserved, and more willing to risk the idle remarks of the usual town gossips, Wickham's elopement with Lydia (certainly his constant reception at Longbourn) would almost surely have been avoided. Had he been less careful of his own reputation and more aware of his responsibilities to the society of which he is a part, the Bennets need not have been so threatened.

It is only through the events surrounding Lydia's elopement, then, that we arrive at the final adjustment of the relations between sociability and reserve. For with her usual good sense, Jane Austen realizes that however important it is to maintain one's dignity in the world, such dignity cannot be an end in itself. The final step Darcy takes towards an involvement in society, therefore, goes beyond the simple candour he learns when he begins to meet people like the Gardiners halfway. It includes being actively engaged in a society where to be a responsible, feeling, and discriminating adult means to risk at times the exposure to laughter.

For Darcy this means stepping down off the pedestal where his pride has kept him aloof in Grandisonian perfection, and joining the mass of men who, as Elizabeth will teach him, are laughing and laughed at. For whatever else it is, laughter is the great equalizer in Jane Austen's novels. And though it may vary in profundity from the vulgar "fun" of Lydia to the sociable playfulness of Elizabeth to the moral consciousness of Jane Austen herself, laughter is there as an eternal reminder that we are all part of one community, and not even the best of men can be totally beyond the responsibility and the reproach of belonging to it.

Notes

1. *The English Novel: Form and Function* (New York: Rinehart, 1953), p. 100.

2. *Jane Austen: A Study of Her Artistic Development* (New York: Oxford Univ. Press, 1965), p. 105.

3. *The Improvement of the Estate* (Baltimore: Johns Hopkins Univ. Press, 1971), p. 118. I am indebted to Duckworth and particularly to the note which accompanies the passage I have quoted for first suggesting to me the prevalence of the "individual-society" interpretation of *Pride and Prejudice*.

4. All quotations from Jane Austen's novels are from the standard Chapman edition [*The Novels of Jane Austen*] (London: Oxford Univ. Press, 1971).

5. *Scrutiny*, 8 (1940), 346-62.

6. *Jane Austen's Letters to Her Sister Cassandra and Others*, 2nd edn., ed. R. W. Chapman (London: Oxford Univ. Press, 1952), p. 32.

7. See the exchange between Charlotte Lucas and Elizabeth about Darcy's pride, p. 20.

8. We are told, for instance, that the Bingley sisters can be agreeable when they wish to be. And in fact we see them turn on their charm more or less when they will. Their reserve seems to be under their own control. In Darcy's case, reserve is a part of his character, and it is by no means clear that he will ever be entirely comfortable in society. Yet Jane's remark, early in the novel, before we have had a chance to know Darcy, makes it almost impossible for us to interpret Darcy's reserve in this way. "'Miss Bingley told me,' said Jane, 'that he never speaks much unless among his intimate acquaintance. With *them* he is remarkably agreeable'" (19). This again seems to make Darcy and the Bingley sisters all of a kind.

9. See Marvin Mudrick, *Jane Austen: Irony as Defense and Discovery* (Princeton: Princeton Univ. Press, 1952), pp. 94-126, and D. W. Harding, "Jane Austen and Moral Judgment," in *From Blake to Byron*, ed. Boris Ford (Baltimore: Penguin Books, 1957), pp. 51-59.

10. Mudrick, p. 100.

11. In a letter to her sister, Jane Austen lamented the contemporary loss of reserve, asking, "What is become of all the Shyness in the World?" (8 Feb. 1808). This letter is usually quoted apropos of Fanny Price's remark in *Mansfield Park*, "'There must be a sort of shyness'" (*MP* [*Mansfield Park*]: 197). But it applies equally well to Lydia's case and perhaps suggests that there is a greater sense of continuity between the two novels than is usually recognized.

12. Critics have in fact so long complained about the second half of the novel (and particularly Lydia's elopement) that Joseph Wiesenfarth devoted an entire chapter of his book on Austen to answering the charge. For the arguments on both sides, see his *The Errand of Form* (New York: Fordham Univ. Press, 1967), pp. 60-85.

13. I am referring of course to Henry Tilney's celebrated comparison of marriage and dancing in *Northanger Abbey*, pp. 76-77.

14. I use the word "practicing" advisedly. For as Elizabeth demonstrates to Darcy at Rosings, sociability, like piano-playing, is an acquired art (175).

Karen Newman (essay date winter 1983)

SOURCE: Newman, Karen. "Can This Marriage Be Saved: Jane Austen Makes Sense of an Ending." *ELH* 50, no. 4 (winter 1983): 693-710.

[*In the following essay, Newman evaluates the parodic elements in the novel's conclusion. Newman suggests that Austen employed irony as a means of subverting the patriarchal underpinnings of literary language.*]

You agree with me in not liking Corinne, then?

I didn't finish the book, said Maggie. As soon as I came to the blond-haired young lady reading in the park, I shut it up and determined to read no further. I foresaw that the light-complexioned girl would win away all the love from Corinne and make her miserable. I'm determined to read no more books where the blond-haired women carry away all the happiness. If you could give me some story now, where the dark woman triumphs, it would restore the balance.

The Mill on the Floss

Despite Maggie Tulliver's plea for novels in which the dark woman triumphs, many feminists have not been kind in their judgment of such plots. Marriage, almost inevitably the narrative event that constitutes a happy ending, represents in their view submission to a masculine narrative imperative that has traditionally allotted women love and men the world. Ironically, perhaps, such readers have preferred novels that show the destructive effects of patriarchal oppression, for they complain that Austen's endings, her happily-ever-after marriages, represent a decline in her protagonists: "as in much women's fiction, the end, the reward, of women's apprentice-ship to life is marriage . . . marriage which requires [Elizabeth Bennet] to dwindle by degrees into a wife."[1]

The question I want to address is, can this marriage be saved? That question poses a larger and more theoretical question about how we read endings generally. In his foreword to a recent number of *Nineteenth-Century Fiction* devoted to endings, Alexander Welsh suggests that "endings are critical points for analysis in all examinations of plot; quite literally, any action is defined by its ending."[2] Many readers of Austen have taken just this attitude toward her endings. Either the critic reads an Austen novel as a romantic love story in which social and economic realities of nineteenth-century women's lives are exposed but undermined by comedy, irony, and most tellingly marriage, or she reads marriage as a metaphor for self-knowledge, the overcoming of egoism and the mark of psychic development: in Austen's *Emma,* for example, marriage "is most significant as a social ritual which ratifies a transformation in Emma herself . . . [just as] the union of Jane Eyre and Rochester . . . takes its meaning from the heroine's own psychic growth."[3] Neither approach seems satisfactory, for both ignore important aspects of these texts and their historical context. The event, marriage, does after all refer to a real social institution that, in the nineteenth century particularly, robbed women of their human rights.[4] The most cursory look at the legal and cultural history of women makes it clear that these narrative events reflect the social and legal limitations that women of the eighteenth and nineteenth centuries faced and that in turn reflect the way a patriarchal society has manipulated biological roles for its own advantage. To read marriage as metaphor is not a sufficient answer.

Nor can we accept the feminist judgment that Austen's endings undermine her critique of social and economic forces and their effects on women.[5] The assumptions of such a reading bear scrutiny, for they read the novel as an object to be consumed by the dominant culture. As

D. A. Miller observes in his recent book on narrative closure, "once the ending is enshrined as an all-embracing cause in which the elements of a narrative find their ultimate justification, it is difficult for analysis to assert anything short of total coherence."[6] By reading an Austen novel as a unity with romantic marriage as its final statement, we impose a resolution on her work that makes it conform to the very expectations for women and novels that Austen's irony constantly undermines. Such a habit of reading, which, as Welsh puts it, defines any action by its ending, falls prey to a teleological prejudice that contemporary criticism has called into question. As critics and feminists, we must refuse the *effect* of her endings; instead of simply accepting the text as it presents itself, we must investigate the contradictory, disparate elements from which it is made: the psychological paradigms, the raw materials of ideology and of women's place in culture. An Austen novel and indeed any fashioned work of art conceals and diverts attention from the visible seams where these contradictory materials are joined; the critic's task is to analyze how this diversion takes place, to investigate *how* the text produces its meaning and effect.[7]

If instead of assuming that endings define the action of a novel (an enterprise we would never even attempt in reading poetry) we assume that our sense of an ending is a function of the principles of structure by which the novel is generated or according to which one element follows another, in the case of Austen our sense of closure is markedly different from the one a teleological reading provides. Austen exposes the fundamental discrepancy in her society between its avowed ideology of love and its implicit economic motivation. But her response to this conflict is more complex than the simple juxtaposition of the languages of love and money so often remarked by her critics since Dorothy Van Ghent and Mark Schorer in the early fifties.[8] Her consistent use of economic language to talk about human relations and her many portraits of unsatisfactory marriages prevent us from dismissing her novels as romantic love stories in which Austen succumbs uncritically to the "rewards" her culture allotted women. Even more important, however, are the unresolved contradictions between romantic and materialist notions of marriage and human relationships that govern the production of meaning in her texts.[9] Austen's novels provide us with rival versions of a single set of facts that coexist without final reconciliation or resolution, and the text displays these gaps or disjunctions on the levels of both plot and sentence.

Nancy Miller has called attention to the usefulness of formalist approaches, particularly the work of Gérard Genette, for reading women's fiction.[10] In his essay "Vraisemblance et Motivation," Genette defines *vraisemblance* in a literary text as action that conforms to the maxims, presuppositions, or received opinions of the public or society: "Real or assumed, this opinion is pretty much what today would be called ideology, that is to say, a body of maxims and prejudices which constitute both a vision of the world and a system of values."[11]

For Genette, texts solve the problem of *vraisemblance* in three ways. In the first kind of text, "the relationship between a plausible narrative and the system of plausibility to which it subjects itself . . . is essentially mute." Such works conform to the "tacit contract between a work and its public," and this silence indicates the text's conformity to the dominant ideology. The second kind of text is liberated from ideology, but is also silent because it refuses to justify the "motives and maxims of the actions." The silence of the first text is a function of what Genette calls "plausible narrative"; that of the second, a function of "arbitrary narrative." It is only in the third type of narrative that these silences are voiced in what Genette calls the "endless chatting" of the Balzacian novel. Balzac presents the reader with an "artificial plausibility" in which authorial commentary justifies the plot by inventing the missing maxims. I would like to suggest that Jane Austen's novels represent a variant of this third type. *Pride and Prejudice* begins with a maxim on which the ensuing narrative is based—that "it is a truth universally acknowledged that a single man in possession of a good fortune must be in want of a wife."[12] What is the relation of this maxim to the novel and its context? Neither of the young men in possession of a fortune in the novel seems in want of a wife; on the contrary, it is the young women without property—the Bennets, Charlotte Lucas—who are in need of spouses, and not the reverse. The maxim, then, on which the novel is based does not justify the story; its function is not *vraisemblance* but exposure, for it serves as a continual ironic reminder of the discrepancy or gap between social convention and economic necessity.

In *Emma,* maxims serve a somewhat different function. Early in the novel, in talking to Harriet of that lady's farmer suitor, Robert Martin, the heroine announces that "The yeomanry are precisely the order of people with whom I feel I can have nothing to do."[13] This maxim does not function for everyone of Emma's rank and social class but is designed to expose her own snobbery and class prejudice. Knightley has "to do" not only with Robert Martin, but also with William Larkin; the Westons dine with the Coles. The maxim serves to expose the contradiction between Emma's ideas of herself and her class and the actual social relations the novel portrays.

Genette argues that the maxims and generalizations that an author makes are all determined by the *telos*—in this case marriage. In Austen's case, however, the generalization that opens *Pride and Prejudice* in no way explains or justifies the ultimate ending of the novel, for it is not the young men who are in want of spouses, but all those without property. In this novel, then, Austen creates a deliberate disjunction between received opinion and social reality. Her epigrammatic maxims, instead of being designed to justify ends, or simply to create irony, are designed to expose the contradiction between their own pretense of causality and the real economic basis for action in the novel.

There are abundant examples in Austen's novels of her ironic juxtaposition of incongruous elements to satirize a character. One of my favorites is, not surprisingly, a conversational tidbit of Mrs. Bennet's. After lamenting the defection of Bingley and the treachery of the Lucases in gaining Mr. Collins, she says to her sister-in-law, Mrs. Gardiner, "your coming just at this time is the greatest of comforts, and I am very glad to hear what you tell us of long sleeves" (178). The wonderful parallel juxtaposition of "comfort" and "long sleeves," both of which fall at the end of their respective independent clauses, and the superlative "greatest" expose marvelously Mrs. Bennet's characteristic exaggeration of trivialities and corresponding diminution of real values. But there are other moments in the text when Austen's irony does not serve so simple a purpose.

In chapter 3 Austen finally provides us with a description of the Netherfield party that has been the subject of such interest and anxiety in the neighborhood:

> Mr. Bingley was good looking and gentlemanlike; he had a pleasant countenance and easy and unaffected manners; his sisters were fine women with an air of decided fashion. His brother-in-law, Mr. Hurst, merely looked the gentleman; but his friend Mr. Darcy drew the attention of the room by his fine, tall person, handsome features, noble mien; and the report which was in general circulation within five minutes after his entrance, of his having ten thousand a year. The gentlemen pronounced him to be a fine figure of a man, the ladies declared he was much handsomer than Mr. Bingley.

(58)

Here Austen's irony is not directed at a fool but at society, and she does not exclude Elizabeth or Jane Bennet, those characters whom we regard as admirable. On the contrary, she emphasizes that the report was in *general* circulation and uses the generic *ladies* and *gentlemen*. This passage details the way in which wealth determines judgment, not only of character, but also even of appearance. Each member of the Netherfield party, though seemingly rated according to his or her "natural" attributes, is actually rated according to his fortune—Darcy, Bingley, the sisters, Mr. Hurst.[14] Austen's point here is clearly the way in which wealth determines point of view. Traditionally Elizabeth is excluded from this judgment, but as Sir Walter Scott long ago noticed, Elizabeth's change of heart toward Darcy happens at Pemberley in response to his property. I do not mean to denigrate Elizabeth—she is a superior individual, and what impresses her about Pemberley is not simply its wealth but also the taste and judgment it implies.[15] Scott was, of course, wrong in reducing Elizabeth's change of heart to crass materialist motives, but not, I think, entirely, for a close examination of Elizabeth's relation to property reveals a deliberate intention on Austen's part to show us not simply a moral development, Elizabeth's sense that she had not known herself and had misread others in her prejudice, but a growing recognition of her "interest."[16]

Austen is at pains from early in the novel to show us Elizabeth's response to Darcy's wealth. When she is at Netherfield nursing her sister, Austen unfolds a scene in which Elizabeth overhears a conversation between Darcy and Miss Bingley about his property in Derbyshire. The function of the scene is not simply to introduce and describe Darcy's property or to show Miss Bingley's clear interest in it; its function is explained by the description of Elizabeth's behavior that follows the conversation:

> Elizabeth was so much caught by what passed, as to leave her very little attention for her book, and soon laying it wholly aside, she drew near the cardtable and stationed herself between Mr. Bingley and his eldest sister, to observe the game.
>
> (84)

Clearly the motivation for Elizabeth's action is not the ironic one given by the narrator, "to observe the game," but to hear more on the subject of Darcy's estate. Elizabeth was so much *caught* by what passed. Later, when she seeks to discover from Wickham the reason for Darcy's reaction to meeting him, Elizabeth says to him tellingly, unwilling, we are told, to let the subject drop, "he is a man of very large property in Derbyshire, I understand" (121). In her revealing conversation with Mrs. Gardiner about Wickham's affection, she says that "he is the most agreeable man I ever saw—and if he becomes really attached to me—I believe it will be better that he should not. I see the imprudence of it—Oh, that abominable Mr. Darcy" (181). On a syntactic level, Darcy here literally blocks her affections for the impecunious Wickham! Austen voices through Elizabeth herself the fundamental contradiction of the novel: "What is the difference in matrimonial affairs between the mercenary and the prudent motive? Where does discretion end and avarice begin?" (188). No one, particularly no woman who is economically dependent, not *even* Elizabeth, whom we admire, is unmoved by property. We should remember that only the ignorant and imprudent Lydia marries "for love," and then a man whom Darcy has paid to tie the knot.

A close reading of ***Pride and Prejudice*** reveals the contours of the patriarchal ideology from which Austen's

novels emerge and in which women are at the mercy of male control of the means of production. Should we say, as Judith Lowder Newton does, that the range and complexity of the Marxist-feminist problematic the novel poses is blocked or repressed by the fantasy-wish-fulfillment structure of the boy-meets-girl-leads-to-marriage convention? I don't think so, for I think the constant alternation between the fairy tale structure and the materialist language that pervades the novel emphasizes rather than represses or obscures what Terry Eagleton terms the "fault lines" of nineteenth-century English society.[17]

Let us return briefly to the sentence quoted earlier describing Darcy at the ball: "but his friend Mr. Darcy drew the attention of the room by his fine, tall person, handsome features, noble mien; and the report which was in general circulation within five minutes after his entrance, of his having ten thousand a year" (58). Austen juxtaposes the "Prince Charming" description of Darcy—his fine, tall person, handsome features, noble mien—with the final attribute of the series that reports his having ten thousand a year. The juxtaposition of these two clauses represents the two conflicting and independent perspectives that function in the novel—love and money. The tension created by this contrast in which neither perspective is subordinated to the other reveals what the French critic Pierre Macherey would call the "not said" or silence of the novel—the true place of women in a materialist culture in which men control money: this silence "is the juxtaposition and conflict of several meanings which produces the radical otherness which shapes the work; this conflict is not resolved or absorbed, but simply displayed."[18] The happy ending of an Austen novel gives it an apparent unity that is false, for meaning is produced not so much by resolution, but by means of oppositions and contradictions, by the incompatibility of several meanings.

Such an understanding of Austen's art explains the extremes of critical thinking her novels have generated—the claims, such as Marilyn Butler's on the one hand, that Austen's books "belong decisively to one class of novels, the conservative," which criticizes individualism and the unconventional, or those of Van Ghent and more recently Nina Auerbach and Susan Morgan, who read her novels as revolutionary, romantic, or both.[19] Butler is convincing in her claim that Austen works out of the anti-Jacobin tradition, but to conclude that her novels are therefore conservative is problematic. To justify such claims, Butler is forced to infer that the meaning of ***Pride and Prejudice*** "is not precisely or not sufficiently written into the text" and worse, that ***Persuasion*** is "muddle."[20] And however many times we are told that "Austen's subject is perception" or that ***Persuasion*** is about the self imperiled by change and time, we still recognize in Austen's work principles of proportion and social integration quite unromantic and unrevolutionary.[21]

If, instead of taking a partisan view, we admit that culture is not a harmonious and unified whole in which political and social beliefs and institutions are at one with aesthetic productions, whether anti-Jacobin or romantic, we are in a better position to understand Austen's art and its relation to ideology. In his "Letter on Art in Reply to André Daspre," Althusser proposes that art makes us "see" or "perceive" "the ideology from which it is born, in which it bathes, from which it detaches itself as art, and to which it alludes."[22] Art is not a reflection of ideology because this act of seeing, the "view" that art provides, presupposes "an internal distanciation from the very ideology from which such novels [Balzac's] emerged."[23] We are not required, therefore, to argue that Austen abandoned a conservative political position in order to claim that her novels criticize the patriarchal ideology from which they emerged, for her personal political views are only one component of the content of her work.

Instead we must recognize that Austen's artistic achievement in rendering the inner life of her characters, of Elizabeth, Emma, and Anne, wins our sympathy regardless of the ultimate "lessons" these heroines may learn. Our sympathy with their inner lives may even conflict with the author's critical intentions, just as Austen's irony in treating her romantic endings contradicts their conventional claims for the happily-ever-after. These contradictions are not artistic failures or "muddle"; they allow us a view, from a critical distance, of English society and the position of women in the first decades of the nineteenth century.

Oppositions are also evident in the ironic ambiguity of Austen's diction. For example, Johnson defines "to fix" as 1) to make fast, firm or stable; 2) to settle, to establish invariably; 3) to direct without variation; 4) to deprive of volatility; 5) to pierce, to transfix; and finally, 6) to withhold from motion. Austen plays on the polysemous nature of "fix" at various, often significant, moments in her text. The novel's opening maxim, we learn in the second paragraph, "is so well fixed in the minds of the surrounding families" that a single man "is considered as the rightful property of some one or other of their daughters" (51). The second meaning of "fix" occurs so frequently in the novel as not to require example, but those senses concerned with motionlessness deserve quotation: Charlotte judges Jane's composure with Bingley disadvantageous because "If a woman conceals her affection with the same skill from the object of it, she may lose the opportunity of fixing him" (68). Here the entomologist's eye and pin seem fixed on that "single man in possession of a good fortune." In the plot of *Pride and Prejudice,* women try to fix men,

but it is women who are "fixed" in all of Johnson's senses of the word. When Elizabeth stands before Darcy's portrait at Pemberley, she does not fix her eyes on him; instead we find an oddly subjectless clause that inscribes Elizabeth in a scopic economy and highlights her position in a patriarchy:

> Every idea that had been brought forward by the housekeeper was favourable to his character, and as she stood before the canvas, on which he was represented, and fixed his eyes upon herself, she thought of his regard with a deeper sentiment of gratitude than it had ever raised before.
>
> (272)

Here the syntax leads us to expect Elizabeth as the subject of "fixed," but we are brought up short by the possessive pronoun "his." It is Darcy's "regard" that fixes Elizabeth.

The multiple meanings of words in Austen's prose are means for exposing the social contradictions that are the subject of her novels. Johnson defines "amiable" as 1) "pleasing or lovely" and 2) "pretending or shewing love." When Elizabeth thanks Charlotte Lucas for listening to Mr. Collins and thus sparing Elizabeth herself, Charlotte

> assured her friend of her satisfaction in being useful, and that it amply repaid her for the little sacrifice of her time. This was very amiable, but Charlotte's kindness extended farther than Elizabeth had any conception of;—its object was nothing less, than to secure her from any return of Mr. Collins's addresses, by engaging them towards herself. Such was Miss Lucas's scheme.
>
> (162)

As her emphasis on Charlotte's scheming suggests, Austen intends both meanings of "amiable" to work on the reader in this passage. Two chapters later the narrator remarks: "After a week spent in professions of love and schemes of felicity, Mr. Collins was called from his amiable Charlotte" (177). The adjective with its contradictory meanings, here linked with other similarly ambiguous words—"schemes," "professions"—becomes almost an epithet for Charlotte, perhaps even for courtship itself, in this section of the novel.

"Prudent," like "amiable," also has conflicting meanings in *Pride and Prejudice.* In its original sense, *prudentia* was one of the cardinal virtues in pagan and Christian ethics. Prudence was the practical wisdom of moral conduct, but as Glenn Hatfield has pointed out in his discussion of the word in Fielding, in the eighteenth century the term was debased by custom and usage to mean cunning or deceit making for the appearance of virtue.[24] In *Pride and Prejudice* Elizabeth puzzles over the meaning of prudence in matrimonial affairs. Jane deems Charlotte prudent when she endeavors to soften Elizabeth's condemnation of her friend's match with the boorish Mr. Collins, but Elizabeth counters "that selfishness is not prudence" (174).[25] Soon afterward, Mrs. Gardiner warns her of the imprudence of a match with Wickham. Elizabeth admits to her aunt, "I see the imprudence of it" (181). When Wickham begins courting the heiress Mrs. King, the narrator comments:

> Elizabeth, less clear-sighted perhaps in his case than Charlotte's, did not quarrel with him for his wish of independence. Nothing, on the contrary, could be more natural . . . she was ready to allow it a wise and desirable measure for both, and could very sincerely wish him happy.
>
> (186)

The *perhaps* that follows "less clear-sighted" undermines the force of this judgment. We wonder, is Elizabeth really clear-sighted in her condemnation of Charlotte, or is the novel as much about her learning the complexities of "prudence" as those of "pride" and "prejudice"?[26]

Though the meaning of imprudence may be clear enough, prudence in matrimonial affairs is more complex.[27] Charlotte is prudent, and, as the quotation above suggests, scheming in her pursuit of Mr. Collins. Yet the narrator's report of what are admittedly Charlotte's reflections on her choice do not betray Elizabeth's prejudice:

A
Without thinking highly either of men
B
or matrimony, marriage had always been
C
her object; it was the only honourable
provision for well educated young women
A
of small fortune, and however uncertain of
B
giving happiness, must be their pleasantest preservative from want.

(163)

The careful eighteenth-century balance of clauses in this passage emphasizes the conflicting forces women encounter in culture. The negative clause that begins the passage is contrasted with the contradictory "marriage had always been her object," just as the negative clause of the final lines is juxtaposed with the opposed sentiment expressed in the final clause to give us the following scheme: A/B C A/B.[28] The realistic Charlotte has no romantic illusions about marriage, but she nevertheless deems it the best alternative for "well educated young women of small fortune" in her society. The unresolvable conflicts inherent in her situation are expressed in the characteristic Austenian balance the novelist inherits from the Augustans. In Jane Austen,

prudence is not only the practical wisdom of moral conduct; it is also what we might define as acting in one's own interest in accordance with virtue, but with a realistic appraisal of the limits and difficulties life presents. When she visits Charlotte, Elizabeth is compelled, we recall, to meditate "upon Charlotte's degree of contentment, to understand her address in guiding, and composure in bearing with her husband, and to acknowledge that it was all done very well" (193).

That this technique of exploiting the connotations or variations in meaning of key words is central to Austen's irony and meaning is evident in the titles of her novels. In those with paired words, this opposition is clear, but even in the late novel **Persuasion** variation in meaning is important.[29] Johnson's dictionary defines "persuade" as 1) "to bring to any particular opinion" and 2) "to influence by argument." So in **Persuasion** Anne Elliott "was persuaded to believe the engagement a wrong thing—indiscreet, improper, hardly capable of success, and not deserving it" by Lady Russell's influence on her pliant will.[30] Now that Anne is more mature, however, even after considering every argument against her engagement to Wentworth,

> She was persuaded that under every disadvantage of disapprobation at home, and every anxiety attending his profession, of all their probable fears, delays and disappointment, she should yet have been a happier woman in maintaining the engagement than she had been in the sacrifice of it.

If we turn to the endings themselves, we find an ironic self-consciousness that emphasizes the contradiction between the sentimentality of Austen's comic conclusions and the realism of her view of marriage and of women's plight.[31] Darcy's second proposal is prompted by Elizabeth's thanking him, despite her aunt's admonitions of secrecy, for his part in effecting the marriage of Lydia and Wickham. In chapter 60, after they are united and reflecting on the past, Elizabeth exclaims: "what becomes of the moral, if our comfort springs from a breach of promise" (389). Here Austen subverts the traditional sentimental ending with a moral. Though often brought about by ironic reversals or miraculous coincidences from which moral lessons can be drawn, reconciliations in eighteenth- and nineteenth-century fiction are not usually dependent on a breach of promise! Darcy counters with his version by claiming that it was not Elizabeth's breach of promise but Lady Catherine's interference that led him to hazard a second proposal.

In Austen's novels, our conventional expectations are often met but at the same time undermined by self-consciousness and parody. Wickham and Lydia are not punished with misery and unhappiness, but live tolerably well given their weaknesses and extravagance; Miss Bingley has no change of heart when acquainted with her brother's happiness—her congratulations "were

39

all that was affectionate and insincere" (391). But perhaps no detail in the final pages better suggests Austen's ironic treatment of her own happy endings than Mr. Bennet's brusque letter to Mr. Collins: "I must trouble you once more for congratulations. Elizabeth will soon be the wife of Mr. Darcy. Console Lady Catherine as well as you can. But, if I were you, I would stand by the nephew. He has more to give" (390).

In *Emma* the heroine despairs over her father's anxiety about her marriage. We are told "she could not proceed" (380). Austen pointedly observes that no "sudden illumination" or "wonderful change" in Mr. Woodhouse's character made the marriage possible; instead a pilfering of poultry yards so frightened the old man that Emma's marriage became desirable (380-81). So also in *Persuasion* she consistently undercuts our expectation of a reconciliation between Anne and Wentworth. The so-called autumnal descriptions of Anne's faded beauty and the overheard conversations between the Musgroves and Wentworth serve to contradict our usual expectations for a comic ending of matrimonial reunion. Austen's comic conclusions neither undermine her heroines by making them dwindle into wives nor institute what has been called a virtual "ideological paradise";[32] they reveal the gap between sentimental ideals and novelistic conventions on the one hand, and the social realities of sexist prejudice, hypocrisy, and avarice on the other.

Austen's novels show us women confronting the limitations imposed by late eighteenth- and nineteenth-century English society. Instead of assuming, as critics so often have, that Austen's respect for limits grows out of eighteenth-century philosophical thought and the conservative anti-Jacobin sentiments of the 1790s we might attribute a part at least of her strong sense of boundaries to her experience of women's limited horizons and opportunities for action.[33] If Jane Austen had not written with a deep sense of those limitations, she would have written utopian fantasy, not novels. What is positive and pleasurable about Austen's or Bronte's novels is that their heroines live powerfully within the limits imposed by ideology. In doing so, they redefine what we think of as power, helping us to avoid the trap that traditional male definitions of power present, arguing that a woman's freedom is not simply a freedom to parody male models of action. These novels of the past and their endings are valuable because they do not assume that what men do is what every human being wants to do. As I suggested earlier, the marriages that solve the narrative problem created by an independent female protagonist are strategies for arriving at solutions that ideology precludes. In *Pride and Prejudice,* everything about Elizabeth—her poverty, her inferior social position, the behavior of her family, her initial preference for Wickham, and her refusal of Darcy's first offer of marriage—all these things ideologically should lead if not to death, at best to genteel poverty and spin-

sterhood. Instead Austen has her marry despite her violations of these accepted norms of female behavior, and in so doing, she distorts the very historical and economic realities of marriage that her novel so forcefully depicts. Bronte does similar things both in *Jane Eyre* and *Villette.* In *Jane Eyre,* traditional critics call Bertha, the madwoman in the attic, a gothic-romantic holdover from Bronte's childhood fantasies of Angria; feminists, however, interpret Bertha as the incarnation of Jane's repressed rage and sexual desire. In terms of narrative, this element of the plot, then, is a device for expressing what cannot be articulated; Bertha is a literary device for circumventing the ideological strictures that prevent Bronte from writing openly about Jane's sexuality.[34]

The literary text's mode of resolving a particular ideological conflict may also produce conflicts on levels of the text other than that of plot, as in Austen's sentence describing Darcy in which the two clauses mediate our understanding of love and money in the novel. A novel's value, then, or indeed the value of any work of art for feminists, is determined not by its progressive picture of woman or by any exhortation to change a sexist society, but rather by its articulation of the conflict, or what is sometimes called the problematic, posed by a sexist ideology, in the background but nevertheless dominant, in which female consciousness is foregrounded. Austen's novels in fact suggest that space, time, and human relations—what we might call ideology—are understandable and controllable, that power is in self-mastery, internal not external. Bronte, on the other hand, implies that circumstances should and can be overcome; her heroines, in fact, change them.

So Austen, as students notice and puzzle over, is both reactionary and revolutionary. She takes women's exclusion from political power and action as she finds it. In the nineteenth century she clearly looked backward, and her sense of order represents in part at least a reaction to the social and political upheaval caused by the revolutions in France and America. But she is also revolutionary in her determination to change our ideal of what power is by arguing that women cannot be excused from power by the limits society imposes on them. She in fact argues that those who succeed are larger than their circumstances, that they control their fate and exercise real power, and from such characters and actions come the claims for Austen's kinship with the Romantics. In *Persuasion,* Wentworth seems to have the power of choice over Anne. He has all the advantages of male power and privilege—travel, the opportunity to make his fortune, the power to choose a wife—but he must return to the limits of the neighborhood of Kellynch Hall and finally wait for Anne to choose him, for her words to pierce his soul. "Only Anne," as Austen introduces her, to whom no one listened and whom no one heard (11). Austen is in this sense revolutionary—she redefines our traditional assumptions about the nature of power.

The feminist critic's rejection of Austen's endings is all too easily subsumed by the old complaints about the smallness of her art, the claims that it is limited because she ignored or even fought against currents of thought released by the French revolution, or in the case of the feminist critic, by Wollstonecraft and the early movements for women's rights. No criticism of Austen's art more effectively reveals the dangers of what has been called "phallocentric" criticism, which privileges the traditional male domains of action and modes of reading, for as the London-based Marxist Feminist Literature Collective points out:

> Austen's refusal to write about anything she didn't know is as undermining to the patriarchal hegemony as Wollstonecraft's demand for a widening of women's choices: the very narrowness of her novels gave them a subversive dimension of which she herself was unaware, and which has been registered in critics' bewilderment at what status to accord them.[35]

I would quarrel with this statement only in its assertion that Austen was unaware of the subversive dimension of her novels, for how can we know?

In closing I want to consider briefly the problem of specificity in women's writing. Feminist critics have been preoccupied with discovering "what, if anything, makes women's writing different from men's."[36] The most common answer is that women's lives and experiences differ from men's, and that the difference is inscribed in their writing—in imagery, and more important, in content. This judgment is ironically consonant with the traditional rejection of Austen's small world, her "little bit (two inches wide) of Ivory," though the feminist critic usually, but not always, recognizes the value of the women's world Austen portrays. Alternatively feminists have hypothesized a feminine or female consciousness different from the masculine that produces a specifically feminine or female style. Both approaches have met criticism from those who point out that male writing often manifests a content or style elsewhere termed feminine or female. Rather than attempt to label particular features of style or units of content as feminine, we would be better served by recognizing common strategies among women and men who are, for whatever reason, excluded or alienated from traditional patriarchal power structures. In Austen's case, irony and parody are subversive strategies that undermine the male hegemony her novels portray and reveal the romantic and materialist contradictions of which her plots and characters are made.

The French feminist psychoanalyst Luce Irigaray claims that women's writing is impossible because men control language. Women's access to language, to the Word, is determined by the cultural constructions of patriarchal power.[37] Their only recourse, according to Irigaray, is mimesis, imitation of male forms, but imitation that is self-conscious or reflexive, what we might call imitation with a difference. Parody is that literary form which most openly declares its status as imitation, its difference.[38] We might say, then, that Austen's parody, particularly her parodic endings, is her means of interrogating patriarchal plots and power. The marriages that end her novels can only be saved by reading them not as statements of romantic harmony or escape, but in the context in which she placed them. Far from acquiescing to women's traditional role in culture, Austen's parodic conclusions measure the distance between novelistic conventions with their culturally coded sentiments and the social realities of patriarchal power.

Notes

1. See Judith Lowder Newton, "*Pride and Prejudice*: Power, Fantasy, and Subversion in Jane Austen," *Feminist Studies* 4 (Fall, 1978), 41; and her more recent *Women, Power, and Subversion* (Athens: Univ. of Georgia Press, 1981), 55ff. See also Nina Auerbach's discussion of "equivocal" female power and Elizabeth's acquiescence to Darcy in *Communities of Women* (Cambridge: Harvard Univ. Press, 1978), 38ff.; and Sandra M. Gilbert and Susan Gubar, *The Madwoman in the Attic* (New Haven: Yale Univ. Press, 1979), 154ff.

2. Alexander Welsh, Foreword, *Narrative Endings, Nineteenth-Century Fiction* 33 (1978), 1; see also D. A. Miller's discussion of the "common assumption of an a priori determination of means by the ends" in twentieth-century narratology in *Narrative and its Discontents* (Princeton: Princeton Univ. Press, 1981), xiiff.

3. Ruth Yeazell, "Fictional Heroines and Feminist Critics," *Novel* 8 (1974), 34.

4. For a survey of the legal and social aspects of marriage and their impact on women in the eighteenth and nineteenth centuries, see Patricia Thomson, *The Victorian Heroine; A Changing Ideal* (London: Oxford Univ. Press, 1956); Duncan Crow, *The Victorian Woman* (London: Allen and Unwin, 1971); Françoise Basch, *Relative Creatures,* trans. Anthony Rudolf (New York: Schocken, 1974); and Jenni Calder, *Women and Marriage in Victorian Fiction* (New York: Oxford Univ. Press, 1976).

5. Newton, "*Pride and Prejudice,*" 27-42; Gilbert and Gubar, 154ff.

6. Miller, xiii.

7. My discussion of the critical enterprise owes a great deal to Pierre Macherey's *Pour une théorie de la production littéraire* (Paris: F. Maspero, 1971).

8. Mark Schorer, "Fiction and the 'Matrix of Analogy,'" *Kenyon Review* 11 (1949), 539-60; Dorothy Van Ghent, *The English Novel* (New York: Rinehart, 1953); and David Daiches, who calls Austen a "Marxist before Marx" ("Jane Austen, Karl Marx and the Aristocratic Dance," *American Scholar* 17 [1948], 289-98).

9. For an interesting discussion of contradiction in literary texts, see Rosalind Coward and John Ellis, *Language and Materialism* (London: Routledge and Kegan Paul, 1977), 87ff.

10. Nancy K. Miller, "Emphasis Added: Plots and Plausibilities in Women's Fiction," *PMLA* 97 (1981), 36-48; my remarks on maxims are based on Miller's discussion.

11. Gérard Genette, "Vraisemblance et Motivation," in *Figures II* (Paris: Seuil, 1969), 71-99; translated by Nancy Miller, 38-39.

12. Jane Austen, *Pride and Prejudice,* ed. Tony Tanner (Harmondsworth: Penguin, 1972), 51; all references are to this edition.

13. Jane Austen, *Emma,* ed. R. W. Chapman (Cambridge: Riverside, 1957), 20. All references are to this edition.

14. In an essay on *Persuasion,* Gene Ruoff points out that at the end of *Pride and Prejudice,* the worth of each character is represented by his or her "proximity and access to Pemberley" ("Anne Eliott's Dowry: Reflections on the Ending of *Persuasion,*" *The Wordsworth Circle* 7 [1976], 343).

15. See Tanner's introduction to the Penguin edition in which he points out that "the grounds, the house, the portrait, all bespeak the man—they represent a visible extension of his inner qualities, his true style" (24).

16. Remember that late in the novel in response to Jane's question, "tell me how long you have loved him," Elizabeth says, "I believe I must date it from my first seeing his beautiful grounds at Pemberley" (382). This sentence is followed by "another entreaty that she should be serious," but Austen's point is clear enough—no one is immune.

17. Terry Eagleton, *Criticism and Ideology* (New York: Schocken, 1978) discusses the way in which novels display the "fault lines" of a particular period or culture. His Marxist perspective is useful to any feminist analysis of literary texts.

18. Macherey, trans. Geoffrey Wall, *A Theory of Literary Production* (London: Routledge and Kegan Paul, 1978), 84. See also Wolfgang Iser's discussion of indeterminacy in *The Implied Reader* (Baltimore: Johns Hopkins Univ. Press, 1974), 29-56.

19. Marilyn Butler, *Jane Austen and the War of Ideas* (Oxford: Clarendon, 1976), 3. For recent examples of the opposing point of view, see Nina Auerbach's "O Brave New World: Evolution and Revolution in *Persuasion,*" *ELH* 39 (1972), 112-28; and Susan Morgan, *In the Meantime* (Chicago: Univ. of Chicago Press, 1980).

20. Butler, 215, 290.

21. Morgan, 10; and William A. Walling, "The Glorious Anxiety of Motion: Jane Austen's *Persuasion,*" *The Wordsworth Circle* 7 (1976), 333-41.

22. Louis Althusser, *Lenin and Philosophy and Other Essays,* trans. Ben Brewster (New York: Monthly Review Press, 1971), 222.

23. Althusser, 222-23.

24. Glenn W. Hatfield, *Henry Fielding and the Language of Irony* (Chicago: Univ. of Chicago Press, 1968), 177-96.

25. See Morgan, who takes Elizabeth's view (92-97). She condemns Charlotte Lucas to the "immoral" company of Isabella Thorpe, Mary Crawford, and Lucy Steele, a singularly ungenerous judgment that distorts the text and ignores both Austen's ironic commentary on Elizabeth's very different judgment of Wickham's engagement and Elizabeth's own changed opinion of Charlotte's situation later during her visit with her friend (see 703).

26. Butler sees Elizabeth's conflicting attitudes toward Charlotte and Wickham as "pointlessly inconsistent" (214). She ignores Austen's emphatic critique of the double standard that condoned such behavior for a man who must, after all, head a household, but condemned a woman who makes similar choices as mercenary.

27. Hatfield claims that Austen insists only on the "original" meaning of the word *prudence* rather than on its increasingly common meaning in eighteenth-century usage, "deceit" or "cunning" (196); however, attention to the various uses of the word in her novels suggests that Austen, like Fielding, plays with the conflicting meanings of the term.

28. For a discussion of style as meaning and of eighteenth-century parallelism and antithesis generally, see W. K. Wimsatt, Jr., *The Prose Style of Samuel Johnson* (New Haven: Yale Univ. Press, 1941).

29. Lloyd W. Brown, *Bits of Ivory* (Baton Rouge: Louisiana State Univ. Press, 1973) presents an interesting discussion of Austen's ambiguous diction in terms of eighteenth-century philosophical and moral writings (15-51). See also K. C. Phillips,

Jane Austen's English (London: Deutsch, 1970); Stuart Tave, *Some Words of Jane Austen* (Chicago: Univ. of Chicago Press, 1973); and most recently, Janice Bowman Swanson, "Toward a Rhetoric of Self: The Art of *Persuasion*," *Nineteenth-Century Fiction* 36 (1981), 1-21.

30. Jane Austen, *Persuasion* (New York: NAL, 1964), 31. All references are to this edition.

31. See also Brown's discussion of Austen's narrative conclusions, 223-35.

32. For Miller in *Narrative and its Discontents,* Austen's fiction enacts a perpetual double bind between "its tendency to disown at an ideological level what it embraces at a constructional one," that is, the moral lapses, blindness, or wayward-ness of her heroines. Despite the richness of his reading of Austen, he fails to see that the "coinci-dence of truth with closure in Jane Austen's nov-els" is undermined by her ironic play with the conventions of the female plot (46, 54).

33. For a detailed and scholarly discussion of Aus-ten's place on the philosophical and political map of the late eighteenth and early nineteenth centu-ries, see Butler, and Tanner's introduction, 42-45.

34. Marxist Feminist Literature Collective, "Women's Writing; *Jane Eyre, Shirley, Villette, Aurora Leigh,*" *Ideology and Consciousness* (Spring, 1978), 34-35. Nancy Miller argues that the fantasy and extravagance of plot in women's fiction is linked to their unsatisfied ambitious wishes or de-sires often concealed in seemingly erotic longing (40-41); see also Gilbert and Gubar, 336ff.

35. "Women's Writing," 31.

36. Annette Kolodny, "Some Notes on Defining a 'Feminist Literary Criticism,'" *Critical Inquiry* 2 (1975), 78.

37. *Ce sexe qui n'en est pas un* (Paris: Minuit, 1977), 134ff.

38. See Froma I. Zeitlin's interesting discussion of parody and mimesis in "Travesties of Gender and Genre in Aristophanes' *Thesmophoriazousae,*" *Critical Inquiry* 8 (1981), 311ff.

Claudia Brodsky Lacour (essay date fall 1992)

SOURCE: Lacour, Claudia Brodsky. "Austen's *Pride and Prejudice* and Hegel's 'Truth in Art': Concept, Reference, and History." *ELH* 59, no. 3 (fall 1992): 597-623.

[*In the following essay, Lacour explores modes of ab-stract and concrete representation in Austen's novel. Lacour argues that* Pride and Prejudice *represents a pivotal work in the history of literary realism.*]

I: Historicisms and Narrative

It is a truth generally acknowledged, that narrative is in need of a new form of analysis. A field of study that not very long ago seemed coherently defined and self-contained is presently undergoing historical change, as interpretative activities of an avowedly partisan stamp all but replace the structuralist and semiotic pursuit of a formal poetics or "science" of narration. The leading notion of a generative "grammar," of a single syntactic pattern abstractable from every narrative text, has been succeeded by a hyperrealist investigation of narrative *context*; the truth of the archive, the labyrinth of quotid-ian detail, has come to command the kind of belief pre-viously accorded to indexical charts and geometrical paradigms, the spare outlines of Chomskian trees and Greimasian rectangles.

Characterized as a change in conceptual models, this shift conforms to a traditional picture of the history of modern literary criticism, and may indeed appear typi-cal. On closer scrutiny, however, a less familiar theo-retical complication emerges, setting this picture askew if not altering it altogether. For the current change in the focus of narrative interpretation also involves a sig-nificant shift of *reference,* a turn from the concerns and terms of literary theory to theories of history. This movement may be viewed in turn as a translation be-tween theoretical genres, or, more often the case, as a closer approximation of literary studies to the real. But the interpretation of narrative fiction by way of contex-tual data organized according to concepts originating in theories of history sets into motion a considerable theo-retical difficulty resembling in certain fundamental re-spects a vicious circle.

At the level of methodology, the shift from the study of the specificity of literary form to the pursuit of a truth embedded in specific historical content inevitably en-gages the interpretation of narrative in an ambiguous conceptual relation to narration itself. The theoretical writings that have served as cognitive models or sup-ports for the contextualist approach make this ambigu-ity conspicuous. For those theories that have largely en-couraged new historicisms of literature often rely in their own conceptualization of history on some version of narrative form. Foucault's layered narrative of suc-cessive perceptual "ages" identified with homogeneous and hegemonic doctrines of "representation," and Lyo-tard's speculative tale of the metahistorical "grand nar-ratives" that have served to "legitimize" cognitive and political practices come to mind most obviously as widely diffused examples of *theoretical* narration whose explicit conceptual aim was to provide a truer under-standing of history, and so of the present, by taking the form and content of narration to task.[1]

In attempting to merge empirical with theoretical or epistemological interests, contemporary historicisms that seek to dispute the claims of historically delimited, ideological fictions derive needed leverage from narrative form and narrative representation. Within the course of abstract formulations aimed at elaborating a general conception of history such ambivalent discursive practices are entirely understandable, if not indeed inevitable, and it may only be in their own claim to operate without narrative means that some current theories of history can most accurately be considered "new." But contextualist studies of *literary* narrative that take up a "post-narrative" historical stance manifest this ambivalence in a different, more literal manner, directly displacing their own field of reference from textual details to external events, from the already-narrated, tainted by the "fictions" of history, to non-literary, historical narration. Such efforts at reconceiving the past or of rediscovering history as it is at once excluded and suggested by literature are less interpretive than they are like narratives themselves, alternatives to, or fresh historical explanations of, stories no longer viewed as merely formal or innocent fictions. In the place of stories once relegated, along with problems of concrete narrative analysis, to the empirically slippery category of artistic expression, appear stories credited with telling the truth about nonfictional agents and occurrences. In substituting the object of historical reality for the representations of literary fiction, contextual studies of narrative fashion other narratives with claims to new referential accuracy. Thus it is that, on a second level of actualization, the turn to empirical, archival history remains—if in displaced form—literary. The new historicisms, like the old historicisms, conceive of history and narrative as reflected in one another, whether it is the right or the left hand of history that writes the text.

The same hand, however, fashions an infinite variety of artifacts, all the made phenomena, self-representations, and fetishes a culture throws up. In this regard contextualist critics may have taken another theoretical cue from the program of an overarching *Kulturkritik* developed by Adorno, without distinguishing, as Adorno himself generally did not, the literary from any other kind of artifact.[2] While Adorno's own purely theoretical writings (on dialectic, epistemology, and aesthetics) were more thoroughly enmeshed in the conceptual logic of idealist and critical philosophy than those of any other philosopher of cultural history since Hegel, his writings on literature tended to take the literary *less,* so to speak, at its word, demonstrating little of the same admirably excessive attention to problems of articulation.[3] That conceptual rigor Adorno reserved for the language of critical philosophy, revealing the social contagion of culture always about to become kitsch.[4] But, as consciously post-philosophical as post-narrational in orientation, new historical or contextualist critics who similarly consider narrative fiction as but another specimen of general cultural production lay no such claim to a rigor dependent—as Adorno never failed to recall—on

a concept of "objective," because negatively constituted, "truth."[5] Their inclusion of narratives and narrative form within a defined field of cultural givens thus operates quite differently, effectively raising narrative to the level of reliable historical evidence and reducing it to the reflection of a transhistorical truth, the tautological (Adorno would say vulgar) power of power to distort perception. Unlike dialectical analyses, the contextualist interpretation of narrative may ascribe either a naively mimetic or a subtly complicitous intention to the historical author. But since all authorship, inscribed *a priori* in history, is conceived to reiterate preexistent relations of power and authority, the interpretative result in either case is an affirmation of discursive culpability, a strangely anthropomorphic view of literary form most frequently expressed in the question of what narrative (a or any narrative) is up to. Here it is the critic of ideology whose gaze indicts as it defines, ultimately miming the self-legitimizing techniques of *surveiller et punir.*

Yet, to gaze is not to read, and to judge narrative is to misjudge literature. By switching the verdict on narrative from (aesthetically) innocent to (ideologically) guilty, proponents of contextualist literary criticism continue to measure the promise of truth in discourse against the writing of fiction, and thus remain within a historiographic tradition which, younger only than the writings of Thucydides, is as old as the conventional division between empirical and conceptual history. Contemporary historical criticism continues to enforce conventional notions of discursive truth by opposing empirical history to *narrative* literature in particular, because narrative more than any other discursive form seems to imply a conceptual manipulation of the empirical, a *mis*representation of the real toward the end of constructing a coherent fiction. Inattentive to the links between truth and fiction formed at every moment by the discourse of narrative fiction, contextualist narratives and appropriations of narrative attempt to distinguish the truth of their own representations, whether factual or theoretical, from the distortions of literature. In so doing they pile fiction upon fiction, telling a story *about* story-telling, a story in which narrative itself already stands convicted of iniquitous activities.[6]

II: HEGEL'S HISTORY OF "TRUTH IN ART"

A closer look at individual narrative constructions routinely wreaks havoc with the contextualist protocol. While almost every narrative can be retold as a series of events, it is only at their most superficial level that narrative fictions may be equated simply with the stories they tell. The hybrid language and dynamic character of narrative call for more complicated forms of analysis, just as the lived experience that historical writings strives to represent literally seems to call forth all the verbal complexity and formal precision of representational literature.[7] Finally, it is in this interaction of history with its verbal analysis that the path of contextual criticism proves most circular. For if the truth of a fictive representation is to be located in concrete historical detail, such detail must first be *abstracted,* for theoretical reasons, from its empirical context. The privileging of concrete particulars *outside* the fiction may yield a theory, which, in seeking to avoid nonreferential abstraction, generalizes the particular.

More than any other theory of history, Hegel's philosophy attempts to navigate this Scylla and Charybdis of the general and the particular. His dialectic describes thought in general as the translation of the particular into the absolute. But, for Hegel, that general translation must also be concretely perceivable. The particular objects which, for Hegel, concretely embody and reveal the general are the fictions of art. As the "sensory embodiment of truth" art precedes both religion and philosophy in Hegel's universal history of spirit.[8] If, as Hegel famously remarked, "art in its highest determination is for us a thing of the past" (1:25), it is also the beginning of the future of all speculation—of religion, of philosophy, and, ultimately, of the overcoming, in absolute spirit, of thought. A theory of art which argues that its fictions make thinking possible by first particularizing the general in concrete form, must itself begin by clearing away theories of art which make thinking impossible, in that they conflate or isolate the abstract and the concrete.

In the section of the Introduction to the *Aesthetics* entitled, "Scientific Modes of Treating the Beautiful and Art" [*Wissenschaftliche Behandlungsarten des Schönen und der Kunst*], Hegel juxtaposes his dialectical thesis that "truth" is "revealed in the sensory form of art" (1:82) to two already existing and "opposed modes" of treating art [*zwei entgegengesetzte Behandlungsweisen*]:

> On the one hand we see the science of art concern itself only externally with real works of art, classing them chronologically in art history, offering observations on the work of art at hand, or sketching theories which should provide the general point of view for judgment as well as for artistic production.
>
> On the other hand we see science independently relegate thought about the beautiful to *itself,* thought that only brings forth the universal, an abstract philosophy of the beautiful which does not touch upon the work of art in its particularity.
>
> Insofar as the first of these is concerned, which takes the *empirical* as its point of departure, this is the necessary path for those who wish to educate themselves as art scholars . . .
>
> In this view each art work belongs to *its time, its people,* and its environment, and depends especially on historical and other representations and aims . . . the individual nature of the work of art is related to the particular.
>
> (1:29-30)

Hegel notes that, while they originate in the historical and the particular, these considerations of concrete works of art give rise historically to more general "theories of the arts." Such "theories" may have much to say "*im einzelnen*"—"in specific"—but, Hegel observes, they become "very trivial reflections" once translated from the "narrow sphere of the work." In their *universality,* they "progress to no determination of the *particular,* which is, after all, the first business of theory of art [*um welches es doch vornehmlich zu tun ist*]" (1:31). Over the course of their own history, then, *historical* treatments of art come to resemble their opposite, that second mode "which strives to recognize the beautiful as such," considering objects "not in their *particularity* but in their *universality*" (1:39). Hegel argues that this abstraction—"the ground of an abstract metaphysics" beginning with Plato—"no longer suffices. We must grasp this [idea of the beautiful] deeper and more concretely, for the contentlessness [*Inhaltslosigkeit*], which clings to the Platonic idea, no longer satisfies the richer philosophical needs of our spirit today" (1:39).

"Today," according to Hegel, the spirit demands another way, a path of reflection which "contains mediated within it both these extremes, in that it unites metaphysical universality with the determination of real particularity" (1:39). This way is Hegel's aesthetics, a historical theory of art that doubles as a theoretical history, the speculative tale of symbolic, classic, and romantic phases in which art forms develop so as to "disclose the truth in art": the particular as prelude to the universal. It is also, however, before Hegel, the way of Austen's ***Pride and Prejudice,*** a fiction of the universal pretensions of the particular which, *as* a fiction, rings changes upon the order of Hegelian history. A narrative fiction, it also marks a change in literary history, a dialectical moment when literature becomes identified with the historical and the particular, the representation (or misrepresentation) of the real classified chronologically by literary scholars as "realism."

III: "REALISM" HISTORICALLY

Before the categorization of "realism," the relationship between the concrete and the abstract—the basis of "truth in art" for Hegel—was the particular linguistic focus of early modern fiction. In eighteenth-century "realist" fictions by such experimenters in prose as Richardson, Diderot, Rousseau, and Goethe, the real is the heterogeneous reality of narrated lived experience.[9] Such fiction we now classify as "psychological," as less intent on representing objective reality than giving voice to personal subjectivity. This retrospective judgment of course is indebted largely to the first-person format of early realist fictions: journal, dialogue, and epistolary novels that purposefully avoided the third-person vehicle of traditional epic, mock-epic and romance.[10] The third-person narratives we now identify as realist appear to circumvent the problem of subjective *versus* objective narration by representing subjectivity "objectively" as a function of "character," a quasi-empirical, describable feature. But before the fiction of objectivity became equated with realism, first-person realist fiction represented not subjectivity as such but the recognition that realism in narration could only begin by representing reality *as it was experienced.* The primary activity narrated in early realist fiction is the act of articulating experience itself, an act combining sensory immediacy with linguistic mediation, discursive understanding and imagination with incomprehensibility, and which effects the actions of the fiction, its story, rather than the other way around. Early realist fiction is "true" to life neither in its power to represent historically delimited "truths," whether deemed subjective or ideological, nor in the level of referential accuracy with which it represents an empirical object world. The distinct categories of truth and reality meet explicitly in the composition of early realist fiction in the only manner in which they meet in reality, which is to say, in the mind's composition of experience.

But if truth in early realist fiction has everything to do with the mental activity of narration, the translation of realism from the first to the third person must introduce another means of representing the truth of experience now attributed to conventionally fictitious, reported individuals. On one level third-person realism displaces the process of articulating experience imitated in first-person realist fiction by conceptualizing its own representations in the articulate form of a plot; events draw their meaning not from the conceptual acts narrated to produce them but from the part they play in a narrated story, much as the writing of history gives narrative shape and meaning to events attributed to the reported dead. But in general third-person realist narrative replaces articulation with representation, conceptual speculation (now limited to stylized interventions of the narrative "voice") with description. To call such narrative "omniscient" or "authorial" is a convenient shorthand for saying that it already knows the reality it represents, as opposed to the immediate vagaries and urgencies of experience its characters may fall prey to. Representing its own omniscience through techniques of emplotment and description, realist narrative written in the third person introduces another dimension and problem of fiction. For such realism would be the fiction of knowing everything about a fiction about which nothing really needs to be known.

IV: ABSTRACT AND CONCRETE LANGUAGE IN AUSTEN

The historical transition between first and third-person narrative fiction, between speculative and representational realism—and the attendant difficulty in reconceiving the category of truth in fiction—are central to the works of Richardson's most important literary descendant, Jane Austen. The very titles of Austen's completed novels reveal the division between notional and concrete language in her understanding of narrative realism, dividing, as it happens evenly, between abstract nouns (**Sense and Sensibility, Pride and Prejudice,** and **Persuasion**) and the names of particular people and places (**Northanger Abbey, Mansfield Park,** and **Emma**; the uncompleted works, **Lady Susan, The Watson,** and **Sanditon,** are also named for fictive particulars). The specific problems involved in relating these two kinds of language—in representing "persuasion," for example, in the form of a realist or nonallegorical story—were never directly addressed by Austen. But the difficulty of translating between abstract and representational language by way of narration and thus of representing an abstraction, truth, in fiction, pervades the structure of the novel often regarded as her purest success.[11] More than any other work by Austen, **Pride and Prejudice** gives free rein to the powers of conceptualization, and it is just this continuous conceptual motion of the novel that Austen considered its structural defect. In a celebrated letter to her sister Cassandra of 4 February 1813, she criticized the recently completely **Pride and Prejudice** for the very qualities that would make it the most popular of her fictions:

> The work is rather too light, and bright, and sparkling; it wants shade; it wants to be stretched out here and there with a long chapter of sense, if it could be had; if not, of solemn specious nonsense, about something unconnected with the story; an essay on writing, a critique on Walter Scott, or the history of Buonaparté, or anything that would form a contrast, and bring the reader with increased delight to the playfulness and epigrammatism of the general style.[12]

Pride and Prejudice, Austen fears, may be overrich in its own verbal brilliance, the quickness and levity of wit that have come to characterize her writings as a whole. For like the curt articulations of opinion that are the hallmark of her dialogues, Austen's narrative voice is often viewed as too knowing, too consistently ironic in tone, her novels (with the possible exception of **Mansfield Park**) as lacking in a regard for the hard facts of reality and moral responsibility of art.[13] In her letter Austen mocks just such a criticism of her fiction, one which esteems that, in order to be read seriously, novels must incorporate kinds of writing which they are not: "an essay on writing, a critique of Walter Scott, or the history of Buonaparté." Yet **Pride and Prejudice,** she reflects, may be so much itself as to impede the reader's "increased delight." In the absence of any objective "contrast"—whether "a long chapter of sense" or "of solemn specious nonsense"—the displays of quicksilver wit that comprise the predominant verbal mode of the novel may be so "sparkling" as to divert the reader from appreciating the "general style" of which they are a part.

Three years later, such an appreciation of Austen's style was written by the same author whose writing she suggested be critiqued so as to provide the wanted contrast to her own. In a review of *Emma* written shortly after that novel's publication in 1816, Walter Scott drew a general comparison between Austen's fiction and the history of the novel from which it departs. Most important for the present analysis is his discussion of Austen's realism, which he describes as a freeing of the novel from the constraints of its "original style," the representation of the "extraordinary" it inherited from romance:

> In its first appearance, the novel was the legitimate child of romance; and though the manner and general tone of the composition were altered so as to suit modern times, the author remained fettered by many peculiarities derived from the original style of romantic fiction. . . . [T]he reader expected to peruse a course of adventures more interesting and extraordinary than those which occur in his own life, or that of his next-door neighbours.[14]

The new style of Austen's fiction recalls the "course" of one's "own life" on two related levels for Scott: as a structured series of mimetic actions ("the studied involution and extrication of the story"[15]) and as internally ruled experience. Not only what people *do* but how they themselves *conceive* their actions compose the scope of the reality Austen represents according to Scott. It is this added dimension of internal comprehension, including, for the first time, the real consequences of misapprehension or mistake, which forever separates, in Scott's analysis, the new novel from the old. I quote from his description of romantic fiction at length because it provides, point for point, a perfect contrast with Austen's own:

> [T]he second broad line of distinction between the novel, as formerly composed, and real life, [is] the difference . . . of the sentiments. . . . In the serious class of novels, the hero was usually
>
> A knight of love, who never broke a vow.
>
> And although, in those of a more humorous cast, he was permitted a license . . . still a distinction was demanded even from Peregrine Pickle or Tom Jones. . . . The heroine was, of course, still more immaculate; and to have conferred her affection upon any other than the lover to whom the reader had destined her from their first meeting, would have been a crime against sentiment which no author . . . would have hazarded, under the old *régime*. . . . We, therefore, bestow no mean compliment upon the author of *Emma,* when we say that, keeping close to common incidents, and to such characters as occupy the ordinary walks of life, she has produced sketches of such spirit and originality, that we never miss the excitation which depends upon a narrative of uncommon events. . . . The narrative of all her novels is composed of such common occurrences as may have fallen under the observation of most folks; and her dramatis personae conduct them-

selves upon the motives and principles which the readers may recognize as ruling their own and that of most of their acquaintances. The kind of moral, also, which these novels inculcate, applies equally to the paths of common life.[16]

Like the new combination of mimetic with conceptual action (proceeding by "motives and principles") in Austen's fiction, Austen's "originality," as described by Scott, sets new standards for our perception of the original. With Austen, originality in prose fiction is no longer a matter of invention but rather a mode of representing the commonplace as it had never been comprehended before, of affording the reader a new medium for "observ[ing]" and "recogniz[ing]" "real life." The idea of originality in recognition may seem a regressive view of innovation in fiction, but only if one underestimates the power of recognition that is meant. According to Scott, the force of recognition that Austen's fiction effects may be so comprehensive as to invert our conception of mimesis itself, making the fiction appear the model for the real, as he illustrates by way of an anecdote relating to *Pride and Prejudice*: "A friend of ours, whom the author never saw or heard of was at once recognized by his own family as the original of Mr. Bennet, and we do not know if he has yet got rid of the nickname."[17]

Fictions that are novel in that they are styled on "real life" rather than "romantic fiction," fictions that would be unthinkable under the "old *régime*" of romance, may read in fact—which is to say in our actual experience of them—as if they weren't novels, or fictions, at all. Lesser wits than Mr. Bennet will be no less recognizably rendered, with the result, Scott complains, that "their prosing is apt to become as tiresome in fiction as in real society."[18] That is to say, instead of experiencing Austen's fictions as artistic or aesthetic objects conventionally expected to afford pleasure, we may experience them with mixed feelings, the feelings of pleasure and displeasure with which we experience living. In a later discussion of *Pride and Prejudice* (a journal entry of 14 March 1826), Scott's appreciation of Austen's ability to achieve "truth" both of "description" and of "sentiment" leads him to regard the reality of the author's own life with just such felt ambivalence:

> That young lady had a talent for describing the involvement and feelings of characters of ordinary life which is to me the most wonderful I ever met with. The Big Bow-wow strain I can do myself like any now going, but the exquisite touch which renders ordinary commonplace things and characters interesting from the truth of the description and the sentiment is denied to me. What a pity such a gifted creature died so early![19]

V: AUSTEN'S HISTORY OF AN IDEA

To say that, unlike the ever-popular "Big Bow-wow strain" in fiction, Austen's fictions represented for the first time popularly recognizable "truth," is to ascribe a very serious purpose to the novel Austen created and to set the realist novel even further apart from any notion of prose literature as pleasurable diversion, a notion typified, traditionally and to this day, in the forms of historical epic and romance.[20] It is to say that general knowledge may be abstracted from the fictive representation of particulars, that part of the "real life" early realist fiction represents is the experience of cognition. Yet **Pride and Prejudice,** Austen's tour-de-force of the life of the mind, was faulted by her for just that mental skillfulness, its cognitive flair. **Pride and Prejudice,** Austen suggests, may appear to present no obstacles to the mind's power of illumination, to cast no shadow where it reflects, to contain no sense of gravity at odds with the novel's levity—nothing which would stretch or extend the fiction by holding the mind in place. The sharp succession of thoughts the novel narrates may appear devoid of any particular weight, and that lack of substance or of seriousness is in fact the first impression the novel gives.[21] For how can we take seriously a novel which begins by speaking about universal knowledge as follows:

> It is a truth universally acknowledged, that a single man in possession of a good fortune, must be in want of a wife.[22]

Not only the claims made by Walter Scott about the special significance of Austen's novels—the distinct moment they constitute in the history of narrative fiction *because of their* "*truth*"—but the universal claim made contemporaneously by Hegel, that the relation of the abstract to the concrete in art embodies the relation of truth to history—both these claims, covering very different registers, make the opening of **Pride and Prejudice** a matter of some theoretical note. Why should a novel ostensibly about the gain of knowledge—that is, the recognition and overcoming of the errors of perception signified by the abstract nouns, "pride and prejudice"—begin by making light of knowledge as these first words of **Pride and Prejudice** famously do? Such a question may seem out of line with the apparently ironic tone of this opening pronouncement, which reads less like the beginning of an omniscient realist fiction than the preface to a domestic comedy based on the propositional philosophy of David Hume.[23] But it does address the peculiar imbalance of sense that this purposefully mundane reference to a "universally acknowledged" "truth"—*unlike* a universally acknowledged truth—effects. While truth provides the ground of knowledge, this statement destabilizes the concept of truth, producing not knowledge but the effort to attain it, which is to say, with Hegel, history. For the imbalance between concept ("truth") and reference ("a single man in possession of a good fortune") enacted in Austen's opening sentence provokes another kind of action, one that unfolds specifically in time. What this experience of uncertainty initiates—as reaction and as counterweight to

it—is a specifically *narrative* activity of understanding, a second moment or movement of thought that entails with it the form of diachrony. Here diachrony is not a form presented to, but rather created by the comprehending mind, whose attempt to understand concretely the meaning of a particular "truth"[24] stated to be acknowledged universally extends dynamically to the following sentence and new paragraph in which, within characteristic Austenian "limits,"[25] a minor revolution in narrative understanding begins:

> However little known the feelings or views of such a man may be on his first entering a neighbourhood, this truth is so well fixed in the minds of the surrounding families, that he is considered as the rightful property of some one or other of their daughters.

Remarkably and almost unnoticeably, universal knowledge begins to be broken down here by the very workings of representation: certain "feelings or views" are admitted as ignored by this universally acknowledged truth—those of "such a man . . . on his first entering a neighbourhood"—and the "truth" itself is said to be "fixed" only in the "minds of the surrounding families," families qualified in addition as having one or more unmarried daughters. In the space of one sentence a kind of mock or ironic maxim has given way to the particular exigencies of narration: persons, actions, and their situation in context, their coordination along the axes of time and place—the demands not of universal knowledge but of the construction of a particular narrative plot. This rapid-fire process of specification continues immediately in the next sentence, which is no longer even a properly narrative sentence but one taken literally out of context, a piece of quoted dialogue spoken at a specific moment to someone named Mr. Bennet and concerning a specific place called Netherfield Park: "'My dear Mr. Bennet,' said his lady to him one day, 'have you heard that Netherfield is let at last?' Mr. Bennet replied that he had not."

What is effected in this simple sequence of sentences is an anatomy, as clearly delineated as each new paragraph division, of the linguistic mental work that is the internal rule of fiction. If in reading **Pride and Prejudice** we read right by them, accepting such conceptual activity as given, that is because Austen had laid out concisely and deftly what we take blindly for granted in reading fiction: that fiction, like history, depends absolutely upon the representation of specifics, and that the relation between such specifics and any universal truth is as disputable and undependable as it is also absolutely necessary. In short, if there is a universal truth governing the writing of fiction, it is that fiction must be composed in concrete and specific rather than universal and abstract terms. Yet the specifics represented in novels would be linguistically indistinguishable from yesterday's news ("Dog Bites Man On Main St.," "Young Man Moves Into Netherfield") if narrative fiction did not also represent the way in which particulars are conceived and known. The fiction of *Pride and Prejudice* does not begin from the premise that the reality it represents can be known objectively as long as its own narrative reality is ignored. Austen's narrator does not opt out of the fiction by beginning with a third-person account of the narrative setting as if such a setting were *not* a beginning, a necessary device of the fiction, but rather an entry *in medias res* reflecting an already surrounding reality. All narratives must name places and agents as if representing a historical object world—this is their fiction. The opening of *Pride and Prejudice* neither conceals nor points to that fact but makes different forms of prose language enact its proof. Beginning with a proposition in the form of a universal truth, a truth already so trivialized and thus ironized in content that it appears at once to pit truth against all novels, including the one now beginning, the narrative takes shape *as* narrative in the moment it relativizes that truth, translating universal knowledge into a type of concrete context. The instability caused by the first sentence of *Pride and Prejudice* seems to settle down into the course of narration by moving "truth," as it were, along with Bingley, into a neighborhood.

By the third sentence, the type becomes fully particular, the neighborhood neighbors on Netherfield, and the neighbors are specific individuals made even more individual by speaking in their own words. But before there is a Mr. Bennet or a Mrs. Bennet who can name him for the reader, there is a statement implying that the fiction in which Mr. and Mrs. Bennet will continue to say and do things has some claim, however "narrow" and "trivial," in Hegel's terms, to the universal. The universal truth stated at the opening of the novel invokes the imagining of a diachronic context in which its immediately uncertain meaning may eventually be understood. The plot of *Pride and Prejudice,* one might say, remains to confirm that universal truth by submitting it to the trial and error of experience, relating an apodictic statement to concrete reality by involving truth in history. Like Hegel's "truth in art," Austen's novel, then, would be the history of an idea its opening sentence states. But the history which should demonstrate that idea, through the representation of narrative particulars, is named for the nonrepresentational causes of conceptual mistakes.

Just as the first sentence of *Pride and Prejudice* at once states a truth and unsettles the claim of truth to universal validity, a true history of "pride and prejudice" would be more like an antihistory, a story of enlightenment never attained. Austen's continuing development of the representational context of the novel certainly suggests as much. The ensuing dialogue between the Bennets, a well-deserving favorite of the novel's devotees, is a touchstone of Austen at her conceptual best. Composing almost the entire remainder of chapter 1, its

subject is the ostensible subject of all Austen's novels: marriage—the implied subject of this novel's opening maxim as well.[26] But in the course of the Bennets' dialogue it soon becomes apparent that its subject does not matter at all: it is not what is said about marriage, that most particular of universals, which matters here at the beginning of the novel (nor, arguably, anywhere else in Austen) but what is revealed about those who say it which sets the terms of the history of "pride and prejudice" to come. When Mrs. Bennet's praise of Mr. Bingley's bachelorhood and wealth ("What a fine thing for our girls!") inspires professions of literal-minded wonder from her husband ("How so? how can it affect them?"), and when her exclamations of exasperation ("My dear Mr. Bennet . . . how can you be so tiresome! You *know* that I am thinking of his marrying one of them") draw only a renewed exercise in disbelief ("Is that his design in settling here?" [3-4]), it is clear that Mr. and Mrs. Bennet, whatever thoughts may occupy them, are not in the habit of thinking along the same lines. Playing the part of the empirical philosopher to his wife's less subtle turn of mind, Mr. Bennet feigns a naivete that only years of experience can teach. Rather than describing that temporal situation as the Bennets' narrator, however, Austen again lets their dialogue do the talking for her. When Mr. Bennet finally accedes to understanding his wife's meaning, which now, or at any other time, is that their daughters must be married, he states flatly: "They have none of them much to recommend them . . . they are all silly and ignorant like other girls; but Lizzy has something more of quickness than her sisters" (5). Mrs. Bennet's protest— "Mr. Bennet, how can you abuse your own children in such a way? . . . You have no compassion on my poor nerves"—invites in turn her husband's elegant and thoroughly devastating reply, a concise survey of the long history of a mismarriage that no moment or chapter of dialogue can correct: "You mistake me, my dear. I have a high respect for your nerves. They are my old friends. I have heard you mention them with consideration these twenty years at least" (5).

Mr. Bennet is so skilled at talking past his wife and his wife so obtuse in talking at him that the idea of communication between them during this or any conversation of "these twenty years" appears a veritable ideal of human communion, an idea whose time has not previously and assuredly will never come. Indeed the uncrossing mental registers of their speech may explain the formal register in which it is undertaken, for Mrs. Bennet regularly addresses her husband as "Mr. Bennet" throughout the novel. The repetition of the proper noun, Bennet, the formal marker of the couple's alliance, may be Austen's means of narrating all that is shared by the couple, and of giving a new mental twist to the cliched sexual meaning of "a marriage in name alone." While the Bennets' daughters indicate their marriage has been consummated in the figurative physical sense, the Bennets' dialogues indicate they will never be linked in any terms less tangible, that as far as their minds go the word "Bennet" is the only linguistic reference they share.

Still this conversation devoid of common understanding may seem a simple comic interlude; as readers of a comic dialogue from which we assume a spectatorial distance, we may laugh at it, as we are certainly meant to, but only until it ends. For after Mr. and Mrs. Bennet have spoken, the voice of the maxim returns, speaking this time, however, and for the very first time, as the novel's third-person narrator. The tenor of that voice is just as definitive as before, but rather than stating a universal truth it narrates some very particular truths about Mr. and Mrs. Bennet, and these historical truths now have the effect (that, again, can only be called revolutionary) of standing the original maxim—both its form and overtly ironic content—on its head. For if marriage may result in the wedding of two such disparate spirits as Mr. and Mrs. Bennet then to follow the maxim may be to embrace a veritable kiss of death. The narrator concludes the opening chapter by declaring succinctly and directly what the preceding dialogue has dramatized at some length:

> Mr. Bennet was so odd a mixture of quick parts, sarcastic humour, reserve, and caprice, that the experience of three and twenty years had been insufficient to make his wife understand his character. *Her* mind was less difficult to develop. She was a woman of mean understanding, little information, and uncertain temper. When she was discontented she fancied herself nervous. The business of her life was to get her daughters married; its solace was visiting and news.
>
> (6)

Now the maxim, it may be objected, refers specifically to "a single man in possession of a good fortune," and surely if Mr. Bennet were so well-fortuned financially his wife's monomania for marrying their daughters to men of good fortune might not exist. Thus the marriage between the Bennets, which could be more accurately described as permanent spiritual divorce, a perfect disunion of dissimilar souls, or, to bastardize Shakespeare instead of John Donne, a marriage of such minds as are each other's true impediment—certainly the Bennets' marriage cannot be considered as an argument against the truth of the maxim, a constraint upon universality issuing from the realm of the concrete. Yet the reader who, having read further, thinks back to the maxim, will realize that the well-born and bred Mr. Bennet was indeed once a single man of good fortune. His mistake may have been to marry Mrs. Bennet but his single misfortune was to have only daughters, and thus to see his estate entailed to the insufferable Mr. Collins, the best argument made anywhere in fiction against the so-called natural right to property of the male. The first impression made by the maxim may be one of mere

Austenian mock-seriousness, but when one realizes that in accordance with it Mrs. Bennet became Mrs. Bennet, it appears upon further inspection a proposition of entirely serious consequence, in the negative sense that this "truth universally acknowledged" might result in a life-long mistake.

The first persons to be represented in this novel, or rather, to present themselves in their own words, are cogent arguments *against* the truth that the novel proposes. Within a few paragraphs of its opening sentence, as the novel moves, by way of representation, from the form of the maxim, to first-person dialogue, and finally, to authorial narration, the gulf it reveals between abstract and representational language steadily grows. Yet marriage, the predicative referent of the maxim, also remains the motor of the story of this novel: not only does the unbearable Collins, for whom any mate will do, pursue (in a manner of speaking) that predicate, but Bingley also wants to marry Jane, and Darcy (remarkably) Elizabeth. From the obsequious Collins to the sternly self-assured Darcy, men of good fortune in *Pride and Prejudice,* as stated by the maxim and represented in the novel's story line, are "in want of a wife." How does the knot get tied in this novel? Since this act of predication is the central action of the novel, to ask this question is the same as asking how abstraction is translated into representation, how the maxim gets made, or tied, into plot.

Marriages in this novel are made when pride and prejudice no longer hold sway. What, then, precisely are pride and prejudice? First of all they are a quotation from a novel well known and admired by Austen, Fanny Burney's *Cecilia,* which closes with a kind of neatly self-canceling repetition of the terms. Pride and prejudice, it is concluded in that novel, are the source of woes and also of their overcoming: "If to PRIDE and PREJUDICE you owe your miseries, so wonderfully is good and evil balanced, that to PRIDE and PREJUDICE you will also owe their termination."[27] Austen knew her audience would recognize the subtext of her title, but *Pride and Prejudice* is not like *Cecilia* precisely because in *Cecilia* pride and prejudice are easily identifiable, and, as the shaping motives of the novel's action, easily known. Here Austen's reference to an earlier text points to the differences rather than similarities of lexical significance that arise when abstract terms are engaged in a representational context. At the same time it points to the further possibility that within her own text these words may also have very different meanings, as, quite literally, in *Pride and Prejudice* they do.[28]

Prejudice, one can say to begin with, is a consequence of pride, a disposition for or against which results from the pride of being disposed in any manner at all. Prejudice indicates an object only in function of a subject who does or does not feel disposed toward it; thus it serves more to reflect and define the self than any particular object to which it refers. Prejudice affirms, negatively, the identity of the prejudger: he or she is someone who thinks something about something else and thinks this without need of external proof. As such prejudice is, most obviously, an inverted form of self-affirmation, or, in other words, pride. But what can be said about pride, an abstract noun which need not take any object? One can be proud of something, as one can be prejudiced for or against something, but in addition one can simply be proud without there being a fixed reference point for one's pride at all. It is Darcy's pride which, in one of the most memorable passages of the novel, is said to transform him within no time from an object of "admiration" to one of "disgust" in the eyes of those gathered at the same ball at which he does in fact judge and reject Elizabeth, after a moment's inspection, as quite beneath him (10). And it is his own "pride" that Darcy himself will condemn as the narrow habit of mind from which Elizabeth, in rejecting him, had forcibly freed him (369). Similarly Elizabeth, so unlike Darcy in temperament, fortune, and circumstance, who would sooner laugh at herself and at Darcy's initial insult than indulge in any form of conceit, eventually attributes her misjudgment of Darcy to the "vanity" of having "prided" herself in her very ability to discern character truly (208). And it is Elizabeth who will finally commend Darcy for his pride once she believes she loves him, a pride she now perceives as well-merited and which she wishes her own sisters had been taught; a "pride" which in Darcy, as she ultimately persuades her father, is not "improper" at all (396). "Pride" is also appealed to by the professional eloper Wickham as the source to which the evil actions he imputes to Darcy "may be traced" (81). Indeed, the abstract notion of pride may be appealed to by just about anyone in this novel, and applied to just about anyone as well. It may be a good or bad thing in ostensibly good or bad people, or it may be a good or bad thing alternately in a single person, persons such as Darcy and Elizabeth themselves. If pride can be applied to anyone in the novel, it can serve any representational end; it is not a concept by which we can judge characters, for even such judgments may then become a source of pride. Like the novel's opening maxim, pride becomes a highly plastic bit of abstraction when imprinted with the particular, a highly malleable concept or verbal bit of clay rather than the tough bit of ivory into which, as Austen once remarked metaphorically, she carefully carved her fictions.[29]

If pride is a word emptied of specific determination in that it is filled with too many determinations, too many particular meanings—meanings that in different contexts serve different and often contradictory ends—then how is the end of knowledge, the overcoming of pride and prejudice, served in a novel named for pride and prejudice, words that hold too many meanings and thus

cannot be said to hold true? How do prejudices become true perceptions in the novel, perceptions that take a shape which holds, as, hypothetically, the shape of marriage should hold instead of changing both shape and object with infinite plasticity? The fickle quality of perception in the novel is reflected not only—if most openly—in the tendency of Lydia and her mother to praise anything in a red coat that walks (Austen's wonderful analogue, from the female perspective, for that time-worn metonymy: anything in a skirt that moves), or in Darcy's unforgettably "mortifying," because unexpectedly "pleasing," second impression of Elizabeth, but also in Elizabeth's own response to Darcy's criticism of the "unvarying" confines of country society, a criticism applicable to Austen's fictions as well.[30] At that early stage of the novel it is Elizabeth who speaks wittily in favor of the inconstancy of human nature: "But people themselves alter so much, that there is something new to be observed in them for ever" (43). Once again the conceits of Shakespeare's Sonnet 116 offer a critical gloss on the novel's steady stream of conceptual fictions: "Let me not to the marriage of true minds / Admit impediment. Love is not love / Which alters when it alteration finds." For something must indeed be *in*alterable, be unlike pride and prejudice in this novel, if Darcy is to marry Elizabeth and her feelings of disregard for him turn sensibly to their opposite. Something must be observable that cannot alter itself in the course of observation, that cannot be submitted to the abstractual alchemy of pride and prejudice, if pride and prejudice, the unreliable notions of the novel, are to be related to truth by representation, to name the history of how they are overcome.

The endless interplay of abstraction and representation in the novel make such a thing hard to fix, yet, as sure as the novel begins with a maxim, it concludes by way of the particular, suggesting what such a thing is. Furthermore, in order to be true not only to Austen's "truth" but to its consequences, the diachronic mental activity involved in understanding her unstable equation of the universal with the particular, such a thing must function as a referent both of mimetic representation and of verbal conceptualization. In addition to concretely plotted appearance it must take conversational form, providing the referent for a remark conceived as ironic *within* dialogue which, ironically, can be no irony for the author of that dialogue at all.

If Darcy, on second observation, notices the "beautiful expression of [Elizabeth's] dark eyes" (23), it is for the intelligence and liveliness reflected in them that he desires to know her better. It is that same liveliness that "bewitched" him when reflected in her retorts (52), the liveliness of any conversation entered into with Elizabeth, the life of language spoken with the inexplicable quickness and grace of an ironic wit. But for Elizabeth to desire Darcy she must see something fixed—something with which she can have no conversation, which cannot be made light, bright, and sparkling by the lively translating power of her mind. One such thing, most obviously, is Darcy's letter, a surprising inclusion in the novel in that it is inordinately long and takes up almost an entire chapter (vol. 2, chapter 12), itself the second longest chapter in the book (yet still not, according to Austen, the needed chapter "of sense"). Darcy's letter is of course made of language, but, like no stretch of language in the novel preceding it, it takes the form of monologue, the recounting of past occurrences that Wickham had already misrepresented in dialogue, a give and take of information and opinion in which Elizabeth had all too eagerly engaged. Dialogues may shape or alter one's thoughts, but there is nothing transformative one can say back to a written letter, nothing, in any case, that can change the writing on the page: that writing is fixed and its author beyond hearing, beyond the reach of our sentiments and beyond our power to change the sentiments which first gave rise to the words on the page. Darcy's letter does not bewitch Elizabeth but rather makes her think that, before reading it, "I never knew myself" (208), and her reading of that letter cannot bewitch Darcy as her conversation with him had done. The solitary writing and the solitary reading of that letter lead instead, as Elizabeth reflects negatively, to knowledge, just as another solitary moment in **Pride and Prejudice** does. But this is a moment of knowledge which makes Elizabeth know Darcy in addition to herself, a knowledge which in her own mind defines another as its object.

In volume 3, chapter 1, the longest chapter in the novel, Elizabeth makes her celebrated visit to Pemberley. For the first and only time she gets to see something that she may admire rather than reshape into something worth seeing by the power of her ironic perspective, make bright by the power of her wit. Much has been made, and should be made, of this visit to Darcy's estate, for it is only in seeing it that Elizabeth begins to imagine herself in possible connection to Darcy—a connection, however, which remains mediated by the tasteful beauty and order of the estate itself.[31] The narrator writes: "At that moment she felt, that to be mistress of Pemberley might be something," continuing, "'And of this place,' thought she, 'I might have been mistress! With these rooms I might now have been familiarly acquainted! Instead of viewing them as a stranger, I might have rejoiced in them as my own'" (245-46). Regardless of one's view of Elizabeth at this moment, the drift of her thoughts stands out markedly from the fiction. For it is a strange thing indeed to regret being a "stranger" to "rooms," to wish to be more "familiarly acquainted" with them, to be able to "rejoice in them as one's own" rather than rejoice in the expressed passion of, or wish to become more familiar with, their owner. Such thoughts appear even stranger when one considers that Elizabeth is *not* experiencing a naive displacement

of feelings; she is freely viewing objects that please her in a way that Darcy's grave and apparently indifferent demeanor never pleased her, objects that, unlike Darcy's pride, condescending proposal, and disturbing letter, need not even be read, let alone responsively or dialogically transformed.

Elizabeth's imaginings about Pemberley leave Darcy quite out of the picture, until she sees Darcy at Pemberley *in* a picture. Walking in the family portrait gallery she is "arrested" by her recognition of Darcy in a painting, "with such a smile over the face, as she remembered to have sometimes seen, when he looked at her" (250). The reader may remember that Darcy is frequently described by the narrator as consciously averting Elizabeth's eyes lest she discern the light of admiration for her in his own. Here in the portrait the very liveliness of mind absent from Darcy's person is represented, and, the narrator observes:

> There was certainly at this moment, in Elizabeth's mind, a more gentle sensation towards the original, than she had ever felt in the height of their acquaintance . . . and as she stood before the canvas, on which he was represented, and *fixed his eyes upon herself,* she thought of his *regard* with a deeper sentiment of gratitude than it had ever raised before; she remembered its warmth, and softened its impropriety of expression.
>
> (250-51; emphasis added)

The "regard" referred to here is Darcy's half-unwilling, improperly expressed proposal of marriage, but, in a semantic irony of the narrative necessarily imperceptible to the mind of the character narrated, it is the painted regard of the arresting face in the portrait, "his eyes fixed upon herself," that Elizabeth now feels the warmth of, and for which she begins to feel particular attachment. "The canvas on which he was represented" represents Darcy better than he represents himself: it makes a truth about Darcy available to perception which his language and manners in conversation hide.[32] In a novel filled with dancing and dialogue, social forms performed in pairs, this meeting between Elizabeth and Darcy requires the absence of one of the parties; in a novel filled with constant motion and conversation, this representation is silent and still: it neither speaks, nor moves, nor can be spoken back to.

The truth that is mimetically fixed, that is inalterable in the portrait is one, however, that Elizabeth will not actually see in its subject. When Elizabeth finally gives voice to the change in her sentiments, Darcy, the narrator reports, "expressed himself on the occasion as sensibly and warmly as a man violently in love can be supposed to do. Had Elizabeth been able to encounter his eye," the narrator continues,

> she might have seen how well the expression of heartfelt delight, diffused over his face, became him; but,

though she could not look, she could listen, and he told
her of feelings, which, in proving of what importance
she was to him, made his affection every moment more
valuable.

(366)

The living rather than represented look that Elizabeth
cannot meet eye-to-eye is not an object of proof of importance, nor of pride, whether negative or positive, nor
of prejudice. Represented by the narrative and read
only by the reader, it is not part of the conversation of
the novel, but an ironic conversational rendering of the
abstract truth we perceive in it is, a truth concerning the
cognitive necessity of representation and fixity of reference. When Jane asks her sister soon after how long
she has loved Darcy, Elizabeth responds that she "must
date it from [her] first seeing his grounds at Pemberley"
(373). This statement, the narrator implies abruptly, was
taken by Jane to have been meant ironically, or, in any
event, not seriously. And indeed the narrator offers no
retort to that perception on Jane's part, stating instead
in the very next sentence: "Another intreaty that she
[Elizabeth] would be serious, however, produced the
desired effect; and she soon satisfied Jane by her solemn assurances of attachment" (373).[33] Elizabeth, it
may be argued, was indeed utterly serious at that moment, as serious as at the precise historical moment oc-
cluded by its own mocking conversational reference,
when she began to know and so to love represented
what she could not perceive or love in life. Or if Elizabeth is *not* serious, being engaged once again in the
dialogue of pride and prejudice and so deflecting a seriousness she knows she cannot fix in words by the brilliance of her ironic wit, then Austen, certainly, is. For
Austen made the character of Elizabeth engaging not by
objectively representing her person or nature but by
giving her all the best lines of dialogue in the novel,
lines which render Elizabeth's liveliness of mind in the
mental medium of liveliness, words, the verbal power
to create relations between the universal and the particular, the abstract and the concrete.

But it is Austen too who narrates a representational fiction in which words themselves are pure fictions, the
insubstantial vehicles of pride and prejudice, abstract
notions that make history because no single representation can make them known; and who sent Elizabeth to
Pemberley to compose within that fiction, in the fixed
form of a necessarily nonverbal representation, a particular moment of the recognition of a universal truth
which no dialogue, no matter how lively, light, bright,
and sparkling can render. The "truth" that is given referential meaning, that is fixed at the end of *Pride and
Prejudice* but never fully represented within it, never
rendered fully present or conceptualized as represent-
able, is an idea that continues—after the end of the
novel as *story*—to distinguish concrete from universal
truths, history from an idea or ideology of history, from

pride and from prejudice, Hegel's "needs" of the spirit
from its teleological, even if dialectical, abstraction: it
is a truth, after all, universally acknowledged, that a
single man, in possession of a good fortune, must be in
want of a wife.

Notes

1. See in particular Michel Foucault's early pivotal
   equation of the "classical age" with a conceived
   transparency of "representation" in *Les mots et les
   choses* (Paris: Gallimard, 1966), 77-80 (trans. Alan
   Sheridan-Smith, *The Order of Things* [New York:
   Vintage, 1973], 63-66); see Jean-François Lyotard,
   "The Narrative Function and the Legitimation of
   Knowledge," and "Narratives of the Legitimation
   of Knowledge," in *The Postmodern Condition: A
   Report on Knowledge,* trans. G. Bennington and
   B. Massumi (Minneapolis: Univ. of Minnesota
   Press, 1984), 27-37.

2. Within Theodor Adorno's *Ästhetische Theorie*
   (Frankfurt: Suhrkamp, 1970), for example, no conceptual formulation distinguishes the literary from
   any other form of artifact, nor does any specific
   consideration distinguish the reflections gathered
   in *Ästhetische Theorie* from his *Noten zur Literatur* (Frankfurt: Suhrkamp, 1971). Whatever the
   medium of its appearance, art, as form of negation
   (precisely of reified historical contexts), presents
   for Adorno the concrete occasion for critical reflection in general. The theoretical consequences
   of this assimilation of the literary to the aesthetic
   are perhaps most tellingly represented in the essay, "Valéry Proust Museum" (*Prisms*, trans. Sam
   Weber and Shierry Weber [Cambridge: MIT Press,
   1984]) in which two modern authors whose
   sharply contrasting practices and conceptions of
   literature might have encouraged a discussion of
   the literary as such are used by Adorno to speak
   not about writing but about the fate of plastic artifacts displaced from their historical context, the
   negative enhancement of art by museums. What
   Adorno does not reflect on is that the fact of alienation rendered explicit by the artificial space of
   museums is one which remains in turn forever
   natural or innate to literature, in that the literary—
   copied, stored, disseminated, but rarely, and certainly never essentially displayed—includes that
   "space" of displacement within the alienated reality of its own medium, the fact of abstraction effected by language discussed further below.

3. A striking exception to this remains Adorno's insight that the inassimilable strangeness of Kafka's
   writing owes precisely to its literal quality, its presentation of the metaphorical, alien or negative as
   positive reality ("Notes on Kafka," in *Prisms* [note
   2], 243-71).

4. For Adorno's counter-critique of philosophies that seek rather to represent language as the mere propadeutic to a truth transcending words, see his *The Jargon of Authenticity,* trans. Knut Tarnowski and Frederic Will (Evanston: Northwestern University Press, 1973).

5. On the hidden but no less "objective" "truth" of art and the "inconceivability of dialectic" without a concept of "objective truth," see especially *Noten zur Literatur* (note 2), 11, 19, 23, 25, 188-89, and "Cultural Criticism and Society," in *Prisms,* 9-34 (28-29 in particular).

6. Outstanding exceptions to this use and abuse of narrative in the service of nonliterary history are the critical investigations of historiographic conventions carried out in the works of Hayden White and Dominick LaCapra. While White, by a turn upon Vico, identifies historical narratives with the functions of tropes, and thereby allies historical with literary theory, LaCapra has emphasized the literary and rhetorical dimensions of all referential (or "informational") histories and their reading. See White, *Metahistory: the Historical Imagination in Nineteenth-Century Europe* (Baltimore: Johns Hopkins Univ. Press, 1973), and *Tropics of Discourse* (Baltimore: Johns Hopkins Univ. Press, 1978); LaCapra, *Rethinking Intellectual History: Texts, Context, Language* (Ithaca: Cornell Univ. Press, 1983), and *History and Criticism* (Ithaca: Cornell Univ. Press, 1985). See also White, "Narrative in Historical Theory," *History and Theory* (23) 1984, for an excellent overview of the historians' debate on the status of narrative within historical writing.

7. See Peter Brooks, *Reading for the Plot* (New York: Knopf, 1984), and Ross Chambers, *Story and Situation: Narrative Seduction and the Power of Fiction* (Minneapolis: Univ. of Minnesota Press, 1984), for cogent readings of the dynamics of narrative form as a motive force in, if not model for, the ordering of empirical experience. For both Brooks and Chambers the pragmatic potential of narrative to effect action through perception offers the most compelling ground for analyzing, rather that indicting, fiction.

8. G. W. F. Hegel, *Vorlesungen über die Ästhetik,* 3 vols. (Frankfurt: Suhrkamp, 1970), 1:140. All translations from the German are my own; all further references to the *Aesthetics* will be given parenthetically in the text by page number.

9. I take my reference to realism here from Diderot's commemorative description of Richardson: "The world where we live is the place of his scene; the depth of his drama is true, his personages have all possible reality; his characters are taken from the midst of society; . . . he shows me the general flow of things that surround me." Diderot's important praise of Richardson's realism as "true" includes his celebrated comparison of the novel and history: "Oh Richardson! I would dare to say that the truest history is filled with lies, and that your novel is filled with truths . . . that often history is a bad novel; and that the novel, as you write it, is good history. Oh painter of nature, it is you who never lie!" (Diderot, "Eloge de Richardson," in *Oeuvres complètes,* ed. J. Assezat, 20 vols. [Paris: Garnier, 1875-1877], 5:213, 221; translation my own).

10. See Lorna Martens, *The Journal Novel* (Cambridge: Cambridge Univ. Press, 1985), for a comprehensive study of the rise and continuing development of the journal novel in modern continental literature. See also *Novel and Romance: 1700-1800,* ed. Ioan Williams (London: Routledge & Kegan Paul, 1970). In *The Origin of the English Novel 1600-1740* (Baltimore: Johns Hopkins Univ. Press, 1987), Michael McKeon describes the change from romance to novel as a generic occurrence grounded in and representing a breakdown of the beliefs and legal ties of the traditional aristocracy. The early realist fiction indicated by the present study, however, is both slightly later than McKeon's (who, in concluding, touches on Richardson) and extends beyond England. In addition, the discussion of the interplay between novel and romance in the following pages does not use the concept of genre as a touchstone for an argument concerning social relations, although one can easily assume that changing social relations are very much involved in what Scott describes in cognitive and perceptual terms (see below) as "real life."

11. See, for example, Saintsbury's stirring praise of *Pride and Prejudice,* in a preface written in 1894, as "the most perfect, the most characteristic, the most eminently quintessential of its author's works"—whose heroine, more than any other in fiction, he would choose "to live with and to marry" (*Jane Austen: The Critical Heritage, 1870-1940, Vol. 2,* ed. B. C. Southam [London: Routledge & Kegan Paul, 1987], 215, 218).

12. *Jane Austen's Letters to Her Sister Cassandra and Others,* ed. R. W. Chapman, 2 vols. (Oxford: Clarendon Press, 1932), 2:299-300.

13. See in particular Marvin Mudrick, *Jane Austen: Irony as Defense and Discovery* (Princeton: Princeton Univ. Press, 1952), for a psychological interpretation of irony as Austen's means of defending against the dangers of untoward passion. Andrew Wright, in *Jane Austen's Novels: A Study in Structure* (London: Chatto & Windus, 1964), especially

24-35, and Jan Fergus, in *Jane Austen: The Didactic Novel* (Totowa: Barnes & Noble, 1983), provide more balanced views both of Austen's use of irony and the critical response to its function in her fiction. See Lionel Trilling, *"Mansfield Park,"* in *The Opposing Self* (New York: Viking, 1955), 206-30, for the seminal interpretation of that novel as a uniquely and unequivocally moral tale requiring Austen to pit irony "against irony itself" (224). For a fuller discussion of the issue and interpretation of irony in Austen see my *Imposition of Form: Studies in Narrative Representation and Knowledge* (Princeton: Princeton Univ. Press, 1987), 141-87.

14. Walter Scott, Review of *Emma, Quarterly Review* (1816), in *Jane Austen: The Critical Heritage,* ed. B. C. Southam (London: Routledge & Kegan Paul, 1968), 59-60. Scott's description of Austen's role in the historical development of the novel is echoed in Richard Whately's important review of *Northanger Abbey* and *Persuasion* in *Quarterly Review* (1821) (Southam, 1968, 87-105). In *The Rambler* No. 4 (1750) Samuel Johnson had offered a similar assessment of the turn of narrative from "heroic romance." Writing after the publication of *Clarissa* and *Tom Jones,* Dr. Johnson was probably responding more to Fielding than to Richardson when he classified new realist fiction under the contrasting category of "the comedy of romance." Still, his view that realist narratives depend upon their authors' "accurate observation of the living world" foresees Scott's later appreciation of Austen. On the influence of Dr. Johnson's periodical writings on Austen, see Frank W. Bradbrook, *Jane Austen and Her Predecessors* (Cambridge: Cambridge Univ. Press, 1967), 10-19.

15. Southam, 1968 (note 14), 62.

16. Southam, 1968, 61-65.

17. Southam, 1968, 64-65.

18. Southam, 1968, 68.

19. Southam, 1968, 106.

20. The purpose of realism to represent truth in fiction is underscored later by William Dean Howells (*Criticism and Fiction,* 1891) in his exclusive identification of the realist novel in England with Austen: "Realism is nothing more and nothing less than the truthful treatment of material, and Jane Austen was the first and the last of the English novelists to treat material with entire truthfulness. Because she did this, she remains the most artistic of the English novelists, and alone worthy to be matched with the great Scandinavian and Slavic and Latin artists" (Southam, 1987 [note 11], 203).

21. I use these words advisedly, as "First Impressions" was Austen's original title for the novel. Whether or not Austen borrowed the term from Richardson or Radcliffe, or from Hume's philosophy, it retains a specific importance with regard to Austen's own critical view of the immediate effect produced by the novel. The connection with Hume is helpfully developed by Tony Tanner in his Introduction to *Pride and Prejudice* (New York: Penguin Books, 1972), especially 11-13.

22. *The Novels of Jane Austen,* 3rd ed., ed. R. W. Chapman, 5 vols. (1967; reprint, London: Oxford Univ. Press, 1932), 2:3. All following quotations will be from this edition; all further references will be given parenthetically in the text by page number.

23. The line has been suggested to derive from a phrase of Addison's (*The Spectator* no. 413) with which, however, it shares only the words "universally acknowledged." See Bradbrook (note 14), 6.

24. Critics and admirers of the novel tend to characterize its unparalleled first sentence as "ironic," without, however, ever specifying precisely what or who the object of its irony is. The point seems to be to move on from the quizzical sentence quickly, which, in a sense, is what I am arguing the sentence itself causes us to want to do. No critic, to my knowledge, has raised the immediate and pragmatic question of what the sentence actually *means,* although all, I think, would universally acknowledge it cannot mean what it says.

25. While the present analysis clearly regards the common view of the limitations of Austen's fiction as a misjudgment based retrospectively on later third-person realist fiction—in which realism becomes equated with the range of representational language rather than the interrelation of representation and speculation in experience—a persuasive refutation of that view on mimetic and generic grounds (that is, drama *vs.* epic) is offered by Donald Greene, "The Myth of Limitation," in *Jane Austen Today,* ed. Joel Weinsheimer (Athens: Univ. of Georgia Press, 1975), 142-75. Greene argues that the "subject matter" we now require of realism (listed by Greene, citing Van Ghent, as "death, sex, hunger, war, guilt, God") is indeed represented in Austen's fictions, and that their presence must be imperceptible only to the most "literal-minded critic" (145, 153). Such literal-mindedness also accounts, Greene suggests, for the widely-held critical assumption that Austen's metaphor for her medium, "two inches wide of ivory," directly indicates her own limited purposes. The phrase is helpfully reinterpreted by Greene within its original epistolary context, an ironic and charitable comparison by Austen of her own novels

with the amateur efforts of the nephew to whom she writes (149-50).

26. It should be noted that as no other of Austen's novels contains more, or more "sparkling," conversation than *Pride and Prejudice,* in no other are the chapters so very short. After the third paragraph in which, unique in Austen's fiction, quoted dialogue rather than third-person narration serves to situate the novel's context, it is as if, for the most part, each chapter were itself but a line, a terse retort in a larger conversation the novel reports.

27. Fanny Burney, *Cecilia, or Memoirs of an Heiress* (1782; reprint, London: Virago Press, 1986), 908.

28. The best discussion I have encountered of the novel's use of the terms occurs in Robert B. Heilman's excellent study, "*E pluribus unum*: Parts and Whole in *Pride and Prejudice,*" in *Jane Austen: Bicentenary Essays,* ed. John Halperin (Cambridge: Cambridge Univ. Press, 1975), 123-43. Arguing that it is "the complex structure of definitions of pride that give both form and life to the story," Heilman compares the changing contextual significance of the term with the power of fiction to make us rethink abstraction: "Art forces us out of the simple omnibus concept of daily life into the conceptual discrimination on which truth depends" (138). By contrast, Julia Kavanagh, in *English Women of Letters* (1862), offered an early allegorical reading of the terms: "Pride assumes the shape of the handsome, haughty Mr. Darcy; and Elizabeth Bennet, the lively, spirited girl, is Prejudice" (see Southam, 1968 [note 14], 187). Just as *Sense and Sensibility* has been recognized critically (by Wright [note 13], 86; Kenneth L. Moler, *Jane Austen's Art of Illusion* [Lincoln: Univ. of Nebraska Press, 1968], 61-73; and Ian Watt, "On *Sense and Sensibility,*" in *Jane Austen: A Collection of Critical Essays* [Englewood Cliffs: Prentice Hall, 1963], 48) to afford no direct correlation of its title with the Dashwood sisters, an allegorical identification of "pride" and "prejudice" with the characters of Darcy and Elizabeth must ignore Austen's conspicuously inconsistent use of the terms.

29. See letter to J. Edward Austen, 16 December 1816, in Chapman ([*Jane Austen's Letters,*] note 12), 469. See also note 25 of this essay.

30. "But no sooner had he made it clear to himself and his friends that she had hardly a good feature in her face, than he began to find it was rendered uncommonly intelligent by the beautiful expression of her dark eyes. To this discovery succeeded some others equally mortifying. Though he had detected with a critical eye more than one failure of perfect symmetry in her form, he was forced to acknowledge her figure to be light and pleasing; and in spite of his asserting that her manners were not those of the fashionable world, he was caught by their easy playfulness" (23).

31. Here I both agree and take issue with Scott's famous statement that Elizabeth "does not perceive that she has done a foolish thing until she accidentally visits a very handsome seat and grounds belonging to her admirer" (Southam, 1968 [note 14], 65). While Scott's observation cannot be considered inaccurate, it clouds the crucial action of Elizabeth's visit, which, as the present analysis argues, takes place in a part of Pemberley from which the estate is not visible, that is, in front of Darcy's picture. Reginald Farrer misses the issue of the visit to Pemberley altogether when he ascribes Elizabeth's "real feeling" for Darcy, like Emma's for Knightly, to a "subconsciously" continuous "love," asserting that because Austen "fumbled" this "psychological situation" in *Pride and Prejudice,* she left "herself open to such a monstrous misreading as Sir Walter Scott's, who believed that Elizabeth was subdued to Darcy by the sight of Pemberley" (see "Jane Austen, *ob.* July 18, 1817," *Quarterly Review* [July, 1917], in Southam, 1987, 260). Saintsbury allowed that Elizabeth "would have married Darcy just as willingly without Pemberley as with it" (Southam, 1987, 218).

32. The opposition proposed in this analysis between the unresting verbal play of the novel and the nonverbal portrait, between perpetual conceptual error and referential recognition, stands in direct contrast to Reuben Brower's conclusion that "playfulness" in the novel gives way of itself to "sound judgments" (see "Light and Bright and Sparkling: Irony and Fiction in *Pride and Prejudice,*" in *Jane Austen: A Collection of Critical Essays,* ed. Ian Watt [Englewood Cliffs: Prentice Hall, 1963], 70). Brower astutely views the novel as "combining . . . the poetry of wit with the dramatic structure of fiction" (62). But noting that, given the irony which pervades the novel's dialogues, "variety or forward movement in the drama will almost surely be difficult," he solves the dilemma he indicates by locating dramatic recognition in the dialogues themselves, displacing the structural narrative problem he had identified by declaratively uniting dramatic movement with wit: "The poetry of wit in *Pride and Prejudice* is completely dramatic" (64, 70). Brower's appeal to Austen's "belief that some interpretations of behavior are more reasonable than others" does little to illuminate how Elizabeth's "new view of Darcy" is achieved by way of narration except to imply, by a rather circular logic, that it is assumed by the novel to be-

gin with: "The assumption that more reasonable interpretations of conduct are attainable provides for the movement toward a decisive change in relationships at the climax of the novel" (70-71).

33. Farrer contends that, contrary to her own words, and despite the important elision here of any authorial commentary, Elizabeth had indeed always loved Darcy. He takes the second reported entreaty as nonironic proof that Elizabeth's original response was "emphatically a joke" (Southam, 1987 [note 11], 260).

Tim Fulford (essay date September 2002)

SOURCE: Fulford, Tim. "Sighing for a Soldier: Jane Austen and Military Pride and Prejudice." *Nineteenth-Century Literature* 57, no. 2 (September 2002): 153-78.

[*In the following essay, Fulford discusses Austen's treatment of military themes in* Pride and Prejudice. *In Fulford's view, the novel's implicit valorization of overseas military action reveals Austen's fundamental belief in British imperial power.*]

Since the 1970s, critical inquiry into Jane Austen's novels has come to focus upon their relationship to the social and political issues of a nation that, in the years during which Austen was writing, was almost continually at war with revolutionary France. Critics have extensively discussed Austen's attitudes toward radicalism and Jacobinism, as well as her references to West Indian slavery, the issue around which many radicals united.[1] Yet it is only in the last few years that they have begun a detailed scrutiny of her part in some of the most urgent debates of the period. These debates, which figure more explicitly in her books than does the abolitionist campaign, concerned the proper role and conduct of the armed forces and of the men who served in them. In *Persuasion* (1818), as Anne K. Mellor and Brian Southam have demonstrated, Austen contributed to a national discussion about the degree of social status and political authority that might be allowed to an expanded class of professional gentlemen—naval officers.[2] In *Pride and Prejudice* (1813), I shall suggest, Austen entered a similar debate about the role of army (specifically militia) officers in a manner that aligned her—at least on this issue—with the public rhetoric not of her Tory neighbors but of radical Whigs.[3]

The debate about the militia grew in stridency over thirty-five years, with particular climaxes in the late 1790s, when Austen was drafting what was to become *Pride and Prejudice,* and again from 1811 to 1812, when she was revising it. A long and complex debate, it requires a detailed elucidation before a critique of the novel's contribution to it can be made. Accordingly, I

begin by focusing on the debate itself before turning, in the second half of this essay, to consider *Pride and Prejudice* in depth.

* * *

In the British countryside of the late eighteenth century the most striking new thing was an officer's coat. The military was in residence for the first time, and its dress was anything but uniform. The red, blue, and green coats shone in a dazzling variety, identifying the wearers not as individuals but as members of different regiments.[4] What splashed regimental color into the countryside was a situation that was to last almost throughout Jane Austen's writing career—war with France. In 1757, and again in 1778 (when the French joined the American colonies in war with Britain), a worried ministry began to raise a militia intended to defend the country from invasion. Landowners as great as Mr. Darcy sprang to the fore—the Duke of Devonshire, for instance, left London to organize and train the militia of his locality. So did other great aristocrats, and their brightly colored uniforms became fashion items.

Despite the alarm about a possible French invasion, the militia impressed the public more as a spectacle than as a fighting force. According to a field officer writing to the *London Chronicle,* the Duke of Devonshire found himself in camp at Coxheath (Kent) together with fifteen thousand men and the "flower of the Nobility." Over three miles long, Coxheath was soon a magnet for sightseers both common and aristocratic. A coach service had to be set up to let Londoners satisfy their curiosity to view what the *Chronicle* calls "one of the most striking military spectacles ever exhibited in this country."[5] The spectators saw brightly dressed men, commanded by dukes, exercising (for some of the time), but they also saw the kind of aristocratic self-indulgence that was normally hidden behind the doors of the great houses. The Duke of Devonshire had several marquees pitched, one acting as his personal kitchen, another as his servants' hall, and another as his entertaining rooms.[6] In the camp at Winchester, Oriental rugs, "festoon-curtains, . . . chintz sophas," and silver candlesticks made the camp a place of opulence.[7] Yet as the *Morning Post* reported, the most glamorous spectacle was the uniforms, the "regimentals," especially when the Duchess of Devonshire redesigned them to clothe herself and the other ladies whom she formed into a female auxiliary corps: "Her Grace the Duchess of Devonshire appears every day at the head of the *beauteous Amazons* on *Coxheath,* who are all dressed *en militaire*; in the regimentals that distinguish the several corps in which their Lords, &c. serve, and charms every beholder with their beauty and affability."[8] Not content with admiring the men's uniforms, the Duchess and other society ladies played at being soldiers, to the admiration of the sightseers. The camp seemed, as Gillian

Russell has noted, a theater of "social and sexual interchange"—or, in the words of the anonymous novel *Coxheath-Camp* (1779), "a masquerade [that] levels all distinction."[9]

All this cross-dressed fashion parade was a long way removed from the horrors—and the glories—of battle, and it seemed still more so when it emerged that the noblemen and noblewomen at Coxheath had played at other games besides soldiering. They had undressed as well as dressed up: "the officers," wrote the *Morning Chronicle,* "were in the practice of conducting their ladies, *pro nocte,* secretly into their marquees."[10] The Duke of Devonshire dallied with Lady Jersey while his wife paraded, Lady Melbourne became pregnant by Lord Egremont, and—in a scandal that fascinated the press—Lady Derby left her husband and children to live with the Duke of Dorset. The militia was making love, not war. As the heroine in *Coxheath-Camp* put it, "General Officers and Cadets, Duchesses and Demoiselles, are alike exposed to the snares of beauty, are alike susceptible to the tender passion."[11] The militia's reputation, after these scandals, would be more about the risks it posed to English ladies' virtue than the threat it made to Frenchmen's lives.

By 1793 Britain was again at war with France, and in 1798, 1803, and 1809, the nation was doing badly enough to face a more severe invasion threat. As Napoleon's fleet waited across the channel, the local militias, by this time swollen to three hundred thousand men under training per year, marched back and forth, camped, and danced at assemblies. For the inhabitants of English villages—especially in the southeast—the militia was, if not overpaid, definitely oversexed and over here. Still, the militia offered new glamour: only recently could soldiers wear their bright uniforms off duty, and only now were they spread across the country. The traditional English fear of a standing army had dissolved in the face of the French menace, and soldiers were now visible across the land as never before. Of course, this gave them a social mobility enjoyed by very few in eighteenth-century England up to that point.

Like Mr. Wickham in *Pride and Prejudice,* a soldier posted away from his home district was free from those who knew him and his reputation. His very identity was changed: he was now an officer by title, and his previous self and his social status were covered by his gaudy regimental dress. But his dress and rank might well have been earned not by experience on the battlefield or parade ground but by influence, and the shiny uniforms masked a variety of characters and origins. Men got commissions in the local militias without needing ever to have owned a residence in the area[12]—thus they could acquire social status regardless of merit or their reputation among those who knew their worth. It was, perhaps, the corrupting effect of this unearned social status

that Jane Austen feared in her brother Henry. In 1796 he tried to obtain an adjutancy in the Oxfordshire regiment, and when he was unsuccessful he tried again in the 86th. In January 1796 Austen wrote to her sister Cassandra: "I heartily hope that he will, as usual, be disappointed in this scheme."[13] It was possibly the dangers that soldiering posed to the character (and the finances), rather than those it posed to the health, that she had in mind.

As contemporary satires suggested, the reputation of Britain's soldiers—as Napoleon loomed and as Jane Austen sketched out the work later to be published as ***Pride and Prejudice***—was not high. It was the navy, not the army, that was having success in battle, despite the vast increase in the army's size (it grew from thirteen thousand men at the outbreak of war to two hundred thousand in 1807). But Britons had traditionally been suspicious of a large standing army: the Militia Act had provoked riots when it first passed in 1757, and in 1808 there was opposition in parliament to Castlereagh's bill, which proposed to conscript the militia by ballot from the population at large and to place it under martial law when on duty. To liberal and radical Members of Parliament, the militia threatened to become a means by which an unrepresentative ministry could oppress the people—a threat that was carried out in 1812, when the militia was used to quell Luddite protesters. Rather than helping to fight Napoleon, the militia seemed to many observers to be turning Britain into a military state, one symbolized by the new barracks in which soldiers were kept separate from their countrymen. By the end of the Napoleonic War no less than 155 barracks had been built all over the kingdom, despite protests in press and parliament. Something of the public unease they engendered can be seen in Keats's 1817 letter from the Isle of Wight: "On the road from Cowes to Newport I saw some extensive Barracks which disgusted me extremely with Government for placing such a Nest of Debauchery in so beautiful a place—I asked a man on the Coach about this—and he said that the people had been spoiled—In the room where I slept at Newport I found this on the Window 'O Isle spoilt by the Mil*a*tary.'"[14] Clearly, soldiers in uniform, whether in barracks or village, put many Britons in mind of the risk of sexual corruption as well as political despotism.

For much of the Napoleonic period, soldiers appeared to be as incompetent in battle as they were dangerous in barracks. Corruption seemed to spread from the top down, and the army seemed dogged by aristocratic self-indulgence just when Britain wanted heroes to prove its power and manliness against the French. In the *Anti-Jacobin* in July 1798 George Canning called for a return to "manlier virtues, such as nerv'd / Our fathers' breasts."[15] But the nation did not find a great warrior among its princes. The Duke of York commanded troops in the French Netherlands in 1799, but he attracted ridicule for marching back and forth, losing soldiers without ever coming into a decisive battle: "O, the grand old Duke o' York, / He had ten thousand men; / He marched them up the hill my boys, / Then marched them down again!"[16] This now-famous nursery rhyme was just one of the satires mocking York as an ineffectual soldier. In the broadside "The Duke of York's New March" he appeared as an absurd parody of a chivalric warrior:

> The gallant Duke shall go,
> And Carmagnals shall know
>   What he can *do*
> He'll give them such a Fright,
> When clad in Armour bright,
> Like some brave ancient Knight,
>   He bolts in view.[17]

While the nation found knightly pretensions in the soldier princes and dukes, it also found sexual and financial corruption. In 1808 a great scandal broke upon Regency Britain, and the Duke of York, by now Commander-in-Chief of the army, was at its center. York's mistress, the longtime courtesan Anna Clarke, had been accepting bribes from army officers seeking promotion: to supplement the inadequate allowance that her royal lover gave her, she accepted cash, in return for which the Duke arranged rapid advancement for the officer concerned. It was also alleged that, as well as sterling, she accepted sexual favors from the more eligible soldiers. The anonymous author of *Military Promotions; or, The Duke and his Dulcinea. A Satirical Poem* (1809) imagined events thus:

> "My Dear",—said *Proserpine* one day
> Whilst with the *Duke* in am'rous play,
>   "Let me a favour ask;"
> "Whate'er it is," replied the Duke,
> Charm'd with her fascinating look
>   "To please,—be mine the task."
>
> "No,—'tis not such a mighty thing,
> 'Tis a Commission from the King,"
>   The Dulcinea cried:
> "'Tis only to oblige a friend,
> And well you know, I recommend
> None whom I have not tried."[18]

When the scandal broke, questions in the House of Commons brought about a full-scale pamphlet war and press campaign. A motion of censure was brought against the Duke as Commander-in-Chief, and sufficient MPs—Tory as well as Whig—condemned him for his resignation to become unavoidable. He was reappointed as early as 1811, however, scandalizing commentators and public alike. Journalists such as Coleridge and Southey were most shocked by the conjunction of three things: aristocratic sexual immorality, financial corruption, and the army on whose strength the fight against Napoleon depended.

The York affair reveals that the sexual mores of the nobility were now a major issue in wartime politics. Many feared that their governors' "libidinous desire" (*Military Promotions,* p. 13) would leave the strength of the army sapped by female wiles, thus leaving the nation vulnerable to French invasion. Redcoats, it seemed, were too busy indulging their mistresses to be an effective fighting force, and York's conduct suggested that the officers were more concerned with enjoying the women impressed by their splendid uniforms than they were with beating Napoleon. The Duke's immoral and unchivalrous behavior discredited the army as an institution, just when it was most necessary to demonstrate Britain's superiority to its republican and revolutionary enemy across the channel. Redcoats seemed vain and craven, especially since the York scandal followed a military debacle: in late 1808, at the Convention of Cintra, the generals fighting the French in Spain and Portugal surrendered their advantage and let Napoleon's army escape.

Austen did not comment directly on the York affair or the Convention of Cintra, but her letters indicate that she both felt horror at the killing of soldiers in battle and, at the same time, maintained an ironic distance from the war. Thus on 31 May 1811 (in the year of York's reinstatement) she wrote to Cassandra about the Battle of Albuera, in which the British took heavy casualties: "How horrible it is to have so many people killed!—And what a blessing that one cares for none of them!" (*Letters* [*Jane Austen's Letters to Her Sister Cassandra and Others*], p. 286). Austen had said as much before, in 1809, when the York scandal was at its height. On 30 January 1809 she wrote to Cassandra, after General Sir John Moore and many troops had died heroically at Corunna: "I wish Sir John had united something of the Christian with the Hero in his death.—Thank Heaven! we have had no one to care for particularly among the Troops" (*Letters,* pp. 261-62). As Warren Roberts has shown, there is a self-protective sardonic humor in these comments that should not be equated with lack of compassion: because Austen can imagine how terrible it would be to lose a loved one, she is glad that she is not suffering personally (and of course having two brothers in the navy, she lived with that prospect constantly).[19] But there is also a hint of criticism, not unrelated to what the army, in the years of the Duke of York scandal, symbolized. Moore had died a brave death but not a Christian one—he had not prayed, or acknowledged his sins and the suffering of his men, on his deathbed. Soldiers, it seemed, displayed little humility or compassion, and the Cintra Convention—when Moore had died trying to protect his troops after his fellow generals had let Napoleon's defeated army escape to fight another day—only seemed to confirm this view. In Wordsworth's verdict, the generals had cast shame on both the army and the nation:

If our Generals had been men capable of taking the measure of their real strength, either as existing in their own army, or in those principles of liberty and justice which they were commissioned to defend, they must of necessity [have rejected the peace terms offered by the French];—if they had been men of common sagacity for business, they must have acted in this manner;—nay, if they had been upon a level with an ordinary bargain-maker in a fair or a market, they could not have acted otherwise.—Strange that they should so far forget the nature of their calling! They were soldiers, and their business was to fight. Sir Arthur Wellesley had fought, and gallantly; it was not becoming his high situation, or that of his successors, to treat, that is, to beat down, to chaffer, or on their part to propose: it does not become any general at the head of a victorious army to do so.[20]

It is significant that in his comment Wordsworth accuses the generals not just of forgetting their duty in a cowardly way, but also of being incompetent as "men of business." Comparing them unfavorably to middle-class and laboring-class tradesmen, Wordsworth implies that their failure stems from their aristocratic rank. Command of the army was traditionally the prerogative of the nobility, but now, Wordsworth implies, the noblemen are too naive and unprofessional, too unschooled in the world of affairs, to be fit for their task. The aristocracy was coming to seem—to conservatives as well as radicals—too self-indulgent to be trusted to conduct the nation's interests.

The Duke of York's reappointment in 1811 reinforced this impression. Coleridge, in a piece that was suppressed from the *Courier,* wrote that reappointing York was "a bold indecent measure" and "a national insult," timed as it was to coincide with the good news of victory at Albuera.[21] It was an insult because it showed that the self-interest of the princes and their ministers dominated policy—they favored themselves and made others dependent on them, monopolizing patronage. The army would again be commanded by a man who had promoted officers on the basis of how much they were prepared to pay his mistress. Successful and tried generals, like Moore, would be overlooked as the Duke promoted those who favored him with money or flattery. Thus the perverted system, which ignored professional competence and rewarded princely and noble vanity, would continue—the very system that had left the army in the hands of the incompetent generals at Cintra.

* * *

There is some question of how much we can read Austen in the light of British attitudes toward the military in this period. After all, she had little to say about foreign wars and Westminster politics, of which she had no direct experience. But as a number of scholars have shown, political and social debates lie just below the surface of Austen's work, and she alludes to them in brief but knowing references.[22] Tracing these allusions gives us a changed picture of her work: no longer does it appear cut off from the great issues of the day, but instead is seen to deal with the way these issues flew from and back to the local level. Austen, that is to say, is a historical novelist who concerns herself not with battles and bills but with the contexts of those battles and bills, away from the public arena, in the country as a whole.

Austen, like Wollstonecraft and Mary Robinson, turned her acute intelligence toward understanding the social causes and effects of the decisions and deeds made by men in the theaters of war and politics. Few men troubled to devote such intelligent and detailed attention to this field, concerned as they were with the public affairs in which they played a direct part. Austen, however, developed a scrutiny so sensitive that it would be fair to call her work a micro-history (in Iain McCalman's sense),[23] were it not for the fact that in delineating the manners and morals of the country gentry she not only puts on record what seemed too small to include in conventional history, but does so on a macro-scale. She examines the social construction of whole strata of England—the contemporary clergy, navy, and aristocracy—and offers analyses of communities as different as Portsmouth, Bath, and Pemberley. In effect she not only exhibits what Raymond Williams calls new structures of feeling (structures that are also, I would add, structures of thinking, speaking, and acting), but she also traces their generation from the inside outward. Her achievement is to transform the romantic story—the woman sighing for a soldier—into a discourse in which politics and history can be seen to begin at home.

In *Pride and Prejudice* Austen brings aristocratic corruption and military immorality home to the shires in the form of soldiers who, after the vast expansion of army and militia, were now living in villages and towns all over the country. And she did so at a time when, as Chris Jones reminds us, the York scandal led her friends and acquaintances to support the radicals' campaign for reform of the army and of parliament.[24]

The militia first appears in chapter 7 of the novel, and Austen's depiction of the officers is colored by their contemporary reputation for sexual dalliance. Catherine and Lydia Bennet are obsessed with the dazzling color of the military uniforms: "They could talk of nothing but officers; and Mr. Bingley's large fortune, the mention of which gave animation to their mother, was worthless in their eyes when opposed to the regimentals of an ensign."[25] And Mrs. Bennet herself says: "I remember the time when I liked a red coat myself very well" (p. 29). From the start the soldiers are seen in terms of the romantic naïveté of the younger sisters and of the nostalgia of Mrs. Bennet, who has learned nothing from her greater experience.

Why is the militia seen in this way? Do the Bennet women's desires simply reflect their own silliness, or do they tell us something about the contemporary reputation of the militia? Austen's narratorial irony suggests that she wishes to play upon that reputation as well as satirize the Bennets, for in chapter 12 she has this to say about the soldiers:

> Much had been done, and much had been said in the regiment since the preceding Wednesday; several of the officers had dined lately with their uncle, a private had been flogged, and it had actually been hinted that Colonel Forster was going to be married.
>
> (p. 60)

Here Austen's free indirect speech ironizes Catherine's and Lydia's indiscriminate admiration of the troops even as it narrates it. The sentence shows military life to be a routine of trivial social engagements and gossip about affairs of the heart, but one in which brutal punishment seems just another amusing and ordinary event in the social round. The inclusion of the detail of the flogging shows the Bennet sisters'—and the militia's—moral sense to be sadly lacking. The sisters view the whipping of an ordinary soldier as an unremarkable detail, a scene appropriate to mention—so used are they to it—along with polite dinners and engagements.

It is worth remembering that the issue of flogging was topical in the years in which Austen was rewriting her novel. In 1809 William Cobbett had seized on a newspaper report in the *Courier* to launch a public attack on the government. On 24 June 1809 the *Courier* noted: "The Mutiny amongst the LOCAL MILITIA which broke out at Ely, was *fortunately* suppressed . . . by the arrival of *four squadrons* of the GERMAN LEGION CAVALRY. . . . Five of the ring-leaders were tried by a Court Martial, *and sentenced to receive 500 lashes each.*"[26] Horrified at the punishment and resentful that hired German troops had been used against Englishmen, Cobbett went on the attack in his radical paper *Cobbett's Weekly Political Register,* writing with heavy sarcasm: "*Five hundred lashes* each! Aye, that is right! Flog them; flog them; flog them! They deserve it, and a great deal more. They deserve a flogging at every mealtime. 'Lash them daily, lash them duly.' . . . O, yes; they merit a double-tailed cat. Base dogs!" He also imagined the impression that the affair made on the people of Ely: "I really should like to know how the inhabitants looked one another in the face, while this scene was exhibiting in their town."[27] For Cobbett the affair revealed a corrupt ministry in action: having made the militiamen pay for their own knapsacks, while their officers dined in plenty, it used foreign troops to lash protesters into submission. The floggings were symbolic of a government that was all too similar to the despotic Napoleonic regime across the channel.

Cobbett's article became famous because the ministry used it to try to silence him, the radical pressman it

feared most. The ministry prosecuted Cobbett for libeling the German troops, but this only protracted the publicity and gave him the chance to reiterate his charges at the trial. On 15 June 1810, during his trial, Cobbett used the flogging to portray the whole militia system as both dangerous to English liberties and inefficient militarily:

> If one of us was in a garrison town, and saw a soldier flogged to death . . . would it be criminal to say any thing, or to write any thing, upon the subject? What! is every man who puts on a red coat, to be from that moment deserted by all the world; and is no tongue, or no pen, ever to stir in his defence? Who were these local militiamen? The greater part were then young fellows, probably in smock frocks, just taken from the plough, and ignorant of that subordination that is practised in the army. I allow that against a serious mutiny severe measures may be necessary; but then by mutiny, I understand taking up arms, and forcibly and violently resisting the officers in the execution of their military duties. I do not think a mere discontent and squabble in a corps . . . should either receive the name or punishment of mutiny. I, and other people, told Lord Castlereagh from the beginning, that it would come to this; that these local militiamen would be made just soldiers enough to be disinclined to return to labour, and that they would be so much of labourers as never to be made effective soldiers.[28]

Cobbett was imprisoned after a Special Jury of middle-class men found him guilty. But he and others kept the militia in the public eye. In 1810 Leigh Hunt responded to Cobbett's trial by publishing a critique of military flogging in *The Examiner.* Titled "One Thousand Lashes," the article lists horrific punishments for trivial offenses and reiterates Cobbett's charge that English militiamen were treated worse than Napoleon's soldiers:

> Bonaparte does *not* treat his refractory troops in this manner: there is not a man in his ranks whose back is seamed with the lacerating cat-o'nine-tails:—*his* soldiers have never yet been drawn up to view one of their comrades stripped naked,—his limbs tied with ropes to a triangular machine,—his back torn to the bone by the merciless cutting whipcord . . . they have never seen the blood oozing from his rent flesh.[29]

Publishing such inflammatory details got Hunt prosecuted too—but he was acquitted (despite the ministry packing the jury) when his defense lawyer, Henry Brougham, showed that flogging had "a direct and inevitable tendency to brutalize the people habituated to the practice of it."[30] Flogging was coming to seem not only cruel, but ineffective (as several serving generals argued in pamphlet publications).[31] A brutalized army was a greater threat to British civilians than to Napoleon's unflogged troops.

What made flogging impinge on Austen's consciousness was its presence in the quiet English countryside. Hunt recorded dreadful whippings inflicted by militia officers in the Kentish towns among which Austen had lived: Canterbury, Chatham, Malling, and Bearstead. Sir Francis Burdett publicized still more incidents in 1811 and 1812, demanding that flogging be abolished and attacking the barrack system and the use of the militia against civilians. His chief opponent was the Duke of York, recently reappointed as army commander, who, as J. R. Dinwiddy reports, "complained in 1826 that since 'Liberalism and Philanthropy' had become the order of the day, there had been a great increase in the amount of military crime, especially insubordination" ("Flogging" ["The Early Nineteenth-Century Campaign against Flogging in the Army"], p. 321).

With the reinstated York determined to whip soldiers into submission, the anti-flogging agitation became one strand of a larger campaign to reform the governmental system that could impose the rule of a corrupt, arbitrary, and callous aristocracy upon parliament, army, and people. Cobbett and his fellow radicals went on tour, attracting support from a scandalized country gentry that normally considered itself loyal to the King's ministers, of whichever party they were. At one Hampshire meeting a motion for reform proposed by Cobbett was signed by members of several families that featured in Austen's circle and that would not formerly have wished to be associated with the firebrand radical—the names included Portal, Powlett, and Mildmay.[32] On the other side, among the Tory opponents of reform whom Cobbett attacked, were William Chute and Sir Thomas Heathcote—figures whom Austen mocked when they stood for parliament.[33] Austen, in her letters and social connections at least, was on the side of those who saw flogging as an aristocratic abuse in need of change—and thus she, like many of the country gentry, was drawn to a cause that radicals and Whigs espoused as part of their attack on the Tory ministry.

In *Pride and Prejudice* Austen is neither Whig nor Tory,[34] but she is a critic of the spread of aristocratic abuses into the gentry by means of the corrupting society of the militia. In other words, she is not a party writer—her fiction is concerned with tracing the social causes and effects of political decisions rather than with repeating the formulations of those causes and effects made in parliament. Austen is not formulaic but oblique, yet she is nevertheless incisive in her deployment of current political and social anxieties in order to organize her readers' responses. In *Pride and Prejudice* the details of flogging and vanity, alluding to a contemporary public issue, have the effect of making readers wary of the militia. They anticipate Mr. Bennet's warning to Elizabeth: "Here are officers enough at Meryton to disappoint all the young ladies in the country. Let Wickham be *your* man. He is a pleasant fellow, and would jilt you creditably" (*Pride and Prejudice*, p. 138). Readers see first that militia officers are poor officers in terms of the latest military standards and are

morally insensitive, and then they see that the officers are unreliable romantic partners who may exploit impressionable young women. Parliament's decision to raise ever-larger militias and station them across the countryside is registered not as a party issue but in terms of a dangerously seductive intrusion of a foreign body, with its own vain codes and loose standards, into the shires.

The details of the flogging at Meryton quietly cast doubt on Wickham's own statements because they make us suspicious of the kind of society offered by the militia—since Wickham joined up in order to enter that society. In chapter 16 he says to Elizabeth: "It was the prospect of constant society, and good society, . . . which was my chief inducement to enter the ———shire. I knew it to be a most respectable, agreeable corps, and my friend Denny tempted me farther by his account of their present quarters, and the very great attentions and excellent acquaintance Meryton had procured them. Society, I own, is necessary to me" (p. 79). As readers we doubt Wickham, and the army that welcomes him, not just because of his blithe indifference to the very purpose of the militia (defending the country against the French), but also because of our already existing concern about the nature of the society that the militia offers. As we read between the lines and remember when (and in what national context) the novel is set, we see that Wickham and his fellow officers are characterized not by duty, discipline, or dedication to the country, but by social and romantic opportunism.

Austen shows, in effect, that political and social circumstances maketh the man (and woman): Wickham is not just a stereotypical romantic charmer but also, in his very desires and fears as well as his assumed attitudes, a specimen created by the social changes that the militia exemplifies. These social changes, in turn, are furthered by men such as Wickham, who are already the product of them. Austen's exact and discriminating understanding of her contemporary England amounts to more than a flair for detailing social nuances, since she constantly makes those nuances revelatory both of the interiority of individuals and groups and of the processes by which those individuals and groups change. What is decided in cabinet, debating chamber, and battlefield, Austen reveals, is the explicit form, the obvious surface of the shifting tensions, anxieties, and ways-of-being that saturate the everyday.

It is the everyday social mobility offered by the new militia, the ability to escape one's past locale and reputation, that makes Wickham dangerous. After Darcy's letter exposes Wickham, Elizabeth reflects on how easily and casually he entered the militia: "She had never heard of him before his entrance into the ———shire Militia, in which he had engaged at the persuasion of the young man, who, on meeting him accidentally in town, had there renewed a slight acquaintance" (pp. 205-6). Obscure to everyone, Wickham is all appearance; only when Elizabeth starts to get some information from Mrs. Gardiner's dim memories of his Derbyshire youth is she forced to question what lies beneath the polished manners and the sleek uniform. Elizabeth realizes that Wickham has flattered her by his polite exterior: what he comes to signify to her is her own vanity in being so easily pleased by his attentions. And his social mobility makes other officers, as well as Lydia, his dupes—when he elopes, it emerges that few in the militia know anything of his past, either. Even his commanding officer appears to lack the kind of knowledge necessary to judge him until it is too late: Colonel Forster is left looking in vain for information about an officer who has absconded—hardly a reassuring picture of military efficiency or of the judgment of men that was expected of a senior officer. The narrator relates the extent of Wickham's obscurity:

> It was not known that Wickham had a single relation, with whom he kept up any connection, and it was certain that he had no near one living. His former acquaintance had been numerous; but since he had been in the militia, it did not appear that he was on terms of particular friendship with any of them. There was no one therefore who could be pointed out, as likely to give any news of him. And in the wretched state of his own finances, there was a very powerful motive for secrecy, in addition to his fear of discovery by Lydia's relations, for it had just transpired that he had left gaming debts behind him, to a very considerable amount. Colonel Forster believed that more than a thousand pounds would be necessary to clear his expences at Brighton. He owed a good deal in the town. . . .
>
> (pp. 297-98)

The anonymity and prestige conferred by the regimental uniform gave Wickham, literally and metaphorically, unwarranted credit—and his fellow soldiers and the townspeople were left to pay the price.

It is Darcy who clears up the resultant mess, stung into using the connections in Derbyshire and London that give him both knowledge of Wickham's past and power with regard to the present. Darcy and—as Austen suggests—the settled network of information and patronage controlled by the landed classes provide a reliable social order that, if used responsibly, is also a moral order. Darcy's fault hitherto has been that he has inherited a position in that network but has not lived up to the responsibility that this position confers on him. He has not met the obligation, recognized by eighteenth-century aristocrats as a justification of their inherited power, to use that power disinterestedly for the good. He has hoarded, but not used, the knowledge of Wickham that his position in the network provided him. By the end of the novel, however, he does use this knowledge, and Austen looks to Darcy and his fellow landowner Bingley, rather than to the new social order of the army, for

a model of social and national government. A landowning class reminded of its responsibilities by interrelationships with the middle classes, rather than an army mimicking aristocratic manners (an army in which gentlemanliness is often no deeper than a shiny uniform), is the institution that Austen looks to for social stability.

The aristocratic vanity of the militia is symbolized throughout by its dress-sense—as a significant passage from the Meryton period reveals. Lydia remarks to Elizabeth:

> "Dear me! we had such a good piece of fun the other day at Colonel Forster's. . . . We dressed up Chamberlayne[35] in woman's clothes, on purpose to pass for a lady,—only think what fun! Not a soul knew of it, but Col. and Mrs. Forster, and Kitty and me, except my aunt, for we were forced to borrow one of her gowns; and you cannot imagine how well he looked! When Denny, and Wickham, and Pratt, and two or three more of the men came in, they did not know him in the least. Lord! how I laughed! and so did Mrs. Forster. I thought I should have died. And *that* made the men suspect something, and then they soon found out what was the matter."
>
> (p. 221)

Here Austen tells readers several things at once. She shows Wickham's and his cronies' discernment to be very limited: they cannot see through the dress to the real person beneath, because they do not look with judgment or penetration. Perhaps Austen is telling us that, being as vain of their uniforms as Lydia is of her caps and gowns, the militia officers can no longer see what it is to be a man. The frivolity of the militia is on parade: Colonel Forster is playing charades rather than disciplining or leading his men, and the childish Lydia imposes her desires on the older commanding officer (a reversal of authority that will have disastrous consequences when Lydia is left under his care in Brighton). And Forster allows a feminization of the military: dressed in women's clothes, Chamberlayne symbolizes a militia in which soldiers act like girls, and girls have them under their command. Forster's game shows that the militia culture of vanity and display makes gentlemen forget their authority. Playing at soldiers turns to playing at dressing up, and lost in the process is the knowledge of how to play—and be—a man.[36] Austen effectively demonstrates the dangers of an aristocratic military culture of masquerade and display: in *Pride and Prejudice,* as in *Mansfield Park* (1814), dressing up and cross-dressing are signs of moral danger when the line between theater and reality is blurred (and as Roger Sales has shown, the *Mansfield Park* theatricals called for Henry Crawford to dress up as a soldier—performing a male part often played on the professional stage by a woman).[37]

The line gets further blurred at Brighton, where Forster loses command and Wickham compromises Lydia in order to get money from her relations. Wickham has tried to play this game before with Darcy's sister, but on that occasion Darcy's connections revealed the plot to him. Yet the mobility and anonymity—the alluring uniform and uniformity—offered by the militia, and by the militia as it functions in camp, let Wickham succeed the second time. Elizabeth greets the move to Brighton with what turns out to be unwitting prophetic irony: "Good Heaven! Brighton, and a whole campful of soldiers, to us, who have been overset already by one poor regiment of militia" (p. 220).

There had actually been a camp at Brighton in 1793 and 1795, featuring the militia defending the country against a mock invasion. Like the camp at Coxheath, it attracted fascinated sightseers and featured in newspapers and illustrations. According to the *Morning Chronicle,* "the firing of cannon and musquetry, and the immense crowds of spectators, were wonderfully pleasing. Every thing had the appearance of festivity and pleasure . . . and displayed as gay and festive a sight, as can possibly be imagined."[38] Perhaps Austen read the newspaper reports, for Lydia looks forward to just such a party in the novel: "She saw all the glories of the camp; its tents stretched forth in beauteous uniformity of lines, crowded with the young and the gay, and dazzling with scarlet; and to complete the view, she saw herself seated beneath a tent, tenderly flirting with at least six officers at once" (**Pride and Prejudice,** p. 232). Like Coxheath, Brighton's bright color conceals a camp of immorality, indiscipline, and show—one in which social and gender hierarchies are overturned and promiscuity is in the air. At the real Brighton Camp in 1795, the *Times* reported, the Prince of Wales patronized a masquerade that featured "a few *lively* Gentlemen in *Petticoats,* their Wives wearing the *Breeches.*"[39] Lydia's penchant for dressing militiamen up as women was, it seems, a trait founded on behavior at the real camp; Colonel Forster presides over the fictional one, and he fails to control either the men or the women in his charge: they are gambling and making love without his knowledge. Austen opposes Brighton Camp to Pemberley, where glittering surfaces are combined with depth: as Elizabeth discovers at Pemberley, order and tradition turn an appealing address into a place of virtue. Brighton Camp, by contrast, is a transitory place with no foundation: while Elizabeth is an enquiring visitor in Derbyshire, Lydia becomes a camp follower in Sussex. From there the road leads to the anonymous streets of that capital of social mobility and immorality, east London.

Yet it is clear that Lydia has learned nothing from her rash elopement to London. When she forces her sisters to hear the story of her wedding, she says of her "dear Wickham": "I longed to know whether he would be married in his blue coat" (p. 319).[40] To the end she is fascinated by the glittering surface that dress repre-

sents—which reminds us, by this stage of the novel, of the hollowness within. By this point Darcy has bought Wickham a place in the regular army, having saved Wickham's honor in the militia by paying his gambling debts to other officers. Darcy's actions let Wickham live a life of ease, able "to enjoy himself in London or Bath" (p. 387), but they scarcely present the regular army in a good light; instead, it seems a useful social dumping ground for the plausible hypocrite who consults only his own pleasure. Once again the military gives Wickham social mobility: he goes to a regiment stationed in the north, where few people will know about the dishonor and embarrassment that surrounds him in Meryton and Derbyshire. And regiments in the north, in 1811-12, were being used to crush the poverty-stricken, machine-breaking handloom weavers.

* * *

Jane Austen could discern the true character beneath the uniform, but, in the figures of Lydia, Wickham, and Forster, she showed her fear that many of her compatriots could not. In other words, she criticized the militia because, as an institution, it seduced too many of her fellow Britons, blurring the difference between true and fake gentlemanliness and giving greater scope than ever before for local vices and weaknesses to grow and move across the country. By spreading seductive surfaces across the land, the militia led many Britons to succumb to novelty and show, and to forget that the real man was known by the history of his deeds—small and large. And the militia, stationed at ease far from the action, had few chances to prove itself by deeds. The regular army, by contrast, did engage in battle, and it was a battle-hardened yet thoughtful regular soldier who came closest to fulfilling Austen's ideal of a true military character. Charles William Pasley was a veteran of war in the Mediterranean when, in 1811, he published his *Essay on the Military Policy and Institutions of the British Empire.* In this work, which achieved considerable popular success, Pasley suggests that the nation's moral and political health would be improved by imperial conquest on land and sea. Pasley argues that conquest would revive Britain's manly vigor, and that the government's initial reluctance to colonize Malta was evidence of its effeminacy:

> Thus, like the nursery maid, who stops the restless child in the midst of his play, by dreadful stories of some phantom that is coming to take him; we have often cramped ourselves in our operations, and have allowed ourselves to be terrified into inactivity, by our apprehension of drawing upon us the resentment of other nations; to which we ourselves ought to have dictated in a lofty tone, if they had presumed to speak one word in disapprobation of our measures.[41]

A more masculine policy, for Pasley, would be more like that of the ancient Romans. He argues for a more "daring spirit" in pursuit of a land empire that would undermine Napoleon and make Britain dominant across Europe, as Rome had once been. Pasley talked tough and wrote in a terse, decisive, no-nonsense style, criticizing the aristocratic politesse that he thought governed the generals and politicians who made policy. For Pasley this politesse amounted to pusillanimity and effeminacy: what was needed instead was a forceful expression of what amounted to an empire of force. Britain had the men, guns, and resources to dominate Europe, and it should use them for "great conquests" rather than "paltry" gains, because the "warlike spirit, by which alone they can be effected, commands respect; and increasing power gradually changes the respect of other states into submission" (pp. 177-78). Pasley's stark message was conquer or be conquered, and he was sure that he had the answer for the previous "bad success of our armies": it was not from lack of valor among the men but from "want of a more daring spirit in our national councils," which preferred negotiation to aggression (p. 119). Essentially, Pasley wanted to turn international politics into single combat, for only then would nations act like men. Chivalry and policy alike were reduced to the image of a fighter squaring up to his opponent.

It seems surprising that Pasley should have impressed Jane Austen, who was normally so wittily wise about male pretensions. But impress her he did, although there are strong elements of irony in her judgment of him.[42] She admired the self-confident and terse masculinity of his style, preferring his compact book to the digressive travel writings that made up the stock of the neighboring subscribing library. In a 24 January 1813 letter to Cassandra, Austen declared Pasley's book "delightfully written & highly entertaining" and, in a wittily sexualized comment, called its author "the first soldier I ever sighed for" (*Letters,* p. 292). In the process she redefined gentlemanly masculinity as a matter of manners and morals tested in (military) action, rather than as an imitation of the self-indulgence and vanity of the great aristocrats.

Pasley was no Wickham, and no York either, but instead a plain-writing man of action who redeemed the army from corruption, self-indulgence, and effeminacy. And he was neither an aristocrat nor an arrivist hiding his inexperience behind a red coat, but instead a man who had seen action. In admiring his masculinity (even if she did not comment on his politics), Austen suggested that imperial war was the arena in which the gentleman—via service in the regular army rather than the militia—could discover the manly authority that the nobility had surrendered, the authority necessary to govern effectively.

Pasley, his sphere of action outside Austen's direct experience, was confined to her letters rather than her fiction. In *Pride and Prejudice,* observing the army at home, Austen portrays no military hero. Only Colonel Fitzwilliam resists the corrupting influence of the militia of which he is part, showing himself to be a sensitive and moral professional gentleman. Yet even he lacks scope to prove his character: it is only when Wickham brings on a crisis that he gains a field on which he carries his politeness into disinterested and effective deeds. Until then, confined to a routine of wining, dining, chit chat (and flogging), their previous history obscure, the militia officers face no test that will allow their mettle to be judged.

As Gary Kelly has argued, through her unheroic officers Austen offered a satire on current trends within the aristocracy and gentry, a satire whose social conservatism did not prevent her from taking up issues that radical Whigs used to attack Tories.[43] Like that other critic of those trends, the aristocrat and radical Whig Lord Byron, Austen looked at masculinity as it was increasingly lived out in the fashionable institutions of Regency Britain and made the "want [of] a hero" the basis of her critique of the spirit of the age. Yet in addition to that critique, she also at least sketched what a proper military man might look like. While Austen finds stature and stability in the great reformed aristocrat Darcy, in Fitzwilliam she looks forward to the kind of professional that the lesser gentry might become in the nineteenth century, if given a field of action. She was to define that new professional gentleman fully in the figure of Captain Wentworth in *Persuasion*—a man whose honor and self-knowledge, although once weak, become reformed and deepened by the trials and opportunities experienced during a career in the war.[44] But Wentworth, like Pasley and like her own sailor brothers, is tested abroad; the militia stayed at home, an institution that in Austen's depiction epitomized the insular frivolity that threatened Britain's governors from within. In both *Pride and Prejudice* and *Persuasion,* then, Austen depicts British society as only semi-adequate to form the character of the nation's ruling class (and sex); instead, the renewal of the gentry must come from the hard school of engagement in action. In showing that such action will occur mostly on the far-flung seas and shores of Britain's empire, Austen anticipates the imperialist novel of the later nineteenth century.

Notes

1. On Jacobinism, see Warren Roberts, *Jane Austen and the French Revolution* (New York: St. Martin's Press, 1979); on slavery, see Edward W. Said, *Culture and Imperialism* (New York: Alfred A. Knopf, 1993).

2. See Mellor, *Mothers of the Nation: Women's Political Writing in England, 1780-1830* (Bloomington: Indiana Univ. Press, 2000); and Southam, *Jane Austen and the Navy* (London and New York: Hambledon and London, 2000).

3. In *Jane Austen and the War of Ideas* (Oxford: Clarendon Press, 1975), pp. 161-299, Marilyn Butler traces the continuation of 1790s anti-Jacobinism into the nineteenth century, but she does not always place sufficient emphasis on the realignment of politics that, beginning at the outset of the Regency, was to lead to the Reform Act of 1832. Like Gary Kelly in *Women, Writing, and Revolution, 1790-1827* (Oxford: Clarendon Press, 1993), p. 182, I take a different view than Butler of the "war of ideas" in which Austen participated. In *Jane Austen and Representations of Regency England* (London and New York: Routledge, 1994), Roger Sales gives a more nuanced picture of Austen's relationship to the shifting political positions of the Regency.

4. The older term for military dress, "regimentals" (the first OED [*Oxford English Dictionary*] citation is from the *London Magazine* in 1742), conveys this sense; the newer term "uniform" (the first OED citation is from 1748) suggests even more strongly that the new coats made the soldiers appear identical. I am grateful to Debbie Lee for her advice on terminology here and throughout this essay.

5. [Anon.], "Extract of a Letter from a Field Officer, dated Coxheath Camp, Kent, June 10," *London Chronicle,* 13-16 June 1778, p. 570.

6. See Gillian Russell, *The Theatres of War: Performance, Politics and Society 1793-1815* (Oxford: Clarendon, 1995), p. 38. My discussion of camp culture is indebted to Russell throughout.

7. See [anon.], "Extract of a Letter from an Auctioneer, dated Winchester, July 9," *Morning Chronicle,* 16 July 1778, p. [4].

8. "Foreign Intelligence," *Morning Post,* 18 July 1778, p. [2].

9. See Russell, *Theatres of War,* p. 44; and *Coxheath-Camp: A Novel in a Series of Letters by a Lady* (1779), quoted in *Theatres of War,* p. 39.

10. "Camp at Cox-Heath Intelligence," *Morning Chronicle,* 18 July 1778, p. [4].

11. *Coxheath-Camp,* quoted in Russell, *Theatres of War,* p. 39.

12. This was true for men below the rank of captain, at least, like Wickham. Above this rank, a local property qualification was applied.

13. Jane Austen, letter to Cassandra Austen, 9 January [1796], in *Jane Austen's Letters to Her Sister Cassandra and Others,* ed. R. W. Chapman, 2d ed. (New York: Oxford Univ. Press, 1952), p. 3 (hereafter cited in the text as *Letters*). I should point out that if the cause of Austen's concern was the fear that Henry would be corrupted, then it was not only soldiering but other professions—including his failed venture into banking—that posed a threat.

14. John Keats, letter to J. H. Reynolds, 17-18 April 1817, in *The Letters of John Keats, 1814-1821,* ed. Hyder Edward Rollins, 2 vols. (Cambridge, Mass.: Harvard Univ. Press, 1958), I, 131-32. I am grateful to Nicholas Roe for alerting me to these remarks.

15. George Canning, "New Morality," in George Canning and John Hookham Frere, *Poetry of the Anti-Jacobin* (1799; rpt. Oxford and New York: Woodstock Books, 1991), p. 140; ll. 454-55.

16. "Duke o' York," in *Mother Goose's Book of Nursery Rhymes and Songs,* rev. ed. (London: J. M. Dent and Sons, 1931), p. 67.

17. "The Duke of York's New March," by "Peter Pension, Esq. Poet Laureat Extraordinary." Broadside, n.d., "sold by R. Lee, at the TREE OF LIBERTY, No. 2 St Ann's Court, Dean Street, Soho."

18. *Military Promotions; or, The Duke and his Dulcinea. A Satirical Poem* (London: printed for the author, 1809), p. 3.

19. See Roberts, *Jane Austen and the French Revolution,* p. 92.

20. Wordsworth, "Concerning the Convention of Cintra" (1809), in *The Prose Works of William Wordsworth,* ed. W. J. B. Owen and Jane Worthington Smyser, 3 vols. (Oxford: Clarendon Press, 1974), I, 257.

21. Coleridge, "The Duke of York I" (1811), in *Essays on His Times in* The Morning Post *and* The Courier, ed. David V. Erdman, 3 vols., vols. 1-3 of *The Collected Works of Samuel Taylor Coleridge* (London: Routledge/Princeton: Princeton Univ. Press, 1978), III, 221. The essay was withdrawn from publication, supposedly for political reasons (see Erdman's headnote, "Suppressed and Rejected Essays on the Duke of York," in *Essays on His Times,* III, 220-21).

22. In addition to the studies already cited in notes 1, 2, and 3, see also Chris Jones, "Jane Austen and Old Corruption," *Literature and History,* 9, no. 2 (2000), 1-16.

23. See Iain McCalman, *Radical Underworld: Prophets, Revolutionaries, and Pornographers in London, 1795-1840* (Cambridge: Cambridge Univ. Press, 1988).

24. See Jones, "Jane Austen and Old Corruption," pp. 2-3.

25. Jane Austen, *Pride and Prejudice,* vol. 2 of *The Novels of Jane Austen,* ed. R. W. Chapman, 3d ed., 5 vols. (Oxford: Clarendon Press, 1965), p. 29. Further quotations are from this edition and are included in the text.

26. *The Courier,* 24 June 1809; quoted in *William Cobbett: Selected Writings,* ed. Leonora Nattrass, 6 vols. (London: Pickering and Chatto, 1998), II, 249.

27. Cobbett, "Summary of Politics," in *Selected Writings,* II, 249-50. The article first appeared on 1 July 1809.

28. Cobbett, quoted in "Law Report. Court of King's Bench, Friday, June 15," in *Selected Writings,* II. 261.

29. [Leigh Hunt], "One Thousand Lashes!!" *The Examiner,* 2 September 1810, p. 557. Thanks to Michael Eberle Sinatra and Morton D. Paley for information on Hunt.

30. Brougham, speaking before the House of Commons, 6 March 1812, in *Parliamentary Debates,* 21 (1812), 1204; quoted in J. R. Dinwiddy, "The Early Nineteenth-Century Campaign against Flogging in the Army," *English Historical Review,* 97 (1982), 325. As Dinwiddy shows (pp. 312-13), John Drakard, the editor who published the original story (which the Hunts reprinted), was not so fortunate: a packed jury at Lincoln convicted him and he was imprisoned for eighteen months.

31. See, for example, Lt.-Gen. John Money, *A Letter to the Right Hon. William Windham, on the Defence of the Country at the Present Crisis* (Norwich, 1806); Brig.-Gen. William Stewart, *Outlines of a Plan for the General Reform of the British Land Forces,* 2d ed. (London, 1806); Lt.-Col. R. T. Wilson, *An Enquiry into the Present State of the Military Force of the British Empire* (London, 1804); all cited in Dinwiddy, "Flogging in the Army" ["The Early Nineteenth-Century Campaign against Flogging in the Army"], p. 310.

32. See Jones, "Jane Austen and Old Corruption," pp. 2-3. See also Leigh Hunt's report of the meeting ("Hampshire Meeting," *The Examiner,* 30 April 1809, pp. 275-77).

33. See Jones, "Jane Austen and Old Corruption," pp. 2-3; and Claire Tomalin, *Jane Austen: A Life* (New York: Alfred A. Knopf, 1997), p. 96.

34. This is not to say, of course, that Austen was unpolitical, but rather to remind ourselves that party discipline and party affiliations at this period were not fixed.

35. Chamberlayne, the tone suggests, may have been a servant rather than a militia officer—but the point here remains the militia's frivolity and lack of discernment. I am grateful to Jill Heydt-Stevenson for her suggestions concerning Austen's innuendos.

36. Mary Wollstonecraft also makes this argument in *A Vindication of the Rights of Woman* (1792), where she sees the gambling and socializing of the soldiers as evidence of their corruption by the kind of vanity that, though usually associated with women, was dangerous in both sexes (see Wollstonecraft, *A Vindication of the Rights of Woman,* ed. Miriam Brody [Harmondsworth: Penguin, 1975], pp. 256-60).

37. See Sales, *Austen and Representations of Regency England,* pp. 118-31, 222-26.

38. "Camp, near Brighton," *Morning Chronicle,* 26 August 1793, p. [3].

39. "Brighton, Oct. 1," London *Times,* 5 October 1795, p. [3].

40. This is probably a reference to the soldier wearing a civilian gentleman's clothes, and looking fine in them.

41. C. W. Pasley, *An Essay on the Military Policy and Institutions of the British Empire,* 2d ed. (London: Edmund Lloyd, 1811), p. 176.

42. On Austen and Pasley, see Roberts, *Austen and the French Revolution,* p. 94.

43. See Kelly, *Women, Writing and Revolution,* p. 182.

44. I argue this point more fully in my "Romanticizing the Empire: The Naval Heroes of Southey, Coleridge, Austen, and Marryat," *Modern Language Quarterly,* 60 (1999), 161-96. See also Roberts, *Jane Austen and the French Revolution,* pp. 104-5.

Sandra Macpherson (essay date spring 2003)

SOURCE: Macpherson, Sandra. "Rent to Own; or, What's Entailed in *Pride and Prejudice.*" *Representations* 82 (spring 2003): 1-23.

[*In the following essay, Macpherson studies Austen's attitude toward British inheritance law in* Pride and Prejudice.]

"'Oh! my dear,'" Mrs. Bennet says to her family over breakfast one morning,

> "I cannot bear to hear that mentioned. Pray do not talk of that odious man. I do think it is the hardest thing in the world, that your estate should be entailed away

from your own children; and I am sure if I had been you, I should have tried long ago to do something or other about it."

> Jane and Elizabeth attempted to explain to her the nature of an entail. They had often attempted it before, but it was a subject on which Mrs. Bennet was beyond the reach of reason; and she continued to rail bitterly against the cruelty of settling an estate away from a family of five daughters, in favour of a man whom nobody cared anything about.[1]

This exchange from the opening chapters of *Pride and Prejudice* is immensely funny, and not only because it marks the entrance into the plot of the "odious" Mr. Collins. The joke would have been apparent to a contemporary readership, but for most of us—even those of us who might be lawyers—it doesn't register clearly. Yet it is impossible to get the full effect of Mrs. Bennet's obtuseness, and thus to comprehend what is wrong with her characteristic way of thinking, unless you know what an entail is, and what it isn't.

Estate law has been, or at least has seemed a significant feature of Austen criticism since Alistair Duckworth's influential 1971 book *The Improvement of the Estate*. Duckworth argued that in Austen, "the estate as an ordered physical structure is a metonym for other inherited structures—society as a whole, a code of morality, a body of manners, a system of language"—in other words, for the entitlements and conventions of English class structure.[2] For him, and for his successors among the "political" critics (most famously, Marilyn Butler), estate law was understood primarily as a vehicle for, if not a version of, politics.[3] It wasn't necessary to analyze laws of inheritance in any detail because one already knew all she needed to know about them: they underwrote in a transparent way class—and for later critics gender—privilege. This commitment to political allegory was for Duckworth a way of avoiding the quietism of the "subversive critics," for whom Austenian irony signaled the author's detachment from the social conventions she described, and in whom "detachment" was synonymous with "autonomous" and "self-responsible moral judgment."[4] Duckworth's reorientation of the critical discussion away from formal and ethical questions constituted a paradigm shift; and in a strange violation of the materialist logic of that shift, few accounts of Austen's novels published since 1971 have engaged the history of English land law in any detail. Only two essays take up the challenge of explaining entailment in *Pride and Prejudice,* and neither is cited in other criticism on the novel.[5] The recent essay by Clara Tuite, whose title, "Decadent Austen Entails," promises an account of entailment, doesn't in the end offer one: Tuite, too, uses "entail" allegorically to register something like "literary succession" or "tradition."[6]

In what follows I want to revisit the question of the Longbourn entail, for it seems to me that in losing—or losing interest in—the acquaintance with land law that

the first readers of *Pride and Prejudice* possessed, we have lost sight of one of the novel's key investments. The entail is not merely a plot device designed to set in motion and to serve the marriage comedy. It is difficult to fully comprehend the way the novel thinks about relationship (dynastic and affective) without understanding with some precision the legal logic of entailment. Land law, rather than marriage or class, is the ground upon which Austen works out the way in which persons are, and ought to be, connected to others.[7] Ultimately entailment is less interesting to her for the way it manages material relations than for the way it imagines ethical ones; but the link between ethics and the law is not, therefore, merely allegorical. What is entailed in *Pride and Prejudice* is an argument about short- and long-term obligations: an argument on behalf of a model of obligation whose durability and impersonality, whose extension through time and social space, is enabled by the technology—at once conceptual and historical—of entailment.

* * *

What's funny about Mrs. Bennet's rant about entails—what Jane and Elizabeth have apparently long tried to explain to her—is that you can't blame anyone for them. Or rather, you can't, as Mrs. Bennet wants to do, blame Mr. Bennet or Mr. Collins: the former *couldn't* have done "something or other" about the disinherision of his five daughters; the latter bears no particular distinction in or responsibility for being "favored" by the inheritance. Mrs. Bennet attempts to particularize, and to make agentive—to make the effect of someone's agency or act of omission—a legal structure that is purely formal, and whose raison d'etre is to make impossible anyone's agency but the original donor of the fee. In order to understand what is ridiculous and impracticable, wrong both logically and ethically with such an attempt, we need to be at least as familiar with English land law as are Jane and Elizabeth—and as is Austen herself.

Acquiring such familiarity is complicated by the fact that legal historians tell different stories about the common law of real property. Or to be more precise, they tell the same story until they get to the question of which modality of property has the better (read: more libertarian) politics. Whiggishness is perhaps inevitable in a discipline organized around the notion that beginning in 1660 (when the Statute of Tenures abolished feudal exactions), and certainly after 1870 (when the Forfeiture Act abolished forfeiture and escheat), one witnesses the progressive erosion of the tenurial system and the unstoppable march "from status to contract." It seems absurd to challenge such a teleology: villeinage, fealty, primer seisin, escheat, are clearly things of the past, and few feel any nostalgia for their passing. Historians of the land law therefore tend to acquiesce in the teleology and preoccupy themselves instead with producing refinements on the political question. As a result, common-law historiography doesn't offer us any easy way out of the allegorical turn in Austen criticism—the tendency to see land law as a species of politics—for it would seem to have helped make such a turn possible in the first place. And so I am going to try to tell my own story about the history of English land law, one that draws heavily upon the breathtaking expertise of legal historians such as J. H. Baker and A. W. B. Simpson, but that subjects their accounts of legal history to a further historicization. In this way I hope to determine not only what Austen could have known about the law but also what she might have known more clearly than we.

The basic unit of feudal tenure in England was the "fee" (*feodum*), which belonged neither to lord nor tenant but was temporally divided into present and future "interests," and into interests of varying duration.[8] The tenant had a life interest in the estate (he possessed the land for his lifetime), but upon his death the inheritable fee reverted to the lord, and the life estate and inheritable fee were the central units of estate law until around 1200. Gradually, however, common lawyers began to think that the fee was not merely a succession of life interests, "but a single estate, owned in its entirety by the tenant in fee," an idea that developed alongside, and helped to shore up, a new conceptual interest in alienation.[9] As Baker puts it, the understanding of the fee as a single estate "arose when the tenant in fee was permitted to alienate to another person in fee in such a way as to disinherit his own heirs."[10] In other words, ownership came to be seen as dependent upon and marked by the capacity to give what one owned away (alienability); and the sign of alienability was one's freedom to violate biological, historical, or juridical imperatives of succession.[11] As J. R. McCulloch described it in 1824, the English fee had developed as an alternative to the strict lineal model of succession central to Greek, Roman, and Saxon law—a model of succession in which, as McCulloch quotes Alexis de Tocqueville saying, "'the machine once set in motion, will go on for ages, and advance, as if self-directed, steadily to a certain end, according to the bias originally impressed upon it.'"[12] Devising property to what McCulloch called one's "natural" or "necessary" heirs severely limited what a donor could give or withhold. The innovation in English law was to dramatically expand the possibilities for giving and withholding; and for McCulloch, this commitment to alienability entailed a corresponding, necessary commitment to disinherision: "for if a man may alienate, or dispose of his property during his lifetime, his heirs at law may be as effectually disinherited as if he were permitted to bequeath his property to others to their exclusion."[13] If lineal succession was anathema to English liberty, it followed that disinherision was the touchstone of that liberty.

We will return to this observation in a moment; for now I want to note that the emerging emphasis on the ethico-juridical value of alienability had interesting consequences for the question of the fee's duration. If the old fee had been a succession of interests with an organic limit (the life span of the donee), the tenant granted this new form of property—called a "pure fee" or "fee simple"—had something very different from a life estate: his estate "was of infinite duration," paradoxically because he could get rid of it whenever and howsoever he liked.[14] That is, the act of alienation—which one might intuitively expect to be a delimited act, an act that takes place once, by one person for one person—was "infinite" because its consequences for the future teleology of the estate were total and unending. (The fee is of course altered by the next act of alienation, but each of these acts affects, inalterably, the causal chain of succession.) The new durability of the estate in turn had interesting consequences for the question of agency. The fee simple's durability presumed and upheld a strong version of the tenant's agency, prolonging the temporality of his actions and elongating the limit of his will. But as McCulloch makes clear, the heir fared rather differently. The wording of the fee simple grant— "To A and his heirs for ever"—"gave no interest to individual heirs but merely defined as inheritable the character of the interest granted."[15] If the ancestor alienated the estate during his lifetime, the heir (the person next in a biological line of succession) had "nothing to inherit and no legal standing," because, as the law put it, "the identity of the heir could not be known until the ancestor's death."[16] The "Tenant in fee-simple," William Blackstone explains, "is he that hath lands, tenements, or hereditaments, to hold to him and his heirs for ever; generally, absolutely, and simply; without mentioning *what* heirs, but referring that to his own pleasure."[17] The development of the fee simple, which became the basis for English estate law from the thirteenth century onwards, thus rested on a contradiction: on the one hand, the guiding principle was an enhancement of alienability; on the other hand, only the donor had agency. Not only did the heir maintain a merely presumptive right to the estate; his very existence as heir was contingent on the actions of another.

There is perhaps nothing very surprising about this: that an heir cannot act—cannot exist—until someone makes him. And yet embedded in the fee simple's privileging of the donor's agency and intentionality at the expense of the heir's *was* a surprising challenge to the instrumentalism of primogeniture or "necessary" succession. Under primogeniture you always already knew yourself to be an heir because you knew yourself to be a first-born son. There's no agency for the heir here either, as Tocqueville's mechanistic rhetoric reveals; but at least you know who you are and who you're likely to be. This tension between fee simple and primogeniture— the way in which the former has seemed both conceptually and historically at odds with the latter—has meant that fee simple has consistently been understood as the more progressive institution. After all, the fee simple could descend to females. Yet the logic of alienability that underwrites fee simple, and the history of its statutory retrenchment, complicates the question of its politics in ways that legal historians have not fully acknowledged. Fee simple, as Blackstone consistently if unselfconsciously points out, is absolutist: the king's "*absolutum et directum dominium*" is transferred to the tenant in fee, who acquires an "absolute inheritance, clear of any condition, limitation, or restrictions to particular heirs, but descendible to the heirs general, whether male or female, lineal or collateral." "In no other sense than this," he asserts, "is the king said to be seised in fee, he being the feudatory of no man."[18]

In 1285 the second statute of Westminster, *De donis conditionalibus* ("of conditional gifts") was devised to shore up the sovereignty of the tenant in fee. According to Blackstone, the statute paid "greater regard to the private will and intentions of the donor, than to the propriety of such intentions, or any public considerations whatsoever"; and Baker agrees that it protected the "intentions of donors from frustration in the most liberal terms" and allowed them to "restrict categories of heirs in ways not possible at common law."[19] One of the first restrictions sought was on female inheritance. As Simpson describes it, *De donis* was a response to a "'fragmentation' of ownership" that had arisen earlier in the century with the development of the *maritagium,* or marriage gift. *Maritagia* were conditional gifts of a freehold in land to an affianced couple and their future heirs, and once the condition (the procreative imperative) attached to the gift "was satisfied by the birth of issue, the donee could alienate." The alienability of the gift meant that it was not a life interest but a fee simple, and this produced a conceptual crisis: for since the fee was not identical to the freehold but represented the "heritable interest" *in* the freehold, it was impossible to envisage a situation in which "two people might simultaneously hold fees in the same land." And yet this was precisely what was required in the case of *maritagia,* which pitted the alienability (and therefore possession) of the donor against that of the donee.[20] In 1258 a group of feudal lords drafted a "Petition of the Barons" to complain of this conundrum, and in particular to complain that "when land is given to a husband and wife jointly in marriage, with a limitation to their issue, wives who survive their husband alienate the land during their widowhood and destroy the reversion [to the grantor]" and "no writ exists to enable the grantor to recover the land from the alienee." The 1285 statute was the response to this complaint: *De donis* laid down "the general principle that in future the will of the donor, as expressed in the *forma doni,* is to prevail"; and established a new remedy—a writ of *formedon in descender*—that allowed the issue of a donor to

recover land if it had been alienated by a donee.[21] *De donis* thus responded to a fragmentation and proliferation in ownership by reinforcing the alienability of donors at the expense of donees. And this ushered in a variation on the conditional or cut-down fee (*feodum talliatum*). Blackstone puts the change most succinctly: "Upon the construction of this act of parliament," he says, "the judges determined that the donee had no longer a conditional fee-simple, which became absolute and at his own disposal, the instant any issue was born; but they divided the estate into two parts, leaving in the donee a new kind of particular estate, which they denominated a *fee-tail*; and vesting in the donor the ultimate fee-simple of the land."[22] The "fee tail" or "entail" created by the statute differed from the conditional fee in two ways: it was not freely alienable, and it could and often did take the form of a donation "To A and B and the heirs *male* of their two bodies."[23]

The possible antifeminism of the entail was the least of its excesses. The entail granted a donor the legal capacity to alienate his property without restraint in perpetuity, and thus to deprive succeeding generations of freedom of alienation. The fee simple, as we've seen, was an estate limited to the feeholder's lifetime but within that lifetime absolutely and unqualifiedly disposable by him. Transmission of the fee tended to follow customary biological or patrilineal lines of succession; but theoretically the heir's alienability (once he was in possession of the fee) was as unrestricted as his ancestor's. The fee tail, on the other hand, allowed a donor to severely restrict the alienability of his heirs: to entail land was to grant limited interests to a number of persons in succession—persons who were often not yet born and would not be for several generations—so that no one possessor was absolute owner, nor could anyone alter the future as it was mapped out by the donor's will. Such gifts were therefore conditional in a radically new way: they contained "successive remainders in tail to different people, each enforceable by *formedon* 'in the remainder'"; and in each case, "the fee simple stayed in the donor."[24]

Baker is typical of common-law historians in assuming that because of its "unattractive" interference with freedom of alienation, the fee tail has "opposite characteristics from the fee simple": it was, he says (quoting S. F. C. Milsom), a "'juridical monster.'"[25] (Blackstone is less hyperbolic: estates tail, he says, "were justly branded . . . mischiefs unknown to the common law; and almost universally considered as the common grievance of the realm.")[26] Yet if, as Baker also says, the idea of "ownership entire" that underwrites fee simple depends upon protecting donors' intentions, and especially their capacity to disinherit or otherwise control their heirs, then entailment is not "opposite" to fee simple but is its logical apotheosis. He admits as much when he asks a question he thinks of as merely rhetorical: "Could freedom of alienation include the freedom to prevent future alienation?"[27] By the 1830s McCulloch had thought that the answer to this was "yes": if disinherision is the touchstone of English liberty, then entailment perfects rather than threatens the logic of possessive individualism. For while the entail certainly vitiated the alienability of the heir, it also assumed that the owner of land in fee was sovereign, and moreover that the individual must not be subject to genetic or historical determinism but must be able to re-imagine family formation—to *make* family, to construct unprecedented networks of affiliation and obligation.

As a result, by the seventeenth century entails were primarily favored by the newly gentried, successful lawyers, merchants, or tradesmen who'd amassed fortune enough to purchase an estate they didn't want to see wasted, mortgaged, or sold by profligate heirs. Entails were not, that is, favored by Tories with whom absolutism is usually associated, but by Whigs who wanted to see acquired land achieve the same durability as land with a centuries-long pedigree. Whig landowners thus dabbled in a "monstrous" juridical absolutism that seemed to contradict their own anti-absolutist politics, constructing elaborate conveyances that punished spendthrift sons by devising property to a series of collateral heirs (who were themselves granted only life-tenancies), or that prevented spending altogether by ensuring that heirs inherited nothing they could really call their own. But the contradiction is only apparent, since it is also true that during the Exclusion Crisis it was to the entail that Whigs looked for a way to bar James's and justify William's succession to the throne. This fact makes the Revolution Settlement—that paradigmatic instance of Whig politics—look less contractarian than even a revisionist might have expected, and reveals the degree to which entailment was once a vehicle for Whig ascendency, rather than, as it became, its antithesis.[28]

When by end of century a similar class of would-be squires found that the preference for entails encouraged an endogamy that prevented *them* from doing what their predecessors had done, a rigorous critique of entailment emerged from the context of—and subsequently became synonymous with—Whig commercialism. "Although it is a praiseworthy thing for someone who has risen from little or nothing . . . to desire the continuance [of an estate] in his name and family," said one of these critics, "when a man endeavours to make it so firm and stable that neither the law of the realm nor the providence of God may alter it, then it is an unlawful thing . . . and if such perpetuities were allowed it would in a short while take away all commerce and contract from the realm, for no one would be able to buy or sell . . . land for any cause, be it never so important."[29] In the *Wealth of Nations,* Adam Smith offered an elaborate defense for this sense of the mutual exclusivity of liberty and entailment. His argument was

grounded on the assumption that "entails are the natural consequence of the law of primogeniture," a claim that is by no means self-evident since, as we've seen, entails are expressly designed to violate the determinism and instrumentalism of primogeniture.[30] Despite the speciousness of its grounding presupposition, however, Smith's conclusion—that entails "are founded upon the most absurd of all suppositions, the supposition that every successive generation of men have not an equal right to the earth, and to all that it possesses; but that the property of the present generation should be restrained and regulated according to the fancy of those who died perhaps five hundred years ago"; and that they thus maintain the "exclusive privilege of the nobility to the great offices and honours of their country"—forever made entailment seem a Tory phenomenon, obscuring its whig-libertarian logic and its Whig politics.[31]

Not only was Smith's attack on entailment somewhat disingenuous, it was, in the context of English law, belated.[32] In the 1680s a precedent had emerged that was meant to counteract the totalizing and monopolistic properties of entailment complained of in the preceding paragraph. Commonly known as the "rule against perpetuities," the *Duke of Norfolk's Case* (1680-83) introduced a relaxation in estate law that favored "complex contingencies" less extensive in duration and remote in time.[33] By the early eighteenth century this relaxed version of entailment—for example, "To A for life with a remainder in tail male to the heirs of B"—took on a structure that lasted three hundred years. Under what came to be called the "strict settlement," the maximum duration allowed for postponing the fee simple (that is for postponing the reversion of the estate to an alienable fee) was the "life in being" of the donee plus a term of twenty-one years.[34] The alienability of both the donor and the heir was thereby preserved: donors could still control the transmission of an estate, but now through only two generations; heirs could alienate the fee, but were limited in what they could do with it by the requirement that the estate descend intact to their heirs. (They could, for example, mortgage the estate to make money on it, but they couldn't sell it or bequeath it to anyone other than the remainderman stipulated in the original settlement.) The strict settlement thus presumed and demanded that there would be a resettlement each generation so as to accommodate changes in family structure. But while this produced a certain kind of flexibility, Smith's anxiety makes it clear that a century later the problems of endogamy and monopoly (and of course the default patriarchalism of succession) were not solved. Indeed, despite a professed commitment to enhanced alienability—one reiterated by legal historians who optimistically claim that strict settlement "limited the patriarchal capacity of fathers by circumscribing their powers over disinheritance" and thus weakened the tradition of patrilineal descent[35]—in substance the strict settlement continued to function "as an entail of unlimited duration."[36]

* * *

My point is that Austen knows all this. And not only is she familiar with the logic and the history of land law, she has a highly articulate position on it. By calling an "entail" what by 1813 could only have been a strict settlement, for example, Austen questions the historical and political distinction that had developed between the two. She recognizes more clearly than legal historians have done, that with respect to the question of the agency and durability of the donor's will—and especially with respect to the question of gender—fee simple, fee tail, and strict settlement are structurally identical. Given the pathos generated by the five Bennet girls' disinherision, it looks as though her position on entailment is that it is bad. But this is an assumption I want us to resist, and ultimately to reject.

Austen takes a great deal of time in the opening pages of the novel laying out the specifics of families' estates. The Miss Bingleys, we're told, "were of a respectable family in the north of England; a circumstance more deeply impressed on their memories than that their brother's fortune and their own had been acquired by trade" (11). Mr. Bingley has inherited the proceeds of this trade "to the amount of nearly an hundred thousand pounds"; and we're informed that his father intended to purchase an estate with this money "but did not live to do it," and that "Mr. Bingley intended it likewise . . . but as he was now provided with a good house and liberty of a manor, it was doubtful to many of those who best knew the easiness of his temper, whether he might not spend the remainder of his days at Netherfield, and leave the next generation to purchase" (11). Bingley rents. And renting—his preference for short- over long-term commitment—becomes a marker of his "easiness of temper": Bingley rents because he's genial.

Sir William Lucas, it seems, also rents. We're told in the next chapter that he "had been formerly in trade in Meryton, where he had made a tolerable fortune and risen to the honour of knighthood by an address to the King, during his mayoralty"; and that like Bingley he's used the money to remove his family "to a house about a mile from Meryton, denominated from that period Lucas Lodge" (13). Austen's use of "denominated" suggests that this is what the estate is *called,* but that in reality it is not *Lucas*—nor *Lucas's*—Lodge at all: it is inhabited rather than owned. And again this eschewing of ownership is aligned with geniality of character: Sir William is "civil to all the world," "all attention to every body," "inoffensive, friendly and obliging" (13). It is as though it is because he rents that he can be civil to "*every body*": because he is not tied to a particular

place or to the particularity of dynastic obligation embodied in the freehold, he can be obliged and obliging to "all the world."

Darcy, on the other hand, has by this point been established as the possessor of a freehold, and simultaneously established as the possessor of a "disgust[ing]" personality. "He was discovered to be proud," the narrator explains, "to be above the company, and above being pleased; and not all his large estate in Derbyshire could then save him from having a most forbidding, disagreeable countenance, and being unworthy to be compared with his friend" (8). Given the ways in which one's character and one's relation to land are lining up, however, the problem for Darcy is not that the Derbyshire feehold cannot *save* him from being disagreeable; rather, it is precisely the ownership of the estate—ownership *per se*—that *makes* him disagreeable. And his "unworthiness" is later confirmed when Mrs. Bennet informs the assembled company that "he would have talked to Mrs. Long. [But] . . . I dare say he had heard somehow that Mrs. Long does not keep a carriage, and had come to the ball in a hack chaise [a rented carriage]"— his lack of sociability signaled by his contempt for those who rent (14).

The only other male character in the novel with any connection to a freehold is Mr. Bennet. "Mr. Bennet's property consisted entirely in an estate of two thousand a year," the narrator again helpfully informs us, "which, unfortunately for his daughters, was entailed in default of heirs male, on a distant relation" (19-20). Austen's syntax here self-consciously echoes the wording of a settlement in tail male; and while we never know where the settlement comes from we can gather that on paper it looks something like this: "To A for life with a remainder in tail male to the heirs of his body, and on failure of such heirs a remainder to B and the heirs male of his body."[37] We know that Mr. Bennet has only a life interest in the estate because otherwise he could alienate the feehold so as to disinherit Mr. Collins. We know that the estate must be remaindered to a male heir of Mr. Bennet's because we are told late in the novel that he had hoped to have a son who would "join in cutting off the entail, as soon as he should be of age" (196). (A son would have become "tenant-in-tail in remainder" and upon his maturity could join his father in a lawsuit that would have barred the entail and made the feehold alienable once more.)[38] And we know that the estate must have been again remaindered to a collateral male heir (Mr. Collins *pere*) and to his heir male— which is how one arrives at Mr. Collins.

The reader arrives at Mr. Collins through the letter that produces the outburst from Mrs. Bennet with which this essay began. Mr. Collins's entrance into the novel's plot—embedded as it is in a rigorous discussion of how entails work—functions as an allegory of his imminent entry into possession of the estate, of the fact that he stands to be "seised of" (literally, entered onto) the freehold. Mrs. Bennet's "bitter railing" against this predicament is met by her husband with a response that at once highlights and ironizes her commitment to blaming the hapless heir: "'It certainly is a most iniquitous affair,' said Mr. Bennet, 'and nothing can clear Mr. Collins from the guilt of inheriting Longbourn'" (42). It is by now *easy* for us to get the joke, since it is absurd to blame Mr. Collins for a state of affairs mapped out long ago by someone neither he nor we have any connection to; and it is equally absurd to attribute malice—to attribute any agency at all—to heirs.

Understanding the precise way in which this joke works helps to explain what is so egregious about Mr. Collins's characteristic investment in apologia. Elizabeth's response to the offending letter is to observe that there is "'something very pompous in his stile'"; for "'what can he mean by apologizing for being next in the entail?—We cannot suppose he would help it, if he could'" (44). Elizabeth comprehends something her mother does not: that by being "next in the entail" Mr. Collins is a mere cog in an elaborate conveyance that preexists him and will outlast him. By apologizing—by "continu[ing] to apologise for about a quarter of an hour" (45) after he arrives in the flesh—he is ascribing to himself a distinction and an agency in relation to entailment that he doesn't in fact possess. It is quite delightful to accumulate instances of this phenomenon: at Mrs. Phillips's whist party we are told that he "apologis[ed] for his intrusion," "repeated his apologies in quitting the room" (50), and on the way home in the carriage "repeatedly fear[ed] that he crouded his cousins" (57). After being rejected by Elizabeth, he responds by telling her baffled parents, "I here beg leave to apologise" (77); and once he embarks upon his courtship of Charlotte Lucas, "he sometimes returned to Longbourn only in time to make an apology for his absence before the family went to bed" (87). At the Netherfield ball he is described as "apologising instead of attending" (61) to his partners on the dance floor; and in the most hilarious example, he earnestly explains to Elizabeth that he is heading over to apologize to Mr. Darcy for not having introduced himself (in violation of a code that says he should be sorry *for* introducing himself to someone to whom he is not known), and to her dismay, from across the room she sees "in the motion of his lips the words 'apology,' 'Hunsford,' and 'Lady Catherine de Bourgh'" (65-66).

Entailment is in part a problem because it makes apologia a social pathology, a compulsively felt and broadly distributed need, and at the same time seems to foreclose the possibility of blame and accountability. We share Collins's sense that he is a necessary cause of the girls' dispossession, and this is true even if we don't know that heirs could, though they very rarely did,

refuse an inheritance.[39] Even had he opted out of the entail, however, the estate would have continued to bypass the Bennet girls. In the context of entailment, refusal is an act without effect, hardly an act at all: remediation does not and cannot happen. If Collins can't be the hero he wants to imagine himself, then, he also can't be the villain Mrs. Bennet (and perhaps the reader) wants to imagine him to be. And if you can't blame anyone for an entail, or can't locate the person who is to blame, a world structured by entailment is a world in which obligation appears largely impossible. Once again, Austen uses Mrs. Bennet's obtuseness about land law to make this point. "'It is a grievous affair to my poor girls, you must confess,'" she tells Mr. Collins; "'Not that I mean to find fault with *you,* for such things I know are all chance in this world. There is no knowing how estates will go when once they come to be entailed'" (44). Mrs. Bennet seems finally to have understood that Mr. Collins has not acted to make and cannot act to unmake the entail; but her understanding remains comically confused. The point about entails, of course, is that there is nothing at all "chancy" about them: one knows all too well "how they will go"; their trajectory through a perpetual series of remaindermen is clear and incontrovertible even if the ontological (as opposed to structural) identity of those men remains obscure. Yet if Mrs. Bennet is wrong about *why* she can't, she's right *that* she can't "find fault" with Mr. Collins. Simpson notes that a "curious characteristic" of entailment was that it "protected against attachment for debts incurred by the tenant in tail."[40] Because the tenant didn't own the freehold, that is, he couldn't be responsible for it—neither for damages to it, nor for improvements. As Francis Bacon enumerated the problem in 1630, "Entayles of Land" "made the Sonne to bee disobedient, negligent, and wastfull"; "made the owners of the land less fearefull to commit Murthers, Felonies, treasons, and Manslaughters"; "hindred men that had intayled lands, that they could not make the best of their lands by fine and improuement"; and "did defraud the Crowne, and many Subjects of their Debts; for that the land was not lyable longer then his owne life-time; which caused that the King could not safely commit any office of accompt to such, whose land were entailed, nor other men trust them with loane of money."[41] This inability to "commit any office of accompt" to tenants in tail begins to explain why Sir William Lucas's capacious sense of responsibility—his commitment to "all the world" and "every body"—is aligned with a refusal to participate in the technologies of landed succession.

But if from one perspective it looks as though the novel is a critique of hereditability on behalf of mobile property—of owning (or possessing) on behalf of renting—from another, renting is as much a threat to the future happiness and domestic stability of the Bennet girls as entailment. When early in their acquaintance Mrs. Bennet tells Mr. Bingley that she hopes he will "'not think of quitting [Netherfield] in a hurry . . . though you have but a short lease,'" his response—"'Whatever I do is done in a hurry'"—is meant to signal to Elizabeth that he has quickly fallen in love with her sister Jane (29). "'You begin to comprehend me, do you?'" he inquires of Elizabeth; and she, immediately conscious of the double entendre, replies approvingly: "'that is exactly what I should have supposed of you'" (29). His description of his tendency to "do things in a hurry," that is, paradoxically is meant as a description of (romantic) commitment. But the exchange also foreshadows Bingley's precipitous abandonment of Netherfield and of Jane at the slightest hint from Darcy; and the irony of Elizabeth's approval is played out in the next chapter as she elevates haste to the status of an ethic. In response to his sister's observation that he "writes in the most careless way," Bingley explains: "My ideas flow so rapidly that I have not time to express them." When Darcy accuses his friend of taking pride in the defects produced by this characteristic precipitancy—"'you consider them as proceeding from a rapidity of thought and carelessness of execution, which if not estimable, you think at least highly interesting'"— Elizabeth responds by insisting that such defects *are* estimable, and moreover that they are part and parcel of Bingley's "sweetness of . . . temper" (33). She chastises Darcy for allowing "'nothing for the influence of friendship and affection,'" thus implicitly establishing haste as sign and signifier of a capacity for affection: "'a regard for the requester,'" she explains, "'would often make one readily yield to a request, without waiting for arguments to reason one into it'" (34). Darcy's commitment to duration (we are told that he writes exceedingly slowly) is contrasted unfavorably with Bingley's precipitancy; and yet given what Bingley's "regard" for his friend does to Jane—a regard that sends him fleeing Netherfield for London—being easily and quickly moved by one's affection for particular people is a dubious virtue.

Jane too is associated with an investment in affective particularity (or "regard") that likewise functions as a sign of her sweetness of temper; but again, particularism is an ambivalent, even dangerous, mode. Jane's tendency to think well of everyone makes it look as though she operates on a principle—one the novel seems to commend—contrary to that governing her mother's behavior: Mrs. Bennet wants to blame people for things for which they are not accountable; Jane wants to let people off the hook even when they are. Yet Mrs. Bennet's willful misunderstanding of entails derives in the end from her own brand of particularism. "'How any one could have the conscience to entail away an estate from one's own daughters I cannot understand; and all for the sake of Mr. Collins too!'" she again complains to her husband. "'Why should *he* have it more than anybody else?'" (88). When she is finally

made to understand that Mr. Collins has not been granted the estate "for his sake"—that is, not for any distinction in his character, not by reason of anyone's affection—she promptly deems his possession illegitimate: "'Well if [the Collinses] can be easy with an estate that is not lawfully their own, so much the better,'" she concludes; "'*I* should be ashamed of having one that was only entailed upon me'" (147). Mrs. Bennet's desire to see property follow affection or moral distinction (character) is satirized here; and this complicates the question of Jane's, and everyone else's, good-natured investment in affective or particularist models of attachment and valuation.

Jane's particularism is consistently couched in the language and the logic of equity. We are told that she is "the only creature who could suppose there might be any extenuating circumstances in the case" of Wickham versus Darcy; and that her "mild and steady candour always pleaded for allowances, and urged the possibility of mistakes" (91-92). Once again her commitment to exculpation is implicitly, and favorably, contrasted with her mother's fondness for invective. "'Blame you! Oh, no,'" Jane responds in horror when, after confessing that she's rejected Darcy's proposal, Elizabeth asks, "'You do not blame me, however, for refusing him?'" (144); and when Elizabeth proceeds to inform her that, as she suspected, things are not as they seem between Wickham and Darcy, Jane is described as "earnestly" laboring to "prove the probability of error," seeking "to clear one, without involving the other" (145). We're meant to hear in Jane's concern with "allowances," "mistakes," and "errors," familiar justifications of the equity courts: Aristotle had described equity as "a means of correcting general laws which in their nature could not provide for every eventuality"; and Lord Ellesmere famously agreed that the need for Chancery arose because "men's actions are so diverse and infinite that it is impossible to make a general law which may aptly meet with every particular and not fail in some circumstances."[42] A popular eighteenth-century treatise put its benefits this way: "Equality is Equity," "Equity prevents Mischief."[43] We're meant, that is, to hear in Jane's characteristic eschewal of blame an anxiety about legal formalism, and also to recall that entailment is the example *par excellence* of such formalism. "A perpetuity is a thing odious in law," asserted one justice involved in establishing the Rule Against Perpetuities, "and is not to be countenanced in equity."[44]

But the value the novel seems to ascribe to Jane's equitable and equanimous temper is complicated by the fact that the other purveyor of equity argument in the novel is Wickham. Wickham's duplicity succeeds precisely by describing Darcy as a cold-hearted formalist in a community in which formalism is excoriated. "'There was just such an informality in the terms of the bequest [from Darcy's father] as to give me no hope from law,'" he tells Elizabeth; "'A man of honour could not have doubted the intention, but Mr. Darcy chose to doubt it—or to treat it as a merely conditional recommendation, and to assert that I had forfeited all claim to it by extravagance, imprudence, in short any thing or nothing'" (54). Wickham's account of his predicament, and of the law, is quite ingenious. He begins by making it look as though the problem he confronts is a lack of formality—the bequest not being formal enough; but quickly shifts ground to say that the greater problem is Darcy's formalism, his caring more for the letter than the spirit of the law. He proceeds to establish an opposition between legal formalism and the "kindness" that prompted the gift in the first place. The late Mr. Darcy, he says, was "excessively attached to me" and "meant to provide for me amply, and thought he had done it"; yet Darcy has read the will as though it were a "conditional" gift (or entail), a misreading that derives not from any ambiguity in the *forma doni* but from Darcy's lack of a capacity for affection, a lack signaled by and through his investment in the tyrannical logic of entailment. Coldness of temper makes it impossible for Darcy to understand either gifts or feelings as unconditional, and as a result, like those seventeenth-century Whigs he entails away the clerical living to a collateral heir as punishment for the presumptive heir's "imprudence." And although Wickham insists he "cannot accuse [himself] of having really done any thing to deserve to lose it," he concludes by attributing his imprudence—as Elizabeth does Bingley's—to a "warm, unguarded temper" (54).

This opposing of "warmth" and formalism, equity and entailment, is a pervasive gesture in the novel: Mrs. Bennet does it, Jane does it, even Elizabeth does it, and Wickham merely exploits its normative coherence. In Wickham's hands we see the problem with thinking gifts and obligations ought to be shot through with feeling; and we begin to see a problem with feeling *per se*. When Bingley's "unguarded temper" sends him off to London and away from Jane, Jane's response is to echo Wickham's exculpatory emphasis on "warmth": "'We must not be so ready to fancy ourselves intentionally injured,'" she tells Elizabeth; "'We must not expect a lively young man to be always so guarded and circumspect'" (90). This is not the last time Jane will claim that heedless indiscretion is something for which one cannot be held accountable. When Wickham's duplicity is finally revealed by his seduction of Lydia, Elizabeth suggests that had they "told what [they] knew of him, this could not have happened"; but Jane asserts with her characteristic equanimity—an equanimity that looks too much like Wickham's self-exoneration for comfort—"'We acted with the best intentions'" (185-86). Elizabeth's reply to this line of argument is, I think, the novel's reply: "'without scheming to do wrong, or to make others unhappy,'" she has earlier told Jane, "'there may be error'" (90). On the face of it, Eliza-

beth's use of "error" is less juridical than ethical: what she wants by invoking the term is a more capacious category of wrong than the law can give. Error thus seems to be an equity category, as it is in Jane's vocabulary. And yet, given the way blame is worked out in the closing chapters of the novel, Elizabeth's "error" functions more precisely as a kind of legal formalism—indeed, like entailment—in the way it understands obligation and accountability as radically prior to and beyond the individual's control: a system one cannot opt out of or be excused from, a system in which one finds oneself tied to persons she has not chosen and for whom she did not know herself to be responsible.[45]

To register the significance of this moment, and of Elizabeth's account of accountability, is to begin to explain the mistake Mrs. Bennet makes about Mr. Collins and that he makes about himself—a point to which I will return. It also helps to explain Darcy's relation to the problem of Lydia. On the one hand, entailment is responsible for the fact that Mr. Bennet can't himself bail Lydia out of her unfortunate predicament. The narrator tells us that he "had very often wished, before this period of his life, that, instead of spending his whole income, he had laid by an annual sum, for the better provision of his children, and of his wife," and explains that he hasn't done this as "economy was held to be perfectly useless; for, of course, they were to have a son" (196)—the son who would bar the entail and make it possible for Mr. Bennet to mortgage or sell the estate. Entailment is here described as a form of estate planning on the part of the original donor that impedes others' ability to plan, indeed to act at all. Lady Catherine's relation to entailment is important in this regard. Although she offers a critique of the patriarchalism of the fee tail male—"'I see no occasion for entailing estates from the female line,'" she says (108)—her investment in the logic of entailment is revealed by her desire to control in minute detail the lives of anyone with even a remote connection to her, a tyrannical extensiveness of self that, as we see in the encounter with Elizabeth (when she attempts to coerce Elizabeth's nonconsent to Darcy's imminent marriage proposal), seeks to deprive others of the freedom to act and to choose.

On the other hand, Mr. Bennet's indolence and inertia, which comes from entailment, is not unlike Bingley's precipitousness, which comes from renting: if being embedded in the structure of landed succession is a problem, so too is not being embedded. In both cases an inability to commit oneself to duration, to extending one's actions in time and ethical space, constitutes a threat to the safety of others. Lady Catherine imagines herself to be connected to and responsible for persons to whom she is not related, and whom she does not like (Mr. Collins, Elizabeth); and while this trait is objectionable in her, in Darcy it works quite differently. Darcy's protection of Lydia, which critics have read as an instance of Austen's general investment in good-old-fashioned noblesse oblige—an investment literally mapped onto the grounds of Pemberley—doesn't in fact depend upon the customary models of affiliation (chivalry, paternalism) that Pemberley is supposed to embody.[46] It doesn't depend upon whether one is connected to or wants to be connected to a *particular* person, in fact it makes irrelevant the question of affiliation and of affect. Darcy saves Lydia not because he cares about Lydia, or about the Bennets—not even because he cares about Elizabeth. Elizabeth acknowledges that Darcy had "done all this for a girl whom he could neither regard nor esteem"; and since she still has trouble thinking of obligation in the absence of "regard," she flirts with the idea that "he had done it for her" (208). But this is merely her own feeling talking ("her heart did whisper" it); for it turns out that Darcy saves Lydia because he feels himself, without having "schem[ed] to do wrong," to be accountable for *Wickham.*

It might make sense to read Darcy's responsibility for Wickham as essentially nostalgic and neofeudalist, deriving, for example, from old common-law actions of trespass for vicarious liability that made masters strictly liable for the acts of their servants. Although she doesn't put it in these terms, Susan Fraiman gestures in this direction when she describes Darcy as "deus ex machina, exerting an implausible power to set everything straight—a power Mr. Bennet conspicuously lacks," thus making Darcy's agency part and parcel of the unencumbered quality of his estate.[47] It might, that is, make sense to argue that fee simple ownership is the novel's ultimate value, the preferred, necessary medium for ethical agency. Something like such a claim is implicit in the line of criticism invoked earlier, which sees Pemberley as a symbol of Darcy's authority and of the conservative, recuperative impulses of marriage comedy *tout court.* It is true that Darcy is the only character seised of an unconditional fee; and this accords him a power of alienation, and thus a capacity for action that others lack. But it is also true that Darcy's responsibility for Wickham in part derives from his having *overinvested* in the aristocratic ethos underwriting the freehold. Darcy's preoccupation with Georgiana's reputation and with the integrity of the family name and estate leads him to suppress what he knows about Wickham's past and thus ensures the success of Wickham's future predations; his fastidiousness about character (and about one character's character in particular) leads him to neglect the interests of the community. This makes it difficult to maintain, as Gilbert Ryle does, that Austen's novels are invested in an ethics of character;[48] and impossible to say of *Pride and Prejudice* that it "affirm[s]" the "majesty of Pemberley" and all that the freehold represents.[49] For Darcy's affirming Pemberley at the expense of larger obligations is a source of, rather than the solution to, the escalating crises of volume three.

It is only to the extent that fee simple works like entailment that it enables ethical action in *Pride and Prejudice.* What distinguished fee simple from fee tail, we recall, was a strong commitment to donor intentionality. Fee tail was what happened to others when the donor got his will. Fee-simple sovereigntism is what Elizabeth means to mark when she describes Darcy as committed to "doing what he likes" (119). "'He likes to have his own way very well,'" agrees Colonel Fitzwilliam; "'But so we all do. It is only that he has better means of having it than many others'" (119). Such intentionalism—and especially an intentionalist account of blameworthiness—is subjected to intense pressure in the novel, and ultimately rejected for the way it allows people like Wickham to continue to think well of themselves. And it is only as Darcy moves from "doing what he likes" to doing what he must, from a fee-simple to a fee-tail model of agency and accountability, that he can embody ethical subjectivity. Darcy's sense of responsibility comes from the logic of entailment, a logic grounded in seeing attachment as radically abstract, extended across time and space, and, in important ways, involuntary. From the perspective of the tenant in tail, allegiance happens without choice or deliberation: one finds oneself connected to others through no act of one's own. From the perspective of the donor, allegiance is again not fully deliberative: one connects oneself to others whom one does not know and who do not yet exist—allegiance happens in the absence of interpersonal connection, perhaps in the absence of (material) persons at all.[50] Inheritance—the dispensing of a gift, the ascription of an obligation—does not on this account derive from preference, prepossession, or "regard": it is not a sign of affection or of desert. Entailment is an escape from sentimental and contractual or volitional models of affiliation. Its role in *Pride and Prejudice* is to suggest a way out of the sentimental economy that has caused so much trouble in the novel: "'How despicably I have acted!'" Elizabeth asserts: "'Pleased with the preference of one, and offended by the neglect of the other . . . I have courted prepossession and ignorance, and driven reason away'" (135).

This famous indictment—of her own feelings, of feeling as a basis for moral action—lays the groundwork for a philosophy and a rhetoric of blame that escalates as the novel reaches its denouement. If Mr. Collins's apologies were unsuccessful because he lacked alienability, it would seem to follow that Darcy alone is equipped to engage in apologia. "'I am sorry, exceedingly sorry,'" he tells Elizabeth; and indeed he is, and can be (234). But Elizabeth's reply—a version of her reply to Jane that there is error and thus accountability even in the absence of "intentional injury"—is to insist that accountability is shared, and moreover that it is something we cannot be sure we've escaped. "'We will not quarrel for the greater share of blame,'" she assures Darcy: "'the conduct of neither, if strictly examined, will be irreproachable'" (236). A novel that begins with Mrs. Bennet "railing" against specific persons for the wrong reasons, ends with Elizabeth holding to account all persons, and for the right ones: not because they are in control of the ways in which they might be tied to others, but precisely because they are not. This is ethics understood as a species of accident—a secular version of the fortunate fall. And it explains, finally, the mistake represented by Mr. Collins. Mr. Collins wants to dispense favors like a fee-simple landlord: he wants to be the kind of agent—the agent *as such*—he thinks the tenancy in tail makes him. He understands his marriage proposal to Elizabeth as a dispensation, at once moral and legal—in other words as a will (which is what marriage settlements were). But the novel rejects the presumptuous sovereigntism of this dispensation, and especially its particularism—his choosing only *one* of the dispossessed girls to redeem. Mr. Collins and Mrs. Bennet think this is what moral action looks like. The mistake they make—the mistake the novel seeks to correct—is thinking that responsibility for others requires or implies the will.

In **Pride and Prejudice,** the ethical subject is willed rather than willing—subject to rather than issuing forth donations. And Darcy, paradoxically, is the exemplary ethical subject. By recognizing his responsibility for Wickham he puts the ethics of entailment to work in a way that the tenant in tail Mr. Collins does not. Darcy's abstract and a posteriori sense of responsibility, detached, in contradistinction to Sir William, from geniality of sentiment, makes possible the social order established in the novel's comic resolution. "When nature has bestowed little sympathy of heart on a person, when he (otherwise an honourable man) is by temperament cold and indifferent," observes Immanuel Kant in the 1798 English translation of his *Groundwork of the Metaphysic of Morals,* "the worth of a character, which is moral and beyond all comparison the highest, begins exactly here, namely, to do good, not from inclination, but from duty."[51] There is no evidence that Austen was familiar with this translation, just as there is no evidence that she was familiar with the legal treatises that proliferated in England after 1760. Yet the similarities between Kant's critique of "pathological" morality and her own are as striking and persuasive as is her obvious legal expertise. "For love as inclination cannot be commanded," Kant continues, "but to do good from duty itself, though no inclination at all incites thereto, nay, even though natural and insuperable aversion opposes, is not pathological, but practical love, which lies in the will and not in the propensity of sensation, in principles of action and not in melting participation."[52] Kant does not mean by "will" here an act of deliberation or volition—he does not meant to describe an act at all. As he puts it, the will is not an action but a "principle of action." Will is not volitional but formal, an effect of a structure of obligation that the individual recognizes but

does not create—and where recognition is not, properly speaking, the same as accession. Will *is* the moral law: like the entail it is a technology into which one finds oneself inserted. It doesn't make sense to describe one's relation to the technology as chosen, as another instance (as Friedrich Nietzsche would have it) of the will to power. The moral law, like the law of entail, is indifferent: indifferent to what an individual might think or feel, indifferent, even, to how she might act since her action will in no way alter the form of the donation. This indifference—indifference as a mode of being and, paradoxically, as a kind of caring—is what Darcy embodies. He comes to function as a model of ethical agency in the novel—of "practical love"—not because he is rich, or because he has a fee-simple estate, or because he is a man, or because he has "reformed" into the "private, emotive individual of modernity"; but because for Austen, as for Kant, we need not care *for* someone to find that we are obliged to take care *of* them.[53] Responsibility, even for "odious" persons, is entailed upon us all. And in the end, Bingley buys.

Notes

1. Jane Austen, *Pride and Prejudice,* ed. Donald Gray, 2d ed. (1813; reprint, New York, 1993), 42; hereafter cited parenthetically in the text.

2. Alistair Duckworth, *The Improvement of the Estate* (Baltimore, 1971), ix.

3. Marilyn Butler, *Jane Austen and the War of Ideas* (Oxford, 1975). Duckworth and Butler were succeeded by a number of other "political" (that is, Marxist, feminist, or postcolonial) critics: R. S. Neale, "Zapp Zapped: Property and Alienation in *Mansfield Park,*" in *Writing Marxist History: British Society, Economy, and Culture since 1700* (Oxford, 1985); Lillian Robinson, "Why Marry Mr. Collins?" in *Sex, Class, and Culture* (New York, 1986); Claudia Johnson, *Jane Austen: Women, Politics, and the Novel* (Chicago, 1988); Beth Fowkes Tobin, "The Moral and Political Economy of Property in Austen's *Emma,*" *Eighteenth-Century Fiction* 2, no. 3 (1990): 229-54; Edward Said, "Jane Austen and Empire," in *Culture and Imperialism* (New York, 1993); and Ruth Perry, "Austen and Empire: A Thinking Woman's Guide to British Imperialism," *Persuasions* 16 (1994): 95-106, to name but a few.

4. Duckworth, *Improvement of the Estate,* 7.

5. P. S. A. Rossdale, "What Caused the Quarrel Between Mr. Collins and Mr. Bennet? Observations on the Entail of Longbourn," *Notes and Queries* 27 (1980): 503-4; Luanne Bethke Redmond, "Land, Law, and Love," *Persuasions* 11 (1989): 46-52.

6. Clara Tuite, "Decadent Austen Entails: Forster, James, Firbank, and the 'Queer Taste' of *Sanditon*

(comp. 1817, publ. 1925)," in *Janeites: Austen's Disciples and Devotees,* ed. Deidre Lynch (Princeton, 2000).

7. Although it is not the one I am telling here, there *is* a story to be told about entailment and eighteenth-century marriage law. One critic of Lord Hardwicke's 1753 clandestine marriage bill said that he "look[ed] upon the Bill only as the prelude to another bill for restoring the old law of intails." The bill became the infamous Marriage Act, legislation that Austen clearly has in mind in the Wickham/Lydia subplot. The act was under heavy attack in the decades during which Austen was at work on *Pride and Prejudice* and was repealed in 1823. In "Radical Marriage," Sarah Emsley argues that the novel is an implicit critique of the statute; but I wonder whether Austen's revisionist defense of entailment might not also entail a commitment to the legal logic of the act—in particular its formalism and anti-intentionalism. See William Cobbett, *The Parliamentary History of England* (1813; reprint, New York, 1966), 15:61; and Sarah Emsley, "Radical Marriage," *Eighteenth-Century Fiction* II, no. 4 (1999): 477-98.

8. J. H. Baker, *Introduction to English Legal History,* 3d ed. (London, 1990), 296.

9. Baker, *Introduction to English Legal History,* 2d ed. (London, 1979), 222.

10. Ibid., 223.

11. A. W. B. Simpson argues, in *A History of the Land Law,* 2d ed. (Oxford, 1986), that "ownership" is an inappropriate category to apply to the fee simple. According to him, the fee is never owned but only "seised." Seisin he distinguishes from possession and from proprietorship, and also from title (to which it is most closely analogous). In a real action—writs that helped to consolidate the category of real property—"what is recovered," he says (somewhat tautologically) "is not the ownership of the land, nor the possession of the land, but the seisin of land" (37-38). The transitive verb "to seize" described the action of a feudal lord in establishing his vassal on the land as tenant; but the noun form denotes "a condition rather than an event, a relationship between person and land" (40). Seisin is the basis of entitlement, and duration is what distinguishes a stronger title from a weaker one: "the person who can base his title upon the earliest seisin is best entitled to recover seisin" (38). This distinction seems very rich to me, but it doesn't substantially affect the issue of agency and alienability; it merely asks that we call freedom of alienation by some other word than "ownership."

12. J. R. McCulloch, *Treatise on the Succession to Property Vacant by Death* (London, 1848), 4.

13. Ibid., 5.

14. Baker, *Introduction* [*Introduction to English Legal History*], 3d ed., 301.

15. Ibid., 300.

16. Baker, *Introduction,* 2d ed., 224.

17. William Blackstone, *Commentaries on the Laws of England* (1766; reprint, Chicago, 1979), 2:104.

18. Ibid., 2:106.

19. Ibid., 2:112; Baker, *Introduction,* 3d ed., 311; Baker, *Introduction,* 2d ed., 232. In the third edition, Baker describes *De donis* this way: "So liberally was the statute construed that donors were able to restrict the inheritance in ways not permissible at common law but deemed to fall within the equity of the statute. Thus, a gift could be restricted to A and the heirs *male* of his body, whereas a gift to A and his heirs male (without words of procreation) at common law passed a fee simple inheritance by females" (312). The change in wording from the second edition is designed to emphasize the structural antifeminism of entailment.

20. Simpson, *History of the Land Law,* 66-67.

21. Ibid., 81-82.

22. Blackstone, *Commentaries* [*Commentaries on the Laws of England*], 2:112.

23. There are, of course, other modalities of property besides fee simple and fee tail. But these are the basic forms of real property (as distinct from copyhold, for example), and legal scholars from Sir Edward Coke to Simpson ground their histories of the common law upon them.

24. Baker, *Introduction,* 3d ed., 312.

25. Ibid., 319.

26. Blackstone, *Commentaries,* 2:116.

27. Baker, *Introduction,* 3d ed., 299.

28. For a discussion of the role of entailment in the Exclusion Crisis, see Howard Nenner, *By Color of Law: Legal Culture and Constitutional Politics in England, 1660-1689* (Chicago, 1977), 179-85.

29. Baker is quoting Dodderidge J., dissenting in *Pells v. Brown* (1620); Baker, *Introduction,* 2d ed., 241.

30. Adam Smith, *An Inquiry into the Nature and Causes of the Wealth of Nations,* ed. R. H. Campbell and R. S. Skinner (1776; reprint, Indianapolis, 1981), 1:384.

31. Ibid., 1:385.

32. Entails were alive and well in Scotland until the mid-nineteenth century, and this in part accounts for the fact that Smith is more worried about them than is Blackstone. Blackstone asserts that developments in conveyancing have "greatly abridged estatestail with regard to their duration" and that they have become "by degrees unfettered." But it was Smith's paranoia rather than Blackstone's sanguinity that governed the rhetoric of entailment in the period: Whig politicians continued, even after the Rule Against Perpetuities, to invoke the specter of entailment wherever and whenever they saw a threat to their "ancient liberties" (the very liberties, I am suggesting, entail helped to perfect); Blackstone, *Commentaries,* 2:119.

33. Baker, *Introduction,* 3d ed., 332.

34. Ibid.

35. Lloyd Bonfield, *Marriage Settlements, 1601-1740: The Adoption of the Strict Settlement* (Cambridge, 1983), 121-122. For a dissenting account of the strict settlement, see Eileen Spring, who calls into question the notion, received from Lawrence Stone, Bonfield, and H. J. Habakkuk, that "the strict settlement raised daughters' portions and that [it] is to be associated with the development of equality in the family"; Eileen Spring, *Law, Land, and Family: Aristocratic Inheritance in England, 1300 to 1800* (Chapel Hill, 1993), 2. Lawrence Stone, *The Family, Sex, and Marriage in England, 1500-1800* (London, 1977); H. J. Habakkuk, "Marriage Settlements in the Eighteenth Century," *Transactions of the Royal Historical Society,* 4th ser. 32 (1950): 15-30.

36. Simpson, *History of the Land Law,* 238. Simpson doesn't elaborate upon this claim, but Redmond's essay on *Pride and Prejudice* helps explain how the strict settlement continued to function like an entail: "A son, coming of age, wanted to take the Grand Tour of the European continent, present himself at the London season, and in general live a more interesting life than could be found in the realm of riding to hounds and assembly balls. In return for sufficient cash for his pursuits, he signed away his interest as tenant in fee tail. A series of documents was drawn up, the effect of which was to settle the land on the father for life, remainder to the son for life, remainder in fee tail to his sons. This moved the fee tail up one generation, since the son's son would be tenant in tail and could do the same when his own sons came of age. The process, like the fee tail itself, could continue indefinitely." The system thus works to postpone indefinitely the possession of a fee simple; Redmond, "Land, Law, and Love," 49-50.

37. For examples of donations in tail, see Sir Frederick Pollock and Frederic William Maitland, *The History of English Law,* 2d ed. (Cambridge, 1968), 1:24.

38. Rossdale makes this point; Rossdale, "What Caused the Quarrel Between Mr. Collins and Mr. Bennet?" 503.

39. I am grateful to Michael Hoeflich, of the Law School at the University of Kansas, for the observation that Collins could have refused the tenancy in tail.

40. Simpson, *History of the Land Law,* 90.

41. Francis Bacon, *The Elements of the Common Lawes of England. The Use of the Law* (1630; reprint, New York, 1969), 54.

42. Baker, *Introduction,* 3d ed., 122.

43. R. Francis, *Maxims of Equity* (London, 1727). Equitable decisions are not necessarily exculpatory ones, but I am less interested in how equity courts actually functioned than I am in the ideology of equity. Proponents of equity assumed, and indeed continue to assume, that equitable laws are ones that take account of extenuating circumstances (where, that is, circumstances are by and large understood as extenuating). For a recent example of this argument, see Peter Goodrich's work on the Courts of Love, in *Law in the Courts of Love: Literature and the Other Minor Jurisprudences* (New York, 1996).

44. Quoted in Baker, *Introduction,* 2d ed., 245.

45. For a different account of Austen's interest in formalism, see Frances Ferguson, "Jane Austen, *Emma,* and the Impact of Form," *Modern Language Quarterly* 61, no. 1 (2000): 157-80.

46. This argument receives its most influential treatment in Butler, whose assertions about *Pride and Prejudice*'s "conservatism" depend in part upon taking seriously Sir Walter Scott's claim that Elizabeth is moved in Darcy's favor when she encounters Pemberley and the social and economic value it represents. Butler notes that Scott has been "teased" for declaring that when Elizabeth sees Pemberley "her prudence" subdues "her prejudice"; and she says we are not supposed to take literally Elizabeth's own joke to Jane that "she must date her love for Darcy from first seeing his beautiful grounds." But she then proceeds to do just this; Butler, *Jane Austen and the War of Ideas,* 214. Sir Walter Scott, "*Emma,*" *Quarterly Review* 14 (1815): 194. For similar arguments about the role Pemberley plays in the novel, see Susan Fraiman, "The Humiliation of Elizabeth Bennet," in *Refiguring the Father: New Feminist*

Readings of Patriarchy, ed. Patricia Yaeger and Beth Kowaleski-Wallace (Carbondale, Ill., 1989); and Karen Newman, "Can This Marriage Be Saved: Jane Austen Makes Sense of an Ending," *ELH* 50 (1983): 693-710. For an interesting variation on the argument, see Claudia Brodsky Lacour, who says that Pemberley becomes the formal marker of Darcy's value not because Austen fetishizes the aristocracy, but because for her, as for G. W. F. Hegel, understanding is only possible in the absence of persons; Claudia Brodsky Lacour, "Austen's *Pride and Prejudice* and Hegel's 'Truth in Art': Concept, Reference, and History," *ELH* 59 (1992): 597-623.

47. Fraiman, "Humiliation of Elizabeth Bennet," 178.

48. Gilbert Ryle, "Jane Austen and the Moralists," in *Collected Papers* (New York, 1971), 1:278. Ryle's argument about Austen's Aristotelianism largely ignores the presence in the novel of the sustained critique of particularism that I have been delineating. "The Aristotelian pattern of ethical ideas," he notes, "represents people as differing from one another in degree and not in kind . . . [and] in respect of a whole spectrum of specific week-day attributes" (284). Aristotle, on this account, is a particularist of the highest order; and so is Austen: "Her descriptions of people mention their tempers, habits, dispositions, moods, inclinations, impulses, sentiments, feelings, affections, thoughts, reflections, opinions, principles, prejudices, imaginations, fancies" (289). Charmed by Austen's realist/particularist aesthetic, Ryle makes this aesthetic identical with an ethical philosophy—missing all the ways and moments in which particularism fails to produce ethical ideas or actions.

49. I am quoting Claudia Johnson, but other critics have made a version of this claim. See Susan Morgan's succinct summary of the work of "all who would locate the embodiment of [the novel's] final harmony among the stately and tasteful grounds of Pemberley"; Susan Morgan, *In the Meantime: Character and Perception in Jane Austen's Fiction* (Chicago, 1980), 78-79. Johnson, *[Jane Austen:] Women, Politics, and the Novel,* 89.

50. In this, the ethics of entailment seem to resemble what William Deresiewicz, in "Community and Cognition in *Pride and Prejudice*," *ELH* 64 (1997): 503-35, calls "density." "The novel," he says, "is structured so as to suggest that its plot emerges from the threshing of communal mechanism more than from the movements of individual will" (516). But for Deresiewicz, density is ultimately sentimental: it is based on the idea that one's. "every action will bear consequences for

people to whom she feels, and feels she ought to feel, significant responsibility" (514).

51. Immanuel Kant, *Essays and Treatises on Moral, Political, and Various Philosophical Subjects* (London, 1798), 1:36. I am grateful to the Spencer Research Library at the University of Kansas for allowing me to consult their copy of the 1798 English edition of Kant's works.

52. Ibid., 1:37.

53. Ryle, "Jane Austen and the Moralists," 279; Duckworth, *Improvement of the Estate,* 535 n. 21. It is frequently argued that both Elizabeth and Darcy reform by the end of the novel, and that the latter in particular becomes endowed with an affective life he did not formerly possess. As I hope to have made clear, I don't think the novel's resolution hinges on this kind of change: Darcy's "coldness," after all—his legal and ethical formalism—was throughout improperly understood and in the end validated. The "private, emotive individual" is the one who comes in for reformation, as Bingley, in the end, puts aside his precipitance in favor of a Darcy-esque duration.

Susan C. Greenfield (essay date spring 2006)

SOURCE: Greenfield, Susan C. "The Absent-Minded Heroine: Or, Elizabeth Bennet Has a Thought." *Eighteenth-Century Studies* 39, no. 3 (spring 2006): 337-50.

[*In the following essay, Greenfield considers the philosophical implications of physical absence in Jane Austen's* Pride and Prejudice. *Greenfield posits that Elizabeth's decision to marry Darcy coincides with the loss of her intellectual autonomy.*]

What should be made of the way Elizabeth Bennet falls in love with Mr. Darcy in his absence? For even if one fondly believes that Elizabeth is attracted to Darcy from the start, it is not until midway through the novel that she begins to know that she is. In the first half of the novel, Elizabeth answers Darcy's proposal by calling him "the last man in the world whom I could ever be prevailed on to marry."[1] It is only in the subsequent months that her "sentiments" undergo "so material a change" that she decides the exact opposite (366). And yet throughout this period of change, Darcy is rarely before her. After he proposes in March, Elizabeth does not see him again until July, when he appears while she is viewing Pemberley; the next morning Darcy waits on Elizabeth at her inn for "above half an hour" (263); Elizabeth goes to Pemberley the following day for a visit "that did not continue long" (270); and Darcy subsequently visits the inn, arriving just as Elizabeth learns of Lydia's elopement and leaving almost immediately thereafter. Even by a generous estimate, Elizabeth has been with him for maybe three hours. Nevertheless, when Elizabeth next sees Darcy in September she is sure of her attachment. She is so, we are meant to understand, because Darcy's absence has ignited new thoughts—because, thanks to his body's disappearance, her own mind is enlarged.

That *Pride and Prejudice* is about the unreliability of physical appearances or of "First Impressions" hardly needs belaboring. That it also aligns absence with productive thought is the subject of this article. In what follows, I argue that Elizabeth is confused in Darcy's presence and thoughtful about him (and much else) in his absence, and that this contrast reflects one of the most basic tensions of early modern epistemology. Elizabeth's confusion suggests that human perception of the material world is necessarily uncertain; thus, when Elizabeth actually sees the object of Darcy she routinely misunderstands him. But her thoughtfulness suggests that the absence—whether of a physical object (like Darcy) or of certainty itself—can be intellectually fruitful and rewarding. Thus, it is precisely when Darcy is missing that Elizabeth is most mindful. Critics have long recognized Austen's interest in epistemology. Susan Morgan writes that all of Austen's novels concern the "relation between the mind and its objects," and Tony Tanner describes *Pride and Prejudice* as a dramatization of the "whole problem of knowledge."[2] My goal is to extend this conversation by considering the particular—and the particularly gendered—relationship between material absence and the mind both in *Pride and Prejudice* and in the broader philosophical and novelistic traditions to which the text alludes.[3]

To clarify, let me offer a few choice examples from Austen's novel. When Elizabeth visits Pemberley, for instance, she does so only after being repeatedly "assured of [Darcy's] absence" from it (256, 241, 246). Nevertheless he suddenly and unexpectedly appears on the lawn. The two greet each other awkwardly, after which Darcy retreats into the house and Elizabeth becomes "[in]sensible" of the surroundings:

> [A]nd, though she . . . seemed to direct her eyes to such objects as they [her aunt and uncle] pointed out, she distinguished no part of the scene. Her thoughts were all fixed on that one spot of Pemberley House, whichever it might be, where Mr. Darcy then was. She longed to know what at that moment was passing in his mind. . . . At length, however, the remarks of her companions on her absence of mind roused her.
>
> (253)

Narratively, Elizabeth's mind fills the space that Darcy exits. "Objects" fade before her "eyes" as she "fix[es]" on the immaterial and indeterminable "spot" in Pember-

ley House into which he has vanished. Her ignorance about Darcy's whereabouts and her "long[ing] to know what . . . was passing" in his unseen "mind" bring Elizabeth's own mind into textual relief. The less she physically "distinguish[es]" of him, the more pensive she becomes. Her "companions" remark on Elizabeth's "absence of mind" because she seems mentally detached from the present "scene." But Elizabeth might just as profitably be called *absent-minded* in that absence fuels her "thoughts."

As the novel's famous opening makes clear, most of Elizabeth's neighbors suffer from the contrasting and deluded belief that they can know the object world. The "truth universally acknowledged, that a single man in possession of a good fortune must be in want of a wife" is "fixed" only in the "minds of the surrounding families." That such a man physically exists is hardly certain. For, as Austen continues, even should an eligible bachelor (like Mr. Bingley) actually enter the neighborhood, "little" can be "known" of his true "feelings or views" (3). On the one hand, a single man raises basic epistemological problems for any person who tries to perceive him.[4]

On the other hand, though, Austen insists that women—especially single ones—are particularly disadvantaged. It is, after all, because they rarely have a "good fortune" that women are far more likely to "want" rich men than the other way around.[5] Families may see a man like Mr. Bingley as the "rightful property of . . . one . . . of their daughters" (3). But "rightful property" is exactly what daughters both lack and need to become for a willing husband. Like countless novels before and after it, *Pride and Prejudice* is structured around women's inability to own objects and around their own objectification. And this, I argue, genders epistemological problems. However difficult it is to know the material world, *Pride and Prejudice* shows that it is more so for women who possess neither worldly goods nor full rights to their own bodies. For a heroine like Elizabeth Bennet, the things outside her are literally less available—and in this way more absent—than they are for a landed hero like Mr. Darcy. Such absence, the novel suggests, places greater restrictions on woman's knowledge.[6]

As consolation, Elizabeth acquires both the freedom of interpretation, and, more dubiously, the provocation to fall in love. The narrative advantage of uncertainty is that it creates the need for thought. Or, to put it oppositely, those who are certain they know things may have little cause to think about them. This helps explain why the dispossessed heroine is such a fixture of the early novel: she epitomizes the doubt that renders a character's mind complex.[7] But their dispossession also helps explain why so many heroines—including, of course, Elizabeth Bennet—are designed to think about men. As objects that women depend upon but never possess, men are ever absent and—at least in many novels—thus likely to occupy the female mind.

In terms of philosophical history, Elizabeth's problems of knowledge are less gender-specific than they are reflective of epistemological skepticism. In the eighteenth century skepticism propelled the very emergence of epistemology as a topic and led Immanuel Kant to declare that "there always remains this scandal for philosophy and human reason in general: . . . that we have to accept merely on *faith* the existence of things outside us (even though they provide us with all the material we have for cognitions)."[8] The skeptical link between absence and uncertainty is especially important for this article. From a skeptical perspective absence does not simply refer to the removal of a previously present object (as when Darcy disappears from Elizabeth's view). It also evokes the difficulty of comprehending any object—whether present or not—when the mind's idea of that object is merely a representation and never the thing itself. In this way, objects are always absent in the mind and the mind is bound to be uncertain about them—bound to be in doubt.

Precisely because of its oft-quoted optimism about human knowledge, John Locke's *An Essay Concerning Human Understanding* (1690) is especially revealing about absence and uncertainty. On the one hand, Locke celebrates the mind's ready reception of the physical world. The mind is a place like "white paper," "wax," an "empty cabinet," a "storehouse," or a "presence-room," that is "imprinted" or "furnished" with the "materials" of ideas "by external things."[9] On the other hand, though, the mind's materials can decompose, just as "print" on paper "wears out" like the moldered "inscriptions" on old "tombs," or a seal "will be *obscure*" when wax is too hard or too soft.[10]

Indeed, the Lockean mind is ultimately divided from external objects, however full its own "storehouse," because its ideas share the same representational failures as language. Because they refer to but never are the things they name, words have "naturally no signification."[11] So too, an idea impressed on the mind by an external body is only "a sign or representation of the thing it considers"; an idea is not the "thing" itself, which is, after all, never literally "present to the understanding." As Charles Landesman explains, "Locke thought it obvious that ideas *are* and bodies *are not* present" to the mind (emphasis added).[12] Thus, external objects are always absent in the mind, whose cumulative furnishings mark empty spots. The problem is exacerbated when an external object is itself absent from view—when, though it may exist elsewhere, an object is missing from the present landscape. Locke explains that "if I saw a . . . *man*, . . . one minute since, and am now alone, I cannot be certain, that the same man exists now. . . .

[A]nd much less can I be certain of the existence of men, that I never saw" (*Essay* [*An Essay Concerning Human Understanding*], 4.11.9). How different from the neighbors in *Pride and Prejudice* who believe universally accepted truths about unseen bachelors!

As an empiricist, convinced that all knowledge is founded on personal experience, Locke disparaged this kind of universal acknowledgment. The "*giving up our assent to the common received opinions,* either of our friends, or party; neighbourhood or country" keeps "more people" in "ignorance, or error" than any other "*measure of probability.*" But Locke also recognized that to privilege personal experience required the rejection of most general truth claims. For if "*general knowledge*" can lie "only in our own thoughts," then "our knowledge goes not beyond particulars."[13]

Nobody impugned the logic of deriving general truths from particular observations more memorably than David Hume. As Frederick Copleston puts it, Hume argued that "we are confined to the world of perceptions and enjoy no access to a world of objects existing independently of these perceptions."[14] Hume's much-noted riddle of induction specifically discredits generalizations made about the future. Even if we have persuasive evidence about a past object or event, Hume writes, it is illogical to extend "this experience . . . to future times, and to other objects" because "the course of nature may change."[15]

Hume also suggested that the mind is itself a particular object about which the mind has no certainty. In the Appendix of *A Treatise of Human Nature* (1739-40) he instructs philosophers to be "reconcil'd to the principle" that "with regard to the mind, . . . *we have no notion of it, distinct from particular perceptions.*"[16] Nor can the mind escape the riddle of induction. Because the mind's perceptions may change its future is independent of its past and unpredictable. As Hume famously puts it, "the mind is a kind of theatre, where several perceptions successively make their appearance; pass, re-pass, glide away, and mingle in an infinite variety of postures." But we have neither the "most distant notion of the place, where these scenes are represented, [nor] of the materials, of which it is compos'd."[17] In Locke, the mind is a storehouse of absent referents, but for Hume the "place" of the mind is itself absent, its "materials" too "distant" for human "notion."

As I have suggested of *Pride and Prejudice,* the early modern novel also associates problems of absence with problems of knowledge. In novel studies, there is a long tradition of attention to the latter. Ian Watt originally defined the genre's "formal realism" as, in part, a response to "Nominalist skepticism about language"; but Watt later adjusted "realism" to include the narrative separation of mental or "inner life" from the "outer world" of "physical objects." Among Watt's many revisionists, Michael McKeon is especially useful here. He argues that the novel registers an "epistemological crisis . . . in attitudes toward how to tell the truth in narrative." The same crisis, McKeon adds, creates the early modern mind: "Henceforth . . . knowing something will consist in having it 'in mind,' and knowing it well will require that we refine the capacity of our ideas for the accurate, inner representation of external objects."[18]

I would stress that novel protagonists, both male and female, are routinely incapable of such refinement. Consider, for instance, the famous moment when Robinson Crusoe is "exceedingly surprized" to see the "print of a man's naked foot on the shore" of his Caribbean island. Though the print leaves an indelible "impression" in the sand, it is only a sign of a now absent object. The more Crusoe thinks about the print's missing referent the less he grasps the material world. Crusoe returns to his fortification "not feeling, as we say, the ground I went on"; he confounds absence and presence, "mistaking every bush and tree, and fancying every stump at a distance to be a man"; and his ideas so supersede reality that he cannot begin to "describe [in] how many various shapes affrighted imagination represented things to me."[19]

Whereas Crusoe suffers from his uncertainty about an absent object, a half century later Tristram Shandy and his uncle Toby suffer when the absence of an object appears too certain. For they suffer when those around them should—but do not—doubt that they have been either partially or fully castrated. Thus the wide-ranging gossip about Toby's wounded groin overpowers Tristram's claim that "nothing was ever better" than "my uncle['s] . . . fitness for the marriage state" (596-7). Similarly, when the sash crashes as little Tristram urinates out the window, Susannah screams that "[n]othing is left" (369). Tristram says the accident was "nothing," but "all the world" believes the worst (419). As his puns suggest, for Tristram even nothing is indeterminable and proves nothing about itself.

At least Crusoe and Tristram own property, which—though no cure for the absence of objects in the mind—offers some modicum of power in the object world. The consolation is clear when Crusoe "march[es]" around the island with a "secret kind of pleasure . . . to think that this was all my own" (113-4). The footprint interrupts this security, but soon enough Friday arrives and reestablishes Crusoe's mastery by setting Crusoe's "foot upon his head."[20] Even Tristram—who fears for his own head—is (thanks to the untimely death of his older brother) "heir-apparent to the Shandy" (332) family. Uncle Toby is not so lucky. As a younger son, he is "born to nothing" (279), his wounded groin and miniature fortifications fitting symbols of male landlessness.

Female characters generally have it worse because, in addition to being "born to nothing," they can be owned by men. For the heroine who both lacks—and is treated as—property, absence is a constitutive condition and the uncertainty accompanying it can be intense. Think of Clarissa Harlowe. She inherits but never commands her grandfather's estate, and first her family and then Lovelace seek possession of her body. The crucial scene where Lovelace abducts her from her father's garden indicates the epistemological hazard of such deficiency. Here, Lovelace is able to seize Clarissa and (as if mimicking her landlessness) to lift her off the land by confusing her about external objects. Though Clarissa's family is absent, Lovelace convinces her otherwise: "Now behind me, now before me, now on this side, now on that, turned I my affrighted face . . . expecting a furious brother here, armed servants there, an enraged sister screaming and a father armed with terror in his countenance." Lacking both knowledge about materiality and material control, Clarissa doubly loses her ground. "I ran," she says, "yet knew not that I ran; my fears at the same time that they took all power of thinking from me adding wings to my feet."[21]

In one sense, the scene closely recalls Crusoe's uncertainty when he ran from the footprint, "not feeling . . . the ground I went on," and "fancying every stump at a distance to be a man" (162). But once he acquires Friday as well as other subjects and slaughters the natives, Crusoe regains his "undoubted right of dominion" (240-1) on the island. The same can never be true for Clarissa after her flight. Rather, her right of dominion contracts as Lovelace's expands, culminating in the rape that completes her dispossession. It is a testament to the uncertainty from which it descends that the rape is famously unrepresented in the novel. As if epitomizing the failures of perception that led Clarissa to the moment, the rape simply is not there.

Elizabeth Bennet also runs—or nearly does, and the oft-quoted scene where this occurs provides a fit return to *Pride and Prejudice.* When Jane is sick at Netherfield and their father cannot spare the carriage, Elizabeth walks there "alone, crossing field after field at a quick pace, jumping over stiles and springing over puddles with impatient activity, and finding herself at last within view of the house, with weary ancles, dirty stockings, and a face glowing with the warmth of exercise" (32). Though she flees no danger (and, in fact, happily glows despite Jane's illness) Elizabeth resembles both Crusoe and Clarissa in barely touching down. Her greater affinity, however, is with the latter. Elizabeth makes enough contact with the ground to have "weary ancles" and "dirty stockings." But this is hardly the kind of impact Crusoe has when he overcomes the footprint by claiming "dominion" of the island. Rather than marking the land she cannot own, Elizabeth, like Clarissa, shares the mark (and the mud) of valuable property. No wonder Darcy is so smitten when she enters Bingley's home.

From its opening chapter, **Pride and Prejudice** coordinates women's lack of property with their lack of knowledge, as if one absence informs the other. Mr. Bingley's arrival in the neighborhood is symptomatic. Since men control both their own—and their female relatives'—bodily movements, the Bennet women can meet Mr. Bingley only if Mr. Bennet visits first and arranges their introduction.[22] That Mr. Bennet visits without telling them and teases his wife by pretending otherwise suggests the magnitude of women's uncertainty. However little Mr. Bennet knows about this particular "single man in possession of a good fortune," Mrs. Bennet is physically bound to know less.

Elizabeth's misunderstanding of Darcy repeats the basic paradigm. Though both she and Darcy initially misperceive and dislike each other, Darcy quickly knows better. A few pages after Elizabeth hears him declare her "not handsome enough to tempt *me*" (12), Darcy "discover[s]" that her "uncommonly intelligent" eyes, her "light and pleasing" figure, and her "easy playfulness" are indeed tempting. "Wish[ing] to know more of her"—and using her outer appearance as his gauge—Darcy begins to discern her inner character. While Elizabeth remains "perfectly unaware" of his attraction and continues to misperceive him, he accurately appraises her personal worth (23-4).

And yet such accuracy is of virtually no narrative interest, for the mind the novel clearly prefers is the unknowing one. The only time Austen uses free indirect discourse to recount Darcy's perspective, for instance, is when he is confused. Thus, we learn that he is "mortif[ied]" to recognize the beauty of Elizabeth's eyes and that her walk to Netherfield leaves him torn between attraction and "doubt as to the occasion's justifying her coming so far alone" (23, 33). But as soon as Darcy falls entirely in love—as soon as what he perceives of Elizabeth's body begins to correspond with her delightful character—all passages from his consciousness vanish, as if only misperception qualifies for narrative thought.

Elizabeth, of course, perfectly meets this skeptical standard, and she does so, in part, because she is misled by language. This is hardly surprising given that news, gossip, secrets, disagreements, misunderstandings, and lies saturate her social world. Indeed the detachment of language and meaning is so pervasive that Mr. Collins can ridiculously claim to be "run away with by my feelings" when proposing to Elizabeth and then can dismiss her sincere rejection of him as "merely words of course" (105, 108). As with other epistemological problems, however, women are particularly susceptible to linguistic imprecision. It is telling, for instance, that

Elizabeth first emerges as the novel's heroine only after overhearing Darcy's insult. Though for Darcy the comment ultimately has no signification, as Locke would say, Elizabeth long believes it an accurate account of his view. Along with other female characters, she is also easy prey for lies. Thus, while Mrs. Bennet is deceived by her husband and Jane suffers from false reports about Bingley's indifference, Elizabeth is readily seduced by Wickham's distortion of Darcy's history, much like Georgiana Darcy and Lydia are seduced by Wickham's lies about loving them. Elizabeth's gravest mistakes occur when she takes language too literally—when she assumes words are really true.

At other times, though, Elizabeth not only recognizes but also makes a virtue of language's misdirection. She may overestimate Darcy's insult, but she also repeats the story with such incongruously "great spirit" that—publicly at least—Darcy's words become "ridiculous." Indeed, it is her "deligh[t]" in the "ridiculous" that makes Elizabeth so delightful (12). Laughing "whenever [she] can" at "[f]ollies and nonsense, whims and inconsistencies" (57), she at least finds "absurdities" amusing (152). Austen's celebrated irony takes linguistic advantage of such moments. In that it concerns the divorce between language and reality, irony invokes—but also exploits—the skeptical difficulty of representing the external world. Words are ironic when their patent nonsense, ridiculousness, or inconsistencies become significant, when the gap between what is said and what is real is where meaning itself inheres. To enjoy irony, as Elizabeth often does, is to make comic sense of the absence of literal truth. Or, to put it another way, the absence in irony leads the capable mind to new thought.[23]

Elizabeth becomes most thoughtful in the novel's second half when she is faced not simply with the inevitable and general absence of literalism, but also with the particular and literal absence of Darcy. Here the peculiar benefits of uncertainty become especially apparent. Could Elizabeth simply grasp Darcy as an external object she would have little need to think about him. Her detachment from Darcy is advantageous in alerting her to her lack of knowledge, which ironically elevates her mind by forcing it to work.

The elevation begins after Elizabeth rejects Darcy's first proposal and he disappears. Having routinely misunderstood him in his presence, Elizabeth is now left with only signs—first Darcy's letter, then his Pemberley estate, and finally, her aunt's second-hand account of his help with Lydia. As she interprets one piece of evidence and then another, Elizabeth is almost always alone. Her isolation suggests both the general subjectivity of any interpretive act and Elizabeth's particular and growing capacity to resist what Locke calls the "ignorance, or error" of *common received opinions*" (which, in this case, involves the neighborhood's disdain for Darcy and admiration of Wickham).[24]

That the process reflects both her epistemological limits and her mental growth becomes clear when she reads Darcy's letter and experiences a "contrariety of emotion" and "perturbed state of mind" (204, 205). As when she visited Jane at Netherfield, Elizabeth walks restlessly as she reads. But whereas the earlier scene described her feet jumping over stiles and puddles—here it is her "thoughts that could rest on nothing" (205). The object world recedes as Elizabeth reads and re-reads "every line" of Darcy's account of Wickham's perfidy, her own "thoughts" becoming a "line" to be re-read and reinterpreted (205, 208).[25] Hume describes a mental theater where perceptions "pass, re-pass, glide away, and mingle in an infinite variety of postures and situations."[26] Similarly, Elizabeth "see[s] [Wickham] instantly before her," but "[h]ow differently did everything now appear." His solicitude now cast as impropriety, Elizabeth watches as "[e]very lingering struggle in his favour grew fainter and fainter" (206, 207).

In recognizing the "variety" (209) and instability of thought, Elizabeth makes her most extraordinary and "humiliating" discovery. When she famously declares "Till this moment I never knew myself" (208), her mind becomes its own uncertain object—uncertain because it can change without warning and uncertain because it can be unknown. Arguing that the mind's perception of itself is as dubious and disconnected as any other perception, Hume insists *we have no notion of it, distinct from the particular perceptions*" (*Treatise* [*A Treatise of Human Nature*], 677). Elizabeth Bennet may be more optimistic (she never knew herself but now she thinks she does). Nevertheless, she learns that her own thoughts can be as deceptive and inaccessible as Wickham and Darcy, that, like the external reality they so easily misinterpret, thoughts can misread themselves. Thus, Elizabeth concludes that although she had "prided" herself on her "discernment" of Darcy, she was actually so "offended by" his "neglect" that she drove "reason away." She now sees herself as "blind, partial, prejudiced, [and] absurd" because what she thought she was thinking was not what she really thought—or at least not entirely (208). If such a formulation prefigures the Freudian unconscious it does so because Austen makes the mind ironic. As with the linguistic absurdities Elizabeth so enjoys, there is a difference between what the mind articulates and what it really means.[27]

When, a few months later, Elizabeth agrees to visit Pemberley in Darcy's absence, she arrives knowing enough of her own "ignorance" (208) to be free for new perceptions. Her notorious attraction to Darcy's "large, handsome" and clearly phallic property ("standing well on rising ground" [245]) suggests that even in a non-referential world his material power is reasonably certain. But Elizabeth's ability to know his character from it is not. Still, Pemberley does have an advantage all of Elizabeth's previous information lacked. Until now she has depended either on direct perceptions of Darcy or on testimonies about him (supplied by Wickham, her neighbors, and Darcy in his letter). With its varied grounds, "trees," "rooms," "furniture," and, of course, portraits, Pemberley is the first space to provide objects that represent him in his absence (246). Together they constitute what Ian Hacking would call "the evidence provided by *things*"—the distinctly modern concept at the heart of probability theory.[28]

Elizabeth also receives new testimony, this time from Darcy's housekeeper, Mrs. Reynolds, who has "known him ever since he was four years old." Convinced that she speaks "the truth, and what every body will say that knows him," Mrs. Reynolds remembers Darcy as "the sweetest-tempered, most generous-hearted, boy in the world." Now, she claims, he is "the best landlord, and the best master," and the best brother "that ever lived." In another context Elizabeth might, like her uncle Mr. Gardiner, be "highly amused" by this "excessive"—arguably even ridiculous—praise; but here (as she once did with Wickham) Elizabeth listens trustingly (248-50).

Earlier, Elizabeth had seen miniatures of both Wickham and Darcy. Now she ascends to the gallery where she sees the "finer, larger picture" (247) of only Darcy (perhaps painted by the artist to whom Mrs. Reynolds's name alludes).[29] The servant's words repeat almost verbatim in her stream of consciousness: "As a brother, a landlord, a master, [Elizabeth] considered how many people's happiness were in his guardianship!" The experience is both empirical and subjective. Mrs. Reynolds knows her master but she is biased; the portrait, in which Elizabeth sees "a striking resemblance of Mr. Darcy," is more than five years old (250, 200).

Ultimately, the material reality—both of the portrait and of its absent referent—proves less important than Elizabeth's passing thoughts. "There was certainly at this moment, in [her] mind, a more gentle sensation towards the original, than she had ever felt in the height of their acquaintance." Replacing the "original" Darcy with her own idea of him, Elizabeth Bennet makes a man. She thinks of Darcy's "regard with a deeper sentiment of gratitude than it had ever raised before," and, as if *she* were the painter, "soften[s] its impropriety of expression" (250-1). That such command depends on Darcy's absence is made clear when Elizabeth subsequently leaves the house and meets him on the lawn. Unlike with her inspection of the portrait, now she "scarcely dared lift her eyes to his face" (251). The detachment typifies Elizabeth's material deficiency in Darcy's presence. Darcy often looks at her; she rarely does the same.[30]

The next night Elizabeth's "thoughts were at Pemberley," and she lies "awake two whole hours, endeavouring" to decipher her feelings for Darcy (265). Her confusion is resolved once she becomes convinced she cannot have him. Lydia elopes with Wickham, Darcy is present when Elizabeth hears the news, and "never had she so honestly felt that she could have loved him, as now, when all love must be in vain" (278). "When it was no longer likely they should meet" (311), her love for Darcy is the one thing Elizabeth knows. In *Pride and Prejudice* absence makes the heart grow fonder in particularly gendered terms.[31] Darcy first falls in love with Elizabeth when watching her body. But for Elizabeth, who cannot appraise objects as Darcy does, male absence is a prerequisite for love. As if confirming the paradigm, Darcy responds to Lydia's elopement by telling Elizabeth "I am afraid you have long been desiring my absence" (278). Elizabeth may not literally desire Darcy's absence at this moment (though at others she does [268]), but she must think about his absence to desire him. For a woman like Elizabeth (and also Jane) to love is to fixate on a missing man; to love is the consummation of missing that man.

Incidentally, other female characters develop alternative approaches to male absence. After marrying Mr. Collins, for instance, Charlotte wisely cultivates his absence by choosing an unattractive room as her parlor so as to discourage his attendance (168). Lydia, on the other hand, depends upon male presence. Whereas Elizabeth philosophically accepts her apparent loss of Darcy, Lydia can so little tolerate the idea of the officers leaving the neighborhood that she literally follows them to Brighton, from where she follows Wickham to London.

In one extraordinary passage preceding Lydia's departure for Brighton, there is a full paragraph rendered from her mind:

> She saw with the creative eye of fancy, the streets of that gay bathing place covered with officers. She saw herself the object of attention, to tens and to scores of them at present unknown. She saw all the glories of the camp; its tents stretched forth in beauteous uniformity of lines, crowded with the young and the gay, and dazzling with scarlet; and to complete the view, she saw herself seated beneath a tent, tenderly flirting with at least six officers at once.
>
> (232)

The vivid physical detail (the camp "dazzling with scarlet," tents "stretched forth in beauteous . . . lines," crowds of the "young and the gay") is unusual for Aus-

ten and speaks to the material basis of Lydia's near ruin. Lydia's mistake is to imagine that her visions can become "realities" (232). In a world where women are "object[s]," Lydia truly believes that—like the master of a harem—she will sit "beneath a tent," and control "scores" of "unknown" men.[32]

Not only does Elizabeth have no such illusions, but it is also finally thanks to Lydia's pursuit of Wickham and to her own continued separation from Darcy that she completes the mental work of loving him. For Elizabeth secures her final evidence of Darcy's virtue when she learns about his success in arranging Lydia's marriage.[33] As earlier, the information arrives in the form of a testimonial letter—now from Mrs. Gardiner, who has herself only second-hand access to the details of Darcy's rescue. That report is enough for Elizabeth who, upon reading the letter, overcomes her "vague and unsettled . . . uncertainty" about Darcy and concludes that what had seemed "an exertion of goodness [in him] too great to be probable" had "proved" to the "greatest extent to be true!" (326).

But even this truth about Darcy's "goodness" raises epistemological problems—this time about continuity and change. For Hume, past experience has no bearing on the future for the "course of nature may change" (*Enquiry* [*An Enquiry Concerning Human Understanding*], 4.2.21). Similarly, we might ask whether Darcy's heroism marks the emergence of his fixed and essential goodness (which Elizabeth simply needed to discover) or whether time has altered him. Mrs. Reynolds would claim the former. "I have always observed, that they who are good-natured when children, are good-natured, when they grow up; and he was always the sweetest-tempered, most generous-hearted, boy in the world" (249). Yet Darcy later confesses to Elizabeth:

> I have been a selfish being all my life, in practice, though not in principle. As a child I was taught what was *right,* but I was not taught to correct my temper. . . . I was spoilt by my parents, . . . allowed, encouraged . . . to be selfish and overbearing, to care for none beyond my own family circle, to think meanly of all the rest of the world.
>
> (369)

For Mrs. Reynolds, Darcy has the same, coherent good-nature that he demonstrated when "four years old" (248). But Darcy insists that he was selfish "from eight to eight and twenty" and that Elizabeth has reformed him: "such I might still have been but for you, dearest, loveliest Elizabeth!" (369).[34] Perhaps Mrs. Reynolds and Darcy are both right. Darcy may have always had some goodness and still have needed to improve. And Mrs. Reynolds's account of her master's history (in his "family circle") may be just as true for her as Darcy's account is true for him. What their conflicting perceptions preclude, however, is the possibility of reaching an absolute truth about Darcy (or indeed anyone) at any time—past, present or future.

Elizabeth's romantic victory is to decide that such truth is irrelevant when one can be absent-minded. Affirming what Susan Morgan calls Austen's "optimistic skepticism," the heroine finally assumes that it is not the mind's certainty about either the external world or internal thoughts that matters.[35] Happiness is born in imaginative selection. Thus, at the conclusion of the novel, when she and Darcy disagree about the spirit in which he wrote his letter, Elizabeth tells him to "[t]hink no more of the letter. . . . You must learn some of my philosophy. Think only of the past as its remembrance gives you pleasure" (368-9). By the end of the nineteenth century, Freud will describe forgetting as a form of repression and neurosis. But for Elizabeth, to forget is to relish uncertainty and incompleteness and to enjoy mental health.[36]

To put it another way, Elizabeth achieves the "pleasure" of loving Darcy by ridding her mind of certain memories—she achieves it via absence. Darcy rejects Elizabeth's forgetfulness, telling her "with *me,* it is not so." But then again, as a man Darcy has never much needed to console himself for—or with—absence. He declares that the "contentment arising" for Elizabeth from her retrospections "is not of philosophy, but what is much better, of ignorance" (369). And perhaps he has a point. For if, as I have argued, Elizabeth's experience of absence generates her intellectual triumph—if the dispossessed heroine epitomizes the uncertainty that renders a protagonist's mind complex—then her final "pleasure" in obliterating memories is a kind of defeat.[37] Elizabeth enlarged her mind in Darcy's absence. Now that she is again in his presence, she willfully absents her own thoughts. Though they are "merely words" (108), of course, what for Darcy requires "ignorance" and for Elizabeth "philosophy" we might just as well call "wifehood."

Notes

1. Jane Austen, *The Novels of Jane Austen, Pride and Prejudice,* ed. R. W. Chapman, 5 vols. (Oxford and New York: Oxford Univ. Press, 1966-9), 2: 193. Hereafter *Pride and Prejudice* is cited parenthetically in the text.

2. Susan Morgan, *In The Meantime: Character and Perception in Jane Austen's Fiction* (Chicago and London: Univ. of Chicago Press, 1980), 4. Tony Tanner, *Jane Austen* (Cambridge: Harvard Univ. Press, 1986), 105. For specific discussions of epistemological uncertainty in *Pride and Prejudice* see Martha Satz, "An Epistemological Understanding of *Pride and Prejudice*: Humility and Objectivity," in *Jane Austen: New Perspectives,* ed. Ja-

net Todd (New York and London: Holmes and Meier Publishers, 1983), 171-86; Tara Ghoshal Wallace, *Jane Austen and Narrative Authority* (New York: St. Martin's Press, 1995), 45-58; and Felicia Bonaparte, "Conjecturing Possibilities: Reading and Misreading Texts in Jane Austen's *Pride and Prejudice,*" *Studies in the Novel* 37 (2005): 141-61. On Austen's response to the politically progressive implications of—and the stigma attached to—the word "philosophy" in the wake of the French Revolution see Claudia L. Johnson's superb *Jane Austen: Women, Politics, and the Novel* (Chicago and London: Univ. of Chicago Press, 1988), 10-14, 78.

3. I have written elsewhere about absence and the creation of the unconscious in Austen's *Emma.* See my *Mothering Daughters: Novels and the Politics of Family Romance, Frances Burney to Jane Austen* (Detroit: Wayne State Univ. Press, 2002), 145-68. I make a related argument about absence and the mind in "Money or Mind? *Cecilia,* the Novel, and the Real Madness of Selfhood," *Studies in Eighteenth-Century Culture* 33 (2004): 49-70.

4. The syntax suggests that even the single man may not know his own "feelings or views." For excellent discussions of the epistemological problems reflected in the opening lines see Tanner, *Jane Austen,* 110-11 and Claudia Brodsky Lacour, "Austen's *Pride and Prejudice* and Hegel's 'Truth in Art': Concept, Reference, History," *ELH* 59 (1992): 607-10.

5. Lady Catherine De Bourgh and her daughter are unusual in having independent fortunes.

6. Mary Wollstonecraft specifically uses the term "absence of mind" to describe women's ignorance in a world that commodifies their bodies and lets their "mind[s] . . . lie fallow"; *A Vindication of the Rights of Woman,* ed. Carol H. Poston (New York and London: Norton, 1988), 192.

7. On the popularity of "dispossession in the [eighteenth-century] rhetoric of authorship"—especially of female authorship—see Catherine Gallagher, *Nobody's Story: The Vanishing Acts of Women Writers in the Marketplace, 1670-1820* (Berkeley and Los Angeles: Univ. of California Press, 1994), xxi. On how eighteenth-century epistemological problems influenced the development of the romantic mind see M. H. Abrams *The Mirror and the Lamp: Romantic Theory and the Critical Tradition* (New York: Oxford Univ. Press, 1953), 57-69; and James Engell, *The Creative Imagination: Enlightenment to Romanticism* (Cambridge, MA and London: Harvard Univ. Press, 1981), 3-10.

8. Immanuel Kant, *Critique of Pure Reason: Unified Edition,* trans. Werner S. Pluhar (Indianapolis and Cambridge: Hackett, 1996), Bxl, note. On how skepticism influenced the emergence of epistemology see Charles Landesman, *Skepticism: The Central Issues* (Oxford: Blackwell Publishers, 2002), 70. Also see David Bates, "Idols and Insight: An Enlightenment Topography of Knowledge," *Representations* 73 (2001): 17. Though space prohibits elaboration, eighteenth-century skepticism anticipates both Marxist and Freudian accounts of human detachment from external objects. See, for instance, Richard Terdiman on the "*de*-valorization of the object in a world [of mass production] in which objects are counted by the trillions" and on "the power of psychical presentations . . . to displace the reality of the material world"; *Present Past: Modernity and the Memory Crisis* (Ithaca and London: Cornell Univ. Press, 1993), 52, 258.

9. John Locke, *An Essay Concerning Human Understanding,* ed. Roger Woolhouse (London: Penguin, 1997), 1.2.15, 2.1.2, 2.3.1, 2.10.2. Locke suggests that certain "simple ideas" or sensory impressions can be fully and entirely known; see, for instance, 2.2.25. For more on Locke's distinction between "simple" and "complex ideas" see Frederick Copleston, S.J., *A History of Philosophy,* 9 vols. (New York: Doubleday, 1994) 5:79-107.

10. Locke, *Essay* [*An Essay Concerning Human Understanding*], 2.10.5 and 2.29.3. Also see Locke's famous image of the mind as a dark closet (2.11.17). Laurence Sterne offers a hilarious parody of Locke's wax image in *The Life and Opinions of Tristram Shandy, Gentleman,* ed. Graham Petrie (Harmondsworth: Penguin, 1983), 107-8.

11. Locke, *Essay,* 3.9.5. Michel Foucault offers one of the best-known accounts of the early modern crisis in representation that separated things and words; see *The Order of Things: An Archaeology of the Human Sciences* (New York: Vintage Books, 1973), 34-44.

12. Locke, *Essay,* 4.21.4; Landesman, *Skepticism,* 24. As Locke writes elsewhere in the *Essay,* "[t]here is nothing like our ideas, existing in the bodies themselves" (2.8.15).

13. Locke, *Essay,* 4.20.17, 4.6.13, and 4.6.16; also see 4.15.6. On probability in Locke see Bates, "Idols and Insight," 14. On how the problem of generalizing from particulars informed the early modern emergence of probability theory see Ian Hacking, *The Emergence of Probability: A Philosophical Study of Early Ideas about Probability, Induction and Statistical Inference* (London: Cambridge Univ. Press, 1975). On how the same problem in-

formed the "history of the modern fact" see Mary Poovey, *A History of the Modern Fact: Problems of Knowledge in the Sciences of Wealth and Society* (Chicago and London: Univ. of Chicago Press, 1998).

14. Copleston, *History of Philosophy,* 293; also see 291-9. My reading of Hume is much influenced by Copleston; Hacking, *The Emergence of Probability*; Landesman, *Skepticism*; and Poovey, *A History of the Modern Fact.*

15. David Hume, *An Enquiry Concerning Human Understanding,* ed. Tom L. Beauchamp (New York: Oxford Univ. Press, 1999), 4.2.16, 4.2.21; for Hume's famous comments on whether or not the sun will rise see 4.1.2.

16. David Hume, *A Treatise of Human Nature,* ed. Ernest C. Mossner (New York: Penguin Books, 1969), 677.

17. Hume, *Treatise* [*A Treatise of Human Nature*], 301.

18. On formal realism as a response to "Nominalist skepticism about language" see Watt, *The Rise of the Novel: Studies in Defoe, Richardson and Fielding* (Berkeley and Los Angeles: Univ. of California Press, 1957), 27-30. Watt describes realism in more skeptical terms in "Flat-Footed and Fly-Blown: The Realities of Realism," *Eighteenth-Century Fiction* 12 (2000): 157-58. McKeon, *The Origins of the English Novel, 1600-1740* (Baltimore: Johns Hopkins Univ. Press, 1987), 20, 83. Georg Lukács's work remains one of the most lyrical and valuable accounts of the novel's skepticism about human knowledge: "the objectivity of the novel is the mature man's knowledge that meaning can never quite penetrate reality"; *The Theory of the Novel: A Historico-Philosophical Essay on the Forms of Great Epic Literature,* trans. Anna Bostock (Cambridge, Mass.: MIT Press, 1996), 88; also see 60-1, 70-1, 75. Catherine Gallagher describes the novel as an "alternative" to referential truth telling (*Nobody's Story,* xvi).

19. Daniel Defoe, *The Life and Adventures of Robinson Crusoe,* ed. Angus Ross (New York: Penguin, 1983), 162. John Richetti writes that the footprint makes "Crusoe's interior life" appear "to him as mysterious and chaotic as its external provocations"; *The English Novel in History, 1700-1780* (London and New York: Routledge, 1999), 68.

20. Friday puts Crusoe's foot on his head twice (*Robinson Crusoe,* 207, 209).

21. Samuel Richardson, *Clarissa; or, The History of a Young Lady,* ed. Angus Ross (Harmondsworth: Penguin, 1985), 380.

22. Later, Charlotte Lucas says that because Jane cannot control how often or under what circumstances Bingley will see her she must "make the most of every half hour in which she can command his attention" (22).

23. Marvin Mudrick's discussion of Austen's use—and Elizabeth's appreciation—of irony remains valuable; *Jane Austen: Irony as Defense and Discovery* (Princeton, N.J.: Princeton Univ. Press, 1952), 1-4, 94-5, 120-22.

24. Locke, *Essay,* 4.20.17.

25. I am indebted to Jennifer Luongo for some of these observations about Elizabeth's reading.

26. Hume, *Treatise,* 301. For a fuller discussion of Hume's relevance for Austen see Tanner, *Jane Austen,* 108-10, 139-40.

27. Hume arguably anticipates the Freudian unconscious, but Locke explicitly states that it is "hard to conceive, that anything should think, and not be conscious of it" (*Essay,* 2.1.11; also see 2.1.19).

28. Hacking, *The Emergence of Probability,* 32.

29. On the name's "jokey allusion to Sir Joshua Reynolds" see Vivien Jones, ed., *Pride and Prejudice* (Harmondsworth: Penguin, 1996), 332n.

30. See, for instance, 51, 263, 335, 366.

31. In *Persuasion,* Anne Elliot memorably tells Captain Harville "[a]ll the privilege I claim for my own sex (it is not a very enviable one, you need not covet it) is that of loving longest, when existence or when hope is gone"; *The Novels of Jane Austen, Persuasion,* 5: 235.

32. Lydia generally sees men as commodities. When she visits Meryton, her "eyes" wander "in quest" either of the "officers" or of a "very smart bonnet . . . or a really new muslin in a shop window" (72).

33. In keeping with his privileged access to knowledge and material power, only Darcy knows where to find Wickham and he alone satisfies Wickham's financial demands. Darcy also blames himself that "Wickham's worthlessness had not been . . . well known" (321).

34. In an oft-quoted passage Elizabeth anticipates her own transformation when she says that people "alter so much, that there is something new to be observed in them for ever" (43). The uncertainty about whether Elizabeth has uncovered the "real" Darcy or whether he has changed is reflected in critical discussions; for instance, Tanner argues that *Pride and Prejudice* is concerned with "[j]ust what constitutes a person's 'real character'" (*Jane Austen,* 115), whereas Johnson emphasizes the progressive implications of Darcy's improvement (*Jane Austen,* 83-4).

35. Morgan, *In the Meantime,* 10; similarly, Bonaparte argues that "Austen seeks an answer not beyond but within . . . skepticism" by recognizing that "knowledge and understanding are partial, imperfect, and indistinct" ("Conjecturing Possibilities," 152).

36. In his early work on hysteria, co-authored with Josef Breuer, Freud writes that "*[h]ysterics suffer mainly from reminiscences*" that they are "genuinely unable to recollect"; "On the Psychical Mechanism of Hysterical Phenomena: Preliminary Communication" [1893], in *Studies on Hysteria,* ed. Irvin D. Yalom, trans. James Strachey (New York: Basic Books, 2000), 7, 3; for the first use of "repressed" in the psychoanalytic sense see 10. For other accounts of memory in *Pride and Prejudice* see Nicholas Dames, who argues that *Pride and Prejudice* reflects a "modern nostalgic consciousness . . . in which the old is overthrown"; "Austen's Nostalgics," *Representations* 73 (2001): 129; Margaret Anne Doody suggests that the novel shows that "[w]ithout some intelligent check on memory, neither freedom nor love is possible"; "'A Good Memory is Unpardonable': Self, Love, and the Irrational Irritation of Memory," *Eighteenth-Century Fiction* 14 (2001): 94.

37. Forgetting is clearly a problem in earlier passages. The Bingley sisters' "memories," for instance, are "more deeply impressed" with the respectability of their family than with the "circumstance . . . that their brother's fortune and their own had been acquired by trade" (15). Also, after receiving Darcy's letter, Elizabeth realizes how much she has "endeavoured to forget what she could not overlook" of the "impropriety of her father's behavior as a husband" (236).

Michael J. Stasio and Kathryn Duncan (essay date summer 2007)

SOURCE: Stasio, Michael J., and Kathryn Duncan. "An Evolutionary Approach to Jane Austen: Prehistoric Preferences in *Pride and Prejudice*." *Studies in the Novel* 39, no. 2 (summer 2007): 133-46.

[*In the following essay, Stasio and Duncan assess representations of marriage and gender in* Pride and Prejudice.]

While not all scholars of the period agree, some have observed a paradigm shift regarding marriage and gender during the eighteenth century. Thomas Laqueur cogently argues that the two-sex model came into being during this time period, and Lawrence Stone traces the dominance of companionate marriage to the eighteenth century. Anthony Fletcher demonstrates the shift from a medically and theologically based subordination of women to a more secular ideology, while Susan Kingsley Kent claims that notions of inherent gender differences arose out of natural rights ideology. She writes that by the end of the century, women were understood to be passionless and distinct from men biologically. Certainly the most popular and perhaps most important genre of the period, the novel, brings these issues to the forefront with its tendency to focus on mate choice. This near obsession with mate selection and the above paradigm shifts indicate a culture that valued and emphasized companionate marriage both in fact and fiction. In life and print, therefore, we find mating behavior best explained by the genetically influenced method of mate selection that humans adopted in the Pleistocene era, the subject of evolutionary psychology. The rise of the novel, then, represents an expression not only of new ideologies of gender and marriage but also of universal desire explained by evolutionary psychology; nowhere can this be seen more clearly than in the most canonical of domestic novels, Jane Austen's *Pride and Prejudice.*

Unlike neuropsychology or clinical psychology, evolutionary psychology is not a specialized subfield in psychology; rather it represents the viewpoint that functional aspects of the mind such as consciousness and emotion have evolved by natural selection, that is, in a way that best insures reproductive success. Evolutionary theorists attempt to explain why such adaptations may have evolved. For example, starting with D. M. Buss in 1989, cross-cultural research consistently has shown that women value economic resources in a potential mate more than men do. The evolutionary perspective thus seeks to explain why such a gender difference in mate preferences would have evolved.

The key element in evolutionary psychology—the assertion that human sexual mechanisms exist because of evolution by natural selection—is rooted in Charles Darwin's 1871 theory of sexual selection. Sexual selection was proposed as a type of natural selection in which traits that were genetically passed on were those that offered the organism an amount of reproductive advantage that outweighed the potential costs of having the trait. One often cited example of a trait shaped through sexual selection is a peacock's tail. The peacock's long tail and colorful plumage make the bird more noticeable to predators and slow him down when trying to escape threat. However, the characteristics of the tail do solve a very important ecological problem: attracting mates. Thus, while peacocks with very colorful tails will be more vulnerable to predators than birds with less colorful plumage, they will also find mates more

frequently and produce more offspring, which is the goal in evolution: passing one's genes on to the next generation. The fact that peahens are unadorned compared to peacocks supports the notion that sexual selection acts upon the sexes unequally.

What variable may explain how sexual selection acts differentially upon the sexes? R. Trivers argues that the amount of parental investment each sex devotes to an individual offspring and the potential cost of this investment to the parent and other offspring are the key variables in sexual selection in all species. Parental investment is defined as any behavior that increases the likelihood that an individual offspring will survive—and thus reproduce. In humans, as in other mammals, women and men differ in the minimum amounts of parental investment that they must provide for their offspring. Parental investment is necessarily higher for women than for men since women's parental investment involves gestation and lactation at the very least. As the more investing sex, women are necessarily more selective in choosing a mate. While many men also invest in their offspring, their required minimum investment can be only a fraction of that for women. Therefore, women should show mate selection preferences that increase their reproductive success, such as preferences for men who are willing and able to invest economic resources (and ideally emotional commitment). Men also should show mate selection preferences that lead to reproductive success, such as preferences for access to large numbers of fertile women. Differences exist between long-term and short-term mating strategies, but since Austen is interested in the lifelong commitment of marriage, that is our emphasis as well.

A major evolutionary theory of mate selection is Sexual Strategies Theory, proposed by Buss and D. P. Schmitt in 1993 and later elaborated upon by Buss in 1998. A main tenet of this theory holds that mating is strategic, directed toward the goal of successful survival of offspring whether people are conscious of this or not, and that mate preferences exist as solutions to reproductive problems faced by our human ancestors. For example, it would have been reproductively advantageous for ancestral women and men to recognize and avoid mating with people who suffered from diseases or pathogens. Sexual Strategies Theory suggests that those ancestors with evolved preferences or desires for health cues in a mate—such as clear eyes and skin signaling the absence of disease—were more likely to find healthy mates and produce offspring who would survive. According to the sexy son hypothesis, our ancestors also adopted preferences for attractive partners in order to produce more attractive offspring who would be at a reproductive advantage when mating in the future.

Sexual selection has two processes: intrasexual (same-sex) competition and mate choice. When members of the same sex compete with each other, the "victors" are said to increase their preferential access to mates and thus increase the likelihood that their genes will survive. Whatever qualities were important in securing victory in this competition would be selected by evolution; for example, athletic ability, fierce displays of aggression, social skills, or biting humor may deter a potential rival depending on the environment. Another important evolutionary point holds that the more investing sex (women) chooses more selectively while the less investing sex (men) engages in more intrasexual competition. However, if there is an absence of men (or acceptable men), then women will engage in more intrasexual competition. As Anne Campbell has explored, it is also possible that women engage in less obvious intrasexual competition since female strategies are less aggressive than male strategies.

A number of counter-arguments to any analysis involving evolutionary psychology exist, the first being the social construction of ideology. However, laws and ideologies support evolutionary psychology along with other dominant social needs so that social construction and biology work in concert, not opposition. As Brian Boyd explains, "That our minds reflect evolution's design does not mean that all is nature and not nurture, that all is heredity and not environment. In any sophisticated biological thinking these oppositions have been thoroughly discredited" (4). Marriage, for instance, serves the dictates of evolutionary psychology, patriarchy, and the economy, to name a few ideological and biological determinants (see Buss [*Evolutionary Psychology*] 135). Certainly, the actions of the characters in **Pride and Prejudice** can be explained via social concerns and the laws of Austen's era, but these laws and ideology partially owe their being to the inherent principles of evolutionary psychology. In fact, John Tooby and Leda Cosmides's influential work asserts that psychology is the middle link between biology and culture. Their view is that biology has shaped our evolved psychological mechanisms and that this psychology has in turn shaped our culture given the available environmental cues. The authors propose three main assumptions about evolutionary psychology. First, universal human nature originates primarily in our evolved psychological mechanisms (e.g., desire for a healthy partner) and not in cultural expressions of behavior. Second, these psychological mechanisms are adaptations designed by natural selection. Finally, the evolved psychology of the mind reflects adaptations to life experienced by our hunter-gatherer ancestors during the Pleistocene period dating from about two million years ago (5). We mainly explore the authors' first premise in this work. We accept the notion of evolved psychological mechanisms and propose that Austen's era is a particularly useful time period in which to examine psychological mechanisms related to sexuality as well as their cultural expression.[1]

Another objection is that evolutionary psychology can appear as a kind of essentialism, boiling people—or literary characters—down to biological determinism. In fact, though, evolutionary psychology is less deterministic than Freud's theories. Evolutionary psychology consists of preparedness; humans are prepared to make choices, though not at the conscious level, that best ensure that they will reproduce successfully. However, there is still the issue of choice; our evolved psychological dispositions are the primary shapers of culture, but individual choice is inherent in this process. Natural selection would not have designed a human cerebral cortex capable of higher cognitive functions such as thinking and decision-making unless these adaptations conferred reproductive advantages. Therefore, the process by which evolved dispositions create culture must necessarily involve choices among available environmental cues. As Tooby and Cosmides note, the observation that environmental contexts differ around the world helps to explain between-group variability in culture: while preferences for facial symmetry (as a cue to good health) appear to be universally consistent, other preferences thought to be universal may in fact show cultural variation. For example, most data show that men prefer women with a low waist-to-hip ratio (as a cue to reproduction), but one exception is the Hadza, an indigenous group of hunter-gatherers in Tanzania, who prefer women with higher waist-to-hip ratios (Marlow and Wetsman ["How Universal Are Preferences for Female Waist-to-Hip Ratios"] 219). Buss argues that since 1930, women and men have come to value physical attractiveness to a greater degree because attractive models are frequently depicted across a wide range of media (*Evolutionary* [*Evolutionary Psychology*] 148). This is consistent with our argument that evolved psychological mechanisms can shape culture and still produce between-group differences.

In *Evolution and Literary Theory,* Joseph Carroll believes resistance to biologically based approaches to literature often originates from a politically "intellectual prejudice" (27). Carroll accuses poststructuralists of ignoring biology and "reality" out of a political desire to affect social change. In other words, the admission that differences result from biology, not social construction, lays the groundwork for continued discrimination based on such differences. Carroll sees poststructuralism and evolutionary psychology as irreconcilable, arguing in *Literary Darwinism,* for example, against any feminist interpretation of Austen because such a reading is colored by postmodern, radical bias.[2] We disagree. Carroll is correct in saying that

> [o]ften, but not always, they [authors] align themselves with some particular set of species-typical norms, under the rubric of "human nature," and they use these norms as a means of adopting a critical perspective on the conventions of their own cultures. By appealing to elemental dispositions that answer to their own idio-

syncratic psychological organization, they can adopt a critical perspective on species-typical norms, or their own cultures, or both.

(131)

A close examination of Austen's perspective shows that Austen ignores some of the inherent laws and norms of both evolutionary psychology and her culture in a way that opens a feminist reading of her work. For example, according to evolutionary psychology, the best-case scenario for a man is not only a long-term partner who will care for his children but also the opportunity for adultery, that is the spreading further of his genes. Matt Ridley argues, "we are designed for a system of monogamy plagued by adultery" (176). And while the ideology of marriage in Regency England was monogamy, many men enjoyed Ridley's description of the evolutionary psychology ideal. In Austen, though, they do not as she creates a space that upon closer examination often empowers her female characters.

While evolutionary psychology is a powerful explanation of human mate selection, we do not wish to apply it as a heuristic. It is not a mere substitute for a Freudian or Lacanian reading of human behavior. Evolutionary psychology provides insight into the eighteenth and nineteenth centuries because social conditions proved ripe for its ideas to dominate the culture and literature. Stone argues that scientific advances such as the creation of the smallpox vaccine made the eighteenth-century English feel active in determining their fate as they had not before; they no longer felt totally at the mercy of God's will, which extended into how they governed their families: "This sense of control over the environment, and particularly over animal breeding, inevitably led men to choose their wives as one would choose a brood mare, with a great care for their personal genetic inheritance, and to train their children with the same patience and attention as they had long devoted to their horses, dogs or hawks" (234). As personal choice came to the fore, so did the biological basis of selection. What Stone's argument lacks, though, is the female perspective that evolutionary psychology and Austen elucidate.

Evolutionary psychology posits universal, gender-specific traits that each sex would find attractive in the other. Certainly, some of the more general traits apply in a discussion of Austen. Attractive male prospects are capable of supporting and protecting a family. Though Austen is infamous for lack of physical descriptions, she introduces Bingley as "good looking and gentlemanlike" and Darcy as grabbing "the attention of the room by his fine, tall person, handsome features, noble mien" (7), fulfilling the sexy son hypothesis. Desirable female potential mates ideally would be young, healthy, and fertile. But we need to ground our argument in the

historically relevant qualities Austen and her audience would have found most appealing. David and Nanelle Barash observe that men and women universally look for "kindness and intelligence" in a mate so that "[h]ere again, Jane Austen provides a textbook case of sexual selection in action, as her protagonists reveal their intellects—while stimulating the readers'—via their verbal adroitness" (55). True, but Austen's contemporary readers had a specific context for Austen's witty word play and emphasis on manners. As David Monaghan states, "Being a very formal society, eighteenth-century England placed tremendous emphasis on the moral implications of the individual's polite performance, as is indicated by Edmund Burke's assertion that 'Manners are of more importance than laws. . . . According to their quality, they aid morals, they supply them, or they totally destroy them'" (2-3). So while her Pleistocene ancestors probably valued male physical strength more than politeness, Austen recognizes that manners and wit in her tamer eighteenth century are effective weapons for social dominance and evidence of moral superiority. For example, while Mr. Bennet revels in his wit, his barbs are too strongly pointed for our ultimate admiration. His bad manners serve as a warning that Mr. Bennet ultimately is a failed, weak patriarch, beholden to another man to sustain his family's reputation, and hence a poor mate choice. Similarly, Darcy at first appears a poor mate choice to Elizabeth because of his rudeness; it is only when he demonstrates manners and a commensurate generosity that Elizabeth falls in love with and chooses to be with him.

Though in *Northanger Abbey* Henry Tilney tells Catherine that "man has the advantage of choice, woman only the power of refusal" (95), in *Pride and Prejudice,* Austen explores female choice in mate selection.[3] Obviously, Austen values choice as our heroine rejects two proposals and chooses a mate that no one else would have chosen for her. Karen Newman writes:

> In *Pride and Prejudice,* everything about Elizabeth— her poverty, her inferior social position, the behaviour of her family, her initial preferences for Wickham, and her refusal of Darcy's first offer of marriage—all these things ideologically should lead if not to death, at best to genteel poverty and spinsterhood. Instead, Austen had her marry despite her violations of these accepted norms of female behaviour.
>
> (205)

Austen rewards Elizabeth and, to a lesser extent, Charlotte for their active attempts to choose mates. At the same time, Austen recognizes her social context. Elizabeth cannot choose Colonel Fitzwilliam, nor he her, because of their financial situations. She also must wait for Darcy to reintroduce his marriage proposal. And the ever patient Jane, who embodies the contemporary female ideal of passivity in the novel, must pine endlessly for Bingley's return. Note, though, that much as we may wish Jane well in the novel, she is not our heroine, nor is she Austen's ideal. More importantly, evolutionary psychology contends that women in all cultures show more discrimination in mate choice, which is true for all of the mature female characters in the novel. (Lydia and Georgianna are the obvious exceptions, but they are both adolescents duped by Wickham.) Mr. Collins, in a typical pattern of male mating behavior, is willing to marry any of the attractive Bennet daughters, which sadly excludes Mary, but none of the attractive daughters is willing to marry him.

This gendered discretion in choice appears in spite of the number of single women in the novel and the commensurate intrasexual competition: Caroline Bingley rightfully sees Elizabeth as a rival and lies to Jane by claiming that Georgiana is proposed as a match for Bingley, and, of course, Lady Catherine argues that her daughter is betrothed to Darcy (see Gilbert and Gubar [*The Madwoman in the Attic*] 126). One intrasexual competitive tactic specified by evolutionary theory and used by women in *Pride and Prejudice* is derogation of competitors, notably used by Caroline Bingley when she first derogates Jane for her lack of social connections and her incomplete knowledge of London streets. Caroline also derogates Elizabeth a number of times, most pointedly when "in the imprudence of anger, [she] took the first opportunity of saying, with sneering civility, 'Pray, Miss Eliza, are not the——shire militia removed from Meryton? They must be a great loss to *your* family'" (174). Lady Catherine behaves much the same as a kind of substitute competitor for her daughter, telling Elizabeth, "But *your* arts and allurements may, in a moment of infatuation, have made him [Darcy] forget what he owes to himself and to all his family" (231). And like Caroline, she points to Elizabeth's poor social connections, asking, "Are the shades of Pemberley to be thus polluted?" (233), in reference to Lydia and Wickham's hastily arranged marriage. But in spite of the competition for few desirable mates, even Charlotte Lucas who claims, "Happiness in marriage is entirely a matter of chance" (16) carefully considers her mate choice.

Charlotte, of course, marries Mr. Collins purely out of mercenary self-interest, denying any romantic feelings at all. The narrator is blunt: Charlotte accepts Mr. Collins "solely from the pure and disinterested desire of an establishment," labeling marriage the "pleasantest preservative from want" (83). Cultural exigencies and evolutionary psychology work together to explain Charlotte's pragmatic choice, with the shortage of men (and Charlotte's age) forcing her into making a less than perfect but in some ways desirable choice. David Geary would call Charlotte's strategy an example of bounded

rationality, a rational choice that best serves her evolutionarily within a given ecological context. Rational does not mean optimal but weighing "cost-benefit trade-offs" and accepting "good enough" as a way to increase her chances at reproduction (13). Austen makes clear that Charlotte's is not the worst fate for women in the novel. She has the comfort of a home and the adaptability necessary to live with a fool for a husband. As Elizabeth observes when seeing their home, "When Mr. Collins could be forgotten, there was really a great air of comfort throughout, and by Charlotte's evident enjoyment of it, Elizabeth supposed he must be often forgotten" (105). Austen commented in a letter that "single Women have a dreadful propensity for being poor—which is one very strong argument in favor of Matrimony" (qtd. in Sulloway [*Jane Austen and the Province of Womanhood*] 17). Given the negative attitude toward spinsterhood in the period and Austen's own comments, marriage, even to Mr. Collins, appears preferable to being single (see Sulloway 23). And one need only think of Fanny Price's family in *Mansfield Park* to see that Austen by no means punishes Charlotte for her choice of mate. Choosing security over love is preferable to a life of love and poverty.

Elizabeth, of course, is faced with the same choice of mate in Mr. Collins and chooses differently, turning down his proposal in spite of no alternative offers. Evolutionary psychology—as well as good taste and the ideology of companionate marriage—offers an explanation. In choosing a mate who will offer social and financial support, women, as the more investing sex, must consider a man's long-term stability—both as a husband and as a father. Austen's novels almost obsessively discuss the need for marriage between those who are like-minded, and they demonstrate the problems that result with the incompatible and impecunious mate. The Bennets are the obvious example in *Pride and Prejudice,* with Mr. Bennet's rude treatment of his wife and lax parenting resulting in near disaster for the family. Upon Lydia's elopement, Elizabeth "had never felt so strongly as now, the disadvantages which must attend the children of so unsuitable a marriage" as that of her parents (155). She even warns her father before Lydia embarks for Brighton saying, "Our importance, our respectability in the world, must be affected by the wild volatility, the assurance and disdain of all restraint which mark Lydia's character" (151). Mr. Bennet's neglect of his daughters, Austen makes clear, results from his lack of respect and love for Mrs. Bennet, whom he married for her "youth and beauty, and that appearance of good humour, which youth and beauty generally give," temporary qualities that led to "an end to all real affection for her." In a different situation from that created by Austen, this basis of attraction would work well for a male, who would simply move on to another attractive young partner. With the Bennets, we most clearly see Austen's refusal to give her male characters any leeway for their poor mate selection. Mr. Bennet is allowed no possibility of escape, no solace in a mistress, which Austen obliquely mentions: "Mr. Bennet was not of a disposition to seek comfort for the disappointment which his own imprudence had brought on, in any of those pleasures which too often console the unfortunate for their folly or their vice" (155). His only refuge lies in cutting remarks that his wife rarely comprehends—since "the experience of three and twenty years had been insufficient to make his wife understand his character" (4)—and his library, "not the sort of happiness which a man would in general wish to owe to his wife" (155). After watching Mr. Bennet's disdain for his wife and the consequent emotional and patriarchal neglect of his daughters, Elizabeth wisely rejects Darcy's first proposal since it expresses a similar vein of disdain. She recognizes she would be placing herself in the same position as her mother, thereby creating a similarly uncomfortable position for her future children. As the more investing sex, Elizabeth will not do this (see [*The Family, Sex, and Marriage in England*] Stone 457).

The men of Austen's culture could choose more freely than the women, but, in line with evolutionary psychology, the men in the novel perform for the women, engaging in competition to draw female attention to themselves, like peacocks with their tail feathers. Here, instead of male cardinals, we have redcoats using their manners and wit to impress. Austen pointedly notes Wickham's efforts to appear "agreeable" and "amiable" so that when he enters the gathering at Mrs. Philips's, he "was the happy man towards whom almost every female eye was turned. . . . With such rivals for the notice of the fair, as Mr. Wickham and the officers, Mr. Collins seemed likely to sink into insignificance; to the young ladies he certainly was nothing" (52). Unlike Bingley and Darcy, however, Wickham has no property and must, like the female characters, rely solely upon his person and social skills to impress. This is true also of Colonel Fitzwilliam as a younger son whom Austen, with language reminiscent of how she initially presents Wickham, describes as pleasant and agreeable, "in person and address most truly a gentleman" (113). In fact, Wickham and other men in the novel who have no property, in line with evolutionary psychology, are not chosen by women as appropriate long-term mates. Wickham, like Charlotte Lucas, attempts to marry for money and security only to find himself rejected. Fitzwilliam makes clear that he may not choose a mate based upon personal preference but must pay attention to financial security through marriage. In an attempt to let Elizabeth know he finds her attractive but unsuitable as a mate because of her lack of fortune, Colonel Fitzwilliam reminds her, "Younger sons cannot marry where they like. . . . Our habits of expence make us too dependant [sic], and there are not many in my rank of life who can afford to marry without some attention to money" (121; also, see Gilbert and Gubar 167). Elizabeth, therefore, never views Colonel Fitzwilliam as a potential mate and is quick to control her feelings for Wickham upon Mrs. Gardiner's warning "not [to] involve yourself, or endeavour to involve him in an affection which the want of fortune would make so very imprudent" (96).

Of course, this is not true of the other men in the novel who use their property to draw the attention of women. While Mr. Collins fails to gain notice in the intrasexual competition of the drawing room, he is able to attract a wife since he does have material qualities that are desirable in a mate. He eagerly displays this to Elizabeth upon her visit, "as if wishing to make her feel what she had lost in refusing him" (104). When Lady Catherine soon extends an invitation to dine, Mr. Collins feels the thrill of "letting them see her civility towards himself and his wife," which "was exactly what he had wished for" (106). However, Mr. Collins—property, wife, and all—begins and ends the novel as the butt of many jokes because of his poor manners. Austen makes clear his inferiority to Darcy when he ignores Elizabeth's advice that he would be committing an "impertinent freedom" (66) by approaching Darcy at the Netherfield ball. Darcy, of course, responds with "distant civility" and dismisses Mr. Collins with "a slight bow," emphasizing, as Elizabeth acknowledges, Mr. Darcy as being "superior in consequence" (67). Additionally, Mr. Collins's social and financial dependence upon a woman (Lady Catherine De Bourgh) makes him much less attractive as a potential mate to women in the novel. Data from evolutionary psychology support this claim: women consistently place higher value on independence and social dominance in a prospective mate than do men.

Here is the problem for Bingley. One could argue that it is Jane who is temporarily punished for her inability to attract a mate properly. After all, Charlotte Lucas in reference to Jane proclaims, "In nine cases out of ten, a woman had better shew *more* affection than she feels. Bingley likes your sister undoubtedly; but he may never do more than like her, if she does not help him on" (15). Darcy excuses his interference in Bingley's relationship with Jane by arguing that "the serenity of your sister's countenance and air was such, as might have given even the most acute observer, a conviction that, however amiable her temper, her heart was not likely to be touched" (130). However, the real problem here is not Jane but Bingley. After all, Elizabeth is rewarded with the best marriage of the novel in spite of telling Darcy that he is the last man on earth she would marry, clearly a stronger statement than merely appearing calm as Jane does. No, it is Bingley who fails to reach the eventual heroic status of Darcy due to his timidity. Bingley's willingness to be persuaded so easily to give up Jane puts him in some ways on the same plane with Mr. Collins, lacking independence, of will in this case, and social dominance; for though Mr. Bingley's manners are the most agreeable at parties, it is Darcy who commands the most attention.

But even with the competitive advantages of wealth and influence, Darcy must learn to perform—improve his manners—in spite of his protestations to Elizabeth that "[w]e neither of us perform to strangers" (117); and he does perform better when Elizabeth arrives at Pemberley. Elizabeth recognizes, "Never, even in the company of his dear friends at Netherfield, or his dignified relations at Rosings, had she seen him so desirous to please, so free from self-consequence, or unbending reserve as now" (170-171). As Sir Walter Scott joked, it is upon seeing Pemberley that Elizabeth falls in love with Darcy; perhaps, though, the joke is correct and explained by evolutionary psychology: not only does Elizabeth see Darcy's estate, but Darcy recognizes that he must work to attract her as a mate.[4] Much of this "work" involves generosity in welcoming Elizabeth and her aunt and uncle to share the estate during their visit. Clearly, Darcy is sending the signal to Elizabeth that he is willing to share his possessions with her as well as exhibit proper manners by treating them all graciously.

Elizabeth first rejects Darcy because of the issue of generosity. Buss's influential 1989 cross-cultural study clearly showed that women value generosity in a mate more than do men. Men must not only be able to invest in a partner but must also be willing to invest. In *Pride and Prejudice,* it is not enough for Darcy to be wealthy; he also must be willing (or perceived as willing) to share some of these resources with a mate. At first, Darcy is not generous with either money or, perhaps more importantly, his public praise of Elizabeth. On one of their first meetings, Darcy says out loud of Elizabeth, "she is tolerable; but not handsome enough to tempt *me*" (9). As the novel progresses, Darcy is more generous to Elizabeth in terms of both public praise for her "fine" eyes and eventually in the payment of Wickham's debt as part of the deal for his marriage to Lydia. Later, when Elizabeth thanks him for his actions on behalf of her family, Darcy replies, "I thought only of *you*" (239). Since Darcy shows no indication that he is willing to be generous to Elizabeth prior to his first proposal, he is at first less attractive as a mate to Elizabeth. However, as Darcy's generosity increases towards Elizabeth, her attraction to him increases—in line with evolutionary predictions.

In fact, it is Darcy's letter in which he describes his actions to protect Georgianna, then Elizabeth's observations of his protective kindness toward his sister, that first convey Darcy's generous nature to Elizabeth and begin to warm her toward accepting his second offer. And, obviously, Darcy acts as protective patriarch toward Lydia in ways that Mr. Bennet could not. Elizabeth recognizes that Darcy's love for her is essential to long-term mating, and his actions toward his sister—and her own sister—convince her that Darcy will protect not only her but also their future children.

And what attracts Darcy to the financially strapped Elizabeth straddled with an unfortunate family? Her eyes. While poetry may call the eyes windows to the soul, evolutionary psychology, as we noted, postulates that men are attracted to women who appear healthy and able to bear and nurture children. One such sign of health is the eyes. Evolutionary theorists remind us that in early ancestral environments, cloudy or dull eyes may have been a signal of disease or bad genes. The first compliment Darcy pays to Elizabeth, though it is to Caroline Bingley, is on "the very great pleasure which a pair of fine eyes in the face of a pretty woman can bestow" (19). While Darcy questions the propriety of Elizabeth's walk to check on Jane, he simultaneously admires "the brilliancy which exercise had given to her complexion" (23) and tells Caroline that Elizabeth's eyes "were brightened by the exercise" (25). Elizabeth exudes health, whereas Anne De Bourgh, a more suitable match by society's standards, does not (see Wiltshire ["Jane Austen, Health, and the Body"] 125). According to Fraiman, Austen is suggesting "a decline in aristocratic welfare . . . by the sickly Miss De Bourgh. It may well be the enfeeblement of his own class that encourages Darcy to look below him for a wife with greater stamina" (174). Mr. Collins, of course, being far less discerning than Darcy, sees the beauty of Miss De Bourgh as relying entirely on "features which marks the young woman of distinguished birth" (46). In this way, evolutionary psychology and Austen are not conservative at all, displacing the aristocratic Anne De Bourgh in favor of the middle-class healthy and seemingly fertile Elizabeth. Stone contends, "It was generally agreed that the ideal was a pale, languid, and fainting belle, and that 'an air of robustness and strength is very prejudicial to beauty'" (446), making Darcy's choice of Elizabeth much more in line with the principles of evolutionary psychology than the fashion of the time. Though crudely put, perhaps Mrs. Bennet is on target when she proclaims to Jane, "I was sure you could not be so beautiful for nothing!" upon hearing about her daughter's engagement (227).

On its surface, *Pride and Prejudice* may appear conservative, but if one believes that the overriding, nonconscious purpose in humans' lives—both male and female—is to pass our genes forward, then the seemingly conservative marriage ending in fact liberates. Elizabeth's chances of successfully producing and nurturing a family are excellent thanks to a secure marriage to a loyal, caring, and rich husband. Austen's novels create the stability necessary for women to succeed in the evolutionary game, whereas she rejects the male strategy of multiple partners. Seemingly constraining monogamy becomes liberation for the heroines when we read Austen vis a vis evolutionary psychology.

Notes

1. One might logically wonder about the underlying biology that makes the relationship between psychology and culture possible: can preferences for particular mate qualities be transmitted genetically from generation to generation? The short answer seems to be no; mate preferences themselves are unlikely to be directly inherited from one's parents. Evolutionary psychologists argue that the kind of specialized social reasoning involved in mate choice suggests that the mind acts not as a general problem-solving machine, but rather consists of domain-specific modules that facilitate the expression of cognitive adaptations. Cummins argues that what is genetically "innate" is best understood as a biological preparedness for learning evolutionary-relevant cognitive functions, such as social reasoning in mate choice, that develop through interaction with the environment. Thus, biology "puts strong constraints on what types of knowledge or skills can or will be learned, but . . . the environment plays a very large role in how and whether biological predispositions get expressed" (240-241). This notion is entirely compatible with our basic argument that changes in eighteenth-century culture regarding companionate marriage interacted with biologically-prepared adaptations of the mind to influence the human psychology of mate choice.

2. Critics, of course, do not agree on Austen's status as conservative or feminist, as noted by Langland in her useful survey, *"Pride and Prejudice*: Jane Austen and Her Readers." Butler and Fraiman point out the conservatism of Austen's work, while Sulloway sees a feminist intent similar to Wollstonecraft's (15). Duckworth suggests that Austen tends to be all things to all people: conservative, feminist, Romantic, Augustan, etc.

3. We would not go so far as Barash and Barash who claim that "[n]early always, Austen's women are in the driver's seat (and never more so than when they adroitly lead a man to think that *he* is)" (41).

4. Butler says Pemberley represents a turning point not because of its material wealth but because it shows real taste and a lack of pomposity while providing the good opinion of Darcy's housekeeper. Burlin argues much the same, claiming

that the pictures at Pemberley affect Elizabeth and that the chapter is an aesthetic argument in Darcy's favor. See also Polhemus.

Works Cited

Austen, Jane. *Pride and Prejudice.* 1813. New York: W. W. Norton, 2001.

———. *Northanger Abbey.* 1817. Ed. Claire Grogan. Toronto: Broadview, 2002.

Barash, David P. and Nanelle R. Barash. *Madame Bovary's Ovaries: A Darwinian Look at Literature.* New York: Delacorte, 2005.

Boyd, Brian. "Jane, Meet Charles: Literature, Evolution, and Human Nature." *Philosophy and Literature* 22.1 (1998): 1-30.

Buss, D. M. "Sexual Strategies Theory: Historical Origins and Current Status." *Journal of Sex Research* 35.1 (1998): 19-31.

———. *Evolutionary Psychology: The New Science of the Mind.* Boston: Allyn and Bacon, 2004.

———. "Sex Differences in Human Mate Preferences: Evolutionary Hypotheses Tested in 37 Cultures." *Behavioral and Brain Sciences* 12 (1989): 1-49.

Buss, D. M. and D. P. Schmitt. "Sexual Strategies Theory: An Evolutionary Perspective on Human Mating." *Psychological Review* 100.2 (1993): 204-32.

Burlin, Katrin R. "'Pictures of Perfection' at Pemberley: Art in *Pride and Prejudice.*" *Jane Austen: New Perspectives. Women and Literature* Vol. 3. Ed. Janet Todd. New York: Holmes and Meier Publishers, 1983. 155-70.

Butler, Marilyn. *Jane Austen and the War of Ideas.* Oxford: Clarendon, 1975.

Campbell, Anne. *A Mind of Her Own: The Evolutionary Psychology of Women.* Oxford: Oxford UP, 2002.

Carroll, Joseph. *Evolution and Literary Theory.* Columbia: U of Missouri P, 1995.

———. *Literary Darwinism: Evolution, Human Nature, and Literature.* New York: Routledge, 2004.

Cummins, Denise Dellarosa. "Cheater Detection Is Modified by Social Rank: The Impact of Dominance on the Evolution of Cognitive Functions." *Evolution and Human Behavior* 20.4 (1999): 229-48.

Duckworth, Alistair. "Jane Austen and the Conflict of Interpretations." *Jane Austen: New Perspectives. Women and Literature* Vol. 3. Ed. Janet Todd. New York: Holmes and Meier Publishers, 1983. 39-52.

Fletcher, Anthony. *Gender, Sex, and Subordination in England 1500-1800.* New Haven: Yale UP, 1995.

Fraiman, Susan. "The Humiliation of Elizabeth Bennet." *Refiguring the Father: New Feminist Readings of Patriarchy.* Ed. Patricia Yaeger and Beth Kowaleski-Wallace. Urbana: U of Illinois P, 1989. 168-87.

Geary, David C. *The Origin of Mind: Evolution of Brain, Cognition, and General Intelligence.* Washington, DC: American Psychological Association, 2005.

Gilbert, Sandra M. and Susan Gubar. *The Madwoman in the Attic: The Woman Writer and the Nineteenth-Century Literary Imagination.* New Haven: Yale UP, 1984.

Kent, Susan Kingsley. *Gender and Power in Britain, 1640-1990.* New York: Routledge, 1999.

Langland, Elizabeth. "*Pride and Prejudice*: Jane Austen and Her Readers." *A Companion to Jane Austen Studies.* Ed. Laura Cooner Lambdin and Robert Thomas Lambdin. Westport, CT: Greenwood, 2000. 41-56.

Laqueur, Thomas. *Making Sex: Body and Gender from the Greeks to Freud.* Cambridge: Harvard UP, 1990.

Marlow, F. and A. Wetsman. "How Universal Are Preferences for Female Waist-to-Hip Ratios?: Evidence from the Hadza of Tanzania." *Evolution and Human Behavior* 20.4 (1999): 219-228.

Monaghan, David. "Introduction: Jane Austen as a Social Novelist." *Jane Austen in a Social Context.* Ed. David Monaghan. Totowa, N.J.: Barnes & Noble, 1981. 1-8.

Newman, Karen. "Can This Marriage Be Saved: Jane Austen Makes Sense of an Ending." *ELH* 50.4 (1983): 693-710.

Polhemus, Robert M. *Erotic Faith: Being in Love from Jane Austen to D. H. Lawrence.* Chicago: U of Chicago P, 1990.

Ridley, Matt. *The Red Queen: Sex and the Evolution of Human Nature.* New York: Penguin, 1993.

Stone, Lawrence. *The Family, Sex, and Marriage in England, 1500-1800.* New York: Harper & Row, 1977.

Sulloway, Allison G. *Jane Austen and the Province of Womanhood.* Philadelphia: U of Pennsylvania P, 1989.

Tooby, John and Leda Cosmides. "The Psychological Foundations of Culture." *The Adapted Mind.* Ed. Jerome H. Barkow, Leda Cosmides, and John Tooby. New York: Oxford UP, 1992. 19-136.

Trivers, R. "Parental Investment and Sexual Selection." *Sexual Selection and the Descent of Man, 1871-1971.* Ed. B. Campbell. Chicago: Aldine, 1972. 136-179.

Wiltshire, John. "Jane Austen, Health, and the Body." *The Critical Review* 31 (1991): 122-34.

FURTHER READING

Criticism

Belsey, Catherine. "Making Space: Perspective Vision and the Lacanian Real." *Textual Practice* 16, no. 1 (April 2002): 31-55.

    Examines the symbolic importance of landscape and space in Austen's *Pride and Prejudice.*

Bloom, Harold. *Jane Austen's* Pride and Prejudice. New York: Bloom's Literary Criticism, 2007, 246 p.

    Includes a range of critical responses to the novel's characters, language, and themes.

Bonaparte, Felicia. "Conjecturing Possibilities: Reading and Misreading Texts in Jane Austen's *Pride and Prejudice.*" *Studies in the Novel* 37, no. 2 (July 2005): 141-61.

    Discusses themes of miscommunication and misrepresentation in the novel.

Carr, Jean Ferguson. "The Polemics of Incomprehension: Mother and Daughter in *Pride and Prejudice.*" In *Diversifying the Discourse: The Florence Howe Award for Outstanding Feminist Scholarship, 1990-2004,* edited by Mihoko Suzuki and Roseanna Dufault, pp. 1-16. New York: Modern Language Association of America, 2006.

    Analyzes the ways in which patriarchal forms of discourse shape female relationships in *Pride and Prejudice.*

Christie, William. "Pride, Politics, and Prejudice." *Nineteenth-Century Contexts* 20, no. 3 (1997): 313-34.

    Investigates the tension between conservative and progressive values in the novel.

Deresiewicz, William. "Community and Cognition in *Pride and Prejudice.*" *ELH* 64, no. 2 (July 1997): 503-35.

    Assesses the role of community in shaping Elizabeth's character.

Hirsch, Gordon. "Shame, Pride and Prejudice: Jane Austen's Psychological Sophistication." *Mosaic: A Journal for the Interdisciplinary Study of Literature* 25, no. 1 (January 1992): 63-78.

    Explores the thematic importance of shame in the novel.

Litvak, Joseph. "Delicacy and Disgust, Mourning and Melancholia, Privilege and Perversity: *Pride and Prejudice.*" *Qui Parle* 6, no. 1 (fall-winter 1992): 35-51.

    Examines representations of pleasure and revulsion in the novel.

McKeon, Richard. "*Pride and Prejudice*: Thought, Character, Argument, and Plot." *Critical Inquiry* 5, no. 3 (April 1979): 511-27.

Evaluates the tension between artifice and nature in Austen's narrative style.

Morgan, Susan. "Intelligence in *Pride and Prejudice.*" *Modern Philology* 73, no. 1 (August 1975): 54-68.

Addresses the relationship between intelligence and freedom in Austen's portrayal of Elizabeth.

Morrison, Robert. *Jane Austen's* Pride and Prejudice *: A Sourcebook*. edited by Robert Morrison. New York: Routledge, 2005, 172 p.

Provides detailed discussions of the novel's major scenes, as well as an overview of the book's critical reception.

Phelan, James. "Character, Progression, and the Mimetic-Didactic Distinction." *Modern Philology* 84, no. 3 (February 1987): 282-99.

Analyzes the tension between the novel's mimetic and thematic qualities.

Reilly, Susan. "'A Nobler Fall of Ground': Nation and Narration in *Pride and Prejudice.*" *Symbiosis* 4, no. 1 (April 2000): 19-34.

Interprets the novel as a defense of English nationalism in the face of democratic reform movements.

Scott, Steven D. "Making Room in the Middle: Mary in *Pride and Prejudice.*" In *The Talk in Jane Austen,* edited by Bruce Stovel and Lynn Weinlos Gregg, pp. 225-36. Edmonton: University of Alberta Press, 2002.

Offers an in-depth analysis of Mary's character, assessing her symbolic role in the novel.

Searle, Alison. "The Moral Imagination: Biblical Imperatives, Narrative and Hermeneutics in *Pride and Prejudice.*" *Renascence: Essays on Values in Literature* 59, no. 1 (October 2006): 17-32.

Considers the moral attitude of the novel's narrator.

Smith, Johanna M. "The Oppositional Reader and *Pride and Prejudice.*" In *A Companion to Jane Austen Studies,* edited by Laura Cooner Lambdin and Robert Thomas Lambdin, pp. 27-40. Westport, Conn.: Greenwood Press, 2000.

Evaluates the novel's ideological underpinnings, identifying various "opposing paradigms" in the narrative.

Wiesenfarth, Joseph. "The Case of *Pride and Prejudice.*" *Studies in the Novel* 16, no. 3 (October 1984): 261-73.

Studies Austen's portrait of English society within the context of Napoleonic military aggression.

Young, Kay. "Word-Work, Word-Play, and the Making of Intimacy in *Pride and Prejudice.*" In *The Talk in Jane Austen,* edited by Bruce Stovel and Lynn Weinlos Gregg, pp. 57-70. Edmonton: University of Alberta Press, 2002.

Examines the connections between the narrative's conversational style and attitude toward marriage.

Zimmerman, Everett. "Pride and Prejudice in *Pride and Prejudice.*" *Nineteenth-Century Fiction* 23, no. 1 (June 1968): 64-73.

Discusses the relationship between the novel's title and the "moral framework" of the narrative.

Additional coverage of Austen's life and career is contained in the following sources published by Gale: *Authors and Artists for Young Adults,* **Vol. 19;** *Beacham's Guide to Literature for Young Adults,* **Vol. 3;** *British Writers,* **Vol. 4;** *British Writers: The Classics,* **Vol. 1;** *British Writers Retrospective Supplement,* **Vol. 2;** *Concise Dictionary of British Literary Biography, 1789-1832; Dictionary of Literary Biography,* **Vol. 116;** *DISCovering Authors; DISCovering Authors: British Edition; DISCovering Authors: Canadian Edition; DISCovering Authors Modules: Most-studied Authors* **and** *Novelists; DISCovering Authors 3.0; Exploring Novels; Feminism in Literature: A Gale Critical Companion,* **Ed. 1:2;** *Gothic Literature: A Gale Critical Companion,* **Vol. 2;** *Literary Movements for Students,* **Vol. 1;** *Literature and Its Times,* **Vol. 2;** *Literature and Its Times Supplement,* **Vol. 1:1;** *Literature Resource Center; Nineteenth-Century Literature Criticism,* **Vols. 1, 13, 19, 33, 51, 81, 95, 119, 150;** *Novels for Students,* **Vols. 1, 14, 18, 20, 21;** *Twayne's English Authors; World Literature and Its Times,* **Vol. 3;** *World Literature Criticism,* **Vol. 1; and** *Writers for Young Adults Supplement,* **Ed. 1.**

Thomas Hughes
1822-1896

English novelist, biographer, historian, and essayist.

The following entry presents an overview of Hughes's life and works.

INTRODUCTION

Thomas Hughes was a prominent Victorian author and social activist, a vigorous reformer who dedicated his life to promoting the cause of social justice. Along with author Charles Kingsley and others, Hughes is credited with developing the idea of "muscular Christianity," a social ideal that promoted the fusing of physical education with Christian principles. Among modern literary scholars, Hughes is primarily remembered for his 1857 novel *Tom Brown's School Days*. Hughes originally wrote the work for his son, Maurice, as a way of offering him advice on the eve of his departure for public school. The novel proved widely popular upon its publication and quickly became one of the emblematic works of the era; indeed, most modern commentators recognize Hughes as the inventor of the "public school novel," a genre of literature that romanticized virtues of masculinity and moral righteousness. As scholar Douglas Ivison has argued, Hughes's work not only helped shape the transformation of educational practices during the later part of the nineteenth century but also contributed to the emergence of the culture of militarism that defined British imperialism in the Victorian age. In addition to *Tom Brown's School Days,* Hughes published two other novels, including *Tom Brown at Oxford* (1861), as well as several biographies and numerous religious and political essays. Throughout his nonfiction works, Hughes continually promoted the moral and religious ideals that he embraced in his own life, typically in what critics have described as a polemical, earnest style. Although Hughes is not widely read today, many scholars regard his works to be of central importance in the history of Victorian social and political ideas.

BIOGRAPHICAL INFORMATION

Thomas Hughes was born on October 20, 1822, in Uffington, a small village outside of London. His father, John Hughes, was an Oxford University graduate and author who published articles and poems in periodicals, such as *Ainsworth's Magazine* and *Blackwood's,* and coedited *The Boscobel Tracts* (1830), a history of Charles the Second's military adventures. The second of eight children, Hughes enjoyed an especially close relationship with his older brother, George; as scholar George J. Worth has emphasized, George Hughes exerted an inestimable influence on his younger brother, playing a key role in his intellectual and creative development. Hughes later memorialized his brother in his 1873 work *Memoir of a Brother.*

In 1830 Hughes and his brother George left home to attend the Twyford School in Winchester. While at Twyford, Hughes devoured the writings of Sir Walter Scott, committing a number of the great writer's poems to memory. After four years at Twyford, Hughes enrolled in the prestigious Rugby School. At the time he entered Rugby, the school was in the midst of significant reforms under its new headmaster, the pioneering educator Thomas Arnold. Arnold's educational philosophy emphasized the centrality of strict adherence to moral principles, along with a commitment to virtuous action, in a young boy's intellectual development. Arnold's promotion of Christian ideals had a powerful impact on the young Hughes and inspired his dedication to social causes throughout his adult life. According to biographers, Hughes devoted most of his time to athletic pursuits during his time at Rugby, although he did demonstrate a talent for writing during these years. Hughes's Rugby years also played an important role in shaping his future literary work, and many of his most memorable fictional characters were modeled after his classmates.

Upon graduating from Rugby in 1842, Hughes entered Oriel College at Oxford University. In November of his initial term he published his first work, a poem entitled "Milton and the Swedish Lord," in *Ainsworth's Magazine.* Although a good student, Hughes, who excelled at cricket and rowing, was again more committed to sports than academics at Oriel. When he completed his B.A. in 1845, Hughes decided to embark on a career in law; after leaving Oxford he entered Lincoln's Inn, a prominent society of barristers in London. In 1847, shortly before taking his bar exam, he married Frances Ford, the niece of the author Richard Ford. Their first son, Maurice, was born a year later; in all, Hughes and his wife had nine children, two of whom died in childhood. While living in London, Hughes became friends with a number of promising young lawyers and writers, among them J. M. Ludlow, Charles Kingsley, and Frederick

Denison Maurice. Together they helped form the Christian Socialist Movement, an organization that emerged in reaction to the violent political upheavals taking place throughout Europe in 1848. Dedicated to improving the lives of England's working classes, the Christian Socialists espoused a nonviolent approach to reform, one based on ideals of cooperation and shared sacrifice among different social groups.

As Douglas Ivison has pointed out, Hughes was a tireless and dedicated member of the movement; he helped found various organizations, including the Society for Promoting Working Men's Associations, and edited the group's short-lived *Journal of Association.* Hughes also wrote prolifically on behalf of the movement, publishing several influential political tracts during the early 1850s, among them *History of the Working Tailors' Association* (1850), *A Lecture on the Slop-System, Especially As It Bears Upon the Females Engaged in It* (1852), and *King's College and Mr. Maurice* (1854). In 1854 Hughes and Ludlow moved with their families into a communal house in Wimbledon. An 1896 article published in the *Economic Review* quotes Ludlow recalling the living arrangement as a "communistic experiment"; indeed, for the next three years the home also served as the headquarters of Christian Socialist activities.

In 1856, as Maurice was preparing to enter school for the first time, Hughes became inspired to write a short story for his eldest son. Based on Hughes's personal reminiscences of the Rugby School, the story eventually became the novel *Tom Brown's School Days.* The book was an instant success; it ran through six printings in its first year, in addition to appearing in two American editions. In 1858 Hughes published a second novel, *The Scouring of the White Horse; or, the Long Vacation Ramble of a London Clerk. Tom Brown at Oxford,* a sequel to *Tom Brown's School Days,* appeared serially in *Macmillan's Magazine* between November 1859 and July 1861 and was published in book form a short time later. During these years Hughes also published two new nonfiction works, *Account of the Lock-out of Engineers, 1851-2* (1860) and *Religio Laici* (1861), an essay voicing support for the Church of England in the face of criticism from nonconformists. At the onset of the American Civil War, Hughes became actively involved in the abolitionist movement; in 1862 he helped form the London Emancipation Society. He published two important works supporting the Northern cause against the Confederacy, "The Struggle for Kansas" (1862) and *The Cause of Freedom: Which Is Its Champion in America, The North or the South?* (1863).

Hughes was elected in 1865 to the House of Commons, where he lobbied on behalf of the working class. Serving in government for the next nine years, he worked for the royal commission on trade unions and acted for

a period as the Queen's Counsel. In the midst of these activities, he continued to write, publishing his first biography, *Alfred the Great,* in 1869. In 1870 Hughes founded the Church Reform Union, an organization dedicated to making the Church of England open to a broader demographic of parishioners. That year he also traveled to America for the first time, at the invitation of the poet James Russell Lowell. Hughes remained in the House of Commons until 1874, when he received a royal appointment to examine the legal framework behind a number of recent reforms, including the Master and Servant Act of 1867 and the Criminal Law Amendment Act of 1871. By the late 1870s Hughes had once again begun writing prolifically, producing such works as the *Lecture on the History and Objects of Co-operation* (1878), *The Old Church: What Shall We Do with It?* (1878), and *The Manliness of Christ* (1879).

Returning to the United States in 1880, Hughes founded a Christian commune in Tennessee. He called the settlement Rugby, and he devoted the bulk of his financial resources to launching the experiment. The community was poorly managed, however, and it failed in 1882. That year Hughes returned to England to accept an appointment as a county judge in the town of Chester. He continued to write steadily over the next decade, publishing numerous biographies and other prose works. Hughes died in Brighton, England, on March 22, 1896.

MAJOR WORKS

Most scholars agree that *Tom Brown's School Days* is Thomas Hughes's most lasting contribution to English literature. First published anonymously in 1857, the novel originated as a short story Hughes wrote for his son Maurice. The story quickly evolved into a series of tales revolving around a fictional public school student, Tom Brown. Through the narrative of Tom's education, Hughes described the maturation of the boy's character, from his early years defying the school rules to his discovery of his athletic prowess. As George J. Worth has suggested, the novel represents more than a simple portrayal of public school life. In Hughes's vision, Rugby is a broad, all-encompassing community with its own laws and codes dedicated to shaping the moral character of the students. *Tom Brown's School Days* is thus in many respects an instructive work, one intended to illustrate the process by which English boys become morally righteous men—a theme that is also central to many of Hughes's other writings.

Hughes published two other novels in his career, *The Scouring of the White Horse* and *Tom Brown at Oxford*; neither work enjoyed the same critical appreciation as his debut work of fiction, however. He also published a number of noteworthy works of nonfiction, most of them dedicated to exploring political and moral issues. Hughes's passion for social reform is evident in many of his early writings, notably his *History of the Working Tailors' Association, A Lecture on the Slop-System, Especially As It Bears Upon the Females Engaged in It,* and *Account of the Lock-out of Engineers, 1851-2.* Ideals of social justice also play a key role in Hughes's spiritual writings. In *The Manliness of Christ,* Hughes attempted to promote an idea of masculinity that eschewed violence while still embracing qualities of self-discipline, physical strength, and vigorous action. Works such as *Religio Laici* (later republished as *A Layman's Faith,* 1868) and *The Old Church: What Shall We Do with It?* offer a spirited defense of the Church of England and, at the same time, advocate a number of critical reforms primarily designed to make the national religion more tolerant and inclusive.

CRITICAL RECEPTION

Hughes's novel *Tom Brown's School Days* enjoyed great popular and critical success upon its original publication. A contemporary reviewer for the *Quarterly Review* applauded the work's mixture of "plain, unvarnished" storytelling with the "highest themes." In a private letter to Hughes written shortly after the book's publication, Charles Kingsley commended the work's "manly" qualities, praising the novel as a vital antidote to the "effeminate" tendencies of the younger generation. As early as 1861, a writer for *Blackwood's Edinburgh Magazine* lauded Hughes for inventing the character of the "British Schoolboy," also noting that the novel had already spawned several imitators. Scottish author Margaret Oliphant made a similar observation in her 1892 study *The Victorian Age of English Literature,* remarking that Hughes was primarily responsible for creating the figure of the "ideal young man of Victorian romance." Sir Joshua Fitch introduced a note of doubt in his 1897 work *Thomas and Matthew Arnold and Their Influence on English Education,* however, lamenting what he perceived to be the anti-intellectual prejudice of Hughes's work.

Although most nineteenth-century commentators focused their attention on *Tom Brown's School Days,* a few authors recognized Hughes's other works. Writing in the *Dictionary of Literary Biography* in 1901, Reverend J. Llewelyn Davies described Hughes's religious writings as the work of a "simple and devout mind," one "intolerant of deceit or meanness." In the twentieth century scholars devoted greater attention to some of the larger historical and cultural contexts surrounding Hughes's work; for example, Henry Harrington examines depictions of adolescent sexuality in *Tom Brown's School Days,* while Ian Watson interprets the novel against the backdrop of England's shifting economic and political landscape in the Victorian era.

PRINCIPAL WORKS

History of the Working Tailors' Association (history) 1850

A Lecture on the Slop-System, Especially As It Bears Upon the Females Engaged in It (essay) 1852

King's College and Mr. Maurice (essay) 1854

Tom Brown's School Days [published anonymously] (novel) 1857; also published as *Schooldays at Rugby,* 1857

The Scouring of the White Horse; or, the Long Vacation Ramble of a London Clerk (novel) 1858

Account of the Lock-out of Engineers, 1851-2 (essay) 1860

Religio Laici (essay) 1861; also published as *A Layman's Faith,* 1868

*Tom Brown at Oxford. 3 vols. (novel) 1861

"The Struggle for Kansas" (essay) 1862; published in *A Sketch of the History of the United States*

The Cause of Freedom: Which Is Its Champion in America, The North or the South? (essay) 1863

Alfred the Great (biography) 1869

Memoir of a Brother (biography) 1873

Lecture on the History and Objects of Co-operation (essay) 1878

The Old Church: What Shall We Do with It? (essay) 1878

The Manliness of Christ (essay) 1879

Rugby, Tennessee: Being Some Account of the Settlement Founded on the Cumberland Plateau by the Board of Aid to Land Ownership (essay) 1881

Memoir of Daniel Macmillan (biography) 1882

Church Reform and Defence (essay) 1886

Life and Times of Peter Cooper (biography) 1886

Co-Operative Production (essay) 1887

James Fraser, Second Bishop of Manchester: A Memoir, 1818-85 (biography) 1887

David Livingstone (biography) 1889

Co-Operative Faith and Practice [with E. Vansittart Neale] (essay) 1890

Vacation Rambles (autobiography) 1895

Early Memories for the Children (autobiography) 1899

*This work was originally published in 17 monthly parts by Ticknor & Fields between 1859 and 1861.

CRITICISM

Quarterly Review (review date October 1857)

SOURCE: Review of *Tom Brown's School Days. Quarterly Review* 102, no. 204 (October 1857): 330-54.

[*In the following excerpts, the reviewer assesses the distinctively English aspects of Tom Brown's character and praises the book for being "singularly free from all sickly sentimentalism."*]

This attractive and suggestive book [***Tom Brown's School Days***] is singularly free from all sickly sentimentalism. Tom's plain, unvarnished tale is told in simple language, but the highest themes are often touched on, and with an earnestness so natural and unaffected that the serious tone never jars. The book will be read with general pleasure. We have all been boys in our time, and a fellow interest pervades any faithful record of the associations of a starting-point in common. As years glide on, we recur with a satisfaction tinged with sadness to the pleasures of memory of a moment when every organ of mind and body offered, in all the freshness of vitality, new inlets of delight.

The family of the Browns were of the *juste milieu,* and removed alike from the scum that often froths on the social surface as from the dregs that sink to the bottom; the members—true Britons—for centuries have been the working bees of the community, and, sturdy in mind and stalwart in frame, have in their quiet homespun way subdued the earth at home and abroad, evincing a pugnacious propensity; all their opinions are downright beliefs; they have a testimony to deliver and a work to do, which they will speak out and maintain to the death, however counter to common opinion. Thus carrying their lives in their hands, and getting hard knocks and work in plenty, they have won our battles from Crecy to Trafalgar.

Tom, the son of a Berkshire squire, was reared near the healthy downs of the Vale of the White Horse, where the hardy spirit of Alfred still lingers, and here he early imbibed that fresh love of Nature which he has so closely observed and so truly described. Impatient of petticoat rule, he soon emancipated himself—never, however, to forget the early religious views instilled by a careful mother, and we can have, as Gray said, but one. His father, although a Churchman and a Tory of the old country gentleman school, was strongly imbued with the specious doctrines of the equality of man. These, when espoused and expounded by well-intentioned philanthropists of Young England, in white waistcoats, have evaporated in Christian socialism; but under the ancient régime of France, and when worked out to their logical conclusion by the disciples of Voltaire, naturally led to revolution and to la Sainte Guillotine.

Equality of man seems to us to be the child of conceit and egotism, and diametrically opposed to the first principle and great law which pervades the system of human economy established by the Creator. There, however the balance of actual happiness and compensation may be adjusted, variety, infinite and inexhaustible, forms the rule. The 'diversity of the gifts' of Providence, mental and physical, those of fortune and condition, are as plainly evinced as the difference in the faces of their respective subjects. The identical similarity of the two Dromios is no less a fiction of the poet than this equality, bodily or intellectual, which is contended for by a political Procrustes.

Tom's father, who reasoned better on breeding bullocks and crossing cattle, coincided with Burns in points of blood and pedigree in the human species, and holding them as 'leather and prunella' in lords and ladies, maintained that, while the rank only marked the guinea stamp, the man was the thing for all that. It mattered not a straw to him whether his son, in whom these social views sunk deeply, associated with the sons of peers or of ploughmen. Nor was much harm done to the muscles of the young squire by the rough exercises of rustic playmates, while his grammar was rescued by a timely removal from smock-frocks, although many think the separation of classes to be one of the worst signs of the times. Tom soon passed from a seminary for young gentlemen into a larger sphere of existence at Rugby. We quote his racy record of his first step into life on the top of a fast coach—one of the institutions of those pre-macadamite days, and still so delectable to old stagers. But first we may quote the Squire's parental and parting counsels, the excellent *sermo pedestris,* which he elaborated after protracted ponderings, aided by a reflective cheroot, and by his own *crassa Minerva* and sound common-sense. Those manly, honest thoughts, expressed in plain words, and no mistake, will, we trust, long find an echo in thousands of English hearts:—

> 'And now, Tom, my boy, remember you are going, at your own earnest request, to be chucked into this great school, like a young bear with all your troubles before you—earlier than we should have sent you perhaps. If schools are what they were in my time, you'll see a great many cruel, blackguard things done, and hear a deal of foul bad talk. But never fear. You tell the truth, keep a brave and kind heart, and never listen to or say anything you wouldn't have your mother and sister hear, and you'll never feel ashamed to come home, or we to see you.'

> To condense the Squire's meditation, it was somewhat as follows: 'I won't tell him to read his Bible, and love and serve God; if he don't do that for his mother's sake and teaching, he won't for mine. Shall I go into the sort of temptations he'll meet with? No, I can't do that. Never do for an old fellow to go into such things with a boy. He won't understand me. Do him more harm than good, ten to one. Shall I tell him to mind his work, and say he's sent to school to make himself a good scholar? Well, but he isn't sent to school for that—at any rate not for that mainly. I don't care a straw for Greek particles, or the digamma, no more does his mother. What is he sent to school for? Well, partly because he wanted so to go. If he'll only turn out a brave, helpful, truth-telling Englishman, and a gentleman, and a Christian, that's all I want,' thought the Squire; and upon this view of the case framed his last words of advice to Tom, which were well enough suited to his purpose.

The turn-out of the Tally-ho—the sketch of the road, its ways and worthies, are touched with the truth and local colour of the Nimrods and the Hieovers of the past; the detail sparkles with a nicety and fidelity that marks the observant spirit of the age, and which finds utterance in the immortal works of Dickens, and expression in the pictures of Millais. . . .

The solitary traveller, cast on the wide world of New-Boydom, is plunged into its mysteries and miseries. Sad, indeed, and sinking are the first sensations of those who, delicate in mind and body, when torn from the affections of home, are abruptly exposed to the buffetings and want of sympathy of public schoolboy nature; when every cause of annoyance, personal and private, and all that is most avoided in after life, is most harped on; when every weak blot is hit, and followed up with the pain-inflicting, curious felicity of nicknaming. Tom finds a friend of his family, and is let by his ''cute chum' into the secrets of the prison-house, and, thus piloted, steers safely through shoals in which the unprotected are too often swamped. Strong in body and heart, quick in eye and hand, companionable and courting danger with true English schoolboy love, he soon settled into his place. He details the different phases of his new life with an accuracy that rivals his record of the stages of the road, and gives a peep behind the curtain that is hung over the sanctum sanctorum of the educational system of our 'upper ten thousand' class—a system so utterly inaccessible and unintelligible to our ten-pounders and to foreigners who 'don't understand us.' The new boy, well broken-in by his rough rustic antecedents, plunges at once into the 'scrimmage' of football, and our Brown comes out of the fight black, blue, and bruised, with a capital character for courage, and there is no quality which boys are quicker to estimate or appreciate higher. Tom's first and most successful appearance is crowned by certain sausages, with which he, a fresh boy, with money in his pocket, regales his brother combatants—long broziers; these he is taught to toast, and eats with an appetite that surpasses the best sauce concocted by Soyer. The scholastic Saturnalia and the peristaltic motions are enlivened by tossings—so delectable to bulls and bullies; but our Tom cares as little for the blanket as the best broken-in farthing minds a chuck. The result is, that he wins golden opinions, and passes for a regular trump.

Charles Kingsley (letter date 1857)

SOURCE: Kingsley, Charles. "To Thomas Hughes, Esq." In *Charles Kingsley: His Letters and Memories of His Life.* Vol. 2, pp. 25-8. London: Henry S. King & Co., 1877.

[In the following excerpt from a letter originally written in 1857, Kingsley compares Tom Brown's School Days *to a "good wine," while deeming it the "jolliest book" he's ever read.]*

Eversley, 1857

I have often been minded to write to you about *Tom Brown* [*Tom Brown's School Days*], so here goes. I have puffed it everywhere I went, but I soon found how true the adage is that good wine needs no bush, for every one had read it already, and from every one, from the fine lady on her throne, to the red-coat on his cock-horse, and the school-boy on his forrum (as our Irish brethren call it), I have heard but one word, and that is, that it is the jolliest book they ever read. Among a knot of red-coats at the cover-side, some very fast fellow said, 'If I had had such a book in my boyhood, I should have been a better man now!' and more than one capped his sentiment frankly. Now isn't it a comfort to your old bones to have written such a book, and a comfort to see that fellows are in a humour to take it in? So far from finding men of our rank in a bad vein, or sighing over the times and prospects of the rising generation, I can't help thinking they are very teachable, humble, honest fellows, who want to know what's right, and if they don't go and do it, still think the worse of themselves therefore. I remark now, that with hounds, and in fast company, I never hear an oath, and that, too, is a sign of self-restraint. Moreover, drinking is gone out, and, good God, what a blessing! I have good hopes, and better of our class, than of the class below. They are effeminate, and that makes them sensual. Pietists of all ages (George Fox, my dear friend, among the worst), never made a greater mistake (and they have made many), than in fancying that by keeping down manly θυμός, which Plato saith is the root of all virtue, they could keep down sensuality. They were dear good old fools. However, the day of 'Pietism' is gone, and *Tom Brown* is a heavy stone in its grave.

Blackwood's Edinburgh Magazine (essay date February 1861)

SOURCE: "School and College Life: Its Romance and Reality." *Blackwood's Edinburgh Magazine* 89, no. 544 (February 1861): 131-48.

[In the following excerpt, the reviewer evaluates the heroic qualities of the book's protagonist.]

If any type of human being might have seemed likely to escape being made the hero of romance, it was the British Schoolboy. His existence was an admitted necessity, and that was all. He was tolerated by civilised society as it tolerates poor relations or cynical maiden aunts—either for the sake of antecedents or future expectations. Parents knew that in that strange lump of shyness and impudence there lay the personal identity of that darling child of past years, so clever and so engaging; and that from that unhewn material was to start, in due time, the strength and grace of hopeful manhood. But, meanwhile, society in general voted him a bore, and he returned the compliment. Apologies, kindly meant, were tendered for him and accepted, as having come to "that disagreeable age." Even fond mamma looked at him reproachfully, because he grew so big, and sighed to think that this rough creature was all that remained of her lost pet in sash and petticoat; while his father, as he cast his eye over the last half-year's bills, groaned inwardly because he grew so expensive. Even in his coming home for the holidays his anxious family did but "snatch a fearful joy." While he was within sight and hearing, some suffering domestic animal—cat or dog, or younger brother or sister—was pretty sure to give token of his presence; and whenever he was out of the way, or unusually quiet, his friends felt certain he was in some more serious mischief. Beyond this, nobody showed much interest in him, except by occasional gifts of a half-sovereign or a crown-piece; a sort of black-mail which relations and friends of the afflicted family gladly paid to escape his nearer acquaintance, and which contributions he was understood to employ in the worship of an idol known and reverenced by all schoolboys, in all places, under the various names of "sock," "tuck," "grub," and "guttle." Society dealt with him, in short, as a weak but well-meaning parish clergyman deals, in his parochial visitations, with some of his flock whom he finds both morally and physically unsavoury: rather reversing apostolic precedent, he has recourse to gold and silver as the easiest, and; as appears to him, the only intelligible expression of goodwill; any higher circulating medium seems impossible under the circumstances. Those, indeed, who had never possessed a schoolboy of their own, regarded the whole species with unmitigated horror; and nothing less than a severe course of Aristotle could have persuaded such persons of the truth of the physiological paradox, that parents could love their own productions when they took *that* shape. So that even the best friends of *Tirunculus* [young beginner] were content to keep him a good deal out of sight; putting him by, as an entomologist does some hideous chrysalis, in the hope that he is to come out better by-and-by. There was, no doubt, another presentment of the character, in the persons of smart youths from the higher forms of Eton and Harrow, who put on all the worst airs of grown-up men, and were an abomination even more eschewed by all except very young, or very would-be-young, ladies.

We have changed all this, and a very remarkable change it is. The British Schoolboy has become a hero. His slang has been reproduced in print, more or less successfully, until it has become almost as classical as the Scotticisms of Burns, or the French that passes muster in polite society. Talk which would have made our respectable grandmothers' very china rattle with horror at its "vulgarity," is quoted unrebuked by the lips of very correct young ladies. The professional story-tellers re-

joice in the addition of another new figure to their repertory of ready-made characters; and they put in the sharp public-school boy side by side with the clever governess and the muscular parson.

The discovery is due to the author of ***Tom Brown's School Days***. Let it be no derogation to a work of such established and well-deserved reputation to say, that the main elements of its great success lay in the selection of ground at once so fresh and so commonplace—a story familiar to so many, and yet told by none—and in the bold and honest truthfulness with which every detail of schoolboy life is given, without any attempt to overlay it with the conventional graces of the novelist. It is no mean triumph to have been the Columbus of the world of schoolboy romance. It lay within easy reach, indeed, but was practically undiscovered. And it is remarkable that, out of the many who have made the voyage thither since ***Tom Brown***'s [***Tom Brown's School Days***'s] appearance, scarce one has brought back anything like a trustworthy account. We have had abundance of narratives, professing to be the true and faithful records of eyewitnesses—some of them dealing largely in the marvellous, the horrible, and the grotesque, and therefore, of course, highly popular with a certain portion of the reading public; but, like most of the tales brought back from the mysterious Cathay, they are but travellers' stories after all.

It was to be supposed that such a popular and successful story would soon find its imitators. Not to speak of the professional book-makers, who were sure to seize on such an opening for a new line of "Standard Works adapted for Christmas Presents," there were other and higher impulses stirred. There was an opening for didactic charity, which saw a new mode of influencing *Tirunculus,* by the medium of good little novelets. Hitherto these had been chiefly of a feminine character. There was already in existence volume upon volume in which young ladies might see the mirror held up to nature for their warning and their edification; presenting, on the one side, the scapegrace of Mrs———'s establishment, who cheats her teachers, steals her companions' pocket-money, and gets into all kinds of disgrace, until she is finally either reformed by an angelic half-boarder, or dismissed to her friends, or (in one instance we remember) marries a drunken dancing-master—an awful example; and, on the other hand, the pattern school-girl, who passes through a furnace of unjust suspicions and jealousies, never does wrong, wins all the prizes, always knows where to find her gloves, is crowned by her schoolfellows at the last half-yearly ball with a laurel-wreath as the "reward of virtue," and withdraws from the scene gracefully, amidst a tumult of applause, into the bosom of grown-up society, to make, we should conceive (though we are bound to say the story never gives a hint of it), a highly-accomplished and rather disagreeable wife. But very little moral literature of this sort was there for the benefit of poor *Tirunculus*. Whatever attempts of the kind had been made, were either of the high evangelical and impossible type, or they were written by women—quite enough to insure their missing their mark. If any public-school boy ever read Miss Edgeworth's well-meant attempts to moralise Eton, he probably condensed his criticism into some such emphatic formula as "rot," or "bosh." What could be done in the moral-story line for a young gentleman who used such language as that? But when Tom Brown's Rugby experiences were found to have touched the right note,—when boys—not good and religious boys only, but boys with many of the faults of boyhood strongly marked—were known to read them, and to admire Tom beyond all boys, and not to vote him a "muff" because he told the truth and feared God, then it was very natural and very commendable that others should try to influence the mind of boyhood—so readily touched, and yet so difficult to touch successfully—by means which promised to transform the pandemonium of school into a paradise with such delightful facility. Perhaps, also, there was some natural and laudable jealousy of Arnold and Rugby. There was a wish to show that the reformation of school morals need not be confined to that place, or that particular teacher, or that particular phase of religious teaching which Arnold and his disciples were supposed to represent. Neither of the two great Church parties counted him amongst their adherents; and in spite of Tom Brown's popularity, the elders of both shook their heads doubtingly upon the question of his orthodoxy. So the improved schoolboy speedily reappeared in other forms, High Church and Evangelical; and the private-school interest made praiseworthy though rather feeble attempts to show that they could grow the article also, if there was a demand for it. It must be a malicious comfort to Mr Hughes to read these performances of his followers, and to observe how almost entirely all that is really captivating to an English boy is borrowed or adapted from the original, and how comparatively weak and poor are all attempts on the part of the writers to strike out into a line of their own, and to polish up their hero into their own notions of school-boy perfection. It seemed, too, as if the school-novelist could only be safe so long as he confined himself to Rugby and the days of Arnold; for the only public-school sketches which we can remember as marked by anything like reality are the *Experiences of a Fag* and the opening chapters of *Guy Livingstone*—both written by Rugbæans.

Still, there are some points in Tom Brown's Rugby reminiscences, genuine and delightful as they are, which go far to leave a false impression on the mind of the reader. In his honest zeal to hold up to public admiration the master whom he loved and honoured, the writer has unconsciously been guilty of something like injustice towards others. We are no iconoclasts, and least of

all would we write a word that could be fairly construed into depreciation of such a character as Arnold's. If any name could afford, living or dead, to cast aside every iota of partial or overstated praise, it is his who "changed the face of public education throughout England." Happily, his memory holds too firm a place in the hearts of all who knew him to be shaken by any word of honest truth, any more than by the whisper of slander; and, loving truth as he did, they honour him best who speak it. To imply, as we hear it apparently implied in the book of which we are speaking, that before "Arnold's manly piety had begun to leaven the school" no boy could venture to kneel at his bedside to say his prayers without subjecting himself to outrage and insult, is to present a picture of the Rugby of former days which many living know to be untrue. No doubt such a thing required some strength of purpose at all times; and whether it could be done in peace and without fear of interruption, in a large room occupied by a dozen boys, would depend very much, under any headmaster's government, on the character of the præpostor, or other head boy who slept there. If he were a bad boy, and others in the room were like him, no doubt to a little boy the thing was almost impossible. We very much doubt whether there were not some rooms in Rugby in which it was felt practically to be so, even in the best days of Arnold. There will always be a difficulty and a discouragement to boys under such circumstances; and so strongly has this been felt in later years by the authorities themselves, that in at least one of our old public schools the plan has been adopted of portioning off the dormitory into "cubicles"—divisions like the boxes of an old coffee-house—so that each boy has all the practical advantage of a private bedroom: an admirable system, first introduced into some of our middle-class training colleges, and which we believe the modern schools of Radley and Bradfield deserve the credit of having set the example of adopting. But to assume that under former headmasters the general tone of Rugby was such as to deter of necessity a boy from such acts of private devotion, and that under Arnold it totally changed, is to do a very serious injustice, and to exalt, by unfair comparison, a great man who did a great work, but who would have been the last to desire praise at the expense of others. So, again, to state that he "found the school and school-house in a state of monstrous licence and misrule"[1] is to state what, in the first place, the writer could himself only know from hearsay: it is to bring forward a very serious charge, in very unmeasured language, against Dr Arnold's immediate predecessor—a name which, though Mr Hughes may not know it, is still held by many of his old pupils in great and deserved respect; and a charge which the facts of the case would be found quite insufficient to justify. Every man of energy and ability who is appointed to the headship of a great place of public education, when his predecessor's rule has been a long one, will probably find—some would consider it almost part of their duty to find—abuses which call for remedy. A man like Arnold was sure to find much of this work to do at Rugby; and none need be told how well he did it. But we need no further testimony than his own, that he had not that Augean stable to cleanse which Mr Hughes supposes. In a letter to a friend, written soon after his entrance upon his duties, he expresses his "generally favourable impression of it," and records that he had as yet found "surprisingly few irregularities."[2] He also expressed to one of the masters personally his satisfaction at the state in which he found the school. It is to be regretted that Mr Hughes did not remember, in this particular instance, that his admirable sketch of Rugby could not be regarded as wholly a work of fiction: it dealt with real names and real facts, openly and without disguise; and that if there were many of his readers to whom these circumstances made the book additionally delightful, there were also some to whom they might give pain. We have such a hearty appreciation of the writer and his story, that we should be rejoiced if, in the future editions which the coming generation of schoolboys are sure to call for, he could find it in his heart to modify some two or three of these sweeping sentences of praise or censure.

Notes

1. *Tom Brown's School Days,* p. 141.

2. Letter to Blackstone (*Life and Correspondence,* i. 250).

Margaret Oliphant (essay date 1892)

SOURCE: Oliphant, Margaret. "Of the Younger Novelists." In *The Victorian Age of English Literature,* pp. 460-506. New York: Dodd, Mead and Company, 1892.

[*In the following excerpt, Oliphant briefly discusses the role of* Tom Brown's School Days *in popularizing the character of the "English Schoolboy" in Victorian literature.*]

We may add to this list, though his one remarkable book can scarcely be called a novel, the name of Mr. Thomas Hughes, now Judge Hughes, whose **Tom Brown** [**Tom Brown's School Days**] was the beginning of that interest of the general public in public schools which has never flagged since then, and which made the remarkable reign of Dr. Arnold at Rugby, and his ideal of the English Schoolboy better known than the more legitimate medium of biography and descriptive history could ever have made it. **Tom Brown at Oxford** was not equally successful, but the introduction of the ideal young man of Victorian romance, the fine athlete, moderately good scholar, and honest, frank, muscular, and

humble-minded gentleman, of whom we have seen so many specimens, is due to Judge Hughes more than to any other. If circumstances have occurred since to make us a little tired of that good fellow, and disposed to think his patronage of the poorer classes somewhat artificial, it is not Judge Hughes' fault.

Thomas Hughes (essay date 1893)

SOURCE: Hughes, Thomas. Preface to *Tom Brown's School Days,* pp. vii-xviii. New York: Macmillan and Co., 1893.

[*In the following preface to the 1893 edition of* Tom Brown's School Days, *Hughes defends the work's underlying seriousness. Hughes also insists that "moral thoughtfulness" is a critical aspect of every young boy's education.*]

Several persons, for whose judgment I have the highest respect, while saying very kind things about this book [**Tom Brown's School Days**], have added, that the great fault of it is, "too much preaching"; but they hope I shall amend in this matter should I ever write again. Now this I most distinctly decline to do. Why, my whole object in writing at all was to get the chance of preaching! When a man comes to my time of life and has his bread to make, and very little time to spare, is it likely that he will spend almost the whole of his yearly vacation in writing a story just to amuse people? I think not. At any rate, I wouldn't do so myself.

The fact is, that I can scarcely ever call on one of my contemporaries now-a-days without running across a boy already at school, or just ready to go there, whose bright looks and supple limbs remind me of his father, and our first meeting in old times. I can scarcely keep the Latin Grammar out of my own house any longer; and the sight of sons, nephews, and godsons, playing trap-bat-and-ball, and reading *Robinson Crusoe,* makes one ask oneself, whether there isn't something one would like to say to them before they take their first plunge into the stream of life, away from their own homes, or while they are yet shivering after the first plunge. My sole object in writing was to preach to boys: if ever I write again, it will be to preach to some other age. I can't see that a man has any business to write at all unless he has something which he thoroughly believes and wants to preach about. If he has this, and the chance of delivering himself of it, let him by all means put it in the shape in which it will be most likely to get a hearing; but let him never be so carried away as to forget that preaching is his object.

A black soldier, in a West Indian regiment, tied up to receive a couple of dozen, for drunkenness, cried out to his captain, who was exhorting him to sobriety in future, "Cap'n, if you preachee, preachee; and if floggee, floggee; but no preachee and floggee too!" to which his captain might have replied, "No, Pompey, I must preach whenever I see a chance of being listened to, which I never did before; so now you must have it all together; and I hope you may remember some of it."

There is one point which has been made by several of the Reviewers who have noticed this book, and it is one which, as I am writing a Preface, I cannot pass over. They have stated that the Rugby undergraduates they remember at the Universities were "a solemn array," "boys turned into men before their time," "a semi-political, semi-sacerdotal fraternity," &c., giving the idea that Arnold turned out a set of young square-toes, who wore long-fingered black gloves and talked with a snuffle. I can only say that their acquaintance must have been limited and exceptional. For I am sure that every one who has had anything like large or continuous knowledge of boys brought up at Rugby from the times of which this book treats down to this day, will bear me out in saying, that the mark by which you may know them, is, their genial and hearty freshness and youthfulness of character. They lose nothing of the boy that is worth keeping, but build up the man upon it. This is their *differentia* as Rugby boys; and if they never had it, or have lost it, it must be, not because they were at Rugby, but in spite of their having been there; the stronger it is in them the more deeply you may be sure have they drunk of the spirit of their school.

But this boyishness in the highest sense is not incompatible with seriousness,—or earnestness, if you like the word better.[1] Quite the contrary. And I can well believe that casual observers, who have never been intimate with Rugby boys of the true stamp, but have met them only in the every-day society of the Universities, at wines, breakfast-parties, and the like, may have seen a good deal more of the serious or earnest side of their characters than of any other. For the more the boy was alive in them the less will they have been able to conceal their thoughts, or their opinion of what was taking place under their noses; and if the greater part of that didn't square with their notions of what was right, very likely they showed pretty clearly that it did not, at whatever risk of being taken for young prigs. They may be open to the charge of having old heads on young shoulders; I think they are, and always were, as long as I can remember; but so long as they have young hearts to keep head and shoulders in order, I, for one, must think this only a gain.

And what gave Rugby boys this character, and has enabled the School, I believe, to keep it to this day? I say fearlessly,—Arnold's teaching and example—above all, that part of it which has been, I will not say sneered at, but certainly not approved—his unwearied zeal in creating "moral thoughtfulness" in every boy with whom he came into personal contact.

He certainly *did* teach us—thank God for it!—that we could not cut our life into slices and say, "In this slice your actions are indifferent, and you needn't trouble your heads about them one way or another; but in this slice mind what you are about, for they are important"—a pretty muddle we should have been in had he done so. He taught us that in this wonderful world, no boy or man can tell which of his actions is indifferent and which not; that by a thoughtless word or look we may lead astray a brother for whom Christ died. He taught us that life is a whole, made up of actions and thoughts and longings, great and small, noble and ignoble; therefore the only true wisdom for boy or man is to bring the whole life into obedience to Him whose world we live in, and who has purchased us with His blood; and that whether we eat or drink, or whatsoever we do, we are to do all in His name and to His glory; in such teaching, faithfully, as it seems to me, following that of Paul of Tarsus, who was in the habit of meaning what he said, and who laid down this standard for every man and boy in his time. I think it lies with those who say that such teaching will not do for us now, to show why a teacher in the nineteenth century is to preach a lower standard than one in the first.

However, I won't say that the Reviewers have not a certain plausible ground for their dicta. For a short time after a boy has taken up such a life as Arnold would have urged upon him, he has a hard time of it. He finds his judgment often at fault, his body and intellect running away with him into all sorts of pitfalls, and himself coming down with a crash. The more seriously he buckles to his work the oftener these mischances seem to happen; and in the dust of his tumbles and struggles, unless he is a very extraordinary boy, he may often be too severe on his comrades, may think he sees evil in things innocent, may give offence when he never meant it. At this stage of his career, I take it, our Reviewer comes across him, and, not looking below the surface (as a Reviewer ought to do), at once sets the poor boy down for a prig and a Pharisee, when in all likelihood he is one of the humblest and truest and most childlike of the Reviewer's acquaintance.

But let our Reviewer come across him again in a year or two, when the "thoughtful life" has become habitual to him, and fits him as easily as his skin; and, if he be honest, I think he will see cause to reconsider his judgment. For he will find the boy, grown into a man, enjoying every-day life as no man can who has not found out whence comes the capacity for enjoyment, and who is the Giver of the least of the good things of this world—humble, as no man can be who has not proved his own powerlessness to do right in the smallest act which he ever had to do—tolerant, as no man can be who does not live daily and hourly in the knowledge of how Perfect Love is for ever about his path, and bearing with and upholding him.

Note

1. "To him (Arnold) and his admirers we owe the substitution of the word 'earnest' for its predecessor 'serious'"—*Edinburgh Review,* No. 217, p. 183.

Charles D. Lanier (essay date May 1896)

SOURCE: Lanier, Charles D. "Thomas Hughes and 'Tom Brown.'" *Review of Reviews* 13, no. 5 (May 1896): 567-71.

[*In the following excerpt, Lanier addresses the lasting influence of* Tom Brown's School Days. *Lanier suggests that the work's enduring appeal lies in its espousal of basic Christian values.*]

All peoples who can read English, and some who cannot, have fallen under the spell of ***Tom Brown's School Days,***—generally in those plastic years of the early teens when the deepest and most lasting impressions may result from such winning sermons as Judge Hughes cunningly worked into that classic. *Robinson Crusoe* and ***Tom Brown*** [***Tom Brown's School Days***] are our boy epics. Critics who can be suspected of no envy have found that Mr. Hughes' masterpiece was "thin," that its humor was false, that its style was naught, that the standards of boy-excellence were beefy and unfeeling; but after forty years, the story of Rugby life still furnishes the one pre-eminent example of the schoolboy in fiction. It has even been translated into French—how the pupils of a *lycée* can understand it, much less like it, is a mystery; and if any final evidence is needed of its triumphant and irresistible veracity, one need only add that the English boys of the rival public schools admit its sovereignty.

TOM WAS THE TYPICAL ENGLISH BOY

It is right to begin a sketch of the bright, earnest life just ended with a retrospect of this tale,—in the face of the fact that the extraordinary popularity of the one book has veiled from the general public the other manifold activities of Thomas Hughes. For the story of Tom Brown was not only his *magnum opus*; it embodied the very essence of his creed of life, a creed to which all his work as educator, social reformer, colonizer, pamphleteer, theologian, conformed with an exceedingly rare degree of consistency. Perhaps there was never a more consistent life, in the best sense, than Hughes', and the key to it is in the simply told adventures of Tom Brown at Rugby which have delighted and inspired the English-speaking boys of four decades. The Tom in the book,—who, despite the author's assurances to the contrary, is clearly the same Thomas who wrote Hughes, Q.C., after his name,—was one of "the great

family of Browns," an average healthy English boy, "born and raised" amid the quaint village surroundings of that Berkshire whose rustic games and ceremonies Mr. Hughes never tired of describing. Tom's earliest education corresponded closely with that short curriculum prescribed for the Persian youth, and after an unsatisfactory experience with a private school, the youngster boards the tally-ho for famous Rugby. Doctor Arnold is master; he is Mr. Hughes' ideal teacher of men and boys, and his character is confessedly drawn from "real life." His ways of trying to make the savage boy a manly Christian are Mr. Hughes' ways; the very strong ethical teaching of the story has its centre in the Master of Rugby, who is, by force of simple boy-like enthusiasm for good things, invested with the attributes of the unfailing hero and ruler within his little kingdom.

THE FOOTBALL HERO

Just as it would be impossible to make another story which would so wholly convince the ever critical boy,—even if all the novelists in the world were to combine their wits and energies,—so it is impossible to suggest the fresh, wholesome flavor, the naïve unconsciousness, the honest boy barbarism, of *Tom Brown's School Days* to those mortals who have not read it. But to the boy who has in this book lived at Rugby with Tom and "Scud" East, a mention of the landmarks in the careers of these two veritable youngsters is an instant reminder that they have furnished him with his most powerful impressions of things good to do at school, and the way a self-respecting boy ought to do them. Did any battle description ever exceed in moral enthusiasm, in high loyalty, and reckless bravery, that stupendous football struggle which initiated young Tom in the most sacred rite of schoolboy sports? Was there ever a more undeniable hero than Old Brooke, or one surer of the worship of all boys, young and old? The career and downfall of Flashman the bully; that memorable, that Homeric combat between Tom Brown and Slogger Williams in the defense of weak Arthur; the thrilling race of hare-and-hounds; the treeing of Tom by Velveteens; and the final cricket match when the hero, having passed through the harassing vicissitudes of successive "forms," seems to have attained the very last glory of nineteen years, a set of whiskers and the captaincy of the school cricket team—these are memories to conjure with!

THE RUGBY IDEAL

But besides being one of the stories—which can be counted on one's fingers—that immediately capture and hold the attention of the universal boy, and leave him gasping in eagerness after fine, true, manly, forceful things,—there is in *Tom Brown's School Days* the whole round of sympathies for which Mr. Hughes lived. He himself was a Rugby boy, under Dr. Arnold. He believed that the life at a great English public school served to bring out the best virtues of the average Englishman. He was himself a notable feature on the football and cricket fields, and held that they were the surest foundations of health, happiness and manliness in a boy. He loved out-of-door country life with an eager, buoyant strength, which led him to regard it as the greatest regenerating influence on earth for stale minds, hearts and bodies. His faith was implicitly fixed in the Rugby system of self-government, where the bigger and wiser boys were in rather despotic charge of the smaller ones. He hated bullying worse than any other form of sin, whether it was from a hulking boy at school or grinding social conditions in London. And finally Judge Hughes was throughout his life blessed with an untroubled belief in the tenets of the Established Church. This faith was inextricably blended with his mighty friendships for Arnold, Maurice and Kingsley, and it was an integral portion of the great Rugby master's system of training his boys.

"Tom" Hughes as a Muscular Christian

Tom Brown's School Days was written in 1857, when Mr. Hughes was a young lawyer of thirty-four. He was in politics an advanced Liberal; his public activities were always concentrated on measures which promised to affect the moral and material standards of workingmen and the poor. He threw himself passionately into a struggle to brighten and better the lives of his poorer brethren with just the spirit that brought Tom Brown to fight for his weak little Rugby friend, Arthur. "Tom" Hughes was a busy and fairly successful lawyer. Bound to his office from ten till five, he and his chosen band of workers met at six in the morning and eight in the evening to found a society for the promotion of workingmen's associations. Mr. Hughes saw revolutionary possibilities in the idea of co-operation, and so persistently did he follow this belief that it was necessary for him at one time to maintain membership in no less than eighteen different co-operative associations. The group of devoted men among whom he was easily the most restlessly active were peculiarly favored by temperament and creed to bring conviction to the hearts of the poor people they tried to help. Beautifully loyal to the church, they were mutineers against the idea which had gradually tainted England, that piety and decency were to be expressed only by meditative and timid lives protected from the rough contact of the world. This effeminate ideal of the righteous life could not, of course, be appreciated by the people, and there was a general hunger extant for the heathen virtues when Hughes and Kingsley came on the scene with their "Christian Socialism" and "Muscular Christianity." This mighty cricketer, this broad shouldered, fresh faced athlete, this cheery, sympathetic man, almost too "tolerant of the intolerable," this Tom Hughes, who loved the things that boys loved, who was too true to believe that another man would lie—such a man was as good as any heathen of them all, and neither he nor the doctrines of Christ lost through his interpretation of them to the masses.

The Triumphs of the Christian Socialists

At the end of the century we may have grown a little weary of the phrase "Muscular Christianity," or, rather, of the vulgarities which have sometimes masqueraded under it, but in the fifties it was not only a new and wholesome ideal; its devoted disciples had the fine true ring which comes from glorious earnestness and self-forgetfulness. At any rate, where the "Chartists" had failed, the "Christian Socialists," with their Rugby standards and methods, won in no indecisive measure. In one of their meetings where the National Anthem was hissed, "Tom" Hughes arose and insisted that the scoffer should settle the disagreement between their respective views personally with him. The hissing ceased, and the form of Christian earnestness appealed to the people.

Sir Joshua Fitch (essay date 1897)

SOURCE: Fitch, Sir Joshua. "Chapter Five." In *Thomas and Matthew Arnold and Their Influence on English Education,* pp. 75-109. New York: Charles Scribner's Sons, 1897.

[*In the following excerpt, Fitch explores Hughes's idealization of the English schoolboy in* Tom Brown's School Days. *While Fitch praises the book's energy and humor, he argues that the work's anti-intellectual bias ultimately illustrates a "low standard of civilization" and a "false ideal of manliness."*]

Tom Brown's School Days is a manly and spirited book, and is pervaded throughout with a sense of humour, a sympathy with boyhood, and a love of righteousness and truth. The story is well and vigorously told, and has been deservedly admired. But as Matthew Arnold once said to me, it has been praised quite enough, for it gives only one side, and that not the best side, of Rugby school life, or of Arnold's character. It leaves out of view, almost wholly, the intellectual purpose of a school. It gives the reader the impression that it is the chief business of a public school to produce a healthy animal, to supply him with pleasant companions and faithful friends, to foster in him courage and truthfulness, and for the rest to teach as much as the regulations of the school enforce, but no more. It is to be feared that Hughes' own boyhood was not spent with the best set at Rugby. There were in his time Lake, C. J. Vaughan, Arthur Stanley, Bradley, Lushington, the two Walronds, Matthew and Thomas Arnold, but of these, and of the intense intellectual strain in the sixth form and the upper schoolhouse set, and of the aims by which they were inspired, Hughes appeared to have little or no knowledge. His typical school-boy is seen delighting in wanton mischief, in sport, in a fight, and even in a theft from a farm-yard, distinguished frequently by insolence to inferiors, and even by coarseness and brutality, but not by love of work or by any strong interest in intellectual pursuits. It is after all a one-sided and very imperfect view of ethical discipline, which while it seeks to make a boy sensitive on the point of honour, refusing to "blab" or tell tales of a schoolfellow, is yet tolerant of "cribs" and "vulguses" and other devices by which masters could be hoodwinked or deceived.

This picture of a public school, in spite of its attractive features and of its unquestionable power and reality, will probably be quoted in future years as illustrating the low standard of civilization, the false ideal of manliness, and the deep-seated indifference to learning for its own sake which characterized the upper classes of our youth in the early half of the nineteenth century. In short, the book will be held to explain and justify the famous epithet of "Barbarians" which Matthew Arnold was wont to apply to the English aristocracy and to that section of society which was most nearly influenced by the great public schools.

W. D. Howells (essay date 1911)

SOURCE: Howells, W. D. Introduction to *Tom Brown's School-Days*, pp. ix-xii. New York: Harper and Brothers, 1911.

[*In the following introduction, Howells lauds the book's magnanimity of spirit. Howells suggests that the novel has the potential to exert a positive influence on the moral development of American schoolboys.*]

It is not often that in later years one finds any book as good as one remembers it from one's youth; but it has been my interesting experience to find the story of *Tom Brown's School Days* even better than I once thought it, say, fifty years ago; not only better, but more charming, more kindly, manlier, truer, realler. So far as I have been able to note there is not a moment of snobbishness in it, or meanness of whatever sort. Of course it is of its period, the period which people call Middle Victorian because the great Queen was then nearly at the end of the first half of her long reign, and not because she personally characterized the mood of arts, of letters, of morals then prevalent.

The author openly preaches and praises himself for preaching; he does not hesitate to slip into the drama and deliver a sermon; he talks the story out with many self-interruptions and excursions; he knows nothing of the modern method of letting it walk along on its own legs, but is always putting his hands under its arms and helping it, or his arm across its shoulder and caressing it. In all this, which I think wrong, he is probably doing quite right for the boys who formed and will always form the greatest number of his readers; boys like to have things fully explained and commentated, whether they are grown up or not. In much else, in what I will not say are not the great matters, he is altogether right. By precept and by example he teaches boys to be good, that is, to be true, honest, clean-minded and clean-mouthed, kind and thoughtful. He forgives them the follies of their youth, but makes them see that they are follies.

I suppose that American boys' schools are fashioned largely on what the English call their public schools; and so far as they emulate the democratic spirit of the English schools, with their sense of equality and their honor of personal worth, the American schools cannot be too like them. I have heard that some of our schools are cultures of unrepublican feeling, and that the meaner little souls in them make their account of what families it will be well to know after they leave school and restrict their school friendships accordingly; but I am not certain this is true. What I am certain of is that our school-boys can learn nothing of such baseness from the warm-hearted and large-minded man who wrote *Tom Brown's School Days*. He was one of our best friends in the Civil War, when we sorely needed friends in England, and it was his magnanimous admiration which made our great patriotic poet known to a public which had scarcely heard of James Russell Lowell before.

But the manners and customs painted in this book are the manners and customs of the middle eighteen-fifties. It appears from its witness that English school-boys then freely drank beer and ale, and fought out their quarrels like prize-fighters with their naked fists, though the beer was allowed and the fighting disallowed by the school. Now, however, even the ruffians of the ring put on gloves, and probably the quarrels of our own school-boys are not fought out even with gloves. Beer and ale must always have been as clandestine vices in our schools as pitched battles with fists in English schools; water was the rule, but probably if an American boy now went to an English school he would not have to teach by his singular example that water was a better drink for boys than beer.

Our author had apparently no misgiving as to the beer; he does not blink it or defend it; beer was too merely a matter of course; but he makes a set argument for fighting, based upon the good old safe ground that there always had been fighting. Even in the heyday of muscular Christianity it seems that there must have been some question of fighting and it was necessary to defend it on the large and little scale, and his argument as to fisti-cuffs defeats itself. Concerning war, which we are now hoping that we see the beginning of the end of, he need only have looked into *The Biglow Papers* to find his idolized Lowell saying:

> Ez fur war I call it murder;
>   There ye hev it plain an' flat;
> An' I don't want to go no furder
>   Then my Testament fur that.

I feel it laid upon me in commending this book to a new generation of readers, to guard them, so far as I may, against such errors of it. Possibly it might have been cleansed of them by editing, but that would have taken much of the life out of it, and would have been a grievous wrong to the author. They must remain a part of literature as many other regrettable things remain. They are a part of history, a color of the contemporary manners, and an excellently honest piece of self-portraiture. They are as the wart on Cromwell's face, and are essentially an element of a most Cromwellian genius. It was Puritanism, Macaulay says, that stamped with its ideal the modern English gentleman in dress and manner, and Puritanism has stamped the modern Englishman, the liberal, the radical, in morals. The author of *Tom Brown* [*Tom Brown's School Days*] was strongly of the English Church and the English State, but of the broad church and of the broad state. He was not only the best sort of Englishman, but he was the making of the best sort of American; and the American father can trust the American boy with his book, and fear no hurt to his republicanism, still less his democracy.

It is full of the delight in nature and human nature, un-patronized and unsentimentalized. From his earliest boyhood up Tom Brown is the free and equal comrade of other decent boys of whatever station, and he ranges the woods, the fields, the streams with the joy in the sylvan life which is the birthright of all the boys born within reach of them. The American school-boy of this generation will as freshly taste the pleasure of the school life at Rugby as the American school-boys of the two generations past, and he can hardly fail to rise from it with the noble intentions, the magnanimous ambitions which only good books can inspire.

Henry R. Harrington (essay date fall 1973)

SOURCE: Harrington, Henry R. "Childhood and the Victorian Ideal of Manliness in *Tom Brown's School-days*." *Victorian Newsletter,* no. 44 (fall 1973): 13-17.

[*In the following essay, Harrington analyzes representations of childhood sexuality in the novel. In Harrington's view, Hughes's conception of manliness is inextricably connected to an ideal of sexual purity.*]

The Eucharistic vision of the Holy Grail that is revealed to Galahad and denied to Lancelot in *Idylls of the King* (VIII, 464-484) divides the Knights of the Roundtable into the sexually pure and impure. Purity in Galahad's vision is rendered as "the fiery face as of a child," and eventually Galahad himself merges with that vision in an apocalyptic ascension "when the heavens open'd and blazed." That salvation should be a consequence of chastity explains the angelic appearance of the children of Victorian literature from John Bold, Jr., in *Barchester Towers* to Mowgli in *The Jungle Book.* Yet, staring sullenly across library stacks at these cherubic faces are the dark faces of their contemporaries, the Artful Dodger and Heathcliff. Whereas Mowgli and his spiritual brothers embody untrammelled natural innocence, the Artful Dodger's fraternity are characterized by their shrewdness and, as Arnold Kettle has demonstrated, their rebelliousness.[1] The worldly consciousness of these children protests against the characterization of their interest in women simply as mothers; the sexuality of Nancy and Cathy is as undeniably real as the rebellious energy of the Artful Dodger and Heathcliff. One set of children seems to confirm Victorian piousness, the other, by dint of its vitality, to deny it. The child's "fiery face," then, is more ambiguous than Tennyson admits: the price of childhood's sexual innocence is an inability to confront the harsh social world beyond the playpen or the perimeter of the friendly jungle.

Steven Marcus, in *The Other Victorians,* discovers the same ambiguous response to children in William Acton's *The Functions and Disorders of the Reproductive Organs* (1857), an "objective" account of human sexuality barely distinguishable from pornography. It seems that Acton is unable to discover anything "to mediate between these two extreme states [sexual innocence and sexual 'precocity'], no middle ground or connection between them. And the contradiction that children are both at once remains altogether unconscious."[2] Both visions of childhood are the products of the "logic of fantasy" and can admit no bridge of consecutive thought or of realism. But a bridge, a third state of childhood sexuality, did exist in Victorian literature and coincidently appeared the same year as Acton's work. *Tom Brown's Schooldays,* by Thomas Hughes, reveals an ethical middle ground between supra-ethical innocents and the subethical rebels. Allowing little room for fantasy of the kind his contemporaries were indulging, Hughes set himself to the task of describing manliness as it was acquired and embodied in the Victorian child. With a realistic technique remarkable only for its application to childhood, Hughes seriously addressed Wordsworth's dictum, "the child is father to the man."

I

From the beginning of Hughes's novel it is apparent that he shares the peculiar and largely dominant attitude of other contemporary writers that moral growth and sexual energy are exclusively male phenomena. Even at ten years, Tom wants to be free from his mother and her maids in order to develop his athletic and masculine skills, which they try to discourage as unmannerly. Tom Brown, from the moment he escapes from his nurse, begins "fraternizing with all the village boys." Hughes makes clear, however, that this descent into the lower classes is a prelude to manliness rather than an initiation into sexual experience: "The village boys were full as manly and honest and certainly purer than those in a higher rank." With this disclaimer Hughes balances democratic and pastoral "purity" against imputations of sodomitic "impurity" among lower class youth.[3] So Tom continues to play at "wrestling, running, and climbing" with the village boys free from the taint of both women and the lower classes' childhood knowledge of sex.

Still lacking moral discipline, but sharing the animal vitality of the Artful Dodger and the innocence of Mowgli, Tom travels from his Berkshire home to a private school. Tom is singularly unsuited for the close supervision and limited muscular activities there. The fault Hughes found with private schools lay in their "constant supervision," a theory that was doomed in practice to deteriorate into "bullying" and "talebearing" that "sapped all the foundations of school morality." While far less cruel and repressive than Mr. Squeers's institution in Dickens' *Nicholas Nickleby* (1839), the school seems to cultivate secrecy and suspicion. Hughes almost certainly would have agreed with the Rev. John Chillingly, in Bulwer-Lytton's novel *Kenelm Chillingly* (1870), who arrived at the conclusion regarding private schools that "There is not manliness enough in those academies; no fagging and very little fighting. . . . Nothing muscular in the system."[4] Fully aware of his hero's difficulties, then, Hughes removes Tom from private school by an honored convention of Victorian fiction; a fever breaks out in the town where the school is located and Tom is removed to a higher sphere, Rugby School, where the rest of the novel is set.

The difference between the private school and the public one that Tom now attends is largely of increased freedom and arises out of Hughes's Protestant mistrust of imposed systems (religious as well as educational) that restrict human behavior by defining human nature too narrowly. Hughes recognized, as perhaps no other of his contemporaries did, that the complexity of human nature involved children no less than adults. In *Tom Brown's Schooldays* the relationships between the characters assume social as well as sexual configurations, and indeed, as we might expect, the two are closely related. The corollary of freedom in Hughes's writings is democracy (before he wrote *Tom Brown's Schooldays,* Hughes was a member of the Christian Socialist group that gathered around F. D. Maurice and after that became a Radical member of Parliament). He

tended, therefore, to regard public school education as an education in democracy. Nor was he far from one of the fundamental tenets of British public schools in the nineteenth century: Walter Bagehot described the leveling process that occurred as "removeable inequality."[5] The inequality was certainly between all classes, but the only ones affected by public schools were the old upper classes, the new rich merchant and industrial classes, and the ambiguously defined clergy. Tom Brown belongs to the squirearchy and is thus placed in a mediate position among his fellows, which allows him the kind of interior anonymity that his name suggests. Below him in social class rank is Arthur, the son of a poor Low Church clergyman and "Freethinker" who died treating the poor of his typhus-ridden parish. By virtue of his wealth and "adroit toadyism," Flashman looms menacingly above Tom. Whether the source of Flashman's wealth is new or old money is not clear, but the point of the wealth, that it defines a social extreme, is very clear. Both Arthur and Flashman appear to define sexual extremes as well, and in proportion to their relation to their wealth: the one with the most money is an overt sadist, the one with the least sublimates sexual desire in religious devotion. Tom Brown, as we shall see, experiences sex on a level between these extremes by means of his participation in athletics. The effect on England of the kind of aversion to extremes that operates in *Tom Brown's Schooldays* is described tersely by Mrs. Leavis:

> The upper and middle classes, affected by the modern Public School system, which has replaced the famous "eccentric" Englishman of the Augustan and Georgian ages by the "simple but virile" type, imposed upon a nation whose governing class had been for several centuries noted as having pronounced (because highly developed) personalities and keen intellectual interests, an ideal whose bywords were correctness and sport. This ideal has had the effect of arresting the development of whole generations at adolescence.[6]

To give perspective to Mrs. Leavis' opprobrium it should be noted that, while Hughes is undeniably turning his back on the "eccentric" Englishman, he is at the same time facing up to the real threats posed by social and sexual extravagances.

II

When the narrator cries in the passion of a rugby game, "Meet them like Englishmen and charge them home," school spirit and national spirit become indistinguishable. This is precisely the effect of games that Charles Kingsley, Hughes's close friend, had anticipated four years earlier when he was arguing shorter working hours for factory laborers:

> You may smile; but try the experiment, and see how as the chest expands, the muscle hardens . . . and sound sleep refreshes the lad for his next day's work, the

temper will become more patient, the spirits more genial; there will be less tendency to brood angrily over
inequalities of fortune, and to accuse society for evils
which she knows not as yet how to cure.[7]

Athletics, in short, stem revolution. No less did they
stem the anti-social threat of prostitution: the only way,
said Bulwer-Lytton in *England and the English,* to correct prostitution was to "banish thought" by entering
athletic contests.[8] Hughes's faith in athletics coupled
with his distrust of extremes, then, was by no means
particularly original. Yet, he did place athletics in the
one context, the public school, where they could almost
completely dominate "thought." So, Tom learns, as
Kingsley would have the workers do, to accept the status distinctions based on athletic ability and finds his
"respect increases" for those players ahead of him in
rank. Rendered in Freudian terms, this security, derived
from Tom's confirmed social position in the hierarchy
of and in games, is the result of "transferring the instinctual aims into such directions that cannot be frustrated by the other world."[9]

The concept of manliness as it occurs in Hughes's writings is inextricably bound up with these two fundamental presumptions: that one's place in society should be
related more to ability than birth and that "instinctual"
energy (for which we may read sexual energy) can be
channelled into nondisruptive social activities. The word
manliness has a venerable history in English literature,
but underlying all of its modern meanings is the common theme of sociality. When Coleridge originally appended to the title, *Aids to Reflection,* the phrase *in the
Formation of a Manly Character* (1825), "manly"
seemed to denote a quality based on man's ability to reflect on "a higher good" that would distinguish him
from the animals. There is something of Tillich's "ultimate concern" in Coleridge's "manliness" in that both
terms are expressive of a fundamental, yet central component of religious life. Much of Coleridge's definition
survives in Hughes so that he could write a book in
1889 called *The Manliness of Christ* and could write
in *Tom Brown* [*Tom Brown's Schooldays*]:

> . . . [Rugby] was no fool's or sluggard's paradise into
> which [Tom] had wandered by chance, but a battlefield
> ordained from old, where there are no spectators, but
> the youngest must take his side, and the stakes are life
> and death.

But there is another voice implicit in this description of
Rugby, that of Thomas Arnold, who was Hughes's headmaster at Rugby and a major figure in his novel. Arnold
acknowledged Coleridge's influence on his thought but
narrowed Coleridge's definition of manliness to mean a
quality that could only be achieved at the expense of
the moral irresponsibility of the juvenile. Rugby school
boys found favor with headmaster Arnold only when
they ceased to be boys in spirit or character. In *Tom
Brown* this attitude is softened somewhat so that we
find Arnold "with all his heart and soul and strength,
striving against whatever was mean and unmanly and
unrighteous in our little world." At work here is Hughes's ideal of manliness, which opposes not so much
childishness as "effeminacy." Still manliness was a
moral and religious quality but now with sexual connotations aimed at redirecting rather than denying sexual
desires in children. To again quote Kingsley, "The day
of 'Pietism' is gone, and Tom Brown is a heavy stone
in its grave."[10] Men, by virtue of manliness, are accountable not only to God but to their fellow men.

The measure of manliness is the ability to withstand
pain. The very existence of pain in Tom Brown's world
marks it off from the world of primal innocence that
was Mowgli's. And the experience of pain overshadows
all other childish emotional experiences that if indulged
might appear "effeminate": "Don't ever talk about
home, or your mother and sisters" is Tom's warning to
Arthur. This fear of emotional excess eventually became endemic to the English character: "It is not that
the Englishman can't feel," writes E. M. Forster, "it is
that he is afraid to feel. He had been taught at his public school that feeling is bad form."[11] Feeling, as a result
of this attitude, is not expressed and thus manliness begins to resemble masochism.

The turning point of the novel occurs in the famous
"roasting scene," where Tom finally confronts and refuses to yield to the sadistic torture of Flashman: "'Very
well then, let's roast him,' cried Flashman, and catches
hold of Tom by the collar. . . . His shoulders are
pushed against the mantlepiece, and he is held tight by
main force before the fire, Flashman drawing his trou-
sers tight by way of extra torture." The immediate cause
of the roasting is the money that Tom has won in a
horse lottery; Flashman tries to extort the lottery ticket.
The relation of money to sex is common to the Victorian novel but somewhat surprising in this particular
context. What it seems to acknowledge here is the intimate connection of the manly ability to withstand pain
and the powerful attraction of money; for in this crucial
scene Tom completes the journey to independence that
began with his break from women. Here he becomes
independent of the power of Flashman that originated
in his wealth and found expression in his sadism. But
Tom's independence here finds expression not in rebellion as it occurs in Heathcliff, for example, but in passivity and, to a certain extent, depersonalization. The
relation of money and manliness is founded on the deliberate rejection of a particularized identity, of eccentricity. Tom's denial of painful emotions, as he refuses
to cry out, is in a way a symbolic death followed by a
second birth; indeed his first words as consciousness returns is "Mother!" This scene is quite literally an initia-

tion into the mysteries of sex and money, the one being tied to the other, and the state beyond initiation is manly independence.

If the roasting passage demonstrates through Flashman the danger of not maintaining a strict control on the psychic economy of the libido, it also indicates that there is a very thin line even among school children separating repressed and overt sexual desire. Generally, the athletic life at Rugby (which Flashman significantly avoided) appears to be designed to hold that line by translating sexual energy into socially acceptable forms, but sublimation also occurs for the same purpose. Thus, avoiding the obvious problems with having Tom actually enjoy his pain during recovery, Hughes conveniently substitutes a verse from a hymn in Tom's mind: "Where the wicked cease from troubling / And the weary are at rest."

With the timing of Cordelia as she takes over the Fool's role of companion for Lear, Arthur replaces Flashman, who has been expelled from the school. Arthur, appointed by Arnold as Tom's ward, is perfectly suited to Tom's hymnic state of mind, but Hughes clearly was not comfortable with the subliminal influence of Arthur. For Arthur, even in his unquestionable innocence, has the look of a masturbator about him, fearing as he does "sleeping in the room with strange boys" and preferring contemplative solitude to fellowship with his mates. So despite the fact that Arthur in prayer reflects "Arnold's manly piety," he is advised by Arnold to take in "some Rugby air, and cricket, and . . . some good long walks." Arthur soon becomes athletic, and Tom in his manliness comes to value piety and sports. Hughes's faith in God was second to his faith in cricket when matters of sex were at stake.

III

Marcus in his discussion of the literature of flagellation describes as one of its characteristics that the dialogue "is unmistakably the language of the public school."[12] This literature reverts to childhood experiences of caning, but such experiences must be distinguished from Tom's at the hands of Flashman. Flashman's sadism manifests a dangerous anti-social impulse that belongs to a category of sexual expression that includes revolution and prostitution. But caning as it occurs in **Tom Brown** is an overt expression of social order that opposes such chaos. Thus Arnold asks the sixth former, Holmes, to beat a boy in another house because the sixth former in that house lacked the muscles to cause real pain: "Holmes has plenty of strength," observed Arnold. "I wish all the sixth had as much. We must have it here, if we are to keep order at all." Flagellation and pain, when backed by moral authority such as Arnold's, promote manliness; as Kingsley put it, "pain [is] necessary to bring out the masculine qualities."[13] The

most curious aspect of the masculinity of manliness, of course, is its implicit fear of overt sexuality. To young schoolboys, Hughes warned:

> Let me urge you, by all that you hold most sacred, to avoid secret sins of impurity—*scelus onanis*—the source of the most fatal results in after years, and the destruction of all that is pure in a young man's heart and life. I could tell you of souls hopelessly besmirched and befouled, and of lives utterly ruined and lost, by this deadly habit.[14]

Although, as we have seen, manliness has a sexual orientation, it is a covert one. In a sense this hidden meaning of manliness as a youthful ideal addresses the "secret sins" on their own level, the unconscious. While the outward forms of manliness, especially athletics, were eminently public, the meaning was essentially private. While it is easy to dispose of this attitude toward sex as prudish, it is more enlightening to take Hughes at his word: masculinity is essentially a social condition. To regard it as anything else is to fall in one or the other antithetical positions of his contemporaries: either masculinity is to be ignored in children altogether, in which case they depart from the ranks of male humanity and join the angels, or masculinity is given no moral quotient and is debased into pure animality like the schoolboy fraternity in Rudyard Kipling's *Stalky and Co.* What Hughes proposes instead is that "strength, courage, and endurance, the products of athletic sports, ought to be cultivated, for they are given to us to protect the weak, to subdue the earth, to fight for our homes and country, if necessary."[15]

By transforming sexual energy into social, public commitment, Hughes was affirming a human communion that has largely disappeared. That the basis for the communion should be the common experience of pain is surprising only in its modernity. But it would be a mistake to regard pain in **Tom Brown's Schooldays** out of its public school context; it is not a metaphor for existence as it is for Sartre, for example. One has only to look at the fate of the black Earl of Clydesdale in G. A. Lawrence's *Barren Honour* (1862) to see the importance of the public school setting: "If any ordinary social danger had presented itself, he would scarcely have quailed before it. . . . But it so happened (he had not been at a public school) that in all his life he had never seen a blow stricken in anger."[16] The Earl simply lacks the experience of public school to put pain and anger within the security of a public school reference, the result being that he is unable to "protect the weak," as Hughes would have it. The Victorian experience of the world was divided, as Masao Miyoshi has demonstrated in *The Divided Self,* into various configurations of public and private. Regarded in terms of its effects, manliness was a public virtue that was intended to fit into the Victorian intellectual impulse toward social reform; but in terms of its cause, it was a private virtue that offered substitutive gratification for the sexual desire that might otherwise be expressed in masturbation, sadism, or other prohibited sexual activities.

Yet, despite the straightforwardness of manliness, a problem remained. How long could Tom Brown uphold an implicit vow of chastity and remain physically fit? With Flashman removed from the picture and Arthur turned into a cricket player, athletics absorbs all the random energy of the schoolboys, but how long could Tom Brown uphold his implicit vow after he left Rugby? Not long, barring such an ascension as Galahad's. The cult of manliness was inevitably a cult of youth. Its emphasis on athletics as a means of diminishing sexual anxiety left out of account middle and old age, not to mention certain eventual contact with the opposite sex.

Lewis Mumford regards the devotion to sports that was an outgrowth of the cult of manliness as altering the whole conception of a well-balanced environment.[17] His point is not difficult to see if one takes seriously Mrs. Leavis' judgment, mentioned above, that development of whole generations of Englishmen was arrested at adolescence. But even so, this judgment is somewhat misleading given the obvious fact that Englishmen continued to reproduce despite an alarming increase of professional athletics. Hughes was aware of the obvious limitations of his alternative to sexual innocence and sexual precocity, and his concessions to these limitations is interesting for the light it casts on the Victorian institution of marriage.

In *Tom Brown at Oxford* (1861), the sequel to *Tom Brown's Schooldays,* Tom finally confronts the opposite sex as desirable. But his rhetorical question, "Can there be any true manliness without purity?" suggests that the ending of the novel, Tom's marriage, is also the ending of manliness. For much of the novel Hughes is able to uphold in his hero the ideal of chaste manliness by giving women an ideal status that operates as the spiritual corollary of manliness. But Tom's fall is adumbrated when he carries his ideal in his arms: "For the credit of muscular Christianity, one must say that it was not the weight, but the tumult in his own inner man which made her bearer totter." No amount of athletic training could cover such a situation; while contact lasted, sexual excitement overrode Tom's carefully programmed circuits. And predictably, sexual excitement is characterized as physical weakness, the diminution of the most characteristic physical quality of manliness, strength. The crisis of sex does not pass until Tom is safely married at which point the tone of the novel shifts completely away from the heartiness of the earlier novel to a kind of mellowness tokened by the recognition of the "darkness in one and around one." The implication here as in most Victorian literature that deals with the topic is that marriage, though it contains

sexual desire in a social institution, diminishes manliness. Like Tennyson's Arthur, Tom Brown must abandon in marriage the child's "fiery face" and settle for a compromised manliness upon which heterosexuality has intruded. In marriage, sexual precocity and sexual innocence, though presumably either is possible, lose their meaning. Manliness does not so much lose its meaning as its energy. It provides Tom with a vision of the "new world," but that vision turns out to be a fallen one: the "new world" is "the old, old world after all, and nothing else."

Notes

1. *An Introduction to the English Novel* (London, 1953), pp. 123-139.

2. *The Other Victorians* (New York, 1966), p. 15.

3. Marcus notes that in such balancing efforts "a good deal of collective amnesia must have taken place, and a good deal of folk-knowledge and traditional rural lore been repressed or denied" (p. 15).

4. Knebworth edition (London, 1892), XXX, 21.

5. Harold Nicholson, *Good Behaviour: Being a Study of Certain Types of Civility* (London, 1955), p. 263.

6. Q. D. Leavis, *Fiction and the Reading Public* (London, 1932), p. 190.

7. *Sanitary and Social Lectures and Essays* (London, 1889), pp. 210-212.

8. (London, 1833), I, 233.

9. Sigmund Freud, *Civilization and its Discontents* (London, 1955), p. 32.

10. Letter to Hughes, 1857, quoted in Francis Kingsley, *Charles Kingsley: His Letters and Memories of His Life,* 2 vols. (London, 1877), II, 27.

11. *Abinger Harvest* (London, 1936), p. 6.

12. Marcus, p. 263.

13. *Letters [Charles Kingsley: His Letters and Memories of His Life],* II, 316.

14. Thomas Hughes, *Notes for Boys on Morals, Mind and Manners* (London, 1855), p. 65.

15. Thomas Hughes, *The Scouring of the White Horse* (London, 1892), p. 249.

16. 2 vols. (London, 1862), I, 207.

17. *The Culture of Cities* (London, 1940), pp. 428-429.

Ian Watson (essay date 1981)

SOURCE: Watson, Ian. "Victorian England, Colonialism and the Ideology of *Tom Brown's Schooldays*." *Zeitschrift fur Anglistik und Amerikanistik* 29, no. 2 (1981): 116-29.

[*In the following essay, Watson examines the novel within the context of shifting political and economic conditions in early Victorian England. Watson describes the book as a "bible for the ideology of colonialism."*]

Of the various literary and historical questions thrown up by Thomas Hughes' still widely-read **Tom Brown's Schooldays** (1857), this study seeks to concentrate on the novel as a reflection of a contradictory process of social re-alignment by Britain's hereditary ruling class. The Reform Bill of 1832 represented a central advance in political power by the industrial bourgeoisie, and heralded legislation to curb the power of the squires. In 1835 the Municipal Corporations Act made the newly-appointed magistrates—although in many cases actually the former squire—responsible to the elected representatives of the newly enfranchised. The history of the old hereditary ruling class after 1832 is, *on the surface,* a story of reaction. Louis Cazamian has pointed out that the greater part of the post-1830 interventionist movement stemmed from groupings which had their source in the old ruling class.[1] These "interventionists" reproached industrialism for creating a "class society", by which they meant, in the limited sense, that the new social order had produced an alienation between social classes, and resultant class conflict. This, they claimed, had not existed in pre-industrial Britain, where everyone knew his place and the squire was fully aware not only of his hereditary rights but also of his paternal responsibilities. Their call was for political and spiritual regeneration, in which, since the "new rulers" had shown themselves incapable of responsible government, the old, "natural" ruling class must have a new role. In its most reactionary form, it may have included a harking-back to pre-industrial times; but in its later and more complex form it meant an acceptance of the technological necessity of industrial capitalism as an irrevocable progress.

It is all too easy to see the "old rulers", for reasons of outrage, fear or spite, putting their weight behind industrial legislation such as the Ten Hours Bill; or to view this as an "act of revenge" against the Repeal of the Corn Laws.[2] For the story is much more complex; not a struggle of blind reaction, but in effect an attempt at *rehabilitation.*

Cazamian stresses too much the idea of two distinct ruling classes. The land-owners, increasingly capitalist since the 17th century, infiltrated early by (finance-) capitalist "gentlemen", and gelling themselves in the 19th century into the farming *industry,* did have differing interests and a different history from the industrial bourgeoisie. Yet their interests were converging. Issues like Corn Law Repeal (which, in any case, brought benefits to the landed interest in the form of impulses for the rationalisation of agricultural production), or factory legislation, were less of a confrontation between two classes than a give-and-take re-alignment of *two lobbies inside what had become a single ruling class,* uniting before a common enemy: the working class, and its political expression in Chartism. The divergent spheres of production of these two groups, (coupled with their different historical sources, have tended to distract from a social contract, a political division of labour between what were originally two classes. The class compromise of 1688 left the progressive sections of the gentry in charge of England's administrative superstructure. The Whig aristocracy administered justice and charity on behalf of the new capitalist forces. In the meantime, the bourgeoisie got on with its work of accumulation and the fulfillment of its historical task. The whole period of the Industrial Revolution was its era of consolidation. As long as this phase was incomplete, economic clashes of interest could still produce political turbulence, both with the old rulers and with the working class. The industrial explosion created the friction which led to parliamentary reform; the economic crisis of 1837-42 brought forth Chartism. The economic boom which superceded the "hungry forties" represented the final enthronement of industrial capitalism in England. The era between 1848 and 1866 is signified by important new developments: the second wave of the Industrial Revolution (the unfolding of heavy industry); and the confirmation of Britain as the "workshop of the world". This monopoly position had its consequences for the social and political structure of the country, the creation of the hegemony of the industrial capitalist class. On the industrial front, this economic supremacy meant a turning away from confrontation to conciliation. The working class' *partial* share in the new wealth was reflected in the defusing of Chartism and the promotion of New Model Unionism by the bourgeoisie.[3] But the new policy was not only made *possible* by the boom; it had been made *necessary* by the growing threat of working-class strength in Chartism. The industrialists' relationship to the landed interest shifted too. For the land-owning section of the ruling class profited just as much from industrialism and Free Trade.[4] Indeed, the strength and persistence of the hegemony of the British industrialist class can be traced back not only to its successful conciliation of significant sections of the working class at a crucial period of the latter's formation, but to its productive coexistence with the landed interest. The old rulers saw their own economic interests ensured by such co-operation; the industrialists viewed it largely in terms of ideological strategy, especially in the context of expanding colonialism and imperialism. The policy of industrial concession, with its economic base of world supremacy and the ideological acceptance of "laissez faire" by key working-class groups, had a counterpoint which enabled the absorption of the interventionist trends which had been at odds with the inhuman effects of utilitarianism, before the prosperity which became *par excellence, the Victorian Age*".[5] This study is an attempt to look at **Tom Brown's Schooldays** as a documentation of ideological adjustment and compromise between the two wings of the ruling bloc; and to set into historical context the view that Hughes' career was an attempt to reconcile three often contradictory factors:

> his love of the common man; his feeling that perhaps workers were not quite ready to handle their own affairs; and his desire to save his own class from being considered useless or pernicious.[6]

In the spirit of the appeal by Carlyle in the opening paragraph of *Chartism* (1839) on the "Condition of England" and the "condition and disposition of the Working Classes"[7], a whole generation of the English gentry began to busy itself with the affairs of the working class. By 1850 the phrase "Christian Socialism" had been coined to describe one group, which began in the forties and had reached a climax in their support of moral-force Chartism against the physical-force faction in 1848. On 10th April, 1848, the day on which the last Chartist petition was presented to Parliament, Kingsley, Maurice and J. M. Ludlow met to form the group later to found Christian Socialism; and Hughes was acting as a special constable in the face of feared revolution. Although he had earlier flirted with moral-force Chartism, he was actually arrested in the afternoon for causing a disturbance by heckling a Chartist speaker.[8] The group around Kingsley worked quickly during these events, publishing on the following day a moral appeal to the workers:

> The Charter is not bad *if the men who use it are not bad* . . . There will be no true freedom without virtue, no true science without religion, no true industry without the fear of God and love to your fellow citizens. Workers of England, be wise and then you *must* be free, for you will be fit to be free.[9]

Christian Socialism linked class fear with a pragmatism necessary to avoid the class war rendered apparently inevitable by the anarchy of industrial capitalism; to save society, they must be realistic and run with the tide:

> The new element is democracy in Church and State. Waiving the question of its evil or its good, we cannot stop it. We must Christianise it instead.[10]

Compare this manifesto with that written months earlier by Marx and Engels:

> Nichts leichter, als dem christlichen Asketismus einen sozialistischen Anstrich zu geben. Hat das Christentum nicht auch gegen das Privateigentum, gegen die Ehe,

gegen den Staat geeifert? Hat es nicht die Wohltätigkeit und den Bettel, das Zölibat und die Fleischesertötung, das Zellenleben und die Kirche an ihrer Stelle gepredigt? Der christliche Sozialismus ist nur das Weihwasser, womit der Pfaffe den Ärger des Aristokraten einsegnet.[11]

Hughes and Kingsley took Christian Socialism and its paternalism into the Trade Union movement, which began to flourish as Chartism died; and especially into the Cooperative movement. Hughes later put his neo-Owenite ideas into practice with disastrous results in Tennessee, where he founded a colony based on the twin principles of cooperation and paternalistic leadership. As a result of his Co-op connections he was commissioned to look into the wave of strikes in 1858 and to investigate the activities of trade unions. In the course of this work he got to know many of the more conservative union leaders, and agreed to become their legal adviser. Hughes argued in his report that legal recognition of all union activity would avert tendencies to class war and stop strikes, since many of the workers' grievances were justified. His union contacts also brought him, in 1865, the parliamentary seat of Lambeth, an area with a large number of enfranchised small craftsmen. Despite his supporters, he followed an individualistic line, often going against trade-union policy.[12] He also became increasingly tempted by the idea of profit-sharing as a remedy to class war, and threw himself into various projects, despite opposition from within the Cooperative movement. After the Sheffield "outrages" of 1867, which involved intimidation of strike-breakers, Hughes conducted a successful defence of the unions, but a coolness in his relationship to the Labour Movement was increasingly apparent. In 1868 he became M. P. for the small country town of Frome, where he could become a government representative in strike arbitration without having to worry about a working-class electorate, which was what the male population of Lambeth had become after the 1867 Reform Act. In the course of this activity he quickly lost working-class support; his policies displayed increasingly "cold feet" and a break with union aims. In 1871 he supported the Criminal Law Amendment Act, which allowed up to three years for picketing. When the unions attacked his beloved Church of England as a class institution, he retaliated sharply. He also invoked the anger of working people when he declared in 1873:

> Work is not the same as it had been twenty years ago. You do not put the same honest vigour into it, nor do you have the same delight in it, nor do you turn it out as well as you possibly can.[13]

Hughes was eventually broken by the irreconcilability of his belief in paternalistic leadership, which presupposed passive, unselfsufficient workers, with the cooperative trends which were one reflection of precisely this growing independence and self-confidence in the working class. He drew his own consequences: he became a county court judge in 1882, resigned from the Co-op movement and "drifted into a conservatism of the sentimental".[14]

These biographical notes and his relationship to the organised working class are important factors in setting the tone of his philosophy of life, which was fully formed by 1857. Its main features were hatred of industrial chaos and its related class war, and a longing for class harmony, which he believed had existed in a previous, principally rural and paternalistic form of society. This Golden Age finds ample expression in *Tom Brown's Schooldays,* especially in the opening chapters, which are little more than a summary of Hughes' class beliefs and prejudices. Tom's idyllic childhood at the feet of the two old faithful family servants, and his apparently classless play environment provide a picture of a regrettably disappearing world where the squire set the tone of village life, where those who knew their place showed their gratitude, and where squire and poacher played cricket together on the village green. Hughes comments with an almost audible sigh:

> I suppose that on the whole, people were worked less then than they are now.[15]

The Veast of the second chapter is Hughes' most extensive glorification of "old England". After descriptions of idyllic village life, with its banter and its biblical names, comes the first note of regret for the death of this social order, and—more interestingly—the clear reasons for its demise. The Veast, even when it included excessive drinking, had had an effect that was "humanising and Christian":

> In fact, the only reason why this is not the case still, is that gentlefolk and farmers have taken to other amusements, and have as usual forgotten the poor. They don't attend the feasts themselves, and call them disreputable, whereupon the steadiest of the poor leave them also, and they become what they are called.
>
> (*TBS* [*Tom Brown's Schooldays*], 33)

All this he sees as the result of the increasing division of classes:

> Class amusements, be they for dukes or ploughboys, always become nuisances and curses to a country. The true charm of cricket and hunting is that they are still more or less sociable and universal; there's still a place for every man who will come and take his part.
>
> (*TBS,* 33)

Towards the end of the chapter Hughes makes his class-division argument more concrete, in his condemnation of farmers who no longer subscribe to the country feasts, which are "much altered for the worse":

> Is this a good or a bad sign? I hardly know. Bad, sure enough, if it only arises from the further separation of classes consequent of twenty years of buying cheap and selling dear, and its accompanying over-work.
>
> (*TBS,* 42)

These farmers, too, have succumbed to the cash nexus.

Hughes' antidote to this tendency seems simple; the readers of his novel, the future leaders of the country, should try in the course of making acquaintances to seek friends from all classes of society, including

> three or four out of the working classes, tailors, engineers, carpenters, engravers—there's plenty of choice. Let them be men of your own ages, mind, and ask them to your homes; introduce them to your wives, and sisters, and get introduced to theirs: give them good dinners, and talk to them about what is really at the bottom of your hearts, and box, and run, and row with them, when you have a chance.
>
> (*TBS,* 44)

In a purely idealistic way, Hughes could transfer the paternalistic mentality which he believed to have existed in pre-industrial society on to the changed face of England, a country now contaminated by "too much over-civilisation, and the deceitfulness of riches".

In his picture of this idyll in the novel, Hughes calls as witnesses *not* the agricultural proletariat, but *untypical* representatives of the working class: servants. The spirit of paternalism is incorporated in Benjy and Noah, the old family retainers who are responsible for Tom's first boyhood education. Noah proudly wears the wig of a deceased Brown whom he had valeted, and

> talked to Tom quite as if he were one of his own family, and indeed had long completely identified the Browns with himself.
>
> (*TBS,* 30)

Benjy, in his discourses to Tom about the "doings of deceased Browns" also identifies himself completely with the squire's family, proudly expounding on how Tom's grandfather had dispelled the mob (in 1795?) (*TBS,* 31). Benjy has inherited the very coat he had cleaned regularly a generation before (*TBS,* 34).

As to paternalism, charity and class harmony in agrarian England, there is much evidence to the contrary. In Hughes' (and, we can assume, in Tom Brown's) second year at Rugby (1834), the Tolpuddle Martyrs were transported for seven years to Australia for "conspiracy", that is, for trying to organise an agricultural trade union, a "blow against the weakest front of the working-class movement"[16] which showed little spirit of class harmony. The Hammonds have described in *The Village Labourer* the intensive class struggle in agriculture: from the food riots of 1795, where the rioters "did not rob: they fixed prices" and "did not use their strength to plunder the shops: they organised distribution, selling food they seized at whatever they considered fair rates, and handing the proceeds over to the owners";[17] to the Last Labourers' Revolt of 1830. As a result of this latter, which spread over all of Southern England from August to December, "most of the agricultural population of Hampshire had made itself liable to the death penalty, if the authorities cared to draw the noose".[18] Tom Brown's home, Berkshire, was a major county of disturbance: 162 cases were heard, one rioter was hanged, and 123 were jailed or transported.[19] All this contrasts sharply with the fictional villagers' affection for little Tom at the Veast:

> And elders come up from all parts to salute Benjy, and girls who have been Madam's pupils to kiss Master Tom. And they carry him off to load him with fairings; and he returns to Benjy, his hat and coat covered with ribands, and his pockets crammed with wonderful boxes . . .
>
> (*TBS*, 35)

Generosity indeed, towards the grandson of the man who had quelled the food-riot mob, especially at a time when the village labourers were "living on roots and sorrel; in the summer of 1830 four harvest labourers were found under a hedge dead of starvation, and . . . this was not an exceptional case".[20]

The aspect of the spiritual regeneration movement with which *Tom Brown's Schooldays* is most widely associated was the reform of the public schools. This field has been too often documented[21] to warrant any repetition in these pages, but the most important element which must be stressed, is the fact that the public school reform of the 1830s was not a bourgeois reform. It was not an attempt to make moral or curricular concessions to the needs of the industrial capitalist class through broader admission or the expansion of new natural-science subjects. The sons of "trade" did form a negligible minority at public schools before this time, but the industrial bourgeoisie still tended to send its sons to schools where the skills necessary to buying, selling and engineering were to be more easily acquired; only in the second round of public school reform (at State level this time) in the 1860s did the portals of these institutions begin to open freely to the ideology and curriculum of the technological age.[22]

In *Signs of the Times* (1829) Carlyle had propagated the correction of "Mechanics", as the doom of mankind, by the principle of "Dynamics", which rested on Christian faith, love and the knack of happiness, all of which could be achieved only by a moral rearmament of the old aristocratic order. By the time he wrote *Past and Present* fourteen years later, Thomas Arnold had already gone a long way to introducing at Rugby the qualities which Carlyle demanded, and the values which influenced Hughes and his generation so profoundly.[23] The purpose of the reformed Rugby was to produce from the ranks of the hereditary rulers of the nation the future leaders who would display the strength of char-

acter necessary to guide the country. They were to be an utterly dependable, tightly-knit ruling caste, whose steadfastness was matched only by their arrogance and their confidence in their own superiority.

These qualities are apparent in the very pores of ***Tom Brown's Schooldays***; in the treatment of gamekeepers and coachmen, and above all in the way the young gentlemen react to servants and "louts", as Hughes refers to members of the working class who appear. Tom meets this attitude and reflects on it during his first minutes in the school, when he meets Harry East, later to become his bosom friend.

> Tom was somewhat inclined to resent the patronising air of his new friend, a boy of just about his own height and age, but gifted with the most transcendent coolness and assurance, which Tom felt to be aggravating and hard to bear, but couldn't for the life of him help admiring and envying—especially when young my lord begins hectoring two or three long loafing fellows, half porter, half stableman, with a strong touch of the blackguard; and in the end arranges with one of them nicknamed Cooey, to carry Tom's luggage up to the school-house for sixpence.
>
> "And heark'ee Cooey, it must be up in ten minutes, or no more jobs from me. Come along, Brown." And away swaggers the young potentate, with his hands in his pockets, and Tom at his side.
>
> "All right, sir", says Cooey, touching his hat, with a leer and a wink at his comrades.
>
> (*TBS*, 78)

It is worthwhile quoting this passage in full, as it reveals several crucial attitudes and tensions underlying the Rugby idyll which Hughes is about to present. Firstly, there is the attitude of Harry East, his "patronising air" and his "transcendent coolness and assurance". On the following page he is described as being "frank, hearty and good-natured, well satisfied with himself and his position": surely the Carlylean superman in miniature. Then, there is Tom's reaction to East; he finds his new friend's air aggravating, but can't help admiring it. But if East's peer Tom is galled, if only momentarily, by the former's attitude, the tension produced by his arrogance in the members of the working class can be imagined. (Indeed, this simmering tension, which seldom finds explicit expression elsewhere in the novel, is hinted at in the closing sentence of the passage.) Thirdly, and most expressive, is the treatment of the workers by East and the description of them by the narrator, which is amazing in its compression of so many upper-class prejudices towards the working class into such a short space. Finally, East's remark ". . . it must be up in ten minutes, or no more jobs from me . . .", displays eloquently a crucial class attitude in microcosm. It is the veiled threat of one who has the power to hire and fire those who possess nothing but their labour power. East has learned his social role at an early age.

The reference to the porter in question only by his nickname is also significant, and is echoed in a later chapter. On the morning of his first full Rugby day, Tom awakes to find the school servant at work collecting dirty shoes at the foot of the beds; he

> watched the movements of Bogle (the generic name by which the successive shoe-blacks of the School-House were known).

(TBS, 111)

The servant is without identity, merely the bearer of a "generic name", the fulfiller of a function—a "hand". The portrayal of the lower orders as semi-idiots finds expression in the description of Stumps, the shoemaker husband of the school tuck-shopkeeper, and his treatment by the boys. Stumps could be mentally tortured at will by the pupils, until his pain would explode and he would attempt to have his revenge; but even then he was "easily pacified by two-pence to buy beer with" *(TBS,* 97). If Stumps can be bought off like a child with a tantrum, so too are the lower classes to be viewed as children. This view is expressly represented in Tom's remark to the young master, who has said of East that he will "make a capital officer".

> "Aye, won't he!" said Tom, brightening; "no fellow could handle boys better and I suppose soldiers are very like boys."

(TBS, 276)

Whereas the industrial bourgeoisie was, by the 1850s, only sceptically coming to terms with interventionist legislation at home, it supported, indeed demanded, full State backing—military and administrative—in the colonies, which British industry needed both as sources of raw materials and as markets for finished goods. It was on the colonial front that the ideological training and attitudes of the old rulers could best be harnessed to the needs of the new, within the hierarchical structure of military and administrative organisations; and it is within the context of colonial expansion that the values and attitudes of Tom Brown's Rugby are best understood. The "curacy, chambers and regiment" of the Browns *(TBS,* 15) became the fort and the diplomatic outpost. The systematic exploitation of India, for example, necessitated increased penetration into the hinterland, and involved vast military deployment and an administrative class whose function it was to appease and corrupt the native ruling class, and impose a system of "feudalism at second hand" (Hill). The social system of pre-British India was wrecked in the nineteenth century and replaced by a heritage of vagrancy and starvation which still persists. But the twin method of military brutality and "buying off" the native rulers was unskilfully carried out and engendered resistance not only among the broad population but also among the ruling castes themselves, who—although many had been pro-British—saw their privileges threatened by British military and technological advance. The climax came in 1857, significantly the year in which *Tom Brown's Schooldays* was published. While this was largely a revolt engineered by the indigenous rulers, in some areas the population exploited the situation to stage a popular uprising against their landlords.

The main result of the Indian "Mutiny" was that it showed up clearly the weaknesses of the British administration in India: too much crude military oppression and too little diplomatic, administrative and ideological skill. The demand in India and in Whitehall was for an extended, professionally run colonial army and above all for a tightening up of civil service administration. Hughes' dream of a new role for the squire class was coming true.

The relationship between ideology and the material basis of social reality is richly complex; but at the risk of short-cutting many of the dialectics of this process, we might safely say that the British bourgeoisie legitimised colonial exploitation by means of an ideological camouflage which was necessary *within* the ruling class as much as within the country as a whole.[24] The ideology of the industrial capitalist class (or rather, the class compromise of which we have spoken) after midcentury welded what we may call "capitalist" values of competition, individual achievement, the survival of the fittest and social mobility; with older, loosely "feudal" ideas of honour, social obligation to the less-well-off and social hierarchy. This is a vitally important factor which still merits a more intensive study by the social historians. This class compromise (with certain parallels to 1688) brought with it, in ideological terms, a peculiarly British set of dominant social values which exist to the present day. The rehabilitation of the seemingly redundant squirearchy, made necessary by the colonial requirements of administration and by the strategy of the skilfully organised domestic class warfare recognised by Engels,[25] was instrumental in this class coalition. *Tom Brown's Schooldays* is an excellent literary documentation of this ideology.

In this set of values, the underdog plays an important role. The Brown family and the pupils of the fictional Rugby were well versed in the unswerving protection of the weak. In his eulogy to the Browns, Hughes presents his squire class as unstintingly charitable and constant prey to plebeian ingratitude:

> Jem and his whole family turn out bad, and cheat them one week, and the next they are doing the same thing for Jack; and when he goes to the treadmill, and his wife and children to the workhouse, they will be on the look-out for Bill to take his place.

(TBS, 15)

As the domestic working class increasingly rejected such paternalistic ideas, it was useful, in the context of the beginnings of serious international colonialist competition, to portray Britain as *protecting* defenceless colonial peoples from the expansionist aggression of other colonial powers.[26]

* * *

Bullying plays a central role in *Tom Brown's School-days,* as indeed it was a problem for the real Dr. Arnold in his Rugby reforms; the novel is permeated with such injustice, and the one negative character is a bully. Flashman must be one of Victorian literature's most telling of telling names; it represents everything cruel and showy, both the relics of aristocratic decay and the gaudiness of the nouveau riche that Carlyle had condemned with equal vigour in *Past and Present.* The Flashmans had allowed the old paternalism to decline through abuse; they were cowardly, lazy, spendthrift and, above all, unjust rulers and bullies. The Flashman of the novel was

> big and strong for his age. He played well at all games where pluck wasn't much wanted, and managed generally to keep up appearances where it was; and having a bluff, off-hand manner, which passed for heartiness and considerable power of being pleasant when he liked, went down with the school in general for a good fellow enough. Even in the School-house, by dint of his command of money, the constant supply of good things which he kept up, and his adroit toadyism, he had managed to make himself not only tolerated but rather popular amongst his own contemporaries.
>
> (*TBS,* 141)

He also administers "sly blows and taunts" (*TBS,* 148). Flashman is one of the clique who, when the "natural leaders" like Old Brooke have left Rugby, threaten to lead the School-house "into darkness and chaos again"; under their "no-government the School-house began to see bad times"; they were "a sporting and drinking set" and "soon began to usurp power and to fag little boys" and "bully and oppress" (*TBS,* 133). The "roasting" of Tom Brown is the climax of this rule of terror (*TBS,* 145ff.). In stark contrast stand those who represent the new spirit of Rugby: Old Brooke, whose speech (*TBS,* 100ff.) stands alongside Arnold's sermon (*TBS,* 115ff.) as the expression of the Arnoldian ideology; Harry East, who matures from a "young potentate" (*TBS,* 78) to a boy with a "hatred of everything cruel, or underhand, or false" (*TBS,* 256); and finally Tom Brown himself, who,

> besides being very like East in many points of character, had largely developed in his composition the capacity for taking the weakest side. This is not putting it strongly enough; it was a necessity with him, he couldn't help it any more than he could eating and drinking. He could never play on the strongest side with any heart at football or cricket, and was sure to make friends with any boy who was unpopular, or down on his luck.
>
> (*TBS,* 256)

Hughes hammers home his message in a long narrative comment, which includes the moral commandment:

> But you are brave gallant boys, who hate easy chairs, and have no balances or bankers. You only want to have your heads set straight to take the right: so bear in mind that majorities, especially respectable ones, are nine times out of ten in the wrong; and that if you see man or boy striving earnestly on the weak side, however wrong-headed or blundering he may be, you are not to go and join the cry against him. If you can't join him and help him, and make him wiser, at any rate remember that he has found something in the world which he will fight and suffer for, which is just what you have got to do for yourselves, and so think and speak of him tenderly.
>
> (*TBS,* 153f.)

Linked to the view of Britain as the paternal protector of weaker peoples was a stout nationalism which developed throughout the 19th century, as British overseas involvement grew by necessity, from Palmerston's adventurism of the forties and fifties, to the period before 1914. This nationalism was the product of three centuries of the bourgeois nation state which England had been. In *Tom Brown's Schooldays* nationalism is propagated both directly and in microcosm, as house-loyalty and school-loyalty. The direct nationalism exists throughout the novel: the contribution of the Browns in the opening passage to the "fleets and armies of England" (*TBS,* 13); the narrator's appeal to his readers, "Young England" (sic!), to get to know the lanes and by-ways of their own "Dulce domum" (*TBS,* 16); or the communal singing of "The British Grenadiers", "The Siege of Seringapatan" and a "prolonged performance of 'God Save the King'" (*TBS,* 99/106).

More directly problematical than the direct appeal to national feeling, but a vital corollary of it, is the group-identification, a kind of nationalism in miniature, which is fostered in the school. This is essentially an exercise in class solidarity, the definition of the political and cultural/ideological affinities of an élite. Equals stand by equals: school versus "louts"; rebellious fags versus bullies; house versus the rest of the school. Thus the social patterns are formed which define the relationship which these boys will have in their leader-roles with the "louts" they will employ, administer or sentence at home, and with whom they must seem to have a common interest overseas. Hughes recognises this training in fellowship in "the best house in the best school in England" (*TBS,* 103) as a link to the national and international role of the pupils. Speaking of his own school memories, the narrator writes:

> As the old scenes became living, and the actors in them became living too, many a grave in the Crimes and distant India, as well as in the quiet church-yards of our dear old country, seemed to open and send forth their dead, and their voices and looks and ways were again in one's ears and eyes as in the old School-days.
>
> (*TBS,* 262)

It was sport which played the most significant role in the service of this spirit. Team games were especially suited to training the very dialectical relationship which was fostered between competition and fellowship; physical courage, strength, fitness and endurance were seen as the pillars of the Empire. From the Browns as a "fighting family" (*TBS,* 14) we are given a panorama of backswording and wrestling, the combative pastimes of rural England, "something to try the muscles of men's bodies, and the endurance of their heart, and to make them rejoice in their strength" (*TBS,* 43) Linked to the physical courage of sports and fighting is

> the consciousness of silent endurance, so dear to every Englishman—of standing out against something, and not giving in.
>
> (*TBS,* 67)

Thus Tom on the coach to Rugby. Soon he is to have a glimpse of his future companions as they run alongside the coach. Before he even reaches the school, Tom is offered a foretaste of the Rugby ideology; the coach-man remarks proudly on one runner:

> I do b'lieve too as that there un'd sooner break his heart than let us go by him at the next milestone.
>
> (*TBS,* 76)

The first sporting contest which Tom experiences is the great football match, where military images rule the day. The leader is Old Brooke,

> absolute as he of Russia, *but wisely and bravely ruling over willing and worshipping subjects,* a true football king. His face is earnest and careful as he glances a last time over his array, but full of pluck and hope, the sort of look I hope to see in my general when I go out to fight.
>
> (*TBS,* 88; my emphasis)

The martial allusions of these few pages are too numerous to mention. It is sufficient to summarise them in the auctorial comment:

> My dear sir, a battle would look much the same to you, except that the boys would be men, and the balls iron; but a battle would be worth your looking at for all that, and so is a football match.
>
> (*TBS,* 89)

Endurance appears again in Brooke's speech as "learning to stand it, and to take your own parts, and fight it through" (*TBS,* 101f.) Tom does not have to waste much time before testing his powers of endurance; on the same evening he is tossed in a blanket and is "called a young trump for his pains" (*TBS,* 110).

But it is to Dr. Arnold himself that the main task falls of instilling the fighting spirit into the pupils. His sermon in the novel is a literary monument to Hughes'

philosophy of "muscular Christianity", as it was later to be dubbed. At the feet of the master the boys learn the meaning of life:

> That it was no fool's or sluggard's paradise into which he had wandered by chance, but a battle-field ordained from of old, where there are no spectators, but the youngest must take his side, and the stakes are life and death.
>
> (*TBS,* 116)

Arnold is the shepherd, the general, the example; he stands before his pupils as

> their fellow-soldier and the captain of their band. The true sort of captain too for a boys' army, one who had no misgivings and gave no uncertain word of command, and, let who would yield or make truce, would fight the fight out (so every boy felt) to the last gasp and the last drop of blood.
>
> (*TBS,* 117)

Of course the supreme hymn to fighting in the novel is the whole fifth chapter, which indeed bears the title "The Fight". It starts with a warning to lily-livered readers:

> . . . let those young persons whose stomachs are not strong, or who think a good set-to with the weapons which God has given us all, an uncivilised, unchristian, or ungentlemanly affair, just skip this chapter at once, for it won't be to their taste.
>
> (*TBS,* 217)

So the tone is set: boxing is described as a thrice-weekly routine in the School-house. Then comes a passage which has earned a central place in the discussion of the novel and its author. In his praise of fighting, Hughes outlines a whole view of life which became a class cult, as Britain's colonial army spread swiftly over the world in the nineteenth century:

> After all, what would life be without fighting, I should like to know? From the cradle to the grave, fighting, rightly understood, is the business, the real, highest, honestest business of every son of man. Every one who is worth his salt has his enemies, who must be beaten, be they evil thoughts and habits in himself, or spiritual wickedness in high places, or Russians, or Border-ruffians, or Bill, Tom or Harry, who will not let him live his life in quiet till he has thrashed them.
>
> It is no good for Quakers, or any other body of men, to uplift their voices against fighting. Human nature is too strong for them, and they don't follow their own precepts. Every soul of them is doing his own piece of fighting, somehow and somewhere. The world might be a better world without fighting for anything I know, but it wouldn't be our world; and therefore I am dead against crying peace when there is no peace, and isn't meant to be. I'm as sorry as any man to see folk fighting the wrong people and the wrong things, but I'd a deal sooner see them doing that, than that they should have no fight in them.
>
> (*TBS,* 218)

Closely related to the fighting spirit and the support of the underdog, both of which seemed to shed new light on the unpleasant job the British colonial forces were carrying out, was a strong sense of missionary purpose, a vision which also permeates the pages of *Tom Brown's Schooldays*. The British Empire was seen to be won by men carrying bibles, rifles and spanners. The spreading of technology and the Christian religion were seen as bringing light and civilisation to a pagan, backward world. The military defence of this splendidly praiseworthy idea seemed to be self-evident. According to the colonial pioneers, the natives of India and elsewhere had no respectable God, were therefore hostile to technological improvement and fought dirty. In their striving to "civilise" India, the British had, by 1850, the railway at their disposal and by about 1870 the machine-gun.

Squire Brown's only wish for his son is that he will turn out to be

> a brave, helpful, truth-telling Englishman and a gentleman and a Christian,
>
> (***TBS,*** 66)

> . . . striving against whatever was mean and unmanly and unrighteous in our little world.
>
> (***TBS,*** 116)

On three occasions Tom has experiences which involve the discussion of the meaning of life and of the necessity of fulfilling one's life through a mission of some kind. Indeed he is given a mission to fulfil, when Arnold puts in his charge the shy new boy, George Arthur. Through his care of Arthur, Tom sees a real aim in life and benefits from Arthur's stories of his clergyman father, who had given his life for his parishioners in a typhus epidemic. Later, Arthur's grave illness leads to a strengthening of the bonds between the two boys. Arthur admits that the motivation which kept him alive was the thought that

> to die without having fought, and worked, and given one's life away, was too hard.
>
> (***TBS,*** 243)

By the end of the novel, Tom has a clearer perspective of his future, which he discusses with his form-master.[27]

> I want to be at work in the world . . . I mean real work; one's profession; whatever one will have really to do, and make one's living by. I want to be doing some good, feeling that I am not only at play in the world.
>
> (***TBS,*** 277)

The master accuses Tom of confusing "earning a living" and "doing good in the world", and advises him to

> Keep the latter before you as your one object, and you will be right, whether you make a living or not.
>
> (***TBS,*** 277)

and to set his sights a little lower, on the "place you find yourself in, and try to make things a little better and honester there" (***TBS,*** 277). After the lean years of Utilitarianism, this is an interesting shift away from the Puritan calling towards an early ideal of charity, albeit pragmatic.

Flying in the face of the "social mobility" and "rags-to-riches" ideology of British 19th-century industrialism, the colonies offered a social structure which was, in the main, rigid. The public school mentality, as represented by Arnold's reformed Rugby, acted as a safety-valve for both, justifying and combining individual performance, achievement and social climbing with hierarchy and the rule of "natural leaders". This skilful working-out of a social contradiction was to play an important ideological function not only in the colonies but later at home in Britain, as social mobility decreased with monopolisation. All this is reflected in the novel, where, on the one hand, progress upwards through the school depends on academic ability (witness the "great stupid boys" with "incipient down on their chins of the lower fourth form", ***TBS,*** 129); and, on the other hand, a strong hierarchy and insistence on respect for ordained authority reign supreme. Indeed, the Arnold administration is openly quoted as a model for the Empire:

> Perhaps ours is the only little corner of the British Empire which is thoroughly wisely and strongly ruled just now.
>
> (***TBS,*** 272)

Not only Arnold but the daunting Old Brooke act as figureheads of kindly despotism. The transfer of these hierarchical values from school to career is embodied in Harry East; when he has left Rugby, the form-master wishes for him that he will find a replacement for Arnold as guide in a good commanding officer

> . . . but I hope East will get a good colonel. He won't do if he can't respect those above him. How long it took him even here, to learn the lesson of obeying.
>
> (***TBS,*** 277)

Even those who rule must learn to obey: that was the watchword of Rugby. For Hughes, hierarchy is God-given and natural: the young, the weak and the foolish need guidance and strong leaders to look up to. The boys, resentfully at first, respond instinctively to the "strong man over them, who would have things his own way" (***TBS,*** 104). And the instinct must be right and proper:

> Such stages have to be gone through, I believe, by all young and brave souls, who must win their way through hero-worship, to the worship of Him who is the King and Lord of heroes.
>
> (***TBS,*** 288)

Tom Brown, the six-former, leaves the school moulded after two intellectual giants:

> And so after . . . sorrowful adieus to his tutor, from whom he received two beautifully-bound volumes of the Doctor's Sermons as a parting present, he marched down to the School-house, a hero-worshipper, who would have satisfied the soul of Thomas Carlyle himself.

(*TBS,* 280)

By the mid-fifties, Hughes was propagating the ideas of the later Carlyle. Yet these ideas—above all, the hero-worship of paternalism—were being overhauled historically *inside* Britain by the "humanized Utilitarianism"[28] of J. S. Mill, based, as it was, on the recognition of growing working-class independence and self-confidence.[29] As British capitalism began to export its inherent contradictions, *Tom Brown's Schooldays* was to become a bible for the ideology of colonialism.

Notes

1. Louis Cazamian, *The Social Novel in England 1830-1850* (1903), London, Routledge and Kegan Paul 1973.

2. Cf. for example Cazamian, op. cit., p. 73.

3. Wage struggles still play a central role in the fifties, but no longer predominantly geared to political aims of social change, rather in the words of Elizabeth Gaskell's Higgins in *North and South* (1855): ". . . for justice and fair play. We help to make their profits, and we ought to help spend 'em." For the discussion on the fifties, I am especially indebted to Susanne Klein, whose unpublished Bremen exam thesis has linked Elizabeth Gaskell to Mill and the political strategy of the bourgeoisie after Chartism.

4. Cf. A. L. Morton, *A People's History of England,* London, Lawrence and Wishart 1971, pp. 405ff.

5. Morton, op. cit., p. 407.

6. E. C. Mack and W. H. G. Armytage, *Thomas Hughes: the Life of the Author of "Tom Brown's Schooldays",* London, Ernest Benn, n. d., p. 156.

7. Thomas Carlyle, "Chartism". In *The Works of Thomas Carlyle,* London, Chapman and Hall, vol. 29, p. 118.

8. Cf. Mack and Armytage, op. cit., pp. 54f.

9. Quoted in Mack and Armytage, op. cit., p. 56. This foreshadows similar ideas expressed almost twenty years later by George Eliot in *Felix Holt,* and especially in her "Address to Working Men, by Felix Holt" (1868).

10. Charles Kingsley, *His Letters and Memories of his Life,* edited by his Wife, London, 1877, vol. I, p. 141.

11. *MEW [Marx Engels Werke],* vol. 4, p. 484.

12. He opposed, for example, the secret ballot, which he held to be "unmanly". He attacked as an "impediment to progress" the unions' attempt to fight mechanisation, and he was against compulsory arbitration.

13. Quoted in Mack and Armytage, op. cit., p. 200.

14. Mack and Armytage, op. cit., p. 260.

15. Thomas Hughes, *Tom Brown's Schooldays*; with an introduction by Naomi Lewis. Harmondsworth, Penguin/Puffin 1971, p. 31. Henceforth, references to the novel appear in brackets in the text, with the abbreviation *TBS.*

16. Jürgen Kuezynski, *Die Geschichte der Lage der Arbeiter unter dem Kapitalismus,* Berlin, Akademie Verlag 1964, vol. 24, p. 52 (my translation).

17. J. L. and Barbara Hammond, *The Village Labourer 1760-1832,* London, Longman 1920, p. 97; cf. also Eric Hobsbawm and George Rudé, *Captain Swing,* Harmondsworth, Penguin 1973 etc.

18. Hammonds [J. L. and Barbara], op. cit., p. 256.

19. Hobsbawm/Rudé, op. cit., p. 202 and Appendix II. Another area of class warfare was poaching. From 1827-30 more than 8,500 men and boys were convicted under the Game Laws. The sentence for being found at night with a rabbit net was seven years in Van Diemen's Land. Armed poachers could be hanged. Man-traps were made illegal only in 1826 and in 1831 the House of Lords voted to reintroduce them. For discussion on this point, cf. A. L. Lloyd, *Folk Song in England,* London, Lawrence and Wishart 1967, pp. 223-233, Morton, op. cit., p. 372, and Hammonds, op. cit., p. 295.

20. Hammonds, op. cit., p. 218.

21. E.g. the relevant passages in E. C. Mack, *Public Schools and British Opinion,* London 1938; Curtis and Bouldwood, *An Introductory History of English Education since 1800,* London 1966; John Lawson and Harold Silver, *A Social History of Education in England,* London 1973; Brian Simon, *The Two Nations and the Educational Structure 1780-1870,* London 1974; Ian Bradley and Brian Simon, *The Victorian Public School,* Dublin 1975.

22. On this point, cf. especially Simon, op. cit., pp. 299f.

23. Cf. A. P. Stanley's *Life and Correspondence of Thomas Arnold,* London 1846. I refer here only to the fictional Arnold of the novel.

24. It was not until the Boer War (1899-1902)—the first war which was conducted largely with the aid

of civilian "recruits" rather than professional soldiers—that the British workers, forced through unemployment to volunteer, could draw parallels between the domestic and the overseas exploitation of British capitalism.

25. "Of all the national bourgeoisies in the various countries, it is the English that has undoubtedly up to now preserved a keener class sense, that is, political sense, than any other. . . . The English bourgeoisie is neither as greedily stupid as the French, nor as pusillanimously stupid as the German. During the period of its greatest triumphs it has constantly made concessions to the workers . . . ." Engels, "The Abdication of the Bourgeoisie". In Marx and Engels, *Articles on Britain,* Moscow 1971, p. 395.

26. This view is of course far from dead in British schools: "To nationalists and constitutionalists alike it seemed intolerable that this despotic, aggressive Power, Russia, should pose as a sort of guardian of the Turkish Empire, with vague and convenient rights of interference . . ." D. Thomson, *England in the Nineteenth Century,* Harmondsworth, Pelican 1963, p. 157; on the entry of Britain into the Crimean War.

27. Mack and Armytage, op. cit., p. 21, have identified the "young master" as Cotton, later headmaster of Marlborough and bishop of Calcutta.

28. Raymond Williams, *Culture and Society,* Harmondsworth 1963, p. 79.

29. Cf. e.g. his chapter on "The Probable Future of the Labouring Classes": "The working classes have taken their interests into their own hands, and are perpetually showing that they think the interests of their employers not identical with their own, but opposite to them." And: ". . . the patriarchal system of government is one to which [the working class] will not again be subject." J. S. Mill, *Principles of Political Economy* (1848), Harmondsworth, Pelican 1970, pp. 122, 121.

George J. Worth (essay date 1984)

SOURCE: Worth, George J. "Writings about America." In *Thomas Hughes,* pp. 68-91. Boston: Twayne Publishers, 1984.

[*In the following essay, Worth investigates Hughes's attitudes toward the United States through an analysis of his nonfiction writings. In Worth's view, Hughes's impressions of American political events were predominantly shaped by his own deep-seated religious and social beliefs.*]

Hughes's attitudes toward the momentous events that were occurring in the United States before and during the Civil War were deeply colored by the same Christian commitment that marked his other work of the 1850s and early 1860s. What may be less obvious is that even after the emancipation of the slaves and the cessation of hostilities his continuing interest in America grew out of religious, social, and political convictions that also found expression in his writings about his own country.

SLAVERY AND THE AMERICAN CIVIL WAR

Three pieces of printed prose best exemplify Hughes's hatred of slavery and his advocacy of the Northern cause in the years before 1865: **"Opinion on American Affairs"** (1861), an article cast as a lengthy letter to the editor of *Macmillan's Magazine*; **"The Struggle for Kansas"** (1862), a sixty-two-page supplement to Ludlow's *A Sketch of the History of the United States*; and *The Cause of Freedom: Which Is Its Champion in America, The North or the South?* (1863), a pamphlet divided equally between the text of an important speech and some "Introductory Remarks" that expand on what he had said orally. They are of interest not only for the views they espouse but also for the mode of argument that Hughes employed.

"Opinion on American Affairs." When news of the Confederate triumph in the first Battle of Bull Run, the initial major engagement of the Civil War, reached England in August 1861, Hughes was on holiday at the Norfolk fishing village of Cromer. Even in this placid setting, he felt compelled to set down his own reaction because "all our leading journals . . . with the single exception of the *Spectator*" had been taking an unseemly delight in the rout of the Union army.[1] The resulting **"Opinion on American Affairs"** was Hughes's first published pronouncement on the Civil War; in it, he made a number of points that were to recur in his writings during the next four years.

First, Hughes insists that the widespread derision with which the outcome of the battle was greeted by significant organs of opinion in his country has "been ungenerous and unfair, and has not represented the better mind of England" (**"Opinion"** [**"Opinion on American Affairs"**], 414). The North had not been prepared for war. Nevertheless, when the Union's patient hopes for some sort of "amicable arrangement" with the seceding states finally proved unfounded, "at the word of the President the whole North rose as one man" in "as grand, as noble, a national act, as any which we have seen, or are likely to see, in our generation" (**"Opinion,"** 415), and the English people approved and admired the Northern resolve. Hughes never tired of pointing out to his audiences, first in England and later in the United States, that the establishment press and establishment politicians did not necessarily speak for the nation in their utterances on the Civil War.

Hughes grants that there had indeed been instances of dereliction of duty and panic on the Northern side, as English journalists rather smugly reported, but he points out that many of these troops "had been hastily thrown together, and half drilled" ("**Opinion**," 415) and that the general standard of conduct in General McDowell's army had been at least as high as one had any right to expect given the circumstances under which it fought at Bull Run. He reminds his readers that the Northern command had yielded to political and journalistic pressures in committing its troops to battle and attempting to advance on Richmond, the Confederate capital, before the men were properly trained. The press, particularly the English press, cannot be trusted to write responsibly of affairs about which it knows nothing. "On the news of the defeat, all the best of the Northern papers have acknowledged their error, and formally undertaken to refrain from military criticism. Our own papers are so little in the habit of acknowledging themselves in the wrong, or of abstaining from criticism, however ill-judged, on any matter under the sun, that I confess to being rather struck by this action of the American journalists" ("**Opinion**," 416).

By the late summer of 1861, relations between England and the Union were in a sorry state. Britain had declared her neutrality in the Civil War. Though there was virtually no proslavery sentiment and the government had refrained from recognizing the Confederacy, there was also very little support in England for the idea of keeping the American Union together by force of arms. Many in the North found the English position incomprehensible, and the New York press made things worse by attributing it to "low material considerations," "base selfishness," and "canting hypocrisy."[2] As Hughes notes, these fantasies of unscrupulous Northern journalists were duly reported by their equally unscrupulous London counterparts. The result of all this irresponsible scribbling was an exacerbation of feelings on the English side, and this doubtless had some bearing on the way the news from Virginia was received. Interrupting his summer vacation to write to *Macmillan's* on a matter that concerned him deeply, Hughes assumed a role he was to play on many more formal occasions during the next two decades: that of the man in the middle, trying to bring about better Anglo-American understanding by urging each nation to judge the other at its best and not at its worst. "I quite admit that the tone of the Government and people of the North has been such as deeply to grieve and disappoint every right-minded Englishman; but don't let us saddle them with the frantic slanders of the *New York Herald*" ("**Opinion**," 416).

But Hughes's fundamental point in the article is that one must look beyond the shifts in the fortunes of war and the resulting shifts in the tides of public opinion to the principle that is at stake in this conflict. "If the North were right before, they are right now, though de-

feated" ("**Opinion**," 415). That they were, and are, right—that they are engaged in a fight against slavery and for freedom, which is God's fight—there is no doubt whatever in Hughes's mind. If the North is defeated in that fight, "it will be a misfortune such as has not come on the world since Christendom arose," "the greatest misfortune which can happen to us and to mankind." Therefore, "God grant that they may hold on, and be strong! God grant that they may remember that the greatest triumphs have always come, and must always come, to men through the greatest humiliations" ("**Opinion**," 416).

* * *

"**The Struggle for Kansas**." During the late summer and autumn of 1861, J. M. Ludlow delivered a series of lectures on American history at the London Working Men's College. When these were published by Macmillan the next year as *A Sketch of the History of the United States,* the volume also contained Hughes's "**The Struggle for Kansas**," which was based on two lectures he had given to the same audience after Ludlow had concluded his.

This joining of Hughes's work to Ludlow's in one book was highly appropriate. Both of them were much less interested in detailing historical facts, dates, and personalities than they were in expounding a point of view about the direction that American history had taken from Colonial times to Secession. In their judgment as religious men who had agreed ever since their collaboration in the Christian Socialist movement on the supreme importance of applying the Gospel to political and social questions, slavery was immoral and contrary to the teachings of Jesus. They saw the Civil War, which was still in its first year, as a climactic contest in which that evil of long standing would surely be expunged, and the will of God would inevitably prevail in the victory of the North.

In launching into "**The Struggle for Kansas**," Hughes is quite explicit about his partisanship and the reason for it. "I hate slavery of every kind,—of the body, of the intellect, of the spirit,—with a perfect hatred. I believe it to be the will of God that all men should be free, and that Christ came into the world to do God's will, and to break *every* yoke."[3] The "struggle" in Kansas from its organization as a territory in 1854 until its admission to the Union as a state in January 1861 had been between the free-soilers and the proponents of slavery, and Hughes makes it plain from the outset that all his sympathies lie with the former, though he insists that he will base his argument on facts, suppressing none that might damage his case.

Why devote well over 20 percent of a book dealing with the history of the United States to the agony of a single territory during the seven bloody years it took to achieve statehood? In Hughes's view, Kansas had been a microcosm of the whole American republic, its "struggle" not only foreshadowing the issues of that much vaster "struggle which is now raging," but also illustrating "remarkably the strength and the weakness of the great nation engaged in that struggle" (**"Struggle"** [**"The Struggle for Kansas"**], 322). Though far from democratic, the government of the United States throughout the first eight decades of the nation's existence had been reasonably responsive to the will of the electorate, such as it was. This was a strength. That the electorate did not always act from the highest motives and that the conflicting interests of its component segments could be reconciled, if at all, only through political maneuvering and not on principle was a grave weakness.

Never in American history did this weakness lead to more lamentable results than in the matter of slavery, specifically with regard to the perceived need to maintain some kind of balance between the number of free states and the number of slave states in the Union. Though he might have gone back even farther, Hughes discerns the origins of the troubles of Kansas in the Missouri Compromise of 1820, by which, after weeks of wrangling, Congress finally agreed to admit Missouri as a slave state, and Maine as a free state, on the explicit understanding that slavery would be excluded from the rest of the Louisiana Purchase north of 36° 30'. Whatever the political advantages of this disposition of such a huge stretch of land between the Mississippi and the Rocky Mountains might have been, it ignored the will of "the Lord of the whole earth," and, in Hughes's judgment, that was a fatal flaw: "one of the lessons which stand out in letters of sunlight on the face of History is, that He is against all such compromises,—that He will allow no system of wrong or robbery to be fixed on any part of His earth" (**"Struggle,"** 323). Any attempt to reach a compromise between good and evil is doomed to fail sooner or later—not only because of God's displeasure with it, but also because of the deviousness and rascality of the forces of evil, which will lead them to violate its terms. As Hosea Biglow points out in a line of Lowell's of which Hughes was especially fond: "Conciliate? it jest means *be kicked.*"[4]

And indeed the Missouri Compromise did not remain "fixed" much longer than a single generation. The Kansas-Nebraska Act of 1854, rather than barring slavery from those territories as the Missouri Compromise had guaranteed, provided for "popular sovereignty," leaving it up to the people of each territory to determine on what basis they would organize their system. To the dismay of such United States senators as Charles Sumner and Salmon P. Chase at the time, and of Thomas Hughes later, this piece of legislation totally disregarded the principled arguments against slavery.

Worse than that, at least as far as the Kansas Territory was concerned, it led to a period during which each side tried by all means at its command to gain control of the territorial government so that it might make its views on the slavery question prevail. Hughes's characterizations of the contending parties make it clear which has his sympathy. The proslavery men, he remarks, had found it easy to cross over to Kansas from the neighboring slave state of Missouri. A considerable number of them came only to harass their adversaries and vote in elections, returning home when their missions were accomplished. The free-soilers, by contrast, were genuine settlers, often sponsored by high-minded emigrant aid societies as far away as New England. They were "very unlike the usual coon-hunting, whisky-drinking pioneers of the West," but rather "educated and intelligent men" who "brought with them not only civilised habits, but saw-mills, capital, and other material aid" (**"Struggle,"** 329).

Hughes devotes some fifty pages of **"The Struggle for Kansas"** to a circumstantial account of the contest that afflicted the territory following passage of the Kansas-Nebraska Act, a contest whose nature is well indicated by the term "Bleeding Kansas," which was often used by journalists and politicians during the 1850s.[5] Virtually from the start, the free-soilers enjoyed a numerical majority, but, as Hughes tells the story, their forbearance and high-mindedness put them at a disadvantage against the fraud and violence to which the proslavery side habitually resorted. Each party convened its own legislature and drew up its own constitution, so that it was difficult to tell, especially from some distance, who was actually in charge in Kansas.

Certainly in Washington the Kansas free-soilers received little understanding and less support. Two successive presidents paid no attention to their claims that they and not the intruders from Missouri represented "popular sovereignty" in the territory. When the Topeka legislature applied for the admission of Kansas as a free state in 1855, President Pierce came out in opposition, "declaring that the people of Kansas had no right to organise as a state without a previous enabling Act of Congress" (**"Struggle,"** 344). Even after the people endorsed the Topeka constitution at the polls, Pierce remained unmoved, "sanctioning the territorial (bogus) legislature which had been elected by the Missouri invaders, and declaring that the territorial (bogus) laws would be sustained by the whole force of the Government" (**"Struggle,"** 350). Federal troops from Fort Leavenworth, acting under Pierce's orders, dispersed the free-state legislature when it attempted to hold its first scheduled meeting on July 4, 1856. James Buchanan, who succeeded Pierce in the presidency in 1857, did not look any more kindly on the free-soilers than his predecessor had. Though it should have been abundantly clear by then that the prevailing sentiment in

Kansas was hostile to slavery, Buchanan accepted the proslavery Lecompton constitution, which had not been ratified by the voters, rather than the free-state Topeka one, which had. When the acting governor, Frederick P. Stanton, convened the legally elected legislature, Buchanan dismissed him.

All the considerable power of the executive branch of the federal government was thus arrayed against the opponents of slavery in the Kansas Territory. So was the judiciary: United States District Court Judge Samuel D. Lecompte was an ardent proslavery man and frequently ruled against the free-soilers. As to the United States Congress, only after years of debate that had little to do with the moral principles at issue did it finally approve the admission of Kansas as a free state in January 1861—less than a year before Hughes lectured to the London workmen on this subject.

Despite such hostility and indifference in Washington, and a great deal of chicanery and brute force close to home, the antislavery cause in Kansas did prevail, giving the lie to the old saw that might makes right. In God's world, Hughes insists, that cannot be so, certainly not in the long run. Shortly after "the free-state settlers of Kansas had reached the lowest point of their humiliation" (**"Struggle,"** 363) in July 1856, when a United States Army contingent prevented the Topeka legislature from meeting, the tide began to turn in their favor. Though sporadic guerrilla warfare continued, by the end of that year there was no doubt that they would win.

Long before the achievement of statehood and the start of the Civil War in 1861, "the struggle for Kansas" had served a salutary purpose. "The border ruffian bands had failed in their special object, but had effected much, for they had opened the eyes of the North to the meaning of 'squatter sovereignty' in the territories in Southern mouths; they had converted thousands of Democrats in Kansas and Missouri into free soilers; they had proved the truth of [Senator William H.] Seward's words, that compromise between freedom and slavery was thenceforth impossible, and had opened the great contest" (**"Struggle,"** 367).

Not only was this struggle "the beginning of the present war" (**"Struggle,"** 378), but it also helped to define the terms according to which the conflict would be waged. The Democratic party split over the proslavery Lecompton constitution "when [Senator Stephen A.] Douglas ratted" (**"Struggle,"** 379), unable to reconcile that document with his advocacy of "popular sovereignty"; this internal division led to the election of the Republican Abraham Lincoln in 1860.[6] The platform on which Lincoln ran and won, calling for "the limitation of slavery, the deliverance of all the remaining territories from the curse which had cost Kansas four years' war"

(**"Struggle,"** 379), would not have been so widely accepted in the North had it not been for the somber lessons of "the struggle for Kansas."

It must be said to Hughes's credit that, despite his strong antislavery feeling, he is not blind to the faults of the free-soilers. They were no more respectful of the rights of the Indians than the proslavery party was (**"Struggle,"** 330). Their Topeka constitution contained an article, "commonly known as the 'black law,' by which coloured people were excluded from the territory" (**"Struggle,"** 342). This was weakened in the Wyandotte state constitution of 1859 into a provision that "disfranchised the resident coloured people" (**"Struggle,"** 376), in Hughes's eyes a deplorable failure "to be thoroughly generous and liberal" (**"Struggle,"** 377). They occasionally committed atrocities, like the so-called Pottawatomie Massacre, but these were exceptional cases, occurring after severe provocation by the border ruffians.

Despite such serious blemishes, however, to a Christian like Hughes the cause of the Kansas free-soilers was undeniably just and that of the proslavery forces was undeniably evil. In this important respect, Hughes points out, "the struggle for Kansas" was exactly like the much greater struggle that is now raging. During the 1850s there was a great deal of pious talk in the United States about "popular sovereignty," but this was largely a smokescreen intended to obscure the moral issue at stake in Kansas. In 1861 the skillful propaganda of Confederate agents and their domestic supporters seeks to persuade the English, who are already indignant about such affronts as the Morrill tariff and the *Trent* affair, that the American Civil War is basically an economic and social conflict. Like Ludlow in his *History* [*A Sketch of the History of the United States*], Hughes urges his compatriots to reject such specious arguments: the truth is that "the Confederate states have seceded because they found that the North would no longer permit the extension of slavery in the territories of the United States" (**"Struggle,"** 379-80) and that the result of a Southern victory would be the perpetuation of that institution, which almost everyone in Hughes's English audience agrees in regarding as a sin before God and a crime against humanity.

* * *

The Cause of Freedom. However cogent and eloquent the arguments of Northern sympathizers like Hughes and Ludlow may have been, an influential school of thought in England continued to hold that slavery was not the main issue in the American Civil War and that it was the Union rather than the Confederacy that was trampling on liberty. On January 19, 1863, for example, an editorial in the *Times* made precisely these points. After chiding the North for the insincerity of its professed views about slavery, the writer declared "that, hating slavery, but being all unmoved by the stage tricks of Mr. LINCOLN and his friends in this matter, we look upon the American contest as a purely political quarrel, and tacitly hold our opinion that, as the cause of Italy against Austria is the cause of freedom, so also the cause of the South gallantly defending itself against the cruel and desolating invasion of the North is the cause of freedom."[7]

This editorial gave Hughes the text for a speech that he delivered ten days later before a large and enthusiastic meeting sponsored by the London Emancipation Society. Hughes insisted that, far from defending "the cause of freedom" as the *Times* argued, the Confederacy is fighting for "the cause of the most degrading and hateful slavery that has been before the world for thousands of years."[8]

Look at the leadership of the South, Hughes suggests to his audience. The blatantly proslavery and antiblack convictions of the Confederate president and vice-president, Jefferson Davis and Alexander H. Stephens, are matters of record. Particularly galling to the author of **"The Struggle for Kansas"** was Davis's role in that conflict of the previous decade. As Pierce's secretary of war, "he sent troops, turned out the free legislators, and had it not been for John Brown, and such men as he, slavery would have been established in Kansas by Mr. Jefferson Davis" (*Cause* [*The Cause of Freedom*], 11). As late as 1860, while serving as United States senator from Mississippi, Davis introduced a constitutional amendment that would have required all states to recognize that owning slaves was legal. As for Stephens, he is a man who asserts that the inferiority of the black race to the white is a "'natural and normal condition'" sanctioned by God (*Cause,* 12). Another prominent Southerner well known in England, where he has been spreading Confederate propaganda for the past year, Commissioner James M. Mason, is the same politician who drafted the Fugitive Slave Act in 1850 while representing Virginia in the United States Senate.

With such leaders, how can the Confederacy possibly be advocating "the cause of freedom"? It stands for no such noble goal but only the degraded and un-Christian motives of its inhabitants. As evidence that the Southern people as a whole are (to use a term from our own age) racists, Hughes cites the dispatches of the well-known *Times* correspondent William Howard Russell. "He and all other trustworthy witnesses describe both the people and the Government to be as deliberately hostile to freedom as any men that ever lived on the face of this earth. . . . I challenge any friend of the South to name one single leader there who is not pledged over and over again to slavery. I ask them to name one public act, one single Southern Confederate State, which is in favor of human freedom" (*Cause,*

15). Certainly the clamor in the South in favor of re-opening the slave trade, prohibited by Congress more than a half-century ago, does not sound as if it comes from champions of liberty.

No matter what the editorial writer in the *Times* and like-minded Englishmen may say, then, the Confederate cause is *not* "the cause of freedom"; rather, the conclusion is inescapable that it is the cause of tyranny.

The list of speakers at Exeter Hall on that January evening in 1863 was a long one, and Hughes was allotted only twenty minutes for his address (*Cause,* 9). As delivered, therefore, the speech could not be "a full statement of the case against the Confederate States" (*Cause,* 3); instead of amending the text when it appeared in print, however, Hughes prefaced it with some "Introductory Remarks" in order to make several additional points that he was anxious to lay before his readers.

First, Hughes alludes to the deviousness and manipulativeness of the Southern leaders, their highhandedness, "their avowed designs on Mexico, Cuba, and other possessions of neighbouring powers," and their bringing about "the ever increasing degradation, morally and intellectually, of the whole black, and two-thirds of the white population of the Southern states" (*Cause,* 4). These are points that must at least be touched on if the enormity of the Confederate position is to be properly understood.

Next, he reiterates an argument he had made at the conclusion of **"The Struggle for Kansas."** Those Englishmen who believe that the Southern cause is "the cause of freedom" need to ask themselves what the result of a Confederate victory would be. There is ample evidence in the statements of Southern leaders to indicate that such an outcome would lead to the extension of slavery "over half a continent" (*Cause,* 6). Not only would the Union break up irretrievably in that unhappy event, but the North American republic, except for the New England states, would turn "into a great confederacy, ruled by a fierce and proud oligarchy, and with slavery for its corner-stone. How will England like standing in a few years face to face with such a power as this?" (*Cause,* 8).

As delivered at Exeter Hall, *The Cause of Freedom* was a fighting speech. Hughes's "Introductory Remarks" do not soften the force of his spoken words, but they do serve to absolve him of the charge of demagoguery implicit in a hostile *Saturday Review* article about the Emancipation Society meeting.[9] He does not advocate fighting for its own sake now any more than he did in **Tom Brown's School Days** six years earlier. "War and bloodshed, blazing towns and villages, and starving people, are fearful sights. Every man must shrink from them, must long to see an end to them. But there are times when nations have to endure these things, when the stake at issue is so precious that the truest men and the gentlest women are the foremost to never their hearts to brave all miseries, to undergo all sacrifices, so that it be not lost. The present contest in America is of this kind" (*Cause,* 7).

Nor does Hughes align himself with those fiery abolitionists on both sides of the Atlantic who made freeing all the slaves the foremost of their war aims. Hughes's are much more modest. "I call any peace premature which shall not at least secure the Mississippi boundary, and shut up slavery within the Gulf States" (*Cause,* 7). A timorous abandonment of principle? Certainly not, if this statement of Hughes's is taken in the context of his whole outlook on the slavery question. Fighting as they are for this immoral institution and not for freedom, the Confederates will surely lose. God will see to that and to the ultimate destruction of slavery, which will inevitably come about once the expansionist goals of the South have been checked once and for all.

RECONCILIATION AND COLONIZATION

Hughes's efforts on behalf of rapprochement between his country and the United States did not end with the Civil War. Much as that conflict had deeply scarred the American body politic, it left a strong residue of ill feeling between Britain and America. To mention just one vexing dispute, the charges and countercharges over the heavy damage done to Union shipping by Confederate vessels built in British ports—the so-called *Alabama* claims—went on for years before the matter was finally settled by arbitration in 1872. During this troubled postwar era, Hughes did his best to induce each side to come to a more sympathetic grasp of the other's position.

* * *

Selected Minor Writings. In a magazine article published during the first Christmas season following the cessation of hostilities, Hughes strove to make English readers aware of how much their kinsmen in the North, and particularly in New England, had suffered and sacrificed on the long and tortuous path to victory. Whatever faults the Union might have been guilty of, its society had been transfigured by this ordeal, which "must ever, to my mind, rank amongst the most noble, the most sublime pieces of history of the century in which we are living," demonstrating triumphantly "the metal of which English-speaking men are made." At Christmas it was especially appropriate to show the survivors of this ordeal "that we honour, as it deserves, the work they have done for the world since the election of 1860, and can sympathize with their high hopes for the future of their continent with no jealousy or distrust, as brethren of the same stock, and children of the same Father."[10]

On the American side, there was lingering resentment of British neutrality, which had at times seemed suspiciously pro-Southern, during the conflict. Hughes's attempts to persuade the North that neutrality did not signify indifference and that the noisy English voices attacking the Union and defending the Confederacy had not spoken for the nation began as early as 1864, before the war had ended.

In that year, Hughes was asked to donate a manuscript to a fair held in New York to raise funds for the Union cause. Not only did he comply, but he also wrote an eloquent letter to the editor of the newspaper published by the fair in which, after expressing his own sympathy with the North, he argued that, with the one prominent exception of his old hero Carlyle (he might have mentioned his old friend Kingsley as well), "'almost the whole weight of English thought has been on the side of freedom.'" Largely because of the influence wielded by anonymous journalists, Hughes concedes, "'the lion's share'" of the blame for the "'estrangement and bitterness which have arisen between our countries since the war broke out'" is England's; but he does complain, in the most tactful way conceivable, "'that even the best and fairest men amongst you have never yet done justice, either to the conduct of our Government, beset as they have been with questions of no common difficulty on all sides, or to the attitude of the thinking portion of our community.'" In closing, Hughes expresses his hope for "'a closer and more hearty alliance between my country and yours, as soon as this war is over, than has been possible since we parted in last century.'"[11] When peace finally came, Hughes worked tirelessly for such an alliance.

His first trip to the United States, from late August to October 1870, gave Hughes a golden opportunity to pursue this work. Feted and lionized by his hosts wherever he went, he spent "the greater part of my time in showing them how mistaken they must be in their views as to England, else how is it that we didn't interfere and get to war."[12] In his private conversations with Americans, Hughes wanted to "help to heal wounded pride and other sorely irritating places in the oversensitive, but simple and gallant Yankee mind";[13] and, though he fended off "numerous and urgent" requests that he deliver public lectures in which he might expound his views to even more people, he finally came to believe "that I ought not to leave the country without giving one at any rate, and all my friends said that the Music Hall in Boston was the place if I only spoke once."[14]

Hughes addressed a distinguished and appreciative Boston audience on October 11.[15] His calling the speech **"John to Jonathan"** was an obvious reference to Lowell's "Jonathan to John" (1862), a statement of the Northern case directed to John Bull in the wake of the

Trent affair; and the whole lecture may be taken as a belated response to that poem, particularly to the reproach voiced in ll. 91-94:

> We know we've got a cause, John,
>   Thet's honest, just, an' true;
> We thought 't would win applause, John,
>   Ef nowheres else, from you.

It was Hughes's thesis that the Union "cause" did "win applause" in England, far more than Lowell and his compatriots realized at the time. Though there were swings in public opinion during the war, the great majority of Englishmen "were the staunch friends of the North from the very outset" (**"John"** [**"John to Jonathan"**], 84). As for the English government, its actions were not anti-Northern: the queen's proclamation of neutrality a month after the firing on Fort Sumter may have been premature and somewhat tactless, but it had been urged on her by friends of the North who "wanted to stop letters of marque and to legitimize the captures made by your blockading squadron" (**"John,"** 88). Certainly neutrality was preferable to the only feasible alternative, recognition of the Confederate States, and that the government would not accept. Now, the war having ended, England was prepared to submit the troublesome *Alabama* claims to arbitration; in any case, he reminded his audience, "the *Alabama* was the only one of the rebel cruisers of whose character our Government had any notice, which escaped from our harbours" (**"John,"** 89).

Hughes concluded the Boston address with his answer to a question raised by his "very dear and old friend" Lowell in "Jonathan to John" (ll. 109-10):

> Shall it be love, or hate, John?
>   It's you thet's to decide. . . .

England has decided, Hughes asserted. "It will be love and not hate between the two freest of the great nations of the earth, if our decision can so settle it." Apparently alluding to the general election of July 1865, three months after Appomattox, which made Members of Parliament of Hughes and John Stuart Mill and otherwise strengthened the radical wing of the Liberal party, Hughes said: "In England the dam that had for so many years held back the free waters burst in the same year that you sheathed your sword, and now your friends there are triumphant and honoured; and if those who were your foes ever return to power you will find that the lesson of your war has not been lost on them." He foresaw a time, not far distant, when these two "great nations," sharing the same heritage as well as the same language, would work together in amity to establish "free and happy communities" around the earth "in which the angels' message of peace and good-will amongst men may not be still a mockery and delusion" (**"John,"** 91).

Before a decade had passed, Hughes himself was to play a major role in founding what he hoped would be one such community.

Rugby, Tennessee. The complicated and bittersweet story of the rise and fall of the Rugby settlement in northeastern Tennessee and of Hughes's part in it has been told in considerable detail elsewhere.[16] Here we must concentrate on the one text into which Hughes poured all of his high hopes for the colony, a rather short book with a very long title: ***Rugby, Tennessee: Being Some Account of the Settlement Founded on the Cumberland Plateau by the Board of Aid to Land Ownership, Limited, a Company Incorporated in England, and Authorised to Hold and Deal in Land by Act of the Legislature of the State of Tennessee, with a Report on the Soils of the Plateau by the Hon. F. W. Killebrew, A.M. Ph.D., Commissioner of Agriculture for the State.*** Like ***The Old Church*** of three years earlier, ***Rugby, Tennessee*** (1881) was something of a pastiche, consisting largely of essays already published and speeches already delivered. It probably owed its appearance in volume form chiefly to Hughes's desire to raise funds for this American venture, his longtime publisher Macmillan having agreed to give Hughes "all the profits but a 'modest percentage to pay costs out of pocket,' in order that he might use the money for 'needed public buildings and improvements at Rugby.'"[17]

Our consideration of ***Rugby, Tennessee*** is enriched if we recall that Hughes had long entertained the notion that young Englishmen who had reached a dead end at home should think about going abroad to make a fresh start in life. Twenty years before this book was published, in chapter 35 of ***Tom Brown at Oxford,*** Tom and Hardy discussed "the advantages of emigration," which here seemed to mean getting away from old England in the company of "graceful women" and "beautiful children" and literally carving out a new and idyllic existence in some far-off primeval wilderness. Though the obviously amused narrator dismissed this utopian talk by a couple of undergraduates as "castle-building," the passage does contain an uncanny foreshadowing of Hughes's later vision of the Tennessee Rugby, especially in these two sentences: "The log-houses would also contain fascinating select libraries, continually reinforced from home, sufficient to keep all dwellers in the happy clearing in communion with all the highest minds of their own and former generations. Wondrous games in the neighbouring forest, dear old home customs established and taking root in the wilderness, with ultimate dainty flower gardens, conservatories, and pianofortes—a millennium on a small scale, with universal education, competence, prosperity, and equal rights!" (*Oxford* [*Tom Brown at Oxford*], 387).

About ten years later, during the same American journey on which he delivered his **"John to Jonathan"** speech, Hughes again reflected on the subject of emigration, this time viewing it somewhat less fancifully than he had done in **Tom Brown at Oxford.** After returning home, he contributed to *Macmillan's Magazine* a series of obviously autobiographical sketches describing an Englishman's trip by train from Niagara Falls to Sioux City along the same route that Hughes himself had followed. In the first of these pieces, the narrator asks one of his traveling companions—another Englishman, who here sounds very much like Hughes—if the fact that he has been poring over some brochures designed to lure foreign settlers to various western states means that he himself might emigrate.

No, no; my roots are too deep in the old soil. The fact is, I have several long-legged, strapping boys growing up, and, like most of the youngsters in the Old World, they won't take kindly to the beaten ways of life. Somehow, our atmosphere is electric, and the whole of society is slipping away from its moorings. Latin and Greek for ten or twelve years, and the three learned professions to follow, won't hold English boys. They will swarm off, and I, for one, can't say they're wrong. So the point is, to find where they can light with the best chances.[18]

These passages—one from the early 1860s and the other from the early 1870s—anticipate two of the major themes of **Rugby, Tennessee.** One is idealistic: life under the right conditions in the new world can satisfy the frustrated aspirations of ardent youths like Tom Brown. The other is more practical: emigration, again under the right conditions, will drain off from England an ominously growing surplus of highly educated but underutilized men. **Rugby, Tennessee** also enunciates a third important theme, which might be called political, and which builds on Hughes's earlier emphasis on the need to forge secure links between Britain and the United States: for the sake of closer understanding and friendship between the two countries, England should send "all that can be spared of our best blood into the United States."[19]

Of the three parts into which **Rugby, Tennessee** is divided, only the first consists of new material by Hughes. Appropriately for someone who contributed from time to time to the *Spectator,* Hughes named this section "Our Will Wimbles," after a character in the early eighteenth-century periodical essays by the same title. Joseph Addison's original Will Wimble, descended from an ancient family, was an accomplished, amiable, and popular man who had nothing worthwhile to occupy his time. He was "wholly employed in trifles," typical in that respect "of many a younger brother of a great family, who had rather see their children starve like gentlemen, than thrive in a trade or profession."[20]

In the final quarter of the nineteenth century, Hughes points out, England is full of Will Wimbles. There has been a "vast increase of public schools in England" and also a resurgence "of the old grammar schools . . . into new life." Such establishments are attracting not only the offspring of the aristocracy and the squirearchy, but also "sons of professional men, manufacturers, merchants," and "the aims and methods of the education they are giving have improved as rapidly as the numbers requiring it have increased" (**Rugby** [Rugby, Tennessee], 4). In Hughes's judgment, these schools have succeeded admirably not only in imparting classical learning but also in building character.

What is to be done with all the well-educated and well-trained young men they have produced? There is not room for them in "the three learned professions, the public service, and the press. Art and science . . . offer at present too few and too special careers" (**Rugby,** 5). Of those who come from the aristocracy or the landed gentry, the great majority cannot, as younger sons, hope to succeed to their fathers' titles or estates. That leaves only three other obvious possibilities, each unattractive for one reason or another: trade, manual labor, or idleness.

Whatever the virtues of commerce may be in the abstract, in practical terms it is not an appealing option for these young men. In an age when, in Hughes's not unbiased view, Carlyle's denunciations of the "Gospel of Mammonism" have been widely influential and the idea that cooperation should replace competition in business and manufacturing is gaining more and more adherents, "it is plain that the spirit of our highest culture and the spirit of our trade do not agree together" (**Rugby,** 5). At school the modern Will Wimble, even if he is himself the son of a businessman, has been taught to honor "scrupulousness—a scorn of anything like sharpness or meanness—in money matters . . . and so he is as rapidly becoming as averse to, and as unfitted for, the practices of ordinary competitive trade as the son of a squire or parson" (**Rugby,** 12). Besides, there are not as many opportunities in trade as there were in earlier, economically more buoyant, times. W. H. G. Armytage explains Hughes's glancing reference to "these last few years of deep depression" (**Rugby,** 6) by remarking that "the rise of Germany, the consequent slump of 1878-79 in England, and the shrinkage of the British share in the world markets lessened the number of outlets for the public schoolmen produced in ever-increasing numbers on the Tom Brown pattern."[21]

As to manual labor, which Hughes—following Emerson, from whose "Man the Reformer" he quotes at length—praises warmly, that is not for the Will Wimbles either, at any rate in the England of the present day. Still voicing some of his Christian Socialist convictions, Hughes does predict that the future belongs to those whom he calls "our handicraftsmen," and he concedes that "it seems not improbable that the Will Wimbles in another generation may find their best chance of satisfactory daily bread, and general usefulness, in some form of manual labour at home." Until that time arrives, however, "the handicraftsman's career is not really open to anyone not born in the ranks," because of "the jealousy and distrust of the working class, and the prejudice of their own against what would be considered loss of caste" (***Rugby,*** 20).

As unacceptable as trade or manual labor, though for different reasons, is enforced idleness. Hughes is saddened and appalled by the growing number of "fine strong fellows" with no appropriate work to do: "hopeful still, ready to do *anything,* so that they may only be independent and a burthen to nobody," instead "of first-rate human material going helplessly to waste, and in too many cases beginning to turn sour, and taint, instead of strengthening, the national life" (***Rugby,*** 6).

Having outlined the problem in the first three chapters of part I of ***Rugby, Tennessee,*** Hughes proceeds in the fourth to explain the solution he has in mind. The only course open to the Will Wimbles of Victorian England is to follow Emerson's advice and "begin the world anew, as he does who puts the spade into the ground for food."[22] Because "the present caste prejudice against manual labour is too strong" to allow them to take spade in hand at home, and because "land here is too costly a luxury" to allow them to work English ground, they "must begin, then, across the seas somewhere—the sooner the better" (***Rugby,*** 25). This means emigration, preferably to a carefully chosen setting where they can live by the values they have learned: "a place where what we have been calling the English public-school spirit—the spirit of hardiness, of reticence, of scrupulousness in all money matters, of cordial fellowship, shall be recognised and prevail" (***Rugby,*** 25-26).

As its name is meant to suggest, the Rugby settlement in Tennessee is just such a place, where an educated young Englishman will find ready access to rewarding and respected labor and to inexpensive housing and land. He will live there amid conditions that Hughes—ever the advocate of the cooperative movement and the national church—is convinced will redound to his moral and spiritual welfare, buying what he needs at a community-owned commissary devoid of "the old tricks and frauds of trade" characteristic of shops run for profit, and attending "one church which is open to all, and which invites to a common worship, being the property of no single denomination, but of the community" (***Rugby,*** 27). This community will mold the individual by bringing out the best that is in him, just as he by his exertions will help to build a stronger community.

If the above summary of part I makes Hughes's vision of the Rugby scheme sound more austere than it really is, there is no such problem in part II, "A New Home—First Impressions." This consists of reprints of eight predominantly lighthearted essays that Hughes sent to the *Spectator* in the late summer and autumn of 1880 from Tennessee, where he had gone for the official opening of the colony in his capacity as president of the Board of Aid to Land Ownership. Here, he stresses the conviviality of the community, the beauty of its setting, and the attractive qualities of the natives, and expresses optimism that his dream of a "public-school paradise" in the mountains of Tennessee will come true.

That life in this remote Rugby can be jolly is impressed on Hughes as soon as he arrives there. He is met at the little railway station some seven miles from the town site by a small band of cheerful Englishmen, unmistakably public-school products despite the frontier garb they wear, and they make a merry party of their rough ride to the settlement. This is still only a "city of the future" (***Rugby,*** 41), but the food he is served there is plentiful and the company is excellent. Hughes is astonished to find a beautifully groomed tennis court ready for play in the midst of unfinished houses and public buildings—one symbol of the settlers' determination to carry with them to Tennessee as many of the amenities of English life as they could.

The rugged, isolated Cumberland Plateau is no White Horse Vale, but this only adds to its charms for Hughes. He is enchanted by "the new flora and fauna" (***Rugby,*** 56) he encounters in the woods, and he finds that "you can't live many days up here without getting to love the trees even more, I think, than we do in well-kempt England" (***Rugby,*** 54). Having recently left "the great heat of New York, Newport, and Cincinnati," he rejoices at "the freshness and delight of this brisk mountain air" (***Rugby,*** 36).

Hughes's attitude toward the mountaineers of northeastern Tennessee is oddly ambivalent. He concedes that they are shiftless and too fond of illegally distilled "moonshine" whiskey for their own good, and he calls their women "dreadful slatterns" (***Rugby,*** 65); but he considers it "a pleasure" to get to know them, and indignantly rejects the frequent references to them as "'mean whites,' 'poor white trash' and the like, in novels, travels, and newspapers" (***Rugby,*** 61). What, then, are their redeeming features? For one thing, they were staunchly pro-Union during the Civil War. Moreover, though mostly very poor, they are hospitable and honest, and their wit—their adeptness at "quaint and ready replies" (***Rugby,*** 66)—is appealing. A late-twentieth-century reader is likely to wince at Hughes's blithe depictions of the blacks in the area as grinning darkies, but he does point out that in his experience they are marginally less lazy than the local whites and much less willing to sell their votes. There is nothing backhanded in Hughes's praise of the blacks' determination to get their children educated.

Hughes's faith in the future of this colony is perhaps best expressed in part II of **Rugby, Tennessee** in the final chapter, "The Opening Day," an account of the festivities associated with the dedication of the settlement on October 5, 1880. Presided over by the Episcopal Bishop of Tennessee, the ceremony is a most impressive one, despite a number of mishaps. When it is over and the distinguished visitors have left, those who remain behind are imbued with "a sense of strength gained for the work of building up a community which shall know how to comport itself in good and bad times, and shall help, instead of hindering, its sons and daughters in leading a brave, simple, and Christian life" (**Rugby,** 91).

As it turned out, of course, the Rugby settlement was unable to survive "bad times," but it would not be quite fair to use our hindsight to condemn Hughes for the buoyant optimism of part II or accuse him of engaging in the sort of "castle-building" for which he had teased Tom Brown and Hardy twenty years earlier. It is true that Hughes was always rather too prone to indulge in wishful thinking about his visionary schemes. To do him justice, however, we must recall that he was aware of this trait in himself. In the third chapter, for example, he raises a troubling question and immediately answers it in characteristic fashion, with ruefully qualified self-confidence. "The thought occurs, are our swans—our visions, already so bright, of splendid crops, and simple life, to be raised and lived in this fairy-land—to prove geese? I hope not. It would be the downfall of the last castle in Spain I am ever likely to build" (**Rugby,** 46).

In the final part of **Rugby, Tennessee** the tone shifts again. It consists of four chapters, alternately inspirational and practical in nature, but each making essentially the same main point: there is every reason to suppose that, if everyone does his part, this settlement can be, not a "castle in Spain," but a new Jerusalem.

Hughes begins with the text of the address he gave, as president of the Board of Aid, on the opening day of the Tennessee Rugby. Its mission, he says, is an exalted one. Uniting as it does the labors of English settlers on American soil with the financial and moral backing of men on both sides of the Atlantic, it is an outgrowth of the deep conviction "that the future of our own race; and indeed of the world, in which our race is so clearly destined to play the leading part; can never be what it should be, until the most cordial alliance, the most intimate relations, have been established firmly, without any risk or possibility of disturbance or misunderstanding between its two great branches" (**Rugby,** 93). In this "swarming time of the race," "a time of great movement of population" (**Rugby,** 95), it is especially important that this mission be carried out in accordance with carefully defined principles, and these Hughes proceeds to list.

To proclaim that Rugby will be a community is not very helpful. Such a statement may suggest, misleadingly, that it will embody the features of the kind of centralized communism advocated in Europe by Marx and Lassalle "and on this continent by very inferior, and even more violent and anarchic, persons." Nothing could be further from the truth. Throughout his involvement with the Christian Socialist, cooperative, and trade-union movements, Hughes advocated a very minimal role for government in economic life, and so he is being perfectly consistent in disavowing state socialism here, as well as in his subsequent rejection of "a paternal state, the owner of all property, finding easy employment and liberal maintenance for all citizens, reserving all profits for the community, and paying no dividends to individuals." Nor does he want anyone to associate Rugby with earlier utopian "communistic experiments here or in Europe" (**Rugby,** 96), experiments that have regularly failed.

The members of a community must have something in common, and it is necessary to explain what that something—that common spirit behind Rugby—is. In Hughes's view, it means taking "this lovely corner of God's earth which has been entrusted to us," treating "it lovingly and reverently," and using it for "the common good" (**Rugby,** 96-97). By the latter phrase, as any reader of this study will readily infer, Hughes means far more than material well-being. The development and use of land and the design and construction of buildings must be such as to educate "the eye and mind" (**Rugby,** 98). In order to get "rid once for all of the evils which have turned retail trade into a keen and anxious and, generally, a dishonest scramble in older communities" (**Rugby,** 101), business must be conducted along cooperative lines, not only in the commissary but also in the thriving cattle industry that Hughes envisages. The essential religious life of the community, too, must foster harmony and fellowship among the residents: though there will be one church, holding Anglican services, members of other denominations will be welcome to use the building "as a pledge of Christian brotherhood and an acknowledgment that, however far apart our courses may seem to lie, we steer by one compass and seek one port" (**Rugby,** 104). In short, "our aim and hope are to plant on these highlands a community of gentlemen and ladies"—not "the joint product of feudalism and wealth" one finds in a traditional aristocratic society, but rather dedicated men and women who are proud to live "by the labour of their own hands" (**Rugby,** 106) in pursuit of their common goals.

By contrast with this lofty statement, the second chapter of part III concerns itself with some very down-to-earth matters. Reprinted from an article, also called **"Rugby, Tennessee,"** in the February 1881 number of *Macmillan's Magazine,* it answers such practical questions as who should consider going to the colony, what he should take, how he can get there from England most cheaply and expeditiously, and what he can expect to find once he arrives.

But it too contains an idealistic strain. Life in Rugby will be hard, Hughes warns, but when the settler's daily work is done he will find much to occupy his mind and spirit. In a probably unconscious echo of the reference to "fascinating select libraries" in the passage from *Tom Brown at Oxford* quoted earlier in this chapter, Hughes points with special pride to the "good library" already in existence in the infant settlement. He again adverts to the contribution Rugby will make to Anglo-American friendship, adding that its location in the American South will contribute to another political goal for which all Englishmen should work. "What we English want, looking to the future, is, not only that England and America should be fast friends, but that the feeling of union in the States themselves should be developed as soundly and rapidly as possible—that all wounds should be healed, and all breaches closed, finally and for ever—for the sake of our race and of mankind. Much still remains to be done for this end, and I am convinced that a good stream of Englishmen into the Southern States may and will materially help on the good cause" (*Rugby,* 118).

Part III of *Rugby, Tennessee* also contains the text of another speech by Hughes, this one delivered at the English Rugby School on April 7, 1881. This third chapter combines the inspirational tone of the first (explaining the ethos behind the Tennessee settlement) and the practical tone of the second (explaining what life there is like), and bases its argument on the thesis of part I: that emigrating to a place like the new Rugby is the best thing a young Englishman can do if he is unable to find any appropriate outlet for his talents and his training at home after leaving an institution like the old Rugby. The fact that Hughes, now nearly sixty years of age, has returned there to address an audience of schoolboys accounts for a certain playful cast to his remarks, especially near the beginning; but it also lends a certain solemnity to his message. Abandoning for the moment his several roles as a prominent public figure, Hughes makes it clear that he is staking his reputation as an Old Rugbeian on the integrity of the vision he depicts.

Especially right after this moving speech, chapter 4 of part III may seem something of an anticlimax. Entitled "Colonel Killebrew's Report," it is a detailed account by the Tennessee commissioner of agriculture—who is, in a sense, also staking his reputation on what he is saying—of what he believes to be the economic potential of the region chosen for the Rugby colony. Marguerite B. Hamer's characterization of this report as "none too flattering" tells only part of the story.[23] What Killebrew says, in prose that is remarkably measured and matter-of-fact, is that, though the soil of the Cum-

berland Plateau is "comparatively thin and infertile," "it is far superior to any soils found in New England outside the valleys" (*Rugby,* 138); with proper cultivation and due attention to which crops will flourish there, it can be made highly productive. Moreover, because of its rail connections with Cincinnati, Atlanta, and the larger towns of Tennessee, Rugby and its environs could serve those markets with advantage. Given the abundance of timber and mineral deposits around the settlement, it might well turn into a manufacturing as well as an agricultural center. Implicit in Killebrew's statement, however, there is one very important proviso: "patient labour, guided by skill and intelligence" (*Rugby,* 159), must be lavished on this rugged virgin area if its potential is to be realized. His report indicates very clearly what "great errors and mistakes" (*Rugby,* 158) must be avoided if Rugby is to prosper.

That it ultimately failed does not detract from the soundness of Killebrew's advice—or, for that matter, from the nobility of Hughes's dreams for it.

Notes

1. "Opinion on American Affairs," *Macmillan's Magazine* 4 (September 1861): 414. Subsequent page references will be given parenthetically in the text.

2. Donaldson Jordan and Edwin J. Pratt, *Europe and the American Civil War* (Boston: Houghton Mifflin, 1931), p. 13.

3. "The Struggle for Kansas," in J. M. Ludlow, *A Sketch of the History of the United States* (Cambridge, 1862), p. 321. Subsequent page references will be given parenthetically in the text.

4. "Latest Views of Mr. Biglow," 1. 45.

5. For reliable modern accounts, see chapter 5, "'Bleeding Kansas'—the Territorial Period," pp. 61-78, in Robert W. Richmond, *Kansas: A Land of Contrasts* (St. Charles, Mo.: Forum Press, 1974); and chapter 6, "Bleeding Kansas, 1854-1859," pp. 67-79, in William Frank Zornow, *Kansas: A History of the Jayhawk State* (Norman: University of Oklahoma Press, 1957).

6. Hughes is probably overstating his case here. As the *Encyclopedia of American History* (ed. Richard B. Morris [New York: Harper, 1961], p. 227) puts it, even if the two Democratic candidates, Stephen A. Douglas and John C. Breckenridge, and the Constitutional candidate, John Bell, had "combined on a fusion ticket," Lincoln would have lost only eleven electoral votes and been left with more than enough to win.

7. *Times* (London), January 19, 1863, p. 8.

8. *The Cause of Freedom* (London [1863]), p. 10. Subsequent page references will be given parenthetically in the text.

9. "Exeter Hall and Emancipation," *Saturday Review* 15 (January 31, 1863): 141-42.

10. "'Peace on Earth,'" *Macmillan's Magazine* 13 (January 1866): 201. This article was published in the United States in pamphlet form by the Old South Work of Boston (Old South Leaflets, no. 181, n.d.).

11. Nelson F. Adkins, "Thomas Hughes and the American Civil War," *Journal of Negro History* 18 (July 1933): 328, 329.

12. *Vacation Rambles* (London, 1895), p. 146.

13. Ibid., p. 169.

14. Ibid., p. 177. Cf. pp. 169-70, 178.

15. This speech was reprinted in *Macmillan's Magazine* 23 (December 1870): 81-91; the following quotations are taken from that version.

16. Marguerite Bartlett Hamer, "Thomas Hughes and His American Rugby," *North Carolina Historical Review* 5 (October 1928): 390-412; M. B. Hamer, "The Correspondence of Thomas Hughes Concerning His Tennessee Rugby," *North Carolina Historical Review* 21 (July 1944): 203-14; W. H. G. Armytage, "New Light on the English Background of Thomas Hughes' Rugby Colony in Tennessee," *East Tennessee Historical Society's Publications* 21 (1949): 69-84; W. H. G. Armytage, "Public School Paradise," *Queen's Quarterly* 57 (Winter 1950-51): 530-36; W. Hastings Hughes, *The True Story of Rugby,* ed. John R. DeBruyn (Jackson, Tenn.: n.p., n.d.); John R. DeBruyn, "Letters to Octavius Wilkinson: Tom Hughes' Lost Uncle," *Princeton University Library Chronicle* 34 (Autumn 1972): 33-52; Brian L. Stagg, *The Distant Eden: Tennessee's Rugby Colony* (Rugby, Tenn.: Paylor Publications, 1973); W. H. G. Armytage, Introduction to Thomas Hughes, *Rugby, Tennessee* (London, 1881; repr. Philadelphia: Porcupine Press, 1975), 8 pp. unpaginated; and John R. DeBruyn, "Thomas Hughes on Eduard Bertz," *Notes and Queries,* n.s. 23 (September 1976): 405-6.

17. [Edward C.] Mack and [W. H. G.] Armytage, *Thomas Hughes* [London, 1952], p. 236.

18. "A Week in the West," *Macmillan's Magazine* 24 (August 1871): 246.

19. *Rugby, Tennessee,* p. 117. Subsequent page references will be given parenthetically in the text.

20. Joseph Addison, *Spectator* No. 108, July 4, 1711.

21. Armytage, "New Light on the English Background," p. 76.

22. "Man the Reformer," *Essays and Poems of Emerson,* ed. Stuart P. Sherman (New York: Harcourt, Brace, 1921), p. 309.

23. Hamer, "Thomas Hughes and His American Rugby," p. 408.

George J. Worth (essay date 1984)

SOURCE: Worth, George J. "Of Muscles and Manliness: Some Reflections on Thomas Hughes." In *Victorian Literature and Society: Essays Presented to Richard D. Altick,* edited by James R. Kincaid and Albert J. Kuhn, pp. 300-14. Columbus: Ohio State University Press, 1984.

[*In the following essay, Worth considers themes of "muscular Christianity" and "manliness" in* Tom Brown's School Days. *According to Worth, the novel remains noteworthy to modern scholars as a social document rather than as a work of literature.*]

In February 1858, ten months after the publication of *Tom Brown's School Days,* a writer in a respected British quarterly referred to it as "a work which everybody has read, or means to read."[1] The early publishing history of Thomas Hughes's novel seems to confirm this characterization: by the time the remark appeared in print, *Tom Brown's School Days* had already attained its sixth edition in England and come out under two different titles in the United States.[2] Reviewers, as well as readers, found the novel to be highly pleasing and highly instructive,[3] and throughout the rest of the century there was no doubt about its status as a minor classic.

In our own day, however, it can claim no such distinction. Though obviously one cannot say that *Tom Brown's School Days* is "a work which *nobody* has read," there is considerable evidence to indicate that the book is ignored by that elusive creature, the late twentieth-century common reader. To be sure, the 1981 American and British *Books in Print* do list nine currently available editions of *Tom Brown's School Days,* but closer inspection reveals that these are by and large intended for the juvenile market, bearing such imprints as Puffin Books and Dent's Illustrated Children's Classics. The suspicion that adult readers of Victorian fiction, most of whom these days seem to inhabit universities and colleges, disregard *Tom Brown's School Days* is reinforced by a perusal of the recent annual bibliographies in *Victorian Studies:* during the entire decade of the 1970s, for instance, these show only two brief articles concentrating on Hughes's novel, and one of these was published in the journal *Children's Literature in Education.*

Contemporary scholars have not totally overlooked *Tom Brown's School Days,* of course; but on the whole they have viewed it less as a novel worthy of consideration—

let alone enjoyment—in its own right than as a document in the history of something: public-school fiction, or the public school itself, or physical fitness, or the revival of the chivalric ideal.[4] Even more striking is the fact that modern critics with no visible pretensions to scholarship but with ready access to highly regarded periodicals for the expression of their opinions have heaped on *Tom Brown's School Days* a kind of abuse that can have had few parallels in the long and honorable tradition that induces men and women of letters to subject cherished books to periodic reassessment. And so Richard Usborne has exclaimed in the *Spectator* "What a thoroughly unpleasant book *Tom Brown's Schooldays* is!" and gone on to dismiss it as "generally being painful, or mawkish, or snobbish."[5] Not to be outdone, Kenneth Allsop, writing in *Encounter,* calls Hughes's novel "humid drivel" brimming over with "cruelty, conformity, and homosexuality," and Hughes himself a fool or a knave (it is impossible to be sure which) afflicted with "thick-headed self-satisfaction, fluctuating between a facetious smugness and a creepy piety."[6]

Why this neglect? Why this abuse? Such questions are, of course, impossible to answer conclusively, but there are several possible explanations. For one thing, *Tom Brown's School Days,* like the rest of Hughes's writings, is obviously dated, heavily didactic, and clumsily constructed; but then so are many other mid-Victorian novels that we continue to read, or at least to teach, and to write about with every indication of affection and respect. A more promising line of inquiry might lead us away from aesthetics into the even trickier terrain of twentieth-century British social and political history to examine the following hypothesis: because many British intellectuals, especially of the Labor and lately the Social Democratic persuasions, deplore the effect that they are sure the public schools have had in perpetuating the class system and perverting the communal life of their country, and because *Tom Brown's School Days* can be shown to have played a major role in elevating the public schools to a prominent place in the national consciousness, Hughes's modest little novel makes an irresistible target for them—all the more so because his religious convictions happen to be quite unfashionable among the majority of those who mold opinion in postwar, post-Imperial, post-Christian Britain.

This brings me to my own thesis. I shall not defend the artistic merits of *Tom Brown's School Days* (though I believe they are considerable), and I shall avoid sociopolitical pronouncements (though I am sorely tempted to slip them in). Rather, my task is a much more restricted one: I shall argue that one important reason for the low esteem in which Hughes is generally held today is that *Tom Brown's School Days,* and by extension the rest of his work, is closely associated with two interrelated mid-Victorian concepts that few now take seriously and many ridicule or condemn: "muscular Chris-

tianity" and "manliness"; that Hughes did indeed deal with both concepts, frequently and respectfully; but that he regarded them in ways that are quite different from, and much subtler than, the simpleminded attitudes often ascribed to him by those who have read him with certain biases, a long time ago, or not at all.

I

The phrase "muscular Christianity" appears to have been coined by the author of a February 1857 review of Charles Kingsley's novel *Two Years Ago*: "We all know by this time what is the task that Mr. Kingsley has made specially his own—it is that of spreading the knowledge and fostering the love of a muscular Christianity. His ideal is a man who fears God and can walk a thousand miles in a thousand hours—who, in the language which Mr. Kingsley has made popular, breathes God's free air on God's rich earth, and at the same time can hit a woodcock, doctor a horse, and twist a poker round his fingers."[7] Two months later, *Tom Brown's School Days* was published, and it was not long before reviewers of this novel began to link Hughes's work with that of his close friend. The *Literary Gazette,* for example, pointed to "the remarkable affinity" between *Tom Brown's School Days* and "the writings of Mr. Kingsley," particularly in its celebration of "the true Saxon delight in exercise, combat, and every manifestation of physical strength."[8] The *Times,* going further, applied the label "muscular Christianity" to the ideas of both novelists, but, in a generally favorable notice, did take Hughes to task for his praise of the spiritual dimensions of fighting: "We cannot but regret that everything high and holy should be invoked to the aid of the vulgar instinct of pugnacity, and that what Christianity commands should be so recklessly confounded with that which it prohibits."[9] Writing about the novel in the *Edinburgh Review,* James Fitzjames Stephen took a somewhat different line. Though he called *Tom Brown's School Days* "a very charming book" and "heartily congratulate[d] Mr. Kingsley on a disciple who reproduces so vigorously many of his own great merits," Stephen worried about one aspect of the Kingsleyan doctrine it professed: "not content with asserting the value of bodily strength, it throws by implication a certain slur on intellectual strength, which, when all is said and done, is much more important."[10] Such misgivings about the allegedly irreligious or anti-intellectual tone of its muscular Christianity did nothing to diminish the acclaim with which Hughes's novel was initially greeted, but they were indicative of much that was to come in its subsequent critical history.

Hughes had certainly given ammunition to censorious critics, of his day or ours. There is no question about it: when Tom Brown arrives at Rugby School at the age of ten,[11] he is a little animal, much more partial to outdoor sports and games and physical exercise than to studying.[12] Even earlier, he is fascinated by "the noble old game of back-sword" that is still in vogue in his native Berkshire. As Allsop reminds his readers in 1965, the players' object "is simply to break one another's heads" with the "good stout ash stick" each of them wields (1:2). Among Hughes's frequent sermon-like digressions (in themselves objectionable to post-Jamesian students of fiction), the most notorious in the eyes of Allsop and like-minded critics is his widely quoted praise of fighting: "After all, what would life be without fighting, I should like to know? From the cradle to the grave, fighting, rightly understood, is the business, the real, highest, honestest business of every son of man" (2:5).

But reading to prove a point and selective quotation fail to do justice to Hughes or to *Tom Brown's School Days.* That Tom is, and to a large extent remains, a physical rather than a spiritual or an intellectual being is undeniable. It is equally clear from a judicious reading of the novel, however, that—under the tutelage of Thomas Arnold, of the teachers at Rugby (especially the one referred to as "the young master"), and even of his fellow-pupils—Tom does develop in significant ways spiritually, intellectually, and morally while at the school, and that he goes up to Oxford with a social conscience as well. The nature of that social conscience may be beyond our comprehension today, combining as it does a full-blown Carlylean hero-worship of Arnold with an incipient Christian Socialism; but this does not alter the fact that it is manifestly there. A close look at the last two chapters of the novel should remove any doubts on that score.

As to the supposedly brutal game of back-swording, it is necessary to do two things if Hughes's feelings about it are to be properly assessed: to place his more hair-raising remarks in context, and to understand that he himself viewed this sport with considerable ambivalence.

The picture of back-swording as relentless mutual bludgeoning that Allsop paints with such relish is appreciably modified if one reads on beyond the point where he chooses to stop quoting. In Hughes's text, the phrase "to break one another's heads" is followed by a colon and not by a period as in Allsop's *Encounter* piece; the sentence continues: "for the moment that blood runs an inch anywhere above the eyebrow, the old gamester to whom it belongs is beaten, and has to stop." And the next sentence, omitted by Allsop, reads: "A very slight blow with the sticks will fetch blood, so that it is by no means a punishing pastime, if the men don't play on purpose, and savagely, at the body and arms of their adversaries" (1:2).

They do not in fact ordinarily play in order to inflict pain, either in *Tom Brown's School Days* or in Hughes's second novel, *The Scouring of the White Horse*

(1858), but rather to demonstrate their remarkable agility. And they are doing more than that. Back-swording and wrestling are traditional amusements in the Vale of the White Horse, where Tom Brown spends his early childhood and which the protagonist of Hughes's next novel visits to his great edification; by the second quarter of the nineteenth century, such diversions are indulged in ritualistically at the great feasts that periodically draw the entire community together in fellowship, and they are rich in historic associations, which the participants carry on into an age that is too rapidly becoming commercialized and in a society that is increasingly held together by a cash-payment nexus rather than by more meaningful bonds.

These celebrations, the Parson in *The Scouring of the White Horse* insists, are essentially religious observances: God intended them to be "feasts for the whole nation—for the rich and the poor, the free man and the slave." The games that have, he concedes, given rise to considerable controversy play an important role in such divinely sanctioned festivals. "The object of wrestling and of all other athletic sports is to strengthen men's bodies, and to teach them to use their strength readily, to keep their tempers, to endure fatigue and pain. These are noble ends, my brethren. God gives us few more valuable gifts than strength of body, and courage, and endurance—to you labouring men they are beyond all price. We ought to cultivate them in all right ways, for they are given us to protect the weak, to subdue the earth, to fight for our homes and our country if necessary."[13]

But these sports need to be more strictly regulated, the Parson goes on to stress. Under the surveillance of resolute umpires, the participants must subordinate their animal instincts to rules that guarantee fair play. To suppress such drives, which are necessary and healthy, would turn them into less than men; to give these impulses free rein, on the other hand, by resorting to excessive violence or outright brutality, would lead to anarchy. In this sense, the stage where back-swording and wrestling contests are held is not really very different from the playing fields of Rugby or, for that matter, from the arena in which the social and political life of the nation runs its course.

Like those contests between aging rustics, the fighting between schoolboys that Hughes depicts is also something quite distinct from what critics have read into his work. The locus classicus is chapter 5 of part 2 of *Tom Brown's School Days,* where Tom comes to the aid of his frail young friend George Arthur after the smaller boy is picked on by "Slogger" Williams, one of the duller and more brutish members of their class. Tom manages to battle this bully to a draw in a free-form contest that combines bare-knuckle boxing with West Country wrestling before Dr. Arnold's arrival on the scene puts a stop to the proceedings. Far from being an everyday event, however, this is in fact "Tom's only single combat with a school-fellow" during his nine years at Rugby; "it was not at all usual in those days for two School-house boys to have a fight."

Before the battle begins, Hughes makes the famous statement about fighting being "the real, highest, honestest business of every son of man" that hostile critics like Allsop have held against him. But Hughes's next sentence makes it clear that according to his definition "fighting" means far more than fisticuffs or brawling, taking in moral as well as physical combat and sometimes combining the two, as in patriotic or Abolitionist fervor. (If the former is in ill repute in the 1980s, the latter certainly is not.) "Every one who is worth his salt has his enemies, who must be beaten, be they evil thoughts and habits in himself, or spiritual wickednesses in high places, or Russians, or Border-ruffians, or Bill, Tom, or Harry, who will not let him live his life in quiet till he has thrashed them."

Far from advocating physical combat for its own sake, Hughes takes pains to point out that it should normally be avoided, but that there are situations in which there is no acceptable alternative. When the Slogger lays violent hands on the smaller and weaker Arthur, Tom must rescue him, even if this means a fight, or else stand by and watch Arthur absorb a beating that he has done nothing to deserve. Those who accuse Hughes of arguing in favor of blind pugnacity need to look again at the final paragraph of the chapter:

> As to fighting, keep out of it if you can, by all means. When the time comes, if it ever should, that you have to say "Yes" or "No" to a challenge to fight, say "No" if you can—only take care you make it clear to yourselves why you say "No." It's a proof of the highest courage, if done from true Christian motives. It's quite right and justifiable, if done from simple aversion to physical pain and danger. But don't say "No" because you fear a licking, and say or think it's because you fear God, for that's neither Christian nor honest. And if you do fight, fight it out; and don't give in while you can stand and see.

As Mark Girouard has noted recently,[14] one of Hughes's immediate predecessors in his praise of fighting was Carlyle; like Hughes, he gave the term a broad, and at least largely unobjectionable, meaning. In *Past and Present,* a book Hughes read while an undergraduate at Oriel and much admired,[15] Carlyle had written: "Man is created to fight; he is perhaps best of all definable as a born soldier; his life 'a battle and a march,' under the right General. It is forever indispensable for a man to fight: now with Necessity, with Barrenness, Scarcity, with Puddles, Bogs, tangled Forests, unkempt Cotton;—now also with the hallucinations of his poor fellow Men."[16] That Thomas Hughes—the school and college

athlete, the outdoorsman, the boxing and gymnastics coach at the London Working Men's College, the vigorous man of action—should be thought of as an advocate of mindless bodily strength and pugnaciousness is understandable, though wrong; to think of his idol and inspiration Thomas Carlyle, the perpetually ailing Sage of Chelsea, in that light is ludicrous.

Like Kingsley,[17] Hughes was uncomfortable wearing the mantle of the muscular Christian. In his view the term was unfortunate because it carried, then as now, certain misleading connotations. If this designation is to be applied to him, Hughes urges more than once, let it at least be defined appropriately and distinguished from that which it is not. In the eleventh chapter of *Tom Brown at Oxford,* for instance, he sets down some wry observations on the confusion that has arisen regarding the whole subject of muscular Christianity:

> Our hero on his first appearance in public some years since, was without his own consent at once patted on the back by the good-natured critics, and enrolled for better or worse in the brotherhood of muscular Christians, who at that time were beginning to be recognised as an actual and lusty portion of general British life. . . . I am speaking of course under correction, and with only a slight acquaintance with the faith of muscular Christianity, gathered almost entirely from the witty expositions and comments of persons of a somewhat dyspeptic habit, who are not amongst the faithful themselves. Indeed, I am not aware that any authorized articles of belief have been sanctioned or published by the sect, Church, or whatever they may be. . . .
>
> But in the course of my inquiries on the subject of muscular Christians, their works and ways, a fact has forced itself on my attention, which . . . ought not to be passed over. I find, then, that, side by side with these muscular Christians, and apparently claiming some sort of connexion with them . . . have risen up another set of persons, against whom I desire to caution my readers and my hero. . . . I must call the persons in question "musclemen," as distinguished from muscular Christians; the only point in common between the two being, that both hold it to be a good thing to have strong and well-exercised bodies. . . . Here all likeness ends; for the "muscleman" seems to have no belief whatever as to the purposes for which his body has been given him, except some hazy idea that it is to go up and down the world with him, belabouring men and captivating women for his benefit or pleasure, at once the servant and fomenter of those fierce and brutal passions which he seems to think it a necessity, and rather a fine thing than otherwise, to indulge and obey. Whereas, so far as I know, the least of the muscular Christians has hold of the old chivalrous and Christian belief, that a man's body is given him to be trained and brought into subjection, and then used for the protection of the weak, the advancement of all righteous causes, and the subduing of the earth which God has given to the children of men. He does not hold that mere strength or activity are in themselves worthy of any respect or worship, or that one man is a

bit better than another because he can knock him down,
or carry a bigger sack of potatoes than he.

Described in this way, seriously but not solemnly, muscular Christianity actually sounds rather engaging. Though it may be difficult for us to accept it, it should be even more difficult to rail against it or ridicule it.

II

Walter Houghton and other chroniclers of "the Victorian frame of mind" have correctly identified manliness as an important mid-nineteenth-century touchstone of virtue. Houghton himself conceives of it as part of the tradition "of the English squirearchy, both at home and at the public schools and universities, with its cult of games and field sports, and its admiration for physical strength and prowess," and calls *Tom Brown's School Days* "the classic text" of manliness.[18] There are, however, several difficulties here.

In the first place, that numerous band of Englishmen to which an admiring Hughes refers collectively as "The Brown Family" in the title of the opening chapter of *Tom Brown's School Days* contains representatives of several classes, and so one cannot really say, as Houghton does, that "the Browns are the squires of England." Second, games, field sports, and displays of physical strength and prowess, though undeniably important in *Tom Brown's School Days* and elsewhere in Hughes's work, are not all-important, as we have seen. And finally, an examination of *Tom Brown's School Days* itself reveals that Hughes's use of the terms *manly* and *manliness* is neither frequent nor specific.

Hughes calls the village boys—certainly not members of the squirearchy—with whom Tom Brown plays before he begins his schooling "fully as manly and honest, and certainly purer, than those in a higher rank" (1:3). Old Brooke, the sixth-form hero during Tom's early days at Rugby, admonishes the younger boys in their house that, though they "'get plenty of good beer here,'" "'drinking isn't fine or manly'" (1:6). In one of Hughes's numerous asides, he urges "boys who are getting into the upper forms" to remember that their juniors will view them as what we now call role models: "Speak up, and strike out if necessary, for whatsoever is true, and manly, and lovely, and of good report" (1:8). In another, he remarks on the beneficent influence of "Arnold's manly piety" (2:1) in so softening the mood of the school that boys were no longer ashamed of being seen and heard to say their prayers kneeling at their dormitory bedsides. Tom's "young master" tells him as he is about to leave Rugby that the headmaster's goal had been to enable Tom to acquire "manliness and thoughtfulness" (2:8).

My list of five examples may not be complete, but it is certainly representative, and it suggests that for Hughes in *Tom Brown's School Days* manliness may be equated with such general concepts as moral virtue and strength of character.[19] Though its first syllable doubtless grates on the ears of some, the term could conceivably be applied to right-living girls and women as well as to right-living boys and men, and it certainly goes beyond mere bodily strength or athletic prowess much as the muscular Christian excels over the mere muscleman.

Those who question Hughes's conception of manliness sometimes read back into *Tom Brown's School Days* the title, if not the contents, of a somewhat disconcertingly named work he published twenty-two years later, *The Manliness of Christ.* They might find instructive a little confession that one writer inserted into a review of *The Manliness of Christ* shortly after it appeared. Having been put off by the title, this critic went ahead and read the book anyway, and was much relieved to discover that "our feeling of dislike has entirely passed away" and that "'manliness' is not the old 'muscular Christianity,' only under a new name; but that it is humanity at its best."[20]

Despite its relatively late date, *The Manliness of Christ* is worth bringing into the present discussion because it is the one place where Hughes provides an extended definition of manliness as he understands it.[21] Having begun by praising Jesus for displaying courage and manliness, Hughes devotes some twenty pages to differentiating between those terms before launching into the chronological account of Christ's life and ministry that comprises the body of the work. Put simply, manliness is more comprehensive than courage, and neither attribute is necessarily connected with physical strength or athletic skill. Manliness, which includes such ingredients as "tenderness and thoughtfulness for others,"[22] is a distinctly human quality, though it does bear out the fact that mankind at its best both reflects and aspires to divinity. Ordinary physical courage, on the other hand, admirable and necessary though it may be at times as a component or accompaniment of manliness, is really "an animal quality" (p. 22). As for "athleticism," with which Hughes has so often been identified, he insists that it is worthless in itself—"a good thing if kept in its place," but one that "has come to be very much over-praised and over-valued among us" (p. 24)—and that, unlike manliness, it can be turned to vicious purposes: "a great athlete may be a brute and a coward, while the truly manly man can be neither" (p. 26).

There are three other important characteristics of manliness, in Christ or in the ordinary mortals for whom he serves as the supreme example. The first and most obvious is the readiness to bear pain or even death—not in the form of self-gratification we call masochism, but unselfishly, for the sake of one's fellow humans. A second attribute of manliness is unswerving loyalty to truth, which is, according to Hughes, "the most rare and difficult of human qualities," especially when we are forced to bear this witness, as Christ did, not only against the establishment but also "against those we love, against those whose judgments and opinions we respect, in defence or furtherance of that which approves itself as true to our inmost conscience" (pp. 34-35). Finally, manliness is marked by the subordination of the human will to one's sense of duty, ultimately duty to one's God: "'to do the will of my Father and your Father'" (p. 40).

Though the subject and the aim of *The Manliness of Christ* are clearly loftier than those of Hughes's three novels, it is not difficult to see how the definition of manliness it articulates is implicit in those earlier works, as they deal with Tom Brown's development at school and at college or with Richard's growth during his Berkshire holiday in *The Scouring of the White Horse.* Clearly, there is far more involved in all four books than "games and field sports," than "physical strength or prowess."

III

At the end of *The Healthy Body and Victorian Culture,* Bruce Haley points out that the "manly ideal" was a product of the Victorian age but also that "Victorian intellectuals initiated the protest against it. They did so, not because it equated health and manliness, but because it envisioned both of these so narrowly."[23] *The Manliness of Christ* could hardly be called a "protest" against "the manly ideal," but certainly it is an attempt—a largely successful one, I would maintain—to broaden it, in much the same way that *Tom Brown at Oxford* contains a telling attempt to correct and expand the popular perception of muscular Christianity.

Our understanding of what a mid-Victorian like Thomas Hughes meant by muscular Christianity and manliness is necessarily much cloudier than that of his contemporaries, partly because some of our recent reading has befogged rather than clarified our thinking and partly because in these *autres temps* we observe *autres moeurs.* To the extent that we believe we comprehend those old-fashioned ideals, many of us regard them as naive, objectionable, or risible. We are, after all, products of a culture in which a series of novels by George Macdonald Fraser celebrating the later exploits of Flashman, the odious arch-bully at Tom Brown's Rugby, has achieved considerable popularity since the late 1960s. In a few strategic places, this outrageous anti-hero openly expresses his profound contempt for Hughes, for Arnold, for Arnold's school, and for the "manly" set there, and all of his ultimately triumphant misadventures implicitly mock their values.

Thomas Hughes did indeed praise muscular Christianity and manliness, the former reluctantly and the latter with increasing precision as his career continued. If we are

to read *Tom Brown's School Days* and his other work aright, we must try to free those terms of the overtones and connotations they have taken on over the past century and a quarter, by doing what we can to recover the meanings that he himself assigned to them. If we are successful at this task, a return to, or a first acquaintance with, his writing should yield some pleasant surprises.

Notes

1. "Arnold and His School," *North British Review* 28 (February 1858): 139.

2. Edward C. Mack and W. H. G. Armytage, *Thomas Hughes* (London, 1952), p. 294.

3. See, for example: *"Tom Brown's Schooldays,"* Spectator* 30 (2 May 1857): 477-78; "Books of the Week," *Examiner,* 2 May 1857, p. 278; *"Tom Brown's School Days,"* Literary Gazette,* 20 June 1857, pp. 587-88; *"Tom Brown's School Days,"* Saturday Review* 4 (3 October 1857): 313-14; *"The Book of Rugby School, Its History and Its Daily Life* and *Tom Brown's School Days by an Old Boy,"* Quarterly Review* 102 (October 1857): 330-54; and *"Tom Brown's School Days* (Third Edition),"* Times,* 9 October 1857, p. 10.

4. John R. Reed, *Old School Ties: The Public Schools in British Literature* (Syracuse, 1964), pp. 17, 26-27; cf. Reed's "The Public Schools in Victorian Literature," *NCF* [*Nineteenth-Century Fiction*] 29 (1974): 67-69; David Newsome, *Godliness & Good Learning* (London, 1961), passim; Bruce Haley, *The Healthy Body and Victorian Culture* (Cambridge, Mass., 1978), pp. 145-55; and Mark Girouard, *The Return to Camelot: Chivalry and the English Gentleman* (New Haven, Conn., 1981), pp. 166-68.

5. Richard Usborne, "A Re-reading of 'Tom Brown,'" *Spectator* 197 (17 August 1956): 229.

6. Kenneth Allsop, "A Coupon for Instant Tradition: On 'Tom Brown's Schooldays,'" *Encounter* 25 (November 1965): 60-63. Allsop was answered by A. L. LeQuesne in "Defending Tom Brown," *Encounter* 26 (June 1966): 93-94; and by A. J. Hartley in "Christian Socialism and Victorian Morality: The Inner Meaning of *Tom Brown's Schooldays,"* Dalhousie Review* 49 (1969): 216-23. I agree with both LeQuesne and Hartley, but my discussion of muscular Christianity and manliness goes considerably beyond them. (There may be some significance in the fact that, unlike Usborne and Allsop, neither LeQuesne [an Australian] nor Hartley [a Canadian] is English.)

7. "Two Years Ago," *Saturday Review* 4 (21 February 1857): 176.

8. *Literary Gazette,* 20 June 1857, p. 587.

9. *Times,* 9 October 1857, p. 10.

10. James Fitzjames Stephen, "*Tom Brown's Schooldays.* 4th edition," *Edinburgh Review* 107 (January 1858): 193.

11. The time scheme of *Tom Brown's School Days* is neither clear nor consistent. In the first chapter of part 1, the reader is told that Tom "went first to school when nearly eight years of age," but two chapters later Tom is shown setting out for that establishment, a private school, "when he was nine years old." If the second statement is correct, Tom would have to be ten when he goes to Rugby, for he leaves his first school "in the middle of his third half-year, in October, 183-" (1:3) and is sent to Rugby almost immediately, "in the early part of November 183-" (1: 4). The statement that Tom has "grown into a young man nineteen years old" when he leaves Rugby occurs in 2:8, but the text yields no persuasive evidence that nine years have in fact passed since his arrival there. Subsequent quotations from *Tom Brown's School Days* will be documented parenthetically, with part numbers followed by chapter numbers.

12. Tom's "boyishness" is defined as consisting of "animal life in its fullest measure, good nature and honest impulses, hatred of injustice and meanness, and thoughtlessness enough to sink a three-decker" (1:7).

13. "The Sermon Which the Parson Sent to Mr. Joseph Hurst, of Elm Close Farm, in Fulfilment of His Promise," *The Scouring of the White Horse* (Cambridge, 1859), pp. 203 and 210.

14. Girouard, *The Return to Camelot,* p. 130.

15. Mack and Armytage, *Thomas Hughes,* p. 35.

16. *Past and Present,* ed. Richard D. Altick (Boston, 1965), p. 191.

17. Robert B. Martin, *The Dust of Combat: A Life of Charles Kingsley* (London, 1959), p. 219.

18. *The Victorian Frame of Mind 1830-1870* (New Haven, Conn., 1957), p. 202.

19. In *Tom Brown at Oxford,* Hughes works from essentially the same definition. For instance, in chapter 15, while sliding into an irresponsible affair with a barmaid, Tom hears "the still small voice appealing to the man, the true man, within us, which is made in the image of God—calling on him to assert his dominion over the wild beast" and bringing out his better nature, his "true strength, and nobleness, and manliness." I find Henry R. Harrington's equation of Tom's emerging manliness with sublimated sexual energy interesting but reductive and ultimately unpersuasive. See his "Childhood and the Victorian Idea of Manliness in *Tom Brown's Schooldays,*" *VNL* [*Victorian Newsletter*] 44 (Fall 1973): 13-17.

20. "Mr. Hughes on the Manliness of Christ," *Spectator* 53 (3 April 1880): 437.

21. Mention should be made here of a curious volume of extracts from Hughes's writings that was published in the United States a year after *The Manliness of Christ: True Manliness,* ed. E. E. Brown (Boston, 1880). Except for a fifteen-page autobiographical letter by Hughes, prefaced with a "Preliminary Note" by his friend James Russell Lowell, to whom the letter had been written, the book contains nothing that had not previously appeared in print. It seems clear that the American publisher, who included *True Manliness* in his uplifting "Spare Minute Series," was trading on the popularity of *The Manliness of Christ,* from which long passages are included. Hughes had nothing to do with the publication of *True Manliness* and apparently did not even see a copy until 1894. See Mack and Armytage, *Thomas Hughes,* pp. 289-91.

22. Thomas Hughes, *The Manliness of Christ* (London, 1879), p. 21. Subsequent quotations from *The Manliness of Christ* will be documented parenthetically.

23. Haley, *The Healthy Body and Victorian Culture,* p. 261.

Jeffrey Richards (essay date 1988)

SOURCE: Richards, Jeffrey. "The Making of a Muscular Christian: *Tom Brown's Schooldays.*" In *Happiest Days: The Public Schools in English Fiction,* pp. 23-69. Manchester, England: Manchester University Press, 1988.

[*In the following excerpts, Richards studies the novel's ideological underpinnings.*]

Tom Brown's Schooldays is the most famous school story ever written. It has been continuously in print since its publication in 1857 and its influence has been enormous, J. J. Findlay, Professor of Education at Manchester University, observed in 1897, 'With the exception of Pestalozzi's *Leonard and Gertrude,* **Tom Brown** [*Tom Brown's Schooldays*] is the only work of fiction which has exercised a worldwide influence on the development of education.'[1] This influence lay in the reflection, mythification and propagation of what was to become a dominant image of the public school, a place which trained character and produced Christian gentlemen. Bernard Darwin, devoting to *Tom Brown* an entire chapter in a book on the public schools in the 'English Heritage' series in 1929, wrote, 'It is often said . . . that Dickens created Christmas. In that sense it may be permissible to suggest that Hughes created . . . the public school spirit.'[2]

Precursors of *Tom Brown's Schooldays* are regularly disinterred and examined, the merits of Harriet Martineau's *The Crofton Boys* (1841) or Frank Smedley's *Frank Fairlegh* (1850) canvassed. Diligent research has even turned up two earlier schoolboy heroes called Tom Brown. But none of these books created anything like the impact that *Tom Brown's Schooldays* did.[3] Its place as the *fons et origo* of the school story remains secure. With *Tom Brown* the school story as *genre* effectively began. As early as 1861 *Blackwood's Magazine* could declare:

> The British schoolboy has become a hero. His slang has been reproduced in print . . . until it has become almost as classical as the Scotticisms of Burns, or the French that passes muster in polite society . . . The professional storytellers rejoice in the addition of another new figure to their repertory of ready-made characters; and they put in the sharp public-school boy side by side with the clever governess and the muscular parson. The discovery is due to the author of *Tom Brown's Schooldays* . . . It is no mean triumph to have been the Columbus of the world of schoolboy romance . . . It lay within easy reach, indeed, but was practically undiscovered.[4]

The ideological significance of *Tom Brown's Schooldays* is threefold, as it looks to the past, to the present and to the future. Firstly, it recalls, records and mythifies the Rugby of Dr Arnold, creating a selective image of Arnoldianism which was to be highly influential, and eclipsing the somewhat different reality. But on to his image of Arnoldianism Thomas Hughes grafted other concepts dear to himself and not especially associated with Arnold, the ideals of Christian Socialism, the ideas of Carlyle (work, hero worship) and a strongly marked English nationalism. In due course the work was to receive an additional and most potent imprint—that of Victorian chivalry. With the passing of time the pronounced religious element of the second half of the book, which had been Hughes's avowed object in writing it, was downgraded in favour of the games-playing and character formation of the first half, which were adduced in support of the later nineteenth-century cults of athleticism and imperialism. For *Tom Brown* is more than just a school story: it is a mirror of the changing nature and structure of Victorian values, a vital point of intersection between ideas that had been dominant and ideas that were to become so. It exists on two levels of distortion. Arnold's concept of 'Godliness and Good Learning' is passed through the filter of Hughes's commitment to muscular Christianity, and this in its turn feeds into the games mania and Empire worship of later decades.

The changing values and preoccupations of society and in particular the receding of the tide of religious faith led to the development of a critical view of the novel, summed up characteristically by P. G. Wodehouse in a piece for *The Public School Magazine* in 1902.[5] He claimed that the two halves of *Tom Brown* were written by two different authors. In Part 2, in the final cricket match, Tom Brown does a whole range of inconceivable things—he puts the visiting M.C.C. in to bat first, allows comic songs to be sung during the luncheon interval and admits including Arthur in the first eleven not on his merit as a player but because it will do him good. For Wodehouse, who took his cricket seriously, this proved conclusively that Hughes could not have written Part 2. Wodehouse reveals that in fact it was written by the committee of the Secret Society for Putting Wholesome Literature within the reach of Every Boy and Seeing that he Gets it. They had objected to Part 1 ('It contained no moral. There are scenes of violence and your hero is far from perfect') and so took over the writing of the rest of the book, apart from the fight with Slogger Williams, interpolated by Hughes as a concession by the society. This amusingly encapsulates the much debated view that something happened to Hughes between the writing of the two parts of the book. J. M. Ludlow suggested that the death of Hughes's eldest daughter half-way through affected him so deeply as to cause him to adopt a different tone in the second half of the book, and subsequent commentators have taken up this interpretation.[6] But it is a misconceived view and one which entirely overlooks the purpose Hughes had in writing it.

Patrick Scott's researches in the Macmillan papers have put the whole subject in perspective. He uncovered Hughes's plan for the book, which shows that he had already written several of the key religious episodes before his daughter's death (Arthur praying in the dormitory and being abused, Tom getting some new ideas about the Bible, Arthur's illness and recovery, East and Tom discussing religion). The change of mood and tone had always been part of Hughes's scheme.[7] For, as he said in the preface added to the sixth edition, in response to those critics who chided him for preaching, 'My sole object in writing was to preach to boys.'

Scott argues convincingly that the book is entirely coherent and consistent if seen in terms of Tom's moral evolution from feckless and thoughtless eleven-year-old to thoughtful, mature Christian gentleman. Scott does much to eliminate the false dichotomy between the idea of Part 1 as realistic and Part 2 as pious fiction. But he perhaps overstates his case when he says that:

> The piety and highmindedness of Part 2 of *Tom Brown's Schooldays* was a true presentation of Arnold's Rugby as Hughes would have experienced it, while the gentlemanly philistinism of the first part, au-

thentic enough in its outline, is much closer to previous literary simplification of life at Rugby School. The historian will find safer evidence of Arnold's Rugby in Part Two than in Part One, splendid as that is.[8]

It would be truer to say that the two conventions existed side by side. Many boys passed through the school uninfluenced by Dr Arnold. Bullying, drinking and poaching continued and there were punitive expulsions aimed at eliminating it.[9] Indeed, Thomas Hughes's idolised elder brother George was one of those expelled because as a prefect he had failed to punish those who had broken an Italian's plaster casts. Arnold explained to George's father that he believed that 'those praeposters who had been more active in enforcing the school routine have been unjustly treated with contempt and insult by a larger party of the boys—in fact, either bullied or cut.'[10] Gentlemanly philistinism remained a feature of some Rugby circles and indeed is celebrated by a younger contemporary of Tom Hughes, George Alfred Lawrence, who entered Rugby in 1841 and published in 1857, the same year as ***Tom Brown's Schooldays,*** his novel *Guy Livingstone.* The hero, first seen at Rugby, is a hard-riding sportsman, who lays an enemy out with a brass candlestick, does as little work as possible and flirts with the headmaster's wife. *Blackwood's Magazine* singled out these opening scenes at Rugby for praise for their realism.[11]

Hughes's novel needs to be seen as part of the continuing ideological battle to secure the victory of Christian gentlemanliness over other forms, particularly the Regency sporting tradition epitomised by Lawrence. In writing ***Tom Brown*** Hughes was consciously using the novel as a vehicle for ideas, as did so many eminent Victorians, among them F. D. Maurice (*Eustace Conway*), John Henry Newman (*Loss and Gain*), Cardinal Wiseman (*Fabiola*), James Anthony Froude (*Nemesis of Faith*), Benjamin Disraeli and Charles Kingsley. Novels were in the nineteenth century, in a way they no longer are, part of the intellectual and moral debate. . . .

Three parallel themes are explored in ***Tom Brown*** and they are central to Victorian culture and society. The first is Tom's socialisation into the institution, his acceptance of hierarchy, privilege and responsibility; the second is the inculcation of manliness, and the third his religious awakening. ***Tom Brown*** is, first of all, a classic exposition of the socialisation of the English public school boy, a detailed account of the moral and spiritual education of an ideal and idealised Christian gentleman. It fits precisely the model of socialisation outlined by Ian Weinberg.

Socialisation. In Weinberg's model the new boy is subject initially to *rites de passage,* systematic humiliations involving compulsory singing, bullying and fagging.[12]

This serves 'to erase all of his former statuses, whether of family, class or preparatory school. He loses his means of defence against the institution and is a *tabula rasa* for a new "total identity" to be imprinted by the public school. Any confidence or rebelliousness is drubbed out of him.' The new boy is also instructed in the layout, lore and slang of the school, which signals his acceptance into the new community.

Once the new boys have become established they enter the middle phase of their school existence, when they have integrated into the school but not yet achieved the authority of the prefectorial elite. It is at this stage that they rebel against the authority of the older boys and the masters, and bully smaller boys. Weinberg observes, 'The boys in the middling stratum are the most troublesome because they are gaining their full physical strength and they wish to test their independence in an environment which is now familiar.' Rebellion can take different forms—withdrawal into oneself and out of the system, breaking the rules (against smoking, bounds, sexual activity) or withdrawal into intellectual pursuits and eccentricity, something which Weinberg notes is 'tolerated and perhaps even respected'.

The school has ways of dealing with rebellion, however. One is close supervision and the enforcement of rules by prefects and masters. Another is 'emphasising *superordinate* goals in daily activities', in particular loyalty to the school and house in sporting and academic competition. But it is also helped in part by the boys themselves, who develop a set of codes in order to survive, codes which 'serve to protect the inmate's self against authority, and make it easier to live a nonprivate life among peers'. This involves not stealing from or cheating other boys, bearing irritation with self-control, not 'squealing' on other boys and asserting 'manliness' via sport in order to define oneself as a male at a time of segregation from the opposite sex. But these norms have the effect of stabilising rather than disrupting traditional rules and procedures, and because the norms are a form of social control imposed by the boys on each other they enable headmaster and staff to keep aloof from the petty details of routine and discipline.

In due course the rebellious phase ends with acceptance into the elite, the prefects. For, despite the rebellion, the boy in general 'accepts the institution's view of him and conforms to its demands'. Boys recognise and accept the hierarchy of school society in the expectation of eventual accession to the elite.

Tom Brown thus begins with Tom's emancipation from the family and the protection of womenfolk and his emergence into a world of boys, first by playing with the village boys and then attending a private school, characterised by bullying, tale-telling, inadequate supervision and a defective educational philosophy which contrasts with that of Rugby: 'The object of all schools is not to ram Latin and Greek into boys but to make them good English boys, good future citizens.'[13]

When the private school closes on account of fever, Tom is sent to Rugby (the year is 183-). His father, Squire Brown, meditates on what to tell Tom:

> Shall I tell him to mind his work, and say he's sent to school to make himself a good scholar? Well but he isn't sent to school for that—at any rate, not for that mainly. I don't care a straw for Greek particles or the digamma; no more does his mother . . . If he'll only turn out a brave, helpful, truthtelling Englishman and a gentleman and a Christian, that's all I want.[14]

So his advice to Tom is 'Tell the truth, keep a brave and kind heart and never listen to or say anything you wouldn't have your mother and sister hear, and you'll never feel ashamed to come home or we to see you.' So the agenda for education is clearly set out and parallels exactly Dr Arnold's statement that his avowed aim was to create 'a school of Christian gentlemen'. Arnold sought to instil in his pupils 'first, religious and moral principle; second, gentlemanly conduct; third, intellectual ability'.[15] Arnold intended that the list should be in ascending order of importance, the first two being an essential preparation for the third. Hughes, however, takes it in descending order of importance, with intellect seen as much less important than conduct. This in a sense encapsulates the distortion of Arnoldianism which *Tom Brown's Schooldays* represents.

By the end of the book Tom has reached an acceptance and understanding of his father's educational goals for him, as he tells Arthur:

> I want to be A1 at cricket and football and all other games . . . I want to carry away just as much Latin and Greek as will take me through Oxford respectably . . . I want to leave behind me the name of a fellow who never bullied a little boy or turned his back on a big one.[16]

His process of socialisation follows exactly the pattern laid down by Weinberg. First there are the *rites de passage*. East takes Tom round the school, explaining rules and practices, dress regulations and *mores*. Then there is house singing, with each new boy placed on the table in turn and made to sing a song on penalty of drinking a large mug of salt and water if he resists or breaks down. There is fagging, into which Tom enters cheerfully, and bullying, with Tom tossed in a blanket by Flashman and company on his first day, but pluckily taking it.

The middle-school phase of rebellion comes next. Discipline in School House breaks down once Old Brooke leaves. The new praeposters are either small, clever boys with neither the strength of body or character to

govern (i.e. intellect without character) or big boys of the wrong sort with no sense of responsibility (i.e. strength without character). So there is bullying, as fifth-form boys of the sporting and drinking set who have age and experience but not yet authority join forces with irresponsible praeposters to tyrannise over younger boys. This leads to the celebrated roasting of Tom. But Tom and East organise resistance to the fagging, take on and fight Flashman and the bullying declines, particularly after Flashman is expelled for being found hopelessly drunk.

But Tom and East not only rebel against bullying, they also rebel against rules and authority in that demonstration of independence and muscle-flexing that Weinberg postulates. Tom and East become outlaws, 'Ishmaelites, their hands against everyone and everyone's hands against them'. They break bounds, fish illegally and, when caught, are flogged.

The eccentrics also fulfil the role perceived by Weinberg. At Rugby Diggs and Martin are loners, pursuing their interests (naturalism, chemistry) outside the usual schoolboy range, and are left alone. They also intervene, Diggs to protect Tom and East from Flashman and Martin to defend Arthur.

The school's way of dealing with rebellion are all implemented. The inculcation of house loyalty begins on the first day, when Tom participates in the big game between the School House and the rest of the school, post-game feast and sing-song. He witnesses the keynote speech of house captain, Old Brooke, with the toast: 'dear old School House—the best house of the best school in England'. This prompts one of Hughes's many homiletic asides to his reader, apologising for his excessive school patriotism, but adding, 'Would you, any of you, give a fig for a fellow who didn't believe in and stand up for his own house and his own school,' assuming a common experience in his readers.[17] The boys' code is seen in force with Tom admired for not sneaking to the masters on his ill treatment by Flashman. Indeed, Tom's conduct in the face of gross ill treatment, his acceptance and silence about it, help shame some of the bullies. Finally, there is magisterial supervision. The Doctor watches over the career of Tom and East, warns them that they are in danger of expulsion if they carry on as they are doing and rescues Tom from perdition by assigning the frail and timid new boy George Arthur to his care, causing him to blossom into a new sense of responsibility. Tom ends up as captain of cricket, pillar of the school and exponent of all the virtues and values of the public school system.

Manliness. Hughes was well aware of the boy's need to assert and demonstrate his masculinity, and his book therefore sought to advocate a particular form of manliness. The form which Hughes espoused was that which was satirically labelled 'muscular Christianity' and of which he and Charles Kingsley were the most celebrated exponents. Kingsley disliked the term but Hughes willingly embraced it, providing a very careful definition of it in *Tom Brown at Oxford,* distinguishing muscular Christians from those whom he calls mere 'musclemen':

> The only point in common between the two being, that both hold it to be a good thing to have strong and well-exercised bodies, ready to be put at the shortest notice to any work of which bodies are capable, and to do it well. Here all likeness ends; for the 'muscleman' seems to have no belief whatever as to the purposes for which his body has been given him, except some hazy idea that it is to go up and down the world with him, belabouring men and captivating women for his benefit or pleasure, at once the servant and fomenter of those fierce and brutal passions which he seems to think it a necessity, and rather a fine thing than otherwise, to indulge and obey. Whereas, so far as I know, the least of the muscular Christians has hold of the old chivalrous and Christian belief, that a man's body is given him to be trained and brought into subjection, and then used for the protection of the weak, the advancement of all righteous causes and the subduing of the earth which God has given to the children of men.[18]

This clearly points to the context within which Hughes was preaching, an ideological contest between rival versions of manliness. It was one in which indeed Hughes can be said to have joined battle with an influential fellow Rugbean, George Alfred Lawrence.

Few areas of Hughes's writing have become so controversial as Part 2, chapter 5, of *Tom Brown,* with its graphic account of the fight between Tom and Slogger Williams and its long disquisitions on the value of fighting. But passages from this chapter are regularly taken out of context to demonstrate that Hughes was progenitor of a brutal philistinism.[19] The most celebrated are:

> After all, what would life be without fighting, I should like to know? From the cradle to the grave, fighting, rightly understood, is the business, the real, highest, honestest business of every son of Man.[20]

and:

> Boys will quarrel and when they quarrel, they will sometimes fight. Fighting with fists is the natural and English way for English boys to settle their quarrels. What substitute for it is there, amongst any nation under the sun?[21]

But critics of Hughes almost invariably omit his qualifications. 'Fighting, rightly understood' is the key phrase. He goes on to give a broad definition of fighting: 'Everyone who is worth his salt has his enemies who must be beaten, be they evil thoughts and habits in himself or spiritual wickednesses in high places, or Russian or border-ruffians, or Bill, Tom or Harry, who will not let him live his life in quiet till he has thrashed them.'[22]

'Struggle' might be a better word than fighting, for Hughes's fighting includes self-conquest, moral crusading, imperial defence and self-defence. His second passage continues:

> As to fighting, keep out of it if you can by all means. When time comes, if it ever should, that you have to say 'Yes' or 'No' to a challenge to fight, say 'No' if you can . . . It's proof of the highest courage and one from true Christian motives. It's quite right and justifiable if done from a simple aversion to physical pain and danger. But don't say 'No' because you fear a licking, and say or think it's because you fear God, for that's neither Christian nor honest.[23]

Now this is very far from being an unqualified endorsement of brutishness. It is a clear desire to direct man's natural aggressive instincts into proper, productive channels. Hughes advocated boxing as much for its efficacy in keeping men fit as for its use in fighting. He was himself a keen exponent and taught it at the Working Men's College. In his definition of fighting he was following his mentor, Carlyle, who wrote:

> Man is created to fight; he is perhaps best of all definable as a born soldier; his life 'a battle and a march' under the right General. It is for ever indispensable for a man to fight: now with Necessity, with Barenness, Scarcity, with Puddles, Bogs, tangled Forests, unkempt Cotton—now also with the hallucinations of his poor fellow Men.[24]

The idea that Hughes advocated merely physical courage and athletic proficiency is wholly bogus: that was the ethic of his rivals. That great set piece, the fight between Tom and Slogger Williams, is provoked by the bullying of Arthur and ends with the combatants shaking hands—the quintessence of muscular Christianity, fighting for a just cause and as a last resort. It is the promotion of an ethic of fighting which seeks to civilise and humanise the sheer brutality and cruelty of life in the unreformed public school and to counteract the neo-Regency aristocratic philistinism of Lawrence and his school of writers.

Hughes elaborated further on manliness in *The Manliness of Christ,* which he defined not just as physical courage or athletic proficiency. He defined it as tenderness and thoughtfulness for others, readiness to bear pain and even death, unswerving loyalty to truth, subordination of the human will to one's sense of duty. Tom Brown embodies these qualities exactly. Hughes adds; 'True manliness is as likely to be found in a weak as in a strong body . . . a great athlete may be a brute or a coward, while a truly manly man can be neither'.[25] Nor is manliness an exclusive attribute of the upper class. Hughes gives examples of it from all classes: imperial episodes of self-sacrifice by ordinary soldiers in the storming of Badajoz and the sinking of the *Birkenhead,* miners at Pontypridd working day and night to rescue friends, a gambler at St Louis losing his life rescuing women and children from a fire. In ***Tom Brown*** the village boys Tom plays with are described as 'manly' and so too are Dr Arnold and Arthur's clergyman father.

This is Christian Manliness, whose emergence has been sensitively and sympathetically traced by Norman Vance.[26] It emerged from the religious upheavals of the mid-Victorian period, in particular the dispute between Kingsley and John Henry Newman about the nature of Christianity. Kingsley could not accept the rejection of the physical world that Newman was advancing, stressing instead the importance of direct Christian action in the world. He was equally opposed to the promotion of celibacy, asceticism and what he saw as 'fastidious, maundering, die-away effeminacy'. So Kingsley articulated a comprehensive alternative world view in his novels, where discussions of contemporary social and political problems rubbed shoulders with satire, moralising and *mens sana in corpore sano* propaganda. The principal elements in this world view were the promotion of physical strength, courage, health, the importance of family life and married love, the elements of duty and service to mankind and the scientific study of the natural world to discover the divine pattern of the moral universe. Hughes differed in some respects from Kingsley, and Kingsley himself differed from the mainstream of manliness advocates by laying stress on the particular importance of married love, something which undoubtedly proceeded from his own highly sexed nature. He placed rather less emphasis on the romantic male friendships that figured strongly in other manly writings, such as those of Hughes.

The ideas of Christian manliness were derived from various intellectual influences, notably Samuel Taylor Coleridge, Thomas Carlyle, Thomas Arnold and F. D. Maurice, whom Vance calls 'traditionalist Radicals'. They rejected the triumphalist gospel of material progress associated with Macaulay and asserted more important moral, spiritual and cultural values, based on the gospel of work, the worship of heroes, the celebration of God in nature, an idealised vision of the past, the promotion of cross-class sympathy. They were not revolutionaries. Arnold's prescription for revolutionaries was 'Flog the rank and file and fling the ringleaders from the Tarpeian rock'.[27] In sum, the aim of Christian Socialists was the regeneration, purification and redirection of the nation through a loving, committed and socially active Christianity, creating the kingdom of God on earth.

Christian manliness was, however, up against an older ideal of manliness, that of the Regency sporting ethic, celebrated by Pierce Egan, which involved physical prowess, courage and endurance but also drinking, gambling and brutality.[28] It was centred on such cruel pursuits as prizefighting, cock-fighting and dog-fighting.

Appealing as they did to all classes, these pursuits were seen as democratic, patriotic and the source of national strength. This ethic, which linked the aristocracy and the lowest classes, was the ethic characterising the unreformed public school. It was to be driven underground by the purification of society under the impact of Evangelical respectability, but it maintained its hold, with a chivalric veneer, in the novels of G. A. Lawrence, which highlighted war, sport and fighting, and featured hard-riding, hard-drinking, two-fisted, anti-intellectual, godless aristocratic snobs. *The Saturday Review* (12 September 1857) described Guy Livingstone as 'a hero of the iron kind, unequalled for strength of body, will and temper—in boxing and riding, a demigod to his sporting set, and heroically and Byronically overbearing and insolent to the world in general': the epitome of the muscle man.

Games. A vital role in the creation of the muscular Christian was taken by sports and games, properly organised and played.[29] This is the second key element of the book. Early on, Hughes sings the praises of backswording and wrestling, old country pursuits, which are falling into desuetude but which he wants to preserve as bulwarks of manliness, to 'try the muscles of men's bodies and the endurance of their hearts, to make them rejoice in their strength'.[30] But sport also promotes qualities of character. Hughes shows strutting, arrogant Joe Willis beaten by an older man who demonstrates the athletic skill, discipline and moderation in victory that Hughes wants to see in public school sport.

Hughes praises the old stagecoach rides at the expense of the soft and safe train travel boys now enjoy. Those rides tested endurance. Tom's endurance is also tested by the tossing and roasting he uncomplainingly endures. But, more important, he takes part in games, from the very day of his arrival and immediate participation in the rugby match between the School House and the rest of the school.

> 'Are you ready?' 'Yes.' And away comes the ball kicked high in the air, to give the School time to rush on and catch it as it falls. And here they are amongst us. Meet them like Englishmen, you Schoolhouse boys, and charge them home. Now is the time to show what mettle is in you—and there shall be a warm seat by the hall fire, and honour, and lots of bottled beer tonight, for him who does his duty in the next half-hour. And they are well met. Again and again the cloud of their players-up gathers before our goal and comes threatening on, and Warner or Hedge, with young Brooke and the relics of the bulldogs, break through and carry the ball back; and old Brooke ranges the field like Job's warhorse, the thickest scrummage parts asunder before his rush, like the waves before a clipper's bows; his cheery voice rings over the field, and his eye is everywhere. And if these miss the ball, and it rolls dangerously in front of our goal, Crab Jones and his men have seized it and sent it away towards the sides with

the unerring drop-kick. This is worth living for; the whole sum of schoolboy existence gathered up into one straining, struggling half-hour, a half-hour worth a year of common life.[31]

Old Brooke's farewell speech to the School House at the sing-song is an important statement of the value of team games:

Why did we beat em? . . . It's because we've more reliance on one another, more of a house feeling, more fellowship than the School can have. Each of us knows and can depend on his next-hand man better—that's why we beat 'em today. We've union, they've division—there's the secret. (Cheers.)[32]

Games promote team spirit and fellowship. Brooke wants this unity kept up and therefore denounces the evils in School House, which are clearly the opposite of healthy games-playing and team spirit; bullying ('There's nothing breaks up a house like bullying'), drinking ('drinking isn't fine or *manly,* whatever some of you may think of it'; my italics) and opposition to the Doctor's attempts to suppress disreputable old customs.

The same theme recurs at the end of the book in the description of the climactic cricket match. Tom, now nineteen, is captain of cricket, a praeposter, and he talks to the Young Master about cricket:

'It's more than a game. It's an institution,' said Tom.

'Yes,' said Arthur, 'the birthright of British boys old and young, as *habeas corpus* and trial by jury are of British men.'

'The discipline and reliance on one another which it teaches is so valuable, I think . . . it merges the individual in the eleven; he doesn't play that he may win but that his side may.'[33]

The genuinely joyous celebrations of sport were one of the reasons for the book's continuing popularity.

Arnoldianism. The third key aspect of the book, perhaps the most significant in Hughes's eyes, was the religious and moral education of Tom under the guidance of Dr Arnold. As Hughes noted in the preface to the sixth edition, 'He taught us that life is a whole, made up of actions and thoughts and longings, great and small, noble and ignoble; therefore the only true wisdom for boy or man is to bring the whole life into obedience to Him whose world we live in, and who has purchased us with His blood.'[34]

When Tom first arrives at Rugby the Doctor's power is still not fully established. He is unpopular because of his attempts to eradicate old customs. 'There are no such bigoted holders by established forms and customs, be they never so foolish and meaningless, as English school boys,' says Hughes. There was a minority, 'often

so small a one as to be countable on the fingers of your hand', totally in sympathy with the doctor's message. But 'he was looked upon with great fear and dislike by the great majority even of his own house.'[35]

But Arnold's success with Tom is to be the measure of his success with the school at large. The Doctor's first substantive appearance in the book is when he preaches in chapel and his sermon is a crucial and vivid setpiece, the first step in Tom's spiritual awakening:

What was it that moved and held us, the rest of the three hundred reckless, childish boys, who feared the Doctor with all our hearts, and very little besides in heaven and earth; who thought more of our sets in school than of the Church of Christ and put the traditions of Rugby and the public opinion of boys in our daily life above the laws of God.

The Doctor's success lay in the image he presented, not of a man giving advice and warning from above, but:

the warm, living voice of one who was fighting for us and by our sides and calling on us to help him and ourselves and one another.[36]

He fought against 'whoever was mean and unmanly and unrighteous in our little world' and brought home steadily to a boy the meaning of his life, depicting life as:

a battlefield, ordained from of old, where there are no spectators but the youngest must take his side, and the stakes are life and death. And he who roused this consciousness in them, showed them at the same time, by every word he spoke in the pulpit, and by his whole daily life, how that battle was to be fought, and stood there before them their fellow soldier and the captain of their band . . . it was this thoroughness and undaunted courage which more than anything else won his way to the hearts of the great mass of those on whom he left his mark and made them believe first in him, and then in his Master. It was this quality above all others which moved such boys as our hero, who had nothing whatever remarkable about him, except excess of boyishness: by which I mean animal life in its fullest measure, good nature and honest impulses, hatred of injustice and meanness, and thoughtlessness enough to sink a three-decker.[37]

As a result of these sermons, Tom 'hardly ever left chapel on Sunday evenings without a serious resolve to stand by and follow the doctor'. This certainly provides justification for Arnold's decision to make the chapel central to school life, to take on the chaplaincy himself and to stress Christian principles as the basis of life.

The image Arnold presented was a stern one. As an Old Rugbeian, Theodore Walrond, recalled, 'In his government of the school he was undoubtedly aided by a natural sternness of aspect and manner,' which made 'all his relations with his pupils rest on a background of awe'.[38]

But Hughes also contrived to soften and humanise the Doctor. His very first appearance in the book is when he and his family attend the House game and cheer the team, seeming 'as anxious as any boy for the success of the School House'. Arnold certainly encouraged games and sports for exercise and fitness but was not especially interested in them and certainly not associated with the cult of athleticism. But his appearance here was to lead to his association with the cult in later years. When Tom and 'Tadpole' Hall are lost at 'hare and hounds' and return to the school late, bedraggled and anticipating punishment, Arnold greets them kindly and concernedly, and does not punish them. Arnold is seen in the bosom of his family, carrying a wooden boat, a scene that was 'kindly and homely and comfortable'. Later still Tom joins the Arnold family for tea, and, when the Doctor arrives, 'how frank and kind and *manly* was his greeting'.[39] All this serves to round out the preacher and pedagogue as family man, sports-lover and mentor.

The Doctor is seen in action, working with the sixth form. In one vignette a gross case of bullying occurs, deserving expulsion. The Doctor sends for Holmes, a praeposter, and invokes his aid. Holmes lectures the house on bullying and the bully is beaten. Years later the bully thanks him for making a man of him by the beating, 'the turning point in his character'. He intervenes similarly and also by indirect means to save Tom.

The Doctor, who makes it his business to know about all the boys in the school, their appearance, habits, companions, becomes concerned about Tom and East in their rebellious phase. His solution is to put Tom in charge of George Arthur, a delicate, fatherless child of thirteen new to the school. The second phase of Tom's spiritual education now begins. Tom protects Arthur from bullying and is much mocked for it. When the homesick Arthur kneels to pray in the dormitory and a slipper is thrown at him, Tom retaliates on his behalf. Later Tom himself starts to pray and other boys follow suit. Hughes comments:

> It was no light act of courage in those days, my dear boys, for a little fellow to say his prayers publicly, even at Rugby. A few years later when Arnold's *manly* piety had begun to leaven the school, the tables turned; before he died, in the school-house at least, and I believe in the other house, the rule was the other way. [Italics mine.][40]

Arthur reads his Bible daily, and Tom and East start to do so too. When Arthur is recovering from a near fatal bout of fever he appeals to Tom not to use cribs in his lessons because it is not honest; Tom agrees.

The role of Arthur, much mocked in later, more secular years, is in fact crucial, for it provides the complement to Tom's healthy boyishness. Just as Arthur's influence on Tom and East is spiritually beneficial (Bible-reading, prayer), so theirs on him is physically improving (cricket, swimming, running). Arthur symbolises adult responsibility, spirituality, commitment, the necessary counterbalance to the sturdy manliness, decent instincts and robust common sense of Tom. He is almost the Soul to Tom's Body.

Arthur's influence on Tom is reflected and extended in Tom's influence on East. East admits that he has never been confirmed and does not take the sacrament. Tom persuades him of the value of the sacrament, something that makes you feel part of the great struggle for good. He sends him to see the Doctor and East returns transfigured:

> 'You can't think how kind and gentle he was, the great grim man, whom I've feared more than anybody on earth . . . I can hardly remember what he said, yet; but it seemed to spread round me like healing and strength and light, and to bear me up, and plant me on a rock, where I could hold my footing and fight for myself.'[41]

So by a combination of the Doctor's teachings, the influence of Arthur, his family background and his own innate decency Tom is transformed into an ideal Christian gentleman, unable to do anything but fight for the underdog: 'It was a necessity with him, he couldn't help it any more than he could eating or drinking. He could never play on the strongest side with any heart at football or cricket, and was sure to make friends with any boy who was unpopular or down on his luck.'[42]

At the very end of his career Tom learns from the Young Master that all along Arnold has watched over and guided him, and that separating him from East and putting him with Arthur was his means of ensuring that Tom would get 'manliness and thoughtfulness':

> Up to this time, Tom had never wholly given in to, or understood the Doctor. At first he had thoroughly feared him. For some years, he had learnt to regard him with love and respect and to think him a very great and wise and good man. But, as regarded his own position in the School, of which he was no little proud, Tom had no idea of giving anyone credit for it but himself; and truth to tell, was a very self-conceited young gentleman on the subject . . . It was a new light to him to find that, besides teaching the sixth and governing and guiding the whole school, editing classics, and writing histories, the great Headmaster had found time in those busy years to watch over the career, even of him, Tom Brown, and his particular friends—and, no doubt, of fifty other boys at the same time; and all this without taking the least credit to himself, or seeming to know, or let anyone else know, that he ever thought particularly of any boy at all. However, the Doctor's victory was complete from that moment over Tom Brown at any rate . . . there wasn't a corner of him left which didn't believe in the Doctor.[43]

Soon after, the Doctor dies and the book ends with Tom's moving visit to his tomb and his grief over the loss of the hero who had made him realise his true mission in life.

So the book enshrines the picture of Arnold as the great apostle of the Christian life. How accurate was Hughes's depiction of Arnold's views? Dean Stanley, Arnold's biographer and one of his most famous pupils, claimed that he did not recognise the life of Rugby depicted by Hughes.[44] One of Arnold's masters, James Prince Lee, later Bishop of Manchester, was horrified by the misrepresentation of Arnold's mode of dealing with boys.[45] Matthew Arnold, the Doctor's son, said, 'It gives only one side, and that not the best side, of Rugby School life, or of Arnold's character. It leaves out of view, almost wholly, the intellectual purpose of a school.'[46]

Arnold was unquestionably the most celebrated headmaster of the nineteenth century, thanks to the success of *Tom Brown's Schooldays*. But he had little to do with many of the principal changes affecting the public school during the course of the nineteenth century—the broadening of the curriculum, the introduction of compulsory games, uniformity of dress and stricter social discipline. Nor is it true that he transformed Rugby from barbarism to civilisation. The school was neither as bad under his predecessor nor as good under Arnold as apologists claimed.[47] The extent of his influence was always limited. Dean W. C. Lake, one of his elite, recorded, 'It would be a mistake to suppose that his influence materially changed the character of school life for the ordinary boy.'[48] Arthur Hugh Clough, another of the elite, wrote while there, 'Even here at Rugby . . . there is a vast deal of bad.'[49] Arnold himself was only too aware that conditions in school varied according to the character and capabilities of the prefects. In his last sermon he declared his anxiety 'that our good seems to want a principal stability: to depend so much on individuals. When everything in past years has been most promising, I have seen a great change suddenly produced after a single vacation; and what we hoped had been the real improvement of the school, was proved to have been no more than the present effect produced by a number of individuals.'[50] But even if the full weight of his 'Godliness and Good Learning' fully touched only an elite, his moral influence and character training reached further. Theodore Walrond insisted, 'Not in the universities only, but in the army and elsewhere, it came more and more to be observed that Arnold's pupils were, to a degree unusual at that time, thoughtful, manly-minded, and conscious of duty and obligation.'[51] The very evidence of the conversion of the ordinary and unintellectual Tom Hughes lends credence to that claim.

Arnold did lay stress on the training of character, and, as Jonathan Gathorne-Hardy puts it, 'School as a place to train character—a totally new concept so far—was what came to distinguish the English public school from all other Western school systems. It was what amazed and impressed foreigners—and amazes them still.'[52] Arnold's principal means of doing this was to make the chapel the focus of school life, to stress Christian values and to gear the school to the production of Christian gentlemen, with the emphasis on the Christian: 'He is not well educated who does not know the will of God or knowing it, has received no help in his education towards being inclined and enabled to do it.'[53] He was the first headmaster to take on the school chaplaincy. His ideas were set out in his sermons which became a high point of schoolboy life and were aimed at the improvement and shaping of character and outlook. He quoted with approval John Bowdler's description of public schools as 'the very seats and nurseries of vice':

That is properly a nursery of vice where a boy unlearns the pure and honest principles which he may have received at home, and gets in their stead, others which are utterly low and base and mischievous—where he loses his modesty, his respect for truth, and his affectionateness, and becomes coarse, and false and unfeeling. That too is a nursery of vice, and most fearfully so, where vice is bold, and forward, and presuming; and goodness is timid and shy, and existing as if by sufferance—where the good, instead of setting the tone of society, and branding with disgrace those who disregard it, and themselves exposed to reproach for their goodness, and shrink before the open avowal of evil principles, which the bad are trying to make the law of the community. That is a nursery of vice where the restraints laid upon evil are considered as so much taken from liberty, and where, generally speaking, evil is more willingly screened and concealed, than detected and punished. What society would be, if men regarded the laws of God and man as a grievance, and thought liberty consisted in following to the full their proud, and selfish, and low inclination—that schools to a great extent are; and therefore, they may be well called 'the seats and nurseries of vice'.[54]

In another sermon he specifies the evils existing in schools as direct sensual wickedness, such as drunkenness, the systematic practice of falsehood, cruelty and bullying, a spirit of active disobedience, general idleness, a spirit of combination in evil.[55] Of these Arnold felt that lying and the spirit of combination were the most serious sins at Rugby, but that there was also some evidence of bullying and idleness.

The principal remedy for all this was of course religion. But, coupled with religion, he believed also in the cultivation of the intellect. He believed it to be a moral duty. 'I am quite sure that it is a most solemn duty to cultivate our understanding to the uttermost . . . I am satisfied that a neglected intellect is far oftener the cause of mischief to a man than a perverted or overvalued one,' he wrote in a letter.[56] In a sermon he said, 'You are called upon like all other persons to make yourselves, as far as you can, strong and active and healthful and patient in your bodies, yet your especial call is rather to improve your minds because it is with your minds that God calls you to work hereafter.'[57] He sought to instil a love of learning and was always most at home and most comfortable with his intellectual elite, boys like Arthur Penrhyn Stanley, Charles James Vaughan, Arthur Hugh Clough, William Charles Lake and his son, Matthew Arnold, who went on to distinguished scholarly and ecclesiastical careers, though in some cases also to loss of faith.[58]

Arnold's special efforts were reserved for his intellectual elite: 'I do enjoy the society of youths of seventeen or eighteen, for they are all alive in limbs and spirits at least, if not in mind, while in older persons the body and spirits often become languid without the mind gaining any vigour to compensate for it.'[59] But critics of Arnold, including some of the elite in later life, felt that he pushed bright boys too hard, leading to overstrain and intellectual burn-out. Dean Lake suggested, 'I have always thought that it was the average idle boy, such as those whom *Tom Brown* describes, who were most improved, and more in their after life than at school, by Arnold's training and example,' and he himself bitterly regretted in later life abandoning his friends of the cricket and football fields and devoting himself exclusively to intellectual companions like Vaughan and Stanley.[60]

Apart from the chapel, Arnold utilised existing institutions to pursue his aims. He made great use of the prefectorial system, using the sixth form as his allies, to allow his ideas to filter down. He raised the prestige, increased the salaries and improved the conditions of the teaching staff, securing their support as well. He used corporal punishment sparingly, and then only on the younger boys and for moral offences (lying, drinking, sloth). But he made regular use of punitive expulsions ('It is not necessary that this should be a school of three hundred, or even one hundred boys, but it *is* necessary that it should be a school of Christian gentlemen').[61] He encouraged games and sports, as well as nature rambles, for exercise, but not the cult of athleticism.

Arnold's significance was that he symbolised the new tone that was taking over society. His view can be summed up as 'Godliness and Good Learning' and it was a view that others besides Arnold were advancing. But his articulation of it, promoted by Dean Stanley's life, which Sir Joshua Fitch, Her Majesty's Inspector of Training Colleges, called 'one of the best biographies in our language',[62] and popularised with variations by Hughes, made Arnold the standard-bearer of the new moral earnestness and commitment to personal and social improvement which was the characterising hallmark of early and mid-Victorian society. Certainly his

disciples, Vaughan, Cotton and Prince Lee, who all became headmasters, consciously advocated 'Arnoldian' ideas. The intellectual leaders of the movement were, as David Newsome put it, 'a single class stamped with an unmistakable mint mark: a combination of intellectual toughness, moral earnestness and deep spiritual conviction'.[63] This earnestness, the product of the Evangelical revival, gave Victorian England its philanthropy, its missionary zeal, its paternalism, its reformist impulse and its puritanism. As Newsome says, 'The application of the doctrine of godliness and good learning to the upbringing of boys in the public schools did much to create that breed of diligent, earnest, intellectual eminent Victorians which has left its impress on almost every aspect of the age.'[64]

Arnold's celebrated encapsulation of his aim—to instil religious and moral principle, gentlemanly conduct and intellectual ability—has been much misunderstood. Taken at face value, it has been alleged to mean an order of priorities with intellect coming last. But this is a clear contradiction of his oft-stated commitment to intellectual activity. It is an order of priority which recognises the reality of the situation. Without the first two qualities, intellectual ability is useless. But also the first two needed to be instilled as part of the campaign against the unreformed public school which Arnold found—the system of boy republics with masters and boys in open warfare, boys ruling themselves and perpetuating savagery, bullying and drunkenness. Arnold was perfectly clear about the situation he faced. He outlined it in his sermons, and if the sermons are read in conjunction with Hughes's book it is clear that in some respects the latter is almost a dramatisation of the former. Hughes vividly illustrates drunkenness, lying, bullying and the spirit of combination. The battle between good and evil Arnold discerned is fought in those terms in *Tom Brown,* with Tom epitomising the modesty, affectionateness and respect for truth that Arnold admires. In more general terms, the other aspects of Arnold's regime come out fully. The centrality of chapel and the impact of the Doctor's sermons are brought home. The value of the prefectorial system is illustrated, with Brooke and Holmes supporting and furthering the Doctor's work and with the prefectorial duties making a man of East ('he rose to the situation and burnt his cigar-cases, and gave away his pistols and pondered on the constitutional authority of the sixth and his new duties . . . ay, and no fellow ever acted up to them better').[65] The expulsion of wrongdoers is graphically demonstrated.

There are, however, some differences of emphasis. The Doctor wanted fighting stopped. But Hughes approved of it, when necessary. Rather more significant is the fact that intellectual life plays a minor role in the book, and this reflects Hughes's own experience. He was not an academic boy; his critics (Stanley, Matthew Arnold) were. So godliness plays a much greater role than good learning in *Tom Brown.* When Old Brooke says, 'I know I'd sooner win two school-house matches running than get the Balliol scholarship,' he is reflecting a feeling common among the generality of boys.[66] Hughes gave voice to it himself in an address at Rugby in 1894 at the unveiling of a memorial to William Cotton Oswell:

> Though we small boys were proud in a way of Stanley and Vaughan, of Clough and Burbidge, and other scholars and poets, we looked on them more as providential providers of extra half-holidays than with the enthusiasm of hero-worship. This we reserved for the kings of the Close, round whom clustered legends of personal encounters with drovers at the monthly cattle-fairs . . . or the navvies who were laying down the first line of the London and North Western Railway or the gamekeepers of a neighbouring squire with whom the school was in a state of open war over the right of fishing in the Avon.[67]

Academic work appears only in a short passage dealing with methods of doing the *vulgus,* a short exercise in writing a Latin or Greek verse on a set subject or in a discussion of the ethics of cribbing between Tom and East.[68] As for the rest, there is none of the joy in scholarship, intellectual enquiry or book learning that characterised the true Arnoldian. But the true Arnoldian was probably as rare as George Arthur, who goes rapidly up the school and is at its head by sixteen, but is 'no longer a boy, less of a boy in fact than Tom', who is a year older. This serious, intense intellectual, old beyond his years, is the authentic Arnoldian. But he is not the book's hero.

Hero worship. Aside from the three main threads of the story, *Tom Brown's Schooldays* has received the impress of many of the intellectual and ideological movements of the era, which Hughes himself embraced and embodied, and it is this which makes *Tom Brown's Schooldays* one of the most representative books of its age. First, there is hero worship. The nineteenth century was pre-eminently the age of hero worship, the cult defined and promoted by Thomas Carlyle, who believed that:

> Universal History, the history of what man has accomplished in this world, is at bottom the History of the Great Men who have worked here. They were the leaders of men, these great ones; the modellers, patterns, and in a wide sense creators, of whatsoever the general mass of men contrived to do or to attain; all things that we see standing, accomplished in the world are properly the outer material result, the practical realization and embodiment, of Thoughts that dwelt in the Great Men sent into the world: the soul of the whole world's history, it may justly be considered, were the history of these.[69]

It was, according to Walter E. Houghton, the product of the combination of the enthusiastic temper, the concept of the superior being, the revival of Homeric mythology and medieval balladry, the popularity of Scott and Byron, the experience of Napoleon and his age.[70] It flourished as a bulwark against the dominance of the commercial spirit, to meet the need for moral exemplars to resist or promote change, to provide symbols of an Age of Industry and Empire.

Hughes was a hero worshipper, his worship in turn being directed towards his elder brother George, Dr Arnold and F. D. Maurice. The latter he variously described as 'the best and wisest Englishman who ever lived' and 'the greatest figure since St Paul'. He wrote hero-worshipping biographies of, among others, his brother George, Dr David Livingstone and Alfred the Great. He also penned encomia to two former schoolfellows who went on to become heroes of the empire. One was William Hodson of Hodson's Horse, a hero of the Indian Mutiny, who died in action in 1857. Hughes remembered him as 'a bright, pleasant boy, fond of fun, and with abilities decidedly above the average, but of no very marked distinction, except as a runner, in which exercise . . . he was almost unequalled and showed great powers of endurance'.[71] But his heroic service and death in India made him 'a glorious Christian soldier and Englishman'. Hughes was embodying contemporary public opinion when he wrote of the Mutiny, 'In all her long and stern history, England can point to no nobler sons than these, the heroes of India in 1857.'[72]

William Cotton Oswell was a hero of Hughes's at school and after, and when he addressed Rugby on the subject of Oswell in 1894 he began by saying, 'I hope you boys in this last decade of the century are as great hero-worshippers as we were in the fourth.' Oswell struck the young Hughes as standing out from the rest 'as Hector from the ruck of Trojan princes'. It was the rare mixture of kindliness and gentleness with marvellous strength, activity and fearlessness, which made him *facile princeps* among his contemporaries. 'I don't believe he ever struck a small boy here, or even spoke to one in anger.'[73] Six feet tall, perfectly developed, a sporting hero, nicknamed 'The Muscleman', he served in India as collector and judge, then travelled to Africa as explorer, big game hunter and friend and companion to Livingstone. Sir Samuel Baker dubbed Oswell 'the Nimrod of South Africa, without a rival and without an enemy, the greatest hunter ever known in modern times, the truest friend and most thorough example of an English gentleman'.[74] The Old Etonian Lord Rendel described him as 'manliness without coarseness, polish without complacency, nobility without caste. May Rugby keep the mould and multiply the type.' To which Hughes adds, 'amen'.[75] It was these men of principle and action that Hughes held up as role models for the youth of Britain. They were the sort of men that Tom Brown would have grown into.

Like his creator, Tom Brown is also a hero worshipper. In the village he is devoted to handsome, intelligent

Harry Winburn ('the quickest and best boy in the parish . . . the Crichton of our village'), who can wrestle, climb and run better than anyone else and gives Tom valuable wrestling lessons. At private school he has an unnamed schoolfellow hero, whom he partners in many scrapes. He looks up at Rugby to Old Brooke, and finally ends up worshipping Arnold as 'a hero-worshipper who would have satisfied the soul of Thomas Carlyle'.

Ruralism. Hughes saw the true source of national strength as residing in the countryside.[76] He expressed in the opening chapters of **Tom Brown** his distaste for the transformation of the countryside in particular and society in general by industrialisation and its agent, the railways. The railways had decisively altered the old static, stable life: 'We are a vagabond nation now, that's certain . . . The Queen sets us the example—we are moving on from top to bottom.'[77] This is said in tones of deep regret, and it is perhaps one reason why he made his childhood reminiscences so vibrant. As Raymond Chapman points out, so many of the great Victorians had been children in the Regency period, and when they grew up to live in a transformed world they looked back with regret to that era, which became suffused with innocence, and imbued with qualities which the modern age seemed to be losing—order, calm, stability, unhurriedness.[78] Like Dickens, Hughes celebrates the stagecoach age, and rejoices in the old coaching days, penning an exhilarating account of Tom's journey to school by coach which remains one of the great coaching passages.

His love of the countryside, country sports and pursuits, of rural myths and legends, coupled with his regret about change, its agencies and effects, is encapsulated in one of many passages apostrophising his young readers:

Oh, young England! young England! You who are born into these racing railroad times, when there's a Great Exhibition, or some monster sight, every year; and you can get over a couple of thousand miles of ground for three pounds ten, in a five weeks' holiday; why don't you know more of your own birth-places? You're all in the ends of the earth, it seems to me, as soon as you get your necks out of the educational collar, for Midsummer holidays, long vacations or what not . . . And when you get home for a quiet fortnight, you turn the steam off, and lie on your backs in the paternal garden, surrounded by the last batch of books from Mudie's library, and half bored to death . . . Now, in my time, when we got home by the old coach, which put us down at the cross-roads with our boxes, the first day of the holidays, and had been driven off by the family coachman, singing 'Dulce Domum' at the top of our voices, there we were, fixtures, till black Monday came round. We had to cut out our own amusements within a walk or a ride of home. And so we got to know all the country folk, and their ways and songs and stories, by heart; and went over the fields, and woods, and hills, again and again, till we made friends of them all. We

were Berkshire, or Gloucestershire, or Yorkshire boys; and you're young cosmopolites, belonging to all counties and no countries.[79]

But there is more than mere nostalgia here. He sees rural sports and customs as essential to the cultivation of manliness, both physical and moral, and also to class harmony. He describes wrestling and back-swording—fighting with sticks—and laments its decline. He lovingly evokes the 'veast', the Berkshire equivalent of the Lancashire wakes, the anniversary of the local church's dedication, celebrated with eating, drinking, sports and shows. This allows him to castigate the exclusiveness of other pastimes, 'class amusements, be they for dukes or ploughboys', which 'always become nuisances and curses to a country. The true charm of cricket and hunting is, that they are still more or less sociable and universal; there's a place for every man who will come and take part.'[80]

He sees the decline of rural sports, then, as a threat both to democracy and to manliness, and he fears that overly intellectual and refined efforts to reform the working classes will fail, increasing class division. His answer is, of course, the inculcation of muscular Christianity, as much a recipe for a moral working class as for a moral gentry:

Don't let reformers of any sort think that they are going to lay hold of the working boys and young men of England by any educational grapnel whatever, which hasn't some *bona fide* equivalent for the games of the old country 'veast' in it; something to try the muscles of men's bodies and the endurance of their hearts, to make them rejoice in their strength. In all the new fangled comprehensive plans which I see, this is all left out; and the consequence is that your great Mechanics' Institutes end in intellectual priggism and your Christian Young Men's Societies in Religious Pharisaism . . . Life isn't all beer and skittles—but beer and skittles, or something better of the same sort, must form a good part of every Englishman's education.[81]

The proper way to approach the working class is 'to talk to them about what is really at the bottom of your hearts, and box, and run, and row with them, when you have a chance'.[82] Tom is taught rural lore by two old villagers and plays happily with village boys, 'full as manly and honest, and certainly purer, than those in a higher rank'.[83]

Squire Brown is held up as the model of a Tory populist. He believed in social hierarchy and thought loyalty and obedience to it were men's first duties. But he held other social principles, first and foremost:

The belief that a man is to be valued wholly and solely for that which he is in himself . . . As a necessary corollary to this belief, Squire Brown held further that it didn't matter a straw whether his son associated with lord's sons or ploughman's sons, provided they were brave and honest.[84]

The squire himself had played football and gone birds-nesting with farmers and labourers, so had his father and grandfather. Tom therefore played with the village boys freely. This philosophy, of course, feeds directly into Hughes's Christian Socialism.

But there is more to Hughes's ruralism even than manliness and class harmony. This part of rural Berkshire was closely associated with and inextricably bound up in England's past, historical and mythical. It was the area where St George slew the dragon, where Wayland Smith had his cave, where Alfred defeated the Danes at the battle of Ashdown. So we have a potent combination of chivalry, Anglo-Saxon folk heroes and the victory of a Christian warrior over the forces of paganism. Together these ideas were potent in the national ideology and in Hughes's thinking. It is no coincidence that he wrote both a biography of Alfred the Great and *The Scouring of the White Horse,* devoted entirely to his native heath.

He expatiates on Saxon place names, traditions and his pride in being a West Saxon, 'I was born and bred a West Countryman, thank God! A Wessex man, a citizen of the noblest Saxon kingdom of Wessex . . . There's nothing like the old countryside for me, and no music like the fresh twang of the real old Saxon tongue.'[85] This lines Hughes up with the exponents of Anglo-Saxonism like Charles Kingsley, J. A. Froude and E. A. Freeman, who saw the Anglo-Saxons as the source of Britain's democratic institutions (Parliament, the common law), national religion (the Protestant temper) and the fighting and leadership qualities of the British race.[86] It was a central interpretative strand in English history, explaining the impulse to world rule. There is therefore a direct link between the green hills of Berkshire and the far-off foreign shores that constitute Britain's overseas empire.

On one level Hughes conforms to the influential thesis advanced by Martin Weiner that Britain's industrial decline can be traced to a state of mind best described as ruralism. Weiner sees this as the glorification of the countryside and all things rural in a deliberate rejection of urban and industrial reality by a non-industrial, non-innovative, anti-materialist patrician culture, endorsed by a gentrified bourgeoisie. The myth of England as essentially rural and essentially unchanging appealed across party lines to Conservatives and Socialists alike, and counted among its adherents such disparate figures as Rudyard Kipling, William Morris, Robert Blatchford and John Ruskin, all of whom in their different ways castigated the evils of technology, capitalism and an acquisitive industrial society. For some, however, the countryside was not only the antithesis of capitalism, it was also the antithesis of imperialism, part of the Little Englandism which saw the true destiny of the nation lying in a return to the pre-imperial rural Eden.

Not everyone saw it like that, however. For some the English inheritance of character, leadership, moral strength and democratic traditions, so rooted in the rural past of Merrie England, led inevitably to expansion overseas. It was one of the principal sources and inspirations of imperialism. Thus the English countryside, alive with the associations and lore of the past, represents stability, tradition, inspiration, home, family, history, the place from which to start forth in the divinely ordained British mission to govern the world and spread the virtues and values of Englishness and to return thence when the burden was laid down. So the two aspects of ruralism and imperialism, far from being antithetical, are mutually supportive and complementary.[87] Hughes is the perfect exemplar of this. For him there is no distinction between nation and empire, between rural England and Greater Britain.

Imperialism. Hughes was a fervent patriot, declaring proudly in Boston, Massachusetts, 'I am before all things an Englishman—a John Bull, if you will—loving Old England and feeling proud of her.'[88] He therefore saw no contradiction in praising the rich traditions of rural Wessex and the expanding empire overseas. For his closest identification is with the squirearchy, which he sees as equally the backbone of England and of the empire. 'The great army of Browns who are scattered over the whole empire on which the sun never sets and whose general diffusion, I take to be the chief cause of that empire's stability.' Why? Because 'for centuries, in their quiet, dogged, homespun way, they have been subduing the earth in most English counties, and leaving their mark in American forests and Australian uplands. Wherever the fleets and armies of England have won renown, there stalwart sons of the Browns have done yeoman's work.'[89] So empire is the context within which Hughes's heroes function. He lovingly exalts the qualities of the Browns, their fighting spirit, clannishness, quixotic temper and optimism, exactly the qualities needed to run an empire. All this struck the right chords later in the century when imperialism had become the dominant ideology, and the public schools were the nurseries of imperial administrators and officers.

At the end of *Tom Brown* Harry East departs to join a regiment in India. The Young Master tells Tom of Rugby, 'Perhaps ours is the only little corner of the British Empire which is thoroughly, wisely and strongly ruled just now.'[90] thus suggesting a model for future imperial rule, a model which was indeed followed, so that in looking back we can see that all relationships between officers and men, rulers and ruled, can be construed in the mould of teachers, prefects and fags, with the empire as Eton, Harrow and Rugby writ large.[91] Rugby itself contributed those imperial heroes lauded by Hughes, William Hodson and William Cotton Oswell, as well as the Doctor's son, William Delafield Arnold, who became Director of Education in the Punjab.

Imperialism ran like a scarlet thread through Hughes's thought. In *The Manliness of Christ* he cited the wreck of the *Birkenhead,* one of the great imperial myths, to illustrate self-sacrifice, and in his defence of fighting when necessary he included 'Russians and border-ruffians'.

Chivalry. For Arnold chivalry was synonymous with feudalism, tyranny and class arrogance, all that was re-actionary and needed eliminating. In 1829 he wrote, 'If I were called upon to name what spirit of evil predomi-nantly deserved the name of Antichrist, I should name the spirit of chivalry.'[92] But by 1917 Sir Henry Newbolt was claiming that the public school system was essen-tially based on the codes and structures of chivalry and in 1898 J. H. Skrine, Warden of Trinity College, Glena-lmond, wrote, 'With all its glory and its faults, chivalry it is again.'[93]

What happened in between was the simultaneous pro-motion of athleticism, muscular Christianity and chiv-alry by a whole raft of influential figures in literature, education and society as a code for living, and for coun-teracting the violence, godlessness and aristocratic self-ishness of the old unreformed public school. Games, chapel and missions to the slums became key elements in the new public schools, and by the 1870s chivalry was in the air. As Mark Girouard has written:

> Actual knights in armour appear as school trophies, and abound in the form of statues or stained glass fig-ures, especially as memorials to the Crimean, Boer or Great Wars . . . In school magazines, the articles inter-spersed among the ever increasing accounts of school games include ones on muscular Christianity, Kingsley, King Arthur, Tennyson's *Idylls,* chivalry and the Niebe-lungenlied.[94]

Hughes was steeped in the works of Walter Scott, who had been a friend of his grandmother. Indeed, Mary Ann Hughes had supplied Scott with the details of the legend of Wayland Smith's cave which he used in *Ken-ilworth.*[95] Arnold had used Scott's novels to teach from at Rugby. Hughes himself loved to allude to the old Spanish legend of Durandarte at Roncesvalles, which represented for him 'the beau ideal of knighthood summed up in a few words'.

> Kind in manners, fair in favour,
> Mild in temper, fierce in fight—
> Warrior, purer, gentler, braver,
> Never shall behold the light.[96]

This is the beau ideal of the public schoolboy too. Hughes installed stained glass pictures of Guinevere, Vivian, Elaine and Enid, the heroines of Tennyson's *Idylls of the King,* in his house.

Although the language of chivalry is not as prominent in *Tom Brown* as it might have been later in the cen-tury, the story was firmly annexed to the chivalric tradi-tion by the illustrated edition of Arthur Hughes, pub-lished in 1889. The capital letter of chapter 1 had the infant Tom in helmet, sword and buckler as St George fighting the dragon. The capital of Part 2, chapter 7, had a knight in full armour kneeling to pray. The chap-ter dealt with East's struggle with his religious feelings and was headed by six lines from James Russell Low-ell's *Vision of Sir Launfal.* The poem, by one of Hugh-es's favourite poets, told of a knight setting out to seek the Holy Grail and learning in a dream that the Grail is really to be found in sharing all he has with his fellow men. In Part 2, chapter 9, the illustration of Tom's visit to Arnold's tomb gives him, as Mark Girouard has pointed out, a knightly air; 'the rug over his shoulder suggests a military cloak and his attitude—pensive, bareheaded, one leg forward—is in the tradition of West's Black Prince and Watts's recent Sir Galahad'.[97]

Christian Socialism. Chivalry was a key element in Christian Socialism and a strong element in the ideol-ogy of Kingsley and Hughes. Kingsley described him-self as 'a joyous knight errant' and Hughes as 'a knight of the Round Table'. Preaching before Queen Victoria, Kingsley declared, 'The age of chivalry is never past so long as there is a wrong left unredressed on earth or a man or woman left to say, "I will redress that wrong or spend my life in the attempt."'[98]

Christian Socialism, one of Hughes's abiding enthusi-asms, inevitably left its imprint on *Tom Brown's Schooldays.*[99] So great was F. D. Maurice's influence on *Tom Brown,* which he read in draft, that Macmillan's reader observed that Arnold was presented as preaching Mauricean doctrines.[100] Christian Socialists sought to re-christianise the masses by promoting fellowship, human dignity and, where necessary, social reform. In particu-lar they believed in 'co-operation, not competition' and were proposing an alternative to *laissez-faire.* They arose in response to the events of 1848. Alarmed by the revolutionary elements in Chartism, with whose broad aims they were in sympathy, they tried to propose a peaceful and constructive alternative. This alternative aimed to bring to the working classes four types of ben-efit: a renewal of Christian commitment, better living and working conditions and an improved education. It was hoped that this would improve cross-class sympa-thy and avert violent outbreaks.

The group centred on F. D. Maurice, Charles Kingsley, J. M. Ludlow and Hughes, and found practical expres-sion in the Working Men's College, of which Maurice was the first and Hughes the second Principal. *Tom Brown's Schooldays* has been described by one com-mentator as 'the most important document in Christian Socialist literature . . . a social document depicting a polity in miniature as a model for national society'.[101] This is confirmed by Hughes's words in the preface to the first edition, where he quotes approvingly from the

Rugby Magazine: 'We must bear in mind that we form a complete social body . . . a society in which by the nature of the case we must not only learn but act and live; and act and live not only as boys but as boys who will be men.'[102] So Hughes depicts both good and evil at Rugby and shows that evil can be conquered by faith, truth, manliness, co-operation and brotherly love.

When Arthur talks to Tom of his father it is clear that the Rev. Arthur was an archetypal Christian Socialist. His father had been a clergyman in a Midland town, oppressed by economic recession, strikes and crime. He had arrived there aged twenty-five, a young man, newly married, full of faith, hope and love, and inspired with 'a real wholesome Christian love for the poor, struggling, sinning men, of whom he felt himself one'. He earned 'a *manly* respect wrung from the unwilling souls of men who fancied his order their natural enemies; the fear and hatred of everyone who was false or unjust in the district, were he master or man' (my italics). He acted as mediator between master and man and strove to improve conditions, supported always by his wife. When he died during a typhus epidemic, which he characteristically strove to combat, working men carried his coffin to its grave. 'For many years afterwards the townsfolk felt the want of that brave, hopeful, loving parson and his wife, who had lived to teach them mutual forbearance and helpfulness, and had *almost* at last given them a glimpse of what this old world would be if people would live for God and each other instead of for themselves.'[103] It is evident too that George Arthur has the spirit of his father in him and becomes in a way a symbol of adult Christian Socialist responsibility. This is finally confirmed by the vision that Arthur has when seriously ill, a vision which draws on the imagery and ideas of Carlyle that so inspired the Christian Socialists—of fellowship, work and common effort. He dreams that he has died and gone to heaven and finds himself on the bank of a great river:

> On the other bank of the great river I saw men and women and children rising up pure and bright and the tears were wiped from their eyes, and they put on glory and strength, and all weariness and pain fell away. And beyond were a multitude which no man could number, and they worked at some great work; and they who rose from the river went on and joined in the work. They all worked and each worked in a different way, but all at the same work. And I saw there my father, and the men in the old town whom I knew when I was a child; many a hard stern man, who never came to church, and whom they called atheist and infidel. There they were, side by side with my father, whom I had seen toil and die for them, and women and little children, and the seal was on the foreheads of all. And I longed to see what the work was, and could not . . . Then . . . I saw myriads on this side, and they too worked, and I knew that it was the same work; and the same seal was on their foreheads. And though I saw that there was toil and anguish in the work of these . . . I longed . . . more and more to know what the

work was. And as I looked, I saw my mother and my sisters, and I saw the Doctor, and you, Tom, and hundreds more whom I knew; and at last I saw myself too, and I was toiling and doing ever so little a piece of the great work.[104]

The great work is clearly that work which Arthur's father had died while performing and which Arnold also preached, the improvement of the lot of the poor, the spreading of Christian values and the improvement of class harmony. All this recalls Carlyle:

> There is a perennial nobleness, and even sacredness, in Work . . . It has been written, 'an endless significance lies in Work'; a man perfects himself by working . . . properly speaking, all true Work is Religion . . . Older than all preached Gospels was this unpreached, inarticulate, but ineradicable, forever-enduring Gospel: Work and therein have wellbeing . . . What is immethodic, waste, thou shalt make methodic, regulated, arrable; obedient and productive to thee. Wheresoever thou findest Disorder, there is thy eternal enemy; attack him swiftly, subdue him; make Order of him, the subject not of Chaos, but of Intelligence, Divinity and Thee . . . But above all, where thou findest Ignorance, Stupidity, Brute-Mindedness . . . attack it, I say; smite it wisely, unweariedly, and rest not while thou livest and it lives.[105]

Here is the same visionary quality, the same equation of work and godly purpose, the same injunction to struggle.

Notes

1. J. J. Findlay, *Arnold of Rugby,* Cambridge, 1914, xiii.

2. Bernard Darwin, *The English Public School,* London, 1929, 157-8. Cf. also Harold Child, 'The public school in fiction', in *The Public Schools from Within,* London, 1906, 295.

3. On Brown's precursors see, for instance, P. W. Musgrave, *From Brown to Bunter,* London, 1985, 21-46; Margaret Maison, 'Tom Brown and company: scholastic novels of the 1850s', *English,* 12 (1958), 100-3; Gerald Redmond, 'Before Hughes and Kingsley: the origins and evolution of "Muscular Christianity" in English children's literature', in Charles Jenkins and Michael Green (ed.), *Sporting Fictions,* Birmingham, 1981, 8-35. The earlier Tom Browns appear in Dorothy Kilner's *First Going to School* (1804) and *The Good Child's Delight* (1819), see Redmond, p. 21.

4. *Blackwood's Magazine,* 89 (February 1861), 132.

5. Reprinted in P. G. Wodehouse, *Tales of St Austin's,* London, 1972, 157-62.

6. W. H. G. Armytage and E. C. Mack, *Thomas Hughes,* London, 1952, 88.

7. Patrick Scott, 'The school and the novel: *Tom Brown's Schooldays*', Brian Simon and Ian Bradley (ed.), *The Victorian Public School*, Dublin, 1975, 34-57.

8. Scott, 'The school and the novel', 48.

9. On conditions at Arnold's Rugby see T. W. Bamford, *Thomas Arnold*, London, 1960, Edward C. Mack, *Public Schools and British Opinion, 1780-1860*, London, 1938, 238-9; Armytage and Mack, *Thomas Hughes*, 16-17.

10. Thomas Hughes, *Memoir of a Brother*, London, 1873, 34.

11. *Blackwood's Magazine*, 89, 133.

12. Ian Weinberg, *The English Public Schools*, New York, 1967, 97-126. Cf. also John Wakeford, *The Cloistered Elite*, London, 1969, 128-59.

13. Thomas Hughes, *Tom Brown's Schooldays* (1857), London, 1889, 52.

14. Hughes, *Tom Brown's Schooldays*, 59.

15. Vivian Ogilvie, *The English Public School*, London, 1957, 145.

16. Hughes, *Tom Brown's Schooldays*, 255-6.

17. Hughes, *Tom Brown's Schooldays*, 102.

18. Hughes, *Tom Brown at Oxford*, 99.

19. This controversy is surveyed by George Worth, 'Of muscles and manliness: some reflections on Thomas Hughes', in James R. Kincaid and Albert J. Kuhn, *Victorian Literature and Society*, Ohio, 1984, 300-14. Cf. also Harold Nicolson's statement that Hughes believed in 'indiscriminate combat', *Good Behaviour*, London, 1956, 259.

20. Hughes, *Tom Brown's Schooldays*, 231.

21. Hughes, *Tom Brown's Schooldays*, 246.

22. Hughes, *Tom Brown's Schooldays*, 231.

23. Hughes, *Tom Brown's Schooldays*, 246.

24. Thomas Carlyle, *Past and Present*, London, 1905, 163-4.

25. Thomas Hughes, *The Manliness of Christ*, London, 1880, 21, 22, 25-6.

26. Norman Vance, *The Sinews of the Spirit*, Cambridge, 1985.

27. Matthew Arnold, *Culture and Anarchy* (1869), Cambridge, 1978, 203.

28. See J. C. Reid, *Bucks and Bruisers*, London, 1971.

29. On this whole subject see Bruce Haley, *The Healthy Body and Victorian Culture*, Cambridge, Mass., 1978.

30. Hughes, *Tom Brown's Schooldays*, 33-4.

31. Hughes, *Tom Brown's Schooldays*, 89-90.

32. Hughes, *Tom Brown's Schooldays*, 100.

33. Hughes, *Tom Brown's Schooldays*, 289.

34. Hughes, *Tom Brown's Schooldays*, xv. On Arnold and his views see Arthur P. Stanley, *The Life and Correspondence of Thomas Arnold*, 2 Vols., London, 1845; Findlay, *Arnold of Rugby*; Joshua Fitch, *Thomas and Matthew Arnold and their Influence on English Education* (1897), London, 1905; T. W. Bamford, *Thomas Arnold*; David Newsome, *Godliness and Good Learning*, London, 1961.

35. Hughes, *Tom Brown's Schooldays*, 103.

36. Hughes, *Tom Brown's Schooldays*, 115.

37. Hughes, *Tom Brown's Schooldays*, 115-16.

38. *Dictionary of National Biography*, I, 587.

39. Hughes, *Tom Brown's Schooldays*, 126, 180.

40. Hughes, *Tom Brown's Schooldays*, 184-5. William Gover recalls being pelted with shoes when kneeling to pray. *Parents Review*, 6 (1895-96), 834.

41. Hughes, *Tom Brown's Schooldays*, 177-8.

42. Hughes, *Tom Brown's Schooldays*, 272.

43. Hughes, *Tom Brown's Schooldays*, 298-9.

44. Rowland E. Prothero, *Life and Letters of Dean Stanley*, I, London, 1894, 68.

45. Arthur Westcott, *Life and Letters of Brooke Foss Westcott*, London, 1903, I, 248.

46. Fitch, *Thomas and Matthew Arnold*, 105.

47. Bamford, *Thomas Arnold*, 175-90.

48. [Katherine] Lake, *Memorials of Dean [William Charles] Lake [of Durham*, London, 1901], 17.

49. A. H. Clough, *Poems and Prose Remains*, I, London, 1896, 56.

50. Thomas Arnold, *Sermons*, V. London, 1878, 341.

51. *Dictionary of National Biography*, I, 587.

52. Jonathan Gathorne-Hardy, *The Public School Phenomenon*, Harmondsworth, 1979, 85.

53. Thomas Arnold, *Sermons*, III, 131.

54. Thomas Arnold, *Sermons*, II, 82-3.

55. Thomas Arnold, *Sermons*, V, 48-54.

56. Fitch, *Thomas and Matthew Arnold*, 90.

57. Fitch, *Thomas and Matthew Arnold*, 90.

58. On the careers of four of his disciples see Frances J. Woodward, *The Doctor's Disciples,* Oxford, 1954.

59. Newsome, *Godliness and Good Learning,* 50.

60. Lake, *Memorials of Dean Lake,* 12.

61. Fitch, *Thomas and Matthew Arnold,* 83-4. Expulsion was a favoured weapon of Arnold, his firm belief being 'the first, second and third duty of the master of a great public school is to get rid of unpromising boys', Thomas Hughes, 'Rugby School', *Great Public Schools,* London, 1889, 158.

62. Fitch, *Thomas and Matthew Arnold,* 1.

63. Newsome, *Godliness and Good Learning,* 25.

64. Newsome, *Godliness and Good Learning,* 48.

65. Hughes, *Tom Brown's Schooldays,* 296.

66. Hughes, *Tom Brown's Schooldays,* 100.

67. Hughes, *Manliness of Christ,* London, 1894, appendix, 232.

68. Hughes, *Tom Brown's Schooldays,* 211-13 (*vulgus*); 264-9 (cribbing).

69. Thomas Carlyle, *Lectures on Heroes and Hero-worship,* London, 1905, 1, 2.

70. [Walter E.] Houghton, *Victorian Frame of Mind* [(1957), New Haven, Conn., 1979], 310.

71. Thomas Hughes, 'Hodson of Hodson's House', *Fraser's Magazine,* 59 (February 1859), 128.

72. Thomas Hughes, 'Hodson', 127.

73. Hughes, *Manliness of Christ,* appendix, 231, 233.

74. Hughes, *Manliness of Christ,* appendix, 240-1.

75. Hughes, *Manliness of Christ,* appendix, 251-2.

76. On ruralism see Martin Weiner, *English Culture and the Decline of the Industrial Spirit, 1850-1980,* Cambridge, 1981, and Raymond Williams, *The Country and the City,* London, 1985.

77. Hughes, *Tom Brown's Schooldays,* 15.

78. Raymond Chapman, *The Sense of the Past in Victorian Literature,* London, 1986, 145.

79. Hughes, *Tom Brown's Schooldays,* 45.

80. Hughes, *Tom Brown's Schooldays,* 23.

81. Hughes, *Tom Brown's Schooldays,* 33-4.

82. Hughes, *Tom Brown's Schooldays,* 20-1.

83. Hughes, *Tom Brown's Schooldays,* 50.

84. Hughes, *Tom Brown's Schooldays,* 42-3.

85. Hughes, *Tom Brown's Schooldays,* 13.

86. On Anglo-Saxonism see J. W. Burrow, *A Liberal Descent,* Cambridge, 1981; Hugh McDougall, *Racial Myth in English History,* Montreal, 1982; Asa Briggs, 'Saxons, Normans and Victorians', *Collected Essays,* 2, Brighton, 1985, 218-39.

87. This is persuasively argued by J. S. Bratton, '"Of England, Home and Duty": the image of England in Victorian and Edwardian juvenile fiction', *Imperialism and Popular Culture,* Manchester, 1986, 73-93.

88. Quoted in W. E. Winn, 'Tom Brown's Schooldays and the Development of "Muscular Christianity"', *Church History,* 29 (1960), 71.

89. Hughes, *Tom Brown's Schooldays,* 1-2, 4.

90. Hughes, *Tom Brown's Schooldays,* 290.

91. This argument is developed in Jeffrey Richards, *Visions of Yesterday,* London, 1973.

92. Stanley, *Life of Arnold* [*The Life and Correspondence of Thomas Arnold*], I, 255.

93. Mark Girouard, *The Return to Camelot,* New Haven, Conn., 1981, 170.

94. Girouard, *Return to Camelot,* 169.

95. S. M. Ellis, *Wilkie Collins, Lefanu and Others* (1931), Freeport, Conn., 1968, 217.

96. Vance, *Sinews of the Spirit,* 136.

97. Girouard, *Return to Camelot,* 168.

98. Girouard, *Return to Camelot,* 130.

99. On Christian Socialism see Torben Christensen, *Origin and History of Christian Socialism,* Aarhus, 1962, and Edward Norman, *The Victorian Christian Socialists,* Cambridge, 1987.

100. Vance, *Sinews of the Spirit,* 53.

101. A. J. Hartley, 'Christian Socialism and Victorian morality: the inner meaning of *Tom Brown's Schooldays*', *Dalhousie Review,* 49 (1969), 216, 223.

102. Hartley, 'Christian Socialism and Victorian morality', 216.

103. Hughes, *Tom Brown's Schooldays,* 195-7.

104. Hughes, *Tom Brown's Schooldays,* 259-60.

105. Carlyle, *Past and Present,* 168, 172-3. Arnold would certainly have endorsed this vision of work. *Quarterly Review,* 102 (1857), 338, stressed Arnold's dedication to work, 'of which he was a worshipper, holding labour—which of itself formed his best pleasure—to be his appointed lot on earth'.

Paul M. Puccio (essay date fall 1995)

SOURCE: Puccio, Paul M. "At the Heart of *Tom Brown's Schooldays*: Thomas Arnold and Christian Friendship." *Modern Language Studies* 25, no. 4 (fall 1995): 57-74.

[*In the following essay, Puccio identifies qualities of intimacy in the novel's depictions of public school friendships. Puccio argues that for Hughes, religious devotion was the foundation of Victorian masculinity.*]

Early in Evelyn Waugh's *Brideshead Revisited* (1945), Cara, Lord Marchmain's Italian mistress, says to Charles Ryder:

> I know of these romantic friendships of the English and the Germans. They are not Latin. I think they are very good if they do not go on too long . . . It is a kind of love that comes to children before they know its meaning. In England it comes when you are almost men; I think I like that. It is better to have that kind of love for another boy than for a girl.
>
> (101-02)

The romantic friendships to which Cara refers most often developed between boys who met at boarding schools and universities. In canonical Victorian and Edwardian fiction, these friendships occasionally occupy a chapter or two—for example, in *David Copperfield* (1850), *The Way of All Flesh* (1903), and *Of Human Bondage* (1915). Only in the genre of the school-boy novel, however, does friendship typically take center stage, and it is to this genre that we must turn if we wish to study the conventions of romantic friendship, which lasted, at least in fiction, as late as the Second World War.

The novel generally considered to mark the debut of this genre is Thomas Hughes's ***Tom Brown's Schooldays*** (1857).[1] Focusing on this novel, I will delineate some of the narrative conventions that came to shape schoolboy novels, as well as other *bildungsromane* that include events set in English boarding schools; I will also argue that schoolboy friendships, like those in ***Tom Brown's Schooldays,*** reveal some of the ways in which religious ideology, articulated and enacted in a boarding school setting, created ideals of middle-class masculinity and intimate, though non-sexual, relations between men.

Readers typically remember ***Tom Brown's Schooldays*** as a sporting adventure story. However, most of the football and cricket matches, the fishing and hunting expeditions, the episodes of bullying and fisticuffs occur in the *first* part of the novel. In that part, Tom's friendships are vigorous but lawless; he and his chum East use cribs for their schoolwork and devote most of their energies to getting into trouble: fishing out of bounds, poaching, attending the prohibited town fair, carving their names on the minute hand of the school clock.

In an attempt to guide Tom back toward virtue and gentlemanly good form, his Headmaster, "the Doctor" (a fictional depiction of Thomas Arnold, Headmaster at Rugby School, 1828-42), puts in Tom's charge a new boy, George Arthur[2]—the delicate, bookish, earnest orphan of an Evangelical minister. Arnold trusts that Tom and Arthur will become friends, and that while Tom offers Arthur physical protection from the masses of boys who generally make life hell for delicate, bookish, earnest orphans, Arthur will provide for Tom spiritual protection from the corrupting influences of those same boys.

Indeed, the historical Thomas Arnold believed that highly emotional friendships, based on shared Christian values, could redeem boys from the naturally evil state of boyhood and induce an Evangelical passion for personal salvation. Arnold writes in March of 1828, six months before settling into the Headmastership at Rugby School: "my object will be, if possible, to form Christian men, for Christian boys I can scarcely hope to make; I mean that, from the natural imperfect state of boyhood, they are not susceptible of Christian principles in their full development upon their practice, and I suspect that a low standard of morals in many respects must be tolerated amongst them" (Stanley [*Life and Correspondence of Thomas Arnold*] 68). In a Rugby Chapel sermon Arnold explains that "[A] great protection to the principles of a young man, is to connect himself closely with Christian friends. Two men of the same age, intimate with one another, and both in earnest in their desire to please God, are a strength and support to each other" (Sermons II [*Christian Life at School*] 217). Elsewhere, he writes, "I love to think that Christian friendships may be a part of the business of eternity" (qtd. in Stanley 260).[3]

Like F. D. Maurice, the Christian Socialist, Arnold believed that God's incarnation in Christ, sacramentalized in the act of Christian Communion, both engendered and pledged an intimate relationship between God and "man." In another sermon, Arnold maintains that participation in the Communion service represents and improves the human communion with God as well as the fraternal communion of the boys with one another:

> What is the first and outward thing of which . . . [the Communion service] reminds us? Is it not that last supper in Jerusalem, in which men—the twelve disciples, the first members of our Christian brotherhood,—were brought into such solemn nearness to God, as seems to have begun the privileges of heaven upon earth? They were brought near at once to Christ and to one another; united to one another in Him, in that double bond which

is the perfection at once of our duty and of our happiness. And so in our communion we, too, draw near to Christ and to each other; we feel—who is there at that moment, at least that does not feel?—what a tie there is to bind each of us to his brother, when we come to the table of our common Lord.

(Sermons IV [*Christian Life Its Course, Its Hindrances, and Its Helps*], 171-72)

Norman Vance explains that this spiritual relationship shaped the Evangelical perception of human relationships: "[t]his acceptance of Christ involved accepting the fact of human solidarity with Christ: in a sense all men were sons of God as He was, so all men were brothers in Christ and Christ himself could be regarded as the elder brother of the human race" (55).[4]

Tom and Arthur's friendship, the focal point for the second part of the novel, illustrates Arnold's ideal of a Christian and Christianizing brotherhood. The epigraph to this second part promises moral rejuvenation:

I [hold] it truth, with him who sings
　To one clear harp in divers tones,
　That men may rise on stepping-stones
Of their dead selves to higher things.

(214)

These lines from *In Memoriam* (1850), perhaps the greatest Victorian testimony to friendship between men, anticipate Tom's friendship with Arthur, through which he rises to higher things: because of Arthur's companionship, Tom's emotional restraint gives way to earnest expressiveness, his boyish barbarism evolves into adult responsibility, and his unprincipled muscularity matures into Christian manliness.

Through his close association with Arthur, Tom learns to value decency, courtesy, and tenderness—standards of conduct that eventually replace the more common schoolboy standards, which he had earlier come to accept:

East and he had made up their minds to get this study, and then every night from locking-up till ten they would be together to talk about fishing, drink bottled-beer, read Marryat's novels, and sort birds' eggs. And this new boy would most likely never go out of the close, and would be afraid of wet feet, and always get laughed at, and called Molly, or Jenny, or some derogatory feminine nickname.

(218)

Although Tom's first reaction to Arthur is anything but cordial, he ultimately agrees to befriend the boy when he is told that "his father's dead, and he's got no brothers . . . and . . . one of his sisters [is] like to die of decline" (218). Rather like one of W. S. Gilbert's Pirates of Penzance, Tom cannot resist the plea of an "or-

phan boy." This appeal to his "warm heart" moves Tom to accept his new charge; doing so assures not only Arthur's protection, but Tom's salvation.

Both in protecting Arthur from the bullying of the more vicious boys in the School and in learning to respect Arthur's self-confident goodness, Tom comes to recognize his own potential for mentorship and influence; according to Arnold, "middle-aged boys," such as Tom, constitute a

class of persons . . . whose station in the school is high, but yet does not invest them with actual authority, while their age is often such as to give them really an influence equal to that of those above them, or it may be superior. . . . They forget that, if they have not authority, they have what really amounts to the same thing; they know that they are looked up to,—that what they say and do has its effect on others; they know, in short, that they are of some consequence and weight in the school. . . . And as it is most certain that you have an influence and power, and you well know it; so remember that where there is power, there is ever a duty attached to it; if you can influence others,—as beyond all doubt you can, and do influence them daily,—if you do not influence them against evil and for good, you are wasting the talent entrusted to you, and sinning against God.

(Sermons V [*Christian Life, Its Hopes, Its Fears, and Its Close*], 44-45)

Before Tom shows signs of assimilating Arnold's conception of proper influence, however, he exercises his seniority in inevitably superficial and ultimately inappropriate ways. At first, Tom fancies himself the cicerone to the younger, less experienced boy, and he provides him with the "survival skills" necessary for life at Rugby: "You must answer straight up when the fellows speak to you, and don't be afraid. If you're afraid, you'll get bullied. And don't say you can sing; and don't you ever talk about home, or your mother and sisters" (223).

Needless to say, this is not in the least the sort of guidance that the Doctor has in mind. Indeed, in one sermon Arnold specifically denounces the very attitude Tom endorses:

you sometimes learn to feel ashamed of indulging your natural affections, and particularly of being attached to your mothers and sisters, and fond of their society. You fancy it is unmanly to be thought to be influenced by them, and you are afraid of being supposed to long too much for their tenderness and indulgent kindness towards you. Thus you affect a bluntness and hardness which, at first, you cannot put on without an effort; but the effort is made, and that from a false shame of being laughed at for seeming too fond of home. The effort is made . . . till, sometimes I fear, it ceases to be an effort, and the coldness, which was at first merely put on, becomes at last a natural temper.

(Sermons II, 59)

Arnold admits in this sermon that this domestic alienation results inevitably from the fact that most boys at public school leave their homes for several months of the year in order to live at school; yet, boys must struggle against the impulse to "become ashamed of speaking of [their] homes and relations in the natural language of a good heart" (60).

He believed that anything good in a boy originated in his home-life; to encourage a boy to erase this home-life from his speech, and, presumably, from his consciousness, would to Arnold have represented the most corrupt and ignoble objectives. In "The Discipline of Public Schools," he writes:

> Boys, in their own families, as the members of the natural and wholesome society of their father's household, may receive its lessons and catch its spirit, and learn at a very early age to estimate right and wrong truly. But a society formed exclusively of boys, that is, of elements each separately weak and imperfect, becomes more than an aggregate of their several defects: the amount of evil in the mass is more than the sum of the evil in the individuals . . . while the amount of good, on the contrary, is less in the mass than in the individuals, and its effect greatly weakened.
>
> (*Miscellaneous* [*The Miscellaneous Works of Thomas Arnold*] 365-66)

Thomas Hughes puts in Tom Brown's mouth the very sentiments that Thomas Arnold was committed to eradicate; for Arnold was convinced that if boys ignored their home-lives upon entering public schools, they risked the integrity of their moral and spiritual welfare.

Hughes's fiction, however, grants Arnold a victory. Not only does Tom fail to convince Arthur of the appropriateness of this schoolboy mandate, Arthur succeeds in challenging Tom's own acceptance of it. Upon hearing Tom's interdiction on domestic affection,

> Poor little Arthur looked ready to cry.
>
> "But please," said he, "mayn't I talk about—about home to you?"
>
> "Oh yes, I like it. But don't talk to boys you don't know, or they'll call you home-sick, or mamma's darling, or some such stuff."
>
> (223)

It is Tom's willingness—not, in the end, all that difficult to elicit—to talk with Arthur about his home and family that reveals his own potential for moral purity and spiritual strength. In Part II of ***Tom Brown's Schooldays,*** Tom realizes this potential through the redemptive powers of Arthur's virtuous companionship.

Of course, young boys do not always appreciate the value of virtuous companionship, and earnest friendships occasionally come under fire. Early in the second part of the book, we find East teasing Tom for "coddling" Arthur; employing a series of discursive tags that feminize Tom, he calls him Arthur's "dry nurse" (231), and insists that "[Arthur will] never be worth a button if you go on keeping him under your skirts" (232). Yet East accepts and respects Tom's determination to help Arthur: "[East] slapped him on the back and then put his arm round his shoulder, as they strolled through the quadrangle together. 'Tom,' said he, 'blest if you ain't the best old fellow ever was—I do like to see you go into a thing'" (232-33). With this blustering affability, East restores Tom's masculinity ("best old fellow ever was") and re-constructs his "coddling" of Arthur as unquestionably moral and thoroughly manly.

Before Hughes depicts this virtuous friendship, however, he provides, as contrast, a misalliance between two boys that reveals the depths to which schoolboy companionship could sink. Just after East throws his arm around Tom's shoulder, giving him the schoolboy stamp of approval, they encounter the white-handed boy: "He was one of the miserable little pretty white-handed curly-headed boys, petted and pampered by some of the big fellows, who wrote their verses for them, taught them to drink and use bad language, and did all they could to spoil them for everything in this world and the next" (233). Hughes defends the vehemence of this malediction in a footnote that suggests that schoolboys and old boys alike knew what he was talking about and that they too recognized significant differences between high-minded friendships and sordid relations:

> A kind and wise critic, an old [Rugbeian] notes here in the margin: "The small friend system was not so utterly bad from 1841-1847." Before that, too, there were many noble friendships between big and little boys, but I can't strike out the passage; many boys will know why it is left in.
>
> (233)[5]

Such pointed equivocation betrays the sexual nature of the subject; after all, if the sins were merely plagiarism, drinking, and bad language, why would Hughes make such a fuss? One might say that here he drops the penny, admitting that there were sexual acts between boys at Rugby—if not acts of sodomy then mutual masturbation, the distinctions between which were probably meaningless to Thomas Hughes, Thomas Arnold, or, for that matter, Thomas Brown.[6]

Although his characterization of the white-handed boy demonstrates Hughes's awareness of schoolboy sexuality, Tom and East's response to this boy reveals, far more than the provocative footnote, Hughes's condemnation of boyhood sensuality. As soon as the miserable little creature bids Tom and East to fag for some older boys of another house, our "heroes" react swiftly and furiously: "The youth was seized and dragged struggling out of the quadrangle"; "Tom gave the prisoner a shake-up"; "East . . . quietly tripped him up, and deposited him on the floor"; "Tom walked up to him and jerked him on to his legs"; and, finally, East "sent the young gentleman flying into the quadrangle, with a parting kick" (233-35). That Hughes never names the white-handed boy suggests that he functions as a "type" of schoolboy: the type who attaches himself to older, more powerful boys who do their work and teach them the less ingratiating qualities of late male adolescence, in return for unquestioning devotion, servility, and sexual favors. The violence of Tom and East's abuse transparently indicates that they not only disapprove of the white-handed boy, they want to stamp out the type entirely—to "exterminate the brutes." The only other character in this novel attacked two-to-one is Flashman, who is older and larger than the two boys fighting him and is, moreover, an unregenerate bully who takes his pleasure in roasting young boys before a fire.[7] The white-handed boy may be no Flashman, but we cannot doubt that Hughes believes that he receives the treatment he deserves.

Modern readers may question the justice of Hughes's feelings. After all, if the boy is, indeed, "little," "pretty," "white-handed," and "pampered," why does it take both East and Tom, two strong, athletic boys, to overpower him? Are Tom and East asserting not only their ascendency over this boy and his older friends, but also their own compelling masculinity, a masculinity that might be challenged by the tenderness they both show towards Arthur? In many uncomfortable ways, this scene does resemble a modern-day gay-bashing, with two strong (presumably heterosexual) males bullying an effeminate (presumably homosexual) one. Eve Kosofsky Sedgwick identifies this kind of behavior as homosexual panic:

> the historically shifting . . . arbitrary and self-contradictory . . . nature of the way *homosexuality* . . . has been defined in relation to the rest of the male homosocial spectrum has been an exceedingly potent and embattled locus of power over the entire range of male bonds, and perhaps especially over those that define themselves, not *as* homosexual, but *as against* the homosexual. Because the paths of male entitlement, especially in the nineteenth century, required certain intense bonds that were not readily distinguishable from the most reprobated bonds, an endemic and ineradicable state of what I am calling male homosexual panic became the normal condition of male heterosexual entitlement.

("Beast" ["The Beast in the Closet"] 151)

According to this formulation, Tom and East affirm their "heterosexual entitlement" by demonstrating, redundantly and violently, that they are not like the white-handed boy and, what's more, that they can beat up his type.

While I find Sedgwick's theoretical structures both riveting and provocative, especially in regard to late Victorian and Modern culture, I question their validity as an interpretive guide for such early Victorian figures as Arnold and Hughes, who would not have found Christian friendship and homosexual intimacy *anything but* "readily distinguishable." Indeed, a conversation at the end of this scene demonstrates that Hughes means to distinguish Tom, and by implication Arthur, from the likes of the carnal white-handed boy and his patrons:

> "Nice boy, Tommy," said East, shoving his hands in his pockets and strolling to the fire.
>
> "Worst sort we breed," responded Tom, following his example.
>
> "Thank goodness, no big fellow ever took to petting me."
>
> "You'd never have been like that."

(235)

East's rejoinder, "You'd never have been like that"—employing a negative conditional past perfect construction—summarily denies that Tom is, was, or ever could be a white-handed boy—and that although some big fellows take to petting younger ones, Tom is a big fellow of an altogether different stamp.

While this episode affirms Tom's manly virtue, it also speaks for Arthur's purity. Arthur and the white-handed boy are, after all, superficially similar: both are the delicate younger friends of athletic older boys. Arthur, moreover, conforms to a type then considered morally dubious, at least by the more hysterical. William Acton, in *The Functions and Disorders of the Reproductive Organs,* published the same year as *Tom Brown's Schooldays,* warns that frail, bookish boys, like Arthur, are prone to sexual vices, both solitary and otherwise: "as any one may observe, it is not the strong athletic boy, fond of healthy exercise, who thus early shows marks of sexual desire, but your puny exotic, whose intellectual education has been fostered at the expense of his physical development" (qtd. in Pearsall [*Public Purity, Private Shame*] 20). The momentum of contrast established in this chapter distinguishes Arthur from the white-handed boy, just as it dissociates the virtuous friendship from the wicked dalliance. By opposing respectable intimacies and "beastly" ones, Hughes shows that Tom and Arthur's friendship is more than irreproachable, it is ennobling. For they not only avoid those behaviors which Hughes cannot bring himself to name, they also inspire in one another a respect for all that is virtuous and decent, especially "natural affections" for home-life and for one another. They become, in short, the kinds of boys Thomas Arnold hoped to produce at Rugby.

The structure of the chapter reinforces the opposition between venal intimacies and rewarding ones, by placing the appearance of the white-handed boy between two episodes concerned with Tom and Arthur's friendship. We have already examined the initial episode, in which East first teases and then praises Tom for his affectionate concern for Arthur; the second episode allows us to see this affection enacted. Tom discovers Arthur in their shared study, weeping copiously; he is so moved that he "shut the door at once and sat down on the sofa by Arthur, putting his arm around his neck" (236). Arthur explains that he is despondently recalling that his family always read the Bible together after tea—a custom he was finding difficult to continue in the dormitories at school. Tom responds in two significant ways: he asks Arthur to call him "Tom," instead of "Brown," and he invites him to talk about his home life:

> Arthur had never spoken of his home before, and Tom hadn't encouraged him to do so, as his blundering schoolboy reasoning made him think that Arthur would be softened and less manly for thinking of home. But now he was fairly interested, and forgot all about chisels and bottled beer.
>
> (237)

Not only does this reverse his earlier admonition against talking about one's family at school, it also shows that Tom himself feels drawn to, even *into,* Arthur's family: "From this time Arthur constantly spoke of his home, and, above all, of his father . . . [whom] Tom soon got to love and reverence almost as much as his own son did" (237-38). The language of familial closeness and fraternity provides Hughes, and later writers of the genre as well, with a means for understanding and articulating the intimacy of these friendships.[8] In schoolboy fiction, metaphorical brotherhood establishes an affective structure for emotionally charged bonds between unrelated males of roughly the same age, merging in this metaphor the familial use of *brothers* and the Evangelical use of *brethren.*

Family configurations and re-configurations, more generally, appear consistently in representations of these friendships. Few pairs of schoolboy friends have a full complement of parents. Arthur has no father or brothers, and Tom's friendship might be said to fill a male affectional void in his life. In varying degrees nearly all schoolboy heroes are, to quote David Copperfield's memorable phrase, "posthumous children." Edwin Russell, in F. W. Farrar's *Eric* (1858), has no parents; in J. E. C. Welldon's *Gerald Eversley's Friendship* (1895), Gerald has no mother; in Horace A. Vachell's *The Hill* (1905), John Verney has no father, and Harry Desmond no mother; in Farrar's *Julian Home* (1860), Julian and DeVayne are fatherless while their friend Kennedy is motherless; in E. F. Benson's *David Blaize* (1916), David has no mother, while his friend Maddox has no father; Charles Ryder, in *Brideshead Revisited* (1945), is motherless and, for all of the support and love his father

gives him, would be better off fatherless, as well. The high parent-mortality rate in this genre reflects more than the prevalence of fatal disease in Victorian England; to be without parents was, indeed, the experience of all of these boys—shipped off at age 12 or 13 for the better part of the year to live with one another rather than with their families. Moreover, as boarding preparatory schools multiplied and expanded during the nineteenth century, an increasing number of middle-class boys left home by the age of seven or eight (Honey 126).

This separation from home naturally shaped the relationships boys formed at school; as late as 1958, Fraser Harrison writes about the void he experienced as an institutional orphan at Shrewsbury:

> the development of special friendships was a natural response to the highly unnatural circumstances in which we had all been brought up since the age of eight or so. They were the only available substitute for the relationships that had been cut short, starved or forgotten as a result of our being sent to school. Without either side being more than vaguely aware of it, friends were required to compensate for the absence of parents, brothers and sisters, grandparents, aunts, [and] uncles.
>
> (125)

Inevitably, the public school system itself, while providing the means for boys to leave behind their homes and families, was often conceptualized as a kind of family. In the 1840s Stephen Hawtrey started a private school at Windsor, St. Mark's, which by the end of the century developed into a public school; its "principle was to promote, on the analogy of the family, personal contact between 'human living souls'—the fraternal relationship between boys, the filial relationship between boys and masters" (Honey 20).

Tom's invitation for Arthur to call him by his Christian name, likewise, represents an attempt to mitigate school-life with an intimacy characteristic of home-life. Isabel Quigly reports that Victorian and Edwardian schoolboys took the custom of addressing one another by surname very seriously; she notes that by the turn of the century, most boys demanded that their mail be addressed to them at school with surname and initials only—so that no one could even accidentally discover their Christian names, which were reserved for family and the very closest of friends (73). Harold Nicolson, writing of his school days at the turn of the century, attests to this: "In my own youth, had I been addressed by my Christian name at my private or even my public school, I should have blushed scarlet, feeling that my privacy had been outraged and that some secret manliness had been purloined from me" (272). This boundary, marked by the names by which boys are known, is clearly important as early as **Tom Brown's Schooldays,** a mid-century novel; only East and Arthur call the hero "Tom," and

Tom invites Arthur to do so as a gesture of affection and comfort in a moment of great distress. Inviting a friend to use one's Christian name, in essence, invited that friend into the circle of home and family.

In fiction, this custom is honored both in the breach and the observance. In Benson's *David Blaize* (1916), the hero is mortified when his father reveals David's given name while visiting his school: "every boy in the school would know what his Christian name was. . . . Christian names at Helmsworth were hidden secrets: if you liked a boy very much you might tell him what your Christian name was, but to have it publicly shouted out, so that every one knew, was quite horrible" (66-67). Compton Mackenzie's *Sinister Street* (1913), the *bildungsroman* that captured the imagination of several writers during the first half of the century (including Benson and Evelyn Waugh), presents a wistful *précis* of the schoolboy friendship that encapsulates the significance of a boy's home-life in the formation of such friendships:

> Michael formed a great friendship. He and Buckley were inseparable for sixteen whole weeks. During that time they exchanged the most intimate confidences. Buckley told Michael that his Christian names were Claude Arnold Eustace, and Michael told Buckley that he was called Charles Michael Saxby, and also that his mother was generally away from home, that his father was dead, that his governess was called Miss Carthew, that he had a sister who played the piano and that one day when he grew up he hoped to be an explorer and search for orchids in Borneo.
>
> (94-95)

This genre is full of such attempts to merge family life with school life, "adoptions" of a kind that perhaps represent the means by which the schoolboy novel shares the broader generic impulse of the novel form: middle-class concerns about births, marriage, and property. If the protagonists in this genre can't give birth to children or marry one another, they *can* form other social alliances that establish or reinforce middle-class values. In place of the strictly heterosexual events of birth and marriage, we see other forms of family coalescence: a boy spending the holidays with his friend's family; a mother exchanging letters with her son's "particular friend"; a sister professing that this boy is, by virtue of his friendship, a member of the family. Incipient forms of many of these tropes appear in ***Tom Brown's Schooldays***. When Tom meets Arthur's mother, Arthur arranges the two of them on the same sofa, as if in a portrait, and exclaims, "[N]ow . . . I have realized one of the dearest wishes of my life—to see you two together" (321).

Such a fusion of family and friends can also be accomplished through the romantic (i.e., sexual) attachment between a boy and his friend's sister. In view of the public schools' integral role in the class-defined social network, such a scenario makes perfect sense. Public school friendships not only offer boys companionships with one another, they provide families with the means by which presumably compatible men and women from the same or neighboring classes can meet. What could be more convenient than introducing a sister to one's good friend? The sister is assured of a husband who is a gentleman, and the friend is assured of at least one member of the family of whom he is already fond. This pattern was so established by the end of the century that E. F. Benson could parody it in *The Babe, B.A.* (1897): "One is supposed to fall in love with each other's sisters in May week . . . But the sisters either die of consumption or else the Dean snaps them up, and so it doesn't come off" (85).[9]

Typically the sisters are not only agreeable and available, they also bear a striking resemblance to their brothers. We should recall Charles Ryder's frank admission to Sebastian's sister Julia that Sebastian was, after all, her "forerunner" (Waugh [*Brideshead Revisited*] 303). Not even the young Tom Brown is immune from this partiality for his friend's female relatives. When he meets Arthur's mother, Tom recognizes her face: "the eye that he knew so well, for it was his friend's over again and the lovely tender mouth that trembled while he looked" (320). Tom thinks Mrs. Arthur a good and beautiful woman, but at age 38 she is hardly an appropriate choice for his rather sudden enthusiasm for female goodness and beauty; perhaps realizing this, "[h]e couldn't help wondering if Arthur's sisters were like her" (321). Family resemblances, Tom Brown fervently hopes, will tell.

Later writers can be surprisingly candid about this identification of brother and sister "lovers": in A. W. Clarke's *Jaspar Tristram* (1899), Jaspar finds Nita compelling mainly because "she had in her something of a boy. . . . it was always of her brother that she reminded him" (216). We might explain this triad of brother, sister, and friend with reference to Sedgwick's schema for gender asymmetry and erotic triangles. In *Between Men*, Sedgwick identifies such triangles as relationships in which the primary bond exists between the two men, while the woman serves as the "traffic" through which the men's bonds are cemented (21-27). This vicarious consummation is made explicit in Welldon's *Gerald Eversley's Friendship* (1895), when Gerald considers his affections for Ethel Venniker, his friend Harry's sister:

> [T]here was . . . a presentiment of love in Gerald Eversley's relation to Miss Venniker. It lay in his old affection for her brother. . . . Miss Venniker was endowed in Gerald Eversley's view not only with her own charm, rare as it was, but with her brother's too. To be linked to her was to be linked to him, to him perpetually. The old schoolboy friendship would be consolidated, nay, it

would be sanctified by a deeper and holier sympathy. . . . Have I not known elsewhere instances of men who have loved the brother first, and then—with a still stronger love—his sister? And can there be any guarantee more beautiful for the perfectness of married life than this meeting, this blending of the old love and the new in one deep, holy, peaceful current of devotion?

(293)

Friendships like Tom and Arthur's were more than unexceptional, they were conventional—conventional because they shared many of the cultural ideals of the mid-Victorian middle class. David Newsome reminds us that a yearning for passionate friendships was inseparable.

from the spirit of the age . . . the spirit supplying the passion, the intensity, the rapture of love and the bitterness of hate which we meet at every turn. In the long run, they perished together, killed by the same foe. Of the revelations that were to come from the pens of Freud and Havelock Ellis, these generations were blissfully unaware. No exception was taken to boys linking arms or to men occasionally showing deep affection by embraces. . . . There is really nothing odd about the attitude of these early and mid-Victorians to friendship save in comparison with later standards of outward conduct.

(88)

Tom and Arthur's affection epitomizes the passion, the tenderness, and the piety of such friendship: they read the Bible together; they pray together, rather conspicuously, on their knees in a crowded dormitory; they inspire decent behavior in others, even encouraging East to prepare for Confirmation; and they recognize their love for one another, without a shred of embarrassment or inner turmoil. When Arthur falls ill with a fever, Tom visits him and realizes that "his little chum had twined himself round his heart-strings"; "he stole gently across the room and knelt down, and put his arm round Arthur's head on the pillow" (308). For Hughes and Arnold, as well as their readers, this love was emphatically Christian and undeniably manly. Their affection for one another makes neither boy puny or exotic. In fact, Tom teaches Arthur the importance of exercise and team sports; by the end of the novel, Arthur is playing on the cricket eleven.

Hughes explicates such "Muscular Christianity" more distinctly in *Tom Brown at Oxford* (1861):

the muscular Christian . . . has hold of the old chivalrous and Christian belief that a man's body is given him to be trained and brought into subjection, and then used for the protection of the weak, the advancement of all righteous causes, and the subduing of the earth. . . . He does not hold that mere strength or activity are in themselves worthy of any respect or worship or that one man is a bit better than another because he can knock him down, or carry a bigger sack of potatoes than he.

(119)

Although Hughes celebrates boyish stamina in football, cricket, fishing, even fist-fighting, he doesn't allow readers to ignore the spiritual and emotional lives of his characters—at least his male characters. And those emotional lives included, if the men were fortunate, Christianizing friendships, which both Arnold and Hughes dignified. Towards the end of *Tom Brown's Schooldays,* Hughes writes:

a time comes in every human friendship, when you must go down into the depths of yourself, and lay bare what is there to your friend and wait in fear for his answer. A few moments may do it; and it may be (most likely will be, as you are English boys) that you will never do it but once. You must find what is there, at the very root and bottom of one another's hearts; and if you are at one there, nothing on earth can, or at least ought, to sunder you.

(335)

Despite the "stiff-upper-lip" quality of this passage, it allows for emotional depths which can, at least on occasion, be fathomed. Canonical Victorian and Edwardian novels reveal several intimate male friendships: Pip and Herbert Pocket, Mortimer Lightwood and Eugene Wrayburn, Sherlock Holmes and Dr. Watson, Ratty and Mole (*The Wind in the Willows*). The lesser read novels of this period yield other illustrations: *The Bachelor of the Albany* (Marmion Wilmo Savage, 1847), *Julian Home* (F. W. Farrar, 1860), *Jack Raymond* (E. L. Voynich, 1901), *Keddy: A Story of Oxford* (H. N. Dickinson, 1907), *Sinister Street* (Compton Mackenzie, 1913), and the countless schoolboy novels written between the 1860s and the Great War.

All of this suggests that middle-class Victorian men were, by and large, comfortable with intense, occasionally affectionate, earnestly sentimental friendships. In our own age, when many American men seem to express non-sexual passion only for the rituals of the playing field or the beating of tribal drums, we might learn about more than cricket when we look at the heart of *Tom Brown's Schooldays.*

Notes

1. Before the appearance of *Tom Brown's Schooldays,* other fictions, most of them written by women with elevated purposes, were set at boys' schools; these include Maria Edgeworth's "The Barring Out" and "Tarlton" (1796), Dorothy Kilner's *First Going to School; Or, the Story of Tom Brown and His Sisters* (1804), and Harriet Martineau's *The Crofton Boys* (1841). Most critics short-sightedly dismiss them in their considerations of the development of the genre, which they place, instead, in the hands of male writers.

2. Many characters in this genre have surnames that are actually Christian names (e.g., Arthur, Will-

iams, Russell, Stanley, and, for that matter, Arnold). This can result in some confusion—but a significant confusion. These complexities in the naming of characters can be seen to reflect the unstable identities of the characters, boys and young men who are discovering themselves during the course of the events in these fictions. I refer to characters with the names most regularly used by their narrators.

3. A letter from Thomas Arnold to J. T. Coleridge, 17 September 1832. John Taylor Coleridge (1790-1876), nephew to the poet, was a close friend of Arnold's from their time together in Oxford.

4. Christian brotherhood was at the root of Christian Socialism, a movement largely associated with F. D. Maurice (1805-72), who believed that it was cooperation and not competition that formed the foundation of a Christian society. Preaching a universal brotherhood that crossed class boundaries, Maurice founded the Working Men's College in London in 1854. Thomas Hughes was principal of the College (1872-83), taught Bible classes there, and commanded its volunteer corps.

5. The campaign against the potentially dangerous friendships between older and younger boys raged throughout the latter years of the century. In 1882, the *Journal of Education* printed a correspondence addressing the issue of schoolboy sex, in which the Rev. J. M. Wilson, headmaster of Clifton, argued that all schoolboy sexuality was evil and bound to lead to adult promiscuity and other ruinous side-effects. To counter those claims, the pseudonymous "Olim Etonensis" endeavored to reassure the public by explaining that these morally compromising relationships "exist . . . in all large schools": "it would be wiser to regard the habit with contempt than with horror. A friend of mine—a peer, the Lord Lieutenant of his county, and the father of a public school boy—told me that when he was at school he was 'taken up' . . . by boys bigger than himself, and petted—he supposed because of his good looks; that before he received such notice he was an 'untidy, slovenly little ruffian,' and that he dated his conversion to gentlemanly habits and refined manners from the time when he was so patronised" (qtd. in Honey [*Tom Brown's Universe*] 178-81). I doubt that "Olim Etonensis" offered much consolation to the burgeoning middle classes—the major supplier of boys for public schools—who were not particularly eager for their sons to acquire the more voluptuous manners of the aristocracy, especially when they were purchased at such a price.

6. That mid-Victorian schoolboys did, on occasion, engage in sexual activities with one another is made explicit in John Addington Symonds's *Mem-oirs*; Symonds writes, arguably with more interest than he admits to, that, at Harrow at least, "one could not avoid seeing acts of onanism, mutual masturbation, the sports of naked boys in bed together" (94). Symonds was at Harrow 1854-58; his memoirs—written in 1892—were kept secret until Phyllis Grosskurth published them in 1984.

7. George MacDonald Fraser's irreverent Flashman novels continue the boy-villain's experiences after his expulsion from Rugby, re-casting Harry Flashman as a robust and impulsive, if also rakish and womanizing, anti-hero. Although Fraser is intent on portraying Arnold as a hypocrite and a prig, his portrayal of Flashman's family conforms to Arnold's own theories about the significance of a boy's home-life. In *Flashman* (1969), the first novel in the series, we learn that Harry Flashman's father is a hunting, drinking, whoring Clubman, whose vast family wealth was made in the slave trade; his virtuous mother, of course, is long dead. Without an appropriately Christian family model, Flashman would, in Arnold's eyes, be doomed to less than principled behavior.

8. Just as Hughes's associate F. D. Maurice repeatedly used the language of brotherhood in his religious discourse (see Vance [*The Sinews of the Spirit*] 55).

9. On the tendency to reinforce old-school ties through intermarriage to sisters and daughters, see Honey 161.

Works Cited

Arnold, Thomas. *The Miscellaneous Works of* . . . New York: Appleton, 1845.

———. *Christian Life at School.* [Sermons, Volume II.] Ed. Mrs. W. E. Forster. London: Longmans, 1878.

———. *Christian Life, Its Course, Its Hindrances, and Its Helps.* [Sermons, Volume IV.] Ed. Mrs. W. E. Forster. London: Longmans, 1878.

———. *Christian Life, Its Hopes, Its Fears, and Its Close.* [Sermons, Volume V.] Ed. Mrs. W. E. Forster. London: Longmans, 1878.

Benson, Edward F. *The Babe, B.A.* New York: Garland, 1984.

———. *David Blaize.* London: Hogarth, 1989.

Clarke, A. W. *Jaspar Tristram.* New York: Garland, 1984.

Fraser, George MacDonald. *Flashman: From The Flashman Papers 1839-1842.* London: Jenkins, 1969.

Harrison, Fraser. *Trivial Disputes.* London: Collins, 1989.

Honey, J. R. de S. *Tom Brown's Universe: The Development of the English Public School in the Nineteenth Century.* New York: Quadrangle, 1977.

Hughes, Thomas. *Tom Brown at Oxford.* New York: American News, n.d.

————. *Tom Brown's Schooldays.* Oxford: Oxford UP, 1989.

Mackenzie, Compton. *Sinister Street.* London: Macdonald, 1949.

Newsome, David. *Godliness and Good Learning: Four Studies on a Victorian Ideal.* London: Cassell, 1961.

Nicolson, Harold. *Good Behaviour: Being a Study of Certain Types of Civility.* Boston: Beacon, 1955.

Pearsall, Ronald. *Public Purity, Private Shame: Victorian Sexual Hypocrisy Exposed.* London: Weidenfeld and Nicolson, 1976.

Quigly, Isabel. *The Heirs of Tom Brown: The English School Story.* London: Chatto and Windus, 1982.

Sedgwick, Eve Kosofsky. *Between Men: English Literature and Male Homosocial Desire.* New York: Columbia UP, 1985.

————. "The Beast in the Closet: James and the Writing of Homosexual Panic." *Sex, Politics, and Science in the Nineteenth-Century Novel.* Ed. Ruth Bernard Yeazell. Baltimore: Johns Hopkins UP, 1986. 148-186.

Stanley, Arthur Penrhyn. *Life and Correspondence of Thomas Arnold.* London: Fellowes, 1852.

Symonds, John Addington. *The Memoirs of . . .* Ed. Phyllis Grosskurth. New York: Random House, 1984.

Vance, Norman. *The Sinews of the Spirit: The Ideal of Christian Manliness in Victorian Literature and Religious Thought.* Cambridge: Cambridge UP, 1985.

Waugh, Evelyn. *Brideshead Revisited.* Boston: Little Brown, 1945.

Welldon, J. E. C. *Gerald Eversley's Friendship: A Study in Real Life.* London: Smith, Elder, 1895.

Robert Dingley (essay date summer 1996)

SOURCE: Dingley, Robert. "Shades of the Prison House: Discipline and Surveillance in *Tom Brown's Schooldays.*" *Victorian Review* 22, no. 1 (summer 1996): 1-12.

[*In the following essay, Dingley addresses representations of disciplinary action in* Tom Brown's Schooldays.]

> The delight with which . . . he regarded even the unsightliness of the great Birmingham Railway, when it was brought to Rugby, was very characteristic of him.—"I rejoice to see it", he said, as he stood on one of the arches, and watched the train pass on through the distant hedgerows,—"I rejoice to see it, and think that feudality is gone for ever".
>
> (Stanley, *Life of Arnold* [*Life and Correspondence of Thomas Arnold*], 507n.)

I

When Tom Brown first leaves his Berkshire home to begin his schooldays at Rugby [in ***Tom Brown's Schooldays***], he travels up by coach, and Hughes lavishes several pages of nostalgic evocation on the details of his journey—on "the music of the rattling harness", on "the cheery toot of the guard's horn", even on the bitterly cold weather, which is relished as a test of "silent endurance, so dear to every Englishman" (76; Part One, Ch. 4). Some eight years later, his schooldays ended, Tom leaves Rugby for the last time: by midday, we are curtly informed, he "was in the train, and away for London" (367; Part Two, Ch. 8).

Hughes makes no direct comment on the crucial shift that has taken place in transport and communication during the relatively brief course of Tom's school career, but the way in which that career is framed by two such starkly contrasted journeys is one among many textual hints that the book's preoccupation with historical change extends far beyond the transformation of a single school by a uniquely gifted headmaster. Thomas Arnold's educational reforms of the 1830s are construed by Hughes both as symptomatic of, and as partly responsible for, a more general adaptation in the structure of English life. In common with other mid-nineteenth century novelists—the most obvious examples are Thackeray in *Vanity Fair* and George Eliot in *Middlemarch*—he seeks to locate in the comparatively recent past the origins of the distinctive present inhabited by himself and his readers. All three writers, indeed, select a pivotal, partly symbolic and partly instrumental, event—the Battle of Waterloo, the coming of railways and reform to a country town, the arrival of Arnold at an ancient foundation—in which it is possible to locate the tentative establishment of a new order, or in which, at least, a momentum for change becomes demonstrably irreversible.

And, in the case of ***Tom Brown's Schooldays,*** the nature of that change seems clearly defined. When Tom first enters Rugby, Arnold has been there only a short time and has already made himself deeply unpopular by insisting on the abolition of cherished and time-honored traditions. The school he has set out to reform appears (both to its inmates and to Hughes's readers) to be regulated largely through displays of violence, and the nature and extent of that violence to be dependent on the personal qualities of the senior pupils rather than on the authority of the more or less invisible teaching staff.

The regular replacement of each sixth form by its successor means that no stability or continuity can be assured from year to year, and there is always, consequently, a potential for anarchy—for what Hughes calls "no-government" (167; Part One, Ch. 8)—in which corruption and cruelty go unchecked. The systematic torture of small boys by larger ones—tossing in blankets, scorching before the fires in Hall—is presented in Hughes's narrative as aberrant and is carefully ascribed to the influence of individual sadists like Flashman, but it is also visibly part of a nexus of customary practice which has developed over centuries and it is not readily isolable (either in narrative or in ethical terms) from a culture where beatings, fist-fights, and football matches during which little boys can be knocked unconscious by big ones, receive not only institutional sanction but fulsome endorsement.

At one revealing point, indeed, it is even suggested that bullying itself forms part of the educational curriculum: in his valedictory address to School House, the exemplary old Brooke concedes that "there's a deal of bullying going on" but reassures the younger boys that "You'll be better football players for learning to stand it, and to take your own parts, and fight it through" (123; Part One, Ch. 6). Quite apart from its implicit acknowledgment of a continuum between the activities of Flashman and those of the playing-field, Brooke's remarks attest the degree to which the life of the boys is assumed to be self-regulating; for all his concession that the Doctor will prove "an awkwardish customer" (124; Part One, Ch. 6), it simply never occurs to Brooke that the "deal of bullying" he has noticed might be a matter of concern for Rugby's headmaster, let alone for his staff.

This, then, is the situation which Arnold inherits and over which he seeks to impose his own centralized control. Initially, he tries to dominate the school by appropriating its existing violence as a disciplinary prerogative. Examining Tom's form, the Doctor loses patience with a "luckless youngster" who is unable to construe his Latin exercise:

> he made three steps up to the construer and gave him a good box on the ear. The blow was not a hard one, but the boy was so taken by surprise that he started back; the form caught the back of his knees, and over he went on to the floor behind.
>
> (165-6; Part One, Ch. 8)

After this "terrible field-day", however, "never again while Tom was at school did the Doctor strike a boy in lesson" (166; Part One, Ch. 8).

Indeed, following this incident, Arnold becomes increasingly remote from the school's daily life, and for minatory presence he substitutes a largely invisible surveillance, occasionally issuing from his "turret" (297; Part Two, Ch. 5) to quell by his mere appearance some outbreak of disorder. From the "highest round tower" at the end of the "long line of gray buildings" (89; Part One, Ch. 5), however, his gaze—and thus his moral authority—is unresting. He has "long had his eye on Flashman" (194; Part One, Ch. 9), for example, and so expels him from the school at the earliest available opportunity; when Tom and East become ringleaders of indiscipline, "his eye, which was everywhere, was upon them" and Tom comments ruefully that "It's all his look . . . that frightens fellows" (199; Part One, Ch. 9). Tom, indeed, has already had some experience of the Doctor's wrathful countenance and "wouldn't have met his eye for all he was worth" (165; Part One, Ch. 8). Arnold, we are later told, "knew everything" (250; Part Two, Ch. 3) and Hughes rings the changes on this assertion of omniscience elsewhere, when he rhetorically enquires: "What didn't the Doctor know?" (221; Part Two, Ch. 1). Even so, this absolute power is exercised with tact and discretion: "He knows better than any one when to look, and when to see nothing" (130; Part One, Ch. 6).

But the conclusive affirmation of Arnold's moral and political ascendancy occurs in the book's penultimate chapter. After the last cricket match of his school career, Tom and a junior master sit together over tea and cake and discuss the former's progress during his time at Rugby. Tom mentions the "lucky chance" that sent George Arthur to the school "and made him my chum", but the young master reveals to him that no chance has been entailed here, that Arnold entrusted the withdrawn Arthur to Tom's care so that Tom would become "a little steadier" and acquire "manliness and thoughtfulness":

> And I can assure you he has watched the experiment ever since with great satisfaction. Ah! not one of you boys will ever know the anxiety you have given him, or the care with which he has watched over every step in your school lives.
>
> (364-5; Part Two, Ch. 8)

For Tom, this comes as a revelation. He has hitherto believed, not only that he has been responsible for his own moral regeneration, but that "the great reform in the School had been owing quite as much to himself as to any one else" (365; Part Two, Ch. 8). Now, however, he becomes "a hero-worshipper, who would have satisfied the soul of Thomas Carlyle himself" because he sees that:

> the great Headmaster had found time . . . to watch over the career, even of him, Tom Brown and his particular friends,—and, no doubt, of fifty other boys at the same time; and all this without taking the least credit to himself, or seeming to know, or let any one else know, that he ever thought particularly of any boy at all.
>
> (366-7; Part Two, Ch. 8)

The disclosure of this unseen but all-seeing vigilance has on Tom the effect of a religious conversion: he now, we are told, has "the blindest faith" and "there wasn't a corner of him left which didn't believe in the Doctor" (366-7; Part Two, Ch. 8). Indeed, in the book's final chapter, when Tom returns to Rugby after Arnold's death to pay homage to his mentor, the Doctor and God become more or less interchangeable in his mind, and Hughes excuses the elision as a necessary phase in the individual's progression towards spiritual truth:

> And let us not be too hard on him, if at that moment his soul is fuller of the tomb and him who lies there, than of the altar and Him of whom it speaks. Such stages have to be gone through, I believe, by all young and brave souls, who must win their way through hero-worship to the worship of Him who is the King and Lord of Heroes.

(376; Part Two, Ch. 9)

II

Tom's education at Rugby begins in the rough community of the football field; it ends with solitary meditation in the chapel. The novel's closing paragraphs thus affirm the radical recentering that has taken place not only in Tom's own moral being but in the constitution of the school itself. And the nature of that transformation, as Hughes represents it in his novel, bears, I would suggest, a striking general resemblance to the paradigm-shift in Western penal systems which Michel Foucault chronicles in *Discipline and Punish*. At the commencement of Tom's school career, power is expressed through public, and often ritualized, displays of physical violence, and these displays have less to do with justice or moral reform than with the maintenance in place of an hierarchical system founded on seniority.[1] By the end of the novel, however, the Doctor has substituted for that earlier disciplinary structure a new model based on the healing of souls rather than on the torture of bodies and instrumented through the power of his gaze; as he occupies his "turret", invisible and unresting in his care, his role is closely analogous to that of the gaoler in the watchtower at the centre of Bentham's radiating Panopticon.[2]

But while Foucault's argument seems applicable in broad terms to the transition Hughes describes, there are also significant discrepancies. Most importantly, I think, Arnold's mission does not consist in the subjection of his school to a uniform disciplinary regime (the Benthamite ideal) but rather in tailoring his treatment (and the term, like Arnold's title, seems apposite here) to the specific needs of each pupil. Tom's tendency to transgression, for example, derives from boyish high spirits rather than real vice, so it is effectively tempered by the Doctor's provision of George Arthur as a spiritually elevating room-mate; conversely, Arthur's withdrawn reticence finds itself healthily adjusted by expo-

sure to Tom's more clubbable personality. While, then, Arnold's structural *position* within the school is—and almost explicitly—that of the omniscient watcher in the Panopticon, his *actions* bear a closer resemblance to those of the Enlightenment thinkers described in the second Part of Foucault's book who devised increasingly elaborate procedures for the adaptation of penal measures to the moral reformation of individual offenders.

Our need to adjust the Foucaultian model if it is to be appropriate to Hughes's presentation of Arnold derives, I think, from two possible sources. In the first place, as Michel de Certeau has suggested in a brilliant critique of *Discipline and Punish,* Foucault presents what is essentially a linear, sequential, even panoptic, progression—from torture in the public square to the numbing anonymity of the reformatory—which allows for very little overlap between different phases in the narrative or for moments in which a plurality of practices or, indeed, a mixed practice, is not only possible but inevitable (185-192). The discrepancy (in terms of Foucault's thesis) between Arnold's structural position in the school (and, indeed, the text) and his individuating practice may thus derive in large measure from his status (or rather from Hughes's implicit recognition of his status) as an historically transitional figure.

At a less general level, however, I want to suggest that the friction which results from attempting to impose a Foucaultian schema on Hughes's narrative is generated by an obvious difference in the institutions which each writer describes. Foucault's examples—prisons, reform schools, charity wards, and so on—are all, by and large, premised on a clear distinction in social class between governors and governed—a fact which receives only muted acknowledgement in *Discipline and Punish* because Foucault's theoretical concern is broadly with the epistemology of power rather than with its local histories. Hughes's Rugby, however, is marked by no such social division—its purpose, indeed, is precisely to educate a new generation of governors and legislators. And that, in turn, means that, unlike the Panopticon, the public school cannot be devoted solely to the production of obediently conforming citizens; it must balance its standardizing function with the nurturance of independent initiative and judgment, with the creation of fully constituted subjects who will themselves be capable of exercising power creatively rather than becoming merely inert objects of surveillance.[3]

However attractive, then, a Benthamite model of streamlined efficiency may seem as an image for Arnold's systematic reform, it operates in Hughes's text rather as a figurative index of the distance Rugby has travelled between Tom's arrival and his departure than as a sign of the specific direction which that reform has taken. Rugby has become the nursery not only of efficient servants of the state but also of its future masters (whose service, indeed, is perfect freedom), and the extent to which that process has been successful is, I would suggest, exemplified as much in the book's narrative procedures as in the bare history of Tom's career.

Tom Brown's Schooldays, its early editions insisted, was written not by "Thomas Hughes" but by "An Old Boy", whose soubriquet lays claim to representative status. What kind of book, therefore, does a typical product of Arnold's Rugby write? By most conventional criteria, the answer to that question would have to be (indeed, has been) unfavorable.[4] Hughes's novel, set against the fictions of his major contemporaries, seems formless, episodic, poorly proportioned, and, above all, remorselessly digressive. Its narrator's habit of breaking off, whenever the impulse moves him, in order to lecture—hector, even—his audience on any subject which takes his fancy has become notorious and it is tempting to attribute it simply to Hughes's naive ebullience. But I want to suggest here that, on the contrary, the novel's narrative voice is a deliberate and purposeful construct. It is, for one thing, buoyantly self-aware. Responding to charges of "too much preaching" in the Preface to the sixth edition, the author exclaims:

> Why, my whole object in writing at all was to get the chance of preaching! . . . I can't see that a man has any business to write at all unless he has something which he thoroughly believes and wants to preach about. If he has this, and the chance of delivering himself of it, let him by all means put it in the shape in which it will be most likely to get a hearing; but let him never be so carried away as to forget that preaching is his object.
>
> ("Preface", xl)

But "preaching" for the "Old Boy" entails no concomitant assumption of authority; it is rather to be construed as a kind of amiable impulsiveness, a spontaneous overflow of powerful earnestness which requires an immediate outlet no matter what the consequences may be for the structure or consistency of the text. Chapter One thus ends with a cheery admission:

> So having succeeded in contradicting myself in my first chapter (which gives me great hopes that you will all go on, and think me a good fellow notwithstanding my crotchets,) I shall here shut up for the present, and consider my ways; having resolved to "sar" it out", as we say in the Vale, "holus bolus", just as it comes, and then you'll probably get the truth out of me.
>
> (19-20; Part One, Ch. 1)

Much later in the novel, a similar confession of narratorial eccentricity occurs when the book presents the history of George Arthur's saintly father:

> What has all this to do with our story? Well, my dear boys, let a fellow go on his own way, or you won't get anything out of him worth having. I must show you

what sort of a man it was who had begotten and trained little Arthur, or else you won't believe in him, which I am resolved you shall do . . .

> (241; Part Two, Ch. 2)

Such intrusions are partly designed to establish a tone of avuncular familiarity which will ingratiate the book with juvenile readers.[5] But they also serve, I would suggest, another and more central purpose in Hughes's narrative simply by parading their own artless neglect of conventional decorum. *This* narrative voice, clearly, has not been reduced to conformist anonymity by his education; however clumsily, he thinks for himself, and his formal shortcomings are so much evidence that he represents in his own person the same forthright independence he everywhere champions. In Chapter Two, for example, the novel provides an account of a country fair in Berkshire (an incident which Hughes later expanded into his novella *The Scouring of the White Horse* (1859)) and characteristically admits its failure to impose a due order and control; but this very loss of proportion enables the whole description to mime—even to participate in—the carnival freedom of the event itself:

> How my country fair is spinning out! I see I must skip the wrestling, and the boys jumping in sacks, and rolling wheelbarrows blindfolded . . .
>
> (40; Part One, Ch. 2)

Even after this recognition of his own untidiness, however, the narrator cannot bring himself to close the chapter without inserting some polemical remarks on precisely the kinds of deadening reform which are most perfectly exemplified in the Panopticon and which seek to eradicate traditional practices like the fair in favor of "new-fangled comprehensive plans" (41; Part One, Ch. 2). His impatience with such measures is not therefore expressed simply in the content of his "preaching", but in his assertive disruption of his own book's economy:

> Only I have just got this to say before I quit the text. Don't let reformers of any sort think that they are going really to lay hold of the working boys and young men of England by any educational grapnel whatever, which hasn't some *bona fide* equivalent for the games of the old country "veast" in it . . .
>
> (41; Part One, Ch. 2)

By foregrounding his own blunt, no-nonsense persona, the narrator aligns himself here with the "healthy sound" (41; Part One, Ch. 2) Englishness that the fair represents and against the stifling uniformity which "reformers of any sort" seek to impose in its place. And that same display of "crotchets", that same parade of defiant idiosyncracy, operates throughout the novel as a whole to refute any suspicion that an "Old Boy" who has emerged from Arnold's reformed Rugby will have had his intellectual self-reliance crushed rather than fostered.

The narrator's habit of "preaching" has, then, as one of its principal effects, the vindication of the public school as an institution capable of turning out tough-minded subjects rather than passively acquiescent objects. But the more the "Old Boy" advertises, indeed glories in, his opinionated bluffness, the less he can credibly assert objective narratorial authority. And this, I would like to suggest, has the effect of displacing omniscient narrative control from the speaker to the Doctor. Arnold's plot for each of his pupils is formulated by an author whose invisible labors resemble those of a shaping providence, and which become discernible only in retrospect and when the desired ending has been achieved. When the "Old Boy" preaches about his "preaching", he presents himself as endearingly partisan, offering to his reader provocations which are fully open to assent or to disagreement; when, however, he describes Arnold's preaching in Chapter Seven, he presents the Doctor as a medium for the transmission of absolute, because divine, knowledge:

> The tall, gallant form, the kindling eye, the voice, now soft as the low notes of a flute, now clear and stirring as the call of the light infantry bugle, of him who stood there Sunday after Sunday, witnessing and pleading for the Lord, the King of righteousness and love and glory, with whose Spirit he was filled, and in whose power he spoke.
>
> (141; Part One, Ch. 7)

The co-existence of these two types of preacher—of crotchety narrator and omniscient headmaster—at different but homologous levels of the same text, is, I have been arguing, designed to forestall the emergence of a potential contradiction in Hughes's presentation of school-life. Arnold's centralized authority can be presented as absolute, but it has been (implicitly) directed towards the encouragement rather than the repression of his pupils' autonomy. The reformist model of the Panopticon can thus be enlisted as an enhancing analogy for Arnold's achievement without entailing the totalitarian consequences of its Benthamite origin.

Bourgeois individualism, then, is happily reconciled with the imperative need for civic cohesion not only within the enclosed world of the school (where, as Dennis W. Allen has recently emphasized, what is presented as a social microcosm is in fact an exclusively middle class preserve (125)) but within the enclosed world of the text. But this comfortably symbiotic relationship between Rugby and the book which celebrates it can survive only within carefully self-imposed parameters, and any hint of what lies outside the purview of either threatens to expose the limitations of both. In the penultimate chapter, Tom talks to the young master about his friend East. East has left Rugby to join his regiment in India, so that his future is now beyond the bounds both of school and narrative. Tom reminisces that East was

"always a people's man—for the fags and against constituted authorities" (362; Part Two, Ch. 8). The most Powerful of those "constituted authorities", of course, has been the Doctor himself, but East, we are given to understand, has cheerfully surrendered to his headmaster's invincible moral (rather than to his merely political) power. This, however, leaves a note of uncertainty about his future conduct as a regimental officer: the young master worries:

> . . . I hope East will get a good colonel. He won't do if he can't respect those above him. How long it took him, even here, to learn the lesson of obeying.
>
> (362; Part Two, Ch. 8)

The problem of adjustment that is foreshadowed here—between East's sturdily independent interrogation of authority and his soldier's duty of submission—and the problem of what exactly happens if he *cannot* respect his colonel as he has respected Arnold, are problems that the book does not, and on its own terms need not, address because they lie beyond its closely defined limits.[6] But their fugitive presence at least serves to suggest that the issues of discipline and surveillance which Hughes has been addressing may be less tractable outside, than they have proved to be within, the privileged discursive space of public schools and public school novels.

Notes

1. *Discipline and Punish* argues, of course, that public executions are intended primarily as displays of the sovereign's authority; nevertheless, Foucault stresses the importance of public assent or dissent to these exhibitions of state-power, the readiness of spectators to intervene, often in direct (and potentially subversive) opposition to the official sentence (57-65). Such assertions of popular "justice" against the absolutist state might be seen as analogous to the internal autonomy claimed by the pupils of unreformed Rugby in Hughes's novel.

2. Norman Vance is describing very much the same transition when he writes that "halfway through the book Hughes has to go beyond the framework of robust autonomous boy-society, with some regret, and introduce Arthur and Rugby Chapel to perfect Tom and East in Christian manliness" (148), but his account fails, I think, to place sufficient emphasis on the crucial importance of Arnold himself in this development.

3. A. J. Hartley makes a similar point when he observes that "though, ideally, the individual works within the group for the good of all, independence of thought and action are needed for balance" (220). That this problem of "balance" is not con-

fined to Hughes's text, but troubled Victorian educational thinkers, is suggested by A. C. Benson's concern, later in the century, that public schools were turning out "well-groomed, well-mannered, rational, manly boys, all taking the same view of things, all doing the same things" (qtd. Briggs, 152).

4. The view that *Tom Brown's Schooldays* is "three or four times as long as it has any right to be, due in great part to the author's irritating habit of interrupting his deadly tale to harangue the reader with his views on any subject that creeps into his reactionary and conventional mind" (Brophy, Levey, Osborne, 83), is, of course, an extreme one, but even the more sympathetic George Worth concedes that the book is "obviously dated, heavily didactic, and clumsily constructed" (301). Dominic Hibberd may well be unique in his conviction that Hughes has written "a surprisingly neat story" with a "careful narrative plan" (72).

5. As Isabel Quigly perceptively notes, Hughes seems to have been characteristically uncertain about the age and sophistication of the audience he was trying to address, and his narrative mode is consequently inconsistent (48-9); nevertheless, what I have described as his "avuncular" voice is fairly prominent among the book's various (and conflicting) tones.

6. A large part of Hughes's difficulty, of course, is that he wants to portray Arnold both as *representative* of centralized authority and as *unique* in his personal, moral qualities. This surfaces, for example, earlier in the same chapter when the young master sees the Doctor as a type of the imperial proconsul—"the Doctor as a ruler!"—but then adds that "perhaps ours is the only little corner of the British empire which is thoroughly, wisely, and strongly ruled just now" (355; Part Two, Ch. 8).

Works Cited

Allen, Dennis W. "Young England: Muscular Christianity and the Politics of the Body in *Tom Brown's Schooldays*". *Muscular Christianity: Embodying the Victorian Age*. Donald E. Hall (ed.). Cambridge: Cambridge UP, 1994. 114-132.

Briggs, Asa. *Victorian People. A Reassessment of Persons and Themes, 1851-67.* 1954. Harmondsworth: Penguin B, 1965.

Brophy, Brigid, Michael Levey, and Charles Osborne. *Fifty Works of English Literature We Could Do Without.* London: Rapp and Carroll, 1967.

de Certeau, Michel. *Heterologies: Discourse on the Other.* Trans. Brian Massumi. Minneapolis: U of Minnesota P, 1986.

Foucault, Michel. *Discipline and Punish: The Birth of the Prison.* Trans. Alan Sheridan. 1977. Harmondsworth: Penguin B, 1979.

Hartley, A. J. "Christian Socialism and Victorian Morality: The Inner Meaning of *Tom Brown's School-days*". *Dalhousie Review* 49 (1969): 216-223.

Hibberd, Dominic. "Where There Are No Spectators: A Rereading of *Tom Brown's Schooldays*." *Children's Literature in Education* 21 (1976): 64-73.

Hughes, Thomas. *Tom Brown's Schooldays.* 1857. Andrew Sanders (ed.). Oxford: Oxford UP, 1989.

Quigly, Isabel. *The Heirs of Tom Brown: The English School Story.* 1982. Oxford: Oxford UP, 1984.

Stanley, Arthur Penrhyn. *Life and Correspondence of Thomas Arnold, D.D.* 1844. London: Ward Lock, n.d.

Vance, Norman. *The Sinews of the Spirit: The Ideal of Christian Manliness in Victorian Literature and Religious Thought.* Cambridge: Cambridge UP, 1985.

Worth, George J. "On Muscles and Manliness: Some Reflections on Thomas Hughes". *Victorian Literature and Society: Essays Presented to Richard D. Altick.* James R. Kincaid and Albert J. Kuhn (eds.). Ohio: Ohio State UP, 1985. 300-314.

FURTHER READING

Biography

Mack, Edward C., and W. H. G. Armytage. *Thomas Hughes.* London: Ernest Benn, 1952, 302 p.

Explores the role of Hughes's moral character in shaping his literary sensibility.

Criticism

Allen, Dennis W. "Young England: Muscular Christianity and the Politics of the Body in 'Tom Brown's Schooldays.'" In *Muscular Christianity: Embodying the Victorian Age,* edited by Donald E. Hall, pp. 114-32. Cambridge: Cambridge University Press, 1994.

Discusses the relationship between national pride and athletic prowess in the novel.

Beatty, C. J. P. "Thomas Hardy and Thomas Hughes." *English Studies: A Journal of English Language and Literature* 68, no. 6 (December 1987): 511-18.

Examines the importance of English geography in the two authors' works.

Briggs, Asa. "Thomas Hughes and the Public Schools." In *Victorian People,* pp. 150-77. Chicago: University of Chicago Press, 1955.

> Analyzes Hughes's depiction of English public school education and culture in *Tom Brown's School Days.*

Cordery, Gareth. "*Tom Brown's Schooldays* and *Foreskin's Lament*: The Alpha and Omega of Rugby Football." *Journal of Popular Culture* 19, no. 2 (October 1985): 97-105.

> Studies the connections between athletics and character development in Hughes's novel.

Haley, Bruce. "Growing up Healthy: Images of Boyhood." In *The Healthy Body and Victorian Culture,* pp. 141-60. Cambridge: Harvard University Press, 1978.

> Assesses the relationship between physical and moral health in *Tom Brown's School Days.*

Hall, Donald E. "Muscular Anxiety: Degradation and Appropriation in *Tom Brown's Schooldays.*" *Victorian Literature and Culture* 21 (1993): 327-43.

> Evaluates the importance of heterosexuality in Hughes's view of masculinity.

Harrison, Eric. "The Englishry of Tom Brown." *Queen's Quarterly* 50 (1943): 37-52.

> Investigates the author's attitudes toward Victorian morality and educational ideals in *Tom Brown's School Days.*

Hartley, A. J. "Christian Socialism and Victorian Morality: The Inner Meaning of *Tom Brown's School-Days.*" *Dalhousie Review* 49 (1969): 216-23.

> Considers thematic connections between Hughes's portrait of the Rugby School and his ideals concerning British national identity.

Martin, Maureen M. "'Boys Who Will Be Men': Desire in *Tom Brown's Schooldays.*" *Victorian Literature and Culture* 30, no. 2 (2002): 483-502.

> Analyzes manifestations of sexual desire in Hughes's depictions of English schoolboys.

Musgrave, P. W. "*Tom Brown* and *Eric.*" In *From Brown to Bunter: The Life and Death of the School Story,* pp. 47-82. London: Routledge and Kegan Paul, 1985.

> Discusses the importance of *Tom Brown's School Days* in the emergence of the nineteenth-century English school novel.

Proctor, Mortimer R. "Growth of Realism." In *The English University Novel,* pp. 88-117. Berkeley: University of California Press, 1957.

> Critiques Hughes's novel *Tom Brown at Oxford,* asserting that the book lacks the "spontaneity and enthusiasm" of its predecessor, *Tom Brown's School Days.*

Quigly, Isabel. "The School Story as Moral Tale: Hughes and Farrar." In *The Heirs of Tom Brown: The English School Story,* pp. 42-76. London: Chatto and Windus, 1982.

> Evaluates Hughes's depictions of English public school life in *Tom Brown's School Days.*

Worth, George J. *Thomas Hughes.* Boston: Twayne Publishers, 1984, 142 p.

> Offers a comprehensive critical overview of Hughes's fiction and nonfiction.

Additional coverage of Hughes's life and career is contained in the following sources published by Gale: *Beacham's Guide to Literature for Young Adults,* **Vol. 3;** *Dictionary of Literary Biography,* **Vols. 18, 163;** *Literature and Its Times,* **Vol. 2;** *Literature Resource Center;* *Reference Guide to English Literature,* **Ed. 2; and** *Something About the Author,* **Vol. 31.**

Henry David Thoreau
1817-1862

(Born David Henry Thoreau) American essayist, poet, letter and journal writer, and translator.

The following entry presents an overview of Thoreau's life and works. For discussion of "Civil Disobedience" (1849), see *NCLC*, Volume 21; for discussion of *Walden; or, Life in the Woods* (1854), see *NCLC*, Volume 61; for discussion of *A Week on the Concord and Merrimack Rivers* (1849), see *NCLC*, Volume 138; and for information on Thoreau's complete career, see *NCLC*, Volume 7.

INTRODUCTION

Thoreau is considered a foundational figure in nineteenth-century American letters. Along with Ralph Waldo Emerson, Thoreau was a leading member of the transcendentalist movement and played a central role in what critic F. O. Matthiessen dubbed the "American Renaissance," a period during the 1850s that saw the emergence of a distinctive national literature in the United States. In such works as *A Week on the Concord and Merrimack Rivers* (1849) and *Walden; or, Life in the Woods* (1854), Thoreau combined astute observations of nature with spiritual meditations on the character of human existence; in other writings, notably "Resistance to Civil Government" (1849; later republished as "Civil Disobedience"), he argued passionately in defense of individual freedom, which he regarded as under constant threat by the political power of an uninformed and conformist majority. Like other iconoclastic figures in world literature, Thoreau is often mythologized by modern readers, who regard him as a freethinker who abandoned society and material gain to live an uncorrupted existence in the woods. In truth, throughout his career Thoreau remained deeply engaged with the vital political issues of his age and was an outspoken opponent of slavery and the Mexican-American War. Indeed, Thoreau's conviction that philosophical principles must have practical applications in society anticipated the Pragmatist philosophy of John Dewey, and his ideas have assumed a central place in the work of reformers and social activists throughout the twentieth and twenty-first centuries. Mahatma Gandhi drew inspiration from Thoreau's "Civil Disobedience" when fighting on behalf of Indian independence from British rule in the early twentieth century. Decades later, Martin Luther King Jr. cited the essay as one of the key sources behind his doctrine of nonviolent confrontation with authority.

BIOGRAPHICAL INFORMATION

Thoreau was born on July 12, 1817, in Concord, Massachusetts, the third of four children. His father, John, was an itinerant shopkeeper and schoolteacher who changed jobs frequently; Thoreau's mother, Cynthia Dunbar, has been described by biographers as an energetic and sociable woman with a passion for nature that exerted a profound influence on her youngest son. As a child Thoreau also developed a close bond with his older brother, John, whose gregarious, extroverted personality complemented Thoreau's quiet stoicism. Thoreau and his family moved several times during his early years, settling for brief periods in Chelmsford and Boston before returning to Concord permanently in 1823. That year Thoreau's father established a successful pencil-manufacturing business, providing the family with financial stability for the first time.

In 1833 Thoreau entered Harvard College, receiving financial assistance not only from his parents but also from his older siblings and several aunts. A gifted student, he followed a rigorous program of Greek, Latin, and modern languages, while spending much of his free time in the college library. During these years Thoreau discovered Ralph Waldo Emerson's essay "Nature," which left an indelible impression on him. According to Thoreau authority Walter Harding, the scholar enjoyed his years at Harvard, joining a fraternity and participating in the school debating society. He was also plagued by continual financial difficulties, however, and in the winter of 1835 he briefly left college to teach school in the town of Canton, Massachusetts. Shortly after returning to Harvard, Thoreau contracted tuberculosis and was forced to take a second leave of absence. In spite of these setbacks, he earned his degree in 1837 and was selected to present an oration at his class's commencement ceremonies; as Harding relates, Thoreau's address, in which he advocated for a one-day workweek, caused a small scandal among the faculty and students.

After graduation Thoreau returned to Concord, where he joined a philosophical society, the Hedge Club, whose members included the leading figures in the burgeoning transcendentalist movement, among them Emerson, Bronson Alcott, Elizabeth Palmer Peabody, and

Margaret Fuller. Thoreau became particularly close friends with Emerson, whom he regarded as an intellectual and a spiritual mentor and whose writings helped shape Thoreau's own emerging literary sensibility. Shortly after his return to Concord, Thoreau began teaching at the Center School; he resigned two weeks later, however, after refusing to administer corporal punishment to his students. At around this time Thoreau began keeping a journal, a practice he would maintain for much of his life. He also reversed his first and middle names and became known as Henry David Thoreau. In 1838 he and his brother, John, founded a private school, basing their educational philosophy and curriculum on progressive principles; the school proved successful, attracting a number of students from the surrounding towns. A year after launching their school, Thoreau and his brother embarked on a canoe trip along the Concord and Merrimack Rivers, an experience that would later form the basis of his first published book. In 1840 Thoreau began publishing poems and articles in the *Dial,* a prominent transcendentalist journal.

Thoreau and his brother operated their school until 1841; after the school's closure, Emerson invited Thoreau to live in his home. A turning point in Thoreau's life came a year later, when his brother, John, died of lockjaw. According to scholars, John's death deeply traumatized Thoreau and haunted him for the remainder of his life. In 1843 Emerson tried to help his young friend by finding him work as a private tutor in Staten Island, New York. While living in New York, Thoreau met the newspaper editor Horace Greeley, who soon became an important source of support for his literary career, helping him place his essays in journals and publishing favorable reviews of his work in the *New York Tribune.* Thoreau grew tired of life in the city, however, and returned to Concord after only six months. After a year working at menial jobs, Thoreau decided to devote himself to writing full-time. In 1845, he determined that he should live self-sufficiently and more deliberately and so built a small cabin near the shore of Walden Pond. Far from being a hermit, Thoreau visited Concord frequently, and received a number of visitors in the woods. He lived at the cabin for more than two years, and completed drafts of two manuscripts that would become *A Week on the Concord and Merrimack Rivers* and *Walden; or, Life in the Woods.* At one point while living at Walden, Thoreau was forced to spend a night in the Concord jail after refusing to pay a poll tax; this experience inspired the essay "Resistance to Civil Government," which appeared in the first and only issue of Elizabeth Palmer Peabody's journal *Aesthetic Papers*; the essay was later renamed "Civil Disobedience."

In 1847 Thoreau left his cabin at Walden Pond and moved back to Emerson's house, where he lived while his literary mentor was on a lecture tour of England.

Over the next two years Thoreau published several of his best-known early works, notably the essays "The Ascent of Ktaadn" (1848) and "Resistance to Civil Government," as well as *A Week on the Concord and Merrimack Rivers.* In 1849 he made his first trip to Cape Cod; that same year, his older sister, Helen, died of tuberculosis. For the next year Thoreau traveled extensively before eventually settling into his parents' home in the summer of 1850. For the next several years he supported himself as a lecturer while continuing to keep copious notes in his private journals. In 1854 he published the essay "Slavery in Massachusetts," in which he protested the state's adherence to the Fugitive Slave Law of 1850; that year he also published *Walden,* which enjoyed limited success. Walter Harding attests that many commentators dismissed Thoreau's writing as imitative of Emerson's work, a charge that vexed the younger author.

During the second half of the 1850s Thoreau traveled extensively throughout New England while continuing to lecture and publish essays. In his later years Thoreau also became deeply involved in the antislavery movement; many of his later essays, among them "A Plea for Captain John Brown" (1860), deal with issues of social justice. In late 1860 Thoreau once again developed symptoms of tuberculosis; he died on May 6, 1862, after a protracted illness. A number of his works, including *The Maine Woods* (1864) and *Cape Cod* (1865), were published in the years immediately following his death.

MAJOR WORKS

Most scholars regard Thoreau's *Walden; or, Life in the Woods* as his most important work. The book details Thoreau's experiences while living in a cabin on Walden Pond, where he stayed from 1845 to 1847. In one respect the work is a straightforward chronicle of Thoreau's life and routines at Walden; it offers a comprehensive account of the practical concerns involved with living outside of conventional society while also providing meticulous descriptions of the author's observations from nature. In a broader sense, however, the work is also a philosophical treatise, a plea for individual freedom in the face of the conforming forces of mainstream culture. In Thoreau's view the solitary, self-sufficient individual finds continual confirmation of his beliefs in the natural world, which he regarded as more honest, joyful, and "immortal" than the artificial constructs of society. These ideals find their clearest expression in the chapter titled "Higher Laws," in which Thoreau implores the reader to heed "the faintest but constant suggestions of his genius," trusting his own impulses and beliefs "over the arguments and customs of mankind." Numerous scholars have pointed out that the underlying philosophy of *Walden* owes a great deal to the writings of Emerson, in particular his essays "Nature" and "Self-Reliance." In the eyes of many commentators, *Walden* also represents a scathing indictment of the prevailing culture; Thoreau levels his criticisms with irony and wit, however, and the overall sense of the work is life-affirming rather than cynical.

In the estimation of modern critics, Thoreau's "Civil Disobedience" is one of the most influential political essays in the history of American literature. The work was inspired by Thoreau's night in a Concord jail in 1846, when he was arrested for refusing to pay a poll tax. He believed that paying the tax was equivalent to supporting what he deemed unjust political causes, in particular war and slavery. In this sense the work reflects Thoreau's growing dissatisfaction with the power of government majorities to infringe on the rights of the individual. The issue was fundamentally a moral one for Thoreau; in refusing to participate in the established order, he reasoned, he was simply following the dictates of his own conscience. He elaborated these ideas even further in his essay "A Plea for Captain John Brown," a passionate defense of the antislavery radical who advocated and practiced armed rebellion.

Although not as critically acclaimed as some of Thoreau's other writings, *A Week on the Concord and Merrimack Rivers* offers valuable insight into Thoreau's early development as a writer while also serving as a poignant memorial to his brother, John.

CRITICAL RECEPTION

Thoreau's writings elicited mixed reactions from his contemporaries. In a review of *A Week on the Concord and Merrimack Rivers* published in the *New York Tribune* in 1849, George Ripley praised the book's power of observation, calling Thoreau's descriptions "as genial as Nature herself"; Ripley was less sympathetic toward Thoreau's philosophical musings, however, dismissing them as typical examples of the "Pantheistic egotism vaguely characterized as transcendental" and ultimately a "bad specimen of a dubious and dangerous school." Reviewing *Walden* shortly after its publication, a writer for *Graham's Magazine* praised the work's originality, hailing it as "racy and stimulating." Nathaniel Hawthorne responded quite differently to the work; in a letter dated November 1854, he described Thoreau as a misanthrope and an "intolerable bore."

After World War II a number of scholars began to reevaluate Thoreau's body of work, as well as its impact on twentieth-century literature and thought. In his 1949 essay "Thoreau's 'Civil Disobedience,'" John Haynes Holmes argued that Thoreau's political philosophy, especially his ideas concerning individual freedom, had

particular resonance in the wake of the devastation caused by World War II. A decade later Vincent Buranelli offered a dissenting view in his essay "The Case against Thoreau," censuring Thoreau's belief that the individual should pursue the dictates of his own genius as contrary to the basic needs of the community as a whole. Writing in 1969, John A. Christie examined the relationship between individual freedom and self-sacrifice in Thoreau's "Civil Disobedience"; other commentators, notably Jonathan Bishop, have analyzed qualities of spirituality in Thoreau's writings. In recent years critics have paid closer attention to Thoreau's prose style; describing his writing as "concrete, clear, straightforward, and precise," Walter Harding has asserted that Thoreau was one of the true innovators of nineteenth-century American literature. In Harding's view *Walden* in particular contains "some of the most poetic prose in our language." Early twenty-first century scholars began to examine Thoreau's writings in new social and political contexts. In his 2002 essay "'They Locked the Door on My Meditations': Thoreau and the Prison House of Identity," Jason Haslam discusses the relationship between Thoreau's style of discourse and postmodern dialogues concerning social and political control. James J. Donahue offers his evaluation of the problematic role of violence that was an underpinning of Thoreau's political radicalism in his 2007 essay, "'Hardly the Voice of the Same Man': 'Civil Disobedience' and Thoreau's Response to John Brown."

PRINCIPAL WORKS

"The Ascent of Ktaadn" (essay) 1848; published in journal *Sartrain's Union Magazine*

"Resistance to Civil Government" (essay) 1849; published in journal *Aesthetic Papers*; also published as "Civil Disobedience" in *A Yankee in Canada, with Anti-Slavery and Reform Papers,* 1866

A Week on the Concord and Merrimack Rivers (essays) 1849

"Slavery in Massachusetts" (essay) 1854; published in journal *Liberator*

Walden; or, Life in the Woods (essays) 1854

"A Plea for Captain John Brown" (essay) 1860; published in *Echoes of Harper's Ferry* (edited by James Redpath)

"Walking" (essay) 1862; published in magazine *Atlantic Monthly*

Excursions (essays) 1863

"Life without Principle" (essay) 1863; published in magazine *Atlantic Monthly*

The Maine Woods (essays) 1864

Cape Cod (essays) 1865

Letters to Various Persons (letters) 1865

CRITICISM

Raymond W. Adams (essay date 1929)

SOURCE: Adams, Raymond W. "Thoreau and Immortality." *Studies in Philology* 26 (1929): 58-66.

[*In the following essay, Adams ponders Thoreau's views on death, God, and the afterlife.*]

Ever since James Russell Lowell undertook to blue-pencil Thoreau's essay **"Chesuncook"** in the July, 1858, *Atlantic Monthly* and removed the objectionable sentence about the pine tree ("It is as immortal as I am and perhaps will go to a higher heaven, there to tower above me still"[1]) someone has been meddling with Thoreau's ideas of immortality. And no one has done much more than meddle.

While Thoreau was still alive (but not very much so) an intimate friend asked him if he had thought about the other world; he replied that he preferred to think about one world at a time. When his death became imminent, his aunt Louisa Dunbar, as maiden aunts will, asked if he had "made his peace with God." Henry replied with practically the last flash of his delicious humor, "I did not know that God and I had ever quarrelled."

This apparent unconcern was, however, more apparent than real. Thoreau, like all of us, but more than most of us, assumed an unconcern toward the very things that he most hungered for. His preference of "one world at a time" is to be compared with many of his poses that misled Robert Louis Stevenson, as he confessed, to call Thoreau a skulker. Thoreau was centripetal. One looks

in vain among the writings he left for publication for even a slight reference to his brother's death or to his own disappointment in love. To the world he paraded unconcern.

But within himself he had eternal longings well matured. Aunt Louisa wanted some kind of shriving known as "making one's peace with God." Her nephew knew of other shrivings and had no fear of the future. To a closer friend than Aunt Louisa (Edmund Hosmer), who came one day early in the spring of Thoreau's death and described his coming through the country and across a field where the first robin had alighted, Thoreau remarked, "Yes. This is a beautiful world; but I shall see a fairer." The note of certainty is here. It is in many places in the writings of Thoreau, for immortality is no uncommon theme in his private journal.

The journal now is published, but there are other paragraphs about immortality. In one bundle of unclassified Thoreau manuscript in the Harvard College Library is an essay on death and graveyards and immortality, a probable product of Thoreau's reading of Sir Thomas Browne. And there are unpublished bits of journal and unpublished poems that seem more cogent arguments that Thoreau did think of more than one world at a time than any of the quotations to be gleaned from the published works.

In common with most Transcendental and Hindu philosophers, Thoreau draws almost no line of demarkation between the present and the eternal; the two merge and become one. The body, the soul, do not cease existence in this world but rise to higher and more perfect articulation with the world of nature.

The body but changes form and continues its existence, as Thoreau says,

> . . . in some other form; in corn for fodder, in wood for fuel; in grain or flowers, for use or beauty. Every wind blows the last trump which shall call the lost atoms together.[2]

Nature is of more consequence than any of its physical aspects, and more eternal too, and more unalterable. The bodies, the forms of nature, revert to elements and are reassembled in other forms, but nature does not change. The whole notion is expressed by Thoreau in a letter to Emerson written on March 11, 1842 (a letter not included in the Walden edition of Thoreau's writings), in which he says:

> Nature is not muffled by the hardest blast—the hurricane only snaps a few twigs in some nook of the forest. . . . How plain that death is only the phenomenon of the individual. Nature does not recognize it, she finds her own again under new forms without loss. Yet death is beautiful when seen to be a law and not an ac-

cident. . . . We are partial and selfish when we lament the death of an individual, unless our plaint be a paean to the departed soul.[3]

We are led to the belief that Thoreau held that the soul suffered a different fate from that of the body. The soul seems not to lose its identity.

Thoreau's brother John had died on the first of the month preceding the letter to Emerson; and this, the first instance of death that had come close home (and none came closer), had turned his thoughts almost entirely to the meaning of death. He wrote, a week earlier, to Mrs. Lucy Brown, Mrs. Emerson's sister,

> What right have I to grieve who have not ceased to wonder.[4]

At the same time Emerson's boy Waldo died, and the two deaths affected Thoreau profoundly. It will be worth while to quote some sentences from Thoreau's journal and his letters of that spring. They reveal much of the growth of Thoreau's eschatology and need no comment.

On February twenty-first, 1842, Thoreau writes:

> My soul and body have tottered along together of late, tripping and hampering one another like unpracticed Siamese twins.[5]

On March second there are two statements:

> I do not wish to see John ever again,—I mean him who is dead,—but that other . . . of whom he was the imperfect representative.[6]

and:

> The same everlasting serenity will appear in this face of God (i. e. nature), and we will not be sorrowful if he is not.[7]

On March eighth Thoreau identifies himself with nature:

> I live in the perpetual verdure of the globe. I die in the annual decay of nature.[8]

and he holds the same idea on the eleventh:

> Why, God, did you include me in your great scheme? Will you not make me a partner at last?[9]
>
> If Nature is our mother, is not God much more?[10]

By March twelfth, 1842, Thoreau has settled much in his own mind and says:

> There is no continuance of death. It is a transient phenomenon.[11]

And by the fourteenth there seems to be no doubt left, nothing but optimism:

> Life is grand, and so are its environments of Past and Future. Would the face of nature be so serene if man's destiny were not equally so?[12]

To Thoreau, the body itself was a poor enough thing and utterly despicable. Denied a healthy body himself, though endowed with a tough fiber that made some amends, Thoreau decided early that we, as he says,

> should strengthen and beautify and industriously mould our bodies to be fit companions of the soul,—assist them to grow up like trees.[13]

Here is the **"Chesuncook"** kinship with trees, the brotherhood with every living object, the identification of soul with life—on however low a plane—that is Hindu in its origin, but that runs through the whole of Thoreau's thinking on the subject of immortality.

The body changes its form, though it too endures. It would have been better, he says, had his soul been bestowed "on some antelope of the plains than upon this sickly body."[14] But, having a sickly and sluggish body, one can try to immerse it in nature and enjoy purely physical ecstacies like an antelope and so make the body an object of nature to endure in the metamorphosis of nature forever. The body matters little. He says in a scrap of manuscript,

> The last thing I should want to preserve is an old man's body which now for thirty years has been wracked with gout and rheumatism. Waste no time at funerals.

The physical immortality of the elements that compose the body is naturally a very small item in Thoreau's idea of immortality. It is the soul or spirit or mind that must be considered chiefly, for it (the three are used interchangeably) alone matters and endures as a self. The soul is housed in the body but is not of it. To Thoreau the two were related as they are in the thought of Plato. Even so weak a thing as sleep may release the soul and send it for a time to its heavenly home.

> At night we recline and nestle and infold ourselves in our being. Each night I go home to rest. Each night I am gathered to my fathers. The soul departs out of the body and sleeps in God, a divine slumber. As she withdraws herself, the limbs droop and the eyelids fall and nature reclaims her clay again.[15]

And death is but a deeper sleep that sends the soul about its business without a "wracked" body. He has expressed this thought in his comment upon the corpse strewn beach in *Cape Cod,* speaking of the bodies,

> Their owners were coming to the New World, as Columbus and the Pilgrims did; they were within a mile of its shores; but, before they could reach it, they emi-

grated to a newer world than ever Columbus dreamed of, yet one of whose existence we believe there is far more universal and convincing evidence—though it has not yet been discovered by science—than Columbus had of this: not merely mariners' tales and some paltry driftwood and seaweed, but a continual drift and instinct to all our shores. I saw their empty hulks that came to land; but they themselves, meanwhile, were cast upon some shore yet farther west, toward which we are all tending, and which we shall reach at last, it may be through storm and darkness, as they did. . . . It is hard to part with one's body, but, no doubt, it is easy enough to do without it when once it is gone. All their plans and hopes burst like a bubble! Infants by the score dashed on the rocks by the enraged Atlantic Ocean! No, no! If the St. John did not make her port here, she has been telegraphed there. The strongest wind cannot stagger a Spirit; it is a Spirit's breath. A just man's purpose cannot be split on any Grampus or material rock, but itself will split rocks until it succeeds.[16]

Death, then, but releases the soul from its human body and sends it on about its business. What did Thoreau conceive that business to be?

It was chiefly to become attuned to Nature and the soul that dwells in Nature—God. It is an upward climb. Though, as he says, "The form of the soul is eternal," yet it must abide in various bodies before it can attain perfection and rest. The soul flies in the bird because it has crawled in the beast. It is in the *Journal*;

Methinks the hawk that soars so loftily and circles so steadily and apparently without effort, has earned this power by faithfully creeping on the ground as a reptile in a former state of existence.[17]

Up from the reptile to the bird, from bird to man, from man to man unto perfect harmony, and then out into nature and eternity—that is the course of the soul. That conception explains much; the peculiar sympathy of Thoreau with beasts and even with plants may be considered to have come partly from a belief that his soul had once inhabited a plant or an animal. Emerson's Oriental library seems to have made an impression upon the young reader who spent the summer of 1841 with Menu and the Vedas. Thoreau had come to see all history as contemporary with him and said,

Hawthorne, too, I remember as one with whom I sauntered, in old heroic times, along the banks of the Scamander, amid the ruins of chariots and heroes.[18]

Once, looking into a spring pool with its teeming life of insect metamorphosis and tadpole recapitulation, he remarks, musingly,

Yes, I feel positive beyond a doubt, I *must* pass through *all* these conditions, one day and another; I must go the whole round of life, and come full circle.[19]

And, having come full circle, having risen upon the stepping-stones of its dead bodies, the soul now ma-

tured and perfect, released "through storm and darkness" from its final earthly form "makes the safest port in heaven."

A skillful pilot comes to meet him, and the fairest and balmiest gales blow off that cost, his good ship makes the land in halcyon days, and he kisses the shore in rapture there, while his old hulk tosses in the surf here.[20]

One of the early poems, written in June, 1837, while Thoreau was a student at Harvard, voices the great patience that marked the man. It begins,

The blossoms on the tree
Swell not too fast for me.
God does not want quick work but sure,
Not to be tempted by so cheap a lure.[21]

Neither was Thoreau to be tempted by the cheap lure of speed. Time meant nothing with eternity to work in. He seemed impatient at twenty-two when he wrote **"The Poet's Delay,"** but there is no impatience twelve years later when, six days after his thirty-fourth birthday, he expresses his idea of eternity in his *Journal* in a paragraph that certainly suggests Browning:

May not my life in nature, in proportion as it is supernatural, be only the spring and infantile portion of my spirit's life? Shall I turn my spring to summer? May I not sacrifice a hasty and petty completeness here to entireness there? If my curve is large, why bend it to a smaller circle? My spirit's unfolding observes not the pace of nature. The society which I was made for is not here. Shall I, then, substitute for the anticipation of that this poor reality? I would (rather) have the unmixed expectation of that than this reality. If life is a waiting, so be it. I will not be shipwrecked on a vain reality. What were any reality which I can substitute? Shall I with pains erect a heaven of blue glass over myself, though when it is done I shall be sure to gaze still on the true ethereal heaven far above, as if the former were not,—that still distant sky o'erarching that blue expressive eye of heaven? I am enamored of the blue-eyed arch of heaven.[22]

What is time if one be enamored of the blue-eyed arch of heaven? What is a mere body but a vain reality, one which cannot hinder the soul on its progress to the ethereal heaven far above?

Among other earthly forms Thoreau sees hints and types of the final disembodying of the soul. The moth puts off its wintry chrysalis, the bird migrates toward summer in more pleasant tropics, and Thoreau himself is impelled to say,

Today I feel the migratory instinct strong in me. . . . This indefinite restlessness and fluttering on the perch do, no doubt, prophesy the final migrations of souls out of nature to a serener summer.[23]

He describes the "serener summer" in an unpublished paragraph of his *Journal* for 1843 (a year that is omitted from the published *Journal*),

The future will no doubt be a more natural life than this. We shall be acquainted and shall use flowers and stars, and sun and moon, and occupy this nature which now stands over and around us. We shall reach up to the stars and planets fruit from many parts of the universe. We shall *purely* use the earth and not abuse it—God's in the breeze and whispering leaves and we shall then hear *him*. We live in the midst of all the beauty and grandeur that was ever described or conceived. We have hardly entered the vestibule of nature. It was here, be assured, under these heavens that the gods intended our immortal life should pass—these stars were set to adorn and light it—these flowers to carpet it.[24]

He has made his heaven the perfected image of his world—Nature. He had said,

The truest account of heaven is the fairest, and I will accept none which disappoints expectation. It is more glorious to expect a better, than to enjoy a worse.[25]

Thoreau had been protesting against the conventional heaven since he had been told, at the age of three, that sometime he too must die and go to heaven and had replied that he "did not want to go to heaven, because he could not carry his sled with him, for the boys said it was shod with iron, and therefore not worth a cent." He had given up the sled for another hobby now; the boys of Concord still said his hobby was not worth a cent. But he no longer shied at heaven on that account. He made himself a heaven that included the hobby.

Indeed, he considered that he was already in the vestibule of heaven while yet in Concord. Eternity was not postponed but was, if the body were properly merged into nature, already attained in the woods of Concord. For him "Wilderness were paradise enow," and he remarked:

I can see nothing so proper and holy as unrelaxed play and frolic in this bower God has built for us. The suspicion of sin never comes to this thought. Oh, if men felt this they would never build temples even of marble or diamond, but it would be sacrilege and profane, but disport them forever in this paradise.[26]

Heaven lies about us long after our infancy; it is with us whenever we are heavenly enough to begin to see it, thinks Henry Thoreau.

The young Concord radical who renounced the church still thought much about his soul and immortality, and wrote much about it too. It happens that little of that part of his thinking got into his books. Most of it remained in manuscript until the **Journals** were published in 1906. And some of it has remained so until now.

Notes

1. The sentence is restored in the Walden edition of Thoreau's *Writings*, Boston, 1906, III, 135. See also VI, 395-6, and Channing's *Thoreau the Poet-Naturalist*, Boston, 1902, p. 17.

2. MS. in Harvard Library. Bundle labelled "Miscellaneous MS. Material."

3. Letter of March 11, 1842. Copy in New York Public Library.

4. Walden edition of Thoreau's *Writings*, VI, 41.

5. *Writings* (Walden edition), VII, 322.

6. *Ibid.*, VI, 41.

7. *Ibid.*, VI, 41.

8. *Ibid.*, VII, 324.

9. *Ibid.*, VII, 327.

10. *Ibid.*, VII, 326.

11. *Ibid.*, VII, 327-8.

12. *Ibid.*, VII, 330.

13. *Ibid.*, VII., 176.

14. *Writings* (Walden edition), VII, 176.

15. This is from a *Journal* entry dated October 5, 1840. It is not in the Walden edition but is in *Autumn* (Boston, 1892), p. 69.

16. *Writings* (Walden edition), IV, 12-13.

17. *Ibid.*, IX, 108.

18. *Writings* (Walden edition), VI, 93. See also *ibid.*, VI, 179.

19. Channing, *Thoreau the Poet-Naturalist*, Boston, 1902, p. 271.

20. *Writings* (Walden edition), IV, 13.

21. Quoted in the American Art Association, Wakeman Catalog, No. 977.

22. *Writings* (Walden edition), VIII, 316-317.

23. *Writings* (Walden edition), VII, 176.

24. A MS. dated Aug. 26, 1843, owned by Mr. George S. Hellman.

25. *Writings* (Walden edition), IX, 232.

26. *Writings* (Walden edition), VII, 302.

John Brooks Moore (essay date December 1931)

SOURCE: Moore, John Brooks. "Thoreau Rejects Emerson." *American Literature* 4, no. 3 (November 1932): 241-56.

[In the following essay, first read at the December 1931 meeting of the Modern Language Association, Moore investigates Emerson's influence on Thoreau. In Moore's view, Thoreau and Emerson differed most dramatically on the subjects of God and religion.]

I

That Emerson exercised a considerable influence upon Thoreau, who was fourteen years younger, from the time when they became acquainted in 1837, for many years, is almost certain. Almost certain, I say, because Thoreau might have viewed Nature, man, and God in something the way he did if there had never been an Emerson. Contemporaries report that Thoreau was looked upon not seldom as an imitator of Emerson in speech and gait as well as in ideas. But Thoreau was a more strongly marked individual than Emerson himself and it would not be surprising to find that Thoreau's peculiar attitudes revived, as something of his awe for Emerson and Emersonism dwindled. A curious witness to the comparative dominance of Thoreau in their relationship is to be found in their journals. There are over sixty important references to Thoreau in Emerson's *Journals*; while in Thoreau's *Journal* there are only between twenty and thirty really significant references to Emerson, most of them very brief. Further, it ought to be noted, Thoreau's references to Emerson are often ironic and entirely lack the tone of discipleship. Emerson, however, ordinarily quotes a choice remark from Thoreau and commends it. Thoreau is clearly something of a marvel to Emerson, though a perplexing and often a positively irritating marvel. Emerson admires and praises Thoreau in his magnanimous fashion, only causing Thoreau to complain:

> I should value E's. praise more, which is always so discriminating, if there were not some alloy of patronage and hence of flattery about [it] . . .[1]

> (1852)

Professor Moore died in Honolulu on May 1 without completing his revision of this article and without seeing the proofs. It was read before the American Literature Group at the December, 1931, meeting of the Modern Language Association.

Emerson probably felt no condescension in the matter at all, but Thoreau was jealous of his complete independence. He could not endure following any master lest he should lose himself.

Of the Transcendental Emersonian attitude toward Nature and God not a great deal takes permanent lodgment in Thoreau. To be sure, Thoreau says in his journal as late as 1851:

> My profession is to be always on the alert to find God in nature, to know his lurking-places, to attend all the oratorios, the operas, in nature.[2]

Other equally vivid passages from a Thoreau ten years younger might be cited to enforce the point that Thoreau sought and expected to find his God in Nature. But instead of bringing a conviction that Thoreau was clinging to Emersonism these passages may more plausibly be interpreted as individual Thoreauvian doctrine; for Nature seems to be Thoreau's only road to God;—whereas, Nature is one road, but not the straightest road, to the Over-Soul. Emerson's God antedates Nature and they are never to be confused, though the Over-Soul does inform and flow through Nature. The truest knowledge of God always reached Emerson through intuition—or, in its most perfect manifestation, through a mystic experience. This sort of illumination is always just around the corner in Emerson's life and writing. He was deeply mystical. Nature was a healthy aid to the understanding of God, for him; yet it was not essential. Revelation of the Over-Soul could come to the mystic even if he were locked in jail or walking the crowded streets of a city. Nature is a sort of divine by-product, not the main clue nor the God-in-Itself. Now Thoreau is as unmystical as a man may well be who still hovers about the fringe of Transcendentalism. In the section of **Walden** named "Solitude," Thoreau records what was very likely his nearest approach to a mystical experience. He tells of a few terrible moments of loneliness when he first went to live alone at Walden, and then goes on to explain how a glow of mild reassurance—not attaining to ecstasy—came over him. In the journal for 1856, Thoreau again tells of being "expanded and infinitely and divinely related for a brief season."[3] He remarks revealingly, in 1857, that men are all infidels "except in the rarest moments when they are lifted above themselves by an ecstasy."[4] The interesting phrase is "in the rarest moments," for the fourteen volumes of his **Journal** bear witness that such moments were so infrequent in Thoreau's experience that it is doubtful whether or not he deserves the name of genuine Transcendentalist. While Emerson and Alcott do not give full accounts of mystical trances (such as those of Jonathan Edwards, for example), they contrive to make their readers continually aware of their reception of intuitional revelations. Emerson is obviously reaching for communion with God through Nature in his daily walks. Many passages witness the success of his efforts.

To put the matter bluntly, God is not a preoccupation of Thoreau. Something else fills his mind so completely most of the time that God is shut out:—by God, I mean, of course, the Transcendental God, the Emersonian Over-Soul. He does not often dwell directly upon the divine as he probably would have done, if he had found himself the recipient of constant quasi-electric messages. Such revelations he seems to have respected and desired. They were the final seal upon a Transcendentalist. The messages appear, however, not to have come constantly enough to control the daily life of Thoreau, and his attention may be expected to have centered itself elsewhere. It was too difficult for a man of Thoreau's temperament to follow Emerson into the mystic realm of the Over-Soul. Hence the deep-laid divergence of their attitudes.

The way in which each man responded to Nature may be partly foreseen by one who appreciates their attitudes toward God. In Thoreau, there is a sort of struggle between what may be called his acquired Emersonian tendency to look chiefly *through* Nature to the underlying Over-Soul, and what possibly his native—at least his inbred—tendency to look *at* Nature or to look *into* Nature with no wish to pass through to that uniform, subtending divinity. It would be a mistake to say that Nature was not full of poetic suggestion to Thoreau in his native mood, when he looked upon it and hearkened after it, with full delight of the senses and of the imagination, though this does not alter the likelihood that he was usually content to rest upon the opaque objects of his senses instead of upon the transparent film (affording glimpses of God, the Over-Soul) which rejoiced Emerson. Emerson loved God and Thoreau loved Nature. Still, Emerson may have lavished considerable incidental love upon Nature, partly impelled by Thoreau; and Thoreau may have dwelt with occasional enthusiasm upon the super-sensuous Over-Soul.

What did Thoreau reveal when he wrote at the age of twenty-four the following justification of himself?

> I seem to see somewhat more of my kith and kin in the lichens on the rocks than in any books. It does seem as if mine were a peculiarly wild nature, which so yearns towards all wildness. I know of no redeeming qualities in me but a sincere love for some things, and when I am reproved I have to fall back on to this ground.[5]

There is little room for doubt that these "things" which he loved so sincerely that they seemed sufficient warrant for his unconventional life were natural objects which stimulated first of all Thoreau's acute senses—senses astonishingly acute, to Emerson's way of thinking. His imagination was alert to make the most of the rich sensuous material at its disposal; and his intellect, even, seemed to operate with greater ease among sensations than among unsensuous abstractions. When Emerson noted in his journal, the year after Thoreau's death, the vigor of the images by which the latter enforced his thoughts, Emerson was on the verge of expressing the very reality in Thoreau.

> He has muscle, and ventures on and performs feats which I am forced to decline. In reading him, I find the same thought, the same spirit that is in me, but he takes a step beyond, and illustrates by excellent images that which I should have conveyed in a sleepy generality.[6]

The "step beyond" which Emerson attributed here to Thoreau could well be interpreted (though Emerson did not mean it so) as that most rare of steps—when a man seems to think with his senses, so perfect is the articulation of thought and sensation. The strain of music, the touch of damp earth, the glance of a darting fish, the fragrance of a pond-lily—they were to Thoreau the instant materials of thought. Thoreau was not "performing feats" by his "excellent images," he was thinking according to his own constitution. What might have been a stylistic feat to Emerson was native to Thoreau and perhaps uncalculated. No wonder he loved what his senses brought to perception, for his senses brought him more and deeper information than our senses ordinarily bring to us about what we call the world of Nature. The region of thought is, thus, to Thoreau a place not remote from the world of the concrete, but necessarily and intimately attached to that world. He could not think on any other terms. While Thoreau's constitution in this way set him apart from Emerson, it seemed to make him only the more fascinating and significant to Emerson. In this connection, a student of their journals and essays comes first to feel Thoreau bulking large on the Emersonian horizon; while, to Thoreau, Emerson seems retreating and always less engrossing.

Representative passages from Emerson's journal lucidly expressing his wonder at Thoreau are not difficult to find. Emerson is, however, struck more by the way in which Thoreau deals successfully and practically with every-day persons and things, his self-dependence in face of the physical world, his capacities for action and for doing things—more struck with all this than with what is perhaps the basis of it—Thoreau's genius for apprehending the world sensuously. For example, Emerson writes in his journal for 1838 (the second year of his association with Thoreau):

> My good Henry made this else solitary afternoon sunny with his simplicity and clear perception.[7]

And this was only one of several such "afternoons," all of them impressive to Emerson. In an entry of 1839, there is a tone of more specific approbation:

> My brave Henry here who is content to live now, and feels no shame in not studying any profession, for he does not postpone his life, but lives already,—pours contempt on these cry-babies of routine and Boston.[8]

The next year comes the following entry, merely (as often with Emerson) the enthusiastic quotation of a sample of what he called Henry's mother-wit:

> I like Henry Thoreau's statement on Diet: "If a man does not believe that he can thrive on board nails, I will not talk with him."[9]

Among the many references, from 1838 till 1843, Emerson reveals in his journal an unflawed admiration for Thoreau. Then, when Emerson was forty and Thoreau twenty-six, creeps in the first note of discontent from Emerson, but apparently such offense as there was originated with Thoreau.

II

Before considering the discord between Emerson and Thoreau, the three early publications of Emerson in which he seems most deliberately to be commending the qualities of Thoreau demand attention. The three forces which shape the American Scholar for his high task are Nature, the Past—mainly great books—and Action. Nature was a shaping force in Thoreau's life even more surely than in Emerson's own, for Thoreau was country-bred; only he, unlike the ordinary farmer's son, was informed by a deep passion for the wild in all its manifestations. If ever a man was educated by Nature, the man was Thoreau. Emerson achieved his intimate enthusiasm (never so intimate as Thoreau's) for natural beauty only after he was well over twenty. Before that, he may be viewed as a city-bred boy. Of course, Cambridge and Boston were much more like country towns then than we can easily realize, and Emerson often visited the villages round about; yet his journal before 1833 (the year after he resigned from his pastorate in Boston) shows relatively slight concern over the significance of Nature. Emerson's genuine love of Nature was something acquired in his maturity or at least greatly augmented then. He learned to appreciate and depend upon it, partly from living in the country at Concord, partly from Thoreau and others who possessed the seeing eye. Thoreau may, consequently, be thought to exemplify the man schooled by Nature more precisely than Emerson.

The influence of the past, in the form of books, was easily traceable in Thoreau, too, though Emerson himself seems a somewhat more perfect instance of the one who makes the thoughts in books his own without any servile subjection to the minds of the past.

In the man who wins to deep wisdom only through action, a reader feels he can recognize distinctly Henry Thoreau, the man whose capacity to do things frequently drew admiring exclamations from Emerson, to judge by his journal. But "The American Scholar" was an address delivered in 1837, the year in which Emerson became acquainted with Thoreau. Now Emerson's first reference to Thoreau in his journal appears in 1838, and, is to be sure, very interesting.

> I delight much in my young friend [Thoreau], who seems to have as free and erect a mind as any I have ever met.[10]

Strong as this praise may be, it offers no evidence that Thoreau could have been in Emerson's mind the preceding year as a sort of model for "The American Scholar" who attains to the truth of profound thought only by the way of action. The probability is that Emerson described his ideal American in 1837, only to have the incredible good fortune to find his ideal come to life in young Thoreau, right there in Concord. Another apparent reference to Thoreau has often been pointed out in Emerson's poem "Woodnotes."[11] Students of Emerson can not easily forget those lines celebrating the Forest-seer:

> You ask, he said, what guide
> Me through trackless thickets led,
> Through thick-stemmed woodlands rough and wide.
> I found the water's bed.
> The watercourses were my guide;
> I travelled grateful by their side,
> Or through their channel dry;
> They led me through the thicket damp,
> Through brake and fern, the beavers' camp, . . .
> The falling waters led me,
> The foodful waters fed me,
> And brought me to the lowest land,
> Unerring to the ocean sand.
> The moss upon the forest bark
> Was pole-star when the night was dark;
> The purple berries in the wood
> Supplied me necessary food; . . .[12]

Surely these lines celebrate Thoreau. They ought to; but Edward Emerson in *Emerson in Concord* says that his father

> . . . delighted in being led to the very inner shrines of the wood-gods by this man (i.e., Thoreau), clear-eyed and true and stern enough to be trusted with their secrets, who filled the portrait of the Forestseer of the Woodnotes, although those lines were written before their author came to know Thoreau.[13]

The real significance of the passage here as of those in "The American Scholar" just mentioned comes from the fact that it shows what sort of man Emerson was longing to see. From this, we can guess at the greatness of his gratification when Thoreau presented himself in the late 1830's. Thoreau incarnated some of Emerson's most precious dreams; he might almost be called Emerson's truest wish-fulfillment. Emerson needed him.

Emerson's address of January 25, 1841, was written in the period when the relations between himself and Thoreau were more cordial (if we are to accept the evidence of the journals, especially Emerson's journal) than in the later years. In sketching the feelings and the way of life of this Man-the-Reformer in that address, Emerson gives a rather fervent and partly-idealized view of the Henry Thoreau whom he persuaded that very year to take a hand at gardening and grafting of fruit trees on Emerson's own small "farm." Thoreau lived at the Emerson house for the period from 1841 to 1843, endearing himself, at any rate, to Emerson's children, though it is easy to suspect that he was not always a docile conversationalist with Emerson. It is necessary to recall only one or two passages of the great address of 1841 to see how relevant Thoreau probably was to the development of Emerson's ideas.

> The young man, on entering life, finds the way to lucrative employments blocked with abuses. The ways of trade are grown selfish to the borders of theft and supple to the borders (if not beyond the borders) of fraud. The employments of commerce are not intrinsically unfit for a man, or less genial to his faculties, but

these are now in their general course so vitiated by derelictions and abuses at which all connive, that it requires more vigor and resources than can be expected of every young man, to right himself in them; he is lost in them; he cannot move hand or foot in them. Has he genius and virtue? the less does he find them fit for him to grow in, and if he would thrive in them, he must sacrifice all the brilliant dreams of boyhood and youth as dreams;[14] . . . and must take on him the harness of routine and obsequiousness. If not so minded, nothing is left him but to begin the world anew, as he does who puts the spade into the ground for food.[15] . . . It happens therefore, that all such ingenuous souls as feel within themselves the irrepressible strivings of a noble aim, who by the law of their nature must act simply, find these ways of trade unfit for them, and they come forth from it.[16] . . .

Never again did Emerson quite so eloquently recommend the basic ideas of Thoreau's life. Were they Emerson's ideas or Thoreau's? They became Thoreau's more truly than Emerson's—wherever they originated—because, according to Emerson's own requirement, Thoreau acted the part which Emerson merely sketched. With that magnanimous readiness to praise the deed beyond his own capacities, often observed in his journal, Emerson pushed his theme still further, insisting that the true man must learn by practical efforts and must often completely care for himself with his own hands that he may keep clear of the smirch of corrupt commerce and that he may—by supplying a Spartan minimum of wants—preserve the many hours of leisure from physical toil requisite to the work of the thinker or the artist.

> . . . he only is a sincere learner, he only can become a master, who learns the secrets of labor, and who by real cunning extorts from nature its sceptre.[17]

Unmistakably Thoreau is the man, the inspiration, the subject. Emerson makes this more inescapable when he adds:

> . . . that man ought to reckon early with himself, and, respecting the compensations of the Universe, ought to ransom himself from the duties of economy, by a certain rigor and privation in his habits. For privileges so rare and grand, let him not stint to pay a great tax. Let him be a caenobite, a pauper, and if needs be, celibate also. Let him learn to eat his meals standing, and to relish the taste of fair water and black bread. He may leave to others the costly conveniences of housekeeping, and large hospitality, and the possession of works of art. . . . He must live in a chamber, and postpone his self-indulgence, forewarned and forearmed against that frequent misfortune of men of genius,—the taste for luxury.[18]

Emerson would have no disciples; discipleship is the betrayal of Self-Reliance. Thoreau would have no master and carried about in his brain a sleepless suspicion that someone might dominate or control his thought and his life. Emerson would allow no disciple, but he himself at least this once was half-dazzled by perhaps the most competent, most observant, and most independent human being he ever encountered. Emerson finds the young man as he should be; and on him Emerson pours the vials of his benevolence and profound approval. Thoreau soon began to bristle apprehensively; let no man touch him to teach or tame him. He sufficed to himself.

III

That Thoreau was less preoccupied than Emerson with thoughts of God is soon felt by the student; that he ordinarily viewed nature rather sensuously and concretely where Emerson viewed it as the veil through which God was half-visible is not difficult to discover. The two men were also frequently at odds in their attitude toward, and opinions of, mankind. There is the unconfirmed story that a farmer objected to conversing with Emerson, because the beaming eye of the great man suggested that he expected jewels of divine revelation to drop from the lips of a man who spent his days in intimacy with Nature. This silenced the farmer. Men were the vehicles of God's revelation, repositories of intuitions from the Over-Soul at any favorable moment. Thoreau took his farmers very differently. In his journal, he once affirmed that farmers reminded him of oxen, their sons of bullocks, their daughters of heifers.[19] Many of the villagers also he prodded with his sharpened doubts of the worth of their daily businesses. He held them either in derision or in a sort of enmity. And in another mood he looked upon his fellow men as a species among the many zoological species to be observed and reported upon. The resentment of villagers can easily be guessed.

> As I walked in the woods to see the birds and squirrels, so I walked in the village to see the men and boys; instead of the wind among the pines I heard the carts rattle. In one direction from my house there was a colony of musk-rats in the river meadows; under the grove of elms and buttonwoods in the other horizon was a village of busy men, as curious to me as if they had been prairie dogs, each sitting at the mouth of its burrow, or running over to a neighbor's to gossip. I went there frequently to observe their habits.[20]

Compared with himself, why should Thoreau not find most men stupid and many of them knavish? This attitude which Thoreau based on observation and experience harmonized badly with the abstract goodness of man that followed from Emerson's ideas about the Over-Soul in men. To be sure, Thoreau indicated that property and certain other institutions twisted and tormented men out of their natural shape; yet in his contacts with individuals, he seems to have been little inclined to palliate human failings. Probably "misanthrope" is too strong a word to fasten upon Thoreau, though a misanthrope he seems in the presence of Emerson.

With these several divergences in ideas, taste, and pre-occupation, the event is what might be foretold. The journals reveal a discord between them that Emerson dwells upon occasionally after about 1843, and that colors more or less nearly every one of the sparse references to Emerson by Thoreau. Emerson was the troubled and outraged admirer of Thoreau even after Thoreau's death—as appears in the measured praise of Emerson's funeral address upon Thoreau. Thoreau was the one who withdrew and opposed and argued and rejected the friendship or rather the powerful influence of Emerson. That censure should fall upon Thoreau for this need not be maintained. He probably found himself Emerson's equal in the realm of thought, and it could not have escaped him that thought became true wisdom with him because he was magnificently able to put his thoughts in practice. By this test, he was Emerson's ideal and thus vastly his superior. Emerson's comparative inability to observe nature accurately—while it made Thoreau a precious companion to him—may have made him seem inferior to Thoreau. Emerson's all-embracing benignity must also have irked the man who studied men and muskrats almost indifferently.

Thoreau's strictures upon Emerson can be represented by two or three quotations from his journals after 1850. He was a very exacting critic, and it may be well to quote one favorable mention of Emerson as foil to the later condemnation or faint praise. Though undated, the following extract can be rather confidently assigned to the middle twenties of Thoreau's life.

> Emerson has special talents unequalled. The divine in man has no more easy, methodically distinct expression. His personal influence upon young persons [is] greater than any man's. In his world every man would be a poet, Love would reign, Beauty would take place, Man and Nature would harmonize.[21]

In 1852, there are obvious signs that Thoreau no longer feels the deference toward Emerson that he used to feel. Their talks are generally disagreements. They disagree about Margaret Fuller one day; another day they wrangle over architecture, Thoreau maintaining that architectural ornamentation (as such) should not even be considered. As Thoreau reads Emerson on one occasion, he reports opening the book at random "to try what a chance sentence out of that could do for me."[22] To his disappointment, he finds that he had *thought the same thing myself twenty times during the day, and yet had not been contented with that account of it, leaving me thus to be amused by the coincidence, rather than impressed as by an intimation out of the deeps.*"[23] Such intimations were evidently what Thoreau had once looked for—not in vain—from Emerson. We recall that once Emerson's disapproval had been enough to make Thoreau destroy his early verses. Now their Transcendental friendship may be drawing to the close which Emerson in his essay on friendship contemplated as the

necessary end of most friendships. The friends (if we can believe Thoreau's journal) no longer inspire one another; fresh thoughts do not spring up between them; instead, disagreements and arguments. Thoreau condemns Emerson for what he is not, no longer praising him for what he is; and Emerson is nettled at the persistent opposition from a friend so much younger and one whom he wishes to esteem highly.

Later in the year 1852, while Thoreau was still thirty-five and Emerson was forty-nine, Thoreau voices a complaint of significance.

> One must not complain that his friend is cold, for heat is generated between them.[24]

> I doubt if Emerson could trundle a wheelbarrow through the streets, because it would be out of character. One needs to have a comprehensive character.[25]

Was Thoreau finding satisfactions in Emerson? Evidently not on that day. The next year matters were still worse between them.

> Talked, or tried to talk, with R. W. E. Lost my time—nay, almost my identity. He, assuming a false opposition where there was no difference of opinion, talked to the wind—told me what I knew—and I lost my time trying to imagine myself somebody else to oppose him.[26]

Lest anyone should suppose that the benevolent Emerson was unaware of Thoreau's discontent with him, or unaware of his systematic conflict in conversation, here is Emerson's own report on Thoreau in that same year:

> Henry is military. He seemed stubborn and implacable; always manly and wise, but rarely sweet. One would say that, as Webster could never speak without an antagonist, so Henry does not feel himself except in opposition. He wants a fallacy to expose, a blunder to pillory, requires a little sense of victory, a roll of the drums, to call his powers into full exercise.[27]

Edward Emerson in commenting on this passage suggests that Thoreau (for whom Edward Emerson always showed a sensitive affection almost as great as that for his father) "was on his guard not to be over-influenced." But this kindly surmise takes no account of some derisive references to Emerson in Thoreau's journal of this period, references indicating that Thoreau was in no danger of being over-influenced.

> I was amused by R. W. E.'s telling me that he drove his own calf out of the yard, as it was coming in with the cow, not knowing it to be his own, a drove going by at the time[28] (1853).

> Emerson is gone to the Adirondack country with a hunting party. Eddy says he has carried a double-barrelled gun, one side for shot, the other for ball, for Lowell killed a bear there last year. But the story on the Mill-Dam is that he has taken a gun which throws shot from one end and ball from the other.[29]

(1858)

Such excerpts suggest the delicate derision of one who sees his great man compromised, his great man who endeavors to do that for which he is unfit. A tone of veiled superiority is implicit in Thoreau's report of Emerson's activities on the Adirondack trip. He concludes the account scornfully:

> Think of Emerson shooting a peetweet (with shot) for Agassiz, and cracking an ale-bottle (after emptying it) with his rifle at six rods! They cut several pounds of lead out of the tree. It is just what Mike Saunders, the merchant's clerk, did when he was there.[30]
>
> (1858)

Perhaps Thoreau was too implacable ever to forgive a friend like Emerson for such a lapse. At any rate, there are no references after 1858 to Emerson in Thoreau's *Journal* which can be taken to indicate a genuine cordial exchange of ideas between the two. Thoreau talks of Emerson in the matter of a "flock of ducks," bluebirds on March 7, white-pine seed, windfall pears, and white-oak acorns. The signs point to an association supported mainly by a common taste for nature, not by the exchange of ideas.

The corroboration of Thoreau's rejection of, or at least his withdrawal from, Emerson, is to be found, of course in Emerson's journal.

> Thoreau wants a little ambition in his mixture. Fault of this, instead of being the head of American engineers, he is captain of a huckleberry party.[31]

Here Emerson pretty completely loses touch with Thoreau. He does not comprehend the fundamental delight of Thoreau in the sensuous richness of huckleberry parties—a richness not by any means paralleled in the activities of engineers. In spite of misconceptions, Emerson obviously finds something his nature requires and admires in Thoreau. The "something" is probably the astonishing acuteness of Thoreau's senses, and his equally astonishing powers of manipulating the material world of which those senses informed him. Emerson speaks the praises of Thoreau in many passages of the Journal, long years after Thoreau was clearly the one who withdrew as though he felt nothing more were to be gained by the association, more self-sufficient than the author of "Self-Reliance." But the passages of irritation crop up occasionally in the later journals of Emerson. In 1856 occurs an overt condemnation of Thoreau, which seems to mark a change in their relation to one another.

> If I knew only Thoreau, I should think co-operation of good men impossible. Must we always talk for victory, and never once for truth, for comfort, and joy? Centrality he has, and penetration, strong understanding, and the higher gifts,—the insight of the real, or from the real, and the moral rectitude that belongs to it; but all

this and all his resources of wit and invention are lost to me, in every experiment, year after year, that I make, to hold intercourse with his mind.[32]

This might well be taken to mark the expiration of their Transcendental friendship, the intercourse of mind with mind which each of them had always cherished as his explicit ideal human relationship. But Emerson continues to quote profound comments of Thoreau.

In 1858, some circumstance or other wrings from Emerson a hopeless cry:

> It needs the doing hand to make the seeing eye, and my imbecile hands leave me always helpless and ignorant, after so many years in the country.[33]

Almost immediately after that passage is one expressing wonderment at Thoreau's capacity for dealing with wild creatures. These passages recall that part of "The American Scholar" where Emerson expounds the idea that one man may be a delegated mind (Man Thinking), another may be a delegated hand or foot, or what not, to serve the rest of mankind. Experience had brought this pre-Thoreauvian theory to the test. We find Emerson frequently repeating the botanical lore and the zoological lore imparted to him by Thoreau. Their later walks tended to concentrate on flowers where their early walks apparently often led almost to the presence of the Over-Soul. Thoreau, nevertheless, would not serve as the practical hand and the seeing eye for Emerson. Emerson discovered, furthermore, that Thoreau was not inviting ideas nor offering them. Thoreau had always been Man-Thinking himself, Emerson or no Emerson. But Emerson's imbecile hands never improved. As always, Emerson finally appears in a gracious light, a wistful one, in the *Journal* for 1862—the year of Thoreau's death. Thoreau, for any signs that I can discover, chose to remain in his last year essentially out of Emerson's reach, perhaps not intentionally so much as through an indifference of slow growth. Some say that Thoreau was jealous of the great man with whom he was so long associated. I believe incipient jealousies might be discovered but they hardly account for the intellectual schism in the Church of Walden. The readers of Thoreau's *Journal* have long noted that the later volumes read frequently more like the records of a naturalist than the reflections of a philosopher. It is not impossible that philosophically Thoreau had hardened—perhaps all that side of things was settled to his satisfaction—and if it was a satisfaction to have settled philosophy, it probably was because it left him free to study the sense phenomena of the world. Objects of sense he loved, and who shall say confidently that the sensuous life was not Thoreau's most private and passionate approach to thought? Feeling the trees or rocks might have been Thoreau's way of thinking.

Notes

1. *The Writings of Thoreau* (Boston and New York, 1906), 20 vols. Fourteen of these constitute the *Journal.—Journal*, III, 256.

2. *Ibid.*, II, 472.

3. *Ibid.*, VIII, 294.

4. *Ibid.*, IX, 217.

5. *Ibid.*, I, 296.

6. Edward Waldo Emerson and Waldo Emerson Forbes (eds.), *Journals of Ralph Waldo Emerson* (Boston and New York, 1908-1914), 10 vols., IX, 522.

7. *Ibid.*, IV, 397.

8. *Ibid.*, V, 208.

9. *Ibid.*, V, 414.

10. *Ibid.*, IV, 395.

11. *Works*, IX, 44-48.

12. *Ibid.*, IX, 47-48.

13. E. W. Emerson, *Emerson in Concord* (Boston and New York, 1889), p. 111.

14. Emerson, *Journals* [*Journals of Ralph Waldo Emerson*], I, 230-231.

15. *Ibid.*, I, 231.

16. *Ibid.*, I, 233.

17. *Ibid.*, I, 241.

18. *Ibid.*, I, 242-243.

19. Thoreau, *Journal*, I, 432-433.

20. Thoreau, *Walden* [in *The Writings of Thoreau*], II, 185.

21. Thoreau, *Journal*, I, 432-433.

22. *Ibid.*, III, 134.

23. *Ibid.*, III, 135.

24. *Ibid.*, III, 250.

25. *Ibid.*, III, 250.

26. *Ibid.*, V, 188.

27. Emerson, *Journals*, VIII, 375.

28. Thoreau, *Journal*, VI, 15.

29. *Ibid.*, XI, 77.

30. *Ibid.*, XI, 120.

31. Emerson, *Journals*, VIII, 228.

32. *Ibid.*, IX, 15-16.

33. *Ibid.*, IX, 153.

Donald Culross Peattie (essay date spring 1938)

SOURCE: Peattie, Donald Culross. "Is Thoreau a Modern?" *North American Review* 245, no. 1 (spring 1938): 159-69.

[*In the following essay, Peattie evaluates the enduring relevance of Thoreau's writings in the twentieth century.*]

Sinclair Lewis writes of Henry David Thoreau that he

> conducted a one-man revolution and won it. . . . We aren't within seventy-five years of catching up with him. He wanted, more than anything else, to buy his own time. . . . He did it. . . . He built his own warm shack, and in it he lived with a dignity vaster than any harassed emperor. He was popular in his social set . . . composed . . . of swallows and chipmunks and sunfish, and other swift, elegant and shining notabilities.
>
> All this with gaiety and warmth, he wrote out in *Walden*. . . . published in 1854 and more modern than Dos Passos. . . . His *Walden* and all that is important from his other books, with notes and biography by Henry Seidel Canby, in an 848-page volume handsomely published by Houghton Mifflin at five dollars is the book-buy of the year.

And so it is. Mr. Lewis wishes that one hundred thousand copies will have been sold in the Christmas season just past. And though I would not, like Mr. Lewis, care to set up Thoreau as a supreme *Duce* for this sick world, I could wish that everyone capable of understanding Thoreau who has never read him, should meet him in this new year.

Mr. Canby, like Mr. Lewis, claims that Thoreau is modern where most of his contemporaries are dated. And the proposition is worth examining. With this republication of Thoreau, especially if it does become the best-seller it deserves to be, the man and his thoughts are shorn of the limp-leather immunity accorded to unread classics, to Scripture, to saintly lives of the past. He is bruited; his pages are flung wide open. They will be read, I hope with Mr. Lewis, by those who acknowledge no fealty to the grace of things past, but judge every writer by today's standards. By high-school boys who think of chemistry as the touchstone of Cosmos, by students in New York City College who look at the world sociologically. By persons not less fanatically conscientious than Thoreau, who believe it their first duty to picket for the garment-workers' strike, and by others whose conscience dictates that they shall bash the heads of such picketers. And by countless more whose persuasions, trainings, emergencies were undreamed of in Concord in 1838. What will they find in Thoreau?

First let us take a swallow-flight over the table of contents, representing Mr. Canby's preferences among the works of his master. We open with some selections from the great poetic and philosophic quarry of the *Journals.* They are selections rather carefully dissected out of Thoreau's natural tissue of sheer nature writing. For Mr. Canby believes that "much damage has been done to his [Thoreau's] reputation as a writer to be read, by the still current belief that he was only a nature writer." (And of course he wasn't only a nature writer.) And "while he was a nature writer *à outrance* as he was a protestant *à outrance,* and paid the penalty of all those whose ambition is infinitely to know, that is not the way to begin to read him."

Mr. Canby does give us some of the nature essays, not the immediate, Thoreau-afoot of the diaries, but for the most part the reworked and highly finished products which he either sent to the printer or must have been nearly ready so to do. The one called *Wild Apples* is especially Thoreauvian, and for myself I could wish that it led off the book.

The second big item is *A Week on the Concord and Merrimac Rivers.* Mr. Canby, like a flattering tailor, has slimmed the portly girth of this, Thoreau's first book. Even so it is one of the most leisurely, digressive books ever written by an American and it is be-gemmed with a wealth of classical allusion and references to thoughts in others' books.

But *Walden* comes next, and since it is a work so nearly perfect, and probably immortal, no comment is needed on its inclusion or its better-than-modernity. Next come a few poems, and then selections from the travel books (and it did Thoreau a world of good to travel, in spite of his reluctance to leave Concord). Then follow essays on friendship, civil disobedience and on John Brown's execution. The last indeed was an oration, probably Thoreau's only really successful speech, and it closes the book like a trumpet blast.

The purchaser also has the benefit of Mr. Canby's own comments. They represent, though so admirably concise, years of scholarship, a restrained but vital enthusiasm, and some little distinguished prose on their own account. One of the lasting impressions of this omnibus is that of gratitude to Mr. Canby for his work and guidance, and respect for his opinion, a respect that does not preclude, we may hope, the right to prefer, sometimes, one's own way of reading Thoreau.

Three preoccupations had the man of Walden, Mr. Canby points out. They were Nature, Himself, and Criticism (that is, social criticism, comment, even satire and open scorn). Proper to all philosophers are these concerns, for they tackle the age-old problems: Where am I, Who am I, and What shall I do? For himself, a hundred years ago, Thoreau knew all the answers. He is definite as a right angle. How does that clear voice ring in 1938?

"We have the Saint Vitus dance, and cannot possibly keep our heads still." He begs us to "simplify, simplify." Verily, verily, he says unto us:

> Our life is frittered away by detail. . . . The nation itself, with all its internal improvements, which, by the way, are all external and superficial, is . . . cluttered with furniture . . . ruined by luxury and heedless expense. . . . It lives too fast. Men think that it is essential that the *Nation* have commerce, and export ice, and talk through a telegraph, and ride thirty miles an hour . . . but whether we should live like baboons or like men, is a little uncertain.

"Must every squirrel turn a coffee mill?"

It stings sharper than ever; the finger he points through Concord identifies ourselves.

He visits an Irishman in his miserable shanty, surrounded by his brats and under the thumb of his old wife. Why should Paddy swink and sweat to get his hot morning coffee? Thoreau has the solution: he can go without coffee, and drink pure spring water.

If you take the railroad to Fitchburg and he walks it, he will be there afore ye. He means by this that while you are earning the fare to Fitchburg, he, penniless, will have set out the day before. And will have lived more, on the way. True, though he may have walked to Fitchburg, Thoreau took the trains to Philadelphia.

He demands to know what good word was ever sent by cable? What are we likely to hear? Why, that the little Princess Adelaide has whooping cough. But one brave and eternal thing, never. We can fancy his opinion of airplanes and automobiles. One doubts whether even for radio concerts he would have had any use. The opera was caterwauling to him, but he listened with pleasure to a child banging a tin spoon in an old pot.

I believe there is no pose anywhere in the man, that a soul never spoke who meant more literally what he said.

But are we in our Babylon all hypocrites and Pharisees, softies and fools? It is easy to proclaim that Middletown should learn from Tepoztlan; can it assimilate the knowledge, and apply it? Perhaps Thoreau would still have preferred only a thrush on the air to a broadcast of Brahms's *First*. He may like best, as he says, to sit alone on a pumpkin. But for good or ill we are not, most of us, born under his lonely planet. You cannot get away from the neighbors by crossing the Mississippi today. You cannot even, always and anywhere, hear a thrush. But you can find a sort of skill and self-reliance and nerve in men who can bring a Diesel locomotive in on time, even if they cannot build a shack. There is the brotherhood of man in a free medical clinic, is there not? And even if we should admit that we were sick now with the maladies of Thoreau's times in a virulent degree, in a pandemic that has spread from the foci of industrial civilization to the ultimate isles, it is then, alas, only too likely that we are too far gone now for the simple cures that Thoreau proposed.

But his own needs Thoreau perfectly comprehended, as he could in himself satisfy them.

His self-exploration was accomplished well nigh to perfection. It is clearer than Whitman's, and to my taste more decent than Tolstoi's. To be what he wished, even in the face of social opposition and ridicule, was his right and his great triumph. When we ask whether his splendid disobedience and his affirmations and doubts are widely applicable to moderns, we are asking his biographers to tell us what befell him. Mr. Canby answers that question when he says that the solutions worked out in *Walden* are not for family men. He might have added that, on the whole, they are not for women. Or children. Thoreau chose to have no personal ardors, and underwent no great personal griefs. He was sheltered from most hard-bought human knowledge, so that he can say, "I have heard no bad news." Thank God that it was so.

But he knew Nature. By Nature he means of course Cosmos. He means the nature of Nature, the fundamental structure of the Universe that shall manifest itself in the revolution of the moons of Jupiter, and the six-sided crystals of a snowflake, and the hiving of bees and the curious ways of women. When he speaks of the surface of Nature, of a terrestrial, a New England view of it, he writes as a poet and a lover. But to be a Transcendentalist, particularly Thoreau's especial brand, is to seek through all Nature for some higher law, some reality transcending that which the senses proclaim.

This idea is inherent in Greek philosophy of which Greek science is but a department. It reached Christian theology early, and came to New England, no doubt, in the sermons to which Thoreau listened, as a child under compulsion, and, as a man tramping past the meeting house, with horror. Platonic realism or Scholastic Aristotelianism in Thoreau's youth, enjoyed a recrudescence in the sciences. Beginning in Germany as romantic Natural Philosophy, it had spread to other nations briefly. Coleridge brought it to the Lake poets, Wordsworth brought it to the world. Alcott and, if I am not mistaken, Emerson brought it to Concord. Thoreau, the only naturalist among them, made it peculiarly his own:

Jan. 21, 1853. A fine still warm moonlight evening. . . . I am somewhat oppressed and saddened by the sameness and apparent poverty of the heavens, that these irregular and few geometrical figures which the constellations make are no other than those seen by the Chaldaean shepherds. I pine for a new world in the heavens as well as on the earth, and though it is some consolation to hear of the wilderness of stars and systems invisible to the naked eye yet the sky does not make that impression of variety and wildness that even the forest does. . . . It makes an impression rather of simplicity and unchangeableness, as of eternal laws. . . . I seem to see it pierced with visual rays from a thousand observatories. It is more the domain of science than of poetry. It is the stars as not known to science that I would know, the stars which the lonely traveler knows. . . . The classification of the stars is old and musty. . . . A few good anecdotes is our science, with a few opposing statements respecting distance and size, and little or nothing about the stars as they concern man. It teaches how he may survey a country or sail a ship, and not how he may steer his life. Astrology contained the germ of a higher truth than this . . . the sun is ninety-five millions of miles distant . . . a statement which never made any impression on me because I never walked it, and which I cannot be said to believe. . . . Though observatories are multiplied, the heavens receive very little attention. The naked eye may easily see farther than the armed. Man's eye is the true star-finder, the comet-seeker. No superior telescope to this has been invented. . . . The astronomer's eye . . . does not see far beyond the dome of the observatory.

Transcendentalism is here very clearly and consistently expressed; one might even say, nobly. But it declares its profound difference from modern science, or even indeed from the best science of Thoreau's time, which he took many occasions to deride and belittle. Out of love for Thoreau, I do not quote them; they are, I think, best passed over.

Nor are we to blame Thoreau for not being a scientist. Any educated man, however, can understand some science if he will, and Thoreau understood it quite enough to utilize it. But he distrusts it; he claims that its findings are less important than those which Transcendentalism will presently divine.

And even in his own times the sciences were discovering the structure, behavior, and nature of protoplasm, which is the very seat of life and ought to have interested a Transcendentalist transcendingly. There was already current a body of knowledge about chlorophyll, perhaps the most significant single substance in the world, the very link between cosmic energy and terrestrial life. But I can find no reference in Thoreau to these facts. While the Transcendentalists were proclaiming the mystery of life, science has rather beat them to a solution of many of those mysteries at the despised gait of the tortoise. Nor has this been accomplished at any great monetary advantage to the scientist, nor in a scramble for fame, but in an incorruptible search for the truth. As for the Transcendental truths, they have never been advanced since Thoreau did what was just possibly all that could be done for them.

Is Thoreau then a modern? It seems hard to prove it; the gap between his century and ours is one of the greatest in the history of the human structure, greater perhaps than the change from classic civilization to barbarian romanticism. It asks too much of him to bridge it.

But were it any great compliment to say that he is modern? Would he himself be pleased to hear it? Would he not prefer to be "dated?" So, he might say, is the *Iliad* dated, so far as siege tactics, or the picture of the human soul in war-time are concerned. But the poetry of the *Iliad* is timeless. And so is the poetry of **Walden.** As Nature's lover, Henry David Thoreau is the greatest in the English language.

And it is as a Nature writer that I hope he will be read forever.

Let us listen to him first on winter. For he himself is so wintry—stinging, chaste, and white-paged. No heavy leafage about him. He brings the blood to our cheeks.

> A cold and dark afternoon, the sun being behind clouds in the west. The landscape is barren of objects, the trees being leafless, and so little light in the sky for variety. Such a day as will almost oblige a man to eat his own heart. A day in which you must hold on to life by your teeth. You can hardly ruck up any skin on Nature's bones. The sap is down; she won't peel. Now is the time to cut timber for yokes and ox-bows, leaving the tough bark on—yokes for your own neck. Finding yourself yoked to Matter and to Time. Truly a hard day, hard times these! Not a mosquito left. Not an insect to hum. Crickets gone into winter quarters. Friends long since gone there, and you left to walk on frozen ground, with your hands in your pockets. Ah, but is not this a glorious time for your deep inward fires?

Note the economy of the style, the continence of adjectives, the passionless diction, like the season itself. Now let him speak for autumn:

> It is pleasant to walk over the beds of these fresh, crisp, and rustling leaves. How beautifully they go to their graves! how gently lay themselves down and turn to mould!—painted of a thousand hues, and fit to make the beds of us living. So they troop to their last resting-place, light and frisky. They put on no weeds, but merrily they go scampering over the earth, selecting a spot, choosing a lot, ordering no iron fence, whispering all through the woods about it—some choosing the spot where the bodies of men are mouldering beneath, and meeting them half-way. How many flutterings before they rest quietly in their graves! They that soared so loftily, how contentedly they return to dust again, and are laid low, resigned to lie and decay at the foot of the trees, and afford nourishment to new generations of their kind, as well as to flutter on high! They teach us how to die.

But no Thoreau enthusiast can long be put off a gloat over **Walden.** The sheer Nature writing first breaks away for a splendid dash around the track of Thoreau's mind in his description of Walden Pond. This begins on page 360 of the present omnibus, and runs on for eighteen breath-taking pages. I have space here for a sample but Walden Pond will ever after linger in the memory not as the individual lake it is but as a jewel whose reputation may outlive that of the greatest diamond:

> In such a day, in September or October, Walden is a perfect forest mirror, set round with stones as precious to my eye as if fewer or rarer. Nothing so fair, so pure, and at the same time so large, as a lake, perchance, lies on the surface of the earth. Sky water. It needs no fence. Nations come and go without defiling it. It is a mirror which no stone can crack, whose quicksilver will never wear off, whose gilding Nature continually repairs; no storms, no dust, can dim its surface ever fresh;—a mirror in which all impurity presented to it sinks, swept and dusted by the sun's hazy brush—this the light dust-cloth—which retains no breath that is breathed on it, but sends its own to float as clouds high above its surface, and be reflected in its bosom still.

At last he settles into the now-famous shack:

> At length the winter set in in good earnest, just as I had finished plastering, and the wind began to howl around the house as if it had not had permission to do so till then. Night after night the geese came lumbering in in the dark with a clangor and a whistling of wings, even after the ground was covered with snow, some to alight in Walden, and some flying low over the woods toward Fair Haven, bound for Mexico. Several times, when returning from the village at ten or eleven o'clock at night, I heard the tread of a flock of geese, or else ducks, on the dry leaves in the woods by a pond-hole behind my dwelling, where they had come up to feed, and the faint honk or quack of their leader as they hurried off. . . . The snow had already covered the ground since the 25th of November, and surrounded me suddenly with the scenery of winter. I withdrew yet farther into my shell, and endeavored to keep a bright fire both within my house and within my breast. My employment out of doors now was to collect the dead wood in the forest, bringing it in my hands or on my shoulders, or sometimes trailing a dead pine tree under each arm to my shed. An old forest fence which had seen its best days was a great haul for me. I sacrificed it to Vulcan, for it was past serving the god Terminus. How much more interesting an event is that man's supper who has just been forth in the snow to hunt, nay you might say, steal, the fuel to cook it with! His bread and meat are sweet.

Thoreau is on his Pegasus now, he is off on the wings of lyricism; these are the happiest moments of his life, and I think some of the happiest moments that were ever lived on the North American continent; certainly the most delicately perceptive. From this point to the end of the book we are borne like leaves on the sunlit brook of Thoreau's spirit and his style. The passage on the deserted farmyard, which begins on page 418, has no equal in American literature, for my tastes, unless it is the essay on arrowheads which begins on page 617.

This is the voice that was stilled by an early death. The sadness that this thought evokes is not consolable. Of the silence one can only hope that it is true that "The gods delight in stillness; they say, 'st—st.'"

John Haynes Holmes (essay date 29 June 1949)

SOURCE: Holmes, John Haynes. "Thoreau's 'Civil Disobedience.'" *Christian Century* 46 (29 June 1949): 787-89.

[*In the following essay, Holmes examines the influence of Thoreau's essay on twentieth-century social and political activism. Holmes asserts that Thoreau's concept of individual liberty had particular resonance in the post-World War II era.*]

Thoreau's essay on civil disobedience, published just a hundred years ago, is usually thought of as a native New England product, and at the most as a permanent part of our American literature. Yet it has gone around the world. It reached, among others, the soul of Gandhi. The great Indian has told us with some precision of the books which were determining factors in the fashioning of his thought and life. These were the Bhagavad-Gita, the Scripture of his Hindu faith, the New Testament, especially the "Sermon on the Mount," John Ruskin's *Unto This Last,* Leo Tolstoi's *The Kingdom of God Is Within You,* and—Henry David Thoreau's **"Civil Disobedience."**

This book, or rather pamphlet, thus had its decisive place in the greatest revolution of modern times, and in the mind of one of the half-dozen supreme historical figures of all times. Gandhi extended and deepened Thoreau's gospel into the potent weapon of soul-force, which achieved Indian independence. He made it not the lone protest against tyranny of the single individual, but the massed revolt of disciplined multitudes of men. But the seed was of Thoreau's planting.

Product of a Tumultuous Time

"Civil Disobedience" was first published, under its original title of **"Resistance to Civil Government,"** in Miss Elizabeth Peabody's *Aesthetic Papers.* Prepared in the beginning as a lecture, it may have been written in 1848. In 1866, it appeared with another essay, **"Life Without Principle,"** in a volume entitled *A Yankee in Canada, with Anti-Slavery and Reform Papers.* (See Henry Seidel Canby's *The Works of Thoreau.*)

In its first form as published in 1849, it appeared midway between the Mexican War (1846-47) on the one hand, and the Fugitive Slave Law (1850) on the other.

In both these fights—the former on the field of battle, the latter in the arena of public opinion—the right of civil disobedience was loudly and widely proclaimed. It was the antislavery epoch, and it was under the stimulus of this tumultuous period that Thoreau's essay was written. Resentment and resistance against the war, and later on against the law, sprang fundamentally from the same furious seething of emotion stirred up by the iniquity of legalized human bondage. Thoreau put by emotion, though he felt the situation keenly, and attempted calmly and soberly to think through the question of slavery in relation to the state. Here was a chance, a challenge, to present the reason for civil disobedience, and therewith justify the widespread rebellion of the times. So he set down the argument for this deliberate defiance of government, and did it so clearly and convincingly that his essay of less than twenty pages became and still remains the classic in its field.

It is usually assumed that **"Civil Disobedience"** presents the case for philosophical anarchism and thus urges opposition to government for its own sake. And it is true that Thoreau wrote sentences, indeed whole passages, which seem to sustain this idea. Thus he quotes Jefferson's famous statement, "That government is best which governs least," and caps it with his own declaration, "That government is best which governs not at all." He asserts that "the objections which have been brought against a standing army, and they . . . deserve to prevail, may also at last be brought against a standing government." "Government never of itself furthered any enterprise, but by the alacrity with which it got out of its way. *It* does not keep the country free. *It* does not settle the west. *It* does not educate. The character inherent in the American people has done all that has been accomplished, and it would have done somewhat more if the government had not sometimes got in its way."

Not "No Government," but "Better Government"

But he is soon making distinction between himself and "those who call themselves no-government men." What he wants, at least for the present, is "not at once no government, but at once a better government." Before he gets through, he is talking about "the authority of government, even such as I am willing to submit to," and "imagining a state . . . which can afford to be just to all men, . . . which even would not think it inconsistent with its own repose if a few were to live aloof from it, not meddling with it, nor embraced by it." Even as things are, he thinks "the Constitution, with all its faults, is very good, the law and the courts very respectable, even this state and this American government . . . very admirable."

It is obvious that what Thoreau had in mind, in his essay, was bad government in contrast to good, and the right, nay the duty, of citizens to resist evil in the state even to the point of open and deliberate disobedience to its laws. There were two prodigious evils present when he was writing, as we have seen—the Mexican War, and the institution of slavery in the interest of which he believed the war was being fought—and these absolved all true citizens from allegiance to existing government. "This people," he wrote, "must cease to hold slaves, and to make war on Mexico, though it cost them their existence as a people."

SERVING THE STATE WITH ONE'S CONSCIENCE

Indeed, they must go farther, and resist the government which recognizes and protects these abominations. "I do not hesitate to say that those who call themselves Abolitionists should at once effectually withdraw their support, both in person and property, from the government of Massachusetts." For men should "serve the state with their consciences." No citizen can, "in the least degree, resign his conscience to the legislator. . . . We should be men first, and subjects afterward. It is not desirable to cultivate a respect for the law, so much as for the right." All of which means that the individual and not society is primary.

Thoreau was not an anarchist but an individualist. He would not have the government impose its law upon the citizen, but rather the citizen impose his will upon the government. As a matter of fact, the state rules the citizen only because it exercises "superior physical strength." It confronts a man not with "superior wit or honesty," but with force, as in an army where men are "on a level with wood and earth and stone." But "I was not born to be forced," cries Thoreau; "I will breathe after my own fashion."

Then he goes on to lay down his philosophy. Government, he writes in the concluding page of his essay, "can have no pure right over my person and property but what I concede to it. The progress from an absolute to a limited monarchy, from a limited monarchy to a democracy, is progress toward a true respect for the individual. . . . There will never be a really free and enlightened state until the state comes to recognize the individual as a higher and independent power, from which all its own power and authority are derived, and treats him accordingly." Such a state is "not yet anywhere seen." It can only be "imagined." Meanwhile, Thoreau will go his way. If this means prison, so be it. Prison is the place for "just men" until the government "gives up war and slavery."

A PRECIOUS SYMBOL

The one method of civil disobedience which Thoreau advocates, and affirms by his example, is refusal to pay taxes. He states that he has "never declined paying the highway tax," nor the school tax, "because I am as de-

sirous of being a good neighbor as I am of being a bad subject." But he will not pay general taxes which help to support war and slavery. He knows that his refusal is ineffectual, but as a symbol it is precious. "I wish to refuse allegiance to the state, to withdraw and stand aloof from it." When neighbors paid his tax for him, and thus released him from jail, he was displeased. And he dreams of the "peaceful revolution" that would come "if a thousand men were not to pay their taxes this year."

It is interesting to read, in these so different times, this uncompromising declaration of the rights of the individual as over against the sovereignty of society. Herbert Spencer's *The Man Versus the State* and John Stuart Mill's *Essay on Liberty* make good supplementary reading on the same theme. Likewise it is exciting to recall how advocates of "non-violent resistance," to use Gandhi's phrase, carried over into action their sentiments of protest.

THEODORE PARKER'S CONTEMPORARY COURSE

Theodore Parker, Thoreau's contemporary, is a supreme example. On the occasion of the Mexican War, which he abominated as the long arm of slavery dragging the country into conflict with its neighbors, Parker asked, "What shall we do?" and answered, "In regard to this present war, we can refuse to take any part in it; we can encourage others to do the same; we can aid men, if need be, who suffer because they refuse. Men will call us traitors: what then? That hurt nobody in '76! We are a rebellious nation; our whole history is treason. . . . Though all the governors in the world bid us commit treason against man, . . . let us never submit. Let God only be a master to control our conscience!"

More dramatic was Parker's statement in the pulpit of the Music Hall on a Sunday morning (October 6, 1850) following the enactment of the Fugitive Slave Law as a part of Henry Clay's omnibus bill. Denouncing the law and pointing out that it placed in jeopardy escaped slaves in Boston and even in his own church, Parker exclaimed: "Shall I stand by and see some of my own flock carried off into bondage, and do nothing to hinder it? . . . To law framed in such iniquity I owe no allegiance. Humanity, Christianity, manhood revolt against it. . . . For myself—I say solemnly—I will shelter and I will help the fugitive with all my humble means and power. I will act with any body of serious and decent men, as the head, or the foot, or the hand, in any mode not involving the use of deadly weapons, to nullify and defeat the operation of this law; and I feel confident there is enough of manhood and true Christianity in Boston to protect every fugitive amongst us, without the shedding of blood or even the rending of a garment."

As to whether Parker ever read **"Civil Disobedience,"** there is no evidence. In all the fifteen large volumes of his collected works, only one reference to Thoreau appears, and that a purely casual one. In the ten volumes of Emerson's *Journals* the essay is not mentioned, though Thoreau's sojourn in jail for not paying his taxes is recorded. "On him," writes Emerson, "they could not calculate." The fact is that **"Civil Disobedience"** seems to have attracted little attention and less comment when it appeared. Yet it defined the principle upon which heroic action was basing itself, and remains therefore a permanent contribution to the literature of man's thought.

DANGERS OF THE NEW DEMOCRACY

In the century that has passed since the publication of **"Civil Disobedience,"** conditions of life have vastly changed. Especially has government been transformed, or rather the relation of government to its citizens. Democracy at the start meant deliverance from the undue intrusion of society upon the individual. This was freedom! Thoreau dramatized the idea in his retreat to Walden. But today we think of democracy in terms of cooperation—the joining together of many free men in some common enterprise for the common good. Society enters into the lives of men in a way and to a degree which would horrify Thoreau were he still alive.

We justify this change of relationship between man and the state by emphasizing that government in this new function is accepted not as a rod to subdue the people, but as an instrument to equip them for the work they have to do together. Government in this sense is an indispensable tool to achieve for society as a whole what could be done by no one man or group of men. But in this very process, government takes on power, and is thus ever tempted to use this power at the expense of the people and in its own corporate interest. Bureaucracy, red tape, rule from above rather than from below, dictatorship, tyranny—all these are perils in waiting for a socialized democracy. At the end of this dangerous road, in other words, if we take the wrong turn, lies totalitarianism of left or right.

It is this fact, now inwrought in a world situation, which makes the revival of Thoreau's essay so timely. Woe to the society which forgets that the state was made for man, and not man for the state! And double and treble woe to the society which no longer breeds men to rise up, at the cost of their lives, their fortunes and their sacred honor, to resent and rebel against any attempt to subordinate them as individuals to the dominance of the state! The individual must at all times and in all places be the very core of social being.

This is the principle which is in such danger at the present hour. We thought that we had won the battle for liberty. But this ideal was never as firmly established in men's minds as we had so fondly imagined. The blast of war has shaken it loose, and in some cases swept it away. We must build anew the rights of man. And in this task there can be no more useful aid than Thoreau's **"Civil Disobedience."**

Nina Baym (essay date April-June 1965)

SOURCE: Baym, Nina. "Thoreau's View of Science." *Journal of the History of Ideas* 26, no. 2 (April-June 1965): 221-34.

[*In the following essay, Baym explores the tension between poetic inspiration and scientific rationalism in Thoreau's writings on nature.*]

One of the crucial intellectual events of the Nineteenth Century was the rapid expansion of scientific knowledge. The accompanying problems of man's view of himself in relation to the new universe occupied scientists, clergymen, and laymen alike, and the positions then defined remain with us in many ways today. In that century, perhaps few stances towards science are as interesting as that of the transcendentalist, which began in scientific radicalism and ended totally opposed to scientific aims, methods, and assumptions. Among the Transcendentalists, the most seriously concerned with the question of science, because the most dedicated to a life in nature, was Thoreau.

Thoreau's attitudes towards nature cannot be wholly considered apart from his views on science, since he constantly illuminated his approach to nature by contrasts and parallels to science; hence, full-scale studies of Thoreau invariably consider these views and attitudes. In his biography of 1873 William Ellery Channing used the phrase "poet-naturalist" to resolve the dichotomy in Thoreau's work between subjective interpretation and objective reporting. Yet the dichotomy persisted. Naturalists continued to be appalled at the inaccuracy of the reporting, humanists to be exasperated at its inclusion at all.

At the present time there seem to be three readings of Thoreau's science, the ecological, humanist, and symbolist. A minority of critics finds him a true scientist ahead of his time, an ecologist before ecology existed.[1] But this reading ignores a pronounced anti-scientific bias in Thoreau's writings which becomes stronger as he becomes more obviously scientific. This puzzle—that his late journals are at once more scientific in content and more opposed to science in comment—has been solved by no interpretation.

The humanist view understands Thoreau as unalterably opposed to science but lapsing into it through loss of inspiration.[2] It ignores the enigma's converse, the many cordial remarks about science in the earlier writings. The third and most widely held view of Thoreau, the symbolist, believes that he was always a poet, never a scientist by lapse or choice. The late journals are unutilized storehouses which testify to the continuity of Thoreau's attitudes throughout life.[3]

I would like to suggest that Thoreau has a far more complex attitude towards science, and to suggest its origins. His basic difficulty may be summarized thus: he believed in 1842 that he could be a Transcendentalist and a scientist simultaneously. In **"The Natural History of Massachusetts"** (1842), his first nature essay, he was convinced that science must lead to transcendental ends, and he accepted it enthusiastically. The untenability of this position gradually became clear to him in two ways, and this gradual clarification is the history of his scientific thought. First, his approach failed. He could not prove what he had intended to prove with the facts he had gathered. Second, he learned that the assumptions of his approach were not accepted by science.

Thoreau, as everyone knows, became interested in nature because of Emerson, but it is not noted often enough that Emerson brought Thoreau to nature through scientific writing. Writing to Margaret Fuller on April 10, 1842, he notes:

> I read a little lately in the "Scientific Surveys of Massachusetts." . . . I went, when I was in Boston last time, to the Secretary's office at the state house and begged of him this series of Reports . . . and this day I have, as I hope, set Henry Thoreau on the good track of giving an account of them in the *Dial.*[4]

Why did Emerson choose this way to interest Thoreau in the Concord landscape? First, Emerson is introducing Thoreau to method as well as subject. Second, Emerson's own excitement about nature had been aroused by science.

Emerson, attempting to save religion from dogmatism, institutionalism, and error, tested everything for its expediency in furthering his urgent aim. Though rejecting revealed religion, with its source in the Bible and support in the churches, he had felt no need to abandon natural religion. He needed a substitute for the Bible, and nature had long been so used. But conventional natural theology used nature to support revealed religion by stressing the limitations of human life and knowledge. However, Swedenborg, introduced into New England by Sampson Reed, suggested a more optimistic interpretation of nature. He said that the mind was destined to expand to divinity through increased knowledge of nature. Reed's work stressed science heavily.[5] But his assertions remained unfelt by Emerson until his European trip in the summer of 1833.

The moment of awakening came in the Jardin des Plantes in Paris, where Emerson looked, not on the face of nature wild, but on nature arranged and methodized. The vast scope of the collection told him that "the universe is a more amazing puzzle than ever"; the orderly display told him at the same time of the capacity of man's mind to encompass and understand this universe; and his own deep emotion in the presence of this combination of mind and matter assured him that science was the key to the religion of the future.[6] This vision inspired, the following winter, a number of lectures on science, for which Emerson read widely and enthusiastically. He saw the science of the Jardin as a dictionary of the language of nature. "Nature is a language and every new fact we learn is a new word. . . . I wish to learn this language, not that I may know a new grammar, but that I may read the great book which is written in that tongue."[7] He wanted science to advance at full speed, for every discovery teaches Divinity and cements our connection to God. He had no conventional fears of scientific impiety. No fact could shake his religious certainty, for his conception of Deity was vaster than fact. "I am not impressed by solitary marks of designing wisdom; I am thrilled by the choral harmony of the whole. Design! It is all design. It is all beauty. It is all astonishment."[8]

In his fight against established religion Emerson found science an ally and a key to understanding the universe in the way he was predisposed to understand it. Here were the mind and the universe merging. Here were progress and optimism. He was better prepared than some scientists of his own day to accept a number of discoveries, such as the great age of the earth, because, being completely non-materialistic, he found nothing disturbing in the ability of secondary causes to explain material effects. How else, he might ask, were material effects to *be* caused? But what animates the causes? "Life," or "spirit." This non-materialism, which led him to equate "life" with "spirit," blinded him entirely to the possibility that secondary causes might ever be extended to account for the existence of life itself. Thus secure in his definition of ends, he cautioned scientists against forgetting ends in their natural delight over means.[9]

Emerson turned Thoreau to nature study, then, not through his *Nature,* a decidedly non-scientific work, but through scientific documents. It seems fair to surmise that he was trying to move Thoreau in the same way and by the same means as he had been moved. "I say I will listen to this invitation. I will be a naturalist,"[10] he had written nine years before. Now he was passing this invitation on to Thoreau.

Thoreau reviewed the surveys in an essay entitled **"The Natural History of Massachusetts,"** which shows his happy acceptance both of nature and science. The surveys are welcomed to the select company of books which "restore the tone of the system," contrasted to the irrelevant "din of literature, religion, and philosophy." The scientific method which they proceed from is "admirable training . . . for the more active warfare of life." Linnaeus is compared to Napoleon. Nature repays the most exacting scrutiny; she "invites us to lay our eye level with the smallest leaf, and take an insect view of its plain."[11] The only criticism he offers is of the unavoidable incompleteness of the surveys. "These volumes deal much in measurements and minute descriptions, not interesting to the general reader. . . . But the ground was comparatively unbroken; and we will not complain of the pioneer, if he raises no flowers with his first crop" (p. 130). The surveys are inadequate because they are first efforts. But they are ground-breaking, full of healthy promise. There is no distrust in Thoreau's welcome.

Thoreau was not, of course, simply a copy of Emerson, and he worked into his welcome of science his own ideas. As religious as Emerson, he was as anxious to define man's proper relationship to a Power assumed to have created the universe and still actively sustaining it. As transcendental as Emerson, he believed that this Power could be directly known by man through intuitions arising from his own internal divinity. These intuitions are supported by the evidences of nature around him, which, as it was created by the Mind he shares, can be perceived and understood by him. But, more Calvinist than Emerson, Thoreau had a strong sense of man estranged from God. So, when he accepted the scientific approach, he turned the scientific life into a holy life of great effort and infinite challenge. In Thoreau's relationship with nature, then, we do not find Emerson's pacific certainty. To study nature becomes the program of an action which achieves the reconciliation of man and God. The naturalist lives a saintly life because he must obey the laws he learns to know them, and these laws explain him and his place in the universe, being spiritual as well as material laws. It is quite scientific, then, to plant beans for the sake of parables; through beans spiritual truths are revealed.

Thoreau's word for this program of nature study, which was identical with the quest for personal salvation, is his famous "anticipation," and we may find the seeds of anticipation in various semi-scientific works which he read in his formative years. There is, first of all, Emerson's early lecture, "The Uses of Natural History," delivered during the winter of 1833-1834. The fourth in an ascending quintet of uses is the effect of nature study on the student—the production of quickness, reverence, love for truth, bravery. These qualities develop because the naturalist "commands nature by obeying her."[12] The highest use is the extension of man's self-knowledge, by which Emerson means knowledge of man's "true place in the system of being." Though man is a spiritual creature, he must learn his spiritual laws in a material world, because that world is the only language (p. 24).

A second seminal work is William Howitt's *Book of the Seasons, or The Calendar of Nature*.[13] Thoreau reviewed this undistinguished work in his youth, and referred to it sporadically throughout his life.[14] Its format, observations and meditations arranged by months and accompanied by tables of migrating birds, blooming flowers, budding trees, and emerging insects, was the prototype for his own unrealized calendar. Howitt held that delight in nature is useless if not instructed; using Linnaeus as his authority, he urged his readers to make tables like his, watching for the dates of bloom and decay. For, he says, "we see trees open their buds and expand their leaves, from whence we conclude that spring approaches; and experience supports us in the conclusion; but nobody has, as yet, been able to show us what trees Providence has intended shall be our calendar, so that we might know on what day the countryman ought to sow his corn." The noting of when leaves fall will teach us "to guess at the approach of winter." Indeed, Howitt concludes, "the hints of Linnaeus constitute a universal rule for the whole world" (p. 101). Howitt is thinking of strictly practical uses for his tables, but his language is virtually identical to Thoreau's; one needs only to make a correspondence between material and spiritual corn.

A third scientific source (Howitt is not science, but he rests his case on Linnaeus) is Thoreau's natural history text, Smellie's *Philosophy of Natural History*.[15] This book explains in its chapter on instinct that some animal behavior proceeds from powers similar to man's—reasoning, judgment, volition—but "the prudence and anticipation of remote consequences so often exhibited by animals can only come from instinct" (p. 109). In **"The Natural History of Massachusetts,"** Thoreau sees the complete scientist as a man who has reacquired instincts. "The true man of science will know nature better by his finer organization; he will smell, taste, see, hear, feel better than other men. . . . The most scientific will still be the healthiest and friendliest man, and possess a more perfect Indian wisdom" (V, 131). What is this Indian wisdom? Thoreau's writings on the Indian show that Indian wisdom is instinct. "Often, when an Indian says, 'I don't know,' in regard to the route he is to take, he does not mean what a white man would by these words, for his Indian instinct may tell him still as much as the most confident white man knows" (III, 203).

The laws of the universe are a great rhythm, to which man at his most fulfilled moments marches. If a sense for this universal rhythm is implanted in the creature, he always moves with the music. Such a sense is instinct, possessed by animals and possibly by Indians. In most men, rhythm is not implanted, and there is substituted a capacity to learn the music. This substitution is man's curse and challenge; it is the sign that he has been expelled from the garden of Eden, but in true Miltonic fashion it is the sign that there is a peculiarly human, and therefore superior, way to regain it. The way back is through learning, which ultimately approaches instinct. When man has learned the music so thoroughly that he can anticipate it, when he knows what comes next, he will be able to keep time.

Thoreau devoted the rest of his life to learning nature well enough to "anticipate" her. In her cyclical organization he saw assurance that anticipation was possible, for in repetition lay the hope of learning, correcting, refining, and profiting from past error. Certain patterns obtruded immediately: the alternation of day and night, the succession of the seasons. These broad patterns could be quickly learned so that man might keep his life in some rough harmony, such that his ignorance did not destroy him. The next step was to sharpen perception and make out finer patterns and more precise regularities. Spring certainly follows winter, but when? This question subdivides—where, on what day, does the first crocus spring? When do the geese fly over Concord?

The sequence of Thoreau's work, from the breezy acceptance of challenge in **"The Natural History of Massachusetts"** to the bird lists of the late journals, can be seen as the attempt to find nature's laws in increasing detail. The so-called scientific entries of the late journals invariably organize themselves around the all-important question of time and are permeated by the repeated refrain, "How long?"

> Hear of bluets found on Saturday, the 17th; how long? . . . The benzoin yesterday and possibly the 19th, so much being killed. It might otherwise have been earlier yet. . . . I receive today *Sanguinaria Canadensia* from Brattleboro, well in bloom,—how long? . . . At Clamshell Ditch, one *Equisetum sylvaticum* will apparently open tomorrow. Strawberries are abundantly out there; how long? Some *Saleix trisit*, bank near baeomyces. Did I not put it too early in last year's list of willows? . . . Storrow Higginson plucked the uva-ursi fully out the 25th; perhaps two or three days, for it was nearly out, he says, the 18th!! . . . Componia well out, how long? *Viola occullata,* how long?[16]

These notes, extending over years, were the raw material for his calendar, which is thus different from Thoreau's other works only in the detailed nature of the material it assembles to anticipate nature. It contains that same assertion of human possibility and responsibility which illuminates **Walden.** Nature invites us and will not disappoint our expectations. Nature can be anticipated, and therefore man has his work to do.

But, reading the late journals and seeing what Thoreau finally did with the material he had collected for the calendar, one senses that Thoreau approached, if he did not accept, the realization that the task, as he had defined it, was impossible. Partly, he needed instruments and manuals to see what could be seen and know what he saw; partly, too, nature was simply not as regular as he had assumed. The arrangements of his calendars were continually being upset by a continuously baffling and erratic factor—the weather. Surveyor of the seasons, Thoreau occupied himself with rendering the boundary line in time between spring and winter with absolute precision, learning day by day the tiny signs that told time,[17] only to find that precision was impossible because the boundary line was unstable. "Though you walk every day, you do not foresee what kind of walking you will have the next day. Skating, crusted snow, slosh, etc., are wont to take you by surprise."[18] Cold winters, long winters, winter thaws, spring frosts, great snows, floods, draughts, heat spells—the calendar seemed at times less a chronicle of repetition than of aberrations.

There are two interpretations for this weather. One may concede that nature is irregular, repeating herself only roughly, more an average of probabilities than an exact system. Such an interpretation incorporates chance into the system, equivalent for Thoreau to taking God out of it, so closely did he, following Emerson, identify God with law. Thus this interpretation is impossible for him.

Second, one may insist that nature is perfectly regular but decide that one's measuring instruments—for the Transcendentalist necessarily the almost unaided senses sharpened by self-discipline and confined to the term of a single life—are not properly designed to record the precision. "It takes us many years to find out that Nature repeats herself annually. But how perfectly regular and calculable all her phenomena must appear to a mind that has observed her for a thousand years!"[19] But the pattern that can be discerned only with microscope and telescope is not a human pattern, and the mind that has observed for a thousand years is not a human mind. Now the whole point of anticipation was its use for man. If the laws of the universe exist in a way not knowable or perceptible by the individual, not only does the study of nature seem pointless but the whole man-centered cosmos comes into question. Thoreau believed that the world was God's text-book; its source was divine, its intention human. The universe in its vast regularity may still be divine, but it has lost its human purpose. God and the creation are taken away from man, opening the very gap anticipation was meant to close. God's intelligence and human intelligence are sharply distinguished, while the Transcendentalist based his faith on a human participation in the divine mind.

The problem of the irregular universe does not arise in **Walden** because the correspondence of the protagonist's life to the seasons is on the largest and most general levels only. The hero must anticipate the limit of winter, believe in the return of spring, know when to plant beans and when to sound the pond. From the vantage point of the late journals, *Walden* is but the roughest blocking out. By 1859, though, it would begin to seem that *Walden*'s roughness was the limit of accuracy. The hero of an 1859 *Walden* would have nothing to do with all the knowledge he had acquired in the intervening years.

In the essays prepared for publication immediately before his death, Thoreau seems to have been concerned to find another use for his storehouses. Accepting, at long last, the fact that God would not make him a partner, he contents himself with learning nature for pleasure. The end of such essays as **"Autumnal Tints"** and **"Wild Apples"** is simply the increased enjoyment of the rigorous observer. "But of much more importance than a knowledge of the names and distinctions of color is the joy and exhilaration which these colored leaves excite."[20] Fine discrimination and detailed knowledge is to be cultivated as an aid to appreciation; the transcendental position towards nature must be that of the informed amateur. This is a failure, to be sure, but the failure is not in Thoreau. It is in the program, which has been followed as far as it can reasonably be followed, and which issues in a kind of conservatism towards science far from the radical enthusiasm which motivated it.

As Thoreau was pursuing his way through this difficulty, science too had come to recognize that nature had a temporal as well as a spatial existence, and accepted a non-human scale for that existence. But the intelligibility or usefulness of the universe was not thereby negated, because for science the unit of knowability was not the single, unaided perceiver. Thus the internal logic of science pushed it on its path while Thoreau went a different way. Following, then, his program of anticipation with great fidelity, Thoreau found that he had set himself an impossible task. At the same time he was also becoming aware of another sort of disturbing fact. The ends he was seeking in nature were increasingly rejected as legitimate scientific ends. Science was changing, and its happy ministration to transcendental idealism was proving to have been a vision. What had seemed inevitable to Emerson in 1833 seemed ridiculous in 1853, as Thoreau defensively acknowledged in his journals. While in 1833, when Emerson had discovered science, scientists were still fretting about the Flood, they were in 1853 bracing themselves for Darwin. These developments created repercussions and difficulties not merely in the relations between science and other disciplines and philosophies, but within science itself. Historians of nineteenth-century science have shown to what great extent scientists were troubled, confused, and divided, and to what great extent general philosophical and religious attitudes colored scientific controversy on all professional levels.[21]

There are perhaps four separable conflicts, none of which oppose religious to nonreligious minds, as they derive rather from different notions of deity and of the legitimate rôle of science in explaining deity than from degrees of piety. All sides used religious arguments.

One argument centered on the question of how God made and sustained the universe. Did he intervene in its functioning? Lyell's *Principles of Geology* was dismaying, to be sure, because it contradicted the Bible, but more disturbing was the fact that it made God's constant supervision of the earth unnecessary. Lyell was doing for the earth what Newton had done for the cosmos—suggesting that God worked by immutable and uniform laws which ran the universe without him, for which he had been directly necessary only once, and which he himself could no longer abrogate. What Lyell suggested for the planet, Darwin was soon to posit for the life on it.

The notion that earth and its life were created and altered by specific, disconnected fiats, and sustained by constant overseeing, died very hard. But the opponents of the notion appealed to religious sentiment as vigorously as its adherents. In his *Vestiges of Creation,* Robert Chambers insisted "when all is seen to be the result of law, the idea of an Almighty Author becomes irresistible, for the creation of a law for an endless series of phenomena—an act of intelligence above all else that we can conceive—could have no other imaginable source."[22] Just this notion of the whole world working by uniform law had excited Emerson, for to him the fact that anything worked at all was miracle enough. Thoreau agreed. "Though I do not believe that a plant will spring up where no seed has been, I have great faith in a seed,—a, to me, equally mysterious origin for it."[23]

In this argument Emerson and Thoreau agreed with the more radical scientists of their own time, opposed, for example, to Agassiz, who wrote in his zoology text, "There is nothing like parental descent connecting [the different species]. . . . The link by which they are connected is of a higher and immaterial nature, and their connection is to be sought in the view of the Creator himself."[24] But in another argument Emerson and Agassiz were firmly aligned. This was the question of whether discussions of first causes are appropriate at all in science. Emerson certainly agreed with the train of thought which led Agassiz up from nature to God. Discussion of secondary causes without reference to the first cause was impious or meaningless. But others felt that to presume to speak with authority for God's intentions was more impious and meaningless still. "The geologist sadly mistakes both the object of his science and the limits of his understanding, who thinks it his business to explain the means employed by INFINITE WISDOM for establishing the laws which now govern the world."[25] Most of those who believed in uniform law also believed that first causes should be kept out of science; the Transcendentalists were in the less usual position of insisting both on uniform law and on constant reference to first cause.

A second pair of questions revolved around the nature of man. What is his place on earth? One view enjoined man to be humble; the other encouraged his pride. "In view of all these facts," Emerson proclaimed, "I conclude that other creatures reside in particular places . . . but the residence of man is the world. It was given to him to possess it."[26] We have already seen that Emerson accepted science largely because it answered his vast conceptions of man and God. To him it implied a rebellion against conservative pessimism. "But I think the paramount source of the religious revolution was Modern Science. . . . Astronomy taught us our insignificance in Nature; showed that our sacred as our profane history had been written in gross ignorance of the laws, which were far grander than we knew; and compelled a certain extension and uplifting of our views of the Deity and his Providence. This correction of our superstitions was confirmed by the new science of Geology, and the whole train of discoveries in every department."[27]

But that conservative pessimism decried by Emerson had been and continued to be supported by science also. Paley, who conventionalized the application of science to religious argument, used science to show the insufficiency of life on earth and imply the need for Revelation. Pope's *Essay on Man* brought scientific knowledge to the support of a view of man as a poor, circumscribed creature whose life was "good" only in terms of a vast divine plan beyond his powers to comprehend. This view is echoed into the nineteenth century in such standard works as Smellie's *Natural History*: "Let man therefore be contented with the powers and the sphere of action assigned him. There is an exact adaptation of his powers, capacities, and desires, both bodily and intellectual, to the scene in which he is destined to move. . . . Let him fill up his rank here with dignity, and consider every partial evil as a cause, or an effect, of general ultimate good" (p. 311).

The second question about man's nature came to be epitomized, for Thoreau, in the question of the relation of the scientist to the material he was discovering and the laws he was deriving. The question at issue is in a sense the question of the set of concepts used to understand nature. Pre-Newtonian science used for its concepts the Aristotelian qualities, which described attributes perceptible to the senses, qualities which were as much responses in the perceiver as inherent characteristics of the object. Thus the perceiver is central in this set of measuring terms; he is the instrument specifically designed to register the nature of objects. It is easy enough then to hold that the purpose of the perceived object is exactly the perception of it by man, and the question of whether man or nature is then studied has no meaning.

Newton, besides creating a universe that required God only once, explained it by a set of concepts which shut men's normal perceptions away from an operational understanding of the world, and made their observations seem irrelevant to the cosmic organization.[28] The distinction between mind and matter, "the strongest distinction of which we have an idea,"[29] and the preoccupation of many post-Newtonian philosophers with epistemology, can be understood at least partly as developments from these explanations which made man's view of the world seem literally "superficial." Now Emerson had attempted to solve the problem of epistemology by a kind of platonic intuitive idealism. He had also attempted to negate the dualism by insisting that what man knows through his senses is *also* real. The world is both as men intuit it to be and as it appears to them. In short, Emerson had bridged the Cartesian dualism by returning to a pre-Newtonian vocabulary, thus insisting that nature is designed for human perception and action, and that its only meaningful description is in terms of human perception of it and responses to it. At the heart of Emerson's system of understanding nature is the perceiver.[30]

This perceiver turned active is the heroic scientist in Thoreau's system, and it was for the scientist himself, as Thoreau understood it, that the whole set of observations had, ultimately, meaning. "Will you be a reader, a student merely, or a seer?"[31] Unwilling even to use spy glasses, he held that "the naked eye may easily see farther than the armed."[32] He held these views because to him the scientist was not engaged in a professional activity, but a symbolic one in which he stood for all men. But science was coming more and more to eliminate the personality and the capacities of the investigator from the investigation, to objectify observation, refine it with instruments, and ultimately to make it as little as possible dependent on the perceiving sense of the scientist. The self-centeredness of Thoreau's investigation, the question of what the scientist personally underwent in the course of his investigations—in short, the whole philosophical point of Thoreau's quest—was deliberately excised. "I think that the man of science makes this mistake, and the mass of mankind along with him: that you should coolly give your chief attention to the phenomenon which excites you as something independent of you, and not as it is related to you."[33] But mistaken science flourished while "anticipation" floundered.

For Thoreau the meaning of every fact was the purpose it served in human education, a purpose not subjective in the sense of idiosyncratic, but decreed by God and accessible to all men in nature—subjective, however, in requiring a personal participation to be known. A man cannot know the significance of a fact if he does not allow his response to the fact to enter into his observations. In Thoreau's study, the searcher stood for all searchers, and in this sense was impersonal; but he was also necessarily subjective because the meaning of the fact became known subjectively. The meaning of every fact in the world is thus "human." The fact means what it is felt to mean by human intelligence when it is seen by human perception. The aim of science, as Thoreau saw it developing, was to study sound divorced from the ear which heard it. But to him the sound was only meaningful to the hearing ear, which must therefore be included in a description of the sound.

> What is the relationship between a bird and the ear that appreciates its melody, to whom, perchance, it is more charming and significant than to any else? Certainly they are intimately related, and one was made for the other. It is a natural fact. If I were to discover that a certain kind of stone by the pond-shore was affected, say partially disintegrated, by a particular natural sound, as a bird or insect, I see that one could not be completely described without describing the other. I am that rock by the pond-side.[34]

That there are on the one hand sounds and on the other ears capable of hearing them is Thoreau's proof that the entire world has been constructed with man at its center.

By 1853, a decade after he had so willingly undertaken his Emersonian burden, Thoreau had become aware of the split between himself and science, and it bothered him so much that when he received a questionnaire from the American Association for the Advancement of Science he reacted with a quite uncharacteristic peevishness.

> I felt that it would be to make myself the laughing stock of the scientific community to describe or attempt to describe to them that branch of science which specially interests me, inasmuch as they do not believe in a science which deals with the higher law. So I was obliged to speak to their condition and describe to them that poor part of me which alone they can understand. The fact is I am a mystic, a transcendentalist, and a natural philosopher to boot. . . . How absurd that, though I probably stand as near to nature as any of them, and am by constitution as good an observer as most, yet a true account of my relation to nature should excite their ridicule only.[35]

The uneasiness betrayed in this passage increased with years. Thoreau's own belief in the intentional shape of the universe, though too firm to be shaken, received shocks within his own symbolic world: the "vast, and dread and inhuman" chaos on Mt. Ktaadn, where "was clearly felt the presence of a force not bound to be kind to man,"[36] for example, and the savage ocean so painfully dealt with in *Cape Cod.* But he clung to his faith all the more fiercely for the difficulties it gave him, and it was alarming to see science so serenely discarding man's centrality.

He could only insist that science was missing the point, and he did, but here he ran into the trouble that although he could call science "wrong" he could not call it "false." Scientific facts could not be dismissed like "facts" in the newspapers or the post office, because they were the facts with which he himself worked. To dismiss science as man-made, a shallow manipulation of artificial nomenclature, became a common attack in the late journals. "Whatever aid is to be derived from the use of a scientific term, we can never begin to see anything as it is so long as we remember the scientific term which always our ignorance has imposed on it."[37] But his dilemma is well shown by the fact that these passages occur in the midst of observations in which he himself was using the scientific terminology he deplored. Elsewhere he admitted this dependence that he always covertly acknowledged. "With the knowledge of the name comes a distincter recognition and knowledge of the thing. . . . My knowledge was cramped and confined before, and grew rusty because not used,—for it could not be used. My knowledge now becomes communicable and grows by communication."[38] That he ever wrote **"The Succession of Forest Trees,"** a late (1860) and deliberately scientific essay, betrays the same ambivalence.

In general, by the end of his life, Thoreau no longer saw scientists as pioneers, but as members of the reactionary fraternity along with, for example, missionaries. In the *Maine Woods* he was delighted at the inexplicable (as he hoped) mystery of the will o' the wisp, clinging to it as something which, by defying scientific explanation, proved the religious character of the universe (III, 200-201). This is a complete reversal of the position taken in **"The Natural History of Massachusetts."** In his late journals he frequently compared the early naturalists, quaint, credulous, unable to tell fact from fable, but with a sense of wonder and miracle fully playing over the world—he compared these legendary figures with the modern scientist, to the latter's disadvantage. "So far as natural history is concerned, you often have your choice between uninteresting truth and interesting falsehood."[39] This he said in 1860; in 1842 he had said that to know is to know what is good.

The growth of the number of strictures against science in the late journals records his realization that science was not what he had taken it to be, and is a separate development from the private collapse of his "anticipation" enterprise. There is no evidence that he brought these two developments together in his own mind, and yet together they pointed to the same thing—the irrelevance of man in the universe. It was inconceivable that Thoreau could ever come to accept, even remotely, the position against which his whole life had been aimed. Hence, he turned on the men who were apparently able to accept it, for if it was horrible to imagine a world in which men were irrelevant, it was perhaps almost as horrible to watch the spread of a type of men who thought they were irrelevant; for we always lead, do we not, the life we imagine we are leading? Yet Thoreau could hardly, with his deep devotion to truth, have urged his world-view on others as a comforting or sustaining illusion. And so he turned against his early pioneers, dissociated himself from their efforts even as he acknowledged that what they are saying is true, and went back to his old naturalists, to whom "gorgons and flying dragons were not incredible."[40]

Notes

1. See, e.g., Raymond Adams, "Thoreau's Science," *Scientific Monthly,* LX (1945), 379-382; Charles Metzger, "Thoreau on Science," *Annals of Science,* XII (1956), 206-211; Leo Stoller, *After Walden* (Stanford, 1957); Kathryn Whitford, "Thoreau and the Woodlots of Concord," *New England Quarterly,* XXIII (1950), 291-306; Kathryn Whitford and Peter Whitford, "Thoreau; Pioneer Ecologist and Conservationist," *Scientific Monthly,* LXXIII (1951), 291-296.

2. See, e.g., Brooks Atkinson, *Henry Thoreau, the Cosmic Yankee* (New York, 1927); Henry Seidel Canby, *Thoreau* (Boston, 1939); Joseph Wood Krutch, *Thoreau* (New York, 1948); Mark Van Doren, *Thoreau, a Critical Study* (Boston, 1916).

3. The best example is Sherman Paul, *The Shores of America* (Urbana, 1958).

4. Ralph Waldo Emerson, *Letters,* edited by Ralph L. Rusk (New York, 1939), III, 47.

5. See Sampson Reed, *Observations on the Growth of the Mind* (Boston, 1826), 42-59; also his "Oration on Genius" in Perry Miller, ed., *The Transcendentalists* (Cambridge, Mass., 1950), 51-53.

6. Ralph Waldo Emerson, *Journals,* ed. E. W. Emerson and W. E. Forbes, (Boston, 1909-1914), III, 161-164. Also H. H. Clark, "Emerson and Science," *Philological Quarterly,* X (1931), 225-260.

7. "The Uses of Natural History," in *The Early Lectures of Ralph Waldo Emerson,* ed. Stephen Whicher and George Spiller (Cambridge, Mass., 1959), 24.

8. "On the Relation of Man to the Globe," *Early Lectures* [*The Early Lectures of Ralph Waldo Emerson*], *op. cit.,* 49.

9. "The Naturalist," *Early Lectures,* 29.

10. *Journals,* III, 164.

11. *The Writings of Henry David Thoreau* (Boston, 1906), V, 105, 107. All references to Thoreau unless otherwise identified are to this edition, the *Walden,* which includes the *Journals.*

12. *Early Lectures,* 25, 20.

13. London and Philadelphia, 1831.

14. See Wendell Glick, "Three New Early Mss. by Thoreau," *Huntington Library Quarterly,* XV (1951), 59-71.

15. Revised by John Ware (Boston, 1824).

16. *Journals,* X, 379-395 passim. The volume number of the journals is given, not the number of the volume in the *Writings* [*The Writings of Henry David Thoreau*].

17. For an example, see *Journals,* XIII, 218-229, where March has a daily time table.

18. *Journals,* XIII, 108.

19. *Journals,* XIII, 279.

20. "Autumnal Tints," V, 274.

21. See, e.g., Charles Gillispie, *Genesis and Geology* (Cambridge, Mass., 1951); Bentley Glass, ed., *Forerunners of Darwin* (Baltimore, 1959).

22. (London, 1844²), 158.

23. "The Succession of Forest Trees," V, 203.

24. L. Agassiz and A. A. Gould, *Principles of Zoology* (Boston, 1848), 417-418.

25. John Playfair, *Illustrations of the Huttonian Theory of the Earth* (Edinburgh, 1802), 132. Emerson read this for his early lectures. (*Letters,* I, 403.)

26. "On the Relation of Man to the Globe," *Early Lectures,* 49.

27. "Historic Notes of Life and Letters in New England," *The Transcendentalists,* 499.

28. See E. A. Burtt, *The Metaphysical Foundations of Modern Science* (New York, 1925; Anchor, 1954), 26-27, 89-90, 236-239.

29. Emerson, "The Uses of Natural History," *Early Lectures,* 24.

30. Sherman Paul, *Emerson's Angle of Vision* (Cambridge, Mass.), 1952.

31. *Walden,* II, 122.

32. *Journals,* IV, 471.

33. *Journals,* X, 164-165.

34. *Journals,* IX, 274-275.

35. *Journals,* V., 4-5.

36. *Maine Woods,* III, 77-78.

37. *Journals,* XIII, 141.

38. *Journals.* XI. 137.

39. *Journals.* XIII. 181.

40. *Journals.* XIII. 180.

Jonathan Bishop (essay date March 1966)

SOURCE: Bishop, Jonathan. "The Experience of the Sacred in Thoreau's *Week*." *ELH* 33, no. 1 (March 1966): 66-91.

[*In the following essay, Bishop analyzes the relationship between Thoreau's artistic subjectivity and qualities of the sacred in* A Week on the Concord and Merrimack Rivers. *In Bishop's opinion, Thoreau's ambivalence toward the spiritual dimension of the self derives from his profound distrust of traditional notions of God and religion.*]

Discussions of Thoreau often begin with a review of the various identities his life and work offer a reader: naturalist, social philosopher, artist. The history of Thoreau criticism includes the rise and fall of Thoreau the naturalist; more recently, the critic of society has enjoyed a briefer vogue. But the Thoreau who seems to have become most prominent within the present critical generation is a figure quite different from either. This is Thoreau the hero of the self, or athlete of subjectivity, and therefore—the connection seems intrinsic—Thoreau the artist.

Such a double definition is argued, for instance, in Sherman Paul's massive *The Shores of America,* the book which has deservedly made the strongest of recent impressions. For Paul it is pre-eminently the subjective idealist in Thoreau whose pains and joys count. The emergence, toils, triumphs, and decline of this egotistical sublime constitute the major plot of a life moving from the glad narcissism of youth to the stoic egotism of middle age. The works that life produced appear accordingly as more or less complex "conceits" of this development. And Thoreau's experience of nature is correspondingly seen as fuel for the fires of self-transcendence. "Thoreau's relation to nature . . . was . . . self-reflexive; he never studied nature apart from the self."[1]

This conclusion can stand as typical of a climate of opinion which Paul's book helps us bring into focus. The other most influential of recent voices would presumably be Perry Miller's; and the introduction to the latter's edition of the lost journal is a curiously exasper-ated and self-involved attack on the depth of Thoreau's self-involvement. Miller depicts a perilously diseased Thoreau, as giddily absorbed in the intricacies of his own consciousness as any Stephen Dedalus.[2] And Alfred Kazin, reviewing Miller's work as man of letters at large, adds his representative note of agreement: Thoreau "really had no subject but himself."[3] Such judgments, elaborate or occasional, triangulate a preference no one writer can be said to have originated, though learning and sensitivity will now sanction it among students eager to respect their author in an approved idiom.[4]

To be sure this subjectivistic Thoreau is not entirely new-fashioned. Thoreau has always attracted readers with a bias toward aggressive individualism, political and philosophical, who not unnaturally end by exaggerating the value for Thoreau himself or for his work of the self they find. This has proved true for those who dislike him as well: the obverse of a sympathetic elaboration of the convolutions of consciousness would be the brisk judgment, "he is an impossible egotist."[5] After such a repudiation, it is even more necessary to fall back on the triumphs of the art.

For the currency of the subjectivistic Thoreau has oddly coincided with the growth in modern respect for Thoreau the artist. From Mattheissen's discovery of an organic structure in ***Walden*** to the latest explication of rebirth rituals, the implicit argument has snowballed: Thoreau escapes from solipsism as a man of letters, a creator of complex metaphor and multiple irony. Such logic may reflect our concerns better than it describes Thoreau. It is a peculiarly modern tendency to divide the world into a lonely self on the one hand and on the other a barren chaos within which only works of art have value. We can positively enjoy seeing the artist as a damned and privileged soul exploiting otherwise worthless experience for material out of which to build images.

The historical evidence will not support the literary side of this contemporary tendency—the Transcendentalists were not New Critics—but it can apparently substantiate the charge of solipsism. Is it not a truism to say of Transcendentalism that it "made the self the center of existence and all beyond it its horizon? The self was called into the world to realize itself."[6] This is Sherman Paul again, making what must seem a fair rendering of the lesson Thoreau learned from Emerson. The rhetoric of that age, abstracted from the experience which once underlay it, does indeed seem to define self-culture in terms of liberation from society and tradition to enjoy the heights of possibility in communion with an accomplice nature. The Thoreau who responded to and repeats such impulses and affirmations would be coincident with at least the surface intention of much which we know influenced him.

At the same time there is, even in Emerson, much to suggest that this kind of self-expansiveness could be a disease as well as a triumph. The self was the Soul—but it was also the consecrations of the failed ego, and to affirm one's ordinary identity obtusely was to betray one's potential life. In any case there remains an obvious element within the standard Transcendentalist creed which can relieve us from any need to eddy long among the ambiguities of the Emersonian self. Freedom and autonomy was one half of the message—the other half, more crucial to the experiencers themselves, was Nature. Even in Emerson's most vatic and (to hostile eyes) solipsistic moments, Nature is never left out of the equation.

If Emerson requires some explanation on this point, Thoreau should not. Words aside, his way of life is inexplicable except on the supposition that Nature was not merely real for him, but more real than the self his present readers are alternately attracted to and repelled by. Why else would he have spent a lifetime of afternoons looking for whatever it was he was looking for? If he were merely the literary consciousness we are to identify, he might have gone up garret immediately and never come downstairs, much less outdoors. Nature must be counted in; and the minute we do this, the figure he presents profoundly alters; he becomes a man seeking to understand and to formulate, to be sure, but first of all to encounter, a reality above him on the scale of being and antecedent to all words about it.

To recollect, though, that Nature must have been a genuine object for Thoreau, and that the Self and its language are better considered starting point and result respectively than final cause of his characteristic activity, will not orient us completely. The term "nature" is too ambiguous. Thoreau's devotion to the particulars of Concord ecology—nature in lower case—is so plentifully exemplified in the words we admire that the sympathetic fellow-naturalist easily concludes the goal of his desire to be simply a more living knowledge of the actual world. On this level Thoreau would represent the "effort of the human spirit to make itself at home in our universe."[7] His art would then become a way of rendering that which is distinctly there to the senses back to the imagination. Such a Thoreau can be reasonably linked with Jeffries and Burroughs, as has been done.

There has been something autumnal, not to say cozy, about much of the criticism which has appreciated Thoreau and Thoreau's nature after this empiricist fashion, and subjectivistic and aesthetic criticism has patronized the results. Yet even the most relaxed commentator of the naturalist school has somewhere registered an awareness that nature, for Thoreau if not for his critic, is also Nature: that the particulars are interesting not only for the sake of the pleasures they offer the senses and the mind, but because they mediate a reality still more objective than the objects which present it. What brought Thoreau out, says Norman Foerster, already repeating a conclusion that goes back in one form or another to Channing and Emerson, was the "mystic's hope of detecting" reality; Thoreau's excursions were a repeated "quest."[8] And this formulation recurs more recently in Ethel Seybold's insufficiently influential book on Thoreau's debt to the classics. "The truth, the quite incredible truth about Thoreau, the truth that we resist in spite of his own repeated witness, is that he spent a quarter of a century in a quest for transcendental reality, in an attempt to discover the secret of the universe."[9]

If Thoreau is an objectivist, then, as well as a subjectivist, and if the object in which he believed was a Nature that included more than the "natural" alone, we should find ourselves more comfortable in our character as literary historians, if not as close critics or existentialists. For it is a matter of the most conventional literary history that the Romantics did believe in the existence of Nature, and were prepared to affirm that the encounter with Nature could become, for certain souls at certain moments, an encounter with God. We are familiar with this "Natural Supernaturalism," in Carlyle's phrase, and would even be able to put the notion into place in a rough history of the relevant ideas.[10] Our apprehension of the cultural evolution of the idea, though, too rarely descends into our response to individual cases. Yet a Natural Supernaturalist would by definition be someone whose experience of the sacred was mediated by the most local kind of natural particulars; and whose testimony to the possibility of such experience was in turn mediated to us through equally concrete details of language. The "other" world would reveal itself not as such, or in so many words, but through some idiosyncratic perception of *this* world. The elements that functioned as instances of "nature" and those which functioned as "super-nature" could differ considerably from writer to writer. For it is of the essence of the Romantic predicament that there can be no general rules distinguishing the two realms in advance of the experience which incorporates them. Each case of Natural Supernaturalism would therefore be unique, and its vocabulary local, not to say eccentric.[11]

Next to Blake and Wordsworth, Thoreau is probably the most interesting such case we have; certainly the most important American example. The obvious place to go for demonstrative evidence of how he could find the supernatural in the natural would be *Walden,* or more justly, all the writings together. And there is a book to be written on Thoreau's total experience of the sacred. But I should like to concentrate here on *A Week on the Concord and Merrimack Rivers.* Criticism has too often condescended to this book. The opinion is only now beginning to go out that it is merely a young man's compendium of essays and poems strung on the thread of a voyage narrative not itself of the first interest. Yet though simple in comparison with *Walden,* or even the *Journal,* the *Week* [*A Week on the Concord and Merrimack Rivers*] is not without independent subtleties which may be taken with some seriousness. It has the advantage of presenting in simple outline a sequence of confrontations between the self and the natural universe, many of which are sufficiently developed to interest a reader looking for a common structure. Here then one might expect to find at least the early Thoreauvian doctrine respecting the possibilities of natural experience. The *Week* is a convenient arena in which to test the suspicion that Thoreau is more than a solipsist, and his art more than imaginative play.

When one sets oneself to become attentive to the kinds of experience of Nature which are given in this book, marking off separate encounters, and staying open to such parallels of situation and language as offer themselves, a common structure and a common direction do seem to emerge. The encounters vary much in detail and degree of expansion, but they are alike. What they share can be read as Thoreau's special version of the Romantic quest. When Thoreau faces Nature, he does indeed seem to find within it special relationships which for him appear to represent the "natural" and the "supernatural."

The most inclusive of these structural relationships has attracted some critical notice. John C. Broderick has pointed out that the typical physical and spiritual action in a Thoreauvian excursion or paragraph is a movement "from the mundane known to the transcendent knowable and back again," a rhythm of adventure and return.[12] The movement may be imagined, another writer argued, as a practical version of the Emersonian "circle."[13] This circular motion would then be a general frame for all lesser contrasts between the profane and the sacred. We need, though, to appreciate the detail of these, since they constitute what is idiosyncratic in Thoreau's approach to reality, and determine the specifics of his experience and language. It will be convenient to summarize the principal polarities before we look at passages.

The first manifestation of the way in which Thoreau distinguishes the "mundane" from the "transcendent" is literally spatial. For him the *near* is associated with the profane; the *remote* with the sacred. Within any specific experience of the natural scene entities at a distance from the eye—whatever they may be—are for the Thoreauvian protagonist always symbols of divinity; while objects physically close correspondingly represent that aspect of nature which addresses the secular intelligence alone. This contrast of far and near is sufficiently prevalent and determinative to establish the "style" of a Thoreauvian confrontation; someone who wished to parody him, for instance, would have to imitate it.

There are other polarities with essentially the same meaning. The temporal complement of the spatial difference between the near and the remote is a contrast between the *present* and the *past.* What Thoreau sees in the present is always banal; what he can recall from the past always sacred. The past of the individual is recovered from his memory; the past of the race from old books or tradition. Thoreau is fascinated by both modes of recovery, which for him work together: the life of each individual recapitulates that of the race, and vice versa. Thoreau shares the Emersonian prejudice against the *near* past, which includes everything which inhibits the original relation to the universe; but unlike Emerson, does not confound this with the *remote* past, from which we derive, he thought, the most valuable hints respecting the reality with which we seek to have that original relation.

Besides space and time, other contexts involving significant polarities are the day and the season. *Noon* is secular; *dawn* (and to some degree sunset) is sacred; though occasionally the ratios are reversed, and midday is paradoxically associated with the divine. *Surface* is profane, *depth* sacred. Ordinary noises, including human speech, are secular; silence is sacred, and so is music, or any sound which can be heard as music, especially if heard from a distance. The same meaning holds for the generic differences between prose and poetry, science and mythology, history and fable; and therefore the difference between the literal and the imaginative generally. Throughout such large polarities as the *cultivated* and the *wild,* the *social* and the *solitary, labor* and *leisure,* have the same import, pervading experiences where they need not be mobilized explicitly, since the intention of the book presupposes them.

Several of these polarities have separately received attention in articles or books. As autonomous images, though for the most part only as such, they are all familiar. One general reminder is perhaps worth making before proceeding to specifics: not every description of an encounter with Nature in the *Week* involves all the possible polarities. The striking instances, though, invariably incorporate more than two or three, and once one is alerted to the full range of possibilities, to the grammar as it were of the Thoreauvian imagination, it is easy to detect vestigial references to contrasts not overtly in use, and so make sense of brief turns of phrase that would otherwise appear accidental.

We are now finally free to examine cases. And for the first let me choose, not a category like near and far, but an episode. All readers of the *Week* will remember the interpolated tale of the excursion to the top of Mt. Greylock. The independence of this story in its context and the unusual elaboration of detail alike qualify this encounter for special attention.

To climb a mountain is of itself a most concrete and traditional way in which to dramatize the journey from the profane to the sacred. The literal action is already ritualistic, whether or not the person who performs it is conscious of the fact. Thoreau may therefore take for granted that his reader will understand his general intention. His opening paragraphs stay close to the profane details of the climb and the circumstances of the night in the open spent at the top of the mountain. Some of these details are interesting in themselves, but the structure of the anecdote invites the reader to pass on directly to the climax.

This occurs when he wakes in the morning to find the whole earth covered with mist. He climbs on the roof of an observatory above the surface of the fog and gazes out upon

> the new world into which I had risen in the night, the new *terra firma* perchance of my future life. There was not a crevice left through which the trivial places we name Massachusetts or Vermont or New York could be seen. . . . All around beneath me was spread for a hundred miles on every side, as far as the eye could reach, an undulating country of clouds, answering in the varying swell of its surface to the terrestrial world it veiled. It was such a country as we might see in dreams, with all the delights of paradise.[14]

The long climb and the night in the open have been an *ascesis* preparing him for the vision of the sacred to which he wakes. To call this new "country" a "paradise" is not merely rhetorical, though the reader is as usual left free to suppose that Thoreau is only using metaphors. Literally the view is of a portion of *this* world, for a mist is as much a natural fact as the land it conceals. But in the context of the experience a portion of nature is as it were set apart to represent that which is beyond nature; the clouds exemplify the invisible. Thoreau *sees* what in ordinary life one "dreams" of; dreaming and waking experience constituting another polarity frequent in the book.

It is typical of the Thoreauvian encounter that "Massachusetts, Vermont, and New York" should disappear, for the giving of distinct names to separate objects is a function of experience within the profane world. It is also worth noticing that the clouds "answer" proportionately to the contours of the landscape below. The sacred, though separate from the profane, is related to it by analogy. What is here a relationship in space is elsewhere repeated in intellectual terms in the form of the familiar "correspondence" between fact and truth, vehicle and tenor, literal and imaginative so characteristic of Transcendental epistemology.

So far the idiom of the experience is chiefly spatial, but other elements of the Thoreauvian matrix are present. The confrontation takes place at dawn, the most sacred

time of day. The experience as a whole is remembered; which engages the contrast of present and past. And finally, the climactic paragraph brings the adventurer to the verge of an encounter not merely with the sacred realm but with the God who we might expect to inhabit it. Consider the language with which he proceeds; Thoreau finds himself, he says, "in the dazzling halls of Aurora" (199) to which his eyes had so often been raised from the earth below, "in the very path of the Sun's chariot," which presently rose, so that "I saw the gracious god. . . ." Such impersonating language makes the rising sun an obvious analogue for God; though the idiom is so poetical that at first one hardly takes the implication seriously. Or is that idiom itself a disguise? Before one can decide, the experience as a whole lapses away—"owing, as I think, to some unworthiness in myself." The mist rises up above the level of his perch, and "I sank down again into that 'forlorn world,' from which the celestial sun had hid his visage." When Thoreau descends the mountain once more he finds on questioning the people he meets that it had been a "cloudy and drizzling day wholly" (200). He has returned once more to the profane world.

One can use this Greylock experience as a full type against which to match less fully developed experiences employing the same grammar. A comparatively pure though minor example of the latter would be the description, late in the book, of the pleasure he used to take watching ships sail out from New York harbor while staying on Staten Island. In the evening he would count the sails still in sight:

> But as the setting sun continually brought more and more to light, still farther in the horizon, the last count always had the advantage, till, by the time the last rays streamed over the sea, I had doubled and trebled my first number; though I could no longer class them all under the several heads of ships, barks, brigs, schooners, and sloops, but most were faint generic *vessels* only. And then the temperate twilight, perchance, revealed the floating home of some sailor whose thoughts were already alienated from this American coast, and directed towards the Europe of our dreams.
>
> (254)

Here that "other world" which on Greylock Thoreau saw as a landscape of mist has become "the Europe of our dreams." In such a manifestation, it cannot literally be seen, though it may be longed for by an imagined protagonist, the anonymous "sailor" whose thoughts are already "alienated" from the banalities of the nearby "American coast." Thoreau himself is still on the coast, and the time is sunset rather than dawn. Nor is this "Europe" inhabited by any figure that could correspond to the role of the sun in the Greylock memory. The idler on the shore had not undergone such a purgative discipline as would fit him for a fuller vision. But even so, what he does see is not wholly of this world. There is a kind of anticipation of the invisible "Europe" in the gradual illumination by the setting sun of more and more distant ships, which increasingly lose their profane distinctness as "ships, barks, brigs, schooner, and sloops." The evaporation of names and numbers is parallel to the disappearance of Massachusetts, Vermont, and New York; ineffability is one sign of the sacred.

In the Greylock experience Thoreau actually travels to the remote place; on Staten Island he dreams of it, and the point of observation remains well within the boundaries of the profane. This second situation is the more typical; the characteristic Thoreauvian excursion leads the eye or the body in the direction of sacred without quite arriving there. Very occasionally the other world will reveal itself suddenly without the labor of a literal voyage, even of the eye: Thoreau is fascinated by reflections in quiet water, for instance, because they image a reality otherwise too distant for approach. "Wherever the trees and skies are reflected, there is more than Atlantic depth, and no danger of fancy running aground" (47). With a "separate intention of the eye" is it possible to see the sacred "trees and sky"—sacred *because* reflected—in place of the profane "river bottom."

And it is not only by the reflections it occasionally offers that the river gives Thoreau glimpses of another world. A voyage on it, like a walk or a mountain climb, is ritually expressive of the belief that value lies at a distance. There are always vistas ahead and astern; the very position of a rower might well make him appreciate the ambiguous satisfactions of actually penetrating into the region of mystery; the hidden and remote, as the boat moves, turning of itself into the obvious and near, and that in turn becoming remote again. A voyager is perpetually "eager to double some distant cape, to make some great bend as in the life of man, and see what new perspective would open," thus "looking far into a new country, broad and serene. . . ." (245) And a river allows, as a path, even self-made, does not, for an indispensable passivity of the will: "we seemed to be embarked on the placid current of our dreams, floating from past to future as silently as one awakes to fresh morning or evening thoughts" (17).

A river is a natural symbol of travel in time as well as space; its waters, like memory, bringing the past into the present. The first extended description of the voyage develops this latent combination of spatial and temporal import. Thoreau describes in close knowledgable details the late summer flowers the boat passes on the river banks. The point of view is literal and quasi-scientific, to correspond with the closeness of the boat to the objects observed. The description comes to a climax, though, with the mention of a flower which is not present, which must be remembered; and that flower is important less for its visible attributes than as the final goal of a recollected excursion:

> We missed the white water-lily, which is the queen of river flowers, its reign being over for this season. He makes his voyage too late, perhaps, by a true water clock who delays so long. Many of this species inhabit our Concord water. I have passed down the river before sunrise on a summer morning, between fields of lilies still shut in sleep; and when, at length, the flakes of sunlight from over the bank fell on the surface of the water, whole fields of white blossoms seemed to flash open before me, as I floated along. . . .
>
> (19)

The immediate qualities of this recollected experience are all characteristic of the sacred: dawn, the rarity of the sight, the preparatory removal from the social world. The power of these signals is reinforced by the contrast already established between the lily and the other flowers, the past and the present, the remembered and the observed, the mysterious and the well-known.

It is clear that such contrastings of sacred and profane do not depend upon the particular features of nature subsumed; water lilies are not in themselves more sacred to Thoreau than polygonum or arrowhead. It is possible to imagine other circumstances which would establish these flowers too as instances of the extraordinary, though here they represent the ordinary. Indeed, something like such a shift occurs in the paragraph just following this description, which notes how the brothers saw on the bank the hibiscus in bloom. They desired to tell one of their friends back in the village, that he might pick this "somewhat rare and inaccessible flower" in time. They speak to a farmer in a nearby field, so that he may convey the news at church the next day, and thus ensure that "while we should be floating on the Merrimack, our friend would be reaching to pluck this blossom on the bank of the Concord" (19). The interposition of distance in space and time, together with the creation of a protagonist not the speaker, gives a sacral character in advance to a flower which, though "rare," remains on the whole a profane fact for the brothers at the time.

The discussion on the fish of the Concord that immediately follows is structured in the same fashion as the description of the flowers. Some pages are devoted to a thorough survey of the different species as Thoreau the naturalist knows them. Each kind of fish is beautiful; each may be known in detail close to, and named.

Yet there are limits to such knowledge. What the naturalist can learn of fish by abstracting them from their proper environment is profane. Their true life is hidden beneath the surface of the water; from the dark depths of which they occasionally emerge, thereby becoming authentic representatives of Nature. Because fish are symbols of what we cannot know about them, the pursuit of them by the fisherman is a "solemn sacrament" whether he knows it or not. "The cork goes dancing down the swift-rushing stream, amid the weeds and sands, when suddenly, by a coincidence never to be remembered, emerges this fabulous inhabitant of another element, a thing heard of but not seen, as if it were the instant creation of an eddy, a true product of the running stream" (28). The tone here is almost teasing, but the metaphor makes the fish virtually personal, almost the God of the depths. Subhumanity is, half seriously, an emblem of superhumanity. "Fabulous" is a key word for such beings, however perfunctory its connotations in this context; the relation between fable and history is elsewhere a serious vehicle for the essential contrast of sacred and profane.

In fact the fish rises from the depth of the water as the sun rose above the clouds on Greylock; as the shad, in the climatic meditation of the sequence on fish, do *not* rise past the new dams to their old spawning ground. Structurally all these images are equivalent. All are presented in elaborately fanciful language; from all we derive a hint that the complete experience of the sacred would develop through the various polarities toward some half-recognition of a sacred presence inhabiting the sacred realm.

All these episodes are chiefly visual, as one would expect of experiences where the major polarities are spatial. The role of the searching eye is so prominent in these experiences of Nature that it is easy to ask what that eye is searching for—would it not be some sort of answering glance?—and therefore to take notice of a series of ocular encounters extending through the book. On Sunday, for instance, the two brothers pass some idle young men who taunt the travellers from a bridge. Thoreau reports that he discomforted the most forward with a glance of his eye. This meeting is followed by a "just and equal encounter of the eyes, as between two honest men" (80), enjoyed with a particularly "serene and liberal-minded" lockkeeper at Middlesex. A later anecdote of a recollected excursion into a Berkshire valley culminates in the "gleam of true hospitality and ancient civility, a beam of pure and even gentle humanity" (218), that Thoreau managed to cozen from a truculent old farmer. The look they finally exchanged was "more intimate with me, and more explanatory, than any words of his could have been if he had tried to his dying day." And on Tuesday the voyagers meet a boy at Bedford, who wishes to go on with them; "as he looked up the river, many a distant cape and wooded shore was reflected in his eye. . . ."(248)

There is a kind of climax for this sequence of ocular imagery (I have not quoted all the instances), in a meditation upon a bittern in "Wednesday":

> As we shoved away from this rocky coast, before sunrise, the smaller bittern, the genius of the shore, was moping along its edge, or stood probing the mud for its

food, with ever an eye on us, though so demurely at work, or else he ran along over the wet stones like a wrecker in his storm-coat, looking out for wrecks of snails and cockles. Now away he goes, with a limping flight, uncertain where he will alight, until a rod of clear sand amid the alders invites his feet; and now our steady approach compels him to seek a new retreat.

(249)

Up to this point the description is still largely of mere fact, as the condescension in the tone attests. It is the smaller bittern only. Yet there are hints already that it is more; the time of day is propitious, the bird is also "the genius of the shore" for all its absurdity, and though the brothers have shoved off, they follow the bittern, forcing it to fly further and further away. The narrative voice rises a degree:

> It is a bird of the oldest Thalesian school, and no doubt believes in the priority of water to the other elements; the relic of a twilight antediluvian age which yet inhabits these bright American rivers with us Yankees. There is something venerable in this melancholy and contemplative race of birds, which may have trodden the earth while it was yet in a slimy and imperfect state. Perchance their tracks, too, are still visible on the stones.

(249-250)

The tone is humorous still, but awed as well. The individual bird dissolves into its species, and that in turn into a consciousness as profound as it is ancient:

> It still lingers into our glaring summers, bravely supporting its fate without sympathy from man, as if he looked forward to some second advent of which *he* has no assurance. One wonders if, by its patient study of rocks and sandy capes, it has wrested the whole of her secret from Nature yet. What a rich experience it must have gained, standing on one leg and looking out from its dull eye so long on sunshine and rain, moon and stars! What could it tell of stagnant pools and reeds and dank night fogs! It would be worth the while to look closely into the eye which has been open and seeing at such hours, and in such solitudes, its dull, yellowish, greenish eye. Methinks my own soul must be a bright invisible green.

(250)

The bird ends by becoming a Presence worth encountering, whose eye conveys a true answering glance, more than fulfilling the promise implicitly made by all the slighter human encounters. But this transcendent identity, given with one hand, is taken away with the other. The bittern represents the mysterious past of Greece, geology, and the two testaments as well, and to look into its eye would be to learn the secret of Nature and of one's own soul. At the same time its God-like eye is "dull, yellowish, greenish"; the knowledge it transmits is only of stagnant pools and dank night fogs. This ambivalence is not resolved; the paragraph ends on a deliberately banal note which returns us to the profane bittern:

I have seen these birds stand by the half dozen together in the shallower water along the shore, with their bills thrust into the mud at the bottom, probing for food, the whole head being concealed, while the neck and body formed an arch above the water.

(250)

There is no symbolic overtone to *these* facts. The narrator seems to dismiss his own half discovery of a sacred meaning with contempt.

Why, we are bound to ask, need the experience of the sacred abort in this curious fashion? If the sun or a fish or a bird is fit to suggest the presence of God, why may they not equally reveal Him? We may be inclined at first to think a partial answer lies in the limits of visual experience as such: the eye, gazing upon nature, necessarily converts the objects of its regard into entities subservient to itself, and there might well be a degree of embarrassment in attributing more than a fanciful and self-consciously anthropomorphic life to phenomena which are merely observed. But Thoreau's knowledge of the sacred is transmitted to him through other senses beside the eye. Indeed, like most Romantics, he believed sound a more trustworthy vehicle for the truth of Nature than sight. An answer to the general question can be postponed until we have noticed one or two of the aural experiences.

For if flowers, fish, and bitterns are mute, the depths and distances of Nature can sometimes speak to the listening ear. Late on the first evening of the voyage the brothers saw a light on the horizon from a fire in Lowell, and they

> heard the distant alarm-bells, as it were a faint tinkling music borne to these woods. But the most constant and memorable sound of a summer's night, which we did not fail to hear every night afterwards, though at no time so incessantly and so favorably as now, was the barking of the house-dogs, from the loudest and hoarsest bark to the faintest aerial palpitation under the eaves of heaven. . . .

(39-40)

Typically the most distant sounds are the least dog-like; a profane "bark" close to is a sacred "aerial palpitation" far off. It is an advantage of sound over sight that no voyage is required to experience this music; a wisely passive ear suffices, which indeed hears best in absolute dark, when the ordinary world is shut out. "Even in a retired and uninhabited district like this, it was a sufficiency of sound for the ear of night, and more impressive than any music." Of course; the sound of the dogs *was* music. Such sounds are "the evidence of nature's health or *sound* state," a language beyond language, or Voice of truth, and the contrast between what they convey and the profane words of men, even the most imaginative, can elsewhere become explicit: "After sitting in my chamber many days, reading the poets, I have been out early on a foggy morning and heard the cry of an owl in a neighboring wood as from a nature beyond the common, unexplored by science or by literature" (56).

The dogs were heard most distinctly on the first night, Saturday; "Monday" affords another nocturnal meditation on the supernatural meaning of natural sound which arises out of hearing "some tyro beating a drum incessantly, in preparation for a country muster" (181). This first description is in day light terms, and the tone is contemptuous, as befits the critic of military folly. From a distance, though, and in darkness, the profane identity of the drummer disappears. A social noise becomes true music. "And still he drummed on in the silence and the dark. This stray sound from a far-off sphere came to our ears from time to time, far, sweet, and significant, and we listened with such an unprejudiced sense as if for the first time we heard at all." So far the sound, like that of the dog barking, is sacred without being personal; but the hint embodied in the word "significant" is picked up and continued in the movements of mind which follow, arriving at an abrupt climax:

> I stop my habitual thinking, as if the plow had suddenly run deeper in its furrow through the crust of the world. How can I go on, who have just stepped over such a bottomless skylight in the bog of my life? Suddenly old Time winked at me,—Ah, you know me, you rogue,—and news had come that IT was well. That ancient universe is in such capital health, I think undoubtedly it will never die. Heal yourselves, doctors; by God I live. . . . I see, smell, taste, hear, and feel, that everlasting Something to which we are allied, at once our maker, our abode, our destiny, our very Selves . . . the actual glory of the universe: the only fact which a human being cannot avoid recognizing, or in some way forget or dispense with.

(181-182)

This is a high moment indeed. The language is almost as confessional as it is cryptic. The sound of the drum was already music; it very nearly becomes a Voice. Indeed, it does become a voice; which says, though, no more than "ah, you know me, you rogue." A Presence appears to exchange the very answering glance for which Thoreau has apparently been looking, and which he fails to find adequately embodied in old farmers or bitterns; but that glance is only a "wink" of "old Time," a fictional gaffer to whom Thoreau mockingly condescends. The "Something" with which he is in touch is still, however capitalized, our "abode" rather than our "maker," an environment rather than a person. Once again Thoreau inhibits himself, checking the drift of his own experience. As on Greylock the end of the ecstatic moment is therefore sad. When we hear such music, he says, "we feel a sad cheer . . . perchance because we that hear are not one with that which is heard" (183). The comment diagnoses his own situation. Aural experience of the sacred has apparently the same limits as visual.

"Music," he says in summary, "is the sound of the universal laws promulgated. It is the only assured tone" (184). But the voice of the "gods," audible through drum or bark or hum of telegraph wire, can also be overheard in human language. The "assured tone" speaks through the myths which we inherit from the remote past. Books as well as unmediated Nature can thereby bring us to the verge of the sacred. "When we read [mythology] . . . we are not concerned about the historical truth . . . but rather a higher poetical truth. We seem to hear the music of a thought. . . ." (58) Through the varying tones of ancient stories—which for Thoreau include the histories of the colonists as well as the poems of the Greeks and the scriptures of the East—we "approach to that universal language which men have sought in vain" (59). In them a Voice speaks on the level of culture in the same accents as the casual sounds of Nature; and like Nature, in riddles to the superficial.

Thoreau's affirmation of the vocal content of myth is still firmer than his recognition of voice in sacred sounds. "To some extent, mythology is only the most ancient history and biography. So far from being false or fabulous in the common sense, it contains only enduring and essential truths, the I and you, the here and there, the now and then, being omitted" (60). To be sure the generalization sometime stops a little short of his true belief; "to some extent," for instance, functions in this sentence like "perchance" before a poetical flight to create a protective mock-identity. The student of curious lore can parallel the fanciful poet as a tonal disguise for Thoreau. And the inhibition that interrupts the progress of his natural experiences appear in the context of myth too. Myth contains a Voice announcing "universal laws"; but the moment it is necessary to imagine a Presence to own that voice, resistance begins. The principal locus for the conflict within the dimension of myth appears in the discussion of Christianity.

The paragraphs devoted to Christianity in "Sunday" proved offensive enough to contemporary readers to ensure the book's failure, and Thoreau's constricted tone shows that this response was not wholly unanticipated. In general he rejects the religion of New England on the ground that it is not sacred at all. "It seems to me that the god that is commonly worshipped in civilized countries is not at all divine, though he bears a divine name, but is the overwhelming authority and respectability of mankind combined" (65-66). This makes Jehovah profane, a nickname for secular facts only. The surface reason why the God of the Christians cannot be a cultural analogue to the presence half-discovered in Nature is clear enough. For a fact to be social was enough to make it imaginatively impenetrable for Thoreau; on this side he was as limited to surfaces as the village philistine of his abhorrence was in the woods. As far as he is concerned the sacred is available only to

solitary individuals. Groups know only the profane; and Christianity is thoroughly gregarious. By the definition the polarities enforce, then, it is entirely banal.

One would not have the difficulties his respectable contemporaries had with this judgment if it were made simply and consistently. But Thoreau is ambivalent, as other elements of his response besides the muffled tone reveal. The Calvinist God is firmly rejected; but Jesus remains obscurely acceptable as a "fable" poeticized by time. The specifics of the Christian story are a "dream" Thoreau half-permits himself. The Gospels, indeed, pass a major test for the sacred; they are full of vocal sentences which have power to leave no meeting-house stone upon another. But bad faith is obvious in the imagery as well as in the mixture of opinions. A last paragraph briskly repudiates the religion of the Church as only "pagoda worship. It is like the beating of gongs in a Hindoo subterranean temple" (78), in unhealthy contrast to the "broad daylight" of American freedom and sanity. The sound of Sunday bells is a "twanging." But if in the rest of the *Week* music, remoteness in time, depth, and darkness are always signs of the sacred, Thoreau is not free to use the same images as terms of abuse; especially on behalf of the "able-souled man," a figure who in every other context is clearly the profane figure Thoreau refuses to recognize here. The presence of such self-contradictory imagery betrays an underground attraction to a "mythology" otherwise too nearby to seem valid.

It seems fair to associate Thoreau's uneasiness about Christianity with the inhibition that prevents him from acknowledging the full presence of God in Nature. For Christianity raises immediately in terms of "mythology" the same question which the encounters with the sun or drum music end by raising on the level of sense experience. Thoreau's resistance is more anxious in proportion to the traditional explicitness of the challenge and to the significance of the cultural generally as opposed to the physical; alone in Nature, it is possible to indulge a fanciful anthropomorphism which must be severely restrained in the village, where people take you literally. In the light of this connection and the conflict it reveals it can be ironic beyond Thoreau's intended irony to read his scornful references to those other writers who "feel it to be incumbent on them, sooner or later, to prove or to acknowledge the personality of God" (79).

In any case it is possible for Thoreau to dismiss Christianity as only a white man's importation; America has no valid mythology of its own, except the lost life of the Indians and the tales of the first settlers, and it is clearly a relief for Thoreau to fall back from the claims of myth altogether, and return to Nature and sensation alone. In this mood he will affirm that pot holes in old river beds "must be our antiquities, for lack of human vestiges" (264); such signs can suit the sensitive imagination all the better because in Nature the present *is* the past. "Here is the gray dawn for antiquity. . . . There are the red maple and birchen leaves, old runes which are not yet deciphered; catkins, pine cones, vines, oak leaves, and scorns; the very things themselves, and not their forms in stone—so much the more ancient and venerable" (266). In the woods meditations can be allowed to lead toward a hint of a creative Presence without loss of ease. "And even to the current summer that has come down tradition of a hoary-headed master of all art, who once filled every field and grove with statues and godlike architecture, of every design which Greece has lately copied. . . . Carnac! Carnac! Here is Carnac for me" (267). Such an apprehension of the past in the present converts the human past of myth, remote as it is, into something comparatively profane, a mere vehicle for a Natural tenor.[15]

But though Nature is frequently affirmed as more mythical than myth, Thoreau does not abandon human vestiges when he can find them. The need to find a variant of the sacred within cultural as well as natural experience, frustrated on the side of Christianity, is satisfied in his classical studies, his readings in Eastern religion, and above all in his effort to recover the lost Indian and colonial past of his own country. The best version of a valid and acceptable myth Thoreau finds develops from the contrast between the white man, whose entire two hundred years in America constitutes a kind of extended present, and the Indian whose much longer history runs back into that of Nature herself. The white man, "knowing well what he knows, not guessing but calculating; strong in community, yielding obedience to authority; of experienced race; of wonderful, wonderful, common sense" (53) is an obvious type of the profane, with attributes explicitly opposite to those of the Indian and implicitly in as strong a contrast with Thoreau's own rebellious, solitary, imaginative way of life. The essence of the white man's activity is a large scale alteration of Nature; of the Indian's, such an unconscious but absolute piety as has left scarcely a trace behind. Yet even the banal New England countryside of farms and villages can become transparent to reveal another world inhabited by another race, whose arrowheads and pestles, though sunk in the mud of the rivers, are still visible to the poet.

What the profane eye sees is civility; what the instructed memory recalls is savagery; and savagery is Thoreau's chief cultural metaphor for spirituality, as fish and flowers and sounds in the dark are principal physical metaphors. The "wary independence and aloofness" of the Indian stands for Thoreau's own ambition to be "admitted from time to time to a rare and peculiar society with Nature" (55), to have "glances of starry recognition to which our saloons are strangers." As the Indian is conventionally below civilization, so the solitary searcher

is above it; from their mutual point of view the labor of the farmer is "something vulgar and foul" (56), to be used if at all only as a source of tropes. It is subversive in the strictest sense to make "wildness" emblematic of holiness, the brutal a more accurate image of the sacred than the humanly worthy and normally respectable, and the apparent contradiction can trouble Thoreau too, as the chapter on "Higher Laws" in *Walden* shows; but for all the risks, rhetorical and spiritual, this version of pastoral succeeds. The meditations on Indian facts are a convincing part of Thoreau's total experience of the sacred, filling a space in the spiritual spectrum that would otherwise, Christianity being refused, remain vacant.

The theme of Indian life is necessarily connected with the more general theme of time, and the climactic episode involving Indian material is also a prime instance of the present as a scene for the re-enactment of the past. This is the tale of Hannah Dustan, the one extended story on the level of myth which is developed as fully as one of the major excursions into Nature. In this tale we have an opportunity to see what happens to the question of the Presence in the context of a myth which Thoreau fully accepts.

The episode begins as the brothers are on their way down the Merrimack once more, returning home to Concord. As they go Thoreau recalls another and less peaceful descent of the same river, "one hundred and forty-two years before this, probably about this time in the afternoon" (341). It was then that "Hannah Dustan, and her nurse, Mary Neff, both of Haverhill, eighteen miles from the mouth of this river, and an English boy, named Samuel Lennardson" (342) paddled hastily down with the scalps of their erstwhile captors in the bottom of the stolen canoe. The specifics attest to actuality with an emphasis that obliges the mind to go beyond it. The fabulous event was as real, the meditation continues, as the stumps on the bank, once trees which "perchance" shaded the fugitives. A shift to the present tense transports the mind into the past: "early this morning the deed was performed, and now, perchance, these tired women and this boy, their clothes stained with blood, and their minds racked with alternate resolution and fear, are making a hasty meal of parched corn and moose-meat. . . ." (343) In structure this experience of the sacred is like many others, but the content is more enigmatic than usual. "Wildness" is in this instance no paradox. Here are human beings—heroic, as befits a myth, but still plain English people—behaving like Indians indeed.

The implications are impressive, and we might as well make use of them, since no other story in the *Week* deals in mythological material so specifically. This episode includes no Voice to announce "universal law," but something better. The exceptional contact from which these people in actuality and Thoreau in imagination are withdrawing is more than the usual glimmerings of a Presence; it is a "deed," an act of war against concrete enemies, a murder. "They are thinking," Thoreau continues, extending the composition of place on which he is embarked as he identifies with his imagined protagonists, "of the dead whom they have left behind on that solitary isle far up the stream, and of the relentless living warriors who are in pursuit." We are invited to conclude that a fully articulated encounter with the Presence in the heart of the sacred wood involves destruction as well as life. To meet Him or his multiplied avatars is not only to see or hear but to kill—or die. If this hint is acceptable, something new is added to our knowledge of the sacred.

The close of this tale is not all dark, but it continues a riddle. "The family of Hannah Dustan all assembled alive once more" (345) to live the civil life of white men again, whatever their memories of that other life in which they had briefly participated; all except "the infant whose brains were dashed out against the apple tree" at the beginning of the adventure; "and there have been many in later times have lived to say that they have eaten of the fruit of that apple tree"; among them, after a fashion, Thoreau himself. This can be read as a partial restoration of the balance which the distrustful references to Christianity and the scornful talk about graveyards upset. When the lines of thematic interest coincide, myth can indeed tell more of the truth than bare nature, and Thoreau can find himself after all "competent to write the poetry of the grave" (179).

What then is the significance of death as a part of the experience of the sacred, a part so largely omitted from the other episodes, so inescapable in this? Death is to be feared as a threat to the self. Would acknowledgment of the Presence of God involve a threat, then, to the ego of the searcher? It is universal testimony that the life of God is offered only on condition that the self of the inquirer first die. But this is of course precisely the part of the tradition which Transcendentalism most expressly rejected. Besides, it is everywhere obvious that Thoreau had exceptional pride of self to reinforce the strictures of the ideology he inherited. The figure with whom contemporary criticism has identified the whole of Thoreau is very real—though as an obstacle as much as an achievement. A solitary pleased with his independence and delighting in an environment which made no immediate resistance to movements of his mind might well interpret a personal God as a threat to his integrity. And a tenacious attachment to self would account for the refusal to carry out the logic of experiences which lead in the direction of that recognition; even if this meant that he was forced to repeat the initial stages of what is essentially the same experience over and over.

Attachment to self occurs on other levels besides the explicitly religious. The recoil of feeling with which Thoreau backs away from the dangers of discovering a personal God can remind us of the prickly attitude he showed his fellow men. There are many anecdotes showing his fear of people who threatened his time and freedom. Mixed with that rigor was evidently a longing for a special intimacy which never found entire satisfaction. This conflict between rejection and frustration appears in the *Week* throughout the essay on **"Friendship"** to which so many pages of "Wednesday" are devoted.

The ideal Friend would be one more manifestation of the Presence, all the more satisfying because entirely human, and no risk to his integrity. But an actual friend is hard to find. "The Friend is some fair floating isle of palm eluding the mariner in Pacific seas. . . . Who would not sail through mutiny and storm, even over Atlantic waves, to reach the fabulous retreating shores of some continent man?" (278). Such language assimilates the ideal Friend to all the other instances of the impossibly remote. Real acquaintances are by contrast frustratingly profane; we discover what was most valuable in our friend only after we have lost him. "After years of vain familiarity, some distant gesture or unconscious behavior, which we remember, speaks to us with more emphasis than the wisest or kindest words" (275). Such references are as melancholy as they are abstract. "There goes a rumor that the earth is inhabited, but the shipwrecked mariner has not seen a footprint on the shore" (280).

Thoreau is then perfectly justified when in this superficially separable essay he calls Friendship the "secret of the universe—" and simultaneously observes that its history is always a "tragedy" (281). For in this context too death appears, as well as the teasing absence of a Presence. The particular "history" he would have had most in mind as he wrote was certainly tragic. For the concealed point of the disquisition, the secret concrete that gives the generalizations their silent meaning, is surely John Thoreau. His brother was one Other who *was* real; who had not to be searched for and evaded, since he was present all the time.[16] But John had died in agony from lockjaw between the time of the voyage and time of writing. Thoreau was left alone, to mourn and celebrate a past made sacred by loss. It is wholly typical of the essay, and of the strategy of the book generally, that John should never appear directly in the text. He disappears into the "we" who together constitute the anonymous sensibility of the narrator. This inexpressiveness seems in inverse proportion to the strength of the feelings involved. "My Friend, . . . is my real brother" (302). The remark might well be reversed. The only place where Thoreau speaks in so many words of his brother is in the brief poetical epigraphs at the beginning. There John is identified with that "only permanent shore, / The cape never rounded, nor wandered o'er" which the prose goes on to supply so many metamorphoses. John is the "muse" who precedes the poet to "loftier" hills and "fairer" rivers; who died, as it were, in his stead, to become identified with the Presence he himself half desired, half feared. But these references are placed so as to be virtually meaningless at first reading. The instinct toward concealment is nowhere more perversely satisfied.

The concluding pages of the **Week** do not significantly alter our sense of the meaning of these several themes and episodes. We hear again, now in valedictory generality, of that "OTHER WORLD which the instinct of mankind has so long predicted" (412) and again learn how difficult it is to actually discover that realm, "to go within one fold of this which we appear to know so well" (409). To be sure "there is only necessary a moment's sanity and sound senses" to assure us that our hopes are legitimate, that "we live on the outskirts of that region," though "carved wood, and floating boughs, and sunset skies are all that we know of it." Thoreau liked to end all his books affirmatively. What is unsatisfying about these concluding pages is not so much the literal falsity of these statements as our memory of the incompleteness of the experiences they interpret. His summations are a little more positive than the implication of his experiments will support; they might better serve as hypotheses for some new explorer to test than as conclusions from the man of experience himself. Occasionally the discrepancy will jar attention. The question, "is not Nature, rightly read, that of which she is commonly taken to be the symbol merely" (408) anticipates, deservedly, a positive answer. The other questions which precede this, though, "may we not *see* God? Are we to be put off and amused in this life, as if it were with a mere allegory?" are, as we have seen, susceptible to a negative or at least ambiguous reply. But to the writer at the moment they must have all seemed rhetorical in the same degree.

We are left, then, with an expression of faith; a faith which the encounters described have "to some extent" justified. To pursue the changes of faith and inhibition alike one would have to continue beyond the **Week** to **Walden** and beyond; indeed the principal story is there, and not, as any critic must agree, in Thoreau's first book. But the **Week** is enough to give us an outline of Thoreau's endeavor, and to fill it up too, somewhat better than literary custom has always allowed us to suppose.

Notes

1. Sherman Paul, *The Shores of America* (Urbana, 1958), p. 59.

2. Perry Miller, *Consciousness in Concord* (Boston, 1958), p. 30.

3. Alfred Kazin, "Thoreau's Lost Journal," *Contemporaries* (Boston, 1963), pp. 47 and 49.

4. Even Joseph Wood Krutch, whose own sympathies must be assumed to lie with Thoreau the naturalist, can be found to have affirmed that Thoreau's "principal achievement was . . . the creation of himself, and his principal literary work was, therefore, the presentation of that self. . . ." See his *Henry David Thoreau* (New York, 1948), p. 11. Similar summary remarks may be found in Canby and Van Doren as well.

5. Theodore Baird, "Corn Grows in the Night," *The Massachusetts Review,* IV (Autumn, 1962), 96. No doubt this succinct judgment has been more often thought than addressed to a class or written down.

6. Paul, p. vii.

7. Reginald L. Cook, *Passage to Walden* (Boston, 1949), p. 181.

8. Norman Foerster, *Nature in American Literature* (New York, 1923), p. 101.

9. Ethel Seybold, *Thoreau: the Quest and the Classics* (New Haven, 1951), p. 7. One reason why modern criticism has been imperceptive about or uneasy with that side of Thoreau which was oriented toward nature, and through nature to Nature, may lie in an inability to suspend a deep seated if unconscious disbelief in his object. If we are not willing to credit Nature with a mode of being which permits, indeed obliges, us to encounter it—or her—rather than simply to "sense," "define," or "explain" inert phenomena, obviously we will not be in any position to appreciate the ways in which one man did. To save our respect for that man and his art, we will then fall back on the self and its words; for these, after our fashion, we do believe in and can prove to exist, as we say, "on the page."

10. Such a history might begin from the scholastic distinction between the realms of Nature and Grace, and come (for the purposes of criticism) rapidly down to the Enlightenment. For if one interprets the Enlightenment as an unconscious cultural decision to end the cold war of the traditional categories by assigning to Nature the whole of the real, instead of, as before, "one half" of it, then we should not be surprised to find that the Nature of the scholastics would gradually expand to take in aspects of reality hitherto segregated under a separate name. The several affirmations of the Romantic phase in this metaphysical dialectic can be understood as intimations that such an expansion of reference had in fact begun to take place. For Romanticism in all its developments, Nature includes at least some "supernatural" elements as well as "natural" ones.

11. Recent studies of the "sacred" and "profane" in primitive and civilized experience presume that in both these contexts the distinctions will be more or less disguised; the ignorance of the participant is the opportunity of the savant. The dichotomy itself has been made familiar to students of literature by the continental tradition in anthropology and sociology, especially by the works of Mircea Eliade, though Roger Caillois and J. Huizinga are also relevant names.

12. John C. Broderick, "The Movement of Thoreau's Prose," *AL* [*American Literature*], XXXIII (May, 1961), 136.

13. J. S. Bois, "Circular Imagery in Thoreau's 'Week,'" *College English,* XXVI (February, 1965), 350.

14. *The Writings of Henry David Thoreau* (Boston, 1906), I, 197-198. All quotations are from this edition.

15. The Thoreauvian distinction between the present and near-past, which together are profane, and the remote natural or mythological past which is sacred, may be found again in contemporary abstractions in Roger Caillois, *Man and the Sacred,* trans. Meyer Barash (Glencoe, Illinois, 1959), pp. 103-107. Caillois observes that the "festival" reenacts the events of sacred time in terms of ordinary time; a phenomenon of all religious traditions which has a parallel in the Thoreauvian "excursion."

16. John is surely more exemplary for the *Week* [*A Week on the Concord and Merrimack Rivers*] than Emerson—or Lidian, who has also been suggested as the figure behind the disquisition on "Friendship."

John Aldrich Christie (essay date first quarter 1969)

SOURCE: Christie, John Aldrich. "Thoreau on Civil Resistance." *ESQ: A Journal of the American Renaissance,* no. 54 (first quarter 1969): 5-12.

[*In the following essay, Christie examines the revolutionary elements in Thoreau's "Civil Disobedience." Christie argues that the essay's most radical quality lies in its demand for personal sacrifice in the cause of social justice.*]

I was in India lecturing to teachers from Indian universities on the writings of Henry David Thoreau when I received notice from my home institution not to offer a proposed undergraduate course on the Concord writer. The decision also prompted a colleague to write me a conciliatory word, suggesting that my absence from the country might have put me out of touch with the current attitudes of American undergraduates and that in his view I might be grateful not to be teaching them Thoreau just now. Whatever else the reassurance revealed of the state of mind on the American campus today, it reflected the unmistakable growth of a relatively new posture on the part of my countrymen towards an American writer whose impact in the past has been most pronounced on ornithologists and the Sierra Club. I was now being "warned" of Thoreau's peculiar relevance not for the potential conservationists among the young but for an unquieting generation of political activists, youthful militants, and social revolutionists.

My correspondent could not have foreseen how the context in which his warning found me cushioned the shock of a suggestion that Thoreau could have a profoundly disrupting influence. India has taken Thoreau with deadly seriousness as a social philosopher ever since Mahatma Gandhi first commenced offering extracts from **"Civil Disobedience"** in his revolutionary journal *Indian Opinion*[1] on September 7, 1907. Thoreau's absence until recently from syllabi of American literature courses at the post-graduate level in Indian universities stemmed not from his exclusion from the literary pantheon but from his solid inclusion in India's more reputable one of philosophers. Not only has Indian thought taken his views on civil resistance to heart; it has had no difficulty in accommodating the whole man, accepting his views on simplification and the values of life and nature as integral parts of the specific challenge proposed in his most famous essay. Gandhi's Satyagraha, which preceded both Gandhi's and India's exposure to Thoreau's views,[2] furnished congenial soil for the nourishment of those features of Thoreau's message most often resisted by Americans: his agrarianism, his stress upon material simplification, his reverence for life, his Ideal reading of nature, his emphasis upon absolute moral truths and the pre-eminence of spiritual reality, even his inclinations toward vegetarianism. The spinning wheel and the loincloth have long symbolized for India the relationship between a way of life and the freedom to practice civil resistance. Unlike another American colleague of mine, a social scientist, who finds Thoreau's natural history "distracting," Indian readers have no difficulty in finding correlation between the primacy of spiritual laws as manifested in nature and the primacy of moral truth determined by the individual conscience. In short, the intellectual schizophrenia so often required of American readers of Thoreau has no parallel in the Indian response.[3] For months I had been conditioned to take Thoreau with a seriousness to match any which an American undergraduate could conceive. I had been encouraged to maintain a healthy respect for the power and stability of the man's mind. My context had fostered a personal outlook considerably more congenial to confrontation than caution.

I now even found it easy to believe that a classroom of students in 1968 might be inclined to take seriously the words of an author of four preceding generations even if he had been over thirty years of age when he voiced them.

So an American writer long familiar to another continent in travail now enjoys a new contemporaneity on similar grounds in his own country. The fact does not, unfortunately, guarantee that either continent has done all its homework with respect to Thoreau's views on civil "disobedience." Supporters of both Gandhi and Martin Luther King, Jr., have looked to him as the American spokesman for massive non-violence, and they have been mistaken. A current contender for the American Vice-Presidency expresses the view that his civil disobedience rejects all law and order; a "free-speech" advocate at Berkeley cites him in defense of the right of the individual to any private preference; and admirers of the "professional agitator"[4] Saul Alinsky presume his support for a national institute to train social revolutionaries; and all three are mistaken. At a moment in our history when judges, ministers, college presidents, and contenders for the highest offices of the land are defining "civil disobedience" for us with more or less tentativeness, I suggest the relevance of allowing Thoreau to speak his own position. It is not altogether as some have supposed.

One is constrained to begin with the title of Thoreau's essay and the first misunderstanding. Characteristic of so many matters attributed to writers no longer able to testify in their own behalf, a phrase made famous has been attributed to an author who did not use it. The essay which Thoreau wrote and published in 1849 in Elizabeth Peabody's *Aesthetic Papers* offers the only title Thoreau ever gave it: **"Resistance to Civil Government."** The article was essentially the lecture Thoreau delivered a year earlier on the subject **"The Relation of the Individual to the State."** The latest title, **"Civil Disobedience,"** was the invention of his posthumous editors, substituted for Thoreau's when they published the essay in 1866 in a collection titled *Yankee in Canada, with Anti-Slavery and Reform Papers.*

The change of title was not a fortunate one, principally because it lacked the exactitude of Thoreau's own titles. Authority's rejoinder to "disobedience" is "punishment," but its response to "resistance" is simply "force"—and Thoreau knew the moral impact of the difference upon an adult conscience. Punishment implied a guilt which enforcement did not; resistance to force placed the kind of initiative and responsibility upon the "enforcer" which Thoreau intended to dramatize. "I was not born to be forced. I will breathe after my own fashion. Let us see who is the strongest. What force has a multitude? They can only force me who obey a higher law than I" (IV, 367).[5] Gandhi too understood the difference,

although he did not appreciate the affinity he thereby shared with the essay's author. With only the substitute title of Thoreau's editors to go on, he wrote to Kodanda Rao of the Servants of India Society on September 10, 1935: "When I saw the title of Thoreau's great essay, I began to use his phrase to explain our struggle to the English readers. But I found that even 'Civil Disobedience' failed to convey the full meaning of the struggle. I therefore adopted the phrase Civil Resistance."[6] Even Thoreau's latest critics and biographers, while acknowledging his original title, appear to set the current pattern by settling for the editor's choice rather than the author's.

Let us turn to some features of Thoreau's view of civil resistance which would seem to need particular acknowledgement today. His concept had both conservative and radical dimensions, and a clarification of his position requires that they be recognized and to some extent distinguished.

On its conservative side, Thoreau's essay offered no clear call to anarchy. Thoreau conceived of such resistance as challenging an unjust requirement of some specific nature, a requirement that forced individual concurrence or support for an immoral end. On the occasion of his arrest in July, 1846, he resisted the government's "requirement" of his support, through its poll tax, for the waging of a foreign war in support of human slavery at home, which he regarded as profoundly immoral. Thoreau was not inclined to bog down in fine distinctions as to the exact degree of immediacy with which his taxes actually supported the invading army or the slaveholder; "I do not care to trace the course of my dollar, if I could, till it buys a man or a musket to shoot with,—the dollar is innocent,—but I am concerned to trace the effects of my allegiance" (IV, 380). It was sufficient that the tax was the means by which the government forcibly sought his support. But while he did not qualify his resistance to this particular "requirement" of him, he went to considerable lengths to make clear that his resistance was not to the concept of law itself or to the principle of order. Although he opened his 1849 essay voicing the "ideal of no government at all" (upon which the Jefferson compromise of a government that governs least was ultimately based), he disassociated himself from "those who call themselves no government men," declaring that he spoke "as a citizen" asking "not at once for no government, but *at once* a better government. Let every man make known what kind of government would command his respect, and that will be one step toward obtaining it" (IV, 357).

It is hard to find anything in Thoreau's utterances which differs in basic principles from the ideals of government upon which his American democracy had been founded. He did not see himself as an opponent of them. He was not opposing the "authority" of the State but emphasizing that its power was empty without the consent of the governed. He did not oppose taxation (he went to pains to point out that he paid his highway tax [IV, 380]), but only its misuse for unjust purposes. He insisted that law be the means by which an interested citizenry make certain its government act in accord with moral principles by resisting the law that did not. He could, in a later essay, turn such resistance around to reveal the bases of order it presumed, by declaring, "The law will never make men free; it is men who have got to make the law free. They are lovers of law and order who observe the law when the government breaks it" (IV, 396). As President Harris Wofford recently reminded us, this form of civil resistance "seeks not to undermine the law, but to perfect it, 'not to abolish the law but to fulfill it.'"[7] It actually expects a great deal from the law, as Thoreau made clear when confronted with Massachusetts' Fugitive Slave Law: "No matter how valuable law may be to protect your property, even to keep soul and body together, if it do not keep you and humanity together" (IV, 461). Thoreau's belief in the doctrine of a fundamental "higher law" (a belief, it should be recalled, which he shared with radicals and conservatives alike in the 1850s)[8] presumed an exacting moral order for the maintenance of which governments and laws were originated.

Equally conservative, perhaps, was the stress which Thoreau placed so exclusively upon individual action, rather than on group or organized social action of any nature. By temperament and conviction he viewed responsibility as an individual rather than a social matter, just as he remained basically disinterested in all mechanisms and motives for manipulating people *en masse,* in groups or social entities of any shape or persuasion.[9] The *raison* for all moral action lay with the individual alone: "It is not so important that many should be as good as you, as that there be some absolute goodness somewhere; for that will leaven the whole loaf." When twelve Massachusetts men, led by Thoreau's friend Thomas Wentworth Higginson, were arrested in Boston for interfering with the Fugitive Slave Law—they had made an abortive attempt to free the negro Anthony Burns from jail where he waited "legal" return to his Virginia owner—they were urged by the Abolitionists to plead not-guilty and seek a jury trial for better publicizing the moral case against the law. Thoreau's advice would have been otherwise: that they proudly acknowledge their action and expose the law's "power" by leaving the consequences of the State's action against them to the conscience and determination of the State. We know that the Burns episode brought Thoreau as close as any event ever did to active support of the Abolitionist's resort to organized social protest. Even then, however, he refused to join any anti-slavery society or turn his attention to the social dimensions of his protest beyond a personal exhortation to others to look to their own individual consciences. When Concord's constable

Sam Staples appealed to Thoreau for an alternative to arresting him on that famous July evening, Thoreau's only suggestion was that Staples resign his office.

When an anonymous donor paid the taxes which Thoreau had deliberately withheld, and thereby secured Thoreau's release from jail, although Thoreau appears to have resented such release,[10] he was later to express an attitude which his more aggressive apostles today may find hard to tolerate. In the first place, he separated the integrity of his own act completely from that by another, no matter how that other person's affected the outcome of his own. And in the second place, he conceded the other person an absolute right to his own act of conscience, even though he regarded that act mistaken and even morally unsound.

> If others pay the tax which is demanded of me, from a sympathy with the State, they do but what they have already done in their own case, or rather they abet injustice to a greater extent than the State requires. If they pay the tax from a mistaken interest in the individual taxed, to save his property, or prevent his going to jail, it is because they have not considered wisely how far they let their private feelings interfere with the public good.

> (IV, 381)

As neither State nor neighbor had the slightest authority over his conscience, so neither did they or he have such over his neighbor's. The power of Thoreau's posture on civil resistance stemmed from its absolute requirements for individual action, not from any call to missionary duty. This he could dramatize in a statement apt to offend both dedicated social reformer and moral zealot: "It is not a man's duty, as a matter of course, to devote himself to the eradication of any, even the most enormous wrong; he may still properly have other concerns to engage him; but it is his duty, at least, to wash his hands of it, and, if he gives it no thought longer, not to give it practically his support." Then bringing the moral test back to rest squarely where he felt it belonged, the *only* place where he felt it belonged, Thoreau concluded, "If I devote myself to other pursuits and contemplations, I must first see, at least, that I do not pursue them upon another man's shoulders. I must get off him first, that he may pursue his contemplations" (IV, 365).

Behind the reservations of Thoreau's stress upon individual, conscionable action lay the more radical implication of its social effectiveness, of course, as Thoreau himself was quick to point out. He found "little virtue in the action of masses of men. When the majority shall at length vote for the abolition of slavery, it will be because they are indifferent to slavery, or because there is but little slavery left to be abolished by their vote" (IV, 363). At the same time, he regarded individual action from moral principle "essentially revolutionary."

> I know this well, that if one thousand, if one hundred, if ten men whom I could name,—if ten *honest* men only,—ay, if *one* HONEST man, in this State of Mas-

sachusetts, *ceasing to hold slaves,* were actually to withdraw from the copartnership, and be locked up in the county jail therefor, it would be the abolition of slavery in America. For it matters not how small the beginning may seem to be; what is once done well is done forever. . . . If the alternative is to keep all just men in prison, or give up war and slavery, the State will not hesitate which to choose.

(IV, 370)

It is not really possible to push Thoreau beyond this point with regard to questions of social effectiveness. He settled, rightly or wrongly, for faith in the unaided power of individual moral persuasion.

Thoreau's emphasis upon the moral premises of civil resistance dictated a further reservation regarding its practice. Such action was reserved for clear-cut issues of profound and universal moral principles, principles whose case one could not possibly assert too strongly. The discrimination was important to Thoreau. Governments, like all machines, had their "frictions," most of which "it would be a great evil to make a stir about." "If the injustice is part of the necessary friction of the machine of government, let it go, let it go: perchance it will wear smooth,—certainly the machine will wear out. If the injustice has a spring, or a pulley, or a rope, or a crank, exclusively for itself, then perhaps you may consider whether the remedy will not be worse than the evil" (IV, 368). The test for resistance was whether the law *required* injustice of one, whether the friction had created its own machine for producing "oppression and robbery": "Then I say, break the law. Let your life be a counterfriction to stop the machine." For Thoreau, civil resistance was not to be practiced indiscriminately or nonchalantly. He did not advocate peering into every act of the government with a myopic moral eye, as his rejection of the issue of import tariffs confirms. As he put his reservations, "I do not wish to quarrel with any man or nation. I do not wish to split hairs, to make fine distinctions, or set myself up as better than my neighbors. I seek, rather, I may say, even an excuse for conforming to the laws of the land" (IV, 362). The moral issue prompting civil resistance from one holding a moderate and accommodating stand should speak loud and clear, so irrefutably as to warrant a virtually inevitable personal commitment.

Because of such reservations, Thoreau offers little support to those demonstrators who throw themselves into postures of civil resistance for superficial causes. He would mark the difference between the defiance of an ordinance for marching in opposition to a war and for securing later dormitory visiting hours for coeds. On the other hand, the very magnitude of the "test" Thoreau requires offers a more radical dimension to his stand, for it is frequently responsible for the failure of such civil resistance to meet the simple one-to-one rela-

tionship between specific law and cause which Justice Abe Fortas would make the *sine qua non* for any act of such resistance in this country.[11] It is understandably tempting for lawyers to reduce the "legitimacy" of civil resistance to another step in the legal process, for on the legal level it *is* that. But for Thoreau, as one must acknowledge for a good number of our contemporary demonstrators, it was not only that. Thoreau was not "testing" the constitutionality of the government's right to tax him when he refused to pay his tax, any more than we can presume that all draft-card burners opposed to the Viet Nam war are resisting the government's right to draft its armed forces from a civilian population.

To the extent that a moral issue assumes dimension, it tends to transcend a particular law which only in some degree relates to it. This was reflected in Thoreau's confession that it was for no particular item in his poll tax that he refused to pay it (IV, 380); the whole had become symbol of the part. To the extent that the South saw the crusade of Martin Luther King as truly "revolutionary" (a term Thoreau uses frequently), it can be assumed it sensed the breadth and inclusiveness of King's challenge to basic inequities beyond those embodied in any single ordinance or segregation law. Particular statutes became means for "refusing allegiance," as Thoreau put it, to the larger power behind them, whether that power was the local magistrate, the southern legislature, the southern white majority, or even the Federal government as it might have appeared to be an active supporter of injustice. In Thoreau's day, it should be noted, the symbol of attack eventually became the Constitution of the United States itself so long as it embodied a specific sanction of slavery.[12] In recommending civil resistance when a government's "tyranny or its inefficiency are great and unendurable," Thoreau recognized that such resistance might extend to different arms of that government's authority. Although he limited his own resistance to the poll tax, he abetted those who extended it openly to the Fugitive Slave Act and ultimately to the original slave laws of the southern states, just as he expressed support for the young men who refused to serve in the Mexican War. His test was a moral one, and only secondarily a constitutional one; but he saw such appeal as a thoroughly responsible one for a democracy, addressed to those who were the true sources of any authority properly expressed through law, an appeal "first and instantaneously from them to the Maker of them, and secondly, from them to themselves."

Those who whiff the smell of anarchy in Thoreau's position often trace the source to yet another cornerstone of his case: his insistence upon the individual conscience as the inviolable yardstick for judgment of the law. Certainly his view of civil resistance rests unabashedly upon the primacy of the individual conscience.

The only value he saw in political freedom was its means to moral freedom, and when it came to the test of the latter, he declared he would much rather "trust to the sentiment of the people" than to judges or courts of law. That "sentiment" was indeed an individual matter with each person. But we tend to forget that Thoreau found civil resistance effective precisely to the extent that these individual "sentiments" accorded with very broadly accepted moral values. A distinguishing feature of the concepts of virtue which Thoreau and his mid-nineteenth-century peers held was the breadth of their intellectual base. Individual conscience was measured by universal moral laws and the "truths" which that conscience was expected to confirm were never less occult, parochial, or idiosyncratic. Far from resting upon the untried truth of the private inner voice, moral philosophers like Thoreau gave most of their service to the cause of testing those truths against the broadest and longest experience of the greatest number of men, testing them against the whole of western man's, and some of eastern's, intellectual heritage. A posture of civil resistance, in Thoreau's eyes, was a reaffirmation of moral values for which one could presume near unanimity on the part of all people; only the application in a particular case found some persons blind, just as the need of acting upon the obvious dictates of one's conscience found others slumbering. Today, as in the mid-nineteenth century in American history or the early twentieth in India's, it is not generally in the moral premises back of conscionable acts of civil resistance that their "radical" dimension resides.

Perhaps the most conservative feature of Thoreau's stance was his insistence on withholding civil resistance until compelled to offer it. Those who today search deliberately for such confrontations with the State find little comfort in Thoreau's position. Judge Charles E. Wyzanski, Jr., chief judge for the U.S. District Court for Massachusetts, referring to Sir Thomas More's response to Henry VIII's legal challenge to him, labels such delayed civil resistance "heroic," "the most likely to give peace of mind and to evidence moral courage" even today.[13] Whatever one calls it, Thoreau practiced and defended it: "It is not for a man to *put himself* in such an attitude to society [of civil resistance], but to maintain himself in whatever attitude he finds himself through obedience to the laws of his being, which will never be one of opposition to a just government. Cut the leather only where the shoe pinches. Let us not have a rabid virtue that will be revenged on society,— that falls on it, not like the morning dew, but like the fervid noonday sun, to wither it." While his decision not to pay his poll tax, following the example set by his neighbor Bronson Alcott three years earlier, represented a deliberate decision on Thoreau's part to defy the State's authority, the latter's quiet avoidance of enforcing its authority saw no move on Thoreau's part to identify his gesture further or to force the State to con-

front him.[14] When the State finally did, Thoreau confessed, "It is true, I might have resisted forcibly with more or less effect, might have run 'amok' against society; but I preferred that society run 'amok' against me, it being the desperate party" (II, 190). His resistance was required when the State "fatally interfered with my lawful business," having "not only interrupted me in my passage through Court Street on errands of trade," but having "interrupted me and every man on his onward and upward path, on which he had trusted to leave Court Street far behind" (IV, 406). The role of civil resistance required that the State be the original initiator of the action and that such action in turn be decisive for compelling conscientious resistance.

We must also acknowledge that for Thoreau the form and degree of such compulsion could vary considerably without contradicting the principle. Judge Wyzanski observes that this readiness ("even an excuse" Thoreau called it) to conform to the laws of the land offers the civil resister maximum assurance of the "relevance" of his application of moral principle. No doubt Thoreau would have agreed with Sir Thomas More that it was not man's business to seek destruction of the law but rather to live within it. "Each year," he observed, "as the tax-gatherer comes around, I find myself disposed to review the acts and position of the general and State governments, and the spirit of the people, to discover a pretext for conformity" (IV, 383).[15] But it is doubtful that once Thoreau made up his mind about a moral issue, he would have gone to the lengths of extenuation suggested by Judge Wyzanski, who considers any resistance to military service prior to actual embarkation on military transport for South Vietnam too premature to represent a "relevant" decision to refuse participation in that war. In 1859 Thoreau saw in John Brown a man of faith and religious principle "who did not wait till he was personally interfered with or thwarted in some harmless business before he gave his life to the cause of the oppressed"; because he made such cause his business, Brown would have been suspect "had he acted in any way so as to be let alone by the government" (IV, 424).

We recognize a wide swing of degree between Thoreau's overstated desire for accommodation in his review of the acts and spirit of the government in regard to its poll tax in 1849, and his defense of the unavoidable character of Brown's resistance to that government's military authority on the side of the slaveholder in 1859. Issues and responses had become clearer, more "just" men had faced jail, the tests of conscience had proved more immediate and conspicuous for Thoreau as well as for his neighbors in ten years. Inevitably the stages of "relevant" resistance were advancing forward rapidly. But contrary to some who have written of Thoreau's later views of the Burns' incident and John Brown's revolt,[16] I do not find Thoreau changing any of the basic principles of his approach. The case he makes is still that for compelled resistance dictated by individual conscience responding to a clear-cut and profoundly important moral principle, calling on other individuals to act similarly and thereby force the government's support of justice.

Readers who see a shift in Thoreau's position are apt to be responding to his changing attitude toward a subsidiary feature of his concept of civil resistance: namely, the role of violence in its expression. Here we encounter a radical dimension of Thoreau's views which has been wishfully ignored. We must note two things about it. In the first place, nowhere in Thoreau's 1849 essay, let alone in his later ones, is there any deliberate eschewal of violence as necessarily inappropriate on moral grounds in connection with civil resistance. Nowhere does Thoreau make passivism an essential concomitant of such action. He defined the prospects for a "peaceable revolution" in his 1849 essay: "If a thousand men were not to pay their tax-bills this year, that would not be a violent and bloody measure, as it would be to pay them, and enable the State to commit violence and shed innocent blood. This is, in fact, the definition of a peaceable revolution, *if any such is possible.*" The italics are mine, to give warning to those who have found herein too quick support for a doctrine solely of passive resistance. For Thoreau immediately adds, "But even suppose blood should flow? Is there not a sort of blood shed when the conscience is wounded? Through this wound a man's real manhood and immortality flow out, and he bleeds to an everlasting death. I see this blood flowing now" (IV, 371-372).

In the second place, we have to recognize that Thoreau's view of the degree of violence which one may be compelled to show in one's resistance, undergoes conspicuous change with the times and circumstances. We forget that he reminded us that he might have resisted "forcibly" his own arrest "with more or less effect," but chose then for good reasons not to. The Sims episode in 1851 provoked him to acknowledge greater sympathy with violent resistance, as he reaffirmed three years later with the Burns case. He now found his thoughts "murder to the State"; rather than settle for obedience to the laws of slavery until North and South were eventually "persuaded" of their injustice, he confessed he "need not say what match I would touch, what system endeavor to blow up" (IV, 401). With the incident at Harper's Ferry and his neighbors' fearful responses to the violence of John Brown's stand, Thoreau declared outright his approval of force if such proved necessary to resist the tyranny of the majority in behalf of gross injustice. He found determining significance in the character of the violence offered, asking his countrymen to consider carefully "what sort of violence is that which is encouraged, not by soldiers, but by peaceable citizens, not so much by laymen as by ministers of

the Gospel, not so much by the fighting sects as by the Quakers, and not so much by Quaker men as by Quaker women?" He concluded with as unequivocal a statement on the subject as one could ask for, one which deserves to be quoted in its entirety. It anticipated the military measures which were soon to rend North and South, and forecast his support of them. It also distinguished honestly the degree of Brown's concern from Thoreau's own, thus defining the common consistency of their respective actions on common moral grounds.

> It was his [Brown's] peculiar doctrine that a man has a perfect right to interfere by force with the slaveholder, in order to rescue the slave. I agree with him. They who are continually shocked by slavery have the same right to be shocked by the violent death of the slaveholder, but no others. Such will be more shocked by his life than his death. I shall not be forward to think him mistaken in his method who quickest succeeds to liberate the slave. I speak for the slave when I say that I prefer the philanthropy of Captain Brown to that philanthropy which neither shoots me nor liberates me. At any rate, I do not think it is quite sane for one to spend his whole life in talking and writing about this matter, unless he is continuously inspired, and I have not done so. A man may have other affairs to attend to. I do not wish to kill nor to be killed, but I can foresee circumstances in which both of these things would be by me unavoidable. We preserve the so-called peace of our community by deeds of petty violence every day. Look at the policeman's billy and handcuffs! Look at the jail! Look at the gallows! Look at the chaplain of the regiment! We are hoping only to live safely on the outskirts of *this* provisional army. So we defend ourselves and our hen-roosts, and maintain slavery. I know that the mass of my countrymen think that the only righteous use that can be made of Sharp's rifles and revolvers is to fight duels with them, when we are insulted by other nations, or to hunt Indians, or shoot fugitive slaves with them, or the like. I think that for once the Sharp's rifles and the revolvers were employed in a righteous cause. . . . The question is not about the weapon, but the spirit in which you use it.

> (IV, 433-434)

The history of the impact of Thoreau's essay is that of a revolutionary document, so revolutionary that we must presume, with all its smoke, a very hot fire at its core. It is not to its implicit or explicit acceptance of resistance by force, however, that we should look for a primary source of this flame. Thoreau identified it when he reminded his readers that the moral bases for the action he recommended rendered all matters of expediency essentially irrelevant. He well recognized that herein lay an ultimate potential for power and threat in his proposed resistance. It was a posture which ruled out all those comfortable compromises with effects to which most of us are prone with respect to most of our acts most of the time, a posture fully justifying our "uneasiness" over a recourse so unmitigatingly to moral conscience. On this issue Thoreau was uncompromising: "There is no such thing as accomplishing a righteous reform by the use of expediency," he declared categorically. Taking issue with the position of William Paley, the British philosopher, in his chapter on "Duty of Submission to Civil Government" from his *Principles of Moral and Political Philosophy,* wherein all civil obligation was resolved into expediency, Thoreau ranked civil resistance under those acts where the rule of expediency did not apply, an act in which "a people, as well as an individual, must do justice, cost what it may. If I have unjustly wrested a plank from a drowning man, I must restore it to him though I drown myself. This, according to Paley, would be inconvenient. . . . The people must cease to hold slaves and to make war on Mexico, though it cost them their existence as a people" (IV, 361-362).

This cardinal premise is the most radical ramrod in Thoreau's stance.[17] The immediate "success" or "failure" of civil resistance was not to determine either its appropriateness or its essential value. Thoreau distrusted fame because "she considers not the simple heroism of an action, but only as it is connected with its apparent consequences. She praises till she is hoarse the easy exploit of the Boston tea party, but will be comparatively silent about the braver and more disinterestedly heroic attack on the Boston Courthouse, simply because it was unsuccessful" (IV, 403). Tolstoy, who read Thoreau, wrote his letter to the desperate young Hessian candidate for conscription, demolishing the arguments he so frantically offered of loved ones dependent, of life at stake, of future service canceled, insisting uncompromisingly that the young man had no alternative but to resist and face the penalty (which both knew, in this case, to be execution) rather than betray his passivist principles.[18] To rule out expediency was to place such resistance above legal considerations: "The lawyer's truth is not Truth," asserted Thoreau, "but consistency or a consistent expediency" (IV, 384). The same exclusion prompted Thoreau's concern for those participants in such resistance who found themselves top-heavy with material encumbrances and dependencies upon the State they wished to resist; they were bound to dread most the consequences to their properties and families of their "disobedience" (the one time Thoreau used the term in his 1849 essay) (IV, 373). To the extent this prompted them to weigh their actions by their losses, in a situation wherein measurement of what one had to lose was basically irrelevant, the moral ground was taken out from under their feet. Thoreau's stand was and is extremely strong advocacy, too strong for the uncommitted or the defensive. It is not a form of resistance for week-end protestors or evasive insurgents. Its winning card has always been personal cost, the strength to "take the consequences."

Notes

1. *The Collected Works of Mahatma Gandhi* (Ahmedabad, 1962), VII, 217-218, 228-230, 305.

2. I am indebted to an article soon to be published in India by my colleague G. Seshachari of Osmania University and the Indian Institute of American Studies, for corrections of assumptions summarily drawn in this country regarding Thoreau's influence on Gandhi. Gandhi read Thoreau's essay for the first time in 1907, well after he had launched his *Satyagraha* campaign in his famous Empire Theatre speech in Johannesburg on September 11, 1906 (misdated by a year by George Hendrick, "The Influence of Thoreau's 'Civil Disobedience' on Gandhi's Satyagraha," *New England Quarterly,* XXIV [Dec., 1965], 465ff.). Gandhi reported that he thereafter went on to read *Walden* and other pieces by Thoreau (letter of Oct. 12, 1929, to Henry S. Salt, "Gandhi and Thoreau," *The Nation and Athenaeum,* XLIV (March, 1930), 72).

3. Paul Lauter ("Thoreau's Prophetic Testimony," in *Thoreau in Our Season,* ed. John Hicks, University of Massachusetts, 1962, pp. 80-90) stresses this wholeness to Thoreau's social stand.

4. "Alinsky to Train White Militants," New York *Times,* Aug. 7, 1968, Sec. 1, p. 27.

5. Citations from Thoreau are from the standard *Writings* (Boston, 1906), 20 vols.

6. Louis Fischer, *The Life of Mahatma Gandhi* (New York, 1950), pp. 87-88.

7. "Another Opinion," New York *Times,* Aug. 11, 1968, Sec. 4, p. 11.

8. See Richard Drinnon, "Thoreau's Politics of the Upright Man," in *Thoreau in Our Season,* pp. 154-168. On the basis of a syllogism that "Belief in higher law plus practice of individual direct action equal anarchism," Drinnon finds Thoreau a "theoretical" anarchist. We are reminded that Jefferson, with Locke, found in a higher natural law the premises of certain inalienable rights. The end aimed at by such idealists was seldom lawlessness, as Drinnon recognizes (p. 157).

9. Cf. Emerson, whose New York address on "The Fugitive Slave Law" on March 7, 1854, made a direct call to political action through organization and predicted a general rush to join the Anti-Slavery Society.

10. Walter Harding, *The Days of Henry Thoreau,* New York, 1965, pp. 204-205. I can not agree at all with Harding that it "had been the whole purpose of [Thoreau's] refusal to pay taxes to get arrested."

11. Abe Fortas, *Concerning Dissent and Disobedience,* New York, 1968. See also "The Limits of Civil Disobedience," New York *Times,* May 12, 1968, Sec. 6, p. 29.

12. Thoreau vigorously attacked Webster's defense of the Constitution's "original compact" with the

slaveholder, in the key address titled "Slavery in Massachusetts" which Thoreau delivered at a rally on July 4, 1854, at which William Lloyd Garrison publicly burned a copy of the U. S. Constitution. Congress was not as quick to rush through legislation legally "protecting" its symbols of authority as it has proved to be in the face of current American protests.

13. Charles E. Wyzanski, Jr., "On Civil Disobedience," *Atlantic* (Feb., 1968), CCXXII, 58-60. Judge Wyzanski alludes to Thoreau only superficially, which may be one reason his analysis sounds so equivocal.

14. Leo Stoller ("Civil Disobedience: Principle and Politics," *Thoreau in Our Season,* pp. 40-43) describes Thoreau's act of civil resistance in 1846 as "an act of desperation, chosen because political circumstances had not yet allowed him a more effective one." Effectiveness was not the primary measure of his stand, as Thoreau made clear; and it is difficult to believe that he saw any such "desperation" in his action. We are reminded that Thoreau considered it "a characteristic of wisdom not to do desperate things."

15. The verse from George Peele which appears following this statement (IV, 382) and voices a yet more moderate tone for an expression of defiance of one's government, appears only in the posthumous version of Thoreau's essay.

16. See, for example, Stoller's "Civil Disobedience: Principle and Practice," *loc. cit.* (above, note 14).

17. This does not, in my opinion, justify the view of Drinnon ("Thoreau's Politics of the Upright Man," *loc. cit.* [above, note 8]) that "in those crucial matters in which expediency was not applicable [Thoreau's position] added up to anarchism," unless one accepts Paley's contention, which Thoreau rejected, that for man in society "the justice of every particular case of resistance is reduced to a computation of the quantity of the danger and grievance on one side, and of the probability and expense of redressing it on the other" (IV, 361).

18. Leo Tolstoy, "Advice to a Draftee," *Atlantic* (Feb., 1968), CCXXII, 56-57.

Stephen Railton (essay date May 1972)

SOURCE: Railton, Stephen. "Thoreau's 'Resurrection of Virtue!'" *American Quarterly* 24, no. 2 (May 1972): 210-27.

[*In the following essay, Railton discusses the tension between nature and society in Thoreau's writings.*]

"There are two worlds," wrote Henry Thoreau, surveyor, "The post-office and nature. I know them both." The first is the world of the village, of institutions and laws, of man and society; one whose measure he has taken and found wanting: "doubtless, if our senses were once purified and educated by a simpler and truer life, we should not consent to live in such a neighborhood" (*J* [*The Journal of Henry David Thoreau*], I, 481).[1] For his part, Thoreau quit the neighborhood whenever he could, preferring to walk across lots and through swamps, careful even to shut farmhouse windows with an apple tree. What most offended him in man's world is implied in the quotation just above, and numerous others could be offered to make the offense explicit: it is the impurity of human life that spoils all of its potential satisfactions. Instead of marrying or prospering in the traditional sense, Thoreau invested all of his emotional energy in the other world—nature. "I love Nature partly *because* she is not man, but a retreat from him" (*J*, IV, 445). But nature was not merely a retreat, it was a goal; not simply to leave the town behind did he go into the woods: "I would be as clean as ye, O woods. I shall not rest till I be as innocent as you. I know that I shall sooner or later attain to an unspotted innocence, for when I consider that state even now I am thrilled" (*J*, I, 302). This knowledge, based upon the capability of expectation, reminds one of the ontological proof of the existence of God. "Even now" was December 1841, not too early in his life to point up the religious nature of Thoreau's enterprise, and how it differed from his friend Emerson's. Although Thoreau showed little interest in the God of his Puritan forefathers, or the thinner God of the Unitarians who congregated in the center of Concord, he did posit a deity, one older than the others: the natural world as it presented itself to his senses— "Olympus is the outside of the earth everywhere" (*J*, V, 200). This pantheism is preached most optimistically in his first book, *A Week on the Concord and Merrimack Rivers*: "We need pray for no higher heaven than the pure senses can furnish, a *purely* sensuous life. Our present senses are but the rudiments of what they are destined to become. . . . May we not *see* God? Are we to be put off and amused in this life, as it were with a mere allegory? Is not Nature, rightly read, that of which she is commonly taken to be the symbol merely?" (*W* [*The Writings of Henry David Thoreau*], I, 408).

Unlike Emerson, Thoreau did not locate the godhead within the self. Nature was not merely a set of phenomena which could be applied to the human condition, not simply hieroglyphics, but the incarnation of the divinity. The way to heaven led not only into the self, but out to the world of nature, and man's task in this world is to make himself wholly fit to assume his place within this divine unity: "Man flows at once to God as soon as the channel of purity, physical, intellectual, and moral, is open" (*J*, II, 4). Like all religious men, Thoreau was anxious to find an alternative to mortality; immortality, he believed, was the reality that nature offered him; he hoped to "have my immortality now, that it be in the *quality* of my daily life" (*J,* III, 351). As Thoreau drew the boundaries, the human world was impure, the divine world of nature, pure. The one offered death (business, he said, "is a negation of life" [*J,* IV, 162]), the other, eternity. His personal enterprise was originally to purify himself, through attention to his employment, his relationships and, most particularly, his body,[2] until he had attained a state of unspotted innocence, merged his self with nature and promoted himself into the ranks of the divine. The success of this enterprise obviously depended upon the absolute purity of nature. At the beginning of his career, fresh from the heady words of Emerson's *Nature* and the Romantic poets, Thoreau never doubted the sanctity of his visible god— "Nature will bear the closest inspection" (*J,* I, 92). (The case was the same when, in *A Week* [*A Week on the Concord and Merrimack Rivers*], Thoreau watched the day break from Saddleback Mountain while the fog covered the ground below him: "As there was wanting the symbol, so there was not the substance of impurity, no spot nor stain" [*W,* I, 198].)

But Emerson's "man of Concord" brought to his task a quality that the other Transcendentalists lacked: Thoreau was thorough. When he was at Harvard, Thoreau began Alexander Chalmers' *The English Poets,* and got practically through the anthology's 21 large volumes before finally putting it down. It was also as an undergraduate that he read *Nature* and found his life's work. Emerson had written, "let us inquire, to what end is nature?" And following up that inquiry became Thoreau's "every-day business." After 1849, for at least three hours every day he visited and revisited the Concord countryside,[3] and for as many hours each night he transcribed his penciled "field notes" into well-formed sentences which were entered into his journal in ink. The goal of this labor lay not at the end but along both sides of his path. Like the cabalist, Thoreau believed that the divine mysteries could be penetrated and that the character of his god could be read, not in the Scriptures, but in the landscape. He ordered his wants and needs to allow himself time to walk in nature; he directed his walks to allow himself to study each natural fact, to discover its significance in the vast scheme and to find his place there as well:

> Why should just these sights and sounds accompany our life? Why should I hear the chattering of blackbirds, why smell the skunk each year? I would fain explore the mysterious relation between myself and these things. I would at least know what these things unavoidably are, make a chart of our life, know how its shores trend, that butterflies reappear and when, know why just this circle of creatures completes the world. Can I not by expectation affect the revolutions of nature, make a day to bring forth something new?
>
> (*J,* III, 438)

The impurity of nature, however, was the one discovery that he did not expect to make, and one that he never directly published; Bradford Torrey did. The reader of Thoreau's *Journal* discovers a half of nature that no reader of *A Week,* and none but the most perceptive reader of *Walden,* could have suspected. I will discuss its place in the second book after following the development of this problematic element in Thoreau's thought through the *Journal,* and before examining the form of its final resolution.

Certainly Thoreau did not pick the concept of this dark side of the natural world out of any of Emerson's pockets—in *Nature* nature is defined as "the integrity of impression made by manifold natural objects." Emerson might have written this: "There seem to be two sides to this world, presented us at different times, as we see things in growth or dissolution. . . . If we see Nature as pausing, immediately all mortifies and decays; but seen as progressing, she is beautiful" (*J,* I, 328). Thoreau wrote it shortly after his brother John died; that event shook his faith in the absolute benevolence of the cosmos, but he makes it clear that this is a subjective failure, a case of faulty eyesight that Emerson would have understood. The two worlds—decaying and progressing—are mutually exclusive, the impression remains integral. Nine years later, once Thoreau has begun his program of daily observation, the impression begins to disintegrate. How, for example, can he explain the fact of the "white and sound teeth" of a decayed hog unless he accepts the conclusion that "this animal succeeded by other means than temperance and purity" (*J,* II, 36)? The lower jaw of this hog, which Thoreau picked up on one of his walks, is the first real evidence of objective impurity in nature that he admits into his *Journal* (and it affected him sufficiently to merit inclusion in *Walden* [*W,* II, 242]). But like the "mephitic eructations" of the frogs in pond-holes that trouble him later (cf. *J,* II, 299-300 and *J,* IV, 31), the impurity can be traced to animal nature, and thus mitigated.

The nature where Thoreau hoped to see God was primarily the plant kingdom, the woods and flowering fields, and although he did study the habits of the birds, fish and muskrats in no little detail, he was much more interested in the local flora. But even these proved impure as his observations grew more precise. We can fix June of 1852 as the month when Thoreau takes full cognizance of the inconsistent nature of flowers; "all things in this world must be seen with . . . youthful, early-opened, hopeful eyes," he writes on June 13th, not because man's senses grow coarser as he grows older, but because "Nature imitates all things in flowers. They are at once the most beautiful and the ugliest objects, the most fragrant and the most offensive to the nostrils, etc., etc." (*J,* IV, 96). The theory of correspondence has been stood on its head—"To correspond to man completely, Nature is even perhaps unchaste her-self" (*J,* III, 255). If, however, the natural world is merely a copy of the human, what is the incentive for renouncing the latter? and what reward can the former offer? "Is not Nature, rightly read, that of which she is commonly taken to be the symbol merely? May we *not* see God?" (my emphasis). But the only way he can ac-count for the carrion flower (or the adder's tongue arethusa [*J,* IV, 126]) is to see nature as a symbol of man, not God: "All things, both beautiful and ugly, agreeable and offensive, are expressed in flowers,—all kinds and degrees of beauty and all kinds of foulness. For what purpose has nature made a flower to fill the lowlands with the odor of carrion? Just so much beauty and virtue as there is in the world, and just so much ug-liness and vice, you see expressed in flowers. Each hu-man being has his flower, which expresses his charac-ter" (*J,* IV, 149-50). It appears that Thoreau, conscious now of imperfection in nature, has been forced to re-duce its significance, to shrink its horizon to an earthly one.

But Thoreau's most damning discoveries were yet to come. The flowers, whatever their smell, were at least blooming; they were still emblems of life, albeit merely human life; though its purity was suspect, the immortal-ity of nature was secure. Thoreau, however, did not confine his walks to the spring or his attention to the flowers. Inevitably he was forced to confront the exist-ence of the full year's phenomena, some of which re-sisted his attempts to "chart" them: "What mean these orange-colored toadstools that cumber the ground, and the citron-colored (ice-cream-like) fungus? Is the earth in her monthly courses?" (*J,* IV, 288). If Mother Nature menstruates, she is indeed a complete imitation of hu-man life, with all its impurities. Does the imitation—and here is the vital question—extend to human mortal-ity? The answer nature offers him in August 1853 is not encouraging:

> In the low woodland paths full of rank weeds, there are countless great fungi of various forms and colors. . . . The ground is covered with foul spots where they have dissolved, and for *most* of my *walk* the air is tainted with a musty, carrion-like odor, in some places very of-fensive, so that I at first suspected a dead horse or cow. They impress me like humors or pimples on the face of the earth, toddy-blossoms, by which it gets rid of its corrupt blood. A sort of excrement they are.
>
> (*J,* V, 374-75)

While the thought of pimples where Thoreau had lo-cated Olympus is itself a disillusioning one, I think it represents a repression of Thoreau's real concern—the fungi may look like acne or excrement, but they smell like death. Horses and cows are expected to die, but not nature. I think that the association Thoreau really makes when he smells the fungi is revealed in his next ***Jour-nal*** entry, made two days later, by the latent transition between these paragraphs:

> Yesterday also in the Marlborough woods, perceived everywhere that offensive mustiness of decaying fungi.
>
> How earthy old people become,—mouldy as the grave! Their wisdom smacks of the earth. There is no fore-taste of immortality in it.
>
> (*J,* V, 377)

And none, we are left to conclude, in the Marlborough woods.

The next day's entry is again organized around that one human event which most resisted transcendentalizing—death. And again it is obvious that natural phenomena, in which he had once hoped to find eternity, are respon-sible for reminding Thoreau of his mortality: "The year is full of warnings of its shortness, as is life. The sound of so many insects and the sight of so many flowers af-fect us so. . . . They say, 'For the night cometh in which no man may work'" (*J,* V, 379). It is understand-ably unbearable to be affected so, and within a week Thoreau severely reminds himself of his higher pur-pose. Taking the pokeweed, which "is the emblem of a successful life, a not premature death," as his natural text (since he had forsworn the Scriptures), he reads himself a sermon:

> Open all your pores and bathe in all the tides of Na-ture, in all her streams and oceans, at all seasons. Mi-asma and infection are from within, not without. . . . [This despite the odor of the Marlborough woods!] For all Nature is doing her best each moment to make us well. She exists for no other end. With the least incli-nation to be well, we should not be sick. . . . Why, "nature" is but another name for health [and yet he has seen her in her monthly courses], and the seasons are but different states of health. Some men think that they are not well in spring, or summer, or autumn, or win-ter; it is only because they are not *well in* them.
>
> (*J,* V, 394-95)

Like any preacher whose faith is unsteady, Thoreau works a little too hard to sound convincing. In the middle of August this passage sounds like a whistle in the dark. In 1841 he could sincerely write: "It is not a true apology for any coarseness to say that it is natural. The grim woods can afford to be very delicate and per-fect in the details" (*J,* I, 299). By 1853 he is too con-scious of the indelicate details to ignore them, nor has he yet found an apology for nature's coarseness. The grim woods have become much grimmer, and the end for which nature exists is by no means as obvious to him as it had been. Although he again offers to take the blame upon himself, the gesture belies the objective facts. He *has* opened his pores, and perceived too much miasma and impurity without to prescribe "*all* the tides of Nature." But unless he is willing to abandon his en-tire enterprise, or turn transcendental Manichean and posit an Over- and an Under-Soul, he must find a way to reunite the good and the evil, the pure and the im-pure.

Since Thoreau considered himself a poet even when he wrote prose, since, in fact, writing was only one of his credentials for the title of poet, and not the most important one—he conceived of his entire life as poetry—we can discuss his search for a theodicy, for a justification of the existence of impurity in the natural world, as the search for a successful metaphor. Naturally, this metaphor would have to be found among the phenomena of nature; as an authority on this point Thoreau could have cited Emerson: "nature is already, in its forms and tendencies, describing its own design." What he hoped to do was what he said the "sensitively bred man" could not—"How far he has departed from the rude vigor of nature, that he cannot assimilate and transmute her elements!" (*J*, IV, 195). "Transmute" replaces "transcend" as the key verb in his vocabulary. The fact of impurity required a new attitude toward nature, and the hum produced by the wind blowing across the telegraph wire, the "Telegraph Harp," taught him a valuable lesson: "I put my ear to one of the posts, and it seemed to me as if every pore of the wood was filled with music, . . . as if every fibre was affected and being seasoned or timed, rearranged according to a new and more harmonious law . . . as if its very substance was transmuted" (*J*, III, 11). Thoreau needed "a new and more harmonious law" with which to judge the offensive elements of nature he had observed, and a natural example which would provide the transmutation of the substance of natural impurity into something better, if possible something pure. One metaphor that he discovered creates the climax of *Walden,* which, we know, is for the most part a mosaic, pieced together out of various *Journal* entries. The individual items are assembled with genius: the book attains a complex unity of its own, and at no point, unless you are familiar with the *Journal,* can you smell the glue, even when it binds two halves of a sentence written years apart. But *Walden* is not just a skillfully edited version of the *Journal*—it is a carefully censored one. While he was writing the book Thoreau was also keeping the *Journal.* The latter, as we have seen, questions more than a few of the natural phenomena it describes; Thoreau is startled, puzzled and discouraged by his discoveries of manifest impurity in nature. In *Walden* neither his discomfort nor nature's ambiguities find direct expression; quite the contrary, they are both explicitly denied:

> After a still winter night I awoke with the impression that some question had been put to me, which I had been endeavoring in vain to answer in my sleep, as what—how—when—where? But there was dawning Nature, in whom all creatures live, looking in at my broad windows with serene and satisfied face, and no question on *her* lips. I awoke to an answered question, to Nature and daylight. . . . Nature puts no questions and answers none which we mortals ask.
>
> (*W,* II, 312)

And we can follow Thoreau's policy of censorship in specific cases by comparing an original *Journal* entry with its published version, for example this one from 1840:

> The lake is a mirror in the breast of nature, as if there were nothing to be concealed. All the sins of the wood are washed out in it. The sun dusts its surface every morning by evaporation. . . . I love to consider the silent economy and tidiness of nature, how after all the filfth of the wood and the accumulated impurities of the winter have been rinsed herein, this liquid transparency appears in the spring.
>
> (*C* [*Consciousness in Concord*], p. 185)[4]

This tidy economy corresponds to that Thoreau adopted as his own; he sought to have his sins "evaporated." In the book *Walden* the pond functions as a larger symbol: "Nothing so fair, so pure, and at the same time so large, as a lake, perchance, lies on the surface of the earth." And again the image of the mirror is employed—"a mirror in which all impurity presented to it sinks, swept and dusted by the sun's hazy brush" (*W,* II, 290). But now there is something to be concealed; Thoreau repeats the idea of the mirror, but omits the exact references to the "sins" and "filfth of the wood" or the "impurities of winter," which by 1854 had become much more problematic than they had been in 1840. But by this time the problem of impurity in nature occupied too large and unsettling a place in his thought to be dismissed in his prose—he could leave all "muck of any kind" out of Walden (where unquestionably it did not belong), but not out of *Walden*—in fact, he introduced it at the book's most dramatic moment.

Some of *Walden* was written while Thoreau was actually living at the pond (1845-47), and a version of it was ready for publication in 1849, when *A Week* appeared. But the failure of his first book delayed the publication of his second for five more years, and he continued to work on it until April 1854. J. Lyndon Shanley, who examined the manuscripts and has established the original version and six successive ones that preceded the "clean copy" Thoreau sent to the printer, decided that the time he took with it gave us a greater book, but still the same one he originally planned to write: ". . . the essential nature of *Walden* did not change from first to last. Much material was added over the years, but it did not introduce a new element and create a new strain; it was absorbed by and used according to the nature of the original piece."[5] But as we have seen, the essential nature of nature itself as it figures in the *Journal* changed between 1845 and 1854, and I think that this change is reflected in the published *Walden,* that Thoreau reworked more than his style. To prove this I would like to focus on the lengthy passage which describes the "sand foliage." If we follow Shanley's editing, this phenomenon comprises only half a paragraph in the text Thoreau wrote in his cabin:

> As I go back and forth over the rail-road through the deep cut I have seen where the clayey sand like lava had flowed down when it thawed and as it streamed it assumed the forms of vegetation, of vines and stout pulpy leaves—unaccountably interesting and beautiful—which methinks I have seen imitated somewhere in bronze—as if its course were so to speak a diagonal between fluids and solids—and it were hesitating whether to stream in to a river, or into vegetation—for vegetation too is such a stream as a river, only of slower current.
>
> (p. 204)

In the *Walden* that we read, this incident is expanded to six pages. According to Shanley, the rest of the material (paragraphs 6-10 of "Spring") was added to the manuscript between the end of 1853 and March 1854;[6] it is the last significant addition that Thoreau made. To understand the addition's significance we must follow his interest in the sand foliage through the pages of the *Journal.*

It is mentioned on eleven days over four years, first on the last day of 1850, at which time Thoreau thinks exclusively of its geological implications (*J,* II, 133). Exactly one year later he revisits the scene to observe the process again. By this time he was already conscious of impure elements in nature, and now his description acknowledges this other side:

> The earth I tread on is not a dead, inert mass. It is a body, has a spirit, is organic, and fluid to the influence of its spirit, and to whatever particle of that spirit is in me. She is not dead, but sleepeth. It is more cheering than the fertility and luxuriance of vineyards, this fundamental fertility near to the principle of growth. To be sure, it is somewhat foecal and stercoral. . . .

Not, this time, "like lava"—this last sentence reflects Thoreau's visits to mephitic pond-holes: the body of the earth has bowels as well as a spirit. But he proceeds, after an intriguing comparison of "women's poetry" as "mere diarrhoea" with the true "creative moment" as having "something pass brain and heart and bowels, too," to gather this fecal quality under nature's great and maternal wing: "There is no end to the fine bowels here exhibited,—heaps of liver, lights, and bowels. Have you no bowels? Nature has some bowels. And there again she is mother of humanity" (*J,* III, 165). Later, in January, he again sees "the artist at work in the Deep Cut" (*J,* III, 161). And again, although "this clay is faecal in its color also," "even the color of the subsoil excites me" (*J,* III, 248). And again in March he makes mention of it, this time specifically as an excretory process: "I see where the banks have deposited great heaps, many cartloads, of clayey sand, as if they had relieved themselves of their winter's indigestions" (*J,* III, 343). In all of this winter's descriptions (also *J,* III, 348-49), the motion of the sand, employed as a metaphor for the living law of nature, for the primitive forces of the earth, for the creative stream of the divine artist, is by simile located in the bowels. But when we remember what it was about the world of man that most offended Thoreau—"What have we to boast of? We are made the very sewers, the cloacae, of nature" (*J,* II, 9)—and how fastidiously he attended to his diet, to what he allowed to pass through his own body, it is possible to see why he could conceptualize this flowing sand in only that one way. He was too acutely conscious of his own bowels to ignore its excremental character.

The next year, 1853, he does not mention the sand foliage. Although he is steadily reworking the text of *Walden,* he makes no record of a visit to the Cut, suggesting that he had not decided upon the important position the event would have in the book, a hypothesis supported by Shanley's dating of the manuscripts. Its absence from the *Journal* could be accounted for simply by the surveying he did in December 1852 and January and February 1853 (that is, he did not have a chance to see it), but I think the omission is more telling than that. It was in the summer of 1852 that Thoreau first recorded the offensiveness of certain flowers and fungi. Nature had abruptly become too much "the mother of humanity." Perhaps in this frame of mind the fecal nature of the sand foliage overbalanced its emblematic vigor, perhaps he did not now want to insist that "Nature has some bowels." At any rate, he does know that *Walden*'s year will conclude with the spring. On March 8th he enters a passage that he could have used to describe another kind of thaw: "Waters are at length, and begin to reflect, and, instead of looking into the sky [or the Deep Cut!], I look into the placid reflecting water for the signs and promise of the morrow. . . . Now, when the sap of the trees is probably beginning to flow, the sap of the earth, the river, overflows and bursts its icy fetters. This is the sap of which I make my sugar after the frosty nights, boiling it down and crystallizing it" (*J,* V, 11). The implication of the two events is essentially the same—nature is flowing again. And here also the connection between the inanimate and the vegetable is metaphorically made. But the sap of the river is infinitely purer than the sap of the Deep Cut, from which he would not think of making his sugar. The melting ice is one promise of the morrow: "Walden was dead, and is alive again," he says in the book (*W,* II, 344), but there the climax of the year, the breaking up of winter, is most dramatically and vitally symbolized in the thawing of the earth. It appears that Thoreau once considered this purer alternative, but, as we know, he later rejected it in favor of the excremental sand.

The *Journal* entries from the following year explain the use he finally made of it. On February 5, 1854, half a year before *Walden* was published, he apparently returns to the embankment and sees—"That sand foliage! It convinces me that Nature is still in her youth. . . .

There is nothing inorganic. The earth is not, then, a mere fragment of dead history, strata upon strata, like the leaves of a book, . . . but living poetry, like the leaves of a tree. . . . These florid heaps lie along the bank like the slag of a furnace, showing that nature is in full blast within" (*J*, VI, 99-100). Now the flow is attributed not to the bowels, but the fire, within. In the analogy between the living and dead leaves Thoreau recalls the one he had made in 1845-47, and has begun to shape the metaphor he will eventually use. Three days later he retrospectively develops it further: "On the 2d I saw the sand foliage in the Cut; pretty good. This is the frost coming out of the ground; this is spring. It precedes the green and flowery spring, as mythology does ordinary literature and poetry" (*J*, VI, 109). Let me only note that the entry for February 2nd contains no mention of what he saw—was it that he could not write about the event until the 5th, when he had realized the way to translate it from something fecal into something fabulous?—and pass on to the final pre-*Walden* entry on this topic. It is a long one dated March 2, and since he does not indicate a trip to the Cut, he is probably giving his thoughts a last phrasing before incorporating them into his manuscript:

> The sand foliage is vital in its form, reminding me [of] what are called the vitals of the animal body. . . .
>
> On the outside all the life of the earth is expressed in the animal or vegetable, but make a deep cut in it and you find it vital; you find in the very sands an anticipation of the vegetable leaf. No wonder, then, that plants grow and spring in it. . . . Let a vegetable sap convey it upwards and you have a vegetable leaf. No wonder that the earth expresses itself outwardly in leaves, which labors with the idea thus inwardly. The overhanging leaf sees here its prototype.

> (*J*, VI, 148)

And thus we have the metaphorical significance of the process as it appears in the book. Thoreau is still reminded of animal bowels, but can translate that reminder into an anticipation of the green and flowery spring of the vegetable leaves. The description in *Walden* follows exactly this pattern. Thoreau begins by emphasizing the fecal quality of the sand: "As it flows it takes the forms of sappy leaves or vines, making heaps of pulpy sprays a foot or more in depth, . . . you are reminded of coral, or leopard's paws, or bird's feet, of brains or lungs or bowels, and excrements of all kinds" (*W*, II, 336-37). Four pages later he explains that, though "true, it is somewhat excrementitious in its character," the natural phenomenon is actually a manifestation of divine omnipotence: "Its throes will heave our exuviae from their graves. You may melt your metals and cast them into the most beautiful moulds you can; they will never excite me like the forms which this molten earth flows into. And not only it, but the institutions upon it, are plastic clay in the hands of the potter"

(*W*, II, 340-41). The sand foliage represents the most complete renewal of life. Even the inorganic, despised institutions of man are threatened by this vital force—perhaps, with a little help from Thoreau, they can even be toppled. Here is the truest artist at work, the greatest potter, shaping clay into organic life. In spite of winter, the earth melts and is made alive again from within. In spite of man, nature is not dead; even his railroads have "greatly multiplied" the studios in which this artist can exhibit his work (*W*, II, 336).

Walden is both autobiographical and hortatory: it is the record of Thoreau's own rebirth and an attempt to stir his neighbors into awakening from their lives of quiet desperation. One of its most striking characteristics is its Yankee honesty. Without insisting that his is the only way, Thoreau does offer his fellow men an example of a successful life ("a not premature death"). At the center of that life is nature, and Thoreau must present the complete natural case as his paradigm. He cannot omit the side of nature that is superficially offensive, and so he went back through the *Journal* and rediscovered the Deep Cut, where he found an opportunity to transmute the impure into the organic. But if the imagery of the sand foliage can poetically assimilate impurity into vigor, it cannot actually transmute it into purity. Perry Miller has a valid point when he takes a hard look at *Walden* and concludes: "The pages by which Henry Thoreau—deliberately, we may be sure!—brings his book about Walden Pond to its climax in a slime of sand demand more analysis than they have received. Once more, every reader is on his own. But none can blink the fact that in this return to fertility the scene is predestined to sterility. Anticipation is the cause for living, and for beating the game, but also the assurance of failure."' As Thoreau knew very well, no vegetable leaf would grow in the Deep Cut. It is but the "*overhanging leaf*," and though it may see its prototype in the leaves of sand flowing out of the earth, it cannot put its roots into that sand. The metaphor is really a conceit, a case of poetic, not natural, transmutation. The phenomenon, as Miller points out, anticipates the flowery spring only; if immortality is hard to accommodate within the cramped space of daily life, immortality now and immortality tomorrow are completely incompatible. Thoreau did not have to read Miller to recognize that "one grain of realization, of instant life, on which we stand, is equivalent to acres of the leaf of hope hammered out to gild our prospect" (*J*, III, 263). If he was content to conclude *Walden* with the promise that "there is more day to dawn," the *Journal*, which after all is the record of every day that did dawn, makes it clear that Thoreau would not be happy until he had fulfilled that promise and realized his hopes.

What he lacked was an example of nature's ability to transmute its baser elements into virtuous (i.e., pure) ones. He found it in the flower of the water lily, and although the discovery came too late to be worked into the text of **Walden,** Thoreau made the most of it for his life. As in the case of the sand foliage, the knowledge of the lily's existence preceded the apprehension of its significance. When it first blossoms in 1852 he writes: "The *Nymphoea odorata,* water nymph, sweet water-lily, pond-lily, in bloom. A superb flower, our lotus, queen of the waters. . . . How sweet, innocent, whole-some its fragrance! How pure its white petals, though its root is in the mud!" (*J,* IV, 147). The "though" de-termines the meaning of this passage: the lily is pure in spite of the mud and the slimy frogs that lie on the pads (cf. *J,* IV, 125). And though he writes on the first of July that "I wished to breathe the atmosphere of lilies, and get the full impression which lilies are fitted to make" (*J,* IV, 168), he did not take that deep a breath for two more years. The first year Thoreau attended to the phenomenon of the lily was 1852, and this attention resulted in an interesting experiment in the first week of July. It is perhaps going too far to speculate that Tho-reau could not accept the lily's natural location, but that week he did pick a dozen "*perfect* lily buds" and bring them home and place them in "a large pan of water." Like Walden, this body of water had no mud at its bot-tom. But although the buds did open and bloom for a while like their counterparts outside, they soon decayed. Thoreau concluded that in this domestic environment "their vitality" is "too little to permit them to perform their regular functions" (*J,* IV, 167 ff). He does not overtly conclude that the lily is inseparable from the slime, but he has proven that that is in fact the case. A few weeks later he revisits the wild lilies and is again struck by their fragrance: "No one has ever put into words what the odor of the water-lilies expresses. A sweet and innocent purity. The perfect purity of the flower is not to be surpassed" (*J,* IV, 235). But not a word about the mud—he seems unable to confront both ends of the plant.

The following summer brought another uncultivated crop of lilies. And Thoreau, ceaselessly walking and observing, was there:

> Found two lilies open in the very shallow inlet of the meadow. Exquisitely beautiful, and unlike anything else that we have, is the first white lily just expanded in some shallow lagoon . . . How admirable its purity! how innocently sweet its fragrance! How significant that the rich, black mud of our dead stream produces the water-lily,—out of that fertile slime springs this spotless purity! It is remarkable that those flowers which are most emblematical of purity should grow in the mud.
>
> (*J,* V, 283)

More aware now of the impure aspects of the rest of the natural world, he was getting closer to finding the place which the lily will eventually assume in it. Tho-reau did not bring home any lilies this year; he did not,

as this passage reveals, deny the slime from which they spring. Yet although this year the phenomenon is sig-nificant and remarkable, it occupies only this one para-graph. Next year it will blossom at the very center of his thought, but not before he had conducted one fur-ther experiment. On November 30, 1853, he went to the spot on the river where the lilies grow "to examine roots." Presumably from his boat, he inspected the life that had died down to await the spring: "There is a vast amount of decaying vegetable matter at the bottom of the river, and what I draw up on my rake emits a very offensive odor" (*J,* V, 529). Fully conscious now of both the "innocently sweet" fragrance of the lily and the "offensive odor" of the river bottom, Thoreau was ready to comprehend the full significance of them both.

That discovery would be very timely. Around Concord the lily blossoms in June, and in 1854 Thoreau both an-ticipated and awaited it, for the psychological and his-torical events that preceded its flowering had darkened the landscape ominously. On May 24th he went boating on the Concord River, where a seemingly innocuous observation forced from him the conclusion that "we soon get through with Nature"—

> How many springs shall I continue to see the common sucker (*Catostomus Bostoniensis*) floating dead on our river! Will not Nature select her types from a new fount? The vignette of the year. This earth which is spread out like a map around me is but the lining of my inmost soul exposed. In me is the sucker that I see. No wholly extraneous object can compel me to recog-nize it. I am guilty of suckers. I go about to look at flowers and listen to the birds. There was a time when the beauty and the music were all within, and I sat and listened to my thoughts, and there was a song in them. . . . Man *should be* the harp articulate.
>
> (*J,* VI, 294)

This passage marks the lowest ebb in Thoreau's rela-tionship with nature. He has long and diligently ob-served the objects of nature—he can even name them in Latin—and the knowledge he has gained has rendered his formerly infinite and pure divinity impure, finite and banal. His enterprise has not prospered at the personal level either: after years of continence and chastity he remains impure and guilty, and has become dissipated and, he thinks, parasitic. Equally threatening was the intrusion into his life of the actions of Massachusetts (which despite his divine aspirations had remained his sublunary home) in the case of a runaway slave named Anthony Burns. Complying with the Fugitive Slave Law, the state decided to return Burns to the South. Thoreau made his opinion of the law clear shortly after it was added to the Compromise of 1850, writing in his ***Journal***: "I hear a good deal said about trampling this law under foot. Why, one need not go out of his way to do that. This law lies not at the level of the head or the reason. Its natural habitat is in the dirt. It was bred and has its life only in the dust and mire" (*J*, II, 177). He made no compromise, contemptuously disobeying the law by assisting several escaped slaves toward Canada and freedom. But now the official action of the Governor, though Thoreau had voted neither for nor against him, could not be ignored:

> For my part, my old and worthiest pursuits have lost I cannot say how much of their attraction, and I feel that my investment in life here is worth many per cent. less since Massachusetts last deliberately and forcibly restored an innocent man, Anthony Burns, to slavery. I dwelt before in the illusion that my life passed somewhere only *between* heaven and hell, but now I cannot persuade myself that I do not dwell wholly within hell. The sight of that political organization called Massachusetts is to me morally covered with scoriae and volcanic cinders. . . .
>
> (*J*, VI, 355-56)

It is interesting that Thoreau does not say covered with fungi or slime, as he usually did earlier when he wished to condemn man for his moral impurity (cf. *J*, IV, 472 for one example, or his comment on the Slave Law just above); the terms he now uses are not examples of imperfect life, but rather of death, of the absence of all life.

This difference can be explained. On June 16, 1854, in the midst of his despair about both the finitude of nature and the turpitude of man, the lily, bred in the mire, blossoms. This year he was watching for it so anxiously that he managed to pick the very first one, and with it its fullest impression:

> Again I scent the white water-lily, and a season I had waited for is arrived. How indispensable all these experiences to make up the summer! It is the emblem of purity, and its scent suggests it. Growing in stagnant and muddy [water], it bursts up so pure and fair to the eye and so sweet to the scent, as if to show us what purity and sweetness reside in, and can be extracted from, the slime and muck of earth. I think I have plucked the first one that has opened for a mile at least.

This year the lily is not white and fragrant in spite of the mud, but *because of* it. Unlike the overhanging leaf and the sand foliage, the lily does indeed spring out of the slime—Thoreau has the perfect metaphor for the transmutation of impurity, of slime and muck, not merely into life, but "the emblem of purity" itself. Nature reveals to him the paradigm on which to pattern his life, by which his life can be saved: "What confirmation of our hopes is in the fragrance of the waterlily! I shall not so soon despair of the world for it, notwithstanding slavery, and the cowardice and want of principle of the North." The purity of the lily asserts itself despite the injustice of the human world, and even offers the possibility that all men may be improved: "It suggests that the time may come when man's deeds

will smell as sweet. Such, then, is the odor our planet emits." It succors the man who has bemoaned the stale repetition of nature and his own guilt; if the dead sucker evoked these two responses from Thoreau, the lily reasserts nature's wildness and vigor, and his own virtue: "Who can doubt, then, that Nature is young and sound? If Nature can compound this fragrance still annually, I shall believe her still full of vigor, and that there is virtue in man, too, who perceives and loves it. It is as if all the pure and sweet and virtuous was extracted from the slime and decay of earth and presented thus in a flower. The resurrection of virtue!"

Earlier there had been nothing "pure and sweet and virtuous" in the "slime and decay of earth"; that is why its existence was so painful a truth for Thoreau to recognize. Decaying fungi, the earth's pimples, had been its only extractors, and could serve as pejorative appositives for men and ideas that Thoreau loathed, for they provided no transmutation of impurity, only its assimilation. But with the lily, impurity is transmuted, resurrecting virtue and completely redeeming nature. Now impure man is equated not with fungi, but with inorganic lava and cinders. It is this complete and perfect transmutation that makes the lily so important, so welcomed: "I scent no compromise in the fragrance of the white water-lily. In it, the sweet, the pure, and innocent are wholly sundered from the obscene and baleful. . . . The foul slime stands for the sloth and vice of man; the fragrant flower that springs from it, for the purity and courage which springs from its midst." Human virtue no longer requires the elimination of vice, nor human purity the elimination of impurity, but the energy and courage to accept vice and impurity and to transmute them into higher ends. Finally, the quintessential goal of Thoreau's enterprise—immortality now—is also resurrected with the flowering of this first lily, which blooms (not dies) to redeem the sins of nature: "It is these sights and sounds and fragrances put together that convince us of our immortality. No man believes against all evidence." And the evidence against him had been mounting; but now—"Our external senses consent with our internal. This fragrance assures me that, though all other men fall, one shall stand fast; though a pestilence sweep over the earth, it shall at least spare one man. The genius of Nature is unimpaired. Her flowers are as fair and as fragrant as ever" (*J*, VI, 352-53).

While the lily, like the bug at the end of *Walden,* anticipates the time when all men's deeds will be pure, it provides one man with the realization of that dream. The one man who can reach heaven even from the depths of hell is of course Henry Thoreau, who has remained true to his enterprise and constant in his dedication to nature and is rewarded with the scent of the lily. Its fact has flowered into a beautiful truth, and a useful one. The conflict between purity and impurity, which is probably the most extensively handled moral issue of the first half of the *Journal,* disappears entirely from the last eight volumes. The polarity was resolved on the day that dawned June 16th, 1854.

In this essay I have tried to describe Thoreau's "everyday business" with nature, one that was saved from spiritual bankruptcy by the particular flower that certified that the other flowers were "as fair and as fragrant as ever." But the concept of transmutation, so successfully demonstrated by the water lily, is central to Thoreau's imaginative activity in other contexts. "From impure to be becoming pure" was the direction in which he had originally aimed his life, but it had proved unviable. In the "Higher Laws" chapter of *Walden,* which Shanley tells us was another late (1852-53) addition to the manuscript,[8] Thoreau confesses: "We are conscious of an animal in us, which awakens in proportion as our higher nature slumbers. It is reptile and sensual, and perhaps cannot be wholly expelled" (*W,* II, 242). On Thoreau's terms, physical purity, however desirable, was unattainable—he could not but "live this slimy, beastly kind of life, eating and drinking" (*J,* II, 9; *W,* II, 243). Yet in *Walden* he is already conscious of an alternative to perfect physical chastity: "the spirit can for the time pervade and control every member and function of the body, and transmute what in form is the grossest sensuality into purity and devotion" (*W,* II, 243). But he remains unable to accept the lower aspects of his nature: "By turns our purity inspires and our impurity casts us down." It should be noted that Thoreau had written this same sentence in the early '40s in an unpublished essay titled **"A Sister"**;[9] a fundamental tenet of Thoreau's thought before 1854 was that "purity and courage" could not coexist with the "sloth and vice of man." In that year, three months after the lily blossomed, he endorsed a different ethic: "I sometimes seem to myself to owe all my little success, all for which men commend me, to my vices. . . . It would seem even as if nothing good could be accomplished without some vice to aid in it" (*J,* VII, 48). When we recall what he wrote in 1841 and repeated in *A Week*—"We are double-edged blades, and every time we whet our virtue the return stroke straps our vice. And when we cut a clear descending blow, our vice on tother edge rips up the work" (*J,* I, 208; *W,* I, 236)—we can clearly see the change in his attitude toward his own impurity. Like the lily, he can grow from his root in the mud.

I suggested earlier that the value of the water lily for Thoreau was that it provided him with a successful metaphor: it resurrected the virtue of nature and redeemed the vices of man. But we can also use it to attempt to explain his literary practice, his definition of poetry. Here again, the operative verb is not "transcend," but "transmute":

> I have a commonplace-book for facts and another for poetry, but I find it difficult always to preserve the vague distinction which I had in my mind, for the most interesting and beautiful facts are so much the more poetry and that is their success. They are *translated* from earth to heaven. I see that if my facts were sufficiently vital and significant,—perhaps transmuted more into the substance of the human mind,—I should need but one book of poetry to contain them all.
>
> (*J,* III, 311)

The familiar assertion of Thoreau's specificity, made by most scholars and supported by hundreds of *Journal* pages, takes on a fuller meaning if we look closely at what he was doing in the *Journal.* When he sees a "farmer driving into his barn-yard with a load of muck," Thoreau concludes that "he is doing like myself. My barn-yard is my journal" (*J,* III, 207). And, we can conclude for him, the muck which he transports into his *Journal* is the accumulation of raw fact provided by his observations. The *Journal* becomes increasingly factual after 1854. A number of commentators have decided that these lengthy descriptive passages prove that Thoreau's creative powers decayed, or slackened, after he finished *Walden,* that the Transcendentalist capitulated to the naturalist. But they do not take into account the importance of the lily in Thoreau's thought: it had shown him the possibility of success on the earth he was then walking on. Nor, I think, do they fully understand the way that Thoreau "created"—as a poet, his genius was closest to "the genius of Nature": the one could produce the fragrant and shapely lily from the formless, excremental slime; the other sought the ability to assimilate his perceptions and to transmute them into significance: "It is a rare qualification to be able to state a fact simply and adequately, to digest some experience cleanly, . . . to conceive and suffer the truth to pass through us living and intact, even as a waterfowl an eel . . . thus stocking new waters . . . taste the world and digest it" (*J,* III, 85).

Perry Miller inverted the correct order when he wrote that Thoreau "applied himself to working away from abstract doctrine toward passionate appropriation of the concrete"[10]—that sequence may roughly reflect the chronology of Thoreau's life (he did read *Nature* before he wrote "The Succession of Forest Trees"), but at any one creative moment he began with unformed fact and made it flower into flawless prose: "As you *see,* so at length will you *say*" (*J,* III, 85). "Each human being has his flower," Thoreau had written, "which expresses his character"; Thoreau's, beyond all doubt, was the lily, symbol of perfect transmutation.

Notes

1. Most of the quotations are from *The Writings of Henry David Thoreau* (Boston: Houghton Mifflin, 1906)—abbreviated in my text with a "*W*" and followed by the volume and page numbers. Vols. VII-XX of this edition are *The Journal of Henry David Thoreau,* which I have renumbered I-XIV

for convenience, and abbreviated with a *"J,"* followed by volume and page numbers. Another source is Perry Miller's edition of *Thoreau's Hitherto "Lost Journal" (1840-1841),* published under the title *Consciousness in Concord* (Boston: Houghton Mifflin, 1958). Miller's volume fits roughly in the middle of Vol. I of Bradford Torrey's and Francis H. Allen's 1906 edition; it is indicated with a *"C"* and the page number. There is also one quote from J. Lyndon Shanley's *Text of the First Version* of *Walden,* which is appended to *The Making of Walden* (Chicago: Univ. of Chicago Press, 1957). I note the page number in parentheses in the text.

2. "The whole duty of man may be expressed in one line,—Make to yourself a perfect body" (*J,* I, 147). For Thoreau, perfection's most important prerequisite was purity: "What more glorious condition of being can we imagine than from impure to be becoming pure? . . . May I not forget that I am impure and vicious. May I not cease to love purity. . . . What temple, what fane, what sacred place can there be but the innermost part of my own being?" (*J,* II, 314-15). The innermost part of Thoreau's being, unlike Emerson's, was not the seat of the godhead, but its temple, and his personal purity—his dietary continence, his bathing, his fastidious attention to daily acts—was his effort to preserve and improve the sanctity of the altar, to open the channel to God.

3. This year is suggested by the evidence of the *Journal,* which resumes in 1850 after a lapse of three years, and a letter written in November 1849, describing Thoreau's daily life to a friend: "Within a year my walks have extended themselves, and almost every afternoon . . . I visit some new hill, or pond, or wood, many miles distant" (*The Familiar Letters of Henry Thoreau,* ed. F. B. Sanborn [Boston: Houghton Mifflin, 1909], p. 210).

4. Although Torrey and Allen emended the spelling in their edition of the *Journal,* Perry Miller points out that Thoreau always wrote filth as "filfth"—"that is the way Thoreau wrote it and the way he thought of it" (Miller, p. 186 n).

5. Shanley, p. 6.

6. Shanley, pp. 72-73.

7. Miller, p. 127.

8. Shanley, pp. 72-73.

9. Quoted in Joseph Wood Krutch, *Henry David Thoreau* (New York: William Sloane, 1948), p. 66.

10. *The American Transcendentalists* (Garden City, N.Y.: Doubleday, 1957), p. 1.

Raymond Tatalovich (essay date January 1973)

SOURCE: Tatalovich, Raymond. "Thoreau on Civil Disobedience: In Defense of Morality or Anarchy?" *Southern Quarterly* 11, no. 2 (January 1973): 107-13.

[*In the following essay, Tatalovich addresses Thoreau's attitude toward organized government in "Civil Disobedience." In Tatalovich's view, Thoreau's notion of "extreme individualism" is incompatible with the moral demands of the community.*]

My intention in this article is to extract from Henry David Thoreau's essay **"Civil Disobedience"** the implications of his argument for a theory of obligation.[1] As his objective in writing these views was to justify a given political tactic in protesting conditions in America—slavery and the Mexican War—little attention is given to specifying the prerequisites for one's obedience to law. Consequently, the theory of obligation being formulated here is extrapolated from his notions on civil disobedience. After defining his obligation theory, I will turn to the problem of obedience versus disobedience as it relates to secular governments.

At the outset, it is clear that the instrument by which an individual undertakes to obey a state is contractual, meaning that no government—regardless of its moral content—can command one's obedience unless he voluntarily consents to it. Moreover, Thoreau is no Hobbesian, for it does not appear that Thoreau contemplates any situation wherein the individual consents for time immemorial. Rather, he strongly implies that the individual has the right to withdraw that consent if he so desires:

> The authority of government, even such as I am willing to submit to . . . is still an impure one: to be strictly just, it can have no pure right over my person and property but what I concede to it.
>
> (37)

> But to speak practically and as a citizen, unlike those who call themselves no-government men, I ask for, not at once no government, but *at once* a better government. Let every man make known what kind of government would command his respect, and that will be one step toward obtaining it.
>
> (10)

Herein he does acknowledge the possibility of some sort of organized community under law. But it begs the questions: What will command Thoreau's obedience to government? Why should he obey? This theme is encountered numerous times in the essay, but perhaps the strongest declaration is embodied in his attack on majority rule:

> After all, the practical reason why, when the power is once in the hands of the people, a majority are permitted, and for a long period continue, to rule is not be-

cause they are most likely to be in the right, nor because this seems fairest to the minority, but because they are physically the strongest. But a government in which the majority rule in all cases cannot be based on justice, even as far as men understand it. Can there not be a government in which majorities do not virtually decide right and wrong, but conscience?—in which majorities decide only those questions to which the rule of experience is applicable? Must the citizen ever for a moment, or in the least degree, resign his conscience to the legislator? Why has every man a conscience, then? I think that we should be men first, and subjects afterward. It is not desirable to cultivate a respect for the law, so much as for the right. The only obligation which I have a right to assume is to do at any time what I think right.

(10-11)

Thus, minimally Thoreau argues that government may become involved in questions of "expedience," and that human beings should act as men first and subjects second, meaning that the only obligation which Thoreau will assume is an obligation to do "right." Thoreau's good government is one in which the individual's obligation to abide by the right is insured; he argues, therefore, for an extreme libertarian position and we must take seriously his demands that some people be permitted to remain "aloof" from the state. This would insure his ability to maintain an obligation to the "right." Other citations strongly reaffirm this interpretation:

> Is it not possible to take a step further towards recognizing and organizing the rights of man? There will never be a really free and enlightened State until the State comes to recognize the individual as a higher and independent power, from which all its own power and authority are derived, and treats him accordingly. I please myself with imagining a State at last which can afford to be just to all men, and to treat the individual with respect as a neighbor; which even would not think it inconsistent with its own repose if a few were to live aloof from it, not meddling with it, nor embraced by it, who fulfilled all the duties of neighbors and fellowmen. A State which bore this kind of fruit, and suffered it to drop off as fast as it ripened, would prepare the way for a still more perfect and glorious State, which also I have imagined, but not yet anywhere seen.

(37)

The condition which would validate Thoreau's theory of obligation in the ideal state I interpret to be the individual's "right" of civil disobedience. In effect, Thoreau is protesting not just the immorality of society—as sanctioned by government—but also the fact that he must go to jail for standing against that wrong (not paying taxes!). Such a circumstance would not prevail if the majority acknowledged his viewpoint. There would hardly be any problem if Thoreau admitted the state's right to punish him for civil disobedience, for such circumstance would realize his status as a subject. Rather, he desires the role of civil disobedience without punish-

ment, as a right; this condition would deny him any subject status in real polities but establish for him such a status under an ideal government. Therefore, Thoreau's theory of obligation would become null and void under either of the following conditions: (1) when the individual is obligated to obey a bad government, one which does not permit him to decide questions of right and wrong, and (2) when the individual is not obligated to obey a good government, one which does permit him to decide freely questions of right and wrong. In no case does Thoreau, in his discussion, deny the logical imperative of these constraints.

Thoreau's appraisal of secular (American) government serves to reaffirm the theoretical construction offered; furthermore, it brings into relief the problems which his theory of obligation poses for the maintenance of any political society. Clearly, Thoreau has a poor estimation of real governments. At best government is "an expedient; but most governments are usually, and all governments are sometimes, inexpedient." (9) He condemns the American government for its involvement in the Mexican War (9) and for its maintenance of slavery (13). Our government does not further any enterprise; it "does not keep the country free," "does not settle the West," "does not educate." "The character inherent in the American people has done all that has been accomplished; and it would have done somewhat more, if the government had not sometimes got in its way." (10) And the minds in government are hardly the best: "If we were left solely to the wordy wit of legislators in Congress for our guidance, uncorrected by the seasonable experience and the effectual complaints of the people, America would not long retain his rank among the nations." (36) Nonetheless, these deficiencies have not transformed Thoreau into a no-government man; let me reinforce this proposition here:

> I seek rather, I may say, even an excuse for conforming to the laws of the land. I am but too ready to conform to them. Indeed . . . as the tax-gatherer comes round, I find myself disposed to review the acts and position of the general and State governments, and the spirit of the people, to discover a pretext for conformity.

(33)

Previously, it was observed that "expedience" was a legitimate province of governmental action; Thoreau does go further, permitting some minor intrusion into morality.

> All machines have their friction; and possibly this does enough good to counterbalance the evil. At any rate, it is a great evil to make a stir about it. But when the friction comes to have its machine, and oppression and robbery are organized, I say, let us not have such a machine any longer. In other words, when a sixth of the population of a nation which has undertaken to be the refuge of liberty are slaves, and a whole country is un-

justly overrun and conquered by a foreign army, and subjected to military law, I think that it is not too soon for honest men to rebel and revolutionize.

(13)

If the injustice is part of the necessary friction of the machine of government, let it go, let it go: perchance it will wear smooth,—certainly the machine will wear out. If the injustice has a spring, or a pulley, or a rope, or a crank, exclusively for itself, then perhaps you may consider whether the remedy will not be worse than the evil; but if it is of such a nature that it requires you to be the agent of injustice to another, then, I say, break the law. Let your life be a counter friction to stop the machine. What I have to do is to see, at any rate, that I do not lend myself to the wrong which I condemn.

(20)

It is not a man's duty, as a matter of course, to devote himself to the eradication of any, even the most enormous wrong; he may still properly have other concerns to engage him; but it is his duty, at least, to wash his hands of it, and, if he gives it no thought longer, not to give it practically his support. If I devote myself to other pursuits and contemplations, I must first see, at least, that I do not pursue them sitting upon another man's shoulders. I must get off him first, that he may pursue his contemplations too.

(17)

Thus, he brings to the fore the pertinent considerations with regard to one's appraisal of governmental impact on morality: (1) some unavoidable friction is tolerable, (2) the balance of good from reform versus the evil from non-reform must be weighed to see the net effect on morality, and (3) immorality should be resisted when two general conditions are in force—(a) when immorality is excessive (slavery) or (b) when immorality forces the individual to be an agent for its advancement. The arena in which Thoreau argues for moral autonomy can be defined, consequently, as being concerned with non-expedient acts (by definition "moral") which are characterized by the two attributes under (3).

Let me present Thoreau's conception of civil disobedience:

Cast your whole vote, not a strip of paper merely, but your whole influence. A minority is powerless while it conforms to the majority; it is not even a minority then; but it is irresistable when it clogs by its whole weight. If the alternative is to keep all just men in prison, or give up war and slavery, the State will not hesitate which to choose. If a thousand men were not to pay their tax-bills this year, that would not be a violent and bloody measure, as it would be to pay them, and enable the State to commit violence and shed innocent blood. This is, in fact, the definition of a peaceable revolution, if any such is possible.

(23)

Civil disobedience becomes necessary because society does not provide for the correct settlement of moral questions. In this light, he is particularly critical of ma-

jority rule and political processes. Not only does Thoreau deny that moral questions can be determined by majoritarianism but he denies that one should even try to build up majority support:

I do not hesitate to say, that those who call themselves Abolitionists should at once effectually withdraw their support, both in person and property, from the government of Massachusetts, and not wait till they constitute a majority of one, before they suffer the right to prevail through them. I think that it is enough if they have God on their side, without waiting for that other one. Moreover, any man more right than his neighbors constitutes a majority of one already.

(21)

He even questions the moral integrity of the masses: "How many *men* are there to a square thousand miles in this country? Hardly one." (17) Reform is compounded by the inadequacies of normal procedures: "As for adopting the ways which the state has provided for remedying the evil, I know not of such ways. They take too much time, and a man's life will be gone." (20) And he lists some deficiencies:

Even voting *for the right is doing* nothing for it. It is only expressing to men feebly your desire that it should prevail.

(16)

But in this case [slavery] the state has provided no way: its very Constitution is the evil.

(20)

It is not my business to be petitioning the Governor or the Legislature any more than it is theirs to petition me; and if they should not hear my petition, what should I do then?

(20)

Others—as most legislators, politicians, lawyers, ministers, and officeholders—serve the state chiefly with their heads; and, as they rarely make any moral distinctions, they are likely to serve the Devil, without *intending* it, as God.

(12)

The task, at this juncture, is to show that Thoreau advocates civil disobedience as a "right," something not to be exercised at the price of imprisonment. It is logically necessary, given his construction of the ideal state, that he deny to government any right to punish him for "moral" wrongs, for such questions *a priori* remain outside the realm of state action and of state redress. Not only does he state his desire to remain "aloof," but Thoreau implicitly reveals a contempt for being jailed for non-payment of taxes.

Thus, the State never intentionally confronts a man's sense, intellectually or moral, but only his body, his senses. It is not armed with superior wit or honesty, but with superior physical strength. I was not born to be forced. I will breathe after my own fashion.

(27)

He suggests that jail serves no function. By attacking his body rather than his mind, it will never alter his views or deny him his freedom. So, why have it? Thoreau's conception of freedom is singularly interesting, and it is revealed elsewhere:

> It is not many moments that I live under a government, even in this world. If a man is thought-free, fancy-free, imagination-free, that which *is not* never for a long time appearing *to be* to him, unwise rulers or reformers cannot fatally interrupt him.
>
> (34)

However, I take exception to his enunciation of a "subjective" freedom, for I am not convinced that he truly believes in it. Rather than preach to the slaves that they should feel free and thereby be free, he is attacking a real political situation. Moreover, if he could be a "free" moral agent and ignore the state, why does he ask to be left aloof? The fact is that Thoreau does comprehend reality (the jail) and it displeases him, and no subjective notion of freedom will entirely satisfy him, in spite of his verbiage. At any rate, it is his denial to the state of any redress which makes Thoreau's libertarianism much more extreme than that espoused by more contemporary civil disobedients, namely Mahatma Gandhi and Dr. Martin Luther King.

Finally, Thoreau's position would not be so untenable if the moral sphere was subject to definition. On one issue, citizens do become men, for all "recognize the right of revolution; that is, the right to refuse allegiance to, and to resist, the government, when its tyranny or its inefficiency are great and unendurable." But while Thoreau finds such conditions presently applicable, "almost all say that such is not the case now." (13) He offers no other suggestions to this critical dilemma, yet he does acknowledge disagreement on interpretations. "If one were to tell me that this was a bad government because it taxed certain foreign commodities brought to its ports, it is most probable that I should not make an ado about it, for I can do without them." (13) For this reason, his extreme individualism is also incompatible with the requirements of contemporary society as we know it. For any government denied the power to police civil disobedients, when they cannot themselves define the boundaries of morality, is subject to the forces of anarchy. One can only wonder if Thoreau would enjoy greater moral autonomy in such a community, the kind dictated by the precepts of his theory of obligation.

Note

1. Pages refer to his essay in the following volume: Henry David Thoreau, *Thoreau: Philosopher of Freedom,* edited by James Mackaye (New York; 1930). guard Press. 1930).

Theodore Haddin (essay date May 1976)

SOURCE: Haddin, Theodore. "Fire and Fire Imagery in Thoreau's *Journal* and *Walden*." *South Atlantic Bulletin* 41, no. 2 (May 1976): 78-89.

[*In the following essay, Haddin describes the thematic and symbolic importance of fire in Thoreau's work.*]

Because Thoreau made conscious use of personal experience in his writing, his life and art are essentially related to each other.[1] Whatever the student of Thoreau may think in general of the critical significance of biographical evidence, he cannot leave this evidence out of account in dealing with this author. One experience that has gone almost unnoticed by Thoreau's critics is the part he had in accidentally burning about one hundred acres of woods which belonged to his Concord neighbors, April 30, 1844.[2] It was the most important single incident in Thoreau's life in which he knew he was in the wrong. One can appreciate, as have Walter Harding, Perry Miller, and H. S. Canby, Thoreau's six-year delay in writing about the incident in his *Journal* on May 31, 1850.[3] The fire had been a dramatic event in Thoreau's life for the wrong reason. It broadcasted his guilt, leaving him little room for public expression of other feelings he experienced at the time. But while the specter of Thoreau's guilt has lingered on in the critical commentaries, what has not been recognized is that his grief and his interest in the phenomenon of the fire underwent a creative metamorphosis resulting in important expressions in his writing after 1844.

The extent of Thoreau's grief is quite evident, as when he wrote in *Walden,* "As though I had been the Lord Warden himself . . . if any part was burned, though I burned it myself by accident, I grieved with a grief that lasted longer and was more inconsolable than that of the proprietors" (*W* [*The Writings of Henry David Thoreau*], II, 276). Thoreau's expressions of friendship associated with fire, fire-worship, the natural force of fire, and fire as spectacle after 1844 are not mere rationalizations of a guilty woods burner, but honest attempts of a literary artist to describe in a variety of ways his interest in and respect for fire. We shall understand these attempts better if we focus on Thoreau's determination from the start to make use of an attitude of aesthetic distance, or of what Edward Bullough has called "psychical distance."[4] Aesthetic distance enabled Thoreau to give way to the full range of his perceptions of fire during and after 1844 and through this process to transform his feelings about fire into art. Discussion of how he made use of his experience of fire and fire imagery in **"Civil Disobedience,"** in the *Journal,* and in *Walden* illuminates his method as a literary artist.

I

As the story goes, Thoreau and his friend Edward Hoar, on an exploratory trip up the Sudbury River, had stopped along the bank of Fair Haven Pond to cook a mess of fish for their dinner, when their fire ignited the dry grass nearby, rapidly causing a ground fire and then the fire that burned up the woods.[5] Thoreau gave a deliberate tone of distance to his *Journal* six years later by sandwiching the entire five pages describing the fire between a paragraph about the pasturing of cows and a placid description about the beginning of summer. He ends by saying, "This has been a cool day, though the first of summer" (*J* [*Journal*], II, 25), as though the whole memory of the 1844 fire were merely part of another springtime observation.

In discussing Thoreau's attempts to get rid of his guilt about the fire, Perry Miller says that Thoreau had only two choices: "He could declare himself perfect and so never apologize; or he could so inure himself against his own vices as never to let himself be shocked by them."[6] These choices preclude the possibility that Thoreau might have done something more positive with his experience of the fire. Thoreau gives us more than a hint about the positive direction he took in his May 31, 1850, entry:

> Hitherto I had felt like a guilty person,—nothing but shame and regret. But now I settled the matter with myself shortly. I said to myself: "Who are these men who are said to be the owners of these woods, and how am I related to them? I have set fire to the forest, but I have done no wrong therein, and now it is as if the lightning had done it. These flames are but consuming their natural food."

> (*J*, II, 23)

From one point of view, this is open rationalization; from quite another, Thoreau is clearly attempting to objectify his experience of the fire. In this instance, Thoreau's thinking anticipates "the sudden view of things from their reverse, usually unnoticed side," which may ultimately affect him like the revelation of art.[7] That Thoreau moved in this direction is clear a few lines further, where he states, "So shortly I settled it with myself and stood to watch the approaching flames. It was a glorious speculate, and I was the only one there to enjoy it" (*J*, II, 23-24). A page later he makes the bold pronouncement, "I at once ceased to regard the owners and my own fault,—if fault there was any in the matter,—and attended to the phenomenon before me, *determined to make the most of it*" (*J*, II, 25, italics mine). These statements suggest that Thoreau's real intention was to experience the full effect of the fire for its own sake. Thus from the beginning he had an aesthetic purpose, and since it involved the contemplation of the object itself, Thoreau's experience constituted the essential ingredient of psychical distance.[8] As Bullough has discussed it, psychical distance "is obtained by separating the object and its appeal from one's own self, by putting it out of gear with practical needs and ends. Thereby the 'contemplation' of the object becomes alone possible."[9]

But a significant corollary of Bullough's definition is that such contemplation "does not mean that the relation between the self and the object is broken to the extent of becoming 'impersonal.'"[10] It is highly unlikely that Thoreau, or anyone involved in burning up the woods as he had been, could completely expunge guilt feelings from himself. It is thus pointless to speak here of a *pure* kind of aesthetic contemplation. What is relevant for our understanding of Thoreau is that his attempt at psychical distance would allow for his feeling of grief (which he had said was extensive) or for any other feelings he had. They would not just disappear.[11] The most important qualification for the artist (and in this instance Thoreau) is that "he will prove artistically most effective in the formulation of an intensely *personal* experience, but he can formulate it artistically only on condition of a detachment from the experience *qua personal*."[12] He may be personal, but not too personal; he may see himself in relation to the object of his contemplation, but he must not put too much of himself into his work that results from it; otherwise it will not be art. This was the precondition of Thoreau's experience at the time the woods caught fire in 1844. The May 31, 1850, *Journal* entry shows that he had determined on a course of aesthetic distance, which to his neighbors must have seemed hopelessly out of place. But as will be shown, his intent was not just to contemplate the fire as an aesthetic object. In order to "make the most of it," he would have to write about it.

Between the fire of 1844 and the *Journal* entry of May 31, 1850, Thoreau's references to fire are few, though they suggest that his earlier experience with fire had entered and been transformed by other areas of his thinking, especially the political ones of his essay **"Civil Disobedience"** (1848, 1849). In the "Tuesday" section of *A Week* [*A Week on the Concord and Merrimac Rivers*] he had ventured a description of a noontide fire, but it was a far cry from the noontide fire that had wreaked so much damage in 1844:

> When we made a fire to boil some rice for our dinner, the flames spreading amid the dry grass, and the smoke curling silently upward and casting grotesque shadows on the ground, seemed phenomena of the noon, and we fancied that we progressed up the stream without effort, and as naturally as the wind and tide went down, not outraging the calm days with unworthy bustle or impatience.

> (*W*, I, 235)

The rhetorical demands of his essay **"Civil Disobedience,"** however, drew upon Thoreau's interest in fire imagery in two instances. In the first, a rhetorical defense of his individual civil disobedience, he compared the State to "an overwhelming brute force" and drew upon fire as a natural force in order to make his point. When the individual could make no appeal to "other millions," he asked:

Why expose yourself to this overwhelming brute force? You do not resist cold and hunger, the winds and the waves, thus obstinately; you quietly submit to a thousand similar necessities. You do not put your head into the fire. But just in proportion as I regard this as not wholly a brute force, but partly a human force, and consider that I have relations to those millions as to so many millions of men, and not of mere brute or inanimate things, I see that appeal is possible, first and instantaneously, from them to the Maker of them, and secondly, from them to themselves. But if I put my head deliberately into the fire, there is no appeal to fire or to the Maker of fire, and I have only myself to blame. . . .

(*W*, IV, 381-382)

Thoreau's distinction between natural force (like fire) and the State (which is "not wholly a brute force") also served another important purpose. It enabled him to appeal to the State in a humane and personal way.

In the second instance, he made a moving appeal for humaneness by casting the narrative of his night in jail as an idyl of friendship.[13] Thoreau celebrates what the State had forgotten and indirectly condemned—friendship such as men reveal when they respect one another and meet each other's needs honestly. But the extent of Thoreau's sympathy is evident when he refers to his cellmate in the scene in jail as a man accused of burning a barn. Thoreau plainly identifies with him. It is no mere coincidence that this man is a "clever man," "my comrade," "quite domesticated and contented," and a man who "thought himself well treated." He was accused, but as he said, "I never did it." In a telling statement Thoreau says, "As near as I could discover, he had probably gone to bed in a barn when drunk, and smoked his pipe there; and so a barn was burnt" (*W*, IV, 377, 379). Thoreau's tone is one of deliberate forgiveness, and he obviously had no rancor toward this neighbor.

In this second instance Thoreau brought his now submerged feelings about the fire and reconciliation with his fellow man together in the same passage. When he felt the experience in himself, he knew the opportunity to turn an important moment into art. Here significant personal involvement had made a significant demand upon his art. In **"Civil Disobedience"** the ideal friendship he celebrated answered the critics of his individual freedom, and the barn-burning friend had made the burning of a barn or woods seem not such a serious crime after all.

Between 1845 and 1849 Thoreau was struggling to find himself as a writer. After he had published **"Civil Disobedience"** and *A Week* in 1849, he had become a public, if not yet a successful, writer. Having indirectly defended himself in a case involving his cellmate's accidently setting a fire, Thoreau could at last tell the story of the 1844 fire in the *Journal* in 1850.

II

The *Journal* entry of May 31, 1850, had a salutary effect on Thoreau, for it indeed opened up the variety of ways he was to describe fire and use fire imagery for the next ten years, through October, 1860. The stimulus that fire gave to his imagination provided a full range of aesthetic possibilities. Canby was right when he said, "Press further and you come again and again to this fire in the woods."[14]

Only five days later, in a *Journal* entry on June 4, 1850, Thoreau records that he attended a burning in the woods, in which one Ray had been employed to burn brush. Thoreau took the opportunity to report his observations and to learn about burning. His words still recall the former fire and the truth he had learned about it, but he is composed in his treatment of Ray and therefore in his sympathy with himself:

One man had sent Ray as the one who had had the most experience in setting fires of any man in Lincoln. He had experience and skill as a burner of brush. . . . It fortunately happens that the experience acquired is oftentimes worth more than the wages. When a fire breaks out in the woods, and a man fights it too near on the side, in the heat of the moment, without the systematic cooperation of others, he is disposed to think it a desperate case, and that this relentless fiend will run through the forest till it is glutted with food.

(*J*, II, 27-28)

The ensuing references Thoreau makes in the *Journal* through September 7, 1851 (*J*, II, 479), show how he resumed his sympathetic appreciation of the working of fire through the example of Ray. Thoreau writes several paragraphs of sober advice about how to burn brush (*J*, II, 28, June 4, 1850), and makes up an effectual system for firefighting (*J*, II, 34, June 9, 1850). In these pages occur several sharply drawn perceptions of fire, such as Thoreau's experience of its sound (*J*, II, 29), of its movement (*J*, II, 29-30), or of its reincarnating effect on a snake (*J*, II, 31-32).

Before he had finished writing about it all, Thoreau had touched upon religious references to fire, quoting Layard on the Yezidis and writing that "For fire, as symbolic, they have nearly the same reverence (as for the sun); they never spit into it, but frequently pass their hands through the flame, kiss them, and rub them over their right eyebrow, or sometimes over the whole face" (*J*, II, 35). He then speaks of the natural advantages which such forest fires provide, in that they generate "some of the noblest natural parks"; because the fire cleans the forest floor, it becomes "inspiriting to walk amid the fresh green sprouts of grass and shrubbery pushing upward through the charred surface with more vigorous growth." In walking by night men do not see butterflies but "fireflies, winged sparks of fire! who

would believe it? What kind of life and cool deliberation dwells in a spark of fire in dewy abodes? Every
man carries fire in his eye, or in his blood, or in his
brain" (*J*, II, 40, 41). In describing the northern lights
Thoreau found a subject for his accumulated imagery,
by which the natural phenomenon is strikingly transformed. If, as Perry Miller asserts, Thoreau relived the
1844 fire in cold blood in his May 31 entry, here he
wrote about it imaginatively in a context that is aesthetically distanced:

> The northern lights now, as I descend from the Conan-
> tum house, have become a crescent of light crowned
> with short, shooting flames,—or the shadows of flames,
> for sometimes they are dark as well as white. . . .
> Now the fire in the north increases wonderfully, not
> shooting up so much as creeping along, like a fire on
> the mountains of the north seen afar in the night. The
> Hyperborean gods are burning brush, and it spread
> from west to east over the crescent hill. . . . It has
> spread into their choicest wood-lots. Now it shoots up
> like a single solitary watch-fire or burning bush, or
> where it ran up a pine tree like powder, and still it con-
> tinues to gleam here and there like a fat stump in the
> burning, and is reflected in the water.

> (*J*, II, 479, September 7, 1851)

Such creative passages become more frequent up to the
time Thoreau published *Walden* in 1854. The more he
observed the spectacle of fire the more imaginative and
even poetic his descriptions became. The extent to
which he identified his own role as a literary artist with
fire during this time is also evident, as when he gave
away, as he says, a "secret":

> Write while the heat is in you. . . . The writer who
> postpones the recording of his thoughts uses an iron
> which has cooled to burn a hole with. He cannot in-
> flame the minds of his audience.

> (*J*, III, 293)

Thoreau went on in his *Journal* to employ fire imagery
in further expressions of friendship, of purification, of
wonder and fire-worship, and of the presence of spring
fires in the woods. He never tired of making and using
fresh observations about what had become a significant
subject of his artistic stock-in-trade. In the *Journal* passages above Thoreau tried to draw significance out of
fire from many angles—from rationalization to sympathy, myth, and art. He recognized reverence for fire. His
imagination took hold of fire and fire imagery, and he
metamorphosed his earlier experience into imagery that
suited his own vision.

III

Thoreau's greatest success in this regard came in certain passages of *Walden*. To be sure, he developed his
interest in fire, associated with friendship, by giving
over his entire "House-warming" chapter (*W*, II, 263-

281) to expressions of friendship and fire-worship.[15] The
chapter is a charming interlude in his writing about
Walden. He says he "lingered most about the fireplace,
the most vital part of the house" (*W*, II, 266-267), and
"endeavored to keep a bright fire both within my house
and within my breast" (*W*, II, 275), sacrificing old wood
to Vulcan and warming himself twice with the stumps
he chopped up from his field. In this chapter also occurs his propitiatory poem **"Smoke,"** in which he asks
the goods to "pardon [the] clear flame" of his fire (*W*,
II, 279). If he went out for a walk, he said, "My house
was not empty though I was gone. It was as if I had left
a cheerful housekeeper behind. It was I and Fire that
lived there" (*W*, II, 279). Here, the 1844 fire looked
small when he recalled the time when he thought he
would look in to see if his house was not on fire ("the
only time I remember to have been particularly anxious
on this score"), and finding a spark had caught his bed,
he went in and extinguished it (*W*, II, 279). Otherwise,
he wrote, "I could afford to let the fire go out in the
middle of almost any winter day" (*W*, II, 279). Fire dispelled his loneliness, too, for "You can always see a
face in the fire" (*W*, II, 281).

More significant for this discussion of *Walden*, however, is Thoreau's development of his interest in fire as
spectacle. This interest is important because it ultimately demonstrates how he linked himself with other
spectators at fires, how, in effect, he joined his fellow-
townsmen through his art. "Determined to make the
most of it," he went back to his *Journal* description of
May 31, 1850, (and immediately thereafter) more than
once for material he would incorporate into *Walden*.

As has been amply demonstrated in the first part of this
paper, spectacle engaged Thoreau from the beginning.
To repeat, in the May 31, 1850, *Journal* entry he says,
"So shortly I settled it with myself and stood to watch
the approaching flames. It was a glorious spectacle, and
I was the only one there to enjoy it" (*J*, II, 23-24). But
only a paragraph later occurs the statement, "I could
not help noticing that the crowd who were so ready to
condemn the individual who had kindled the fire did
not sympathize with the owners of the wood, but were
in fact highly elate and as it were thankful for the opportunity which had afforded them so much sport" (*J*,
II, 24). Thoreau was *not* the only one who had enjoyed
it, and rationalization or no, he identifies his own and
his neighbors' interest in the spectacle as parts of the
same human desire for excitement.

A few pages further, in his June 4 entry, he developed
his observation of his townsmen's interest in spectacle:

> Men go to a fire for entertainment. When I see how ea-
> gerly men will run to a fire, whether in warm or in cold
> weather, by day or by night, dragging an engine at their
> heels, I am astonished to perceive how good a purpose

the love of excitement is made to serve. What other force, pray, what disinterested neighborliness could ever effect so much? No these are boys who are to be dealt with, and these are the motives that prevail. There is no old man or woman dropping into the grave but covets excitement.

(J, II, 30)

Here Thoreau is perhaps a little unconscious of himself in relation to this excitement, for fires are only the sport of "boys"; but he is clearly aware of the unity of purpose which the force of fire brings about. He was drawing closer to an appreciation of his townsmen's interest in spectacle. In a passage in the second chapter of **Walden,** ostensibly about "the hurry and waste of life," he again describes the excitement of the spectacle of fire (in make-believe), implying much from his own earlier experience with fire. If this sounds dangerously close to self-expiation, Thoreau now, nevertheless, includes himself in "we." He had known by then both the excitement of the spectacle and the shared victory of putting fires out:

> If I should only give a few pulls at the parish bellrope, as for a fire, that is, without setting the bell, there is hardly a man on his farm in the outskirts of Concord, notwithstanding that press of engagements which was his excuse so many times this morning, nor a boy, nor a woman, I might almost say, but would forsake all and follow that sound, not mainly to save property from the flames, but, if we will confess the truth, much more to see it burn, since burn it must, and we, be it known, did not set it on fire,—or to see it put out, and have a hand in it, if that is done as handsomely; yes, even if it were the parish church itself.

(W, II, 103-104)

Yet Thoreau went further with this elation, this attention to spectacle. In his later chapter, "Former Inhabitants and Winter Visitors," recalling the history of "Breed's location" near Concord, Thoreau turned his experience of fire-fighting and the elation of his townsmen into one of the most humorous passages in **Walden.** The burning of Breed's hut is a new story in his hands, significantly including himself, presumably added to **Walden** sometime after the first version of 1846-47 (**W,** II, 285-286).[16]

The passage is important for Thoreau because he had consciously identified himself and his townsmen in the same matter that had after all, from different points of view, been everyone's interest in 1844—the fire as spectacle. By implication Thoreau turns the joke upon himself, for Breed's hut "was about the size of mine," and the "mischievous boys" have not done this out of carelessness but as a practical joke. The fire is woefully small compared to the one Thoreau had started. Thoreau's 1844 fire had occurred on Town Meeting day; this was Election night. Everybody is involved in the pursuit of the fire, Thoreau "among the foremost," for he "had leaped the brook," and "rearmost of all, as it

was *whispered,* came they who set the fire" (italics mine). There is no talk here of "damned rascal," as some had called Thoreau earlier. The parallel with Thoreau's experience in the earlier fire is evident by contrast. In lower tone the firefighters mention "the great conflagrations which the world has witnessed, including Bascom's shop," but conspicuously fail to mention Thoreau's woods fire, now buried, in this great episode, under Thoreau's humor. The fire-fighters retreat "without doing any mischief." As humor the passage is successful in itself.

The discussion here of the creative changes Thoreau effected in his use of fire imagery would not be complete without a further reference to his grief, mentioned in the introduction of this paper. In discussing Thoreau's writing Lawrence Bowling has rightly drawn attention to Robert Frost's assertion that griefs, not grievances, are the proper subjects of poetry.[17] Grievances have to do with impatience; griefs, with patience, according to Frost. Thoreau's grief, such as it was initially, and as he generalized it thereafter to include any loss of the woods, is of the second kind. It bespeaks a deeper feeling proper to the poet, proper to his perception and use of fire imagery in the years after his inadvertent firing of the woods in 1844. We have proof of this grief when Thoreau tells us he "grieved with a grief that lasted longer and was more inconsolable than that of the proprietors" (**W,** II, 276). Grief underlies Thoreau's treatment of the woods fire in the "Spring" chapter of **Walden**—only we are not likely to recognize it as such, so changed is it under Thoreau's hand. In one passage of this chapter Thoreau's grief becomes the grief of all men, the universal one about death. It is thus an existential grief which, transformed by the alembic of Thoreau's life and art—indeed by his conscious revisions—culminates in his famous symbol of grass as the hope of eternity:

> The grass flames up on the hillsides like a spring fire,— "et primitus oritur herba imbribus primoribus evocata,"—as if the earth sent forth an inward heat to greet the returning sun; not yellow but green is the color of its flame;—the symbol of perpetual youth, the grass-blade, like a long green ribbon, streams from the sod into the summer, checked indeed by the frost, but anon pushing on again, lifting its spear of last year's hay with the fresh life below. It grows as steadily as the rill oozes out of the ground. It is almost identical with that, for in the growing days of June, when the rills are dry, the grass-blades are their channels, and from year to year the herds drink at this perennial green stream, and the mower draws from it betimes their winter supply. So our human life but dies down to its root, and still puts forth its green blade to eternity.

(W, II, 343)

Thoreau's grief, then, in this instance, came to poetry. Through an attitude of aesthetic distance he went beyond the accidental burning of his neighbors' woods.

For Thoreau, the end was art. In creating his symbol of eternity he metamorphosed his fire into the flame that had been at the root of much of his inspiration through all the years after 1844.[18] Thoreau's green flames grew out of the spectacle and out of the loss; and the pasturing herds of his May 31, 1850, *Journal* account could now drink at the "perennial green stream." Although his account in 1850 of the woods fire in 1844 is after the fact, we can now see the true relation of his feelings concerning the two informing events. Thoreau needed parts of **"Civil Disobedience"** and the ***Journal*** to explore the possibilities of fire and fire imagery in aesthetic distance. *Walden,* containing the best of his attempts to employ fire imagery after 1844, symbolizes— for us and for Thoreau—the perennial possibility of aesthetic perception on a higher level, in this instance one where rationalization is nowhere to be seen, but instead, literary art.

Notes

1. Paul Lauter has put this well: "As the value of [Thoreau's] art is an earnest of the value of his life, so it may be that the testimony of his art cannot succeed beyond the testimony of his life. We shall only learn, in Thoreau's case, as both testimonies are studied together." John H. Hicks, editor, *Thoreau in Our Season* (Amherst: Univ. of Massachusetts Press, 1966), p. 90.

2. Thoreau, *The Writings of Henry David Thoreau* (Boston: Houghton Mifflin Company, 1906), VIII, pp. 21-25. References to this edition are designated by *W.* The *Journal* volumes (VII-XX) are renumbered and designated hereafter as *J.* Thoreau reports (*J,* II, 24, May 31, 1850) that over one hundred acres burned. Walter Harding, in *The Days of Henry Thoreau* (New York: Alfred Knopf, 1965), p. 160, indicates that possibly more than 300 acres were destroyed. In his *A Thoreau Handbook* (New York: New York University Press, 1959), p. 7, he says that "Even today [Thoreau] is known by some Concordians as 'the man who burned the woods.'"

3. Commentators on the fire have included Walter Harding (n. 2 above); H. S. Canby, *Thoreau* (Boston: Houghton Mifflin Company, 1939), pp. 211-212; Perry Miller, *Consciousness in Concord* (Boston: Houghton Mifflin Company, 1958), pp. 119-121; and Joel Porte, *Emerson and Thoreau* (Middletown, Connecticut: Wesleyan University Press, 1966), pp. 29-30.

4. See Edward Bullough, "Psychical Distance as a Factor in Art and an Aesthetic Principle," reprinted in Eliseo Vivas and Murray Krieger (eds.), *The Problems of Aesthetics: A Book of Readings* (New York: Rinehart and Company, 1953), pp. 396-405. Bullough's definition of psychical distance refers to the capacity of the individual to maintain a suitable balance of mental and emotional feelings between himself and the object of his perception, in what he calls "Distance"—that which "lies between our own self and such objects as are the sources or vehicles of such affections" (p. 397). Since the publication of Bullough's article in 1912 several commentators have attempted further to define this concept. Lester Longman, "The Concept of Psychical Distance," *JAAC [Journal of Aesthetics and Art Criticism]*, VI (September, 1947), pp. 31-36, essentially amplifies Bullough, emphasizing the experience of the object for its own sake; Monroe C. Beardsley, in *Aesthetics: Problems in the Philosophy of Criticism* (New York: Harcourt, Brace and World, 1958), p. 62, affirms that any object can be an aesthetic object if we give it "attitudinal definition"; James L. Jarrett, "On Psychical Distance," *Personalist,* LII (Winter, 1971), pp. 61-69, asserts that distance is not a sufficient conceptual tool; Allan Casebier, "The Concept of Psychical Distance," *Personalist,* LII (Winter, 1971), pp. 70-91, prefers the distinctions of "attentional distance" and "emotional distance." In view of the philosophical disagreement about the aesthetic term, but upon which there is some agreement, I prefer the term "aesthetic distance" in referring to Thoreau. Emmett L. Phillips' unpublished doctoral dissertation, "A Study of Aesthetic Distance in Thoreau's *Walden*" (Oklahoma, 1969), while not concerned with the specific approach of this paper, is acutely aware of the problems in defining aesthetic distance.

5. See the account in Harding, *Days [The Days of Henry Thoreau]*, pp. 159-162.

6. Miller, *Consciousness in Concord,* p. 123.

7. Edward Bullough, "Psychical Distance as a Factor in Art and an Aesthetic Principle," in Vivas and Krieger, *The Problems of Aesthetics,* p. 398.

8. Bullough and most subsequent commentators make "the object for itself" the main requirement.

9. Bullough, in *Problems of Aesthetics,* p. 399.

10. *Ibid.,* p. 399.

11. Bullough says (p. 399) that distance "describes a *personal* relation, often highly emotionally colored, but of a peculiar *character.* Its peculiarity lies in that the personal character of the relation has been, so to speak, filtered. It has been cleared of the practical, concrete nature of its appeal, without, however, thereby losing its original constitution."

12. Bullough, in *Problems of Aesthetics,* p. 401.

13. Thomas Carper, "The Whole History of 'My Prisons,'" *ESQ [Emerson Society Quarterly]* 50

(Supplement, 1968), pp. 35-38. Thoreau's description of his night in jail may be found in the middle, or second part of "Civil Disobedience" (*W,* IV, 377-380).

14. Canby, *Thoreau,* p. 213.

15. See also *Walden* (*W,* II, 75-76) for Thoreau's discussion of the religious ceremony of the "busk," well-known to readers of Thoreau.

16. Thoreau extends this account in the following paragraph, telling how he "discovered the only survivor of the family . . . who alone was interested in this burning . . . looking over the cellar wall at the still smouldering cinders beneath. . . . He was soothed by the sympathy which my mere presence implied, and showed me, as well as the darkness permitted, where the well was covered up" (*W,* II, 287). Here Thoreau shows his obvious sympathy for a person who has experienced great loss by fire.

17. "Thoreau's Social Criticism as Poetry," *Yale Review,* LV (Winter, 1966), pp. 259-260.

18. See J. Lyndon Shanley, *The Making of Walden* (Chicago: Univ. of Chicago Press, 1957), pp. 204-205. Thoreau had already written a version of this passage in his first version of *Walden,* 1846-47. Thoreau's use of the "spring fire" places his grief closer to his fire experience of 1844 and the night in jail in 1846. With revision and especially the addition of the word "perennial," the passage was significantly retained in the 1854 edition of *Walden.* In his *Journal* (IV, 18) for May 5, 1852, he had written, "Fires in the woods will now rage. . . . Nature invites fire to sweep her floors, for purification." Again (*J,* V, 73), on March 30, 1853, he wrote, "Now commences the season for fires in the woods." The partial metamorphosis of the "spring fire" in *Walden* (1854) is also indicated by an entry (*J,* III, 469) on April 25, 1852:

> Lay on the dead grass in a cup-like hollow sprinkled with half-dead low shrub oaks. As I lie flat, looking close in among the roots of the grass, I perceive that its endless ribbon has pushed up about one inch and is green to that extent,—such is the length to which the spring has gone here,—though when you stand up the green is not perceptible.

Michael West (essay date winter 1984)

SOURCE: West, Michael. "Thoreau and the Language Theories of the French Enlightenment." *ELH* 51, no. 4 (winter 1984): 747-70.

[*In the following essay, West analyzes the ways in which Thoreau's study of languages shaped his writing style.*

According to West, Thoreau's interest in linguistics was rooted in his desire to invent a new form of literary expression.]

A consuming interest in words drove Thoreau to study seven European languages in college before turning casually in later years to the American Indian dialects. During a life dedicated to the elimination of impedimenta he nonetheless saw fit to accumulate no fewer than seventeen dictionaries. As his friend, confidant, and early biographer, the feckless poet Ellery Channing observed, "In much that Mr. Thoreau wrote there was a *philological* side—this needs to be thoughtfully considered."[1] A distinct stylistic rationale is implicit in his tentative but penetrating musings on language: "How shall we account for our pursuits, if they are original? We get the language to describe our various lives out of a common mint."[2] In 1851, while revising the manuscript that emerged as *Walden* (1854), Thoreau confided to his *Journal* that he "dreamed of" writing a book that would be "a return to the primitive analogical and derivative sources of words" (September 5, 1851).

A rich but representative passage from *Walden*'s chapter "House-Warming" may help us understand some of his stylistic aims and their results:

> It would seem as if the very language of our parlors would lose all its nerve and degenerate into *palaver* wholly, our lives pass at such remoteness from its symbols, and its metaphors and tropes are necessarily so far fetched, through slides and dumb-waiters, as it were; in other words, the parlor is so far from the kitchen and workshop. The dinner even is only the parable of a dinner, commonly. As if only the savage dwelt near enough to Nature and Truth to borrow a trope from them. How can the scholar, who dwells away in the North West Territory or the Isle of Man, tell what is parliamentary in the kitchen?[3]

This passage criticizes Concord's social discourse for having lost touch with reality; by contrast a crackle of wordplay exemplifies the concretely rooted language that Thoreau craves. Linguistic degeneracy is dramatized by setting the slang term *palaver* against the genteel term *parlor* so that an alert reader can think about how both descend from the same French root, *parler,* to talk, as does the word *parliamentary.* How, Thoreau asks, can we truly understand these words if ignorant of their etymology? What does it tell us about Victorian culture that its houses contain a separate room crowded with conversation pieces and consecrated to "talking?" What might it tell us about modern American culture that its ranch houses contain a separate room dominated by a spectral TV set and dedicated to "living?" As Thoreau complains that our figurative language risks forgetting its origins, his own metaphor simultaneously literalizes the abstract meaning of the phrase *far fetched,* just as we are invited to realize the radical irony of having the talking room serviced by a *dumb*-waiter. Whatever the lax gabble in the parlor, Thoreau's own language has certainly not lost its nerve. Indeed, by the end of the passage we may think it has rather too much, for a contorted pun ridicules scholars as idlers (literally those who do no physical work, from the Greek *scholē*, leisure) who dwell on the Isle of Man, i. e., insist on an abstract conception of man artificially isolated from the rest of Nature (*isola*ted = islanded, from Latin *insula*, isle).

Is such punning prose truly muscular or merely nervous? To anatomize its intellectual sinews properly is to trace their connections with the tradition of linguistic speculation that Thoreau inherited and in a sense perfected. Many of Thoreau's puns escape notice because they are essentially learned jokes about the radical meanings of words. The Harvard Class of 1837 upon whom Emerson urged the role of the American Scholar had received an education dominated by the study of language to a degree difficult to imagine today, when most American university graduates cannot read their diplomas. Emerson's central term *scholar* then connoted specifically a student of classical antiquity in the original languages. Thoreau used his Harvard education not only to become one of the best classicists among the Transcendentalists but to acquire some ability in a half-dozen languages. If his erudition never matched that of Theodore Parker, who learned some twenty languages to disqualify himself for the Unitarian ministry, Thoreau's devotion to language study exceeded that of most in his class. In ways previously unrealized it shaped not only his style but his thought.

The achievements of comparative philology in the later nineteenth century were so revolutionary and definitive that they have eclipsed the earlier tentative blunderings toward a science of language. But before the concept of a distinct Indo-European language family was firmly established, a host of scholars noted similarities between languages and tried to explain them by postulating various forms of *ur*-language. We need reminding that many men applied phonetics to etymology with varying plausibility long before the brothers Grimm clarified the laws of phonological change. Thoreau's demonstrable indebtedness to eighteenth-century speculation on this topic was massive. French sources exercised a particular influence upon him, and the unfamiliarity of this material makes it well worth retracing in detail.

Thoreau's ideas about language were shaped to a considerable extent by the previous century because the Enlightenment enjoyed an unusually long half-life in the nascent United States. When Thoreau graduated from Harvard Boston was still Federalist in spirit and rather eighteenth-century in tone. Not surprisingly, our essentially provincial culture tended to lag behind intellectual fashions on the continent. Just as Calvinism lingered in America long after losing its European impetus, so the rationalistic Unitarianism that had officially replaced it as the regnant religion in early nineteenth-century Boston was essentially a holdover from the Enlightenment spirit. The philosophical curriculum at Thoreau's Harvard was dominated by Locke and the Scottish common-sense philosophers. In seeking to challenge what Emerson stigmatized as "the corpse-cold Unitarianism of Brattle Street," the Transcendentalists looked to European Romanticism for inspiration, to be sure, but eighteenth-century authors figured heavily in Emerson's omnivorous reading. Rather colorless, abstract, and balanced, Hawthorne's prose style, so curiously at odds with his material, is only one of the more obvious examples of how the Enlightenment legacy continued to shape mid-century American literature. "In all the dissertations on language, men forget the language that is, that is really universal, the inexpressible meaning that is in all things, everywhere," the young Thoreau complained in his journal (August 23, 1845), and his reference to what he casually lumped together as "all the dissertations on language" testifies to his familiarity with the Enlightenment tradition of linguistic speculation.

In the *Cratylus* Plato had discussed whether the relation between words and the objects they denoted was natural or only conventional, but the fountainhead for such speculation in the eighteenth century was of course the *Essay Concerning Human Understanding* (1690), the third book of which Locke entitled "Of Words." As the apostle of representative government and religious toleration, Locke was enormously influential in America, and the *Essay* [*Essay Concerning Human Understanding*] long remained a key text in almost all college curricula, where it served to link epistemology firmly with semantic inquiry: "When I first began this Discourse of the Understanding, and a good while after, I had not the least thought that any consideration of words was at all necessary to it. But when, having passed over the original and composition of our ideas, I began to examine the extent and certainty of our knowledge, I found it had so near a connection with words, that, unless their force and manner of signification were first well observed, there could be very little said clearly and pertinently concerning knowledge."[4] For Locke, language, like government, issues from a social contract: "*Words* . . . came to be made use of by men as the signs of their ideas; not by any natural connexion that there is between particular articulate sounds and certain ideas, for then there would be but one language amongst all men; but by a voluntary imposition, whereby such a word is made arbitrarily the mark of such an idea" (3.2.1). Just as language is only conventionally associated with ideas, so Lockean doctrine holds that mental ideas themselves are at least one step removed from external reality. But "because men would not be thought to talk barely of their own imagination, but of things as really they are; therefore they often suppose the *words to stand also for the reality of things*" (3.2.5). Locke inveighs tirelessly against this tendency as the origin of philosophical and social confusion.

But while his labors thus tend to set language at a double remove from reality, his sensationalism leads him to "remark how great a dependence our words have on common sensible ideas; and how those which are made use of to stand for actions and notions quite removed from sense, have their rise from thence, and from obvious sensible ideas are transferred to more abstruse significations, and made to stand for ideas that come not under the cognizance of our sense. . . . *Spirit,* in its primary signification, is breath; *angel,* a messenger: and I doubt not but, if we could trace them to their sources, we should find, in all languages, the names which stand for things that fall not under our senses to have had their first rise from sensible ideas" (3.1.5). The result is a certain ambivalence about the relation between language and physical reality, for by means of the dogma of sensationalism "we may give some kind of guess what kind of notions they were, and whence derived, which filled their minds who were the first beginners of languages, and how nature, even in the naming of things, unawares suggested to men the originals and principles of all their knowledge" (3.1.5).

In his *Curiosities of Literature, and the Literary Character Illustrated* (New York: Leavitt, 1846), an edition of which Thoreau owned, J. C. D'Israeli could joke about the "Lock on the human understanding" that this philosophy had come finally to represent (5). But to the eighteenth century the Englishman seemed to furnish the key. His impact upon philosophy of language in France was especially marked, and imaginatively reconstructing the primitive genesis of speech along quasi-Lockean lines became a European intellectual pastime. In his *Essai sur l'origine des connaissances humaines* (1746) Condillac followed Locke's hint in making the origin of language the cornerstone of his entire philosophy. According to Condillac, "the only way to acquire knowledge is to trace our ideas back to their origin, to observe their genesis . . . to compare them under all possible relations" (*Essai* 1.1.7.67), and this analysis is essentially linguistic, for as he proclaimed in the Preface to *La Langue des calculs* (1798), "every language is an analytic method and every analytic method is a language."[5]

But to Condillac Locke's extreme conventionalism seemed untenable: "Let us imagine a totally arbitrary language, such that analogy had determined neither the choice of words nor their different senses. That language would be a gibberish that nobody could learn" (*Language des calculs,* 2.1). He therefore postulated a radical language of gesture and expression, which he

styled the language of action: "The elements of the language of action are born with man, and those elements are the organs that the author of our nature has given us. There is thus an innate language although there are no innate ideas. Indeed, it was necessary that the elements of some language, prepared in advance, should precede our ideas, for without signs of some kind it would be impossible for us to analyze our thoughts" (*La logique, ou les premiers développemens de l'art de penser* [1780], 2.2.) Primitive man expressed himself involuntarily in this radical language of action in response to such emotional stimuli as desire and pain. When the first observer found himself spontaneously "reading" such behavior, language was born—or rather discovered, since for Condillac, unlike Locke, the roots of language lie in a biological need for sheer self-expression independent of any communicative aim. From this natural language of action and the accidental discovery of its utility, men evolved the more complex symbolic system of articulate speech. Since men were always guided by a necessary principle of analogy in doing so, all signs are ultimately natural; but in the course of linguistic development arbitrary social agreement comes to play an increasingly important role in determining the meanings of words. Ordinary languages today are vitiated for Condillac by the fact that so much of their vocabulary derives remotely from other languages in a way that obscures the radical physical analogies underlying all words. If the principle of analogy could have had free play in ordinary language, then "one would reason as nature teaches us to reason, and move effortlessly from discovery to discovery" (*Langue des calculs,* 2.1). As it is, philosophy lacks *une langue bien faite*; and our best hope lies in devising for the individual sciences well-made languages like mathematics or like the rigorous terminology that Condillac inspired Lavoisier to invent successfully for chemistry.

Throughout the French Enlightenment philosophical speculation about language revolved boisterously and erratically within the orbit of Condillac's logical empiricism. In *Réflexions philosophiques sur l'origine des langues et la signification des mots* (1748) Maupertuis began by hypothesizing how a solitary man might invent language and emerged with a metaphysic that resembled Berkeley's. For assuming that a solitary man would invent language to differentiate perceptions he was vigorously criticized by Diderot, Voltaire, and Turgot, who insisted that words are used primarily in a social situation to designate objects. Rousseau's early *Essai sur l'origine des langues* rejected both Condillac and the assumptions of a private language of perception. Although it was only published posthumously, his ideas about language colored several of his works. As the natural foci for a pastoral society of herdsmen, watering-places gave birth to language, Rousseau asserted, and speech was first developed beside ponds by primitive swains as a means of seducing girls busy dipping their jugs. This charming myth was rather confused, since he argued simultaneously that our first languages were "filles du plaisir et non du besoin," but also that the cooperative labor involved in digging wells necessarily made man linguistic.[6] But emotion remained for Rousseau the essence of language. In *Émile* (1762) he postulated a vocal parallel to Condillac's language of action, claiming that a natural language common to all men survives in the cries of infants. Regrettably children forget the expressive natural speech that is their birthright, and only nursemaids retain any skill at communicating through it.

While Rousseau dreamed of primitive languages bubbling up by still waters, Poisinet de Sivry imagined that our first speech was forged in fire. In *Origines des premiers sociétés . . . et des idiomes anciens et modernes* (1770) he endeavored to prove that the Celts were the first to form a civil society—a step to which they were prompted by a vast conflagration that destroyed the forests in which they had previously roamed as wild brutes. This theory happily confirmed France in her role as the mistress of civilization *par excellence,* for he held that all other human societies had been inspired to coalesce by the example of the Celts. Poisinet de Sivry grounded his entire historical theory in philology, because inspection had convinced him that all existing languages were derived from the Celtic, with the most marked analogies evident in terms denoting fire and heat.

This effort to establish Celtic as the original language was seconded by other patriotic Frenchmen like Jacques LeBrigand, the author of *Observations fondamentales sur les langues anciennes et modernes* (1787). Of course any attempt to discover the first form of speech necessarily intertwined or collided with the centuries-old tradition of learned Christian speculation about the primitive tongue.[7] Did traces of Adamic speech survive in Hebrew, or had they all been confounded at Babel? If God was the Word, what role did he play in the genesis of language? In eighteenth-century France Rousseau was not alone in feeling some uneasiness about the way in which Condillac's sensationalism seemed to leave no room for the supernatural. Despite the generally skeptical tenor of Diderot and d'Alembert's *Encyclopédie,* the anonymous author of its article "Langue" concluded that the chicken-and-egg riddle concerning the priority of society or language could only be solved by postulating a God who created both simultaneously. If any irony attaches to this judgment, that may be a natural consequence of handling a question as exhaustively controverted in the eighteenth century as whether the origin of language was divine—a topic that inspired savants to spawn dissertations by the score. Irony certainly characterizes Herder's treatment of the theme in his *Über den Ursprung der Sprache* (1772), where he answers the question propounded by the Berlin Academy in such as way as to mock both extreme positions, and winds up

doubting "that the origins of the first human language, even though it were Hebrew, can ever be completely elaborated."[8]

Herder's effort to dismiss the venerable problem as senseless was in the long run to carry the day, so that when the Linguistic Society of Paris was founded in 1866 its charter forbade the acceptance of any communication concerning the origin of language. But speculation on the topic was too inveterate to be quickly extinguished. Herder's prize essay was immediately attacked by his master Johann Georg Hamann in the *Philologische Einfälle und Zweifel* (1772), as part of the latter's campaign against the Enlightenment philosophy of language. Proudly Protestant, pre-romantic, and indeed proto-existentialist (Kierkegaard was in his debt), Hamann poured forth a flood of cryptic essays and tracts like the *Kreuzzüge des Philologen* (1762), in which he dramatized himself as "the Philologian" crusading against the presumptions of Enlightenment "philosophers." To love wisdom as a true philosopher should was in his view to revere the *logos,* the word, reason as embodied in the ordinary language that the *philosophes* rather distrusted but which God had chosen as the vehicle of divine revelation. For their ideal of a purified, artificial language he had only contempt, stressing instead the embodied human wisdom of natural language as the ultimate criterion of philosophical validity. He shrewdly criticized his fellow Königsberger Immanuel Kant for ignoring the topic of language and attempting to philosophize in a technical, abstract terminology that often violated the normal conditions for understanding human discourse: "Metaphysics misuses all the figures and word-signs and figures of speech of our empirical knowledge as mere hieroglyphs and types of ideal relations and as a result of this learned mischief transforms the straightforwardness of language into such a senseless, whirling, unsteady, indeterminable something (= x), that nothing remains but a windy murmuring, a magical shadow-play, at best . . . the talisman and rosary of a transcendental superstition regarding *entia rationis,* their empty sacks and slogan."[9] Oscillating between sarcastic eloquence and ironic obscurity, tinged with religious mysticism, and influential for the succeeding generation of German Romantics, Hamann's verbalism, as he termed his disorganized philosophy, pointed to the multivalence of ordinary language as a deep reservoir of spiritual truth. At the same time the stylistic opacities in which, like Carlyle, he delighted forced his audience to become more consciously involved in the hermeneutic process. Lurking murkily in his work was the implication that Christianity could be intellectually refurbished were theology reconceived in radical terms as the linguistic rules that govern talk about God.

Like Hamann the savant Charles de Brosses questioned the practicality of creating an artificial universal language for philosophic purposes, but in other respects he was quintessentially representative of the Enlightenment mentality that the German assailed. His two-volume *Traité mécanique de la formation des langues et des principes physiques de l'étymologie* (Paris: Saillant, 1765) was devoted to showing that "the basis of universal language already exists" (1:xxii, my translation). Downplaying Condillac's germinal language of action but retaining his deductively empirical approach, he argued that names were first attached to things by a process in no way arbitrary and conventional but rather through "a true system of necessity determined by two causes. One is the formation of the vocal organs, which can only render certain sounds analogous to their structure; the other is the nature and property of the real objects that one wishes to name. This obliges us to employ for their name sounds that portray them, to establish between the word and the thing a rapport by which the word can excite an idea of the thing" (1:xii-xiii). The result was a classic bow-wow theory, for according to de Brosses the essence of all language is onomatopoetic imitation of external reality. Since "there are few things that do not make noise," they acquired their original names as the cuckoo is called from its cry (1:7). Savages today display the same process when they christen a cannon POUTOUE, not NIZALIE. This primary principle accounted for most names in aboriginal speech, de Brosses believed (without apparently perceiving that it left primitive man inhabiting a pastoral pandemonium fit to drown out the hubbub of Paris).

As for objects that make no noise, "the organ assumes, as much as it can, the very appearance of the object that it wishes to paint with the voice: it gives a hollow sound if the object is hollow, or rough if the object is rough; so that the sound that results from the natural form and movement of the organ put in that state becomes the name of the object, a name that resembles it by the rough or hollow sound that the chosen pronunciation carries to the ear." Thus the voice employs organs that properly represent "either the thing or some quality or effect of the thing that it wishes to name" (1:8). Therefore de Brosses concludes that "there exists a primitive language, organic, physical, and necessary, common to the entire human race, which no people in the world either knows or practices in its first simplicity; but which all men speak nonetheless and which constitutes the first foundation of the language of all countries; a foundation that the immense superstructure of accessories built upon it hardly lets one perceive" (1:14-15). To his credit he did not really seek to romanticize this language, admitting elsewhere that it must have been "fort pauvre," but in enthusiastically pursuing his argument he tended to lose hold of this reservation (2:84).

Neglecting any systematic inventory of objects, de Brosses left somewhat vague and incomplete the question of how many might be said to have naturally corresponding sounds. But that did not really flaw his theory logically, for granted the assumption that an original working vocabulary was phonetically determined, the rest of language could be imagined to derive from it metaphorically through a similarly materialistic process: "Since the fundamental system for human language and the first fabrication of words is in no way arbitrary, but rather of a necessity determined by nature itself, it is impossible that the accessory system of derivation should not share the nature of the primary system from which it emerged as a second order, impossible that it not resemble it in being more necessary than conventional, at least in part of its branches" (1:xvi). Hedging at times almost as if frightened by the deterministic implications of his argument, he claimed like a good Cartesian that his treatise dealt with "the material operation of the voice, not with the spiritual operation of the soul that directs it," then added in the next breath that since we can often infer causes from effects, language allows us to understand "the completely spiritual operation of the human soul that directs the play of the machine" (1:24-26). Locating the truth of both words and ideas referentially "in their conformity with things," he sought to erect a mechanical theory of etymology into the philosopher's heuristic *par excellence*. As he reasoned with cheerful circularity, "the art of deriving words was named *etymology*, that is to say, truthful discourse; ἔτυμος *verus*, λογος, *sermo* (from ἐτος, *verus, quod est* or from ἐιμι, *sum*)" (1:27).

Devoting nearly a thousand pages to this theme, de Brosses possessed just enough erudition to render it plausible, for his knowledge of the European languages permitted him to buttress it selectively with numerous examples while his relative ignorance of non-Indo-European data left him serenely untroubled by doubts. His theory involved him, of course, in the claim that phonemes, which he called germs, have inherent semantic meanings. A rapid global survey of several score languages convinced him that similar labials and dentals were always used "to express the first childish words *Papa* and *Mama*," after which atypical paradigm case he confined himself largely to the Indo-European family (1:222). "The voice of disgust and aversion is labial: it strikes on top of the instrument at the end of the cord, on the elongated lips, *Fi! vae! pouah!*" he explained a few pages earlier, but he failed to see the implications of that claim for his child psychology (1:205).

He contented himself instead with haphazard illustrations of the meanings supposedly inherent in sounds: "The voice of grief strikes on the bass cords: it is drawn out, aspirated, and profoundly guttural, *heu! hélas!*" while the voice of surprise ("Ah Ah! Eh! oh oh!") and joy ("Ha Ha Ha! Hi Hi Hi Hi!") are higher up the scale and more rapid. "The voice of doubt and dissent is spontaneously nasal *hum, hom, in, non*: with the difference that doubt is prolonged, being an uncertain feeling, while pure dissent is brief, being a totally determinate movement" (2:204-5). Thus he merrily located the value of vowel sounds in man's emotional make-up like Rousseau, without worrying much lest this jeopardize the more passive, mechanical and mimetic theory that he generally expounded concerning consonants and the relation between words and things. Admittedly the articulation *fr* became associated with *fear* through "an infraction of the radical analogy," since "its derivatives *frango, fragor, fracas,* which onomatopoetically depict sudden noise and rupture, do not paint the feeling of surprise and fear that it inspires." But though he conceded that the process of derivation might result in "actual opposition . . . between term and idea" psychologically speaking, he generally ignored the problems this posed for his theory (2:91). It seemed evident that "man spontaneously forms the names that he gives to each speech organ from the character or inflection proper to that organ: as *gorge, langue, dent, bouche,* or *babine,*" and "though men have been able to agree to give other names also to these organs, nature has been the guide that most often determined these words mechanically, which one must therefore regard as words almost necessarily belonging to the primitive language" (1:226-27). Citing Leibnitz's similar speculations, he wonders why the character *st* so frequently denotes firmity, fixity, and immobility ("Examples: *Stare, stabilite, stips, stupide . . . stamen, stagnum . . . stella . . . strenuus, stapia, structure, estat, consistence, estime, stuc, sterile . . . stay, stead, stone* etc."), while hollowness and excavation are represented by *sc* ("ϛκάλλω, ϛκάπτω, ϛκαδη, ϛκέλλω, scutum, scaturire, scabies, scyphus, sculpere, scrobs, scrutari, secare, scolto, ecu, ecol, ecuelle, scarifier, scier, scabreux, sculpture, scop, screw, schinden, schall,* etc."). The answer is furnished by his phonetic semantics, for "the teeth being the most immobile of the six vocal organs, the firmest dental letter, namely *t*, was mechanically employed to designate fixity, just as to designate hollowness and cavity one employs *k* or *c*, the guttural, the gorge being the most hollow and cavernous of the six vocal organs. As for the *s* or nasal, which joins freely with other articulations, it is here, as often elsewhere, like a more marked augmentative, tending to make the painting more forceful" (1:238-40).

De Brosses's penchant for digressing from his materials to draw philosophic conclusions meant that after an initial inventory of palatals, gutturals, labials, nasals, liquids, and dentals he never completed any systematic classification of all significant sonal combinations. But his theory may indeed have gained in persuasiveness from that fact. He did provide lengthy lists of European words supposedly explaining why *n*, the most liquid of letters, designates anything like *navis* that acts upon liquid; why *fl* naturally designates fluid motion in air, fire or water; and why other phonemes and consonantal clusters like *sl, sw, r, g, sr, h, s,* and *sm* have various inherent meanings that form the basis of the primitive universal language. Like most other literate Americans Thoreau owned a copy of Hugh Blair's *Lectures on Rhetoric and Belles Lettres* (1783), a massively influential work that went through at least thirty-seven American editions by 1853. Summarizing de Brosses's theories with some skepticism but qualified approval, Blair referred to him as "the Author, who has carried his speculations on this subject the farthest."[10] Thoreau must have read Blair's two lectures "Rise and Progress of Language" with close attention, and he probably accepted the invitation of Blair's footnote to consult the *Traité mécanique.*

Though many of its etymologies were erroneous, perhaps the majority were true and illuminating. As an example of what Thoreau might have learned from it, consider again his discussion of the language of our parlors (above). While sporting with the French root of *parlor, palaver,* and *parliamentary* to demonstrate that our words are fetched too far from the kitchen, Thoreau interjects, "The dinner even is only the parable of a dinner, commonly." Why this slightly strained locution? As de Brosses admirably explained,

> *Parler* can come from παραλαλείν *obloqui* or from παραβαλλείν *conferre, conjicere.* I must choose between these two etymologies: the meaning of both is relevant but that of the first more directly so, and it would at first appear preferable in many respects. . . . But I know that simple verbs often take a very different sense when compounded with a preposition . . . like *iacere* and *conjicere.* Moreover in examining the words that express the same idea as *parler* I immediately find the Greek παραβολη . . . and the Latin *parabola,* of which Quintillian determines the sense, 1. 5, chap. 11. . . . Here is the word *parabola* become almost a synonym for the word *discourse;* and I see that the centuries of late Latinity (according to DU-CANGE) took it in this sense. . . . If I experience any remaining difficulty over the two elements *b* and *o,* which the Greek παραβολη contains but which the French *parler* lacks, I need only compare the words of parallel dialects; I will find the two missing elements, the one in the Spanish *palabra;* the other in the French *parole,* and I shall see that all the elements of the original word reappear in one dialect or another. . . . Thereby I can be sure that the French *parler* and all its derivatives come from παραβολὴ and παραβαλλέιν, words composed from the primitive βαλλω which itself derives from the root *Bal,* which has produced numerous other branches very distant from this one and which has itself no connection of any kind with the idea expressed by the word *parler.*

(2:436-38)

Even a good classical scholar might not recognize that French *parler* = talk is cognate with English *parable* = symbolic representation, both deriving through late

Latin from Greek *parabole* = comparison and ultimately from Greek *paraballein* = throw together. The standard English dictionaries available to Thoreau, such as Johnson's and Webster's, exhausted their ingenuity in tracing our Romance derivatives to the French *parler,* then gave up the chase, leaving no hint of the relationship to the classical roots and their more direct descendants. That Thoreau could consciously exploit this rather recondite etymological connection corroborates the likelihood that he had read de Brosses, and it certainly testifies to his considerable interest in comparative philology.

When de Brosses derived *parler* from a primitive root *Bal,* he was relying on the work of his friend, the Protestant scholar Antoine Court de Gebelin, who collaborated with Benjamin Franklin in publications advancing the cause of American independence. Influenced reciprocally by de Brosses, Court de Gebelin conceived the ambitious plan of his *Monde primitif analisé et comparé avec le monde moderne,* the prospectus of which appeared with the first volume in 1773. For his subscribers he promised to compile what today might be called an anthropological encyclopedia. All knowledge about primitive culture he classified under two divisions: the first concerned words while the second dealt with things. Envisioning etymology as the main key to prehistory, he proposed to devote the bulk of his enterprise to elucidating the development of languages by composing an introductory treatise on the physical principles of language and writing, a universal grammar, a dictionary of the primitive language, a comparative dictionary of languages, individual etymological dictionaries for French, Latin, Greek, and Hebrew, an etymological onomasticon, and a bibliography of etymological authorities. Fortified with a battery of such reference works establishing Celtic as the most primitive European language and God as its ultimate author, he would then undertake a multi-volume exegesis of ancient history and religious mythology as well as ancillary dissertations on primitive arts, sciences, and folkways like poetry, mathematics, agricultural laws, and the calendar. The project was a grandiose tribute to the Enlightenment's fascination with early man: Court de Gebelin assured subscribers that it would be "the key to all centuries and to all human knowledge. It will demonstrate that remotest antiquity, transitional periods, and present times are inseparable from each other and form one continuous whole" (1:7). When death came to the savant in 1784, he had managed to complete only nine volumes; but these five thousand labyrinthine pages sufficed to earn their author a deserved reputation for great learning.

Not, alas, a lasting reputation. Like his pre-scientific linguistics, his literary anthropology was soon outmoded, and today his huge quartos seem artifacts more remote than the primitive world. Few read them now; indeed, few subscribers probably read them even then. But one who did plunder this storehouse of misinformed wisdom was Thoreau. By happy coincidence there exists a holograph dated November 14, 1836, in which a young Harvard senior isolated in the primitive culture of Massachusetts records an encounter with the *Monde primitif.* Since Thoreau apparently whipped up this hasty pudding as a report to the Institute of 1770, it gives us an intimate glimpse of the dissipations then favored by his college fraternity:

> A discussion having arisen in our famous club (Grex Epicuri, etc.—"quae vivit ut edet, non edit ut vivat,"), respecting the origin of the word *ballot,* some affirming that it was derived from the Greek, while others stopped short at the French *ballotte,* it was thought advisable to settle the question at once by a reference to suitable authorities.
>
> Bal was a Celtic monosyllable, and primitive and radical word, which signified the sun; and consequently, 1st all that is beautiful and brilliant like the sun; 2ndly all that is elevated; 3rdly all that is round. Under each of these heads, this word has become the source of a multitude of words in the French language; being pronounced by different people, Bal, Bel, Bol, and with the lision of the vowel, Bla, Blo, etc.
>
> Hence result 10 branches derived from that single root, and from these a cinquantaine of divisions.
>
> Under the 1st branch are found the names of some plants and animals.

2nd Bel, meaning beauty.

3rd Bal, become Bla, the name of different colors,—of the words blanc, bleu, blond, blason, etc.

4th Bail, a name relating to power, to preservation and protection.

5th Bal, relating to elevation, whence Balcon, Balustrade.

6th Bal, signifying to protectect [sic] with an envelope, whence Bale, Baline, Baldaquin, etc.

7th Bal, relating to the physical action de s'elever en s'elancant; whence Bal, Balet, Balade, Baladoire, Baliste, etc.; whence also the Greeks have made βαλλω.

8th Bal, signifying greatness, whence Baleine, Bloc.

9th Bal, signifying rotundity; whence Bale, Balon, Balote, Boule, etc.

10th Some words compounded of Bal, joined to others.[11]

Thoreau has faithfully summarized the entry "Bal" in Court de Gebelin's *Dictionnaire etymologique François-Celte,* where philological insights jostle drastic oversimplifications. *Ballot* is indeed descended from an Indo-European root signifying rotundity (*bhel-*, blow, swell up), as the entry illuminatingly suggests; and that root might conceivably be connected to a similar root (*bhel-*, shine) reflected in Beltane, the Celtic Mayday celebration. But possessing a fertile mind and few laws restricting phonetic development, Court de Gebelin expounded the various branches of this root, prolific enough in itself, with an anagogic passion, tracing them ultimately to one solar divinity together with the derivatives of several other distinct Indo-European roots (e.g., *Bel*, beauty, from I. E. *deu-*, do, via Latin *bonus, bene; Bal,* envelope, from I. E. *pel-*, skin; *Bal,* throw, from I. E. *gwel-*, throw, via Greek *ballein, ballizein,* to throw, dance). Since in his view all languages were one, for lagniappe he also added unrelated Semitic derivatives like *balsamum.* But if his analogizing habit of mind often betrays him into howlers, it also scores enough real triumphs to dignify his naive methodology; for to one ignorant of the phonetic laws governing linguistic evolution in the Indo-European family, the conceptual analogies underlying his mistakes seem no more far-fetched than the conceptual analogies underlying genuine and plausible derivations.

Brewed from equal parts of fantasy and far-sightedness, Court de Gebelin's etymologies were heady stuff for a young man with Thoreau's literary ambitions. If *parler* derives from the root *Bal* as de Brosses demonstrated, what then is the essence of our common *parlance*? In Court de Gebelin Thoreau found an authority for regarding speech itself as physical activity, a balancing act, as it were, the beautiful jugglery of tossing words about, a form of verbal ballet. Since modern American education takes for granted a vital link between throwing the ball and throwing the bull, we tend to forget what foreign-language study could mean to a child of the Puritans in early Victorian Massachusetts. By speaking a man might essentially be performing an ecstatic dance to worship the sun. Indeed, almost all speech is inherently parabolic insofar as Court de Gebelin's primitive language consisted of a limited number of monosyllables designating only physical objects, which necessarily developed through metaphorical extension. The ancients naturally adopted allegorical modes of expression, for these "were necessitated primarily by the nature of language" and congruent with the multivalent nature of words themselves (1:16). As the Frenchman explained in his treatise *Génie allégorique des anciens,* "however one imagines antiquity, one cannot deny that to paint its ideas it was forced to rely on figures, on Emblems, on Metaphors, on Symbols of every kind." Therefore, exegeses of the hermetic forms in which the ancients allegedly embodied their wisdom bulked large in the *Monde primitif.*

What Thoreau could thus imbibe from its pages was a paradoxical vision of primeval truths obvious to all and yet somehow hidden from sight. He certainly read more widely in Court de Gebelin than the dispute before his debating society demanded. As the young Harvard senior copied out, carefully though not without misspellings, "From the primitive word Ver, signifying water, a monosyllable [sic] frequently occurring in the names of rivers—as Var, Varine, Varna, Veresis, Vere, Vir, Vire) is derived the word verité; for as water, by reason of its transparency and limpidness, is the mirror of bodies—of physical êtres, so also is truth equally the mirror of ideas—of intellectual êtres, representing them in a manner faithful and clear, as the water does a physical body, Gebelin—Monde Primitif.—Dictionnaire Etymol. Francoise." And he probably retained this mistaken belief years later when his chapter "The Ponds," that elaborate paean to their purity, made Walden the moral and symbolic center of his great book. "After all, man is the great poet . . . not Homer," observed Thoreau in *A Week on the Concord and Merrimack Rivers,* "and our language itself . . . his work." (1:97-98). Thus the early book records an ecstatic moment when the poetic voyagers "are reminded by interior evidence of the permanence of universal laws." Sitting on the bank contemplating the sunset limpidly "reflected on the water," they transcend "faith" and "faintly remembered . . . knowledge" in "sublimer visions"—"when we do not have to believe, but come into actual contact with Truth, and are related to her in the most direct and intimate way" (1:309-10). Paradoxically but understandably enough, the young writer who could cultivate such symbolic obliquity chose "to build my lodge on some southern slope and there take the life the gods send me" (April 5, 1841) because he felt that his life required "a greater baldness," greater perhaps than words themselves could afford: "I seek a directer relation to the sun" (April 11, 1841).

Often quoting de Brosses, the *Monde primitif* refined and systematized his semantic phonetics. In the volume *Historie naturelle de la Parole, ou l'origine du langage et de l'écriture* Court de Gebelin explained that the seven vowel sounds represented distinct ideas. Thus short *a* "always denoted the sensation of the state in which we find ourselves and which is proper for us, possession and domination" (2:289). Long *e* "designated the sensation of life and all that contributes to life: the earth, for example," while short *e*, by contrast, "was consecrated to existence, to the feeling that one has of it, and to everything concerning existence" (3:290). Such Delphic generalities possessed just enough specificity to obscure the fact that each might be applied indifferently to almost any phenomena. His treatment of other vowels was more definite and bolder. Implicitly challenging de Brosses's equation between vowel sounds and the emotions, he sought instead to link each to a distinct sense. "The sound *i* relates to the hand, to everything about the sense of touch, and to the concerns and uses that result from it," while "the sound *o* designates the sensation of sight, the eye, and all its effects . . . the sound *u,* the action of inhaling or swallowing, taste and the sense of smell . . . and finally the sound *ou,* hearing, the ear, and all their effects." Somewhat nervously he admitted that "these rapports, to tell the truth, will not be conserved with the same simplicity by all peoples," but "despite all these inconveniences, and in the middle of all these ruins . . . our principle remains intact and unshakeable."

Nonetheless he was generally persuaded that "vowels count for nothing in comparing words" (3:47), enunciating the total intraconvertibility of all vowels as his Tenth Etymological Commandment. The values of the various consonants he characterized somewhat like de Brosses, concluding that "sweet and agreeable objects will be painted by labials; sonorous ones will be the lot of the dentals; repulsive objects, that of the nasal *n.* They will employ the lingual *l* for everything liquid and flowing; and the lingual *r* for whatever is rough or rolling; objects that are deep and hollowed into concavities will be the prerogative of gutturals; the sibilant will be for whistling things, etc." (3:335). Haunted by fancied correspondences between sounds and objects, he sought to extend this principle by showing how it shaped the sixteen written characters of the first primitive alphabet. In his view all letters were pictographs representing either a bodily organ somehow associated with the sound in his elaborate scheme (e.g., most vowels, *g, c, s, r,* and *l*) or a symbolic object intimately related to the value of the sound. Thus the character *m* designating "in all languages the idea of Mother, of maternity, of a productive and fruitful being" was really a shorthand sketch of a tree, which primitive man had selected as the hieroglyph of these qualities (3:410).

"Talk of learning our letters and being literate!" exclaimed Thoreau. "Why the roots of our letters are things" (October 16, 1859). He shared the romantic era's fascination with Egyptian hieroglyphics and was aware of Champollion's successful decipherment of them; but occult and garbled theories like those of Court de Gebelin probably did more to shape his conception of them as the radically physical basis of a primitive secret language that could serve as a model for concretizing stylistic innovations.[12] "Shall I be indebted to another man's thought?" he asked himself while laboring over **Walden.** "Shall I not have words as fresh as my thoughts? A genuine thought can find expression if it have to invent hieroglyphics" (September 7, 1851). Similarly Diderot had conceived of the highest works of literary genius as "a tissue of hieroglyphs stacked one upon another," painting thought rather than merely expressing it through sophisticated onomatopoetic correspondences between the syllables of words and the subjects they denoted.[13] In this respect his beliefs were largely congruent with the *Monde primitif,* which held that "every Art answering primary needs," such as language and writing, "contains today both what it has always been and what it has become through human industry" (1:5). Thoreau would surely have agreed.

Condorcet had claimed that intellectual progress made possible the development of language, but Court de Gebelin sought to reverse the relation. Arguing that "ideas could only develop when languages began to perfect themselves and rise above their primitive state" (1:79), he thus envisioned language itself as the dynamic of human progress. The relation of language to thought was a central topic for Destutt de Tracy, Cabanis, and de Gérando, the *idéologues* who dominated French philosophy in the last decade of the eighteenth century. Often cited by the Scottish commonsense philosophers, their work was avidly read by Emerson, and it was at his instigation that in 1838 the young Thoreau dutifully set about transcribing portions of de Gérando's *Histoire comparée des systèmes de philosophie,* which included a section devoted to the development of language. In his *Des Signes et de l'art de penser, considerés dans leurs rapports mutuels* (Paris, 1800) the French philosopher exhaustively explored the question of language. In his doctrine of signs he gave quasi-linguistic status to the function of physical sensations themselves, arguing that "the smell of a rose is the sign of the ideas of color and form that the smell excites."[14] Conventional linguistic signs like the word *rose* are relatively transparent, pointing less to themselves than to the objects they serve to signify, de Gérando felt; but such natural signs continue to obtrude themselves on the mind *per se* even as they excite other ideas in it. He did not push this notion to Keats's romantic extreme and cry, "O for a Life of Sensations rather than of Thoughts!" But disagreeing somewhat with his fellow *idéologues,* he did question whether the individual sciences could be greatly advanced simply by constructing well-made artificial languages for them, since their construction in his view presupposed the scientific advance that one desired to secure.

Defining the philosopher's task as the analysis of sensations and ideas, de Gérando called instead for a thoroughgoing scrutiny of the ways in which natural language reflects our actual learning processes:

> We have felt the need of remaking the language in its entirety and, in some sense, recommencing the education of the human mind. The surest and perhaps the most truly efficacious means of accomplishing this great project would be, I think, the formation of a philosophical dictionary truly worthy of the name—one, that is to say, that would in some sense be a genealogical tree of our ideas and of the signs we use. Such a dictionary would be a sequence of definitions strictly bound to one another. Each notion would be defined in it by showing how it was acquired, or at least how it should have been acquired. The mind would find itself naturally led to *create* the words rather than seeking merely to *explain* them to itself. . . . In it one would seek to explain not so much how we speak as how we think; the conventions of the language would be presented in it as *results,* not as *principles.* . . . The order of facts would be the only order in it. It would not . . . be de-

signed to be consulted occasionally, but it would have to be the object of a connected reading. . . . A definition would never be offered in it except in accordance with one general rule—that of determining an idea by means of tracing it back to the ideas that must have preceded it in the age when language was instituted among men. . . . The dictionary would in some sense embrace the history of mankind and would serve as a natural introduction to all the sciences. The study of it would be necessary for all who wished to think well, and its formation would be one of the noblest undertakings of philosophy.

(4:88ff., tr. Kretzmann, 289)

Since this noble undertaking was never undertaken, its outlines remain somewhat hazy, though echoes of de Gérando's project reverberated through some nineteenth-century texts. Insofar as the *Monde primitif* was organized, its leading categories were linguistic, and its etymological dictionaries classified roots alphabetically. Instead of a linguistically grounded encyclopedia with strong philosophical implications, de Gérando apparently wanted a conceptual dictionary drawing upon linguistic evidence. Ordered not alphabetically but genetically, this enlightened synopticon was to constitute an account of the evolution of human consciousness that would be both historical and psychological. By subjecting our moral concepts to analysis, we could rediscover the sources of our ideas, until we recaptured the magic moment when an inspired brute grunted the first primitive *cogito*. How could such a dictionary of ideas help but clarify all the philosophical issues burning in revolutionary France?

Like belling the cat, de Gérando's project left only the question of which philosophers would want to carry it out. With the *idéologues* neoclassic speculation about language exhausted itself in France. Except for throwbacks like Fabre d'Olivet, whose speculations about the universal language in *La langue hébraique restituée* (Paris, 1815-16) borrowed heavily from de Brosses and a century later were to spark the interest of the American linguist Benjamin Whorf, the next generation of French intellectuals was less obsessed with linguistic questions, which were pursued more vigorously in Germany, England, and America. But it is worth emphasizing Thoreau's indebtedness to French Enlightenment thought about language. There is reason to think that he consulted specimens of French scholarship ranging from Ménage's *Dictionnaire étymologique* (1694) to Morin's *Dictionnaire étymologique des mots francois derivés du grec* (1803).[15] He recorded in his notebooks observations on language apparently culled from an eighteenth-century French translation of Christian Garve, the German disciple of Monboddo. He even withdrew from the Harvard library a volume containing the landmark work of Guillaume Postel, *De originibus seu de Hebraicae linguae et gentis antiquitate, deque linguarum variarum affinitate* (1538), a sixty-page Renaissance tract with long lists of lexical parallels between a dozen languages that is often regarded as the first halting step toward a genuine comparative philology. As Thoreau's comments in *Cape Cod* show, though he was amused by the Frenchman's geographical naiveté and chauvinism, he declined, with a wry pun, to dismiss his theories altogether: "But let us not laugh at Postel and his visions. He was perhaps better posted than we" (4:250).

Even where no direct source can be demonstrated, Thoreau's linguistic ideas often echo those of the *philosophes*. In his fascination with the origin of language he is very much their intellectual heir, just as his thinking also reflects Mme. de Staël's emphasis on national languages as the quasi-organic embodiment of collective consciousness both inspiring and limiting all individual thought and expression. When the Vicomte de Bonald cast a jaundiced eye back over the Enlightenment's philosophical dreams from the conservative vantage point of the French Restoration, the second chapter of his *Recherches philosophiques sur les premiers objets de nos connoissances morales* (1818) argued that no man nor men could ever have "invented" language, which together with society must have characterized human existence from its beginnings (divine, as de Bonald thought). In his view all eighteenth-century speculation about language was dominated and flawed by abstract fantasies of primitive man as an isolated individual, a cardboard figure whom the Enlightenment metaphysicians barmily substituted for the social being created by God. As Guy Harnois has observed, de Bonald's characterization of the *philosophes'* linguistic mentality was a shrewd one.[16] And in some respect it also applies to Thoreau. When he went to Walden Pond to write, he said that he wished to transact some private business. But he might as well have claimed to be conducting an experiment to learn whether a solitary man would invent words for his perceptions, to see what kind of speech might actually be generated at a watering-place. Viewed from this angle Thoreau's *Journal* musings about the difficulty of finding words to express original pursuits (above) may remind us of the autobiographical sketch in which a cantankerous young Frenchman of Protestant extraction proclaimed his need a century earlier for "un langage aussi nouveau que mon projet."[17] Indeed, the Yankee's Walden adventure would probably have seemed natural enough to an eighteenth-century French savant.

Notes

1. William Ellery Channing, Jr., *Thoreau the Poet-Naturalist,* ed. F. B. Sanborn (1902; rpt. New York: Biblo and Tannen, 1966), 77n. In a series of articles I have tried to accord this subject the thoughtful consideration Channing suggested: "Charles Kraitsir's Influence upon Thoreau's Theory of Language," *ESQ* [*Emerson Society*

Quarterly] 19 (1973): 262-74; "*Walden's* Dirty Language: Thoreau and Walter Whiter's Geocentric Etymological Theories," *Harvard Library Bulletin* 22 (1974): 117-28; "Scatology and Eschatology: The Heroic Dimensions of Thoreau's Wordplay," *PMLA* 89 (1974): 1043-64. Most recently Philip F. Gura, *The Wisdom of Words: Language, Theology and Literature in The New England Renaissance* (Middletown: Wesleyan Univ. Press, 1981), has rewardingly studied some of the material relevant to Thoreau. But his limited focus on the linguistic thought of the New England Renaissance rather misrepresents the more venerable, cross-cultural tradition of European linguistic speculation that actually influenced Thoreau, as I hope the present article will suggest; see my review in *Modern Philology* 81 (1983): 81-85. I am grateful to the American Council of Learned Societies for a fellowship during 1978-79 that enabled me to conduct the research upon which this article together with further work forthcoming on the topic is based.

2. Letter to B. B. Wiley of April 26, 1857, in *The Writings of Henry David Thoreau,* ed. Bradford Torrey (Boston: Houghton, 1906), 6:301. Subsequent references to Thoreau's *Journal* are by date of entry in this ed., except for entries in the "lost" journal of 1840-41, ed. Perry Miller as *Consciousness in Concord* (Cambridge: Harvard Univ. Press, 1958). Other works cited by volume and page.

3. [*Walden*] 2:270. With J. Lyndon Shanley, ed., *Walden* (Princeton: Princeton Univ. Press, 1971), 401, I believe that as the manuscripts suggest, the first edition's *parlaver* is not an unhappy attempt at humorous coinage but a simple typographical error that marred the etymological relationships Thoreau was concerned to suggest.

4. *An Essay Concerning Human Understanding,* ed. Alexander Campbell Fraser (1894; rpt. New York; Dover, 1959), 3.9.21. On Thoreau's youthful reactions to Locke see J. J. Kwiat, "Thoreau's Philosophical Apprenticeship," *New England Quarterly* 18 (1954): 51-69; for Locke's continuing influence on him see Joel Porte, *Emerson and Thoreau: Transcendentalists in Conflict* (Middletown: Wesleyan Univ. Press, 1966).

5. Cited from *Oeuvres philosophiques de Condillac,* ed. Georges Le Roy (Paris: Presses Universitaires, 1947), 3 vols., my translation. Thoreau's college philosophy text by Dugald Stewart contained a brief notice of Condillac's language theory.

6. Cited by Pierre Juliard, *Philosophies of Language in Eighteenth-Century France* (Hague: Mouton, 1970), 24.

7. On this subject see Russell A. Fraser, *The Language of Adam* (New York: Columbia Univ. Press, 1977).

8. Johann Gottfried Herder, *Essay on the Origin of Language,* tr. Alexander Gode (New York: Ungar, 1966), 151. On the literary implications of Herder's and Hamann's linguistic theories, see esp. Eric A. Blackall, *The Emergence of German as a Literary Language 1700-1775* (Cambridge: Cambridge Univ. Press, 1959), chs. 13 and 14.

9. Tr. Norman Kretzmann, "History of Semantics," *Encyclopedia of Philosophy,* ed. Paul Edwards (New York: Macmillan, 1967), 7:387. In the curious absence of any more comprehensive treatment of the subject, I have relied heavily throughout on Kretzmann's excellent article, 7:358-406.

10. Ed. Harold F. Harding (Carbondale: Southern Illinois Univ. Press, 1965), 102n. For books owned by Thoreau see Walter Harding, *Thoreau's Library* (Charlottesville: Univ. of Virginia Press, 1957). Harvard Library records show Thoreau definitely reading other works by de Brosses in his senior year; see Kenneth Walter Cameron, *Emerson the Essayist* (Hartford: Transcendental Books, 1945), 2:200.

11. Pierpont Morgan MS MA.594, reprinted by Wendell Glick; "Three New Early Manuscripts by Thoreau," *Huntington Library Quarterly* 12 (1951): 68-70. In view of Thoreau's demonstrable acquaintance with Court de Gebelin and de Brosses, Gura's claims for the pivotal importance of Kraitsir's similar work, 126-36, seem implausible.

12. On this subject see John T. Irwin, *American Hieroglyphics: The Symbol of the Egyptian Hieroglyphics in the American Renaissance* (New Haven: Yale Univ. Press, 1980), esp. 3-40, 213. During Thoreau's senior year at Harvard his debating society sponsored a lecture on Egyptian hieroglyphics; see Kenneth W. Cameron, *The Transcendentalists and Minerva,* (Hartford: Transcendental Books, 1958) 1:83.

13. Denis Diderot, "Lettre sur les sourds et muets," *Diderot Studies* 7 (1965): 70.

14. 1:62-63, tr. Kretzmann, 388. For Thoreau's transcriptions from de Gérando see Cameron, *The Transcendentalists and Minerva,* 1:248-53. On the significance of the *idéologues* see H. B. Acton, "The Philosophy of Language of Revolutionary France," *Proceedings of the British Academy* 45 (1959): 199-219.

15. See Glick, 70. For the circulation of Postel's tracts in Transcendental circles see Cameron, *Transcendentalists and Minerva,* 1:24. See also 1:264, for

Thoreau's transcription from Christian Garve; the source of this extract from "Sur la manière d'écrire l'histoire de la philosophie," which Cameron was unable to identify, may have been the translation of Garve's commentary on the lectures of his master Christian Fürchtegott Gellert, *Leçons de Morale* (Utrecht: Schoonhoven, 1772).

16. See *Les théories du language en France de 1660 à 1821* (Paris: Société d'Edition "LES BELLES LETTRES," 1927), ch. 4.

17. Jean-Jacques Rousseau, "Ébauches de Prologue des *Confessions,*" *Oeuvres complètes,* ed. Jean Fabre and Michel Launay (Paris: Editions du Seuil, 1967), 1:70. In *The New Thoreau Handbook* (New York: New York Univ. Press, 1980), 97-98, 115-16, Walter Harding and Michael Meyer point out that there is no evidence that Thoreau read Rousseau; but they are perhaps too ready to minimize the intellectual affinities of the two writers. There is at least incontrovertible evidence that Thoreau wished to read Rousseau, for in 1838 the young college graduate, then very much under Emerson's influence, jotted down as works to be read *La nouvelle Heloise* and *Émile* together with de Staël's *De l'Allemagne*; see Cameron, *Transcendentalists and Minerva,* 2:360, for the list of *legenda* in Thoreau's copy of *Phelps and Squires Travellers' Guide* (1838). Moreover major works by Rousseau and de Staël stood on Emerson's bookshelves where Thoreau often browsed. On Thoreau's relation to Rousseau see, in addition to the comparative studies listed in *The New Thoreau Handbook,* Frederic Garber, *Thoreau's Redemptive Imagination* (New York: New York Univ. Press, 1977), 16-31, 153-57.

Leonard N. Neufeldt (essay date summer 1987)

SOURCE: Neufeldt, Leonard N. "Thoreau's Enterprise of Self-Culture in a Culture of Enterprise." *American Quarterly* 39, no. 2 (summer 1987): 231-51.

[*In the following essay, Neufeldt considers ideas of vocation and "self-culture" in Thoreau's* Walden. *Neufeldt suggests that Thoreau's philosophy of language originated in his hostility toward mainstream notions of economic enterprise.*]

Were we to consider the prevalence of the subject of enterprise in Henry David Thoreau's writings apart from his cultural environment, we might conclude that in his literary performances a hard Yankee business head and literary inventiveness found each other and decided to live together in a self-constructed and self-regulated house of art. Such a view would privilege a formalist

reading of Thoreau's language while admitting biographical data to the extent that these could be translated into aesthetic considerations. Thoreau scholars will recognize that, allowing for qualifications that acknowledge individual differences, I have just characterized the bulk of Thoreau scholarship in the 1960s and 1970s. A close analysis of Thoreau's texts, however, takes us to the heart of his culture, and to major new dynamics and new developments in cultural discourse. Yet his texts should be read with reference not only to the times but also to a personal agenda: they constitute an ongoing personal narrative about an autobiographical problem that overshadowed all other concerns in his life and that throws considerable light on the intertextuality of culture and literary works in his case—the question of his literary vocation in an age of enterprise.

Why is the problem of vocation the major ligature between culture and literary text in Thoreau's case? First, he identified vocation with self-culture or what the narrator of **Walden** calls the "art of life." Second, in defining self-culture for himself he equated it with a literary career, albeit an unusual one that, in the language of Walden, reregistered *business* as a moral-aesthetic term, *commerce* as the profitability of resistance to mass culture, and *profit* as "virtue" and "*extra-vagance.*" In other words, the art of life and the life of art were from early on two sides of the same fact, and both were identified with means as with ends and with cause as with effect. One of Thoreau's reasons for conducting his two-year "experiment" at Walden Pond was to drive his vocational ideals into a corner in order to determine whether his art of life could be secured by terms tolerable to his society yet compatible with his aspirations as a writer. But the move to Walden was not without precedent. Already in February 1841, less than a year after he published his first literary work (a poem), he reported that he was thinking of purchasing or renting a site in retirement in which the art of life and the life of art could meet under one roof. Both Emerson and Fuller seemed to have understood his desire to find a writer's studio and succeed in his career. In this context Emerson's role in persuading Thoreau to compose **"Natural History of Massachusetts"** for *The Dial* (1842) takes on special significance in that the essay Thoreau produced is, among other things, the manifesto of a would-be writer.

The third point to be made—for the last two sections of this essay the most important one—is that the spirit of enterprise exerted powerful pressures on Thoreau's idea of vocation as well as on his practice of a literary career. What he understood as the enterprise of vocation was increasingly at odds with the vocation of enterprise. To be sure, most of his lexicon on self-culture, vocation, and enterprise belongs to the discourse of his culture. Yet he also quarreled with the contemporary language and assumptions of enterprise, and he was more unrelenting in his criticism of new and narrow conceptions of enterprise than he was of slavery, territorial expansion, political institutions and processes, reformers, and a threatened wilderness. His response to enterprise as defined and practiced by his contemporary culture is an important element in the intellectual, social, and economic history of his America.

I

The more one examines the lexical and semantic forms of thought, attitude and behavioral tendencies of American culture in the years spanning Thoreau's youth, early adulthood, and literary career, the more massively the evidence mounts that Thoreau's age represents a new departure. For good reasons it has been described as the beginning of industrial capitalism in America. A more appropriate characterization might be the age of enterprise. That term *enterprise* houses suggestions of a range of altering and altered assumptions, values, beliefs, agendas, and language. It also registers both the ambiguities of the new age and the ambivalences with which many literary artists viewed it.

Although Thoreau's age has been studied extensively and specifically in socioeconomic terms, these studies, instructive as they are, have focused on economic history, social history, economic activities and transformations, the social impact of economic changes, and the ideological dimensions of the age of enterprise. To date no study of the economic lexicon and discourse of the times has been conducted, which is to say that the spirit of the age of enterprise has not as yet been examined at the level of language and linguistic shifts. This essay assumes that studies in socioeconomic thought and behavior and examinations of lexicon and meaning can richly inform one another and that the latter kind of examination is particularly useful in illuminating Thoreau's literary language on enterprise. Both changes in economic lexicon and in the meaning of key terms, moreover, offer insights into his vocational agenda.

As preamble to the subject of linguistic changes, let me offer a brief summary statement on the new behavioral tendencies of the age of enterprise. As historians have noted, the new economic activities and behavior represented an unprecedented transformation in American economic and social life. Communally and state-controlled manufacturing, external trade and commerce, and internal trade (all of these centered in island communities that competed with one another) were either crowded out or drawn into the dynamic center of a new economic age by an astonishing growth not only in what we today refer to as private enterprise but also in new forms of private enterprise, including individual and group investment and speculation in numerous fields of new economic development.[1]

According to economic historian George Taylor, the chief signs of the new era were the rapid development of regional and national transportation networks, unprecedented technological advances, increased division of labor, greater specialization and interrelatedness of commercial, financial, and industrial activities, phenomenal land development, the development of corporations and rapid increase of money investors and investments, a society that regarded the economic developments as instruments for meeting regional and local needs, and *laissez faire* principles applied to corporations, companies and entrepreneurs in order to promote economic success and prevent the disastrous failures in many state enterprise initiatives in earlier decades.[2] Bray Hammond has succinctly described the spirit and practice of the age: "People were led as they had not been before by visions of moneymaking. Liberty became transformed into *laissez faire*. A violent, aggressive, economic individualism became established."[3] Rush Welter's view is both less pejorative and less vivid: "An expansive economic orientation well in evidence by the 1840s . . . involved a national predisposition to increase individual wealth by any acceptable means even if it also meant sacrificing some of the scruples of the past. The paths by which Americans arrived at enterprise, and the measures they took to be acceptable, were key facts in the intellectual history of the epoch."[4]

Many clergymen in New England and New York, the pillars of their congregations, and their parishioners were caught up in the restive dynamism of the age. On the whole the middle- and upper middle-class religious communities adjusted to the rapid economic transformation as well as any other sector. "We of the East," Horace Hosmer of Acton and friend of the Thoreau family wrote with his customary bluntness, "have a commercial look even at heavenly things."[5] The list of eastern liberal ministers and transcendentalists with impressive business acumen is long, and includes notables like Theodore Parker, Ralph Waldo Emerson, George Ripley, Cyrus Bartol, Henry Bellows, and James Freeman Clarke. One recalls Bartol's moral benedictions on his newly gotten wealth through real estate transactions and Emerson's inspection of the Fitchburg Railroad depot that was being constructed in Concord in the spring of 1844 (at least some of his interest is to be explained by his investment in the new company, an investment that in short order had already gone up ten percent).[6] Publishing records of the 1830s to the 1850s also disclose that shrewd investments by clergymen writing popular and profitable books were hardly limited to Unitarian and transcendentalist ministers. Ann Douglas has attempted to explain in historical and social terms what the book trade records reveal: an unprecedented number of ministers of liberal and conservative theological persuasion lived economically and vocationally by the immediate aid of their books, and cooperated closely with editors and publishers whose role and influence were defined largely by transactions between demand and supply, consumer and producer.[7] Thus ministers joined others in producing formulaic sentimental romances (promoted for their virtuous influence), vaguely edifying and clearly sentimental religious books and tracts, exotic travel literature, profiles of the newly and venerable rich, etiquette books for young women, treatises on domestic economy, and, especially, success manuals for young men (the latter are discussed in the last section of this essay in relation to Thoreau's *Walden*).

II

As noted earlier, neither historians nor literary critics have investigated at the level of language the cultural shift just summarized.[8] The last two sections of this essay suggest that Thoreau was keenly aware of the vigorous and powerfully influential language of enterprise and of the extent to which it contested language and values that he regarded as crucial to self-culture and to the fortunes of the American culture. Whether he was more right than wrong or more wrong than right in his assessments, whether he was modernist or antimodernist in his stance on American culture, or progressive or conservative in his economic assumptions, is not the issue here. What is at issue is the lexical and semantic changes discernible in the language of enterprise, the confirmation of the meaning of these linguistic shifts by cultural behavior, and both Thoreau's vocational agenda and his literary linguistic forms within the context suggested by the dynamic new forces registered in cultural language and frenetic economic activity. Concord, as Robert Gross has carefully documented, presented Thoreau with a local version of the age and spirit of enterprise.[9] Thus he saw fit to travel a good deal in Concord as well as in the history of economic vernacular.

Both the language and the sometimes uneasy consensus that had served a mercantile-agrarian society from the beginning of nationhood to the administration of John Quincy Adams underwent rapid transformation in the next several decades. Perhaps the clearest indicators of this transformation are the speeches made by a succession of presidents to their government and nation. Consider, for example, the speeches that bracketed each administration—the "Inaugural Address" and the "Fourth Annual Message" (in Andrew Jackson's case his inaugural speech and "Farewell Address"). On the whole, the inaugural speeches are couched in a ritualistic, formulaic, and somewhat archaic language whereas the final address, and for that matter every annual address, is much more steeped in the current political-economic terminology. As one might expect, the economic terminology manifests the kind of economic preoccupations totally or largely absent from the inaugural speeches. Moreover, a chronological review of the final annual addresses of the presidents from J. Q. Adams to Millard Fillmore reveals not only an increasing degree of specificity in the economic review and proposals but also an increasing domination of the speech by economic considerations. (In the speeches of Franklin Pierce and James Buchanan, as one might expect, the immediate and explosive issues of slavery, sectional conflict, and the federal union overshadow all other issues.)

A more telling change in the speeches from Adams to Fillmore is the shift in moral assumptions and tone on the subject of America's new economic vigor. Adams registered traditional republican values in his warnings against wealth, pursuit of luxuries, and the equation of prosperity with spiritual fulfillment.[10] Andrew Jackson, however, celebrated the national march to prosperity and spoke honorifically of "our free institutions" which offer every citizen the opportunity to attain "prosperity and happiness without seeking to profit themselves at the expense of others" (*Presidents* [*A Compilation of the Messages and Papers of the Presidents*], 4:1513, 1517). Indeed, the individual should look forward to sharing in the blessings of a national prosperity. Yet Old Hickory also intoned in his strange farewell address that the "planter, the farmer, the mechanic, and the laborer all know that their success depends upon their own industry and economy, and that they must not expect to become suddenly rich by the fruits of their toil" (*Presidents*, 4:1524). In this speech, dark with references to the evil coercion of "monied corporations," "monopoly," "exclusive privilege," speculation, paper money, and paper stocks, the overseer of the early halcyon days of enterprise appealed to the producing groups of the old order to recover the rights they had allowed to slip away. As in the case of several more recent presidential farewells, Jackson's address is marked by expressions of private reflection, regret, censure (including self-censure), nostalgia, and warnings against potentially evil new geniuses countenanced and perhaps even encouraged by the current administration. One is inclined to conclude that the nation was as nostalgically ready for the Jacksonian moralisms of his farewell address as for the vigorous enterprise of the Jacksonian era. Martin Van Buren, whose administration had been bitten in the heels by the 1837 economic panic, repeated Jackson's chastisements for "capitalists" (Van Buren's term), speculators, and monopolists, and warned against a return to the past—a reference, it appears, to the Jacksonian boom. On the other hand, he regarded the nation's top priority as a program of economic stabilization and strong advance (*Presidents*, 5:1823-33).

One of the features distinguishing Polk's addresses from those of his predecessors is his enthusiastic endorsement of all forms of enterprise, the direct connection in his thinking between a vigorous expansion of agricultural, industrial, commercial, and business production and manifest destiny (*Presidents*, 6:2496-2500), and the absence of any doubt or ambivalence in his soporifically long-winded speeches over the country's program of economic expansion. Fillmore is an even more enthusiastic apologist for enterprise than Polk. Luxuries and wealth are referred to favorably, the "progress of the people" reveals itself economically, and the responsibility of the government is to "keep pace with the progress of the people" by fostering and protecting industry and lending powerful governmental assistance toward the further promotion of "our internal commerce" (*Presidents* [*A Compilation of the Messages and Papers of the Presidents*], 6:2717).

Semantically the ideological-economic transformation can be traced through gradual alteration of key terms such as *commerce, business, profit, industry* and *corporation,* and changes in their conjunction with other terms, or, one might say, in their valency. John Quincy Adams used a conventional triangulation of terms to describe the nation's economic life—the "agricultural, commercial, and manufacturing" interests (*Presidents,* 3:979). *Commerce* denoted international trade to Adams, Jackson, Van Buren, and Polk, but was extended to internal exchange of goods and services in the speeches of Fillmore. Thus a term that originally meant "dealings" came gradually to be associated with commercial port cities in the East and, by Thoreau's time, with international and especially domestic exchange of goods and services, for profit. *Profit,* both a moral and economic term in the speeches of Adams, Jackson, and Van Buren, came to signify simply financial profit. *Industry* in the early nineteenth century a synonym for diligence, self-discipline, concentrated effort, and perseverance, gradually replaced the traditional "manufactures," thereby, like *profit,* shedding much of its moral meaning. As for *business* and *corporation,* not until the speeches of Jackson did they emerge as key economic referents with close affinities to our modern use of the terms. *Business* had dual meanings for Jackson: "ordinary business" signified traditional, individual, and collective undertakings for profit (entrepreneurship, farming, mechanic arts, merchant activities, etc.) whereas the insidious new business of "corporations," "monopoly," "exclusive privilege," and "speculation" subverted the "independent spirit," "love of liberty," "intelligence," and "moral character" of the citizens conducting "ordinary business" (*Presidents,* 4:1520-21). Van Buren referred to the promoters of the new business as "capitalists" and warned of "the bitter fruits of that spirit of speculative enterprise to which our countrymen are so liable" (*Presidents,* 5:1832-33). Polk's updated terminology for the domestic production system aside from farming was not the conventional "manufactures" but "business and industry" (*Presidents,* 6:2498). Indeed, business is his most frequent and multifaceted term, referring to activities such as agriculture; manufacturing; construction, expansion, and maintenance of transportation systems; building trades; the merchant's functions; the corporations; and investment capital. Neither Polk nor Fillmore registered moral or

other concerns about the direction America's "business" development was taking.

Probably the richest register of lexical and semantic shifts linked to economic developments is contained in the history of the term *enterprise.* By the 1840s *enterprise* had pretty much disengaged itself from its much earlier associations with moral discipline, courage, and self-sacrifice, characteristics that might be summed up as a conflation of the Greek *oikonomia,* the Latin *virtus,* and the Late Latin *interprendere.* As the presidential addresses reveal, in Thoreau's era *enterprise* contained both negative and positive connotations. In its negative sense the term recalled seventeenth- and eighteenth-century usage, especially of the adjectival form "enterprising": misadventurous, unduly ambitious, scheming, self-aggrandizing, usurpational, compulsive, distorted (ethically crippled and morally impotent). Some of these associations have survived to our day as secondary meanings in the French cognate and most recent ancestor of the English term, especially in the verb *entreprendre* and its past participial form *entrepris,* the adjective *entrepris/entreprise,* and the noun *entreprise.*

By Thoreau's time, however, *enterprise* had also firmly established a favorable connotation which was rapidly crowding out the negative. In its positive sense the term referred to an admirable risk-taking, a venturesome spirit, the shrewdness and diligence to conceive a design and follow through with it. This was the kind of enterprise celebrated by Freeman Hunt in his influential *Hunt's Merchant's Magazine* and in his financially successful books, *Worth and Wealth* (1856) and *Lives of American Merchants* (1856). President Van Buren's finger-pointing at the "spirit of speculative enterprise" invokes a history of negative connotation whereas Fillmore's panegyric to the "exuberance of enterprise" and his ringing declaration that "the whole country is full of enterprise" (*Presidents,* 6:2717) invokes the favorable connotation.[11]

A second point to be made about *enterprise* is that a term whose seventeenth- and eighteenth-century history indicates multiple and general applications (see *Oxford English Dictionary*) was increasingly being appropriated by economic discourse and thus was undergoing transformation into a term that in one of its primary usages was specifically associated with business and the rapid expansion and systematic change in industry, business, corporations, trade, and commerce. For instance, in Francis Bowen's *Political Economy,* the major economic text to appear in the 1850s, *enterprise* is employed throughout in both its general (and favorable) meaning and in its specifically economic sense. On the one hand, the term stands as the opposite to "indolence, feebleness, gayety, and *insouiance,*" it is defined as "industrious, and adventurous habits," and it is associated with "the restlessness, the feverish anxiety to get on," the "effective desire of accumulation," and the "unceasing energy and activity in the pursuit of wealth, . . . which actually generate enthusiasm of character." In his general use of the term, the Harvard-trained, politically conservative Bowen followed his economic mentors, Adam Smith, J. B. Say, and John Rae. Yet *Political Economy* also uses *enterprise* specifically as a referent to agriculture, commerce, trade, manufacturing, shop and factory production, canal or railroad building and investment, finance, and corporation stockholding.[12] Kate McKean's *Manual of Social Science* (1864), a popular, abbreviated, and simplified version of Henry C. Carey's pioneering, three-volume *Principles of Political Economy* (1840; the *Manual* went through at least eight editions by 1888), agrees with Bowen in the general and specific use of enterprise. Bowen's text also contains the earliest American usage I have been able to find of the terminology private enterprise in its modern sense. According to the *Oxford English Dictionary,* "private enterprise" was first used in 1844 in a report on activities the British East India Company (a virtual monopoly) had left to others. Bowen distinguishes between private enterprise and government monopolies in industry, commerce, business, and finance,[13] and strongly links the former with the cultivation and manifestation of "character."

Bowen's association of "enterprise" and "character" invites another observation on the term *enterprise* as a general and specific signifier of economic desire and activity. The industrious and adventurous habits reported by the term and its synonyms were justified in terms of the individual by the moral doctrine of self-culture and in terms of the body politic by the national expansionist doctrine of manifest destiny. Moralist-minded eastern Whigs, especially Unitarian moralists, tended to view favorably the expansionism of the age of enterprise, for, as Daniel Howe has noted, "only a man of secure economic position could really lead the rewarding life of self-development and refinement idealized by the Unitarians." This argument became something of a cliche in the sermons of Unitarian ministers from the time of William Ellery Channing to the post-Civil War sermons of clergymen like Henry Bellows, James Freeman Clarke, and some of their younger colleagues. In the words of Howe: once the individual "had achieved a competence of material things," he was "expected to turn to spiritual development. Furthermore, the habits acquired in the process of material advancement—prudence, industriousness, sobriety, and the like—ought to serve as the foundation for this higher, moral development."[14]

Congressman Robert C. Winthrop of Boston understood such a doctrine of self-culture in social terms when he declared the paramount symbol of the time to be "the rapid and steady progress of the influence of Commerce upon the social and political condition of man."[15] Vigor-

ous enterprise, Winthrop argued before his receptive Boston Mercantile Library Association audience, was renovatingly virtuous and thus was certain to improve American civilization. This direct descendant of Governor John Winthrop of the Bay Colony linked his enterprising view of progress to the work of God's kingdom when he addressed religious groups. As one would expect, extracts of Winthrop's speech to the Mercantile Library Association were reprinted in *Hunt's Merchant's Magazine* (February 1846).

A more secular millennial rationale for enterprise was the exuberant mid nineteenth-century version of enlightenment as articulated by Polk and Fillmore in their invocations of manifest destiny. The principal theme of Polk's annual messages on the state of the Union can be summarized by a statement made at the Texas Convention in 1845. The destiny of enterprising Americans, a Mr. Volney Howard offered, was to "force back the savage and carry civilization into the useless and unproductive wilderness."[16]

A final point to be made here about *enterprise* and its allied terms is that they developed into prominent lexical signifiers in the culture at large, as evidenced in the samples of rhetoric of politicians, clergy, and economists already discussed and in other kinds of documents such as governmental reports, journalism, and popular as well as high-brow literary art. A "Report to the Special Commissioner of the Revenue" in the late 1860s announced and documented approvingly to the federal government a "spirit of enterprise," by which it meant vigorous economic activity, "which seems to redouble its energy with every burden placed upon it."[17] A House of Representatives Executive Document produced about the same time used *enterprise* to designate "channels of trade" and trading policies. Just over a decade later the "Resolutions of the Chicago Convention for the Promotion of Commerce," a special-interest document presented to the House of Representatives, noted the "pushing enterprise of the American merchant" and observed patronizingly that "in material enterprise [business and commerce] the South may look to the North." Indeed, American "business and commerce" are lauded as the "greatest of all enterprises." As a witness in a series of written and oral depositions to the House in the same year on the topic of "Depression in Labor and Business," journalist and labor specialist Charles C. Coffin of Boston repeatedly used the term *enterprise,* both in its general and specific applications, precisely as Francis Bowen had done in his economic writings.[18]

In two extraordinarily popular new kinds of publications, the sentimental romance precursor to the Horatio Alger economic/moral success stories and the success manuals for young men, *enterprise* is a watchword, the age of enterprise the backdrop, and the spirit of enterprise the principle of action and source of moral victory. Since success manuals will be treated in relation to **Walden** toward the end of this essay, let me cite Timothy Shay Arthur here as a sterling example of the economic possibilities of exploiting the theme of enterprise for sentimental romances. For many generations now a certified member of the gallery of national lampoon for his *Ten Nights in a Bar Room,* Arthur was actually just as successful with his business and money romances of the 1840s and 1850s, in which his fascination with prosperity as the crowning glory of enterprise was properly dressed up in moral concern over the perilous seductions of evil enterprise. The nine editions of his *Making Haste to be Rich; or, the Temptation and Fall* brought him quick financial returns, as did his morally tongue-clicking *Nothing But Money* (at least seven editions).[19]

"It is natural that we should be enterprising," Thoreau noted in an enigmatic journal entry in 1852. The speaker of **Walden** manipulates the language of enterprise so as to acknowledge, parody, and counter the current language and behavior of America, to define his vocation with a logic of opposition, and to justify his art and life with the principle of *"extra-vagance"* (standing outside the circle of extravagant enterprise). "I have always endeavored to acquire strict business habits" is the kind of statement in **Walden** that registers both linguistic and vocational agendas and suggests the inseparability of the two. And **Walden** concludes with a declaration that focuses the theme of *"extra-vagance"* while reminding the readers of its cultural connection: "I delight to come to my bearings, . . . not to live in this restless, nervous, bustling, trivial Nineteenth Century, . . . to travel the only path I can, and that on which no power can resist me."[20]

III

Let me state explicitly what has been suggested implicitly throughout the first two sections: that our understanding of Thoreau's texts is enriched if we recognize both the new cultural vernacular of enterprise with its range of semantic differentiations and shifts and Thoreau's language of enterprise as the record of a developing alternative to the language and values of his culture.

"Explain the phrases,—a man of business, a man of pleasure, a man of the world": here is the topic sentence of one of Thoreau's earliest surviving compositions. One should not confer on this piece an exaggerated status. It was one of those writing exercises deemed by Harvard College and E. T. Channing to be a prerequisite for the more advanced and largely interchangeable programs of manhood, true citizenship, worthy service, professional success, and, more immediately, graduation from Harvard. Thoreau walked through the

assignment with the stilted clichés of a second-year student. He also used the opportunity to demonstrate some etymological expertise. A "man of business" is defined as "energetic," "persevering," "always on the lookout," "ever awake to his interest," "well calculated": in short, one who possesses "despatch . . . method and perseverance, industry and activity, united with prudence and foresight."[21] Thus Thoreau runs his bow across old and new saws about the enterprising man and offers a glissando of details provided by the French and English history of *enterprise* and his cultural environment, which is placing new claims on the term.

Another writing assignment, this one included in Thoreau's commencement obligations, addresses "The commercial spirit of modern times," which Thoreau discusses in terms of behavior, attitude, and value. By averring that "the spirit we are considering is not altogether and without exception bad" he introduces a moral judgment and principle not evident in the earlier assignment. Commerce, traditionally the most touted form of economic enterprise in eastern Massachusetts, is usually bad in that it is a materialistic running for luck that has turned means into ends. Thoreau also envisions the redemption of that spirit when "men, true to their natures, cultivate the moral affections, lead manly and independent lives; . . . make riches the means and not the end of existence." His conclusion recalls William Ellery Channing's sermons linking enterprise and prosperity to self-culture and the moral philosophy of Thoreau's Harvard mentors, who, as Daniel Howe has described, linked frenetic materialistic enterprise to self-culture and, for that matter, to national moral maturation by a principle of means and end.[22] Thoreau rejoices—at least rhetorically—in the "avarice . . . din and bustle" of the times because they are the preliminary means to a higher end that he defines as "a more intellectual and spiritual life." Thus, although America's "ruling principle" is "counting [financial] gains," "We [he assumes the consent of his Harvard readers] glory in those very excesses which are a source of anxiety to the wise and good, as an evidence that man will not always by the slave of matter" (**EEM** [*Early Essays and Miscellany*], 115-18). Clearly Thoreau was more thoroughly trained by Harvard than he was willing to admit in later years when his views had changed.

Specifying the extent to which Thoreau's manipulations of language in later writings register altered meanings and convictions is problematical. For instance, in **"Life Without Principle"** he borrows a pronouncement from his 1852 **Journal**: "I think that there is nothing, not even crime, more opposed to poetry, to philosophy, ay, to life itself, than this incessant business." Yet the essay also describes New Englanders as "warped and narrowed by an *exclusive* devotion to trade and commerce and manufactures and agriculture and the like" (emphasis mine).[23] What at first appears to be an elaboration of the sentiment in the first statement exists in a contestatory relation to it by apparently implying an updated version of the principle Thoreau had espoused in his commencement assignment. The adjective *exclusive* strongly suggests that devotion to enterprise is not in and of itself evil or always to be disparaged. Other statements in the essay invite the same inference: "The ways by which you may get money *almost without exception* lead downward" (emphasis mine); "I wish to suggest that a man may be very industrious, and yet not spend his time well"; "Even if we grant that the American has freed himself from a political tyrant, he is still the slave of an economical and moral tyrant" (*RP [Reform Papers]*, 158, 160, 174).

If the reader must reconcile the incompatibilities between these two kinds of statements ("**Life Without Principle**" with its dialectics of opposition does not attempt to make them compatible), one can, for instance, privilege the second kind of statement and paraphrase it as a call to direct *enterprise* toward moral ends. One could also privilege the former pronouncement and regard the essay as an unrelenting jeremiad against America's spirit and practice of enterprise. Or one might attend to Thoreau's manipulations of "Life" and "living," for both of which the term *enterprise* is at times a richly suggestive synonym. Enterprise with principle is itself a generative principle in the essay, but enterprise is a term of multiple intentions and sometimes good ends. So are related terms in the essay such as *labor, value, profit, invest, business, commerce, success, wealth,* and *culture.* Thus one should not treat too narrowly the speaker's interest in "the comparative demand which men make on life" (161) and the comparative demand which he and his countrymen make on the language of enterprise. As he notes toward the end of the essay, the "same ear is fitted to receive" more than one communication (172). The renovating virtue proposed in this wary essay on enterprise is "wariness" (173).

That wariness is not sharper but more narrowly focused in a *Journal* passage that acknowledges the importance of enterprise even while resisting it with a negative example. "It is natural that we should be enterprising," Thoreau declares, "for we are descended from the enterprising, who sought to better their fortunes in the New World." The immediate preamble to this observation suspends the apparent endorsement of enterprise in ambiguity and draws on both the positive and negative potential of the term:

> The race that settles and clears the land has got to deal with every tree in the forest in succession. It must be resolute and industrious, and even the stumps must be got out—or are. It is a thorough process, this war with the wilderness—breaking nature, taming the soil, feeding it on oats. The civilized man regards the pine tree as his enemy. He will fell it and let in the light, grub it up and raise wheat or rye there.
>
> (*J [Journal]*, 3:269-70)

What begins as an apparently affirmative discussion of land-clearing suddenly shifts into an ascerbic comment on civilized man's war against trees, the kind of turn one finds in "**Chesuncook**" and "**The Allegash and East Branch**," especially in their treatment of the effects of a voracious logging enterprise. The *Journal* passage implicates a number of key terms in the potential ironies produced by its shift: "descended," "better," "fortunes," and "new world." Thoreau's use of the predicate adjective *natural* in conjunction with *enterprise* after describing the enterprise as one of "breaking nature" is perhaps the most complicated reregistration of any term in the passage. In *Walden,* for instance, caveman interests, housebuilding, Greek literary classics, nature, the sound of church bells, the lowing of the cow, Alek Therien, the stones in the bean-field, the Walden shore, rabbits and partridges, virtue, business, and commerce are all described as "natural."

Walden, completed in the same year as the first lecture version of "**Life Without Principle**," is also centrally concerned with enterprise. A word frequency check alone is revealing. *Enterprise,* in most cases with reference to business enterprise, risk, or undertaking, occurs nineteen times, the same number as for trade and traders. The term *business* in reference to business enterprise or designs occurs more frequently than *enterprise.* *Economy* as noun and adjective occurs ten times; *the railroad,* a principal avatar of economic expansion, occurs forty times. Related word usages are: *commerce* five times (also the number for banks as for factories); *profit* in a financial sense three times; *expense(s)* fourteen times; *success* as related to enterprise more frequently than *expense(s); interest* as a financial term more frequently than economy, venture and undertaking (as connected to enterprise) ten times; and *industry* in the sense of diligence eight times. One might also note that in the first chapter of *Walden* alone, *money* appears eleven times.

More revealing than these figures is the compositional history of *Walden,* a history that provides a context of significance for the numbers. The evidence of the *Walden* worksheets suggests that the "Economy" chapter was originally drafted as a separate lecture essay designed, in part, as a personal definition of self-culture and perhaps as a comic-serious parody of success manuals for young men (also known as "copy-books").[24] Before Thoreau turned to revising and expanding his *Walden* account, he decided to use the "**Economy**" manuscript as the opening section, although in his second version (*Walden* B), he debates in the "Economy" pages whether to use the terminology "this lecture" and "audience" and alters "I require of a writer" by adding the words "or lecturer." In the successive versions of *Walden* one of the emerging patterns is the gradual extension of the theme of economy to materials other than the "Economy" pages while also adding a considerable amount of material to "Economy," only some of which survived to the final draft. In the second version of *Walden,* the surviving worksheets for "Economy" actually outnumber the surviving leaves for the rest of his account. In the third version of *Walden,* the "Economy" pages have been revised sufficiently to mesh with the rest of the work. In versions four to six the lexicon and theme of economy are expanded in the chapters after "Economy," and by version seven the theme of "*extravagance*" by means of economy (higher means to higher ends) has emerged as a principal motif, supported by the parables on vocation and enterprise that now help to frame the work: the anecdote early in the opening chapter about the Indian basket-weaver-seller with its self-reflexivity and pointed autobiographical application and the exotic parable in the final chapter about the artist of Kouroo who would not make any compromises with his culture and times and so surprised himself by out-enterprising and outliving them through his art.

IV

The most immediate lesson of the richly suggestive parable of the Indian's unsuccessful venture into business enterprise is offered by the narrator, speaking autobiographically for Thoreau: "I too had woven a kind of basket of a delicate texture, but I had not made it worth any one's while to buy them, and instead of studying how to make it worth men's while to buy my baskets, I studied rather how to avoid the necessity of selling them. The life which men praise and regard as successful is but one kind. Why should we exaggerate any one kind at the expense of the others?" (*Walden,* 19). This reflection raises three significant issues: career, economic success, and vocation. Unfortunately, what the entrepreneurial Indian was capable of producing did not match what his successful neighbors needed or wanted. Whether the Indian's baskets were "of a delicate texture" isn't clear, but the narrator has "woven a basket of a delicate texture"—Thoreau's literary productions to 1852 when he added this parable to *Walden* and, above all, *A Week* [*A Week on the Concord and Merrimack Rivers*], which had turned into a business fiasco (in 1853 Thoreau wheelbarrowed home more than 700 unsold and virtually all unbound copies of the 1000 copies James Munroe had printed three years earlier). Like the Indian, the narrator has failed to market his products. With a shrewd entrepreneurial expertise and patronizingly pedagogical tone the narrator explains the Indian's fundamental business mistakes by identifying three alternative actions that the Indian failed to recognize and pursue: "make it worth the other's while to buy them, or at least make him think that it was so, or make something else."

The narrator's explanations are not without irony, the irony directed at the community, the Indian, and himself. All three alternatives are addressed in the autobio-

graphical reflection "I had not made it worth anyone's while to buy them." These alternatives are then rejected: "I studied rather how to avoid the necessity of selling them." Throughout, the narrator employs a language of production, promotion, and economic returns even while undermining the popular assumptions and values behind the language. Even in his deliberate decision to free himself from the anxious demands and expectations of financial success in his line of work, he speaks with the aplomb and calculated idiom of a shrewd entrepreneur who has evaluated his market, his circumstances, and his career interests. He will not jeopardize his best interests; he will merely reject popular interpretations of enterprise and reward. As abrupt as the "well-known lawyer" in the parable is toward the Indian (one suspects that the less than reverent reference is to Judge Samuel Hoar and his equally distinguished sons Ebenezer Rockwood Hoar and George Frisbee Hoar), and with an understatement characteristic of his discussion of vocation here and elsewhere in *Walden,* the narrator concludes that "the life which men praise and regard as successful is but one kind." Central to the parable and its function in "Economy" is this reversal of status by which the authority of presence and worth passes from those whom the business-minded Indian admired and hoped to emulate to the narrator and his unusual enterprise.

Like the moralist who must emphasize the principle of what he has just declared through an extended example, the narrator asks rhetorically, "Why should we exaggerate any one kind [of living] at the expense of the others?" The logic of the parable and the question allows for several intentions in the question and, by extension, in the telling of the *Walden* story. *Walden,* in fact, confirms three intentions: in an age that defines career success in narrow materialistic terms to argue the legitimacy of many alternatives (many kinds of lives); in an age characterized by money-making careerism and the unprecedented popularity of career manuals to add "one kind" more (the narrator's vocation) to the reader's inventory; and in a work that plays serious games to turn an apparent injunction against exaggerating his kind of life into an injunction to exaggerate. This "exaggeration" is justified at length in the final chapter of *Walden*; indeed, the speaker declares in the paragraph in which he distinguishes his "*extra-vagance*" from the "extravagance" of his age, "I am convinced that I cannot exaggerate enough" (*Walden,* 324).

An examination of the preamble to the parable of the Indian will reveal that the rhetorical question concluding the parable is also directed at the four paragraphs immediately preceding the parable, paragraphs in which the narrator offers an obviously satirical career manual; he introduces himself as a "reporter to a journal, of no very wide circulation," a "self-appointed inspector of snow storms," a "surveyor of forest paths," a "custodian of the wild stock of the town" that has escaped its owners and yards, and a nurseryman to red huckleberries, sand cherries, nettle trees, and other varieties of customarily ignored or depreciated flora in the vicinity of Concord. In the minds of "my Townsmen" the entire range of employment belongs not only to the unconventional but also, as the narrator concedes, to the unacceptable (*Walden,* 18). Thus the question of why one would want to "exaggerate any one kind" of career or living "at the expense of the others" is concerned, above all, with the theme of vocation as a private enterprise of self-culture. In addressing this theme the narrator presents himself as an anomaly but not an anachronism. While the parable on the artist of Kouroo celebrates the magical achievement of the artist totally devoted to his vocation regardless of his cultural environment, the parable of the Indian and *Walden* as a whole represent an important contribution by Thoreau to a historically weakening and culturally battered idea of vocation seeking in the age of enterprise to authorize itself and threatened not so much by overt hostility (as the opening sections of the essay have demonstrated) as by neglect in a frenetic society reassured by the dynamism of its enterprise.

Both the concept of vocation and its religious rationale had been pushed to the margins of personal and cultural relevance by Thoreau's time, but his age witnessed the publication of many published sermons and treatises on particular occupations (the popular new term *professions* for what was once called *offices* signals the change). These sermons and treatises often presumed to speak on vocation whereas their interest in most cases was morally acceptable and above all economically successful occupations.

By Thoreau's time the Protestant debate over vocation had been settled among enlightened New Englanders, as Daniel Howe and David Robinson have shown in their examinations of early nineteenth-century New England Unitarianism.[25] To follow the history of the idea of vocation in America, I suggest, is to trace a line from the quarrel between John Cotton and Ann Hutchinson in which both parties claimed authority and justified their behavior by invoking precisely the same argument of having been called by God to perform God's special work.[26] The line of development can be traced through the writings of figures like Cotton Mather to Benjamin Franklin and Thomas Jefferson with their ideal of the *homo oeconomicus.* Early nineteenth-century Unitarianism, as David Robinson has carefully documented, fostered the concept of *homo oeconomicus* as a religious doctrine, or we might say, as a moral-aesthetic religion, of self-culture in which "the moral life was transformed from a sign, or an adjunct, of the religious life, into a religion in itself."[27]

An important reminder to be extrapolated from Howe's and Robinson's examinations of Unitarianism in Tho-

reau's time is that Thoreau invented neither his language nor his general understanding of self-culture. Thus to note the equation in *Walden* and **"Life Without Principle"** between vocation and self-culture and to see this equation confirmed by biographical evidence is to underscore the obvious about Thoreau and his circle. Not even Thoreau's characterization of self-culture as an enterprise in *Walden* is unique, a point that a review of Unitarian sermonizing in his time and region will drive home with monotonous repetition. What is unique is his equation of self-culture with his highly unusual literary vocation and the version of enterprise inherent in it. While hardly denying that self-culture or the "art of life" is a principal theme in a work like *Walden,* I suggest that greater significance should be attached to the fact that the narrator's agenda of self-cultivation and his artistic labors become interchangeable in his vocational "experiment" and that the two became interchangeable in Thoreau's enterprise of vocation.

It is this fusion of self-culture, literary career, and enterprise that throws into intelligible relief Thoreau's "career" decisions and the evidence that he composed *Walden,* among other things, as a serious parody of the highly popular success manuals for young men. Thoreau's actions as a young writer are ambiguous predictors of his future in that they point to both a conventional and unconventional career. Certainly his decision shortly after graduating from Harvard in 1837 to start a writer's journal could point either way. By 1839-40 he was attempting publishable essays. In 1840 he published his first poem and tried, unsuccessfully, to place a lengthy, idiosyncratic, and somewhat unconventional essay with Margaret Fuller and *The Dial* and to understand her reasons for rejecting it. In 1841 he published additional poems, but also reported his desire to purchase or rent living quarters, preferably a farm, that would offer solitude outside Concord. This desire did not conform to conventional expectations for Harvard graduates or for literary writers in Concord. (If Concord had not known what to expect of its literary sons, it now had answer in Emerson.)

At Emerson's encouragement, however, Thoreau made a more conventional move in 1843, settling on Staten Island in the hope of securing a literary career in New York. By 1844, however, he was putting the New York disappointments behind him and filling an oversized notebook in Concord with preliminary drafts of material for *A Week,* a work that he had planned at least as early as 1841[28] but had postponed. His move to Walden Pond and his extraordinary productivity there as a writer reveal signs of an unorthodox career taking shape on his terms (four *Journal* notebooks, two lyceum lectures on why he was living alone at the Pond, the highly unusual travel book *A Week,* and an idyllic evocation of an unconventional experiment at Walden [his first draft of *Walden*]; he also wrote **"Thomas Carlyle,"** **"Ktaadn,"** two somewhat diffuse and unfinished compositions on reform (the basis for **"Reform and the Reformers"**), and began, like the entrepreneurial Indian of *Walden,* to search out angels who might minister to his business of *A Week.*

It is probably no coincidence that his first major literary effort after returning to Concord and while seeking to place his manuscript of *A Week* was to draft **"Resistance to Civil Government,"** in which he conferred the highest moral and aesthetic claims to the principle of resistance. In the 1850s his two major literary enterprises were *Walden* and a *Journal* "of no very wide circulation, whose editor," in the words of *Walden,* "has never yet seen fit to print the bulk of my contributions. . . . However, in this case my pains were their own reward" (*Walden,* 18). "Speak—though your thought presupposes the non-existence of your hearers," Thoreau exhorted himself on December 25, 1851 (*J,* 3:158), the winter when he became aware that the *Journal* was his unique form and began to refer to it as his most important literary enterprise. From the time that he negotiated a contract with James Munroe for the publication of *A Week,* Thoreau's life is marked by carefully calculated employment decisions and regimen to "avoid the necessity of selling" his works of "a delicate texture" and to allow him to exaggerate "one kind [of vocation] at the expense of the others."

Walden, I have already noted, not only rejects popular contemporary assumptions about occupations and economic success but parodies one of the most lucrative forms of plagiarism in his day, a new industry of ballyhoo commonly known as guidebooks, success manuals for young men, or copy-books. William Alcott's title *The Young Man's Guide* is an appropriate collective title for this genre. Such guidebooks were not unfamiliar to Thoreau. Included in his personal library were four such works, listed here by the date of their first printing: *Addresses to Young Men* by James Fordyce (1777), *Letters Addressed to a Young Man* by Mrs. [Jane] West (1801), *The Life of [Dr. Benjamin] Franklin* by Franklin and his friend Dr. Stueber (1796), and *Lectures Addressed to the Young Men of Hartford and New Haven* by Joel Hawes (1828). The Fordyce text was autographed by Thoreau's father, the West guidebook was presented as a gift to Thoreau's brother in his twentieth year and eventually came into Thoreau's possession. Both the British (Fordyce and West) and the American guidebooks were popular in America, and, taken together, can be regarded as a harbinger of the success manuals for young men that emerged as a well-received and lucrative publication in Jacksonian and post-Jacksonian America.

Mid nineteenth-century self-help manuals with their avowed aim of assisting young men in moral growth and getting a living present a large and complicated

topic of inquiry; an examination of *Walden* in terms of this genre compounds the difficulty. My generalizations here grow out of a preliminary effort in a separate essay to gather evidence on the success manual, identify its antecedents, its American context, and its principal generic characteristics (including lexical and semantic features) and to demonstrate one of the achievements of *Walden* as a parody (both irreverent and serious) of the "copy-book" genre.

Most of the success manuals offered a template for behavior (hence "copy-book" and the traditional British designation of "conduct book") and advice on how to succeed economically, professionally, and socially (hence "success manual"). Only a few of them invoke turn-of-the-century republican values and lament the degeneracy of the times (e.g., John Abbott and Charles Butler); most seek to redeem the times in the economic sense of redemption. The latter encourage the development of good business habits as a means to moral development and a sign of good character. With few exceptions the chronological progression of the manuals reveals a shift in cultural values from right living as the basis of the *res-publica* to economic success and the cultivation of taste (the latter an expensive proposition made feasible by prosperity). Those that celebrate the new age of enterprise usually envision a harmonious and prosperous society composed of gentle and civilized businessmen amassing wealth by virtuous industry. Although piously distinguishing between manhood and mammon, the practical effect of the guidebooks is to link the two. In other words, most of the authors accept the new lexicon, meanings, and values of economic enterprise. At the same time, virtually all of them presume to be interested in self-culture and freely employ the moral language of self-culture. As one might expect, these manuals are directed to a limited readership—the middle and upper classes of rural and urban America, especially the Northeast. Of the examples I have found, the majority of the authors are ministers. That they updated the age-old Christian imperative to cast one's bread upon the waters and expertly acted out their own advice could not have been lost on Thoreau if he read many of them.[29]

In any event, success manuals and their popularity among educated readers provided Thoreau with opportunities he would have found difficult to resist: aggressively second-rate authorial minds, a nervous enthrallment with enterprise and profit, invocations of traditional terms and sage old advice in the service of a brave new culture, devoutly extroverted expression, ritual advice and rules on right living, and the equation of enterprise with the profit motive, self-culture with self-discipline and diligence, vocation with moneymaking career, and success with economic prosperity. Recurrent themes in the manuals, as in *Walden,* are economy, industry, idleness, success, poverty, philanthropy, reading, conversation, literature, diet, self-cultivation and renewal. These themes recur in work after work but also within the various chapters—a thematic repetitiousness that, as in *Walden,* is a principle of progressive definition and relatedness. Rhetorically the manuals usually follow one of two progressions: statement-clarification-maxim and statement-numerous examples-maxims, both of which are key rhetorical features of *Walden.*

Above all, almost every manual establishes a first-person narrator within its first few pages who is both self-effacing and authoritative, who speaks from much "experience," and who is middle-aged or older. The somewhat younger speaker of *Walden* appears to disqualify himself on the grounds of inadequate experience: "I should not talk so much about myself if there were any body else whom I knew as well. Unfortunately, I am confined to this theme by the narrowness of my experience" (*Walden,* 3). Yet his narrowness disqualifies an insidious kind of narrowness: "Age is no better, hardly so well, qualified for an instructor as youth, for it has not profited so much as it has lost. . . . Practically, the old have no very important advice to give the young, their own experience has been so partial. . . . I have yet to hear the first syllable of valuable or even earnest advice from my seniors. They have told me nothing, and probably cannot tell me anything, to the purpose. . . . If I have any experience which I think valuable, I am sure to reflect that this my mentors said nothing about" (89).

The strategy in Thoreau's serious parody, I suggest, is to deauthorize the success manual and its personae while authorizing a new manual and persona. Rather than repudiating the genre, *Walden* transforms it by offering a new model: "I address myself now to those of my readers who have a living to get" (60). It is an "impertinent" strategy, he concedes, but only to "those of my readers" who do not recognize its "pertinence." Such readers, the speaker recognizes, will "feel no particular interest in me" (3). That word "interest" refers here to a reader-narrator understanding or misunderstanding, but it is also a key lexical device in *Walden* to distinguish between *Walden*'s enterprise and America's nervous enterprise.

The culture of enterprise in which Thoreau endeavored to find his place and language helped to focus his vocation and concentrate his energies. His dedication to his private enterprise of vocation offers no legitimate basis for mythologizing him as a misplaced, tragic, or pathetic literary figure. To say of Thoreau, as Emerson did, that "with his energy and practical ability he seemed born for great enterprise" is an index of what "enterprise" meant to this extraordinarily successful patron, who in his eulogy at Thoreau's funeral repeated the disappointment in Thoreau's lack of enterprise that

he had been noting for more than a decade.[30] It is much more difficult to explain and assess the precise nature of Thoreau's relation to his culture than it is to explain why so many of his contemporaries ridiculed his enterprise of self-culture and questioned his literary production, and why a culture dedicated to its powerful new version of enterprise would ignore his writings for decades to come.

Notes

1. Both the subject and the scholarship are richly diverse. Rush Welter has provided the fullest intellectual history of the era in *The Mind of America 1820-1860* (New York, 1975); and Marvin Meyer and Harry Watson the most thorough studies of Jacksonian ideology and policies and their national and local implications, in *The Jacksonian Persuasion: Politics and Belief* (Stanford, 1957), and *Jacksonian Politics and Community Conflict* (Baton Rouge, 1981), respectively. In Part II and Part III of *Business in American Life* (New York, 1972), Thomas Cochran offers the best examination of how business ideology became basic to American thought and action in these years. John Cawelti's *Apostles of the Self-made Man* (Chicago, 1965), chaps. 2-3; Richard Weiss' *The American Myth of Success from Horatio Alger to Norman Vincent Peale* (New York, 1969), chap. 1; and Irvin Wyllie's *The Self-made Man in America* (New Brunswick, N.J., 1954) study the success myth of the self-made man that captured the individual and collective imagination. On various sectors of the economy the following scholars have offered the most informative surveys and analyses: on agriculture, Paul Gates, *The Farmer's Age: Agriculture, 1815-1860* (New York, 1951); on industrialization, Marvin Fisher, *Workshops in the Wilderness: The European Response to American Industrialization: 1830-1860* (New York, 1967), chaps. 5-8; and Edward C. Kirkland, *Industry Comes of Age: Business, Labor, and Public Policy, 1860-1897* (Chicago, 1961), chaps. 1-2; on transportation, George Taylor, *The Transportation Revolution, 1815-1860* (New York, 1951); on the canal-building boom in New York State, Nathan Miller, *The Enterprise of a Free People* (Ithaca, 1962); on railroads, Alfred Chandler, *The Railroads: The Nation's First Big Business* (New York, 1965), Parts I and II; on technology, John Kasson, *Civilizing the Machine: Technology and Republican Values in America, 1776-1900* (New York, 1976), chaps. 2-4; on changes in the American work force, Stanley Lebergott, *Manpower in Economic Growth: The American Record Since 1800* (New York, 1964), Part I *passim,* Part II; on banking and finance, Bray Hammond, *Banks and Politics in America from the Revolution to the Civil War* (Princeton, 1957), 286-499, 605-30; on pat-

terns of income and wealth, Edward Pessen, *Riches, Class and Power Before the Civil War* (Lexington, Mass., 1973); on publishing and the book trade, William Charvat, *The Profession of Authorship in America, 1800-1870* (Columbus, Ohio, 1968), chaps. 4, 10, 14, 15; and Charles A. Madison, *Book Publishing in America* (New York, 1966), Part I.

Regional socioeconomic studies have also appeared. The most notable: on the South, William R. Taylor, *Cavalier and Yankee: The Old South and American National Character* (New York, 1961), chap. 3; on southern communities, Watson, *Jacksonian Politics and Community Conflict*; on New England and Massachusetts, Oscar and Mary Handlin, *Commonwealth,* rev. ed. (Cambridge, Mass., 1969), chaps. 7-10. On Thoreau's town of Concord, see Robert Gross, "Culture and Cultivation: Agriculture and Society in Thoreau's Concord," *Journal of American History* 69 (June 1982): 42-61. See also Townsend Scudder, *Concord: American Town* (Boston, 1947), chaps. 11-14; and George Hendrick, ed., *Remembrances of Concord and the Thoreaus* (Urbana, 1977), *passim.*

Daniel Walker Howe has commented on the economic beliefs of the moral philosophers at Harvard and among Unitarian clergymen trained by them. See *The Unitarian Conscience: Harvard Moral Philosophy, 1805-1861* (Cambridge, Mass., 1970), chaps. 8-10. Ann Douglas has explored the changing role and behavior of the congregational clergyman in Massachusetts in the age of enterprise, in *The Feminization of American Culture* (New York, 1977), chaps. 1-4 and *passim.* Finally, Robert Gross, William Heath, and Leo Stoller have examined the influence of the new era on particular New England transcendentalists. See Gross, "'The Most Estimable Place in All the World': A Debate on Progress in Nineteenth-Century Concord," *Studies in the American Renaissance, 1978,* ed. Joel Myerson (Boston, 1978), 1-15; and idem, "Transcendentalism and Urbanism: Concord, Boston, and the Wider World," *Journal of American Studies* 18 (Dec. 1984):261-63; William G. Heath, Jr., "Cyrus Bartol's Transcendental Capitalism," *Studies in the American Renaissance, 1979,* ed. Joel Myerson (Boston, 1979), 399-408; and Leo Stoller, *After Walden: Thoreau's Changing Views on Economic Man* (Stanford, 1957), *passim.*

2. Taylor has been summarized by Meyer, *The Jacksonian Persuasion,* 88-89. My list abbreviates and slightly modifies Meyer's summary.

3. Hammond, *Banks and Politics in America,* 327.

4. Welter, *The Mind of America 1820-1860,* 129.

5. Hendrick, *Remembrances of Concord and the Thoreaus,* 5.

6. On Bartol, see Heath, "Cyrus Bartol's Transcendental Capitalism"; on Emerson's investment in the Fitchburg Railroad, see Scudder, *Concord: American Town,* 190. On the impact of the spirit of enterprise on the clergy, Daniel Howe's assertion that the basic values of Unitarian moralists and the ministers they trained did not essentially change needs to be qualified. See Howe, *The Unitarian Conscience,* 205.

7. Douglas, *The Feminization of American Culture,* chaps. 3-4.

8. The only study I am aware of that acknowledges changes in the cultural discourse that are closely tied to the economic transformation is Welter, *The Mind of America 1820-1860,* in his chapter titled, simply, "Enterprise." He briefly examines the etymology and nineteenth-century American usage of the word *enterprise* (156-59).

9. Gross, "Culture and Cultivation" and "'The Most Estimable Place in All the World.'"

10. For Adams, see "Inaugural Address" and "Fourth Annual Message," *A Compilation of the Messages and Papers of the Presidents* (New York, 1897), 2:860-65 and 3:973-87, respectively. For Jackson, see especially his "First Inaugural Address" (3:999-1001) and "Farewell Address" (4:1511-527). Other speeches included in this survey are Martin Van Buren, "Inaugural Address" (4:1530-537) and "Fourth Annual Message" (5:1819-837); James Polk, "Inaugural Address" (5:2223-232) and "Fourth Annual Message" (6:2479-521); Zachary Taylor, "Inaugural Address" (6:2542-544); Millard Fillmore, "Third Annual Message" (6:2699-3718); Franklin Pierce, "Inaugural Address" (6:2730-736) and "Fourth Annual Message" (7:2930-950). Hereafter cited in text as *Presidents.*

11. Frederika Bremer captures key aspects of the term *enterprise* in its positive connotation in the vernacular. Her description of the "enterprising" young American citizen of the 1850s is "a young man (no matter if he be old) who makes his own way in the world in full reliance on his own power, stops at nothing, shrinks from nothing, finds nothing impossible, tries everything, has faith in everything. . . . If he is unsuccessful, he says 'Try again!' 'Go ahead!' and he begins over again, undertaking something else, and never stopping until he succeeds." *America of the Fifties,* ed. Adolph A. Benson (New York, 1924), 92-93.

12. Francis Bowen, *The Principles of Political Economy* (Boston, 1856), 107; chaps. 8-10; 93, 122, 123. On specifically economic uses of *enter-*

prise see entire text but esp. chaps. 7-10 and, for typical examples: agriculture, 88, 108; commerce, 108; trade, 88; manufacturing, 88, 91, 126; shops and factories, 129; railroads and canals, 101; finance, 108; and corporation stockholding, 130.

13. Ibid., 116. The history of American dictionaries confirms the exceedingly conservative character of dictionary writing until the 1960s. Not until the past few decades, when lexicographers and linguists changed from prescriptive to descriptive principles of lexicography, was the specifically economic usage of *enterprise, private enterprise,* and related terms acknowledged. Thesauruses, in contrast, have acknowledged the economic meanings since early in this century. As for economic lexicons, *Palgrave's Dictionary of Political Economy* (London, 1894) uses the term *enterprise* in its general sense but Horton's *Dictionary of Modern Economics* (Washington, D.C., 1948), a lexicon designed to describe well-entrenched American economic vernacular largely ignored by Palgrave, defines *enterprise* as a "business venture undertaken for profit. . . . More specifically, it may be conceived of as the activities involved in initiating and operating a business venture" (115).

14. Howe, *The Unitarian Conscience,* 227, 231-32.

15. Robert C. Winthrop, *An Address Delivered Before the Boston Mercantile Library Association . . . Oct. 15, 1845* (Boston, 1845), 22.

16. *Debates of the Texas Convention,* William F. Weeks, reporter (Austin, 1845), 645; quoted in Welter, *The Mind of America 1820-1860,* 133.

17. Quoted in Kirkland, *Industry Comes of Age,* 3.

18. House of Representatives Executive Document No. 78, 39th Congress (1867), *United States Government Documents,* Serial 1293, 27-28; House of Representatives Miscellaneous Document No. 15, 45th Congress (1879), ibid., Serial 1861, 5-6; House of Representatives Miscellaneous Document No. 29, 45th Congress (1879), ibid., Serial 1863, 515-42.

19. Several other sample titles from Timothy Shay Arthur's storehouse of formulaic romances and tales about money, morals, and success are: *Keeping Up Appearances; A Tale for the Rich and Poor* (at least eleven editions); *Retiring From Business; or The Rich Man's Error* (at least eight editions); *Rising in the World; or, A Tale for the Rich and Poor* (at least seven editions); *True Riches and Other Tales* (at least thirteen editions); and *The Way to Prosper* (at least nine editions).

Louisa Tuthill's inspirational romances on the theme of enterprise were fewer in number, but were extraordinarily profitable. *I Will Be A Gentleman,* for example, appeared in close to forty editions and the just-as-mellifluously-platitudinous *Onward! Right Onward!* passed through at least twenty-one editions. Her heroes, like Arthur's, are naturally enterprising. Yet they must earn their successes in an environment of corruption and dangerous evils, where enterprise is not a natural expression.

20. *Journal* 3:270 of *The Writings of Henry David Thoreau* (Boston, 1906), also numbered Volume 9 in the 20-volume *Writings; Walden,* ed. Lyndon Shanley, *The Writings of Henry D. Thoreau* (Princeton, 1971), 20, 329. Hereafter *Journal* volumes 3 and beyond in *Writings* are cited in the text as *J* and the Princeton *Walden* as *Walden.*

21. *Early Essays and Miscellanies,* ed. Joseph Moldenhauer and Edwin Moser, *The Writings of Henry D. Thoreau* (Princeton, 1975), 13-14. Hereafter cited in text as *EEM.*

22. Howe, *The Unitarian Conscience,* 226-35.

23. *Reform Papers,* ed. Wendell Glick, *The Writings of Henry D. Thoreau* (Princeton, 1975).

24. The opening pages of Thoreau's first draft of a *Walden* narrative, later enlarged and titled "Economy," are independently numbered, as a check of his worksheets (Huntington Library CSmH HM924) will confirm. The bulk of them (probably to page 30 verso), were originally composed as a lecture that Thoreau presented on 10 Feb. 1847 and again on 17 Feb. at the Concord Lyceum. Pages 31 recto to 35 verso appear to be redrafts of preliminary worksheets. The sequence for "Economy" runs 1 to 51. At least twelve leaves, including most of the concluding pages of "Economy," were subsequently added, very likely when Thoreau began to work toward a functional linguistic and thematic transition from the lecture manuscript to his growing *Walden* account. Whether these leaves were added after Thoreau had essentially completed a first draft of *Walden* cannot be ascertained. The rest of the first draft, beginning with what eventually became "Where I Lived and What I Lived For," starts a new numbering sequence, which raises the strong possibility that Thoreau originally began *Walden* with what we know as the second chapter.

25. Howe, *The Unitarian Conscience,* 100-20, 226-35; David Robinson, *Apostle of Culture: Emerson as Preacher and Lecturer* (Philadelphia, 1982), 7-29 and *passim.*

26. Vocation, from *vocatio, vocationis,* originally referred to the irresistibility of a divine summons. As understood by conservative Catholic scholars of the Renaissance and the majority of the leading

Protestant reformers, this summons to exercise a special function, perform a special work, or take up a particular life's calling, was contrary to man's inclinations and will. Both in Protestantism and in conservative Catholicism the term gradually accommodated both the sense of an arbitrary divine call and the humanist's concept of the way of life (*genus vitae*), in which individual choice, based on the weighing of alternatives, is central. The latter view was held by liberal Catholics like Erasmus and many of the Arminian Protestant sects. The idea of a man called by a sovereign God to perform God's designated work is a concept not easily reconciled with a religious version of the *homo oeconomicus,* a concept usually associated with the humanist's understanding of *vocatio,* but the ambitions of a Cotton Mather constrained him to attempt to reconcile the two. In colonial America the Puritans emphasized the former view, the liberal Anglicans, the Quakers, and some of the Anabaptists the latter. A much less frequent use of the term in early American religious writing equates vocation with the state of grace in God's economy. Here the term is directly linked to a processive state of salvation and the harmony with God realized in this state. Texts directly or indirectly addressing vocation, calling, and appointed task include: William Bradford's *Of Plymouth Plantation*; Edward Johnson's *Wonder-Working Providence*; John Cotton's *The Way of Life*; Cotton Mather's *A Christian at his Calling* and *Agricola*; John Flavel's *Husbandry Spiritualized* and *Navigation Spiritualized*; Richard Steele's *The Husbandman's Calling* and *The Religious Trademan*; Samuel Sewall's *Diary*; John Woolman's *Journal*; Benjamin Franklin's *Autobiography* and "Poor Richard"; Jean de Crevecoeur's *Letter from an American Farmer*; and Thomas Jefferson's *Notes on the State of Virginia.* Instructive noncomformist English texts on the topic include William Perkins, *A Treatise of the Vocations, or Callings of Men* (first printed separately in 1605) and George Swinnock, *The Christian-Mans Calling* (1665). For an excellent discussion of *vocatio* as understood and used in early modern Europe see Richard M. Douglas, "Talent and Vocation in Humanist and Protestant Thought," in *Action and Conviction in Early Modern Europe,* ed. Theodore K. Rabb and Jerrold E. Seigel (Princeton, 1969), 261-98. I am indebted to Professor Douglas for the primary distinction between the conservative and enlightened humanist views of vocation.

27. Robinson, *Apostle of Culture,* 10.

28. *The Correspondence of Henry David Thoreau,* ed. Walter Harding and Carl Bode (New York, 1958), 57.

29. By no means do I presume to have gathered all of the titles or even all of the popular titles of success manuals for young men published from the early 1830s to the early 1850s. Nevertheless, the following list is provisionally offered both as a representative sampler and a fairly complete roster of success manuals for young men to appear in these years: John S. C. Abbott, *The School-Boy: A Guide for Youth to Truth and Duty* (1839); William A. Alcott, *The Young Man's Guide* (1833) and *Familiar Letters to Young Men* (1849); Timothy Shay Arthur, *Advice to Young Men on their Duties and Conduct in Life* (1847); Henry Ward Beecher, *Lectures to Young Men on their Duties and Conduct in Life* (1844); Nathan S. Beman, *The Claims of our Country on Young Men* (1843); Charles Butler, *The American Gentleman* (1836); Dorus Clarke, *Lectures to Young People in Manufacturing Villages* (1836); John Frost, *The Young Merchant* (1840) and *The Young Mechanic* (1843); William T. Hamilton, *The Responsibilities of American Youth* (1851); Joel Hawes, *Letters Addressed to the Young Men of Hartford and New-Haven* (1828); John Todd, *The Student's Manual Designed, by Specific Directions, to Aid in Forming and Strengthening the Intellectual and Moral Character and Habits of the Students* (1835) and *The Foundations of Success* (1843); William H. Van Doren, *Mercantile Morals; or Thoughts for Young Men Entering Mercantile Life* (1852); Daniel Wise, *The Young Man's Counsellor; or, Sketches and Illustrations of the Duties and Dangers of Young Men* (1850).

30. *Lectures and Biographical Sketches,* in *The Complete Works of Ralph Waldo Emerson,* ed. Edward E. Emerson (Boston and New York, 1903), 10:430.

Henry Golemba (essay date October 1988)

SOURCE: Golemba, Henry. "Unreading Thoreau." *American Literature* 60, no. 3 (October 1988): 385-401.

[*In the following essay, Golemba evaluates Thoreau's mixing of diverse literary forms in* Walden. *Golemba believes that the ambivalence and indeterminacy of Thoreau's prose style reflect an underlying preoccupation with "process over product."*]

When readers encounter **Walden**'s opening pages, they are immediately struck by a clash of rhetorical modes. The first paragraph seems straightforward enough and reads rather conventionally as a journalistic record or as an autobiographical account. Although its facts may have been bent to achieve narrative purposes, the paragraph is expressed in a plain style communicating information directly. Its meaning is clear, whether that meaning is meant to serve creative or simply factual ends—whether creatively signaling the reader to receive the event as an experiment and to imagine the author as a sojourner in civilized life, or when bluntly describing the locale and duration of the experiment. The rhetorical mode of this paragraph is rooted in the American tradition, reminding one of William Bradford's early attempt to record history simply and earnestly in a plain style.[1]

The third paragraph is likewise clear in meaning and traditional in form, yet its tone differs greatly from the first paragraph. Its satirical material sounds harsh, and the plain style has been transformed, invoking exaggeration and hyperbole, and introducing exotic Oriental and Classical references. Still, the paragraph's intent is sharply defined: a forceful criticism of normal routine in which men misspend their lives almost masochistically. Rhetorically, its most interesting point is its treatment of the reading audience. The first paragraph had located its readers as the main point of address and had invited them to partake directly of the message almost as though sharing a meal, but the third paragraph situates the reader in the margin of the text, as it were, as though asking the reader to hold Thoreau's coat while he rolls up his sleeves and wades into battle. The text posits those "who are said to live in New England" or even "in this town" as the principal point of address, thus freeing its readers to choose when they wish to place themselves safely at the author's elbow in the margin of the text and when to see themselves as the target of one of Thoreau's attacks. Although clever, this rhetorical strategy is nevertheless conventional, a technique long established as a staple in the genre of satire. Every reader would be sure about how a reader is intended to receive this paragraph's messages and how to respond to its rhetorical signals.

Although different in tone and intent, the first and third paragraphs are identical in that they emerge from established literary modes and present messages clearly. However, the intervening paragraph is markedly different. While the first paragraph may sound as traditional as Bradford's history and the third may be as familiar as Swift's satire, this middle paragraph is a completely different mode. It is unconventional, puzzling, ambiguous. It seems to retract a statement as soon as it is made, to withdraw a declaration as soon as it is uttered, to qualify an assertion to the extent that the reader doubts an assertion has been made. In sharp contrast to the clarity and what Thoreau likes to call "sincerity" of the other two paragraphs, this one seems intent on making everything not just contrary and oxymoronic but indeterminate, leaving readers to guess insecurely about how literally and sincerely they should take any given sentence. The first paragraph may make a literary scholar feel that speech-act theory, which emphasizes

the idea that a writer has a definite message to convey, would be quite appropriate, and the third may seem to call for an analysis like Bakhtin's of Menippean satire or Bercovitch's of the American Jeremiad, but this second paragraph sounds like the kind that has caused Lawrence Buell to describe Thoreau as sounding sometimes like a post-structuralist in a department full of New Critics.[2]

Indeterminacies abound from the paragraph's first sentence even when considering only one rhetorical essential such as how one is to imagine oneself as the reader in one's relationship to the text. *Walden*'s readers are regretfully informed that they must be told details of the author's affairs, the autobiographical record that has proved most endearing to the majority of readers from Thoreau's day to the present, and yet the text suggests that its best readers are "those of my readers" who are superior to autobiographical details, those "who feel no particular interest in me" and who are allowed a privileged reading relationship to the author by being empowered to pardon him—all this despite the fact that the author has obviously taken great pains and, as the record of the reading response has demonstrated, has wonderfully succeeded in making this account of life in the woods intriguing, fascinating, and delightful. Although *Walden*'s principal audience may be variously suggested in later paragraphs as those who are shackled to materialism and their possessions by "golden and silver fetters" or possibly the "mass of men" who lead lives of quiet desperation, a very different but explicit audience is defined in this second paragraph: "Perhaps these pages are more particularly addressed to poor students." However, in contrast to the distinct and memorable descriptions of other possible audiences in other paragraphs, this sentence is more slippery; it begins with a qualifying "Perhaps" and ends with "poor students," which could mean poor in economic terms as a financially strapped version of Emerson's American scholar, or it might mean poor, as Michael West has observed, in an intellectual sense as those who might try to warp the text to fit their own theses.[3] Finally, the paragraph concludes with the Carlylean metaphor of Thoreau's coat. In this trope for *Walden*'s philosophy, Thoreau trusts "that none will stretch the seams in putting on the coat, for it may do good service to him whom it fits." But readers cannot be sure just how big this makes them, whether the metaphor presents the author as modestly assuming that some of his readers may be larger than he, or whether the author is safe to trust since we might be that race of pygmies described in *Walden*'s conclusion who could never stretch the seams of Thoreau's woven work. The latter seems all the more possible since it has been preceded by the author's complaint—when the author describes himself as a reader—that he has never read a true book of a true life. But even that interpretation is slippery, for one is not positive which lack the author-reader more laments, whether it is the absence of "a simple and sincere account" or of a man who "has lived sincerely," whether the complaint is more aesthetic or philosophical.

Despite this swirl of indecision, complexity, and indeterminacy, one point remains clear. The paragraph offers an implied promise that Thoreau will either speak from or fill that gap of a "sincere account," and that he will make some of his readers feel that they are being treated as if they were his "kinsmen" who are being addressed from a far "distant land," a distance necessitated by time and space and, much more significantly in rhetorical matters, a distance represented by the pages of the text which stand between reader and author and simultaneously provide the bridge by which reader and author can entertain the illusion of kinship, communion, communication. Thus, in a paragraph which seems so thoroughly to dissolve itself, one message emerges clearly, and yet that message emerges from an absence, a lack, an existing gap. Thoreau's promise of a sincere account of a life sincerely lived remains precisely that—a promise, a possibility which can be entertained only in the transitory act of reading.

These initial three paragraphs with their intermixture of rhetorical modes resemble in one sense Hawthorne's idealization of a remarkable new kind of writing which he adumbrates, apparently at the time when he and Thoreau were close friends: "To write a dream, which shall resemble the real course of a dream, with all its inconsistency, its eccentricities and aimlessness—with nevertheless a leading idea running through the whole. Up to this old age of the world, no such thing has ever been written."[4] *Walden* proffers many "leading ideas" that are confidently asserted and clearly articulated. Its author does believe firmly that many waste their lives, that the railroad rides upon us, that nature can be rejuvenating and beautiful, that materialism exacts a dear price, that thought and self-discovery are worthwhile pursuits. Still, these "leading ideas" are often wrapped within cloaks of obscurity and ambiguity. Certainty is frequently interwoven with uncertainty. Even simplicity can become highly complex. *Walden*'s longest chapter might detail in extreme precision how economically and cheaply one may live, but the post-structuralist Thoreau advises no one to undertake his dietary regimen unless that reader already has "a well stocked larder" in reserve. *Walden* clearly extols the crucial value of leading a virtuous life and praises the desire to sow the seeds of "sincerity, truth, simplicity, faith, innocence, and the like," but "The Bean-Field" chapter confesses, "Alas! I said this to myself; but now another summer is gone, and another, and another, and I am obliged to say to you, Reader, that the seeds which I planted, if indeed they *were* the seeds of those virtues, were worm-eaten or had lost their vitality, and so did not come up." More than one reader has remarked the jarring note felt when Thoreau writes that he "caged"

himself in the woods, or the sense of uneasiness when the author describes how a cat takes to the woods like Thoreau, but becomes a wild cat and "a dead cat at last," and Walter Benn Michaels has argued that the anecdote in *Walden*'s conclusion about the boy who misleads a traveler into becoming mired in a bog casts doubt on all of Thoreau's other assertions that there is a solid bottom everywhere if only we dive down deeply enough to find it. In fact, while the leading idea of *Walden*'s "Conclusion" is clearly meant to inspire readers to step to the music which they hear and to lead more heroic lives, the inspirational message is mixed. Precisely how much is one meant to be encouraged when at the mid-point of the concluding chapter one encounters the sentiment: "Love your life, poor as it is. . . . It is not so bad as you are"?[5]

Moreover, one could argue that the sentence that most extremely represents Thoreau's ultimate confrontation with the limits and indeterminacy of language is the one which introduces his famous aphorism about building castles in the air. Although his renowned air-castle image definitely and clearly urges readers simultaneously to dream and to work hard to place solid foundations under their dreams, this inspirational passage is prefaced by the sentence: "In proportion as he simplifies his life, the laws of the universe will appear less complex, and solitude will not be solitude, nor poverty poverty, nor weakness weakness." A radical interpretation of this statement would say that words do not mean what they say; if poverty does not equal poverty, then love does not mean love; x does not equal x, nor y, y. Even a more conservative translation would have to interpret the sentence to mean that the author's language is a private language independent of the public language which his culture has composed, and dictionaries, thesauri, or other repositories of cultural discourse will not help much in translating its meaning. Fittingly, Thoreau begins the next paragraph, "It is a ridiculous demand which England and America make, that you shall speak so that they can understand you. Neither men nor toad-stools grow so."

This interweaving of rhetorical modes, particularly the blending of "leading ideas" with dream-like dissolves, of assertions with infinite qualifiers, of clear sentences with the perpetual sense of their imminent erasure, is the crux of that writing which we call Thoreau's. Essentially this interweaving consists of three rhetorical strands. Some statements are confidently urged, maxims forcefully proposed. Other passages are more suggestive, less explicit; the concluding image of the sun as a morning star is one such example. Still other sections seem to dissolve as they are read; seemingly crystal-clear sentiments melt into obscuring fogs. Some statements are said, others unsaid, still others unsaid, and often all three types of rhetorical effect are deployed together. Seemingly in anticipation of this modern critical language, Thoreau called the said, the unsaid and the un-said the "halloo, the whisper, and silence" (*Journal 1,* 61).

A more conventional writer less interested than Thoreau in the boundaries and limits of language—whether naturalist, social reformer, satirist, moralist—might attempt to avoid this last rhetorical mode in order to seem as explicit and clear as possible, but Thoreau revelled in experimenting with the possibilities of language, more so in *Walden* than in works like **"Slavery in Massachusetts"** and his John Brown essays, less so in *Walden* than in essays like **"Moonlight"** and his first book, *A Week on the Concord and Merrimack Rivers.* Linck C. Johnson has recently demonstrated that in its earliest drafts *A Week* [*A Week on the Concord and Merrimack Rivers*] was far more structured, coherent, and accessible than the final published version.[6] Much of Thoreau's effort in revising *A Week* was directed at making it less conventional, less easy to follow, less easily comprehensible. With respect to *Walden,* I would argue that the reader may be fairly blamed for these narrative dissolves, for the un-saying of meaning, for the pains Thoreau spent in his revisions making his message at once more sincere and more elusive. Of course, by "reader" I mean Thoreau's conception of his reader or, to put it more accurately, his attempt to create an idealized process of reading.

Therefore, in the remainder of this essay I wish to clarify Thoreau's conception of his idealized reader, the one whom Thoreau makes responsible for the dissolving rhetorical technique in *Walden.* I choose to triangulate this conception by briefly examining two related concerns of Thoreau's day: the debate over the most effective communicative form of language, and Thoreau's interpretation of nature as text.

Over the past decade, scholars have done much to explain the intense discussion of language's role, especially with respect to biblical exegesis. Philip F. Gura, for one, has admirably described the evolution of linguistic concerns from James Marsh to Horace Bushnell and Charles Kraitsir. Bushnell in particular illustrates a profound shift in the definition of language's supreme function. Strongly influenced by Kant, Coleridge, and others, Bushnell theorized about the rhetorical value of inexplicit language. As Gura explains: "'Writing became, in this manner, to a considerable extent, *the making of a language,* and not a going to the dictionaries' [Gura's italics]. Feeling a new exhilaration in the choice and use of his vocabulary, he became aware of how, as [Bushnell] put it, 'the second, third, the thirteenth sense of words—all but the physical first sense—belong to the empyrean, and are given, as we see in the prophets, to be inspired by.'"[7] Bushnell was one of many composing a movement which redefined the priorities of linguistic communication, shifting emphasis from the

literal to the figurative, from the exact to the metaphorical, from the explicit to the suggestive. Opposed to Hegel, who perceived a fusion of antithetical postulates, these philosophical linguists stressed a "liquidation," a flowing together of opposites into a suspended truth. Or as Bushnell says, again as Gura interprets him: "The creative use of language involved a powerful dialectic process: 'as form battles form, and one [word] neutralizes another, all [their] insufficiencies are filled out' and 'the contrarieties liquidated,' allowing the mind to 'settle into a full and just apprehension of the pure spiritual truth.' Man never comes as close to absolute truth, Bushnell declared, 'as when it is offered paradoxically,' under 'contradictions'; that is, 'under two or more dictions, which taken as dictions, are contrary one to the other.'" Only through paradox can language approach an absolute truth, only through linguistic expression of contrary dictions can a sense of "sincerity" be conveyed, only through a series of harmonies which neutralize each other like the harmonic motion of waves can a writer approach that fullest expression of sound and sense wherein the grandest sense of sound is silence.

As I will soon show, Thoreau's language theory was more radical than that represented by philologists like Bushnell and Kraitsir, but what I should make clear at this point is that Thoreau's similar theory antedates theirs. Publishing their most influential books in 1846 and 1849 respectively, Kraitsir and Bushnell may have reinforced and encouraged Thoreau's own linguistic developments as he paused for several months before undertaking the final three revisions of *Walden,* but he had settled many of their crucial issues for himself by 1842 when he published **"Natural History of Massachusetts"** in *The Dial,* writing that "Nature is mythical and mystical always, and works with the license and extravagance of genius. She has her luxurious and florid style as well as art." Pushing beyond the Kantian or Hegelian need to yoke opposites in synthesis, Thoreau went so far as to suggest an equation of chaos with beauty, of wildness with aesthetic pleasure. By the time he had prepared **"Walking, or The Wild"** as a lecture in 1851, he began to suspect what he would confidently assert in the published version of **"Walking"**: "In literature it is only the wild that attracts us. Dullness is but another name for tameness. It is the uncivilized free and wild thinking in *Hamlet* and the *Iliad,* in all the scriptures and mythologies, not learned in the schools, that delights us. . . . A truly good book is something as natural, and as unexpectedly and unaccountably fair and perfect, as a wild-flower discovered on the prairies of the West or in the jungles of the East. Genius is a light which makes the darkness visible, like the lightning's flash, which perchance shatters the temple of knowledge itself. . . ." This language theory ranges far beyond Kraitsir's and Bushnell's with their emphasis on metaphor, paradox, and oxymoron. Rather than seeking a synthesis of multiple dictions, Thoreau's theory involved a true contra-diction: a use of language to create the impression of meaning which is immediately called into question or rendered into unmeaning; a positing of a temple of knowledge which is promptly shattered. Others may have reasoned that paradoxical language could convey the highest meaning, but Thoreau had developed the idea that the highest rhetoric created meaning which provided gaps in its own significance. As he wrote in a letter to Emerson for 12 February 1843, friends communicate most effectively when "We communicate like the burrows of foxes, in silence and darkness, under ground. . . . How much more full is Nature where we think the empty space is than where we place the solids!—full of fluid influences. Should we ever communicate but by these? The spirit abhors a vacuum more than Nature." By deliberately placing "silence," "darkness," and "empty space" in his text, the literary artist could more forcefully provoke the reader's spirit to attempt to fill the text's vacuum, to strive to span its gaps. The highest rhetoric offers "solids" of meaning which the reader can study and understand but also "empty space" which the reader struggles to fill with material whose provenance is outside the text.[8]

Walden is as much a language experiment in a "natural style" as it is a record of "Life in the Woods." A natural style, like nature itself, speaks in many dictions, in a variety of styles. It can sound florid and plain, Egyptian and New English. At another rhetorical level it involves an eloquent silence, "the silence of a dense pine wood" as Thoreau told Daniel Ricketson. On that level, a natural style resembles the most artificial of aesthetic forms; the writer goes to nature for the same reason that "Men go to the opera because they hear there a faint expression of this news which is never quite distinctly expressed." Thoreau admired this natural style even in the speech of children, representing them as those closest to nature's speech, furthest from a learned diction. As he told Emerson in a letter for 10 February 1843, his young daughter was already proficient in this natural style.

> And like the gypsies she talks a language of her own while she understands ours. While she jabbers Sanskrit, Parsee, Pehlvi, say "Edith go bah!" and "bah" it is. No intelligence passes between us. She knows. It is a capital joke,—that is the reason she smiles so. How well the secret is kept! She never descends to explanation. It is not buried like a common secret, bolstered up on two sides, but by an eternal silence on the one side, at least. It has been long kept, and comes in from the unexplored horizon, like a blue mountain range, to end abruptly at our door one day. (Don't stumble at this steep simile.) Query: what comes of the answers Edith thinks, but cannot express? She really gives you glances which are before this world was. You can't feel any difference of age, except that you have longer legs and arms.[9]

In describing Edith's natural style, Thoreau emphasizes many points. Untutored Edith already intuits the bases of all languages, speaks a private language which antedates all public discourse, speaks most provocatively in silent glances, and enjoys her unspoken rhetoric in good humor. Or, more properly, Thoreau does all this, for it is after all his own interpretations of Edith's silent meanings and stylistic gifts which he presents as hers. In entertaining Edith as "author," Thoreau makes himself his own idealized reader, a reader who is co-author, filling Edith's silent glances with meaning.

A point that should be emphasized is how Thoreau intrudes upon his own presentation of Edith's rhetoric by means of parenthetical remark, a technique which he would develop in his published works. After describing this young child's silent meanings and natural style in metaphors borrowed from nature, he jokes and puns. After creating a beautiful simile, he calls attention to the fact that it is a simile, labels it "steep," and warns Emerson not to stumble over it. After conveying a very difficult, abstract idea in graphic terms, he chooses to give three signals which cast doubt upon how seriously one is to take the idea. That is, after narrating how Edith's inscrutable secret is rhetorically effective because it seems "bolstered up" by "an eternal silence on the one side, at least," Thoreau adds his joking parenthesis which succeeds in unmaking the statement by removing the end wall of his paragraph and substituting what he might call a bolstering silence. In modern critical terms, one would say that after Thoreau carefully describes the rhetorical power of Edith's indeterminacy, he renders even that idea of indeterminacy indeterminate. To achieve a similar effect, he often uses varieties of intrusion throughout *Walden.* Perhaps the most famous is his Artist of Kouroo sketch in the "Conclusion." Thoreau's ideal artist has transcended many commonplace cares and distractions, the chief of which is time: "As he made no compromise with Time, Time kept out of his way, and only sighed at a distance because he could not overcome him." But in the midst of this ideal sketch of his time-transcendent artist, Thoreau interrupts to ask, "But why do I stay to mention these things?" Impatience intrudes upon patience, a care for time upon timelessness. The "leading idea" of the perfect artist has been qualified by an interruptive practicing artist. The temple of a thought has been cracked, if not shattered.

The logical question to be posed is why should Thoreau be so concerned about unmaking assertions? Why should he strive with such pains to become the "Unsayer of Concord" in an age of Melvillean nay-saying and Emersonian aye-saying? What purpose is served in spending ten years rendering indeterminate texts like *Walden* and *A Week* which seem so confident and self-assured? Several reasons apply. The most obvious is the Transcendental commitment to thinking over thought, to process over product, to being over system; the sort of phenomenon which has caused the editor of Thoreau's poetry to remark that he was much more interested in the theory of poetry than he was in the production of poems.[10] That poets should be "liberating gods" became a Transcendental maxim soon after Emerson first uttered the aesthetic goal. Proverbs like "every thought is a prison" imply that even that thought is a prison. With the Transcendental stress upon intuitive reason over analytical understanding, a Thoreau could proclaim the seemingly mystical statement: "Give me a sentence which no intelligence can understand." He would concur with Emerson that Man Thinking is superior to the mere thinker, and Thoreau would go on in his belief that, although it is a profound service to mankind to proffer noble precepts to live by and to pinpoint the errors of life's normal routine, liberation from any settled thought, even the most noble, is the highest morality.

Admittedly this explanation is obvious, almost a textbook definition of Transcendental aesthetics, but it leads to a more profound point. When discussing Kraitsir and Bushnell's theory of language, I stated that their emphasis was biblical exegesis. Thoreau did not share their orientation. While the Bible was their text, Thoreau's was nature, and Thoreau had concluded early in his writing career that nature, inspiring though it may be, was so vast and complex that it stood apart from human systems of meaning, and it eluded attempts to understand it. In trying to console Emerson over the death of his son, Thoreau (who had recently lost his brother) wrote that "the old laws" of nature prevail in spite of pestilence and famine, genius and virtue. "Nature is not ruffled by the rudest blast—the hurricane only snaps a few twigs in some nook of the forest." To H. G. O. Blake a few months before *Walden* was published, he explained that there was "no up nor down in nature," only expansion. In **"Walking, or The Wild,"** he wrote that "Nature is a personality so vast and universal that we have never seen one of her features."[11] In *Walden,* he attempted to present the reader with a text that mirrored the nature which Thoreau believed he perceived. A pine tree might inspire, and so might a proverb; a frozen sandbank might melt, and so might a thought; a fog might evaporate into air, and so an idea; a bog might mire a traveler, and so might an exhortation the reader. Looking into the text of *Walden* fluidly reflects the vision Thoreau experienced when looking into nature.

And, as Thoreau delighted in the intense aesthetic pleasure of being the reader of nature's text, so he felt an equally intense need to imagine idealized readers of his own texts. He enjoyed reading a loon, a chipmunk or a battle between ants, but he could not expect them to read him. As he says in *A Week*: "It takes two to speak the truth,—one to speak, and another to hear. How can one treat with magnanimity mere wood and stone?"[12]

I do not mean to ascribe a psychological motive to Thoreau, being more focused here on his rhetorical ambitions. The need for a reader and the compulsion to work painstakingly on a text like *Walden* for ten years, even declining early publication in 1849 in order to present it to the public in what Thoreau considered its best form, were philosophically and aesthetically motivated. As suggested in the quotation from *A Week,* in order to express meaning, reading is as necessary as writing; reader and writer are collaborators in attempting to express a thought through words especially when their communication transcends the dictionary meaning of those shared words. One of Thoreau's most poignant expressions of literacy as a communal act occurs in his *Journal* for the Summer of 1845: "When I play my flute tonight earnest as if to leap the bounds that narrow fold where human life is penned, and range the surrounding plain—I hear echo from a neighboring wood a stolen pleasure occasionally not rightfully heard—much more for other ears than ours for tis the reverse of sound. It is not our own melody that comes back to us—but an amended strain. And I would only hear myself as I would hear my echo—corrected and repronounced for me. It is as when my friend reads my verse" (*Journal* 2 [Princeton Edition], 167). Thoreau's emphases on "echoes," "other ears," the "reverse of sound," "amended strains," and "repronouncements," attest to the importance he grants the reader/listener. Without another reading, the message does not communicate, indeed does not exist. Without the reader/listener, the writer cannot, as Thoreau seriously puns, "leap the bounds that narrow fold where human life is penned." By a free, not a literal translation, the reader can enable the writer finally to "range the surrounding plain" and not pigeonhole the writer's meaning as an explicit statement. As Thoreau expresses in his earliest *Walden* journal, the reader can help free the text from literal meaning in order to achieve a universal language using the ineffability of words to suggest "the inexpressible meaning that is in all things" (2, 178). By believing in a loving Echo, the text may be rescued from Narcissus' fate. Or, to express the idea less pretentiously, the conception of a reader who reads, as it were, beyond the words enabled Thoreau to feel justified in un-saying his statements in the interest of suggesting a more abstract truth than could a didactic message or an image of moral signification. That "universal language," of course, meant communication as Thoreau intended the term, a constant looking through words (in both meanings of "through") as opposed to the settled perception of an idea, a perpetual process of interpretation and translation of possible meaning. As he wrote in his *Journal* for Spring 1846 in terms that echo his request in *Walden*'s second paragraph that readers pardon him when he undertakes to respond to autobiographical questions, "If you would not stop to look at me,—but look whither I am looking and further—then my education could not dispense with thy company" (2, 239).

It is therefore no surprise that so much of **Walden** should be preoccupied with descriptions of Thoreau's conceptions of a variety of his imagined readers: its first two dozen pages, many intermittent references, an entire chapter titled "Reading." Just as *Moby-Dick* may be approached as an intermixture of various writing styles, **Walden** may be studied as an interweaving of different reading experiences. At its most contrasted, the reader's relationship with the writer can be described as warfare or as communion; in "Visitors" as a hostile activity where the author threatens to put a "bullet" of thought into the listener's ear, in "Winter Visitors" as a friendly relationship with reader and writer peacefully wading "so gently and reverently" that "the fishes of thought were not scared from the stream," but "came and went grandly, like the clouds which sometimes form and dissolve there." Perhaps the most profound of these reading experiences is presented in one of **Walden**'s most famous passages: "I long ago lost a hound, a bay horse, and a turtle dove, and am still on their trail. Many are the travellers I have spoken concerning them, describing their tracks and what calls they answered to. I have met one or two who had heard the hound, and the tramp of the horse, and even seen the dove disappear behind a cloud, *and they seemed as anxious to recover them as if they had lost them themselves*" (italics mine). As the most glossed passage in all of Thoreau's works, it testifies to the power of Thoreau's "leading idea." Scholars have searched diligently to discover what these three animals represent. Treating these animals as emblems in a personal equation, many have tried to make them stand for explicit losses, approaching them as allegories much like Thoreau's coat representing fashion and Walden Pond itself as "earth's eye." When one of Thoreau's contemporary readers asked the "meaning" of this parable, he responded, "I suppose we all have our losses."[13]

He supposed much more than that. The text invites readers to read this parable as an allegory, but it also presents a metaphor of desire. The passage seems autobiographical and specific, and yet it is simultaneously a universal and abstract intimation of that generalized sense of a revelation always imminent but never quite realized, a discovery always promised but never quite grasped by the words which have pointed toward it. Yet a crucial significance is one seldom glossed: the miracle of attempted communication, the fact that anonymous others, readers who are technically strangers, should express an anxiety as intense as the author's to recover losses, to reach toward an understanding. It is a marvel

sufficient sheerly to contemplate. It is as "telling" as one of Edith's silent glances, as eloquent as the hush of a pine woods.

Lest this conclusion seem too serene, too settled, too conclusive, Thoreau's miracle of communication should be balanced by its darker side, should preserve its dynamic tensions. If communication as he defines it is a miracle, then it is an agonized miracle. Discovering that others share one's losses may cause a sense of communion, but it is an aching community of unsatisfied and unsatisfiable desire. Asking readers to "look whither I am looking and further" may articulate a rhetorical ideal, but it clearly involves anxiety over the loss of an author's control and authority. Silence may be offered as the supreme mode of discourse, but it would take a determined reader not to associate silent communication with an ultimate and total silence, a transcendent meaning with meaninglessness, and Thoreau was as intelligent a reader as any. To illustrate this closing point, I refer to Thoreau's *Journal* entry for 21 January 1853, an entry recorded when he was putting the final touches to **Walden.** In **Walden** where he, as he tells us, has put "the best face on the matter," reasonably straightforward statements tend to lead to bright and pleasant imagery. Simple criticisms of routine life tend to result in positive depictions, such as when he takes the dank and warped boards and lays them in the sun to be straightened and purified before building his cabin. In those simpler rhetorical modes where an explicit message need only be articulated clearly, even potentially sinister events can be treated amusingly and delightfully, whether wanting to devour chipmunks raw or to spit Mexicans with relish or describing how a soldier killed by a cannonball might not care much about fashion.

In marked contrast, Thoreau's deliberations upon silence can often lead to more anxiety-ridden delineations. His "natural style" can direct him to a state of mind like that silent nature he discovers on top of Ktaadn in **The Maine Woods,** an ultimate blankness which he regards not in terror nor despair but in puzzlement, a final wall of nature and language with which he knows not what more to do except to turn his back on it and begin his descent. "Man was not to be associated with it. It was Matter, vast, terrific,—not his Mother Earth that we have heard of, not for him to tread on, or be buried in,—no, it were being too familiar even to let his bones lie there—the home this of Necessity and Fate."[14] As with nature, so with Thoreau's natural style when it turns to a discussion of silence in his *Journal.* Beginning positively enough by referring to "a fertile and eloquent silence," he continues to praise silence as a supreme rhetoric. "I wish to hear the silence of the night, for the silence is something positive and to be heard," he records, insisting even more emphatically that "Silence alone is worthy to be heard. Silence is of various depth and fertility, like soil." And he concludes this paragraph with quite joyful sentiments: "The silence rings; it is musical and thrills me. A night in which the silence is audible. I hear the unspeakable." But these thoughts, uplifting though they seem, are followed in the very next paragraph with darker intimations. The silence which is deep and fertile "like soil" leads him to contemplate the grave, the beauty of the night calls forth thoughts of ultimate night, the purity of silence makes him think of "the rottenness of human relations." Boasting that he "can easily read the moral of my dreams," his praise for eloquent and beautiful silence transforms into visions "full of death and decay" as he narrates how "In the night I dreamed of delving amid the graves of the dead, and soiled my fingers with their rank mould. It was *sanitarilly, morally,* and *physically* true."[15] It was also the ultimate wall of language.

Notes

1. Ever since J. Lyndon Shanley made public the lecture version of *Walden* thirty years ago, the manuscripts have been the subject of intense scholarship—*The Making of Walden* (Chicago: Univ. of Chicago Press, 1957); see also Shanley's "The Successive Versions of *Walden,*" *Critical Essays in American Literature: Romanticism,* eds. James Barbour and Thomas Quirk (New York: Garland, 1986). The Princeton Edition of Thoreau's *Journal, Volume 2: 1842-48* (ed. Robert Sattelmeyer, 1984) has necessitated some reconsideration of *Walden*'s genesis since it demonstrates that *Walden* was begun much earlier than previously supposed.

2. Speech-act theory is most classically represented in the writings of J. L. Austin and John Searle. Bercovitch, *The American Jeremiad* (Madison: Univ. of Wisconsin Press, 1978); Buell, *New England Literary Culture: From Revolution through Renaissance* (New York: Cambridge Univ. Press, 1986), p. 62.

3. "Scatology and Eschatology: The Heroic Dimensions of Thoreau's Word Play," *PMLA,* 89 (1974), 1043; reprinted in *Critical Essays in American Literature: Romanticism,* p. 99.

4. *The American Notebooks by Nathaniel Hawthorne,* ed. Randall Stewart (New Haven: Yale Univ. Press, 1932), p. 99.

5. Michaels, "*Walden*'s False Bottoms," *Glyph* I (Baltimore: Johns Hopkins Univ. Press, 1977), p. 136. *Walden,* ed. John C. Broderick (Princeton: Princeton University Press, 1971): worm-eaten seeds, pp. 163-64; well-stocked larder, p. 61; caged, p. 85; dead cat, p. 44; poverty not poverty, p. 324.

6. *Thoreau's Complex Weave: The Writing of* A Week on the Concord and Merrimack Rivers (Charlottesville: Univ. Press of Virginia, 1986).

7. *The Wisdom of Words: Language, Theology, and Literature in the New England Renaissance* (Middletown, Conn.: Wesleyan Univ. Press, 1981), p. 53; next quotation, p. 63. On p. 184 Gura cites other critics (Michael West, David Skwire, Richard Poirier, Stanley Cavell) who have studied Thoreau's language. See also Robert D. Richardson, Jr., *Henry Thoreau: A Life of the Mind* (Berkeley: Univ. of California Press, 1986), pp. 292-95.

8. "Natural History of Massachusetts" (p. 125) and "Walking" (p. 231) in *The Writings of Henry David Thoreau* (Boston: Houghton Mifflin, 1906), V; *The Correspondence of Henry David Thoreau,* eds. Walter Harding and Carl Bode (New York: New York Univ. Press, 1958), to Emerson (12 Feb. 1843), p. 87.

9. *Correspondence* [*The Correspondence of Henry David Thoreau*], to Ricketson (4 Nov. 1860), p. 599; to Blake on opera (27 Feb. 1853), p. 300; to Emerson (10 Feb. 1843), pp. 83-84.

10. *Collected Poems of Henry Thoreau: Enlarged Edition,* ed. Carl Bode (Baltimore: Johns Hopkins Press, 1965), p. vii.

11. *Correspondence,* letter to Emerson (11 March 1842), p. 64; to Blake (19 Dec. 1853), p. 311; "Walking," *Writings,* V, 242.

12. *The Illustrated* A Week on the Concord and Merrimack Rivers, eds. Carl Hovde et al. (Princeton: Princeton Univ. Press, 1983), "Wednesday," p. 267.

13. For glosses on the horse-hound-dove parable, see Walter Harding, *The Variorum Walden* and *The Variorum Civil Disobedience* (New York: Washington Square Press, 1969), pp. 259-62, and Edward Wagenknecht, *Henry David Thoreau: What Manner of Man?* (Amherst: Univ. of Massachusetts Press, 1981), p. 178.

14. *The Maine Woods,* ed. Joseph J. Moldenhauer (Princeton: Princeton Univ. Press, 1972), p. 70.

15. *The Journal of Henry Thoreau,* eds. Bradford Torrey and Francis H. Allen (Boston: Houghton Mifflin, 1906), IV, 471-72.

John Lowney (essay date June 1992)

SOURCE: Lowney, John. "Thoreau's *Cape Cod*: The Unsettling Art of the Wrecker." *American Literature* 64, no. 2 (June 1992): 239-54.

[*In the following essay, Lowney studies themes of exploration and manifest destiny in Thoreau's* Cape Cod. *Lowney regards the work as a deliberate subversion of the conventional travel narrative.*]

But are we not all wreckers contriving that some trea-
sure may be washed up on our beach, that we may secure it, and do we not infer the habits of these Nauset
and Barnegat wreckers, from the common modes of
getting a living?

—Henry David Thoreau, *Cape Cod*

"I wished to see that sea-shore where man's works are
wrecks," wrote Henry David Thoreau about his excursions to Cape Cod, and indeed **Cape Cod** remains a
rarely salvaged wreck in nineteenth-century American
literary studies.[1] Because it was not published complete
in Thoreau's lifetime, and because its loose, disjunctive
form is aesthetically closer to the *Journal* than to
Walden, it has not received the recognition accorded to
Thoreau's other extended travel narratives, *A Week on
the Concord and Merrimack Rivers* and *The Maine
Woods. Cape Cod*'s survey of the geography and historiography of a region marginal to nineteenth-century
New England culture has struck many readers as excessively "digressive."[2] Moreover, the question of whether
Cape Cod is a dissociative narrative of failed transcendence or an ironic critique of Transcendentalist idealism
has divided readers, for its tone is as disjunctive as its
form. Unlike *Walden* or *A Week, Cape Cod* is not structured as a romantic spiritual quest; its loose form is
closer to conventional modes of aesthetic travel writing
still popular in antebellum America.[3] Yet, *Cape Cod*'s
preoccupation with problems of representation suggests
that its digressive structure cannot be attributed solely
to Thoreau's appeal to a popular audience hungry for
travel information. This study will examine how *Cape
Cod* attempts to salvage a mode for New World "discovery" that is critical of the prevailing nationalist ideology of manifest destiny. Thoreau rhetorically exploits
the Cape's "frontier" marginality to unsettle conventional expectations of aesthetic travel narratives. But by
identifying the narrator's method with the "salvage" art
of the "regular Cape Cod man" (45), the wrecker, *Cape
Cod* reveals its own problematic implication within the
commercialist, expansionist ideology it challenges.

Thoreau's characterization of the wrecker as an emblematic figure for the "common modes of getting a living" epitomizes his ambivalent stance toward his own
profession, or more specifically, toward the "mode of
getting a living" dramatized in *Cape Cod*—travel writing.[4] Moreover, this universalization of the wrecker's
work also suggests his uncertain stance toward the subject of his travel narrative, the stance of an urbane representative of an increasingly centralized metropolitan
culture toward a peripheral rural region. To an "inlander," the Cape Cod wrecker was most frequently
perceived as a disreputable figure, one who makes a
business of watching for and plundering wrecked vessels, if not one who intentionally lures ships into wreck
with deceptive signals or lights. To those who earned
their living by the sea, however, the wrecker was more

likely a figure of patient industry or even heroism, hired
to undertake the perilous task of salvaging and repair-
ing wrecked or endangered vessels. Throughout **Cape
Cod** the wrecker alternately signifies for Thoreau a laudable figure of responsible, self-reliant husbandry and its
repellent perversion, a figure of predatory laissez-faire
capitalism. Not only the figure of Cape Cod's geo-
graphic and cultural marginality, the wrecker is also a
transitional figure for antebellum American national
identity. Neither wholly outlaw nor certified professional, the shifty figure of the wrecker conflates the
writer in the emergent marketplace with the archetypal
frontiersman.

Cape Cod explicitly invokes the nationalist myth of the
frontier, the myth of manifest destiny that translates
"*Ne plus ultra* (no more beyond)" into "*plus ultra* (more
beyond)" (141), legitimating the process of pulling up
roots and leaving behind one's local past. As Donald
Pease argues, the "doctrine of manifest destiny was, on
one level, intended to convert this anxiety accompanying cultural displacement into a national mission. And
the figure of the frontiersman was intended to give this
experience of uprootedness a heroic appearance."[5]
Rather than asserting such freedom from a local past in
order to nationalize his identity, the shoreline frontiersman who narrates *Cape Cod* instead enacts his dissent
from a fallen national mission in order to affirm the significance of the local. *Cape Cod*'s failed narrative strategy for "capturing" the alien landscape furthermore
dramatizes the unviability of a prototypical frontier
hero like Cooper's Hawkeye, whose ability to separate
himself from any roots enables his protean imperson-
ation of local landscapes, cultures, and characters. In
his quest to discover an appropriate mode for depicting
the ever-shifting "Wonder-Strand" landscape, Thoreau
digressively appeals to prior travel narratives to confirm
his observations. In doing so he inverts the narrative
pattern of *Walden,* the pattern most often associated
with American discovery narratives, which, as summarized by Wayne Franklin, "has at its verbal center figures whose prime act is a departure (whether actual or
rhetorical), but whose departure is rendered as a deeply
resonant and ritualistic reenactment of the first voyage
west."[6] Thoreau's "reenactment of the first voyage west"
in *Cape Cod* is actually a voyage east, to the geographical and narrative site of previous discovery narratives.
In his departure from familiar geographical and epistemological grounds, Thoreau tests the rhetorical strategies of these narratives, as well as of the "exploratory"
and "settlement" narratives Franklin distinguishes from
narratives of discovery. Franklin explains that the discovery narrative is less narrative than declaratory, less
concerned with the details of the journey than with the
spiritual meaning of the discovery of the New World. In
such narratives America is depicted as a superabundant
landscape compared to the "wasteland" of Europe, a
"vast emblem of rejuvenation" transcending history, in

which "the discoverer achieves through perception alone a communion with the eternal sources of life."[7] The exploratory narrative, on the other hand, filters experience through the colonialist design of the explorer. It formulates the abundance of details into an organized plot to cohere with the tangible objective of colonization. The New World is depicted as a void to be filled, described in "negative participles: unmarked, unplowed, unsettled, unsung."[8] Finally, the settlement narrative contrasts earlier accounts of the landscape with its survey of the actual world. Franklin notes the ironic "realism" of the settlement narrative compared to the "vague predications of the discoverer" and the "more designing ones of the explorer."[9]

Cape Cod is a settlement narrative which compares earlier travel narratives with Thoreau's own experience. Although often skeptical about earlier discovery and exploratory narratives, Thoreau most harshly questions the settlement narratives that center the origins of American history in New England and, more specifically, in the New England village. Concurrent with the socioeconomic transformation of antebellum New England village life resulting from the growth of technology, urbanization, and immigration was an increase in regional historiography which celebrated the traditional values of the village. As Lawrence Buell points out, Thoreau echoes but inverts the "lococentric" historiography of such earlier writers as Timothy Dwight.[10] Thoreau agrees with Dwight in "prescribing a closer rapport with one's immediate surroundings as a better alternative to the spirit of restlessness than an indulgence of wanderlust,"[11] but he satirizes religion, progress, and village life—the "civilizing" forces Dwight values—while celebrating the wilderness and marginal social types. Although Thoreau, like Dwight, surveys Cape Cod with a scientific eye for detail, he "unsettles" the progressivist assumptions behind the sequence of discovery, exploration, and settlement. He portrays Cape Cod as a "dreary" wasteland not with the explorer's intention of filling this void with civilization but with the discoverer's rapt wonder for the "eternal sources of life." Through his critique of earlier discovery narratives, he undercuts any notion of original historical discovery that precludes further "discoveries." The experience of the "mirage" landscape of Cape Cod itself undermines any sense of fixed perspective, historiographic or visual, resulting in a continual questioning of narrative centers and intentions—including his own—that determine which worlds are "new" and which are "old." He enacts this interrogative mode through the juxtaposition of diverse modes of discourse and through semantic and syntactic wordplay. Thoreau's "unsettlement" narrative—which celebrates the "stranger" who "may easily detect what is strange to the oldest inhabitant, for the strange is his province" (152)—establishes such a province for discovery in *Cape Cod.*

The opening chapter of *Cape Cod,* "The Shipwreck," is a microcosmic illustration of the techniques Thoreau uses throughout the book to decenter the New England historical perspective, his own visual perspective, and the reader's interpretive perspective. He unsettles the reader with wordplay, with, for example, his unfamiliar use of words and his etymologies. In the first paragraph he mentions his "excursions" in Concord in the same sentence as his "excursions" to the seashore. An *excursion* can be a relatively short journey in one's hometown as well as a journey of several days to an unfamiliar place; it depends on the traveler's attitude. Thoreau then traces the etymological origins of *Cape Cod,* although he qualifies his explanations with "I suppose" and "perhaps," questioning his own philological authority. He traces *cape* to Latin *"caput,* a head," and *"capere,* to take," and he speculates that *cod* is derived from "the Saxon word *codde,* 'a case in which seeds are lodged'" (3), "perhaps" related to "coddle,—to cook green like peas" (4). This apparent linguistic playfulness actually adumbrates the unsettlement method of the book: *Cape Cod* is indeed "a case in which seeds are lodged" for the receptive, perceptive mind; at the same time the Cape constantly "cooks" Thoreau "green," reminding him of his outsider's perspective, a perspective which nonetheless keeps his vision "fresh."

Thoreau's diversion to Cohasset to see the wreck of the *St. John* introduces us to the array of excursions inscribed in *Cape Cod.* Thoreau (with Ellery Channing, his unnamed companion) compares the Irish immigrants whose bodies were washing up on the shore to "Columbus and the Pilgrims." These immigrants, however, end up in "a newer world than ever Columbus dreamed of, yet one of whose existence we believe that there is far more universal and convincing evidence—though it has not yet been discovered by science—than Columbus had of this" (10). The "New World" Thoreau studies in "The Shipwreck" and throughout *Cape Cod* syncretizes several new worlds: the new world discovered by Columbus and the Pilgrims, the mythical and geographical new world the immigrant Irish sail to, and the new world which science was discovering in Thoreau's time, a new world challenging the assumptions of the spiritual new world "not yet . . . discovered by science." The new worlds the immigrant Irish and the scientists represent, the forces of social and intellectual change in mid-nineteenth century America, underlie Thoreau's "sympathy" for the "winds and the waves, as if to toss and mangle these poor human bodies was the order of the day" (9). This bleak proto-naturalistic vision makes the affirmation of the sublime a more desperate, and hence more necessary, act for Thoreau.

This consideration of new worlds provokes Thoreau's reminiscence about a later excursion to Cohasset. In this recollection he focuses on his vision in Hull of "the isles rapidly wasting away, the sea nibbling voraciously

at the continent" (12). This vision of dissolution corresponds with the narcotic properties of the thorn-apple,
Thoreau's emblem for commerce and "its attending
vices," the emblem which links outer with inner dissolution. On the other hand, "these wrecks of isles were
being fancifully arranged into new shores" (12). This
state of flux, where "everything seemed to be gently
lapsing into futurity," from dissolution to the vision of
reformation and regeneration, foreshadows the conclusion of this reminiscence, the journey through the poly-
glot linguistic landscape of the "South Shore," from the
township of Hull to an old French fort, from Nantasket
beach to Jerusalem village, from Irish moss to Cohasset
rocks. This diversion concludes on the same rocky shore
upon which the *St. John* was wrecked, "Pleasant Cove,
on some maps" (14). The irony of the name is sharp,
but the maps have no consentaneous authority.

"The Shipwreck" ends with a seemingly straightforward
but ultimately perplexing remark: "But to go on with
our first excursion" (14). This "first excursion" recalls
the first use of *excursion,* which contrasts excursions in
Concord with those to the seashore. Yet the first excursion mentioned, the purpose for the book, is the trip to
Cape Cod, a trip intentionally rerouted to view the
wreck in Cohasset, a digression which leads to considerations of other "excursions" to new worlds, including
the author's own later excursion to the same locale he
is discussing. This return to the "first excursion"—after
an opening chapter consisting entirely of pre-Cape digressions—directs the reader's attention to what is
"first," undercutting any absolute notion of "first" as it
suggests a multiplicity of "new worlds." Likewise, the
nature of *excursion* becomes complicated in light of the
numerous journeys already mentioned. An *excursion* is
most familiarly a "journey from home with the intention of returning." Yet the *OED* [*Oxford English Dictionary*] points out an early use of *excursion* as "the action
of running out; escape from confinement; progressions
beyond fixed limits; running to extremes"; such are
Thoreau's excursions from Concord village, in both his
townspeople's eyes and his own. Related to this definition is the notion of *excursion* as "something that runs
out or projects; an extension, offshoot, branch, projection"; Cape Cod is a geographical excursion from Massachusetts and New England. Finally, Thoreau is punning on the rhetorical term *excursus*; "The Shipwreck"
digresses from the journey to Cape Cod, but it is hardly
incidental to the design of **Cape Cod.** Thoreau, the eccentric Concord excursionist, begins his literary excursion to the geographical excursion of New England
with an excursion to the scene of a shipwreck, the result of an excursion to the New World he compares to
previous New World excursions. Interestingly, the
OED's first citation for *excursion* is from the late sixteenth century, the beginning of the English colonization period Thoreau considers. Thoreau, the writer experienced in excursions through philology as well as

ponds and seashores, unsettles any reader who expects
an account of Cape Cod which praises its villages and
ministers and bypasses its shipwrecks and wreckers.

Cape Cod is dominated by the dramatic tension between Thoreau's desire for initiation into the Cape Cod
world and his desire to differentiate his narrative from
previous accounts of initiation. He wants to experience
the Cape from an insider's perspective, but the alien-
ness of the Cape Cod landscape and economy continually reminds him of his "inlander's" point of view. The
problem of linguistic relativism informs both his initiation into and his alienation from the Cape Cod world.
As Thoreau unsettles the reader through wordplay, Cape
Cod unsettles *his* semantic presuppositions. For example, Cape Cod "soil" is actually "sand" from his
point of view: "All an inlander's notion of soil and fertility will be confounded by a visit to these parts" (28).
Similarly, "all sands here are called 'beaches,' whether
they are waves of water, or of air that dash against
them, since they commonly have their origin on the
shore" (28). The stoical Cape Cod disposition challenges Thoreau's presuppositions as much as the landscape does; the "Charity-houses" or "Humane-houses"
hardly fulfill his conceptions of charity and humaneness. This question of linguistic relativism similarly un-
derscores Thoreau's attempt to distinguish his descriptive method from previous chroniclers. In fact, Thoreau
most frequently describes the Cape by showing what it
is *not*. He demonstrates the relativism of descriptive
discourse by revealing the intentions and selective
blindnesses of previous travel narratives.[12] He juxtaposes a variety of languages and speech types, incorporating various genres (for example, travel narratives, regional historiography, religious sermons, lyric poems,
scientific studies, and newspaper articles), with representations of diverse professional, social, and regional
discourses. In juxtaposing such discourses, Thoreau is
experimenting to find the appropriate means for depicting the alien landscape. But he is also undercutting notions of an authoritative "discovery" of America, an authoritative history of Cape Cod, or an authoritative
definition of "travel narrative." He questions the minister's or the state historiographer's authorized versions
of history by representing the voices of marginalized
figures on Cape Cod. The spokesmen whom Thoreau
represents are not only figures who emblematize their
landscapes, like Wordsworth's solitary figures in *Lyrical
Ballads*; they are also figures whose oral histories challenge the "official" histories Thoreau quotes from. Thoreau's discoveries on Cape Cod and the reader's discoveries in **Cape Cod** take place through this dialogical
process of exposing the designs of the published settlement narratives, a process which inevitably makes the
reader wary of the rhetoric of all such narratives, including Thoreau's.

Cape Cod undermines the Anglo-American claims for the Pilgrims' settlement as the origin of American history by tracing their footsteps in Truro and Provincetown and comparing their "green" travel accounts to subsequent accounts of the Cape and to Thoreau's own experiences. His final chapter discusses at length the "Ante-Pilgrim" history of New England by comparing Puritan accounts with other discoveries of America: "Indeed, the Englishman's history of *New* England commences, only when it ceases to be, *New* France" (183). Yet this consideration does not replace the Anglocentric history with a Francocentric alternative. Instead Thoreau travels back to the early sixteenth century, considering the possible discoveries of Cabot, Verrazano, and Gomez. He does not make scientific claims for their journeys; he speculates while questioning the ethnocentric assumptions behind such claims as "Cape Cod is commonly said to have been discovered in 1602" (190). His speculative journey takes him back to Viking explorations of America, to the expedition to "Vinland" in 1007 by Thorfinn, "one of the same family" as "Thoreau" (151), but even this speculation is qualified by "unless," followed by a consideration of an earlier journey. The comparison of these "Ante-Pilgrim" accounts leads Thoreau to conclude that history "for the most part . . . is merely a story agreed upon by posterity" (197). This assertion of a historical relativism that makes the Pilgrims' arrival "quite recent" (197) finally decenters written history itself and affirms the aboriginal world of Cape Cod, the world that existed even when "Cape Cod lay in utter darkness to the civilized world" (197). If this prehistoric world was "even then Cape and Bay,—ay, the Cape of *Codfish,* and the Bay of the *Massachusetts,* perchance" (197), the correspondence of name and place is only somewhat less arbitrary than that of date and discovery, "perchance" the projection of colonist, or philologist, whose access to any aboriginal "Cape and Bay" is no less limited to subsequent written representations.

In addition to discovery narratives, Thoreau questions regional historiography throughout his journey, initially comparing his wry observations with descriptions of "beautiful" Cape villages from *The Collections of the Massachusetts Historical Society*: "I have no great respect for the writer's taste, who talks easily about *beautiful* villages. . . . Such spots can be beautiful only to the weary traveller; or the returning native—or, perchance, the repentant misanthrope; not to him who, with unprejudiced senses, has just come out of the woods, and approaches one of them, by a bare road, through a succession of straggling homesteads where he cannot tell which is the alms-house" (16). Although contrasting his own "taste" with this historian's, Thoreau stresses both the geographical and psychological circumstances of the writer's perspective in composing travel narratives. In foregrounding the site of vision, either the train in which "I could not read as fast as I

travelled" (16) or "that almost obsolete conveyance, the stage" (15), he emphasizes the effects of the technological means of perception on historiography. And in drawing attention to the perceiver's psychological relation to the village—"the weary traveller, or the returning native"—he mocks his own claims for the possibility of someone "with unprejudiced senses." Similarly, Thoreau quotes extensively from the ecclesiastical history of Eastham as he wanders across the rain-swept plains to "make the reader realize how wide and peculiar that plain was, and how long it took to traverse it" (43). The quoted selections begin and end with satirized accounts of settlers' encounters with local Indians. In recounting the Pilgrims' original appropriation of Indian territory, Thoreau quotes the Indians' reported response to the question of who owned the land as "there was not any who owned it": "The Pilgrims appear to have regarded themselves as Not Any's representatives. Perhaps this was the first instance of that quiet way of 'speaking for' a place not yet occupied, or at least not as improved as much as it may be, which their descendants have practiced, and are still practicing so extensively" (33). The ultimate selection to characterize both the physically empty landscape and the morally empty position of the apologists for "Not Any" is the quote from the "Rev. Ephraim Briggs" in an Indian language, "which, not being interpreted, we know not what it means" (42). In situating the Puritan appropriation of Indian lands within the contemporary repetition of this process in the West, Thoreau challenges the grounds of the dominant culture's interpretation of history. By assuming the silenced outsider's perspective, his account decenters the white man's colonialist discourse. However, even this scathing satire of the Puritan appropriation of Indian lands calls attention to Thoreau's own act of "speaking for a place." The image of the travellers walking the plains of Nauset, "reading under our umbrellas as we sailed" (40), comically precludes any pretense toward an unassailable position of epistemological or moral authority.

Thoreau implicitly acknowledges that his perspective can be neither that of the "Indian" nor one "with unprejudiced senses," but he does not easily relinquish the desire for representing the "primal" landscape. The Cape he seeks is the "dreary" landscape dominated by the "grand and sublime" ocean, the Romantic landscape which reminds him of the presumed origins of Western poetry in Homer and Ossian, and the naturalistic landscape which represents the origins of human life, the "sea-slime" of which we "are the product" (147). Thoreau cites the studies of geological and biological evolution by Darwin and other natural scientists to confirm his own shoreline observations. But although he is least likely to undercut these scientific perspectives on the "laboratory of continents" (100), the Cape Cod landscape ultimately resists empirical measurement and analysis. Because of geological and atmospheric conditions, the Cape is a "place of wonders" (137).[13] The land itself is constantly shifting, and the interaction of land and sea continually creates "mirages." Both the "desert" and the ocean distort objects into "grotesque" images; the observer has continually to question his vision. Thoreau finally sees the Cape itself as a mirage when he departs: ". . . like a filmy sliver of land lying flat on the ocean, and later still a mere reflection of a sand-bar on the haze above. Its name suggests a homely truth, but it would be more poetic if it described the impression which it makes on the beholder" (206). The fact that Thoreau does not consider that the name would have to keep changing to fit the ever-shifting "impression which it makes on the beholder" suggests the limits of his linguistic relativism; corresponding with the decentered commonplace name is an underlying belief that a more "poetic" name can convey an idea more "truthfully."

If Cape Cod's "mirage" landscape continually provokes Thoreau to pause and reflect on what he sees, the manners of its inhabitants are only slightly less disconcerting to him. The word *mirage*—a nineteenth-century import from the French *(se) mirer,* "to be reflected, to look at oneself in the mirror"—was an apt Romantic trope for dramatizing Kantian questions about perception. The "mirages" of the Cape provoke Thoreau to consider the "mirror" of his mind, to confront his own reasons for visiting Cape Cod. In "unsettling" the Cape to "discover" its elemental "dreariness," in decentering man from the universe, he approximates an amoral, naturalistic vision. To counteract the potential egocentrism or even solipsism of this vision, Thoreau identifies with the Cape Cod natives who seem most representative of their environment. Like other travel writers portraying regional manners, however, Thoreau's stance toward Cape Codders does not entirely avoid condescension. The character sketches Thoreau develops most fully in **Cape Cod** evince the divisions Buell attributes to regional literature in general, divisions between "the impulse nostalgically to identify with the bygone or simplified life-style depicted and the cosmopolitan impulse to mock it as clownish or repressive."[14]

Upon leaving Cape Cod Thoreau concludes that he "liked the manners" of the Cape inhabitants "very much":

> They were particularly downright and good-humored. The old people appeared remarkably well preserved, as if by the saltness of the atmosphere, and after having once mistaken, we could never be certain whether we were talking to a coeval of our grandparents, or to one of our own age. They are said to be more purely the descendants of the Pilgrims than the inhabitants of any other part of the State. We were told that "sometimes, when the court comes together at Barnstable, they have not a single criminal to try, and the jail is shut up."
>
> (202-03)

This generally favorable impression of Cape Codders does not totally suppress Thoreau's uneasiness about what remained, from his outsider's perspective, an alien "culture." The narrative gap between the description of "the descendants of the Pilgrims" and the quotation of their proud claims about the Cape's lack of crime is especially telling, as Thoreau's experience with the Wellfleet oysterman dramatizes. The account of the oysterman and his family follows the pattern of this descriptive summary almost exactly. A characteristic product of the landscape he inhabits, "deeply impressed with a sense of his own nothingness" (64), the Wellfleet oysterman is a "downright and good-humored" conversationalist whom Thoreau "took to be sixty or seventy years old" (63), but who turns out to be "almost ninety." If not one of the "descendants of the Pilgrims," he is a fourth-generation inhabitant of Wellfleet who "heard the guns fire at the battle of Bunker Hill" (63), and his Biblical rhetoric certainly affects the peculiar combination of admiration and repulsion Thoreau feels for him. As much as Thoreau tries to empathize with the oysterman and his family, he cannot bridge the distance which their distrust of outsiders creates, a distance which conflates the "fool's" description of Thoreau and Channing as "Damn book-peddlers,—all the time talking about books" (71), with the oysterman's suspicion that his guests were the robbers of the Provincetown Bank (79). As the narrative later substantiates, the oysterman's suspicion is typical of his fellow Cape Codders, for the lack of any discernible utilitarian purpose for their foot-travel makes the two outsider/writers presumed outlaws (139-40). The ardent attempt to immerse themselves in the Cape world, to "associate with the Ocean until it lost the pond-like look which it wears to a countryman" (140), itself makes them suspect to those they impersonate.

The tension between the Thoreau who seeks the "dreary," empty landscape and the Thoreau who empathetically identifies with the Cape inhabitants is never abated in **Cape Cod.** This tension is embodied most cogently in his commentary on shipwrecks in "The Highland Light":

> The stranger and the inhabitant view the shore with very different eyes. The former may have come to see and admire the ocean in a storm; but the latter looks on it as the scene where his nearest relatives were wrecked. When I remarked to an old wrecker partially blind . . . that I supposed he liked to hear the sound of the surf, he answered: "No, I do not like to hear the sound of the surf." He had lost at least one son in "the memorable gale," and could tell many a tale of the shipwrecks which he had witnessed there.
>
> (125-26)

This wrecker's contradiction of Thoreau concludes Thoreau's ongoing attempt to identify with this "true monarch of the beach" (46) and exemplifies **Cape Cod**'s dialectical dynamic of presupposition and "discovery." Thoreau's repeated encounters with wreckers show the contradictions underlying his desire for initiation into the Cape Cod world. The wrecker is the elemental man of Cape Cod; his face "was like an old sail endowed with life—a hanging-cliff of weather-beaten flesh—like one of the clay boulders which occurred in that sandbank" (45). His attitude is as harsh as the alien landscape, "too grave to laugh, too tough to cry; as indifferent as a clam" (45). His visage has an ageless quality which links Thoreau's Cape with the Puritans': "He may have been one of the Pilgrims—Peregrine White, at least—who has kept on the back side of the Cape, and let the centuries go by" (45). If the mention of Peregrine White, the first Puritan born in the New World, pays tribute to the Puritans' ability to sustain a community in a harsh environment, this identification represents less admirable characteristics as well. The wrecker is Thoreau's idealized mythical figure for perseverance in the face of adversity, a sand-covered Sisyphus. As the amorally opportunistic salvager of any disaster, even an intentional shipwreck like the Franklin (56, 84), or as the "cold-hearted" wrecker who would turn his back on a ship signalling distress (82), this omnipresent (if not always visible) figure of the shoreline also epitomizes entrepreneurial capitalism. In the guise of the mythologized historical figure of Puritan New England settlement, Peregrine White, the wrecker is a walking reminder of the unfulfilled promise of New World discovery and, more specifically, of the fallen state of the national covenant.

Thoreau most explicitly identifies with the wrecker when he actually mimics his "salvage" art. In doing so, he simultaneously criticizes and affirms the wrecker's "contriving" art of "securing" a living by monumentalizing the objects which are his lifeline: "From time to time we saved a wreck ourselves, a box or barrel, and set it on its end, and appropriated it with crossed sticks; and it will lie there perhaps, respected by brother wreckers, until some more violent storm shall take it, really lost to man until wrecked again" (91-92). This seemingly trivial moment of celebrating the wrecker's art is instead a vortex of the historical currents which compel *Cape Cod*'s digressive narrative form. Thoreau's "appropriation" mocks the exhortatory function of monuments most prevalent in the early nineteenth-century United States, monuments which immortalize a specific religious or political origin in history, such as those commemorating the Revolution. Denoting an occasion on which a covenant was made, they remind their observers of the obligation they have incurred, whether to a great public figure, event, or declaration. While conferring a kind of immortality to the past figure or event, such monuments simultaneously direct the community's future course of action. If Thoreau's empty box or barrel confers immortality on the wrecker, then the interpretive code it violates blocks the appro-

priate future course of action of his "brother wreckers." As *Cape Cod* parodies the various historical claims for "original" settlement, this transitory monument similarly mocks the covenant which legitimates the wrecker's property claims for what he discovers. But Thoreau's monument to the wrecker anticipates a different kind of commemorative mode, one that celebrates his "common mode of getting a living." Rather than the traditional monument of a heroic figure or event, Thoreau's structure resembles monuments of representative anonymous figures more prevalent after the Civil War, such as the Lexington Green Minuteman and the Gloucester Fisherman. As the cultural geographer J. B. Jackson explains, such monuments neither remind observers of a specific obligation nor suggest a particular line of conduct but instead celebrate a vernacular past.[15] Jackson attributes this transition in American monumental art primarily to the changing attitude toward the past that *Cape Cod* dramatizes, an attitude that eschews names, dates, and places of political and legal origins for the evolutionary view of "Human Culture," with its legendary, half-forgotten origins in the natural world. Thoreau's appropriation of box or barrel is, however, hardly an unqualified tribute to the anonymous wrecker. This gesture, while reaffirming *Cape Cod*'s celebration of vernacular history, is certainly ironic in its display of the wrecker's "mode of getting a living" as a "natural" prototype for explaining—or justifying—such predatory socioeconomic relations in a laissez-faire market economy.

Thoreau's "appropriation" of the wrecker's art represents not just his initiation into the Cape Cod world but an act of literary possession, a symbolic act of colonization, as well. Signifying neither exclusive possession nor specific purpose, this appropriation of box or barrel mocks the authority or right to claim "salvage" as property, whether by official wreck-master or by illicit wrecker. Thoreau's "crossed sticks" indeed "lie" to his "brother wreckers." An outsider throughout *Cape Cod,* the suspected bank robber indirectly acknowledges the implications of his "speaking for" Cape Cod: "But the only bank that we pried into was the great Cape Cod sand-bank, and we robbed it only of an old French crown piece, some shells and pebbles, and the materials of this story" (140). His gesture of solidarity with the wrecker suggests the cost of robbing and representing "the materials of this story." In aestheticizing the work of the marginalized figure, he simultaneously mocks his own economic dependence on the art he practices. The wrecker is a "mirage" or mirror image for Thoreau, the writer who must translate his *Journal* into marketable forms and the idealistic social critic of an economic system in which he finds himself inescapably implicated.

The wrecker is more than an image of Thoreau; he is the paradoxical emblem of the uneasy marriage between *Cape Cod*'s contradictory visions: the Romantic vision of the idealized noble savage reigning over a wild, unsettled landscape and the proto-naturalistic vision of the ignoble savage salvaging a living in an economy of scarcity. Thoreau's description of the Cape as "wild and solitary as the Western Prairies—used to be" (107), the dash accentuating the passing of the Western wilderness, situates his travel narrative in the threshold position in American literary history that the figure of the wrecker dramatizes. Thoreau's art of the wrecker—the found-object aesthetic which confronts and makes the most of whatever the ocean "vomits up," whether it be a dead body or a gold coin—was indeed unsettling to the audience of his day.[16] It challenged genteel expectations of literature, exemplified by the quotation of Longfellow's "Seaweed" (53-54), with its embracing acceptance of weeds wrecked ashore by the ocean, the weeds that are "the symbols of those grotesque and fabulous thoughts which have not yet got into the sheltered coves of literature" (54). It remains unsettling today because its hybrid form resists easy classification into "a sheltered cove of literature." *Cape Cod* is unsettling furthermore because it critiques the genre it represents; it is an act of literary criticism which questions its own rhetoric. Finally, the unsettling questions *Cape Cod* raises are not exclusively "literary" questions at all. They are questions about the relations of travel narrative to place, of place to the histories which define it, and of histories to the ideologies which inform them. These very questions foreground the socioeconomic implications of Thoreau's narrative stance as well, of which he was prophetically aware: "The time must come when this coast will be a place of resort for those New-Englanders who really wish to visit the sea-side" (214). Real estate and travel agents have indeed been far less reluctant to salvage *Cape Cod* than literary critics have been.

Notes

1. Henry David Thoreau, *Cape Cod,* ed. Joseph J. Moldenhauer (Princeton: Princeton Univ. Press, 1988), 50. Hereafter quotations from this work will be noted parenthetically within the text.

2. Walter Harding's overview of *Cape Cod* is representative of this position: "Except for a few digressions on the history of the Cape, it is purely and simply a report on his various excursions to the peninsula . . ."; *The Days of Henry Thoreau: A Biography,* rev. ed. (Princeton: Princeton Univ. Press, 1982), 361. For a brief overview of *Cape Cod*'s reception, see William Howarth, *The Book of Concord: Thoreau's Life as a Writer* (New York: Viking, 1982), 116-17. For a reading of *Cape Cod* which argues that Thoreau's "historical digressions," like his empirical methods, act as "supplements" to his vision of an alien environment, see Thomas Couser, *American Autobiography: The Prophetic Mode* (Amherst: Univ. of Massachusetts Press, 1979), 72-79. Joan Burbick compares Thoreau's "uncivil history" to other modes of Romantic historiography in *Thoreau's Alternative History: Changing Perspectives on Nature, Culture and Language* (Philadelphia: Univ. of Pennsylvania Press, 1987). See especially pages 83-100, where she examines his rhetorical use of historical materials in *Cape Cod.*

3. See Stephen Adams and Donald Ross Jr., *Revising Mythologies: The Composition of Thoreau's Major Works* (Charlottesville: Univ. Press of Virginia, 1988), 127-42, for an analysis of *Cape Cod*'s generic features. Specifying *Cape Cod*'s place in Thoreau's intellectual development, they argue that rather than refuting the Transcendentalist vision of *Walden, Cape Cod* is "addressing a middle-class audience within traveling distance of the Cape who were more interested in concrete details than in mythic, poetic transformation" (141).

4. For a provocative essay that examines the aesthetic and epistemological implications of the writer as wrecker, see Mitchell Robert Breitwieser, "Thoreau and the Wrecks on Cape Cod," *Studies in Romanticism* 20 (1981): 3-20. Breitwieser's analysis of *Cape Cod*'s formal strategies for representing the "murderous sublime" is especially incisive.

5. Donald Pease, *Visionary Compacts: American Renaissance Writings in Cultural Context* (Madison: Univ. of Wisconsin Press, 1987), 20.

6. Wayne Franklin, *Discoverers, Explorers, Settlers: The Diligent Writers of Early America* (Chicago: Univ. of Chicago Press, 1979), 183. Franklin briefly discusses *Walden* as an exemplary "reenactment of the first voyage west." He does not discuss *Cape Cod.*

7. Franklin, *Discoverers, Explorers, Settlers,* 23. See also Bruce Greenfield, "Thoreau's Discovery of America: A Nineteenth-Century First Contact," *ESQ* 32 (1986): 81-95, on Thoreau's rhetoric of discovery in "Ktaadn."

8. Franklin, *Discoverers, Explorers, Settlers,* 76.

9. Franklin, *Discoverers, Explorers, Settlers,* 123.

10. Lawrence Buell, *New England Literary Culture: From Revolution Through Renaissance* (New York: Cambridge Univ. Press, 1986), 319-34.

11. Buell, *New England Literary Culture,* 328.

12. See Burbick, *Thoreau's Alternative History,* 90-94, where she concentrates on the ironic transitions between Thoreau's first-person narration and his representations of other Cape Cod travel narratives.

13. Naomi J. Miller and Richard J. Schneider consider aspects of Thoreau's *Cape Cod* "vision" in "Seer and Seen: Aspects of Vision in Thoreau's *Cape Cod*," *ESQ* 29 (1983): 185-96 and "*Cape Cod*: Thoreau's Wilderness of Illusion," *ESQ* 26 (1980): 184-96, respectively. Miller's article is especially useful for its emphasis on Thoreau's narrative technique for "opening up" the reader's perception of the ambiguity of perspective in *Cape Cod.* Barton Levi St. Armand discusses the similarities of Thoreau's aesthetic with that of mid-nineteenth-century American painting in "Luminism in the Work of Henry David Thoreau: The Dark and the Light," *Canadian Review of American Studies* 11 (1980): 13-30. St. Armand argues convincingly that luminism, both in painting and in literary works like *Cape Cod* and *Walden,* is the "missing link between late Romantic idealism and early literary Naturalism."

14. Buell, *New England Literary Culture,* 335.

15. J. B. Jackson, "The Necessity for Ruins," in *The Necessity for Ruins and Other Topics* (Amherst: Univ. of Massachusetts Press, 1980), 89-102.

16. The first four chapters of *Cape Cod* were published in *Putnam's* despite the editors' expressed worries that some of Thoreau's remarks about Christianity and Cape inhabitants might offend some readers. *Putnam's* broke off publication of the Cape Cod pieces after three installments were published. See Moldenhauer, "Historical Introduction" to *Cape Cod,* 259-77, for a summary of the book's publication history.

Morris B. Kaplan (essay date 1995)

SOURCE: Kaplan, Morris B. "Civil Disobedience, Conscience, and Community: Thoreau's 'Double Self' and the Problematic of Political Action." In *The Delegated Intellect: Emersonian Essays on Literature, Science, and Art in Honor of Don Gifford,* edited by Donald E. Morse, pp. 37-63. New York: Peter Lang, 1995.

[*In the following essay, Kaplan investigates concepts of resistance in Thoreau's political writings. Kaplan contends that the ambiguity of Thoreau's ideas lends his work its emotional and moral power.*]

Henry David Thoreau's **"Civil Disobedience"** has had extraordinary influence on the emancipatory politics of the twentieth century. Gandhi credited it with providing important support for his own doctrine of *Satyagraha.* He translated portions of the essay as early as 1907 for publication in South Africa in his journal *Indian Opinion* and later sponsored its distribution in pamphlet

form (Hendrick). Later, Martin Luther King, Jr. studied Thoreau's work at Morehouse College, and early cited Thoreau along with Gandhi, Tolstoy, Jesus, and Socrates, as a source of his own form of non-violent civil disobedience. Indeed, he claimed that his college reading of Thoreau helped him to see that the Montgomery bus boycott was not simply an economic pressure tactic, but at bottom, a refusal to cooperate with the evil of racial segregation (Oates [*Let the Trumpet Sound*] 62). As Don Gifford pointed out in unpublished lectures delivered at the height of the activist Sixties, there is an anomaly here: Thoreau's essay describes a persistent dilemma which confronts the individual in the context of all collective action. Gifford argued that ". . . the essay is disturbing and unsettling, puzzling and ambiguous, and that is why so many who quote the essay . . . have the impulse to transform the questions into answers, to treat the essay, in Gandhi's phrase, as a 'grammar of action,' instead of as a *grammar of questions*" (Gifford 1970). Thoreau's own uneasy relationship with contemporary abolitionists points up the extent to which he is an unlikely sponsor of mass political actions, no matter how sympathetic he might have been to their objectives. The text of **"Civil Disobedience,"** originally titled **"Resistance to Civil Government,"** alternates importantly between urging the individual to withdraw from the corporate contexts in which he is immersed and recognizing that such withdrawal is necessarily a tactical retreat to be followed by return to the exigencies of action. The argument of the essay is framed by the founding doctrines of American democracy: individual rights and the consent of the governed. The movement of the essay is a radicalization of these assumptions toward affirming the sovereignty of "the majority of one." The democratic individual is necessarily engaged in the business of politics to some extent, partially immersed in a network of social and natural relations. However, such persons are also capable of transcending these relationships in the direction of an authentic realization of their own ultimate possibilities. The duty of resistance to civil government becomes important insofar as the political context may make it impossible to "mind one's own business," to live one's life fully and deliberately.

In this reading of Thoreau, I hope to re-awaken the questioning inherent in the multiple gestures of resistance that comprise his teaching on civil disobedience. In contemporary terms, Thoreau's essay serves to problematize the concept of political action as such and of the self which engages in it; in the process, his argument unsettles the very distinctions by which it proceeds—between conscience and expediency, spectator and agent, individual integrity and collective consequences.

I

Everyone knows the story of Thoreau's refusal to pay his poll tax because of his opposition to slavery and the

Mexican War, and of the night he spent in Concord jail as a result. However, Thoreau's ironic and deflationary presentation of his own conduct reveals the essentially problematic character of all political action for him. The episode is recounted quite late in the essay, and its presentation is hardly heroic.

It is a commonplace that Thoreau's actions in refusing to pay his tax and spending a night in jail were politically without visible effect; his account of the events invites the suspicion that a comedy of sorts was enacted in Concord that day. Rather, as Gifford points out, the effective locus of Thoreau's action is the lecture delivered at the Concord Lyceum and the essay subsequently published in 1849 in a volume surprisingly called *Aesthetic Papers,* edited by Elizabeth Peabody:

> The real answer is not in the gestures described or in the arguments contained in the essay; the real answer is the essay itself: the essay is the dramatic gesture which transforms a minor squabble about the payment of a poll tax and a larger squabble about a concluded war into effective individual dissent.
>
> (Gifford, "Address" ["Address to the Danforth Graduate Fellows' Conference"] 7)

When Thoreau delivered the lecture in February, 1848, the Mexican War was practically settled. Moreover, Thoreau's was a modest voice in the advocacy of civil disobedience as a form of resistance to slavery. Wendell Philips led the Abolitionist call for resistance to illegitimate authority, denouncing the United States Constitution itself as "a covenant with death."[1] Advocacy of civil disobedience in the name of a higher law was characteristic of the anti-slavery movements of the time; even Thoreau's radical individualism and pervasive anti-institutionalism had roots in Quaker teachings of the "inner light" which informed some branches of abolitionism (Lynd [*Intellectual Origins of American Radicalism*] 100-29). Perry Miller has traced some of these themes back through Jonathan Edwards to the antinomianism of Anne Hutchinson and to earlier Quaker incursions in Puritan New England (Miller). Finally, Thoreau got the specific idea of refusing to pay his poll tax from his Concord neighbor Bronson Alcott, who had refused for several years previously but who had permitted himself to be deprived of even one night in jail when friends paid the tax on his behalf.[2]

What, in the face of these facts, accounts for the continuing influence of Thoreau's essay and for its ability to move us even today? I will argue that its very ambiguity is an important source of its power. Thoreau defines the contours of the modern self, divided between a heightened feeling of personal responsibility for social wrong and a sense of impotence over against the machinery of a complex society. This "double self" is not only a spectator of the world, but also engaged to act within it, responsible both for living deliberately and being responsive to the claims of the world. Rather than offering a theoretical solution of these dilemmas, Thoreau constructs narratives in which the individual alternates experimentally between withdrawal into a judging consciousness and returning to the network of relations within which one must shape a continuing life.

II

Thoreau's essay both deploys and radicalizes the rhetoric of the American democracy: "I heartily accept the motto,—'That government is best which governs least'; and I should like to see it acted up to more rapidly and systematically" (224). This Jeffersonian creed, which figures also in Emerson's "Politics," is immediately under pressure from an insistent "I" to become "That government is best which governs not at all," undercut a bit by ". . . when men are prepared for it, that will be the kind of government which they will have" (224). Thoreau separates himself from the "no-government" men, while leaving open the possibility that at some point, "no government" may indeed be the best. At the same time, he raises the question, "What kind of government might command the respect of the author of **'Resistance to Civil Government'**?" If making known one's views of the matter is a step toward obtaining such government, the essay itself must be analyzed as such a civic act.

Thoreau develops his critique in terms of a distinction between expediency and conscience, treating government strictly as a tool enabling individuals to pursue their separate and concerted activities. Even the principle of majority rule is derived from an expedient acknowledgment of the superior force of greater numbers. The majority has no claim to superior judgment of right and wrong:

> Can there not be a government in which majorities do not virtually decide right and wrong, but conscience?—in which majorities decide only those questions to which the rule of expediency is applicable? Must the citizen even for a moment, or in the least degree, resign his conscience to the legislator? Why has every man a conscience then?
>
> (225)

The limitation of government to the domain of expediency is accompanied by a similar derogation of law and legal obligation: "I think that we should be men first and subjects afterwards. It is not desirable to cultivate a respect for the law so much as for the right. The only obligation which I have a right to assume is to do at any time what I think right" (225). Undue respect for law at the expense of conscience makes one a machine in the service of the state, ". . . a mere shadow and reminiscence of humanity, a man laid out alive and standing . . . buried under arms with funereal accompaniments . . ." (226). What right requires is not, however, simply a rejection of society and withdrawal from political life. Conscience calls one to a higher service: "A very few, as heroes, patriots, martyrs, reformers in the great sense, and men, serve the State with their consciences also, and so necessarily resist it for the most part . . ." (226). The duty of resistance is both a form of civic virtue and an assertion of individual *life*. The paradox is that to serve one's fellow men fully, with one's entire self, is to risk becoming an enemy to one's government: "I cannot for an instant recognize that political organization as *my* government which is the slave's government also" (227).

In the United States, especially, "all men recognize the right of revolution . . ." (227). With Locke and Jefferson behind him, Thoreau's general claim is not so radical. What heightens his rhetoric is the assertion of its pertinence to his contemporary circumstances. He denies legitimacy to the governments of his day because they authorize slavery and the conduct of aggressive war in Mexico: ". . . when a sixth of the population of a nation which has undertaken to be the refuge of liberty are slaves, and a whole country is unjustly overrun . . . , I think it is not too soon for honest men to rebel and revolutionize" (227). The deliberation which determines one's duty is not a calculation of expediency, but a demand of conscience: "If I have unjustly wrested a plank from a drowning man, I must restore it to him though I drown myself" (227). Thoreau's radicalism consists in the claim that the conscience which determines his duty to his fellows may require him to take actions which threaten actually existent political communities: "This people must cease to hold slaves, and to make war on Mexico, though it cost them their existence as a people" (228).

The political action called for here is not necessarily violent revolution. The "existence of a people" in a democratic polity is constituted by the consent of the governed. The government which supports slavery and wages unjust war must forfeit the consent of persons of conscience. Thoreau urges his fellow citizens to refuse to cooperate with those who perpetuate slavery: "I quarrel not with far-off foes, but with those who, near at home, cooperate with, and do the bidding of those far away . . ." (228). Indeed, for Thoreau, those who fail to act under such circumstances are themselves enslaved. Contrary to a later insistence on first exhausting lawful methods before resorting to civil disobedience,[3] Thoreau urges resistance through law breaking both to assert one's freedom in refusing evil and to articulate opposition to one's fellow citizens. Civil disobedience for Thoreau essentially appeals from the government to the citizenry and from the opinion of the majority to the conscience of the individuals who make up that majority. He rejects political means, like voting as ". . . a sort of gaming, like chequers or backgammon, with a

slight moral tinge to it, a playing with right and wrong, with moral questions . . ." (228). Thoreau believes that trusting to ordinary politics divests moral matters of their inherent urgency: "The character of voters is not staked. I cast my vote, perchance, as I think right; but I am not vitally concerned that right should prevail. I am willing to leave it to the majority" (229). Matters of expediency may be safely left to government and to the rule of the majority; while matters of conscience are of such vital concern to individuals that they may not be delegated to others. Rather, Thoreau insists: "Cast your whole vote, not a slip of paper merely, but your whole influence" (233).

The assertion of the claims of conscience at the expense of political institutions, of "the existence of a people," is an attempt at founding a new community of conscience, of those who ". . . serve the state with their consciences also. . . ." The argument by which Thoreau thus links the personal with the political turns on the ways in which the individual self is situated within social and political contexts. Ironically, the very importance which Thoreau attaches to individual integrity leads to recognition of the extent to which the democratic citizen may be implicated in social injustice:

> It is not a man's duty . . . to devote himself to the eradication of any, even the most enormous wrong; he may still properly have other concerns to engage him; but it is his duty, at least, to wash his hands of it, and, if he gives it no thought longer, not to give it practically his support. If I devote myself to other pursuits and contemplations, I must first see, at least, that I do not pursue them sitting upon another man's shoulders. I must get off him first, that he may pursue his contemplations too.
>
> (229-30)

The argument moves quickly from the apparent ease and indifference of "washing one's hands" to the rather more difficult task of "getting off another's shoulders."

Thoreau shows people, in apparent innocence, comfortably enjoying the protection of a system of government founded upon the exclusion and exploitation of others. The principle of justice at work is demonstrably egalitarian: Thoreau does not pause to consider whether those on whose shoulders others pursue their contemplations may be properly employed as caryatids. Indeed, he insists that they have a right to pursue contemplations of their own. To understand the situation is to see the necessity for withdrawing support from the system and resisting the inertia by which well-meaning citizens may become party to injustice. Thoreau thus advances no new arguments against slavery or the aggressive war in Mexico; he does not even trouble to rehearse the old ones. Rather he is concerned to show those in agreement with his views just what consistency requires of them:

Action from principle,—the perception and the performance of right,—changes things and relations: it is essentially revolutionary and does not consist wholly with anything which was. It not only divides states and churches, it divides families; aye, it divides the individual, separating the diabolical in him from the divine.

(230-31)

To place principle above expediency in determining actions is not simply an assertion of superior virtue. Authentic resistance results from inner struggle. The active refusal to cooperate with social wrong is also a gesture of self-overcoming. Taking a stand may also force neighbors and the representatives of government to reassess their own moral positions. The actions of one "honest man" may occasion a transformation of social attitudes. In part, Thoreau sees evil and injustice as perpetuated as much by inertia and inattention as by deliberate malevolence. In part, he understands acts of conscientious resistance as ends in themselves: "For it matters not how small the beginning may seem to be: what is once well done is done forever" (233).

The most wholehearted acts of resistance may land a person in prison. That is part of the point. Thoreau does not emphasize the importance of the civil disobedient's acceptance of his punishment as a sign of his fidelity to the law, of his acceptance of the general legitimacy of the system. That point, which has been so important to contemporary theorists, is quite foreign to the spirit of Thoreau's argument. Indeed, he joins the abolitionists in denying legitimacy to a Constitution fatally compromised by its tolerance of slavery. For Thoreau, acceptance of punishment by the conscientious actually serves to *delegitimate* the government which is forced to punish its most morally engaged citizens. The fact of his imprisonment grants the resister a considerable rhetorical advantage: "Under a government which imprisons any unjustly, the true place for a just man is also a prison . . . how much more eloquently and effectively he can combat injustice who has experienced a little in his own person." (233)

Much of Thoreau's appeal to Gandhi and to King lies here: the challenge posed by non-violent resistance to the moral authority of the state derives from the willingness of civil disobedients to risk themselves wholly in making their case and to endure suffering for their beliefs. But Thoreau's specific concern is not with such victims of injustice. The teaching of "Civil Disobedience" is directed at those otherwise comfortable citizens who become aware of injustice perpetrated in their names. Free citizens concerned for justice should voluntarily go to prison to challenge their fellows and the officials charged with the business of government to change their course: "It is there that the fugitive slave, and the Mexican prisoner on parole, and the Indian come to plead the wrongs of his race should find them

. . ." (233). It was the genius and radicality of Gandhi and King to translate Thoreau's politics of conscience into a program of resistance for the oppressed, for precisely those whom the state has excluded from its community of consent. In terms defined by the distinct but complementary arguments of John Rawls and Hannah Arendt, they moved from conscientious refusal as an individual moral imperative to civil disobedience as a collective, political act. For Thoreau, political action as such may generate problems for conscientious participants quite similar to those raised by the implication of the citizen in the acts of the democratic state. The demands of solidarity with the victims of injustice, or with one's own group as it asserts its common claims, may conflict with the integrity of the "majority of one." Thus, Thoreau could write of his fellow advocate of civil disobedience, the abolitionist Wendell Philips: he ". . . does himself an injustice when he reminds us of the American [Anti-slavery] Society which he represents; really he stands alone" (Rosenblum, "Thoreau"). Thoreau approaches anarchism in his insistence on the moral autonomy of citizens of free societies, but he does not address directly the victims of oppression as they attempt to combat the injustices they suffer.

Thoreau's account of his own confrontation with the state and its representatives appears as somewhat of an anti-climax: "I have paid no poll-tax for six years. I was put into jail once on this account, for one night . . ." (236). He emphasizes the state's inadequacy in locking him up, confining his body when it could not persuade his soul. His thought remained free, and freely divested the state of its last vestige of authority: "I saw that the State was half-witted, that it was timid as a lone woman with her silver spoons, and that it did not know its friends from its foes . . ." (236). Thoreau presents himself as remaining a friend to the State, calling it to its own highest aspirations. But there is something of Chanticleer crowing in his portrayal of the state in its enmity:

> It is not armed with superior wit or honesty, but with superior physical strength. I was not born to be forced. I will breathe after my own fashion. Let us see who is the strongest. What force has a multitude? They only can force me who obey a higher law than I.
>
> (236)

Compare his earlier question: "Why does it [the state] always crucify Christ, and excommunicate Copernicus and Luther, and pronounce Washington and Franklin rebels?" The strain on Thoreau's rhetoric reveals a profound ambivalence in his relation to the question of power. A night in the Concord jail appears a small price for the moral and rhetorical advantage it provided.

The bragging disappears when Thoreau later comes to write about the forcible return of Anthony Burns to enslavement in Virginia or the condemnation of John

Brown to death by hanging. The confrontation of those men with the state's full repressive force raises the question of power in its starkest form; the problematic of political action is fused with the problematic of violent resistance.[4] Thoreau's night in jail resembles comedy more than it does these tragedies.[5] Nevertheless, the experience of punishment at the hands of the state is instructive. Thoreau's action becomes an experiment through which he comes to see differently his relation to the state and to his neighbors. But there is profound ambiguity in this vision. Leading some of these same neighbors in a huckleberry party on the afternoon of his release, he discovers ". . . the State was nowhere to be seen" (239). Although he never abandons the pressure on himself "to trace the effects of my allegiance," Thoreau systematically undercuts the heroic stance: ". . . I quietly declare war with the State, after my fashion, though I will still make what use and get what advantage of her as I can, as is usual in such cases" (239).

The ironic detachment[6] which informs Thoreau's presentation of his own acts of resistance may in part explain what Emerson identified as simple lack of ambition: ". . . instead of engineering for all America, he was the captain of a huckle-berry-party" (Emerson ["Thoreau"], 9). But Thoreau appears to have anticipated such complaints; his refusal of conventional ambition is intrinsic to his view of the relation between the individual and the state: "I am not responsible for the successful working of the machinery of society. I am not the son of the engineer" (236-37). These comments echo his earlier insistence that government is a matter of expediency. However, his ironic intelligence must acknowledge in his own conscientious actions a resemblance to those "patrons of virtue" he earlier satirized: "They hesitate, and they regret, and sometimes they petition; but they do nothing in earnest and with effect. They will wait, well disposed, for others to remedy the evil, that they may no longer have it to regret" (228). The problem is not easy to resolve. In part, it is a matter of perspective: one man's earnest engagement may appear to another as no more than regret. Thoreau cannot avoid the subjective implications of a conception of conscience which depends so decisively on the intensity of individual commitment. To ask for effectiveness as well is to open the panoply of questions concerning the calculation of consequences which Thoreau's rhetoric of resistance seeks to avoid. All political action occurs within at least two distinct forums, that of the individual conscience and that of the public to whom it is in part directed and by which it is perceived and interpreted. To be both earnest and effective may not be possible; how actions are received is not within an individual's control. The matter cannot be settled in principle, but only through a dynamic inter-action between the individual and the world. Hence, the irony and paradox manifested by Thoreau's oscillation between apparent contraries. He sees individuals as situated in the midst of shifting perspectives and relations through which they must experimentally make their ways. At the very least, individuals are both active participants engaged in a social and natural context and critical spectators capable of withdrawing to judge both themselves and others. Perhaps unexpectedly, the essay on **"Civil Disobedience"** moves through these oscillations toward reconciliation. In the final paragraph, Thoreau both re-asserts the continuity of his views with the individualism inherent in democracy and emphasizes his hope for a transcendence of the forms of common life. The establishment of a society based on justice and respect for the individual becomes a preparation for ". . . a still more perfect and glorious State, which also I have imagined, but not yet anywhere seen" (243). Thoreau appears thus to envision the founding of a new America, a community of sovereign individuals.

III

Thoreau's rhetoric of resistance identifies a "double movement" by which the individuals first recognize the extent to which they are implicated in the wrongs perpetuated by their society and then actively dissociate themselves from such by refusing to cooperate. However, the movement of withdrawal from society is necessarily temporary and incomplete. Withdrawal may salve the individual conscience to some extent, but resistance also marks an attempt "to get off the shoulders" of the oppressed. Not only the earnestness of the actor, but also the effectiveness of the action contributes to its moral worth. This is the problematic of political action: civil disobedience originates in individual conscience, but seeks to have a social impact even as it rejects the normal workings of politics. Resistance must define its own objectives, primarily to awaken one's fellow citizens to the wrongs in which they collaborate and inspire them to undertake their own gestures of conscientious refusal. Thoreau does not permit a person simply "to wash his hands of it"; action initiates further consequences for which one bears some specific responsibility. We cannot elude our history. For Thoreau, there is no action, no living, without risk. We are moved to act because of our involvements with the world, and our actions further involve us with that world. Neither calculation of consequences nor invocation of principle is an adequate guide to action. By our actions we shape who we are and what we become. Thoreau's ethics are both contextual and transcendent. The life of the self is at least double, alternating between the historical context in which we are situated and the inner awareness through which the surrounding world is perceived and transformed.

Thoreau's essays are attempts to effect the common life by showing his fellow citizens the world in which they live. If they come to see it differently, as he does, they may be moved to act. The writing is itself a political action through which he seeks to awaken his neighbors. As the crisis of the United States in the 1850s became more acute, Thoreau's essays more urgently, almost desperately, probe the limits of political action and the responsibilities of the "divided self." Importantly, most of them originated as public lectures, delivered at the Concord Lyceum and elsewhere. They are crystallizations of a man speaking to men, addressing the circumstances of history.[7] **"Slavery in Massachusetts"** was provoked by the furor in Massachusetts over the use of state courts and agencies to enforce the Fugitive Slave Law by returning Anthony Burns to his "master" in Virginia. This event caused considerable public protest, bringing slavery home to Massachusetts. Thoreau called attention to the role of his own local government in enforcing slavery. He rejected the alibi that state officials did only what the law required. For Thoreau, that was precisely the problem: "What is wanted is men, not of policy, but of probity—who recognize a higher law than the Constitution, or the decision of the majority" (**"Slavery"** [**"Slavery in Massachusetts"**] 257). To those for whom this demand went against the grain, he admonished: "I would remind my countrymen that they are to be men first, and Americans only at a late and convenient hour" (256). Thoreau denied himself the invocation of transcendent, universal principles, secured by reason or religious authority; rather, he proceeds by appealing directly to the experience of his fellow citizens and conjuring the claims of a more ambitious patriotism:

> The effect of a good government is to make life more valuable, of a bad one, to make it less valuable . . . but suppose that the value of life itself should be diminished. How can we make a less demand on man and nature, how live more economically in respect of virtue and all noble qualities, than we do? I have lived for the last month . . . with the sense of having suffered a vast and indefinite loss. I did not know at first what ailed me. At last it occurred to me that what I had lost was a country.
>
> (259)

The vision evoked by these last sentences has its source deep in the collective aspiration of Americans to build a "city upon a hill," to create a community of conscience as well as convenience. The energy and urgency of Thoreau's appeal is drawn from the shared expectation that "our community" is better than that. The perpetual risk of democratic politics is that government will exceed its mandate of expediency and compromise the citizenry instead. The acts of officials are matters of personal urgency for the citizens, because they act in our names: ". . . the State has fatally interfered with my lawful business. It has not only interrupted me in my passage through Court Street on errands of trade, but it has interrupted me and every man on his inward and upward path . . ." (260).

The spectacle of slavery enforced in the courts and on the streets of Massachusetts is a direct threat to the individual's sense of his own moral stature: "If we would save our lives, we must fight for them" (260). The politics of the Fugitive Slave Law constitute a moral crisis for all conscientious Americans: "Who can be serene in a country where both the rulers and the ruled are without principle? The remembrance of my country spoils my walk. My thoughts are murder to the State, and involuntarily go plotting against her" (260). The force of this essay is to bring home the extent to which Thoreau and his fellow citizens of Massachusetts are implicated directly in the wrong of slavery. But such a perception requires that one separate one's self not only in one's opinions, but through action. The tone of frustration and bitterness which pervades the essay results in part from Thoreau's inability to propose any resolution of the problem. Even in more narrowly literary terms, its conclusion is unsatisfactory. Thoreau reformulates the categorical imperative to the command "Behave so that the odor of your actions may enhance the general sweetness of the atmosphere . . ." (261). He goes on to develop this trope into a reflection on slavery and the stench of death. The preciosity of the figure cannot disguise the desperation of the conclusion. Thoreau has forcefully rejected an ethic based on the calculation of political consequences as a kind of gambling with morality. His invocation of "higher law" is independent of providential authority, and he has anatomized the narcissistic "regret" of those who stand by and witness the triumph of injustice. The aesthetic resolution attempted in this essay fails not only figuratively but historically. Thoreau is silent throughout the essay about the efforts of his fellow citizens to save Anthony Burns through direct action. In fact, his friend Thomas Wentworth Higginson and a group of sympathetic Bostonians mounted an armed attack on the courthouse in an effort to rescue Burns; they were turned back, but a deputy marshal was killed in the episode. The major consequence of this action was that President Pierce sent federal troops to Boston to ensure that state authorities enforced the law (McPherson [*Battle Cry of Freedom*] 119). Although he does confront the political realities directly, Thoreau is too sensitive to the stakes to let himself off completely. What is to be done when one's thoughts have become "murder to the State?"

Thoreau confronts the challenge of direct action most explicitly in his essays on John Brown. Delivered as a lecture originally in Concord on October 30, 1859, and subsequently in Boston on November first and Worcester on November third, **"A Plea for Capt. John Brown"** was published in a collection of anti-slavery essays, *Echoes of Harper's Ferry,* in 1860. John Brown presents both a challenge and an opportunity. The challenge derives from the appeal of direct action to overcome the sense of impotence and personal loss charted in **"Slavery in Massachusetts."** Brown was for Thoreau a man who acted in accord with "higher law," with his own convictions as to the right. As such he becomes one of the few men whom Thoreau would acknowledge as commanding obedience. But his actions were bloody. The raid on Harper's Ferry was necessarily violent and almost certainly futile in terms of worldly success. Even to Brown's admirers, these actions spoke of madness. In the background were the questions of conscience raised by the massacre at Pottawatomie. But for Thoreau, with his distrust of both normal politics and the abstract rhetoric of universal principle, Brown's life and conduct presented an opportunity for displaying exemplary political action. In figuring someone other than himself as the hero of these essays, Thoreau escapes the irony and deflation of **"Civil Disobedience."** John Brown appears as a man capable of more than words and gestures, but his militant actions resulted in the shedding of the blood of innocents. A deeper irony comes to shape Thoreau's essays in praise of John Brown, as the man of action is transformed into the practitioner of a higher rhetoric. John Brown's life becomes "a trope for parable-makers."

Thoreau praises Brown as revolutionary, humanist, transcendentalist, truth-teller, and martyr. He is a representative of America at its best, the heir of both Puritan and Revolutionary founders. In the rhetoric of these essays, Brown's aggressive actions themselves come to figure as elements in Thoreau's rhetoric of resistance. As revolutionary, Brown is even "firmer and higher principled" than the fighters at Concord Bridge: "They could bravely face their country's foes, but he had the courage to face his country herself when she was in the wrong" (**"Plea"** [**"A Plea for Captain John Brown"**] 212). Thoreau contrasts Brown's lack of formal education with his "public practice of Humanity" in the conduct of his life: "Such were *his humanities* and not any study of grammar. He would have left a Greek accent slanted the wrong way and righted up a falling man" (272-73).[8] Thoreau goes on to praise Brown as ". . . a transcendentalist above all, a man of deeds and principles. . . . Not yielding to a whim or transient impulse, but carrying out the purpose of a life" (274). Strikingly, in an essay composed before the trial, Thoreau emphasizes Brown's qualities as a speaker:

> . . . he did not overstate anything, but spoke within bounds. I remember particularly, how, in his speech here, he referred to what his family suffered in Kansas without giving the least vent to his pent-up fire. It was a volcano with an ordinary chimney-flue . . . He was not in the least a rhetorician, was not talking to Buncombe or his constituents anywhere, but to tell the simple truth and communicate his own resolution: therefore, he appeared incomparably strong. . . .
>
> (274)

In an inversion at least as old as Plato's *Apology of Socrates,* the simple truth-teller becomes the practitioner of a consummate rhetoric: "It was like the speeches of Cromwell compared with those of an ordinary king" (274). Thus, the heroism of John Brown comes to consist in his effectiveness in communicating the demands of conscience to his fellows. Brown's life itself becomes an exercise in the rhetoric of resistance. Like the heroes of old, this hero depends on the appearance of a bard who will immortalize the message of his actions. Thoreau explicitly compares Brown's virtue with the physical courage manifest in the charge at Balaclava:

> . . . the steady and for the most part successful charge of this man, for some years, against the legions of slavery, in obedience to an infinitely higher command, is much more memorable than that, as an intelligent and conscientious man is superior to a machine. Do you think that will go unsung?
>
> (278)

John Brown's conduct meets the prophetic demand of **"Civil Disobedience"** and **"Slavery in Massachusetts"** for citizens strong enough to represent in resistance to their government the highest aspirations of their countrymen. Thoreau's John Brown is the hero of a distinctly American epic:

> He did not recognize unjust human laws, but resisted them as he was bid. For once we are lifted out of the trivialness and dust of politics into the region of truth and manhood. No man in America has ever stood up so persistently and effectively for the dignity of human nature, knowing himself for a man, and the equal of any and all governments. In that sense, he was the most American of us all.
>
> (282)

Brown in his individuality exemplifies the paradoxical aspiration of the American democracy to nourish citizens strong enough to say "no" to their country in its errancy and to found a community of conscience.

To see Brown as representative of America's higher destiny is to redefine the terms of our political order: "We talk about *representative* government: but what monster of government is that where the noblest faculties of the mind and the whole *heart* are not represented" (285). Militant resistance calls forth a higher politics. But the persistent emphasis on Brown's *rhetoric* reveals Thoreau's ambivalence in celebrating acts whose reality includes violence against the innocent. In this passage, the apotheosis of Brown is also his disarmament:

> No, he was not our representative in any sense. He was too fair a specimen of man to represent the like of us. Who then *were* his constituents? . . . Truth is his inspirer, and earnestness the polisher of his sentences. He could afford to lose his Sharp's rifles, while he retained his faculty of speech, a Sharp's rifle of infinitely surer and larger range.
>
> (284)

Thoreau does not simply ignore the issue of violence but rather seeks to displace it in the context of slavery: "We preserve the so-called 'peace' of our community by deeds of petty violence everyday. . . . We are hoping only to live safely on the outskirts of *this* provisional army. So we defend ourselves and our roosts, and maintain slavery" (288-89). The problem of violence is further deflected by emphasizing Brown's courage in risking his own death for the sake of his principles. Indeed, Thoreau renders Brown's resoluteness as the rare, authentic human death: ". . . in order to die you must first have lived. . . . Only a half-dozen or so have died since the world began" (289-90). Echoing an earlier undertaking of death for the salvation of others, Thoreau suggests that the passion of John Brown teaches us to re-evaluate our own relations to death and to life:

> These men, in teaching us how to die, have at the same time taught us how to live. If this man's acts and words do not create a revival, it will be the severest possible satire on the acts and words that do. It is the best news that America has ever had.
>
> (290)

Brown is not only the Puritan prophet and true American revolutionary, but Thoreau's account of his life is to become the new gospel for a people nourished on the Book.

The hagiographic tendencies of **"A Plea for Capt. John Brown"** culminate in **"The Last Days of John Brown,"** which Thoreau prepared as a speech for delivery at funeral services for Brown on July 7, 1860 and published in *The Liberator* of July 27, 1860. Brown's martyrdom is likened not only to the passion of Jesus but also to the execution of Socrates. Thoreau's language recalls the concluding words of Plato's *Phaedo*: "Our thoughts could not revert to any greater or wiser or better man with whom to contrast him, for he, then and there was above them all. The man this country was about to hang appeared the greatest and best of them all" (170-71). The execution of Brown is expected to administer the kind of shock which forces a complacent society to take stock of itself and to recognize the difference between conventional and genuine piety. Thoreau transforms the hanging of Brown into an instant symbol:

> The North, I mean the *living* North, was suddenly all transcendental. It went behind the human law, it went behind the apparent failure, and recognized eternal justice and glory. Commonly, men live according to a formula, and are satisfied if the order of law is observed, but in this instance, they to some extent returned to original perceptions, and there was a slight revival of the old religion. They saw what they called order was confusion, what they deemed justice, injustice, and that the best was deemed the worst. This attitude suggested

a more intelligent and generous spirit than that which actuated our forefathers, and the possibility . . . of a revolution on behalf of another and an oppressed people.

> (178)

The events are taken as a text with a vital message for those who read it properly. That message is both a revival of the old religion, and an inspiration to complete and fulfill the promise of the American Revolution. Further, this message announces what Nietzsche called a "transvaluation of values." Brown's teaching calls us to see the need to set an inverted world right side up. In his martyrdom, Brown becomes a successful emancipator: "He has liberated many thousands of slaves, both North and South. They seem to have known nothing about living or dying for a principle" (174). Again, as in the earlier essay, Brown's directness and composure in the face of death are presented as a rhetorical teaching: "The art of composition is as simple as the discharge of a bullet from a rifle, and its masterpieces imply an infinitely greater force behind them" (175). Brown's death is almost welcomed as the means of transfiguring violence into spirit, into the kind of speech or writing which figures the truth:

> . . . he was not to be pardoned or rescued by men. That would have been to disarm him, to restore to him a material weapon, a Sharp's rifle, when he had taken up the sword of the spirit,—the sword with which he has really won his greatest and most memorable victories.
>
> (176)

The confrontation with death which was taken in the **"Plea"** as a warrant for the authenticity of his life now becomes the means of his immortality. The "good news" is complete as Thoreau announces the passage from passion to resurrection:

> Of all men who were said to be my contemporaries, it seemed to me that John Brown was the only one who *had not died* . . . I meet him at every turn. He is more alive than ever he was . . . He is no longer working in secret. He works in public, and in the clearest light that shines in this land.
>
> (176-77)

By the end of the 1850s, Thoreau's frustration in the effort to define political action that was both earnest and effective led him to transform John Brown's militant action into a text calling men to change themselves and the world. However, when war finally came, Thoreau was appalled by the reality of its violence.

IV

Resistance is inscribed in texts; reading them, students are challenged to become seers. Vision requires revision; a heightened conscience seeks expression through actions which are essays in self-transformation. The social world in which we are immersed provides the context for self-making. But the self is not merely expressive; it seeks to meet others on a higher ground than the daily grind of politics, to discover them as neighbors and as friends. Thoreau's political teaching insists on the individual transcending the terms of ordinary politics. However, he also calls for the founding of a new order in which equals can meet and inter-act without sacrificing the integrity of their personal quests. Indeed, he projects a conception of friendship in which sovereign selves are seen as agonistically engaged in challenging each other to renewed efforts at self-making.[9]

Nonetheless, Thoreau's contempt for the calculations of expediency leads him often to minimize the importance of ordinary politics for the business of deliberate living. He is not a celebrant of civic virtue as necessary for human fulfillment. Yet his vision of the social context of our lives leads him to urge militancy rather than quietism or conformity. One is implicated in the doings of democratic society; its wrongs diminish each of us. Thus, the duty of resistance to civil authority is derived from the individual's aspiration to live integrally and deliberately. In place of calculations of political expediency or the appeal to divine or rational law, Thoreau proposes an essentially aesthetic standard for judging human actions. The magnitude and intensity of such a project is the subject of **Walden.** I can do no more than indicate partially the ways in which the complex portrait of human individuality figured there bears on Thoreau's politics.

As with Kierkegaard, Nietzsche, and Heidegger, the emphasis on individual vision in Thoreau's conception of political action raises questions as to the extremes which may be justified in the name of self-formation. Thoreau's explicitly political essays contain little in the way of general argument to provide reassurance on this score. Rather, they employ rhetorical devices to contain the more explosive implications in the sovereignty of individual choice: irony in **"Civil Disobedience,"** self-conscious mythmaking in the John Brown essays. The texts in which they are inscribed function to transform the acts described from political program to personal problematic. Thoreau's essays are maieutic in their efforts, which include paradox and provocation, to elicit reflection and self-examination in the attentive reader. The political objective of Thoreau's writing is to awaken a slumbering polity to the demands of deliberate living. Thoreau's engagement with the political issues of his time places him squarely on the side of liberty and justice. His circumstance and judgment have insulated his work from the sort of anxiety generated in the cases of Nietzsche and Heidegger. However, the politics of the twentieth century force us to scrutinize with care any view which emphasizes self-formation without attending to the risks that self-assertion may be

pursued with unjustified costs to others. Further, Thoreau's critique of conventional morality and invocation of aesthetic norms in judging human individuality may leave him without resource in the face of moral extremes.

Thoreau's writing evinces a deep awareness of the moral ambiguities of self-formation. Indeed, a major pressure on his literary effort is the need to portray the dynamics by which the individual must negotiate his way between the risks of self-abnegation and those of self-aggrandizement. Thoreau adopts and transforms the contemporary rhetoric of "higher law" as a guide to conscientious action; at the same time, he rejects any recourse to legalism or rationalism. At the heart of Thoreau's portrayal of human individuality in **Walden** is the "double self," divided between community and solitude, action and reflection, goodness and wildness.

In **Walden,** the section called "Higher Laws" presents some of the deepest puzzlements in that deeply puzzling text. The chapter begins with the narrator's observation of a woodchuck, which occasions ". . . a strange thrill of savage delight, and [I] was strangely tempted to seize and devour him raw, not that I was hungry then, except for that wildness which he represented" (139-40). Thoreau embraces this impulse as integral to himself, although it co-exists with competing desires which point in an opposite direction: ". . . I found in myself, and still find, an instinct toward a higher, or, as it is named, spiritual life, as do most men, and another toward a primitive rank and savage one, and I reverence them both. I love the wild not less than the good" (140). These divided desires reveal fundamental ambiguities in man's relation to nature. We are not only travelers, spectators, and students of nature, but hunters, fishermen, and woodchoppers. These diverse engagements with the natural world form the subject of most of the chapter. Thoreau rejects the easy moralizing which urges an unequivocal embrace of spirituality and rejection of all carnal desire and exploitative activity. He affirms rather a progressive sublimation of the savage desires by which hunters and fishermen in their youth grow up to become naturalists and poets. But such development does not mark a complete break with its ambiguous origins:

> There is unquestionably this instinct in me which belongs to the lower orders of creation; yet with every year I am less a fisherman though without more humanity or even wisdom: at present I am no fisherman at all. But I see that if I were to live in a wilderness I should again be tempted to become a fisher and hunter in earnest.

> (142)

The struggle which Thoreau portrays is toward purity, but he conveys a Nietzschean sense that the only chastity worth winning is a victory over contrary desires deep within the self. It is not just a matter of forbearance, but of recognizing and overcoming the wildness within.

This aspect of the "double self" recalls both classical and Christian notions of humanity as divided between the animal and the divine: "We are conscious of an animal in us, which awakens in proportion as our higher nature slumbers. . . . It is reptile and sensual, and perhaps cannot be wholly expelled, like the worms which, even in life and health, occupy our bodies" (146). This division determines the context of our striving toward purity: "I fear that we are such gods or demigods only as fauns and satyrs, the divine allied to beasts, the creatures of appetite, and that to some extent, our very life is our disgrace . . ." (146). Purity cannot be attained simply by turning our backs on our embodied animal nature. Rather, the project of living is to shape a significant form from these very materials: "We are all sculptors and painters, and our material is our own flesh and blood and bones" (147). It is through our bodies that we find ourselves immersed in a social and natural world, subject to the rule of expediency. The dynamic inter-action between spiritual shaping and material circumstance repeats the relation between conscientious action and social context which informs the political essays.

The familiar dualisms of mind and body, spirit and flesh, individual and society, provide important dimensions of the experiment in deliberate living reported in *Walden*. In a critical passage, Thoreau brings them together in a vision for which "doubleness" becomes definitive of the human condition:

> With thinking we may be beside ourselves in a sane sense. By a conscious effort of the mind we can stand aloof from actions and their consequences, and all things, good and bad, go by us like a torrent. We are not wholly involved in nature . . . I only know myself as a human entity; the scene, so to speak, of thoughts and affections; and am sensible of a certain doubleness by which I can stand as remote from myself as from another . . . [a] spectator sharing no experience, but taking note of it. This doubleness may easily make us poor neighbors and friends sometimes.
>
> (90-91)

This rich description must evoke for the contemporary reader a plethora of modern attempts to portray the alienations of reflective self-consciousness. For Thoreau, the project of living deliberately becomes aesthetic in a dual sense: the self becomes a theater in which both actor and spectator are engaged. Each of us is charged both as an artist, making the most we can of the materials of life, and as a judge, evaluating critically the results of that ongoing effort. Though Thoreau sees the spectator in us as characterized by impersonal-

ity—"It is no more I than it is you"—it does not have access to a Kantian domain of transcendental reason. In viewing one's life, it beholds "a kind of fiction, a work of the imagination only" (91). We cannot avoid, in the important questions of life, the need to risk judgment without transcendental support. Thoreau recasts Kant's categorical imperative in terms which aestheticize morality and recognize the centrality of a self divided between actor/artist and spectator/judge: "To affect the quality of the day, that is the highest of arts. Every man is tasked to make his life, even in its details, worthy of the contemplation of his most elevated and critical hour" (61).[10] Morality cannot be reduced to law or convention, reason or calculation. The ambiguities of Thoreau's political essays reflect the pervasive ambiguity of our situation in the world. However, we are not without resource, for life itself becomes an exercise in both acting and judging. Moreover, we are not alone: "I think that I love society as much as most, and am ready enough to fasten myself like a bloodsucker for the time to any full-blooded man that comes my way" (94). Although the conventions of social life and ordinary politics may coarsen and trivialize our interaction, Thoreau adumbrates forms of friendship in which the highest in each may reach out to the other. Such community is as hard to achieve as any deliberate living, and Thoreau imagines intimate conversation across a pathos of distance:

> . . . if we speak reservedly and thoughtfully, we want to be farther apart, that all animal heat and moisture may have a chance to evaporate. If we would enjoy the most intimate society with that in each of us which is without, or above, being spoken to, we must not only be silent, but commonly so far apart bodily that we cannot hear each other's voice in any case. Referred to this standard, speech is for the convenience of those who are hard of hearing; but there are many fine things that we cannot say if we have to shout.
>
> (94-95)

The conversation which Thoreau paradoxically commends is not simply that of the "soul with itself," but of the reader with his texts. Not shouting, but writing, is the vehicle of profound communication: ". . . the noblest written words are commonly as far behind or above the fleeting spoken language as the firmament with the stars is behind the clouds . . ."(69). Whereas the orator is bound by his occasion and the conversationalist by his interlocutor, the writer addresses himself to the thinker in all of us, to any who would make the effort to understand. The written work both symbolizes the fullest life, and establishes a community among those seeking to achieve it: "A written word . . . is something at once more intimate and more universal than any other work of art. It is the work of art nearest to life itself. It may be translated into every language, and not only be read, but actually breathed from all human lips . . ." (69).

Thoreau's writing "prescribes no rules to strong and valiant natures," but rather seeks to show us a text in which we may read ourselves. In *Walden,* the cycles of the day and of the year frame his experiment. Living itself is characterized by rhythms of withdrawal and return, ascent and descent. Our double nature can be negotiated only through the active and attentive exploration of its polarities. Thoreau insists that the search for foundations, for a ground from which to undertake our enterprise, leads us both deep within ourselves and to the most distant horizons: "Why has man rooted himself thus firmly in the earth, but that he may rise in the same proportion into the heavens above?" (117). We pursue the business of living within the contexts of our bodies, our neighborhoods, our society, our natural environment; they provide both the setting and the material of our self-making. The project is enacted in time. At its heart is the paradox of our "double-ness" and the rhythms by which we repeatedly seek to make a divided self whole. In the text of *Walden,* immediately before recounting the episode of his arrest and imprisonment that figures in **"Civil Disobedience,"** Thoreau indicates the "farther shore" of his political and moral vision:

> Every man has to learn the points of the compass again as often as he awakes, whether from sleep or any abstraction. Not till we are lost, in other words, not till we have lost the world, do we begin to find ourselves, and realize where we are and the infinite extent of our relations.

(115)

Notes

1. Thoreau wrote an essay favorable to Philips after the abolitionist's appearance at the Concord Lyceum in 1845.

2. On the other hand, when he first returned to live in Concord after graduating from Harvard, Thoreau objected to paying a village tax the proceeds of which went to support the local church.

3. See John Rawls, sections 55-59.

4. See section III below.

5. "When I came out of prison . . . a change had to my eyes come over the scene,—the town, and State and country,—greater than any than mere time could effect. I saw more distinctly the State in which I lived. I saw to what extent the people among whom I lived . . . were a distinct race from me by their prejudices and superstitions, as the Chinamen and Malays are; that, in their sacrifices to humanity, they ran no risks, not even to their property . . ." (238).

6. Although Nancy Rosenblum, "Thoreau" ["Thoreau's Militant Conscience"], makes a powerful case for the "militant" and "heroic" aspects of Thoreau's conception of individuality, she overlooks the recurrent irony which undercuts these features of his self-portrayal. Similarly, she treats his use of paradox and contradiction solely in terms of rhetorical aggression, neglecting the extent to which these devices have been instruments of maieutic education since Socrates.

7. See F. O. Matthiesen for a discussion of the importance of formal rhetoric in the education of Thoreau's day. This context bears importantly on Thoreau's distinction between speech and writing discussed in section III of this essay.

8. In an essay with explicit reference to Brown's experience in Kansas, Thoreau is silent about the men fallen at Pottawatomie.

9. See Thoreau's essay on "Friendship" in Glick [*Great Short Works of Henry David Thoreau*].

10. In the context of *Walden,* the presentation of morality in aesthetic terms succeeds rhetorically whereas it failed dismally in the political context of "Slavery in Massachusetts," discussed in section III. This movement in Thoreau's thought is reminiscent of Hannah Arendt's appropriation of Kant's Third *Critique.* She discusses Thoreau in her essay on "Civil Disobedience," but I find no reference to him in *The Life of the Mind,* despite the affinities between their analyses of thinking, conscience, and judging.

Works Cited

Arendt, Hannah. "Civil Disobedience." *Crises of the Republic.* New York: Harcourt, Brace, 1972.

———. *The Life of the Mind.* Ed. Mary McCarthy. New York: Harcourt, Brace, Jovanovich, 1978.

Cavell, Stanley. *The Senses of Walden.* Expanded edition. San Francisco: North Point Press, 1981.

Emerson, Ralph Waldo. "Thoreau." *Thoreau.* Thomas.

Gifford, Don. "Address to the Danforth Graduate Fellows' Conference." Danforth Graduate Fellows' Conference. South Lee, MA, 1967.

———. "Thoreau on Civil Disobedience." Address. Essex, England: University of Essex, 1970.

———. *The Farther Shore: A Natural History of Perception.* New York: Atlantic Monthly Press, 1990.

Hendrick, George. "The Influence of Thoreau's 'Civil Disobedience' on Gandhi's Satyagraha." *Thoreau.* Thomas.

Kateb, George. "Democratic Individuality and the Claims of Politics." *Political Theory* 12 (August 1984): 331-360.

————. "Democratic Individuality and the Meaning of Rights." *Liberalism and the Moral Life.* Ed. Nancy Rosenblum. Cambridge, MA: Harvard University Press, 1989: 207-226.

Lynd, Staughton. *Intellectual Origins of American Radicalism.* New York: Random House Vintage, 1969: 100-129.

McPherson, James M. *Battle Cry of Freedom.* New York: Oxford University Press, 1988.

Matthieson, F. O. *American Renaissance: Art and Expression in the Age of Emerson and Whitman.* New York: Oxford University Press, 1941.

Miller, Perry. "From Edwards to Emerson." *Errand Into the Wilderness.* Cambridge, MA: The Belknap Press of Harvard University Press, 1981.

Oates, Stephen B. *Let the Trumpet Sound: The Life of Martin Luther King, Jr.* New York: Penguin Books, 1982.

Rawls, John. *A Theory of Justice.* Cambridge, MA: Harvard University Press, 1971.

Rosenblum, Nancy. "Thoreau's Militant Conscience." *Political Theory* 9 (February 1981): 81-110.

————. *Another Liberalism.* Cambridge, MA: Harvard University Press, 1989).

Thoreau, Henry David. "The Last Days of John Brown." *Thoreau: The Major Essays.* Ed. Jeffrey L. Duncan New York: E. P. Dutton & Co., 1972.

————. "Slavery in Massachusetts." *Great Short Works of Henry David Thoreau.* Ed. Wendell Glick. New York: Harper & Row Perennial Library, 1982.

————. "A Plea for Captain John Brown." *Great Short Works of Henry David Thoreau.* Ed. Wendell Glick. New York: Harper & Row Perennial Library, 1982.

————. *Walden and Civil Disobedience.* Ed. Owen Thomas. New York: W. W. Norton & Co., 1966.

Robert Fanuzzi (essay date June 1996)

SOURCE: Fanuzzi, Robert. "Thoreau's Urban Imagination." *American Literature* 68, no. 2 (June 1996): 321-46.

[*In the following essay, Fanuzzi examines themes of "utopian space" in Thoreau's* Walden.]

A second look at **Walden** suggests that Thoreau went to the country to find the city. He admits that his seclusion is motivated by necessity, since the opportunities for "beautiful living" once characteristic of civilized society are now found only "out of doors, where there is no house and no housekeeper." Thus secluded, he finds "a good port" from which to conduct his "private business," a railroad line to link a "citizen of the world" to national and international market-places, a cosmopolitan alternative to Concord's unlettered, "provincial" culture, and even—through Ellery Channing's companionship—the bonhomie of Broadway. Perhaps most important, he determines that by cultivating Catonian civic virtue, he has reacquired the integrity to "sustain . . . the manliest relations to men" forfeited by his neighboring yeomen.[1] In sum, every historic association of the city was present at Walden Pond—except, of course, the city itself.

The city is indeed both present and absent in **Walden.** It exists through references and allusions to city life, which is to say it exists as metonymy. This city has no geographical equivalent and in fact disclaims its status as locality, for Thoreau's intent is to use historically identified conventions of urbanism to conceive a space that corresponds to his imagination. Still retaining his sense of place, he wants this space to be habitable. When he asks in the midst of the woods, "What sort of space is that which separates a man from his fellows and makes him solitary?" (89), his metaphor adumbrates a sphere of autonomy bounded only by the means of its articulation. Throughout **Walden,** he deliberately designates those activities proper to this sphere—thinking, walking, writing, reading, thinking—and circumscribes them as art, which he defines as the "struggle to free himself from this low state" (25). Like other contemporary utopian reforms, his artistic realization contains the promise of a living space in which one may find the virtue, prosperity, and liberty not found in other environs. With a "mission" that Benjamin terms "the emancipation from experiences," Thoreau strolls through the woods as the flaneur: an aesthetic consciousness whose individualized perception and mode of expression constitute his experience of place.[2]

If Thoreau had lived in Boston, it would be easier to endow him with an urban imagination, though as my opening paragraph suggests, it is surely possible to contrast his project with pastoralism. The greater challenge that **Walden** poses is to see the imagination that Thoreau exercised so freely not only as spatial logic but as a construction of social space and, even more particularly, as a historical incidence of urbanism. In **Walden,** Thoreau creates what urbanists call a development history for the imagination, accounting for the creation of avowedly figural forms by the same changes in social morphology that were transforming the built and unbuilt landscape of eastern Massachusetts into centers or subsidiaries of an equally new social form, the urban-industrial complex.[3] He attributes the liberation of the imagination directly to urbanization, but the same process provided the negative conditions for artistic production. Indeed, describing the emergence of the imagination as a spatialized form for Thoreau meant projecting an invisible space existing only as traces or inferences of representation. In *Walden,* this prospect is realized as an imagined city symbolizing a civic tradition with its attendant social spaces that was disappearing from Concord's increasingly urbanized environs. Though Thoreau stood by this tradition and detested its compromise, he did not resist the processes of historical and morphological change. On the contrary, he exploited them, transforming mutable civic space into its timeless utopian representation. Thoreau's civic project was, in fact, to intensify the awareness of artistic representation—a prospect which Paul Ricoeur defines as the operation of the utopian—in order to mark a disjunction in the progress of liberalism between the material development of cities and its invisible moral and political abstractions.[4] Because Thoreau situated himself in the midst of this conflict, *Walden* describes not just an imagined city but *how* cities became imaginary. We can consider this event to be as crucial to the emergence of Thoreau's artistic consciousness as to the future of urban space, keeping in mind Benjamin's judgment of Baudelaire: "He envisioned blank spaces which he filled in with his poems. His work cannot merely be categorized as historical like anyone else's, but it intended to be so and understood itself as so."[5]

* * *

Thoreau's aspiration towards idiosyncrasy notwithstanding, the unique history that *Walden* tells is the emergence of aesthetic forms from the conventions and traditions of civic life. Indeed, his determination to recreate this life in the midst of the woods lays bare the enabling assumption of an artistic sensibility: that a city is a construct of consciousness, imagined through the awareness of individuality, if not alienation, that city life engenders.[6] While urbanism thus defined is central to our conception of modernism, the tendency to interpret urban space as the medium of the imagination is already extant in the place names for many of the locales of nineteenth-century literature: in addition to Baudelaire's Paris, Whitman's New York, Crane's Bowery, Dickens's London, and so on.[7] The distinctiveness of Thoreau's Walden Pond among these "unreal cities" is that it brings to the fore the contradiction between the experience of place and the actual place, so that both the imaginative processes and the means of representation are defamiliarized. That is, they are foregrounded and thematized as locales in themselves. For Thoreau, this defamiliarization promises an unprecedented and unbounded sphere of experience, but he will also insist that this "sort of space" shares the structure, conditions, and even the history of a spatialized social form.

We are introduced to this contradiction early in *Walden,* when Thoreau quite deliberately juxtaposes associations of city and country. After berating his townsmen for their industriousness, he announces that his "purpose in going to Walden Pond was . . . to transact some private business" (13). Then he invites a comparison between his solitary life of rustic simplicity and the far-flung, multitudinous affairs of the international mercantile trader. In assuming this identity, Thoreau is also borrowing its native habitat. According to political historian Gary Nash, the international merchant would have been a politically active Whig or Federalist, committed to liberalizing developments in government and trade and usually situated in an Atlantic port city like Boston, Baltimore, New York, or Philadelphia.[8] Thoreau contends that Walden Pond is likewise "a good place for business" because of its "good port and good foundation," as well as its ice-trade-convenient railroad connection (14). In "Sounds," he will say that the railroad, transporting exotic goods from free and distant markets, makes him akin to the international merchant, a "citizen of the world" (80). He evidently wants to build not just a city on a hill but a commercial society by a pond, "the germ," he says, "of something more" (175).

In borrowing an urban locale, Thoreau is also reclaiming a political history. Through their alliance with restive manufacturers and disenfranchised artisans, the liberal Whig traders of the eighteenth century made the Atlantic commercial city into the center of political resistance against monopolies, mercantilism, and colonialism. By comparing himself to the urban merchant, Thoreau perpetuates a complementary vision of freedom: the autonomy promised the urban commercial classes in a postcolonial, laissez-faire economy.[9] We may read his intention "to transact some private business with the fewest obstacles" as a similar link between political and economic freedom. This linking would have been compatible with his reigning ambition in *Walden* and in many of his essays, which was to establish the relevance of the nation's democratic revolution to antebellum America; but here he seeks to recreate the appropriate social space for continued struggle through detailed historical references to the eighteenth-century commercial city. In the spirit of the urban Whigs Trenchard and Gordon, Thoreau envisions this space as a free society of trade and commerce, politically and geographically beyond the reach of an intrusive state. The taxation that he seemed to oppose so capriciously represented what these liberals feared most: the intervention of statist policies—whether they financed trade monopolies, the slave trade, or a system of railroads—in the properly private affairs of civil society.[10]

For Thoreau, this kind of uncivil, neomercantilist economy signifies a structural change in the polity, a reorganization of social space that gives the state its own space, the all-inclusive yet personalized space of the nation.[11] He detects the expansion of this space in the sentiments of citizens who "think it essential that the *Nation* have commerce, and export ice, and talk through a telegraph, and ride thirty miles an hour" (62), but he will protect an ideal of civil autonomy rooted in eighteenth-century urban liberalism. When he says that such citizens are "content to live like baboons," he applies a venerable term of moral opprobrium—corruption—to Jefferson's laboring yeomen.

Thoreau's praise of the cosmopolitan merchant, on the other hand, is unstinting; he affects envy, almost wonder, for what amounts to "a demand for universal knowledge" (13). But he is determined to let neither the location of Walden Pond nor the passage of time deprive him of the intelligence, freedom, and prosperity available to the eighteenth-century urban bourgeoisie. He builds his identification with this class by undermining both the pastoral tradition of American letters and the nationalist history it projected. Whereas Bryant and even Emerson celebrated nature as the extension and progress of positive sovereignty, Thoreau represents nature according to the self-negating provisions of civil society. That is, he considers Walden Pond to be natural insofar as it is a completely privative realm, free of superfluous obstacles and unconditioned by an intrusive alien power. Thoreau calls life in this realm "primitive and frontier life" not because it is wild but precisely because it is governed by "the essential laws of man's existence," which he finds recorded in "the old day books of the merchants." Not surprisingly, these laws instruct Thoreau in the ways of bourgeois society: what is natural and necessary is "all that man obtains by his own exertions" (7). Under this condition, he disqualifies the labor of his neighboring farmers, who work not for themselves but for the holders of their mortgages on their homes and farms. So he is forced to commend the unencumbered wigwam, the virtues of uncultivated fields, and the political economy of squirrels. His deprecation of baboons notwithstanding, animals furnish Thoreau with perhaps his most explicitly self-justifying image of the bourgeoisie: their orderly yet consummately free lives follow only the dictates of natural, invisible laws. He makes special allowances when he adds Fuel and Clothing to the animals' necessities of Food and Shelter, but he considers any life that obeys intrinsic imperatives to be both a moral and material improvement over that of Concord townsmen.

Walden ultimately recommends that the conscientious citizen devote himself to "more sacred laws," but Thoreau's attachment to a legally constituted dominion in heaven or on earth perpetuates a historically urban form of society in the absence of a corresponding urban space. Thoreau was well aware of the historical discrepancy, but he means the invocation of an antecedent social form to annul the influence of the state by providing a permanent haven from positive law. In this sense, he is using the pastoral to revive, replay, and infinitely extend eighteenth-century urbanization, which created not only the infrastructure of public dissent but an invisible realm called civil society, which, as Habermas says, was governed by "anonymous laws functioning in accord with an economic rationality immanent, so it appears, in the market." Though Habermas does not historicize the urban development that created this realm, he does make the rise of a "town" consciousness, in opposition to that of a "court," coincident with the codification of civil laws that have exclusive administrative jurisdiction over economic and social exchanges.[12] Thoreau places himself under these "more liberal laws" and hopes that they can again convene an autonomous society in the midst of the woods (214). In commending Walden Pond for its "good port," he is making a glancing reference to the shared history of liberal capitalism and urban development, though he maintains that the commercial city rising from Walden Pond would be built "on piles of your own driving" (14).

Thoreau repeatedly argues a classically liberal ideal of individual autonomy, but he does not abstract even the discussion of inward nature from the infrastructure and institutions of an urbanized social form. His conception of a morally guided subject, obedient to "the laws of his own being," is derived from the self-governing commercial society, while his concern for the state of "true integrity" links him more particularly to the Whig-Federalist city's civic sphere, which fused the republican politics of disinterested virtue with an economically constituted social space. From the Revolution to the antebellum era, the commercial city was indeed the sphere in which the new nation's republican pretensions were given institutional form, often most effectively translated by the Whig-Federalist commercial classes. The lyceums, atheneums, libraries, and salons that composed the antebellum era's "republican institutions" were first developed in Atlantic port cities; with no attempt to disguise the city's principal indigenous activity, their wealthy patrons celebrated them as "cultural ornaments to mercantile society."[13] In conjunction with Federalist architecture's French neoclassicism, these "cultural ornaments" fueled the post-Revolutionary city's comparison of itself to the classical polis, although this was more true for Philadelphia and Boston than for single-mindedly mercantile New York; the former two competed with one another for the title "Athens of America."[14] Within the institutions of this civic sphere, self-seeking burghers could transcend their interests and exercise their rational faculties. Perhaps even more importantly, an unruly populace would learn how to govern itself by the laws of reason.

The Jacksonian era may have envisioned a form of society in the image of the rural majority, but in *Walden* the Whig-Federalist city plan is recovered and extended. In "Reading," Thoreau proposes that Concord proper be developed along the lines of a classically Federalist city, replete with indigenous salons, galleries, libraries, lyceums, and other educational facilities. He exhorts the citizens of Concord not to adopt a "provincial" life but to "act collectively in the spirit of our [prospective] institutions" and "take the place of the noblemen in Europe" (74). This ambition to create "noble villages of men" is in keeping with a principal objective of the early republic, which was to authorize its sovereignty through the education of a rational public capable of governing itself. But in practical terms, this imperative is also an impetus for city-building, for the republican project of political education entailed the development of a cosmopolitan center capable of receiving information, influences, and goods, as Thoreau insists, from distant ports. "Reading" resituates republicanism in an urban tradition and suggests that the Transcendentalists' project of self-culture derives from its plans for civic development.

Jefferson's abhorrence of cities has led us to equate republicanism with the country, but politics and geography are often difficult to equate, especially during the early national period in New England. If agrarianism was celebrated as a republican ideal, it was promoted by the same Federalist urban merchants who were building and promoting the port city. In Boston, a group known as the Essex Junto was particularly effective in investing rural life with the same power to inculcate virtue that the urban institutions aimed at. The country seats and adjoining farms that dotted the eastern Massachusetts landscape were considered not as alternative economies in their own right but as necessary adjuncts to market exchanges that guaranteed the exchanges' virtue and their contribution to the public good. Agrarianism served urban commercial interests even more explicitly when it was accompanied by a program of political education. In lectures such as "The Duty of the Farmer to his Calling" and "Why a Massachusetts Farmer Should Be Content," farmers were told by an urban elite that they were the pillars of the republic and that their thrift, frugality, and increasingly unprofitable industry furnished the moral basis of a predominantly commercial society.[15]

Thoreau may have sought respite from modern society in natural environs, but his plans for Walden Woods and vicinity reflect the traditional land-use patterns of the urban Federalist. In "Where I Lived, and What I Lived for," he reports that he roamed the countryside as a self-appointed real-estate broker, financier, and landscape architect of imaginary country seats; he then reinterprets this conventional pattern of subdivision as the simple experience of sitting. To further link his *"sedes"* to the development plans of the commercial class, he speculates that "the future inhabitants of this region, wherever they may place their houses, may be sure that they had been anticipated" (55).

Like the urban Federalist, Thoreau does not mean to associate himself with present or future farmers. His dedication to husbandry, on display in "The Bean Field," is in fact inspired by a civic tradition cultivated in the eighteenth century by the Anglo-American urban bourgeoisie. As J. G. A. Pocock reports, Whig liberals adopted the Catonian ideal of an agrarian republic to argue that virtue, the selfless participation of a citizen in the life of his polity, could be exercised by the members of an urbanized commercial society whose profits advanced the interests of the public. Their inspiration for an actively moral citizenry came from the classical polis, though as first developed in the seventeenth century, "country" ideology did attempt to secure England's status as a republic by invoking a natural basis for virtue in nondependent landholding.[16] But as Britain evolved into an international trading empire, "country" signified an opposition political party whose model republic was less associated with nature than with free commerce. Against speculative, debt-inducing, and state-sponsored monopolist ventures, proponents of a liberalized marketplace envisioned a virtuous society governed by laws of just commerce, of wide distribution of capital, and of equitable exchange. To ameliorate the influence of financial interests in the government, to mitigate the power of the state, and to establish the authority of the public, *Cato's Letters* proposed "agrarian law or something like it."[17] The polity entailed by these laws corresponded not to a farm but to an idealized commercial society whose market exchanges exemplified classical ideals of citizenship.

We readily accept Thoreau's investment in classical politics as determining his relation to pastoralism and agrarianism; as Horkheimer says, his "escape into the woods was conceived by a student of the Greek polis rather than by a peasant."[18] What we should add to this truism is that his understanding of the civic tradition is mediated by the civil discourse of the urban bourgeoisie. Thoreau likewise refuses to distinguish between virtue and commerce, arguing instead that the value of rural life comes from its contribution to civil commerce. In this sense, he too pursues agrarianism, "or something like it." In "The Bean Field," he archly notes the derision his bastardized husbandry elicited from locals and reserves his pride not for his agricultural expertise and certainly not for his noble toil but for $8.72, "the result of my experience in raising beans" (109). This narrowly economic assessment might seem at variance with the disinterested ideals of agrarian republicanism, but Thoreau's interest in farming is to prove Cato's dictum: "the profits of agriculture are particularly pious or just" (111). Such profits are conducive to virtue because they can be obtained without debt, without state capitalization, and particularly without submission to the "slave-driver" within. To the extent that husbandry allows him to maintain his independence from a neomercantilist, slave-driving economy, Thoreau has fulfilled the promise of urban liberalism and made commerce into a medium of virtuous citizenship. In this context, "country" does not denote a natural setting or even a natural economic order. On the contrary, Whigs used agrarian republicanism to place the imprimatur of the civic ideal on their commercial city. By Thoreau's time, this city does not exist in nature, so he is in the strange position of having to imagine a civic space *as* nature—or, to use an important eighteenth-century distinction, as *second* nature. Through his ersatz agriculture—indeed, through an imitation of nature—Thoreau wants his readers to look beyond his immediate environs and imagine the unrealized, nonlocalizable realm of the commercial city, wherein profit was in proportion to virtue. There they would find not only the advantages of civilization but the evidence of their own imagination.

* * *

Is the model for Walden Pond then an economically productive urban society or a counter-social pastoral? Perhaps we should answer yes. Thoreau appropriates the historic associations of the Whig-Federalist commercial city for the representation of nature, but nature thus represented is neither pastoral nor agrarian; it is symbolic of an idealized sphere of civil commerce. To be more specific: Thoreau adopts historically identified urban forms for the purposes of representation. He evidently wants the juxtaposition of city and country to transcend their status as localities and to signify their metaphorical relations. Indeed, when he says in "The Bean Field" that he ploughs the ground "for the sake of tropes and expression" (108), we sense that the intended reference for Walden Pond is always self-reference. Although Thoreau is committed to the formal innovation this entails, he means the ceaseless transformations of language and the unfettered significations of symbols to project a lived sphere of activity in which the value of human, specifically civic interactions obtains irrespective of social space. Social planning and artistic formalism can in this sense be dismissed as false opposites, which is to say that the "civic consciousness" manifested in the opening chapters of **Walden** persists throughout the work.[19] Thoreau in fact means his social and political agenda to be grasped at the textual level.

If only for this reason, we should not minimize Thoreau's growing investment in an explicitly figural discourse that leads beyond political satire—such as the allegory of the ant battle—into a sophisticated philosophical playfulness and finally, according to Gilmore, into the reification of both language and his intellectual labor into unmarketable fetishes.[20] By the middle of **Walden,** Thoreau has assembled a Transcendentalist idiom of self-consciousness full of extended metaphors of foundations, fathoming, reflections, and bottoms; in "The Pond," Walden Pond is inevitably apostrophized as a Cartesian subject. When he says, "I am thankful that this pond was made deep and pure for a symbol" (189), we may read not merely an expression of artistic indebtedness but an ascending level of figuration—this

time, a metafigural discourse. As **Walden** nears its end, Thoreau leaves behind any sense of place and dissolves himself in this increasingly self-aware discourse, which becomes his horizon of experience. In the "Conclusion," he describes his "experiment in living" as the aspiration toward hyperbole: "I fear chiefly lest my expression may not be *extra-vagant* enough" (214). He says he wants to exceed the limits of language and awaken his contemporaries to the truth of an unsaid "residual statement," but the effect of this and the other figures of **Walden** is to make them a "literal monument"—that is, through such self-reflexive puns to make language an irreducible experience and the ultimate reward for his retreat (215). In the end, he subordinates his preference for either city or country to the desire "to speak somewhere *without* bounds" (214).

The intensified consciousness of language in **Walden** coincides with the displacement of Walden Pond as an actual locale, indeed with the abolition of space per se. As Thoreau says, a discourse transparent to itself is "somewhere *without* bounds." Yet, as we have seen, the elaborate use of tropes and figures, so successful in projecting a horizon of experience beyond the existing forms of society, has the quite perverse effect of preserving, even recreating, a particular social form—the eighteenth-century commercial city. So historically inflected is Thoreau's artistic discourse that he cannot represent this city without the intervening effects of time. That is, he recreates an earlier social form in a way that attests to its own absence in antebellum society. For Thoreau as well as for readers of **Walden,** the urban space of the eighteenth century can exist only invisibly, as a nonlocalizable symbol of everything good and profitable about a civil society. To the extent that the meaningfulness of this symbol is contingent on the absence of the urban site, Thoreau uses the impermanence of social space to discover the criterion for the validity of artistic representation in itself. In hypostasizing its own space, this artistic discourse can ignore the conditions for material existence while constituting itself through detailed historical urban references. This paradox is precisely to Thoreau's point: he intends the self-realization of language not only to create a medium of historicism but to force a moment of historical awareness.

The synchronicity of artistic form is something that has been claimed for culture as a whole, which, like Thoreau's formalism, creates contemporary, endlessly renewable meaning from an orientation toward tradition.[21] In **Walden,** the eighteenth-century commercial city and its liberal capitalist rhetoric serve not only as the material for figural representation but as the inspiration for a transtemporal universal aesthetic experience. The vanishing urban space is thus preserved in perpetuity through and as art. At least, this seems to be the argument of Thoreau's concluding meta-allegory of artistic creation: the city of Kouroo becomes "a hoary ruin," but while time passes and the artist toils he makes a "world with full and fair proportions" and discovers that "the former lapse of time had been an illusion" (216-17).

Yet the conditions for artistic realization as they are laid down in *Walden* are somewhat more complicated. Tradition is recreated for present understanding in an avowedly symbolic form, but it exists in no time and no place but in the medium of that understanding. Fredric Jameson has identified this negative condition for artistic representation as an ideologeme, the trace of a dated social paradigm or an obsolete collective narrative.[22] The proliferation of these traces in *Walden*—the allusions to and reminders of an absent urban environment—raises the kind of question that the social theorist John Brenkman finds inscribed in the horizon of aesthetic experience: "how is aesthetic experience implicated in the historical continuities and discontinuities between the social site of an artwork's genesis and the social site of our reception of it?"[23] Thoreau makes this conflicted position, which here refers to the possibility of an aesthetic understanding, a necessary condition of artistic production. In *Walden,* the aesthetic forms conceived through the recapitulation of an urban tradition also signal a rift in urban history that forbids its reappearance.

The understanding of art as the evidence of discrepancy and discontinuity between historical contexts is suggestive of another concept from Jameson's critical vocabulary, the "ideology of form." In claiming that Thoreau's artistic discourse functions not only as a marker of historical crisis but as an ideological instrument, I am including the insight that the production of art is the objectification of the imaginary as the field of conflicting forces, considered not only diachronically but also dialectically.[24] These antagonisms could be attributed to the process of urbanization that was transforming the built and unbuilt landscape of eastern Massachusetts, but in *Walden,* these conflicts are found only as they generate a symbolic register that transcends the particular social context that is in "real contradiction." Precisely because these conflicts enter *Walden* as an "absent cause," we should not look outside Walden Pond or Thoreau's verbal sophistication for the disruptions of urbanization. Especially at its most symbolic and prospective, Walden Pond is their exact site. We might press the point with Thoreau's example in mind and say that his utopian representation, divorced from a specific place but inclusive of distant settings, contains the "determinate contradictions" that constitute the social. Indeed, the self-sufficiency promised by his artistic discourse establishes his claim on the eighteenth-century civic tradition, which suggests that the transcendence of either social sites or historical context in an avowedly formalist representation has an effect opposite to what we might expect: it generates an irreducible medium of experience through which the social is articulated. Jameson refers to this function as the "symbolic enactment of the social," but we should not conclude that Thoreau's or any other artistic form mitigates the effect of either social conflict or historical discontinuity.[25] Rather, the conclusion that Walden Pond forces upon us is that utopian representation and social-historical realities coexist and are in fact inseparable.

We need only observe the result of Thoreau's artistic project to realize that his most useful allies are the most destructive aspects of urbanization. Walden Pond is in this sense a socially symbolic form created by the same manifest contradictions that organized antebellum society. From the "vantage ground" of this symbol, Thoreau can observe that the intensified patterns of labor and capitalization required for industrial development are incompatible with the civil commerce he associates with the eighteenth-century civic tradition to which, he would argue, a thriving local agricultural economy belongs. His oft-heard conclusion is that citizens like his neighbors are deprived of both their virtue and prosperity, but Thoreau uses their common misfortune to conceive the possibility of an imagined city, a permanent locus of autonomous action and expression. Changes in the land-use, landscape, settlement, and especially labor patterns of eastern Massachusetts can be said to constitute a creative process that provides for the utopian construction of society. Thoreau's eagerness to identify his civic utopia as a figural representation means that a further outcome of urbanization is the recognition of the imagination as a medium of redemptive social existence in lieu of a corresponding social form. Reading and/or writing *Walden* could be said to be an original source of this recognition, but Thoreau also wants his "experiment in living" to demonstrate the autonomy of the imagination as a mode of life.

Thoreau's interest in the imaginary as a historical social form leads him to account for the exercise of the imagination as it pertains to the material prospects for living space. According to *Walden,* the most decisive factor in this determination is the mortgage (perhaps a numbing truism for encumbered aesthetes). For Thoreau, the proliferation of mortgages upon homes and family farms brings misery to the farmers, "toiling . . . that they may become the real owners of their farms" (21), but even more importantly, mortgages direct the course of municipal development towards either utopian or dystopian forms. The evidence of the latter is easily observed in the punishing regimen of Concord farmers, while the scarcely less easily observed sign of the former is the unfettered capacity to imagine a medium of thought and expression as a space in itself—in other words, to make tropes. Although Thoreau's civic ambitions will lead him to distinguish sharply the one course from the other, he argues consistently that their dual emergence is the result of the changing disposition of property. Consequently, he narrates a development history of Concord in which the sphere of the imagination and its avowedly figural forms are seen to share the conditions of land use.

We have seen Thoreau's imagination create a physiocratic society of possessive individuals and animals at Walden Pond, but however fanciful that prospect seems and with whatever hyperbole he identifies it—you can be "richer than the richest are now," he tells us—it is still possible in **Walden** to situate his tropes in the history of spatialized social forms. Thoreau directs our attention toward "'the wealthy and principal men in New England'" (26) who founded the towns of eastern Massachusetts. The urban historian Sam Bass Warner has described their role in the origin and design of the traditional New England town with the concept of "fee-simple land tenure"—property-holding families declaring a covenant with each other and forming a municipal corporation. This entity then had the power to disperse property, at first according to need and then, as descendants of these families sought income through subdivision, according to profit. This process expanded the geographical limits of the municipality and added to the population, but it also ensured that both intrafamily concerns and a low-density agglomeration of farms would be necessary for the town's economic prosperity.[26] For Thoreau, this history, recalled for him by Edward Johnson's "Wonder-Making Providence" and a seventeenth-century real estate prospectus, suggests that building a simple house with a deep storage cellar is the first principle of town planning, one which he would obey at Walden Pond. As in the past, this act frees citizens to pursue more remunerative pursuits, out of whose profits a stronger municipality can be built. It is a simple story of building a "city on a hill," though Thoreau attempts to continue this city plan without brick and mortar.

Although he intends his own shack, "bought and paid for," to contrast positively with the encumbered homes of his townsmen, Thoreau clearly understands that the consolidation of capital in central lending institutions is harmful not just to private prosperity but to the existence of incorporated communities such as Concord. He gives eloquent testimony to the feudalizing effects of merchant capitalism when he describes the subjugation of the Concord farmer to one of the most powerful "institutions of commerce": "On applying to the assessors, I am surprised to learn that they cannot at once name a dozen in the town who own their farms free and clear. If you would know the history of these homesteads, inquire at the bank where they are mortgaged" (21). With this insight, Thoreau presciently describes the land-use pattern that would transform Concord and other New England towns into either urban centers or their satellites: the disproportionate ownership of land by merchant cooperatives and corporations. One scholar has identified the testamentary trust as the legal innovation particularly instrumental in the progress of nineteenth-century urbanization. Capital placed in trust was disengaged from family farms and, hence, family concerns; it was subsequently freed for investment in local, regional, or national commercial enterprises. The inevitable consolidation of these enterprises formed a merchant capitalist class with unprecedented capitalizable wealth, as well as a geometrically expanded marketplace. Capital helped to create those markets when it was invested in the construction of transportation (like the Fitchburg railroad through Concord) and other commercial infrastructures. The result of these efforts was "a coherent network of institutions of commerce and culture that had an intrinsic advantage over traditional forms of organization [that is, family farms] for the production of goods and services."[27] So essential was this network to the concentration of capital that historians have referred to the development of hierarchically managed markets and the organization of regionalized and national marketplaces in the early nineteenth century as a stage of "proto-industrialization."[28]

Thoreau's bitter apothegm that "trade curses everything it handles" (80) is directed against the particular kind of economic transactions that merchant capitalism fosters, not against the civil commerce practiced by his imaginary international merchant or the unencumbered farmer. He is clear in associating the unremunerative toil of his townsmen with the necessity "to acquire the usual capital" (12), with the speculation on nonexistent profits, and with the valuation of commodities by distant marketplaces. But we would still be missing his point if we did not recognize that his rigorously observed economic critique presumes the emergence of a new urban form, the industrial city. To be sure, Concord never developed the manufacturing system that made eastern Massachusetts the historic source of the industrial city, but the financial instruments of urbanization, as well as its constituent labor patterns, were clearly visible to Thoreau, even from his secluded outpost. As we know, Walden Woods was the uncultivated fringe of Emerson's estate, about a mile and quarter from the town's center. As was typical of older Massachusetts towns, this estate was part of the necklace of family-owned farms that ringed a residential and commercial center. But with the consolidation of capital in anonymous "institutions of commerce," New England towns were metamorphosed in both form and function; they assumed a distinctively urban spatial arrangement. Encumbered family farms became peripheral to an economic center, where one found the mercantile and financial institutions of a new urban order: banks, and insurance, investment, and trading companies.[29] As Robert Gross reports, the land and economy of Concord were changing in just this manner as Emerson and Thoreau developed their careers, though he notes the emergence of a suburban form. From Thoreau's perspective, from the margins of this economic and social development, Concord was being urbanized.

Perhaps we should expect that Thoreau's definition of urban space would disregard locale, but his critique of urbanization suggests that the transcendence of place is neither completely self-willed nor artistically motivated, though he uses the conceit of an invisible city to indicate the sphere of the imagination. Neither selfhood nor aestheticism can be invoked as causes for this transcendence because they are among the outcomes of the spatial and social reorganization that transformed Concord. Thoreau's insistence that the urban is found in social logics and behaviors and his refusal to equate the absence of industrial infrastructure with the absence of the urban in fact anticipate urban history, which likewise displaces technological determinism from contemporary antebellum urbanization. In Eric Lampard's deconstructive analysis, the early-nineteenth-century industrial city manifests capital accumulation patterns created by a convergence of factors: local marketplaces, population shifts, agricultural cycles, land uses, and electoral politics, as well as transportation and technological innovation. The human enterprise suited to this pattern entails an unprecedented concentration and organization of labor, which either transforms a commercial city into a densely populated urban center or creates new factory cities. The labor patterns that constructed cities and that cities in turn inculcated in their inhabitants is for Lampard the constituent activity of industrialization:

> City-building activity manifested a population's acquired faculty for capitalizing a particular site in the course of integrating its transactions over a widening social space. Urbanization, or relative preponderance of city building, was thus the ecological condition of certain nineteenth-century populations institutionalizing their adaptive capability to conserve and augment the net (balance) of their numbers and "goods." The term "industrial" in this institutionalizing context is used with reference to increasing ratios of material to human capital and, in particular, to the profitable substitution of modes of embodied capital (practical arts, knowledge, etc.) for given amounts of labor or natural resources in any output.[30]

As Thoreau observes, the "unfolding profit regimen and the logic of 'industrial behavior'" can urbanize all social forms. He pointedly includes Concord, even though the "Mill-dam" that he mentions was one of those traditional small manufacturers rendered obsolete by the combination of higher product volume and lower cost that only industrialization could provide.[31]

Its antiquity notwithstanding, Concord's economy did manifest the quantification of time that the urban-industrial order institutionalizes in its labor patterns. In *Walden* Thoreau has cause to note the rationalization of social intercourse whenever he observes the effect of

the railroad on the life of farmers: "The startings and arrivals of the cars are now the epochs of the village day. They go and come with such regularity and precision, . . . that the farmers set their clocks by them, and thus one well conducted institution regulates a whole country. . . . To do things 'railroad fashion' is now the by-word" (79-80). With farmers reduced to dependent participants in the regional economy, the town can be said to possess at least two of the three characteristics with which Lewis Mumford defines the industrial city: the railroad, the slum (the farmers' fields), and the factory.[32] To Thoreau, even the last seems to be present; the everyday bustle within Concord sounds like "the hammer laying the foundation of another Lowell."[33] Even more indexically urban to him are the railroad shacks of the Irish, whose influx into Concord represents the unwelcome arrival of a floating laboring class. Taken together, the indebted native farmer and the propertyless immigrant who roam through Walden Woods are the denizens of a new urban form that encompasses Concord as much as nearby Boston.

Although Thoreau is determined to rouse his townsmen and readers to consider alternative forms of living, the destructive effects of urbanization are as central to his utopian project as they are to his dystopian critique. That is, they both argue that social space can be and has been reoriented so that it exists solely through certain practicable modes of activity. Thoreau capitalizes on the possibility of a deterritorialized sense of place to sever the experience of place from locale and, ultimately, to reterritorialize that experience as the synchronous, yet practical sphere of the imagination. But we would be omitting the historical process that gave rise to this possibility if we did not observe the effect of this deterritorialization on the place known as Concord. For Thoreau, there was no more immediate or essential condition for his artistic realization.

Once again, Thoreau's criterion for the existence or nonexistence of any locale is derived from his observation of its inhabitants. To Thoreau, the Concord citizens' punishing regimen of scarcely remunerative labor signals the end not only of Concord's economic independence but its existence as a *civitas* or, as he would say, a "noble village." He drew many such images of morally redemptive community life from his conversations with Concord natives such as George Minot, who claimed never to have sullied himself by participating in the market.[34] Yet the fact that Massachusetts farmers such as Minot were producing cash crops for the regional marketplace even before the Revolutionary War suggests that Thoreau's regard for the family farm proceeds not from his love of rural life but from the same commitment to civil, virtuous commerce that his attachment to urban liberalism betrays. Although self-sufficiency was constantly touted as an economic ideal for the family farmer, the preindustrial agrarian society actually constituted a profitable commercial society that, in Thoreau's estimation, was completely compatible with the sphere of virtuous citizenship.[35] Indeed, an important revision of the Massachusetts yeoman farmer ideal by Betty Hobbes Pruit states that "the traditionally sharp distinction between subsistence and commercial agriculture can be set aside as inapplicable to an agrarian economy in which production for home consumption and production for sale or exchange were complementary, not mutually exclusive objectives."[36] Within this system, surpluses were typically traded for necessities, so that a farmer gave his excess grain to the farmer with hungry livestock in exchange for the cattle's labor in his fields. Similarly, a successful landholder with urban professional sons frequently depended on the families of smaller farmers. Individual farmers were not averse to cash exchanges or even to keeping credit, but the result of the shared quest for economic well-being was a social interdependence in which producers who were also traders advanced one another's interests.

In retrospect, the opprobrium that Thoreau and Minot heap upon market exchanges may have been directed at the organized, capitalized marketplace instituted and supervised by an urban mercantile elite, not at the equitable commerce that ameliorated differences in condition. In this sense, for Thoreau the best aspects of rural life are those that further the ends of civic life. A vigorous economy of family farms bound enterprising equals in an ethical contract creating an autonomous community whose shared investment in their municipality makes them a civic body. When one considers the adverse course of local development decreed by urbanization, Thoreau can be said to be arguing that local farmers' best chance for virtue and prosperity came from Concord's incarnation as a city.

This was a highly unlikely prospect, and Thoreau knew it. Not only were existing Atlantic commercial cities being transformed into urban-industrial centers, but by the 1840s, urbanization would have been recognized in Concord as the wholesale destruction of its civic community. Whereas the family farmer might once have participated in a commercial marketplace in conjunction with a domestic and local economy, the Concord farmer of the 1840s and 1850s had only one market: the burgeoning city. Boston had consumed its arable land and was now dependent on external supply, but with the creation of an organized distribution system, a liberalized marketplace, and an efficient commercial infrastructure for the growing city, local farmers played their appointed role. Native grains and corn were replaced with new cash crops such as fruits and vegetables that were transported along improved roads; with the arrival of the train, dairy products from the farthest reaches of Massachusetts could be consumed in Boston. The farmers' patterns of land use and labor now responded exclusively to the desires and demands of remote nonresidents. Within towns, the links between producers and merchants, between rural laborers and the enfranchised elite were broken, as the wealthy mercantile class identified their interests only with the exponentially growing urban marketplace.[37]

As Thoreau observed, the dependent farmer now grew for a specialized agricultural market and brought his produce to a professional merchant or a centralized marketplace like the Middlesex Cattle Show, whose "*éclat*" Thoreau despised (22). Consequently, goods and services that might have been produced by, between, or for local farmers now came from elsewhere and were for sale. In **Walden** Thoreau describes the arrival of the marketplace into Concord with a keen knowledge of its causes and consequences:

> The whistle of the locomotive penetrates my woods summer and winter, . . . informing me that many restless city merchants are arriving within the circle of the town, or adventurous country traders from the other side. As they come under one horizon, they shout the warning to get off the track to the other, heard sometimes through the circles of two towns. Here come your groceries, countries; your rations, countrymen! Nor is there any man so independent on his farm that he can say them nay. And here's your pay for them! screams the countryman's whistle.
>
> (78)

Specialized farming might have provided the farmer with his income, but it propelled him into a monetary economy in which he could not compete. Cash was not only rather scarce in Concord, but it was also a connection to a marketplace that depreciated agricultural labor. Thoreau sees very clearly the diminishing returns that specialization has brought the Concord farmer: "Every New Englander might easily raise all his own breadstuffs in this land of rye and Indian corn, and not depend on distant and fluctuating markets for them. . . . For the most part the farmer gives to his cattle and hogs the grain of his own producing, and buys flour, which is at least, no more wholesome, at a greater cost, at the store" (43). As Thoreau's comments suggest, the commodification of labor and produce involved the subservience of Concord's citizens to an urban mercantile exchange where value was determined by remote interests. For Thoreau, there is nothing more antithetical to the commercial society that had sustained the citizens of Concord in their orientation to the municipality.

Thoreau further argues that the reorientation of the agrarian economy toward the urban marketplace stipulates a shape and fate for the town, so that with the dissolution of its civic community the destruction of Concord is axiomatic. His condemnation of the farmers' "worship of Plutus" shows the intimate connection between his moral-economic critique and his understanding of land use: "By [the farmer's] avarice and selfishness, and a groveling habit, from which none of us is free, of regarding the soil as property, or the means of acquiring property chiefly, the landscape is deformed, husbandry is degraded with us, and the farmer leads the meanest of lives. He knows Nature but as a robber" (111). The Massachusetts farmers' "grovelling habit" had left ninety percent of Concord deforested by the time Thoreau published **Walden.** This was the result of competition. The local farmer's principal rival in the urban marketplace was not his neighbor but the farmer of western lands who sent tons of cheap grain eastward. The Concord farmer could change his crop and take his chances in another specialized marketplace, or he could stubbornly face the challenge of an undervalued market and expand his holdings. The latter course, aggressive cultivation, was pursued by many, but it had two distinct liabilities: it was debt-producing and labor intensive. To make matters worse, agrarian depressions led to depopulation, which depleted the labor force of able sons and daughters. The farmer was then forced to redouble his own labor and/or to hire the unpropertied immigrant, that is, Irish, population. The apparently random insight that neither party was capable of maintaining "the manliest relations to men" thus proceeded from a comprehensive local history whose stunning conclusion was that Concord, its subject, no longer existed.

* * *

It should not surprise us that, as Gross reports, Concord embarked upon a prolonged period of prosperity that has persisted to the present day just as Thoreau was bemoaning the destruction of its economically productive civic community.[38] On the contrary, the very form of that prosperity—the growth of educational and cultural institutions—should alert us to the negative conditions that Thoreau suggests for the development of an aesthetic sphere. If his artistic realization was indeed coincident with Concord's institutional development, then we can say that the persistence of civic life, manifesting itself through various forms of cultural life, was in both cases premised on the absence of a corresponding social form. Thoreau's distinction is that unlike Concord elites—or agrarian and utopian reformers, for that matter—he never attempted to rectify that absence and in fact made negation his positive goal: "I did not wish to live what was not life" (61). This oft-quoted rationalization, so informed by the most provincial effects of urbanization, also projects something called the "essential facts of life," which are by definition universal.

That Thoreau looks forward to the abstraction of experience from social space may justify every nasty thing said about affirmative culture, especially since his version of a "civic consciousness" displaces the sphere of autonomy from a lived environment to figural forms representing city life. But Thoreau's contribution to this discourse is precisely in demonstrating that only "the sort of space" created by the imagination is politically, even historically, continuous with the socially redemptive urban form of eighteenth-century liberalism. To the extent that he imbues this imaginary form with the same opportunities for human progress that the earlier commercial city inspired, he is linking the civic republicanism of the eighteenth century to the philosophies of modernism in a unique and shared history of urbanisms. Walden Pond can be included in that history as the critical site where the promise of a civic utopia gave way under the pressure of urban development and Thoreau's own rhetorical ambitions to the utopian possibilities of artistic expression. We may question or even reject this outcome, but Thoreau asks us to assess those possibilities by their moral and, he hopes, their practical relation to a socially symbolic living space. It is through this relation that he utilizes language as space—that is, as tropes—that circumscribe the realm of the imagination or, rather, that denominate the imagination as a realm unto itself. Through this same relation, we can use Thoreau, as Benjamin used Baudelaire, to find the origin of an artistically defined inward state in the permutation of urban space. What emerged at Walden Pond was not just an imaginary city but something even more incongruous with the American pastoral tradition—an urban imagination.

We might recoil at the period designation this conclusion forces upon Thoreau, but the success of his artistic enterprise depends not upon modernist categories of individualism and the aesthetic but upon the already established currency of an urban imaginary. When the "Conclusion" to **Walden** exhorts the individual to "live the life which he has imagined," Thoreau is only claiming the potential inherent in civic discourse to generate its own utopian space. The refusal to equate the social with either empirical reality or sheer numbers, the tendency to route the representation of society through moral and political ideals, the incessant creation of a counter-social are in indeed not original with Thoreau; the political philosopher Claude Lefort characterizes these aspects as "the symbolic dimension" of liberal society that defies the existence of the "real."[39] But we can add to our understanding of both liberalism and the emergence of liberal culture if we understand what was at stake in the particular conflicts that Thoreau mediated. Those conflicts were not just between competing forms of society but also, at their most crucial, between any social form and the social imaginary. Thoreau situated himself and Walden Pond at this critical interstice, "the real site," Benjamin says, "of poetic excitation."[40] His determination to liberate the imaginary from its social determinations might have decreed a separate course for utopian representation, but it also created for liberal society the intractable and continuing problem of its own legitimation.

Notes

1. Henry David Thoreau, *Walden,* in *"Walden" and "Civil Disobedience,"* ed. Owen Thomas (New York: W. W. Norton, 1966), 26, 14, 13, 80, 74, 3. All further citations are from this edition and are cited parenthetically within the text.

2. Walter Benjamin, "On Some Motifs in Baudelaire," in *Illuminations,* ed. Hannah Arendt (New York: Schocken Books, 1969), 162.

3. The term *urban-industrial complex* and its signification as a network of social intercourse, social planning priorities, and economic organization are taken from Thomas Bender, *Toward an Urban Vision: Ideas and Institutions in Nineteenth-Century America* (Baltimore: Johns Hopkins Univ. Press, 1982), 28-51.

4. Paul Ricoeur, "Imagination in Discourse and Action," in *Rethinking Imagination: Culture and Creativity,* ed. Gillian Robinson and John Rundell (London: Routledge, 1994), 129-35.

5. Benjamin, 162.

6. This formulation is distilled from William Sharpe and Leonard Wallock, "From 'Great Town' to 'Nonplace Urban Realm': Reading the Modern City," in *Visions of the Modern City: Essays in History, Art, and Literature,* ed. Sharpe and Wallock (Baltimore: Johns Hopkins Univ. Press, 1987), 2-5; and Raymond Williams, *The Country and the City* (New York: Oxford Univ. Press, 1973), 233-47.

7. See elaborations of such subjectivized urban space in Phillips Collins, "Dickens and the City," in *Visions of the Modern City,* 101-21; William Sharpe, *Unreal Cities: Urban Figurations in Wordsworth, Baudelaire, Whitman, Eliot and Williams* (Baltimore: Johns Hopkins Univ. Press, 1990); and Allan Trachtenberg, "Experiments in Another Country: Stephen Crane's City Sketches," in *American Realism: New Essays,* ed. Eric Sundquist (Baltimore: Johns Hopkins Univ. Press, 1982), 138-52.

8. For an analysis of the urban bourgeoisie that pays close attention to social stratification, see Gary B. Nash, *The Urban Crucible: Social Change, Political Conflict and the Origins of the American Revolution* (Cambridge: Harvard Univ. Press, 1979), 341-42.

9. Eighteenth-century urban political and economic agendas are described in Nash, 236-342. The moral and political virtues that American Federalists attached to an urban commercial economy are explicated in Janet A. Reisman, "Money, Credit, and Federalist Political Economy," in *Beyond Confederation: Origins of the Constitution and American National Identity* (Chapel Hill: Univ. of North Carolina Press, 1987), 128-61; Charles Sellers, *The Market Revolution: Jacksonian America, 1815-1846* (New York: Oxford Univ. Press, 1991), 3-69; Tamara Plakins Thornton, *Cultivating Gentlemen: The Making of Country Life Among the Boston Elite, 1785-1860* (New Haven: Yale Univ. Press, 1989), 7-19.

10. My source for this and the following discussion of eighteenth-century Whig liberalism is J. G. A. Pocock, *The Machiavellian Moment: Florentine Political Thought and the Atlantic Republican Tradition* (Princeton: Princeton Univ. Press, 1975), 423-505. From Jurgen Habermas we also derive the notion of a separate public space thematized as cosmopolitan, urbane, and above all profitable; Habermas, *The Structural Transformation of the Public Sphere: An Inquiry into a Category of Bourgeois Society,* trans. Thomas Burger (Cambridge: MIT Press, 1989), 23-31.

11. Thoreau's statist theories anticipate those of Henri Lefebvre, which are the subject of M. Gottdiener, *The Social Production of Urban Space* (Austin: Univ. of Texas Press, 1985), 132-47. The political economy of antebellum American-style state capitalism is the subject of Sellers, 34-69; and George Thomas, *Revivalism and Cultural Change: Christianity, Nation-Building, and the Market in Nineteenth-Century United States* (Berkeley and Los Angeles: Univ. of California Press, 1989), 34-51.

12. Habermas, 46-47, 29-30.

13. The Federalists' project of civic development is celebrated in Beatrice Garden, *Federal Philadelphia 1785-1825: The Athens of the Western World* (Philadelphia: Philadelphia Museum of Art, 1987). The phrase "[c]ultural ornaments" is quoted in Thornton, 16. Particularly during the antebellum era, these "republican institutions" were instrumental in administering civic pedagogy; see Linda Kerber, *Federalists in Dissent: Imagery and Ideology in Jeffersonian America* (Ithaca: Cornell Univ. Press, 1970), 67-134; and Robert T. Oliver, *The History of Public Speaking in America* (Boston: Allyn and Bacon, 1965), 430-65.

14. James Spear Loring took special pride in noting that the title "Athens of America" had been bestowed upon Boston by the *Philadelphia Bulletin.* See Loring, *The Hundred Boston Orators . . . Comprising Historical Gleanings, Illustrating the Principles and Progress of Our Republican Institutions* (Boston: John P. Jewett, 1853), 720. New York, on the other hand, did not aggressively develop its civic institutions and consciousness until

the rise of the industrial capitalist class and of the City Beautiful movement at the end of the nineteenth century; see Edward K. Spann, *The New Metropolis: New York City, 1840-1857* (New York: Columbia Univ. Press, 1981).

15. See Thornton, 19-56, 186.

16. See Pocock, 446-505. For Thoreau's relation to this tradition, see Leonard Neufeldt, "Henry David Thoreau's Political Economy," *New England Quarterly* 57 (1984): 359-83.

17. "Cato" quoted in Pocock, 468.

18. Max Horkheimer, "Rise and Decline of the Individual," in *Eclipse of Reason* (New York: Continuum Publishing, 1974), 131. The best account of Thoreau's classical education is of course Edith Sybold, *Thoreau: The Quest and the Classics* (New Haven: Yale Univ. Press, 1951).

19. Cf. Michael Gilmore, "Walden and the 'Curse of Trade,'" in *Ideology and Classic American Literature,* ed. Sacvan Bercovitch and Myra Jehlen (Cambridge: Cambridge Univ. Press, 1986), 293-308. Gilmore sees a civic project with direct applicability to Concord derailed in successive drafts and in the second half of *Walden.*

20. Gilmore, 307.

21. Gadamer's version of this cultural theory is recapitulated and critiqued in John Brenkman, *Culture and Domination* (Ithaca: Cornell Univ. Press, 1987), 26-44.

22. Fredric Jameson, *The Political Unconscious: Narrative as a Socially Symbolic Act* (Ithaca: Cornell Univ. Press, 1981), 76, 185.

23. Brenkman, 34.

24. Jameson, 56, 76-85. His account of formal and narrative structure, which I incorporate throughout this paragraph, makes thorough use of the Levi-Strauss paradigm of socially symbolic forms, though I am not as sure what "mediation" would mean in this sense.

25. Jameson, 77.

26. Sam Bass Warner Jr., *The Urban Wilderness: A History of the American City* (New York: Harper and Row, 1972), 8-18.

27. Peter Dobkin Hall, "Family Structure and Economic Organization: Massachusetts Merchants, 1700-1850," in *Family and Kin in Urban Communities, 1700-1930,* ed. Tamara K. Hareven (New York: New Viewpoints, 1977), 47-55; see also Hall, *The Organization of American Culture, 1700-1900: Private Institutions, Elites, and the Making of American Nationality* (New York: New York Univ. Press, 1984), 79-124.

28. Henry C. Binford, *The First Suburbs: Residential Communities on the Boston Periphery* (Chicago: Univ. of Chicago Press, 1985), 35. Lewis Mumford also considers the commercial city to have provided the resources for industrialization and thus its own eclipse; see Mumford, *The City in History: Its Origins, Its Transformations, and Its Prospects* (New York: Harcourt, Brace, Jovanovich, 1961), 419.

29. See Robert Gross, "Transcendentalism and Urbanism: Concord, Boston and the Wider World," *Journal of American Studies* 18 (1984): 361-81.

30. Eric Lampard, "The Nature of Urbanization," in *Visions of the Modern City,* 65-66.

31. The prehistory of Massachusetts industrialization is told in Jonathan Prude, *The Coming of the Industrial Order: Town and Factory Life in Rural Massachusetts, 1810-1860* (Cambridge: Cambridge Univ. Press, 1983), 34-142.

32. Mumford, 446.

33. Henry David Thoreau, *A Week on the Concord and Merrimack Rivers,* in *"A Week on the Concord and Merrimack Rivers," "Walden," "Maine Woods," "Cape Cod,"* ed. Robert Sayre (New York: Library of America, 1985), 200.

34. These conversations are given considerable weight in Robert Gross, "'The Most Estimable Place in All of the World': A Debate on Progress in Nineteenth-Century Concord," *Studies in the American Renaissance* 2 (1978): 7-26; and Leo Stoller, *After Walden: Thoreau's Changing Views of Economic Man* (Stanford: Stanford Univ. Press, 1957), 15-25.

35. See Robert Gross, "Culture and Cultivation: Agriculture and Society in Thoreau's Concord," *Journal of American History* 69 (1982): 42-61.

36. Betty Hobbes Pruitt, "Self-Sufficiency and the Agricultural Economy of Eighteenth-Century Massachusetts," *William and Mary Quarterly* 41 (1984): 335.

37. For the development of Boston's commercial infrastructure, see Binford, 30-34. The preceding and following account of local agricultural economic transformation were culled from Gross, "Transcendentalism" ["Transcendentalism and Urbanism"] 363-81; "Culture and Cultivation," 50-55; Thornton, 108-30; and Warner, 65-73.

38. Gross, "Transcendentalism," 380.

39. See Claude Lefort, "Outline of a Genesis of Ideology in Modern Societies," in *The Political Forms*

of *Modern Society: Bureaucracy, Democracy, and Totalitarianism,* ed. John Thompson (Cambridge: MIT Press, 1987), 192-209.

40. Benjamin, 164.

Ning Yu (essay date December 1996)

SOURCE: Yu, Ning. "Thoreau's Critique of the American Pastoral in *A Week.*" *Nineteenth-Century Literature* 51, no. 3 (December 1996): 304-26.

[*In the following essay, Yu analyzes Thoreau's mixing of history, satire, and pastoral elegy in* A Week on the Concord and Merrimack Rivers. *Yu argues that the work represents a "critique of the American pastoral tradition."*]

Largely because of Thoreau's statement that he wrote *A Week on the Concord and Merrimack Rivers* as a "paean to the departed soul," few critics question a consensus that Thoreau's first book is a pastoral elegy to his brother John.[1] Sherman Paul reads *A Week* [*A Week on the Concord and Merrimack Rivers*] as Thoreau's attempt to achieve a "communion with the eternal" and to be part of the tradition of "the eternally timeless." Reading *A Week* as Thoreau's "memorial tribute to John," Walter Harding identifies the timeless tradition with "the tradition of the pastoral elegy." Linck C. Johnson, more recently, compares *A Week* with Milton's "Lycidas" and argues that Thoreau's book is "one of the most ambitious of all pastoral elegies, in which Thoreau, like Milton, sought to assuage his grief for the loss of a companion of his youth." To do this, Thoreau used a "basic strategy of the pastoral elegy," placing John's "sudden and seemingly 'accidental'" death "within the annual cycle of the decay and regeneration." For Richard Lebeaux, *A Week* is "in part an affectionate elegy to John" attempting to resolve John's death in the pastoral "golden age," and in part self-therapy attempting to relive "the lost Eden of the pre-rivalry and pre-oedipal past." H. Daniel Peck postulates that in *A Week* Thoreau tries to redeem his brother's death by "killing time."[2]

That *A Week* contains pastoral elements does not necessarily mean it is a pastoral book. As a generic category, the pastoral elegy tends to limit Thoreau's first book to a personal scope. Read as such, *A Week* seems consistent with Thoreau's request for every author to write "a simple and sincere account of his own life" in spite of, or perhaps because of, "the narrowness of [his] experience."[3] Yet such a reading conflicts with another aspect of Thoreau's writing: his commitment to the role of a "lusty Chanticleer" whose job is to wake up his fellow New Englanders from a smug yet unenlightened existence. More specifically, approaching *A Week* as a pastoral elegy one can hardly explain why Thoreau includes in it pages upon pages of indignant and satirical comments on the dispossession of the Native Americans and on the industrialization of the Merrimack. *A Week* is not unrolled in a timeless Eden but in the historicized landscape of New England.

Analyzing the complex landscape representation in Thoreau's first book, I wish to argue that *A Week* is a critique of the American pastoral tradition. I read the book from a geographical perspective, for according to Henry C. Darby, a twentieth-century British geographer, "to explain the landscape" is "the purpose of geography."[4] However, critics who traditionally regard Thoreau as not only a major voice in American literature but also "an heir of . . . the emerging natural sciences" usually treat him as a natural historian; none, to my knowledge, has examined Thoreau's knowledge and use of the geography of his time.[5] In this essay I will explain why geography as a scientific subject may shed new light in our effort to understand Thoreau better.

Geography, according to Robert E. Dickinson and O. J. R. Howarth, two renowned geographers of the twentieth century, is both the description of the earth and the science about the interrelation between nature and humans. "As the description of the earth," they point out, geography "is the oldest" science in the record of civilization; "as the science of the interrelations between man and his environment," however, it is still "one of the youngest . . . sciences" of our time.[6] By both its oldest and newest definitions, geography is one of the main concerns of Thoreau. His major works—*A Week, Walden, Maine Woods,* and *Cape Cod*—can be read as, among other things, geographical descriptions of nineteenth-century New England. Running through these works is his attempt to experience nature directly so as to attain and represent a transcendental vision of the ideal interrelation between humankind and the natural environment. Rather proud of his geographical activities, Thoreau claims that he "travelled a good deal in Concord," portrays himself as "self-appointed inspector of snow storms and rain storms," and "surveyor . . . of forest paths and all across-lot routes" (*Walden,* pp. 4, 18). Indeed, he surveyed land, lakes, and rivers; went on excursions; drew maps himself and commented on maps drawn by his predecessors and contemporaries; and read carefully works by such geographers as Humboldt, Guyot, and Lewis and Clark.

Geography as a scholarly discipline was undergoing a paradigm shift in Thoreau's lifetime. As Richard Hartshorne argues, modern geography began with Alexander von Humboldt and Carl Ritter, two German scientists who, in the early half of the nineteenth century, established their theoretically self-conscious "new geography" in a number of monumental works.[7] Their geography was "new" in that they refused to take geography as a mere collection of sketches of unconnected places on the earth. They wanted "to comprehend all the phenomena of physical objects in their general connexions and to represent nature as one great whole."[8] Their emphasis on interconnection, their world picture in which humankind is but a part, and their insight that landscape is shaped by human activities as well as natural forces all appealed strongly to Thoreau the transcendentalist. Their theory supplemented what Thoreau felt was lacking in the naturalist's narrower perspective.

Thoreau was especially familiar with the work of Alexander von Humboldt. About a decade before Mrs. Sabine translated into English Humboldt's first multivolume work, *Personal Narrative,* Thoreau showed some knowledge about the German geographer's work in the Andes. Later, in 1848, the year before *A Week* was published, Thoreau copied long passages from the *Personal Narrative.* Sometime in the 1850s Thoreau acquired and read Humboldt's most comprehensive work, *Cosmos,* and between 1850 and 1853 he read at least two versions of Humboldt's *Aspects of Nature. Aspects* was so important to Thoreau that when he felt necessary to explain his relation with the emerging sciences, he named it as one of the two sources of scientific influence on himself:

> I am an observer of nature generally, and the character of my observations, so far as they are scientific, may be inferred from the fact that I am especially attracted by such books of science as White's Selborne and Humboldt's *Aspects of Nature.*
>
> (*Correspondence* [*The Correspondence of Henry David Thoreau*], p. 310)[9]

Despite Thoreau's own acknowledgment of his indebtedness to Humboldt, I am not interested so much in a source / influence study here as in an interdisciplinary attempt to examine Thoreau's *A Week* from a geographical perspective and to see how Thoreau appropriated the most advanced geographical theory of his time in his effort to discover, or dismiss, the possibility of resolving his problem with John's sudden death in the pastoral tradition.

* * *

In his formalistic analysis of *A Week* Sherman Paul skips over the opening chapter, "Concord River." Yet the chapter is rich in suggestions, and it provides a "map" of Thoreau's meandering prose about the river voyage he and John made in 1839. A survey of Thoreau's representation of the New England aquatic landscapes may very well start with this "map."

"Concord River" can be regarded as a map because of its detailed description of the river valley's physical geography. It is also a thematic map of the book, offering clues to Thoreau's insightful social study of transforma-tion of the Native-American, Colonial, and modern-industrial landscapes. Furthermore, as a map, it leads to some early hints about where Thoreau's personal faith lies concerning possible resolutions about the untimely death of his brother and best friend, John.

In the very first paragraph of the chapter, Thoreau identifies the sources of Sudbury River and Assabeth River, two major tributaries of the Concord, traces them to their confluence at the south part of the town of Concord, and then describes the course of the river through Bedford, Carlisle, and Billerica until it "empties into the Merrimack at Lowell."[10] In this opening chapter Thoreau demonstrates prowess at solidifying the foundation of the factual before building the symbolic upon it.

Thoreau does not stop at the physical level in his geographical description. Soon the cultural implications of the watershed landscapes emerge in a meaningful spatial relationship: located around the town of Concord is a landscape typical of an agricultural community, with some scenes reminiscent of the pastoral ideal. Near Sudbury, the next town upstream to the southwest of Concord, there are "great hills, and a hundred brooks, and farm-houses, and barns, and hay-stacks" (p. 7). Farther upstream, in the southwest backcountry of Sudbury, we see a landscape of wild nature evoking the American West with broad meadows that look "like a smaller Lake Huron" (p. 6).

Downstream from Carlisle through Billerica, however, a series of dams along the river and the factories at Lowell lend the landscape an industrial feature. Yet, sometimes in the midst of and sometimes underneath the agricultural and industrial landscapes, we see traces of "an extinct race" that has a stronger claim to the river valley because originally this place was "where they hunted and fished" (p. 5). The Concord itself is compared to "an Indian warrior" whose "moccasined tread" is the metaphor for the quiet flow of the river "ceaselessly rolling through the plains and valleys of the substantial earth" (p. 11).

The spatial relation among the three cultural landscapes—agricultural Concord at the center, facing the industrial growth downstream and leaning on the wild nature upstream in Sudbury and Wayland for support, and both the agricultural and industrial *over* the aboriginal—is highly suggestive. In the light of new geography, Thoreau sees the various stages of cultural development as parts of the larger network of nature. Against the interplay of the natural and man-made landscapes, Thoreau conducts an original kind of geographical study that twentieth-century geographers later named the study of "sequent occupance."[11]

* * *

In *A Week* the pastoral is a prominent feature of the Concord plain. The way Thoreau positions the topographical entities in the opening chapter is typically pastoral: the river flows through "great hills, and a hundred brooks, and farm-houses, and barns, and haystacks" (p. 7); the houses of the inhabitants, "gray and white" in color (p. 10) and scattered "along the Sudbury shore, which rises gently to a considerable height, command fine water prospects" (p. 6). This picture has many parallels with what Leo Marx describes in *The Machine in the Garden* as "the cardinal image" of the American pastoral since the Jeffersonian age:

> Although it probably shows a farmhouse or a neat white village, the scene usually is dominated by natural objects: in the foreground a pasture, a twisting brook with cattle grazing nearby, then a clump of elms on a rise in the middle distance and beyond that, way off on the western horizon, a line of dark hills.
>
> (p. 141)

Thoreau uses the pastoral tradition deliberately. In a reminiscence about a summer trip in the Berkshire Hills he evokes the tradition by quoting a passage from Spenser's *The Faerie Queene* as an illustration of his own experience of the pastoral scene at the western terminus of the Shelburne Falls Valley, which is located at Greenfield, Massachusetts (see p. 203).

In addition to sketching the pastoral scenery Thoreau humorously presents his neighbors, Emerson and Hawthorne, as poetic shepherds in the idealized garden landscape. Quoting Emerson's "North Bridge," Thoreau refers to his mentor as "a Concord poet" who has elevated the "peaceful pasture ground" of Concord village to the poetic height of any Arcadia (pp. 17-18). And as the conventions of the pastoral prescribe, in Concord too the "aged shepherd" is assured of the perpetuation of his virtue and talent by the emergence of a new poet-shepherd, "our Hawthorne in the dale" (pp. 18-19).

Not all the people who spend their lives in the pastoral scenery are able to see the world as a bucolic paradise, however, where they can stay free from the drudgery of the mundane life and enjoy their pastoral existence in the light of poetry. In the paradisiacal valley in Mount Greylock, Thoreau encounters someone who at first looks like an old poet-shepherd but turns out to be a hypocrite. At first glance the old man of Mount Greylock is reminiscent of the older Concord poet, yet when Thoreau asks him for help, rather than practicing the fundamental Christian doctrine of charity that one should help a lost traveler, the old man recites biblical dogmas to get rid of Thoreau (see pp. 208-9).

That the idealized rustic environment does not guarantee ideal inhabitants of a pastoral vision is already foreshadowed in the opening chapter, in a passage where Thoreau describes the daily lives of the Concord farmers, echoing Thomas Gray's "Elegy Written in a Country Churchyard":

> [They could be] greater men than Homer, or Chaucer, or Shakespeare, only they never got time to say so; they never took to the way of writing. Look at their fields, and imagine what they might write, if ever they should put pen to paper. Or what have they not written on the face of the earth already, clearing, and burning, and scratching, and harrowing, and plowing, and subsoiling, in and in, and out and out, and over and over, again and again, erasing what they had already written for want of parchment.
>
> (p. 8)

This passage can be divided into two parts, the first speculating upon what the farmers could have done on paper, the second describing what they have done in the fields. The first part is a clear echo from Gray and encourages readers to understand it as a praise of the silent but nonetheless poetic farmers of Concord; the rhetorical scheme of the second part, however, challenges the pastoral theme in the preceding lines, urging readers to interpret Thoreau as a social satirist who questions the same farmers' obsessions with the earthly endeavor and thereby their failure to fulfill their higher potentials; they are almost soulless in their relation with God. Thoreau's exaggerated use of polysyndeton subverts the simple lifestyle in the pastoral world: the ridiculous proliferation of conjunctions, present participles, and adverbs slows down the movement of the sentence to the degree of boredom, forcing readers to question whether the farmers deliberately choose a monotonous lifestyle or passively remain in a "quiet desperation" because, having been corrupted by their own greed for more profit from commercial farming, they know no other use for their lives.

Of course, in what Leo Marx calls the "complex" pastoral tradition there is always a counter-element to balance the reader's appreciation of an idealized world.[12] Yet Thoreau's presentation of the dwellers in the American Arcadia as dumb and hypocritical challenges the pastoral ideal to an unprecedented degree from within that tradition. His presentation of the New England pastoral as laid on top of and thus burying the Native-American landscape challenges the tradition itself. It undermines the validity of the American pastoral typically presented by Crevecoeur and critically analyzed by Leo Marx.

Underneath the rustic topography of New England lies a landscape filled with memories of the values of another race—the Native Americans.[13] The existence of such a landscape, or rather Thoreau's unearthing of it, poses a moral question about the agricultural landscape as the site of the pastoral Utopia.

In the first sentence of the first chapter of his first book, Thoreau refers to his hometown river by its Indian name, which had been suppressed since the advent of the colonial agriculture: "The Musketaquid, or Grass-ground River, though probably as old as the Nile or Euphrates, did not begin to have a place in civilized history, until the fame of its grassy meadows and its fish attracted settlers out of England in 1635, when it received the other but kindred name of Concord from the plantation on its banks" (*A Week,* p. 5). Thoreau's message is clear: by highlighting the relation between the Euramerican's geography and territorial expansion, he shows that the white settler's advance in North America means the displacement of the natives; the Grass-ground River disappears the minute it is written into the "civilized history," though both the grass-ground and the river survive under another name to become owned property of the newcomers.

In the conflict between the aboriginal race and the agricultural society, Thoreau from the beginning sides with the indigenous people, first on the level of language: he thinks that the river is more "properly named Musketaquid, or Meadow River, by the Indians" (p. 9). To support this statement Thoreau cites the 1831 official "valuation" that "there were in Concord two thousand one hundred and eleven acres, or about one-seventh of the whole territory, in meadow" (p. 9). Because the indigenous name of the river is closer to natural facts, Thoreau, using the language of the Indian treaties, suggests that it would outlast the European name: "It will be Grass-ground River as long as grass grows and water runs here; it will be Concord River only while men lead peaceable lives on its banks" (p. 5). The appropriateness of the native name is almost unconditional; as "a transcendentalist, and a natural philosopher to boot"[14] Thoreau has ultimate faith in the regenerating power of nature, and for him water will always run and grass will always grow. By contrast, the colonial name is culturally conditioned; it is subjected to two questions: have the farmer-settlers ever lived peaceable lives? and how long can they stay in peace and harmony with nature and themselves? In his attempt to answer these questions Thoreau converts a relatively static pastoral representation into a dynamic landscape study.

The native landscape is often suppressed and buried underneath what looks like the pastoral geography of the white settlers. Gliding "over the broad bosom of the Merrimack, between Chelmsford and Dracut" (p. 80), the Thoreau brothers learn from their gazetteer that they are passing through "an old battle and hunting ground" of the Indians (p. 82). Yet no apparent traces are left about that "ancient dwelling-place of a race of hunters and warriors." Thoreau has to use his talent in field exploration to unearth relics of the aboriginal tribes in that area: "Their weirs of stone, their arrowheads and hatchets, their pestles, and the mortars in which they pounded Indian corn before the white man had tasted it, lay concealed in the mud of the river bottom" (p. 82).

There is another kind of excavation Thoreau has to perform, however, before he can recover the suppressed aboriginal landscape. The native name for Billerica, for instance, is Shawshine, but the white settlers simply ignored it and renamed the place "from the English Billericay" (p. 50). Here I must quote Thoreau at length in order to delineate adequately his attitudes toward the white man's erasure of the native landscape from the surface of the region. In "Sunday" Thoreau depicts the "Saxon pioneer[s]" (p. 54) as invaders who changed the landscape and chased away the natives:

> Some spring the white man came, built him a house, and made a clearing here, letting in the sun, dried up a farm, piled up the old gray stones in fences, cut down the pines around his dwelling, planted orchard seeds brought from the old country, and persuaded the civil apple tree to blossom next to the wild pine. . . . And thus he plants a town. The white man's mullein soon reigned in Indian corn-fields, and sweet scented English grasses clothed the new soil. Where, then, could the Red Man set his foot? The honey bee hummed through the Massachusetts' woods, and sipped the wild flowers round the Indian's wigwam, perchance unnoticed, when, with prophetic warning, it stung the Red child's hand, forerunner of that industrious tribe that was to come and pluck the wild flower of his race up by the root.
>
> (pp. 52-53)

The founder of the New England Eden is presented as a proverbial greedy person who would ask for a mile if you gave him an inch: he came and built a house, and then cleared and dried a farm, expanding the space he "owned"; and then he "planted a town," covered the land with "English grasses," and named it Billerica so that the native place, Shawshine, no longer existed on his map. In contrast to "the young pines springing up in the corn-fields" (p. 55), which symbolizes the wild strength of the native way of life, the farmer planted the apple trees in the Indian's hunting ground and thus symbolically preconditioned his second fall, from the Eden of North America.

In the conflict between the native's and the settler's efforts to shape New England topography according to their different cultures, Thoreau is again sympathetic to the native. We can sense Thoreau's anger at the white man through his rhetorical question: "Where, then, could the Red Man set his foot?" Native Americans could only go farther north and west, of course. In an emphatic pattern of repetition, Thoreau describes how the aboriginal hunters lost their grounds to the settlers:

> The white man comes, pale as the dawn, with a load of thought, with a slumbering intelligence as a fire raked up, knowing well what he knows, not guessing but calculating. . . . He buys the Indian's moccasins and baskets, then buys his hunting grounds, and at length forgets where he is buried, and plows up his bones. And here town records, old, tattered, time-worn, weather-

stained chronicles, contain the Indian sachem's mark, perchance, an arrow or a beaver, and the few fatal words by which he deeded his hunting grounds away.

(p. 53)

As soon as they turned the native's hunting ground into a pastoral garden, the settlers reinforced the dominance of their version of New England geography through language, signing legal documents and assigning European names to places that already had native names ages before their own arrival:

> He comes with a list of ancient Saxon, Norman, and Celtic names, and strews them up and down this river,—Framingham, Sudbury, Bedford, Carlisle, Billerica, Chelmsford,—and this is New Angle-land, and these are the New West Saxons, whom the Red Men call, not Angle-ish or English, but Yengeese, and so at last they are known for Yankees.

(p. 53)

Thoreau's record of the white man's verbal possession of the land allows readers to see the conflict between the pastoral and the native landscapes as a result of the farmers' invasion of native territory and their remapping of America.

The settlers' possession of America was more than verbal. Physical landmarks along the rivers, too, reminded Thoreau of the "extinct race" and how their land was wrested away from them. On the bank of the Merrimack near the village of Nashville there is "the figure of an Indian's head" carved in the trunk of "a large tree." This is how Thoreau reads the artificial landmark:

> It is related in the History of Dunstable, that on the return of Farwell the Indians were engaged by a fresh party, which they compelled to retreat, and pursued as far as the Nashua, where they fought across the stream at its mouth. After the departure of the Indians, the figure of an Indian's head was found carved by them on a large tree by the shore, which circumstance has given its name to this part of the village of Nashville,—the "Indian Head."

(pp. 167-68)

Thoreau also presents a picture of the landscape before the incident: "As late as 1724 there was no house on the north side of the Nashua, but only scattered wigwams and gristly forests between this frontier and Canada" (p. 166). He thus puts the battle in the perspective of territorial conflicts between the settlers and the natives; linking it to King Philip's War, which according to Puritan settlers was fought in the name of God against the pagans, Thoreau challenges the validity of the pastoral myth fabricated out of the violent enterprise of the white colonists. Thoreau quotes a white local historian:

> It was observed by some judicious . . . that at the beginning of the war, the English soldiers made a nothing

of the Indians, and many spake words to this effect; that one Englishman was sufficient to chase ten Indians; many reckoned it was no other but *Veni, vidi, vici.*

(p. 168)

The "judicious" may be wrong about the natives' ability as warriors, but they faithfully represent the *Veni-vidi-vici* attitude of the "Englishman," an attitude that conflicts with the myth of the peaceful garden. Since the Native Americans were by no means "peaceably" exterminated, by Thoreau's definition the farmers' way of life can never be called truly pastoral. The Concord River and the seemingly "peaceable" communities representing pastoral Utopia never existed in the real sense. Nor can the myth last very long, for there is another threat to the presence of the pastoral: the threat from industrialization.[15]

* * *

Prominent topographical symbols in *A Week* of the growing industry are the dams scattered along the Concord River at Concord, Bedford, Carlisle, Billerica, and Lowell, and many more on the Merrimack. These dams signal the beginning of the end of the so-called pastoral in New England landscape: "Its farmers tell me that thousands of acres are flooded now, since the dams have been erected . . . and they look sadly round to their wood-lots and upland as a last resource" (p. 6). The farmers of that area have every reason to feel "sad" because the growing industrialization threatens to erase the bucolic completely by taking away open land, the matter that makes the pastoral ideal possible in the first place.

The "Corporation with its dam" formed an artificial landmark on the Concord at Billerica, flooding farmers' meadows and keeping the shad from "revisiting their old haunts" (p. 37). Soon "it would seem that the interests, not of the fishes only, but of the men of Wayland, of Sudbury, of Concord, demand the levelling of that dam" (p. 38). Frequently in vain "the farmers stand with scythes whet, waiting the subsiding of the waters, by gravitation, by evaporation or otherwise" (p. 38), but it does not take them too long to realize that it is not enough for them just to wait; they must do something to the dam (with "a crowbar," Thoreau advises [p. 37]) against the conspiring "dam proprietors" who used a wider float-board to increase "their already too high privileges" (p. 38).

The pun reveals Thoreau's anger at the greed of the damn proprietors. Yet he soon shows us that dams and locks on the Concord and Merrimack rivers represent but the older and perhaps milder form of industry. Nature, with the help of time, has been able to absorb the damage that the dams brought to the landscape. Therefore, despite the several dams, the pastoral along the

Concord River, though challenged, has not given up its dominant presence in landscape; instead the old dams are given a vernal look by mosses and other creeping plants and thus mingle with the rest of the environment. The true triumph of the industrial landscape begins at the point where the Concord and the Merrimack merge—at Lowell, the factory city that Thoreau calls the "Manchester of America" (p. 83). At this spot, imagining how the river issues "from the iron region of Franconia" (p. 86), Thoreau depicts for his readers a panoramic view of the whole river valley, which to Thoreau's chagrin has been much industrialized:

> Standing at its mouth, look up its sparkling stream to its source,—a silver cascade which falls all the way from the White Mountains to the sea,—and behold a city on each successive plateau, a busy colony of human beaver around every fall. Not to mention Newburyport and Haverhill, see Lawrence, and Lowell, and Nashua, and Manchester, and Concord, gleaming one above the other. When at length it has escaped from under the last of the factories it has a level and unmolested passage to the sea, a mere *waste water,* as it were, bearing little with it but its fame; its pleasant course revealed by the morning fog which hangs over it, and the sails of the few small vessels which transact the commerce of Haverhill and Newburyport. But its real vessels are railroad cars, and its true and main stream, flowing by an iron channel further south. . . .
>
> (p. 87)

From its Anglo-Puritan beginning, as Sacvan Bercovitch points out, American geography "in one sense . . . was historical, in another sense prophetic."[16] Here Thoreau appeals to both the historical and the prophetic meanings of American geography by evoking the image of a city (or here a series of cities) on a height. The irony is that these actual cities do not really carry the prophetic significance that the Puritans assigned to New England. The cities are not established according to the word of God but built upon the principle of minimum cost for maximum profits. This is no Massachusetts Bay Colony but "a busy colony of human beaver around every fall." The word "fall" is, again, a pun, suggesting that with this second fall the new occupants of the American Eden have not only demeaned themselves into mindless beasts (beavers) but also disgraced nature by "molesting" the beautiful river and turning it into "a mere *waste water.*"

Yet in another sense, in the dynamic process of landscape evolution, Thoreau's description of the geography of the Merrimack area is truly prophetic. At that particular spot on the river he sees that only a small section of the pastoral riverscape remains "level and unmolested." And even on this small section "small vessels" transact commerce on the water and the true vessels, the railroad cars, shuttle along the "iron channel" between Lowell and Boston. In contrast, the major part of the river has been transformed into a corridor for industry and commerce, characterized by the "iron region"—the dams, locks, canals, canal boats, railroads, and factories.

As the industrialization process accelerated in nineteenth-century New England, new images appeared on the rivers to compete for the domination of the landscape. In this competition, pastoralism in and of itself was no match for the powerful and violent industrialism; the pastoral landscape receded as industry advanced, and it was reduced to a smaller area by the speedy appearance (and disappearance) of the canals, canal boats, and steamboats that commercialized the riverscape. Finally, the railroad replaced the other industrial landmarks as well as the pastoral ones. Thoreau had noticed on the Merrimack what Mark Twain noticed on the Mississippi decades later:

> Since our voyage the railroad on the bank has been extended, and there is now but little boating on the Merrimack. All kinds of produce and stores were formerly conveyed by water, but now nothing is carried up the stream. . . . The locks are fast wearing out, and will soon be impassable, since the tolls will not pay the expense of repairing them, and so in a few years there will be an end of boating on this river. The boating, at present, is principally between Merrimack and Lowell, or Hooksett and Manchester.
>
> (p. 213)

In addition to the revolution in transportation, new factories mushroomed in the Merrimack valley to help change the appearance of the river. In the summer of 1848, one year before he published *A Week,* Thoreau made a walking tour in southern New Hampshire with Ellery Channing, covering some of the areas that he and John had traveled through nine years before. Thoreau incorporated into the final draft of *A Week* some of the materials he collected during this tour, which reflected how fast the river had changed since 1839. With John, Thoreau noticed the beginning of an industrial town at the mouth of Piscataguoag, which emptied into the Merrimack: "Just above the mouth of this river we passed the artificial falls where the canals of the Manchester Manufacturing Company discharge themselves into the Merrimack" (p. 245). Not liking what they saw there, the Thoreau brothers "did not tarry to examine [the scene] minutely" but made "haste to get past the village here collected, and out of hearing of the hammer which was laying the foundation of another Lowell on the banks."

Nevertheless, the image of the incipient manufacturing center stuck in Thoreau's mind, and he compared this early picture with the look of the full-grown industrial town nine years later when he revisited it with Channing:

> At the time of our voyage Manchester was a village of about two thousand inhabitants, where we landed for a

moment to get some cool water. . . . But now, as I have been told, and indeed have witnessed, it contains fourteen thousand inhabitants.

(p. 245)

These new factories, together with the dams, locks, canals, canal boats, and railroads along both rivers, form an emerging but powerful landscape, crowding the banks and threatening to squeeze the pastoral out of the picture. As the agricultural settlements had replaced the aboriginal hunting and fishing grounds, modern industry was rapidly replacing the agricultural presence along the rivers. If the conflict between the so-called pastoral landscape and the native one shows that from the start the European settlers' agricultural community was not peaceably established and that its pastoral appearance was achieved by violent deeds as well as violent words, the fast-expanding industrial landscape indicates that the myth of the American pastoral cannot last very long.

Such a doomed fabrication can hardly help Thoreau resolve his problem of human mortality; hence a fundamental question about the nature of Thoreau's first book: despite his use of the pastoral conventions, can we rightfully regard *A Week* as a pastoral book? It is more accurate to call the book a counter-pastoral work, for on the one hand, in the actual geography of New England, Thoreau shows us that the pastoral landscape has no true past because its violent beginnings contradict the definition of the pastoral; on the other hand, he foresees no future for a pastoral myth that is quickly disappearing before the encroachment of industrialization.

Thoreau did not trust the cultural institution of the pastoral but dramatized the conflicts of three types of New England landscape and sought a resolution of the conflicts in a fourth and by far the most powerful landscape, a wild nature before which the native, pastoral, and industrial models contest for a dominant presence. In *A Week* the force of wild nature represented by the high flood of the rivers eventually would swallow up human dramas and render them petty and irrelevant.

* * *

Nature in *A Week* does not exist in a separate space from the pastoral, the industrial, or the native; it exists, instead, securely behind all three contending landscapes, temporarily giving in to human encroachment but ultimately promising a triumph over human problems. The Great Meadows area of Concord, for instance, is a place where the three cultural landscapes clash but nature reclaims with final serenity: the swampy lowland in the northeast corner of Concord had been the fishing ground for the Indians, but the white farmer bought and owned it as property; the "dam proprietors," however, encroached upon the farmer's "right" by flooding it with an extra-wide "new float-board." Yet when the Thoreau brothers paddled round "the neighboring bend" from Concord village into the Great Meadows in 1839, they found that nature still had the upper hand there; whether used as fishing ground or meadow or flooded by the dam proprietors, Great Meadows remained a level, "fertile and juicy place in nature" (p. 19).

The natural landscape is omnipresent in the book, and readers feel its presence not only in Concord, where Thoreau's journey started, but also in "New Concord," the farthest spot the boat carried the brothers. At "the limit of our voyage" (p. 299) Thoreau describes a personal experience in a water-saturated landscape similar to the Great Meadows: "I can fancy that it would be a luxury to stand up to one's chin in some retired swamp a whole summer day, scenting the wild honeysuckle and bilberry blows, and lulled by the minstrelsy of gnats and mosquitoes! . . . Surely one may as profitably be soaked in the juices of a swamp" (p. 300). Thoreau's study of a healthy and reassuring nature helps him and his readers to expand their view of life from an anthropocentric perspective to a broader, "new geographical" one that takes into account both the organic and inorganic kingdoms. The element that Thoreau chooses to represent the vitality of wild nature is water, the source of all forms of life and a connecting symbol in the holistic picture of "new geography." Thoreau's actual trip to New Hampshire took two weeks, one of which was spent in the White Mountains. In his literary representation of the journey, however, he focuses on the rivers but leaves out the week in the mountains. Through the dominant presence of water in his natural landscape Thoreau resolves not only his personal problem of the death of a brother but also the disappearance of a race and its culture.

Thoreau supports his confidence in nature by emphasizing the profusion of lives in the two rivers: "It enhances our sense of the grand security and serenity of nature, to observe the still undisturbed economy and content of the fishes of this century, their happiness a regular fruit of the summer" (p. 26). After listing all the fishes in the Concord he ponders on the disappearance of salmon, shad, and alewives, whose migration is blocked from the Concord by the dam and canal at Billerica and the factories at Lowell. Unlike the fishermen of Concord who complain about the improper construction of the "fish-ways" in the dams, Thoreau looks further and trusts that nature will eventually, "after a few thousands of years" (p. 34), overcome industry and restore the normal migratory route for the fishes all the way to the source of the Concord River.

In addition to hoping for nature's ultimate triumph, Thoreau depicts some of the ever-going renaturalizing processes on the Concord and Merrimack rivers. Near Bedford on the Merrimack the brothers have to move through some ancient-looking locks that are already somewhat naturalized by erosion: "These old gray structures, with their quiet arms stretched over the river in the sun, appeared like *natural* objects in the scenery, and the king-fisher and sand-piper alighted on them as readily as on stakes or rocks" (p. 238; emphasis added). Water can renaturalize industrial scenes in a more powerful manner, and "the works of man are every where swallowed up in the immensity of Nature" (p. 316). This is best shown in Thoreau's expectation of the highest freshet of the Merrimack.

At Tyngsborough, Thoreau sees a nail in an old apple tree behind a farmer's house, marking "one of the greatest freshets on this river [that] took place in October, 1785" (pp. 355-56). Thoreau is pleased to "learn that there has since been a freshet which rose within nine inches of the rails at Biscuit Brook, and such a freshet as that of 1785 would have covered the railroad two feet deep" (p. 356). Such a freshet would indicate the beginning of nature's triumph and attest that water in *A Week* functions as something more than the emblem "of human life" (p. 124); it also functions as a powerful agent of nature's self-rejuvenation.

In *A Week* the process of rejuvenation takes place not so much in the seasonal or diurnal cycle as in the geographical cycle, a term coined by William Morris Davis toward the end of the nineteenth century. But the basic concept of the cycle of geographical transformation is already present in the first book by Thoreau, who probably assimilates it from Charles Lyell's *Principles of Geology*.[17] Passing "a large and densely wooded island this forenoon, between Short's and Griffith's Falls" (p. 243), Thoreau contemplates how the river erodes the banks along its course and deposits the debris somewhere down the stream and thus makes an island. He sees the process of aqueous reproduction as a symbol of the perpetual cycle in which nature renews itself:

> An island always pleases my imagination, even the smallest, as a small continent and integral portion of the globe. . . . There is commonly such a one at the junction of two rivers, whose currents bring down and deposit their respective sands in the eddy at their confluence, as it were the womb of a continent. By what a delicate and far-fetched contribution every island is made! What an enterprise of Nature thus to lay the foundations of and to build up the future continent, of golden and silver sands and the ruins of forests.
>
> (p. 243)

Thoreau has "a fancy for building my hut on [a small island]" (p. 243), because it enables him to see the "earth" constantly "created or destroyed" (p. 244). Through this specific fact Thoreau sees a general truth of nature's perpetual regeneration: when nature "destroys" something, she is actually using it to "create" the world anew; thus, perhaps after nature levels down

the dams "a few thousands years later," she will use the chunks of concrete as foundations of a new continent. Treating human affairs as part of the geographical cycle, Thoreau comments:

> There is, indeed, a tide in the affairs of men, as the poet says, and yet as things flow they circulate, and the ebb always balances the flow. All streams are but tributary to the ocean, which itself does not stream, and the shores are unchanged but in longer periods man can measure. Go where we will, we discover infinite change in particulars only, not in generals.
>
> (p. 124)

The aqueous causes transform the face of earth in a larger cycle than days and seasons. This larger cycle has the power to absorb the human impact on the earth, and it redeems the death of individuals by including human beings in the whole, organic process of life-death-regeneration. By enacting the dramas of the conflicting cultures in the natural landscape, Thoreau emphasizes the power of nature over that of cultural traditions, including the pastoral elegy. For Thoreau, nature is the "true benefactress, the secret of [whose] service is unchangeableness" (p. 114). Thoreau turns to this ultimate unchangeableness as a source of comfort for the loss of a brother, and he criticizes the pastoral tradition in a larger, geographical representation of the shaping of New England. The two New England rivers symbolize for Thoreau something that functions in its own way, something that cannot be reduced to the generic category of the pastoral elegy nor to any other human category. Reading *A Week* as an Americanized pastoral elegy prevents us from seeing the larger issues in Thoreau's first book; considering *A Week* as held together only by the "days of the week" (again a cultural category) leads readers to see the book's structure as flawed. In contrast, considering the larger cycles of "sequent occupance" and geographical rejuvenation as major warp and weft in the "complex weave" of *A Week,* we have reason to argue that Thoreau's first book is, like *Walden,* a well-structured cultural critique as well as the private resolution of a personal tragedy.

Notes

1. See *The Correspondence of Henry David Thoreau,* ed. Walter Harding and Carl Bode (New York: New York Univ. Press, 1958), p. 65. The American pastoral tradition discussed in this essay refers to a tendency to view America as an idealized place of pure and carefree existence in rural settings. In *The Machine in the Garden: Technology and the Pastoral Ideal in America* (New York: Oxford Univ. Press, 1964), Leo Marx studies this tendency as two distinct types of pastoralism: the sentimental and the imaginary. This trend has also been discussed under different names such as "agrarianism," "rural values," "the agrarian myth,"

the "Old Republican idyll," and "the myth of the garden" by such scholars as Richard Hofstadter, Marvin Meyers, Henry Nash Smith, Lawrence Buell, and Glen Love. Often embodied in "an image of a natural landscape, a terrain either unspoiled or, if cultivated, rural" (Marx, p. 9), the American pastoral can be found in the works of scores of American authors with which Thoreau was familiar, including John Smith's promotional description of New England, William Bartram's "little promontory" on the west bank of a Florida river, Jean de Crevecoeur's "too-good-to-be-true" American farms, and Timothy Dwight's "flourishing village" of the idealized Greenfield Hill.

2. See Paul, *The Shores of America: Thoreau's Inward Exploration* (Urbana: Univ. of Illinois Press, 1958), pp. 199, 198; Harding, "Introduction" to *A Week on the Concord and Merrimack Rivers,* ed. Walter Harding (New York: Holt, Rinehart and Winston, 1963), p. viii; Johnson, *Thoreau's Complex Weave: The Writing of* A Week on the Concord and Merrimack Rivers, *with the Text of the First Draft* (Charlottesville: Univ. Press of Virginia, 1986), pp. 41, 44; Lebeaux, *Thoreau's Seasons* (Amherst: Univ. of Massachusetts Press, 1984), pp. 4, 7; and Peck, *Thoreau's Morning Work: Memory and Perception in* A Week on the Concord and Merrimack Rivers, *the* Journals, *and* Walden (New Haven: Yale Univ. Press, 1990), pp. 3-21.

3. Thoreau, *Walden,* ed. J. Lyndon Shanley (Princeton: Princeton Univ. Press, 1971), p. 3.

4. Quoted in Michael Williams, "Historical Geography and the Concept of Landscape," *Journal of Historical Geography,* 15 (1989), 92.

5. Joan Burbick, *Thoreau's Alternative History: Changing Perspectives on Nature, Culture, and Language* (Philadelphia: Univ. of Pennsylvania Press, 1987), p. 3. See also William Ellery Channing, *Thoreau the Poet-Naturalist, with Memorial Verses, New Edition,* ed. F. B. Sanborn (Boston: Charles E. Goodspeed, 1902); James McIntosh, *Thoreau as Romantic Naturalist: His Shifting Stance toward Nature* (Ithaca: Cornell Univ. Press, 1974); John Hildebidle, *Thoreau: A Naturalist's Liberty* (Cambridge, Mass.: Harvard Univ. Press, 1983); and Robert D. Richardson, Jr., "Thoreau and Science," in *American Literature and Science,* ed. Robert J. Scholnick (Lexington: Univ. Press of Kentucky, 1992), pp. 110-27. Joan Burbick, however, anticipated me in noticing the importance of landscape description in *A Week.* She argues in *Thoreau's Alternative History* that *A Week* is both a geographical description and historical narrative about the small corner of northeastern Massachusetts and southern New Hampshire. As early as in

his first book, Burbick argues, Thoreau develops "the art of description as the only means to present a correct history of the landscape" (p. 11). But while Burbick emphasizes Thoreau's "alternative" representation of history, I also stress Thoreau's geographical insight in his study of "sequent occupance" of the two river valleys. William Rossi's study of Thoreau's poetic appropriation of Lyell's geological principles is ground-breaking (see Rossi, "Poetry and Progress: Thoreau, Lyell, and the Geological Principles of *A Week,*" *American Literature,* 66 [1994], 275-300). Yet Rossi's focus on geology does not include the important impact of new geography on Thoreau's mind.

6. R. E. Dickinson and O. J. R. Howarth, *The Making of Geography* (Oxford: Clarendon Press, 1933), p. 138. I am aware of the sexist language in this quotation and other quotations in the present essay from Thoreau and other nineteenth-century authors. While I avoid using gender specific pronouns, I don't attempt to make anachronistic corrections of older texts.

7. See Hartshorne, *The Nature of Geography: A Critical Survey of Current Thought in the Light of the Past* (Lancaster, Penn.: Association of American Geographers, 1939), esp. pp. 38-61.

8. Alexander von Humboldt, preface to *Cosmos,* quoted in Dickinson and Howarth, *Making of Geography,* p. 146.

9. Noticing the important role *Natural History of Selborne* plays in the shaping of Thoreau's attitude toward science, Robert D. Richardson, Jr., chooses Gilbert White as one of the major figures in his study of Thoreau and science. For some reason, Richardson excludes from his list of twenty-odd scientists Alexander von Humboldt, whose influence on Thoreau is as great as that of White, whom Richardson lists (see "Thoreau and Science"). In this paragraph and the two paragraphs preceding it, I draw on Ning Yu, "Thoreau and the New Geography: The Hydrological Cycle in 'Ktaadn,'" *ESQ: A Journal of the American Renaissance,* 40 (1994), 113-38.

10. Thoreau, *A Week on the Concord and Merrimack Rivers,* ed. Carl F. Hovde, William L. Howarth, and Elizabeth Hall Witherell (Princeton: Princeton Univ. Press, 1980), p. 6. Further references to this work appear in the text.

11. In 1929 Derwent Whittlesey described the geographical study of the processes of change in an area caused by human occupance as the study of "sequent occupance." It is interesting that his focus was also New England: "Each generation of human occupance is linked to its forbear and to its

offspring, and each exhibits an individuality expressive of mutations in some elements of its natural and cultural characteristics. Moreover, the life history of each discloses the inevitability of the transformation from stage to stage" ("Sequent Occupance," *Annals of the Association of American Geographers,* 19 [1929], 163). Of course, there is an essential difference between Thoreau's landscape study and the twentieth-century study of sequent occupance. Whittlesey and other geographers searched and invented a geographical study against the "environmental determinism" that had dominated American geography since the late nineteenth century. Thoreau, in contrast, depicted the interaction among the cultural landscapes only to show that nature had the final say in the shaping of land.

12. See Marx, esp. pp. 88-89; for the distinction between the two kinds of pastoralism, see Marx, pp. 5-11, 24-33.

13. Though widely recognized as "Concord's leading Indian expert and defender," Thoreau is nevertheless biased by the nineteenth-century stereotype of the Native American only as a hunter and fisherman, especially in *A Week* (see Robert Sayer, *Thoreau and the American Indians* [Princeton: Princeton Univ. Press, 1977], pp. ix, 4, 7). However, because my focus is on Thoreau's metaphorical use of geography rather than on how incorrect he is in understanding and representing Native-American culture, I use the term "Indian landscape" as Thoreau projected it—a favorable alternative to the white man's farm. For a critique of Thoreau's concept of Native Americans, see Sayer.

14. Thoreau, *The Journal of Henry David Thoreau,* ed. Bradford Torrey and Francis H. Allen, 14 vols. (Salt Lake City: Gibbs M. Smith and Peregrine Smith Books, 1984), V, 4.

15. This is Leo Marx's central argument. He remarked, for instance, that "since Jefferson's time the forces of industrialism have been the chief threat to the bucolic image of America" (p. 26). Yet Marx did not notice that Thoreau had made this process a part of his geographical critique.

16. Sacvan Bercovitch, *The American Jeremiad* (Madison: Univ. of Wisconsin Press, 1978), p. 15.

17. See Geoffrey J. Martin and Preston E. James, *All Possible Worlds: A History of Geographical Ideas,* 3d ed. (New York: John Wiley and Sons, 1993). William Morris Davis established the theory of "geographical cycle" or "cycle of erosion" toward the end of Thoreau's century (first announced in 1884 and published in revised form in 1899). Conducting a geographical survey of the Missouri River for the Northern Pacific Railroad, Davis noted some terraces above the river and interpreted their existence "as the result of the removal of an 'unknown thickness of overlying strata,' and the reduction of an earlier surface close to the baselevel of the drainage" (Martin and James, p. 307). Davis invented a useful set of terminology to explain the interesting phenomena he discovered along the Missouri Valley: "When the initial surface is still undissected between the valleys, when the valleys are V-shaped, and when the rivers descend through them turbulently—this is a stage Davis described as *youth.* The greatest amount of relief occurs when the last remnant of the initial surface is dissected. Then the surface is gradually reduced, and the valleys begin to widen. This is the stage Davis described as *maturity.* When the rivers meander across wide valleys and the land between the valleys has been reduced to gently rounded slopes—this he called *old age.* The upheaved block of the earth's crust is worn down almost to a level plain, which Davis called a *peneplain.* The whole cycle, Davis pointed out, could start again with another uplift, resulting in *rejuvenation*" (Martin and James, p. 308). For Lyell's concept of aqueous causes for changes on the surface of the earth, see Rossi, "Poetry and Progress," esp. pp. 279, 297.

Ryan Patrick Hanley (essay date April 2001)

SOURCE: Hanley, Ryan Patrick. "Thoreau among His Heroes." *Philosophy and Literature* 25, no. 1 (April 2001): 59-74.

[*In the following essay, Hanley studies the concept of "heroic magnanimity" in Thoreau's* Walden.]

> To live alone one has to be a beast or a god—says Aristotle. But there's a third case: one has to be both—a *philosopher.*[1]
>
> —Nietzsche

For a book that implores its readers to "simplify, simplify," **Walden** has more than its fair share of obscurity. Lovers of simplicity have long mined it for its clear and comforting maxims, only to leave behind more than a few tough nuts for those who incline towards the esoteric—which, for Thoreau, is the essence of the philosophical. To the former set of readers he offers an apology: "You will pardon some obscurities, for there are more secrets in my trade than in most men's, and yet not voluntarily kept, but inseparable from its very nature."[2] To the latter he offers advice: "Books must be read as deliberately and reservedly as they were written." The mysteries of the best books, Thoreau insists, are revealed only to those who, through their patience and persistence, prove themselves worthy of their teachings. "The heroic books, even if printed in the character of our mother tongue, will always be in a language dead to degenerate times; and we must laboriously seek the meaning of each word and line, conjecturing a larger sense than common use permits out of what wisdom and valor and generosity we have" (p. 83). Thoreau's *Walden,* I mean to show, was both conceived and meant to be read as just such a heroic book, not only because of its author's "epic ambition" to create a national literature,[3] but also because a unique understanding of heroism is the subject of its most esoteric chapters.

A deliberate and reserved reading of chapters eleven and twelve of *Walden* reveals the irony of their titles.[4] The dominant theme of the chapter entitled "Higher Laws" is brutishness; that of "Brute Neighbors," nobility. Where "Higher Laws" examines the savagery inherent in human nature, "Brute Neighbors" examines the nobility inherent in the natural world. Why this inversion? Surely the switch is meant, at least in part, to have us rethink that artificial distinction which Thoreau believes we have drawn between the savage and the noble. But redeeming our oft-denigrated savage nature is only part of his project. In the set piece formed by these two chapters,[5] Thoreau also presents a new understanding of heroic magnanimity, one designed to reconcile his conflicting attractions to natural savagery and to cultivated nobility. Thoreau's sincere conviction that civilization constitutes "a real advance in the condition of man" rendered both Homer's premodern Achilles and Rousseau's noble savage unfit models for the sort of human excellence he sought (p. 27). According to Thoreau, the well-ordered soul belongs neither to him who merely indulges in the primordial elements of his character nor him who merely renounces them, but rather to the man who harmonizes his primitive and polite sides once each has been allowed to flourish. And as we shall see, Thoreau offers his readers a glimpse of this new magnanimity in his homage to Walden's greatest-souled guest, the loon, the embodiment of that philosophic self-sufficiency to which he aspired.

Thoreau's sensitivity to both the spiritual and the savage sides of his nature is evident in the opening of "Higher Laws." "I found in myself, and still find," Thoreau here explains, "an instinct toward a higher, or, as it is named, spiritual life, as do most men, and another toward a primitive rank and savage one, and I reverence them both. I love the wild not less than the good" (p. 170). Thus Thoreau makes his clearest statement of a central teaching of *Walden*: that "the wild" is no less deserving of our love and respect than "the good."[6] And though he believes we are called to the amalgamation of these two sides of our nature, the emphasis of "Higher Laws" is decidedly on the former, our wild and primitive side. The genius of "Higher Laws" is that the

higher law of which Thoreau here speaks is not a transcendent or divine law, but, in the truest sense of the word, a *natural* law—a law which emerges from the nature of our being, and which we need look no further than within to find.

The opening scene of "Higher Laws" offers a hint that the chapter's primary focus is the savage and primitive rather than the civilized or spiritual. Here Thoreau recounts the impulse that besieged him upon spying a woodchuck stealing across his path. The sight of the woodchuck, he tells us, filled him with "a strange thrill of savage delight." Gleefully and impiously, Thoreau recounts how he "was strongly tempted to seize and devour him raw; not that I was hungry then, except for that wildness which he represented" (p. 170). As this episode reveals, there is in Thoreau a passionate appetite—quite literally a "hunger"—to revel and delight in wildness and savagery. That he revels and delights in it there can be no doubt. In recalling the encounter with the woodchuck Thoreau has not the slightest sense of shame or remorse for harboring such a powerful and savage passion; such passions, he understands, are as much a part of his nature as his passion for the *Iliad* and the passions therein depicted.

Throughout "Higher Laws," this fascination with the wild and untamed is sustained. But Thoreau's invocations of wildness in the chapter rarely occur in his discussions of the nature which surrounds him; instead, they occur in his discussions of man. Whatever might be said about the rest of *Walden,* at least in "Higher Laws" it is not man's relationship to nature which principally interests Thoreau, but rather man's relationship to his own nature, to "the animal within him" (p. 47). In *A Week on the Concord and Merrimack Rivers,* Thoreau introduces this theme when he confesses that there "is in my nature, methinks, a singular yearning toward all wildness."[7] Early in *Walden,* he refers to "the natural yearning of that portion of our most primitive ancestor which still survived in us" (p. 25). It is this primitive side of our nature that "Higher Laws" explores—indeed, celebrates—in depth. Far from being ashamed of or repentant for the brutish elements of his nature, Thoreau is proud to proclaim that there "is unquestionably this instinct in me which belongs to the lower orders of creation" (p. 173). Thus, he calls his reader to be mindful of this "most original part of himself," so that self-knowledge might serve as "the seeds of a better life in him" (p. 172).

But Thoreau's celebration of the latent savage within culminates in the following observation:

> We are conscious of an animal in us, which awakens in proportion as our higher nature slumbers. It is reptile and sensual, and perhaps cannot be wholly expelled; like the worms which, even in life and health, occupy

our bodies. Possibly we may withdraw from it, but never change its nature. I fear that it may enjoy a certain health of its own; that we may be well, yet not pure.

(p. 177)

At first glance Thoreau here seems to take a decided step back from his earlier enthusiasm for man's savage nature. "Reptile" and "sensual" are hardly terms of approbation, nor does the comparison of our savage nature to parasitic worms seem kind. Further, what significance should we ascribe to Thoreau's admission that it is not with joy but with fear that he greeted the possibility that we might be "well, yet not pure"? Perhaps Thoreau was simply inclined sometimes to revel in our bestial passions and sometimes to judge them more harshly, according to his mood. Clearly, he was never comfortable with all of our primitive natural passions; witness his almost prudish celebrations of chastity.

More interesting and also more consistent throughout *Walden* than his stance on the passions is Thoreau's insistence that although we might be able to suppress the animal within from time to time, we can "never change its nature." Surely we would be wrong to read Thoreau's comments on the immutability of our animal nature as a resigned assertion of the futility of change, for the hope which drove him to embark on the experiment of *Walden* is evidence enough against that view. Far from simply declaring man a lost cause, and even while realizing that we might never change our nature, Thoreau instead called men to take life seriously, to strive deliberately to make the most of life. Thus, Thoreau suggests that we need not waste our time with efforts to adjust man's nature; perhaps, he hints, our energies are better spent adjusting our standards for evaluating man. In seeking to disabuse us of our conventional distinctions and categories of moral judgment, Thoreau indeed seems "a man who has come back down into the cave to tell the residents there that they are really in chains."[8]

In this vein Thoreau insists that the proper path to greatness lies in the struggle to live a fully human life—a fully human life being that which does not extinguish, but rather develops to its fullest capacities, that ineradicable animal which is in us by nature. Thoreau's quest to establish a firmer foundation for greatness is reminiscent of Montaigne's similar effort. "Greatness of soul," Montaigne insisted, "is not so much pressing upward and forward as knowing how to set oneself in order and circumscribe oneself. . . . There is nothing so beautiful and legitimate as to play the man well and properly, no knowledge so hard to acquire as the knowledge of how to live this life well and naturally; and the most barbarous of our maladies is to despise our being."[9] For both Montaigne and Thoreau, the "life in conformity to higher principles" is not synonymous with the life dedicated to renouncing our base instincts or "despising our

being" (p. 175). By "higher principles" Thoreau instead means an awareness and consciousness of our basic nature, composed as it is of "the wild" along with "the good." Rather than have us suppress these instincts, Thoreau would have us recast our definition of greatness so that the instinctual and natural are glorified. To be superior, according to Thoreau, one must first become the greatest beast, the greatest brute, one can be.

But surely these assertions will strike some as overstated; does not Thoreau himself preach quite the opposite? After all, one could hardly ask for a better vindication of civilized restraint and temperance and general "anti-brutishness" than his insistence that "Nature is hard to be overcome, but she must be overcome" (p. 178). But to read these words as a call to mortify the animal within man is to do their author a disservice. Thoreau has already given us some reason to think that the task of living is not that simple. Rather, in emphasizing that men are called to overcome nature, Thoreau means to tell us that we must never allow ourselves to become the slaves of our animalistic sides. The target of his attack here is not on our natural impulses, but rather on the perversion of our natural impulses—hence his professed repugnance to sensuality. "The fruits eaten temperately need not make us ashamed of our appetites, nor interrupt the worthiest pursuits," he tells us. "But put an extra condiment into your dish, and it will poison you" (p. 174). In this respect Thoreau follows Carlyle: "Enjoying things which are pleasant; that is not the evil: it is the reducing of our moral self to slavery by them that is."[10] Far from advocating the asceticism of a rigid and inflexible self-command, Thoreau, like Carlyle, would have us regulate our passions rather than extirpate them. Indeed, Thoreau advocates struggling for austerity as much as he does succumbing to sensuality—which is to say, not at all. Again following Montaigne, he instead insists that we should strive to live in harmony with our dual nature; by overcoming the most imperious aspects of nature, Thoreau hopes we might better live in accord with the dictates of *human nature,* which encompasses both savage and civilized elements. So even in celebrating our wildest attributes, he never suggests that we should allow ourselves to remain merely brute beasts; thus his invocation of Mencius: "'That in which men differ from brute beasts is a thing very inconsiderable; the common herd lose it very soon; superior men preserve it carefully'" (p. 177). Instead, Thoreau insists we must allow our higher side to manifest itself even as we allow our animal side to flourish. By living in such a manner, giving each side its due, Thoreau suggests that we might achieve our potential. Such a position is underscored by his quotation from Donne's verse letter "To Sire Edward Herbert at Iulyers": "How happy's he who hath due place assigned / To his beasts and disaforested his mind!" (p. 178). In "Higher Laws" Thoreau similarly calls each of us to organize consciously the many facets of our soul and thus "set oneself in order." By so doing, we become the sculptors and painters and builders whose "material is our own flesh and blood and bones," and whose aim is to establish the proper balance of our higher and lower impulses and inclinations (p. 179). By giving each part its "due place," we aim for the whole to strike its mark.

So much for Thoreau's examination of the purely brutish elements of man's character. For insight into the heroic and noble, we must turn to the next chapter, in which Thoreau takes to observing his "brute neighbors" to see what they might teach him about the higher side of his nature. Perhaps it is altogether fitting for him to have done this. In "Higher Laws" Thoreau explains that even fishermen come closer to apprehending nature's truths than do scholars, for the former are "in a peculiar sense a part of Nature themselves." For this reason they are better able to observe and apprehend her, better "than philosophers or poets even, who approach her with expectation. She is not afraid to exhibit herself to them" (p. 170). Such a perspective indicates that those closest to nature will best grasp her teachings—and who better than his brute neighbors to teach Thoreau nature's noble lessons?

In surveying these brute neighbors, Thoreau discovers that several of them have already attained that precarious balance of the primordial and the polite for which he strives himself. Several times in the chapter he deliberately obscures the conventional boundary between the savage and the civilized. Representative of this ambiguity are his thoughts on the housecat he was once surprised to find strolling along Walden's stony shore. Reflecting on the cat's ability to make herself equally at home in the wild as in town, Thoreau is moved to observe that even "the most domestic cat which has lain on a rug all her days, appears quite at home in the woods, and, by her sly and stealthy behavior, proves herself more native there than the regular inhabitants" (p. 188). Here and elsewhere, Thoreau is captivated by the facility with which even the most civilized and domesticated reawaken their typically dormant primordial wildness.

Thoreau finds a similar interweaving of the primordial and the noble in the partridge, which fascinates him because of its ability to exist at once within nature and above it. Twice in the chapter and once elsewhere Thoreau mentions the partridge's ability to appear one with nature, each time describing how it uses the natural camouflage of the forest floor to make itself indistinguishable from the dried and decaying leaves. Yet even as Thoreau the naturalist was fascinated by this simple ability, there was also something about the partridge which commanded the respect of Thoreau the admirer of the heroic. It was this latter side of Thoreau which marveled at the young partridges' stalwart ability to stand before him "obedient to their mother and their in-

stinct . . . without fear or trembling." Like Kierkegaard's Abraham, Thoreau's partridge is possessed of a nobility and a courage which transcend conventional estimations. Both respond instinctively to calls to which reason could never command their assent.

Thoreau's study of the young partridges culminates in a celebration of their transcendent natures. "The remarkably adult yet innocent expression of their open and serene eyes is very memorable," he is moved to observe. "All intelligence seems reflected in them. They suggest not merely the purity of infancy, but a wisdom clarified by experience. Such an eye was not born when the bird was, but is coeval with the sky it reflects" (p. 184). In its naturalness, the partridge's eye, "coeval with the sky it reflects," exhibits a timelessness and immortality suggestive of its primordial origins. In its higher nature, the young partridge exhibits that mixture of purity and self-knowledge sought by John Farmer in the concluding paragraph of "Higher Laws." But where John Farmer struggled to overcome the divide which separated the "mean moiling life" he lived from that "glorious existence" he felt was possible, the partridge and Thoreau's fellow brute neighbors, without conscious intention, beat John Farmer to the punch in achieving that glorious life which seamlessly integrates the noble and the animal, the spiritual and the corporeal, domesticating rather than extirpating wildness (p. 179).

Like the wild mouse he trains to eat from his hand, these partridges—his "hens and chickens"—are the animated embodiments of that balanced ideal of domesticated wildness which Thoreau cultivated in his bean-field. "They were beans cheerfully returning to their wild and primitive state that I cultivated," he tells us, not without some pride. Neither civilized nor barbarous nor half-civilized nor savage, Thoreau's plot of beans was rather "the connecting link between wild and cultivated fields" (p. 128). Like John Farmer and his partridges, the bean-field too evokes the larger contrast between savagery and nobility which concerns Thoreau in these two chapters. Early in the experiment, Thoreau parenthetically wonders whether it might be possible "to combine the hardiness of these savages with the intellectualness of the civilized man" (p. 13). Such is the question at the heart of the myriad enterprises, from nurturing beans to cultivating souls, in which Thoreau was engaged while at Walden.

"Higher Laws" and "Brute Neighbors," as we have seen, ask us to reevaluate our ill-considered, conventional notions of civilization and barbarism. In portraying men actuated by brutish passions and animals actuated by impulses that transcend the merely brutish, Thoreau calls on us to learn to see differently, to apply a new sort of vision to the study of ourselves and our world. By so doing, Thoreau hopes we might come to reevaluate that line of demarcation which we have too hastily drawn between the realm of nature and the kingdom of man. Early in *Walden,* Thoreau laments that "we inhabitants of New England live this mean life that we do because our vision does not penetrate the surface of things. We think that that *is* which *appears* to be" (p. 79). Thoreau effects a similar shift in our perspective in "Brute Neighbors" by opening it with the central epistemological question of *Walden*: "Why do precisely these objects which we behold make a world?" (p. 182). At the heart of this question is another concern: why do we limit our estimation of a man's character to only those exterior qualities which we can readily behold? In posing his questions, Thoreau challenges us to go beyond our all-too-superficial assumptions, and to examine instead the souls of men in order that we might come to a more just evaluation of their essence.

With this we come to the comic interlude of "Brute Neighbors," the "internecine war" of the ants. In his account of the *bellum* waged during the presidency of Polk between those red republicans and their black imperialist foes, Thoreau mounts his strongest challenge yet to our received notions of nobility and savagery, for it is here that he makes his most explicit association of the savage with the heroic. One can hardly miss the echoes of Homeric grandeur in the language Thoreau uses to recount the ferocious exploits of the combatants. Thoreau's flights of fancy are giddy; one can readily imagine the journal-writer chuckling to himself as he composed his depiction of that single red ant late to join the fray, perhaps dispatched Lacedaemonian-like by his mother, who "had charged him to return with his shield or upon it"—or "perchance he was some Achilles, who had nourished his wrath apart, and had now come to avenge or rescue his Patroclus" (p. 186). Yet importantly, even as we join Thoreau in savoring the humor of the mock heroic, it is not heroism that Thoreau mocks here. His comments on John Brown's magnanimity attest to the profound respect in which he held his heroes.

Thoreau's use of humor in describing the ants' exploits was not intended to denigrate heroism, but instead to effect the change of perspective and the reconsideration of our received categories which he asks us to undertake in these chapters. Indeed, Thoreau crafts the entire scene of the ant battle around a series of shifts in perspective. Witness the author, incomparably bigger than the humble ants, lifting the woodchip on which they wage their mortal combat to his windowsill so that he might better see their rage and fury with the aid of his microscope, thus effecting a quite literal change of perspective. Witness also his suggestion that "the results of this battle will be as important and memorable to those whom it concerns as those of the battle of Bunker Hill"—a figurative, but dramatic, shift (p. 187). Indeed, just as our understanding of heroism changes when we apply the language of the heroic to so seemingly insig-

nificant a creature as an ant, our understanding of our own place in the scheme of creation is brought into question through these artful shifts. If an ant might be a hero, in what then does heroic magnanimity consist?

Thoreau provides two answers to this question, one at the end of "Brute Neighbors," and the other in his homage to John Brown. In his eulogy of Brown, Thoreau depicts the rebellious captain as an exceptional individual dedicated to "carrying out the purpose of a life."[11] On several occasions, Thoreau hints at the nature of that purpose, observing that Brown's was a life led in "obedience to an infinitely higher command," and explaining that Brown was "actuated by higher motives."[12] Such lofty language might lead us to think that in hearkening to this higher voice Brown was moved by motives which we lesser modern men, deaf to the calls of apotheosis, are incapable of feeling. But such a view would obscure the reasons why Thoreau admired Brown. Indeed Thoreau takes great pains to show that even in obeying this "higher command," Brown was not primarily motivated by an obsession with the transcendent or the spiritual; rather, it was Brown's aspiration to live a fully human life which principally distinguished him. Brown, Thoreau insists, well understood the nature of his duties to his fellow men—duties which themselves offered him insight into what it means to live the life of the complete individual. In the end, the highest praise Thoreau could bestow on Brown was not that he was driven by a need to become superhuman or a passion for god-like self-sufficiency, but rather that he "stood up so persistently and effectively for the dignity of human nature, *knowing himself for a man,*" and for this reason Thoreau saluted Brown as the "humanest man in all the country."[13] To be a hero is not to be more than a man, Thoreau insists, but to live and act in a manner befitting the dignity of man's nature. In praising Brown for his "humanness" and in emphasizing that "the hero is commonly the simplest and obscurest of men," Thoreau was working toward a decidedly democratic magnanimity.[14]

In the end, however, it was not against the charge that Brown believed himself to be superhuman that Thoreau had to defend his hero, but rather against the charge that in the execution of his plan the misguided Captain showed himself to be subhuman. Thoreau surely had no difficulty convincing his Concord audience that Brown's intentions were laudable. Rather, it was the means Brown employed—means which revealed the other side of his character, that ferocious wildness and passionate intensity—which so appalled his polite townsmen. Five times in his defense of Brown, Thoreau returned to the charges of "wildness" and "insanity" which had been levied against his great-souled man.[15] In defending Brown against these charges Thoreau found himself vindicating precisely that same wild and spirited side of the soul he had praised in *Walden.* "If one listens to the faintest but constant suggestions of his genius, which are certainly true, he sees not to what extremes, or even insanity, it may lead him; and yet that way, as he grows more resolute and faithful, his road lies," he observed in "Higher Laws" (p. 175). Indeed, Thoreau well understood Emerson when the latter called heroism "an obedience to a secret impulse of an individual's character."[16] In Brown, Thoreau found just such a hero, a well-ordered soul capable of listening to its instinctual genius, and possessed of the self-knowledge required to harness his wildest and most savage passions in the service of the highest and most humane ends.

In his fellow Concordians, Thoreau could only find representatives of a fallen and degenerate race of men who, even if they spent their days "reading their Plutarch a little," couldn't "recognize his magnanimity" when it appeared in their midst.[17] That the citizens of Concord were blind to Brown's greatness because of his savagery suggested to Thoreau how incapable we cultivated and civilized moderns are from an accurate assessment of character. Brown indeed was to Thoreau the most recent incarnation of an ancient character which modern society had already been too successful in rendering extinct, and it was all Thoreau could do to persist in the hope "that this bird might continue to dive here when Concord should be no more."[18]

In *Walden,* however, it was not Brown but a heroic bird of a different feather that captivated Thoreau. Thoreau's reflections on savagery and nobility, the principal themes of "Higher Laws" and "Brute Neighbors," culminate in the passage on the loon that closes the latter chapter (pp. 189-91). In two striking paragraphs, Thoreau provides us with a glimpse into the nature of the experiment he carried out at Walden, as well as an opportunity to observe in action an exemplar of the new magnanimity to which he calls democratic man in *Walden.* First, the loon offers an interesting perspective on Thoreau's understanding of himself, for his identification with the loon runs deep. Of all the neighbors, both animal and human, with whom Thoreau had "solid seasons," it is surely to the loon that he feels most akin. From the moment of our introduction to the loon we cannot miss Thoreau's identification with his stately and solitary mentor. "In the fall the loon (*Colymbus glacialis*) came, as usual, to moult and bathe in the pond, making the woods ring with his wild laughter before I had risen." Thus the loon, not unlike his biographer, has come to this majestic molting ground to engage deliberately in the ritual of purification and renewal for which its waters afford him the necessary solitude.[19] Again like Thoreau, the loon professes his manifest delight in his fortune, through his wild laughter proclaiming to all who will listen and bragging as lustily as he can of the glory of his enterprise. How can we miss the fact that the loon, like Thoreau—and indeed like Abraham before them—is an early riser? Even

before the early rising Thoreau has rubbed the sleep from his eyes, the loon is already about his morning work. Finally, like Thoreau the loon is something of an outlaw; both retreat to the pond to evade their pursuers in town. But even given the deep affinities between Thoreau and the loon, the bird is not simply Walden's reflection of Thoreau himself. In many ways the loon represents not so much the man Thoreau was at Walden as he does the self-aware ideal to which Thoreau aspired in *Walden.* The loon, in achieving that balance of the savage and the heroic, "the good" and "the wild," proves the most magnanimous of the book's characters.

Both the loon's savage and noble sides are on display in Thoreau's portrait, yet his wild side is the more conspicuous of the two. In his discussions of the loon's laughter Thoreau repeatedly emphasizes its wildness. More than any other single feature of the loon, it was this "looning"—"perhaps the wildest sound that is ever heard here"—that commanded Thoreau's immediate respect. Surely it is no accident that Thoreau picked the wildest-sounding creature of the wilderness for his hero. Of all his animal neighbors, the loon forms the sharpest contrast with the comparatively staid conventions of civilized sociability. Yet even though the loon is the most "in touch" with his savage nature of the creatures Thoreau encounters on Walden's shores, there is not in the loon a hint of that brutishness, that passionate sensuality, which Thoreau insists degrades the soul's more noble parts. The loon rather eschews barbarism and displays instead something more like the cultivated savagery of the bean-fields: having retained its primordial wildness and having assigned it to its "due place" in the soul, the loon retains its natural savagery without allowing it to tarnish or threaten its inherent dignity.

The loon's lofty superiority is well displayed in the "pretty game" he plays with Thoreau. In describing his adversary's qualities, Thoreau bedecks the loon with all of the attributes of a formidable classical hero. Physically, the "long-winded" and "unweariable" loon is the embodiment of vigor and vitality, the want of which Thoreau so often laments in modern man. Further, the loon is not just a well-conditioned but a skilled competitor. In his facility of movement both underwater and on the surface, the loon proves himself the rival of each realm's native inhabitants. Finally, the loon is invested with certain arts and intellectual powers, consistently "displaying so much cunning." Indeed, in both physical ability and practical wisdom, the elusive loon proves himself Thoreau's superior. Thoreau, in truth, is decidedly the weaker party in this contest, and both contestants know that, literally and metaphorically, the loon is consistently one step ahead. Similarly, Thoreau is perpetually a step behind in grasping the lesson here at stake. Where Thoreau set out to live deliberately, to struggle with life and wrestle it down, the loon, in contrast, lives with abandon and yet with serenity and dignity. "Let everyone mind his own business, and endeavor to be what he was made," Thoreau implores his fellow moderns (p. 261). But the loon understands the lesson better than its professor. Would that we could live with similarly unruffled breast.

The loon is remarkable for several reasons: it has preserved its primordial wildness, cultivated those skills which make it better adapted to the ends for which it was created, fortified itself with an inherent sense of nobility. But the loon also deserves our attention for a final reason. We have already had occasion to remark that Thoreau can consider no man a hero unless he somehow reaches beyond his particularity and, fixing his sight on the highest things, dedicates himself to their pursuit. The loon, no less than Captain Brown, harkens also to the calling of higher laws. As their game ends, Thoreau recalls that the loon "uttered one of those prolonged howls, as if calling on the god of loons to aid him, and immediately there came a wind from the east and rippled the surface, and filled the whole air with misty rain, and I was impressed as if it were the prayer of the loon answered, and his god was angry with me; and so I left him disappearing far away on the tumultuous surface." In drawing upon his wild and primordial nature to send up a call to the heavens, the solitary loon displays his ability to reach out and establish a bond with the transcendent. A sailing hawk will later do the same, also appearing to Thoreau "to have no companion in the universe,—sporting there alone,—and to need none but the morning and the ether with which it played" (p. 254). Glorying in their independence, such birds have no use for conventional companions; only the heroic void is a fair enough friend for such wild divinities.

Few men will find such ethereal friends sufficient company, Thoreau knows. "The morning wind forever blows, the poem of creation is uninterrupted; but few are the ears that hear it" (p. 70). The same might be said of Thoreau's book. Many have valued it, but as its explicit disclaimers attest and its esoteric style suggests, *Walden* is addressed not to all, but to "poor students"—presumably students who have both the time and the talent to read heroic books as they were meant to be read and to profit from them. Its author is not an orator who would be heard by all in his age but rather a writer who would speak "to all in any age who can *understand* him" (p. 84). To these, Thoreau addressed his teachings on human excellence, leaving it to others to titillate the "broad, flapping American ear" (p. 44).

Finishing *Walden* one is thus left wondering whether the great prophet of the "each-to-his-own" style of independence is as egalitarian as he is often assumed. On the one hand, Thoreau extends the hope and promise of excellence to many. Extraordinary abilities, superior wisdom, grandiose ambition, lofty deeds—this is not

the stuff of heroic excellence, he assures us. Just live your life in accord with your nature, however humble that natural stock might be, and that greatness you so desire will surely follow. Thoreau's is thus an active rather than contemplative excellence, founded, importantly, on reflection and self-examination. Greatness might consist in living in accord with the dictates of one's dual nature, bestial and divine as it is, but the pursuit of greatness must begin with a knowledge of the duality of this nature. In choosing self-knowledge rather than extraordinary actions as the foundation of greatness, Thoreau, modern though he is, reveals his debt to the ancients. Gary Borjesson, *contra* Cavell, has called Thoreau "an ancient in spirit" whose philosophy "allies him most closely with the ancient tradition."[20] This is surely right, but there were many ancients and many ancient traditions. To whom and to which was Thoreau indebted? In founding his understanding of heroic magnanimity on contemplative rather than practical wisdom, Thoreau, I have sought to emphasize, ultimately casts himself in the image of the classical philosopher rather than that of the classical epic hero, finding highest inspiration in neither the valor of Hector nor the steadfastness of Priam, but in Socrates' humble and singular self-knowledge. Thoreau's highest magnanimity, perhaps like Aristotle's, is an intellectual as much as it is an ethical virtue.

Thus we come to one of the most mysterious elements of this strange book. In his especially optimistic moments, Thoreau suggests that many would follow him if only they knew how. "With a little more deliberation in the choice of their pursuits, all men would perhaps become essentially students and observers," Thoreau suggests, and presumably *Walden* propounds a method for such deliberation (p. 82). But Thoreau's "perhaps" is pregnant, for in his more pessimistic moments he expresses decided doubts about the capacities of his fellow men. At such times, far from being faithful to the egalitarian project he seems otherwise to support, Thoreau calls attention to the exclusivity of philosophy, reflecting that "there never was and is not likely soon to be a nation of philosophers, nor am I certain it is desirable that there should be" (p. 47). Thoreau knows that, as alluring as his doctrine of greatness may be, even the best among us—even our most upright men—will not readily undertake its challenge. What prudent and upright citizen of the village will so happily forsake his security for the challenge of living outside the city's walls? "To be a philosopher," Thoreau tells us, "is not merely to have subtle thoughts, nor even to found a school, but so to love wisdom as to live according to its dictates, a life of simplicity, independence, magnanimity, and trust" (p. 14). Like Nietzsche's philosopher and his own loon, Thoreau dedicated himself to an exceptional calling, the harmonizing of the bestial and the divine necessary to live independently and in accord with only the highest laws of his nature and his Nature's God. That all are meant to follow seems unlikely.

Notes

1. Friedrich Nietzsche, *Twilight of the Idols, Or, How to Philosophize with the Hammer,* trans. Richard Polt (Indianapolis: Hackett Press, 1997), p. 5.

2. Henry David Thoreau, *Walden, Or, Life in the Woods* (New York: Vintage, 1991), p. 16. Hereafter all references to *Walden* will be given in the text.

3. Stanley Cavell, *The Senses of Walden* (San Francisco: North Point Press, 1981), p. 13.

4. R. W. B. Lewis notes the irony of applying "the phrase 'Higher Laws' to a chapter that, for all its idealism, talks at some length about fried rats." Lewis, *The American Adam: Innocence, Tragedy and Tradition in the Nineteenth Century* (Chicago: University of Chicago Press, 1955), p. 24.

5. As noted in F. O. Matthiessen, *American Renaissance: Art and Expression in the Age of Emerson and Whitman* (Oxford: Oxford University Press, 1968), p. 169.

6. Of course this theme is not limited to *Walden.* Illustrative is the passage from "Walking" in which Thoreau observes, "Ben Jonson exclaims,—'How near to good is what is fair!' So I would say,—'How near to good is what is *wild*!'" See Thoreau, "Walking," in *The Writings of Henry David Thoreau,* vol. 5 (Boston: Houghton Mifflin, 1906), p. 226. [Hereafter *Writings.*]

7. Quoted in Richard Drinnon, "Thoreau's Politics of the Upright Man," *Massachusetts Review* 4 (1962): 133.

8. Lewis, *The American Adam,* p. 21.

9. Montaigne, "Of experience," in *The Complete Essays of Montaigne,* trans. Donald M. Frame (Stanford: Stanford University Press, 1958), p. 852.

10. Carlyle, *On Heroes, Hero-Worship, and the Heroic in History,* in *The Works of Thomas Carlyle,* vol. 5 (London: Chapman and Hall, 1904), pp. 74-75.

11. "A Plea for Captain John Brown," in *Writings,* vol. 4, p. 413.

12. Ibid., pp. 418, 420.

13. Ibid., pp. 425, 439 (my italics).

14. "Walking," in *Writings,* vol. 5, p. 224.

15. As noted in Richard Bridgman, *Dark Thoreau* (Lincoln: University of Nebraska Press, 1982), p.

249. See "A Plea for Captain John Brown," in *Writings,* vol. 4, pp. 418, 420, 422, 423, 426.

16. Emerson, "Heroism," in *The Complete Works of Ralph Waldo Emerson,* vol. 2 (Boston: Houghton Mifflin, 1904), p. 251.

17. "A Plea for Captain John Brown," in *Writings,* vol. 4, pp. 419, 423.

18. "The Last Days of John Brown," in *Writings,* vol. 4, p. 441.

19. Cavell emphasizes the loon's significance as a symbol of metamorphosis and insanity; see *The Senses of Walden,* pp. 42-43. But like those Concordians who castigate Brown, Cavell fails to note Thoreau's distinction between insanity and heroism.

20. Gary Borjesson, "Sounding Walden's Philosophical Depths," *Philosophy and Literature* 18 (1994): 305-6.

Jason Haslam (essay date fall/winter 2002)

SOURCE: Haslam, Jason. "'They Locked the Door on My Meditations': Thoreau and the Prison House of Identity." *Genre: Forms of Discourse and Culture* 35, no. 3/4 (fall/winter 2002): 449-78.

[*In the following essay, Haslam interprets Thoreau's "Civil Disobedience" within the context of the American penal system. Haslam suggests that, paradoxically, Thoreau's rhetorical strategies in the essay both transcend and validate traditional discourses of incarceration and social control.*]

Henry David Thoreau's **"Civil Disobedience"** offers an explicit interplay between incarceration, politics, and identity. The essay, in which Thoreau explains and justifies his refusal to pay his poll tax—which led to his 1846 arrest—has become one of the most influential political statements of the past one hundred and fifty years. Indeed, it would not be an exaggeration to suggest that Thoreau's discussion of nonviolent resistance has helped to shape the current form of American and world politics. Prison authors and political figures such as Mahatma Gandhi, Martin Luther King, Jr., and the British suffragette Constance Lytton, as well as organizations such as the African National Congress, have cited Thoreau's text as a foundation of their own social philosophies.[1] Despite this range of influences, however, Thoreau's essay and his political thought in general are not without detractors. Indeed, discussing the vast amount of critical study on Thoreau's works, Bob Pepperman Taylor bemoans the fact that Thoreau's political ideas have occasionally been figured more as "a symptom of a problem in the American political tradition—an extreme individualism, say, and moral subjectivism—than as a rich, powerful, and helpful resource to inspire and guide us today" (*America's* [*America's Bachelor Uncle*] 2).

Taylor's assertion that the critical interpretations of Thoreau's work are disjoined from its real-world effects can lead to the conclusion that the writings themselves open up the spectre of opposed viewpoints, that they can exist as both symptoms of problems and as inspirational resources. By examining **"Civil Disobedience"** not only in terms of Thoreau's other work and its philosophical and literary contexts, but also in the context of nineteenth-century penological and punitive discourses, the contradiction between Thoreau's transcendental individualism and his more communal political project becomes clear. By tying together his political rebellion and his transcendental subjectivity, Thoreau's essay actually reproduces—even as it attempts to critique—the ontological foundations of what Foucault calls the "carceral city."[2] Despite this reproduction, however, certain dynamic constructions of identity in **"Civil Disobedience"** allow the reader access to a more positive appropriation of Thoreau's rebellious strategies, one that avoids Thoreau's overly deterministic assertion of himself as an ideal.[3]

I. PRISONS, REFORM, AND ALIENATION

The overt connection between **"Civil Disobedience"** and American punitive practices and penological history has been largely ignored by critics of the essay. Only eleven years prior to Thoreau's one-night confinement in a local jailhouse, de Beaumont and de Tocqueville published in France and America their influential treatise, *On the Penitentiary System in the United States, and its Application in France,* detailing the methods and practices of the American prison systems, and cementing America's reputation as the world leader in penology. Orlando F. Lewis, in his foundational study of American penal history, notes that 1844 marked the formation of the Prison Association of New York (327). Moreover, Lewis defines the years between 1844 and 1846, the actual year of Thoreau's arrest, as an especially significant period during "the formative era of American penology" (323). The highly influential nurse and reformer Dorothea Dix published *Remarks on Prisons and Prison Discipline in the United States* in 1845 and, in 1846, Frankfort on the Main hosted the inaugural international congress of penologists (Lewis [*The Development of American Prisons and Prison Customs*] 323). Prisons had become a center of both American debate and transnational efforts.

As has been noted by contemporary critics, American penological practices were defined during this period by the competing, but in many ways similar, Auburn and Philadelphia systems, which were named respectively after prisons opened in the late-eighteenth and early nineteenth centuries at Auburn, New York, and at Walnut Street in Philadelphia, Pennsylvania. The practices of and theories behind these systems, as Lewis writes, had become ingrained in American penology: "principles had become fairly well established; methods were fairly well fixed; traditions had already formed" (324). While one might not expect the jail in the small town of Concord to resemble closely the larger state institutions, Thoreau found himself in a fairly large building which served not just Concord, but the surrounding county as well. Thoreau biographer Walter Harding writes that the jail was "built of granite, three stories high, sixty-five feet long, thirty-two feet wide, and surrounded with a brick wall about ten feet high, mounted with iron pickets. It had eighteen cells, each twenty-six feet long and eight-and-a-half feet high. Each cell had two double-grated windows" (202-03). The county jail may not be much more than a miniature and more localized replica of the imposing institutions at Auburn and Philadelphia, or the notoriously brutal environment of Sing Sing prison, but the cultural discourses informing the practice of imprisonment were becoming entrenched in the American imagination. In other words, despite the fact that "County and local prisons were almost without exception the centers of [. . .] unsystematic [. . .] confinement of inmates" (Lewis 328), these local jails, like the larger prisons, were seen as sites for the punishment of criminals through confinement. Such punishment, moreover, was understood as a means of deterring further criminal activity (both by the inmate and the general population), and the prisons were, at least theoretically, supposed to be institutions designed to reform the criminal into a civil, socially productive individual.[4]

This construction of reformation and productivity as mutually reinforcing categories was, as John M. Sloop writes, reflected practically in the prison system by the use of "silence and hard labour: silence in order to allow reflection and redemption, labor in order to make the criminal 'productive'" (22). Sloop goes on to note that,

> In early debates about criminal justice, the argument was not over whether prisoners should be silent or work at hard labor but instead, whether their hard labor and silence should be practiced in isolation or in the company of other inmates. Hence, in the Auburn system, the prisoners worked in silent groups, while in the Philadelphia system [. . .], the prisoners lived and worked in silence and separate from each other.

(22)

At the root of the use of silence is the assumption that personal reflection can lead to spiritual redemption and concomitant behavioural changes. De Beaumont and de Tocqueville make this clear when they note that "communication between" prisoners "renders their moral reformation impossible," whereas when a prisoner is "thrown into solitude he reflects. Placed alone, in view of his crime, he learns to hate it" (55). This emphasis on the individual's innate ability to change is further discussed by Foucault as a shift in punitive practices which reflects a change in the conception of subjectivity, away from the notion of an embodied subject, which reacts mostly to externally enforced punishments, to a subjectivity constituted by an internalized notion of social hierarchies and authorities. Foucault writes of the Philadelphia system that "it is not [. . .] an external respect for the law or fear of punishment alone that will act upon the convict but the workings of the conscience itself" (238). While Foucault sees a difference between this system and the Auburn system, which, through communal labour, attempted to "rehabilitate the criminal as a social individual" (238), the rule of silence enforced in both systems places the overarching emphasis on the prisoners' individual abilities to reconstitute themselves as socially acceptable beings.

The actual practice of the prisons belies not only the effectiveness of this rule of silence, but also the general notions of human subjectivity that enable it. While the spectacle and practices of corporal punishment did, indeed, diminish in the nineteenth-century, violent physical punishment did not disappear but was reorganized and shifted in emphasis. Rather than using pain as a direct punishment for crime, the American prison system in Thoreau's time used it in part as a means of enforcing a second order of law—the prison rules, including those of silence and labour. Lewis describes these problems in both the Auburn and Philadelphia systems:

> the unbroken silence in Auburn-type prisons could, in most instances, be maintained only by the inflicting of severe corporal punishments. Floggings became so atrocious in Auburn, and especially in Sing Sing, as to stagger public opinion when finally revealed. [. . .] Prisons on the Pennsylvania plan were not without weaknesses. [. . .] the Eastern Penitentiary was with increasing frequency charged with a higher rate of deaths, disease and insanity than was alleged to occur in prisons of the Auburn type.
>
> (326-27)

Peter Oliver supports this view, writing that, when officials from Upper Canada were reviewing the Auburn plan with American prison officials before setting up Kingston Penitentiary, "nothing was said about how men could be forced to work together twelve to fourteen hours a day, month after month, year after year, without ever speaking to each other, or about the punishments that such a system would require" (112). Rather than following through with the protestant rhetoric of the possibility of the individual's reformation through meditation and reliance on conscience, these prisons in fact brutalized and killed more often than they rehabilitated.[5]

The difference between the prisons' theoretical models and their practices begs the question of what the actual relationships were between prison, society, and the inmates whose identities were being actively re-formed. Rather than reconfiguring the inmates' identities from deviants and criminals to "productive citizens" who have authentic relationships with their essential consciences, these prisons consistently brutalized and alienated prisoners, treating them as objects and tools, pointing to the connections between the American prison and slavery.[6] In the Auburn system especially, prisoners' welfare and moral reform were only important insofar as they were valuable as marketable products. The Auburn system's primary goal was to be economically self-sufficient through the exploitation of inmate labour. H. Bruce Franklin notes that such prisons "rapidly shed much of their early pretense of being places of reformation and became frankly acknowledged as places of cheap mass production" (134-35). Oliver elaborates this point in discussing the Canadian support of the Auburn system: "Because they believed convict labour in a congregate institution would make the facility self-supporting, the organization of such labour took priority over every other consideration. All other disciplinary possibilities, such as the inculcation of religious values and the provision of educational training, received lip service at most" (112). Indeed, the Auburn prisons were so profitable that working groups employed at making the same products as the prisoners held strikes and protests, claiming that the prisons were threatening their livelihoods.[7]

However, even though the Auburn system was motivated to a large degree by the desire for profit, hard labour *was* justified within penological theory as a means of rehabilitation. The prisons run on the Philadelphia system were not nearly as profitable as the Auburn prisons, simply because each prisoner was required to remain completely isolated (thus rendering factory-like work impossible), but even in the Philadelphia system hard labour was still one of the central facets of prison life. In other words, while modern-day, and even some nineteenth-century critics easily separated labour as market relation from labour as means for individual salvation, they were not as easily disjoined within the prison context. Auburn proponents could discuss the possibility (and reality) of prisons as profit-making ventures because hard labour as a "rehabilitative activity" (for white men) was generally unquestioned (Davis, "Race" ["Race, Gender, and Prison History"] 40), as was the rule of silence. In the burgeoning industrial society, and in the established republic that was America, both labour and one's innate ability to "further" oneself went hand in hand.

These contradictions between prison practices and penological theory lead to a paradoxical construction of individuality in relation to social control and punishment. The result of the emphasis on people's innate re-formative ability and the use of labour to aid that ability led to a uniformity of punishment that was embodied in the identical rows upon rows of cells in the panoptic structures of the larger prisons. Prisons became man-factories, churning out supposedly rehabilitated citizens. The stress on the power of the individual thus effectively removed any notions of individualized punishment. Martin J. Wiener phrases this contradiction succinctly:

> The advancing individualism of the age had a dark, an-archic side that few failed to sense. Many traditional limitations upon individual freedom of action were be-ing dismantled, while traditional structures of authority were being challenged. [. . .] As the brutality of the law was lessened, its reach was extended to cover more persons and more forms of behavior. [. . .] In tandem with these changes, punishment was reconstructed so that its discretionary, public, and violent character yielded to forms more calculated to promote the devel-opment of inner behavioural controls. In convicted criminals, this reorientation was accomplished through the uniform and impersonal disciplinary regime of the new prisons [. . .]. At all levels prosecution was made easier, punishment more certain, and penalties more predictable, impersonal, and uniform. The guiding vi-sion of this reconstructed system of criminal justice was that of the responsible individual.

(11)

The power of the single person rapidly degenerates into the uniform treatment of "the people" as a civic body, each member of which reacts to, and can thus be disci-plined by, the universally applicable rulings of the State. Wiener is here discussing Victorian England, but in nineteenth-century America these issues were if any-thing more pronounced, thanks to the democratization of the country and to the growing popularity of the fig-ure of the rugged individual.[8] Since the individual, and not the State, is endowed with "certain inalienable rights," uniform, predictable, and specifically de-individualized forms of punishment are seen as neces-sary in order to avoid violating those rights.

Prisons and the legal system are thus situated within the socio-political spectrum between the emphasis on the power and rights of each person, and the theoretically uniform treatment of the entire populace. The difficulty here is that such uniform treatment, especially when combined with industrial capitalism, leads to one's alienation not only from the product of one's labour, but from society at large. The prisons' treatment of in-mates also results in the effective removal of whatever rights those people could claim. In the prison system, as in slavery, the alienation that Marx described as being the result of the forces of commodification becomes distilled into a brutalizing force that denies the very hu-manity of its victims. As Sloop argues, "The prisoner was constituted in some sense as one element of the communal machine, to be taken, repaired, and made to work again, with no question of what the prisoner him-self thought was best, with no imagination that a crimi-nal could have rights. [. . .] The old penology shaped criminal justice and carried with it the assumption of the prisoner as malleable object" (25). While Sloop sees this reification of prisoners as a holdover from earlier forms of punishment, it can also be read as an indirect result of the nineteenth-century emphasis on individual rights and freedoms. Foucault gestures to this under-standing when he writes that, in the Philadelphia sys-tem, "life," here meaning identity, was "annihilated and begun again" (239). Before prisoners can be rehabili-tated as "properly" functioning individuals with "in-alienable" rights, their identities (as the origin of their improper behaviour) must be wiped clean—ideally by silence and hard labour, and practically by brutal and harsh treatment that is (re)enforced by the assertion that a prisoner has very limited rights, or none at all.

In order to retain personal rights within society, people had to act within (self)regulated bounds of propriety; if certain individuals did not do so, it became the State's responsibility *to the individual* to readjust him or her. And those bounds of propriety generally fall within the social behaviour of the upper classes who, since they are enfranchised and control economic power, can help form the law. Thus Wiener, summarizing arguments made by Michael Ignatieff and David Garland, writes that "penal policy has always been determined by unac-knowledged deep structures of power. The point of criminal policy [. . .] has always been to reproduce ex-isting power relations" (7).[9] From an emphasis on de-mocracy and people's power to reform their behaviour, then, we come to the position from which that propriety is defined, and through which individual actions and rights are limited. Within this limitation, the most brutal functioning of a hierarchical society is also apparent, where people who act outside "proper" norms are treated as less than human, and those who are seen as less than human are automatically subject to the prison system.

II. THOREAU, ALIENATION, AND SOCIETY

With my passing reference to Marx and the coinciding language of economic power, I want to suggest that the brutalizing effects of prison are part and parcel of the alienating forces of nineteenth-century American soci-ety. It is in this regard that Thoreau's texts become cen-tral. **"Civil Disobedience"** and the prison-related con-text of its writing offer an opening for the voice of the prisoner to be incorporated into the histories of the prison and of the larger social framework. Specifically, in conjunction with *Walden* and Thoreau's other writ-ings, **"Civil Disobedience"** provides us with a connec-tion between the policies of the seminal nineteenth-century prison and the socializing forces of the time.

Thoreau, occasionally in very proto-Marxist language, sees the prison's alienating forces as part of the larger structures of enculturation in his society.

"Civil Disobedience" was written as a means of protesting the American war against Mexico, which began on May 11, 1846 as a direct result of Texas' entrance into the Union. The addition of Texas as a slaveholding state was felt, in Len Gougeon's words, to "increase substantially the influence of the South in national politics" (200). Because the addition of Texas was seen as an expansion of slavery and because it inevitably resulted in the war with Mexico, many abolitionists and peace advocates opposed it, both before and after Texas achieved statehood in 1845.[10] The year Thoreau's essay was written, 1848, was also an election year, and therefore a pivotal year in the debates that would result in the passing of the Fugitive Slave Law in 1850. This law allowed for the forced return of slaves who had escaped from the South to the supposed "freedom" of the North. In order to protest the war and the related issue of slavery, Thoreau followed the example of his friend Bronson Alcott, who refused to pay his poll tax and was arrested in 1843. Despite his arrest, Alcott was never jailed, because "Squire Hoar, [Concord]'s leading citizen, paid Alcott's taxes himself rather than permit such a blot on the town escutcheon" (Harding 200). Hoar paid the same tax for Alcott's friend Charles Lane, who also refused to pay (200-01). Thoreau, though, perhaps due more to the fact that he was arrested at the end of the day than to the seriousness of his crime, did spend the night in jail in late July, 1846, and when he was to be released the next day after someone else paid his tax, he tried to refuse to leave (204-205).

Thoreau's transformation of his economic protest into a verbal and written form did not occur for a few years. He first delivered an address on the subject at the Concord Lyceum in 1848, and published the essay in Elizabeth Peabody's first and only issue of the journal *Aesthetic Papers* in May, 1849.[11] Rather than focus on the explicit issues that resulted in his refusal to pay the poll tax, Thoreau instead offers a complex denunciation of what he perceived to be the alienating effects of the government and the economy of his time. He saw the State and the market-driven economy as mutually reinforcing entities that separated people's actions from their consciences in order to exploit fully their labour, thus helping the market and the State, as institutions, to reproduce and perpetuate themselves.

The second paragraph of the essay explains this institutional desire for perpetuation explicitly: "This American government,—what is it but a tradition, though a recent one, endeavoring to transmit itself unimpaired to posterity" (63). The institution of the State itself, rather than its officers or leaders, is portrayed as an active force that uses people to sustain itself. This is most obvious for Thoreau in the use of soldiers:

A common and natural result of an undue respect for law is, that you may see a file of soldiers, colonel, captain, corporal, privates, powder-monkeys and all, marching in admirable order over hill and dale to the wars, against their wills, aye, against their common sense and consciences, which makes it very steep marching indeed, and produces a palpitation of the heart. They have no doubt that it is a damnable business in which they are concerned; they are all peaceably inclined. Now, what are they? Men at all? or small moveable forts and magazines, at the service of some unscrupulous man in power? Visit the Navy Yard, and behold a marine, such a man as an American government can make, or such as it can make a man with its black arts, a mere shadow and reminiscence of humanity, a man laid out alive and standing, and already, as one may say, buried under arms with funeral accompaniments [. . .].

(65-66)

Beginning by tying "law" and the military together under the single force of "an American government," this early passage organizes Thoreau's vision of the relationship between the State and the individual: the State, in effect, erases the existence of individuals, replacing them with a homogenous assemblage of tools and parts. In the act of homogenizing them, it removes their ability to act on their own, to match properly their movements with their wills, thus transforming them from "men" to machines that further the State's aim of retaining the slave territories of Texas.

The gothic imagery at the end of the passage, recalling more of *Frankenstein* than of American politics, culminates the description of the alienated, objectified, State-manufactured person, transforming what Thoreau elsewhere calls "the noblest faculties of the mind" (**"A Plea for Captain John Brown,"** 129) into corpse-like automaton. This description of the objectification of people looks forward to Thoreau's description of slavery in **"Slavery in Massachusetts,"** his direct response to the passing of the Fugitive Slave Law.[12] Thoreau sees slavery as an issue simply beyond debate; as the legally and socially sanctioned transformation of human beings into objects, it is the ultimate evil. He writes that,

If I were seriously to propose to Congress to make mankind into sausages, I have no doubt that most of the members would smile at my proposition, and if any believed me to be in earnest, they would think that I proposed something much worse than Congress had ever done. But if any of them will tell me that to make a man into a sausage would be much worse,—would be any worse, than to make him into a slave,—than it was to enact the Fugitive Slave Law, I will accuse him of foolishness, of intellectual incapacity, of making a distinction without a difference. The one is just as sensible a proposition as the other.

(96-97)

Exposing not only the evils of slavery, but also what he sees as the foolishness of debating the issue, Thoreau's "Swiftian modest proposal" (Kritzberg ["Thoreau, Slavery, and 'Resistance to Civil Government'"] 545) further emphasizes his vision of the State-control of the populace as a dehumanizing and even deadly force. Similar arguments allow him to conclude that the citizens of Massachusetts, through passing the Fugitive Slave Law, have turned themselves into slaves of the State: "There is not one slave in Nebraska; there are perhaps a million slaves in Massachusetts" (91). Further, if people who recognize these forces still defend them, they are not only serving the State to their own detriment, but also actively splitting their own vision of the world—they make distinctions where no difference exists.

Military activity and slavery are only the most obvious of the State's alienating powers and, as such, Thoreau does not spend much time actively engaging them. Instead, most of the rhetorical energy of **"Civil Disobedience"** is devoted to more insidious and pervasive dehumanizing and alienating forces within the dominant culture. Keeping with the essay's general theme of explaining the reasons of his arrest, certain taxes are portrayed as State impositions that, when obeyed, result in a splitting of identity, a severance between thought and deed. This is a form of alienation which for Thoreau is the equivalent of a living death. Addressing an audience which he delineates as, in Henry Golemba's words, "'well disposed' to lead a just and moral life," but "who comply with the state even though they disapprove" of it (144), Thoreau reconstitutes the act of paying the poll tax as instead an attack on the taxpayer himself:

> See what gross inconsistency is tolerated. I have heard some of my townsmen say, "I should like to have them order me out to help put down an insurrection of the slaves, or to march to Mexico—see if I would go;" and yet these very men have each, directly by their allegiance, and so indirectly, at least, by their money, furnished a substitute. [. . .] Thus, under the name of order and civil government, we are all made at last to pay homage to and support our own meanness. After the first blush of sin, comes its indifference; and from immoral it becomes, as it were, *un*moral, and not quite unnecessary to that life which we have made.
>
> (71-72)

The exchange of funds between the taxpayer and the State is grounded on an understanding that those funds will help to perpetuate "order and civil government," but that exchange comes at the expense of the taxpayer's ability to act in accordance with his own beliefs and values. Because the equation of the civil government with social order is unquestioned, acts of immorality are not only tolerated, but seem to become part of the foundation of civil society. This unquestioning tolerance of the State's action results, in Thoreau's logic, in the splitting of identity of the individual taxpayer into a passive figure who speaks against the State and the more active subject who supports it by substituting himself with his tax.

Making a distinction between paying taxes which help to make him "a good neighbor," such as the highway tax, and those that are demanded of him as a "subject" of the State, Thoreau writes that "I do not care to trace the course of my dollar, if I could, till it buys a man, or a musket to shoot one with,—the dollar is innocent,—but I am concerned to trace the effects of my allegiance" (84). By highlighting the action involved in the exchange of money, rather than the existence of money and taxes *per se,* Thoreau opens up a space for the possibility of rebellion through a personal refusal of action, while still allowing for the potential of communal, civic behaviour. Thoreau is less concerned about the act of exchange, as Richard Grusin argues, than he is about the alienation which arises from the separation of the exchange from the value of labour within the market economy.

Thoreau further constructs his critique of society by depicting the relationship between owner and owned as one in which people are subordinated to the very objects they supposedly possess. This is one of the central points behind his experiment at Walden Pond. The general condition of society as Thoreau sees it, however, is in direct opposition to his view of the more authentic and direct mode of living dictated by his experiment. Thoreau also makes this point in **"Civil Disobedience."** He writes that "the rich man [. . .] is always sold to the institution which makes him rich. Absolutely speaking, the more money, the less virtue; for money comes between a man and his objects, and obtains them for him; and it was certainly no great virtue to obtain it" (77). While this passage seems to describe a Marxist form of alienation of worker from product which results in a separation of the individual from his or her authentic self, Thoreau does not construct these relations as part of a capitalist market which exists within a chain in a dialectic of history. Rather, he sees this alienation as a singular fact that must be overcome on an individual level.

A better comparison than Marxism for Thoreau's view of society, figured both in the condition of the mass of men and through the image of the State, is the nineteenth-century disciplinary, penological model. Thoreau argues that society, like the prison, attempts to force those under its control to behave in a docile yet productive fashion, removing personal motivations and restructuring those people as socially acceptable automata. Thoreau's portrayal of the State's current economic forces parallels Wiener's early discussion of penal policies, in that both are seen as being "determined by unacknowledged deep structures of power," while at the same time their point is "to reproduce existing social power relations" (7). Individuals in society, like prisoners, are constructed or reduced to a uniform mob, which is then forced to function within dictated bounds of propriety as a means of allowing the institution, or State, to continue to operate.

Thoreau writes that, given this disciplinary functioning of society, the rule of the majority in a democracy is simply a means of forcing on the minority certain codes of behaviour that, in and of themselves, are not tied to justice or right:

> the people must have some complicated machinery or other, and hear its din, to satisfy that idea of government which they have. Governments show thus how successfully men can be imposed on, even impose on themselves, for their own advantage. [. . .] After all, the practical reason why, when the power is once in the hands of the people, a majority are permitted, and for a long period continue, to rule, is not because they are most likely to be in the right, nor because this seems fairest to the minority, but because they are physically the strongest. But a government in which the majority rule in all cases cannot be based on justice, even as far as men understand it.
>
> (63-65)

The "men" referred to in this passage are not individuals of "integrity," the unalienated few who are not owned by their possessions. They are "the mass of men" and so their need to hear the din of government is itself a result of their alienation by the social structures around them. Grammatically, the pronoun in the clause "their own advantage" refers not to the men who are the objects of the sentence, but to the "Governments," which are the agential subjects. Taylor discusses the agency of the State, picking up on a passage in *Walden* which refers obliquely to the construction of the pyramids, noting that "Thoreau sees our economic life as a new incarnation of an old attempt by nations to assure their place in history by building monuments to themselves" (*America's* 84). Or, as Thoreau puts it in **"Civil Disobedience,"** governments use complex disciplinary powers in order to force men to impose on themselves, allowing governments to gain even more advantage, helping the State "to transmit itself unimpaired to posterity" (63).

Because of the hierarchical structure of the disciplinary mechanisms of society, Thoreau's townsmen, like prison inmates, are subject not just to the amorphous structures of power, but to the people who are placed in the upper echelons of the social, or carceral, system. Just as the warden has the ability to decide *exactly* how the discipline of the prison will be enforced, those in positions of power in the government can control the means through which the subjects of the State are controlled. Because the American government "has not the vitality and force of a single living man [. . .] a single man can bend it to his will" (63). Further, as Donald E. Pease details, such seemingly powerful men were gen-

erally idealized in nineteenth-century American popular culture as powerful orators: "The idealization of the characters of the people's representatives [. . .] assumed the early form of a denial of their representative function and in effect reversed the relation between the leaders and the will they were to represent" (34). These men thus reinforce the separation in the "mass of men" between thought and deed, or between will and government.

In his argument, Thoreau does not, however, allow the leaders of government to become simple scapegoats without whom society would improve. The problem, as he sees it, is with the disciplinary functions of the State itself. Those who are in positions of power, such as "legislators, politicians, lawyers, ministers, and office-holders" (66), turn their intellect to solving the problems that impede the functioning of the State, thus helping the State to continue, and so, Thoreau writes, "as they rarely make any moral distinctions, they are as likely to serve the devil, without intending it, as God" (66). Thoreau's use of the word "intending" (which is italicized in the posthumous version of the essay [*Yankee* [*A Yankee in Canada, with Anti-Slavery and Reform Papers*] 126]) reinforces a sense of separation between thought and deed, an alienation which, he implies, affects those at the top of the social hierarchy as much as those on the bottom.

III. Thoreau and the Transcending of Society

The seeming pervasiveness of society's discipline is, however, superficial. For Thoreau, unlike Marx, the means through which to escape the cycle of discipline, monetary exchange, and alienation is not through a communal effort, but through a personal rejection of the power of social forces. Relying on the American rhetoric of the power of the individual, and on the philosophical basis provided by his transcendentalist circle, Thoreau constructs a strategic economic and political philosophy that evades the discipline of the State and the alienating forces of the market through a construction of an interior subjectivity which simply denies the State access to the individual. Thoreau details this subjectivity by emphasizing the importance of a simplified mode of living, which is tied to a heavily Romanticized relationship with Nature, which in turn allows for a more direct relationship between thought and deed.

Walden is, of course, the prime example of Thoreau's doctrine of simplification. The infamous passage which contains the command, "Simplify, simplify," continues,

> Instead of three meals a day, if it be necessary eat but one; instead of a hundred dishes, five; and reduce other things in proportion. [. . .] The nation itself, with all its so called internal improvements, which, by the way, are all external and superficial, is just such an unwieldy

and overgrown establishment, cluttered with furniture and tripped up by its own traps, ruined by luxury and heedless expense, by want of calculation and a worthy aim, as the million households in the land; and the only cure for it as for them is in a rigid economy, a stern and more than Spartan simplicity of life and elevation of purpose.

(91-92)

The entire nation is here depicted as having its integrity destroyed by the objects of material gain. Beyond this critique, Thoreau makes the connection between the simplified life in which these objects are stripped away and an "elevation of purpose." This transcendental vision is the common perception of Thoreau's experiment at Walden Pond; not only by placing himself at a remove from society, but also by removing the trappings that are valued in that society, Thoreau attempts to construct his life as a Romantic ideal, where his connection to Nature and its "Higher Laws" is unimpeded by the alienation brought about by those objects.

Thoreau explicates the personal nature of his transcendence of the everyday, and his connection to a more Platonic notion of the universal right, in a passage in the "Conclusion" of *Walden*:

> I learned this, at least, by my experiment; that if one advances confidently in the direction of his dreams, and endeavors to live the life which he has imagined, he will meet with a success unexpected in common hours. He will put some things behind, will pass an invisible boundary; new, universal, and more liberal laws will begin to establish themselves around and within him; or the old laws will be expanded, and interpreted in his favor in a more liberal sense, and he will live with the license of a higher order of beings. In proportion as he simplifies his life, the laws of the universe will appear less complex, and solitude will not be solitude, nor poverty poverty, nor weakness weakness.

(323-24)

The self-imposition of simplicity is tied to a more complete understanding of "universal" laws, and both are the direct result of acting "confidently," of not allowing anything to come between one's actions and one's conscience or thought. Economic simplification leads to a removal of the danger of market- or State-enforced alienation, thus erasing the personal and ideological boundaries that "unnaturally," in Thoreau's view, separate the individual from the "truly" universal.

The erasure of these enforced boundaries, and the resulting direct relationship between action and conscience, has an immediate and powerful political effect. Shortly following the above passage, Thoreau writes: "It is a ridiculous demand which England and America make, that you shall speak so that they can understand you. [. . .] I desire to speak somewhere *without* bounds; like a man in a waking moment, to men in their waking

moments" (324). The State, for Thoreau, attempts to enforce not only its laws, but also the means and modes of communication. The restrictions placed by the State on people's actions may result in the alienation of those people, but Thoreau argues that each person can learn to speak "*without* bounds;" individuals can remove themselves from the effects of the market through a concerted simplification of their relationships to market and social forces. This removal, in turn, allows the individual to understand higher and more universal laws than those imposed by the State, and thus allows that person to act, with conscience, against earthly laws.

For this reason, Thoreau writes in **"Civil Disobedience"** that "Action from principle,—the perception and the performance of right,—changes things and relations; it is essentially revolutionary, and does not consist wholly with any thing which was. It not only divides states and churches, it divides families; aye, it divides the *individual,* separating the diabolical in him from the divine" (72). While Barry Wood notes that, for Thoreau, "Doing *something* means [. . .] resolving the polarities through action which carries dichotomies to a new level where they can be synthesized in a higher unity" (109), Thoreau here seems to function less in the dialectical form Wood would impose than through a simple binary construction that opposes the degraded society to the principled individual. The step from one to the other may involve a synthesis of action and conscience, but this connection is perceived as a reinstantiation of a pre-existing natural order, not as a progression to a completely new stage of development. Thus, the person of integrity who has a simplified life and a transcendent connection to the right, cannot simply be a subject of the State, or even an ideal synthesis of the contradictions of society which leads to a new evolution of that society, but is instead a permanent ideal, the Platonic form of the revolutionary figure that is always opposed to the impure social world.

Further describing the transcendental figure, Thoreau writes that, while alienated subjects serve the State with their bodies and others serve with their heads, "A very few, as heroes, patriots, martyrs, reformers in the great sense, and *men,* serve the State with their consciences also, and so necessarily resist it for the most part; and they are commonly treated by it as enemies" (66). Only through a denial of alienation and through a transcendent relationship to the law can people truly be patriots, and such people are resisted by the government which would impose "bounds" on the necessarily boundless, universal conscience. James Duban argues a similar point in discussing Thoreau's relationship to Unitarian thought, writing that Thoreau subordinates "civil authority to the voice of God manifest in private conscience" (213). This subordination allows Thoreau to write that John Brown, who attempted to steal weapons to arm an antislavery revolt, was "a transcendentalist above all, a man of ideas and principles" who was not afraid to act on them (**"A Plea for Captain John Brown,"** 115; Duban ["Conscience and Consciousness"] 219). Transcendentalism can therefore simultaneously involve the individual's removal from and replacement into the State. The removal from the State "divides" the person from its alienating effects, and the replacement becomes the necessary rebellion of the transcendentalist against the State. This dual movement is true for Thoreau even if the rebellion takes the form of a passive example of living the "proper" life, because "It is not so important that many should be as good as you, as that there be some absolute goodness somewhere; for that will leaven the whole lump" (**"Civil"** [**"Civil Disobedience"**] 69).

IV. "MY PRISONS"

"Civil Disobedience" dramatizes the process of the Romantic individual's transcendence beyond the State's disciplinary functions in the section dealing with Thoreau's imprisonment, which he refers to as "My Prisons." Offset in a different typeface in most editions, this section explicates Thoreau's disciplinary social model, and the means through which one can escape its imposed alienation, by inverting contemporary penological thought on imprisonment, meditation, and reform.

Thoreau introduces the offset section by describing his arrest, and by creating an explicit synecdochic relationship between the prison and the State as a whole. He writes that "I have paid no poll-tax for six years. I was put into a jail once on this account," which leads him to the conclusion that "the State never intentionally confronts a man's sense, intellectual or moral, but only his body, his senses" (79-80). Thoreau identifies the causal relationship between the tax and the jail, making them both parts of the physical imposition of the State. His continuing references to the State as an alienating force which attempts to deal with people only as physical objects are again stated here, directly reinforcing a previous description of the jail cell: "as I stood considering the walls of solid stone, two or three feet thick, the door of wood and iron, a foot thick, and the iron grating which strained the light, I could not help being struck with the foolishness of that institution which treated me as if I were mere flesh and blood and bones, to be locked up" (80). Introducing the central prison section, this passage sets up the terms on which Thoreau will critique his night in jail. Specifically, the prison, as a figure of the State, attempts to deal with Thoreau as an alienated, purely embodied tool which is in need of correction. Thoreau, as the transcendent individual, sees himself as being beyond such punishment.

Moving from the State's ineffective attempts to punish him, the central description of Thoreau's night in jail details a specific moment of transcendence which ironi-

cally duplicates the reformative rhetoric of the nineteenth-century prison system. This system, especially as perceived in the Philadelphia-style prisons, relied on the assumption that personal reflection could lead to a form of spiritual redemption, which would lead to changes in behaviour that would make the prisoner more amenable to social life. Thoreau plays off of this notion by constructing a moment of personal reflection that *does* lead to a spiritual redemption, but that simultaneously places him at odds with the general social world. Thoreau, after his cell mate blows out the light, felt that "It was like travelling into a far country, such as I had never expected to behold, to lie there for one night." He continues,

> It seemed to me that I never had heard the town-clock strike before, nor the evening sounds of the village; for we slept with the windows open, which were inside the grating. It was to see my native village in the light of the middle ages, and our Concord was turned into a Rhine stream, and visions of knights and castles passed before me. They were the voices of old burghers that I heard in the streets. I was an involuntary spectator and auditor of whatever was done and said in the kitchen of the adjacent village-inn,—a wholly new and rare experience to me. It was a closer view of my native town. I was fairly inside of it. I never had seen its institutions before. This is one of its peculiar institutions; for it is a shire town. I began to comprehend what its inhabitants were about.
>
> (82)

The prison cell does indeed become a place of reflection, but instead of a purely internal vision of the impropriety of his past "criminal" actions, Thoreau's perspective immediately widens, giving him an intimate view of his town and his society. This view is also one in which the society is primitivized, looking backward both temporally and geographically to pre-imperial Europe, a past that America supposedly revolted against. In other words, while privately reflecting in his prison cell, Thoreau has a condemnatory vision of the degraded character of the outside society.

This vision is a dramatization of Thoreau's transcendentalism, which permits him to condemn the State based on his own Romantic connection to and understanding of higher laws. His censure of society is clarified in the penultimate main paragraph of the prison section:

> When I came out of prison,—for some one interfered, and paid the tax,—I did not perceive that great changes had taken place on the common, such as he observed who went in a youth, and emerged a tottering and gray-headed man; and yet a change had to my eyes come over the scene,—the town, and State, and country,—greater than any that mere time could effect. I saw yet more distinctly the State in which I lived. I saw to what extent the people among whom I lived could be trusted as good neighbors and friends; that their friend-

ship was for summer weather only; that they did not greatly purpose to do right [. . .].

(83)

Thoreau employs the rhetoric of the reformatory practice of the prison to condemn the brutalizing and alienating effects of the disciplinary institution, which he sees at work in the whole of society. Thus, he uses the institution of the prison itself to reverse the judgmental gaze. His reflective time in prison does change his outlook on his position in society but, rather than reconstruct him as a productive citizen, it highlights for him the hypocrisy and untrustworthiness of his neighbors, and his country as a whole. A. Robert Caponigri summarizes the philosopher's transcendent, judgmental position, writing that, "To the degree to which" a person achieves this position "he becomes the lawgiver to himself, not subservient to any outer law" (545). Thoreau's prison vision defines the State and its law-abiding citizens as the true criminals, while Thoreau becomes the transcendental patriot.

This reversal, indicative of Thoreau's writing, is evident in his strategic use of the "happy prison" motif, wherein the prison cell becomes an idealized space of freedom. He writes, "I saw that, if there was a wall of stone between me and my townsmen, there was a still more difficult one to climb or break through, before they could get to be as free as I was" (80). Discussing the late eighteenth-century prison writing of British radical John Thelwall, Julia M. Wright notes, "While Victor Brombert suggests that the 'happy prison' in Romantic literature arises from the identification of solitude with transcendence and creativity, the prison [in Thelwall's works] is a 'happy' one insofar as it functions as the site of defiance, and reveals the limits of the state's power" (2).[13] While Thoreau's essay constructs the prison as "happy" for reasons similar to Thelwall's, his reversal of the prison's reformatory rhetoric implies that the State itself is precisely what enables this rebellion, by "stripping" the prisoner of all but his necessities. The construction of the second wall between Thoreau and his neighbors—obviously a moral or transcendental wall—is available to Thoreau precisely because the prison cell offers the preconditions for a transcendental rediscovery of one's own conscience. Like his life at Walden, his prison life is stripped of all but its essentials, "Food and Shelter" (*Walden* 12). And just as his shack is devoid of an excess of furniture that would "trap" its owner, the prison cell is "the whitest, most simply furnished, and probably the neatest apartment in the town" (*Walden* 66; "Civil" 81). The cell offers a life free of the material objects and market relations, which Thoreau sees as the precondition for his transcendent moments at Walden Pond.

V. Thoreau as State

Thoreau's history of "My Prisons" therefore seems to dramatize both the State's methods of alienation and its

impotence in the face of transcendent truths, by ironically deploying the rhetoric of reformation that lies behind the State's prisons. Is Thoreau's use of this rhetoric actually ironic, however? The reformative foundations of the original Philadelphia system and Thoreau's notion of the individual's ability to comprehend and act on universal truths are in many ways similar. Both grow out of a protestant notion of each person's ability to understand and receive divine guidance, and both the prisons and his writings are posited as guides toward a better society. Given this, Thoreau's use of the prison cell as a space of conversion may be ironic in that he uses it to attack the very State that arrests him, but on a philosophical level, Thoreau's advice to "simplify, simplify" in order to reach a more authentic relation to the self actually runs parallel to the prison project. The question that needs to be posed is whether Thoreau's philosophical project, like the prison system, results in the alienation and brutalization of its audience members instead of their reformation.

Many so-called revisionist readings of Thoreau and of the American Romantics in general support an affirmative answer to this question. Grusin discusses such interpretations of Thoreau's economic critique, noting that they "have suggested that the economy Thoreau practiced at Walden was not independent of the ideology of American capitalism but made in its image" (30).[14] Michael T. Gilmore's conclusion about *Walden* provides perhaps the clearest statement on the revisionist position. Gilmore writes that, in Thoreau's critique,

> market society engenders a conflation of history with nature. By presenting its limited, time-bound conventions as eternal, the existing order in effect places itself outside time and beyond the possibility of change. Although Thoreau rigorously condemns his society's "naturalizing" of itself in this fashion, he can be charged with performing a version of the same process on his own life by erasing history from *Walden* and mythologizing his experiment at the pond.

(44-45)

Gilmore argues that Thoreau's rhetorical and compositional methods in *Walden* duplicate the alienating forces of society from which he is avowing to remove himself. By setting up his experiment as an ideal example, Gilmore writes, Thoreau's text assumes the ideological functions of the market. Even critics who set themselves against the revisionist readings occasionally find themselves rehearsing the difficulties these other critics highlight. Despite writing that radicals "dislike Thoreau's individualism" (*Bachelor* [*America's Bachelor Uncle*] 126), Taylor states that, while Thoreau "parodies our political economy in the great first chapter of *Walden,* he is unable to escape the type of self-conscious and exploitative manipulation of the world that he criticizes capitalism for;" because of this, "Thoreau did not solve the problem of how to discipline a free will, how to remain free and yet not fall prey to the vice of pride" ("Henry" ["Henry Thoreau, Nature, and American Democracy"] 60; 61). This vice of pride, or individualism, one might say, is closely related to Gilmore's conclusions about Thoreau's naturalization of his own life.

I argue that we must expand these conclusions. The problem of the reduplication of the dominant culture in Thoreau's writings, be it in terms of economics or politics, is embedded at the very root of Thoreau's worldview, in his construction of his own identity as the basis from which his philosophy evolves. At the beginning of *Walden*, Thoreau defends his use of first-person address, writing: "In most books, the *I*, or first person, is omitted; in this it will be retained. [. . .] We commonly do not remember that it is, after all, always the first person that is speaking" (3). While the wording of this defense may seem to suggest that Thoreau is setting up a subjective narrative, where the viewpoints expressed are only defensible as one person's opinion, Thoreau quickly relates how his viewpoint is a universal one that allows him access to all others. First, he turns his first-person account into one that can speak *for* the reader, offering, "I would fain say something, not so much concerning the Chinese and Sandwich Islanders as you who read these pages, who are said to live in New England; something about your condition" (4). Moving from a focus on his own voice, on his own opinion, Thoreau here elaborates that voice to include the specific readers from his region—his "simple and sincere account" (3) of his life, he implies, will have immediate and important consequences for others.

Thoreau's expanding voice does not stop there. After he enumerates the cost of his shack, he writes, "If I seem to boast more than is becoming, my excuse is that I brag for humanity rather than for myself; and my shortcomings and inconsistencies do not affect the truth of my statement" (49). Despite problems with what he writes, his boasting is still universally true. While this is certainly one of the passages that would cause Taylor's radicals to cringe, Thoreau's unquestioning assumption of the universal applicability of his particular experiences is not simply the braggadocio of an unabashed egotist. Rather, Thoreau is bringing to the surface the ontological assumptions that are inherent in his transcendentalism. Caponigri details the transcendent moment as one that "lends to the vision and to the utterance [. . .] of the individual a range and authority far outreaching his personal capacity; indeed it makes these utterances normative for all men" (544). For Thoreau, everyone has the ability to transcend the particular, to understand the universal laws that are applicable to "all men."[15]

As Sidonie Smith argues, this neo-Platonic Romantic individual is the foundation of a democratic subject which "can claim equal access to the universally human" (*Subjectivity* [*Subjectivity, Identity, and the Body*] 9). Smith goes on to detail the central difficulty with this identity:

> Yet within this claim there is implicit a hierarchy wherein what is and is not appropriate, at any given juncture, to the universal subject gets staked out. Founded on exclusionary practices, this democratic self positions on its border [. . .] that which becomes identified culturally as other, exotic, unruly, irrational, uncivilized, regional, or paradoxically unnatural.
>
> (9-10)

What other critics have termed Thoreau's radical individualism, or what George Hochfield calls an "intense" egotism, the "maggot in Thoreau's head" (435), is instead his own take on the naturalization of the liberal, humanist identity. The problem with such a naturalization, as Smith points out, is that it is grounded on an exclusion of the "other," which generally denotes, in this context, anyone who is not white, male, and of a certain class. As Thomas Augst writes, these conclusions are also tied to the argument that "concepts of self-culture and character were key terms in the formation of a middle-class hegemony, which lent moral justification to patterns of class formation and acquisitive individualism" (89-90).[16] The "others" left out of such formations are then perceived as being lower on the hierarchical valuation of humanity. Ignatieff places this structuring principle in the prison context, writing that nineteenth-century American penal and criminal policy arises from "an increasing intolerance towards 'deviant' minorities" which was itself a characterization of "the advent of democracy" (212). Thus the supposedly democratic, universally accessible, transcendent subject that Thoreau constructs can be seen as a form of further privileging the white, rich, and male subject.

The grounding of Thoreau's transcendent identity and its relation to a specifically racial practice of othering is explicit in **"Civil Disobedience."**[17] After he "came out of prison," having realized the degradation of his townspeople and that they "did not greatly purpose to do right," Thoreau claims "that they were a distinct race from me by their prejudices and superstitions, as the Chinamen and Malays are" (83). Thoreau only recognizes his new and higher position against the backdrop of a racist depiction of the "mass of men;" Thoreau is, indeed, made distinct by "prejudices."[18]

In addition to the construction of an "other" against whom he contrasts his own idealized identity, Thoreau also occasionally describes the transcendental itself in hierarchical terms. Indeed, Thoreau's transcendentalism can be seen to be based on comparisons that exclude and vilify while simultaneously claiming universality. In **"Civil Disobedience,"** these hierarchical implications of Thoreau's transcendentalism are figured in the heavily symbolic ending of the dramatized prison section:

> I was put into jail as I was going to the shoemaker's to get a shoe which was mended. When I was let out the next morning, I proceeded to finish my errand, and, having put on my mended shoe, joined a huckleberry party, who were impatient to put themselves under my conduct; and in half an hour,—for the horse was soon tackled,—was in the midst of a huckleberry field, on one of our highest hills, two miles off; and then the State was nowhere to be seen.

(83-84)

This passage, I argue, must be read as a symbolic pairing with the transcendent moment in the jail cell, when Thoreau sees his town with a "closer view" than ever before, thus gaining a new insight into its functioning and its institutions. That insight immediately places him in a position from which to judge and condemn the State, and therefore remove himself from its power. That movement is figured spatially in this passage, with Thoreau climbing "one of our highest hills," a vantage point from which he escapes the panoptic gaze of the prison and the State. This removal, however, is decidedly not constructed in purely individual terms. Thoreau's exit from prison, his escape from the alienating forces of society, is directly paired to his control over others. The position Thoreau constructs for himself is not the "point of vantage" that lies "at the redemptive margin," the liminal space between society and the wilderness which John Hildebidle argues that *Walden* lauds ("Thoreau at the Edge" 349), but is instead a removal from the State's power, from the town's institutions, and a replication of that power in the figure of Thoreau. People wait for him, "impatient to put themselves under my conduct." Given the energy Thoreau devotes to constructing his audience at the beginning of the essay (as Golemba details), this image of people listening to and following Thoreau's lead should be read as an intradiegetic representation of the "proper" behaviour of the audience. Like the townspeople, the audience members should be impatient to follow Thoreau, reject the State, and gain a more authentic connection to themselves through Nature (symbolized by the huckleberries which, as Thoreau notes in *Walden,* lose their "ambrosial and essential part" when taken to town [173]).[19]

The difficulty with this self representation arises from the problems with the exclusionary nature of Thoreau's "universal" transcendentalism. Moving from the town to the hill, Thoreau's huckleberry party, and any converts in his audience, can be seen as merely exchanging one dominating power for another. Thoreau's inability to see the State from the hill is a duplication of his critique of "Statesmen and legislators, standing so completely within the institution" that they "never distinctly and nakedly behold it" (86). This reading holds espe-

cially true since the essay ends with Thoreau asserting that there is "a still more perfect and glorious State, which also I have imagined, but not yet anywhere seen" (90). Thoreau cannot see the extant State, because he is capable of—and is wrapped up in—the creation of a State of his own, which his transcendent nature allows him to encapsulate, and in a sense rule, in his imagination. And, since Thoreau's transcendentalist rhetoric mirrors the prison's alienating, reformatory rhetoric of "universal" codes of propriety, which in turn support the reproduction of the means of production for the dominant culture, Thoreau's political statement replicates the carceral matrix more than it rebels against that system. D. A. Miller summarizes this problem when he writes that "the difference between liberal and carceral camps is not substantive" (220).

I began this paper with a brief enumeration of the positive political influence that Thoreau's essay has had. To conclude with the assertion that Thoreau's rebellion is a stand-in for State power and carceral discipline would seem to ignore his actual historical impact. The disparity here arises from the two distinct ways in which **"Civil Disobedience"** and Thoreau's opus can be read—both of which are enabled by Thoreau's textual construction of his identity. On the one hand, he becomes the ideal that dictates to people what they "should be," thus reinforcing the dominant values and forces of the State. Olaf Hansen defends Thoreau's construction of himself as authority: "The voice of authority that assumes the burden of setting things right cannot be a disembodied one; it needs an agent" (128). Nevertheless, Hansen's assertion that this mantle of authority is a self-sacrifice in which "Thoreau adopted [. . .] the role of the victim" in a Christ-like attempt to save others rings false given Thoreau's more than occasionally derogatory depiction of those others, and given the ontological baggage of his transcendentalism. On the other hand, Thoreau can be seen as constructing a fictional persona toward which people can aspire, and which can be used strategically as a means of instigating political action. This form of reading allows Hildebidle, in *Thoreau: A Naturalist's Liberty,* to transmute *Walden*'s contradictions into a self-reflexive criticism, and Thoreau's "Transcendental egotism" into a form of "inspiration and reassurance" that Thoreau's audience "may draw from being shown that the goal is attainable" (109). What the goal is, exactly, is left up to those who are "inspired." As a strategic textual example, "Thoreau" is not only separated from the rhetorically persuasive, domineering, and socio-economically specific position of the historical Thoreau, but also from the historically oppressive ontological ramifications of the transcendent identity. Using "Thoreau" as an example, other authors can replace his "universal" laws with different ones, and thereby empty out the danger of replicating the oppressive hierarchies that his works imply.

These strategic uses of Thoreau's essay need to remain aware, however, of the possibility that the ideals or laws they espouse may engage in the same problematic motion of reproduction as Thoreau's essay. While Hildebidle is right in noting that Thoreau does use some contradictory statements intentionally as a means of critique (such as the reversal of criminals and law-abiding citizens), less easy to solve is the overarching contradiction between Thoreau's exclusionary and hierarchical transcendentalism and his political critique of the exclusionary and hierarchical disciplinary functions of the State. Both readings of "Thoreau," one in which he is figured as the domineering, State-like figure, and the other that uses "Thoreau" strategically as idealized textual example, are viable and do not necessarily easily meld together. As Richard F. Teichgraeber III writes about Thoreau's conception of the market, one must recognize that "a number of different paths lead into Thoreau's thinking" (46).[20] The contradictory axes of interpretation arising from these paths are what allow both the revisionist and non-revisionist camps of opinion in Thoreau criticism to continue. Indeed, prison authors often must deal with the difficulty of constructing an account of a rebellion from within prison which functions as an example, but which also seeks not to reproduce the rhetoric, hierarchical ontology, and alienating power of prison. Because this difficulty is such a central one, recognizing the problem in **"Civil Disobedience"** should not cause us to cast the essay aside; nor should we ignore the problem altogether. Rather, recognizing this problem allows readers to appreciate the political and theoretical centrality of Thoreau's attempt, while also highlighting the difficulty—for other prison writers and for people at large—of escaping the carceral matrix.

Notes

1. On Thoreau's political influence on these and other figures, see, for example, Frances B. Dedmond, Stanley Edgar Hyman, Michael Meyer, and Brent Powell. The debate concerning the title of Thoreau's essay rages on. In the standard Princeton edition of [Thoreau's] *Reform Papers,* Wendell Glick reverts to "Resistance to Civil Government," the title used in the essay's original 1849 publication, rather than the still more commonly known title, "Civil Disobedience," which was used in the posthumous publication *A Yankee in Canada, with Anti-Slavery and Reform Papers* (1866). Fritz Oehlschlaeger, however, makes a convincing case not only for the adoption of the posthumous title, but also for the reintroduction of certain material from the 1866 edition which Glick omits. For the ease of referencing, my page citations will be to the standard Princeton edition; however, in keeping with Oehlschlaeger's conclusions, I will be using "Civil Disobedience" as the title.

2. Foucault defines the "carceral city" as a society in which the prison "is not alone, but linked to a whole series of 'carceral' mechanisms which seem distinct enough—since they are intended to alleviate pain, to cure, to comfort—but which all tend, like the prison, to exercise a power of normalization" (307-08).

3. In my longer project on nineteenth- and twentieth-century prison writings (in progress), I argue that King's "Letter from Birmingham Jail" engages, in part, in precisely this form of positive appropriation of Thoreau's text.

4. For discussions of contemporary perceptions of prisons and penitentiaries in North America and Europe, see Lewis (esp. 323-45), Peter Oliver (esp. 105-29), and Martin J. Wiener (1-45).

5. Angela Y. Davis has recently argued that "the penitentiary as an institution for the reformation of criminals was aimed largely at white men," while women and people of color were "excluded from the moral realm within which punishment in the penitentiary was equated with rehabilitation" ("Race" ["Race, Gender, and Prison History"] 37; 38). She then argues that it is when "black people began to be integrated into southern penal systems in the aftermath of the Civil War—and as the penal system became a system of penal servitude—[that] the punishment associated with slavery became integrated into the penal system" ("Race" 39). Davis' assertion of the racialized and gendered nature of assumptions of prison reform are beyond dispute, as are her conclusions regarding the violence perpetrated on prisoners in the postbellum period. However, as both Lewis and Oliver note, the theory of labor as reform in American penitentiaries was belied by its violent practices long before the Civil War. Despite the justifying rhetoric of prison proponents, the earlier prisons did in fact systemically engage in physical punishments which were explicitly related to prisoners' productivity and labour rather than rehabilitation.

6. For discussions of the relationship between slavery and the development of the American prison, see, for example, Davis ("From the Prison" ["From the Prison of Slavery to the Slavery of Prison"] and "Race"), H. Bruce Franklin, and Adam Jay Hirsch (71-111).

7. Like Franklin, Lewis states that, in the Auburn-style prisons such as Sing Sing, "Efforts at reformation were sacrificed to the struggle of the State to make money out of the prisons" (327). Lewis (130-46) and Foucault (239-44) further detail the nineteenth-century market relationships between prison labourers and outside workers.

8. The rugged individual was figured not only in the writings of such authors as Emerson and Thoreau,

but also through the popular image of the frontiersman. See Donald E. Pease (3-48) on the constitution of representative figures of the individual in the nineteenth-century US.

9. Garland argues, for instance, that "penal institutions are functionally, historically and ideologically conditioned by numerous other social relations and agencies, which are, in turn, supported and conditioned by the operation of penal institutions" (*Punishment and Welfare* viii).

10. Gougeon provides a more detailed summary of the issues surrounding the inclusion of Texas, the war with Mexico, and their historical relationship to Thoreau (201-02).

11. On the reception of *Aesthetic Papers,* and specifically of Thoreau's essay, see Steven Fink (206-10).

12. For a description of the events and decisions leading up to the Fugitive Slave Law, and Thoreau's dealings with it, see Barry Kritzberg (540 ff.).

13. Wright's reference is to Brombert (68-69).

14. Grusin refers explicitly to the readings of Thoreau done by Michael T. Gilmore and Sacvan Bercovitch.

15. Caponigri goes on to somewhat overstate, at least for Thoreau, the mediational aspect of the transcendental philosopher: "This self-reliance is not a form of egotism. The transcendentalist is self-dependent precisely because he is not an egotist. He is self-reliant because he humbly recognizes the universal truth which speaks in him and through him, of which he is the bearer but not the source" (545).

16. Augst refutes these claims as they are applied to Emerson. He writes that revisionist readings of Emerson that would situate his philosophy as part of the matrix of oppression "are emblematic of the profound difficulty that modern scholars have in appreciating the degree to which general knowledge about character, of the sort retailed by Emerson in his later lectures, constituted a practical civic pedagogy concerned with the [. . .] challenges of democracy under modern capitalism" (90). Augst's conclusions about the "practical" nature of this civic pedagogy are largely not applicable to Thoreau, as evidenced by the generally negative contemporary reviews of *Walden.* For reprints of reviews of *Walden* and *A Week on the Concord and Merrimack Rivers,* see Myerson (*Emerson* [*Emerson and Thoreau*] 341-415); also see Henry Abelove's excellent essay on Thoreau and queer politics for a summation of some of the reviews (17-19).

17. This racial othering is also apparent in the section of *Walden* dealing with Thoreau's Irish-immigrant neighbour, John Field (204-09). Field is characterized by Thoreau in ways that resonate strongly with David R. Roediger's conclusion that "In the mid nineteenth century, the racial status of Catholic Irish incomers became the object of fierce, extended debate. The 'simian' and 'savage' Irish only gradually fought, worked, and voted their ways into the white race in the US" (*Towards* [*Towards an Abolition of Whiteness*] 184). On the racialized identification of the Irish in nineteenth-century America, also see, for example, Noel Ignatiev and Roediger (*Wages* [*The Wages of Whiteness*]).

18. Anita Goldman's claim that Thoreau, in this passage, claims "a status within a race which is distinct from the white people among whom he lives," and that this status "allows him to speak on behalf of the oppressed" (245) is belied by the grammatical structure of the passage. The "Chinamen and Malays" are equated to Thoreau's neighbors, not to Thoreau.

19. For discussions of this passage of *Walden,* see Gilmore and Grusin.

20. Indeed, Hildebidle recognizes these multiple interpretive possibilities opened up in Thoreau's text when he notes early in his work that Thoreau "can be labeled only partially and tentatively" (*Thoreau* 5).

Works Cited

Abelove, Henry. "From Thoreau to Queer Politics." *Yale Journal of Criticism* 6.2 (1993): 17-27.

Augst, Thomas. "Composing the Moral Senses: Emerson and the Politics of Character in Nineteenth-Century America." *Political Theory* 27.1 (1999): 85-120.

De Beaumont, Gustave, and Alexis de Tocqueville. *On the Penitentiary System in the United States and its Application in France.* Trans. Francis Lieber. 1833. Carbondale: Southern Illinois UP, 1964.

Bercovitch, Sacvan. *The American Jeremiad.* Madison: U of Wisconsin P, 1978.

Brombert, Victor. "The Happy Prison: A Recurring Romantic Metaphor." *Romanticism: Vistas, Instances, Continuities.* Ed. David Thorburn and Geoffrey Hartman. Ithaca: Cornell UP, 1973. 62-79.

Caponigri, A. Robert. "Individual, Civil Society, and State in American Transcendentalism." *Critical Essays on American Transcendentalism.* Ed. Philip F. Gura and Joel Myerson. Boston: G. K. Hall, 1982. 541-60.

Davis, Angela Y. "From the Prison of Slavery to the Slavery of Prison: Frederick Douglass and the Convict

Lease System." *The Angela Davis Reader.* Ed. Joy James. Oxford: Blackwell, 1998. 74-95.

———. "Race, Gender, and Prison History: From the Convict Lease System to the Supermax Prison." *Prison Masculinities.* Ed. Don Sabo, Terry A. Kupers, and Willie London. Philadelphia: Temple UP, 2001. 35-45.

Dedmond, Francis B. "'Many Things to Many People': Thoreau in His Time and Ours." *Forum* 30.3 (1989): 60-69.

Duban, James. "Conscience and Consciousness: The Liberal Christian Context of Thoreau's Political Ethics." *New England Quarterly* 60.2 (1987): 208-22.

Fink, Steven. *Prophet in the Marketplace: Thoreau's Development as a Professional Writer.* Princeton: Princeton UP, 1992.

Foucault, Michel. *Discipline and Punish: The Birth of the Prison.* Trans. Alan Sheridan. New York: Vintage, 1979.

Franklin, H. Bruce. *The Victim as Criminal and Artist: Literature from the American Prison.* Oxford: Oxford UP, 1978.

Garland, David. *Punishment and Welfare: A History of Penal Strategies.* Aldershot: Gower, 1985.

Gilmore, Michael T. *American Romanticism and the Marketplace.* Chicago: U of Chicago P, 1985.

Golemba, Henry. *Thoreau's Wild Rhetoric.* New York: New York UP, 1990.

Gougeon, Len. "Thoreau and Reform." *The Cambridge Companion to Henry David Thoreau.* Ed. Joel Myerson. Cambridge: Cambridge UP, 1995. 194-214.

Grusin, Richard. "Thoreau, Extravagance, and the Economy of Nature." *American Literary History* 5.1 (1993): 30-50.

Hansen, Olaf. *Aesthetic Individualism and Practical Intellect: American Allegory in Emerson, Thoreau, Adams, and James.* Princeton: Princeton UP, 1990.

Harding, Walter. *The Days of Henry Thoreau: A Biography.* 1970. New York: Dover, 1982.

Hildebidle, John. *Thoreau: A Naturalist's Liberty.* Cambridge: Harvard UP, 1983.

———. "Thoreau at the Edge." *Prose Studies* 15.3 (1992): 344-65.

Hirsch, Adam Jay. *The Rise of the Penitentiary: Prisons and Punishment in Early America.* New Haven: Yale UP, 1992.

Hochfield, George. "Anti-Thoreau." *Sewanee Review* 96.3 (1988): 433-43.

Hyman, Stanley Edgar. "Henry Thoreau in Our Times." *The Recognition of Henry David Thoreau: Selected Criticism Since 1848.* Ed. Wendell Glick. Ann Arbor: U of Michigan P, 1969. 334-51.

Ignatieff, Michael. *A Just Measure of Pain: The Penitentiary in the Industrial Revolution, 1750-1850.* New York: Pantheon, 1978.

Ignatiev, Noel. *How the Irish Became White.* New York: Routledge, 1995.

Kritzberg, Barry. "Thoreau, Slavery, and 'Resistance to Civil Government.'" *Massachusetts Review* 30.4 (1989): 535-65.

Lewis, Orlando F. *The Development of American Prisons and Prison Customs: 1776-1845.* 1922. Montclair: Patterson Smith, 1967.

Meyer, Michael. *Several More Lives to Live: Thoreau's Political Reputation in America.* Contributions in American Studies 29. Westport: Greenwood, 1977.

Miller, D. A. *The Novel and the Police.* Berkeley: U of California P, 1988.

Myerson, Joel, ed. *Emerson and Thoreau: The Contemporary Reviews.* American Critical Archives 1. Cambridge: Cambridge UP, 1992.

Oehlschlaeger, Fritz. "Another Look at the Text and Title of Thoreau's 'Civil Disobedience.'" *ESQ* 36.3 (1990): 239-54.

Oliver, Peter. *Terror to Evil Doers: Prisons and Punishments in Nineteenth-Century Ontario.* Toronto: U of Toronto P, 1998.

Pease, Donald E. *Visionary Compacts: American Renaissance Writings in Cultural Context.* Madison: U of Wisconsin P, 1987.

Powell, Brent. "Henry David Thoreau, Martin Luther King Jr., and the American Tradition of Protest." *Magazine of History* 9.2 (1995): 26-29.

Roediger, David R. *Towards an Abolition of Whiteness: Essays on Race, Politics, and Working Class History.* London: Verso, 1994.

———. *The Wages of Whiteness: Race and the Making of the American Working Class.* London: Verso, 1991.

Sloop, John M. *The Cultural Prison: Discourse, Prisoners, and Punishment.* Tuscaloosa: U of Alabama P, 1996.

Smith, Sidonie. *Subjectivity, Identity, and the Body: Women's Autobiographical Practices in the Twentieth Century.* Bloomington: Indiana UP, 1993.

Taylor, Bob Pepperman. *America's Bachelor Uncle: Thoreau and the American Polity.* Lawrence: UP of Kansas, 1996.

———. "Henry Thoreau, Nature, and American Democracy." *Journal of Social Philosophy* 25.1 (1994): 46-64.

Thoreau, Henry David. "Civil Disobedience" ["Resistance to Civil Government"]. Thoreau, *Reform [Reform Papers]* 63-90.

———. "A Plea for Captain John Brown." Thoreau, *Reform* 111-38.

———. *Reform Papers.* Ed. Wendell Glick. *Writings of Henry D. Thoreau.* Princeton: Princeton UP, 1973.

———. "Slavery in Massachusetts." Thoreau, *Reform* 91-109.

———. *Walden.* Ed. J. Lyndon Shanley. *Writings of Henry D. Thoreau.* Princeton: Princeton UP, 1971.

———. *A Yankee in Canada, with Anti-Slavery and Reform Papers.* 1892. New York: Greenwood, 1969.

Teichgraeber, Richard F. *Sublime Thoughts/Penny Wisdom: Situating Emerson and Thoreau in the American Market.* Baltimore: Johns Hopkins UP, 1995.

Wiener, Martin J. *Reconstructing the Criminal: Culture, Law, and Policy in England, 1830-1914.* Cambridge: Cambridge UP, 1990.

Wood, Barry. "Thoreau's Narrative Art in 'Civil Disobedience.'" *Philological Quarterly* 60.1 (1981): 105-15.

Wright, Julia M. "'National Feeling' and the Colonial Prison: Teeling's *Personal Narrative.*" *Captivating Subjects: Writing Confinement, Citizenship, and Nationhood in the Nineteenth Century.* Ed. Jason Haslam and Julia M. Wright. Toronto: U of Toronto P, [2005].

Robert Pinsky (essay date summer 2004)

SOURCE: Pinsky, Robert. "Comedy, Cruelty, and Tourism: Thoreau's *Cape Cod.*" *American Scholar* 73, no. 3 (summer 2004): 79-88.

[*In the following essay, Pinsky assesses the "sardonic, maniacally various" qualities of Thoreau's* Cape Cod.]

Henry David Thoreau's last book, the posthumously published **Cape Cod,** is a sardonic, maniacally various work. Thoreau's barbed, twisty, and contrary nature, his defiantly indecorous comedy, his rage at hypocrisy are clear enough in all his writing. But Thoreau's life was short. The young man who sets out to write **Walden** in 1846 at the age of twenty-nine does not feel the pressure of mortality as did the author of **Cape Cod** only a few years later. Thoreau, who had tuberculosis, entrusted his sister Sophia and his poet friend William Ellery Channing to edit the manuscript. It was published in 1865, nearly three years after his death.

But the book is antic rather than somber. Launching into an opening spectacle of calamity, but full of startling jokes; ambling yet dramatic; shifting rapidly among whimsy, natural history, polemic, diary, research paper, parody, sermon, history, and wisecrack—*Cape Cod* can amaze modern readers with its peculiar freshness. Contemporary books about places have their own excellences, but they don't attain this unpredictable movement or this immediacy. Thoreau's vividness of mind illuminates the Cape in what remains the place's best portrait.

Cape Cod's manner—quirky, scholarly, thorny, clowning—comes partly from the circumstances of its composition: it was written for performance, and in chronological sequence. That is, Thoreau wrote many parts of the book as lectures; and their organization often relies on the order in which events—a storm, a visit to a lighthouse keeper or to the library—actually occurred. The mercurial texture reflects that structure (and Thoreau's mind); but it also reflects a public speaker's relation to a hall full of listeners, different from a writer's relation to readers.

The audience at Thoreau's Cape Cod lectures for the Concord Lyceum "laughed till they cried." Those are the words of Ralph Waldo Emerson, working on the Secretary of the South Danvers Lyceum, to whom Emerson is recommending his friend for a speaking engagement. The prose of both Thoreau and Emerson should be understood in relation to the lecture form. A secular pulpit, an uplifting theater, and an entertaining classroom, for these writers the lecture format was also a source of income.

The history of the lecture in nineteenth-century American life, and behind it the history of the sermon, must go beyond mere oratory to include the performed composition as a communal center, an intellectual base, and a public diversion. The sermon was a social ritual as well as a religious occasion; the secular lecture strove for improvement, for spiritual effect as well as amusement and literary cachet. The political importance of abolitionist oratory reflected and advanced an already highly evolved, central civic form.

The lecturer is an essayist in the old sense of "essaying" through terrain, not bound by assignment or research as is the journalist or the scholar. The lecturer, like the true essayist, is free to wander a bit, if the byways engage his audience and meander eventually back to the main road. Because the form is social and dramatic, the lecturer also plans for immediate response—most readily by being funny, as Emerson's promotion of Thoreau as a speaker suggests. Smiles, chuckles, even the secular "amen" provided by a ripple of guffaws, build participatory confidence and rapport.

For example, an aria of comic variations based on the town of Eastham's 1662 agreement "that a part of every whale cast on shore be appropriated for the support of the ministry":

No doubt, there seemed to be some propriety in thus leaving the support of the ministers to Providence, whose servants they are, and who alone rules the storms; for, when few whales were cast up, they might suspect that their worship was not acceptable. The ministers must have sat upon the cliffs in every storm, and watched the shore with anxiety. And, for my part, if I were a minister, I would rather trust to the bowels of the billows, on the backside of Cape Cod, to cast up a whale for me, than to the generosity of many a country parish that I know. You cannot say of a country minister's salary, commonly, that it is "very like a whale." . . . Think of a whale having the breath of life beaten out of him by a storm, and dragging in over the bars and guzzles, for the support of the ministry! What a consolation it must have been to him!

The deadpan first sentence might seem pious to the unalert, even after the comically pragmatic understatement of its second half. Then the passage extends more and more outrageously, building from the irreverent picture of the ministers perched on the cliff in every storm, anxiously watching for distressed whales. The audience is cued to smile by the alliterative "bowels of the billows" on the Cape's backside, to grin knowingly at the expense of stingy country parishes, then chuckle appreciatively while being flattered by the allusion to *Hamlet*.

This is largely the performative comedy of personality, demonstrated by the rhythmically recurring first person: "I would rather trust the . . . billows"; "many a country parish that I know." Reader and listeners marvel at Thoreau's deliberate nerve, his ability to persist longer than expected, driving the joke ever further until the very silliness itself becomes funny. There's a theatrical effect in how the comedy reaches its peak with the image of the beaten whale, dragging over the bars and guzzles "for the support of the ministry." It is not hard to imagine an audience laughing out loud at "What a consolation it must have been to him!"

* * *

If the texture is sometimes that of performance, the book's structure is that of a diary. *Cape Cod* was written as journal entries and later as lectures, then as magazine articles, then as the book manuscript edited by Sophia Thoreau and William Ellery Channing. Channing had accompanied Thoreau on the first, October 1849, trip to the Cape, which begins the book, and also returned with him on the last of Thoreau's four Cape expeditions, in 1855. On the two intervening journeys, Thoreau was alone. *Cape Cod* artfully presents the material from these separate visits as a single, composite narrative. The organization of parts, meandering yet purposeful, expresses and follows the unpredictable nature of events, most notably violent weather. Even the placement of early historical material at the end of the book reflects the timing of Thoreau's library research, conducted well after all four Cape Cod journeys.

Their first journey was planned as a walking trip from Provincetown at the tip of the Cape all the way back to the mainland, after a steamer crossing from Boston to Provincetown. But a destructive gale and persistent bad weather changed their plans; they went to the beginning of the Cape by rail and continued by stage to Orleans, nearly halfway to Provincetown. The stormy weather also presented the theme of *Cape Cod*'s first chapter:

> On reaching Boston, we found that the Provincetown steamer, which should have got in the day before, had not yet arrived, on account of a violent storm; and, as we noticed in the streets a handbill headed, "Death! 145 lives lost at Cohasset!" we decided to go by way of Cohasset.

The laconic "we decided to go by way of Cohasset," a cool and perhaps startling acknowledgment of the writer's curiosity, represents part of Thoreau's ability to make tourism the material for a deeply engaging work. He is candidly a spectator as well as a wanderer, and he uses the tourist's preoccupations with diversion and observation like probes to touch profound human mysteries. This is no conventional tourist guide, and indeed it challenges and queries the touristic role with ruthless introspection, even as it raises observation to the level of art.

The travelers go toward the Cape by train, along with many mourners, mostly Irish, as were the immigrant passengers of the wrecked brig *St. John*. When the mourners stop at Cohasset, so does the writer, and he gives a masterly description of corpses on the beach, still being found and transported to the graveyard, and "a large hole, like a cellar, freshly dug." Some of what Thoreau writes might suggest that he is interested in pathos, though he maintains in it a clinical element, and a bizarrely fanciful, almost playful metaphorical element as well:

> I saw many marble feet and matted heads as the cloths were raised, and one livid, swollen and mangled body of a drowned girl—who probably had intended to go out to service in some American family—to which some rags still adhered, with a string, half concealed by the flesh, about its swollen neck; the coiled-up wreck of a human hulk, gashed by the rocks or fishes, so that the bone and muscle were exposed, but quite bloodless—merely red and white—with wide-open and staring eyes, yet lustreless, dead-lights; or, like the cabin windows of a stranded vessel, filled with sand.

The passage feints or gestures in several directions, most of them cruel toward the reader or the drowning victim, all of them affecting perspective. One element reminds us of the social context—the Irish immigrants who sailed from Galway to America on the *St. John* would likely have become servants or laborers—an immediate distancing corrective, maybe, to the sympathetic word "girl." That social perspective is submerged in the detailed horror of the descriptive details; and embedded in those particulars, nearly overwhelmed by them, is the word "hulk." That term for a wrecked ship is left behind, effaced by the bone and muscle, then by the speculation about rocks or fishes, then by the equally detailed description of the open but "lustreless" eyes that suddenly return us through "dead-lights" to the image of a wrecked hulk and its windows, in the sentence's devastating monosyllabic climax, "filled with sand."

The shipwreck begins Thoreau's book by chance, because the *St. John* was wrecked in 1849 by an autumn storm that changed the author's travel plans. But the dead on the beach, with their mourners and spectators and cleanup crews, enable Thoreau to establish a central concern: the nature of sightseeing, and the nature of description. Some on the beach where he sees the drowned girl are carting off bodies and belongings, and other men there with carts are "busily collecting the sea-weed which the storm had cast up, . . . often obliged to separate fragments of clothing from it, and they might, at any moment, have found a human body under it." This information comes a few paragraphs after Thoreau's description of the drowned girl, and what he writes about the seaweed-gatherers applies to the literary traveler as well:

> Drown who might, they did not forget that this weed was a valuable manure. This shipwreck had not produced a visible vibration in the fabric of society.

The word "fabric" echoes sardonically the "fragments of clothing" tangled in the seaweed, and the "rags" that "still adhered" to the drowned girl.

The giving of pathos and sympathy and then taking them away is a repeated gesture of *Cape Cod,* keeping the reader off balance, suggesting a conventional sermon and then denying it. Like the comic passage about the ministers dependent on beached whales, this encounter with death is performative and introspective. Thoreau writes about the scene on the beach, which he has evoked impressively, at length:

> On the whole, it was not so impressive a scene as I might have expected. If I had found one body cast upon the beach in some lonely place, it would have affected me more. I sympathized rather with the winds and waves, as if to toss and mangle those poor human bodies was the order of the day.

The casual expressions "On the whole" and "the order of the day," bracketing what I have quoted, call up the realm of ordinary speech in order to put it in its place. This is no more a work in the spirit of conventional piety than it is a conventional guidebook.

A repeated mode of Thoreau's is the mock-sermon, almost a parody-sermon. After his cool disclaimer of much emotion on his part beyond that of the manure-gatherers, he speaks lyrically of the drowned immigrants as "coming to the New World, as Columbus and the Pilgrims did," though instead they "emigrated to a newer world than ever Columbus dreamed of," toward "a shore yet further west, toward which we all are tending. . . . No doubt, we have reason to thank God, that they have not been 'shipwrecked into life again.'" If we begin to feel comfortable on this rhetorical height, the writer unsettles us by a whimsical process of not-quite-conventional exaggeration and specificity:

> The mariner who makes the safest port in Heaven, perchance, seems to his friends on earth to be shipwrecked, for they deem Boston harbor the better place; though, perhaps, invisible to them, a skillful pilot comes to meet him, and the fairest and balmiest gales blow off that coast, his good ship makes the land in halcyon days, and he kisses the shore in rapture there, while his old hulk tosses in the surf here. It is hard to part with one's body, but no doubt, it is easy enough to do without it when once it is gone. All their plans and hopes burst like a bubble! Infants by the score dashed on the rocks by the enraged Atlantic Ocean! No, no! If the St. John did not make her port here, she has been telegraphed there. The strongest wind cannot stagger a Spirit; it is a Spirit's breath. A just man's purpose cannot be split on any Grampus or material rock, but itself will split rocks till it succeeds.

The piety here is tilted by a subtle irony, one that does not so much dispute the Christian commonplaces as make them uneasy. The specificity of "Boston harbor" and the hyperbole of kissing the shore "in rapture" contrast with the deflating "easy enough to do without it," a laconic remark that can be as agnostic or skeptical as religious. (Similarly, the passage ends not with Our Lord, but with the humanistic spirit of "a just man's purpose.") This nuanced undermining becomes more pointed, becomes practically vocal, with the series of exclamations: the plans and hopes did indeed burst, and infants "by the score" have indeed been dashed on rocks, but "No, no!"

That negative cry, making explicit a satirical or skeptical element in the passage, simultaneously asserts a Christian idea of the afterlife and teases the glibness of standard piety. "Telegraphed," like "Boston harbor," embodies a modernizing and temperature-lowering element of the quotidian. And the piety that is most significantly Thoreau's target may not be religious at all, but a journalistic glibness of sympathy. The exclamations about plans burst like bubbles and infants dashed on rocks are, formally speaking, parodic headlines. Part of Thoreau's genius is that he understood modern American life as it was first forming—almost before it formed. The opening chapter of *Cape Cod* is among other things a corrective to the solemn righteousness of the television anchorperson reporting a disaster. Choosing to imagine the wrecked brig *St. John* "telegraphed" to heaven, he brilliantly evokes and inspects the sanctimony of the observer.

* * *

Great writing can be disagreeable where mediocrity goes down easily. After the first four chapters of **Cape Cod** had appeared in the June, July, and August 1855 issues of *Putnam's Monthly,* the arrangement to serialize was broken. Professor Joseph Moldenhauer, in his very useful "Historical Introduction" to the Princeton University Press textual edition of **Cape Cod,** cites an early correspondence with the magazine in which Thoreau alters a passage involving Calvinists and the word "Scripture," because the religious sensibilities of editor, publisher, and readers "had been abraded by Thoreau's apparent 'heresies' of wording or tone on religious matters." The magazine seems to have aborted publication partly because of Thoreau's impolite references to such matters as the stupidity of Cape Cod guidebooks, the unattractiveness of Cape women, and the coarseness of manners in Cape villages. Passages excised in the magazine but present in the book and lectures include references to the seedpod of marine creatures, to the manuring of apple trees, and to an excessively effective sermon. Newspapers mentioned the offense these magazine pieces had given to the residents of Barnstable County.

The idea that Thoreau's book scandalously criticized or mocked the Cape's villages or inhabitants has become literary folklore, more a part of the book's reputation than of a modern reader's experience. But as with all folklore, the notion of Thoreau mocking his subject contains a truth. The book may or may not have upset local feelings or contemporary pruderies, but it surely does undermine conventional expectations.

What Thoreau mocks and questions is not Barnstable County but himself and the reader and the traveler—the greedy, naïve appetite for "beauty" and "interest" and eloquent "reflections," the questing enterprise of moving to and through places in the world. In **Cape Cod** that enterprise perpetually questions itself, by shifting perspective from the personal to the grand, from the historical to the local, from the eternal to the idiosyncratic. It is an enterprise brilliantly pursued a generation later by the travel books of Mark Twain. Some passages, in particular certain gags, feel as if they must have inspired Twain directly: as when Truro's Highland Light shines directly into Thoreau's bedchamber so that he "knew exactly how [it] bore all that night, and I was in no danger of being wrecked."

In another shift of perspective, Thoreau reports something that happened at Cohasset days after he and Channing had interrupted the railroad part of their journey, perhaps after they had already begun their walking tour of the Cape. He says that "something white was seen floating on the water by one who was sauntering"—a characteristic verb—"on the beach." When a boat went to investigate, this white object turned out to be

the body of a woman, which had risen in an upright position, whose white cap was blown back with the wind. I saw that the beauty of the shore itself was wrecked for many a lonely walker there, until he could perceive, at last, how its beauty was enhanced by wrecks like this, and it acquired thus a rarer and sublimer beauty still.

The sublime beauty and the grotesquerie, wrecked and restored and wrecked again, the perspective of one sauntering alone and, also in solitude, the ghostly replication of that sauntering by the body bobbing upright with its white cap lifted back by the wind: this is the writer's echo of the ocean itself, claiming and giving up and reclaiming, peaceful then turbulent, reassuring and then disturbing and then, in a cycle without end, reassuring again. In this image as throughout, a theatrical panache dominates attention before yielding to the immense perspective of eternity, terrible and sublime.

A third characteristic move, like the wisecrack and the mock-sermon, is the rhetorical flight, an extravagant excursus demonstrating how adeptly the writer can contradict himself, or skim from whimsy to tragedy to philosophy and back again. These performances show how far the writer can journey in a few paragraphs: each course of rhetoric itself a feat of travel. One such figurative journey begins with the rhetorical standby that the ocean's vastness dwarfs human life. Particularly horrible is the remoteness of the invisible ocean floor. The ever darker and deeper water, he writes, seemed unrelated to the "friendly land" or to the bottom. He begins with the nightmare of tremendous depth, of drowning without touching the sandy floor:

—of what use is a bottom if it is out of sight, if it is two or three miles from the surface, and you are to be drowned so long before you get to it, though it were made of the same stuff with your native soil?

Then on through quoting the Veda ("there is nothing to give support, nothing to rest upon, nothing to cling to"), and through the first-person "I felt that I was a land animal." Then how, unlike the sailor fathoms above the bottom, a "man in a balloon even may commonly alight on the earth in a few moments." Then, a new admiration for the drowning navigator who cried out to his companions, "We are as near to Heaven by sea as by land." To that brave dying statement Thoreau responds, "I saw that it would not be easy to realize."

And then the passage moves erratically enough to that staple of American humor, inventive exaggeration:

Every Cape man has a theory about George's Bank having been an island once, and in their accounts they gradually reduce the shallowness from six, five, four, two fathoms, to somebody's confident assertion that he has seen a mackerel-gull sitting on a piece of dry land there. It reminded me, when I thought of the shipwrecks which had taken place there, of the Isle of Demons, laid down off this coast in old charts of the New World. There must be something monstrous, methinks, in a vision of the sea bottom from over some bank a thousand miles from the shore, more awful than its imagined bottomlessness; a drowned continent, all livid and frothing at the nostrils, like the body of a drowned man, which is better sunk deep than near the surface.

So, through an astonishing route of digressions, he has navigated from horror of the nearly bottomless, profound depths to the opposite horror of the shallow, visible bottom where an undersea bank rises far offshore. Speeding from the mackerel-gull to a drowned continent "all livid and frothing at the nostrils," we barely notice the complete reversal. In this turn, too, the voyage is through performance to what is enormous and eternal, the spectacle of mortality.

He says of the seashore, "It is even a trivial place." Also, "there is no flattery in it. Strewn with crabs, horseshoes, and razor-clams, and whatever the sea casts up,—a vast *morgue,* where famished dogs may range in packs, and crows come daily to glean the pittance which the tide leaves them." Almost gleefully sardonic, he notes how human and animal carcasses alike "lie stately" as they rot and bleach together, and in one of his inspired, grotesquely extended metaphors, "each tide turns them in their beds, and tucks fresh sand under them. There is naked Nature,—inhumanly sincere, wasting no thought on man, nibbling at the cliffy shore where gulls wheel amid the spray."

Seeing the natural world this way as "sincere" and "without flattery" entitles him to write as a meticulous naturalist, turning to the sand of Provincetown with the informed, analytical eye that inspects the ice of Walden, the abundant details colored, but not distorted, by his personality. The minute, extended, contagiously attentive prose requires a long quotation:

> The highest and sandiest portion next the Atlantic was thinly covered with Beach-grass and Indigo-weed. Next to this the surface of the upland generally consisted of white sand and gravel, like coarse salt, through which a scanty vegetation found its way up. It will give an ornithologist some idea of its barrenness if I mention that the next June, the month of grass, I found a nighthawk's eggs there, and that almost any square rod thereabouts, taken at random, would be an eligible site for such a deposit. The kildeer-plover, which loves a similar locality, also drops its eggs there, and fills the air above with its din. This upland also produced *Cladonia* lichens, poverty-grass, savory-leaved aster (*Diplopappus linariifolius*), mouse-ear, bearberry, &c. On a few hillsides the savory-leaved aster and mouse-ear alone made quite a dense sward, said to be very pretty when the aster is in bloom. In some parts the two species of poverty-grass (*Hudsonia tomentosa* and *ericoides*), which deserve a better name, reign for miles in little hemispherical tufts or islets, like moss, scattered over the waste.

The Linnaean names, the observation, the shapely sentences with their active verbs (the kildeer-plover *loves, drops, fills*; the upland *produced*; the aster *made*: this masterly nature writing is in a different key from the sermonizing, the rhetorical cadenzas, the deliberately cornball wit that says of the wide cart tires demanded by Provincetown's sand roads, "the more tired the wheels, the less tired the horses." Among the various kinds of performances, always deferring eventually to the perspective of eternity, Thoreau's matchless attention to natural detail constitutes a kind of credential. With the emphasis on information, the ingenious personality that thinks poverty-grass deserves a better name, then has it "reign" for miles, remains distinct, but relatively muted. The exhaustive natural history, interrupting the performer's reckless flights and pranks and burlesque preachings, is another way of surprising the reader, another drastic change of perspective.

Natural history, and also history. But history serves mainly as something to be put behind us, a demonstration of the void. Thoreau composed the pages about early European exploration of the Cape not long before his death in 1862. Here near the very end of the book he peers into the past, and his account of it is based in skepticism, advancing the knowledge and skill of the French, Italian, and Portuguese explorers, and elevating the claims of the Vikings, in order to mock the English. The particular objects of his scorn include Governor Winthrop and the Pilgrims. Thoreau questions both their knowledge and the truthfulness of their accounts. But his main point is more general:

> Consider what stuff history is made of,—that for the most part it is merely a story agreed on by posterity. . . . I believe that, if I were to live the life of mankind over again myself, (which I would not be hired to do,) with the Universal History in my hands, I should not be able to tell what was what.

Here the superhuman perspective is treated comically, an effect he emphasizes by alternating Pilgrim descriptions of coming into Provincetown harbor with his own arrangements at Provincetown hotels and conversations. ("The Pilgrims say: 'There was the greatest store of fowl that ever we saw.' *We* saw no fowl there, except gulls of various kinds.")

What does that italicized first-person perspective mean? What is the meaning of the Cape in this book? A kind of haunting and haunted absence, a refutation of the traveler as dilettante. In his final pages he writes: "When we reached Boston that October, I had a gill of Provincetown sand in my shoes. . . . I seemed to hear the sea roar, as if I lived in a shell, for a week afterward." The meaning of that haunting sound is suggested by this book's concluding paragraphs. The Cape is an available remoteness, a rough rebuttal of the traveler's comfortable, habitual viewpoints: "strange and remote," twice as far from Boston as England is from France, yet only hours away by train. In the book's closing passages, he distinguishes the place from the Newport of his day (or the Martha's Vineyard of our own?), saying of Cape Cod:

> At present, it is wholly unknown to the fashionable world, and probably it will never be agreeable to them. If it is merely a ten-pin alley, or a circular railway, or an ocean of mint-julep, that the visitor is in search of,—if he thinks more of the wine than the brine, as I suspect some do at Newport,—I trust that for a long time he will be disappointed here. But this shore will never be more attractive than it is now.

He says of the "bare and bended arm" of the Cape that it makes the bay in which Lynn and Nantasket "lie so snugly." *Cape Cod,* with its terrors and uneasy cackles, its bottomless ironies, is like an obverse of the withdrawal and relatively serene immersion of **Walden.** This book supplies a wintery corrective to an overly soft understanding of that one. In *Cape Cod*'s final sentences Thoreau says:

> A storm in the fall or winter is the time to visit it; a light-house or a fisherman's hut the true hotel. A man may stand there and put all America behind him.

James J. Donahue (essay date winter 2007)

SOURCE: Donahue, James J. "'Hardly the Voice of the Same Man': 'Civil Disobedience' and Thoreau's Response to John Brown." *Midwest Quarterly* 48, no. 2 (winter 2007): 247-65.

[*In the following essay, Donahue considers the ways in which Thoreau reconciles violent resistance with morality in his political writings. In Donahue's view, Thoreau's defense of John Brown illuminates the central tensions between abstract transcendental thought and active political involvement.*]

> How rarely I meet with a man who can be free, even in thought! We live according to rule. Some men are bed-ridden; all, world-ridden.
>
> Henry David Thoreau. *Journal,* May 10, 1857

Henry David Thoreau lived in a society teeming with political strife. In his introduction to *Thoreau: People, Principles, and Politics,* Milton Meltzer writes that "Thoreau was born in time to hear reminiscences of the American Revolution from local survivors of those battles, and he died as the Civil War was creating another generation of veterans" (ix). Thoreau's life was framed by wars that helped to shape the political and cultural borders of America. Further, he was witness to the use of violent action as a means of effecting political change. However, he himself was not an activist, at least not violent; rather, as Michael Meyer points out, his

"his greatest strengths as a social critic was his diagnoses" ("Black Emigration" ["Thoreau and Black Emigration"], 380). Rather than committing himself to any use of physical warfare, Meltzer continues, "[h]e was committed to another war . . . against injustice and slavery" (ix). Meltzer contrasts Thoreau's "inner war" of conscience to the "outer wars" against the Indians and Mexico, wars that Thoreau took no active part in (unless one reads his night in jail for refusing to pay taxes as an overt act). In either case, what is important to note here is the non-confrontational nature of Thoreau's political activism.

Although political injustice was a complaint as old as the country itself, slavery was bringing the country closer to imminent warfare. The Fugitive Slave Law of 1851 increased the outrage of Northern abolitionists—including Thoreau—and helped to strike the match that would eventually help spark the Civil War (1861-1865). An informed and civic-minded thinker who spent much time writing on his own thoughts (often revising his journals into public addresses), Thoreau's writings from the period reflect his own understanding of and responses to various contemporary issues. Specifically, Thoreau's pieces in support of John Brown reflect his views on the issue of slavery in the United States.

However, one cannot simply read **"A Plea for Captain John Brown"** (1859) and **"The Last Days of John Brown"** (1860) and appreciate Thoreau's political and ethical arguments. In order to understand the complexities and contradictions that are often noted in these two pieces, one must read them as a development in his political thinking, specifically with regard to the issue of slavery—a development that runs through **"Civil Disobedience"** (1849) and **"Slavery in Massachusetts"** (1854). Although Thoreau's sympathies to John Brown and his violence are seemingly more extreme than his earlier statements in **"Civil Disobedience,"** such a change reflects not a break with his Transcendental ideals but rather the identification of his metaphysical ideals in the person of John Brown. More specifically, Thoreau's seemingly contradictory attempts to link his ethics to John Brown's acts represent the move from the abstract and more general world of ideas (**"Civil Disobedience"**) to the more concrete world of politics (**"Slavery in Massachusetts"** and **"A Plea for [Captain] John Brown"**), before turning once again to the abstract and universal in **"The Last Days of John Brown."**

Thoreau was not the only public figure to champion Brown. Brown's friend Frederick Douglass voiced his support in a now-famous letter of October 31, 1859, in the *Rochester Democrat* (though widely reprinted). Having fled to Canada for fear of arrest as an accomplice at Harpers Ferry, Douglass states that "I am ever ready to write, speak, publish, organize, combine, and even to conspire against Slavery" (qtd. in Quarles [*Blacks on John Brown*], 9). However, Douglass's letter was inspired primarily to answer a charge of cowardice made by John E. Cook, one of Brown's captured conspirators. Douglass notes that "Mr. Cook may be perfectly right in denouncing me as a coward. I have not one word to say in defense or vindication of my character for courage" (8). Douglass further makes clear that, though ever ready to join forces with those who would topple America's peculiar institution, his "field of labor for the abolition of Slavery has not extended to an attack upon the United States Arsenal" (9). If it here appears that Douglass does not support Brown's efforts, he later states that "every man [should] work for the abolition of Slavery in his own way. I would help all and hinder none" (10). This letter, from one the period's greatest masters of abolitionist rhetoric, evidences a common paradox with regard to Brown: how does one support the motives behind his actions without supporting the violence of the actions themselves? How does one champion abstract notions of sweeping political change without supporting its violent instruments? These questions become particularly interesting with respect to John Brown, whose violence was widely known. By 1856 (three years before Harpers Ferry), as F. B. Sanborn makes clear, "Brown's name had become such a terror, that wherever the enemy were attacked they believed he was in command" (309), and Brown was personally named in many letters as leading parties of abolitionists to murder in Kansas. John Brown, then, created a complex test case for many abolitionists, and especially the Transcendentalists, with respect to their calls for an immediate end to slavery in America.

In her study of Thoreau and Daniel Berrigan (Vietnam-era political activist), Laraine Fergenson argues:

> One problem inherent in Transcendental politics is the contradiction between the inner-spiritual aspect of Transcendentalism and its turning outward, its impetus toward social reform, which sprang paradoxically from the very inwardness of the Transcendentalist philosophy. . . . Another facet of the problem at the heart of Transcendental politics—one that is related to the incongruity between its inner-spiritual-individualistic tendencies and the outer-secular-collective mode of the radical political action it has inspired—is . . . the conflict between reason and passion.
>
> (104-5)

Fergenson would have us believe that not only must the Transcendental political thinker be separate from the Transcendental political activist, but that this is also a problem, seen in her reading of **"Resistance to Civil Government"** as "at once a passionate statement of individual conviction and a reasoned argument calling for unified mass action" (105). However, no justification for the problematic nature of Transcendental political activism is provided, other than the argument that passion and reason exist only as a paradox, as if mutually exclusive. In terms of Thoreau's relationship to Brown, Thoreau would apparently embody reason, and Brown, passion. This relationship is only paradoxical, in terms of Thoreau's defense of Brown, if one understands Brown to be representative of the political ethic outlined in **"Civil Disobedience."** This relationship is not paradoxical, however, if one understands Thoreau's four political essays as developmental, and if one understands Thoreau's relationship to Brown to be complementary.

Leon Edel argues that "[h]is defense of John Brown, with his espousal of violence in that instance, is hardly the voice of the same man" (qtd. in Goodwin ["Thoreau and John Brown"], 156). Though correct, Edel's observation is not as problematic as critics such as Fergenson may be inclined to believe. For as James Goodwin points out:

> in crucial instances [Thoreau's] thought appears to be more closely aligned to a doctrine of individual nihilism than to the philosophy of mass nonviolence. One such instance is contained in Thoreau's response to John Brown.
>
> (156)

In other words, to understand Thoreau's political stance as simply one of "mass nonviolence" is faulty, given that he does not in fact come out and espouse such an understanding in his political writings. Although he did espouse nonviolent protest—for instance in his night spent in jail for refusing to pay taxes, which action later influenced such significant nonviolent protesters as Mahatma Gandhi and Dr. Martin Luther King, Jr.—reading him simply as a proponent of nonviolent activism is an oversimplification of the political tensions found in his work. Instead, Goodwin understands Thoreau to focus on the individual, whatever his response, and as such individual acts of rebellion. And it is in this respect that one can begin to understand Thoreau's defense of Brown. Goodwin writes:

> In John Brown, Thoreau believed he had at last found an individual whose conduct transcended conflicts of conscience and whose action eliminated disparity between the ideal and the real . . . [understood] not as a departure from or a moderation of transcendental individualism but as a further radicalization of its tenets and an escalation of its goals.
>
> (158)

Thoreau's reaction to Brown, then, is not a break from his individualistic political views, but an identification of such values in the figure of Brown. In defining the ideal figure of Transcendental political action, Goodwin further observes:

> The transcendental hero, for Thoreau, is the individual who proves himself to be utterly superior to the com-

mon mass. Here, however, it should be emphasized that in his published statements and letters Brown consistently identifies himself with the multitude suffering in slavery.

(163)

This definition is significant for two reasons. First, nowhere in any of Thoreau's political pieces is there any explicit prohibition of violence as a means to achieve an end, even if such is often read into his own nonviolent actions. This is noted by Michael Meyer when he argues for Thoreau's "having to shift his ground to sustain his faith in moral law," understanding that "nonviolent resistance—practiced individually or collectively—could not effectively further the cause of abolitionism" ("Problem" ["'Civil Disobedience' and the Problem of Thoreau's 'Peaceable Revolution'"], 153). It was the times, not a move away from moral law, that prompted Thoreau to sympathize with Brown's actions, as well as necessitated Brown's actions in the first place. Second, where Thoreau holds Brown to be the ideal embodiment of Transcendental political ethics, Brown considered himself as just a man among the mass of men. It is in this respect that Thoreau can not only discuss Brown's actions in terms of Transcendentalism, but can also construct a reading of Brown as Christ. However, this is only the case if Thoreau's political pieces are read as developing from an abstract discussion of politics to the specific person of Brown and his actions at Harper's Ferry. **"Civil Disobedience"** is a statement against the idea of oppressive government, with local examples for illustration. **"Slavery in Massachusetts"** is a general argument against the institution of slavery, again with local supporting examples. Finally, the John Brown pieces provide at first a focused defense of one particular man in whom Thoreau has identified the solution to slavery, followed by an abstract eulogy for a Transcendental hero. It is with respect to this move from the abstract to the specific and back again that Thoreau's developing political ethic must be read.

Laying the Groundwork: "Civil Disobedience" and "Slavery in Massachusetts"

If **"Civil Disobedience"** works as the cornerstone upon which Thoreau's developing political views are built, then it stands to reason that it should be as general as possible, to allow for the broadest base upon which Thoreau can construct his political ethic. The essay, then, is not so much an anti-slavery tract as an ideological statement outlining the problems with government. One of these problems is, of course, slavery. It is for this reason that critics such as Fergenson can write of **"Civil Disobedience"**:

> Thoreau is a major influence on American political protest, and yet his writings, taken as a whole, are a tissue of self-contradiction. In **"Civil Disobedience"** itself

one does not find a consistent theory but rather a series of brilliant insights and a faint shadow of a program for a "peaceable revolution," which is undercut by other statements made in the same essay.

(115)

To address her first point, one would be oversimplifying Thoreau's political development in taking his writings as a whole, as representative of one ideal. But more importantly is her problematizing of the "unresolved contradiction" she finds between "collective and individual action" (115). This contradiction only exists if one expects the essay to provide such a "program," and the contradiction dissolves if one reads the text as an abstract declaration of personal independence from the idea of oppressive government. In fact, the text is more the statement of a moral facilitator than the outline of a political theorist.

The abstract nature of the piece is evident in its use of general, even at times vague, political claims. At the start Thoreau writes "That government is best which governs least," and follows with "That government is best which governs not at all" (36). Leaving aside the general political theory he begins to map out, the language itself sets off the abstract tone. "That government" can apply to any government. Shortly following, Thoreau rebuts, "[b]ut to speak practically and as a citizen, unlike those who call themselves no-government men, I ask for, not at once no government, but at once a better government" (37-8). Thoreau here writes as a citizen, implicitly a citizen of the United States, but more explicitly a citizen in general, one who is governed. Although he later discusses American government more explicitly—such as when he poses the question: "How does it become a man to behave toward this American government today?" (39), or when he discusses the current situation with Mexico—by opening his piece with abstract gestures toward the idea of government, Thoreau allows for his essay to be read as an abstract piece of moral facilitation, which uses specific examples in American government and history to support its general claims. However, even in his use of American references, he still keeps the tone abstract. This is apparent both in his question mentioned above, generalizing his audience now rather than his subject, and in his references to the American Revolution.

In claiming that "[a]ll men recognize the right to revolution; that is, the right to refuse allegiance to, and to resist, the government" (40)—and note here the generalizing of both subject and object—Thoreau brings the reader back to "the Revolution of '75" (40). He later questions why "government" will "always crucify Christ, and excommunicate Copernicus and Luther, and pronounce Washington and Franklin rebels" (44). Here, the use of specific American figures works to both provide a direct American example for his audience and construct a more mythic chain of morally justified individuals whom history has since glorified (in the same way Thoreau will later expect Brown to be glorified, by adding him to this chain and linking him with Christ). By the time of this piece, the Revolutionary War had become a part of history, and references to it operate more abstractly than references to current politics. By mentioning these specific actors who instigated various "revolutions" against oppressive systems of rule (a list which will later include Brown), Thoreau sets the reader up to then read any man, including himself, in Thoreau's claim that "[w]hen the subject has refused allegiance, and the officer has resigned his office, then the revolution is accomplished" (47). Often taken as a defense of nonviolent revolutionary action, nothing in this statement precludes the type of violence Thoreau will later implicitly defend in his support of Brown. The individual refusal of allegiance can be nothing more than refusal to pay taxes to a government waging unjust war, or it can be the taking up of arms in an effort to free slaves from that same government. It is the state of mind of the subject, not the form of protest he commits himself to, that Thoreau is emphasizing here. And it is from this general, abstract foundation of personal revolutionary measures that one can begin to see the development of Thoreau's later defense of Brown.

"Civil Disobedience" does, however, include a direct appeal to abolish slavery:

> In other words, when a sixth of the population of a nation which has undertaken to be the refuge of liberty are slaves, and a whole country is unjustly overrun and conquered by a foreign army and subjected to military law, I think that it is not too soon for honest men to rebel and revolutionize.
>
> (40)

Even though the United States is implicated, as is the possibility of violent protest, the language remains abstract, indicting any government that tolerates such practices. But within the span of five years, Thoreau will address the American people yet again, only this time discussing the specific issue of slavery for his specific nation.

In **"Slavery in Massachusetts,"** Thoreau more clearly discusses the most significant ethical dilemma facing the United States and ties together the ethical and political strings he begins weaving in **"Civil Disobedience."** Again addressing the place of government in the ethical considerations of the people, Thoreau takes a staunchly individualistic, anti-governmental stand against the sitting government. Speaking of the governor of Massachusetts, Thoreau writes: "I think that I could manage to get along without one" (110), "[h]e is no governor of mine. He did not govern me" (111). These statements regarding his immediate local govern-

ment more clearly articulate his sentiments in **"Civil Disobedience"** regarding the subject's refusal of allegiance, for he clearly shows none to the authority of Massachusetts. Note also the sustained, albeit weakened, abstract nature of his remarks; rather than naming the governor, Thoreau addresses his complaint to the seat of authority, allowing for the reader to associate any governor, any elected official, with this complaint. The abstract nature of Thoreau's piece is furthered by his statement regarding voting:

> The fate of the country does not depend on how you vote at the polls—the worst man is as strong as the best at that game; it does not depend on what kind of paper you drop into the ballot box once a year, but in what kind of man you drop from your chamber into the street every morning.
>
> (119)

Hinting further at the necessity for such a man as Brown, Thoreau keeps his discussion of government institutions abstract. A further abstraction addressed is the idea of law itself:

> The law will never make men free; it is men who have yet to make the law free. They are the lovers of law and order who observe the law when the government breaks it.
>
> (115)

However, even this abstraction is connected to the specific issue of American law in his reference to the Fugitive Slave Law:

> The question is, not whether you or your grandfather, seventy years ago, did not enter into any agreement to serve the devil, and that service is not accordingly now due; but whether you will not now, for once and at last, serve God—in spite of your own past recreancy, or that of your ancestor—by obeying that eternal and only just CONSTITUTION, which HE, and not any Jefferson or Adams, has written in your Being.
>
> (118-9)

Thoreau now addresses not only his explicit audience but also clearly articulates both the problem with the laws imposed by the government and the very foundation of the government itself, with his refusal to accept the Constitution of the United States as the statement of his rights and freedoms.

Near the beginning of his speech, Thoreau brings to the attention of his audience the Thomas Sims case: "Again it happens that the Boston Courthouse is full of armed men, holding prisoner and trying a man, to find out if he is not really a slave. Does any one think justice or God awaits Mr. Loring's decision?" (110). By referring to a specific case, even naming the official involved, Thoreau means his audience to apply the abstract critique of government found in the text to the specific case now in front of them. Further, looking at the development of Thoreau's political ethic, one is able to apply his abstract discussions of politics in **"Civil Disobedience"** to this direct statement against slavery. The result is to see how Thoreau has come to understand the necessity for more direct action, even if he does not take it upon himself to act as Brown does. As Thoreau writes near the end of his speech:

> Show me a free state, and a court truly of justice, and I will fight for them, if need be; but show me Massachusetts, and I refuse her my allegiance, and express contempt for her courts.
>
> (120-1)

Here we have not only a hint at the necessity for more direct action against injustice (now to be understood as the American government's institution of slavery), but the combining of Thoreau's theory of individual revolution and violent action. Where the call in **"Civil Disobedience"** to "refuse allegiance to, and to resist, the government" (40), as well his claim that once "the subject has refused allegiance, and the officer has resigned his office, then the revolution is accomplished" (47), can be read as supporting nonviolent, passive resistance to create the "revolution of one," here the refusal of allegiance to government is linked with direct, possibly violent action. Even if Thoreau entertains this option only hypothetically (stating the sentiment conditionally), the recognition of violence as a possible response to slavery has been made, and it is just such a sentiment that will allow Thoreau to see in Brown the only possible, the only ethical, abolitionist action. By tracing out Thoreau's developing political stance through **"Civil Disobedience"** and **"Slavery in Massachusetts,"** one can now fully appreciate his recognition of Transcendental political ethics in the figure of a violent abolitionist, and the act of a bloody assault.

JOHN BROWN: TRANSCENDENTAL MESSIAH

"A Plea for Captain John Brown" does not simply support the use of violence as a means to end slavery. Rather, it raises Brown's character to a higher moral plateau from which his actions are to be read as ethically superior, and as such out of the bounds of any human consideration of law and order (working more in the Transcendental realm of just vs. unjust). He does this in part, as Kent Ljungquist points out, when he "modifies images from the newspaper accounts (blindness vs. sight, darkness vs. light, coherence vs. inchoateness) to establish Brown's moral preeminence" (678). Another way Thoreau was able to raise Brown to a higher moral plateau was by discussing him in light of the abstract principles he outlined in **"Civil Disobedience"** and more clearly articulated in **"Slavery in Massachusetts."** One such example is when Thoreau says of Brown that "only he was firmer and higher principled," and that "he had the courage to face his country herself when she was in the wrong" (171). In Brown, Thoreau sees a man refusing allegiance to his country, resisting unjust laws, answering only to the "higher law" (175). Thoreau makes this explicit when he argues that Brown had no interest in any aspect of common socio-economic, political ethics:

> Well, no, I don't suppose he could get four-and-sixpence a day for being hung, take the year round; but then he stands a chance to save a considerable part of his soul—and such a soul!—when you do not.
>
> (176)

It is at this point that Thoreau, as in **"Slavery in Massachusetts,"** turns the attention back to his audience. As in his earlier pieces, Thoreau works to establish the moral superiority of his claims by comparing them to the lack of such morals in his audience. In this way, Thoreau attempts to separate Brown from "the common man" as much as possible, and as such remove him and his actions from "common" considerations of law and order.

In an effort to set Brown apart from the common man, Thoreau writes:

> I wish I could say that Brown was the representative of the North. He was a superior man. He did not value his bodily life in comparison with ideal things. He did not recognize unjust human laws, but resisted them as he was bid. For once we are lifted out of the trivialness and dust of politics into the region of truth and manhood. No man in America has ever stood up so persistently and effectively for the dignity of human nature, knowing himself for a man, and the equal of any and all governments. In that sense he was the most American of us all.
>
> (181)

First, note the emphasis on the metaphysical, as opposed to the simply physical that the common man represents. Thoreau then says of Brown: "No man has appeared in America, as yet, who loved his fellow man so well, and treated him so tenderly. He lived for him" (187). Not only is Brown enacting the rights and duties entrusted to Americans as Thoreau defines them in **"Civil Disobedience,"** but he is also the ultimate expression of those values; he is not only "equal" to any government by nature of his being human but he is superior to any American, those who consider themselves to be the most free, as well as the most moral. In fact, Thoreau pays Brown an even higher compliment. Where in **"Civil Disobedience"** he uses himself as the *exemplum* through which one is to understand the workings of moral law under an unjust government, here Thoreau subordinates himself to Brown, clearly the better man: "I rejoice that I live in this age, that I am his contemporary" (181). It is by such subordination that Thoreau is able to express his excitement over his proximity to such a figure, one Thoreau knows will transcend both history as well as the contemporary censure of the common people. He may walk among us, but is certainly not one of us, Thoreau argues: "No, he was not our representative in any sense. He was too fair a specimen to represent the like of us" (152). Where in **"Civil Disobedience"** Thoreau points out that unjust governments will "always crucify Christ, and excommunicate Copernicus and Luther, and pronounce Washington and Franklin rebels" (44), and so ties Brown's revolutionary actions to a larger, now mythical tradition of civil disobedience, **"A Plea for Captain John Brown"** does more than tie Brown to such a tradition; instead, Thoreau identifies Brown with the most powerful figure on that list: Christ.

Following an attack on its failings, Thoreau levies a now-familiar charge against government: "A government that pretends to be Christian and crucifies a million Christs every day!" (184). Now before one is tempted to read this solely as a generalized statement, reading every slave as a Christ-figure (which is certainly one way to read this statement, considering the over-generalizing nature of Thoreau's other works), one must consider the growing trend in Thoreau's writings on slavery away from the abstract, toward the specific. In this light, one is able to understand how this statement works to support Thoreau's identification of Brown with Christ: by playing off of the Christian sympathies of his audience, asking them to read acts of martyrdom as acts of Christ-figures, Thoreau is able to create the tone by which he can identify Brown *as*—not with—Christ. In counting Brown's band of men, Thoreau identifies "as many at least as twelve disciples" (182). Thoreau later reads Brown as Christ by way of symbolic approximation: the "same indignation that is said to have cleared the temple once will clear it again" (187). Further, in discussing the death of the mass of men, he writes that "[n]o temple's veil was rent" (188). By referring to these two instances in Christ's life—his teaching in the temple of Jerusalem and the reaction in that temple to his death on the cross—Thoreau is allowing his audience to understand Brown as the second coming of Christ: the temple will be cleared again as a result of Brown's significant act of disobedience, and Brown's eventual death at the hands of his oppressors will have the same result.

Not only does Brown show "himself superior to nature," but he also "has a spark of divinity in him" (189). Brown is more than "divinely appointed," but is "such a man as it takes ages to make, and ages to understand; no mock hero, nor the representative of any party" (189). And that government which persecutes him has done no more than "pretend to care for Christ crucified" (189). Brown is now linked to Christ directly:

> Some eighteen hundred years ago Christ was crucified; this morning, perchance, Captain Brown was hung. These are the two ends of a chain which is not without its links. He is not Old Brown any longer; he is an angel of light.
>
> (190)

But this linking is not enough to understand the full significance of Brown's fulfillment of Thoreau's developing Transcendental moral and political ethic.

In **"The Last Days of John Brown,"** Thoreau delivers a powerful eulogy for a man he knew would be recognized for his adherence to a higher moral law, even if contemporary America had mixed feelings about his actions. He begins his piece with a bold statement on the nature of Brown's heroism:

> If any person, in a lecture or conversation at that time, cited any example of heroism, such as Cato or Tell or Winkelried, passing over the recent deeds and words of Brown, it was felt by any intelligent audience of Northern men to be tame and inexcusably far-fetched.
>
> (192)

Thoreau recognized that it is only in the North, and even then only among intelligent men, that Brown is justly considered heroic. But Thoreau also knew that such would pass with time, as the legacy of Brown transcended common humanity. Speaking of him now, not in the specific language he employed in his criticism of slavery and plea for Brown's cause, but in the abstract language that is used in **"Civil Disobedience,"** Thoreau says of Brown that "I was so absorbed in him as to be surprised whenever I detected the routine of the natural world surviving still, or met persons going about their affairs indifferent" (192-3). Brown, for Thoreau at least, is an all-encompassing figure, whose legacy operates outside of both human and natural routines. Speaking of him in relation to the purely abstract, Thoreau claims that Brown was one "who actually carried out the golden rule" (194), a simplified, even abstract, name for the "higher law" of Transcendentalism. Even more so, unlike his audience, Brown knew "about living or dying for a principle" (196). And it was specifically in his death that he was fully realized as transcendent.

Goodwin writes of Thoreau's apprehension for the sparing of Brown's life as revealing.

> According to the logic of transcendental individualism, ideal political conduct would necessarily culminate in self-sacrifice. Thus, the most convincing evidence of Brown's integrity is the certainty of his death at the hands of the state.
>
> (160)

Not that Brown's death at the hands of the state was ever in doubt, given the nature and locale of Brown's revolt, but Thoreau—and the abolitionist movement—

needed a martyr. Neither **"The Last Days of John Brown"** nor **"A Plea for Captain John Brown"** were written, as David G. Fuller reminds us, to save him from the gallows: Thoreau's "purpose was to 'plead' Brown's 'cause,' not to plead 'for his life'" (167). Thoreau's celebration of Brown's martyrdom is made clear in the conclusion of **"The Last Days of John Brown"**:

> What a transit was that of his horizontal body alone, but just cut down from the gallows tree! . . . Thus like a meteor it shot through the Union from the Southern regions toward the North! No such freight had the cars borne since they carried him southward alive.
>
> On the day of his translation, I heard, to be sure, that he was *hung,* but I did not know what that meant; I felt no sorrow on that account, but not for a day or two did I even *hear* that he was *dead,* and not after any number of days shall I believe it. Of all who were said to be my contemporaries, it seemed to me that John Brown was the only one who *had not died.* I never hear of a man named Brown now—and I hear of them pretty often—I never hear of any particularly brave and earnest man, but my first thought is of John Brown, and what relation he may be to him. He has earned immortality. He is not confined to North Elba nor to Kansas. He is no longer working in secret. He works in public, and in the clearest light that shines on this land.
>
> (198)

Brown, like Christ, was of such singular character that whoever—or whatever, as with the train cars—came into contact with him was forever changed by the association. Like Christ, Brown did not die, but was "translated" from one mode of existence to another—transcended, in fact, the world of common humanity, with its unjust laws and repressive sense of order, moving on to a higher moral existence. And more importantly, his legend—his spirit, his character, his influence—live on and continue to work. John Brown was the man in whom Thoreau found the ideals of Transcendentalism put into action.

THE MISSING LINK

"But," one may ask after working through Thoreau's texts on John Brown, "why does Thoreau not once discuss the violence, the murder, the bloodshed of the event? Is he blind to the horror of it?" In short, no; and yes. Thoreau was well aware of the violent nature of Brown's assault—he consumed every newspaper he could find on the event (Fuller). But more importantly, it wasn't the most significant aspect of Brown's raid. As Meyer points out, "[b]ecause Thoreau chose moral truth over political expediency, what concerned him was not how slavery was to be ended but that it be ended immediately" ("Black Emigration," 380). Thoreau recognized the importance of ending slavery by whatever means necessary. As Meyer further argues: "Freedom for Thoreau could never be a gift; it had to be earned and established by the person who would be free" ("Black Emigration," 393). This is why Thoreau himself could never effectively take part in the physical war: it was not his freedom at stake. John Brown was just that man, who "would be free" not only in relation to the common laws of humanity—which was the immediate goal for him and the slaves he fought to free—but also in terms of a higher moral freedom, which Thoreau and few others at the time recognized, but which is more universally recognized now. As Barry Kritzberg suggests:

> As a young man, Thoreau had once boastfully claimed that a single individual, if he would but take the simple, sincere first step, might accomplish two-thirds of the world's reform by himself (I, 247). Henry did not propose to do the job himself, but it was his way of emphasizing what he believed to be the inadequacies of cautious reformers who attacked the branches of evil, but never the roots.
>
> (551-2)

Thoreau recognized in Brown one who attacked the roots of the slavery problem, and despite the violent measures used in this attack, it was the effort made—by an individual man of superior moral conscience against an unjust government—that was important to Thoreau, and is arguably the primary reason why history has not forgotten him.

Kritzberg further notes that

> John Brown did, indeed, strike a new chord in Thoreau, but it was not manifested by any marked change in principles. Nearly all of the radical expressions of 1859 have antecedents in his earlier writings.
>
> (536)

Thoreau's writings on Brown, when read not just in light of, but as a development from, **"Civil Disobedience,"** reveal to the reader not only that violence was certainly a foreseeable response to American slavery, but that support of a man who employed such violence to achieve his ends is not antithetical to Thoreau's philosophy. Rather, as a man of superior moral conscience, the rules of law and limiting definitions of order set by common man simply don't apply to Brown. Thoreau avoids discussing the violence of the Harpers Ferry raid for the same reason he avoids discussing the failure of the event. Yes, the revolt failed, the protesters were brought to trial, and Brown was hung. But the importance of this event lay not in the immediate human gains, but in the universal, moral triumph. In terms of Thoreau's politics, Morris B. Kaplan defines the "democratic individual" as

> necessarily engaged in the business of politics to some extent, partially immersed in a network of social and natural relations. However, such persons are also capable of transcending these relationships in the direction of an authentic realization of their own ultimate possibilities.
>
> (38)

He further writes that "Thoreau's writing evinces a deep awareness of the moral ambiguities of self-formation" (57). For Thoreau, Brown was more than simply a "democratic individual." Nor was Thoreau at all morally ambiguous about Brown's self-formation. Where Kaplan may be able to apply these concepts to Thoreau and his work, the importance for Thoreau lay in reading Brown and his work as an admirable progression therefrom. In **"Martyrdom of John Brown,"** his short piece written just prior to **"The Last Days of John Brown,"** Thoreau translated from Tacitus's selections of topical pieces on martyrdom: "[l]et us honor you by our admiration, rather than by short-lived praises, and, if nature aid us, by our emulation of you" (Rosenblum [*Thoreau*], 162).

Works Cited

Douglass, Frederick. "Letter of Monday, Oct. 31, 1859." *Blacks on John Brown.* Ed. Benjamin Quarles. Urbana: University of Illinois Press, 1972. 7-10.

Fergenson, Laraine. "Thoreau, Daniel Berrigan, and the Problem of Transcendental Politics." *Soundings: an interdisciplinary journal,* 65 (Spring 1982), 103-22.

Fuller, David G. "Correcting the Newspapers: Thoreau and 'A Plea for Captain John Brown.'" *The Concord Saunterer,* N. S. 5 (Fall 1997), 165-75.

Goodwin, James. "Thoreau and John Brown: Transcendental Politics." *ESQ: A Journal of the American Renaissance,* 25:3 (1979), 156-68.

Kaplan, Morris B. "Civil Disobedience, Conscience, and Community: Thoreau's 'Double Self' and the Problematic of Political Action." *The Delegated Intellect: Emersonian Essays on Literature, Science, and Art in Honor of Don Gifford.* Ed. Donald E. Morse. American University Studies: Series XXIV—American Literature. Vol. 57. New York: Peter Lang, 1995. 37-63.

Kritzberg, Barry. "Thoreau, Slavery, and 'Resistance to Civil Government.'" *The Massachusetts Review: A Quarterly of Literature, the Arts, and Public Affairs.* Winter 1989, 535-65.

Ljungquist, Kent. "'Meteor of the War': Melville, Thoreau, and Whitman Respond to John Brown." *American Literature: A Journal of Literary History, Criticism, and Bibliography.* 61:4 (December 1989), 674-80.

Meltzer, Milton, ed. *Thoreau: People, Principles, and Politics.* New York: Hill and Wang, 1963.

Meyer, Michael. "Thoreau and Black Emigration." *American Literature: A Journal of Literary History, Criticism, and Bibliography.* 61:4 (December 1981), 380-96.

———. "'Civil Disobedience' and the Problem of Thoreau's 'Peaceable Revolution.'" *Approaches to Teaching Thoreau's* Walden *and Other Works.* Ed. Richard J. Schneider. New York: The Modern Language Association of America, 1996. 150-54.

Rosenblum, Nancy L., ed. *Thoreau: Political Writings.* Cambridge Texts in the History of Political Thought. Cambridge: Cambridge University Press, 1996.

Sanborn, F. B., ed. *The Life and Letters of John Brown: Liberator of Kansas, and Martyr of Virginia.* (1859) New York: Negro Universities Press, 1969.

Warch, Richard, and Jonathan F. Fanton, eds. *John Brown.* Englewood Cliffs, New Jersey: Prentice-Hall, 1973.

Woodson, Thomas. "The Title and Text of Thoreau's 'Civil Disobedience.'" *Bulletin of Research in the Humanities,* 81 (Spring 1978), 103-12.

FURTHER READING

Bibliographies

Allen, Francis H. *A Bibliography of Henry David Thoreau.* Boston: Houghton Mifflin, 1908, 162 p.
    Includes comprehensive lists of Thoreau's book and periodical publications along with a detailed survey of critical writings devoted to his work.

Borst, Raymond R. *Henry David Thoreau: A Descriptive Bibliography.* Pittsburgh: University of Pittsburgh Press, 1982, 232 p.
    Provides an overview of biographical and critical writings dedicated to Thoreau's life and career.

Scharnhorst, Gary. *Henry David Thoreau: An Annotated Bibliography of Comment and Criticism before 1900.* New York: Garland Publishing, 1992, 386 p.
    Offers annotated listings of nineteenth-century responses to Thoreau's writings.

Biographies

Channing, William Ellery. *Thoreau: The Poet-Naturalist.* Boston: Roberts Brothers, 1873, 357 p.
    Paints an intimate portrait of the author's life and work.

Richardson, Robert D. *Henry Thoreau: A Life of the Mind.* Berkeley: University of California Press, 1986, 455 p.
    Examines the origins and development of Thoreau's philosophical convictions.

Sanborn, F. B. *The Life of Henry David Thoreau.* Boston: Houghton Mifflin, 1917, 541 p.

Presents an estimation of Thoreau's character and writings within the context of New England society and culture in the mid-nineteenth century.

Criticism

Abrams, Robert E. "Image, Object, and Perception in Thoreau's Landscapes: The Development of Anti-Geography." *Nineteenth-Century Literature* 46, no. 2 (September 1991): 245-62.

Explores ideas of indeterminate space in Thoreau's nature writings.

Anastaplo, George. "On Civil Disobedience: Thoreau and Socrates." *Southwest Review* 54 (1969): 203-14.

Contrasts Thoreau's doctrine of nonconformity with Socratic ideas concerning the virtues of "simple law-abidingness."

Bode, Carl. "Thoreau: The Double Negative." In *The Young Rebel in American Literature: Seven Lectures,* edited by Carl Bode, pp. 3-22. London: Heinemann, 1959.

Identifies the revolutionary elements in Thoreau's work.

Box, Ian. "A Taste for the Wild: Some Nietzschean Themes in Thoreau." *Canadian Review of American Studies/Revue Canadienne d'Etudes Américaines* 32, no. 2 (2002): 165-91.

Addresses the relationship between physical vigor and individual freedom in the writings of Thoreau and Nietzsche.

Buranelli, Vincent. "The Case against Thoreau." *Ethics* 67, no. 4 (July 1957): 257-68.

Considers the prophetic qualities of Thoreau's writings and ideas.

Conrad, Randall. "'I Heard a Very Loud Sound': Thoreau Processes the Spectacle of Sudden, Violent Death." *American Transcendental Quarterly* 19, no. 2 (June 2005): 82-94.

Evaluates Thoreau's attitude toward death within the context of the 11 September 2001 terrorist attacks on the United States.

Gatta, John. "'Rare and Delectable Places': Thoreau's Imagination of Sacred Space at Walden." In *There before Us: Religion, Literature, and Culture from Emerson to Wendell Berry,* edited by Roger Lundin, pp. 23-48. Grand Rapids, Mich.: William B. Eerdmans Publishing Company, 2007.

Examines the relationship between transcendental philosophy and the natural world in Thoreau's *Walden.*

Gura, Philipo F. "Thoreau's Maine Woods Indians: More Representative Men." *American Literature* 49, no. 3 (November 1977): 366-84.

Discusses Thoreau's idealization of Native Americans in his work *The Maine Woods.*

Harding, Walter. Introduction to *The Variorum Civil Disobedience,* by Henry David Thoreau, pp. 11-28. New York: Twayne Publishers, Inc., 1967.

Assesses the far-reaching effects of Thoreau's "Civil Disobedience" in the twentieth century, including its influence on Mahatma Gandhi's campaign of passive resistance and on the American Civil Rights Movement.

Hourihan, Paul. "Crisis in the Thoreau-Emerson Friendship: The Symbolic Function of 'Civil Disobedience.'" In *Thoreau's Psychology: Eight Essays,* edited by Raymond D. Gozzi, pp. 109-22. Lanham, Md.: University Press of America, 1983.

Includes a range of critical perspectives focusing on the relationship between Thoreau's life experiences and his writings.

Hyde, Lewis. "Henry Thoreau, John Brown, and the Problem of Prophetic Action." *Raritan: A Quarterly Review* 22, no. 2 (October 2002): 125-44.

Considers Thoreau's involvement with political causes in his later career.

Kritzberg, Barry. "Thoreau, Slavery, and 'Resistance to Civil Government.'" *Massachusetts Review* 30, no. 4 (January 1989): 535-65.

Appraises the figure of John Brown as the living embodiment of Thoreau's political principles.

Marks, Barry A. "Civil Disobedience in Retrospect: Henry Thoreau and Norman Mailer." *Soundings: A Journal of Interdisciplinary Studies* 62 (1979): 144-65.

Compares the political convictions and social activism of the two authors.

Meyer, Michael. "Thoreau and Black Emigration." *American Literature* 53, no. 3 (November 1981): 380-96.

Investigates Thoreau's attitudes toward black emigration as a solution to the problem of slavery.

Newman, Lance. "Henry David Thoreau as Wordsworthian Poet." In *Wordsworth in American Literary Culture,* pp. 121-43. New York: Palgrave Macmillan, 2005.

Considers the influence of Wordsworth's nature poetry in shaping Thoreau's literary aesthetic.

Papa, James A., Jr. "Reinterpreting Myths: The Wilderness and the Indian in Thoreau's *Maine Woods.*" *Midwest Quarterly* 40, no. 2 (January 1999): 215-27.

Evaluates the accuracy of Thoreau's descriptions of the wilderness.

Philippon, Daniel J. "Thoreau's Notes on the Journey West: Nature Writing or Environmental History?" *American Transcendental Quarterly* 18, no. 2 (June 2004): 105-17.

Interprets Thoreau's notes chronicling his western travels within the context of American environmental history.

Schneider, Richard J. *Thoreau's Sense of Place: Essays in American Environmental Writing,* edited by Richard J. Schneider. Iowa City: University of Iowa Press, 2000, 310 p.

Offers diverse critical interpretations of Thoreau's nature writings.

Schueller, Malini. "Carnival Rhetoric and Extra-Vagance in Thoreau's *Walden.*" *American Literature* 58, no. 1 (March 1986): 33-45.

Analyzes the relationship between Thoreau's rhetorical style and his philosophy in *Walden.*

Scott, David. "Rewalking Thoreau and Asia: 'Light from the East' for 'A Very Yankee Sort of Oriental.'" *Philosophy East and West: A Quarterly of Comparative Philosophy* 57, no. 1 (2007): 14-39.

Discusses elements of Eastern philosophy in Thoreau's writings.

Van Doren, Mark. *Henry David Thoreau: A Critical Study.* Boston: Houghton Mifflin Co., 1916, 138 p.

Provides a detailed analysis of Thoreau's philosophy, writings, and character.

Additional coverage of Thoreau's life and career is contained in the following sources published by Gale: *American Nature Writers*; *American Writers*; *Authors and Artists for Young Adults,* **Vol. 42;** *Beacham's Guide to Literature for Young Adults,* **Vol. 3;** *Concise Dictionary of American Literary Biography, 1640-1865*; *Dictionary of Literary Biography,* **Vols. 1, 183, 223, 270, 298;** *DISCovering Authors*; *DISCovering Authors: British Edition*; *DISCovering Authors: Canadian Edition*; *DISCovering Authors Modules: Most-studied Authors*; *DISCovering Authors 3.0*; *Literary Movements for Students,* **Vol. 1;** *Literature and Its Times,* **Vol. 2;** *Literature Resource Center*; *Nineteenth-Century Literature Criticism,* **Vols. 7, 21, 61, 138;** *Nonfiction Classics for Students,* **Vol. 3;** *Poetry Criticism,* **Vol. 30;** *Reference Guide to American Literature,* **Ed. 4;** *Twayne's United States Authors*; **and** *World Literature Criticism,* **Vol. 6.**

How to Use This Index

The main references

> **Calvino, Italo**
> 1923-1985 .... CLC **5, 8, 11, 22, 33, 39,**
> **73; SSC 3, 48**

list all author entries in the following Gale Literary Criticism series:

AAL = *Asian American Literature*
BG = *The Beat Generation: A Gale Critical Companion*
BLC = *Black Literature Criticism*
BLCS = *Black Literature Criticism Supplement*
CLC = *Contemporary Literary Criticism*
CLR = *Children's Literature Review*
CMLC = *Classical and Medieval Literature Criticism*
DC = *Drama Criticism*
FL = *Feminism in Literature: A Gale Critical Companion*
GL = *Gothic Literature: A Gale Critical Companion*
HLC = *Hispanic Literature Criticism*
HLCS = *Hispanic Literature Criticism Supplement*
HR = *Harlem Renaissance: A Gale Critical Companion*
LC = *Literature Criticism from 1400 to 1800*
NCLC = *Nineteenth-Century Literature Criticism*
NNAL = *Native North American Literature*
PC = *Poetry Criticism*
SSC = *Short Story Criticism*
TCLC = *Twentieth-Century Literary Criticism*
WLC = *World Literature Criticism, 1500 to the Present*
WLCS = *World Literature Criticism Supplement*

The cross-references

> See also CA 85-88, 116; CANR 23, 61;
> DAM NOV; DLB 196; EW 13; MTCW 1, 2;
> RGSF 2; RGWL 2; SFW 4; SSFS 12

list all author entries in the following Gale biographical and literary sources:

AAYA = *Authors & Artists for Young Adults*
AFAW = *African American Writers*
AFW = *African Writers*
AITN = *Authors in the News*
AMW = *American Writers*
AMWR = *American Writers Retrospective Supplement*
AMWS = *American Writers Supplement*
ANW = *American Nature Writers*
AW = *Ancient Writers*
BEST = *Bestsellers*
BPFB = *Beacham's Encyclopedia of Popular Fiction: Biography and Resources*
BRW = *British Writers*
BRWS = *British Writers Supplement*
BW = *Black Writers*
BYA = *Beacham's Guide to Literature for Young Adults*
CA = *Contemporary Authors*
CAAS = *Contemporary Authors Autobiography Series*
CABS = *Contemporary Authors Bibliographical Series*
CAD = *Contemporary American Dramatists*
CANR = *Contemporary Authors New Revision Series*
CAP = *Contemporary Authors Permanent Series*
CBD = *Contemporary British Dramatists*
CCA = *Contemporary Canadian Authors*
CD = *Contemporary Dramatists*
CDALB = *Concise Dictionary of American Literary Biography*

CDALBS = *Concise Dictionary of American Literary Biography Supplement*

CDBLB = *Concise Dictionary of British Literary Biography*

CMW = *St. James Guide to Crime & Mystery Writers*

CN = *Contemporary Novelists*

CP = *Contemporary Poets*

CPW = *Contemporary Popular Writers*

CSW = *Contemporary Southern Writers*

CWD = *Contemporary Women Dramatists*

CWP = *Contemporary Women Poets*

CWRI = *St. James Guide to Children's Writers*

CWW = *Contemporary World Writers*

DA = *DISCovering Authors*

DA3 = *DISCovering Authors 3.0*

DAB = *DISCovering Authors: British Edition*

DAC = *DISCovering Authors: Canadian Edition*

DAM = *DISCovering Authors: Modules*

    DRAM: *Dramatists Module;* **MST:** *Most-studied Authors Module;*

    MULT: *Multicultural Authors Module;* **NOV:** *Novelists Module;*

    POET: *Poets Module;* **POP:** *Popular Fiction and Genre Authors Module*

DFS = *Drama for Students*

DLB = *Dictionary of Literary Biography*

DLBD = *Dictionary of Literary Biography Documentary Series*

DLBY = *Dictionary of Literary Biography Yearbook*

DNFS = *Literature of Developing Nations for Students*

EFS = *Epics for Students*

EXPN = *Exploring Novels*

EXPP = *Exploring Poetry*

EXPS = *Exploring Short Stories*

EW = *European Writers*

FANT = *St. James Guide to Fantasy Writers*

FW = *Feminist Writers*

GFL = *Guide to French Literature,* Beginnings to 1789, 1798 to the Present

GLL = *Gay and Lesbian Literature*

HGG = *St. James Guide to Horror, Ghost & Gothic Writers*

HW = *Hispanic Writers*

IDFW = *International Dictionary of Films and Filmmakers: Writers and Production Artists*

IDTP = *International Dictionary of Theatre: Playwrights*

LAIT = *Literature and Its Times*

LAW = *Latin American Writers*

JRDA = *Junior DISCovering Authors*

MAICYA = *Major Authors and Illustrators for Children and Young Adults*

MAICYAS = *Major Authors and Illustrators for Children and Young Adults Supplement*

MAWW = *Modern American Women Writers*

MJW = *Modern Japanese Writers*

MTCW = *Major 20th-Century Writers*

NCFS = *Nonfiction Classics for Students*

NFS = *Novels for Students*

PAB = *Poets: American and British*

PFS = *Poetry for Students*

RGAL = *Reference Guide to American Literature*

RGEL = *Reference Guide to English Literature*

RGSF = *Reference Guide to Short Fiction*

RGWL = *Reference Guide to World Literature*

RHW = *Twentieth-Century Romance and Historical Writers*

SAAS = *Something about the Author Autobiography Series*

SATA = *Something about the Author*

SFW = *St. James Guide to Science Fiction Writers*

SSFS = *Short Stories for Students*

TCWW = *Twentieth-Century Western Writers*

WLIT = *World Literature and Its Times*

WP = *World Poets*

YABC = *Yesterday's Authors of Books for Children*

YAW = *St. James Guide to Young Adult Writers*

Literary Criticism Series
Cumulative Author Index

Aeschylus 525(?)B.C.-456(?)B.C. .. **CMLC 11, 51, 94; DC 8; WLCS**
See also AW 1; CDWLB 1; DA; DAB; DAC; DAM DRAM, MST; DFS 5, 10; DLB 176; LMFS 1; RGWL 2, 3; TWA; WLIT 8

Aesop 620(?)B.C.-560(?)B.C. .... **CMLC 24**
See also CLR 14; MAICYA 1, 2; SATA 64

Affable Hawk
See MacCarthy, Sir (Charles Otto) Desmond

Africa, Ben
See Bosman, Herman Charles

Afton, Effie
See Harper, Frances Ellen Watkins

Agapida, Fray Antonio
See Irving, Washington

Agee, James (Rufus) 1909-1955 ...... **TCLC 1, 19, 180**
See also AAYA 44; AITN 1; AMW; CA 108; 148; CANR 131; CDALB 1941-1968; DAM NOV; DLB 2, 26, 152; DLBY 1989; EWL 3; LAIT 3; LATS 1:2; MAL 5; MTCW 2; MTFW 2005; NFS 22; RGAL 4; TUS

A Gentlewoman in New England
See Bradstreet, Anne

A Gentlewoman in Those Parts
See Bradstreet, Anne

Aghill, Gordon
See Silverberg, Robert

Agnon, S(hmuel) Y(osef Halevi) 1888-1970 .... **CLC 4, 8, 14; SSC 30; TCLC 151**
See also CA 17-18; 25-28R; CANR 60, 102; CAP 2; DLB 329; EWL 3; MTCW 1, 2; RGHL; RGSF 2; RGWL 2, 3; WLIT 6

Agrippa von Nettesheim, Henry Cornelius 1486-1535 .... **LC 27**

Aguilera Malta, Demetrio 1909-1981 .... **HLCS 1**
See also CA 111; 124; CANR 87; DAM MULT, NOV; DLB 145; EWL 3; HW 1; RGWL 3

Agustini, Delmira 1886-1914 .... **HLCS 1**
See also CA 166; DLB 290; HW 1, 2; LAW

Aherne, Owen
See Cassill, R(onald) V(erlin)

Ai 1947- .... **CLC 4, 14, 69; PC 72**
See also CA 85-88; CAAS 13; CANR 70; CP 6, 7; DLB 120; PFS 16

Aickman, Robert (Fordyce) 1914-1981 .... **CLC 57**
See also CA 5-8R; CANR 3, 72, 100; DLB 261; HGG; SUFW 1, 2

Aidoo, (Christina) Ama Ata 1942- .... **BLCS; CLC 177**
See also AFW; BW 1; CA 101; CANR 62, 144; CD 5, 6; CDWLB 3; CN 6, 7; CWD; CWP; DLB 117; DNFS 1, 2; EWL 3; FW; WLIT 2

Aiken, Conrad (Potter) 1889-1973 .... **CLC 1, 3, 5, 10, 52; PC 26; SSC 9**
See also AMW; CA 5-8R; 45-48; CANR 4, 60; CDALB 1929-1941; CN 1; CP 1; DAM NOV, POET; DLB 9, 45, 102; EWL 3; EXPS; HGG; MAL 5; MTCW 1, 2; MTFW 2005; PFS 24; RGAL 4; RGSF 2; SATA 3, 30; SSFS 8; TUS

Aiken, Joan (Delano) 1924-2004 ...... **CLC 35**
See also AAYA 1, 25; CA 9-12R, 182; 223; CAAE 182; CANR 4, 23, 34, 64, 121; CLR 1, 19, 90; DLB 161; FANT; HGG; JRDA; MAICYA 1, 2; MTCW 1; RHW; SAAS 1; SATA 2, 30, 73; SATA-Essay 109; SATA-Obit 152; SUFW 2; WYA; YAW

Ainsworth, William Harrison 1805-1882 .... **NCLC 13**
See also DLB 21; HGG; RGEL 2; SATA 24; SUFW 1

Aitmatov, Chingiz 1928-2008 .... **CLC 71**
See Aytmatov, Chingiz
See also CA 103; CANR 38; CWW 2; DLB 302; MTCW 1; RGSF 2; SATA 56

Aitmatov, Chingiz Torekulovich
See Aitmatov, Chingiz

Akers, Floyd
See Baum, L(yman) Frank

Akhmadulina, Bella Akhatovna 1937- .... **CLC 53; PC 43**
See also CA 65-68; CWP; CWW 2; DAM POET; EWL 3

Akhmatova, Anna 1888-1966 ..... **CLC 11, 25, 64, 126; PC 2, 55**
See also CA 19-20; 25-28R; CANR 35; CAP 1; DA3; DAM POET; DLB 295; EW 10; EWL 3; FL 1:5; MTCW 1, 2; PFS 18, 27; RGWL 2, 3

Aksakov, Sergei Timofeevich 1791-1859 .... **NCLC 2, 181**
See also DLB 198

Aksenov, Vasilii (Pavlovich)
See Aksyonov, Vassily (Pavlovich)
See also CWW 2

Aksenov, Vassily
See Aksyonov, Vassily (Pavlovich)

Akst, Daniel 1956- .... **CLC 109**
See also CA 161; CANR 110

Aksyonov, Vassily (Pavlovich) 1932- .... **CLC 22, 37, 101**
See Aksenov, Vasilii (Pavlovich)
See also CA 53-56; CANR 12, 48, 77; DLB 302; EWL 3

Akutagawa Ryunosuke 1892-1927 ... **SSC 44; TCLC 16**
See also CA 117; 154; DLB 180; EWL 3; MJW; RGSF 2; RGWL 2, 3

Alabaster, William 1568-1640 .... **LC 90**
See also DLB 132; RGEL 2

Alain 1868-1951 .... **TCLC 41**
See also CA 163; EWL 3; GFL 1789 to the Present

Alain de Lille c. 1116-c. 1203 .... **CMLC 53**
See also DLB 208

Alain-Fournier .... **TCLC 6**
See Fournier, Henri-Alban
See also DLB 65; EWL 3; GFL 1789 to the Present; RGWL 2, 3

Al-Amin, Jamil Abdullah 1943- ...... **BLC 1:1**
See also BW 1, 3; CA 112; 125; CANR 82; DAM MULT

Alanus de Insluis
See Alain de Lille

Alarcon, Pedro Antonio de 1833-1891 .... **NCLC 1; SSC 64**

Alas (y Urena), Leopoldo (Enrique Garcia) 1852-1901 .... **TCLC 29**
See also CA 113; 131; HW 1; RGSF 2

Albee, Edward (III) 1928- ..... **CLC 1, 2, 3, 5, 9, 11, 13, 25, 53, 86, 113; DC 11; WLC 1**
See also AAYA 51; AITN 1; AMW; CA 5-8R; CABS 3; CAD; CANR 8, 54, 74, 124; CD 5, 6; CDALB 1941-1968; DA; DA3; DAB; DAC; DAM DRAM, MST; DFS 25; DLB 7, 266; EWL 3; INT CANR-8; LAIT 4; LMFS 2; MAL 5; MTCW 1, 2; MTFW 2005; RGAL 4; TUS

Alberti (Merello), Rafael
See Alberti, Rafael
See also CWW 2

Alberti, Rafael 1902-1999 .... **CLC 7**
See Alberti (Merello), Rafael
See also CA 85-88; 185; CANR 81; DLB 108; EWL 3; HW 2; RGWL 2, 3

Albert the Great 1193(?)-1280 ...... **CMLC 16**
See also DLB 115

Alcaeus c. 620B.C.- .... **CMLC 65**
See also DLB 176

Alcala-Galiano, Juan Valera y
See Valera y Alcala-Galiano, Juan

Alcayaga, Lucila Godoy
See Godoy Alcayaga, Lucila

Alciato, Andrea 1492-1550 .... **LC 116**

Alcott, Amos Bronson 1799-1888 ... **NCLC 1, 167**
See also DLB 1, 223

Alcott, Louisa May 1832-1888 . **NCLC 6, 58, 83; SSC 27, 98; WLC 1**
See also AAYA 20; AMWS 1; BPFB 1; BYA 2; CDALB 1865-1917; CLR 1, 38, 109; DA; DA3; DAB; DAC; DAM MST, NOV; DLB 1, 42, 79, 223, 239, 242; DLBD 14; FL 1:2; FW; JRDA; LAIT 2; MAICYA 1, 2; NFS 12; RGAL 4; SATA 100; TUS; WCH; WYA; YABC 1; YAW

Alcuin c. 730-804 .... **CMLC 69**
See also DLB 148

Aldanov, M. A.
See Aldanov, Mark (Alexandrovich)

Aldanov, Mark (Alexandrovich) 1886-1957 .... **TCLC 23**
See also CA 118; 181; DLB 317

Aldhelm c. 639-709 .... **CMLC 90**

Aldington, Richard 1892-1962 .... **CLC 49**
See also CA 85-88; CANR 45; DLB 20, 36, 100, 149; LMFS 2; RGEL 2

Aldiss, Brian W. 1925- .. **CLC 5, 14, 40; SSC 36**
See also AAYA 42; CA 5-8R, 190; CAAE 190; CAAS 2; CANR 5, 28, 64, 121, 168; CN 1, 2, 3, 4, 5, 6, 7; DAM NOV; DLB 14, 261, 271; MTCW 1, 2; MTFW 2005; SATA 34; SCFW 1, 2; SFW 4

Aldiss, Brian Wilson
See Aldiss, Brian W.

Aldrich, Ann
See Meaker, Marijane

Aldrich, Bess Streeter 1881-1954 .... **TCLC 125**
See also CLR 70; TCWW 2

Alegria, Claribel
See Alegria, Claribel
See also CWW 2; DLB 145, 283

Alegria, Claribel 1924- .... **CLC 75; HLCS 1; PC 26**
See Alegria, Claribel
See also CA 131; CAAS 15; CANR 66, 94, 134; DAM MULT; EWL 3; HW 1; MTCW 2; MTFW 2005; PFS 21

Alegria, Fernando 1918-2005 .... **CLC 57**
See also CA 9-12R; CANR 5, 32, 72; EWL 3; HW 1, 2

Aleixandre, Vicente 1898-1984 .... **HLCS 1; TCLC 113**
See also CANR 81; DLB 108, 329; EWL 3; HW 2; MTCW 1, 2; RGWL 2, 3

Alekseev, Konstantin Sergeivich
See Stanislavsky, Constantin

Alekseyer, Konstantin Sergeyevich
See Stanislavsky, Constantin

Aleman, Mateo 1547-1615(?) .... **LC 81**

Alencar, Jose de 1829-1877 .... **NCLC 157**
See also DLB 307; LAW; WLIT 1

Alencon, Marguerite d'
See de Navarre, Marguerite

Alepoudelis, Odysseus
See Elytis, Odysseus
See also CWW 2

Aleshkovsky, Joseph 1929-
See Aleshkovsky, Yuz
See also CA 121; 128

Aleshkovsky, Yuz .... **CLC 44**
See Aleshkovsky, Joseph
See also DLB 317

Alexander, Barbara
See Ehrenreich, Barbara

Alexander, Lloyd 1924-2007 .... **CLC 35**
See also AAYA 1, 27; BPFB 1; BYA 5, 6, 7, 9, 10, 11; CA 1-4R; 260; CANR 1, 24, 38, 55, 113; CLR 1, 5, 48; CWRI 5; DLB 52; FANT; JRDA; MAICYA 1, 2; MAICYAS 1; MTCW 1; SAAS 19; SATA 3, 49, 81, 129, 135; SATA-Obit 182; SUFW; TUS; WYA; YAW

Alexander, Lloyd Chudley
See Alexander, Lloyd

Alexander, Meena 1951- .... **CLC 121**
See also CA 115; CANR 38, 70, 146; CP 5, 6, 7; CWP; DLB 323; FW

Alexander, Samuel 1859-1938 .... **TCLC 77**

Alexeiev, Konstantin
See Stanislavsky, Constantin

Alexeyev, Constantin Sergeivich
See Stanislavsky, Constantin

Alexeyev, Konstantin Sergeyevich
See Stanislavsky, Constantin

Alexie, Sherman 1966- .... **CLC 96, 154;**
NNAL; PC 53; SSC 107
See also AAYA 28; BYA 15; CA 138; CANR 65, 95, 133, 174; CN 7; DA3; DAM MULT; DLB 175, 206, 278; LATS 1:2; MTCW 2; MTFW 2005; NFS 17; SSFS 18

Alexie, Sherman Joseph, Jr.
See Alexie, Sherman

al-Farabi 870(?)-950 .... **CMLC 58**
See also DLB 115

Alfau, Felipe 1902-1999 .... **CLC 66**
See also CA 137

Alfieri, Vittorio 1749-1803 .... **NCLC 101**
See also EW 4; RGWL 2, 3; WLIT 7

Alfonso X 1221-1284 .... **CMLC 78**

Alfred, Jean Gaston
See Ponge, Francis

Alger, Horatio, Jr. 1832-1899 .... **NCLC 8, 83**
See also CLR 87; DLB 42; LAIT 2; RGAL 4; SATA 16; TUS

Al-Ghazali, Muhammad ibn Muhammad
1058-1111 .... **CMLC 50**
See also DLB 115

Algren, Nelson 1909-1981 ..... **CLC 4, 10, 33;**
SSC 33
See also AMWS 9; BPFB 1; CA 13-16R; 103; CANR 20, 61; CDALB 1941-1968; CN 1, 2; DLB 9; DLBY 1981, 1982, 2000; EWL 3; MAL 5; MTCW 1, 2; MTFW 2005; RGAL 4; RGSF 2

al-Hamadhani 967-1007 .... **CMLC 93**
See also WLIT 6

al-Hariri, al-Qasim ibn 'Ali Abu
Muhammad al-Basri
1054-1122 .... **CMLC 63**
See also RGWL 3

Ali, Ahmed 1908-1998 .... **CLC 69**
See also CA 25-28R; CANR 15, 34; CN 1, 2, 3, 4, 5; DLB 323; EWL 3

Ali, Tariq 1943- .... **CLC 173**
See also CA 25-28R; CANR 10, 99, 161

Alighieri, Dante
See Dante
See also WLIT 7

al-Kindi, Abu Yusuf Ya'qub ibn Ishaq c.
801-c. 873 .... **CMLC 80**

Allan, John B.
See Westlake, Donald E.

Allan, Sidney
See Hartmann, Sadakichi

Allan, Sydney
See Hartmann, Sadakichi

Allard, Janet .... **CLC 59**

Allen, Edward 1948- .... **CLC 59**

Allen, Fred 1894-1956 .... **TCLC 87**

Allen, Paula Gunn 1939-2008 . **CLC 84, 202;**
NNAL
See also AMWS 4; CA 112; 143; 272; CANR 63, 130; CWP; DA3; DAM MULT; DLB 175; FW; MTCW 2; MTFW 2005; RGAL 4; TCWW 2

Allen, Roland
See Ayckbourn, Alan

Allen, Sarah A.
See Hopkins, Pauline Elizabeth

Allen, Sidney H.
See Hartmann, Sadakichi

Allen, Woody 1935- .... **CLC 16, 52, 195**
See also AAYA 10, 51; AMWS 15; CA 33-36R; CANR 27, 38, 63, 128, 172; DAM POP; DLB 44; MTCW 1; SSFS 21

Allende, Isabel 1942- ... **CLC 39, 57, 97, 170,**
264; HLC 1; SSC 65; WLCS
See also AAYA 18, 70; CA 125; 130; CANR 51, 74, 129, 165; CDWLB 3; CLR 99; CWW 2; DA3; DAM MULT, NOV; DLB 145; DNFS 1; EWL 3; FL 1:5; FW; HW 1, 2; INT CA-130; LAIT 5; LAWS 1; LMFS 2; MTCW 1, 2; MTFW 2005; NCFS 1; NFS 6, 18; RGSF 2; RGWL 3; SATA 163; SSFS 11, 16; WLIT 1

Alleyn, Ellen
See Rossetti, Christina

Alleyne, Carla D. .... **CLC 65**

Allingham, Margery (Louise)
1904-1966 .... **CLC 19**
See also CA 5-8R; 25-28R; CANR 4, 58; CMW 4; DLB 77; MSW; MTCW 1, 2

Allingham, William 1824-1889 ...... **NCLC 25**
See also DLB 35; RGEL 2

Allison, Dorothy E. 1949- .... **CLC 78, 153**
See also AAYA 53; CA 140; CANR 66, 107; CN 7; CSW; DA3; FW; MTCW 2; MTFW 2005; NFS 11; RGAL 4

Alloula, Malek .... **CLC 65**

Allston, Washington 1779-1843 .... **NCLC 2**
See also DLB 1, 235

Almedingen, E. M. .... **CLC 12**
See Almedingen, Martha Edith von
See also SATA 3

Almedingen, Martha Edith von 1898-1971
See Almedingen, E. M.
See also CA 1-4R; CANR 1

Almodovar, Pedro 1949(?)- .... **CLC 114, 229;**
HLCS 1
See also CA 133; CANR 72, 151; HW 2

Almqvist, Carl Jonas Love
1793-1866 .... **NCLC 42**

al-Mutanabbi, Ahmad ibn al-Husayn Abu
al-Tayyib al-Jufi al-Kindi
915-965 .... **CMLC 66**
See Mutanabbi, Al-
See also RGWL 3

Alonso, Damaso 1898-1990 .... **CLC 14**
See also CA 110; 131; 130; CANR 72; DLB 108; EWL 3; HW 1, 2

Alov
See Gogol, Nikolai (Vasilyevich)

al'Sadaawi, Nawal
See El Saadawi, Nawal
See also FW

al-Shaykh, Hanan 1945- .... **CLC 218**
See also CA 135; CANR 111; CWW 2; DLB 346; EWL 3; WLIT 6

Al Siddik
See Rolfe, Frederick (William Serafino Austin Lewis Mary)
See also GLL 1; RGEL 2

Alta 1942- .... **CLC 19**
See also CA 57-60

Alter, Robert B. 1935- .... **CLC 34**
See also CA 49-52; CANR 1, 47, 100, 160

Alter, Robert Bernard
See Alter, Robert B.

Alther, Lisa 1944- .... **CLC 7, 41**
See also BPFB 1; CA 65-68; CAAS 30; CANR 12, 30, 51, 180; CN 4, 5, 6, 7; CSW; GLL 2; MTCW 1

Althusser, L.
See Althusser, Louis

Althusser, Louis 1918-1990 .... **CLC 106**
See also CA 131; 132; CANR 102; DLB 242

Altman, Robert 1925-2006 .... **CLC 16, 116,**
242
See also CA 73-76; 254; CANR 43

Alurista .... **HLCS 1; PC 34**
See Urista (Heredia), Alberto (Baltazar)
See also CA 45-48R; DLB 82; LLW

Alvarez, A. 1929- .... **CLC 5, 13**
See also CA 1-4R; CANR 3, 33, 63, 101, 134; CN 3, 4, 5, 6; CP 1, 2, 3, 4, 5, 6, 7; DLB 14, 40; MTFW 2005

Alvarez, Alejandro Rodriguez 1903-1965
See Casona, Alejandro
See also CA 131; 93-96; HW 1

Alvarez, Julia 1950- .... **CLC 93; HLCS 1**
See also AAYA 25; AMWS 7; CA 147; CANR 69, 101, 133, 166; DA3; DLB 282; LATS 1:2; LLW; MTCW 2; MTFW 2005; NFS 5, 9; SATA 129; WLIT 1

Alvaro, Corrado 1896-1956 .... **TCLC 60**
See also CA 163; DLB 264; EWL 3

Amado, Jorge 1912-2001 ... **CLC 13, 40, 106,**
232; HLC 1
See also CA 77-80; 201; CANR 35, 74, 135; CWW 2; DAM MULT, NOV; DLB 113, 307; EWL 3; HW 2; LAW; LAWS 1; MTCW 1, 2; MTFW 2005; RGWL 2, 3; TWA; WLIT 1

Ambler, Eric 1909-1998 .... **CLC 4, 6, 9**
See also BRWS 4; CA 9-12R; 171; CANR 7, 38, 74; CMW 4; CN 1, 2, 3, 4, 5, 6; DLB 77; MSW; MTCW 1, 2; TEA

Ambrose c. 339-c. 397 .... **CMLC 103**

Ambrose, Stephen E. 1936-2002 .... **CLC 145**
See also AAYA 44; CA 1-4R; 209; CANR 3, 43, 57, 83, 105; MTFW 2005; NCFS 2; SATA 40, 138

Amichai, Yehuda 1924-2000 .. **CLC 9, 22, 57,**
116; PC 38
See also CA 85-88; 189; CANR 46, 60, 99, 132; CWW 2; EWL 3; MTCW 1, 2; MTFW 2005; PFS 24; RGHL; WLIT 6

Amichai, Yehudah
See Amichai, Yehuda

Amiel, Henri Frederic 1821-1881 .... **NCLC 4**
See also DLB 217

Amis, Kingsley 1922-1995 . **CLC 1, 2, 3, 5, 8,**
13, 40, 44, 129
See also AAYA 77; AITN 2; BPFB 1; BRWS 2; CA 9-12R; 150; CANR 8, 28, 54; CDBLB 1945-1960; CN 1, 2, 3, 4, 5, 6; CP 1, 2, 3, 4; DA; DA3; DAB; DAC; DAM MST, NOV; DLB 15, 27, 100, 139, 326; DLBY 1996; EWL 3; HGG; INT CANR-8; MTCW 1, 2; MTFW 2005; RGEL 2; RGSF 2; SFW 4

Amis, Martin 1949- ... **CLC 4, 9, 38, 62, 101,**
213; SSC 112
See also BEST 90:3; BRWS 4; CA 65-68; CANR 8, 27, 54, 73, 95, 132, 166; CN 5, 6, 7; DA3; DLB 14, 194; EWL 3; INT CANR-27; MTCW 2; MTFW 2005

Amis, Martin Louis
See Amis, Martin

Ammianus Marcellinus c. 330-c.
395 .... **CMLC 60**
See also AW 2; DLB 211

Ammons, A.R. 1926-2001 .. **CLC 2, 3, 5, 8, 9,**
25, 57, 108; PC 16
See also AITN 1; AMWS 7; CA 9-12R; 193; CANR 6, 36, 51, 73, 107, 156; CP 1, 2, 3, 4, 5, 6, 7; CSW; DAM POET; DLB

Apple, Max (Isaac) 1941- .... **CLC 9, 33; SSC 50**
See also AMWS 17; CA 81-84; CANR 19, 54; DLB 130

Appleman, Philip (Dean) 1926- .... **CLC 51**
See also CA 13-16R; CAAS 18; CANR 6, 29, 56

Appleton, Lawrence
See Lovecraft, H. P.

Apteryx
See Eliot, T(homas) S(tearns)

Apuleius, (Lucius Madaurensis) c. 125-c. 164 .... **CMLC 1, 84**
See also AW 2; CDWLB 1; DLB 211; RGWL 2, 3; SUFW; WLIT 8

Aquin, Hubert 1929-1977 .... **CLC 15**
See also CA 105; DLB 53; EWL 3

Aquinas, Thomas 1224(?)-1274 ..... **CMLC 33**
See also DLB 115; EW 1; TWA

Aragon, Louis 1897-1982 .... **CLC 3, 22; TCLC 123**
See also CA 69-72; 108; CANR 28, 71; DAM NOV, POET; DLB 72, 258; EW 11; EWL 3; GFL 1789 to the Present; GLL 2; LMFS 2; MTCW 1, 2; RGWL 2, 3

Arany, Janos 1817-1882 .... **NCLC 34**

Aranyos, Kakay 1847-1910
See Mikszath, Kalman

Aratus of Soli c. 315B.C.-c. 240B.C. .... **CMLC 64**
See also DLB 176

Arbuthnot, John 1667-1735 .... **LC 1**
See also DLB 101

Archer, Herbert Winslow
See Mencken, H(enry) L(ouis)

Archer, Jeffrey 1940- .... **CLC 28**
See also AAYA 16; BEST 89:3; BPFB 1; CA 77-80; CANR 22, 52, 95, 136; CPW; DA3; DAM POP; INT CANR-22; MTFW 2005

Archer, Jeffrey Howard
See Archer, Jeffrey

Archer, Jules 1915- .... **CLC 12**
See also CA 9-12R; CANR 6, 69; SAAS 5; SATA 4, 85

Archer, Lee
See Ellison, Harlan

Archilochus c. 7th cent. B.C.- .... **CMLC 44**
See also DLB 176

Ard, William
See Jakes, John

Arden, John 1930- .... **CLC 6, 13, 15**
See also BRWS 2; CA 13-16R; CAAS 4; CANR 31, 65, 67, 124; CBD; CD 5, 6; DAM DRAM; DFS 9; DLB 13, 245; EWL 3; MTCW 1

Arenas, Reinaldo 1943-1990 .. **CLC 41; HLC 1; TCLC 191**
See also CA 124; 128; 133; CANR 73, 106; DAM MULT; DLB 145; EWL 3; GLL 2; HW 1; LAW; LAWS 1; MTCW 2; MTFW 2005; RGSF 2; RGWL 3; WLIT 1

Arendt, Hannah 1906-1975 .... **CLC 66, 98; TCLC 193**
See also CA 17-20R; 61-64; CANR 26, 60, 172; DLB 242; MTCW 1, 2

Aretino, Pietro 1492-1556 .... **LC 12**
See also RGWL 2, 3

Arghezi, Tudor .... **CLC 80**
See Theodorescu, Ion N.
See also CA 167; CDWLB 4; DLB 220; EWL 3

Arguedas, Jose Maria 1911-1969 .... **CLC 10, 18; HLCS 1; TCLC 147**
See also CA 89-92; CANR 73; DLB 113; EWL 3; HW 1; LAW; RGWL 2, 3; WLIT 1

Argueta, Manlio 1936- .... **CLC 31**
See also CA 131; CANR 73; CWW 2; DLB 145; EWL 3; HW 1; RGWL 3

Arias, Ron 1941- .... **HLC 1**
See also CA 131; CANR 81, 136; DAM MULT; DLB 82; HW 1, 2; MTCW 2; MTFW 2005

Ariosto, Lodovico
See Ariosto, Ludovico
See also WLIT 7

Ariosto, Ludovico 1474-1533 ... **LC 6, 87; PC 42**
See Ariosto, Lodovico
See also EW 2; RGWL 2, 3

Aristides
See Epstein, Joseph

Aristophanes 450B.C.-385B.C. .... **CMLC 4, 51; DC 2; WLCS**
See also AW 1; CDWLB 1; DA; DA3; DAB; DAC; DAM DRAM, MST; DFS 10; DLB 176; LMFS 1; RGWL 2, 3; TWA; WLIT 8

Aristotle 384B.C.-322B.C. .... **CMLC 31; WLCS**
See also AW 1; CDWLB 1; DA; DA3; DAB; DAC; DAM MST; DLB 176; RGWL 2, 3; TWA; WLIT 8

Arlt, Roberto (Godofredo Christophersen) 1900-1942 .... **HLC 1; TCLC 29**
See also CA 123; 131; CANR 67; DAM MULT; DLB 305; EWL 3; HW 1, 2; IDTP; LAW

Armah, Ayi Kwei 1939- . **BLC 1:1, 2:1; CLC 5, 33, 136**
See also AFW; BRWS 10; BW 1; CA 61-64; CANR 21, 64; CDWLB 3; CN 1, 2, 3, 4, 5, 6, 7; DAM MULT, POET; DLB 117; EWL 3; MTCW 1; WLIT 2

Armatrading, Joan 1950- .... **CLC 17**
See also CA 114; 186

Armin, Robert 1568(?)-1615(?) .... **LC 120**

Armitage, Frank
See Carpenter, John (Howard)

Armstrong, Jeannette (C.) 1948- .... **NNAL**
See also CA 149; CCA 1; CN 6, 7; DAC; DLB 334; SATA 102

Arnette, Robert
See Silverberg, Robert

Arnim, Achim von (Ludwig Joachim von Arnim) 1781-1831 .. **NCLC 5, 159; SSC 29**
See also DLB 90

Arnim, Bettina von 1785-1859 ...... **NCLC 38, 123**
See also DLB 90; RGWL 2, 3

Arnold, Matthew 1822-1888 ..... **NCLC 6, 29, 89, 126; PC 5; WLC 1**
See also BRW 5; CDBLB 1832-1890; DA; DAB; DAC; DAM MST, POET; DLB 32, 57; EXPP; PAB; PFS 2; TEA; WP

Arnold, Thomas 1795-1842 .... **NCLC 18**
See also DLB 55

Arnow, Harriette (Louisa) Simpson 1908-1986 ...... **CLC 2, 7, 18; TCLC 196**
See also BPFB 1; CA 9-12R; 118; CANR 14; CN 2, 3, 4; DLB 6; FW; MTCW 1, 2; RHW; SATA 42; SATA-Obit 47

Arouet, Francois-Marie
See Voltaire

Arp, Hans
See Arp, Jean

Arp, Jean 1887-1966 .... **CLC 5; TCLC 115**
See also CA 81-84; 25-28R; CANR 42, 77; EW 10

Arrabal
See Arrabal, Fernando

Arrabal (Teran), Fernando
See Arrabal, Fernando
See also CWW 2

Arrabal, Fernando 1932- ... **CLC 2, 9, 18, 58**
See Arrabal (Teran), Fernando
See also CA 9-12R; CANR 15; DLB 321; EWL 3; LMFS 2

Arreola, Juan Jose 1918-2001 .... **CLC 147; HLC 1; SSC 38**
See also CA 113; 131; 200; CANR 81; CWW 2; DAM MULT; DLB 113; DNFS 2; EWL 3; HW 1, 2; LAW; RGSF 2

Arrian c. 89(?)-c. 155(?) .... **CMLC 43**
See also DLB 176

Arrick, Fran .... **CLC 30**
See Gaberman, Judie Angell
See also BYA 6

Arrley, Richmond
See Delany, Samuel R., Jr.

Artaud, Antonin (Marie Joseph) 1896-1948 .... **DC 14; TCLC 3, 36**
See also CA 104; 149; DA3; DAM DRAM; DFS 22; DLB 258, 321; EW 11; EWL 3; GFL 1789 to the Present; MTCW 2; MTFW 2005; RGWL 2, 3

Arthur, Ruth M(abel) 1905-1979 ..... **CLC 12**
See also CA 9-12R; 85-88; CANR 4; CWRI 5; SATA 7, 26

Artsybashev, Mikhail (Petrovich) 1878-1927 .... **TCLC 31**
See also CA 170; DLB 295

Arundel, Honor (Morfydd) 1919-1973 .... **CLC 17**
See also CA 21-22; 41-44R; CAP 2; CLR 35; CWRI 5; SATA 4; SATA-Obit 24

Arzner, Dorothy 1900-1979 .... **CLC 98**

Asch, Sholem 1880-1957 .... **TCLC 3**
See also CA 105; DLB 333; EWL 3; GLL 2; RGHL

Ascham, Roger 1516(?)-1568 .... **LC 101**
See also DLB 236

Ash, Shalom
See Asch, Sholem

Ashbery, John 1927- ... **CLC 2, 3, 4, 6, 9, 13, 15, 25, 41, 77, 125, 221; PC 26**
See also AMWS 3; CA 5-8R; CANR 9, 37, 66, 102, 132, 170; CP 1, 2, 3, 4, 5, 6, 7; DA3; DAM POET; DLB 5, 165; DLBY 1981; EWL 3; GLL 1; INT CANR-9; MAL 5; MTCW 1, 2; MTFW 2005; PAB; PFS 11, 28; RGAL 4; TCLE 1:1; WP

Ashbery, John Lawrence
See Ashbery, John

Ashbridge, Elizabeth 1713-1755 .... **LC 147**
See also DLB 200

Ashdown, Clifford
See Freeman, R(ichard) Austin

Ashe, Gordon
See Creasey, John

Ashton-Warner, Sylvia (Constance) 1908-1984 .... **CLC 19**
See also CA 69-72; 112; CANR 29; CN 1, 2, 3; MTCW 1, 2

Asimov, Isaac 1920-1992 ..... **CLC 1, 3, 9, 19, 26, 76, 92**
See also AAYA 13; BEST 90:2; BPFB 1; BYA 4, 6, 7, 9; CA 1-4R; 137; CANR 2, 19, 36, 60, 125; CLR 12, 79; CMW 4; CN 1, 2, 3, 4, 5; CPW; DA3; DAM POP; DLB 8; DLBY 1992; INT CANR-19; JRDA; LAIT 5; LMFS 2; MAICYA 1, 2; MAL 5; MTCW 1, 2; MTFW 2005; RGAL 4; SATA 1, 26, 74; SCFW 1, 2; SFW 4; SSFS 17; TUS; YAW

Askew, Anne 1521(?)-1546 .... **LC 81**
See also DLB 136

Assis, Joaquim Maria Machado de
See Machado de Assis, Joaquim Maria

Astell, Mary 1666-1731 .... **LC 68**
See also DLB 252, 336; FW

Bachmann, Ingeborg 1926-1973 ..... **CLC 69; TCLC 192**
See also CA 93-96; 45-48; CANR 69; DLB 85; EWL 3; RGHL; RGWL 2, 3

Bacon, Francis 1561-1626 ..... **LC 18, 32, 131**
See also BRW 1; CDBLB Before 1660; DLB 151, 236, 252; RGEL 2; TEA

Bacon, Roger 1214(?)-1294 ... **CMLC 14, 108**
See also DLB 115

Bacovia, George 1881-1957 .... **TCLC 24**
See Vasiliu, Gheorghe
See also CDWLB 4; DLB 220; EWL 3

Badanes, Jerome 1937-1995 .... **CLC 59**
See also CA 234

Bage, Robert 1728-1801 .... **NCLC 182**
See also DLB 39; RGEL 2

Bagehot, Walter 1826-1877 .... **NCLC 10**
See also DLB 55

Bagnold, Enid 1889-1981 .... **CLC 25**
See also AAYA 75; BYA 2; CA 5-8R; 103; CANR 5, 40; CBD; CN 2; CWD; CWRI 5; DAM DRAM; DLB 13, 160, 191, 245; FW; MAICYA 1, 2; RGEL 2; SATA 1, 25

Bagritsky, Eduard .... **TCLC 60**
See Dzyubin, Eduard Georgievich

Bagrjana, Elisaveta
See Belcheva, Elisaveta Lyubomirova

Bagryana, Elisaveta .... **CLC 10**
See Belcheva, Elisaveta Lyubomirova
See also CA 178; CDWLB 4; DLB 147; EWL 3

Bailey, Paul 1937- .... **CLC 45**
See also CA 21-24R; CANR 16, 62, 124; CN 1, 2, 3, 4, 5, 6, 7; DLB 14, 271; GLL 2

Baillie, Joanna 1762-1851 ...... **NCLC 71, 151**
See also DLB 93, 344; GL 2; RGEL 2

Bainbridge, Beryl 1934- ...... **CLC 4, 5, 8, 10, 14, 18, 22, 62, 130**
See also BRWS 6; CA 21-24R; CANR 24, 55, 75, 88, 128; CN 2, 3, 4, 5, 6, 7; DAM NOV; DLB 14, 231; EWL 3; MTCW 1, 2; MTFW 2005

Baker, Carlos (Heard)
1909-1987 .... **TCLC 119**
See also CA 5-8R; 122; CANR 3, 63; DLB 103

Baker, Elliott 1922-2007 .... **CLC 8**
See also CA 45-48; 257; CANR 2, 63; CN 1, 2, 3, 4, 5, 6, 7

Baker, Elliott Joseph
See Baker, Elliott

Baker, Jean H. .... **TCLC 3, 10**
See Russell, George William

Baker, Nicholson 1957- .... **CLC 61, 165**
See also AMWS 13; CA 135; CANR 63, 120, 138; CN 6; CPW; DA3; DAM POP; DLB 227; MTFW 2005

Baker, Ray Stannard 1870-1946 .... **TCLC 47**
See also CA 118; DLB 345

Baker, Russell 1925- .... **CLC 31**
See also BEST 89:4; CA 57-60; CANR 11, 41, 59, 137; MTCW 1, 2; MTFW 2005

Bakhtin, M.
See Bakhtin, Mikhail Mikhailovich

Bakhtin, M. M.
See Bakhtin, Mikhail Mikhailovich

Bakhtin, Mikhail
See Bakhtin, Mikhail Mikhailovich

Bakhtin, Mikhail Mikhailovich
1895-1975 .... **CLC 83; TCLC 160**
See also CA 128; 113; DLB 242; EWL 3

Bakshi, Ralph 1938(?)- .... **CLC 26**
See also CA 112; 138; IDFW 3

Bakunin, Mikhail (Alexandrovich)
1814-1876 .... **NCLC 25, 58**
See also DLB 277

Bal, Mieke (Maria Gertrudis)
1946- .... **CLC 252**
See also CA 156; CANR 99

Baldwin, James 1924-1987 ...... **BLC 1:1, 2:1; CLC 1, 2, 3, 4, 5, 8, 13, 15, 17, 42, 50, 67, 90, 127; DC 1; SSC 10, 33, 98; WLC 1**
See also AAYA 4, 34; AFAW 1, 2; AMWR 2; AMWS 1; BPFB 1; BW 1; CA 1-4R; 124; CABS 1; CAD; CANR 3, 24; CDALB 1941-1968; CN 1, 2, 3, 4; CPW; DA; DA3; DAB; DAC; DAM MST, MULT, NOV, POP; DFS 11, 15; DLB 2, 7, 33, 249, 278; DLBY 1987; EWL 3; EXPS; LAIT 5; MAL 5; MTCW 1, 2; MTFW 2005; NCFS 4; NFS 4; RGAL 4; RGSF 2; SATA 9; SATA-Obit 54; SSFS 2, 18; TUS

Baldwin, William c. 1515-1563 .... **LC 113**
See also DLB 132

Bale, John 1495-1563 .... **LC 62**
See also DLB 132; RGEL 2; TEA

Ball, Hugo 1886-1927 .... **TCLC 104**

Ballard, J.G. 1930- .... **CLC 3, 6, 14, 36, 137; SSC 1, 53**
See also AAYA 3, 52; BRWS 5; CA 5-8R; CANR 15, 39, 65, 107, 133; CN 1, 2, 3, 4, 5, 6, 7; DA3; DAM NOV, POP; DLB 14, 207, 261, 319; EWL 3; HGG; MTCW 1, 2; MTFW 2005; RGEL 2; RGSF 2; SATA 93; SCFW 1, 2; SFW 4

Balmont, Konstantin (Dmitriyevich)
1867-1943 .... **TCLC 11**
See also CA 109; 155; DLB 295; EWL 3

Baltausis, Vincas 1847-1910
See Mikszath, Kalman

Balzac, Honore de 1799-1850 ... **NCLC 5, 35, 53, 153; SSC 5, 59, 102; WLC 1**
See also DA; DA3; DAB; DAC; DAM MST, NOV; DLB 119; EW 5; GFL 1789 to the Present; LMFS 1; RGSF 2; RGWL 2, 3; SSFS 10; SUFW; TWA

Bambara, Toni Cade 1939-1995 ..... **BLC 1:1, 2:1; CLC 19, 88; SSC 35, 107; TCLC 116; WLCS**
See also AAYA 5, 49; AFAW 2; AMWS 11; BW 2, 3; BYA 12, 14; CA 29-32R; 150; CANR 24, 49, 81; CDALBS; DA; DA3; DAC; DAM MST, MULT; DLB 38, 218; EXPS; MAL 5; MTCW 1, 2; MTFW 2005; RGAL 4; RGSF 2; SATA 112; SSFS 4, 7, 12, 21

Bamdad, A.
See Shamlu, Ahmad

Bamdad, Alef
See Shamlu, Ahmad

Banat, D. R.
See Bradbury, Ray

Bancroft, Laura
See Baum, L(yman) Frank

Banim, John 1798-1842 .... **NCLC 13**
See also DLB 116, 158, 159; RGEL 2

Banim, Michael 1796-1874 .... **NCLC 13**
See also DLB 158, 159

Banjo, The
See Paterson, A(ndrew) B(arton)

Banks, Iain 1954- .... **CLC 34**
See also BRWS 11; CA 123; 128; CANR 61, 106, 180; DLB 194, 261; EWL 3; HGG; INT CA-128; MTFW 2005; SFW 4

Banks, Iain M.
See Banks, Iain

Banks, Iain Menzies
See Banks, Iain

Banks, Lynne Reid .... **CLC 23**
See Reid Banks, Lynne
See also AAYA 6; BYA 7; CN 4, 5, 6

Banks, Russell 1940- . **CLC 37, 72, 187; SSC 42**
See also AAYA 45; AMWS 5; CA 65-68; CAAS 15; CANR 19, 52, 73, 118; CN 4, 5, 6, 7; DLB 130, 278; EWL 3; MAL 5; MTCW 2; MTFW 2005; NFS 13

Banks, Russell Earl
See Banks, Russell

Banville, John 1945- .... **CLC 46, 118, 224**
See also CA 117; 128; CANR 104, 150, 176; CN 4, 5, 6, 7; DLB 14, 271, 326; INT CA-128

Banville, Theodore (Faullain) de
1832-1891 .... **NCLC 9**
See also DLB 217; GFL 1789 to the Present

Baraka, Amiri 1934- .. **BLC 1:1, 2:1; CLC 1, 2, 3, 5, 10, 14, 33, 115, 213; DC 6; PC 4; WLCS**
See Jones, LeRoi
See also AAYA 63; AFAW 1, 2; AMWS 2; BW 2, 3; CA 21-24R; CABS 3; CAD; CANR 27, 38, 61, 133, 172; CD 3, 5, 6; CDALB 1941-1968; CP 4, 5, 6, 7; CPW; DA; DA3; DAC; DAM MST, MULT, POET, POP; DFS 3, 11, 16; DLB 5, 7, 16, 38; DLBD 8; EWL 3; MAL 5; MTCW 1, 2; MTFW 2005; PFS 9; RGAL 4; TCLE 1:1; TUS; WP

Baratynsky, Evgenii Abramovich
1800-1844 .... **NCLC 103**
See also DLB 205

Barbauld, Anna Laetitia
1743-1825 .... **NCLC 50, 185**
See also DLB 107, 109, 142, 158, 336; RGEL 2

Barbellion, W. N. P. .... **TCLC 24**
See Cummings, Bruce F(rederick)

Barber, Benjamin R. 1939- .... **CLC 141**
See also CA 29-32R; CANR 12, 32, 64, 119

Barbera, Jack (Vincent) 1945- .... **CLC 44**
See also CA 110; CANR 45

Barbey d'Aurevilly, Jules-Amedee
1808-1889 .... **NCLC 1; SSC 17**
See also DLB 119; GFL 1789 to the Present

Barbour, John c. 1316-1395 .... **CMLC 33**
See also DLB 146

Barbusse, Henri 1873-1935 .... **TCLC 5**
See also CA 105; 154; DLB 65; EWL 3; RGWL 2, 3

Barclay, Alexander c. 1475-1552 .... **LC 109**
See also DLB 132

Barclay, Bill
See Moorcock, Michael

Barclay, William Ewert
See Moorcock, Michael

Barea, Arturo 1897-1957 .... **TCLC 14**
See also CA 111; 201

Barfoot, Joan 1946- .... **CLC 18**
See also CA 105; CANR 141, 179

Barham, Richard Harris
1788-1845 .... **NCLC 77**
See also DLB 159

Baring, Maurice 1874-1945 .... **TCLC 8**
See also CA 105; 168; DLB 34; HGG

Baring-Gould, Sabine 1834-1924 ... **TCLC 88**
See also DLB 156, 190

Barker, Clive 1952- .... **CLC 52, 205; SSC 53**
See also AAYA 10, 54; BEST 90:3; BPFB 1; CA 121; 129; CANR 71, 111, 133; CPW; DA3; DAM POP; DLB 261; HGG; INT CA-129; MTCW 1, 2; MTFW 2005; SUFW 2

Barker, George Granville
1913-1991 .... **CLC 8, 48; PC 77**
See also CA 9-12R; 135; CANR 7, 38; CP 1, 2, 3, 4, 5; DAM POET; DLB 20; EWL 3; MTCW 1

Beattie, Ann 1947- ..... **CLC 8, 13, 18, 40, 63, 146; SSC 11**
    See also AMWS 5; BEST 90:2; BPFB 1; CA 81-84; CANR 53, 73, 128; CN 4, 5, 6, 7; CPW; DA3; DAM NOV, POP; DLB 218, 278; DLBY 1982; EWL 3; MAL 5; MTCW 1, 2; MTFW 2005; RGAL 4; RGSF 2; SSFS 9; TUS

Beattie, James 1735-1803 .... **NCLC 25**
    See also DLB 109

Beauchamp, Kathleen Mansfield 1888-1923
    See Mansfield, Katherine
    See also CA 104; 134; DA; DA3; DAC; DAM MST; MTCW 2; TEA

Beaumarchais, Pierre-Augustin Caron de 1732-1799 .... **DC 4; LC 61**
    See also DAM DRAM; DFS 14, 16; DLB 313; EW 4; GFL Beginnings to 1789; RGWL 2, 3

Beaumont, Francis 1584(?)-1616 .. **DC 6; LC 33**
    See also BRW 2; CDBLB Before 1660; DLB 58; TEA

Beauvoir, Simone de 1908-1986 .... **CLC 1, 2, 4, 8, 14, 31, 44, 50, 71, 124; SSC 35; WLC 1**
    See also BPFB 1; CA 9-12R; 118; CANR 28, 61; DA; DA3; DAB; DAC; DAM MST, NOV; DLB 72; DLBY 1986; EW 12; EWL 3; FL 1:5; FW; GFL 1789 to the Present; LMFS 2; MTCW 1, 2; MTFW 2005; RGSF 2; RGWL 2, 3; TWA

Beauvoir, Simone Lucie Ernestine Marie Bertrand de
    See Beauvoir, Simone de

Becker, Carl (Lotus) 1873-1945 ..... **TCLC 63**
    See also CA 157; DLB 17

Becker, Jurek 1937-1997 .... **CLC 7, 19**
    See also CA 85-88; 157; CANR 60, 117; CWW 2; DLB 75, 299; EWL 3; RGHL

Becker, Walter 1950- .... **CLC 26**

Becket, Thomas a 1118(?)-1170 .... **CMLC 83**

Beckett, Samuel 1906-1989 ... **CLC 1, 2, 3, 4, 6, 9, 10, 11, 14, 18, 29, 57, 59, 83; DC 22; SSC 16, 74; TCLC 145; WLC 1**
    See also BRWC 2; BRWR 1; BRWS 1; CA 5-8R; 130; CANR 33, 61; CBD; CDBLB 1945-1960; CN 1, 2, 3, 4; CP 1, 2, 3, 4; DA; DA3; DAB; DAC; DAM DRAM, MST, NOV; DFS 2, 7, 18; DLB 13, 15, 233, 319, 321, 329; DLBY 1990; EWL 3; GFL 1789 to the Present; LATS 1:2; LMFS 2; MTCW 1, 2; MTFW 2005; RGSF 2; RGWL 2, 3; SSFS 15; TEA; WLIT 4

Beckford, William 1760-1844 .... **NCLC 16**
    See also BRW 3; DLB 39, 213; GL 2; HGG; LMFS 1; SUFW

Beckham, Barry (Earl) 1944- .... **BLC 1:1**
    See also BW 1; CA 29-32R; CANR 26, 62; CN 1, 2, 3, 4, 5, 6; DAM MULT; DLB 33

Beckman, Gunnel 1910- .... **CLC 26**
    See also CA 33-36R; CANR 15, 114; CLR 25; MAICYA 1, 2; SAAS 9; SATA 6

Becque, Henri 1837-1899 .... **DC 21; NCLC 3**
    See also DLB 192; GFL 1789 to the Present

Becquer, Gustavo Adolfo 1836-1870 .... **HLCS 1; NCLC 106**
    See also DAM MULT

Beddoes, Thomas Lovell 1803-1849 .. **DC 15; NCLC 3, 154**
    See also BRWS 11; DLB 96

Bede c. 673-735 .... **CMLC 20**
    See also DLB 146; TEA

Bedford, Denton R. 1907-(?) .... **NNAL**

Bedford, Donald F.
    See Fearing, Kenneth (Flexner)

Beecher, Catharine Esther 1800-1878 .... **NCLC 30**
    See also DLB 1, 243

Beecher, John 1904-1980 .... **CLC 6**
    See also AITN 1; CA 5-8R; 105; CANR 8; CP 1, 2, 3

Beer, Johann 1655-1700 .... **LC 5**
    See also DLB 168

Beer, Patricia 1924- .... **CLC 58**
    See also BRWS 14; CA 61-64; 183; CANR 13, 46; CP 1, 2, 3, 4, 5, 6; CWP; DLB 40; FW

Beerbohm, Max
    See Beerbohm, (Henry) Max(imilian)

Beerbohm, (Henry) Max(imilian) 1872-1956 .... **TCLC 1, 24**
    See also BRWS 2; CA 104; 154; CANR 79; DLB 34, 100; FANT; MTCW 2

Beer-Hofmann, Richard 1866-1945 .... **TCLC 60**
    See also CA 160; DLB 81

Beg, Shemus
    See Stephens, James

Begiebing, Robert J(ohn) 1946- .... **CLC 70**
    See also CA 122; CANR 40, 88

Begley, Louis 1933- .... **CLC 197**
    See also CA 140; CANR 98, 176; DLB 299; RGHL; TCLE 1:1

Behan, Brendan (Francis) 1923-1964 .... **CLC 1, 8, 11, 15, 79**
    See also BRWS 2; CA 73-76; CANR 33, 121; CBD; CDBLB 1945-1960; DAM DRAM; DFS 7; DLB 13, 233; EWL 3; MTCW 1, 2

Behn, Aphra 1640(?)-1689 .. **DC 4; LC 1, 30, 42, 135; PC 13, 88; WLC 1**
    See also BRWS 3; DA; DA3; DAB; DAC; DAM DRAM, MST, NOV, POET; DFS 16, 24; DLB 39, 80, 131; FW; TEA; WLIT 3

Behrman, S(amuel) N(athaniel) 1893-1973 .... **CLC 40**
    See also CA 13-16; 45-48; CAD; CAP 1; DLB 7, 44; IDFW 3; MAL 5; RGAL 4

Bekederemo, J. P. Clark
    See Clark Bekederemo, J.P.
    See also CD 6

Belasco, David 1853-1931 .... **TCLC 3**
    See also CA 104; 168; DLB 7; MAL 5; RGAL 4

Belcheva, Elisaveta Lyubomirova 1893-1991 .... **CLC 10**
    See Bagryana, Elisaveta

Beldone, Phil "Cheech"
    See Ellison, Harlan

Beleno
    See Azuela, Mariano

Belinski, Vissarion Grigoryevich 1811-1848 .... **NCLC 5**
    See also DLB 198

Belitt, Ben 1911- .... **CLC 22**
    See also CA 13-16R; CAAS 4; CANR 7, 77; CP 1, 2, 3, 4, 5, 6; DLB 5

Belknap, Jeremy 1744-1798 .... **LC 115**
    See also DLB 30, 37

Bell, Gertrude (Margaret Lowthian) 1868-1926 .... **TCLC 67**
    See also CA 167; CANR 110; DLB 174

Bell, J. Freeman
    See Zangwill, Israel

Bell, James Madison 1826-1902 ..... **BLC 1:1; TCLC 43**
    See also BW 1; CA 122; 124; DAM MULT; DLB 50

Bell, Madison Smartt 1957- ..... **CLC 41, 102, 223**
    See also AMWS 10; BPFB 1; CA 111, 183; CAAE 183; CANR 28, 54, 73, 134, 176; CN 5, 6, 7; CSW; DLB 218, 278; MTCW 2; MTFW 2005

Bell, Marvin (Hartley) 1937- ...... **CLC 8, 31; PC 79**
    See also CA 21-24R; CAAS 14; CANR 59, 102; CP 1, 2, 3, 4, 5, 6, 7; DAM POET; DLB 5; MAL 5; MTCW 1; PFS 25

Bell, W. L. D.
    See Mencken, H(enry) L(ouis)

Bellamy, Atwood C.
    See Mencken, H(enry) L(ouis)

Bellamy, Edward 1850-1898 ..... **NCLC 4, 86, 147**
    See also DLB 12; NFS 15; RGAL 4; SFW 4

Belli, Gioconda 1948- .... **HLCS 1**
    See also CA 152; CANR 143; CWW 2; DLB 290; EWL 3; RGWL 3

Bellin, Edward J.
    See Kuttner, Henry

Bello, Andres 1781-1865 .... **NCLC 131**
    See also LAW

Belloc, (Joseph) Hilaire (Pierre Sebastien Rene Swanton) 1870-1953 .... **PC 24; TCLC 7, 18**
    See also CA 106; 152; CLR 102; CWRI 5; DAM POET; DLB 19, 100, 141, 174; EWL 3; MTCW 2; MTFW 2005; SATA 112; WCH; YABC 1

Belloc, Joseph Peter Rene Hilaire
    See Belloc, (Joseph) Hilaire (Pierre Sebastien Rene Swanton)

Belloc, Joseph Pierre Hilaire
    See Belloc, (Joseph) Hilaire (Pierre Sebastien Rene Swanton)

Belloc, M. A.
    See Lowndes, Marie Adelaide (Belloc)

Belloc-Lowndes, Mrs.
    See Lowndes, Marie Adelaide (Belloc)

Bellow, Saul 1915-2005 ...... **CLC 1, 2, 3, 6, 8, 10, 13, 15, 25, 33, 34, 63, 79, 190, 200; SSC 14, 101; WLC 1**
    See also AITN 2; AMW; AMWC 2; AMWR 2; BEST 89:3; BPFB 1; CA 5-8R; 238; CABS 1; CANR 29, 53, 95, 132; CDALB 1941-1968; CN 1, 2, 3, 4, 5, 6, 7; DA; DA3; DAB; DAC; DAM MST, NOV, POP; DLB 2, 28, 299, 329; DLBD 3; DLBY 1982; EWL 3; MAL 5; MTCW 1, 2; MTFW 2005; NFS 4, 14, 26; RGAL 4; RGHL; RGSF 2; SSFS 12, 22; TUS

Belser, Reimond Karel Maria de 1929-
    See Ruyslinck, Ward
    See also CA 152

Bely, Andrey .... **PC 11; TCLC 7**
    See Bugayev, Boris Nikolayevich
    See also DLB 295; EW 9; EWL 3

Belyi, Andrei
    See Bugayev, Boris Nikolayevich
    See also RGWL 2, 3

Bembo, Pietro 1470-1547 .... **LC 79**
    See also RGWL 2, 3

Benary, Margot
    See Benary-Isbert, Margot

Benary-Isbert, Margot 1889-1979 .... **CLC 12**
    See also CA 5-8R; 89-92; CANR 4, 72; CLR 12; MAICYA 1, 2; SATA 2; SATA-Obit 21

Benavente (y Martinez), Jacinto 1866-1954 .... **DC 26; HLCS 1; TCLC 3**
    See also CA 106; 131; CANR 81; DAM DRAM, MULT; DLB 329; EWL 3; GLL 2; HW 1, 2; MTCW 1, 2

Blake, William 1757-1827 . **NCLC 13, 37, 57, 127, 173, 190, 201; PC 12, 63; WLC 1**
See also AAYA 47; BRW 3; BRWR 1; CD-BLB 1789-1832; CLR 52; DA; DA3; DAB; DAC; DAM MST, POET; DLB 93, 163; EXPP; LATS 1:1; LMFS 1; MAICYA 1, 2; PAB; PFS 2, 12, 24; SATA 30; TEA; WCH; WLIT 3; WP

Blanchot, Maurice 1907-2003 .... **CLC 135**
See also CA 117; 144; 213; CANR 138; DLB 72, 296; EWL 3

Blasco Ibanez, Vicente 1867-1928 . **TCLC 12**
See Ibanez, Vicente Blasco
See also BPFB 1; CA 110; 131; CANR 81; DA3; DAM NOV; EW 8; EWL 3; HW 1, 2; MTCW 1

Blatty, William Peter 1928- .... **CLC 2**
See also CA 5-8R; CANR 9, 124; DAM POP; HGG

Bleeck, Oliver
See Thomas, Ross (Elmore)

Bleecker, Ann Eliza 1752-1783 .... **LC 161**
See also DLB 200

Blessing, Lee (Knowlton) 1949- .... **CLC 54**
See also CA 236; CAD; CD 5, 6; DFS 23

Blight, Rose
See Greer, Germaine

Blind, Mathilde 1841-1896 .... **NCLC 202**
See also DLB 199

Blish, James (Benjamin) 1921-1975 . **CLC 14**
See also BPFB 1; CA 1-4R; 57-60; CANR 3; CN 2; DLB 8; MTCW 1; SATA 66; SCFW 1, 2; SFW 4

Bliss, Frederick
See Card, Orson Scott

Bliss, Gillian
See Paton Walsh, Jill

Bliss, Reginald
See Wells, H(erbert) G(eorge)

Blixen, Karen (Christentze Dinesen)
1885-1962
See Dinesen, Isak
See also CA 25-28; CANR 22, 50; CAP 2; DA3; DLB 214; LMFS 1; MTCW 1, 2; SATA 44; SSFS 20

Bloch, Robert (Albert) 1917-1994 .... **CLC 33**
See also AAYA 29; CA 5-8R, 179; 146; CAAE 179; CAAS 20; CANR 5, 78; DA3; DLB 44; HGG; INT CANR-5; MTCW 2; SATA 12; SATA-Obit 82; SFW 4; SUFW 1, 2

Blok, Alexander (Alexandrovich)
1880-1921 .... **PC 21; TCLC 5**
See also CA 104; 183; DLB 295; EW 9; EWL 3; LMFS 2; RGWL 2, 3

Blom, Jan
See Breytenbach, Breyten

Bloom, Harold 1930- .... **CLC 24, 103, 221**
See also CA 13-16R; CANR 39, 75, 92, 133, 181; DLB 67; EWL 3; MTCW 2; MTFW 2005; RGAL 4

Bloomfield, Aurelius
See Bourne, Randolph S(illiman)

Bloomfield, Robert 1766-1823 ..... **NCLC 145**
See also DLB 93

Blount, Roy, Jr. 1941- .... **CLC 38**
See also CA 53-56; CANR 10, 28, 61, 125, 176; CSW; INT CANR-28; MTCW 1, 2; MTFW 2005

Blount, Roy Alton
See Blount, Roy, Jr.

Blowsnake, Sam 1875-(?) .... **NNAL**

Bloy, Leon 1846-1917 .... **TCLC 22**
See also CA 121; 183; DLB 123; GFL 1789 to the Present

Blue Cloud, Peter (Aroniawenrate)
1933- .... **NNAL**
See also CA 117; CANR 40; DAM MULT; DLB 342

Bluggage, Oranthy
See Alcott, Louisa May

Blume, Judy 1938- .... **CLC 12, 30**
See also AAYA 3, 26; BYA 1, 8, 12; CA 29-32R; CANR 13, 37, 66, 124; CLR 2, 15, 69; CPW; DA3; DAM NOV, POP; DLB 52; JRDA; MAICYA 1, 2; MAICYAS 1; MTCW 1, 2; MTFW 2005; NFS 24; SATA 2, 31, 79, 142, 195; WYA; YAW

Blume, Judy Sussman
See Blume, Judy

Blunden, Edmund (Charles)
1896-1974 .... **CLC 2, 56; PC 66**
See also BRW 6; BRWS 11; CA 17-18; 45-48; CANR 54; CAP 2; CP 1, 2; DLB 20, 100, 155; MTCW 1; PAB

Bly, Robert (Elwood) 1926- .... **CLC 1, 2, 5, 10, 15, 38, 128; PC 39**
See also AMWS 4; CA 5-8R; CANR 41, 73, 125; CP 1, 2, 3, 4, 5, 6, 7; DA3; DAM POET; DLB 5, 342; EWL 3; MAL 5; MTCW 1, 2; MTFW 2005; PFS 6, 17; RGAL 4

Boas, Franz 1858-1942 .... **TCLC 56**
See also CA 115; 181

Bobette
See Simenon, Georges (Jacques Christian)

Boccaccio, Giovanni 1313-1375 ... **CMLC 13, 57; SSC 10, 87**
See also EW 2; RGSF 2; RGWL 2, 3; TWA; WLIT 7

Bochco, Steven 1943- .... **CLC 35**
See also AAYA 11, 71; CA 124; 138

Bode, Sigmund
See O'Doherty, Brian

Bodel, Jean 1167(?)-1210 .... **CMLC 28**

Bodenheim, Maxwell 1892-1954 .... **TCLC 44**
See also CA 110; 187; DLB 9, 45; MAL 5; RGAL 4

Bodenheimer, Maxwell
See Bodenheim, Maxwell

Bodker, Cecil 1927-
See Bodker, Cecil

Bodker, Cecil 1927- .... **CLC 21**
See also CA 73-76; CANR 13, 44, 111; CLR 23; MAICYA 1, 2; SATA 14, 133

Boell, Heinrich (Theodor)
1917-1985 ..... **CLC 2, 3, 6, 9, 11, 15, 27, 32, 72; SSC 23; WLC 1**
See Boll, Heinrich (Theodor)
See also CA 21-24R; 116; CANR 24; DA; DA3; DAB; DAC; DAM MST, NOV; DLB 69; DLBY 1985; MTCW 1, 2; MTFW 2005; SSFS 20; TWA

Boerne, Alfred
See Doeblin, Alfred

Boethius c. 480-c. 524 .... **CMLC 15**
See also DLB 115; RGWL 2, 3; WLIT 8

Boff, Leonardo (Genezio Darci)
1938- .... **CLC 70; HLC 1**
See also CA 150; DAM MULT; HW 2

Bogan, Louise 1897-1970 .... **CLC 4, 39, 46, 93; PC 12**
See also AMWS 3; CA 73-76; 25-28R; CANR 33, 82; CP 1; DAM POET; DLB 45, 169; EWL 3; MAL 5; MBL; MTCW 1, 2; PFS 21; RGAL 4

Bogarde, Dirk
See Van Den Bogarde, Derek Jules Gaspard Ulric Niven
See also DLB 14

Bogosian, Eric 1953- .... **CLC 45, 141**
See also CA 138; CAD; CANR 102, 148; CD 5, 6; DLB 341

Bograd, Larry 1953- .... **CLC 35**
See also CA 93-96; CANR 57; SAAS 21; SATA 33, 89; WYA

Boiardo, Matteo Maria 1441-1494 .... **LC 6**

Boileau-Despreaux, Nicolas 1636-1711 . **LC 3**
See also DLB 268; EW 3; GFL Beginnings to 1789; RGWL 2, 3

Boissard, Maurice
See Leautaud, Paul

Bojer, Johan 1872-1959 .... **TCLC 64**
See also CA 189; EWL 3

Bok, Edward W(illiam)
1863-1930 .... **TCLC 101**
See also CA 217; DLB 91; DLBD 16

Boker, George Henry 1823-1890 . **NCLC 125**
See also RGAL 4

Boland, Eavan 1944- ... **CLC 40, 67, 113; PC 58**
See also BRWS 5; CA 143, 207; CAAE 207; CANR 61, 180; CP 1, 6, 7; CWP; DAM POET; DLB 40; FW; MTCW 2; MTFW 2005; PFS 12, 22

Boland, Eavan Aisling
See Boland, Eavan

Boll, Heinrich (Theodor) .... **TCLC 185**
See Boell, Heinrich (Theodor)
See also BPFB 1; CDWLB 2; DLB 329; EW 13; EWL 3; RGHL; RGSF 2; RGWL 2, 3

Bolt, Lee
See Faust, Frederick (Schiller)

Bolt, Robert (Oxton) 1924-1995 ...... **CLC 14; TCLC 175**
See also CA 17-20R; 147; CANR 35, 67; CBD; DAM DRAM; DFS 2; DLB 13, 233; EWL 3; LAIT 1; MTCW 1

Bombal, Maria Luisa 1910-1980 .... **HLCS 1; SSC 37**
See also CA 127; CANR 72; EWL 3; HW 1; LAW; RGSF 2

Bombet, Louis-Alexandre-Cesar
See Stendhal

Bomkauf
See Kaufman, Bob (Garnell)

Bonaventura .... **NCLC 35**
See also DLB 90

Bonaventure 1217(?)-1274 .... **CMLC 79**
See also DLB 115; LMFS 1

Bond, Edward 1934- .... **CLC 4, 6, 13, 23**
See also AAYA 50; BRWS 1; CA 25-28R; CANR 38, 67, 106; CBD; CD 5, 6; DAM DRAM; DFS 3, 8; DLB 13, 310; EWL 3; MTCW 1

Bonham, Frank 1914-1989 .... **CLC 12**
See also AAYA 1, 70; BYA 1, 3; CA 9-12R; CANR 4, 36; JRDA; MAICYA 1, 2; SAAS 3; SATA 1, 49; SATA-Obit 62; TCWW 1, 2; YAW

Bonnefoy, Yves 1923- . **CLC 9, 15, 58; PC 58**
See also CA 85-88; CANR 33, 75, 97, 136; CWW 2; DAM MST, POET; DLB 258; EWL 3; GFL 1789 to the Present; MTCW 1, 2; MTFW 2005

Bonner, Marita . **HR 1:2; PC 72; TCLC 179**
See Occomy, Marita (Odette) Bonner

Bonnin, Gertrude 1876-1938 .... **NNAL**
See Zitkala-Sa
See also CA 150; DAM MULT

Bontemps, Arna(ud Wendell)
1902-1973 ..... **BLC 1:1; CLC 1, 18; HR 1:2**
See also BW 1; CA 1-4R; 41-44R; CANR 4, 35; CLR 6; CP 1; CWRI 5; DA3; DAM MULT, NOV, POET; DLB 48, 51; JRDA; MAICYA 1, 2; MAL 5; MTCW 1, 2; SATA 2, 44; SATA-Obit 24; WCH; WP

Boot, William
See Stoppard, Tom

Booth, Irwin
See Hoch, Edward D.

Booth, Martin 1944-2004 .... **CLC 13**
See also CA 93-96, 188; 223; CAAE 188; CAAS 2; CANR 92; CP 1, 2, 3, 4

Booth, Philip 1925-2007 .... **CLC 23**
See also CA 5-8R; 262; CANR 5, 88; CP 1, 2, 3, 4, 5, 6, 7; DLBY 1982

Booth, Philip Edmund
See Booth, Philip

Booth, Wayne C. 1921-2005 .... **CLC 24**
See also CA 1-4R; 244; CAAS 5; CANR 3, 43, 117; DLB 67

Booth, Wayne Clayson
See Booth, Wayne C.

Borchert, Wolfgang 1921-1947 .... **TCLC 5**
See also CA 104; 188; DLB 69, 124; EWL 3

Borel, Petrus 1809-1859 .... **NCLC 41**
See also DLB 119; GFL 1789 to the Present

Borges, Jorge Luis 1899-1986 ... **CLC 1, 2, 3, 4, 6, 8, 9, 10, 13, 19, 44, 48, 83; HLC 1; PC 22, 32; SSC 4, 41, 100; TCLC 109; WLC 1**
See also AAYA 26; BPFB 1; CA 21-24R; CANR 19, 33, 75, 105, 133; CDWLB 3; DA; DA3; DAB; DAC; DAM MST, MULT; DLB 113, 283; DLBY 1986; DNFS 1, 2; EWL 3; HW 1, 2; LAW; LMFS 2; MSW; MTCW 1, 2; MTFW 2005; PFS 27; RGHL; RGSF 2; RGWL 2, 3; SFW 4; SSFS 17; TWA; WLIT 1

Borne, Ludwig 1786-1837 .... **NCLC 193**
See also DLB 90

Borowski, Tadeusz 1922-1951 .... **SSC 48; TCLC 9**
See also CA 106; 154; CDWLB 4; DLB 215; EWL 3; RGHL; RGSF 2; RGWL 3; SSFS 13

Borrow, George (Henry) 1803-1881 .... **NCLC 9**
See also BRWS 12; DLB 21, 55, 166

Bosch (Gavino), Juan 1909-2001 ..... **HLCS 1**
See also CA 151; 204; DAM MST, MULT; DLB 145; HW 1, 2

Bosman, Herman Charles 1905-1951 .... **TCLC 49**
See Malan, Herman
See also CA 160; DLB 225; RGSF 2

Bosschere, Jean de 1878(?)-1953 ... **TCLC 19**
See also CA 115; 186

Boswell, James 1740-1795 ... **LC 4, 50; WLC 1**
See also BRW 3; CDBLB 1660-1789; DA; DAB; DAC; DAM MST; DLB 104, 142; TEA; WLIT 3

Bottomley, Gordon 1874-1948 ..... **TCLC 107**
See also CA 120; 192; DLB 10

Bottoms, David 1949- .... **CLC 53**
See also CA 105; CANR 22; CSW; DLB 120; DLBY 1983

Boucicault, Dion 1820-1890 .... **NCLC 41**
See also DLB 344

Boucolon, Maryse
See Conde, Maryse

Bourcicault, Dion
See Boucicault, Dion

Bourdieu, Pierre 1930-2002 .... **CLC 198**
See also CA 130; 204

Bourget, Paul (Charles Joseph) 1852-1935 .... **TCLC 12**
See also CA 107; 196; DLB 123; GFL 1789 to the Present

Bourjaily, Vance (Nye) 1922- .... **CLC 8, 62**
See also CA 1-4R; CAAS 1; CANR 2, 72; CN 1, 2, 3, 4, 5, 6, 7; DLB 2, 143; MAL 5

Bourne, Randolph S(illiman) 1886-1918 .... **TCLC 16**
See also AMW; CA 117; 155; DLB 63; MAL 5

Boursiquot, Dionysius
See Boucicault, Dion

Bova, Ben 1932- .... **CLC 45**
See also AAYA 16; CA 5-8R; CAAS 18; CANR 11, 56, 94, 111, 157; CLR 3, 96; DLBY 1981; INT CANR-11; MAICYA 1, 2; MTCW 1; SATA 6, 68, 133; SFW 4

Bova, Benjamin William
See Bova, Ben

Bowen, Elizabeth (Dorothea Cole) 1899-1973 . **CLC 1, 3, 6, 11, 15, 22, 118; SSC 3, 28, 66; TCLC 148**
See also BRWS 2; CA 17-18; 41-44R; CANR 35, 105; CAP 2; CDBLB 1945-1960; CN 1; DA3; DAM NOV; DLB 15, 162; EWL 3; EXPS; FW; HGG; MTCW 1, 2; MTFW 2005; NFS 13; RGSF 2; SSFS 5, 22; SUFW 1; TEA; WLIT 4

Bowering, George 1935- .... **CLC 15, 47**
See also CA 21-24R; CAAS 16; CANR 10; CN 7; CP 1, 2, 3, 4, 5, 6, 7; DLB 53

Bowering, Marilyn R(uthe) 1949- .... **CLC 32**
See also CA 101; CANR 49; CP 4, 5, 6, 7; CWP; DLB 334

Bowers, Edgar 1924-2000 .... **CLC 9**
See also CA 5-8R; 188; CANR 24; CP 1, 2, 3, 4, 5, 6, 7; CSW; DLB 5

Bowers, Mrs. J. Milton 1842-1914
See Bierce, Ambrose (Gwinett)

Bowie, David .... **CLC 17**
See Jones, David Robert

Bowles, Jane (Sydney) 1917-1973 ..... **CLC 3, 68**
See Bowles, Jane Auer
See also CA 19-20; 41-44R; CAP 2; CN 1; MAL 5

Bowles, Jane Auer
See Bowles, Jane (Sydney)
See also EWL 3

Bowles, Paul 1910-1999 ..... **CLC 1, 2, 19, 53; SSC 3, 98; TCLC 209**
See also AMWS 4; CA 1-4R; 186; CAAS 1; CANR 1, 19, 50, 75; CN 1, 2, 3, 4, 5, 6; DA3; DLB 5, 6, 218; EWL 3; MAL 5; MTCW 1, 2; MTFW 2005; RGAL 4; SSFS 17

Bowles, William Lisle 1762-1850 . **NCLC 103**
See also DLB 93

Box, Edgar
See Vidal, Gore

Boyd, James 1888-1944 .... **TCLC 115**
See also CA 186; DLB 9; DLBD 16; RGAL 4; RHW

Boyd, Nancy
See Millay, Edna St. Vincent
See also GLL 1

Boyd, Thomas (Alexander) 1898-1935 .... **TCLC 111**
See also CA 111; 183; DLB 9; DLBD 16, 316

Boyd, William 1952- .... **CLC 28, 53, 70**
See also CA 114; 120; CANR 51, 71, 131, 174; CN 4, 5, 6, 7; DLB 231

Boyesen, Hjalmar Hjorth 1848-1895 .... **NCLC 135**
See also DLB 12, 71; DLBD 13; RGAL 4

Boyle, Kay 1902-1992 .... **CLC 1, 5, 19, 58, 121; SSC 5, 102**
See also CA 13-16R; 140; CAAS 1; CANR 29, 61, 110; CN 1, 2, 3, 4, 5; CP 1, 2, 3, 4, 5; DLB 4, 9, 48, 86; DLBY 1993; EWL 3; MAL 5; MTCW 1, 2; MTFW 2005; RGAL 4; RGSF 2; SSFS 10, 13, 14

Boyle, Mark
See Kienzle, William X.

Boyle, Patrick 1905-1982 .... **CLC 19**
See also CA 127

Boyle, T. C.
See Boyle, T. Coraghessan
See also AMWS 8

Boyle, T. Coraghessan 1948- ..... **CLC 36, 55, 90; SSC 16**
See Boyle, T. C.
See also AAYA 47; BEST 90:4; BPFB 1; CA 120; CANR 44, 76, 89, 132; CN 6, 7; CPW; DA3; DAM POP; DLB 218, 278; DLBY 1986; EWL 3; MAL 5; MTCW 2; MTFW 2005; SSFS 13, 19

Boz
See Dickens, Charles (John Huffam)

Brackenridge, Hugh Henry 1748-1816 .... **NCLC 7**
See also DLB 11, 37; RGAL 4

Bradbury, Edward P.
See Moorcock, Michael
See also MTCW 2

Bradbury, Malcolm (Stanley) 1932-2000 .... **CLC 32, 61**
See also CA 1-4R; CANR 1, 33, 91, 98, 137; CN 1, 2, 3, 4, 5, 6, 7; CP 1; DA3; DAM NOV; DLB 14, 207; EWL 3; MTCW 1, 2; MTFW 2005

Bradbury, Ray 1920- ... **CLC 1, 3, 10, 15, 42, 98, 235; SSC 29, 53; WLC 1**
See also AAYA 15; AITN 1, 2; AMWS 4; BPFB 1; BYA 4, 5, 11; CA 1-4R; CANR 2, 30, 75, 125; CDALB 1968-1988; CN 1, 2, 3, 4, 5, 6, 7; CPW; DA; DA3; DAB; DAC; DAM MST, NOV, POP; DLB 2, 8; EXPN; EXPS; HGG; LAIT 3, 5; LATS 1:2; LMFS 2; MAL 5; MTCW 1, 2; MTFW 2005; NFS 1, 22; RGAL 4; RGSF 2; SATA 11, 64, 123; SCFW 1, 2; SFW 4; SSFS 1, 20; SUFW 1, 2; TUS; YAW

Braddon, Mary Elizabeth 1837-1915 .... **TCLC 111**
See also BRWS 8; CA 108; 179; CMW 4; DLB 18, 70, 156; HGG

Bradfield, Scott 1955- .... **SSC 65**
See also CA 147; CANR 90; HGG; SUFW 2

Bradfield, Scott Michael
See Bradfield, Scott

Bradford, Gamaliel 1863-1932 .... **TCLC 36**
See also CA 160; DLB 17

Bradford, William 1590-1657 .... **LC 64**
See also DLB 24, 30; RGAL 4

Bradley, David, Jr. 1950- ...... **BLC 1:1; CLC 23, 118**
See also BW 1, 3; CA 104; CANR 26, 81; CN 4, 5, 6, 7; DAM MULT; DLB 33

Bradley, David Henry, Jr.
See Bradley, David, Jr.

Bradley, John Ed 1958- .... **CLC 55**
See also CA 139; CANR 99; CN 6, 7; CSW

Bradley, John Edmund, Jr.
See Bradley, John Ed

Bradley, Marion Zimmer 1930-1999 .... **CLC 30**
See Chapman, Lee; Dexter, John; Gardner, Miriam; Ives, Morgan; Rivers, Elfrida
See also AAYA 40; BPFB 1; CA 57-60; 185; CAAS 10; CANR 7, 31, 51, 75, 107; CPW; DA3; DAM POP; DLB 8; FANT; FW; MTCW 1, 2; MTFW 2005; SATA 90, 139; SATA-Obit 116; SFW 4; SUFW 2; YAW

Bradshaw, John 1933- .... **CLC 70**
See also CA 138; CANR 61

Bradstreet, Anne 1612(?)-1672 .... **LC 4, 30, 130; PC 10**
See also AMWS 1; CDALB 1640-1865; DA; DA3; DAC; DAM MST, POET; DLB 24; EXPP; FW; PFS 6; RGAL 4; TUS; WP

Brady, Joan 1939- .... **CLC 86**
See also CA 141

Bragg, Melvyn 1939- .... **CLC 10**
See also BEST 89:3; CA 57-60; CANR 10,
48, 89, 158; CN 1, 2, 3, 4, 5, 6, 7; DLB
14, 271; RHW

Brahe, Tycho 1546-1601 .... **LC 45**
See also DLB 300

Braine, John (Gerard) 1922-1986 . **CLC 1, 3,
41**
See also CA 1-4R; 120; CANR 1, 33; CD-
BLB 1945-1960; CN 1, 2, 3, 4; DLB 15;
DLBY 1986; EWL 3; MTCW 1

Braithwaite, William Stanley (Beaumont)
1878-1962 ...... **BLC 1:1; HR 1:2; PC 52**
See also BW 1; CA 125; DAM MULT; DLB
50, 54; MAL 5

Bramah, Ernest 1868-1942 .... **TCLC 72**
See also CA 156; CMW 4; DLB 70; FANT

Brammer, Billy Lee
See Brammer, William

Brammer, William 1929-1978 .... **CLC 31**
See also CA 235; 77-80

Brancati, Vitaliano 1907-1954 .... **TCLC 12**
See also CA 109; DLB 264; EWL 3

Brancato, Robin F(idler) 1936- .... **CLC 35**
See also AAYA 9, 68; BYA 6; CA 69-72;
CANR 11, 45; CLR 32; JRDA; MAICYA
2; MAICYAS 1; SAAS 9; SATA 97;
WYA; YAW

Brand, Dionne 1953- .... **CLC 192**
See also BW 2; CA 143; CANR 143; CWP;
DLB 334

Brand, Max
See Faust, Frederick (Schiller)
See also BPFB 1; TCWW 1, 2

Brand, Millen 1906-1980 .... **CLC 7**
See also CA 21-24R; 97-100; CANR 72

Branden, Barbara 1929- .... **CLC 44**
See also CA 148

Brandes, Georg (Morris Cohen)
1842-1927 .... **TCLC 10**
See also CA 105; 189; DLB 300

Brandys, Kazimierz 1916-2000 .... **CLC 62**
See also CA 239; EWL 3

Branley, Franklyn M(ansfield)
1915-2002 .... **CLC 21**
See also CA 33-36R; 207; CANR 14, 39;
CLR 13; MAICYA 1, 2; SAAS 16; SATA
4, 68, 136

Brant, Beth (E.) 1941- .... **NNAL**
See also CA 144; FW

Brant, Sebastian 1457-1521 .... **LC 112**
See also DLB 179; RGWL 2, 3

Brathwaite, Edward Kamau
1930- ..... **BLC 2:1; BLCS; CLC 11; PC
56**
See also BRWS 12; BW 2, 3; CA 25-28R;
CANR 11, 26, 47, 107; CDWLB 3; CP 1,
2, 3, 4, 5, 6, 7; DAM POET; DLB 125;
EWL 3

Brathwaite, Kamau
See Brathwaite, Edward Kamau

Brautigan, Richard (Gary)
1935-1984 .... **CLC 1, 3, 5, 9, 12, 34, 42;
TCLC 133**
See also BPFB 1; CA 53-56; 113; CANR
34; CN 1, 2, 3; CP 1, 2, 3, 4; DA3; DAM
NOV; DLB 2, 5, 206; DLBY 1980, 1984;
FANT; MAL 5; MTCW 1; RGAL 4;
SATA 56

Brave Bird, Mary
See Crow Dog, Mary

Braverman, Kate 1950- .... **CLC 67**
See also CA 89-92; CANR 141; DLB 335

Brecht, (Eugen) Bertolt (Friedrich)
1898-1956 ..... **DC 3; TCLC 1, 6, 13, 35,
169; WLC 1**
See also CA 104; 133; CANR 62; CDWLB
2; DA; DA3; DAB; DAC; DAM DRAM,
MST; DFS 4, 5, 9; DLB 56, 124; EW 11;
EWL 3; IDTP; MTCW 1, 2; MTFW 2005;
RGHL; RGWL 2, 3; TWA

Brecht, Eugen Berthold Friedrich
See Brecht, (Eugen) Bertolt (Friedrich)

Bremer, Fredrika 1801-1865 .... **NCLC 11**
See also DLB 254

Brennan, Christopher John
1870-1932 .... **TCLC 17**
See also CA 117; 188; DLB 230; EWL 3

Brennan, Maeve 1917-1993 ... **CLC 5; TCLC
124**
See also CA 81-84; CANR 72, 100

Brenner, Jozef 1887-1919
See Csath, Geza
See also CA 240

Brent, Linda
See Jacobs, Harriet A(nn)

Brentano, Clemens (Maria)
1778-1842 .... **NCLC 1, 191; SSC 115**
See also DLB 90; RGWL 2, 3

Brent of Bin Bin
See Franklin, (Stella Maria Sarah) Miles
(Lampe)

Brenton, Howard 1942- .... **CLC 31**
See also CA 69-72; CANR 33, 67; CBD;
CD 5, 6; DLB 13; MTCW 1

Breslin, James 1930-
See Breslin, Jimmy
See also CA 73-76; CANR 31, 75, 139;
DAM NOV; MTCW 1, 2; MTFW 2005

Breslin, Jimmy .... **CLC 4, 43**
See Breslin, James
See also AITN 1; DLB 185; MTCW 2

Bresson, Robert 1901(?)-1999 .... **CLC 16**
See also CA 110; 187; CANR 49

Breton, Andre 1896-1966 .. **CLC 2, 9, 15, 54;
PC 15**
See also CA 19-20; 25-28R; CANR 40, 60;
CAP 2; DLB 65, 258; EW 11; EWL 3;
GFL 1789 to the Present; LMFS 2;
MTCW 1, 2; MTFW 2005; RGWL 2, 3;
TWA; WP

Breton, Nicholas c. 1554-c. 1626 .... **LC 133**
See also DLB 136

Breytenbach, Breyten 1939(?)- .. **CLC 23, 37,
126**
See also CA 113; 129; CANR 61, 122;
CWW 2; DAM POET; DLB 225; EWL 3

Bridgers, Sue Ellen 1942- .... **CLC 26**
See also AAYA 8, 49; BYA 7, 8; CA 65-68;
CANR 11, 36; CLR 18; DLB 52; JRDA;
MAICYA 1, 2; SAAS 1; SATA 22, 90;
SATA-Essay 109; WYA; YAW

Bridges, Robert (Seymour)
1844-1930 .... **PC 28; TCLC 1**
See also BRW 6; CA 104; 152; CDBLB
1890-1914; DAM POET; DLB 19, 98

Bridie, James .... **TCLC 3**
See Mavor, Osborne Henry
See also DLB 10; EWL 3

Brin, David 1950- .... **CLC 34**
See also AAYA 21; CA 102; CANR 24, 70,
125, 127; INT CANR-24; SATA 65;
SCFW 2; SFW 4

Brink, Andre 1935- .... **CLC 18, 36, 106**
See also AFW; BRWS 6; CA 104; CANR
39, 62, 109, 133, 182; CN 4, 5, 6, 7; DLB
225; EWL 3; INT CA-103; LATS 1:2;
MTCW 1, 2; MTFW 2005; WLIT 2

Brinsmead, H. F(ay)
See Brinsmead, H(esba) F(ay)

Brinsmead, H. F.
See Brinsmead, H(esba) F(ay)

Brinsmead, H(esba) F(ay) 1922- ...... **CLC 21**
See also CA 21-24R; CANR 10; CLR 47;
CWRI 5; MAICYA 1, 2; SAAS 5; SATA
18, 78

Brittain, Vera (Mary) 1893(?)-1970 . **CLC 23**
See also BRWS 10; CA 13-16; 25-28R;
CANR 58; CAP 1; DLB 191; FW; MTCW
1, 2

Broch, Hermann 1886-1951 ... **TCLC 20, 204**
See also CA 117; 211; CDWLB 2; DLB 85,
124; EW 10; EWL 3; RGWL 2, 3

Brock, Rose
See Hansen, Joseph
See also GLL 1

Brod, Max 1884-1968 .... **TCLC 115**
See also CA 5-8R; 25-28R; CANR 7; DLB
81; EWL 3

Brodkey, Harold (Roy) 1930-1996 .. **CLC 56;
TCLC 123**
See also CA 111; 151; CANR 71; CN 4, 5,
6; DLB 130

Brodsky, Iosif Alexandrovich 1940-1996
See Brodsky, Joseph
See also AITN 1; CA 41-44R; 151; CANR
37, 106; DA3; DAM POET; MTCW 1, 2;
MTFW 2005; RGWL 2, 3

Brodsky, Joseph . **CLC 4, 6, 13, 36, 100; PC
9**
See Brodsky, Iosif Alexandrovich
See also AAYA 71; AMWS 8; CWW 2;
DLB 285, 329; EWL 3; MTCW 1

Brodsky, Michael 1948- .... **CLC 19**
See also CA 102; CANR 18, 41, 58, 147;
DLB 244

Brodsky, Michael Mark
See Brodsky, Michael

Brodzki, Bella .... **CLC 65**

Brome, Richard 1590(?)-1652 .... **LC 61**
See also BRWS 10; DLB 58

Bromell, Henry 1947- .... **CLC 5**
See also CA 53-56; CANR 9, 115, 116

Bromfield, Louis (Brucker)
1896-1956 .... **TCLC 11**
See also CA 107; 155; DLB 4, 9, 86; RGAL
4; RHW

Broner, E(sther) M(asserman)
1930- .... **CLC 19**
See also CA 17-20R; CANR 8, 25, 72; CN
4, 5, 6; DLB 28

Bronk, William (M.) 1918-1999 .... **CLC 10**
See also CA 89-92; 177; CANR 23; CP 3,
4, 5, 6, 7; DLB 165

Bronstein, Lev Davidovich
See Trotsky, Leon

Bronte, Anne
See Bronte, Anne

Bronte, Anne 1820-1849 ..... **NCLC 4, 71, 102**
See also BRW 5; BRWR 1; DA3; DLB 21,
199, 340; NFS 26; TEA

Bronte, (Patrick) Branwell
1817-1848 .... **NCLC 109**
See also DLB 340

Bronte, Charlotte
See Bronte, Charlotte

Bronte, Charlotte 1816-1855 ...... **NCLC 3, 8,
33, 58, 105, 155; WLC 1**
See also AAYA 17; BRW 5; BRWC 2;
BRWR 1; BYA 2; CDBLB 1832-1890;
DA; DA3; DAB; DAC; DAM MST, NOV;
DLB 21, 159, 199, 340; EXPN; FL 1:2;
GL 2; LAIT 2; NFS 4; TEA; WLIT 4

Bronte, Emily
See Bronte, Emily (Jane)

Bronte, Emily (Jane) 1818-1848 ... **NCLC 16,
35, 165; PC 8; WLC 1**
See also AAYA 17; BPFB 1; BRW 5;
BRWC 1; BRWR 1; BYA 3; CDBLB
1832-1890; DA; DA3; DAB; DAC; DAM
MST, NOV, POET; DLB 21, 32, 199, 340;
EXPN; FL 1:2; GL 2; LAIT 1; TEA;
WLIT 3

Brontes
See Bronte, Anne; Bronte, (Patrick) Bran-
well; Bronte, Charlotte; Bronte, Emily
(Jane)

Brooke, Frances 1724-1789 .... **LC 6, 48**
See also DLB 39, 99

Brooke, Henry 1703(?)-1783 .... **LC 1**
   See also DLB 39
Brooke, Rupert (Chawner)
    1887-1915 .. **PC 24; TCLC 2, 7; WLC 1**
   See also BRWS 3; CA 104; 132; CANR 61;
   CDBLB 1914-1945; DA; DAB; DAC;
   DAM MST, POET; DLB 19, 216; EXPP;
   GLL 2; MTCW 1, 2; MTFW 2005; PFS
   7; TEA
Brooke-Haven, P.
   See Wodehouse, P(elham) G(renville)
Brooke-Rose, Christine 1923(?)- ..... **CLC 40,
184**
   See also BRWS 4; CA 13-16R; CANR 58,
   118, 183; CN 1, 2, 3, 4, 5, 6, 7; DLB 14,
   231; EWL 3; SFW 4
Brookner, Anita 1928- . **CLC 32, 34, 51, 136,
237**
   See also BRWS 4; CA 114; 120; CANR 37,
   56, 87, 130; CN 4, 5, 6, 7; CPW; DA3;
   DAB; DAM POP; DLB 194, 326; DLBY
   1987; EWL 3; MTCW 1, 2; MTFW 2005;
   NFS 23; TEA
Brooks, Cleanth 1906-1994 . **CLC 24, 86, 110**
   See also AMWS 14; CA 17-20R; 145;
   CANR 33, 35; CSW; DLB 63; DLBY
   1994; EWL 3; INT CANR-35; MAL 5;
   MTCW 1, 2; MTFW 2005
Brooks, George
   See Baum, L(yman) Frank
Brooks, Gwendolyn 1917-2000 .... **BLC 1:1,
2:1; CLC 1, 2, 4, 5, 15, 49, 125; PC 7;
WLC 1**
   See also AAYA 20; AFAW 1, 2; AITN 1;
   AMWS; BW 2, 3; CA 1-4R; 190; CANR
   1, 27, 52, 75, 132; CDALB 1941-1968;
   CLR 27; CP 1, 2, 3, 4, 5, 6, 7; CWP; DA;
   DA3; DAC; DAM MST, MULT, POET;
   DLB 5, 76, 165; EWL 3; EXPP; FL 1:5;
   MAL 5; MBL; MTCW 1, 2; MTFW 2005;
   PFS 1, 2, 4, 6; RGAL 4; SATA 6; SATA-
   Obit 123; TUS; WP
Brooks, Mel 1926-
   See Kaminsky, Melvin
   See also CA 65-68; CANR 16; DFS 21
Brooks, Peter 1938- .... **CLC 34**
   See also CA 45-48; CANR 1, 107, 182
Brooks, Peter Preston
   See Brooks, Peter
Brooks, Van Wyck 1886-1963 .... **CLC 29**
   See also AMW; CA 1-4R; CANR 6; DLB
   45, 63, 103; MAL 5; TUS
Brophy, Brigid (Antonia)
    1929-1995 .... **CLC 6, 11, 29, 105**
   See also CA 5-8R; 149; CAAS 4; CANR
   25, 53; CBD; CN 1, 2, 3, 4, 5, 6; CWD;
   DA3; DLB 14, 271; EWL 3; MTCW 1, 2
Brosman, Catharine Savage 1934- ..... **CLC 9**
   See also CA 61-64; CANR 21, 46, 149
Brossard, Nicole 1943- .... **CLC 115, 169; PC
80**
   See also CA 122; CAAS 16; CANR 140;
   CCA 1; CWP; CWW 2; DLB 53; EWL 3;
   FW; GLL 2; RGWL 3
Brother Antoninus
   See Everson, William (Oliver)
Brothers Grimm
   See Grimm, Jacob Ludwig Karl; Grimm,
   Wilhelm Karl
The Brothers Quay
   See Quay, Stephen; Quay, Timothy
Broughton, T(homas) Alan 1936- ..... **CLC 19**
   See also CA 45-48; CANR 2, 23, 48, 111
Broumas, Olga 1949- .... **CLC 10, 73**
   See also CA 85-88; CANR 20, 69, 110; CP
   5, 6, 7; CWP; GLL 2
Broun, Heywood 1888-1939 .... **TCLC 104**
   See also DLB 29, 171

Brown, Alan 1950- .... **CLC 99**
   See also CA 156
Brown, Charles Brockden
    1771-1810 .... **NCLC 22, 74, 122**
   See also AMWS 1; CDALB 1640-1865;
   DLB 37, 59, 73; FW; GL 2; HGG; LMFS
   1; RGAL 4; TUS
Brown, Christy 1932-1981 .... **CLC 63**
   See also BYA 13; CA 105; 104; CANR 72;
   DLB 14
Brown, Claude 1937-2002 ..... **BLC 1:1; CLC
30**
   See also AAYA 7; BW 1, 3; CA 73-76; 205;
   CANR 81; DAM MULT
Brown, Dan 1964- .... **CLC 209**
   See also CA 217; MTFW 2005
Brown, Dee 1908-2002 .... **CLC 18, 47**
   See also AAYA 30; CA 13-16R; 212; CAAS
   6; CANR 11, 45, 60, 150; CPW; CSW;
   DA3; DAM POP; DLBY 1980; LAIT 2;
   MTCW 1, 2; MTFW 2005; NCFS 5;
   SATA 5, 110; SATA-Obit 141; TCWW 1,
   2
Brown, Dee Alexander
   See Brown, Dee
Brown, George
   See Wertmueller, Lina
Brown, George Douglas
    1869-1902 .... **TCLC 28**
   See Douglas, George
   See also CA 162
Brown, George Mackay 1921-1996 ... **CLC 5,
48, 100**
   See also BRWS 6; CA 21-24R; 151; CAAS
   6; CANR 12, 37, 67; CN 1, 2, 3, 4, 5, 6;
   CP 1, 2, 3, 4, 5, 6; DLB 14, 27, 139, 271;
   MTCW 1; RGSF 2; SATA 35
Brown, James Wllie
   See Komunyakaa, Yusef
Brown, James Wllie, Jr.
   See Komunyakaa, Yusef
Brown, Larry 1951-2004 .... **CLC 73**
   See also CA 130; 134; 233; CANR 117,
   145; CSW; DLB 234; INT CA-134
Brown, Moses
   See Barrett, William (Christopher)
Brown, Rita Mae 1944- .... **CLC 18, 43, 79,
259**
   See also BPFB 1; CA 45-48; CANR 2, 11,
   35, 62, 95, 138, 183; CN 5, 6, 7; CPW;
   CSW; DA3; DAM NOV, POP; FW; INT
   CANR-11; MAL 5; MTCW 1, 2; MTFW
   2005; NFS 9; RGAL 4; TUS
Brown, Roderick (Langmere) Haig-
   See Haig-Brown, Roderick (Langmere)
Brown, Rosellen 1939- .... **CLC 32, 170**
   See also CA 77-80; CAAS 10; CANR 14,
   44, 98; CN 6, 7
Brown, Sterling Allen 1901-1989 ...... **BLC 1;
CLC 1, 23, 59; HR 1:2; PC 55**
   See also AFAW 1, 2; BW 1, 3; CA 85-88;
   127; CANR 26; CP 3, 4; DA3; DAM
   MULT, POET; DLB 48, 51, 63; MAL 5;
   MTCW 1, 2; MTFW 2005; RGAL 4; WP
Brown, Will
   See Ainsworth, William Harrison
Brown, William Hill 1765-1793 .... **LC 93**
   See also DLB 37
Brown, William Larry
   See Brown, Larry
Brown, William Wells 1815-1884 ... **BLC 1:1;
DC 1; NCLC 2, 89**
   See also DAM MULT; DLB 3, 50, 183,
   248; RGAL 4
Browne, Clyde Jackson
   See Browne, Jackson
Browne, Jackson 1948(?)- .... **CLC 21**
   See also CA 120

Browne, Sir Thomas 1605-1682 .... **LC 111**
   See also BRW 2; DLB 151
Browning, Robert 1812-1889 . **NCLC 19, 79;
PC 2, 61; WLCS**
   See also BRW 4; BRWC 2; BRWR 2; CD-
   BLB 1832-1890; CLR 97; DA; DA3;
   DAB; DAC; DAM MST, POET; DLB 32,
   163; EXPP; LATS 1:1; PAB; PFS 1, 15;
   RGEL 2; TEA; WLIT 4; WP; YABC 1
Browning, Tod 1882-1962 .... **CLC 16**
   See also CA 141; 117
Brownmiller, Susan 1935- .... **CLC 159**
   See also CA 103; CANR 35, 75, 137; DAM
   NOV; FW; MTCW 1, 2; MTFW 2005
Brownson, Orestes Augustus
    1803-1876 .... **NCLC 50**
   See also DLB 1, 59, 73, 243
Bruccoli, Matthew J. 1931-2008 .... **CLC 34**
   See also CA 9-12R; 274; CANR 7, 87; DLB
   103
Bruccoli, Matthew Joseph
   See Bruccoli, Matthew J.
Bruce, Lenny .... **CLC 21**
   See Schneider, Leonard Alfred
Bruchac, Joseph 1942- .... **NNAL**
   See also AAYA 19; CA 33-36R; 256; CAAE
   256; CANR 13, 47, 75, 94, 137, 161; CLR
   46; CWRI 5; DAM MULT; DLB 342;
   JRDA; MAICYA 2; MAICYAS 1; MTCW
   2; MTFW 2005; SATA 42, 89, 131, 176;
   SATA-Essay 176
Bruin, John
   See Brutus, Dennis
Brulard, Henri
   See Stendhal
Brulls, Christian
   See Simenon, Georges (Jacques Christian)
Brunetto Latini c. 1220-1294 .... **CMLC 73**
Brunner, John (Kilian Houston)
    1934-1995 .... **CLC 8, 10**
   See also CA 1-4R; 149; CAAS 8; CANR 2,
   37; CPW; DAM POP; DLB 261; MTCW
   1, 2; SCFW 1, 2; SFW 4
Bruno, Giordano 1548-1600 .... **LC 27**
   See also RGWL 2, 3
Brutus, Dennis 1924- ...... **BLC 1:1; CLC 43;
PC 24**
   See also AFW; BW 2, 3; CA 49-52; CAAS
   14; CANR 2, 27, 42, 81; CDWLB 3; CP
   1, 2, 3, 4, 5, 6, 7; DAM MULT, POET;
   DLB 117, 225; EWL 3
Bryan, C(ourtlandt) D(ixon) B(arnes)
    1936- .... **CLC 29**
   See also CA 73-76; CANR 13, 68; DLB
   185; INT CANR-13
Bryan, Michael
   See Moore, Brian
   See also CCA 1
Bryan, William Jennings
    1860-1925 .... **TCLC 99**
   See also DLB 303
Bryant, William Cullen 1794-1878 . **NCLC 6,
46; PC 20**
   See also AMWS 1; CDALB 1640-1865;
   DA; DAB; DAC; DAM MST, POET;
   DLB 3, 43, 59, 189, 250; EXPP; PAB;
   RGAL 4; TUS
Bryusov, Valery Yakovlevich
    1873-1924 .... **TCLC 10**
   See also CA 107; 155; EWL 3; SFW 4
Buchan, John 1875-1940 .... **TCLC 41**
   See also CA 108; 145; CMW 4; DAB;
   DAM POP; DLB 34, 70, 156; HGG;
   MSW; MTCW 2; RGEL 2; RHW; YABC
   2
Buchanan, George 1506-1582 .... **LC 4**
   See also DLB 132
Buchanan, Robert 1841-1901 .... **TCLC 107**
   See also CA 179; DLB 18, 35

Butler, Samuel 1612-1680 .... **LC 16, 43**
    See also DLB 101, 126; RGEL 2

Butler, Samuel 1835-1902 .... **TCLC 1, 33; WLC 1**
    See also BRWS 2; CA 143; CDBLB 1890-1914; DA; DA3; DAB; DAC; DAM MST, NOV; DLB 18, 57, 174; RGEL 2; SFW 4; TEA

Butler, Walter C.
    See Faust, Frederick (Schiller)

Butor, Michel (Marie Francois) 1926- .... **CLC 1, 3, 8, 11, 15, 161**
    See also CA 9-12R; CANR 33, 66; CWW 2; DLB 83; EW 13; EWL 3; GFL 1789 to the Present; MTCW 1, 2; MTFW 2005

Butts, Mary 1890(?)-1937 .... **TCLC 77**
    See also CA 148; DLB 240

Buxton, Ralph
    See Silverstein, Alvin; Silverstein, Virginia B(arbara Opshelor)

Buzo, Alex
    See Buzo, Alexander (John)
    See also DLB 289

Buzo, Alexander (John) 1944- .... **CLC 61**
    See also CA 97-100; CANR 17, 39, 69; CD 5, 6

Buzzati, Dino 1906-1972 .... **CLC 36**
    See also CA 160; 33-36R; DLB 177; RGWL 2, 3; SFW 4

Byars, Betsy 1928- .... **CLC 35**
    See also AAYA 19; BYA 3; CA 33-36R, 183; CAAE 183; CANR 18, 36, 57, 102, 148; CLR 1, 16, 72; DLB 52; INT CANR-18; JRDA; MAICYA 1, 2; MAICYAS 1; MTCW 1; SAAS 1; SATA 4, 46, 80, 163; SATA-Essay 108; WYA; YAW

Byars, Betsy Cromer
    See Byars, Betsy

Byatt, Antonia Susan Drabble
    See Byatt, A.S.

Byatt, A.S. 1936- .... **CLC 19, 65, 136, 223; SSC 91**
    See also BPFB 1; BRWC 2; BRWS 4; CA 13-16R; CANR 13, 33, 50, 75, 96, 133; CN 1, 2, 3, 4, 5, 6; DA3; DAM NOV, POP; DLB 14, 194, 319, 326; EWL 3; MTCW 1, 2; MTFW 2005; RGSF 2; RHW; SSFS 26; TEA

Byrd, William II 1674-1744 .... **LC 112**
    See also DLB 24, 140; RGAL 4

Byrne, David 1952- .... **CLC 26**
    See also CA 127

Byrne, John Keyes 1926-
    See Leonard, Hugh
    See also CA 102; CANR 78, 140; INT CA-102

Byron, George Gordon (Noel) 1788-1824 ..... **DC 24; NCLC 2, 12, 109, 149; PC 16; WLC 1**
    See also AAYA 64; BRW 4; BRWC 2; CD-BLB 1789-1832; DA; DA3; DAB; DAC; DAM MST, POET; DLB 96, 110; EXPP; LMFS 1; PAB; PFS 1, 14, 29; RGEL 2; TEA; WLIT 3; WP

Byron, Robert 1905-1941 .... **TCLC 67**
    See also CA 160; DLB 195

C. 3. 3.
    See Wilde, Oscar

Caballero, Fernan 1796-1877 .... **NCLC 10**

Cabell, Branch
    See Cabell, James Branch

Cabell, James Branch 1879-1958 .... **TCLC 6**
    See also CA 105; 152; DLB 9, 78; FANT; MAL 5; MTCW 2; RGAL 4; SUFW 1

Cabeza de Vaca, Alvar Nunez 1490-1557(?) .... **LC 61**

Cable, George Washington 1844-1925 .... **SSC 4; TCLC 4**
    See also CA 104; 155; DLB 12, 74; DLBD 13; RGAL 4; TUS

Cabral de Melo Neto, Joao 1920-1999 .... **CLC 76**
    See Melo Neto, Joao Cabral de
    See also CA 151; DAM MULT; DLB 307; LAW; LAWS 1

Cabrera Infante, G. 1929-2005 ... **CLC 5, 25, 45, 120; HLC 1; SSC 39**
    See also CA 85-88; 236; CANR 29, 65, 110; CDWLB 3; CWW 2; DA3; DAM MULT; DLB 113; EWL 3; HW 1, 2; LAW; LAWS 1; MTCW 1, 2; MTFW 2005; RGSF 2; WLIT 1

Cabrera Infante, Guillermo
    See Cabrera Infante, G.

Cade, Toni
    See Bambara, Toni Cade

Cadmus and Harmonia
    See Buchan, John

Caedmon fl. 658-680 .... **CMLC 7**
    See also DLB 146

Caeiro, Alberto
    See Pessoa, Fernando

Caesar, Julius .... **CMLC 47**
    See Julius Caesar
    See also AW 1; RGWL 2, 3; WLIT 8

Cage, John (Milton), (Jr.) 1912-1992 .... **CLC 41; PC 58**
    See also CA 13-16R; 169; CANR 9, 78; DLB 193; INT CANR-9; TCLE 1:1

Cahan, Abraham 1860-1951 .... **TCLC 71**
    See also CA 108; 154; DLB 9, 25, 28; MAL 5; RGAL 4

Cain, Christopher
    See Fleming, Thomas

Cain, G.
    See Cabrera Infante, G.

Cain, Guillermo
    See Cabrera Infante, G.

Cain, James M(allahan) 1892-1977 .. **CLC 3, 11, 28**
    See also AITN 1; BPFB 1; CA 17-20R; 73-76; CANR 8, 34, 61; CMW 4; CN 1, 2; DLB 226; EWL 3; MAL 5; MSW; MTCW 1; RGAL 4

Caine, Hall 1853-1931 .... **TCLC 97**
    See also RHW

Caine, Mark
    See Raphael, Frederic (Michael)

Calasso, Roberto 1941- .... **CLC 81**
    See also CA 143; CANR 89

Calderon de la Barca, Pedro 1600-1681 . **DC 3; HLCS 1; LC 23, 136**
    See also DFS 23; EW 2; RGWL 2, 3; TWA

Caldwell, Erskine 1903-1987 ... **CLC 1, 8, 14, 50, 60; SSC 19; TCLC 117**
    See also AITN 1; AMW; BPFB 1; CA 1-4R; 121; CAAS 1; CANR 2, 33; CN 1, 2, 3, 4; DA3; DAM NOV; DLB 9, 86; EWL 3; MAL 5; MTCW 1, 2; MTFW 2005; RGAL 4; RGSF 2; TUS

Caldwell, (Janet Miriam) Taylor (Holland) 1900-1985 .... **CLC 2, 28, 39**
    See also BPFB 1; CA 5-8R; 116; CANR 5; DA3; DAM NOV, POP; DLBD 17; MTCW 2; RHW

Calhoun, John Caldwell 1782-1850 .... **NCLC 15**
    See also DLB 3, 248

Calisher, Hortense 1911- ..... **CLC 2, 4, 8, 38, 134; SSC 15**
    See also CA 1-4R; CANR 1, 22, 117; CN 1, 2, 3, 4, 5, 6, 7; DA3; DAM NOV; DLB 2, 218; INT CANR-22; MAL 5; MTCW 1, 2; MTFW 2005; RGAL 4; RGSF 2

Callaghan, Morley Edward 1903-1990 ..... **CLC 3, 14, 41, 65; TCLC 145**
    See also CA 9-12R; 132; CANR 33, 73; CN 1, 2, 3, 4; DAC; DAM MST; DLB 68; EWL 3; MTCW 1, 2; MTFW 2005; RGEL 2; RGSF 2; SSFS 19

Callimachus c. 305B.C.-c. 240B.C. .... **CMLC 18**
    See also AW 1; DLB 176; RGWL 2, 3

Calvin, Jean
    See Calvin, John
    See also DLB 327; GFL Beginnings to 1789

Calvin, John 1509-1564 .... **LC 37**
    See Calvin, Jean

Calvino, Italo 1923-1985 .... **CLC 5, 8, 11, 22, 33, 39, 73; SSC 3, 48; TCLC 183**
    See also AAYA 58; CA 85-88; 116; CANR 23, 61, 132; DAM NOV; DLB 196; EW 13; EWL 3; MTCW 1, 2; MTFW 2005; RGHL; RGSF 2; RGWL 2, 3; SFW 4; SSFS 12; WLIT 7

Camara Laye
    See Laye, Camara
    See also EWL 3

Camden, William 1551-1623 .... **LC 77**
    See also DLB 172

Cameron, Carey 1952- .... **CLC 59**
    See also CA 135

Cameron, Peter 1959- .... **CLC 44**
    See also AMWS 12; CA 125; CANR 50, 117; DLB 234; GLL 2

Camoens, Luis Vaz de 1524(?)-1580
    See Camoes, Luis de
    See also EW 2

Camoes, Luis de 1524(?)-1580 . **HLCS 1; LC 62; PC 31**
    See Camoens, Luis Vaz de
    See also DLB 287; RGWL 2, 3

Camp, Madeleine L'Engle
    See L'Engle, Madeleine

Campana, Dino 1885-1932 .... **TCLC 20**
    See also CA 117; 246; DLB 114; EWL 3

Campanella, Tommaso 1568-1639 .... **LC 32**
    See also RGWL 2, 3

Campbell, Bebe Moore 1950-2006 . **BLC 2:1; CLC 246**
    See also AAYA 26; BW 2, 3; CA 139; 254; CANR 81, 134; DLB 227; MTCW 2; MTFW 2005

Campbell, John Ramsey
    See Campbell, Ramsey

Campbell, John W(ood, Jr.) 1910-1971 .... **CLC 32**
    See also CA 21-22; 29-32R; CANR 34; CAP 2; DLB 8; MTCW 1; SCFW 1, 2; SFW 4

Campbell, Joseph 1904-1987 .... **CLC 69; TCLC 140**
    See also AAYA 3, 66; BEST 89:2; CA 1-4R; 124; CANR 3, 28, 61, 107; DA3; MTCW 1, 2

Campbell, Maria 1940- .... **CLC 85; NNAL**
    See also CA 102; CANR 54; CCA 1; DAC

Campbell, Ramsey 1946- ... **CLC 42; SSC 19**
    See also AAYA 51; CA 57-60; 228; CAAE 228; CANR 7, 102, 171; DLB 261; HGG; INT CANR-7; SUFW 1, 2

Campbell, (Ignatius) Roy (Dunnachie) 1901-1957 .... **TCLC 5**
    See also AFW; CA 104; 155; DLB 20, 225; EWL 3; MTCW 2; RGEL 2

Campbell, Thomas 1777-1844 .... **NCLC 19**
    See also DLB 93, 144; RGEL 2

Campbell, Wilfred .... **TCLC 9**
    See Campbell, William

Campbell, William 1858(?)-1918
    See Campbell, Wilfred
    See also CA 106; DLB 92

Carver, Raymond 1938-1988 ..... **CLC 22, 36, 53, 55, 126; PC 54; SSC 8, 51, 104**
See also AAYA 44; AMWS 3; BPFB 1; CA 33-36R; 126; CANR 17, 34, 61, 103; CN 4; CPW; DA3; DAM NOV; DLB 130; DLBY 1984, 1988; EWL 3; MAL 5; MTCW 1, 2; MTFW 2005; PFS 17; RGAL 4; RGSF 2; SSFS 3, 6, 12, 13, 23; TCLE 1:1; TCWW 2; TUS

Cary, Elizabeth, Lady Falkland 1585-1639 .... **LC 30, 141**

Cary, (Arthur) Joyce (Lunel) 1888-1957 .... **TCLC 1, 29, 196**
See also BRW 7; CA 104; 164; CDBLB 1914-1945; DLB 15, 100; EWL 3; MTCW 2; RGEL 2; TEA

Casal, Julian del 1863-1893 .... **NCLC 131**
See also DLB 283; LAW

Casanova, Giacomo
See Casanova de Seingalt, Giovanni Jacopo
See also WLIT 7

Casanova, Giovanni Giacomo
See Casanova de Seingalt, Giovanni Jacopo

Casanova de Seingalt, Giovanni Jacopo 1725-1798 .... **LC 13, 151**
See also Casanova, Giacomo

Casares, Adolfo Bioy
See Bioy Casares, Adolfo
See also RGSF 2

Casas, Bartolome de las 1474-1566
See Las Casas, Bartolome de
See also WLIT 1

Case, John
See Hougan, Carolyn

Casely-Hayford, J(oseph) E(phraim) 1866-1903 .... **BLC 1:1; TCLC 24**
See also BW 2; CA 123; 152; DAM MULT

Casey, John (Dudley) 1939- .... **CLC 59**
See also BEST 90:2; CA 69-72; CANR 23, 100

Casey, Michael 1947- .... **CLC 2**
See also CA 65-68; CANR 109; CP 2, 3; DLB 5

Casey, Patrick
See Thurman, Wallace (Henry)

Casey, Warren (Peter) 1935-1988 .... **CLC 12**
See also CA 101; 127; INT CA-101

Casona, Alejandro . **CLC 49; DC 32; TCLC 199**
See Alvarez, Alejandro Rodriguez
See also EWL 3

Cassavetes, John 1929-1989 .... **CLC 20**
See also CA 85-88; 127; CANR 82

Cassian, Nina 1924- .... **PC 17**
See also CWP; CWW 2

Cassill, R(onald) V(erlin) 1919-2002 .... **CLC 4, 23**
See also CA 9-12R; 208; CAAS 1; CANR 7, 45; CN 1, 2, 3, 4, 5, 6, 7; DLB 6, 218; DLBY 2002

Cassiodorus, Flavius Magnus c. 490(?)-c. 583(?) .... **CMLC 43**

Cassirer, Ernst 1874-1945 .... **TCLC 61**
See also CA 157

Cassity, (Allen) Turner 1929- .... **CLC 6, 42**
See also CA 17-20R; 223; CAAE 223; CAAS 8; CANR 11; CSW; DLB 105

Cassius Dio c. 155-c. 229 .... **CMLC 99**
See also DLB 176

Castaneda, Carlos (Cesar Aranha) 1931(?)-1998 .... **CLC 12, 119**
See also CA 25-28R; CANR 32, 66, 105; DNFS 1; HW 1; MTCW 1

Castedo, Elena 1937- .... **CLC 65**
See also CA 132

Castedo-Ellerman, Elena
See Castedo, Elena

Castellanos, Rosario 1925-1974 .... **CLC 66; HLC 1; SSC 39, 68**
See also CA 131; 53-56; CANR 58; CDWLB 3; DAM MULT; DLB 113, 290; EWL 3; FW; HW 1; LAW; MTCW 2; MTFW 2005; RGSF 2; RGWL 2, 3

Castelvetro, Lodovico 1505-1571 .... **LC 12**

Castiglione, Baldassare 1478-1529 ...... **LC 12**
See Castiglione, Baldesar
See also LMFS 1; RGWL 2, 3

Castiglione, Baldesar
See Castiglione, Baldassare
See also EW 2; WLIT 7

Castillo, Ana 1953- .... **CLC 151**
See also AAYA 42; CA 131; CANR 51, 86, 128, 172; CWP; DLB 122, 227; DNFS 2; FW; HW 1; LLW; PFS 21

Castillo, Ana Hernandez Del
See Castillo, Ana

Castle, Robert
See Hamilton, Edmond

Castro (Ruz), Fidel 1926(?)- .... **HLC 1**
See also CA 110; 129; CANR 81; DAM MULT; HW 2

Castro, Guillen de 1569-1631 .... **LC 19**

Castro, Rosalia de 1837-1885 ... **NCLC 3, 78; PC 41**
See also DAM MULT

Castro Alves, Antonio de 1847-1871 .... **NCLC 205**
See also DLB 307; LAW

Cather, Willa (Sibert) 1873-1947 . **SSC 2, 50, 114; TCLC 1, 11, 31, 99, 132, 152; WLC 1**
See also AAYA 24; AMW; AMWC 1; AMWR 1; BPFB 1; CA 104; 128; CDALB 1865-1917; CLR 98; DA; DA3; DAB; DAC; DAM MST, NOV; DLB 9, 54, 78, 256; DLBD 1; EWL 3; EXPN; EXPS; FL 1:5; LAIT 3; LATS 1:1; MAL 5; MBL; MTCW 1, 2; MTFW 2005; NFS 2, 19; RGAL 4; RGSF 2; RHW; SATA 30; SSFS 2, 7, 16; TCWW 1, 2; TUS

Catherine II
See Catherine the Great
See also DLB 150

Catherine, Saint 1347-1380 ..... **CMLC 27, 95**

Catherine the Great 1729-1796 .... **LC 69**
See Catherine II

Cato, Marcus Porcius 234B.C.-149B.C. .... **CMLC 21**
See Cato the Elder

Cato, Marcus Porcius, the Elder
See Cato, Marcus Porcius

Cato the Elder
See Cato, Marcus Porcius
See also DLB 211

Catton, (Charles) Bruce 1899-1978 . **CLC 35**
See also AITN 1; CA 5-8R; 81-84; CANR 7, 74; DLB 17; MTCW 2; MTFW 2005; SATA 2; SATA-Obit 24

Catullus c. 84B.C.-54B.C. .... **CMLC 18**
See also AW 2; CDWLB 1; DLB 211; RGWL 2, 3; WLIT 8

Cauldwell, Frank
See King, Francis (Henry)

Caunitz, William J. 1933-1996 .... **CLC 34**
See also BEST 89:3; CA 125; 130; 152; CANR 73; INT CA-130

Causley, Charles (Stanley) 1917-2003 .... **CLC 7**
See also CA 9-12R; 223; CANR 5, 35, 94; CLR 30; CP 1, 2, 3, 4, 5; CWRI 5; DLB 27; MTCW 1; SATA 3, 66; SATA-Obit 149

Caute, (John) David 1936- .... **CLC 29**
See also CA 1-4R; CAAS 4; CANR 1, 33, 64, 120; CBD; CD 5, 6; CN 1, 2, 3, 4, 5, 6, 7; DAM NOV; DLB 14, 231

Cavafy, C(onstantine) P(eter) .... **PC 36; TCLC 2, 7**
See Kavafis, Konstantinos Petrou
See also CA 148; DA3; DAM POET; EW 8; EWL 3; MTCW 2; PFS 19; RGWL 2, 3; WP

Cavalcanti, Guido c. 1250-c. 1300 .... **CMLC 54**
See also RGWL 2, 3; WLIT 7

Cavallo, Evelyn
See Spark, Muriel

Cavanna, Betty .... **CLC 12**
See Harrison, Elizabeth (Allen) Cavanna
See also JRDA; MAICYA 1; SAAS 4; SATA 1, 30

Cavendish, Margaret Lucas 1623-1673 .... **LC 30, 132**
See also DLB 131, 252, 281; RGEL 2

Caxton, William 1421(?)-1491(?) .... **LC 17**
See also DLB 170

Cayer, D. M.
See Duffy, Maureen (Patricia)

Cayrol, Jean 1911-2005 .... **CLC 11**
See also CA 89-92; 236; DLB 83; EWL 3

Cela (y Trulock), Camilo Jose
See Cela, Camilo Jose
See also CWW 2

Cela, Camilo Jose 1916-2002 .... **CLC 4, 13, 59, 122; HLC 1; SSC 71**
See Cela (y Trulock), Camilo Jose
See also BEST 90:2; CA 21-24R; 206; CAAS 10; CANR 21, 32, 76, 139; DAM MULT; DLB 322; DLBY 1989; EW 13; EWL 3; HW 1; MTCW 1, 2; MTFW 2005; RGSF 2; RGWL 2, 3

Celan, Paul ..... **CLC 10, 19, 53, 82; PC 10**
See Antschel, Paul
See also CDWLB 2; DLB 69; EWL 3; RGHL; RGWL 2, 3

Celine, Louis-Ferdinand .. **CLC 1, 3, 4, 7, 9, 15, 47, 124**
See Destouches, Louis-Ferdinand
See also DLB 72; EW 11; EWL 3; GFL 1789 to the Present; RGWL 2, 3

Cellini, Benvenuto 1500-1571 .... **LC 7**
See also WLIT 7

Cendrars, Blaise .... **CLC 18, 106**
See Sauser-Hall, Frederic
See also DLB 258; EWL 3; GFL 1789 to the Present; RGWL 2, 3; WP

Centlivre, Susanna 1669(?)-1723 .... **DC 25; LC 65**
See also DLB 84; RGEL 2

Cernuda (y Bidon), Luis 1902-1963 .... **CLC 54; PC 62**
See also CA 131; 89-92; DAM POET; DLB 134; EWL 3; GLL 1; HW 1; RGWL 2, 3

Cervantes, Lorna Dee 1954- ..... **HLCS 1; PC 35**
See also CA 131; CANR 80; CP 7; CWP; DLB 82; EXPP; HW 1; LLW

Cervantes (Saavedra), Miguel de 1547-1616 .... **HLCS; LC 6, 23, 93; SSC 12, 108; WLC 1**
See also AAYA 56; BYA 1, 14; DA; DAB; DAC; DAM MST, NOV; EW 2; LAIT 1; LATS 1:1; LMFS 1; NFS 8; RGSF 2; RGWL 2, 3; TWA

Cesaire, Aime
See Cesaire, Aime

Cesaire, Aime 1913-2008 .... **BLC 1:1; CLC 19, 32, 112; DC 22; PC 25**
See also BW 2, 3; CA 65-68; 271; CANR 24, 43, 81; CWW 2; DA3; DAM MULT, POET; DLB 321; EWL 3; GFL 1789 to the Present; MTCW 1, 2; MTFW 2005; WP

Cesaire, Aime Fernand
See Cesaire, Aime

Chesterton, G(ilbert) K(eith)
1874-1936 . **PC 28; SSC 1, 46; TCLC 1,**
6, 64
See also AAYA 57; BRW 6; CA 104; 132;
CANR 73, 131; CDBLB 1914-1945;
CMW 4; DAM NOV, POET; DLB 10, 19,
34, 70, 98, 149, 178; EWL 3; FANT;
MSW; MTCW 1, 2; MTFW 2005; RGEL
2; RGSF 2; SATA 27; SUFW 1

Chettle, Henry 1560-1607(?) .... **LC 112**
See also DLB 136; RGEL 2

Chiang, Pin-chin 1904-1986
See Ding Ling
See also CA 118

Chief Joseph 1840-1904 .... **NNAL**
See also CA 152; DA3; DAM MULT

Chief Seattle 1786(?)-1866 .... **NNAL**
See also DA3; DAM MULT

Ch'ien, Chung-shu 1910-1998 .... **CLC 22**
See Qian Zhongshu
See also CA 130; CANR 73; MTCW 1, 2

Chikamatsu Monzaemon 1653-1724 ... **LC 66**
See also RGWL 2, 3

Child, Francis James 1825-1896 . **NCLC 173**
See also DLB 1, 64, 235

Child, L. Maria
See Child, Lydia Maria

Child, Lydia Maria 1802-1880 .. **NCLC 6, 73**
See also DLB 1, 74, 243; RGAL 4; SATA
67

Child, Mrs.
See Child, Lydia Maria

Child, Philip 1898-1978 .... **CLC 19, 68**
See also CA 13-14; CAP 1; CP 1; DLB 68;
RHW; SATA 47

Childers, (Robert) Erskine
1870-1922 .... **TCLC 65**
See also CA 113; 153; DLB 70

Childress, Alice 1920-1994 .... **BLC 1:1; CLC**
12, 15, 86, 96; DC 4; TCLC 116
See also AAYA 8; BW 2, 3; BYA 2; CA 45-
48; 146; CAD; CANR 3, 27, 50, 74; CLR
14; CWD; DA3; DAM DRAM, MULT,
NOV; DFS 2, 8, 14; DLB 7, 38, 249;
JRDA; LAIT 5; MAICYA 1, 2; MAIC-
YAS 1; MAL 5; MTCW 1, 2; MTFW
2005; RGAL 4; SATA 7, 48, 81; TUS;
WYA; YAW

Chin, Frank (Chew, Jr.) 1940- .... **AAL; CLC**
135; DC 7
See also CA 33-36R; CAD; CANR 71; CD
5, 6; DAM MULT; DLB 206, 312; LAIT
5; RGAL 4

Chin, Marilyn (Mei Ling) 1955- .... **PC 40**
See also CA 129; CANR 70, 113; CWP;
DLB 312; PFS 28

Chislett, (Margaret) Anne 1943- ...... **CLC 34**
See also CA 151

Chitty, Thomas Willes 1926- .... **CLC 11**
See Hinde, Thomas
See also CA 5-8R; CN 7

Chivers, Thomas Holley
1809-1858 .... **NCLC 49**
See also DLB 3, 248; RGAL 4

Choi, Susan 1969- .... **CLC 119**
See also CA 223

Chomette, Rene Lucien 1898-1981
See Clair, Rene
See also CA 103

Chomsky, Avram Noam
See Chomsky, Noam

Chomsky, Noam 1928- .... **CLC 132**
See also CA 17-20R; CANR 28, 62, 110,
132, 179; DA3; DLB 246; MTCW 1, 2;
MTFW 2005

Chona, Maria 1845(?)-1936 .... **NNAL**
See also CA 144

Chopin, Kate   ... **SSC 8, 68, 110; TCLC 127;**
WLCS
See Chopin, Katherine
See also AAYA 33; AMWR 2; AMWS 1;
BYA 11, 15; CDALB 1865-1917; DA;
DAB; DLB 12, 78; EXPN; EXPS; FL 1:3;
FW; LAIT 3; MAL 5; MBL; NFS 3;
RGAL 4; RGSF 2; SSFS 2, 13, 17, 26;
TUS

Chopin, Katherine 1851-1904
See Chopin, Kate
See also CA 104; 122; DA3; DAC; DAM
MST, NOV

Chretien de Troyes c. 12th cent. - . **CMLC 10**
See also DLB 208; EW 1; RGWL 2, 3;
TWA

Christie
See Ichikawa, Kon

Christie, Agatha (Mary Clarissa)
1890-1976 .. **CLC 1, 6, 8, 12, 39, 48, 110**
See also AAYA 9; AITN 1, 2; BPFB 1;
BRWS 2; CA 17-20R; 61-64; CANR 10,
37, 108; CBD; CDBLB 1914-1945; CMW
4; CN 1, 2; CPW; CWD; DA3; DAB;
DAC; DAM NOV; DFS 2; DLB 13, 77,
245; MSW; MTCW 1, 2; MTFW 2005;
NFS 8; RGEL 2; RHW; SATA 36; TEA;
YAW

Christie, Philippa .... **CLC 21**
See Pearce, Philippa
See also BYA 5; CANR 109; CLR 9; DLB
161; MAICYA 1; SATA 1, 67, 129

Christine de Pisan
See Christine de Pizan
See also FW

Christine de Pizan 1365(?)-1431(?) ...... **LC 9,**
130; PC 68
See Christine de Pisan; de Pizan, Christine
See also DLB 208; FL 1:1; RGWL 2, 3

Chuang-Tzu c. 369B.C.-c.
286B.C. .... **CMLC 57**

Chubb, Elmer
See Masters, Edgar Lee

Chulkov, Mikhail Dmitrievich
1743-1792 .... **LC 2**
See also DLB 150

Churchill, Caryl 1938- .... **CLC 31, 55, 157;**
DC 5
See Churchill, Chick
See also BRWS 4; CA 102; CANR 22, 46,
108; CBD; CD 6; CWD; DFS 25; DLB
13, 310; EWL 3; FW; MTCW 1; RGEL 2

Churchill, Charles 1731-1764 .... **LC 3**
See also DLB 109; RGEL 2

Churchill, Chick
See Churchill, Caryl
See also CD 5

Churchill, Sir Winston (Leonard Spencer)
1874-1965 .... **TCLC 113**
See also BRW 6; CA 97-100; CDBLB
1890-1914; DA3; DLB 100, 329; DLBD
16; LAIT 4; MTCW 1, 2

Chute, Carolyn 1947- .... **CLC 39**
See also CA 123; CANR 135; CN 7

Ciardi, John (Anthony) 1916-1986 . **CLC 10,**
40, 44, 129; PC 69
See also CA 5-8R; 118; CAAS 2; CANR 5,
33; CLR 19; CP 1, 2, 3, 4; CWRI 5; DAM
POET; DLB 5; DLBY 1986; INT
CANR-5; MAICYA 1, 2; MAL 5; MTCW
1, 2; MTFW 2005; RGAL 4; SAAS 26;
SATA 1, 65; SATA-Obit 46

Cibber, Colley 1671-1757 .... **LC 66**
See also DLB 84; RGEL 2

Cicero, Marcus Tullius
106B.C.-43B.C. .... **CMLC 3, 81**
See also AW 1; CDWLB 1; DLB 211;
RGWL 2, 3; WLIT 8

Cimino, Michael 1943- .... **CLC 16**
See also CA 105

Cioran, E(mil) M. 1911-1995 .... **CLC 64**
See also CA 25-28R; 149; CANR 91; DLB
220; EWL 3

Circus, Anthony
See Hoch, Edward D.

Cisneros, Sandra 1954- .... **CLC 69, 118, 193;**
HLC 1; PC 52; SSC 32, 72
See also AAYA 9, 53; AMWS 7; CA 131;
CANR 64, 118; CLR 123; CN 7; CWP;
DA3; DAM MULT; DLB 122, 152; EWL
3; EXPN; FL 1:5; FW; HW 1, 2; LAIT 5;
LATS 1:2; LLW; MAICYA 1; MAL 5;
MTCW 2; MTFW 2005; NFS 2; PFS 19;
RGAL 4; RGSF 2; SSFS 3, 13; WLIT 1;
YAW

Cixous, Helene 1937- .... **CLC 92, 253**
See also CA 126; CANR 55, 123; CWW 2;
DLB 83, 242; EWL 3; FL 1:5; FW; GLL
2; MTCW 1, 2; MTFW 2005; TWA

Clair, Rene .... **CLC 20**
See Chomette, Rene Lucien

Clampitt, Amy 1920-1994 .... **CLC 32; PC 19**
See also AMWS 9; CA 110; 146; CANR
29, 79; CP 4, 5; DLB 105; MAL 5; PFS
27

Clancy, Thomas L., Jr. 1947-
See Clancy, Tom
See also CA 125; 131; CANR 62, 105;
DA3; INT CA-131; MTCW 1, 2; MTFW
2005

Clancy, Tom .... **CLC 45, 112**
See Clancy, Thomas L., Jr.
See also AAYA 9, 51; BEST 89:1, 90:1;
BPFB 1; BYA 10, 11; CANR 132; CMW
4; CPW; DAM NOV, POP; DLB 227

Clare, John 1793-1864 .. **NCLC 9, 86; PC 23**
See also BRWS 11; DAB; DAM POET;
DLB 55, 96; RGEL 2

Clarin
See Alas (y Urena), Leopoldo (Enrique
Garcia)

Clark, Al C.
See Goines, Donald

Clark, Brian (Robert)
See Clark, (Robert) Brian
See also CD 6

Clark, (Robert) Brian 1932- .... **CLC 29**
See Clark, Brian (Robert)
See also CA 41-44R; CANR 67; CBD; CD
5

Clark, Curt
See Westlake, Donald E.

Clark, Eleanor 1913-1996 .... **CLC 5, 19**
See also CA 9-12R; 151; CANR 41; CN 1,
2, 3, 4, 5, 6; DLB 6

Clark, J. P.
See Clark Bekederemo, J.P.
See also CDWLB 3; DLB 117

Clark, John Pepper
See Clark Bekederemo, J.P.
See also AFW; CD 5; CP 1, 2, 3, 4, 5, 6, 7;
RGEL 2

Clark, Kenneth (Mackenzie)
1903-1983 .... **TCLC 147**
See also CA 93-96; 109; CANR 36; MTCW
1, 2; MTFW 2005

Clark, M. R.
See Clark, Mavis Thorpe

Clark, Mavis Thorpe 1909-1999 ...... **CLC 12**
See also CA 57-60; CANR 8, 37, 107; CLR
30; CWRI 5; MAICYA 1, 2; SAAS 5;
SATA 8, 74

Clark, Walter Van Tilburg
1909-1971 .... **CLC 28**
See also CA 9-12R; 33-36R; CANR 63,
113; CN 1; DLB 9, 206; LAIT 2; MAL 5;
RGAL 4; SATA 8; TCWW 1, 2

Collier, James Lincoln 1928- .... **CLC 30**
    See also AAYA 13; BYA 2; CA 9-12R;
    CANR 4, 33, 60, 102; CLR 3, 126; DAM
    POP; JRDA; MAICYA 1, 2; SAAS 21;
    SATA 8, 70, 166; WYA; YAW 1

Collier, Jeremy 1650-1726 .... **LC 6, 157**
    See also DLB 336

Collier, John 1901-1980 . **SSC 19; TCLC 127**
    See also CA 65-68; 97-100; CANR 10; CN
    1, 2; DLB 77, 255; FANT; SUFW 1

Collier, Mary 1690-1762 .... **LC 86**
    See also DLB 95

Collingwood, R(obin) G(eorge)
    1889(?)-1943 .... **TCLC 67**
    See also CA 117; 155; DLB 262

Collins, Billy 1941- .... **PC 68**
    See also AAYA 64; CA 151; CANR 92; CP
    7; MTFW 2005; PFS 18

Collins, Hunt
    See Hunter, Evan

Collins, Linda 1931- .... **CLC 44**
    See also CA 125

Collins, Merle 1950- .... **BLC 2:1**
    See also BW 3; CA 175; DLB 157

Collins, Tom
    See Furphy, Joseph
    See also RGEL 2

Collins, (William) Wilkie
    1824-1889 .... **NCLC 1, 18, 93; SSC 93**
    See also BRWS 6; CDBLB 1832-1890;
    CMW 4; DLB 18, 70, 159; GL 2; MSW;
    RGEL 2; RGSF; SUFW 1; WLIT 4

Collins, William 1721-1759 ...... **LC 4, 40; PC
72**
    See also BRW 3; DAM POET; DLB 109;
    RGEL 2

Collodi, Carlo .... **NCLC 54**
    See Lorenzini, Carlo
    See also CLR 5, 120; WCH; WLIT 7

Colman, George
    See Glassco, John

Colman, George, the Elder
    1732-1794 .... **LC 98**
    See also RGEL 2

Colonna, Vittoria 1492-1547 .... **LC 71**
    See also RGWL 2, 3

Colt, Winchester Remington
    See Hubbard, L. Ron

Colter, Cyrus J. 1910-2002 .... **CLC 58**
    See also BW 1; CA 65-68; 205; CANR 10,
    66; CN 2, 3, 4, 5, 6; DLB 33

Colton, James
    See Hansen, Joseph
    See also GLL 1

Colum, Padraic 1881-1972 .... **CLC 28**
    See also BYA 4; CA 73-76; 33-36R; CANR
    35; CLR 36; CP 1; CWRI 5; DLB 19;
    MAICYA 1, 2; MTCW 1; RGEL 2; SATA
    15; WCH

Colvin, James
    See Moorcock, Michael

Colwin, Laurie (E.) 1944-1992 .... **CLC 5, 13,
23, 84**
    See also CA 89-92; 139; CANR 20, 46;
    DLB 218; DLBY 1980; MTCW 1

Comfort, Alex(ander) 1920-2000 .... **CLC 7**
    See also CA 1-4R; 190; CANR 1, 45; CN
    1, 2, 3, 4; CP 1, 2, 3, 4, 5, 6, 7; DAM
    POP; MTCW 2

Comfort, Montgomery
    See Campbell, Ramsey

Compton-Burnett, I(vy)
    1892(?)-1969 .... **CLC 1, 3, 10, 15, 34;
TCLC 180**
    See also BRW 7; CA 1-4R; 25-28R; CANR
    4; DAM NOV; DLB 36; EWL 3; MTCW
    1, 2; RGEL 2

Comstock, Anthony 1844-1915 ...... **TCLC 13**
    See also CA 110; 169

Comte, Auguste 1798-1857 .... **NCLC 54**

Conan Doyle, Arthur
    See Doyle, Sir Arthur Conan
    See also BPFB 1; BYA 4, 5, 11

Conde (Abellan), Carmen
    1901-1996 .... **HLCS 1**
    See also CA 177; CWW 2; DLB 108; EWL
    3; HW 2

Conde, Maryse 1937- .... **BLC 2:1; BLCS;
CLC 52, 92, 247**
    See also BW 2, 3; CA 110, 190; CAAE 190;
    CANR 30, 53, 76, 171; CWW 2; DAM
    MULT; EWL 3; MTCW 2; MTFW 2005

Condillac, Etienne Bonnot de
    1714-1780 .... **LC 26**
    See also DLB 313

Condon, Richard 1915-1996 ...... **CLC 4, 6, 8,
10, 45, 100**
    See also BEST 90:3; BPFB 1; CA 1-4R;
    151; CAAS 1; CANR 2, 23, 164; CMW
    4; CN 1, 2, 3, 4, 5, 6; DAM NOV; INT
    CANR-23; MAL 5; MTCW 1, 2

Condon, Richard Thomas
    See Condon, Richard

Condorcet .... **LC 104**
    See Condorcet, marquis de Marie-Jean-
    Antoine-Nicolas Caritat
    See also GFL Beginnings to 1789

Condorcet, marquis de
    Marie-Jean-Antoine-Nicolas Caritat
    1743-1794
    See Condorcet
    See also DLB 313

Confucius 551B.C.-479B.C. .... **CMLC 19, 65;
WLCS**
    See also DA; DA3; DAB; DAC; DAM
    MST

Congreve, William 1670-1729 ... **DC 2; LC 5,
21; WLC 2**
    See also BRW 2; CDBLB 1660-1789; DA;
    DAB; DAC; DAM DRAM, MST, POET;
    DFS 15; DLB 39, 84; RGEL 2; WLIT 3

Conley, Robert J(ackson) 1940- .... **NNAL**
    See also CA 41-44R; CANR 15, 34, 45, 96;
    DAM MULT; TCWW 2

Connell, Evan S., Jr. 1924- .... **CLC 4, 6, 45**
    See also AAYA 7; AMWS 14; CA 1-4R;
    CAAS 2; CANR 2, 39, 76, 97, 140; CN
    1, 2, 3, 4, 5, 6; DAM NOV; DLB 2, 335;
    DLBY 1981; MAL 5; MTCW 1, 2;
    MTFW 2005

Connelly, Marc(us Cook) 1890-1980 . **CLC 7**
    See also CA 85-88; 102; CAD; CANR 30;
    DFS 12; DLB 7; DLBY 1980; MAL 5;
    RGAL 4; SATA-Obit 25

Connolly, Paul
    See Wicker, Tom

Connor, Ralph .... **TCLC 31**
    See Gordon, Charles William
    See also DLB 92; TCWW 1, 2

Conrad, Joseph 1857-1924 ..... **SSC 9, 67, 69,
71; TCLC 1, 6, 13, 25, 43, 57; WLC 2**
    See also AAYA 26; BPFB 1; BRW 6;
    BRWC 1; BRWR 2; BYA 2; CA 104; 131;
    CANR 60; CDBLB 1890-1914; DA; DA3;
    DAB; DAC; DAM MST, NOV; DLB 10,
    34, 98, 156; EWL 3; EXPN; EXPS; LAIT
    2; LATS 1:1; LMFS 1; MTCW 1, 2;
    MTFW 2005; NFS 2, 16; RGEL 2; RGSF
    2; SATA 27; SSFS 1, 12; TEA; WLIT 4

Conrad, Robert Arnold
    See Hart, Moss

Conroy, Pat 1945- .... **CLC 30, 74**
    See also AAYA 8, 52; AITN 1; BPFB 1;
    CA 85-88; CANR 24, 53, 129; CN 7;
    CPW; CSW; DA3; DAM NOV, POP;
    DLB 6; LAIT 5; MAL 5; MTCW 1, 2;
    MTFW 2005

Constant (de Rebecque), (Henri) Benjamin
    1767-1830 .... **NCLC 6, 182**
    See also DLB 119; EW 4; GFL 1789 to the
    Present

Conway, Jill K. 1934- .... **CLC 152**
    See also CA 130; CANR 94

Conway, Jill Kathryn Ker
    See Conway, Jill K.

Conybeare, Charles Augustus
    See Eliot, T(homas) S(tearns)

Cook, Michael 1933-1994 .... **CLC 58**
    See also CA 93-96; CANR 68; DLB 53

Cook, Robin 1940- .... **CLC 14**
    See also AAYA 32; BEST 90:2; BPFB 1;
    CA 108; 111; CANR 41, 90, 109, 181;
    CPW; DA3; DAM POP; HGG; INT CA-
    111

Cook, Roy
    See Silverberg, Robert

Cooke, Elizabeth 1948- .... **CLC 55**
    See also CA 129

Cooke, John Esten 1830-1886 .... **NCLC 5**
    See also DLB 3, 248; RGAL 4

Cooke, John Estes
    See Baum, L(yman) Frank

Cooke, M. E.
    See Creasey, John

Cooke, Margaret
    See Creasey, John

Cooke, Rose Terry 1827-1892 ...... **NCLC 110**
    See also DLB 12, 74

Cook-Lynn, Elizabeth 1930- .... **CLC 93;
NNAL**
    See also CA 133; DAM MULT; DLB 175

Cooney, Ray .... **CLC 62**
    See also CBD

Cooper, Anthony Ashley 1671-1713 .. **LC 107**
    See also DLB 101, 336

Cooper, Dennis 1953- .... **CLC 203**
    See also CA 133; CANR 72, 86; GLL 1;
    HGG

Cooper, Douglas 1960- .... **CLC 86**

Cooper, Henry St. John
    See Creasey, John

Cooper, J. California (?)- .... **CLC 56**
    See also AAYA 12; BW 1; CA 125; CANR
    55; DAM MULT; DLB 212

Cooper, James Fenimore
    1789-1851 .... **NCLC 1, 27, 54, 203**
    See also AAYA 22; AMW; BPFB 1;
    CDALB 1640-1865; CLR 105; DA3;
    DLB 3, 183, 250, 254; LAIT 1; NFS 25;
    RGAL 4; SATA 19; TUS; WCH

Cooper, Susan Fenimore
    1813-1894 .... **NCLC 129**
    See also ANW; DLB 239, 254

Coover, Robert 1932- .. **CLC 3, 7, 15, 32, 46,
87, 161; SSC 15, 101**
    See also AMWS 5; BPFB 1; CA 45-48;
    CANR 3, 37, 58, 115; CN 1, 2, 3, 4, 5, 6,
    7; DAM NOV; DLB 2, 227; DLBY 1981;
    EWL 3; MAL 5; MTCW 1, 2; MTFW
    2005; RGAL 4; RGSF 2

Copeland, Stewart (Armstrong)
    1952- .... **CLC 26**

Copernicus, Nicolaus 1473-1543 .... **LC 45**

Coppard, A(lfred) E(dgar)
    1878-1957 .... **SSC 21; TCLC 5**
    See also BRWS 8; CA 114; 167; DLB 162;
    EWL 3; HGG; RGEL 2; RGSF 2; SUFW
    1; YABC 1

Coppee, Francois 1842-1908 .... **TCLC 25**
    See also CA 170; DLB 217

Coppola, Francis Ford 1939- ... **CLC 16, 126**
    See also AAYA 39; CA 77-80; CANR 40,
    78; DLB 44

Copway, George 1818-1869 .... **NNAL**
    See also DAM MULT; DLB 175, 183

Creeley, Robert 1926-2005 .... **CLC 1, 2, 4, 8, 11, 15, 36, 78, 266; PC 73**
See also AMWS 4; CA 1-4R; 237; CAAS 10; CANR 23, 43, 89, 137; CP 1, 2, 3, 4, 5, 6, 7; DA3; DAM POET; DLB 5, 16, 169; DLBD 17; EWL 3; MAL 5; MTCW 1, 2; MTFW 2005; PFS 21; RGAL 4; WP

Creeley, Robert White
See Creeley, Robert

Crenne, Helisenne de 1510-1560 .... **LC 113**
See also DLB 327

Crevecoeur, Hector St. John de
See Crevecoeur, Michel Guillaume Jean de
See also ANW

Crevecoeur, Michel Guillaume Jean de 1735-1813 .... **NCLC 105**
See Crevecoeur, Hector St. John de
See also AMWS 1; DLB 37

Crevel, Rene 1900-1935 .... **TCLC 112**
See also GLL 2

Crews, Harry 1935- .... **CLC 6, 23, 49**
See also AITN 1; AMWS 11; BPFB 1; CA 25-28R; CANR 20, 57; CN 3, 4, 5, 6, 7; CSW; DA3; DLB 6, 143, 185; MTCW 1, 2; MTFW 2005; RGAL 4

Crichton, John Michael
See Crichton, Michael

Crichton, Michael 1942-2008 .. **CLC 2, 6, 54, 90, 242**
See also AAYA 10, 49; AITN 2; BPFB 1; CA 25-28R; CANR 13, 40, 54, 76, 127, 179; CMW 4; CN 2, 3, 6, 7; CPW; DA3; DAM NOV, POP; DLB 292; DLBY 1981; INT CANR-13; JRDA; MTCW 1, 2; MTFW 2005; SATA 9, 88; SFW 4; YAW

Crispin, Edmund .... **CLC 22**
See Montgomery, (Robert) Bruce
See also DLB 87; MSW

Cristina of Sweden 1626-1689 .... **LC 124**

Cristofer, Michael 1945(?)- .... **CLC 28**
See also CA 110; 152; CAD; CANR 150; CD 5, 6; DAM DRAM; DFS 15; DLB 7

Cristofer, Michael Ivan
See Cristofer, Michael

Criton
See Alain

Croce, Benedetto 1866-1952 .... **TCLC 37**
See also CA 120; 155; EW 8; EWL 3; WLIT 7

Crockett, David 1786-1836 .... **NCLC 8**
See also DLB 3, 11, 183, 248

Crockett, Davy
See Crockett, David

Crofts, Freeman Wills 1879-1957 .. **TCLC 55**
See also CA 115; 195; CMW 4; DLB 77; MSW

Croker, John Wilson 1780-1857 .... **NCLC 10**
See also DLB 110

Crommelynck, Fernand 1885-1970 .. **CLC 75**
See also CA 189; 89-92; EWL 3

Cromwell, Oliver 1599-1658 .... **LC 43**

Cronenberg, David 1943- .... **CLC 143**
See also CA 138; CCA 1

Cronin, A(rchibald) J(oseph) 1896-1981 .... **CLC 32**
See also BPFB 1; CA 1-4R; 102; CANR 5; CN 2; DLB 191; SATA 47; SATA-Obit 25

Cross, Amanda
See Heilbrun, Carolyn G(old)
See also BPFB 1; CMW; CPW; DLB 306; MSW

Crothers, Rachel 1878-1958 .... **TCLC 19**
See also CA 113; 194; CAD; CWD; DLB 7, 266; RGAL 4

Croves, Hal
See Traven, B.

Crow Dog, Mary (?)- .... **CLC 93; NNAL**
See also CA 154

Crowfield, Christopher
See Stowe, Harriet (Elizabeth) Beecher

Crowley, Aleister .... **TCLC 7**
See Crowley, Edward Alexander
See also GLL 1

Crowley, Edward Alexander 1875-1947
See Crowley, Aleister
See also CA 104; HGG

Crowley, John 1942- .... **CLC 57**
See also AAYA 57; BPFB 1; CA 61-64; CANR 43, 98, 138, 177; DLBY 1982; FANT; MTFW 2005; SATA 65, 140; SFW 4; SUFW 2

Crowne, John 1641-1712 .... **LC 104**
See also DLB 80; RGEL 2

Crud
See Crumb, R.

Crumarums
See Crumb, R.

Crumb, R. 1943- .... **CLC 17**
See also CA 106; CANR 107, 150

Crumb, Robert
See Crumb, R.

Crumbum
See Crumb, R.

Crumski
See Crumb, R.

Crum the Bum
See Crumb, R.

Crunk
See Crumb, R.

Crustt
See Crumb, R.

Crutchfield, Les
See Trumbo, Dalton

Cruz, Victor Hernandez 1949- ... **HLC 1; PC 37**
See also BW 2; CA 65-68, 271; CAAE 271; CAAS 17; CANR 14, 32, 74, 132; CP 1, 2, 3, 4, 5, 6, 7; DAM MULT, POET; DLB 41; DNFS 1; EXPP; HW 1, 2; LLW; MTCW 2; MTFW 2005; PFS 16; WP

Cryer, Gretchen (Kiger) 1935- .... **CLC 21**
See also CA 114; 123

Csath, Geza .... **TCLC 13**
See Brenner, Jozef
See also CA 111

Cudlip, David R(ockwell) 1933- .... **CLC 34**
See also CA 177

Cullen, Countee 1903-1946 ..... **BLC 1:1; HR 1:2; PC 20; TCLC 4, 37; WLCS**
See also AAYA 78; AFAW 2; AMWS 4; BW 1; CA 108; 124; CDALB 1917-1929; DA; DA3; DAC; DAM MST, MULT, POET; DLB 4, 48, 51; EWL 3; EXPP; LMFS 2; MAL 5; MTCW 1, 2; MTFW 2005; PFS 3; RGAL 4; SATA 18; WP

Culleton, Beatrice 1949- .... **NNAL**
See also CA 120; CANR 83; DAC

Cum, R.
See Crumb, R.

Cumberland, Richard 1732-1811 .... **NCLC 167**
See also DLB 89; RGEL 2

Cummings, Bruce F(rederick) 1889-1919
See Barbellion, W. N. P.
See also CA 123

Cummings, E(dward) E(stlin) 1894-1962 .. **CLC 1, 3, 8, 12, 15, 68; PC 5; TCLC 137; WLC 2**
See also AAYA 41; AMW; CA 73-76; CANR 31; CDALB 1929-1941; DA; DA3; DAB; DAC; DAM MST, POET; DLB 4, 48; EWL 3; EXPP; MAL 5; MTCW 1, 2; MTFW 2005; PAB; PFS 1, 3, 12, 13, 19; RGAL 4; TUS; WP

Cummins, Maria Susanna 1827-1866 .... **NCLC 139**
See also DLB 42; YABC 1

Cunha, Euclides (Rodrigues Pimenta) da 1866-1909 .... **TCLC 24**
See also CA 123; 219; DLB 307; LAW; WLIT 1

Cunningham, E. V.
See Fast, Howard

Cunningham, J(ames) V(incent) 1911-1985 .... **CLC 3, 31; PC 92**
See also CA 1-4R; 115; CANR 1, 72; CP 1, 2, 3, 4; DLB 5

Cunningham, Julia (Woolfolk) 1916- .... **CLC 12**
See also CA 9-12R; CANR 4, 19, 36; CWRI 5; JRDA; MAICYA 1, 2; SAAS 2; SATA 1, 26, 132

Cunningham, Michael 1952- .... **CLC 34, 243**
See also AMWS 15; CA 136; CANR 96, 160; CN 7; DLB 292; GLL 2; MTFW 2005; NFS 23

Cunninghame Graham, R. B.
See Cunninghame Graham, Robert (Gallnigad) Bontine

Cunninghame Graham, Robert (Gallnigad) Bontine 1852-1936 .... **TCLC 19**
See Graham, R(obert) B(ontine) Cunning-hame
See also CA 119; 184

Curnow, (Thomas) Allen (Monro) 1911-2001 .... **PC 48**
See also CA 69-72; 202; CANR 48, 99; CP 1, 2, 3, 4, 5, 6, 7; EWL 3; RGEL 2

Currie, Ellen 19(?)- .... **CLC 44**

Curtin, Philip
See Lowndes, Marie Adelaide (Belloc)

Curtin, Phillip
See Lowndes, Marie Adelaide (Belloc)

Curtis, Price
See Ellison, Harlan

Cusanus, Nicolaus 1401-1464 .... **LC 80**
See Nicholas of Cusa

Cutrate, Joe
See Spiegelman, Art

Cynewulf c. 770- .... **CMLC 23**
See also DLB 146; RGEL 2

Cyrano de Bergerac, Savinien de 1619-1655 .... **LC 65**
See also DLB 268; GFL Beginnings to 1789; RGWL 2, 3

Cyril of Alexandria c. 375-c. 430 . **CMLC 59**

Czaczkes, Shmuel Yosef Halevi
See Agnon, S(hmuel) Y(osef Halevi)

Dabrowska, Maria (Szumska) 1889-1965 .... **CLC 15**
See also CA 106; CDWLB 4; DLB 215; EWL 3

Dabydeen, David 1955- .... **CLC 34**
See also BW 1; CA 125; CANR 56, 92; CN 6, 7; CP 5, 6, 7

Dacey, Philip 1939- .... **CLC 51**
See also CA 37-40R, 231; CAAE 231; CAAS 17; CANR 14, 32, 64; CP 4, 5, 6, 7; DLB 105

Dacre, Charlotte c. 1772-1825(?) . **NCLC 151**

Dafydd ap Gwilym c. 1320-c. 1380 ..... **PC 56**

Dagerman, Stig (Halvard) 1923-1954 .... **TCLC 17**
See also CA 117; 155; DLB 259; EWL 3

D'Aguiar, Fred 1960- ..... **BLC 2:1; CLC 145**
See also CA 148; CANR 83, 101; CN 7; CP 5, 6, 7; DLB 157; EWL 3

Dahl, Roald 1916-1990 ...... **CLC 1, 6, 18, 79; TCLC 173**
See also AAYA 15; BPFB 1; BRWS 4; BYA 5; CA 1-4R; 133; CANR 6, 32, 37, 62; CLR 1, 7, 41, 111; CN 1, 2, 3, 4; CPW; DA3; DAB; DAC; DAM MST, NOV,

POP; DLB 139, 255; HGG; JRDA; MAI-
CYA 1, 2; MTCW 1, 2; MTFW 2005;
RGSF 2; SATA 1, 26, 73; SATA-Obit 65;
SSFS 4; TEA; YAW

Dahlberg, Edward 1900-1977 . **CLC 1, 7, 14;**
TCLC 208
See also CA 9-12R; 69-72; CANR 31, 62;
CN 1, 2; DLB 48; MAL 5; MTCW 1;
RGAL 4

Daitch, Susan 1954- .... **CLC 103**
See also CA 161

Dale, Colin .... **TCLC 18**
See Lawrence, T(homas) E(dward)

Dale, George E.
See Asimov, Isaac

d'Alembert, Jean Le Rond
1717-1783 .... **LC 126**

Dalton, Roque 1935-1975(?) ..... **HLCS 1; PC**
36
See also CA 176; DLB 283; HW 2

Daly, Elizabeth 1878-1967 .... **CLC 52**
See also CA 23-24; 25-28R; CANR 60;
CAP 2; CMW 4

Daly, Mary 1928- .... **CLC 173**
See also CA 25-28R; CANR 30, 62, 166;
FW; GLL 1; MTCW 1

Daly, Maureen 1921-2006 .... **CLC 17**
See also AAYA 5, 58; BYA 6; CA 253;
CANR 37, 83, 108; CLR 96; JRDA; MAI-
CYA 1, 2; SAAS 1; SATA 2, 129; SATA-
Obit 176; WYA; YAW

Damas, Leon-Gontran 1912-1978 ... **CLC 84;**
TCLC 204
See also BW 1; CA 125; 73-76; EWL 3

Dana, Richard Henry Sr.
1787-1879 .... **NCLC 53**

Dangarembga, Tsitsi 1959- .... **BLC 2:1**
See also BW 3; CA 163; NFS 28; WLIT 2

Daniel, Samuel 1562(?)-1619 .... **LC 24**
See also DLB 62; RGEL 2

Daniels, Brett
See Adler, Renata

Dannay, Frederic 1905-1982 .... **CLC 11**
See Queen, Ellery
See also CA 1-4R; 107; CANR 1, 39; CMW
4; DAM POP; DLB 137; MTCW 1

D'Annunzio, Gabriele 1863-1938 ... **TCLC 6,**
40, 215
See also CA 104; 155; EW 8; EWL 3;
RGWL 2, 3; TWA; WLIT 7

Danois, N. le
See Gourmont, Remy(-Marie-Charles) de

Dante 1265-1321 .... **CMLC 3, 18, 39, 70; PC**
21; WLCS
See Alighieri, Dante
See also DA; DA3; DAB; DAC; DAM
MST, POET; EFS 1; EW 1; LAIT 1;
RGWL 2, 3; TWA; WP

d'Antibes, Germain
See Simenon, Georges (Jacques Christian)

Danticat, Edwidge 1969- . **BLC 2:1; CLC 94,**
139, 228; SSC 100
See also AAYA 29; CA 152, 192; CAAE
192; CANR 73, 129, 179; CN 7; DNFS 1;
EXPS; LATS 1:2; MTCW 2; MTFW
2005; NFS 28; SSFS 1, 25; YAW

Danvers, Dennis 1947- .... **CLC 70**

Danziger, Paula 1944-2004 .... **CLC 21**
See also AAYA 4, 36; BYA 6, 7, 14; CA
112; 115; 229; CANR 37, 132; CLR 20;
JRDA; MAICYA 1, 2; MTFW 2005;
SATA 36, 63, 102, 149; SATA-Brief 30;
SATA-Obit 155; WYA; YAW

Da Ponte, Lorenzo 1749-1838 .... **NCLC 50**

d'Aragona, Tullia 1510(?)-1556 .... **LC 121**

Dario, Ruben 1867-1916 .... **HLC 1; PC 15;**
TCLC 4
See also CA 131; CANR 81; DAM MULT;
DLB 290; EWL 3; HW 1, 2; LAW;
MTCW 1, 2; MTFW 2005; RGWL 2, 3

Darko, Amma 1956- .... **BLC 2:1**

Darley, George 1795-1846 .... **NCLC 2**
See also DLB 96; RGEL 2

Darrow, Clarence (Seward)
1857-1938 .... **TCLC 81**
See also CA 164; DLB 303

Darwin, Charles 1809-1882 .... **NCLC 57**
See also BRWS 7; DLB 57, 166; LATS 1:1;
RGEL 2; TEA; WLIT 4

Darwin, Erasmus 1731-1802 .... **NCLC 106**
See also DLB 93; RGEL 2

Darwish, Mahmoud 1941-2008 .... **PC 86**
See Darwish, Mahmud
See also CA 164; CANR 133; MTCW 2;
MTFW 2005

Darwish, Mahmud -2008
See Darwish, Mahmoud
See also CWW 2; EWL 3

Daryush, Elizabeth 1887-1977 ...... **CLC 6, 19**
See also CA 49-52; CANR 3, 81; DLB 20

Das, Kamala 1934- .... **CLC 191; PC 43**
See also CA 101; CANR 27, 59; CP 1, 2, 3,
4, 5, 6, 7; CWP; DLB 323; FW

Dasgupta, Surendranath
1887-1952 .... **TCLC 81**
See also CA 157

Dashwood, Edmee Elizabeth Monica de la
Pasture 1890-1943
See Delafield, E. M.
See also CA 119; 154

da Silva, Antonio Jose
1705-1739 .... **NCLC 114**

Daudet, (Louis Marie) Alphonse
1840-1897 .... **NCLC 1**
See also DLB 123; GFL 1789 to the Present;
RGSF 2

Daudet, Alphonse Marie Leon
1867-1942 .... **SSC 94**
See also CA 217

d'Aulnoy, Marie-Catherine c.
1650-1705 .... **LC 100**

Daumal, Rene 1908-1944 .... **TCLC 14**
See also CA 114; 247; EWL 3

Davenant, William 1606-1668 .... **LC 13**
See also DLB 58, 126; RGEL 2

Davenport, Guy (Mattison, Jr.)
1927-2005 . **CLC 6, 14, 38, 241; SSC 16**
See also CA 33-36R; 235; CANR 23, 73;
CN 3, 4, 5, 6; CSW; DLB 130

David, Robert
See Nezval, Vitezslav

Davidson, Avram (James) 1923-1993
See Queen, Ellery
See also CA 101; 171; CANR 26; DLB 8;
FANT; SFW 4; SUFW 1, 2

Davidson, Donald (Grady)
1893-1968 .... **CLC 2, 13, 19**
See also CA 5-8R; 25-28R; CANR 4, 84;
DLB 45

Davidson, Hugh
See Hamilton, Edmond

Davidson, John 1857-1909 .... **TCLC 24**
See also CA 118; 217; DLB 19; RGEL 2

Davidson, Sara 1943- .... **CLC 9**
See also CA 81-84; CANR 44, 68; DLB
185

Davie, Donald (Alfred) 1922-1995 .... **CLC 5,**
8, 10, 31; PC 29
See also BRWS 6; CA 1-4R; 149; CAAS 3;
CANR 1, 44; CP 1, 2, 3, 4, 5, 6; DLB 27;
MTCW 1; RGEL 2

Davie, Elspeth 1918-1995 .... **SSC 52**
See also CA 120; 126; 150; CANR 141;
DLB 139

Davies, Ray(mond Douglas) 1944- ... **CLC 21**
See also CA 116; 146; CANR 92

Davies, Rhys 1901-1978 .... **CLC 23**
See also CA 9-12R; 81-84; CANR 4; CN 1,
2; DLB 139, 191

Davies, Robertson 1913-1995 .. **CLC 2, 7, 13,**
25, 42, 75, 91; WLC 2
See Marchbanks, Samuel
See also BEST 89:2; BPFB 1; CA 33-36R;
150; CANR 17, 42, 103; CN 1, 2, 3, 4, 5,
6; CPW; DA; DA3; DAB; DAC; DAM
MST, NOV, POP; DLB 68; EWL 3; HGG;
INT CANR-17; MTCW 1, 2; MTFW
2005; RGEL 2; TWA

Davies, Sir John 1569-1626 .... **LC 85**
See also DLB 172

Davies, Walter C.
See Kornbluth, C(yril) M.

Davies, William Henry 1871-1940 ... **TCLC 5**
See also BRWS 11; CA 104; 179; DLB 19,
174; EWL 3; RGEL 2

Davies, William Robertson
See Davies, Robertson

Da Vinci, Leonardo 1452-1519 ..... **LC 12, 57,**
60
See also AAYA 40

Davis, Angela (Yvonne) 1944- .... **CLC 77**
See also BW 2, 3; CA 57-60; CANR 10,
81; CSW; DA3; DAM MULT; FW

Davis, B. Lynch
See Bioy Casares, Adolfo; Borges, Jorge
Luis

Davis, Frank Marshall 1905-1987 ... **BLC 1:1**
See also BW 2, 3; CA 125; 123; CANR 42,
80; DAM MULT; DLB 51

Davis, Gordon
See Hunt, E. Howard

Davis, H(arold) L(enoir) 1896-1960 . **CLC 49**
See also ANW; CA 178; 89-92; DLB 9,
206; SATA 114; TCWW 1, 2

Davis, Hart
See Poniatowska, Elena

Davis, Natalie Zemon 1928- .... **CLC 204**
See also CA 53-56; CANR 58, 100, 174

Davis, Rebecca (Blaine) Harding
1831-1910 .... **SSC 38, 109; TCLC 6**
See also AMWS 16; CA 104; 179; DLB 74,
239; FW; NFS 14; RGAL 4; SSFS 26;
TUS

Davis, Richard Harding
1864-1916 .... **TCLC 24**
See also CA 114; 179; DLB 12, 23, 78, 79,
189; DLBD 13; RGAL 4

Davison, Frank Dalby 1893-1970 ..... **CLC 15**
See also CA 217; 116; DLB 260

Davison, Lawrence H.
See Lawrence, D(avid) H(erbert Richards)

Davison, Peter (Hubert) 1928-2004 . **CLC 28**
See also CA 9-12R; 234; CAAS 4; CANR
3, 43, 84; CP 1, 2, 3, 4, 5, 6, 7; DLB 5

Davys, Mary 1674-1732 .... **LC 1, 46**
See also DLB 39

Dawson, (Guy) Fielding (Lewis)
1930-2002 .... **CLC 6**
See also CA 85-88; 202; CANR 108; DLB
130; DLBY 2002

Dawson, Peter
See Faust, Frederick (Schiller)
See also TCWW 1, 2

Day, Clarence (Shepard, Jr.)
1874-1935 .... **TCLC 25**
See also CA 108; 199; DLB 11

Day, John 1574(?)-1640(?) .... **LC 70**
See also DLB 62, 170; RGEL 2

Day, Thomas 1748-1789 .... **LC 1**
See also DLB 39; YABC 1

Day Lewis, C(ecil) 1904-1972 . **CLC 1, 6, 10; PC 11**
See Blake, Nicholas; Lewis, C. Day
See also BRWS 3; CA 13-16; 33-36R; CANR 34; CAP 1; CP 1; CWRI 5; DAM POET; DLB 15, 20; EWL 3; MTCW 1, 2; RGEL 2

Dazai Osamu .... **SSC 41; TCLC 11**
See Tsushima, Shuji
See also CA 164; DLB 182; EWL 3; MJW; RGSF 2; RGWL 2, 3; TWA

de Andrade, Carlos Drummond
See Drummond de Andrade, Carlos

de Andrade, Mario 1892(?)-1945
See Andrade, Mario de
See also CA 178; HW 2

Deane, Norman
See Creasey, John

Deane, Seamus (Francis) 1940- ...... **CLC 122**
See also CA 118; CANR 42

de Athayde, Alvaro Coelho
See Pessoa, Fernando

de Beauvoir, Simone
See Beauvoir, Simone de

de Beer, P.
See Bosman, Herman Charles

De Botton, Alain 1969- .... **CLC 203**
See also CA 159; CANR 96

de Brissac, Malcolm
See Dickinson, Peter (Malcolm de Brissac)

de Campos, Alvaro
See Pessoa, Fernando

de Chardin, Pierre Teilhard
See Teilhard de Chardin, (Marie Joseph) Pierre

de Crenne, Helisenne c. 1510-c. 1560 .... **LC 113**

Dee, John 1527-1608 .... **LC 20**
See also DLB 136, 213

Deer, Sandra 1940- .... **CLC 45**
See also CA 186

De Ferrari, Gabriella 1941- .... **CLC 65**
See also CA 146

de Filippo, Eduardo 1900-1984 ... **TCLC 127**
See also CA 132; 114; EWL 3; MTCW 1; RGWL 2, 3

Defoe, Daniel 1660(?)-1731 .... **LC 1, 42, 108; WLC 2**
See also AAYA 27; BRW 3; BRWR 1; BYA 4; CDBLB 1660-1789; CLR 61; DA; DA3; DAB; DAC; DAM MST, NOV; DLB 39, 95, 101, 336; JRDA; LAIT 1; LMFS 1; MAICYA 1, 2; NFS 9, 13; RGEL 2; SATA 22; TEA; WCH; WLIT 3

de Gouges, Olympe
See de Gouges, Olympe

de Gouges, Olympe 1748-1793 .... **LC 127**
See also DLB 313

de Gourmont, Remy(-Marie-Charles)
See Gourmont, Remy(-Marie-Charles) de

de Gournay, Marie le Jars 1566-1645 .... **LC 98**
See also DLB 327; FW

de Hartog, Jan 1914-2002 .... **CLC 19**
See also CA 1-4R; 210; CANR 1; DFS 12

de Hostos, E. M.
See Hostos (y Bonilla), Eugenio Maria de

de Hostos, Eugenio M.
See Hostos (y Bonilla), Eugenio Maria de

Deighton, Len .... **CLC 4, 7, 22, 46**
See Deighton, Leonard Cyril
See also AAYA 6; BEST 89:2; BPFB 1; CD-BLB 1960 to Present; CMW 4; CN 1, 2, 3, 4, 5, 6, 7; CPW; DLB 87

Deighton, Leonard Cyril 1929-
See Deighton, Len
See also AAYA 57; CA 9-12R; CANR 19, 33, 68; DA3; DAM NOV, POP; MTCW 1, 2; MTFW 2005

Dekker, Thomas 1572(?)-1632 ..... **DC 12; LC 22, 159**
See also CDBLB Before 1660; DAM DRAM; DLB 62, 172; LMFS 1; RGEL 2

de Laclos, Pierre Ambroise Franois
See Laclos, Pierre-Ambroise Francois

Delacroix, (Ferdinand-Victor-)Eugene 1798-1863 .... **NCLC 133**
See also EW 5

Delafield, E. M. .... **TCLC 61**
See Dashwood, Edmee Elizabeth Monica de la Pasture
See also DLB 34; RHW

de la Mare, Walter (John) 1873-1956 ..... **PC 77; SSC 14; TCLC 4, 53; WLC 2**
See also CA 163; CDBLB 1914-1945; CLR 23; CWRI 5; DA3; DAB; DAC; DAM MST, POET; DLB 19, 153, 162, 255, 284; EWL 3; EXPP; HGG; MAICYA 1, 2; MTCW 2; MTFW 2005; RGEL 2; RGSF 2; SATA 16; SUFW 1; TEA; WCH

de Lamartine, Alphonse (Marie Louis Prat)
See Lamartine, Alphonse (Marie Louis Prat) de

Delaney, Franey
See O'Hara, John (Henry)

Delaney, Shelagh 1939- .... **CLC 29**
See also CA 17-20R; CANR 30, 67; CBD; CD 5, 6; CDBLB 1960 to Present; CWD; DAM DRAM; DFS 7; DLB 13; MTCW 1

Delany, Martin Robison 1812-1885 .... **NCLC 93**
See also DLB 50; RGAL 4

Delany, Mary (Granville Pendarves) 1700-1788 .... **LC 12**

Delany, Samuel R., Jr. 1942- .... **BLC 1:1; CLC 8, 14, 38, 141**
See also AAYA 24; AFAW 2; BPFB 1; BW 2, 3; CA 81-84; CANR 27, 43, 116, 172; CN 2, 3, 4, 5, 6, 7; DAM MULT; DLB 8, 33; FANT; MAL 5; MTCW 1, 2; RGAL 4; SATA 92; SCFW 1, 2; SFW 4; SUFW 2

Delany, Samuel Ray
See Delany, Samuel R., Jr.

de la Parra, (Ana) Teresa (Sonojo) 1890(?)-1936 .... **TCLC 185**
See Parra Sanojo, Ana Teresa de la
See also CA 178; HW 2

De La Ramee, Marie Louise 1839-1908
See Ouida
See also CA 204; SATA 20

de la Roche, Mazo 1879-1961 .... **CLC 14**
See also CA 85-88; CANR 30; DLB 68; RGEL 2; RHW; SATA 64

De La Salle, Innocent
See Hartmann, Sadakichi

de Laureamont, Comte
See Lautreamont

Delbanco, Nicholas 1942- ..... **CLC 6, 13, 167**
See also CA 17-20R, 189; CAAE 189; CAAS 2; CANR 29, 55, 116, 150; CN 7; DLB 6, 234

Delbanco, Nicholas Franklin
See Delbanco, Nicholas

del Castillo, Michel 1933- .... **CLC 38**
See also CA 109; CANR 77

Deledda, Grazia (Cosima) 1875(?)-1936 .... **TCLC 23**
See also CA 123; 205; DLB 264, 329; EWL 3; RGWL 2, 3; WLIT 7

Deleuze, Gilles 1925-1995 .... **TCLC 116**
See also DLB 296

Delgado, Abelardo (Lalo) B(arrientos) 1930-2004 .... **HLC 1**
See also CA 131; 230; CAAS 15; CANR 90; DAM MST, MULT; DLB 82; HW 1, 2

Delibes, Miguel .... **CLC 8, 18**
See Delibes Setien, Miguel
See also DLB 322; EWL 3

Delibes Setien, Miguel 1920-
See Delibes, Miguel
See also CA 45-48; CANR 1, 32; CWW 2; HW 1; MTCW 1

DeLillo, Don 1936- ..... **CLC 8, 10, 13, 27, 39, 54, 76, 143, 210, 213**
See also AMWC 2; AMWS 6; BEST 89:1; BPFB 1; CA 81-84; CANR 21, 76, 92, 133, 173; CN 3, 4, 5, 6, 7; CPW; DA3; DAM NOV, POP; DLB 6, 173; EWL 3; MAL 5; MTCW 1, 2; MTFW 2005; NFS 28; RGAL 4; TUS

de Lisser, H. G.
See De Lisser, H(erbert) G(eorge)
See also DLB 117

De Lisser, H(erbert) G(eorge) 1878-1944 .... **TCLC 12**
See de Lisser, H. G.
See also BW 2; CA 109; 152

Deloire, Pierre
See Peguy, Charles (Pierre)

Deloney, Thomas 1543(?)-1600 .... **LC 41; PC 79**
See also DLB 167; RGEL 2

Deloria, Ella (Cara) 1889-1971(?) ..... **NNAL**
See also CA 152; DAM MULT; DLB 175

Deloria, Vine, Jr. 1933-2005 .... **CLC 21, 122; NNAL**
See also CA 53-56; 245; CANR 5, 20, 48, 98; DAM MULT; DLB 175; MTCW 1; SATA 21; SATA-Obit 171

Deloria, Vine Victor, Jr.
See Deloria, Vine, Jr.

del Valle-Inclan, Ramon (Maria)
See Valle-Inclan, Ramon (Maria) del
See also DLB 322

Del Vecchio, John M(ichael) 1947- .. **CLC 29**
See also CA 110; DLBD 9

de Man, Paul (Adolph Michel) 1919-1983 .... **CLC 55**
See also CA 128; 111; CANR 61; DLB 67; MTCW 1, 2

DeMarinis, Rick 1934- .... **CLC 54**
See also CA 57-60, 184; CAAE 184; CAAS 24; CANR 9, 25, 50, 160; DLB 218; TCWW 2

de Maupassant, (Henri Rene Albert) Guy
See Maupassant, (Henri Rene Albert) Guy de

Dembry, R. Emmet
See Murfree, Mary Noailles

Demby, William 1922- ...... **BLC 1:1; CLC 53**
See also BW 1, 3; CA 81-84; CANR 81; DAM MULT; DLB 33

de Menton, Francisco
See Chin, Frank (Chew, Jr.)

Demetrius of Phalerum c. 307B.C.- .... **CMLC 34**

Demijohn, Thom
See Disch, Thomas M.

De Mille, James 1833-1880 .... **NCLC 123**
See also DLB 99, 251

Deming, Richard 1915-1983
See Queen, Ellery
See also CA 9-12R; CANR 3, 94; SATA 24

Democritus c. 460B.C.-c. 370B.C. . **CMLC 47**

de Montaigne, Michel (Eyquem)
See Montaigne, Michel (Eyquem) de

de Montherlant, Henry (Milon)
See Montherlant, Henry (Milon) de

Demosthenes 384B.C.-322B.C. ...... **CMLC 13**
See also AW 1; DLB 176; RGWL 2, 3; WLIT 8

de Musset, (Louis Charles) Alfred
See Musset, Alfred de

Dinesen, Isak ..... **CLC 10, 29, 95; SSC 7, 75**
　　See Blixen, Karen (Christentze Dinesen)
　　See also EW 10; EWL 3; EXPS; FW; GL
　　2; HGG; LAIT 3; MTCW 1; NCFS 2;
　　NFS 9; RGSF 2; RGWL 2, 3; SSFS 3, 6,
　　13; WLIT 2
Ding Ling .... **CLC 68**
　　See Chiang, Pin-chin
　　See also DLB 328; RGWL 3
Diodorus Siculus c. 90B.C.-c.
　　31B.C. .... **CMLC 88**
Diphusa, Patty
　　See Almodovar, Pedro
Disch, Thomas M. 1940-2008 .... **CLC 7, 36**
　　See Disch, Tom
　　See also AAYA 17; BPFB 1; CA 21-24R;
　　274; CAAS 4; CANR 17, 36, 54, 89; CLR
　　18; CP 5, 6, 7; DA3; DLB 8; HGG; MAI-
　　CYA 1, 2; MTCW 1, 2; MTFW 2005;
　　SAAS 15; SATA 92; SATA-Obit 195;
　　SCFW 1, 2; SFW 4; SUFW 2
Disch, Thomas Michael
　　See Disch, Thomas M.
Disch, Tom
　　See Disch, Thomas M.
　　See also DLB 282
d'Isly, Georges
　　See Simenon, Georges (Jacques Christian)
Disraeli, Benjamin 1804-1881 ... **NCLC 2, 39,
　　79**
　　See also BRW 4; DLB 21, 55; RGEL 2
Ditcum, Steve
　　See Crumb, R.
Dixon, Paige
　　See Corcoran, Barbara (Asenath)
Dixon, Stephen 1936- .... **CLC 52; SSC 16**
　　See also AMWS 12; CA 89-92; CANR 17,
　　40, 54, 91, 175; CN 4, 5, 6, 7; DLB 130;
　　MAL 5
Dixon, Thomas, Jr. 1864-1946 ..... **TCLC 163**
　　See also RHW
Djebar, Assia 1936- .... **BLC 2:1; CLC 182;
　　SSC 114**
　　See also CA 188; CANR 169; DLB 346;
　　EWL 3; RGWL 3; WLIT 2
Doak, Annie
　　See Dillard, Annie
Dobell, Sydney Thompson
　　1824-1874 .... **NCLC 43**
　　See also DLB 32; RGEL 2
Doblin, Alfred .... **TCLC 13**
　　See Doeblin, Alfred
　　See also CDWLB 2; EWL 3; RGWL 2, 3
Dobroliubov, Nikolai Aleksandrovich
　　See Dobrolyubov, Nikolai Alexandrovich
　　See also DLB 277
Dobrolyubov, Nikolai Alexandrovich
　　1836-1861 .... **NCLC 5**
　　See Dobroliubov, Nikolai Aleksandrovich
Dobson, Austin 1840-1921 .... **TCLC 79**
　　See also DLB 35, 144
Dobyns, Stephen 1941- .... **CLC 37, 233**
　　See also AMWS 13; CA 45-48; CANR 2,
　　18, 99; CMW 4; CP 4, 5, 6, 7; PFS 23
Doctorow, Edgar Laurence
　　See Doctorow, E.L.
Doctorow, E.L. 1931- . **CLC 6, 11, 15, 18, 37,
　　44, 65, 113, 214**
　　See also AAYA 22; AITN 2; AMWS 4;
　　BEST 89:3; BPFB 1; CA 45-48; CANR
　　2, 33, 51, 76, 97, 133, 170; CDALB 1968-
　　1988; CN 3, 4, 5, 6, 7; CPW; DA3; DAM
　　NOV, POP; DLB 2, 28, 173; DLBY 1980;
　　EWL 3; LAIT 3; MAL 5; MTCW 1, 2;
　　MTFW 2005; NFS 6; RGAL 4; RGHL;
　　RHW; TCLE 1:1; TCWW 1, 2; TUS

Dodgson, Charles L(utwidge) 1832-1898
　　See Carroll, Lewis
　　See also CLR 2; DA; DA3; DAB; DAC;
　　DAM MST, NOV, POET; MAICYA 1, 2;
　　SATA 100; YABC 2
Dodsley, Robert 1703-1764 .... **LC 97**
　　See also DLB 95; RGEL 2
Dodson, Owen (Vincent)
　　1914-1983 .... **BLC 1:1; CLC 79**
　　See also BW 1; CA 65-68; 110; CANR 24;
　　DAM MULT; DLB 76
Doeblin, Alfred 1878-1957 .... **TCLC 13**
　　See Doblin, Alfred
　　See also CA 110; 141; DLB 66
Doerr, Harriet 1910-2002 .... **CLC 34**
　　See also CA 117; 122; 213; CANR 47; INT
　　CA-122; LATS 1:2
Domecq, H(onorio) Bustos
　　See Bioy Casares, Adolfo; Borges, Jorge
　　Luis
Domini, Rey
　　See Lorde, Audre
　　See also GLL 1
Dominique
　　See Proust, (Valentin-Louis-George-Eugene)
　　Marcel
Don, A
　　See Stephen, Sir Leslie
Donaldson, Stephen R. 1947- ... **CLC 46, 138**
　　See also AAYA 36; BPFB 1; CA 89-92;
　　CANR 13, 55, 99; CPW; DAM POP;
　　FANT; INT CANR-13; SATA 121; SFW
　　4; SUFW 1, 2
Donleavy, J(ames) P(atrick) 1926- .... **CLC 1,
　　4, 6, 10, 45**
　　See also AITN 2; BPFB 1; CA 9-12R;
　　CANR 24, 49, 62, 80, 124; CBD; CD 5,
　　6; CN 1, 2, 3, 4, 5, 6, 7; DLB 6, 173; INT
　　CANR-24; MAL 5; MTCW 1, 2; MTFW
　　2005; RGAL 4
Donnadieu, Marguerite
　　See Duras, Marguerite
Donne, John 1572-1631 ... **LC 10, 24, 91; PC
　　1, 43; WLC 2**
　　See also AAYA 67; BRW 1; BRWC 1;
　　BRWR 2; CDBLB Before 1660; DA;
　　DAB; DAC; DAM MST, POET; DLB
　　121, 151; EXPP; PAB; PFS 2, 11; RGEL
　　3; TEA; WLIT 3; WP
Donnell, David 1939(?)- .... **CLC 34**
　　See also CA 197
Donoghue, Denis 1928- .... **CLC 209**
　　See also CA 17-20R; CANR 16, 102
Donoghue, Emma 1969- .... **CLC 239**
　　See also CA 155; CANR 103, 152; DLB
　　267; GLL 2; SATA 101
Donoghue, P.S.
　　See Hunt, E. Howard
Donoso (Yanez), Jose 1924-1996 ... **CLC 4, 8,
　　11, 32, 99; HLC 1; SSC 34; TCLC 133**
　　See also CA 81-84; 155; CANR 32, 73; CD-
　　WLB 3; CWW 2; DAM MULT; DLB 113;
　　EWL 3; HW 1, 2; LAW; LAWS 1; MTCW
　　1, 2; MTFW 2005; RGSF 2; WLIT 1
Donovan, John 1928-1992 .... **CLC 35**
　　See also AAYA 20; CA 97-100; 137; CLR
　　3; MAICYA 1, 2; SATA 72; SATA-Brief
　　29; YAW
Don Roberto
　　See Cunninghame Graham, Robert
　　(Gallnigad) Bontine
Doolittle, Hilda 1886-1961 . **CLC 3, 8, 14, 31,
　　34, 73; PC 5; WLC 3**
　　See H. D.
　　See also AAYA 66; AMWS 1; CA 97-100;
　　CANR 35, 131; DA; DAC; DAM MST,
　　POET; DLB 4, 45; EWL 3; FW; GLL 1;
　　LMFS 2; MAL 5; MBL; MTCW 1, 2;
　　MTFW 2005; PFS 6, 28; RGAL 4

Doppo, Kunikida .... **TCLC 99**
　　See Kunikida Doppo
Dorfman, Ariel 1942- .... **CLC 48, 77, 189;
　　HLC 1**
　　See also CA 124; 130; CANR 67, 70, 135;
　　CWW 2; DAM MULT; DFS 4; EWL 3;
　　HW 1, 2; INT CA-130; WLIT 1
Dorn, Edward (Merton)
　　1929-1999 .... **CLC 10, 18**
　　See also CA 93-96; 187; CANR 42, 79; CP
　　1, 2, 3, 4, 5, 6, 7; DLB 5; INT CA-93-96;
　　WP
Dor-Ner, Zvi .... **CLC 70**
Dorris, Michael 1945-1997 .... **CLC 109;
　　NNAL**
　　See also AAYA 20; BEST 90:1; BYA 12;
　　CA 102; 157; CANR 19, 46, 75; CLR 58;
　　DA3; DAM MULT, NOV; DLB 175;
　　LAIT 5; MTCW 2; MTFW 2005; NFS 3;
　　RGAL 4; SATA 75; SATA-Obit 94;
　　TCWW 2; YAW
Dorris, Michael A.
　　See Dorris, Michael
Dorsan, Luc
　　See Simenon, Georges (Jacques Christian)
Dorsange, Jean
　　See Simenon, Georges (Jacques Christian)
Dorset
　　See Sackville, Thomas
Dos Passos, John (Roderigo)
　　1896-1970 ... **CLC 1, 4, 8, 11, 15, 25, 34,
　　82; WLC 2**
　　See also AMW; BPFB 1; CA 1-4R; 29-32R;
　　CANR 3; CDALB 1929-1941; DA; DA3;
　　DAB; DAC; DAM MST, NOV; DLB 4,
　　9, 274, 316; DLBD 1, 15; DLBY 1996;
　　EWL 3; MAL 5; MTCW 1, 2; MTFW
　　2005; NFS 14; RGAL 4; TUS
Dossage, Jean
　　See Simenon, Georges (Jacques Christian)
Dostoevsky, Fedor Mikhailovich
　　1821-1881 .. **NCLC 2, 7, 21, 33, 43, 119,
　　167, 202; SSC 2, 33, 44; WLC 2**
　　See Dostoevsky, Fyodor
　　See also AAYA 40; DA; DA3; DAB; DAC;
　　DAM MST, NOV; EW 7; EXPN; NFS 28;
　　RGSF 2; RGWL 2, 3; SSFS 8; TWA
Dostoevsky, Fyodor
　　See Dostoevsky, Fedor Mikhailovich
　　See also DLB 238; LATS 1:1; LMFS 1, 2
Doty, Mark 1953(?)- .... **CLC 176; PC 53**
　　See also AMWS 11; CA 161, 183; CAAE
　　183; CANR 110, 173; CP 7; PFS 28
Doty, Mark A.
　　See Doty, Mark
Doty, Mark Alan
　　See Doty, Mark
Doty, M.R.
　　See Doty, Mark
Doughty, Charles M(ontagu)
　　1843-1926 .... **TCLC 27**
　　See also CA 115; 178; DLB 19, 57, 174
Douglas, Ellen 1921- .... **CLC 73**
　　See also CA 115; CANR 41, 83; CN 5, 6,
　　7; CSW; DLB 292
Douglas, Gavin 1475(?)-1522 .... **LC 20**
　　See also DLB 132; RGEL 2
Douglas, George
　　See Brown, George Douglas
　　See also RGEL 2
Douglas, Keith (Castellain)
　　1920-1944 .... **TCLC 40**
　　See also BRW 7; CA 160; DLB 27; EWL
　　3; PAB; RGEL 2
Douglas, Leonard
　　See Bradbury, Ray
Douglas, Michael
　　See Crichton, Michael

Douglas, Michael
See Crichton, Michael

Douglas, (George) Norman
1868-1952 .... **TCLC 68**
See also BRW 6; CA 119; 157; DLB 34, 195; RGEL 2

Douglas, William
See Brown, George Douglas

Douglass, Frederick 1817(?)-1895 .. **BLC 1:1; NCLC 7, 55, 141; WLC 2**
See also AAYA 48; AFAW 1, 2; AMWC 1; AMWS 3; CDALB 1640-1865; DA; DA3; DAC; DAM MST, MULT; DLB 1, 43, 50, 79, 243; FW; LAIT 2; NCFS 2; RGAL 4; SATA 29

Dourado, (Waldomiro Freitas) Autran
1926- .... **CLC 23, 60**
See also CA 25-28R; 179; CANR 34, 81; DLB 145, 307; HW 2

Dourado, Waldomiro Freitas Autran
See Dourado, (Waldomiro Freitas) Autran

Dove, Rita 1952- . **BLC 2:1; BLCS; CLC 50, 81; PC 6**
See also AAYA 46; AMWS 4; BW 2; CA 109; CAAS 19; CANR 27, 42, 68, 76, 97, 132; CDALBS; CP 5, 6, 7; CSW; CWP; DA3; DAM MULT, POET; DLB 120; EWL 3; EXPP; MAL 5; MTCW 2; MTFW 2005; PFS 1, 15; RGAL 4

Dove, Rita Frances
See Dove, Rita

Doveglion
See Villa, Jose Garcia

Dowell, Coleman 1925-1985 .... **CLC 60**
See also CA 25-28R; 117; CANR 10; DLB 130; GLL 2

Downing, Major Jack
See Smith, Seba

Dowson, Ernest (Christopher)
1867-1900 .... **TCLC 4**
See also CA 105; 150; DLB 19, 135; RGEL 2

Doyle, A. Conan
See Doyle, Sir Arthur Conan

Doyle, Sir Arthur Conan
1859-1930 ..... **SSC 12, 83, 95; TCLC 7; WLC 2**
See Conan Doyle, Arthur
See also AAYA 14; BRWS 2; CA 104; 122; CANR 131; CDBLB 1890-1914; CLR 106; CMW 4; DA; DA3; DAB; DAC; DAM MST, NOV; DLB 18, 70, 156, 178; EXPS; HGG; LAIT 2; MSW; MTCW 1, 2; MTFW 2005; NFS 28; RGEL 2; RGSF 2; RHW; SATA 24; SCFW 1, 2; SFW 4; SSFS 2; TEA; WCH; WLIT 4; WYA; YAW

Doyle, Conan
See Doyle, Sir Arthur Conan

Doyle, John
See Graves, Robert

Doyle, Roddy 1958- .... **CLC 81, 178**
See also AAYA 14; BRWS 5; CA 143; CANR 73, 128, 168; CN 6, 7; DA3; DLB 194, 326; MTCW 2; MTFW 2005

Doyle, Sir A. Conan
See Doyle, Sir Arthur Conan

Dr. A
See Asimov, Isaac; Silverstein, Alvin; Silverstein, Virginia B(arbara Opshelor)

Drabble, Margaret 1939- ...... **CLC 2, 3, 5, 8, 10, 22, 53, 129**
See also BRWS 4; CA 13-16R; CANR 18, 35, 63, 112, 131, 174; CDBLB 1960 to Present; CN 1, 2, 3, 4, 5, 6, 7; CPW; DA3; DAB; DAC; DAM MST, NOV, POP; DLB 14, 155, 231; EWL 3; FW; MTCW 1, 2; MTFW 2005; RGEL 2; SATA 48; TEA

Drakulic, Slavenka 1949- .... **CLC 173**
See also CA 144; CANR 92

Drakulic-Ilic, Slavenka
See Drakulic, Slavenka

Drapier, M. B.
See Swift, Jonathan

Drayham, James
See Mencken, H(enry) L(ouis)

Drayton, Michael 1563-1631 .... **LC 8, 161**
See also DAM POET; DLB 121; RGEL 2

Dreadstone, Carl
See Campbell, Ramsey

Dreiser, Theodore 1871-1945 .... **SSC 30, 114; TCLC 10, 18, 35, 83; WLC 2**
See also AMW; AMWC 2; AMWR 2; BYA 15, 16; CA 106; 132; CDALB 1865-1917; DA; DA3; DAC; DAM MST, NOV; DLB 9, 12, 102, 137; DLBD 1; EWL 3; LAIT 2; LMFS 2; MAL 5; MTCW 1, 2; MTFW 2005; NFS 8, 17; RGAL 4; TUS

Dreiser, Theodore Herman Albert
See Dreiser, Theodore

Drexler, Rosalyn 1926- .... **CLC 2, 6**
See also CA 81-84; CAD; CANR 68, 124; CD 5, 6; CWD; MAL 5

Dreyer, Carl Theodor 1889-1968 ...... **CLC 16**
See also CA 116

Drieu la Rochelle, Pierre
1893-1945 .... **TCLC 21**
See also CA 117; 250; DLB 72; EWL 3; GFL 1789 to the Present

Drieu la Rochelle, Pierre-Eugene 1893-1945
See Drieu la Rochelle, Pierre

Drinkwater, John 1882-1937 .... **TCLC 57**
See also CA 109; 149; DLB 10, 19, 149; RGEL 2

Drop Shot
See Cable, George Washington

Droste-Hulshoff, Annette Freiin von
1797-1848 .... **NCLC 3, 133**
See also CDWLB 2; DLB 133; RGSF 2; RGWL 2, 3

Drummond, Walter
See Silverberg, Robert

Drummond, William Henry
1854-1907 .... **TCLC 25**
See also CA 160; DLB 92

Drummond de Andrade, Carlos
1902-1987 .... **CLC 18; TCLC 139**
See Andrade, Carlos Drummond de
See also CA 132; 123; DLB 307; LAW

Drummond of Hawthornden, William
1585-1649 .... **LC 83**
See also DLB 121, 213; RGEL 2

Drury, Allen (Stuart) 1918-1998 .... **CLC 37**
See also CA 57-60; 170; CANR 18, 52; CN 1, 2, 3, 4, 5, 6; INT CANR-18

Druse, Eleanor
See King, Stephen

Dryden, John 1631-1700 ..... **DC 3; LC 3, 21, 115; PC 25; WLC 2**
See also BRW 2; CDBLB 1660-1789; DA; DAB; DAC; DAM DRAM, MST, POET; DLB 80, 101, 131; EXPP; IDTP; LMFS 1; RGEL 2; TEA; WLIT 3

du Bellay, Joachim 1524-1560 .... **LC 92**
See also DLB 327; GFL Beginnings to 1789; RGWL 2, 3

Duberman, Martin 1930- .... **CLC 8**
See also CA 1-4R; CAD; CANR 2, 63, 137, 174; CD 5, 6

Dubie, Norman (Evans) 1945- .... **CLC 36**
See also CA 69-72; CANR 12, 115; CP 3, 4, 5, 6, 7; DLB 120; PFS 12

Du Bois, W(illiam) E(dward) B(urghardt)
1868-1963 .. **BLC 1:1; CLC 1, 2, 13, 64, 96; HR 1:2; TCLC 169; WLC 2**
See also AAYA 40; AFAW 1, 2; AMWC 1; AMWS 2; BW 1, 3; CA 85-88; CANR 34, 82, 132; CDALB 1865-1917; DA; DA3; DAC; DAM MST, MULT, NOV; DLB 47, 50, 91, 246, 284; EWL 3; EXPP; LAIT 2; LMFS 2; MAL 5; MTCW 1, 2; MTFW 2005; NCFS 1; PFS 13; RGAL 4; SATA 42

Dubus, Andre 1936-1999 ..... **CLC 13, 36, 97; SSC 15, 118**
See also AMWS 7; CA 21-24R; 177; CANR 17; CN 5, 6; CSW; DLB 130; INT CANR-17; RGAL 4; SSFS 10; TCLE 1:1

Duca Minimo
See D'Annunzio, Gabriele

Ducharme, Rejean 1941- .... **CLC 74**
See also CA 165; DLB 60

du Chatelet, Emilie 1706-1749 .... **LC 96**
See Chatelet, Gabrielle-Emilie Du

Duchen, Claire .... **CLC 65**

Duck, Stephen 1705(?)-1756 .... **PC 89**
See also DLB 95; RGEL 2

Duclos, Charles Pinot- 1704-1772 .... **LC 1**
See also GFL Beginnings to 1789

Ducornet, Erica 1943-
See Ducornet, Rikki
See also CA 37-40R; CANR 14, 34, 54, 82; SATA 7

Ducornet, Rikki .... **CLC 232**
See Ducornet, Erica

Dudek, Louis 1918-2001 .... **CLC 11, 19**
See also CA 45-48; 215; CAAS 14; CANR 1; CP 1, 2, 3, 4, 5, 6, 7; DLB 88

Duerrenmatt, Friedrich 1921-1990 ... **CLC 1, 4, 8, 11, 15, 43, 102**
See Durrenmatt, Friedrich
See also CA 17-20R; CANR 33; CMW 4; DAM DRAM; DLB 69, 124; MTCW 1, 2

Duffy, Bruce 1953(?)- .... **CLC 50**
See also CA 172

Duffy, Maureen (Patricia) 1933- ...... **CLC 37**
See also CA 25-28R; CANR 33, 68; CBD; CN 1, 2, 3, 4, 5, 6, 7; CP 5, 6, 7; CWD; CWP; DFS 15; DLB 14, 310; FW; MTCW 1

Du Fu
See Tu Fu
See also RGWL 2, 3

Dugan, Alan 1923-2003 .... **CLC 2, 6**
See also CA 81-84; 220; CANR 119; CP 1, 2, 3, 4, 5, 6, 7; DLB 5; MAL 5; PFS 10

du Gard, Roger Martin
See Martin du Gard, Roger

Duhamel, Georges 1884-1966 .... **CLC 8**
See also CA 81-84; 25-28R; CANR 35; DLB 65; EWL 3; GFL 1789 to the Present; MTCW 1

du Hault, Jean
See Grindel, Eugene

Dujardin, Edouard (Emile Louis)
1861-1949 .... **TCLC 13**
See also CA 109; DLB 123

Duke, Raoul
See Thompson, Hunter S.

Dulles, John Foster 1888-1959 .... **TCLC 72**
See also CA 115; 149

Dumas, Alexandre (pere)
1802-1870 .... **NCLC 11, 71; WLC 2**
See also AAYA 22; BYA 3; CLR 134; DA; DA3; DAB; DAC; DAM MST, NOV; DLB 119, 192; EW 6; GFL 1789 to the Present; LAIT 1, 2; NFS 14, 19; RGWL 2, 3; SATA 18; TWA; WCH

Dumas, Alexandre (fils) 1824-1895 ...... **DC 1;
NCLC 9**
See also DLB 192; GFL 1789 to the Present;
RGWL 2, 3

Dumas, Claudine
See Malzberg, Barry N(athaniel)

Dumas, Henry L. 1934-1968 . **BLC 2:1; CLC
6, 62; SSC 107**
See also BW 1; CA 85-88; DLB 41; RGAL
4

du Maurier, Daphne 1907-1989 .. **CLC 6, 11,
59; SSC 18; TCLC 209**
See also AAYA 37; BPFB 1; BRWS 3; CA
5-8R; 128; CANR 6, 55; CMW 4; CN 1,
2, 3, 4; CPW; DA3; DAB; DAC; DAM
MST, POP; DLB 191; GL 2; HGG; LAIT
3; MSW; MTCW 1, 2; NFS 12; RGEL 2;
RGSF 2; RHW; SATA 27; SATA-Obit 60;
SSFS 14, 16; TEA

Du Maurier, George 1834-1896 ..... **NCLC 86**
See also DLB 153, 178; RGEL 2

Dunbar, Paul Laurence
1872-1906 .... **BLC 1:1; PC 5; SSC 8;
TCLC 2, 12; WLC 2**
See also AAYA 75; AFAW 1, 2; AMWS 2;
BW 1, 3; CA 104; 124; CANR 79;
CDALB 1865-1917; DA; DA3; DAC;
DAM MST, MULT, POET; DLB 50, 54,
78; EXPP; MAL 5; RGAL 4; SATA 34

Dunbar, William 1460(?)-1520(?) .... **LC 20;
PC 67**
See also BRWS 8; DLB 132, 146; RGEL 2

Dunbar-Nelson, Alice .... **HR 1:2**
See Nelson, Alice Ruth Moore Dunbar

Duncan, Dora Angela
See Duncan, Isadora

Duncan, Isadora 1877(?)-1927 .... **TCLC 68**
See also CA 118; 149

Duncan, Lois 1934- .... **CLC 26**
See also AAYA 4, 34; BYA 6, 8; CA 1-4R;
CANR 2, 23, 36, 111; CLR 29, 129;
JRDA; MAICYA 1, 2; MAICYAS 1;
MTFW 2005; SAAS 2; SATA 1, 36, 75,
133, 141; SATA-Essay 141; WYA; YAW

Duncan, Robert 1919-1988 ... **CLC 1, 2, 4, 7,
15, 41, 55; PC 2, 75**
See also BG 1:2; CA 9-12R; 124; CANR
28, 62; CP 1, 2, 3, 4; DAM POET; DLB
5, 16, 193; EWL 3; MAL 5; MTCW 1, 2;
MTFW 2005; PFS 13; RGAL 4; WP

Duncan, Sara Jeannette
1861-1922 .... **TCLC 60**
See also CA 157; DLB 92

Dunlap, William 1766-1839 .... **NCLC 2**
See also DLB 30, 37, 59; RGAL 4

Dunn, Douglas (Eaglesham) 1942- .... **CLC 6,
40**
See also BRWS 10; CA 45-48; CANR 2,
33, 126; CP 1, 2, 3, 4, 5, 6, 7; DLB 40;
MTCW 1

Dunn, Katherine 1945- .... **CLC 71**
See also CA 33-36R; CANR 72; HGG;
MTCW 2; MTFW 2005

Dunn, Stephen 1939- .... **CLC 36, 206**
See also AMWS 11; CA 33-36R; CANR
12, 48, 53, 105; CP 3, 4, 5, 6, 7; DLB
105; PFS 21

Dunn, Stephen Elliott
See Dunn, Stephen

Dunne, Finley Peter 1867-1936 ...... **TCLC 28**
See also CA 108; 178; DLB 11, 23; RGAL
4

Dunne, John Gregory 1932-2003 ..... **CLC 28**
See also CA 25-28R; 222; CANR 14, 50;
CN 5, 6, 7; DLBY 1980

Dunsany, Lord .... **TCLC 2, 59**
See Dunsany, Edward John Moreton Drax
Plunkett
See also DLB 77, 153, 156, 255; FANT;
IDTP; RGEL 2; SFW 4; SUFW 1

**Dunsany, Edward John Moreton Drax
Plunkett** 1878-1957
See Dunsany, Lord
See also CA 104; 148; DLB 10; MTCW 2

Duns Scotus, John 1266(?)-1308 ... **CMLC 59**
See also DLB 115

du Perry, Jean
See Simenon, Georges (Jacques Christian)

Durang, Christopher 1949- .... **CLC 27, 38**
See also CA 105; CAD; CANR 50, 76, 130;
CD 5, 6; MTCW 2; MTFW 2005

Durang, Christopher Ferdinand
See Durang, Christopher

Duras, Claire de 1777-1832 .... **NCLC 154**

Duras, Marguerite 1914-1996 . **CLC 3, 6, 11,
20, 34, 40, 68, 100; SSC 40**
See also BPFB 1; CA 25-28R; 151; CANR
50; CWW 2; DFS 21; DLB 83, 321; EWL
3; FL 1:5; GFL 1789 to the Present; IDFW
4; MTCW 1, 2; RGWL 2, 3; TWA

Durban, (Rosa) Pam 1947- .... **CLC 39**
See also CA 123; CANR 98; CSW

Durcan, Paul 1944- .... **CLC 43, 70**
See also CA 134; CANR 123; CP 1, 5, 6, 7;
DAM POET; EWL 3

d'Urfe, Honore
See Urfe, Honore d'

Durfey, Thomas 1653-1723 .... **LC 94**
See also DLB 80; RGEL 2

Durkheim, Emile 1858-1917 .... **TCLC 55**
See also CA 249

Durrell, Lawrence (George)
1912-1990 ..... **CLC 1, 4, 6, 8, 13, 27, 41**
See also BPFB 1; BRWS 1; CA 9-12R; 132;
CANR 40, 77; CDBLB 1945-1960; CN 1,
2, 3, 4; CP 1, 2, 3, 4, 5; DAM NOV; DLB
15, 27, 204; DLBY 1990; EWL 3; MTCW
1, 2; RGEL 2; SFW 4; TEA

Durrenmatt, Friedrich
See Duerrenmatt, Friedrich
See also CDWLB 2; EW 13; EWL 3;
RGHL; RGWL 2, 3

Dutt, Michael Madhusudan
1824-1873 .... **NCLC 118**

Dutt, Toru 1856-1877 .... **NCLC 29**
See also DLB 240

Dwight, Timothy 1752-1817 .... **NCLC 13**
See also DLB 37; RGAL 4

Dworkin, Andrea 1946-2005 ..... **CLC 43, 123**
See also CA 77-80; 238; CAAS 21; CANR
16, 39, 76, 96; FL 1:5; FW; GLL 1; INT
CANR-16; MTCW 1, 2; MTFW 2005

Dwyer, Deanna
See Koontz, Dean R.

Dwyer, K.R.
See Koontz, Dean R.

Dybek, Stuart 1942- .... **CLC 114; SSC 55**
See also CA 97-100; CANR 39; DLB 130;
SSFS 23

Dye, Richard
See De Voto, Bernard (Augustine)

Dyer, Geoff 1958- .... **CLC 149**
See also CA 125; CANR 88

Dyer, George 1755-1841 .... **NCLC 129**
See also DLB 93

Dylan, Bob 1941- .... **CLC 3, 4, 6, 12, 77; PC
37**
See also AMWS 18; CA 41-44R; CANR
108; CP 1, 2, 3, 4, 5, 6, 7; DLB 16

Dyson, John 1943- .... **CLC 70**
See also CA 144

Dzyubin, Eduard Georgievich 1895-1934
See Bagritsky, Eduard
See also CA 170

E. V. L.
See Lucas, E(dward) V(errall)

Eagleton, Terence (Francis) 1943- .. **CLC 63,
132**
See also CA 57-60; CANR 7, 23, 68, 115;
DLB 242; LMFS 2; MTCW 1, 2; MTFW
2005

Eagleton, Terry
See Eagleton, Terence (Francis)

Early, Jack
See Scoppettone, Sandra
See also GLL 1

East, Michael
See West, Morris L(anglo)

Eastaway, Edward
See Thomas, (Philip) Edward

Eastlake, William (Derry)
1917-1997 .... **CLC 8**
See also CA 5-8R; 158; CAAS 1; CANR 5,
63; CN 1, 2, 3, 4, 5, 6; DLB 6, 206; INT
CANR-5; MAL 5; TCWW 1, 2

Eastman, Charles A(lexander)
1858-1939 .... **NNAL; TCLC 55**
See also CA 179; CANR 91; DAM MULT;
DLB 175; YABC 1

Eaton, Edith Maude 1865-1914 .... **AAL**
See Far, Sui Sin
See also CA 154; DLB 221, 312; FW

Eaton, (Lillie) Winnifred 1875-1954 .... **AAL**
See also CA 217; DLB 221, 312; RGAL 4

Eberhart, Richard 1904-2005 ...... **CLC 3, 11,
19, 56; PC 76**
See also AMW; CA 1-4R; 240; CANR 2,
125; CDALB 1941-1968; CP 1, 2, 3, 4, 5,
6, 7; DAM POET; DLB 48; MAL 5;
MTCW 1; RGAL 4

Eberhart, Richard Ghormley
See Eberhart, Richard

Eberstadt, Fernanda 1960- .... **CLC 39**
See also CA 136; CANR 69, 128

Ebner, Margaret c. 1291-1351 ...... **CMLC 98**

**Echegaray (y Eizaguirre), Jose (Maria
Waldo)** 1832-1916 .... **HLCS 1; TCLC 4**
See also CA 104; CANR 32; DLB 329;
EWL 3; HW 1; MTCW 1

Echeverria, (Jose) Esteban (Antonino)
1805-1851 .... **NCLC 18**
See also LAW

Echo
See Proust, (Valentin-Louis-George-Eugene)
Marcel

Eckert, Allan W. 1931- .... **CLC 17**
See also AAYA 18; BYA 2; CA 13-16R;
CANR 14, 45; INT CANR-14; MAICYA
2; MAICYAS 1; SAAS 21; SATA 29, 91;
SATA-Brief 27

Eckhart, Meister 1260(?)-1327(?) .. **CMLC 9,
80**
See also DLB 115; LMFS 1

Eckmar, F. R.
See de Hartog, Jan

Eco, Umberto 1932- .... **CLC 28, 60, 142, 248**
See also BEST 90:1; BPFB 1; CA 77-80;
CANR 12, 33, 55, 110, 131; CPW; CWW
2; DA3; DAM NOV, POP; DLB 196, 242;
EWL 3; MSW; MTCW 1, 2; MTFW
2005; NFS 22; RGWL 3; WLIT 7

Eddison, E(ric) R(ucker)
1882-1945 .... **TCLC 15**
See also CA 109; 156; DLB 255; FANT;
SFW 4; SUFW 1

Eddy, Mary (Ann Morse) Baker
1821-1910 .... **TCLC 71**
See also CA 113; 174

Edel, (Joseph) Leon 1907-1997 .. **CLC 29, 34**
See also CA 1-4R; 161; CANR 1, 22, 112;
DLB 103; INT CANR-22

Eden, Emily 1797-1869 .... **NCLC 10**

Eusebius c. 263-c. 339 .... **CMLC 103**

Evan, Evin
See Faust, Frederick (Schiller)

Evans, Caradoc 1878-1945 ... **SSC 43; TCLC 85**
See also DLB 162

Evans, Evan
See Faust, Frederick (Schiller)

Evans, Marian
See Eliot, George

Evans, Mary Ann
See Eliot, George
See also NFS 20

Evarts, Esther
See Benson, Sally

Evelyn, John 1620-1706 .... **LC 144**
See also BRW 2; RGEL 2

Everett, Percival 1956- .... **CLC 57**
See Everett, Percival L.
See also AMWS 18; BW 2; CA 129; CANR 94, 134, 179; CN 7; MTFW 2005

Everett, Percival L.
See Everett, Percival
See also CSW

Everson, R(onald) G(ilmour)
1903-1992 .... **CLC 27**
See also CA 17-20R; CP 1, 2, 3, 4; DLB 88

Everson, William (Oliver)
1912-1994 .... **CLC 1, 5, 14**
See Antoninus, Brother
See also BG 1:2; CA 9-12R; 145; CANR 20; CP 2, 3, 4, 5; DLB 5, 16, 212; MTCW 1

Evtushenko, Evgenii Aleksandrovich
See Yevtushenko, Yevgeny (Alexandrovich)
See also CWW 2; RGWL 2, 3

Ewart, Gavin (Buchanan)
1916-1995 .... **CLC 13, 46**
See also BRWS 7; CA 89-92; 150; CANR 17, 46; CP 1, 2, 3, 4, 5, 6; DLB 40; MTCW 1

Ewers, Hanns Heinz 1871-1943 ..... **TCLC 12**
See also CA 109; 149

Ewing, Frederick R.
See Sturgeon, Theodore (Hamilton)

Exley, Frederick (Earl) 1929-1992 .... **CLC 6, 11**
See also AITN 2; BPFB 1; CA 81-84; 138; CANR 117; DLB 143; DLBY 1981

Eynhardt, Guillermo
See Quiroga, Horacio (Sylvestre)

Ezekiel, Nissim (Moses) 1924-2004 .. **CLC 61**
See also CA 61-64; 223; CP 1, 2, 3, 4, 5, 6, 7; DLB 323; EWL 3

Ezekiel, Tish O'Dowd 1943- .... **CLC 34**
See also CA 129

Fadeev, Aleksandr Aleksandrovich
See Bulgya, Alexander Alexandrovich
See also DLB 272

Fadeev, Alexandr Alexandrovich
See Bulgya, Alexander Alexandrovich
See also EWL 3

Fadeyev, A.
See Bulgya, Alexander Alexandrovich

Fadeyev, Alexander .... **TCLC 53**
See Bulgya, Alexander Alexandrovich

Fagen, Donald 1948- .... **CLC 26**

Fainzil'berg, Il'ia Arnol'dovich
See Fainzilberg, Ilya Arnoldovich

Fainzilberg, Ilya Arnoldovich
1897-1937 .... **TCLC 21**
See Il'f, Il'ia
See also CA 120; 165; EWL 3

Fair, Ronald L. 1932- .... **CLC 18**
See also BW 1; CA 69-72; CANR 25; DLB 33

Fairbairn, Roger
See Carr, John Dickson

Fairbairns, Zoe (Ann) 1948- .... **CLC 32**
See also CA 103; CANR 21, 85; CN 4, 5, 6, 7

Fairfield, Flora
See Alcott, Louisa May

Fairman, Paul W. 1916-1977
See Queen, Ellery
See also CA 114; SFW 4

Falco, Gian
See Papini, Giovanni

Falconer, James
See Kirkup, James

Falconer, Kenneth
See Kornbluth, C(yril) M.

Falkland, Samuel
See Heijermans, Herman

Fallaci, Oriana 1930-2006 .... **CLC 11, 110**
See also CA 77-80; 253; CANR 15, 58, 134; FW; MTCW 1

Faludi, Susan 1959- .... **CLC 140**
See also CA 138; CANR 126; FW; MTCW 2; MTFW 2005; NCFS 3

Faludy, George 1913- .... **CLC 42**
See also CA 21-24R

Faludy, Gyoergy
See Faludy, George

Fanon, Frantz 1925-1961 ...... **BLC 1:2; CLC 74; TCLC 188**
See also BW 1; CA 116; 89-92; DAM MULT; DLB 296; LMFS 2; WLIT 2

Fanshawe, Ann 1625-1680 .... **LC 11**

Fante, John (Thomas) 1911-1983 .... **CLC 60; SSC 65**
See also AMWS 11; CA 69-72; 109; CANR 23, 104; DLB 130; DLBY 1983

Far, Sui Sin .... **SSC 62**
See Eaton, Edith Maude
See also SSFS 4

Farah, Nuruddin 1945- .. **BLC 1:2, 2:2; CLC 53, 137**
See also AFW; BW 2, 3; CA 106; CANR 81, 148; CDWLB 3; CN 4, 5, 6, 7; DAM MULT; DLB 125; EWL 3; WLIT 2

Fardusi
See Ferdowsi, Abu'l Qasem

Fargue, Leon-Paul 1876(?)-1947 .... **TCLC 11**
See also CA 109; CANR 107; DLB 258; EWL 3

Farigoule, Louis
See Romains, Jules

Farina, Richard 1936(?)-1966 .... **CLC 9**
See also CA 81-84; 25-28R

Farley, Walter (Lorimer)
1915-1989 .... **CLC 17**
See also AAYA 58; BYA 14; CA 17-20R; CANR 8, 29, 84; DLB 22; JRDA; MAICYA 1, 2; SATA 2, 43, 132; YAW

Farmer, Philip Jose 1918- .... **CLC 1, 19**
See also AAYA 28; BPFB 1; CA 1-4R; CANR 4, 35, 111; DLB 8; MTCW 1; SATA 93; SCFW 1, 2; SFW 4

Farquhar, George 1677-1707 .... **LC 21**
See also BRW 2; DAM DRAM; DLB 84; RGEL 2

Farrell, J(ames) G(ordon)
1935-1979 .... **CLC 6**
See also CA 73-76; 89-92; CANR 36; CN 1, 2; DLB 14, 271, 326; MTCW 1; RGEL 2; RHW; WLIT 4

Farrell, James T(homas) 1904-1979 . **CLC 1, 4, 8, 11, 66; SSC 28**
See also AMW; BPFB 1; CA 5-8R; 89-92; CANR 9, 61; CN 1, 2; DLB 4, 9, 86; DLBD 2; EWL 3; MAL 5; MTCW 1, 2; MTFW 2005; RGAL 4

Farrell, Warren (Thomas) 1943- ...... **CLC 70**
See also CA 146; CANR 120

Farren, Richard J.
See Betjeman, John

Farren, Richard M.
See Betjeman, John

Fassbinder, Rainer Werner
1946-1982 .... **CLC 20**
See also CA 93-96; 106; CANR 31

Fast, Howard 1914-2003 .... **CLC 23, 131**
See also AAYA 16; BPFB 1; CA 1-4R; 181; 214; CAAE 181; CAAS 18; CANR 1, 33, 54, 75, 98, 140; CMW 4; CN 1, 2, 3, 4, 5, 6, 7; CPW; DAM NOV; DLB 9; INT CANR-33; LATS 1:1; MAL 5; MTCW 2; MTFW 2005; RHW; SATA 7; SATA-Essay 107; TCWW 1, 2; YAW

Faulcon, Robert
See Holdstock, Robert

Faulkner, William (Cuthbert)
1897-1962 .... **CLC 1, 3, 6, 8, 9, 11, 14, 18, 28, 52, 68; SSC 1, 35, 42, 92, 97; TCLC 141; WLC 2**
See also AAYA 7; AMW; AMWR 1; BPFB 1; BYA 5, 15; CA 81-84; CANR 33; CDALB 1929-1941; DA; DA3; DAB; DAC; DAM MST, NOV; DLB 9, 11, 44, 102, 316, 330; DLBD 2; DLBY 1986, 1997; EWL 3; EXPN; EXPS; GL 2; LAIT 2; LATS 1:1; LMFS 2; MAL 5; MTCW 1, 2; MTFW 2005; NFS 4, 8, 13, 24; RGAL 4; RGSF 2; SSFS 2, 5, 6, 12; TUS

Fauset, Jessie Redmon
1882(?)-1961 ...... **BLC 1:2; CLC 19, 54; HR 1:2**
See also AFAW 2; BW 1; CA 109; CANR 83; DAM MULT; DLB 51; FW; LMFS 2; MAL 5; MBL

Faust, Frederick (Schiller)
1892-1944 .... **TCLC 49**
See Brand, Max; Dawson, Peter; Frederick, John
See also CA 108; 152; CANR 143; DAM POP; DLB 256; TUS

Faust, Irvin 1924- .... **CLC 8**
See also CA 33-36R; CANR 28, 67; CN 1, 2, 3, 4, 5, 6, 7; DLB 2, 28, 218, 278; DLBY 1980

Fawkes, Guy
See Benchley, Robert (Charles)

Fearing, Kenneth (Flexner)
1902-1961 .... **CLC 51**
See also CA 93-96; CANR 59; CMW 4; DLB 9; MAL 5; RGAL 4

Fecamps, Elise
See Creasey, John

Federman, Raymond 1928- .... **CLC 6, 47**
See also CA 17-20R, 208; CAAE 208; CAAS 8; CANR 10, 43, 83, 108; CN 3, 4, 5, 6; DLBY 1980

Federspiel, J.F. 1931-2007 .... **CLC 42**
See also CA 146; 257

Federspiel, Juerg F.
See Federspiel, J.F.

Federspiel, Jurg F.
See Federspiel, J.F.

Feiffer, Jules 1929- .... **CLC 2, 8, 64**
See also AAYA 3, 62; CA 17-20R; CAD; CANR 30, 59, 129, 161; CD 5, 6; DAM DRAM; DLB 7, 44; INT CANR-30; MTCW 1; SATA 8, 61, 111, 157

Feiffer, Jules Ralph
See Feiffer, Jules

Feige, Hermann Albert Otto Maximilian
See Traven, B.

Feinberg, David B. 1956-1994 .... **CLC 59**
See also CA 135; 147

Feinstein, Elaine 1930- .... **CLC 36**
See also CA 69-72; CAAS 1; CANR 31, 68, 121, 162; CN 3, 4, 5, 6, 7; CP 2, 3, 4, 5, 6, 7; CWP; DLB 14, 40; MTCW 1

Feke, Gilbert David .... **CLC 65**

Fitch, John IV
See Cormier, Robert
Fitzgerald, Captain Hugh
See Baum, L(yman) Frank
FitzGerald, Edward 1809-1883 ...... **NCLC 9, 153; PC 79**
See also BRW 4; DLB 32; RGEL 2
Fitzgerald, F(rancis) Scott (Key)
1896-1940 ... **SSC 6, 31, 75; TCLC 1, 6, 14, 28, 55, 157; WLC 2**
See also AAYA 24; AITN 1; AMW; AMWC 2; AMWR 1; BPFB 1; CA 110; 123; CDALB 1917-1929; DA; DA3; DAB; DAC; DAM MST, NOV; DLB 4, 9, 86, 219, 273; DLBD 1, 15, 16; DLBY 1981, 1996; EWL 3; EXPN; EXPS; LAIT 3; MAL 5; MTCW 1, 2; MTFW 2005; NFS 2, 19, 20; RGAL 4; RGSF 2; SSFS 4, 15, 21, 25; TUS
Fitzgerald, Penelope 1916-2000 . **CLC 19, 51, 61, 143**
See also BRWS 5; CA 85-88; 190; CAAS 10; CANR 56, 86, 131; CN 3, 4, 5, 6, 7; DLB 14, 194, 326; EWL 3; MTCW 2; MTFW 2005
Fitzgerald, Robert (Stuart)
1910-1985 .... **CLC 39**
See also CA 1-4R; 114; CANR 1; CP 1, 2, 3, 4; DLBY 1980; MAL 5
FitzGerald, Robert D(avid)
1902-1987 .... **CLC 19**
See also CA 17-20R; CP 1, 2, 3, 4; DLB 260; RGEL 2
Fitzgerald, Zelda (Sayre)
1900-1948 .... **TCLC 52**
See also AMWS 9; CA 117; 126; DLBY 1984
Flanagan, Thomas (James Bonner)
1923-2002 .... **CLC 25, 52**
See also CA 108; 206; CANR 55; CN 3, 4, 5, 6, 7; DLBY 1980; INT CA-108; MTCW 1; RHW; TCLE 1:1
Flaubert, Gustave 1821-1880 .... **NCLC 2, 10, 19, 62, 66, 135, 179, 185; SSC 11, 60; WLC 2**
See also DA; DA3; DAB; DAC; DAM MST, NOV; DLB 119, 301; EW 7; EXPS; GFL 1789 to the Present; LAIT 2; LMFS 1; NFS 14; RGSF 2; RGWL 2, 3; SSFS 6; TWA
Flavius Josephus
See Josephus, Flavius
Flecker, Herman Elroy
See Flecker, (Herman) James Elroy
Flecker, (Herman) James Elroy
1884-1915 .... **TCLC 43**
See also CA 109; 150; DLB 10, 19; RGEL 2
Fleming, Ian 1908-1964 ... **CLC 3, 30; TCLC 193**
See also AAYA 26; BPFB 1; BRWS 14; CA 5-8R; CANR 59; CDBLB 1945-1960; CMW 4; CPW; DA3; DAM POP; DLB 87, 201; MSW; MTCW 1, 2; MTFW 2005; RGEL 2; SATA 9; TEA; YAW
Fleming, Ian Lancaster
See Fleming, Ian
Fleming, Thomas 1927- .... **CLC 37**
See also CA 5-8R; CANR 10, 102, 155; INT CANR-10; SATA 8
Fleming, Thomas James
See Fleming, Thomas
Fletcher, John 1579-1625 . **DC 6; LC 33, 151**
See also BRW 2; CDBLB Before 1660; DLB 58; RGEL 2; TEA
Fletcher, John Gould 1886-1950 .... **TCLC 35**
See also CA 107; 167; DLB 4, 45; LMFS 2; MAL 5; RGAL 4
Fleur, Paul
See Pohl, Frederik

Flieg, Helmut
See Heym, Stefan
Flooglebuckle, Al
See Spiegelman, Art
Flora, Fletcher 1914-1969
See Queen, Ellery
See also CA 1-4R; CANR 3, 85
Flying Officer X
See Bates, H(erbert) E(rnest)
Fo, Dario 1926- .... **CLC 32, 109, 227; DC 10**
See also CA 116; 128; CANR 68, 114, 134, 164; CWW 2; DA3; DAM DRAM; DFS 23; DLB 330; DLBY 1997; EWL 3; MTCW 1, 2; MTFW 2005; WLIT 7
Foden, Giles 1967- .... **CLC 231**
See also CA 240; DLB 267; NFS 15
Fogarty, Jonathan Titulescu Esq.
See Farrell, James T(homas)
Follett, Ken 1949- .... **CLC 18**
See also AAYA 6, 50; BEST 89:4; BPFB 1; CA 81-84; CANR 13, 33, 54, 102, 156; CMW 4; CPW; DA3; DAM NOV, POP; DLB 87; DLBY 1981; INT CANR-33; MTCW 1
Follett, Kenneth Martin
See Follett, Ken
Fondane, Benjamin 1898-1944 ..... **TCLC 159**
Fontane, Theodor 1819-1898 . **NCLC 26, 163**
See also CDWLB 2; DLB 129; EW 6; RGWL 2, 3; TWA
Fonte, Moderata 1555-1592 .... **LC 118**
Fontenelle, Bernard Le Bovier de
1657-1757 .... **LC 140**
See also DLB 268, 313; GFL Beginnings to 1789
Fontenot, Chester .... **CLC 65**
Fonvizin, Denis Ivanovich
1744(?)-1792 .... **LC 81**
See also DLB 150; RGWL 2, 3
Foote, Horton 1916- .... **CLC 51, 91**
See also CA 73-76; CAD; CANR 34, 51, 110; CD 5, 6; CSW; DA3; DAM DRAM; DFS 20; DLB 26, 266; EWL 3; INT CANR-34; MTFW 2005
Foote, Mary Hallock 1847-1938 .. **TCLC 108**
See also CA 194; DLB 186, 188, 202, 221; TCWW 2
Foote, Samuel 1721-1777 .... **LC 106**
See also DLB 89; RGEL 2
Foote, Shelby 1916-2005 .... **CLC 75, 224**
See also AAYA 40; CA 5-8R; 240; CANR 3, 45, 74, 131; CN 1, 2, 3, 4, 5, 6, 7; CPW; CSW; DA3; DAM NOV, POP; DLB 2, 17; MAL 5; MTCW 2; MTFW 2005; RHW
Forbes, Cosmo
See Lewton, Val
Forbes, Esther 1891-1967 .... **CLC 12**
See also AAYA 17; BYA 2; CA 13-14; 25-28R; CAP 1; CLR 27; DLB 22; JRDA; MAICYA 1, 2; RHW; SATA 2, 100; YAW
Forche, Carolyn 1950- .. **CLC 25, 83, 86; PC 10**
See also CA 109; 117; CANR 50, 74, 138; CP 4, 5, 6, 7; CWP; DA3; DAM POET; DLB 5, 193; INT CA-117; MAL 5; MTCW 2; MTFW 2005; PFS 18; RGAL 4
Forche, Carolyn Louise
See Forche, Carolyn
Ford, Elbur
See Hibbert, Eleanor Alice Burford
Ford, Ford Madox 1873-1939 ... **TCLC 1, 15, 39, 57, 172**
See Chaucer, Daniel
See also BRW 6; CA 104; 132; CANR 74; CDBLB 1914-1945; DA3; DAM NOV; DLB 34, 98, 162; EWL 3; MTCW 1, 2; NFS 28; RGEL 2; TEA

Ford, Henry 1863-1947 .... **TCLC 73**
See also CA 115; 148
Ford, Jack
See Ford, John
Ford, John 1586-1639 .... **DC 8; LC 68, 153**
See also BRW 2; CDBLB Before 1660; DA3; DAM DRAM; DFS 7; DLB 58; IDTP; RGEL 2
Ford, John 1895-1973 .... **CLC 16**
See also AAYA 75; CA 187; 45-48
Ford, Richard 1944- .... **CLC 46, 99, 205**
See also AMWS 5; CA 69-72; CANR 11, 47, 86, 128, 164; CN 5, 6, 7; CSW; DLB 227; EWL 3; MAL 5; MTCW 2; MTFW 2005; NFS 25; RGAL 4; RGSF 2
Ford, Webster
See Masters, Edgar Lee
Foreman, Richard 1937- .... **CLC 50**
See also CA 65-68; CAD; CANR 32, 63, 143; CD 5, 6
Forester, C(ecil) S(cott) 1899-1966 . **CLC 35; TCLC 152**
See also CA 73-76; 25-28R; CANR 83; DLB 191; RGEL 2; RHW; SATA 13
Forez
See Mauriac, Francois (Charles)
Forman, James
See Forman, James D.
Forman, James D. 1932- .... **CLC 21**
See also AAYA 17; CA 9-12R; CANR 4, 19, 42; JRDA; MAICYA 1, 2; SATA 8, 70; YAW
Forman, James Douglas
See Forman, James D.
Forman, Milos 1932- .... **CLC 164**
See also AAYA 63; CA 109
Fornes, Maria Irene 1930- .... **CLC 39, 61, 187; DC 10; HLCS 1**
See also CA 25-28R; CAD; CANR 28, 81; CD 5, 6; CWD; DFS 25; DLB 7, 341; HW 1, 2; INT CANR-28; LLW; MAL 5; MTCW 1; RGAL 4
Forrest, Leon (Richard)
1937-1997 .... **BLCS; CLC 4**
See also AFAW 2; BW 2; CA 89-92; 162; CAAS 7; CANR 25, 52, 87; CN 4, 5, 6; DLB 33
Forster, E(dward) M(organ)
1879-1970 ..... **CLC 1, 2, 3, 4, 9, 10, 13, 15, 22, 45, 77; SSC 27, 96; TCLC 125; WLC 2**
See also AAYA 2, 37; BRW 6; BRWR 2; BYA 12; CA 13-14; 25-28R; CANR 45; CAP 1; CDBLB 1914-1945; DA; DA3; DAB; DAC; DAM MST, NOV; DLB 34, 98, 162, 178, 195; DLBD 10; EWL 3; EXPN; LAIT 3; LMFS 1; MTCW 1, 2; MTFW 2005; NCFS 1; NFS 3, 10, 11; RGEL 2; RGSF 2; SATA 57; SUFW 1; TEA; WLIT 4
Forster, John 1812-1876 .... **NCLC 11**
See also DLB 144, 184
Forster, Margaret 1938- .... **CLC 149**
See also CA 133; CANR 62, 115, 175; CN 4, 5, 6, 7; DLB 155, 271
Forsyth, Frederick 1938- .... **CLC 2, 5, 36**
See also BEST 89:4; CA 85-88; CANR 38, 62, 115, 137, 183; CMW 4; CN 3, 4, 5, 6, 7; CPW; DAM NOV, POP; DLB 87; MTCW 1, 2; MTFW 2005
Forten, Charlotte L. 1837-1914 ..... **BLC 1:2; TCLC 16**
See Grimke, Charlotte L(ottie) Forten
See also DLB 50, 239
Fortinbras
See Grieg, (Johan) Nordahl (Brun)
Foscolo, Ugo 1778-1827 .... **NCLC 8, 97**
See also EW 5; WLIT 7

Fosse, Bob 1927-1987
 See Fosse, Robert L.
 See also CA 110; 123
Fosse, Robert L. .... **CLC 20**
 See Fosse, Bob
Foster, Hannah Webster
 1758-1840 .... **NCLC 99**
 See also DLB 37, 200; RGAL 4
Foster, Stephen Collins
 1826-1864 .... **NCLC 26**
 See also RGAL 4
Foucault, Michel 1926-1984 . **CLC 31, 34, 69**
 See also CA 105; 113; CANR 34; DLB 242;
 EW 13; EWL 3; GFL 1789 to the Present;
 GLL 1; LMFS 2; MTCW 1, 2; TWA
**Fouque, Friedrich (Heinrich Karl) de la
 Motte** 1777-1843 .... **NCLC 2**
 See also DLB 90; RGWL 2, 3; SUFW 1
Fourier, Charles 1772-1837 .... **NCLC 51**
Fournier, Henri-Alban 1886-1914
 See Alain-Fournier
 See also CA 104; 179
Fournier, Pierre 1916-1997 .... **CLC 11**
 See Gascar, Pierre
 See also CA 89-92; CANR 16, 40
Fowles, John 1926-2005 .... **CLC 1, 2, 3, 4, 6,
 9, 10, 15, 33, 87; SSC 33**
 See also BPFB 1; BRWS 1; CA 5-8R; 245;
 CANR 25, 71, 103; CDBLB 1960 to
 Present; CN 1, 2, 3, 4, 5, 6, 7; DA3; DAB;
 DAC; DAM MST; DLB 14, 139, 207;
 EWL 3; HGG; MTCW 1, 2; MTFW 2005;
 NFS 21; RGEL 2; RHW; SATA 22; SATA-
 Obit 171; TEA; WLIT 4
Fowles, John Robert
 See Fowles, John
Fox, Paula 1923- .... **CLC 2, 8, 121**
 See also AAYA 3, 37; BYA 3, 8; CA 73-76;
 CANR 20, 36, 62, 105; CLR 1, 44, 96;
 DLB 52; JRDA; MAICYA 1, 2; MTCW
 1; NFS 12; SATA 17, 60, 120, 167; WYA;
 YAW
Fox, William Price (Jr.) 1926- .... **CLC 22**
 See also CA 17-20R; CAAS 19; CANR 11,
 142; CSW; DLB 2; DLBY 1981
Foxe, John 1517(?)-1587 .... **LC 14**
 See also DLB 132
Frame, Janet 1924-2004 ...... **CLC 2, 3, 6, 22,
 66, 96, 237; SSC 29**
 See also CA 1-4R; 224; CANR 2, 36, 76,
 135; CN 1, 2, 3, 4, 5, 6, 7; CP 2, 3, 4;
 CWP; EWL 3; MTCW 1,2; RGEL 2;
 RGSF 2; SATA 119; TWA
France, Anatole .... **TCLC 9**
 See Thibault, Jacques Anatole Francois
 See also DLB 123, 330; EWL 3; GFL 1789
 to the Present; RGWL 2, 3; SUFW 1
Francis, Claude .... **CLC 50**
 See also CA 192
Francis, Dick 1920- .... **CLC 2, 22, 42, 102**
 See Francis, Richard Stanley
 See also AAYA 5, 21; BEST 89:3; BPFB 1;
 CA 5-8R; CANR 9, 42, 68, 100, 141, 179;
 CDBLB 1960 to Present; CMW 4; CN 7;
 DA3; DAM POP; DLB 87; INT CANR-9;
 MSW; MTCW 1, 2; MTFW 2005
Francis, Paula Marie
 See Allen, Paula Gunn
Francis, Richard Stanley
 See Francis, Dick
 See also CN 2, 3, 4, 5, 6
Francis, Robert (Churchill)
 1901-1987 .... **CLC 15; PC 34**
 See also AMWS 9; CA 1-4R; 123; CANR
 1; CP 1, 2, 3, 4; EXPP; PFS 12; TCLE
 1:1
Francis, Lord Jeffrey
 See Jeffrey, Francis
 See also DLB 107

Frank, Anne(lies Marie)
 1929-1945 .... **TCLC 17; WLC 2**
 See also AAYA 12; BYA 1; CA 113; 133;
 CANR 68; CLR 101; DA; DA3; DAB;
 DAC; DAM MST; LAIT 4; MAICYA 2;
 MAICYAS 1; MTCW 1, 2; MTFW 2005;
 NCFS 2; RGHL; SATA 87; SATA-Brief
 42; WYA; YAW
Frank, Bruno 1887-1945 .... **TCLC 81**
 See also CA 189; DLB 118; EWL 3
Frank, Elizabeth 1945- .... **CLC 39**
 See also CA 121; 126; CANR 78, 150; INT
 CA-126
Frankl, Viktor E(mil) 1905-1997 ...... **CLC 93**
 See also CA 65-68; 161; RGHL
Franklin, Benjamin
 See Hasek, Jaroslav (Matej Frantisek)
Franklin, Benjamin 1706-1790 .. **LC 25, 134;
 WLCS**
 See also AMW; CDALB 1640-1865; DA;
 DA3; DAB; DAC; DAM MST; DLB 24,
 43, 73, 183; LAIT 1; RGAL 4; TUS
Franklin, Madeleine
 See L'Engle, Madeleine
Franklin, Madeleine L'Engle
 See L'Engle, Madeleine
Franklin, Madeleine L'Engle Camp
 See L'Engle, Madeleine
**Franklin, (Stella Maria Sarah) Miles
 (Lampe)** 1879-1954 .... **TCLC 7**
 See also CA 104; 164; DLB 230; FW;
 MTCW 2; RGEL 2; TWA
Franzen, Jonathan 1959- .... **CLC 202**
 See also AAYA 65; CA 129; CANR 105,
 166
Fraser, Antonia 1932- .... **CLC 32, 107**
 See also AAYA 57; CA 85-88; CANR 44,
 65, 119, 164; CMW; DLB 276; MTCW 1,
 2; MTFW 2005; SATA-Brief 32
Fraser, George MacDonald
 1925-2008 .... **CLC 7**
 See also AAYA 48; CA 45-48, 180; 268;
 CAAE 180; CANR 2, 48, 74; MTCW 2;
 RHW
Fraser, Sylvia 1935- .... **CLC 64**
 See also CA 45-48; CANR 1, 16, 60; CCA
 1
Frayn, Michael 1933- .... **CLC 3, 7, 31, 47,
 176; DC 27**
 See also AAYA 69; BRWC 2; BRWS 7; CA
 5-8R; CANR 30, 69, 114, 133, 166; CBD;
 CD 5, 6; CN 1, 2, 3, 4, 5, 6, 7; DAM
 DRAM, NOV; DFS 22; DLB 13, 14, 194,
 245; FANT; MTCW 1, 2; MTFW 2005;
 SFW 4
Fraze, Candida (Merrill) 1945- .... **CLC 50**
 See also CA 126
Frazer, Andrew
 See Marlowe, Stephen
Frazer, J(ames) G(eorge)
 1854-1941 .... **TCLC 32**
 See also BRWS 3; CA 118; NCFS 5
Frazer, Robert Caine
 See Creasey, John
Frazer, Sir James George
 See Frazer, J(ames) G(eorge)
Frazier, Charles 1950- .... **CLC 109, 224**
 See also AAYA 34; CA 161; CANR 126,
 170; CSW; DLB 292; MTFW 2005; NFS
 25
Frazier, Charles R.
 See Frazier, Charles
Frazier, Charles Robinson
 See Frazier, Charles
Frazier, Ian 1951- .... **CLC 46**
 See also CA 130; CANR 54, 93
Frederic, Harold 1856-1898 ... **NCLC 10, 175**
 See also AMW; DLB 12, 23; DLBD 13;
 MAL 5; NFS 22; RGAL 4

Frederick, John
 See Faust, Frederick (Schiller)
 See also TCWW 2
Frederick the Great 1712-1786 .... **LC 14**
Fredro, Aleksander 1793-1876 .... **NCLC 8**
Freeling, Nicolas 1927-2003 .... **CLC 38**
 See also CA 49-52; 218; CAAS 12; CANR
 1, 17, 50, 84; CMW 4; CN 1, 2, 3, 4, 5,
 6; DLB 87
Freeman, Douglas Southall
 1886-1953 .... **TCLC 11**
 See also CA 109; 195; DLB 17; DLBD 17
Freeman, Judith 1946- .... **CLC 55**
 See also CA 148; CANR 120, 179; DLB
 256
Freeman, Mary E(leanor) Wilkins
 1852-1930 .... **SSC 1, 47, 113; TCLC 9**
 See also CA 106; 177; DLB 12, 78, 221;
 EXPS; FW; HGG; MBL; RGAL 4; RGSF
 2; SSFS 4, 8, 26; SUFW 1; TUS
Freeman, R(ichard) Austin
 1862-1943 .... **TCLC 21**
 See also CA 113; CANR 84; CMW 4; DLB
 70
French, Albert 1943- .... **CLC 86**
 See also BW 3; CA 167
French, Antonia
 See Kureishi, Hanif
French, Marilyn 1929- .. **CLC 10, 18, 60, 177**
 See also BPFB 1; CA 69-72; CANR 3, 31,
 134, 163; CN 5, 6, 7; CPW; DAM DRAM,
 NOV, POP; FL 1:5; FW; INT CANR-31;
 MTCW 1, 2; MTFW 2005
French, Paul
 See Asimov, Isaac
Freneau, Philip Morin 1752-1832 .. **NCLC 1,
 111**
 See also AMWS 2; DLB 37, 43; RGAL 4
Freud, Sigmund 1856-1939 .... **TCLC 52**
 See also CA 115; 133; CANR 69; DLB 296;
 EW 8; EWL 3; LATS 1:1; MTCW 1, 2;
 MTFW 2005; NCFS 3; TWA
Freytag, Gustav 1816-1895 .... **NCLC 109**
 See also DLB 129
Friedan, Betty 1921-2006 .... **CLC 74**
 See also CA 65-68; 248; CANR 18, 45, 74;
 DLB 246; FW; MTCW 1, 2; MTFW
 2005; NCFS 5
Friedan, Betty Naomi
 See Friedan, Betty
Friedlander, Saul 1932- .... **CLC 90**
 See also CA 117; 130; CANR 72; RGHL
Friedman, B(ernard) H(arper)
 1926- .... **CLC 7**
 See also CA 1-4R; CANR 3, 48
Friedman, Bruce Jay 1930- ...... **CLC 3, 5, 56**
 See also CA 9-12R; CAD; CANR 25, 52,
 101; CD 5, 6; CN 1, 2, 3, 4, 5, 6, 7; DLB
 2, 28, 244; INT CANR-25; MAL 5; SSFS
 18
Friel, Brian 1929- .. **CLC 5, 42, 59, 115, 253;
 DC 8; SSC 76**
 See also BRWS 5; CA 21-24R; CANR 33,
 69, 131; CBD; CD 5, 6; DFS 11; DLB
 13, 319; EWL 3; MTCW 1; RGEL 2; TEA
Friis-Baastad, Babbis Ellinor
 1921-1970 .... **CLC 12**
 See also CA 17-20R; 134; SATA 7
Frisch, Max 1911-1991 ...... **CLC 3, 9, 14, 18,
 32, 44; TCLC 121**
 See also CA 85-88; 134; CANR 32, 74; CD-
 WLB 2; DAM DRAM, NOV; DFS 25;
 DLB 69, 124; EW 13; EWL 3; MTCW 1,
 2; MTFW 2005; RGHL; RGWL 2, 3
Fromentin, Eugene (Samuel Auguste)
 1820-1876 .... **NCLC 10, 125**
 See also DLB 123; GFL 1789 to the Present
Frost, Frederick
 See Faust, Frederick (Schiller)

Gray, Thomas 1716-1771 ..... **LC 4, 40; PC 2, 80; WLC 3**
See also BRW 3; CDBLB 1660-1789; DA; DA3; DAB; DAC; DAM MST; DLB 109; EXPP; PAB; PFS 9; RGEL 2; TEA; WP

Grayson, David
See Baker, Ray Stannard

Grayson, Richard (A.) 1951- .... **CLC 38**
See also CA 85-88, 210; CAAE 210; CANR 14, 31, 57; DLB 234

Greeley, Andrew M. 1928- .... **CLC 28**
See also BPFB 2; CA 5-8R; CAAS 7; CANR 7, 43, 69, 104, 136, 184; CMW 4; CPW; DA3; DAM POP; MTCW 1, 2; MTFW 2005

Green, Anna Katharine
1846-1935 .... **TCLC 63**
See also CA 112; 159; CMW 4; DLB 202, 221; MSW

Green, Brian
See Card, Orson Scott

Green, Hannah
See Greenberg, Joanne (Goldenberg)

Green, Hannah 1927(?)-1996 .... **CLC 3**
See also CA 73-76; CANR 59, 93; NFS 10

Green, Henry .... **CLC 2, 13, 97**
See Yorke, Henry Vincent
See also BRWS 2; CA 175; DLB 15; EWL 3; RGEL 2

Green, Julian .... **CLC 3, 11, 77**
See Green, Julien (Hartridge)
See also EWL 3; GFL 1789 to the Present; MTCW 2

Green, Julien (Hartridge) 1900-1998
See Green, Julian
See also CA 21-24R; 169; CANR 33, 87; CWW 2; DLB 4, 72; MTCW 1, 2; MTFW 2005

Green, Paul (Eliot) 1894-1981 .... **CLC 25**
See also AITN 1; CA 5-8R; 103; CAD; CANR 3; DAM DRAM; DLB 7, 9, 249; DLBY 1981; MAL 5; RGAL 4

Greenaway, Peter 1942- .... **CLC 159**
See also CA 127

Greenberg, Ivan 1908-1973
See Rahv, Philip
See also CA 85-88

Greenberg, Joanne (Goldenberg)
1932- .... **CLC 7, 30**
See also AAYA 12, 67; CA 5-8R; CANR 14, 32, 69; CN 6, 7; DLB 335; NFS 23; SATA 25; YAW

Greenberg, Richard 1959(?)- .... **CLC 57**
See also CA 138; CAD; CD 5, 6; DFS 24

Greenblatt, Stephen J(ay) 1943- ...... **CLC 70**
See also CA 49-52; CANR 115

Greene, Bette 1934- .... **CLC 30**
See also AAYA 7, 69; BYA 3; CA 53-56; CANR 4, 146; CLR 2, 140; CWRI 5; JRDA; LAIT 4; MAICYA 1, 2; NFS 10; SAAS 16; SATA 8, 102, 161; WYA; YAW

Greene, Gael .... **CLC 8**
See also CA 13-16R; CANR 10, 166

Greene, Graham 1904-1991 .. **CLC 1, 3, 6, 9, 14, 18, 27, 37, 70, 72, 125; SSC 29; WLC 3**
See also AAYA 61; AITN 2; BPFB 2; BRWR 2; BRWS 1; BYA 3; CA 13-16R; 133; CANR 35, 61, 131; CBD; CDBLB 1945-1960; CMW 4; CN 1, 2, 3, 4; DA; DA3; DAB; DAC; DAM MST, NOV; DLB 13, 15, 77, 100, 162, 201, 204; DLBY 1991; EWL 3; MSW; MTCW 1, 2; MTFW 2005; NFS 16; RGEL 2; SATA 20; SSFS 14; TEA; WLIT 4

Greene, Robert 1558-1592 .... **LC 41**
See also BRWS 8; DLB 62, 167; IDTP; RGEL 2; TEA

Greer, Germaine 1939- .... **CLC 131**
See also AITN 1; CA 81-84; CANR 33, 70, 115, 133; FW; MTCW 1, 2; MTFW 2005

Greer, Richard
See Silverberg, Robert

Gregor, Arthur 1923- .... **CLC 9**
See also CA 25-28R; CAAS 10; CANR 11; CP 1, 2, 3, 4, 5, 6, 7; SATA 36

Gregor, Lee
See Pohl, Frederik

Gregory, Lady Isabella Augusta (Persse)
1852-1932 .... **TCLC 1, 176**
See also BRW 6; CA 104; 184; DLB 10; IDTP; RGEL 2

Gregory, J. Dennis
See Williams, John A(lfred)

Gregory of Nazianzus, St.
329-389 .... **CMLC 82**

Gregory of Rimini 1300(?)-1358 . **CMLC 109**
See also DLB 115

Grekova, I. .... **CLC 59**
See Ventsel, Elena Sergeevna
See also CWW 2

Grendon, Stephen
See Derleth, August (William)

Grenville, Kate 1950- .... **CLC 61**
See also CA 118; CANR 53, 93, 156; CN 7; DLB 325

Grenville, Pelham
See Wodehouse, P(elham) G(renville)

Greve, Felix Paul (Berthold Friedrich)
1879-1948
See Grove, Frederick Philip
See also CA 104; 141, 175; CANR 79; DAC; DAM MST

Greville, Fulke 1554-1628 .... **LC 79**
See also BRWS 11; DLB 62, 172; RGEL 2

Grey, Lady Jane 1537-1554 .... **LC 93**
See also DLB 132

Grey, Zane 1872-1939 .... **TCLC 6**
See also BPFB 2; CA 104; 132; DA3; DAM POP; DLB 9, 212; MTCW 1, 2; MTFW 2005; RGAL 4; TCWW 1, 2; TUS

Griboedov, Aleksandr Sergeevich
1795(?)-1829 .... **NCLC 129**
See also DLB 205; RGWL 2, 3

Grieg, (Johan) Nordahl (Brun)
1902-1943 .... **TCLC 10**
See also CA 107; 189; EWL 3

Grieve, C(hristopher) M(urray)
1892-1978 .... **CLC 11, 19**
See MacDiarmid, Hugh; Pteleon
See also CA 5-8R; 85-88; CANR 33, 107; DAM POET; MTCW 1; RGEL 2

Griffin, Gerald 1803-1840 .... **NCLC 7**
See also DLB 159; RGEL 2

Griffin, John Howard 1920-1980 ..... **CLC 68**
See also AITN 1; CA 1-4R; 101; CANR 2

Griffin, Peter 1942- .... **CLC 39**
See also CA 136

Griffith, David Lewelyn Wark
See Griffith, D.W.

Griffith, D.W. 1875(?)-1948 .... **TCLC 68**
See also AAYA 78; CA 119; 150; CANR 80

Griffith, Lawrence
See Griffith, D.W.

Griffiths, Trevor 1935- .... **CLC 13, 52**
See also CA 97-100; CANR 45; CBD; CD 5, 6; DLB 13, 245

Griggs, Sutton (Elbert)
1872-1930 .... **TCLC 77**
See also CA 123; 186; DLB 50

Grigson, Geoffrey (Edward Harvey)
1905-1985 .... **CLC 7, 39**
See also CA 25-28R; 118; CANR 20, 33; CP 1, 2, 3, 4; DLB 27; MTCW 1, 2

Grile, Dod
See Bierce, Ambrose (Gwinett)

Grillparzer, Franz 1791-1872 .... **DC 14; NCLC 1, 102; SSC 37**
See also CDWLB 2; DLB 133; EW 5; RGWL 2, 3; TWA

Grimble, Reverend Charles James
See Eliot, T(homas) S(tearns)

Grimke, Angelina (Emily) Weld
1880-1958 .... **HR 1:2**
See Weld, Angelina (Emily) Grimke
See also BW 1; CA 124; DAM POET; DLB 50, 54

Grimke, Charlotte L(ottie) Forten
1837(?)-1914
See Forten, Charlotte L.
See also BW 1; CA 117; 124; DAM MULT, POET

Grimm, Jacob Ludwig Karl
1785-1863 .... **NCLC 3, 77; SSC 36**
See Grimm Brothers
See also CLR 112; DLB 90; MAICYA 1, 2; RGSF 2; RGWL 2, 3; SATA 22; WCH

Grimm, Wilhelm Karl 1786-1859 .. **NCLC 3, 77; SSC 36**
See Grimm Brothers
See also CDWLB 2; CLR 112; DLB 90; MAICYA 1, 2; RGSF 2; RGWL 2, 3; SATA 22; WCH

Grimm and Grim
See Grimm, Jacob Ludwig Karl; Grimm, Wilhelm Karl

Grimm Brothers .... **SSC 88**
See Grimm, Jacob Ludwig Karl; Grimm, Wilhelm Karl
See also CLR 112

Grimmelshausen, Hans Jakob Christoffel von
See Grimmelshausen, Johann Jakob Christoffel von
See also RGWL 2, 3

Grimmelshausen, Johann Jakob Christoffel von 1621-1676 .... **LC 6**
See Grimmelshausen, Hans Jakob Christoffel von
See also CDWLB 2; DLB 168

Grindel, Eugene 1895-1952 .... **PC 38; TCLC 7, 41**
See also CA 104; 193; EWL 3; GFL 1789 to the Present; LMFS 2; RGWL 2, 3

Grisham, John 1955- .... **CLC 84**
See also AAYA 14, 47; BPFB 2; CA 138; CANR 47, 69, 114, 133; CMW 4; CN 6, 7; CPW; CSW; DA3; DAM POP; MSW; MTCW 2; MTFW 2005

Grosseteste, Robert 1175(?)-1253 . **CMLC 62**
See also DLB 115

Grossman, David 1954- .... **CLC 67, 231**
See also CA 138; CANR 114, 175; CWW 2; DLB 299; EWL 3; RGHL; WLIT 6

Grossman, Vasilii Semenovich
See Grossman, Vasily (Semenovich)
See also DLB 272

Grossman, Vasily (Semenovich)
1905-1964 .... **CLC 41**
See Grossman, Vasilii Semenovich
See also CA 124; 130; MTCW 1; RGHL

Grove, Frederick Philip .... **TCLC 4**
See Greve, Felix Paul (Berthold Friedrich)
See also DLB 92; RGEL 2; TCWW 1, 2

Grubb
See Crumb, R.

Grumbach, Doris 1918- .... **CLC 13, 22, 64**
See also CA 5-8R; CAAS 2; CANR 9, 42, 70, 127; CN 6, 7; INT CANR-9; MTCW 2; MTFW 2005

Grundtvig, Nikolai Frederik Severin
1783-1872 .... **NCLC 1, 158**
See also DLB 300

Grunge
See Crumb, R.

Henryson, Robert 1430(?)-1506(?) ..... **LC 20, 110; PC 65**
See also BRWS 7; DLB 146; RGEL 2

Henschke, Alfred
See Klabund

Henson, Lance 1944- .... **NNAL**
See also CA 146; DLB 175

Hentoff, Nat(han Irving) 1925- .... **CLC 26**
See also AAYA 4, 42; BYA 6; CA 1-4R; CAAS 6; CANR 5, 25, 77, 114; CLR 1, 52; DLB 345; INT CANR-25; JRDA; MAICYA 1, 2; SATA 42, 69, 133; SATA-Brief 27; WYA; YAW

Heppenstall, (John) Rayner
1911-1981 .... **CLC 10**
See also CA 1-4R; 103; CANR 29; CN 1, 2; CP 1, 2, 3; EWL 3

Heraclitus c. 540B.C.-c. 450B.C. ... **CMLC 22**
See also DLB 176

Herbert, Frank 1920-1986 ... **CLC 12, 23, 35, 44, 85**
See also AAYA 21; BPFB 2; BYA 4, 14; CA 53-56; 118; CANR 5, 43; CDALBS; CPW; DAM POP; DLB 8; INT CANR-5; LAIT 5; MTCW 1, 2; MTFW 2005; NFS 17; SATA 9, 37; SATA-Obit 47; SCFW 1, 2; SFW 4; YAW

Herbert, George 1593-1633 . **LC 24, 121; PC 4**
See also BRW 2; BRWR 2; CDBLB Before 1660; DAB; DAM POET; DLB 126; EXPP; PFS 25; RGEL 2; TEA; WP

Herbert, Zbigniew 1924-1998 ..... **CLC 9, 43; PC 50; TCLC 168**
See also CA 89-92; 169; CANR 36, 74, 177; CDWLB 4; CWW 2; DAM POET; DLB 232; EWL 3; MTCW 1; PFS 22

Herbst, Josephine (Frey)
1897-1969 .... **CLC 34**
See also CA 5-8R; 25-28R; DLB 9

Herder, Johann Gottfried von
1744-1803 .... **NCLC 8, 186**
See also DLB 97; EW 4; TWA

Heredia, Jose Maria 1803-1839 .... **HLCS 2**
See also LAW

Hergesheimer, Joseph 1880-1954 ... **TCLC 11**
See also CA 109; 194; DLB 102, 9; RGAL 4

Herlihy, James Leo 1927-1993 .... **CLC 6**
See also CA 1-4R; 143; CAD; CANR 2; CN 1, 2, 3, 4, 5

Herman, William
See Bierce, Ambrose (Gwinett)

Hermogenes fl. c. 175- .... **CMLC 6**

Hernandez, Jose 1834-1886 .... **NCLC 17**
See also LAW; RGWL 2, 3; WLIT 1

Herodotus c. 484B.C.-c. 420B.C. .. **CMLC 17**
See also AW 1; CDWLB 1; DLB 176; RGWL 2, 3; TWA; WLIT 8

Herr, Michael 1940(?)- .... **CLC 231**
See also CA 89-92; CANR 68, 142; DLB 185; MTCW 1

Herrick, Robert 1591-1674 .. **LC 13, 145; PC 9**
See also BRW 2; BRWC 2; DA; DAB; DAC; DAM MST, POP; DLB 126; EXPP; PFS 13, 29; RGAL 4; RGEL 2; TEA; WP

Herring, Guilles
See Somerville, Edith Oenone

Herriot, James 1916-1995 .... **CLC 12**
See Wight, James Alfred
See also AAYA 1, 54; BPFB 2; CA 148; CANR 40; CLR 80; CPW; DAM POP; LAIT 3; MAICYA 2; MAICYAS 1; MTCW 2; SATA 86, 135; TEA; YAW

Herris, Violet
See Hunt, Violet

Herrmann, Dorothy 1941- .... **CLC 44**
See also CA 107

Herrmann, Taffy
See Herrmann, Dorothy

Hersey, John 1914-1993 .. **CLC 1, 2, 7, 9, 40, 81, 97**
See also AAYA 29; BPFB 2; CA 17-20R; 140; CANR 33; CDALBS; CN 1, 2, 3, 4, 5; CPW; DAM POP; DLB 6, 185, 278, 299; MAL 5; MTCW 1, 2; MTFW 2005; RGHL; SATA 25; SATA-Obit 76; TUS

Hervent, Maurice
See Grindel, Eugene

Herzen, Aleksandr Ivanovich
1812-1870 .... **NCLC 10, 61**
See Herzen, Alexander

Herzen, Alexander
See Herzen, Aleksandr Ivanovich
See also DLB 277

Herzl, Theodor 1860-1904 .... **TCLC 36**
See also CA 168

Herzog, Werner 1942- .... **CLC 16, 236**
See also CA 89-92

Hesiod fl. 8th cent. B.C.- .... **CMLC 5, 102**
See also AW 1; DLB 176; RGWL 2, 3; WLIT 8

Hesse, Hermann 1877-1962 .. **CLC 1, 2, 3, 6, 11, 17, 25, 69; SSC 9, 49; TCLC 148, 196; WLC 3**
See also AAYA 43; BPFB 2; CA 17-18; CAP 2; CDWLB 2; DA; DA3; DAB; DAC; DAM MST, NOV; DLB 66, 330; EW 9; EWL 3; EXPN; LAIT 1; MTCW 1, 2; MTFW 2005; NFS 6, 15, 24; RGWL 2, 3; SATA 50; TWA

Hewes, Cady
See De Voto, Bernard (Augustine)

Heyen, William 1940- .... **CLC 13, 18**
See also CA 33-36R; 220; CAAE 220; CAAS 9; CANR 98; CP 3, 4, 5, 6, 7; DLB 5; RGHL

Heyerdahl, Thor 1914-2002 .... **CLC 26**
See also CA 5-8R; 207; CANR 5, 22, 66, 73; LAIT 4; MTCW 1, 2; MTFW 2005; SATA 2, 52

Heym, Georg (Theodor Franz Arthur)
1887-1912 .... **TCLC 9**
See also CA 106; 181

Heym, Stefan 1913-2001 .... **CLC 41**
See also CA 9-12R; 203; CANR 4; CWW 2; DLB 69; EWL 3

Heyse, Paul (Johann Ludwig von)
1830-1914 .... **TCLC 8**
See also CA 104; 209; DLB 129, 330

Heyward, (Edwin) DuBose
1885-1940 .... **HR 1:2; TCLC 59**
See also CA 108; 157; DLB 7, 9, 45, 249; MAL 5; SATA 21

Heywood, John 1497(?)-1580(?) .... **LC 65**
See also DLB 136; RGEL 2

Heywood, Thomas 1573(?)-1641 . **DC 29; LC 111**
See also DAM DRAM; DLB 62; LMFS 1; RGEL 2; TEA

Hiaasen, Carl 1953- .... **CLC 238**
See also CA 105; CANR 22, 45, 65, 113, 133, 168; CMW 4; CPW; CSW; DA3; DLB 292; MTCW 2; MTFW 2005

Hibbert, Eleanor Alice Burford
1906-1993 .... **CLC 7**
See Holt, Victoria
See also BEST 90:4; CA 17-20R; 140; CANR 9, 28, 59; CMW 4; CPW; DAM POP; MTCW 2; MTFW 2005; RHW; SATA 2; SATA-Obit 74

Hichens, Robert (Smythe)
1864-1950 .... **TCLC 64**
See also CA 162; DLB 153; HGG; RHW; SUFW

Higgins, Aidan 1927- .... **SSC 68**
See also CA 9-12R; CANR 70, 115, 148; CN 1, 2, 3, 4, 5, 6, 7; DLB 14

Higgins, George V(incent)
1939-1999 .... **CLC 4, 7, 10, 18**
See also BPFB 2; CA 77-80; 186; CAAS 5; CANR 17, 51, 89, 96; CMW 4; CN 2, 3, 4, 5, 6; DLB 2; DLBY 1981, 1998; INT CANR-17; MSW; MTCW 1

Higginson, Thomas Wentworth
1823-1911 .... **TCLC 36**
See also CA 162; DLB 1, 64, 243

Higgonet, Margaret .... **CLC 65**

Highet, Helen
See MacInnes, Helen (Clark)

Highsmith, Patricia 1921-1995 ...... **CLC 2, 4, 14, 42, 102**
See Morgan, Claire
See also AAYA 48; BRWS 5; CA 1-4R; 147; CANR 1, 20, 48, 62, 108; CMW 4; CN 1, 2, 3, 4, 5; CPW; DA3; DAM NOV, POP; DLB 306; MSW; MTCW 1, 2; MTFW 2005; NFS 27; SSFS 25

Highwater, Jamake (Mamake)
1942(?)-2001 .... **CLC 12**
See also AAYA 7, 69; BPFB 2; BYA 4; CA 65-68; 199; CAAS 7; CANR 10, 34, 84; CLR 17; CWRI 5; DLB 52; DLBY 1985; JRDA; MAICYA 1, 2; SATA 32, 69; SATA-Brief 30

Highway, Tomson 1951- ...... **CLC 92; NNAL**
See also CA 151; CANR 75; CCA 1; CD 5, 6; CN 7; DAC; DAM MULT; DFS 2; DLB 334; MTCW 2

Hijuelos, Oscar 1951- .... **CLC 65; HLC 1**
See also AAYA 25; AMWS 8; BEST 90:1; CA 123; CANR 50, 75, 125; CPW; DA3; DAM MULT, POP; DLB 145; HW 1, 2; LLW; MAL 5; MTCW 2; MTFW 2005; NFS 17; RGAL 4; WLIT 1

Hikmet, Nazim 1902-1963 .... **CLC 40**
See Nizami of Ganja
See also CA 141; 93-96; EWL 3; WLIT 6

Hildegard von Bingen 1098-1179 . **CMLC 20**
See also DLB 148

Hildesheimer, Wolfgang 1916-1991 .. **CLC 49**
See also CA 101; 135; DLB 69, 124; EWL 3; RGHL

Hill, Aaron 1685-1750 .... **LC 148**
See also DLB 84; RGEL 2

Hill, Geoffrey (William) 1932- ...... **CLC 5, 8, 18, 45, 251**
See also BRWS 5; CA 81-84; CANR 21, 89; CDBLB 1960 to Present; CP 1, 2, 3, 4, 5, 6, 7; DAM POET; DLB 40; EWL 3; MTCW 1; RGEL 2; RGHL

Hill, George Roy 1921-2002 .... **CLC 26**
See also CA 110; 122; 213

Hill, John
See Koontz, Dean R.

Hill, Susan 1942- .... **CLC 4, 113**
See also BRWS 14; CA 33-36R; CANR 29, 69, 129, 172; CN 2, 3, 4, 5, 6, 7; DAB; DAM MST, NOV; DLB 14, 139; HGG; MTCW 1; RHW; SATA 183

Hill, Susan Elizabeth
See Hill, Susan

Hillard, Asa G. III .... **CLC 70**

Hillerman, Tony 1925-2008 ...... **CLC 62, 170**
See also AAYA 40; BEST 89:1; BPFB 2; CA 29-32R; 278; CANR 21, 42, 65, 97, 134; CMW 4; CPW; DA3; DAM POP; DLB 206, 306; MAL 5; MSW; MTCW 1, 2; MTFW 2005; RGAL 4; SATA 6; TCWW 2; YAW

Hillesum, Etty 1914-1943 .... **TCLC 49**
See also CA 137; RGHL

Holmes, Oliver Wendell
1809-1894 .... **NCLC 14, 81; PC 71**
See also AMWS 1; CDALB 1640-1865;
DLB 1, 189, 235; EXPP; PFS 24; RGAL
4; SATA 34

Holmes, Raymond
See Souster, (Holmes) Raymond

Holt, Victoria
See Hibbert, Eleanor Alice Burford
See also BPFB 2

Holub, Miroslav 1923-1998 .... **CLC 4**
See also CA 21-24R; 169; CANR 10; CD-
WLB 4; CWW 2; DLB 232; EWL 3;
RGWL 3

Holz, Detlev
See Benjamin, Walter

Homer c. 8th cent. B.C.- .... **CMLC 1, 16, 61;**
PC 23; WLCS
See also AW 1; CDWLB 1; DA; DA3;
DAB; DAC; DAM MST, POET; DLB
176; EFS 1; LAIT 1; LMFS 1; RGWL 2,
3; TWA; WLIT 8; WP

Hong, Maxine Ting Ting
See Kingston, Maxine Hong

Hongo, Garrett Kaoru 1951- .... **PC 23**
See also CA 133; CAAS 22; CP 5, 6, 7;
DLB 120, 312; EWL 3; EXPP; PFS 25;
RGAL 4

Honig, Edwin 1919- .... **CLC 33**
See also CA 5-8R; CAAS 8; CANR 4, 45,
144; CP 1, 2, 3, 4, 5, 6, 7; DLB 5

Hood, Hugh (John Blagdon) 1928- . **CLC 15,**
28; SSC 42
See also CA 49-52; CAAS 17; CANR 1,
33, 87; CN 1, 2, 3, 4, 5, 6, 7; DLB 53;
RGSF 2

Hood, Thomas 1799-1845 . **NCLC 16; PC 93**
See also BRW 4; DLB 96; RGEL 2

Hooker, (Peter) Jeremy 1941- .... **CLC 43**
See also CA 77-80; CANR 22; CP 2, 3, 4,
5, 6, 7; DLB 40

Hooker, Richard 1554-1600 .... **LC 95**
See also BRW 1; DLB 132; RGEL 2

Hooker, Thomas 1586-1647 .... **LC 137**
See also DLB 24

hooks, bell 1952(?)- .... **BLCS; CLC 94**
See also BW 2; CA 143; CANR 87, 126;
DLB 246; MTCW 2; MTFW 2005; SATA
115, 170

Hooper, Johnson Jones
1815-1862 .... **NCLC 177**
See also DLB 3, 11, 248; RGAL 4

Hope, A(lec) D(erwent) 1907-2000 .... **CLC 3,**
51; PC 56
See also BRWS 7; CA 21-24R; 188; CANR
33, 74; CP 1, 2, 3, 4, 5; DLB 289; EWL
3; MTCW 1, 2; MTFW 2005; PFS 8;
RGEL 2

Hope, Anthony 1863-1933 .... **TCLC 83**
See also CA 157; DLB 153, 156; RGEL 2;
RHW

Hope, Brian
See Creasey, John

Hope, Christopher 1944- .... **CLC 52**
See also AFW; CA 106; CANR 47, 101,
177; CN 4, 5, 6, 7; DLB 225; SATA 62

Hope, Christopher David Tully
See Hope, Christopher

Hopkins, Gerard Manley
1844-1889 .... **NCLC 17, 189; PC 15;**
WLC 3
See also BRW 5; BRWR 2; CDBLB 1890-
1914; DA; DA3; DAB; DAC; DAM MST,
POET; DLB 35, 57; EXPP; PAB; PFS 26;
RGEL 2; TEA; WP

Hopkins, John (Richard) 1931-1998 .. **CLC 4**
See also CA 85-88; 169; CBD; CD 5, 6

Hopkins, Pauline Elizabeth
1859-1930 .... **BLC 1:2; TCLC 28**
See also AFAW 2; BW 2, 3; CA 141; CANR
82; DAM MULT; DLB 50

Hopkinson, Francis 1737-1791 .... **LC 25**
See also DLB 31; RGAL 4

Hopley-Woolrich, Cornell George 1903-1968
See Woolrich, Cornell
See also CA 13-14; CANR 58, 156; CAP 1;
CMW 4; DLB 226; MTCW 2

Horace 65B.C.-8B.C. .... **CMLC 39; PC 46**
See also AW 2; CDWLB 1; DLB 211;
RGWL 2, 3; WLIT 8

Horatio
See Proust, (Valentin-Louis-George-Eugene)
Marcel

Horgan, Paul (George Vincent
O'Shaughnessy) 1903-1995 .. **CLC 9, 53**
See also BPFB 2; CA 13-16R; 147; CANR
9, 35; CN 1, 2, 3, 4, 5; DAM NOV; DLB
102, 212; DLBY 1985; INT CANR-9;
MTCW 1, 2; MTFW 2005; SATA 13;
SATA-Obit 84; TCWW 1, 2

Horkheimer, Max 1895-1973 .... **TCLC 132**
See also CA 216; 41-44R; DLB 296

Horn, Peter
See Kuttner, Henry

Hornby, Nick 1957(?)- .... **CLC 243**
See also AAYA 74; CA 151; CANR 104,
151; CN 7; DLB 207

Horne, Frank (Smith) 1899-1974 ...... **HR 1:2**
See also BW 1; CA 125; 53-56; DLB 51;
WP

Horne, Richard Henry Hengist
1802(?)-1884 .... **NCLC 127**
See also DLB 32; SATA 29

Hornem, Horace Esq.
See Byron, George Gordon (Noel)

Horne Tooke, John 1736-1812 ..... **NCLC 195**

Horney, Karen (Clementine Theodore
Danielsen) 1885-1952 .... **TCLC 71**
See also CA 114; 165; DLB 246; FW

Hornung, E(rnest) W(illiam)
1866-1921 .... **TCLC 59**
See also CA 108; 160; CMW 4; DLB 70

Horovitz, Israel 1939- .... **CLC 56**
See also CA 33-36R; CAD; CANR 46, 59;
CD 5, 6; DAM DRAM; DLB 7, 341;
MAL 5

Horton, George Moses
1797(?)-1883(?) .... **NCLC 87**
See also DLB 50

Horvath, odon von 1901-1938
See von Horvath, Odon
See also EWL 3

Horvath, Oedoen von -1938
See von Horvath, Odon

Horwitz, Julius 1920-1986 .... **CLC 14**
See also CA 9-12R; 119; CANR 12

Horwitz, Ronald
See Harwood, Ronald

Hospital, Janette Turner 1942- .... **CLC 42,**
145
See also CA 108; CANR 48, 166; CN 5, 6,
7; DLB 325; DLBY 2002; RGSF 2

Hosseini, Khaled 1965- .... **CLC 254**
See also CA 225; SATA 156

Hostos, E. M. de
See Hostos (y Bonilla), Eugenio Maria de

Hostos, Eugenio M. de
See Hostos (y Bonilla), Eugenio Maria de

Hostos, Eugenio Maria
See Hostos (y Bonilla), Eugenio Maria de

Hostos (y Bonilla), Eugenio Maria de
1839-1903 .... **TCLC 24**
See also CA 123; 131; HW 1

Houdini
See Lovecraft, H. P.

Houellebecq, Michel 1958- .... **CLC 179**
See also CA 185; CANR 140; MTFW 2005

Hougan, Carolyn 1943-2007 .... **CLC 34**
See also CA 139; 257

Household, Geoffrey (Edward West)
1900-1988 .... **CLC 11**
See also CA 77-80; 126; CANR 58; CMW
4; CN 1, 2, 3, 4; DLB 87; SATA 14;
SATA-Obit 59

Housman, A(lfred) E(dward)
1859-1936 .... **PC 2, 43; TCLC 1, 10;**
WLCS
See also AAYA 66; BRW 6; CA 104; 125;
DA; DA3; DAB; DAC; DAM MST,
POET; DLB 19, 284; EWL 3; EXPP;
MTCW 1, 2; MTFW 2005; PAB; PFS 4,
7; RGEL 2; TEA; WP

Housman, Laurence 1865-1959 .... **TCLC 7**
See also CA 106; 155; DLB 10; FANT;
RGEL 2; SATA 25

Houston, Jeanne Wakatsuki 1934- .... **AAL**
See also AAYA 49; CA 103, 232; CAAE
232; CAAS 16; CANR 29, 123, 167;
LAIT 4; SATA 78, 168; SATA-Essay 168

Hove, Chenjerai 1956- .... **BLC 2:2**
See also CP 7

Howard, Elizabeth Jane 1923- ..... **CLC 7, 29**
See also BRWS 11; CA 5-8R; CANR 8, 62,
146; CN 1, 2, 3, 4, 5, 6, 7

Howard, Maureen 1930- .... **CLC 5, 14, 46,**
151
See also CA 53-56; CANR 31, 75, 140; CN
4, 5, 6, 7; DLBY 1983; INT CANR-31;
MTCW 1, 2; MTFW 2005

Howard, Richard 1929- .... **CLC 7, 10, 47**
See also AITN 1; CA 85-88; CANR 25, 80,
154; CP 1, 2, 3, 4, 5, 6, 7; DLB 5; INT
CANR-25; MAL 5

Howard, Robert E 1906-1936 .... **TCLC 8**
See also BPFB 2; BYA 5; CA 105; 157;
CANR 155; FANT; SUFW 1; TCWW 1,
2

Howard, Robert Ervin
See Howard, Robert E

Howard, Warren F.
See Pohl, Frederik

Howe, Fanny 1940- .... **CLC 47**
See also CA 117, 187; CAAE 187; CAAS
27; CANR 70, 116, 184; CP 6, 7; CWP;
SATA-Brief 52

Howe, Fanny Quincy
See Howe, Fanny

Howe, Irving 1920-1993 .... **CLC 85**
See also AMWS 6; CA 9-12R; 141; CANR
21, 50; DLB 67; EWL 3; MAL 5; MTCW
1, 2; MTFW 2005

Howe, Julia Ward 1819-1910 . **PC 81; TCLC**
21
See also CA 117; 191; DLB 1, 189, 235;
FW

Howe, Susan 1937- .... **CLC 72, 152; PC 54**
See also AMWS 4; CA 160; CP 5, 6, 7;
CWP; DLB 120; FW; RGAL 4

Howe, Tina 1937- .... **CLC 48**
See also CA 109; CAD; CANR 125; CD 5,
6; CWD; DLB 341

Howell, James 1594(?)-1666 .... **LC 13**
See also DLB 151

Howells, W. D.
See Howells, William Dean

Howells, William D.
See Howells, William Dean

Howells, William Dean 1837-1920 ... **SSC 36;**
TCLC 7, 17, 41
See also AMW; CA 104; 134; CDALB
1865-1917; DLB 12, 64, 74, 79, 189;
LMFS 1; MAL 5; MTCW 2; RGAL 4;
TUS

Author Index

Howes, Barbara 1914-1996 .... **CLC 15**
See also CA 9-12R; 151; CAAS 3; CANR 53; CP 1, 2, 3, 4, 5, 6; SATA 5; TCLE 1:1

Hrabal, Bohumil 1914-1997 ...... **CLC 13, 67; TCLC 155**
See also CA 106; 156; CAAS 12; CANR 57; CWW 2; DLB 232; EWL 3; RGSF 2

Hrabanus Maurus 776(?)-856 .... **CMLC 78**
See also DLB 148

Hrotsvit of Gandersheim c. 935-c. 1000 .... **CMLC 29**
See also DLB 148

Hsi, Chu 1130-1200 .... **CMLC 42**

Hsun, Lu
See Lu Hsun

Hubbard, L. Ron 1911-1986 .... **CLC 43**
See also AAYA 64; CA 77-80; 118; CANR 52; CPW; DA3; DAM POP; FANT; MTCW 2; SFW 4

Hubbard, Lafayette Ronald
See Hubbard, L. Ron

Huch, Ricarda (Octavia) 1864-1947 .... **TCLC 13**
See also CA 111; 189; DLB 66; EWL 3

Huddle, David 1942- .... **CLC 49**
See also CA 57-60, 261; CAAS 20; CANR 89; DLB 130

Hudson, Jeffrey
See Crichton, Michael

Hudson, W(illiam) H(enry) 1841-1922 .... **TCLC 29**
See also CA 115; 190; DLB 98, 153, 174; RGEL 2; SATA 35

Hueffer, Ford Madox
See Ford, Ford Madox

Hughart, Barry 1934- .... **CLC 39**
See also CA 137; FANT; SFW 4; SUFW 2

Hughes, Colin
See Creasey, John

Hughes, David (John) 1930-2005 ..... **CLC 48**
See also CA 116; 129; 238; CN 4, 5, 6, 7; DLB 14

Hughes, Edward James
See Hughes, Ted
See also DA3; DAM MST, POET

Hughes, (James Mercer) Langston 1902-1967 .. **BLC 1:2; CLC 1, 5, 10, 15, 35, 44, 108; DC 3; HR 1:2; PC 1, 53; SSC 6, 90; WLC 3**
See also AAYA 12; AFAW 1, 2; AMWR 1; AMWS 1; BW 1, 3; CA 1-4R; 25-28R; CANR 1, 34, 82; CDALB 1929-1941; CLR 17; DA; DA3; DAB; DAC; DAM DRAM, MST, MULT, POET; DFS 6, 18; DLB 4, 7, 48, 51, 86, 228, 315; EWL 3; EXPP; EXPS; JRDA; LAIT 3; LMFS 2; MAICYA 1, 2; MAL 5; MTCW 1, 2; MTFW 2005; NFS 21; PAB; PFS 1, 3, 6, 10, 15; RGAL 4; RGSF 2; SATA 4, 33; SSFS 4, 7; TUS; WCH; WP; YAW

Hughes, Richard (Arthur Warren) 1900-1976 .... **CLC 1, 11; TCLC 204**
See also CA 5-8R; 65-68; CANR 4; CN 1, 2; DAM NOV; DLB 15, 161; EWL 3; MTCW 1; RGEL 2; SATA 8; SATA-Obit 25

Hughes, Ted 1930-1998 . **CLC 2, 4, 9, 14, 37, 119; PC 7, 89**
See Hughes, Edward James
See also BRWC 2; BRWR 2; BRWS 1; CA 1-4R; 171; CANR 1, 33, 66, 108; CLR 3, 131; CP 1, 2, 3, 4, 5, 6; DAB; DAC; DLB 40, 161; EWL 3; EXPP; MAICYA 1, 2; MTCW 1, 2; MTFW 2005; PAB; PFS 4, 19; RGEL 2; SATA 49; SATA-Brief 27; SATA-Obit 107; TEA; YAW

Hughes, Thomas 1822-1896 .... **NCLC 207**
See also BYA 3; DLB 18, 163; LAIT 2; RGEL 2; SATA 31

Hugo, Richard
See Huch, Ricarda (Octavia)

Hugo, Richard F(ranklin) 1923-1982 .... **CLC 6, 18, 32; PC 68**
See also AMWS 6; CA 49-52; 108; CANR 3; CP 1, 2, 3; DAM POET; DLB 5, 206; EWL 3; MAL 5; PFS 17; RGAL 4

Hugo, Victor (Marie) 1802-1885 .... **NCLC 3, 10, 21, 161, 189; PC 17; WLC 3**
See also AAYA 28; DA; DA3; DAB; DAC; DAM DRAM, MST, NOV, POET; DLB 119, 192, 217; EFS 2; EW 6; EXPN; GFL 1789 to the Present; LAIT 1, 2; NFS 5, 20; RGWL 2, 3; SATA 47; TWA

Huidobro, Vicente
See Huidobro Fernandez, Vicente Garcia
See also DLB 283; EWL 3; LAW

Huidobro Fernandez, Vicente Garcia 1893-1948 .... **TCLC 31**
See Huidobro, Vicente
See also CA 131; HW 1

Hulme, Keri 1947- .... **CLC 39, 130**
See also CA 125; CANR 69; CN 4, 5, 6, 7; CP 6, 7; CWP; DLB 326; EWL 3; FW; INT CA-125; NFS 24

Hulme, T(homas) E(rnest) 1883-1917 .... **TCLC 21**
See also BRWS 6; CA 117; 203; DLB 19

Humboldt, Alexander von 1769-1859 .... **NCLC 170**
See also DLB 90

Humboldt, Wilhelm von 1767-1835 .... **NCLC 134**
See also DLB 90

Hume, David 1711-1776 .. **LC 7, 56, 156, 157**
See also BRWS 3; DLB 104, 252, 336; LMFS 1; TEA

Humphrey, William 1924-1997 .... **CLC 45**
See also AMWS 9; CA 77-80; 160; CANR 68; CN 1, 2, 3, 4, 5, 6; CSW; DLB 6, 212, 234, 278; TCWW 1, 2

Humphreys, Emyr Owen 1919- .... **CLC 47**
See also CA 5-8R; CANR 3, 24; CN 1, 2, 3, 4, 5, 6, 7; DLB 15

Humphreys, Josephine 1945- ..... **CLC 34, 57**
See also CA 121; 127; CANR 97; CSW; DLB 292; INT CA-127

Huneker, James Gibbons 1860-1921 .... **TCLC 65**
See also CA 193; DLB 71; RGAL 4

Hungerford, Hesba Fay
See Brinsmead, H(esba) F(ay)

Hungerford, Pixie
See Brinsmead, H(esba) F(ay)

Hunt, E. Howard 1918-2007 .... **CLC 3**
See also AITN 1; CA 45-48; 256; CANR 2, 47, 103, 160; CMW 4

Hunt, Everette Howard, Jr.
See Hunt, E. Howard

Hunt, Francesca
See Holland, Isabelle (Christian)

Hunt, Howard
See Hunt, E. Howard

Hunt, Kyle
See Creasey, John

Hunt, (James Henry) Leigh 1784-1859 .... **NCLC 1, 70; PC 73**
See also DAM POET; DLB 96, 110, 144; RGEL 2; TEA

Hunt, Marsha 1946- .... **CLC 70**
See also BW 2, 3; CA 143; CANR 79

Hunt, Violet 1866(?)-1942 .... **TCLC 53**
See also CA 184; DLB 162, 197

Hunter, E. Waldo
See Sturgeon, Theodore (Hamilton)

Hunter, Evan 1926-2005 .... **CLC 11, 31**
See McBain, Ed
See also AAYA 39; BPFB 2; CA 5-8R; 241; CANR 5, 38, 62, 97, 149; CMW 4; CN 1, 2, 3, 4, 5, 6, 7; CPW; DAM POP; DLB 306; DLBY 1982; INT CANR-5; MSW; MTCW 1; SATA 25; SATA-Obit 167; SFW 4

Hunter, Kristin
See Lattany, Kristin (Elaine Eggleston) Hunter
See also CN 1, 2, 3, 4, 5, 6

Hunter, Mary
See Austin, Mary (Hunter)

Hunter, Mollie 1922- .... **CLC 21**
See McIlwraith, Maureen Mollie Hunter
See also AAYA 13, 71; BYA 6; CANR 37, 78; CLR 25; DLB 161; JRDA; MAICYA 1, 2; SAAS 7; SATA 54, 106, 139; SATA-Essay 139; WYA; YAW

Hunter, Robert (?)-1734 .... **LC 7**

Hurston, Zora Neale 1891-1960 ..... **BLC 1:2; CLC 7, 30, 61; DC 12; HR 1:2; SSC 4, 80; TCLC 121, 131; WLCS**
See also AAYA 15, 71; AFAW 1, 2; AMWS 6; BW 1, 3; BYA 12; CA 85-88; CANR 61; CDALBS; DA; DA3; DAC; DAM MST, MULT, NOV; DFS 6; DLB 51, 86; EWL 3; EXPN; EXPS; FL 1:6; FW; LAIT 3; LATS 1:1; LMFS 2; MAL 5; MBL; MTCW 1, 2; MTFW 2005; NFS 3; RGAL 4; RGSF 2; SSFS 1, 6, 11, 19, 21; TUS; YAW

Husserl, E. G.
See Husserl, Edmund (Gustav Albrecht)

Husserl, Edmund (Gustav Albrecht) 1859-1938 .... **TCLC 100**
See also CA 116; 133; DLB 296

Huston, John (Marcellus) 1906-1987 .... **CLC 20**
See also CA 73-76; 123; CANR 34; DLB 26

Hustvedt, Siri 1955- .... **CLC 76**
See also CA 137; CANR 149

Hutcheson, Francis 1694-1746 .... **LC 157**
See also DLB 252

Hutchinson, Lucy 1620-1675 .... **LC 149**

Hutten, Ulrich von 1488-1523 .... **LC 16**
See also DLB 179

Huxley, Aldous (Leonard) 1894-1963 .... **CLC 1, 3, 4, 5, 8, 11, 18, 35, 79; SSC 39; WLC 3**
See also AAYA 11; BPFB 2; BRW 7; CA 85-88; CANR 44, 99; CDBLB 1914-1945; DA; DA3; DAB; DAC; DAM MST, NOV; DLB 36, 100, 162, 195, 255; EWL 3; EXPN; LAIT 5; LMFS 2; MTCW 1, 2; MTFW 2005; NFS 6; RGEL 2; SATA 63; SCFW 1, 2; SFW 4; TEA; YAW

Huxley, T(homas) H(enry) 1825-1895 .... **NCLC 67**
See also DLB 57; TEA

Huygens, Constantijn 1596-1687 .... **LC 114**
See also RGWL 2, 3

Huysmans, Joris-Karl 1848-1907 ... **TCLC 7, 69, 212**
See also CA 104; 165; DLB 123; EW 7; GFL 1789 to the Present; LMFS 2; RGWL 2, 3

Hwang, David Henry 1957- .... **CLC 55, 196; DC 4, 23**
See also CA 127; 132; CAD; CANR 76, 124; CD 5, 6; DA3; DAM DRAM; DFS 11, 18; DLB 212, 228, 312; INT CA-132; MAL 5; MTCW 2; MTFW 2005; RGAL 4

Hyde, Anthony 1946- .... **CLC 42**
See Chase, Nicholas
See also CA 136; CCA 1

Jonson, Ben(jamin) 1572(?)-1637 . **DC 4; LC 6, 33, 110, 158; PC 17; WLC 3**
See also BRW 1; BRWC 1; BRWR 1; CD-BLB Before 1660; DA; DAB; DAC; DAM DRAM, MST, POET; DFS 4, 10; DLB 62, 121; LMFS 1; PFS 23; RGEL 2; TEA; WLIT 3

Jordan, June 1936-2002 .. **BLCS; CLC 5, 11, 23, 114, 230; PC 38**
See also AAYA 2, 66; AFAW 1, 2; BW 2, 3; CA 33-36R; 206; CANR 25, 70, 114, 154; CLR 10; CP 3, 4, 5, 6, 7; CWP; DAM MULT, POET; DLB 38; GLL 2; LAIT 5; MAICYA 1, 2; MTCW 1; SATA 4, 136; YAW

Jordan, June Meyer
See Jordan, June

Jordan, Neil 1950- .... **CLC 110**
See also CA 124; 130; CANR 54, 154; CN 4, 5, 6, 7; GLL 2; INT CA-130

Jordan, Neil Patrick
See Jordan, Neil

Jordan, Pat(rick M.) 1941- .... **CLC 37**
See also CA 33-36R; CANR 121

Jorgensen, Ivar
See Ellison, Harlan

Jorgenson, Ivar
See Silverberg, Robert

Joseph, George Ghevarughese .... **CLC 70**

Josephson, Mary
See O'Doherty, Brian

Josephus, Flavius c. 37-100 ..... **CMLC 13, 93**
See also AW 2; DLB 176; WLIT 8

Josiah Allen's Wife
See Holley, Marietta

Josipovici, Gabriel 1940- ...... **CLC 6, 43, 153**
See also CA 37-40R, 224; CAAE 224; CAAS 8; CANR 47, 84; CN 3, 4, 5, 6, 7; DLB 14, 319

Josipovici, Gabriel David
See Josipovici, Gabriel

Joubert, Joseph 1754-1824 .... **NCLC 9**

Jouve, Pierre Jean 1887-1976 .... **CLC 47**
See also CA 252; 65-68; DLB 258; EWL 3

Jovine, Francesco 1902-1950 .... **TCLC 79**
See also DLB 264; EWL 3

Joyaux, Julia
See Kristeva, Julia

Joyce, James (Augustine Aloysius) 1882-1941 .... **DC 16; PC 22; SSC 3, 26, 44, 64, 118; TCLC 3, 8, 16, 35, 52, 159; WLC 3**
See also AAYA 42; BRW 7; BRWC 1; BRWR 1; BYA 11, 13; CA 104; 126; CD-BLB 1914-1945; DA; DA3; DAB; DAC; DAM MST, NOV, POET; DLB 10, 19, 36, 162, 247; EWL 3; EXPN; EXPS; LAIT 3; LMFS 1, 2; MTCW 1, 2; MTFW 2005; NFS 7, 26; RGSF 2; SSFS 1, 19; TEA; WLIT 4

Jozsef, Attila 1905-1937 .... **TCLC 22**
See also CA 116; 230; CDWLB 4; DLB 215; EWL 3

Juana Ines de la Cruz, Sor 1651(?)-1695 ... **HLCS 1; LC 5, 136; PC 24**
See also DLB 305; FW; LAW; RGWL 2, 3; WLIT 1

Juana Inez de La Cruz, Sor
See Juana Ines de la Cruz, Sor

Juan Manuel, Don 1282-1348 .... **CMLC 88**

Judd, Cyril
See Kornbluth, C(yril) M.; Pohl, Frederik

Juenger, Ernst 1895-1998 .... **CLC 125**
See Junger, Ernst
See also CA 101; 167; CANR 21, 47, 106; DLB 56

Julian of Norwich 1342(?)-1416(?) . **LC 6, 52**
See also BRWS 12; DLB 146; LMFS 1

Julius Caesar 100B.C.-44B.C.
See Caesar, Julius
See also CDWLB 1; DLB 211

Jung, Patricia B.
See Hope, Christopher

Junger, Ernst
See Juenger, Ernst
See also CDWLB 2; EWL 3; RGWL 2, 3

Junger, Sebastian 1962- .... **CLC 109**
See also AAYA 28; CA 165; CANR 130, 171; MTFW 2005

Juniper, Alex
See Hospital, Janette Turner

Junius
See Luxemburg, Rosa

Junzaburo, Nishiwaki
See Nishiwaki, Junzaburo
See also EWL 3

Just, Ward 1935- .... **CLC 4, 27**
See also CA 25-28R; CANR 32, 87; CN 6, 7; DLB 335; INT CANR-32

Just, Ward Swift
See Just, Ward

Justice, Donald 1925-2004 ... **CLC 6, 19, 102; PC 64**
See also AMWS 7; CA 5-8R; 230; CANR 26, 54, 74, 121, 122, 169; CP 1, 2, 3, 4, 5, 6, 7; CSW; DAM POET; DLBY 1983; EWL 3; INT CANR-26; MAL 5; MTCW 2; PFS 14; TCLE 1:1

Justice, Donald Rodney
See Justice, Donald

Juvenal c. 60-c. 130 .... **CMLC 8**
See also AW 2; CDWLB 1; DLB 211; RGWL 2, 3; WLIT 8

Juvenis
See Bourne, Randolph S(illiman)

K., Alice
See Knapp, Caroline

Kabakov, Sasha .... **CLC 59**

Kabir 1398(?)-1448(?) .... **LC 109; PC 56**
See also RGWL 2, 3

Kacew, Romain 1914-1980
See Gary, Romain
See also CA 108; 102

Kadare, Ismail 1936- .... **CLC 52, 190**
See also CA 161; CANR 165; EWL 3; RGWL 3

Kadohata, Cynthia 1956(?)- ..... **CLC 59, 122**
See also AAYA 71; CA 140; CANR 124; CLR 121; SATA 155, 180

Kafka, Franz 1883-1924 ... **SSC 5, 29, 35, 60; TCLC 2, 6, 13, 29, 47, 53, 112, 179; WLC 3**
See also AAYA 31; BPFB 2; CA 105; 126; CDWLB 2; DA; DA3; DAB; DAC; DAM MST, NOV; DLB 81; EW 9; EWL 3; EXPS; LATS 1:1; LMFS 2; MTCW 1, 2; MTFW 2005; NFS 7; RGSF 2; RGWL 2, 3; SFW 4; SSFS 3, 7, 12; TWA

Kafu
See Nagai, Kafu
See also MJW

Kahanovitch, Pinchas
See Der Nister

Kahanovitsch, Pinkhes
See Der Nister

Kahanovitsh, Pinkhes
See Der Nister

Kahn, Roger 1927- .... **CLC 30**
See also CA 25-28R; CANR 44, 69, 152; DLB 171; SATA 37

Kain, Saul
See Sassoon, Siegfried (Lorraine)

Kaiser, Georg 1878-1945 .... **TCLC 9**
See also CA 106; 190; CDWLB 2; DLB 124; EWL 3; LMFS 2; RGWL 2, 3

Kaledin, Sergei .... **CLC 59**

Kaletski, Alexander 1946- .... **CLC 39**
See also CA 118; 143

Kalidasa fl. c. 400-455 .... **CMLC 9; PC 22**
See also RGWL 2, 3

Kallman, Chester (Simon) 1921-1975 .... **CLC 2**
See also CA 45-48; 53-56; CANR 3; CP 1, 2

Kaminsky, Melvin .... **CLC 12, 217**
See Brooks, Mel
See also AAYA 13, 48; DLB 26

Kaminsky, Stuart M. 1934- .... **CLC 59**
See also CA 73-76; CANR 29, 53, 89, 161; CMW 4

Kaminsky, Stuart Melvin
See Kaminsky, Stuart M.

Kamo no Chomei 1153(?)-1216 .... **CMLC 66**
See also DLB 203

Kamo no Nagaakira
See Kamo no Chomei

Kandinsky, Wassily 1866-1944 .... **TCLC 92**
See also AAYA 64; CA 118; 155

Kane, Francis
See Robbins, Harold

Kane, Henry 1918-
See Queen, Ellery
See also CA 156; CMW 4

Kane, Paul
See Simon, Paul

Kane, Sarah 1971-1999 .... **DC 31**
See also BRWS 8; CA 190; CD 5, 6; DLB 310

Kanin, Garson 1912-1999 .... **CLC 22**
See also AITN 1; CA 5-8R; 177; CAD; CANR 7, 78; DLB 7; IDFW 3, 4

Kaniuk, Yoram 1930- .... **CLC 19**
See also CA 134; DLB 299; RGHL

Kant, Immanuel 1724-1804 ..... **NCLC 27, 67**
See also DLB 94

Kantor, MacKinlay 1904-1977 .... **CLC 7**
See also CA 61-64; 73-76; CANR 60, 63; CN 1, 2; DLB 9, 102; MAL 5; MTCW 2; RHW; TCWW 1, 2

Kanze Motokiyo
See Zeami

Kaplan, David Michael 1946- .... **CLC 50**
See also CA 187

Kaplan, James 1951- .... **CLC 59**
See also CA 135; CANR 121

Karadzic, Vuk Stefanovic 1787-1864 .... **NCLC 115**
See also CDWLB 4; DLB 147

Karageorge, Michael
See Anderson, Poul

Karamzin, Nikolai Mikhailovich 1766-1826 .... **NCLC 3, 173**
See also DLB 150; RGSF 2

Karapanou, Margarita 1946- .... **CLC 13**
See also CA 101

Karinthy, Frigyes 1887-1938 .... **TCLC 47**
See also CA 170; DLB 215; EWL 3

Karl, Frederick R(obert) 1927-2004 .... **CLC 34**
See also CA 5-8R; 226; CANR 3, 44, 143

Karr, Mary 1955- .... **CLC 188**
See also AMWS 11; CA 151; CANR 100; MTFW 2005; NCFS 5

Kastel, Warren
See Silverberg, Robert

Kataev, Evgeny Petrovich 1903-1942
See Petrov, Evgeny
See also CA 120

Kataphusin
See Ruskin, John

Katz, Steve 1935- .... **CLC 47**
See also CA 25-28R; CAAS 14, 64; CANR 12; CN 4, 5, 6, 7; DLBY 1983

Kerr, M. E.
See Meaker, Marijane

Kerr, Robert .... **CLC 55**

Kerrigan, (Thomas) Anthony 1918- .. **CLC 4, 6**
See also CA 49-52; CAAS 11; CANR 4

Kerry, Lois
See Duncan, Lois

Kesey, Ken 1935-2001 .... **CLC 1, 3, 6, 11, 46, 64, 184; WLC 3**
See also AAYA 25; BG 1:3; BPFB 2; CA 1-4R; 204; CANR 22, 38, 66, 124; CDALB 1968-1988; CN 1, 2, 3, 4, 5, 6, 7; CPW; DA; DA3; DAB; DAC; DAM MST, NOV, POP; DLB 2, 16, 206; EWL 3; EXPN; LAIT 4; MAL 5; MTCW 1, 2; MTFW 2005; NFS 2; RGAL 4; SATA 66; SATA-Obit 131; TUS; YAW

Kesselring, Joseph (Otto) 1902-1967 .... **CLC 45**
See also CA 150; DAM DRAM, MST; DFS 20

Kessler, Jascha (Frederick) 1929- ...... **CLC 4**
See also CA 17-20R; CANR 8, 48, 111; CP 1

Kettelkamp, Larry (Dale) 1933- .... **CLC 12**
See also CA 29-32R; CANR 16; SAAS 3; SATA 2

Key, Ellen (Karolina Sofia) 1849-1926 .... **TCLC 65**
See also DLB 259

Keyber, Conny
See Fielding, Henry

Keyes, Daniel 1927- .... **CLC 80**
See also AAYA 23; BYA 11; CA 17-20R; 181; CAAE 181; CANR 10, 26, 54, 74; DA; DA3; DAC; DAM MST, NOV; EXPN; LAIT 4; MTCW 2; MTFW 2005; NFS 2; SATA 37; SFW 4

Keynes, John Maynard 1883-1946 .... **TCLC 64**
See also CA 114; 162, 163; DLBD 10; MTCW 2; MTFW 2005

Khanshendel, Chiron
See Rose, Wendy

Khayyam, Omar 1048-1131 ... **CMLC 11; PC 8**
See Omar Khayyam
See also DA3; DAM POET; WLIT 6

Kherdian, David 1931- .... **CLC 6, 9**
See also AAYA 42; CA 21-24R; 192; CAAE 192; CAAS 2; CANR 39, 78; CLR 24; JRDA; LAIT 3; MAICYA 1, 2; SATA 16, 74; SATA-Essay 125

Khlebnikov, Velimir .... **TCLC 20**
See Khlebnikov, Viktor Vladimirovich
See also DLB 295; EW 10; EWL 3; RGWL 2, 3

Khlebnikov, Viktor Vladimirovich 1885-1922
See Khlebnikov, Velimir
See also CA 117; 217

Khodasevich, V.F.
See Khodasevich, Vladislav

Khodasevich, Vladislav 1886-1939 .... **TCLC 15**
See also CA 115; DLB 317; EWL 3

Khodasevich, Vladislav Felitsianovich
See Khodasevich, Vladislav

Kidd, Sue Monk 1948- .... **CLC 267**
See also AAYA 72; CA 202; MTFW 2005; NFS 27

Kielland, Alexander Lange 1849-1906 .... **TCLC 5**
See also CA 104

Kiely, Benedict 1919-2007 . **CLC 23, 43; SSC 58**
See also CA 1-4R; 257; CANR 2, 84; CN 1, 2, 3, 4, 5, 6, 7; DLB 15, 319; TCLE 1:1

Kienzle, William X. 1928-2001 .... **CLC 25**
See also CA 93-96; 203; CAAS 1; CANR 9, 31, 59, 111; CMW 4; DA3; DAM POP; INT CANR-31; MSW; MTCW 1, 2; MTFW 2005

Kierkegaard, Soren 1813-1855 ..... **NCLC 34, 78, 125**
See also DLB 300; EW 6; LMFS 2; RGWL 3; TWA

Kieslowski, Krzysztof 1941-1996 .... **CLC 120**
See also CA 147; 151

Killens, John Oliver 1916-1987 ...... **BLC 2:2; CLC 10**
See also BW 2; CA 77-80; 123; CAAS 2; CANR 26; CN 1, 2, 3, 4; DLB 33; EWL 3

Killigrew, Anne 1660-1685 .... **LC 4, 73**
See also DLB 131

Killigrew, Thomas 1612-1683 .... **LC 57**
See also DLB 58; RGEL 2

Kim
See Simenon, Georges (Jacques Christian)

Kincaid, Jamaica 1949- . **BLC 1:2, 2:2; CLC 43, 68, 137, 234; SSC 72**
See also AAYA 13, 56; AFAW 2; AMWS 7; BRWS 7; BW 2, 3; CA 125; CANR 47, 59, 95, 133; CDALBS; CDWLB 3; CLR 63; CN 4, 5, 6, 7; DA3; DAM MULT, NOV; DLB 157, 227; DNFS 1; EWL 3; EXPS; FW; LATS 1:2; LMFS 2; MAL 5; MTCW 2; MTFW 2005; NCFS 1; NFS 3; SSFS 5, 7; TUS; WWE 1; YAW

King, Francis (Henry) 1923- .... **CLC 8, 53, 145**
See also CA 1-4R; CANR 1, 33, 86; CN 1, 2, 3, 4, 5, 6, 7; DAM NOV; DLB 15, 139; MTCW 1

King, Kennedy
See Brown, George Douglas

King, Martin Luther, Jr. 1929-1968 ... **BLC 1:2; CLC 83; WLCS**
See also BW 2, 3; CA 25-28; CANR 27, 44; CAP 2; DA; DA3; DAB; DAC; DAM MST, MULT; LAIT 5; LATS 1:2; MTCW 1, 2; MTFW 2005; SATA 14

King, Stephen 1947- .... **CLC 12, 26, 37, 61, 113, 228, 244; SSC 17, 55**
See also AAYA 1, 17; AMWS 5; BEST 90:1; BPFB 2; CA 61-64; CANR 1, 30, 52, 76, 119, 134, 168; CLR 124; CN 7; CPW; DA3; DAM NOV, POP; DLB 143; DLBY 1980; HGG; JRDA; LAIT 5; MTCW 1, 2; MTFW 2005; RGAL 4; SATA 9, 55, 161; SUFW 1, 2; WYAS 1; YAW

King, Stephen Edwin
See King, Stephen

King, Steve
See King, Stephen

King, Thomas 1943- .... **CLC 89, 171; NNAL**
See also CA 144; CANR 95, 175; CCA 1; CN 6, 7; DAC; DAM MULT; DLB 175, 334; SATA 96

King, Thomas Hunt
See King, Thomas

Kingman, Lee .... **CLC 17**
See Natti, (Mary) Lee
See also CWRI 5; SAAS 3; SATA 1, 67

Kingsley, Charles 1819-1875 .... **NCLC 35**
See also CLR 77; DLB 21, 32, 163, 178, 190; FANT; MAICYA 2; MAICYAS 1; RGEL 2; WCH; YABC 2

Kingsley, Henry 1830-1876 .... **NCLC 107**
See also DLB 21, 230; RGEL 2

Kingsley, Sidney 1906-1995 .... **CLC 44**
See also CA 85-88; 147; CAD; DFS 14, 19; DLB 7; MAL 5; RGAL 4

Kingsolver, Barbara 1955- .... **CLC 55, 81, 130, 216**
See also AAYA 15; AMWS 7; CA 129; 134; CANR 60, 96, 133, 179; CDALBS; CN 7; CPW; CSW; DA3; DAM POP; DLB 206; INT CA-134; LAIT 5; MTCW 2; MTFW 2005; NFS 5, 10, 12, 24; RGAL 4; TCLE 1:1

Kingston, Maxine Hong 1940- .... **AAL; CLC 12, 19, 58, 121; WLCS**
See also AAYA 8, 55; AMWS 5; BPFB 2; CA 69-72; CANR 13, 38, 74, 87, 128; CDALBS; CN 6, 7; DA3; DAM MULT, NOV; DLB 173, 212, 312; DLBY 1980; EWL 3; FL 1:6; FW; INT CANR-13; LAIT 5; MAL 5; MBL; MTCW 1, 2; MTFW 2005; NFS 6; RGAL 4; SATA 53; SSFS 3; TCWW 2

Kingston, Maxine Ting Ting Hong
See Kingston, Maxine Hong

Kinnell, Galway 1927- ..... **CLC 1, 2, 3, 5, 13, 29, 129; PC 26**
See also AMWS 3; CA 9-12R; CANR 10, 34, 66, 116, 138, 175; CP 1, 2, 3, 4, 5, 6, 7; DLB 5, 342; DLBY 1987; EWL 3; INT CANR-34; MAL 5; MTCW 1, 2; MTFW 2005; PAB; PFS 9, 26; RGAL 4; TCLE 1:1; WP

Kinsella, Thomas 1928- .... **CLC 4, 19, 138; PC 69**
See also BRWS 5; CA 17-20R; CANR 15, 122; CP 1, 2, 3, 4, 5, 6, 7; DLB 27; EWL 3; MTCW 1, 2; MTFW 2005; RGEL 2; TEA

Kinsella, W.P. 1935- .... **CLC 27, 43, 166**
See also AAYA 7, 60; BPFB 2; CA 97-100; 222; CAAE 222; CAAS 7; CANR 21, 35, 66, 75, 129; CN 4, 5, 6, 7; CPW; DAC; DAM NOV, POP; FANT; INT CANR-21; LAIT 5; MTCW 1, 2; MTFW 2005; NFS 15; RGSF 2

Kinsey, Alfred C(harles) 1894-1956 .... **TCLC 91**
See also CA 115; 170; MTCW 2

Kipling, (Joseph) Rudyard 1865-1936 . **PC 3, 91; SSC 5, 54, 110; TCLC 8, 17, 167; WLC 3**
See also AAYA 32; BRW 6; BRWC 1, 2; BYA 4; CA 105; 120; CANR 33; CDBLB 1890-1914; CLR 39, 65; CWRI 5; DA; DA3; DAB; DAC; DAM MST, POET; DLB 19, 34, 141, 156, 330; EWL 3; EXPS; FANT; LAIT 3; LMFS 1; MAICYA 1, 2; MTCW 1, 2; MTFW 2005; NFS 21; PFS 22; RGEL 2; RGSF 2; SATA 100; SFW 4; SSFS 8, 21, 22; SUFW 1; TEA; WCH; WLIT 4; YABC 2

Kircher, Athanasius 1602-1680 .... **LC 121**
See also DLB 164

Kirk, Russell (Amos) 1918-1994 .. **TCLC 119**
See also AITN 1; CA 1-4R; 145; CAAS 9; CANR 1, 20, 60; HGG; INT CANR-20; MTCW 1, 2

Kirkham, Dinah
See Card, Orson Scott

Kirkland, Caroline M. 1801-1864 . **NCLC 85**
See also DLB 3, 73, 74, 250, 254; DLBD 13

Kirkup, James 1918- .... **CLC 1**
See also CA 1-4R; CAAS 4; CANR 2; CP 1, 2, 3, 4, 5, 6, 7; DLB 27; SATA 12

Kirkwood, James 1930(?)-1989 .... **CLC 9**
See also AITN 2; CA 1-4R; 128; CANR 6, 40; GLL 2

Kirsch, Sarah 1935- .... **CLC 176**
See also CA 178; CWW 2; DLB 75; EWL 3

Kirshner, Sidney
See Kingsley, Sidney

Kramer, Larry 1935- .... **CLC 42; DC 8**
See also CA 124; 126; CANR 60, 132;
DAM POP; DLB 249; GLL 1

Krasicki, Ignacy 1735-1801 .... **NCLC 8**

Krasinski, Zygmunt 1812-1859 .... **NCLC 4**
See also RGWL 2, 3

Kraus, Karl 1874-1936 .... **TCLC 5**
See also CA 104; 216; DLB 118; EWL 3

Kreve (Mickevicius), Vincas
1882-1954 .... **TCLC 27**
See also CA 170; DLB 220; EWL 3

Kristeva, Julia 1941- .... **CLC 77, 140**
See also CA 154; CANR 99, 173; DLB 242;
EWL 3; FW; LMFS 2

Kristofferson, Kris 1936- .... **CLC 26**
See also CA 104

Krizanc, John 1956- .... **CLC 57**
See also CA 187

Krleza, Miroslav 1893-1981 .... **CLC 8, 114**
See also CA 97-100; 105; CANR 50; CD-
WLB 4; DLB 147; EW 11; RGWL 2, 3

Kroetsch, Robert (Paul) 1927- .... **CLC 5, 23,
57, 132**
See also CA 17-20R; CANR 8, 38; CCA 1;
CN 2, 3, 4, 5, 6, 7; CP 6, 7; DAC; DAM
POET; DLB 53; MTCW 1

Kroetz, Franz
See Kroetz, Franz Xaver

Kroetz, Franz Xaver 1946- .... **CLC 41**
See also CA 130; CANR 142; CWW 2;
EWL 3

Kroker, Arthur (W.) 1945- .... **CLC 77**
See also CA 161

Kroniuk, Lisa
See Berton, Pierre (Francis de Marigny)

Kropotkin, Peter (Aleksieevich)
1842-1921 .... **TCLC 36**
See Kropotkin, Petr Alekseevich
See also CA 119; 219

Kropotkin, Petr Alekseevich
See Kropotkin, Peter (Aleksieevich)
See also DLB 277

Krotkov, Yuri 1917-1981 .... **CLC 19**
See also CA 102

Krumb
See Crumb, R.

Krumgold, Joseph (Quincy)
1908-1980 .... **CLC 12**
See also BYA 1, 2; CA 9-12R; 101; CANR
7; MAICYA 1, 2; SATA 1, 48; SATA-Obit
23; YAW

Krumwitz
See Crumb, R.

Krutch, Joseph Wood 1893-1970 ..... **CLC 24**
See also ANW; CA 1-4R; 25-28R; CANR
4; DLB 63, 206, 275

Krutzch, Gus
See Eliot, T(homas) S(tearns)

Krylov, Ivan Andreevich
1768(?)-1844 .... **NCLC 1**
See also DLB 150

Kubin, Alfred (Leopold Isidor)
1877-1959 .... **TCLC 23**
See also CA 112; 149; CANR 104; DLB 81

Kubrick, Stanley 1928-1999 .... **CLC 16;
TCLC 112**
See also AAYA 30; CA 81-84; 177; CANR
33; DLB 26

Kumin, Maxine 1925- .... **CLC 5, 13, 28, 164;
PC 15**
See also AITN 2; AMWS 4; ANW; CA
1-4R, 271; CAAE 271; CAAS 8; CANR
1, 21, 69, 115, 140; CP 2, 3, 4, 5, 6, 7;
CWP; DA3; DAM POET; DLB 5; EWL
3; EXPP; MTCW 1, 2; MTFW 2005;
PAB; PFS 18; SATA 12

Kundera, Milan 1929- . **CLC 4, 9, 19, 32, 68,
115, 135, 234; SSC 24**
See also AAYA 2, 62; BPFB 2; CA 85-88;
CANR 19, 52, 74, 144; CDWLB 4; CWW
2; DA3; DAM NOV; DLB 232; EW 13;
EWL 3; MTCW 1, 2; MTFW 2005; NFS
18, 27; RGSF 2; RGWL 3; SSFS 10

Kunene, Mazisi 1930-2006 .... **CLC 85**
See also BW 1, 3; CA 125; 252; CANR 81;
CP 1, 6, 7; DLB 117

Kunene, Mazisi Raymond
See Kunene, Mazisi

Kunene, Mazisi Raymond Fakazi Mngoni
See Kunene, Mazisi

Kung, Hans .... **CLC 130**
See Kung, Hans

Kung, Hans 1928-
See Kung, Hans
See also CA 53-56; CANR 66, 134; MTCW
1, 2; MTFW 2005

Kunikida Doppo 1869(?)-1908
See Doppo, Kunikida
See also DLB 180; EWL 3

Kunitz, Stanley 1905-2006 ..... **CLC 6, 11, 14,
148; PC 19**
See also AMWS 3; CA 41-44R; 250; CANR
26, 57, 98; CP 1, 2, 3, 4, 5, 6, 7; DA3;
DLB 48; INT CANR-26; MAL 5; MTCW
1, 2; MTFW 2005; PFS 11; RGAL 4

Kunitz, Stanley Jasspon
See Kunitz, Stanley

Kunze, Reiner 1933- .... **CLC 10**
See also CA 93-96; CWW 2; DLB 75; EWL
3

Kuprin, Aleksander Ivanovich
1870-1938 .... **TCLC 5**
See Kuprin, Aleksandr Ivanovich; Kuprin,
Alexandr Ivanovich
See also CA 104; 182

Kuprin, Aleksandr Ivanovich
See Kuprin, Aleksander Ivanovich
See also DLB 295

Kuprin, Alexandr Ivanovich
See Kuprin, Aleksander Ivanovich
See also EWL 3

Kureishi, Hanif 1954- .. **CLC 64, 135; DC 26**
See also BRWS 11; CA 139; CANR 113;
CBD; CD 5, 6; CN 6, 7; DLB 194, 245;
GLL 2; IDFW 4; WLIT 4; WWE 1

Kurosawa, Akira 1910-1998 ..... **CLC 16, 119**
See also AAYA 11, 64; CA 101; 170; CANR
46; DAM MULT

Kushner, Tony 1956- .... **CLC 81, 203; DC 10**
See also AAYA 61; AMWS 9; CA 144;
CAD; CANR 74, 130; CD 5, 6; DA3;
DAM DRAM; DFS 5; DLB 228; EWL 3;
GLL 1; LAIT 5; MAL 5; MTCW 2;
MTFW 2005; RGAL 4; RGHL; SATA 160

Kuttner, Henry 1915-1958 .... **TCLC 10**
See also CA 107; 157; DLB 8; FANT;
SCFW 1, 2; SFW 4

Kutty, Madhavi
See Das, Kamala

Kuzma, Greg 1944- .... **CLC 7**
See also CA 33-36R; CANR 70

Kuzmin, Mikhail (Alekseevich)
1872(?)-1936 .... **TCLC 40**
See also CA 170; DLB 295; EWL 3

Kyd, Thomas 1558-1594 .. **DC 3; LC 22, 125**
See also BRW 1; DAM DRAM; DFS 21;
DLB 62; IDTP; LMFS 1; RGEL 2; TEA;
WLIT 3

Kyprianos, Iossif
See Samarakis, Antonis

L. S.
See Stephen, Sir Leslie

Labe, Louise 1521-1566 .... **LC 120**
See also DLB 327

Labrunie, Gerard
See Nerval, Gerard de

La Bruyere, Jean de 1645-1696 .... **LC 17**
See also DLB 268; EW 3; GFL Beginnings
to 1789

LaBute, Neil 1963- .... **CLC 225**
See also CA 240

Lacan, Jacques (Marie Emile)
1901-1981 .... **CLC 75**
See also CA 121; 104; DLB 296; EWL 3;
TWA

Laclos, Pierre-Ambroise Francois
1741-1803 .... **NCLC 4, 87**
See also DLB 313; EW 4; GFL Beginnings
to 1789; RGWL 2, 3

Lacolere, Francois
See Aragon, Louis

La Colere, Francois
See Aragon, Louis

La Deshabilleuse
See Simenon, Georges (Jacques Christian)

Lady Gregory
See Gregory, Lady Isabella Augusta (Persse)

Lady of Quality, A
See Bagnold, Enid

**La Fayette, Marie-(Madelaine Pioche de la
Vergne)** 1634-1693 .... **LC 2, 144**
See Lafayette, Marie-Madeleine
See also GFL Beginnings to 1789; RGWL
2, 3

Lafayette, Marie-Madeleine
See La Fayette, Marie-(Madelaine Pioche
de la Vergne)
See also DLB 268

Lafayette, Rene
See Hubbard, L. Ron

La Flesche, Francis 1857(?)-1932 ...... **NNAL**
See also CA 144; CANR 83; DLB 175

La Fontaine, Jean de 1621-1695 .... **LC 50**
See also DLB 268; EW 3; GFL Beginnings
to 1789; MAICYA 1, 2; RGWL 2, 3;
SATA 18

LaForet, Carmen 1921-2004 .... **CLC 219**
See also CA 246; CWW 2; DLB 322; EWL
3

LaForet Diaz, Carmen
See LaForet, Carmen

Laforgue, Jules 1860-1887 . **NCLC 5, 53; PC
14; SSC 20**
See also DLB 217; EW 7; GFL 1789 to the
Present; RGWL 2, 3

Lagerkvist, Paer (Fabian)
1891-1974 ..... **CLC 7, 10, 13, 54; TCLC
144**
See Lagerkvist, Par
See also CA 85-88; 49-52; DA3; DAM
DRAM, NOV; MTCW 1, 2; MTFW 2005;
TWA

Lagerkvist, Par .... **SSC 12**
See Lagerkvist, Paer (Fabian)
See also DLB 259, 331; EW 10; EWL 3;
RGSF 2; RGWL 2, 3

Lagerloef, Selma (Ottiliana Lovisa)
.... **TCLC 4, 36**
See Lagerlof, Selma (Ottiliana Lovisa)
See also CA 108; MTCW 2

Lagerlof, Selma (Ottiliana Lovisa)
1858-1940
See Lagerloef, Selma (Ottiliana Lovisa)
See also CA 188; CLR 7; DLB 259, 331;
RGWL 2, 3; SATA 15; SSFS 18

La Guma, Alex 1925-1985 .. **BLCS; CLC 19;
TCLC 140**
See also AFW; BW 1, 3; CA 49-52; 118;
CANR 25, 81; CDWLB 4; CN 1, 2, 3;
CP 1; DAM NOV; DLB 117, 225; EWL
3; MTCW 1, 2; MTFW 2005; WLIT 2;
WWE 1

Levon, O. U.
See Kesey, Ken

Levy, Amy 1861-1889 .... **NCLC 59, 203**
See also DLB 156, 240

Lewes, George Henry 1817-1878 ... **NCLC 25**
See also DLB 55, 144

Lewis, Alun 1915-1944 .... **SSC 40; TCLC 3**
See also BRW 7; CA 104; 188; DLB 20, 162; PAB; RGEL 2

Lewis, C. Day
See Day Lewis, C(ecil)
See also CN 1

Lewis, Cecil Day
See Day Lewis, C(ecil)

Lewis, Clive Staples
See Lewis, C.S.

Lewis, C.S. 1898-1963 ... **CLC 1, 3, 6, 14, 27, 124; WLC 4**
See also AAYA 3, 39; BPFB 2; BRWS 3; BYA 15, 16; CA 81-84; CANR 33, 71, 132; CDBLB 1945-1960; CLR 3, 27, 109; CWRI 5; DA; DA3; DAB; DAC; DAM MST, NOV, POP; DLB 15, 100, 160, 255; EWL 3; FANT; JRDA; LMFS 2; MAICYA 1, 2; MTCW 1, 2; MTFW 2005; NFS 24; RGEL 2; SATA 13, 100; SCFW 1, 2; SFW 4; SUFW 1; TEA; WCH; WYA; YAW

Lewis, Janet 1899-1998 .... **CLC 41**
See Winters, Janet Lewis
See also CA 9-12R; 172; CANR 29, 63; CAP 1; CN 1, 2, 3, 4, 5, 6; DLBY 1987; RHW; TCWW 2

Lewis, Matthew Gregory
1775-1818 .... **NCLC 11, 62**
See also DLB 39, 158, 178; GL 3; HGG; LMFS 1; RGEL 2; SUFW

Lewis, (Harry) Sinclair 1885-1951 . **TCLC 4, 13, 23, 39, 215; WLC 4**
See also AMW; AMWC 1; BPFB 2; CA 104; 133; CANR 132; CDALB 1917-1929; DA; DA3; DAB; DAC; DAM MST, NOV; DLB 9, 102, 284, 331; DLBD 1; EWL 3; LAIT 3; MAL 5; MTCW 1, 2; MTFW 2005; NFS 15, 19, 22; RGAL 4; TUS

Lewis, (Percy) Wyndham
1884(?)-1957 .. **SSC 34; TCLC 2, 9, 104**
See also AAYA 77; BRW 7; CA 104; 157; DLB 15; EWL 3; FANT; MTCW 2; MTFW 2005; RGEL 2

Lewisohn, Ludwig 1883-1955 .... **TCLC 19**
See also CA 107; 203; DLB 4, 9, 28, 102; MAL 5

Lewton, Val 1904-1951 .... **TCLC 76**
See also CA 199; IDFW 3, 4

Leyner, Mark 1956- .... **CLC 92**
See also CA 110; CANR 28, 53; DA3; DLB 292; MTCW 2; MTFW 2005

Leyton, E.K.
See Campbell, Ramsey

Lezama Lima, Jose 1910-1976 .... **CLC 4, 10, 101; HLCS 2**
See also CA 77-80; CANR 71; DAM MULT; DLB 113, 283; EWL 3; HW 1, 2; LAW; RGWL 2, 3

L'Heureux, John (Clarke) 1934- ...... **CLC 52**
See also CA 13-16R; CANR 23, 45, 88; CP 1, 2, 3, 4; DLB 244

Li Ch'ing-chao 1081(?)-1141(?) .... **CMLC 71**

Liddell, C. H.
See Kuttner, Henry

Lie, Jonas (Lauritz Idemil)
1833-1908(?) .... **TCLC 5**
See also CA 115

Lieber, Joel 1937-1971 .... **CLC 6**
See also CA 73-76; 29-32R

Lieber, Stanley Martin
See Lee, Stan

Lieberman, Laurence (James)
1935- .... **CLC 4, 36**
See also CA 17-20R; CANR 8, 36, 89; CP 1, 2, 3, 4, 5, 6, 7

Lieh Tzu fl. 7th cent. B.C.-5th cent.
B.C. .... **CMLC 27**

Lieksman, Anders
See Haavikko, Paavo Juhani

Lifton, Robert Jay 1926- .... **CLC 67**
See also CA 17-20R; CANR 27, 78, 161; INT CANR-27; SATA 66

Lightfoot, Gordon 1938- .... **CLC 26**
See also CA 109; 242

Lightfoot, Gordon Meredith
See Lightfoot, Gordon

Lightman, Alan P. 1948- .... **CLC 81**
See also CA 141; CANR 63, 105, 138, 178; MTFW 2005

Lightman, Alan Paige
See Lightman, Alan P.

Ligotti, Thomas 1953- .... **CLC 44; SSC 16**
See also CA 123; CANR 49, 135; HGG; SUFW 2

Ligotti, Thomas Robert
See Ligotti, Thomas

Li Ho 791-817 .... **PC 13**

Li Ju-chen c. 1763-c. 1830 .... **NCLC 137**

Liking, Werewere .... **BLC 2:2**
See Werewere Liking; Werewere Liking

Lilar, Francoise
See Mallet-Joris, Francoise

Liliencron, Detlev
See Liliencron, Detlev von

Liliencron, Detlev von 1844-1909 .. **TCLC 18**
See also CA 117

Liliencron, Friedrich Adolf Axel Detlev von
See Liliencron, Detlev von

Liliencron, Friedrich Detlev von
See Liliencron, Detlev von

Lille, Alain de
See Alain de Lille

Lillo, George 1691-1739 .... **LC 131**
See also DLB 84; RGEL 2

Lilly, William 1602-1681 .... **LC 27**

Lima, Jose Lezama
See Lezama Lima, Jose

Lima Barreto, Afonso Henrique de
1881-1922 .... **TCLC 23**
See Lima Barreto, Afonso Henriques de
See also CA 117; 181; LAW

Lima Barreto, Afonso Henriques de
See Lima Barreto, Afonso Henrique de
See also DLB 307

Limonov, Eduard
See Limonov, Edward
See also DLB 317

Limonov, Edward 1944- .... **CLC 67**
See Limonov, Eduard
See also CA 137

Lin, Frank
See Atherton, Gertrude (Franklin Horn)

Lin, Yutang 1895-1976 .... **TCLC 149**
See also CA 45-48; 65-68; CANR 2; RGAL 4

Lincoln, Abraham 1809-1865 .... **NCLC 18, 201**
See also LAIT 2

Lind, Jakov 1927-2007 ... **CLC 1, 2, 4, 27, 82**
See also CA 9-12R; 257; CAAS 4; CANR 7; DLB 299; EWL 3; RGHL

Lindbergh, Anne Morrow
1906-2001 .... **CLC 82**
See also BPFB 2; CA 17-20R; 193; CANR 16, 73; DAM NOV; MTCW 1, 2; MTFW 2005; SATA 33; SATA-Obit 125; TUS

Lindsay, David 1878(?)-1945 .... **TCLC 15**
See also CA 113; 187; DLB 255; FANT; SFW 4; SUFW 1

Lindsay, (Nicholas) Vachel
1879-1931 .... **PC 23; TCLC 17; WLC 4**
See also AMWS 1; CA 114; 135; CANR 79; CDALB 1865-1917; DA; DA3; DAC; DAM MST, POET; DLB 54; EWL 3; EXPP; MAL 5; RGAL 4; SATA 40; WP

Linke-Poot
See Doeblin, Alfred

Linney, Romulus 1930- .... **CLC 51**
See also CA 1-4R; CAD; CANR 40, 44, 79; CD 5, 6; CSW; RGAL 4

Linton, Eliza Lynn 1822-1898 .... **NCLC 41**
See also DLB 18

Li Po 701-763 .... **CMLC 2, 86; PC 29**
See also PFS 20; WP

Lippard, George 1822-1854 .... **NCLC 198**
See also DLB 202

Lipsius, Justus 1547-1606 .... **LC 16**

Lipsyte, Robert 1938- .... **CLC 21**
See also AAYA 7, 45; CA 17-20R; CANR 8, 57, 146; CLR 23, 76; DA; DAC; DAM MST, NOV; JRDA; LAIT 5; MAICYA 1, 2; SATA 5, 68, 113, 161; WYA; YAW

Lipsyte, Robert Michael
See Lipsyte, Robert

Lish, Gordon 1934- .... **CLC 45; SSC 18**
See also CA 113; 117; CANR 79, 151; DLB 130; INT CA-117

Lish, Gordon Jay
See Lish, Gordon

Lispector, Clarice 1925(?)-1977 .... **CLC 43; HLCS 2; SSC 34, 96**
See also CA 139; 116; CANR 71; CDWLB 3; DLB 113, 307; DNFS 1; EWL 3; FW; HW 2; LAW; RGSF 2; RGWL 2, 3; WLIT 1

Liszt, Franz 1811-1886 .... **NCLC 199**

Littell, Robert 1935(?)- .... **CLC 42**
See also CA 109; 112; CANR 64, 115, 162; CMW 4

Little, Malcolm 1925-1965
See Malcolm X
See also BW 1, 3; CA 125; 111; CANR 82; DA; DA3; DAB; DAC; DAM MST, MULT; MTCW 1, 2; MTFW 2005

Littlewit, Humphrey Gent.
See Lovecraft, H. P.

Litwos
See Sienkiewicz, Henryk (Adam Alexander Pius)

Liu, E. 1857-1909 .... **TCLC 15**
See also CA 115; 190; DLB 328

Lively, Penelope 1933- .... **CLC 32, 50**
See also BPFB 2; CA 41-44R; CANR 29, 67, 79, 131, 172; CLR 7; CN 5, 6, 7; CWRI 5; DAM NOV; DLB 14, 161, 207, 326; FANT; JRDA; MAICYA 1, 2; MTCW 1, 2; MTFW 2005; SATA 7, 60, 101, 164; TEA

Lively, Penelope Margaret
See Lively, Penelope

Livesay, Dorothy (Kathleen)
1909-1996 .... **CLC 4, 15, 79**
See also AITN 2; CA 25-28R; CAAS 8; CANR 36, 67; CP 1, 2, 3, 4, 5; DAC; DAM MST, POET; DLB 68; FW; MTCW 1; RGEL 2; TWA

Livius Andronicus c. 284B.C.-c.
204B.C. .... **CMLC 102**

Livy c. 59B.C.-c. 12 .... **CMLC 11**
See also AW 2; CDWLB 1; DLB 211; RGWL 2, 3; WLIT 8

Lizardi, Jose Joaquin Fernandez de
1776-1827 .... **NCLC 30**
See also LAW

Llewellyn, Richard
See Llewellyn Lloyd, Richard Dafydd Vivian
See also DLB 15

Mackenzie, Henry 1745-1831 .... **NCLC 41**
　See also DLB 39; RGEL 2
Mackey, Nathaniel 1947- .... **BLC 2:3; PC 49**
　See also CA 153; CANR 114; CP 6, 7; DLB
　169
Mackey, Nathaniel Ernest
　See Mackey, Nathaniel
MacKinnon, Catharine A. 1946- .... **CLC 181**
　See also CA 128; 132; CANR 73, 140; FW;
　MTCW 2; MTFW 2005
Mackintosh, Elizabeth 1896(?)-1952
　See Tey, Josephine
　See also CA 110; CMW 4
Macklin, Charles 1699-1797 .... **LC 132**
　See also DLB 89; RGEL 2
MacLaren, James
　See Grieve, C(hristopher) M(urray)
MacLaverty, Bernard 1942- ..... **CLC 31, 243**
　See also CA 116; 118; CANR 43, 88, 168;
　CN 5, 6, 7; DLB 267; INT CA-118; RGSF
　2
MacLean, Alistair (Stuart)
　　1922(?)-1987 .... **CLC 3, 13, 50, 63**
　See also CA 57-60; 121; CANR 28, 61;
　CMW 4; CP 2, 3, 4, 5, 6, 7; CPW; DAM
　POP; DLB 276; MTCW 1; SATA 23;
　SATA-Obit 50; TCWW 2
Maclean, Norman (Fitzroy)
　　1902-1990 .... **CLC 78; SSC 13**
　See also AMWS 14; CA 102; 132; CANR
　49; CPW; DAM POP; DLB 206; TCWW
　2
MacLeish, Archibald 1892-1982 ... **CLC 3, 8,**
　　14, 68; PC 47
　See also AMW; CA 9-12R; 106; CAD;
　CANR 33, 63; CDALBS; CP 1, 2; DAM
　POET; DFS 15; DLB 4, 7, 45; DLBY
　1982; EWL 3; EXPP; MAL 5; MTCW 1,
　2; MTFW 2005; PAB; PFS 5; RGAL 4;
　TUS
MacLennan, (John) Hugh
　　1907-1990 .... **CLC 2, 14, 92**
　See also CA 5-8R; 142; CANR 33; CN 1,
　2, 3, 4; DAC; DAM MST; DLB 68; EWL
　3; MTCW 1, 2; MTFW 2005; RGEL 2;
　TWA
MacLeod, Alistair 1936- .. **CLC 56, 165; SSC**
　　90
　See also CA 123; CCA 1; DAC; DAM
　MST; DLB 60; MTCW 2; MTFW 2005;
　RGSF 2; TCLE 1:2
Macleod, Fiona
　See Sharp, William
　See also RGEL 2; SUFW
MacNeice, (Frederick) Louis
　　1907-1963 .... **CLC 1, 4, 10, 53; PC 61**
　See also BRW 7; CA 85-88; CANR 61;
　DAB; DAM POET; DLB 10, 20; EWL 3;
　MTCW 1, 2; MTFW 2005; RGEL 2
MacNeill, Dand
　See Fraser, George MacDonald
Macpherson, James 1736-1796 .... **LC 29**
　See Ossian
　See also BRWS 8; DLB 109, 336; RGEL 2
Macpherson, (Jean) Jay 1931- .... **CLC 14**
　See also CA 5-8R; CANR 90; CP 1, 2, 3, 4,
　6, 7; CWP; DLB 53
Macrobius fl. 430- .... **CMLC 48**
MacShane, Frank 1927-1999 .... **CLC 39**
　See also CA 9-12R; 186; CANR 3, 33; DLB
　111
Macumber, Mari
　See Sandoz, Mari(e Susette)
Madach, Imre 1823-1864 .... **NCLC 19**
Madden, (Jerry) David 1933- .... **CLC 5, 15**
　See also CA 1-4R; CAAS 3; CANR 4, 45;
　CN 3, 4, 5, 6, 7; CSW; DLB 6; MTCW 1
Maddern, Al(an)
　See Ellison, Harlan

Madhubuti, Haki R. 1942- .... **BLC 1:2; CLC**
　　6, 73; PC 5
　See Lee, Don L.
　See also BW 2, 3; CA 73-76; CANR 24,
　51, 73, 139; CP 6, 7; CSW; DAM MULT,
　POET; DLB 5, 41; DLBD 8; EWL 3;
　MAL 5; MTCW 2; MTFW 2005; RGAL
　4
Madison, James 1751-1836 .... **NCLC 126**
　See also DLB 37
Maepenn, Hugh
　See Kuttner, Henry
Maepenn, K. H.
　See Kuttner, Henry
Maeterlinck, Maurice 1862-1949 .... **DC 32;**
　　TCLC 3
　See also CA 104; 136; CANR 80; DAM
　DRAM; DLB 192, 331; EW 8; EWL 3;
　GFL 1789 to the Present; LMFS 2; RGWL
　2, 3; SATA 66; TWA
Maginn, William 1794-1842 .... **NCLC 8**
　See also DLB 110, 159
Mahapatra, Jayanta 1928- .... **CLC 33**
　See also CA 73-76; CAAS 9; CANR 15,
　33, 66, 87; CP 4, 5, 6, 7; DAM MULT;
　DLB 323
Mahfouz, Nagib
　See Mahfouz, Naguib
Mahfouz, Naguib 1911(?)-2006 ..... **CLC 153;**
　　SSC 66
　See Mahfuz, Najib
　See also AAYA 49; BEST 89:2; CA 128;
　253; CANR 55, 101; DA3; DAM NOV;
　DLB 346; MTCW 1, 2; MTFW 2005;
　RGWL 2, 3; SSFS 9
Mahfouz, Naguib Abdel Aziz Al-Sabilgi
　See Mahfouz, Naguib
Mahfouz, Najib
　See Mahfouz, Naguib
Mahfuz, Najib .... **CLC 52, 55**
　See Mahfouz, Naguib
　See also AFW; CWW 2; DLB 331; DLBY
　1988; EWL 3; RGSF 2; WLIT 6
Mahon, Derek 1941- .... **CLC 27; PC 60**
　See also BRWS 6; CA 113; 128; CANR 88;
　CP 1, 2, 3, 4, 5, 6, 7; DLB 40; EWL 3
Maiakovskii, Vladimir
　See Mayakovski, Vladimir (Vladimirovich)
　See also IDTP; RGWL 2, 3
Mailer, Norman 1923-2007 ... **CLC 1, 2, 3, 4,**
　　5, 8, 11, 14, 28, 39, 74, 111, 234
　See also AAYA 31; AITN 2; AMW; AMWC
　2; AMWR 2; BPFB 2; CA 9-12R; 266;
　CABS 1; CANR 28, 74, 77, 130; CDALB
　1968-1988; CN 1, 2, 3, 4, 5, 6, 7; CPW;
　DA; DA3; DAB; DAC; DAM MST, NOV,
　POP; DLB 2, 16, 28, 185, 278; DLBD 3;
　DLBY 1980, 1983; EWL 3; MAL 5;
　MTCW 1, 2; MTFW 2005; NFS 10;
　RGAL 4; TUS
Mailer, Norman Kingsley
　See Mailer, Norman
Maillet, Antonine 1929- .... **CLC 54, 118**
　See also CA 115; 120; CANR 46, 74, 77,
　134; CCA 1; CWW 2; DAC; DLB 60;
　INT CA-120; MTCW 2; MTFW 2005
Maimonides, Moses 1135-1204 ..... **CMLC 76**
　See also DLB 115
Mais, Roger 1905-1955 .... **TCLC 8**
　See also BW 1, 3; CA 105; 124; CANR 82;
　CDWLB 3; DLB 125; EWL 3; MTCW 1;
　RGEL 2
Maistre, Joseph 1753-1821 .... **NCLC 37**
　See also GFL 1789 to the Present
Maitland, Frederic William
　　1850-1906 .... **TCLC 65**
Maitland, Sara (Louise) 1950- .... **CLC 49**
　See also BRWS 11; CA 69-72; CANR 13,
　59; DLB 271; FW

Major, Clarence 1936- ...... **BLC 1:2; CLC 3,**
　　19, 48
　See also AFAW 2; BW 2, 3; CA 21-24R;
　CAAS 6; CANR 13, 25, 53, 82; CN 3, 4,
　5, 6, 7; CP 2, 3, 4, 5, 6, 7; CSW; DAM
　MULT; DLB 33; EWL 3; MAL 5; MSW
Major, Kevin (Gerald) 1949- .... **CLC 26**
　See also AAYA 16; CA 97-100; CANR 21,
　38, 112; CLR 11; DAC; DLB 60; INT
　CANR-21; JRDA; MAICYA 1, 2; MAIC-
　YAS 1; SATA 32, 82, 134; WYA; YAW
Maki, James
　See Ozu, Yasujiro
Makin, Bathsua 1600-1675(?) .... **LC 137**
Makine, Andrei 1957-
　See Makine, Andreï
Makine, Andreï 1957- .... **CLC 198**
　See also CA 176; CANR 103, 162; MTFW
　2005
Malabaila, Damiano
　See Levi, Primo
Malamud, Bernard 1914-1986 .. **CLC 1, 2, 3,**
　　5, 8, 9, 11, 18, 27, 44, 78, 85; SSC 15;
　　TCLC 129, 184; WLC 4
　See also AAYA 16; AMWS 1; BPFB 2;
　BYA 15; CA 5-8R; 118; CABS 1; CANR
　28, 62, 114; CDALB 1941-1968; CN 1, 2,
　3, 4; CPW; DA; DA3; DAB; DAC; DAM
　MST, NOV, POP; DLB 2, 28, 152; DLBY
　1980, 1986; EWL 3; EXPS; LAIT 4;
　LATS 1:1; MAL 5; MTCW 1, 2; MTFW
　2005; NFS 27; RGAL 4; RGHL; RGSF 2;
　SSFS 8, 13, 16; TUS
Malan, Herman
　See Bosman, Herman Charles; Bosman,
　Herman Charles
Malaparte, Curzio 1898-1957 .... **TCLC 52**
　See also DLB 264
Malcolm, Dan
　See Silverberg, Robert
Malcolm, Janet 1934- .... **CLC 201**
　See also CA 123; CANR 89; NCFS 1
Malcolm X . **BLC 1:2; CLC 82, 117; WLCS**
　See Little, Malcolm
　See also LAIT 5; NCFS 3
Malebranche, Nicolas 1638-1715 .... **LC 133**
　See also GFL Beginnings to 1789
Malherbe, Francois de 1555-1628 .... **LC 5**
　See also DLB 327; GFL Beginnings to 1789
Mallarme, Stephane 1842-1898 ...... **NCLC 4,**
　　41; PC 4
　See also DAM POET; DLB 217; EW 7;
　GFL 1789 to the Present; LMFS 2; RGWL
　2, 3; TWA
Mallet-Joris, Francoise 1930- .... **CLC 11**
　See also CA 65-68; CANR 17; CWW 2;
　DLB 83; EWL 3; GFL 1789 to the Present
Malley, Ern
　See McAuley, James Phillip
Mallon, Thomas 1951- .... **CLC 172**
　See also CA 110; CANR 29, 57, 92
Mallowan, Agatha Christie
　See Christie, Agatha (Mary Clarissa)
Maloff, Saul 1922- .... **CLC 5**
　See also CA 33-36R
Malone, Louis
　See MacNeice, (Frederick) Louis
Malone, Michael (Christopher)
　　1942- .... **CLC 43**
　See also CA 77-80; CANR 14, 32, 57, 114
Malory, Sir Thomas 1410(?)-1471(?) . **LC 11,**
　　88; WLCS
　See also BRW 1; BRWR 2; CDBLB Before
　1660; DA; DAB; DAC; DAM MST; DLB
　146; EFS 2; RGEL 2; SATA 59; SATA-
　Brief 33; TEA; WLIT 3

Malouf, David 1934- .... **CLC 28, 86, 245**
See also BRWS 12; CA 124; CANR 50, 76, 180; CN 3, 4, 5, 6, 7; CP 1, 3, 4, 5, 6, 7; DLB 289; EWL 3; MTCW 2; MTFW 2005; SSFS 24

Malouf, George Joseph David
See Malouf, David

Malraux, (Georges-)Andre
1901-1976 .... **CLC 1, 4, 9, 13, 15, 57; TCLC 209**
See also BPFB 2; CA 21-22; 69-72; CANR 34, 58; CAP 2; DA3; DAM NOV; DLB 72; EW 12; EWL 3; GFL 1789 to the Present; MTCW 1, 2; MTFW 2005; RGWL 2, 3; TWA

Malthus, Thomas Robert
1766-1834 .... **NCLC 145**
See also DLB 107, 158; RGEL 2

Malzberg, Barry N(athaniel) 1939- ... **CLC 7**
See also CA 61-64; CAAS 4; CANR 16; CMW 4; DLB 8; SFW 4

Mamet, David 1947- .. **CLC 9, 15, 34, 46, 91, 166; DC 4, 24**
See also AAYA 3, 60; AMWS 14; CA 81-84; CABS 3; CAD; CANR 15, 41, 67, 72, 129, 172; CD 5, 6; DA3; DAM DRAM; DFS 2, 3, 6, 12, 15; DLB 7; EWL 3; IDFW 4; MAL 5; MTCW 1, 2; MTFW 2005; RGAL 4

Mamet, David Alan
See Mamet, David

Mamoulian, Rouben (Zachary)
1897-1987 .... **CLC 16**
See also CA 25-28R; 124; CANR 85

Mandelshtam, Osip
See Mandelstam, Osip (Emilievich)
See also EW 10; EWL 3; RGWL 2, 3

Mandelstam, Osip (Emilievich)
1891(?)-1943(?) .... **PC 14; TCLC 2, 6**
See Mandelshtam, Osip
See also CA 104; 150; MTCW 2; TWA

Mander, (Mary) Jane 1877-1949 ... **TCLC 31**
See also CA 162; RGEL 2

Mandeville, Bernard 1670-1733 .... **LC 82**
See also DLB 101

Mandeville, Sir John fl. 1350- ...... **CMLC 19**
See also DLB 146

Mandiargues, Andre Pieyre de .... **CLC 41**
See Pieyre de Mandiargues, Andre
See also DLB 83

Mandrake, Ethel Belle
See Thurman, Wallace (Henry)

Mangan, James Clarence
1803-1849 .... **NCLC 27**
See also BRWS 13; RGEL 2

Maniere, J.-E.
See Giraudoux, Jean(-Hippolyte)

Mankiewicz, Herman (Jacob)
1897-1953 .... **TCLC 85**
See also CA 120; 169; DLB 26; IDFW 3, 4

Manley, (Mary) Delariviere
1672(?)-1724 .... **LC 1, 42**
See also DLB 39, 80; RGEL 2

Mann, Abel
See Creasey, John

Mann, Emily 1952- .... **DC 7**
See also CA 130; CAD; CANR 55; CD 5, 6; CWD; DLB 266

Mann, (Luiz) Heinrich 1871-1950 ... **TCLC 9**
See also CA 106; 164, 181; DLB 66, 118; EW 8; EWL 3; RGWL 2, 3

Mann, (Paul) Thomas 1875-1955 . **SSC 5, 80, 82; TCLC 2, 8, 14, 21, 35, 44, 60, 168; WLC 4**
See also BPFB 2; CA 104; 128; CANR 133; CDWLB 2; DA; DA3; DAB; DAC; DAM MST, NOV; DLB 66, 331; EW 9; EWL 3;

GLL 1; LATS 1:1; LMFS 1; MTCW 1, 2, 3; SSFS 4, 9; TWA

Mannheim, Karl 1893-1947 .... **TCLC 65**
See also CA 204

Manning, David
See Faust, Frederick (Schiller)

Manning, Frederic 1882-1935 .... **TCLC 25**
See also CA 124; 216; DLB 260

Manning, Olivia 1915-1980 .... **CLC 5, 19**
See also CA 5-8R; 101; CANR 29; CN 1, 2; EWL 3; FW; MTCW 1; RGEL 2

Mannyng, Robert c. 1264-c. 1340 .... **CMLC 83**
See also DLB 146

Mano, D. Keith 1942- .... **CLC 2, 10**
See also CA 25-28R; CAAS 6; CANR 26, 57; DLB 6

Mansfield, Katherine .... **SSC 9, 23, 38, 81; TCLC 2, 8, 39, 164; WLC 4**
See Beauchamp, Kathleen Mansfield
See also BPFB 2; BRW 7; DAB; DLB 162; EWL 3; EXPS; FW; GLL 1; RGEL 2; RGSF 2; SSFS 2, 8, 10, 11; WWE 1

Manso, Peter 1940- .... **CLC 39**
See also CA 29-32R; CANR 44, 156

Mantecon, Juan Jimenez
See Jimenez (Mantecon), Juan Ramon

Mantel, Hilary 1952- .... **CLC 144**
See also CA 125; CANR 54, 101, 161; CN 5, 6, 7; DLB 271; RHW

Mantel, Hilary Mary
See Mantel, Hilary

Manton, Peter
See Creasey, John

Man Without a Spleen, A
See Chekhov, Anton (Pavlovich)

Manzano, Juan Franciso
1797(?)-1854 .... **NCLC 155**

Manzoni, Alessandro 1785-1873 ... **NCLC 29, 98**
See also EW 5; RGWL 2, 3; TWA; WLIT 7

Map, Walter 1140-1209 .... **CMLC 32**

Mapu, Abraham (ben Jekutiel)
1808-1867 .... **NCLC 18**

Mara, Sally
See Queneau, Raymond

Maracle, Lee 1950- .... **NNAL**
See also CA 149

Marat, Jean Paul 1743-1793 .... **LC 10**

Marcel, Gabriel Honore 1889-1973 . **CLC 15**
See also CA 102; 45-48; EWL 3; MTCW 1, 2

March, William .... **TCLC 96**
See Campbell, William Edward March
See also CA 216; DLB 9, 86, 316; MAL 5

Marchbanks, Samuel
See Davies, Robertson
See also CCA 1

Marchi, Giacomo
See Bassani, Giorgio

Marcus Aurelius
See Aurelius, Marcus
See also AW 2

Marcuse, Herbert 1898-1979 .... **TCLC 207**
See also CA 188; 89-92; DLB 242

Marguerite
See de Navarre, Marguerite

Marguerite d'Angouleme
See de Navarre, Marguerite
See also GFL Beginnings to 1789

Marguerite de Navarre
See de Navarre, Marguerite
See also RGWL 2, 3

Margulies, Donald 1954- .... **CLC 76**
See also AAYA 57; CA 200; CD 6; DFS 13; DLB 228

Marias, Javier 1951- .... **CLC 239**
See also CA 167; CANR 109, 139; DLB 322; HW 2; MTFW 2005

Marie de France c. 12th cent. - ..... **CMLC 8; PC 22**
See also DLB 208; FW; RGWL 2, 3

Marie de l'Incarnation 1599-1672 ...... **LC 10**

Marier, Captain Victor
See Griffith, D.W.

Mariner, Scott
See Pohl, Frederik

Marinetti, Filippo Tommaso
1876-1944 .... **TCLC 10**
See also CA 107; DLB 114, 264; EW 9; EWL 3; WLIT 7

Marivaux, Pierre Carlet de Chamblain de
1688-1763 .... **DC 7; LC 4, 123**
See also DLB 314; GFL Beginnings to 1789; RGWL 2, 3; TWA

Markandaya, Kamala .... **CLC 8, 38**
See Taylor, Kamala
See also BYA 13; CN 1, 2, 3, 4, 5, 6, 7; DLB 323; EWL 3

Markfield, Wallace (Arthur)
1926-2002 .... **CLC 8**
See also CA 69-72; 208; CAAS 3; CN 1, 2, 3, 4, 5, 6, 7; DLB 2, 28; DLBY 2002

Markham, Edwin 1852-1940 .... **TCLC 47**
See also CA 160; DLB 54, 186; MAL 5; RGAL 4

Markham, Robert
See Amis, Kingsley

Marks, J.
See Highwater, Jamake (Mamake)

Marks-Highwater, J.
See Highwater, Jamake (Mamake)

Markson, David M. 1927- .... **CLC 67**
See also AMWS 17; CA 49-52; CANR 1, 91, 158; CN 5, 6

Markson, David Merrill
See Markson, David M.

Marlatt, Daphne (Buckle) 1942- .... **CLC 168**
See also CA 25-28R; CANR 17, 39; CN 6, 7; CP 4, 5, 6, 7; CWP; DLB 60; FW

Marley, Bob .... **CLC 17**
See Marley, Robert Nesta

Marley, Robert Nesta 1945-1981
See Marley, Bob
See also CA 107; 103

Marlowe, Christopher 1564-1593 . **DC 1; LC 22, 47, 117; PC 57; WLC 4**
See also BRW 1; BRWR 1; CDBLB Before 1660; DA; DA3; DAB; DAC; DAM DRAM, MST; DFS 1, 5, 13, 21; DLB 62; EXPP; LMFS 1; PFS 22; RGEL 2; TEA; WLIT 3

Marlowe, Stephen 1928-2008 .... **CLC 70**
See Queen, Ellery
See also CA 13-16R; 269; CANR 6, 55; CMW 4; SFW 4

Marmion, Shakerley 1603-1639 .... **LC 89**
See also DLB 58; RGEL 2

Marmontel, Jean-Francois 1723-1799 .. **LC 2**
See also DLB 314

Maron, Monika 1941- .... **CLC 165**
See also CA 201

Marot, Clement c. 1496-1544 .... **LC 133**
See also DLB 327; GFL Beginnings to 1789

Marquand, John P(hillips)
1893-1960 .... **CLC 2, 10**
See also AMW; BPFB 2; CA 85-88; CANR 73; CMW 4; DLB 9, 102; EWL 3; MAL 5; MTCW 2; RGAL 4

Marques, Rene 1919-1979 .. **CLC 96; HLC 2**
See also CA 97-100; 85-88; CANR 78; DAM MULT; DLB 305; EWL 3; HW 1, 2; LAW; RGSF 2

Marquez, Gabriel Garcia
See Garcia Marquez, Gabriel

McGahern, John 1934-2006 .... **CLC 5, 9, 48, 156; SSC 17**
See also CA 17-20R; 249; CANR 29, 68, 113; CN 1, 2, 3, 4, 5, 6, 7; DLB 14, 231, 319; MTCW 1

McGinley, Patrick (Anthony) 1937- . **CLC 41**
See also CA 120; 127; CANR 56; INT CA-127

McGinley, Phyllis 1905-1978 .... **CLC 14**
See also CA 9-12R; 77-80; CANR 19; CP 1, 2; CWRI 5; DLB 11, 48; MAL 5; PFS 9, 13; SATA 2, 44; SATA-Obit 24

McGinniss, Joe 1942- .... **CLC 32**
See also AITN 2; BEST 89:2; CA 25-28R; CANR 26, 70, 152; CPW; DLB 185; INT CANR-26

McGivern, Maureen Daly
See Daly, Maureen

McGivern, Maureen Patricia Daly
See Daly, Maureen

McGrath, Patrick 1950- .... **CLC 55**
See also CA 136; CANR 65, 148; CN 5, 6, 7; DLB 231; HGG; SUFW 2

McGrath, Thomas (Matthew)
1916-1990 .... **CLC 28, 59**
See also AMWS 10; CA 9-12R; 132; CANR 6, 33, 95; CP 1, 2, 3, 4, 5; DAM POET; MAL 5; MTCW 1; SATA 41; SATA-Obit 66

McGuane, Thomas 1939- .. **CLC 3, 7, 18, 45, 127**
See also AITN 2; BPFB 2; CA 49-52; CANR 5, 24, 49, 94, 164; CN 2, 3, 4, 5, 6, 7; DLB 2, 212; DLBY 1980; EWL 3; INT CANR-24; MAL 5; MTCW 1; MTFW 2005; TCWW 1, 2

McGuane, Thomas Francis III
See McGuane, Thomas

McGuckian, Medbh 1950- .... **CLC 48, 174; PC 27**
See also BRWS 5; CA 143; CP 4, 5, 6, 7; CWP; DAM POET; DLB 40

McHale, Tom 1942(?)-1982 .... **CLC 3, 5**
See also AITN 1; CA 77-80; 106; CN 1, 2, 3

McHugh, Heather 1948- .... **PC 61**
See also CA 69-72; CANR 11, 28, 55, 92; CP 4, 5, 6, 7; CWP; PFS 24

McIlvanney, William 1936- .... **CLC 42**
See also CA 25-28R; CANR 61; CMW 4; DLB 14, 207

McIlwraith, Maureen Mollie Hunter
See Hunter, Mollie
See also SATA 2

McInerney, Jay 1955- .... **CLC 34, 112**
See also AAYA 18; BPFB 2; CA 116; 123; CANR 45, 68, 116, 176; CN 5, 6, 7; CPW; DA3; DAM POP; DLB 292; INT CA-123; MAL 5; MTCW 2; MTFW 2005

McIntyre, Vonda N. 1948- .... **CLC 18**
See also CA 81-84; CANR 17, 34, 69; MTCW 1; SFW 4; YAW

McIntyre, Vonda Neel
See McIntyre, Vonda N.

McKay, Claude .... **BLC 1:3; HR 1:3; PC 2; TCLC 7, 41; WLC 4**
See McKay, Festus Claudius
See also AFAW 1, 2; AMWS 10; DAB; DLB 4, 45, 51, 117; EWL 3; EXPP; GLL 2; LAIT 3; LMFS 2; MAL 5; PAB; PFS 4; RGAL 4; WP

McKay, Festus Claudius 1889-1948
See McKay, Claude
See also BW 1, 3; CA 104; 124; CANR 73; DA; DAC; DAM MST, MULT, NOV, POET; MTCW 1, 2; MTFW 2005; TUS

McKuen, Rod 1933- .... **CLC 1, 3**
See also AITN 1; CA 41-44R; CANR 40; CP 1

McLoughlin, R. B.
See Mencken, H(enry) L(ouis)

McLuhan, (Herbert) Marshall
1911-1980 .... **CLC 37, 83**
See also CA 9-12R; 102; CANR 12, 34, 61; DLB 88; INT CANR-12; MTCW 1, 2; MTFW 2005

McMahon, Pat
See Hoch, Edward D.

McManus, Declan Patrick Aloysius
See Costello, Elvis

McMillan, Terry 1951- .. **BLCS; CLC 50, 61, 112**
See also AAYA 21; AMWS 13; BPFB 2; BW 2, 3; CA 140; CANR 60, 104, 131; CN 7; CPW; DA3; DAM MULT, NOV, POP; MAL 5; MTCW 2; MTFW 2005; RGAL 4; YAW

McMurtry, Larry 1936- .... **CLC 2, 3, 7, 11, 27, 44, 127, 250**
See also AAYA 15; AITN 2; AMWS 5; BEST 89:2; BPFB 2; CA 5-8R; CANR 19, 43, 64, 103, 170; CDALB 1968-1988; CN 2, 3, 4, 5, 6, 7; CPW; CSW; DA3; DAM NOV, POP; DLB 2, 143, 256; DLBY 1980, 1987; EWL 3; MAL 5; MTCW 1, 2; MTFW 2005; RGAL 4; TCWW 1, 2

McMurtry, Larry Jeff
See McMurtry, Larry

McNally, Terrence 1939- ... **CLC 4, 7, 41, 91, 252; DC 27**
See also AAYA 62; AMWS 13; CA 45-48; CAD; CANR 2, 56, 116; CD 5, 6; DA3; DAM DRAM; DFS 16, 19; DLB 7, 249; EWL 3; GLL 1; MTCW 2; MTFW 2005

McNally, Thomas Michael
See McNally, T.M.

McNally, T.M. 1961- .... **CLC 82**
See also CA 246

McNamer, Deirdre 1950- .... **CLC 70**
See also CA 188; CANR 163

McNeal, Tom .... **CLC 119**
See also CA 252; CANR 185; SATA 194

McNeile, Herman Cyril 1888-1937
See Sapper
See also CA 184; CMW 4; DLB 77

McNickle, (William) D'Arcy
1904-1977 .... **CLC 89; NNAL**
See also CA 9-12R; 85-88; CANR 5, 45; DAM MULT; DLB 175, 212; RGAL 4; SATA-Obit 22; TCWW 1, 2

McPhee, John 1931- .... **CLC 36**
See also AAYA 61; AMWS 3; ANW; BEST 90:1; CA 65-68; CANR 20, 46, 64, 69, 121, 165; CPW; DLB 185, 275; MTCW 1, 2; MTFW 2005; TUS

McPhee, John Angus
See McPhee, John

McPherson, James Alan, Jr.
See McPherson, James Alan

McPherson, James Alan 1943- . **BLCS; CLC 19, 77; SSC 95**
See also BW 1, 3; CA 25-28R, 273; CAAE 273; CAAS 17; CANR 24, 74, 140; CN 3, 4, 5, 6; CSW; DLB 38, 244; EWL 3; MTCW 1, 2; MTFW 2005; RGAL 4; RGSF 2; SSFS 23

McPherson, William (Alexander)
1933- .... **CLC 34**
See also CA 69-72; CANR 28; INT CANR-28

McTaggart, J. McT. Ellis
See McTaggart, John McTaggart Ellis

McTaggart, John McTaggart Ellis
1866-1925 .... **TCLC 105**
See also CA 120; DLB 262

Mda, Zakes 1948- .... **BLC 2:3; CLC 262**
See also CA 205; CANR 151, 185; CD 5, 6; DLB 225

Mda, Zanemvula
See Mda, Zakes

Mda, Zanemvula Kizito Gatyeni
See Mda, Zakes

Mead, George Herbert 1863-1931 . **TCLC 89**
See also CA 212; DLB 270

Mead, Margaret 1901-1978 .... **CLC 37**
See also AITN 1; CA 1-4R; 81-84; CANR 4; DA3; FW; MTCW 1, 2; SATA-Obit 20

Meaker, M. J.
See Meaker, Marijane

Meaker, Marijane 1927- .... **CLC 12, 35**
See also AAYA 2, 23; BYA 1, 7, 8; CA 107; CANR 37, 63, 145, 180; CLR 29; GLL 2; INT CA-107; JRDA; MAICYA 1, 2; MAI-CYAS 1; MTCW 1; SAAS 1; SATA 20, 61, 99, 160; SATA-Essay 111; WYA; YAW

Meaker, Marijane Agnes
See Meaker, Marijane

Mechthild von Magdeburg c. 1207-c. 1282 .... **CMLC 91**
See also DLB 138

Medoff, Mark (Howard) 1940- .... **CLC 6, 23**
See also AITN 1; CA 53-56; CAD; CANR 5; CD 5, 6; DAM DRAM; DFS 4; DLB 7; INT CANR-5

Medvedev, P. N.
See Bakhtin, Mikhail Mikhailovich

Meged, Aharon
See Megged, Aharon

Meged, Aron
See Megged, Aharon

Megged, Aharon 1920- .... **CLC 9**
See also CA 49-52; CAAS 13; CANR 1, 140; EWL 3; RGHL

Mehta, Deepa 1950- .... **CLC 208**

Mehta, Gita 1943- .... **CLC 179**
See also CA 225; CN 7; DNFS 2

Mehta, Ved 1934- .... **CLC 37**
See also CA 1-4R, 212; CAAE 212; CANR 2, 23, 69; DLB 323; MTCW 1; MTFW 2005

Melanchthon, Philipp 1497-1560 .... **LC 90**
See also DLB 179

Melanter
See Blackmore, R(ichard) D(oddridge)

Meleager c. 140B.C.-c. 70B.C. ...... **CMLC 53**

Melies, Georges 1861-1938 .... **TCLC 81**

Melikow, Loris
See Hofmannsthal, Hugo von

Melmoth, Sebastian
See Wilde, Oscar

Melo Neto, Joao Cabral de
See Cabral de Melo Neto, Joao
See also CWW 2; EWL 3

Meltzer, Milton 1915- .... **CLC 26**
See also AAYA 8, 45; BYA 2, 6; CA 13-16R; CANR 38, 92, 107; CLR 13; DLB 61; JRDA; MAICYA 1, 2; SAAS 1; SATA 1, 50, 80, 128; SATA-Essay 124; WYA; YAW

Melville, Herman 1819-1891 ..... **NCLC 3, 12, 29, 45, 49, 91, 93, 123, 157, 181, 193; PC 82; SSC 1, 17, 46, 95; WLC 4**
See also AAYA 25; AMW; AMWR 1; CDALB 1640-1865; DA; DA3; DAB; DAC; DAM MST, NOV; DLB 3, 74, 250, 254; EXPN; EXPS; GL 3; LAIT 1, 2; NFS 7, 9; RGAL 4; RGSF 2; SATA 59; SSFS 3; TUS

Members, Mark
See Powell, Anthony

Membreno, Alejandro .... **CLC 59**

Menand, Louis 1952- .... **CLC 208**
See also CA 200

Menander c. 342B.C.-c. 293B.C. .... **CMLC 9, 51, 101; DC 3**
See also AW 1; CDWLB 1; DAM DRAM; DLB 176; LMFS 1; RGWL 2, 3

Menchu, Rigoberta 1959- .. **CLC 160; HLCS 2**
See also CA 175; CANR 135; DNFS 1; WLIT 1

Mencken, H(enry) L(ouis)
1880-1956 .... **TCLC 13**
See also AMW; CA 105; 125; CDALB 1917-1929; DLB 11, 29, 63, 137, 222; EWL 3; MAL 5; MTCW 1, 2; MTFW 2005; NCFS 4; RGAL 4; TUS

Mendelsohn, Jane 1965- .... **CLC 99**
See also CA 154; CANR 94

Mendelssohn, Moses 1729-1786 .... **LC 142**
See also DLB 97

Mendoza, Inigo Lopez de
See Santillana, Inigo Lopez de Mendoza, Marques de

Menton, Francisco de
See Chin, Frank (Chew, Jr.)

Mercer, David 1928-1980 .... **CLC 5**
See also CA 9-12R; 102; CANR 23; CBD; DAM DRAM; DLB 13, 310; MTCW 1; RGEL 2

Merchant, Paul
See Ellison, Harlan

Meredith, George 1828-1909 .. **PC 60; TCLC 17, 43**
See also CA 117; 153; CANR 80; CDBLB 1832-1890; DAM POET; DLB 18, 35, 57, 159; RGEL 2; TEA

Meredith, William 1919-2007 ...... **CLC 4, 13, 22, 55; PC 28**
See also CA 9-12R; 260; CAAS 14; CANR 6, 40, 129; CP 1, 2, 3, 4, 5, 6, 7; DAM POET; DLB 5; MAL 5

Meredith, William Morris
See Meredith, William

Merezhkovsky, Dmitrii Sergeevich
See Merezhkovsky, Dmitry Sergeyevich
See also DLB 295

Merezhkovsky, Dmitry Sergeevich
See Merezhkovsky, Dmitry Sergeyevich
See also EWL 3

Merezhkovsky, Dmitry Sergeyevich
1865-1941 .... **TCLC 29**
See Merezhkovsky, Dmitrii Sergeevich; Merezhkovsky, Dmitry Sergeevich
See also CA 169

Merimee, Prosper 1803-1870 ... **NCLC 6, 65; SSC 7, 77**
See also DLB 119, 192; EW 6; EXPS; GFL 1789 to the Present; RGSF 2; RGWL 2, 3; SSFS 8; SUFW

Merkin, Daphne 1954- .... **CLC 44**
See also CA 123

Merleau-Ponty, Maurice
1908-1961 .... **TCLC 156**
See also CA 114; 89-92; DLB 296; GFL 1789 to the Present

Merlin, Arthur
See Blish, James (Benjamin)

Mernissi, Fatima 1940- .... **CLC 171**
See also CA 152; DLB 346; FW

Merrill, James 1926-1995 ...... **CLC 2, 3, 6, 8, 13, 18, 34, 91; PC 28; TCLC 173**
See also AMWS 3; CA 13-16R; 147; CANR 10, 49, 63, 108; CP 1, 2, 3, 4; DA3; DAM POET; DLB 5, 165; DLBY 1985; EWL 3; INT CANR-10; MAL 5; MTCW 1, 2; MTFW 2005; PAB; PFS 23; RGAL 4

Merrill, James Ingram
See Merrill, James

Merriman, Alex
See Silverberg, Robert

Merriman, Brian 1747-1805 .... **NCLC 70**

Merritt, E. B.
See Waddington, Miriam

Merton, Thomas (James)
1915-1968 . **CLC 1, 3, 11, 34, 83; PC 10**
See also AAYA 61; AMWS 8; CA 5-8R; 25-28R; CANR 22, 53, 111, 131; DA3; DLB 48; DLBY 1981; MAL 5; MTCW 1, 2; MTFW 2005

Merwin, W.S. 1927- .... **CLC 1, 2, 3, 5, 8, 13, 18, 45, 88; PC 45**
See also AMWS 3; CA 13-16R; CANR 15, 51, 112, 140; CP 1, 2, 3, 4, 5, 6, 7; DA3; DAM POET; DLB 5, 169, 342; EWL 3; INT CANR-15; MAL 5; MTCW 1, 2; MTFW 2005; PAB; PFS 5, 15; RGAL 4

Metastasio, Pietro 1698-1782 .... **LC 115**
See also RGWL 2, 3

Metcalf, John 1938- .... **CLC 37; SSC 43**
See also CA 113; CN 4, 5, 6, 7; DLB 60; RGSF 2; TWA

Metcalf, Suzanne
See Baum, L(yman) Frank

Mew, Charlotte (Mary) 1870-1928 .. **TCLC 8**
See also CA 105; 189; DLB 19, 135; RGEL 2

Mewshaw, Michael 1943- .... **CLC 9**
See also CA 53-56; CANR 7, 47, 147; DLBY 1980

Meyer, Conrad Ferdinand
1825-1898 .... **NCLC 81; SSC 30**
See also DLB 129; EW; RGWL 2, 3

Meyer, Gustav 1868-1932
See Meyrink, Gustav
See also CA 117; 190

Meyer, June
See Jordan, June

Meyer, Lynn
See Slavitt, David R.

Meyers, Jeffrey 1939- .... **CLC 39**
See also CA 73-76, 186; CAAE 186; CANR 54, 102, 159; DLB 111

Meynell, Alice (Christina Gertrude Thompson) 1847-1922 .... **TCLC 6**
See also CA 104; 177; DLB 19, 98; RGEL 2

Meyrink, Gustav .... **TCLC 21**
See Meyer, Gustav
See also DLB 81; EWL 3

Mhlophe, Gcina 1960- .... **BLC 2:3**

Michaels, Leonard 1933-2003 ..... **CLC 6, 25; SSC 16**
See also AMWS 16; CA 61-64; 216; CANR 21, 62, 119, 179; CN 3, 45, 6, 7; DLB 130; MTCW 1; TCLE 1:2

Michaux, Henri 1899-1984 .... **CLC 8, 19**
See also CA 85-88; 114; DLB 258; EWL 3; GFL 1789 to the Present; RGWL 2, 3

Micheaux, Oscar (Devereaux)
1884-1951 .... **TCLC 76**
See also BW 3; CA 174; DLB 50; TCWW 2

Michelangelo 1475-1564 .... **LC 12**
See also AAYA 43

Michelet, Jules 1798-1874 .... **NCLC 31**
See also EW 5; GFL 1789 to the Present

Michels, Robert 1876-1936 .... **TCLC 88**
See also CA 212

Michener, James A. 1907(?)-1997 . **CLC 1, 5, 11, 29, 60, 109**
See also AAYA 27; AITN 1; BEST 90:1; BPFB 2; CA 5-8R; 161; CANR 21, 45, 68; CN 1, 2, 3, 4, 5, 6; CPW; DA3; DAM NOV, POP; DLB 6; MAL 5; MTCW 1, 2; MTFW 2005; RHW; TCWW 1, 2

Mickiewicz, Adam 1798-1855 . **NCLC 3, 101; PC 38**
See also EW 5; RGWL 2, 3

Middleton, (John) Christopher
1926- .... **CLC 13**
See also CA 13-16R; CANR 29, 54, 117; CP 1, 2, 3, 4, 5, 6, 7; DLB 40

Middleton, Richard (Barham)
1882-1911 .... **TCLC 56**
See also CA 187; DLB 156; HGG

Middleton, Stanley 1919- .... **CLC 7, 38**
See also CA 25-28R; CAAS 23; CANR 21, 46, 81, 157; CN 1, 2, 3, 4, 5, 6, 7; DLB 14, 326

Middleton, Thomas 1580-1627 ...... **DC 5; LC 33, 123**
See also BRW 2; DAM DRAM, MST; DFS 18, 22; DLB 58; RGEL 2

Mieville, China 1972(?)- .... **CLC 235**
See also AAYA 52; CA 196; CANR 138; MTFW 2005

Migueis, Jose Rodrigues 1901-1980 . **CLC 10**
See also DLB 287

Mikszath, Kalman 1847-1910 .... **TCLC 31**
See also CA 170

Miles, Jack .... **CLC 100**
See also CA 200

Miles, John Russiano
See Miles, Jack

Miles, Josephine (Louise)
1911-1985 .... **CLC 1, 2, 14, 34, 39**
See also CA 1-4R; 116; CANR 2, 55; CP 1, 2, 3, 4; DAM POET; DLB 48; MAL 5; TCLE 1:2

Militant
See Sandburg, Carl (August)

Mill, Harriet (Hardy) Taylor
1807-1858 .... **NCLC 102**
See also FW

Mill, John Stuart 1806-1873 ... **NCLC 11, 58, 179**
See also CDBLB 1832-1890; DLB 55, 190, 262; FW 1; RGEL 2; TEA

Millar, Kenneth 1915-1983 .... **CLC 14**
See Macdonald, Ross
See also CA 9-12R; 110; CANR 16, 63, 107; CMW 4; CPW; DA3; DAM POP; DLB 2, 226; DLBD 6; DLBY 1983; MTCW 1, 2; MTFW 2005

Millay, E. Vincent
See Millay, Edna St. Vincent

Millay, Edna St. Vincent 1892-1950 ..... **PC 6, 61; TCLC 4, 49, 169; WLCS**
See Boyd, Nancy
See also AMW; CA 104; 130; CDALB 1917-1929; DA; DA3; DAB; DAC; DAM MST, POET; DLB 45, 249; EWL 3; EXPP; FL 1:6; MAL 5; MBL; MTCW 1, 2; MTFW 2005; PAB; PFS 3, 17; RGAL 4; TUS; WP

Miller, Arthur 1915-2005 ..... **CLC 1, 2, 6, 10, 15, 26, 47, 78, 179; DC 1, 31; WLC 4**
See also AAYA 15; AITN 1; AMW; AMWC 1; CA 1-4R; 236; CABS 3; CAD; CANR 2, 30, 54, 76, 132; CD 5, 6; CDALB 1941-1968; DA; DA3; DAB; DAC; DAM DRAM, MST; DFS 1, 3, 8; DLB 7, 266; EWL 3; LAIT 1, 4; LATS 1:2; MAL 5; MTCW 1, 2; MTFW 2005; RGAL 4; RGHL; TUS; WYAS 1

Miller, Henry (Valentine)
1891-1980 .... **CLC 1, 2, 4, 9, 14, 43, 84; TCLC 213; WLC 4**
See also AMW; BPFB 2; CA 9-12R; 97-100; CANR 33, 64; CDALB 1929-1941; CN 1, 2; DA; DA3; DAB; DAC; DAM MST, NOV; DLB 4, 9; DLBY 1980; EWL 3; MAL 5; MTCW 1, 2; MTFW 2005; RGAL 4; TUS

Miller, Hugh 1802-1856 .... **NCLC 143**
See also DLB 190

Oliphant, Laurence 1829(?)-1888 .. **NCLC 47**
See also DLB 18, 166
Oliphant, Margaret (Oliphant Wilson)
1828-1897 .... **NCLC 11, 61; SSC 25**
See Oliphant, Mrs.
See also BRWS 10; DLB 18, 159, 190;
HGG; RGEL 2; RGSF 2
Oliver, Mary 1935- ... **CLC 19, 34, 98; PC 75**
See also AMWS 7; CA 21-24R; CANR 9,
43, 84, 92, 138; CP 4, 5, 6, 7; CWP; DLB
5, 193, 342; EWL 3; MTFW 2005; PFS
15
Olivier, Laurence (Kerr) 1907-1989 . **CLC 20**
See also CA 111; 150; 129
Olsen, Tillie 1912-2007 .... **CLC 4, 13, 114;
SSC 11, 103**
See also AAYA 51; AMWS 13; BYA 11;
CA 1-4R; 256; CANR 1, 43, 74, 132;
CDALBS; CN 2, 3, 4, 5, 6, 7; DA; DA3;
DAB; DAC; DAM MST; DLB 28, 206;
DLBY 1980; EWL 3; EXPS; FW; MAL
5; MTCW 1, 2; MTFW 2005; RGAL 4;
RGSF 2; SSFS 1; TCLE 1:2; TCWW 2;
TUS
Olson, Charles (John) 1910-1970 .. **CLC 1, 2,
5, 6, 9, 11, 29; PC 19**
See also AMWS 2; CA 13-16; 25-28R;
CABS 2; CANR 35, 61; CAP 1; CP 1;
DAM POET; DLB 5, 16, 193; EWL 3;
MAL 5; MTCW 1, 2; RGAL 4; WP
Olson, Merle Theodore
See Olson, Toby
Olson, Toby 1937- .... **CLC 28**
See also CA 65-68; CAAS 11; CANR 9,
31, 84, 175; CP 3, 4, 5, 6, 7
Olyesha, Yuri
See Olesha, Yuri (Karlovich)
Olympiodorus of Thebes c. 375-c.
430 .... **CMLC 59**
Omar Khayyam
See Khayyam, Omar
See also RGWL 2, 3
Ondaatje, Michael 1943- ..... **CLC 14, 29, 51,
76, 180, 258; PC 28**
See also AAYA 66; CA 77-80; CANR 42,
74, 109, 133, 172; CN 5, 6, 7; CP 1, 2, 3,
4, 5, 6, 7; DA3; DAB; DAC; DAM MST;
DLB 60, 323, 326; EWL 3; LATS 1:2;
LMFS 2; MTCW 2; MTFW 2005; NFS
23; PFS 8, 19; TCLE 1:2; TWA; WWE 1
Ondaatje, Philip Michael
See Ondaatje, Michael
Oneal, Elizabeth 1934-
See Oneal, Zibby
See also CA 106; CANR 28, 84; MAICYA
1, 2; SATA 30, 82; YAW
Oneal, Zibby .... **CLC 30**
See Oneal, Elizabeth
See also AAYA 5, 41; BYA 13; CLR 13;
JRDA; WYA
O'Neill, Eugene (Gladstone)
1888-1953 ... **DC 20; TCLC 1, 6, 27, 49;
WLC 4**
See also AAYA 54; AITN 1; AMW; AMWC
1; CA 110; 132; CAD; CANR 131;
CDALB 1929-1941; DA; DA3; DAB;
DAC; DAM DRAM, MST; DFS 2, 4, 5,
6, 9, 11, 12, 16, 20; DLB 7, 331; EWL 3;
LAIT 3; LMFS 2; MAL 5; MTCW 1, 2;
MTFW 2005; RGAL 4; TUS
Onetti, Juan Carlos 1909-1994 ... **CLC 7, 10;
HLCS 2; SSC 23; TCLC 131**
See also CA 85-88; 145; CANR 32, 63; CD-
WLB 3; CWW 2; DAM MULT, NOV;
DLB 113; EWL 3; HW 1, 2; LAW;
MTCW 1, 2; MTFW 2005; RGSF 2
O Nuallain, Brian 1911-1966
See O'Brien, Flann
See also CA 21-22; 25-28R; CAP 2; DLB
231; FANT; TEA

Ophuls, Max
See Ophuls, Max
Ophuls, Max 1902-1957 .... **TCLC 79**
See also CA 113
Opie, Amelia 1769-1853 .... **NCLC 65**
See also DLB 116, 159; RGEL 2
Oppen, George 1908-1984 ..... **CLC 7, 13, 34;
PC 35; TCLC 107**
See also CA 13-16R; 113; CANR 8, 82; CP
1, 2, 3; DLB 5, 165
Oppenheim, E(dward) Phillips
1866-1946 .... **TCLC 45**
See also CA 111; 202; CMW 4; DLB 70
Oppenheimer, Max
See Ophuls, Max
Opuls, Max
See Ophuls, Max
Orage, A(lfred) R(ichard)
1873-1934 .... **TCLC 157**
See also CA 122
Origen c. 185-c. 254 .... **CMLC 19**
Orlovitz, Gil 1918-1973 .... **CLC 22**
See also CA 77-80; 45-48; CN 1; CP 1, 2;
DLB 2, 5
Orosius c. 385-c. 420 .... **CMLC 100**
O'Rourke, Patrick Jake
See O'Rourke, P.J.
O'Rourke, P.J. 1947- .... **CLC 209**
See also CA 77-80; CANR 13, 41, 67, 111,
155; CPW; DAM POP; DLB 185
Orris
See Ingelow, Jean
Ortega y Gasset, Jose 1883-1955 ...... **HLC 2;
TCLC 9**
See also CA 106; 130; DAM MULT; EW 9;
EWL 3; HW 1, 2; MTCW 1, 2; MTFW
2005
Ortese, Anna Maria 1914-1998 .... **CLC 89**
See also DLB 177; EWL 3
Ortiz, Simon
See Ortiz, Simon J.
Ortiz, Simon J. 1941- . **CLC 45, 208; NNAL;
PC 17**
See also AMWS 4; CA 134; CANR 69, 118,
164; CP 3, 4, 5, 6, 7; DAM MULT, POET;
DLB 120, 175, 256, 342; EXPP; MAL 5;
PFS 4, 16; RGAL 4; SSFS 22; TCWW 2
Ortiz, Simon Joseph
See Ortiz, Simon J.
Orton, Joe ...... **CLC 4, 13, 43; DC 3; TCLC
157**
See Orton, John Kingsley
See also BRWS 5; CBD; CDBLB 1960 to
Present; DFS 3, 6; DLB 13, 310; GLL 1;
RGEL 2; TEA; WLIT 4
Orton, John Kingsley 1933-1967
See Orton, Joe
See also CA 85-88; CANR 35, 66; DAM
DRAM; MTCW 1, 2; MTFW 2005
Orwell, George ...... **SSC 68; TCLC 2, 6, 15,
31, 51, 128, 129; WLC 4**
See Blair, Eric (Arthur)
See also BPFB 3; BRW 7; BYA 5; CDBLB
1945-1960; CLR 68; DAB; DLB 15, 98,
195, 255; EWL 3; EXPN; LAIT 4, 5;
LATS 1:1; NFS 3, 7; RGEL 2; SCFW 1,
2; SFW 4; SSFS 4; TEA; WLIT 4; YAW
Osborne, David
See Silverberg, Robert
Osborne, Dorothy 1627-1695 .... **LC 141**
Osborne, George
See Silverberg, Robert
Osborne, John 1929-1994 .... **CLC 1, 2, 5, 11,
45; TCLC 153; WLC 4**
See also BRWS 1; CA 13-16R; 147; CANR
21, 56; CBD; CDBLB 1945-1960; DA;
DAB; DAC; DAM DRAM, MST; DFS 4,
19, 24; DLB 13; EWL 3; MTCW 1, 2;
MTFW 2005; RGEL 2

Osborne, Lawrence 1958- .... **CLC 50**
See also CA 189; CANR 152
Osbourne, Lloyd 1868-1947 .... **TCLC 93**
Osgood, Frances Sargent
1811-1850 .... **NCLC 141**
See also DLB 250
Oshima, Nagisa 1932- .... **CLC 20**
See also CA 116; 121; CANR 78
Oskison, John Milton
1874-1947 .... **NNAL; TCLC 35**
See also CA 144; CANR 84; DAM MULT;
DLB 175
Ossian c. 3rd cent. - .... **CMLC 28**
See Macpherson, James
Ossoli, Sarah Margaret (Fuller)
1810-1850 .... **NCLC 5, 50**
See Fuller, Margaret
See also CDALB 1640-1865; DLB 1, 59,
73; FW; LMFS 1; SATA 25
Ostriker, Alicia 1937- .... **CLC 132**
See also CA 25-28R; CAAS 24; CANR 10,
30, 62, 99, 167; CWP; DLB 120; EXPP;
PFS 19, 26
Ostriker, Alicia Suskin
See Ostriker, Alicia
Ostrovsky, Aleksandr Nikolaevich
See Ostrovsky, Alexander
See also DLB 277
Ostrovsky, Alexander 1823-1886 .. **NCLC 30,
57**
See Ostrovsky, Aleksandr Nikolaevich
Osundare, Niyi 1947- .... **BLC 2:3**
See also AFW; BW 3; CA 176; CDWLB 3;
CP 7; DLB 157
Otero, Blas de 1916-1979 .... **CLC 11**
See also CA 89-92; DLB 134; EWL 3
O'Trigger, Sir Lucius
See Horne, Richard Henry Hengist
Otto, Rudolf 1869-1937 .... **TCLC 85**
Otto, Whitney 1955- .... **CLC 70**
See also CA 140; CANR 120
Otway, Thomas 1652-1685 ... **DC 24; LC 106**
See also DAM DRAM; DLB 80; RGEL 2
Ouida .... **TCLC 43**
See De La Ramee, Marie Louise
See also DLB 18, 156; RGEL 2
Ouologuem, Yambo 1940- .... **CLC 146**
See also CA 111; 176
Ousmane, Sembene 1923-2007 .... **BLC 1:3,
2:3; CLC 66**
See also AFW; BW 1, 3; CA 117; 125; 261;
CANR 81; CWW 2; EWL 3; MTCW 1;
WLIT 2
Ovid 43B.C.-17 .... **CMLC 7, 108; PC 2**
See also AW 2; CDWLB 1; DA3; DAM
POET; DLB 211; PFS 22; RGWL 2, 3;
WLIT 8; WP
Owen, Hugh
See Faust, Frederick (Schiller)
Owen, Wilfred (Edward Salter)
1893-1918 ... **PC 19; TCLC 5, 27; WLC
4**
See also BRW 6; CA 104; 141; CDBLB
1914-1945; DA; DAB; DAC; DAM MST,
POET; DLB 20; EWL 3; EXPP; MTCW
2; MTFW 2005; PFS 10; RGEL 2; WLIT
4
Owens, Louis (Dean) 1948-2002 .... **NNAL**
See also CA 137, 179; 207; CAAE 179;
CAAS 24; CANR 71
Owens, Rochelle 1936- .... **CLC 8**
See also CA 17-20R; CAAS 2; CAD;
CANR 39; CD 5, 6; CP 1, 2, 3, 4, 5, 6, 7;
CWD; CWP

Oz, Amos 1939- ...... **CLC 5, 8, 11, 27, 33, 54; SSC 66**
See also CA 53-56; CANR 27, 47, 65, 113, 138, 175; CWW 2; DAM NOV; EWL 3; MTCW 1, 2; MTFW 2005; RGHL; RGSF 2; RGWL 3; WLIT 6

Ozick, Cynthia 1928- . **CLC 3, 7, 28, 62, 155, 262; SSC 15, 60**
See also AMWS 5; BEST 90:1; CA 17-20R; CANR 23, 58, 116, 160; CN 3, 4, 5, 6, 7; CPW; DA3; DAM NOV, POP; DLB 28, 152, 299; DLBY 1982; EWL 3; EXPS; INT CANR-23; MAL 5; MTCW 1, 2; MTFW 2005; RGAL 4; RGHL; RGSF 2; SSFS 3, 12, 22

Ozu, Yasujiro 1903-1963 .... **CLC 16**
See also CA 112

Pabst, G. W. 1885-1967 .... **TCLC 127**

Pacheco, C.
See Pessoa, Fernando

Pacheco, Jose Emilio 1939- .... **HLC 2**
See also CA 111; 131; CANR 65; CWW 2; DAM MULT; DLB 290; EWL 3; HW 1, 2; RGSF 2

Pa Chin .... **CLC 18**
See Jin, Ba
See also EWL 3

Pack, Robert 1929- .... **CLC 13**
See also CA 1-4R; CANR 3, 44, 82; CP 1, 2, 3, 4, 5, 6, 7; DLB 5; SATA 118

Packer, Vin
See Meaker, Marijane

Padgett, Lewis
See Kuttner, Henry

Padilla (Lorenzo), Heberto
1932-2000 .... **CLC 38**
See also AITN 1; CA 123; 131; 189; CWW 2; EWL 3; HW 1

Page, James Patrick 1944-
See Page, Jimmy
See also CA 204

Page, Jimmy 1944- .... **CLC 12**
See Page, James Patrick

Page, Louise 1955- .... **CLC 40**
See also CA 140; CANR 76; CBD; CD 5, 6; CWD; DLB 233

Page, P(atricia) K(athleen) 1916- ...... **CLC 7, 18; PC 12**
See Cape, Judith
See also CA 53-56; CANR 4, 22, 65; CP 1, 2, 3, 4, 5, 6, 7; DAC; DAM MST; DLB 68; MTCW 1; RGEL 2

Page, Stanton
See Fuller, Henry Blake

Page, Thomas Nelson 1853-1922 .... **SSC 23**
See also CA 118; 177; DLB 12, 78; DLBD 13; RGAL 4

Pagels, Elaine
See Pagels, Elaine Hiesey

Pagels, Elaine Hiesey 1943- .... **CLC 104**
See also CA 45-48; CANR 2, 24, 51, 151; FW; NCFS 4

Paget, Violet 1856-1935
See Lee, Vernon
See also CA 104; 166; GLL 1; HGG

Paget-Lowe, Henry
See Lovecraft, H. P.

Paglia, Camille 1947- .... **CLC 68**
See also CA 140; CANR 72, 139; CPW; FW; GLL 2; MTCW 2; MTFW 2005

Pagnol, Marcel (Paul)
1895-1974 .... **TCLC 208**
See also CA 128; 49-52; DLB 321; EWL 3; GFL 1789 to the Present; MTCW 1; RGWL 2, 3

Paige, Richard
See Koontz, Dean R.

Paine, Thomas 1737-1809 .... **NCLC 62**
See also AMWS 1; CDALB 1640-1865; DLB 31, 43, 73, 158; LAIT 1; RGAL 4; RGEL 2; TUS

Pakenham, Antonia
See Fraser, Antonia

Palamas, Costis
See Palamas, Kostes

Palamas, Kostes 1859-1943 .... **TCLC 5**
See Palamas, Kostis
See also CA 105; 190; RGWL 2, 3

Palamas, Kostis
See Palamas, Kostes
See also EWL 3

Palazzeschi, Aldo 1885-1974 .... **CLC 11**
See also CA 89-92; 53-56; DLB 114, 264; EWL 3

Pales Matos, Luis 1898-1959 .... **HLCS 2**
See Pales Matos, Luis
See also DLB 290; HW 1; LAW

Paley, Grace 1922-2007 ... **CLC 4, 6, 37, 140; SSC 8**
See also AMWS 6; CA 25-28R; 263; CANR 13, 46, 74, 118; CN 2, 3, 4, 5, 6, 7; CPW; DA3; DAM POP; DLB 28, 218; EWL 3; EXPS; FW; INT CANR-13; MAL 5; MBL; MTCW 1, 2; MTFW 2005; RGAL 4; RGSF 2; SSFS 3, 20

Paley, Grace Goodside
See Paley, Grace

Palin, Michael 1943- .... **CLC 21**
See Monty Python
See also CA 107; CANR 35, 109, 179; SATA 67

Palin, Michael Edward
See Palin, Michael

Palliser, Charles 1947- .... **CLC 65**
See also CA 136; CANR 76; CN 5, 6, 7

Palma, Ricardo 1833-1919 .... **TCLC 29**
See also CA 168; LAW

Pamuk, Orhan 1952- .... **CLC 185**
See also CA 142; CANR 75, 127, 172; CWW 2; NFS 27; WLIT 6

Pancake, Breece Dexter 1952-1979
See Pancake, Breece D'J
See also CA 123; 109

Pancake, Breece D'J .... **CLC 29; SSC 61**
See Pancake, Breece Dexter
See also DLB 130

Panchenko, Nikolai .... **CLC 59**

Pankhurst, Emmeline (Goulden)
1858-1928 .... **TCLC 100**
See also CA 116; FW

Panko, Rudy
See Gogol, Nikolai (Vasilyevich)

Papadiamantis, Alexandros
1851-1911 .... **TCLC 29**
See also CA 168; EWL 3

Papadiamantopoulos, Johannes 1856-1910
See Moreas, Jean
See also CA 117; 242

Papini, Giovanni 1881-1956 .... **TCLC 22**
See also CA 121; 180; DLB 264

Paracelsus 1493-1541 .... **LC 14**
See also DLB 179

Parasol, Peter
See Stevens, Wallace

Pardo Bazan, Emilia 1851-1921 .... **SSC 30; TCLC 189**
See also EWL 3; FW; RGSF 2; RGWL 2, 3

Paredes, Americo 1915-1999 .... **PC 83**
See also CA 37-40R; 179; DLB 209; EXPP; HW 1

Pareto, Vilfredo 1848-1923 .... **TCLC 69**
See also CA 175

Paretsky, Sara 1947- .... **CLC 135**
See also AAYA 30; BEST 90:3; CA 125; 129; CANR 59, 95, 184; CMW 4; CPW; DA3; DAM POP; DLB 306; INT CA-129; MSW; RGAL 4

Paretsky, Sara N.
See Paretsky, Sara

Parfenie, Maria
See Codrescu, Andrei

Parini, Jay (Lee) 1948- .... **CLC 54, 133**
See also CA 97-100; 229; CAAE 229; CAAS 16; CANR 32, 87

Park, Jordan
See Kornbluth, C(yril) M.; Pohl, Frederik

Park, Robert E(zra) 1864-1944 ..... **TCLC 73**
See also CA 122; 165

Parker, Bert
See Ellison, Harlan

Parker, Dorothy (Rothschild)
1893-1967 . **CLC 15, 68; PC 28; SSC 2, 101; TCLC 143**
See also AMWS 9; CA 19-20; 25-28R; CAP 2; DA3; DAM POET; DLB 11, 45, 86; EXPP; FW; MAL 5; MBL; MTCW 1, 2; MTFW 2005; PFS 18; RGAL 4; RGSF 2; TUS

Parker, Robert B. 1932- .... **CLC 27**
See also AAYA 28; BEST 89:4; BPFB 3; CA 49-52; CANR 1, 26, 52, 89, 128, 165; CMW 4; CPW; DAM NOV, POP; DLB 306; INT CANR-26; MSW; MTCW 1; MTFW 2005

Parker, Robert Brown
See Parker, Robert B.

Parker, Theodore 1810-1860 .... **NCLC 186**
See also DLB 1, 235

Parkin, Frank 1940- .... **CLC 43**
See also CA 147

Parkman, Francis, Jr. 1823-1893 .. **NCLC 12**
See also AMWS 2; DLB 1, 30, 183, 186, 235; RGAL 4

Parks, Gordon 1912-2006 . **BLC 1:3; CLC 1, 16**
See also AAYA 36; AITN 2; BW 2, 3; CA 41-44R; 249; CANR 26, 66, 145; DA3; DAM MULT; DLB 33; MTCW 2; MTFW 2005; SATA 8, 108; SATA-Obit 175

Parks, Suzan-Lori 1964(?)- ..... **BLC 2:3; DC 23**
See also AAYA 55; CA 201; CAD; CD 5, 6; CWD; DFS 22; DLB 341; RGAL 4

Parks, Tim(othy Harold) 1954- ...... **CLC 147**
See also CA 126; 131; CANR 77, 144; CN 7; DLB 231; INT CA-131

Parmenides c. 515B.C.-c.
450B.C. .... **CMLC 22**
See also DLB 176

Parnell, Thomas 1679-1718 .... **LC 3**
See also DLB 95; RGEL 2

Parr, Catherine c. 1513(?)-1548 .... **LC 86**
See also DLB 136

Parra, Nicanor 1914- ... **CLC 2, 102; HLC 2; PC 39**
See also CA 85-88; CANR 32; CWW 2; DAM MULT; DLB 283; EWL 3; HW 1; LAW; MTCW 1

Parra Sanojo, Ana Teresa de la
1890-1936 .... **HLCS 2**
See de la Parra, (Ana) Teresa (Sonojo)
See also LAW

Parrish, Mary Frances
See Fisher, M(ary) F(rances) K(ennedy)

Parshchikov, Aleksei 1954- .... **CLC 59**
See Parshchikov, Aleksei Maksimovich

Parshchikov, Aleksei Maksimovich
See Parshchikov, Aleksei
See also DLB 285

Parson, Professor
See Coleridge, Samuel Taylor

Parson Lot
See Kingsley, Charles

Parton, Sara Payson Willis
1811-1872 .... NCLC 86
See also DLB 43, 74, 239

Partridge, Anthony
See Oppenheim, E(dward) Phillips

Pascal, Blaise 1623-1662 .... LC 35
See also DLB 268; EW 3; GFL Beginnings
to 1789; RGWL 2, 3; TWA

Pascoli, Giovanni 1855-1912 .... TCLC 45
See also CA 170; EW 7; EWL 3

Pasolini, Pier Paolo 1922-1975 .. CLC 20, 37,
106; PC 17
See also CA 93-96; 61-64; CANR 63; DLB
128, 177; EWL 3; MTCW 1; RGWL 2, 3

Pasquini
See Silone, Ignazio

Pastan, Linda (Olenik) 1932- .... CLC 27
See also CA 61-64; CANR 18, 40, 61, 113;
CP 3, 4, 5, 6, 7; CSW; CWP; DAM
POET; DLB 5; PFS 8, 25

Pasternak, Boris 1890-1960 ... CLC 7, 10, 18,
63; PC 6; SSC 31; TCLC 188; WLC 4
See also BPFB 3; CA 127; 116; DA; DA3;
DAB; DAC; DAM MST, NOV, POET;
DLB 302, 331; EW 10; MTCW 1, 2;
MTFW 2005; NFS 26; RGSF 2; RGWL
2, 3; TWA; WP

Patchen, Kenneth 1911-1972 .... CLC 1, 2, 18
See also BG 1:3; CA 1-4R; 33-36R; CANR
3, 35; CN 1; CP 1; DAM POET; DLB 16,
48; EWL 3; MAL 5; MTCW 1; RGAL 4

Patchett, Ann 1963- .... CLC 244
See also AAYA 69; AMWS 12; CA 139;
CANR 64, 110, 167; MTFW 2005

Pater, Walter (Horatio) 1839-1894 . NCLC 7,
90, 159
See also BRW 5; CDBLB 1832-1890; DLB
57, 156; RGEL 2; TEA

Paterson, A(ndrew) B(arton)
1864-1941 .... TCLC 32
See also CA 155; DLB 230; RGEL 2; SATA
97

Paterson, Banjo
See Paterson, A(ndrew) B(arton)

Paterson, Katherine 1932- .... CLC 12, 30
See also AAYA 1, 31; BYA 1, 2, 7; CA 21-
24R; CANR 28, 59, 111, 173; CLR 7, 50,
127; CWRI 5; DLB 52; JRDA; LAIT 4;
MAICYA 1, 2; MAICYAS 1; MTCW 1;
SATA 13, 53, 92, 133; WYA; YAW

Paterson, Katherine Womeldorf
See Paterson, Katherine

Patmore, Coventry Kersey Dighton
1823-1896 .... NCLC 9; PC 59
See also DLB 35, 98; RGEL 2; TEA

Paton, Alan 1903-1988 ..... CLC 4, 10, 25, 55,
106; TCLC 165; WLC 4
See also AAYA 26; AFW; BPFB 3; BRWS
2; BYA 1; CA 13-16; 125; CANR 22;
CAP 1; CN 1, 2, 3, 4; DA; DA3; DAB;
DAC; DAM MST, NOV; DLB 225;
DLBD 17; EWL 3; EXPN; LAIT 4;
MTCW 1, 2; MTFW 2005; NFS 3, 12;
RGEL 2; SATA 11; SATA-Obit 56; TWA;
WLIT 2; WWE 1

Paton Walsh, Gillian
See Paton Walsh, Jill
See also AAYA 47; BYA 1, 8

Paton Walsh, Jill 1937- .... CLC 35
See Paton Walsh, Gillian; Walsh, Jill Paton
See also AAYA 11; CA 262; CAAE 262;
CANR 38, 83, 158; CLR 2, 65; DLB 161;
JRDA; MAICYA 1, 2; SAAS 3; SATA 4,
72, 109, 190; SATA-Essay 190; YAW

Patsauq, Markoosie 1942- .... NNAL
See also CA 101; CLR 23; CWRI 5; DAM
MULT

Patterson, (Horace) Orlando (Lloyd)
1940- .... BLCS
See also BW 1; CA 65-68; CANR 27, 84;
CN 1, 2, 3, 4, 5, 6

Patton, George S(mith), Jr.
1885-1945 .... TCLC 79
See also CA 189

Paulding, James Kirke 1778-1860 ... NCLC 2
See also DLB 3, 59, 74, 250; RGAL 4

Paulin, Thomas Neilson
See Paulin, Tom

Paulin, Tom 1949- .... CLC 37, 177
See also CA 123; 128; CANR 98; CP 3, 4,
5, 6, 7; DLB 40

Pausanias c. 1st cent. - .... CMLC 36

Paustovsky, Konstantin (Georgievich)
1892-1968 .... CLC 40
See also CA 93-96; 25-28R; DLB 272;
EWL 3

Pavese, Cesare 1908-1950 .... PC 13; SSC 19;
TCLC 3
See also CA 104; 169; DLB 128, 177; EW
12; EWL 3; PFS 20; RGSF 2; RGWL 2,
3; TWA; WLIT 7

Pavic, Milorad 1929- .... CLC 60
See also CA 136; CDWLB 4; CWW 2; DLB
181; EWL 3; RGWL 3

Pavlov, Ivan Petrovich 1849-1936 . TCLC 91
See also CA 118; 180

Pavlova, Karolina Karlovna
1807-1893 .... NCLC 138
See also DLB 205

Payne, Alan
See Jakes, John

Payne, Rachel Ann
See Jakes, John

Paz, Gil
See Lugones, Leopoldo

Paz, Octavio 1914-1998 . CLC 3, 4, 6, 10, 19,
**51, 65, 119; HLC 2; PC 1, 48; TCLC
211; WLC 4**
See also AAYA 50; CA 73-76; 165; CANR
32, 65, 104; CWW 2; DA; DA3; DAB;
DAC; DAM MST, MULT, POET; DLB
290, 331; DLBY 1990, 1998; DNFS 1;
EWL 3; HW 1, 2; LAW; LAWS 1; MTCW
1, 2; MTFW 2005; PFS 18; RGWL 2, 3;
SSFS 13; TWA; WLIT 1

p'Bitek, Okot 1931-1982 . BLC 1:3; CLC 96;
TCLC 149
See also AFW; BW 2, 3; CA 124; 107;
CANR 82; CP 1, 2, 3; DAM MULT; DLB
125; EWL 3; MTCW 1, 2; MTFW 2005;
RGEL 2; WLIT 2

Peabody, Elizabeth Palmer
1804-1894 .... NCLC 169
See also DLB 1, 223

Peacham, Henry 1578-1644(?) .... LC 119
See also DLB 151

Peacock, Molly 1947- .... CLC 60
See also CA 103, 262; CAAE 262; CAAS
21; CANR 52, 84; CP 5, 6, 7; CWP; DLB
120, 282

Peacock, Thomas Love
1785-1866 .... NCLC 22; PC 87
See also BRW 4; DLB 96, 116; RGEL 2;
RGSF 2

Peake, Mervyn 1911-1968 .... CLC 7, 54
See also CA 5-8R; 25-28R; CANR 3; DLB
15, 160, 255; FANT; MTCW 1; RGEL 2;
SATA 23; SFW 4

Pearce, Philippa 1920-2006
See Christie, Philippa
See also CA 5-8R; 255; CANR 4, 109;
CWRI 5; FANT; MAICYA 2; SATA-Obit
179

Pearl, Eric
See Elman, Richard (Martin)

Pearson, Jean Mary
See Gardam, Jane

Pearson, Thomas Reid
See Pearson, T.R.

Pearson, T.R. 1956- .... CLC 39
See also CA 120; 130; CANR 97, 147, 185;
CSW; INT CA-130

Peck, Dale 1967- .... CLC 81
See also CA 146; CANR 72, 127, 180; GLL
2

Peck, John (Frederick) 1941- .... CLC 3
See also CA 49-52; CANR 3, 100; CP 4, 5,
6, 7

Peck, Richard 1934- .... CLC 21
See also AAYA 1, 24; BYA 1, 6, 8, 11; CA
85-88; CANR 19, 38, 129, 178; CLR 15;
INT CANR-19; JRDA; MAICYA 1, 2;
SAAS 2; SATA 18, 55, 97, 110, 158, 190;
SATA-Essay 110; WYA; YAW

Peck, Richard Wayne
See Peck, Richard

Peck, Robert Newton 1928- .... CLC 17
See also AAYA 3, 43; BYA 1, 6; CA 81-84,
182; CAAE 182; CANR 31, 63, 127; CLR
45; DA; DAC; DAM MST; JRDA; LAIT
3; MAICYA 1, 2; SAAS 1; SATA 21, 62,
111, 156; SATA-Essay 108; WYA; YAW

Peckinpah, David Samuel
See Peckinpah, Sam

Peckinpah, Sam 1925-1984 .... CLC 20
See also CA 109; 114; CANR 82

Pedersen, Knut 1859-1952
See Hamsun, Knut
See also CA 104; 119; CANR 63; MTCW
1, 2

Peele, George 1556-1596 .... DC 27; LC 115
See also BRW 1; DLB 62, 167; RGEL 2

Peeslake, Gaffer
See Durrell, Lawrence (George)

Peguy, Charles (Pierre)
1873-1914 .... TCLC 10
See also CA 107; 193; DLB 258; EWL 3;
GFL 1789 to the Present

Peirce, Charles Sanders
1839-1914 .... TCLC 81
See also CA 194; DLB 270

Pelecanos, George P. 1957- .... CLC 236
See also CA 138; CANR 122, 165; DLB
306

Pelevin, Victor 1962- .... CLC 238
See Pelevin, Viktor Olegovich
See also CA 154; CANR 88, 159

Pelevin, Viktor Olegovich
See Pelevin, Victor
See also DLB 285

Pellicer, Carlos 1897(?)-1977 .... HLCS 2
See also CA 153; 69-72; DLB 290; EWL 3;
HW 1

Pena, Ramon del Valle y
See Valle-Inclan, Ramon (Maria) del

Pendennis, Arthur Esquir
See Thackeray, William Makepeace

Penn, Arthur
See Matthews, (James) Brander

Penn, William 1644-1718 .... LC 25
See also DLB 24

PEPECE
See Prado (Calvo), Pedro

Pepys, Samuel 1633-1703 ... LC 11, 58; WLC
4
See also BRW 2; CDBLB 1660-1789; DA;
DA3; DAB; DAC; DAM MST; DLB 101,
213; NCFS 4; RGEL 2; TEA; WLIT 3

Percy, Thomas 1729-1811 .... NCLC 95
See also DLB 104

Popov, Evgenii Anatol'evich
  See Popov, Yevgeny
  See also DLB 285

Popov, Yevgeny .... **CLC 59**
  See Popov, Evgenii Anatol'evich

Poquelin, Jean-Baptiste
  See Moliere

Porete, Marguerite (?)-1310 .... **CMLC 73**
  See also DLB 208

Porphyry c. 233-c. 305 .... **CMLC 71**

Porter, Connie (Rose) 1959(?)- .... **CLC 70**
  See also AAYA 65; BW 2, 3; CA 142;
  CANR 90, 109; SATA 81, 129

Porter, Gene(va Grace) Stratton .. **TCLC 21**
  See Stratton-Porter, Gene(va Grace)
  See also BPFB 3; CA 112; CWRI 5; RHW

Porter, Katherine Anne 1890-1980 ... **CLC 1,
  3, 7, 10, 13, 15, 27, 101; SSC 4, 31, 43,
  108**
  See also AAYA 42; AITN 2; AMW; BPFB
  3; CA 1-4R; 101; CANR 1, 65; CDALBS;
  CN 1, 2; DA; DA3; DAB; DAC; DAM
  MST, NOV; DLB 4, 9, 102; DLBD 12;
  DLBY 1980; EWL 3; EXPS; LAIT 3;
  MAL 5; MBL; MTCW 1, 2; MTFW 2005;
  NFS 14; RGAL 4; RGSF 2; SATA 39;
  SATA-Obit 23; SSFS 1, 8, 11, 16, 23;
  TCWW 2; TUS

Porter, Peter (Neville Frederick)
  1929- .... **CLC 5, 13, 33**
  See also CA 85-88; CP 1, 2, 3, 4, 5, 6, 7;
  DLB 40, 289; WWE 1

Porter, William Sydney 1862-1910
  See Henry, O.
  See also CA 104; 131; CDALB 1865-1917;
  DA; DA3; DAB; DAC; DAM MST; DLB
  12, 78, 79; MTCW 1, 2; MTFW 2005;
  TUS; YABC 2

Portillo (y Pacheco), Jose Lopez
  See Lopez Portillo (y Pacheco), Jose

Portillo Trambley, Estela 1927-1998 .. **HLC 2**
  See Trambley, Estela Portillo
  See also CANR 32; DAM MULT; DLB
  209; HW 1

Posey, Alexander (Lawrence)
  1873-1908 .... **NNAL**
  See also CA 144; CANR 80; DAM MULT;
  DLB 175

Posse, Abel .... **CLC 70**
  See also CA 252

Post, Melville Davisson
  1869-1930 .... **TCLC 39**
  See also CA 110; 202; CMW 4

Postman, Neil 1931(?)-2003 .... **CLC 244**
  See also CA 102; 221

Potok, Chaim 1929-2002 ... **CLC 2, 7, 14, 26,
  112**
  See also AAYA 15, 50; AITN 1, 2; BPFB 3;
  BYA 1; CA 17-20R; 208; CANR 19, 35,
  64, 98; CLR 92; CN 4, 5, 6; DA3; DAM
  NOV; DLB 28, 152; EXPN; INT CANR-
  19; LAIT 4; MTCW 1, 2; MTFW 2005;
  NFS 4; RGHL; SATA 33, 106; SATA-Obit
  134; TUS; YAW

Potok, Herbert Harold -2002
  See Potok, Chaim

Potok, Herman Harold
  See Potok, Chaim

Potter, Dennis (Christopher George)
  1935-1994 .... **CLC 58, 86, 123**
  See also BRWS 10; CA 107; 145; CANR
  33, 61; CBD; DLB 233; MTCW 1

Pound, Ezra (Weston Loomis)
  1885-1972 .. **CLC 1, 2, 3, 4, 5, 7, 10, 13,
  18, 34, 48, 50, 112; PC 4; WLC 5**
  See also AAYA 47; AMW; AMWR 1; CA
  5-8R; 37-40R; CANR 40; CDALB 1917-
  1929; CP 1; DA; DA3; DAB; DAC; DAM
  MST, POET; DLB 4, 45, 63; DLBD 15;

EFS 2; EWL 3; EXPP; LMFS 2; MAL 5;
MTCW 1, 2; MTFW 2005; PAB; PFS 2,
8, 16; RGAL 4; TUS; WP

Povod, Reinaldo 1959-1994 .... **CLC 44**
  See also CA 136; 146; CANR 83

Powell, Adam Clayton, Jr.
  1908-1972 .... **BLC 1:3; CLC 89**
  See also BW 1, 3; CA 102; 33-36R; CANR
  86; DAM MULT; DLB 345

Powell, Anthony 1905-2000 ... **CLC 1, 3, 7, 9,
  10, 31**
  See also BRW 7; CA 1-4R; 189; CANR 1,
  32, 62, 107; CDBLB 1945-1960; CN 1, 2,
  3, 4, 5, 6; DLB 15; EWL 3; MTCW 1, 2;
  MTFW 2005; RGEL 2; TEA

Powell, Dawn 1896(?)-1965 .... **CLC 66**
  See also CA 5-8R; CANR 121; DLBY 1997

Powell, Padgett 1952- .... **CLC 34**
  See also CA 126; CANR 63, 101; CSW;
  DLB 234; DLBY 01; SSFS 25

Powell, (Oval) Talmage 1920-2000
  See Queen, Ellery
  See also CA 5-8R; CANR 2, 80

Power, Susan 1961- .... **CLC 91**
  See also BYA 14; CA 160; CANR 135; NFS
  11

Powers, J(ames) F(arl) 1917-1999 ..... **CLC 1,
  4, 8, 57; SSC 4**
  See also CA 1-4R; 181; CANR 2, 61; CN
  1, 2, 3, 4, 5, 6; DLB 130; MTCW 1;
  RGAL 4; RGSF 2

Powers, John J(ames) 1945-
  See Powers, John R.
  See also CA 69-72

Powers, John R. .... **CLC 66**
  See Powers, John J(ames)

Powers, Richard 1957- .... **CLC 93**
  See also AMWS 9; BPFB 3; CA 148;
  CANR 80, 180; CN 6, 7; MTFW 2005;
  TCLE 1:2

Powers, Richard S.
  See Powers, Richard

Pownall, David 1938- .... **CLC 10**
  See also CA 89-92; 180; CAAS 18; CANR
  49, 101; CBD; CD 5, 6; CN 4, 5, 6, 7;
  DLB 14

Powys, John Cowper 1872-1963 ... **CLC 7, 9,
  15, 46, 125**
  See also CA 85-88; CANR 106; DLB 15,
  255; EWL 3; FANT; MTCW 1, 2; MTFW
  2005; RGEL 2; SUFW

Powys, T(heodore) F(rancis)
  1875-1953 .... **TCLC 9**
  See also BRWS 8; CA 106; 189; DLB 36,
  162; EWL 3; FANT; RGEL 2; SUFW

Pozzo, Modesta
  See Fonte, Moderata

Prado (Calvo), Pedro 1886-1952 ... **TCLC 75**
  See also CA 131; DLB 283; HW 1; LAW

Prager, Emily 1952- .... **CLC 56**
  See also CA 204

Pratchett, Terence David John
  See Pratchett, Terry

Pratchett, Terry 1948- .... **CLC 197**
  See also AAYA 19, 54; BPFB 3; CA 143;
  CANR 87, 126, 170; CLR 64; CN 6, 7;
  CPW; CWRI 5; FANT; MTFW 2005;
  SATA 82, 139, 185; SFW 4; SUFW 2

Pratolini, Vasco 1913-1991 .... **TCLC 124**
  See also CA 211; DLB 177; EWL 3; RGWL
  2, 3

Pratt, E(dwin) J(ohn) 1883(?)-1964 . **CLC 19**
  See also CA 141; 93-96; CANR 77; DAC;
  DAM POET; DLB 92; EWL 3; RGEL 2;
  TWA

Premchand .... **TCLC 21**
  See Srivastava, Dhanpat Rai
  See also EWL 3

Prescott, William Hickling
  1796-1859 .... **NCLC 163**
  See also DLB 1, 30, 59, 235

Preseren, France 1800-1849 .... **NCLC 127**
  See also CDWLB 4; DLB 147

Preussler, Otfried 1923- .... **CLC 17**
  See also CA 77-80; SATA 24

Prevert, Jacques (Henri Marie)
  1900-1977 .... **CLC 15**
  See also CA 77-80; 69-72; CANR 29, 61;
  DLB 258; EWL 3; GFL 1789 to the
  Present; IDFW 3, 4; MTCW 1; RGWL 2,
  3; SATA-Obit 30

Prevost, (Antoine Francois)
  1697-1763 .... **LC 1**
  See also DLB 314; EW 4; GFL Beginnings
  to 1789; RGWL 2, 3

Price, Edward Reynolds
  See Price, Reynolds

Price, Reynolds 1933- .. **CLC 3, 6, 13, 43, 50,
  63, 212; SSC 22**
  See also AMWS 6; CA 1-4R; CANR 1, 37,
  57, 87, 128, 177; CN 1, 2, 3, 4, 5, 6, 7;
  CSW; DAM NOV; DLB 2, 218, 278;
  EWL 3; INT CANR-37; MAL 5; MTFW
  2005; NFS 18

Price, Richard 1949- .... **CLC 6, 12**
  See also CA 49-52; CANR 3, 147; CN 7;
  DLBY 1981

Prichard, Katharine Susannah
  1883-1969 .... **CLC 46**
  See also CA 11-12; CANR 33; CAP 1; DLB
  260; MTCW 1; RGEL 2; RGSF 2; SATA
  66

Priestley, J(ohn) B(oynton)
  1894-1984 .... **CLC 2, 5, 9, 34**
  See also BRW 7; CA 9-12R; 113; CANR
  33; CDBLB 1914-1945; CN 1, 2, 3; DA3;
  DAM DRAM, NOV; DLB 10, 34, 77,
  100, 139; DLBY 1984; EWL 3; MTCW
  1, 2; MTFW 2005; RGEL 2; SFW 4

Prince 1958- .... **CLC 35**
  See also CA 213

Prince, F(rank) T(empleton)
  1912-2003 .... **CLC 22**
  See also CA 101; 219; CANR 43, 79; CP 1,
  2, 3, 4, 5, 6, 7; DLB 20

Prince Kropotkin
  See Kropotkin, Peter (Aleksieevich)

Prior, Matthew 1664-1721 .... **LC 4**
  See also DLB 95; RGEL 2

Prishvin, Mikhail 1873-1954 .... **TCLC 75**
  See Prishvin, Mikhail Mikhailovich

Prishvin, Mikhail Mikhailovich
  See Prishvin, Mikhail
  See also DLB 272; EWL 3

Pritchard, William H(arrison)
  1932- .... **CLC 34**
  See also CA 65-68; CANR 23, 95; DLB
  111

Pritchett, V(ictor) S(awdon)
  1900-1997 ... **CLC 5, 13, 15, 41; SSC 14**
  See also BPFB 3; BRWS 3; CA 61-64; 157;
  CANR 31, 63; CN 1, 2, 3, 4, 5, 6; DA3;
  DAM NOV; DLB 15, 139; EWL 3;
  MTCW 1, 2; MTFW 2005; RGEL 2;
  RGSF 2; TEA

Private 19022
  See Manning, Frederic

Probst, Mark 1925- .... **CLC 59**
  See also CA 130

Procaccino, Michael
  See Cristofer, Michael

Proclus c. 412-c. 485 .... **CMLC 81**

Prokosch, Frederic 1908-1989 ...... **CLC 4, 48**
  See also CA 73-76; 128; CANR 82; CN 1,
  2, 3, 4; CP 1, 2, 3, 4; DLB 48; MTCW 2

Propertius, Sextus c. 50B.C.-c.
16B.C. .... **CMLC 32**
See also AW 2; CDWLB 1; DLB 211;
RGWL 2, 3; WLIT 8

Prophet, The
See Dreiser, Theodore

Prose, Francine 1947- .... **CLC 45, 231**
See also AMWS 16; CA 109; 112; CANR
46, 95, 132, 175; DLB 234; MTFW 2005;
SATA 101, 149

Protagoras c. 490B.C.-420B.C. ...... **CMLC 85**
See also DLB 176

Proudhon
See Cunha, Euclides (Rodrigues Pimenta)
da

Proulx, Annie
See Proulx, E. Annie

Proulx, E. Annie 1935- ...... **CLC 81, 158, 250**
See also AMWS 7; BPFB 3; CA 145;
CANR 65, 110; CN 6, 7; CPW 1; DA3;
DAM POP; DLB 335; MAL 5; MTCW 2;
MTFW 2005; SSFS 18, 23

Proulx, Edna Annie
See Proulx, E. Annie

Proust, (Valentin-Louis-George-Eugene)
Marcel 1871-1922 ..... **SSC 75; TCLC 7,**
13, 33; WLC 5
See also AAYA 58; BPFB 3; CA 104; 120;
CANR 110; DA; DA3; DAB; DAC; DAM
MST, NOV; DLB 65; EW 8; EWL 3; GFL
1789 to the Present; MTCW 1, 2; MTFW
2005; RGWL 2, 3; TWA

Prowler, Harley
See Masters, Edgar Lee

Prudentius, Aurelius Clemens 348-c.
405 .... **CMLC 78**
See also EW 1; RGWL 2, 3

Prudhomme, Rene Francois Armand
1839-1907
See Sully Prudhomme, Rene-Francois-
Armand
See also CA 170

Prus, Boleslaw 1845-1912 .... **TCLC 48**
See also RGWL 2, 3

Prynne, William 1600-1669 .... **LC 148**

Prynne, Xavier
See Hardwick, Elizabeth

Pryor, Aaron Richard
See Pryor, Richard

Pryor, Richard 1940-2005 .... **CLC 26**
See also CA 122; 152; 246

Pryor, Richard Franklin Lenox Thomas
See Pryor, Richard

Przybyszewski, Stanislaw
1868-1927 .... **TCLC 36**
See also CA 160; DLB 66; EWL 3

Pseudo-Dionysius the Areopagite fl. c. 5th
cent. - .... **CMLC 89**
See also DLB 115

Pteleon
See Grieve, C(hristopher) M(urray)
See also DAM POET

Puckett, Lute
See Masters, Edgar Lee

Puig, Manuel 1932-1990 .... **CLC 3, 5, 10, 28,**
65, 133; HLC 2
See also BPFB 3; CA 45-48; CANR 2, 32,
63; CDWLB 3; DA3; DAM MULT; DLB
113; DNFS 1; EWL 3; GLL 1; HW 1, 2;
LAW; MTCW 1, 2; MTFW 2005; RGWL
2, 3; TWA; WLIT 1

Pulitzer, Joseph 1847-1911 .... **TCLC 76**
See also CA 114; DLB 23

Pullman, Philip 1946- .... **CLC 245**
See also AAYA 15, 41; BRWS 13; BYA 8,
13; CA 127; CANR 50, 77, 105, 134;
CLR 20, 62, 84; JRDA; MAICYA 1, 2;
MAICYAS 1; MTFW 2005; SAAS 17;
SATA 65, 103, 150; SUFW 2; WYAS 1;
YAW

Purchas, Samuel 1577(?)-1626 .... **LC 70**
See also DLB 151

Purdy, A(lfred) W(ellington)
1918-2000 .... **CLC 3, 6, 14, 50**
See also CA 81-84; 189; CAAS 17; CANR
42, 66; CP 1, 2, 3, 4, 5, 6, 7; DAC; DAM
MST, POET; DLB 88; PFS 5; RGEL 2

Purdy, James (Amos) 1923- .... **CLC 2, 4, 10,**
28, 52
See also AMWS 7; CA 33-36R; CAAS 1;
CANR 19, 51, 132; CN 1, 2, 3, 4, 5, 6, 7;
DLB 2, 218; EWL 3; INT CANR-19;
MAL 5; MTCW 1; RGAL 4

Pure, Simon
See Swinnerton, Frank Arthur

Pushkin, Aleksandr Sergeevich
See Pushkin, Alexander (Sergeyevich)
See also DLB 205

Pushkin, Alexander (Sergeyevich)
1799-1837 .... **NCLC 3, 27, 83; PC 10;**
SSC 27, 55, 99; WLC 5
See Pushkin, Aleksandr Sergeevich
See also DA; DA3; DAB; DAC; DAM
DRAM, MST, POET; EW 5; EXPS; PFS
28; RGSF 2; RGWL 2, 3; SATA 61; SSFS
9; TWA

P'u Sung-ling 1640-1715 .... **LC 49; SSC 31**

Putnam, Arthur Lee
See Alger, Horatio, Jr.

Puttenham, George 1529(?)-1590 ...... **LC 116**
See also DLB 281

Puzo, Mario 1920-1999 .... **CLC 1, 2, 6, 36,**
107
See also BPFB 3; CA 65-68; 185; CANR 4,
42, 65, 99, 131; CN 1, 2, 3, 4, 5, 6; CPW;
DA3; DAM NOV, POP; DLB 6; MTCW
1, 2; MTFW 2005; NFS 16; RGAL 4

Pygge, Edward
See Barnes, Julian

Pyle, Ernest Taylor 1900-1945
See Pyle, Ernie
See also CA 115; 160

Pyle, Ernie .... **TCLC 75**
See Pyle, Ernest Taylor
See also DLB 29; MTCW 2

Pyle, Howard 1853-1911 .... **TCLC 81**
See also AAYA 57; BYA 2, 4; CA 109; 137;
CLR 22, 117; DLB 42, 188; DLBD 13;
LAIT 1; MAICYA 1, 2; SATA 16, 100;
WCH; YAW

Pym, Barbara (Mary Crampton)
1913-1980 .... **CLC 13, 19, 37, 111**
See also BPFB 3; BRWS 2; CA 13-14; 97-
100; CANR 13, 34; CAP 1; DLB 14, 207;
DLBY 1987; EWL 3; MTCW 1, 2; MTFW
2005; RGEL 2; TEA

Pynchon, Thomas 1937- .. **CLC 2, 3, 6, 9, 11,**
18, 33, 62, 72, 123, 192, 213; SSC 14,
84; WLC 5
See also AMWS 2; BEST 90:2; BPFB 3;
CA 17-20R; CANR 22, 46, 73, 142; CN
1, 2, 3, 4, 5, 6, 7; CPW 1; DA; DA3;
DAB; DAC; DAM MST, NOV, POP;
DLB 2, 173; EWL 3; MAL 5; MTCW 1,
2; MTFW 2005; NFS 23; RGAL 4; SFW
4; TCLE 1:2; TUS

Pythagoras c. 582B.C.-c. 507B.C. . **CMLC 22**
See also DLB 176

Q
See Quiller-Couch, Sir Arthur (Thomas)

Qian, Chongzhu
See Ch'ien, Chung-shu

Qian, Sima 145B.C.-c. 89B.C. .... **CMLC 72**

Qian Zhongshu
See Ch'ien, Chung-shu
See also CWW 2; DLB 328

Qroll
See Dagerman, Stig (Halvard)

Quarles, Francis 1592-1644 .... **LC 117**
See also DLB 126; RGEL 2

Quarrington, Paul 1953- .... **CLC 65**
See also CA 129; CANR 62, 95

Quarrington, Paul Lewis
See Quarrington, Paul

Quasimodo, Salvatore 1901-1968 .... **CLC 10;**
PC 47
See also CA 13-16; 25-28R; CAP 1; DLB
114, 332; EW 12; EWL 3; MTCW 1;
RGWL 2, 3

Quatermass, Martin
See Carpenter, John (Howard)

Quay, Stephen 1947- .... **CLC 95**
See also CA 189

Quay, Timothy 1947- .... **CLC 95**
See also CA 189

Queen, Ellery .... **CLC 3, 11**
See Dannay, Frederic; Davidson, Avram
(James); Deming, Richard; Fairman, Paul
W.; Flora, Fletcher; Hoch, Edward D.;
Holding, James (Clark Carlisle, Jr.); Kane,
Henry; Lee, Manfred B.; Marlowe,
Stephen; Powell, (Oval) Talmage; Shel-
don, Walter J(ames); Sturgeon, Theodore
(Hamilton); Tracy, Don(ald Fiske); Vance,
Jack
See also BPFB 3; CMW 4; MSW; RGAL 4

Queneau, Raymond 1903-1976 ..... **CLC 2, 5,**
10, 42
See also CA 77-80; 69-72; CANR 32; DLB
72, 258; EW 12; EWL 3; GFL 1789 to
the Present; MTCW 1, 2; RGWL 2, 3

Quevedo, Francisco de 1580-1645 ...... **LC 23,**
160

Quiller-Couch, Sir Arthur (Thomas)
1863-1944 .... **TCLC 53**
See also CA 118; 166; DLB 135, 153, 190;
HGG; RGEL 2; SUFW 1

Quin, Ann 1936-1973 .... **CLC 6**
See also CA 9-12R; 45-48; CANR 148; CN
1; DLB 14, 231

Quin, Ann Marie
See Quin, Ann

Quincey, Thomas de
See De Quincey, Thomas

Quindlen, Anna 1953- .... **CLC 191**
See also AAYA 35; AMWS 17; CA 138;
CANR 73, 126; DA3; DLB 292; MTCW
2; MTFW 2005

Quinn, Martin
See Smith, Martin Cruz

Quinn, Peter 1947- .... **CLC 91**
See also CA 197; CANR 147

Quinn, Peter A.
See Quinn, Peter

Quinn, Simon
See Smith, Martin Cruz

Quintana, Leroy V. 1944- ...... **HLC 2; PC 36**
See also CA 131; CANR 65, 139; DAM
MULT; DLB 82; HW 1, 2

Quintilian c. 40-c. 100 .... **CMLC 77**
See also AW 2; DLB 211; RGWL 2, 3

Quiroga, Horacio (Sylvestre)
1878-1937 ... **HLC 2; SSC 89; TCLC 20**
See also CA 117; 131; DAM MULT; EWL
3; HW 1; LAW; MTCW 1; RGSF 2;
WLIT 1

Quoirez, Francoise 1935-2004 .... **CLC 9**
See Sagan, Francoise
See also CA 49-52; 231; CANR 6, 39, 73;
MTCW 1, 2; MTFW 2005; TWA

Raabe, Wilhelm (Karl) 1831-1910 . **TCLC 45**
See also CA 167; DLB 129

Rabe, David (William) 1940- .. **CLC 4, 8, 33,**
200; DC 16
See also CA 85-88; CABS 3; CAD; CANR
59, 129; CD 5, 6; DAM DRAM; DFS 3,
8, 13; DLB 7, 228; EWL 3; MAL 5

Rabelais, Francois 1494-1553 .... **LC 5, 60; WLC 5**
  See also DA; DAB; DAC; DAM MST; DLB 327; EW 2; GFL Beginnings to 1789; LMFS 1; RGWL 2, 3; TWA

Rabi'a al-'Adawiyya c. 717-c. 801 .... **CMLC 83**
  See also DLB 311

Rabinovitch, Sholem 1859-1916
  See Sholom Aleichem
  See also CA 104

Rabinyan, Dorit 1972- .... **CLC 119**
  See also CA 170; CANR 147

Rachilde
  See Vallette, Marguerite Eymery; Vallette, Marguerite Eymery
  See also EWL 3

Racine, Jean 1639-1699 .. **DC 32; LC 28, 113**
  See also DA3; DAB; DAM MST; DLB 268; EW 3; GFL Beginnings to 1789; LMFS 1; RGWL 2, 3; TWA

Radcliffe, Ann (Ward) 1764-1823 ... **NCLC 6, 55, 106**
  See also DLB 39, 178; GL 3; HGG; LMFS 1; RGEL 2; SUFW; WLIT 3

Radclyffe-Hall, Marguerite
  See Hall, Radclyffe

Radiguet, Raymond 1903-1923 ...... **TCLC 29**
  See also CA 162; DLB 65; EWL 3; GFL 1789 to the Present; RGWL 2, 3

Radishchev, Aleksandr Nikolaevich 1749-1802 .... **NCLC 190**
  See also DLB 150

Radishchev, Alexander
  See Radishchev, Aleksandr Nikolaevich

Radnoti, Miklos 1909-1944 .... **TCLC 16**
  See also CA 118; 212; CDWLB 4; DLB 215; EWL 3; RGHL; RGWL 2, 3

Rado, James 1939- .... **CLC 17**
  See also CA 105

Radvanyi, Netty 1900-1983
  See Seghers, Anna
  See also CA 85-88; 110; CANR 82

Rae, Ben
  See Griffiths, Trevor

Raeburn, John (Hay) 1941- .... **CLC 34**
  See also CA 57-60

Ragni, Gerome 1942-1991 .... **CLC 17**
  See also CA 105; 134

Rahv, Philip .... **CLC 24**
  See Greenberg, Ivan
  See also DLB 137; MAL 5

Raimund, Ferdinand Jakob 1790-1836 .... **NCLC 69**
  See also DLB 90

Raine, Craig 1944- .... **CLC 32, 103**
  See also BRWS 13; CA 108; CANR 29, 51, 103, 171; CP 3, 4, 5, 6, 7; DLB 40; PFS 7

Raine, Craig Anthony
  See Raine, Craig

Raine, Kathleen (Jessie) 1908-2003 .. **CLC 7, 45**
  See also CA 85-88; 218; CANR 46, 109; CP 1, 2, 3, 4, 5, 6, 7; DLB 20; EWL 3; MTCW 1; RGEL 2

Rainis, Janis 1865-1929 .... **TCLC 29**
  See also CA 170; CDWLB 4; DLB 220; EWL 3

Rakosi, Carl .... **CLC 47**
  See Rawley, Callman
  See also CA 228; CAAS 5; CP 1, 2, 3, 4, 5, 6, 7; DLB 193

Ralegh, Sir Walter
  See Raleigh, Sir Walter
  See also BRW 1; RGEL 2; WP

Raleigh, Richard
  See Lovecraft, H. P.

Raleigh, Sir Walter 1554(?)-1618 .... **LC 31, 39; PC 31**
  See Ralegh, Sir Walter
  See also CDBLB Before 1660; DLB 172; EXPP; PFS 14; TEA

Rallentando, H. P.
  See Sayers, Dorothy L(eigh)

Ramal, Walter
  See de la Mare, Walter (John)

Ramana Maharshi 1879-1950 .... **TCLC 84**

Ramoacn y Cajal, Santiago 1852-1934 .... **TCLC 93**

Ramon, Juan
  See Jimenez (Mantecon), Juan Ramon

Ramos, Graciliano 1892-1953 .... **TCLC 32**
  See also CA 167; DLB 307; EWL 3; HW 2; LAW; WLIT 1

Rampersad, Arnold 1941- .... **CLC 44**
  See also BW 2, 3; CA 127; 133; CANR 81; DLB 111; INT CA-133

Rampling, Anne
  See Rice, Anne
  See also GLL 2

Ramsay, Allan 1686(?)-1758 .... **LC 29**
  See also DLB 95; RGEL 2

Ramsay, Jay
  See Campbell, Ramsey

Ramuz, Charles-Ferdinand 1878-1947 .... **TCLC 33**
  See also CA 165; EWL 3

Rand, Ayn 1905-1982 ...... **CLC 3, 30, 44, 79; SSC 116; WLC 5**
  See also AAYA 10; AMWS 4; BPFB 3; BYA 12; CA 13-16R; 105; CANR 27, 73; CDALBS; CN 1, 2, 3; CPW; DA; DA3; DAC; DAM MST, NOV, POP; DLB 227, 279; MTCW 1, 2; MTFW 2005; NFS 10, 16; RGAL 4; SFW 4; TUS; YAW

Randall, Dudley (Felker) 1914-2000 .... **BLC 1:3; CLC 1, 135; PC 86**
  See also BW 1, 3; CA 25-28R; 189; CANR 23, 82; CP 1, 2, 3, 4, 5; DAM MULT; DLB 41; PFS 5

Randall, Robert
  See Silverberg, Robert

Ranger, Ken
  See Creasey, John

Rank, Otto 1884-1939 .... **TCLC 115**

Rankin, Ian 1960- .... **CLC 257**
  See also BRWS 10; CA 148; CANR 81, 137, 171; DLB 267; MTFW 2005

Rankin, Ian James
  See Rankin, Ian

Ransom, John Crowe 1888-1974 .. **CLC 2, 4, 5, 11, 24; PC 61**
  See also AMW; CA 5-8R; 49-52; CANR 6, 34; CDALBS; CP 1, 2; DA3; DAM POET; DLB 45, 63; EWL 3; EXPP; MAL 5; MTCW 1, 2; MTFW 2005; RGAL 4; TUS

Rao, Raja 1908-2006 . **CLC 25, 56, 255; SSC 99**
  See also CA 73-76; 252; CANR 51; CN 1, 2, 3, 4, 5, 6; DAM NOV; DLB 323; EWL 3; MTCW 1, 2; MTFW 2005; RGEL 2; RGSF 2

Raphael, Frederic (Michael) 1931- ... **CLC 2, 14**
  See also CA 1-4R; CANR 1, 86; CN 1, 2, 3, 4, 5, 6, 7; DLB 14, 319; TCLE 1:2

Raphael, Lev 1954- .... **CLC 232**
  See also CA 134; CANR 72, 145; GLL 1

Ratcliffe, James P.
  See Mencken, H(enry) L(ouis)

Rathbone, Julian 1935-2008 .... **CLC 41**
  See also CA 101; 269; CANR 34, 73, 152

Rathbone, Julian Christopher
  See Rathbone, Julian

Rattigan, Terence (Mervyn) 1911-1977 .... **CLC 7; DC 18**
  See also BRWS 7; CA 85-88; 73-76; CBD; CDBLB 1945-1960; DAM DRAM; DFS 8; DLB 13; IDFW 3, 4; MTCW 1, 2; MTFW 2005; RGEL 2

Ratushinskaya, Irina 1954- .... **CLC 54**
  See also CA 129; CANR 68; CWW 2

Raven, Simon (Arthur Noel) 1927-2001 .... **CLC 14**
  See also CA 81-84; 197; CANR 86; CN 1, 2, 3, 4, 5, 6; DLB 271

Ravenna, Michael
  See Welty, Eudora

Rawley, Callman 1903-2004
  See Rakosi, Carl
  See also CA 21-24R; 228; CANR 12, 32, 91

Rawlings, Marjorie Kinnan 1896-1953 .... **TCLC 4**
  See also AAYA 20; AMWS 10; ANW; BPFB 3; BYA 3; CA 104; 137; CANR 74; CLR 63; DLB 9, 22, 102; DLBD 17; JRDA; MAICYA 1, 2; MAL 5; MTCW 2; MTFW 2005; RGAL 4; SATA 100; WCH; YABC 1; YAW

Ray, Satyajit 1921-1992 .... **CLC 16, 76**
  See also CA 114; 137; DAM MULT

Read, Herbert Edward 1893-1968 ..... **CLC 4**
  See also BRW 6; CA 85-88; 25-28R; DLB 20, 149; EWL 3; PAB; RGEL 2

Read, Piers Paul 1941- .... **CLC 4, 10, 25**
  See also CA 21-24R; CANR 38, 86, 150; CN 2, 3, 4, 5, 6, 7; DLB 14; SATA 21

Reade, Charles 1814-1884 .... **NCLC 2, 74**
  See also DLB 21; RGEL 2

Reade, Hamish
  See Gray, Simon

Reading, Peter 1946- .... **CLC 47**
  See also BRWS 8; CA 103; CANR 46, 96; CP 5, 6, 7; DLB 40

Reaney, James 1926-2008 .... **CLC 13**
  See also CA 41-44R; CAAS 15; CANR 42; CD 5, 6; CP 1, 2, 3, 4, 5, 6, 7; DAC; DAM MST; DLB 68; RGEL 2; SATA 43

Reaney, James Crerar
  See Reaney, James

Rebreanu, Liviu 1885-1944 .... **TCLC 28**
  See also CA 165; DLB 220; EWL 3

Rechy, John 1934- ..... **CLC 1, 7, 14, 18, 107; HLC 2**
  See also CA 5-8R, 195; CAAE 195; CAAS 4; CANR 6, 32, 64, 152; CN 1, 2, 3, 4, 5, 6, 7; DAM MULT; DLB 122, 278; DLBY 1982; HW 1, 2; INT CANR-6; LLW; MAL 5; RGAL 4

Rechy, John Francisco
  See Rechy, John

Redcam, Tom 1870-1933 .... **TCLC 25**

Reddin, Keith 1956- .... **CLC 67**
  See also CAD; CD 6

Redgrove, Peter (William) 1932-2003 .... **CLC 6, 41**
  See also BRWS 6; CA 1-4R; 217; CANR 3, 39, 77; CP 1, 2, 3, 4, 5, 6, 7; DLB 40; TCLE 1:2

Redmon, Anne .... **CLC 22**
  See Nightingale, Anne Redmon
  See also DLBY 1986

Reed, Eliot
  See Ambler, Eric

Reed, Ishmael 1938- . **BLC 1:3; CLC 2, 3, 5, 6, 13, 32, 60, 174; PC 68**
  See also AFAW 1, 2; AMWS 10; BPFB 3; BW 2, 3; CA 21-24R; CANR 25, 48, 74, 128; CN 1, 2, 3, 4, 5, 6, 7; CP 1, 2, 3, 4, 5, 6, 7; CSW; DA3; DAM MULT; DLB

2, 5, 33, 169, 227; DLBD 8; EWL 3; LMFS 2; MAL 5; MSW; MTCW 1, 2; MTFW 2005; PFS 6; RGAL 4; TCWW 2

Reed, John (Silas) 1887-1920 .... **TCLC 9**
See also CA 106; 195; MAL 5; TUS

Reed, Lou .... **CLC 21**
See Firbank, Louis

Reese, Lizette Woodworth
1856-1935 .... **PC 29; TCLC 181**
See also CA 180; DLB 54

Reeve, Clara 1729-1807 .... **NCLC 19**
See also DLB 39; RGEL 2

Reich, Wilhelm 1897-1957 .... **TCLC 57**
See also CA 199

Reid, Christopher (John) 1949- .... **CLC 33**
See also CA 140; CANR 89; CP 4, 5, 6, 7; DLB 40; EWL 3

Reid, Desmond
See Moorcock, Michael

Reid Banks, Lynne 1929-
See Banks, Lynne Reid
See also AAYA 49; CA 1-4R; CANR 6, 22, 38, 87; CLR 24, 86; CN 1, 2, 3, 7; JRDA; MAICYA 1, 2; SATA 22, 75, 111, 165; YAW

Reilly, William K.
See Creasey, John

Reiner, Max
See Caldwell, (Janet Miriam) Taylor (Holland)

Reis, Ricardo
See Pessoa, Fernando

Reizenstein, Elmer Leopold
See Rice, Elmer (Leopold)
See also EWL 3

Remarque, Erich Maria 1898-1970 . **CLC 21**
See also AAYA 27; BPFB 3; CA 77-80; 29-32R; CDWLB 2; DA; DA3; DAB; DAC; DAM MST, NOV; DLB 56; EWL 3; EXPN; LAIT 3; MTCW 1, 2; MTFW 2005; NFS 4; RGHL; RGWL 2, 3

Remington, Frederic S(ackrider)
1861-1909 .... **TCLC 89**
See also CA 108; 169; DLB 12, 186, 188; SATA 41; TCWW 2

Remizov, A.
See Remizov, Aleksei (Mikhailovich)

Remizov, A. M.
See Remizov, Aleksei (Mikhailovich)

Remizov, Aleksei (Mikhailovich)
1877-1957 .... **TCLC 27**
See Remizov, Alexey Mikhaylovich
See also CA 125; 133; DLB 295

Remizov, Alexey Mikhaylovich
See Remizov, Aleksei (Mikhailovich)
See also EWL 3

Renan, Joseph Ernest 1823-1892 . **NCLC 26, 145**
See also GFL 1789 to the Present

Renard, Jules(-Pierre) 1864-1910 .. **TCLC 17**
See also CA 117; 202; GFL 1789 to the Present

Renart, Jean fl. 13th cent. - .... **CMLC 83**

Renault, Mary .... **CLC 3, 11, 17**
See Challans, Mary
See also BPFB 3; BYA 2; CN 1, 2, 3; DLBY 1983; EWL 3; GLL 1; LAIT 1; RGEL 2; RHW

Rendell, Ruth 1930- .... **CLC 28, 48**
See Vine, Barbara
See also BPFB 3; BRWS 9; CA 109; CANR 32, 52, 74, 127, 162; CN 5, 6, 7; CPW; DAM POP; DLB 87, 276; INT CANR-32; MSW; MTCW 1, 2; MTFW 2005

Rendell, Ruth Barbara
See Rendell, Ruth

Renoir, Jean 1894-1979 .... **CLC 20**
See also CA 129; 85-88

Rensie, Willis
See Eisner, Will

Resnais, Alain 1922- .... **CLC 16**

Revard, Carter 1931- .... **NNAL**
See also CA 144; CANR 81, 153; PFS 5

Reverdy, Pierre 1889-1960 .... **CLC 53**
See also CA 97-100; 89-92; DLB 258; EWL 3; GFL 1789 to the Present

Rexroth, Kenneth 1905-1982 .... **CLC 1, 2, 6, 11, 22, 49, 112; PC 20**
See also BG 1:3; CA 5-8R; 107; CANR 14, 34, 63; CDALB 1941-1968; CP 1, 2, 3; DAM POET; DLB 16, 48, 165, 212; DLBY 1982; EWL 3; INT CANR-14; MAL 5; MTCW 1, 2; MTFW 2005; RGAL 4

Reyes, Alfonso 1889-1959 .... **HLCS 2; TCLC 33**
See also CA 131; EWL 3; HW 1; LAW

Reyes y Basoalto, Ricardo Eliecer Neftali
See Neruda, Pablo

Reymont, Wladyslaw (Stanislaw)
1868(?)-1925 .... **TCLC 5**
See also CA 104; DLB 332; EWL 3

Reynolds, John Hamilton
1794-1852 .... **NCLC 146**
See also DLB 96

Reynolds, Jonathan 1942- .... **CLC 6, 38**
See also CA 65-68; CANR 28, 176

Reynolds, Joshua 1723-1792 .... **LC 15**
See also DLB 104

Reynolds, Michael S(hane)
1937-2000 .... **CLC 44**
See also CA 65-68; 189; CANR 9, 89, 97

Reznikoff, Charles 1894-1976 .... **CLC 9**
See also AMWS 14; CA 33-36; 61-64; CAP 2; CP 1, 2; DLB 28, 45; RGHL; WP

Rezzori, Gregor von
See Rezzori d'Arezzo, Gregor von

Rezzori d'Arezzo, Gregor von
1914-1998 .... **CLC 25**
See also CA 122; 136; 167

Rhine, Richard
See Silverstein, Alvin; Silverstein, Virginia B(arbara Opshelor)

Rhodes, Eugene Manlove
1869-1934 .... **TCLC 53**
See also CA 198; DLB 256; TCWW 1, 2

R'hoone, Lord
See Balzac, Honore de

Rhys, Jean 1890-1979 .... **CLC 2, 4, 6, 14, 19, 51, 124; SSC 21, 76**
See also BRWS 2; CA 25-28R; 85-88; CANR 35, 62; CDBLB 1945-1960; CD-WLB 3; CN 1, 2; DA3; DAM NOV; DLB 36, 117, 162; DNFS 2; EWL 3; LATS 1:1; MTCW 1, 2; MTFW 2005; NFS 19; RGEL 2; RGSF 2; RHW; TEA; WWE 1

Ribeiro, Darcy 1922-1997 .... **CLC 34**
See also CA 33-36R; 156; EWL 3

Ribeiro, Joao Ubaldo (Osorio Pimentel)
1941- .... **CLC 10, 67**
See also CA 81-84; CWW 2; EWL 3

Ribman, Ronald (Burt) 1932- .... **CLC 7**
See also CA 21-24R; CAD; CANR 46, 80; CD 5, 6

Ricci, Nino 1959- .... **CLC 70**
See also CA 137; CANR 130; CCA 1

Ricci, Nino Pio
See Ricci, Nino

Rice, Anne 1941- .... **CLC 41, 128**
See Rampling, Anne
See also AAYA 9, 53; AMWS 7; BEST 89:2; BPFB 3; CA 65-68; CANR 12, 36, 53, 74, 100, 133; CN 6, 7; CPW; CSW; DA3; DAM POP; DLB 292; GL 3; GLL 2; HGG; MTCW 2; MTFW 2005; SUFW 2; YAW

Rice, Elmer (Leopold) 1892-1967 ...... **CLC 7, 49**
See Reizenstein, Elmer Leopold
See also CA 21-22; 25-28R; CAP 2; DAM DRAM; DFS 12; DLB 4, 7; IDTP; MAL 5; MTCW 1, 2; RGAL 4

Rice, Tim(othy Miles Bindon)
1944- .... **CLC 21**
See also CA 103; CANR 46; DFS 7

Rich, Adrienne 1929- ..... **CLC 3, 6, 7, 11, 18, 36, 73, 76, 125; PC 5**
See also AAYA 69; AMWR 2; AMWS 1; CA 9-12R; CANR 20, 53, 74, 128; CDALBS; CP 1, 2, 3, 4, 5, 6, 7; CSW; CWP; DA3; DAM POET; DLB 5, 67; EWL 3; EXPP; FL 1:6; FW; MAL 5; MBL; MTCW 1, 2; MTFW 2005; PAB; PFS 15, 29; RGAL 4; RGHL; WP

Rich, Barbara
See Graves, Robert

Rich, Robert
See Trumbo, Dalton

Richard, Keith .... **CLC 17**
See Richards, Keith

Richards, David Adams 1950- .... **CLC 59**
See also CA 93-96; CANR 60, 110, 156; CN 7; DAC; DLB 53; TCLE 1:2

Richards, I(vor) A(rmstrong)
1893-1979 .... **CLC 14, 24**
See also BRWS 2; CA 41-44R; 89-92; CANR 34, 74; CP 1, 2; DLB 27; EWL 3; MTCW 2; RGEL 2

Richards, Keith 1943-
See Richard, Keith
See also CA 107; CANR 77

Richardson, Anne
See Roiphe, Anne

Richardson, Dorothy Miller
1873-1957 .... **TCLC 3, 203**
See also BRWS 13; CA 104; 192; DLB 36; EWL 3; FW; RGEL 2

Richardson (Robertson), Ethel Florence Lindesay 1870-1946
See Richardson, Henry Handel
See also CA 105; 190; DLB 230; RHW

Richardson, Henry Handel .... **TCLC 4**
See Richardson (Robertson), Ethel Florence Lindesay
See also DLB 197; EWL 3; RGEL 2; RGSF 2

Richardson, John 1796-1852 .... **NCLC 55**
See also CCA 1; DAC; DLB 99

Richardson, Samuel 1689-1761 ...... **LC 1, 44, 138; WLC 5**
See also BRW 3; CDBLB 1660-1789; DA; DAB; DAC; DAM MST, NOV; DLB 39; RGEL 2; TEA; WLIT 3

Richardson, Willis 1889-1977 .... **HR 1:3**
See also BW 1; CA 124; DLB 51; SATA 60

Richler, Mordecai 1931-2001 .... **CLC 3, 5, 9, 13, 18, 46, 70, 185**
See also AITN 1; CA 65-68; 201; CANR 31, 62, 111; CCA 1; CLR 17; CN 1, 2, 3, 4, 5, 7; CWRI 5; DAC; DAM MST, NOV; DLB 53; EWL 3; MAICYA 1, 2; MTCW 1, 2; MTFW 2005; RGEL 2; RGHL; SATA 44, 98; SATA-Brief 27; TWA

Richter, Conrad (Michael)
1890-1968 .... **CLC 30**
See also AAYA 21; AMWS 18; BYA 2; CA 5-8R; 25-28R; CANR 23; DLB 9, 212; LAIT 1; MAL 5; MTCW 1, 2; MTFW 2005; RGAL 4; SATA 3; TCWW 1, 2; TUS; YAW

Ricostranza, Tom
See Ellis, Trey

Riddell, Charlotte 1832-1906 .... **TCLC 40**
See Riddell, Mrs. J. H.
See also CA 165; DLB 156

Riddell, Mrs. J. H.
See Riddell, Charlotte
See also HGG; SUFW
Ridge, John Rollin 1827-1867 ...... NCLC 82; NNAL
See also CA 144; DAM MULT; DLB 175
Ridgeway, Jason
See Marlowe, Stephen
Ridgway, Keith 1965- .... CLC 119
See also CA 172; CANR 144
Riding, Laura .... CLC 3, 7
See Jackson, Laura (Riding)
See also CP 1, 2, 3, 4, 5; RGAL 4
Riefenstahl, Berta Helene Amalia 1902-2003
See Riefenstahl, Leni
See also CA 108; 220
Riefenstahl, Leni .... CLC 16, 190
See Riefenstahl, Berta Helene Amalia
Riffe, Ernest
See Bergman, Ingmar
Riffe, Ernest Ingmar
See Bergman, Ingmar
Riggs, (Rolla) Lynn
1899-1954 .... NNAL; TCLC 56
See also CA 144; DAM MULT; DLB 175
Riis, Jacob A(ugust) 1849-1914 ..... TCLC 80
See also CA 113; 168; DLB 23
Riley, James Whitcomb 1849-1916 .... PC 48; TCLC 51
See also CA 118; 137; DAM POET; MAI-CYA 1, 2; RGAL 4; SATA 17
Riley, Tex
See Creasey, John
Rilke, Rainer Maria 1875-1926 .... PC 2; TCLC 1, 6, 19, 195
See also CA 104; 132; CANR 62, 99; CD-WLB 2; DA3; DAM POET; DLB 81; EW 9; EWL 3; MTCW 1, 2; MTFW 2005; PFS 19, 27; RGWL 2, 3; TWA; WP
Rimbaud, (Jean Nicolas) Arthur
1854-1891 ... NCLC 4, 35, 82; PC 3, 57; WLC 5
See also DA; DA3; DAB; DAC; DAM MST, POET; DLB 217; EW 7; GFL 1789 to the Present; LMFS 2; PFS 28; RGWL 2, 3; TWA; WP
Rinehart, Mary Roberts
1876-1958 .... TCLC 52
See also BPFB 3; CA 108; 166; RGAL 4; RHW
Ringmaster, The
See Mencken, H(enry) L(ouis)
Ringwood, Gwen(dolyn Margaret) Pharis
1910-1984 .... CLC 48
See also CA 148; 112; DLB 88
Rio, Michel 1945(?)- .... CLC 43
See also CA 201
Rios, Alberto 1952- .... PC 57
See also AAYA 66; AMWS 4; CA 113; CANR 34, 79, 137; CP 6, 7; DLB 122; HW 2; MTFW 2005; PFS 11
Ritsos, Giannes
See Ritsos, Yannis
Ritsos, Yannis 1909-1990 .... CLC 6, 13, 31
See also CA 77-80; 133; CANR 39, 61; EW 12; EWL 3; MTCW 1; RGWL 2, 3
Ritter, Erika 1948(?)- .... CLC 52
See also CD 5, 6; CWD
Rivera, Jose Eustasio 1889-1928 ... TCLC 35
See also CA 162; EWL 3; HW 1, 2; LAW
Rivera, Tomas 1935-1984 .... HLCS 2
See also CA 49-52; CANR 32; DLB 82; HW 1; LLW; RGAL 4; SSFS 15; TCWW 2; WLIT 1
Rivers, Conrad Kent 1933-1968 .... CLC 1
See also BW 1; CA 85-88; DLB 41
Rivers, Elfrida
See Bradley, Marion Zimmer
See also GLL 1

Riverside, John
See Heinlein, Robert A.
Rizal, Jose 1861-1896 .... NCLC 27
Roa Bastos, Augusto 1917-2005 ...... CLC 45; HLC 2
See also CA 131; 238; CWW 2; DAM MULT; DLB 113; EWL 3; HW 1; LAW; RGSF 2; WLIT 1
Roa Bastos, Augusto Jose Antonio
See Roa Bastos, Augusto
Robbe-Grillet, Alain 1922-2008 ..... CLC 1, 2, 4, 6, 8, 10, 14, 43, 128
See also BPFB 3; CA 9-12R; 269; CANR 33, 65, 115; CWW 2; DLB 83; EW 13; EWL 3; GFL 1789 to the Present; IDFW 3, 4; MTCW 1, 2; MTFW 2005; RGWL 2, 3; SSFS 15
Robbins, Harold 1916-1997 .... CLC 5
See also BPFB 3; CA 73-76; 162; CANR 26, 54, 112, 156; DA3; DAM NOV; MTCW 1, 2
Robbins, Thomas Eugene 1936-
See Robbins, Tom
See also CA 81-84; CANR 29, 59, 95, 139; CN 7; CPW; CSW; DA3; DAM NOV, POP; MTCW 1, 2; MTFW 2005
Robbins, Tom .... CLC 9, 32, 64
See Robbins, Thomas Eugene
See also AAYA 32; AMWS 10; BEST 90:3; BPFB 3; CN 3, 4, 5, 6, 7; DLBY 1980
Robbins, Trina 1938- .... CLC 21
See also AAYA 61; CA 128; CANR 152
Robert de Boron fl. 12th cent. - .... CMLC 94
Roberts, Charles G(eorge) D(ouglas)
1860-1943 .... SSC 91; TCLC 8
See also CA 105; 188; CLR 33; CWRI 5; DLB 92; RGEL 2; RGSF 2; SATA 88; SATA-Brief 29
Roberts, Elizabeth Madox
1886-1941 .... TCLC 68
See also CA 111; 166; CLR 100; CWRI 5; DLB 9, 54, 102; RGAL 4; RHW; SATA 33; SATA-Brief 27; TCWW 2; WCH
Roberts, Kate 1891-1985 .... CLC 15
See also CA 107; 116; DLB 319
Roberts, Keith (John Kingston)
1935-2000 .... CLC 14
See also BRWS 10; CA 25-28R; CANR 46; DLB 261; SFW 4
Roberts, Kenneth (Lewis)
1885-1957 .... TCLC 23
See also CA 109; 199; DLB 9; MAL 5; RGAL 4; RHW
Roberts, Michele 1949- .... CLC 48, 178
See also CA 115; CANR 58, 120, 164; CN 6, 7; DLB 231; FW
Roberts, Michele Brigitte
See Roberts, Michele
Robertson, Ellis
See Ellison, Harlan; Silverberg, Robert
Robertson, Thomas William
1829-1871 .... NCLC 35
See Robertson, Tom
See also DAM DRAM; DLB 344
Robertson, Tom
See Robertson, Thomas William
See also RGEL 2
Robeson, Kenneth
See Dent, Lester
Robinson, Edwin Arlington
1869-1935 .... PC 1, 35; TCLC 5, 101
See also AAYA 72; AMW; CA 104; 133; CDALB 1865-1917; DA; DAC; DAM MST, POET; DLB 54; EWL 3; EXPP; MAL 5; MTCW 1, 2; MTFW 2005; PAB; PFS 4; RGAL 4; WP
Robinson, Henry Crabb
1775-1867 .... NCLC 15
See also DLB 107

Robinson, Jill 1936- .... CLC 10
See also CA 102; CANR 120; INT CA-102
Robinson, Kim Stanley 1952- ... CLC 34, 248
See also AAYA 26; CA 126; CANR 113, 139, 173; CN 6, 7; MTFW 2005; SATA 109; SCFW 2; SFW 4
Robinson, Lloyd
See Silverberg, Robert
Robinson, Marilynne 1944- ...... CLC 25, 180
See also AAYA 69; CA 116; CANR 80, 140; CN 4, 5, 6, 7; DLB 206; MTFW 2005; NFS 24
Robinson, Mary 1758-1800 .... NCLC 142
See also BRWS 13; DLB 158; FW
Robinson, Smokey .... CLC 21
See Robinson, William, Jr.
Robinson, William, Jr. 1940-
See Robinson, Smokey
See also CA 116
Robison, Mary 1949- .... CLC 42, 98
See also CA 113; 116; CANR 87; CN 4, 5, 6, 7; DLB 130; INT CA-116; RGSF 2
Roches, Catherine des 1542-1587 ...... LC 117
See also DLB 327
Rochester
See Wilmot, John
See also RGEL 2
Rod, Edouard 1857-1910 .... TCLC 52
Roddenberry, Eugene Wesley 1921-1991
See Roddenberry, Gene
See also CA 110; 135; CANR 37; SATA 45; SATA-Obit 69
Roddenberry, Gene .... CLC 17
See Roddenberry, Eugene Wesley
See also AAYA 5; SATA-Obit 69
Rodgers, Mary 1931- .... CLC 12
See also BYA 5; CA 49-52; CANR 8, 55, 90; CLR 20; CWRI 5; INT CANR-8; JRDA; MAICYA 1, 2; SATA 8, 130
Rodgers, W(illiam) R(obert)
1909-1969 .... CLC 7
See also CA 85-88; DLB 20; RGEL 2
Rodman, Eric
See Silverberg, Robert
Rodman, Howard 1920(?)-1985 .... CLC 65
See also CA 118
Rodman, Maia
See Wojciechowska, Maia (Teresa)
Rodo, Jose Enrique 1871(?)-1917 .... HLCS 2
See also CA 178; EWL 3; HW 2; LAW
Rodolph, Utto
See Ouologuem, Yambo
Rodriguez, Claudio 1934-1999 .... CLC 10
See also CA 188; DLB 134
Rodriguez, Richard 1944- .... CLC 155; HLC 2
See also AMWS 14; CA 110; CANR 66, 116; DAM MULT; DLB 82, 256; HW 1, 2; LAIT 5; LLW; MTFW 2005; NCFS 3; WLIT 1
Roethke, Theodore 1908-1963 ... CLC 1, 3, 8, 11, 19, 46, 101; PC 15
See also AMW; CA 81-84; CABS 2; CDALB 1941-1968; DA3; DAM POET; DLB 5, 206; EWL 3; EXPP; MAL 5; MTCW 1, 2; PAB; PFS 3; RGAL 4; WP
Roethke, Theodore Huebner
See Roethke, Theodore
Rogers, Carl R(ansom)
1902-1987 .... TCLC 125
See also CA 1-4R; 121; CANR 1, 18; MTCW 1
Rogers, Samuel 1763-1855 .... NCLC 69
See also DLB 93; RGEL 2
Rogers, Thomas 1927-2007 .... CLC 57
See also CA 89-92; 259; CANR 163; INT CA-89-92
Rogers, Thomas Hunton
See Rogers, Thomas

Sartre, Jean-Paul 1905-1980 . **CLC 1, 4, 7, 9, 13, 18, 24, 44, 50, 52; DC 3; SSC 32; WLC 5**
See also AAYA 62; CA 9-12R; 97-100; CANR 21; DA; DA3; DAB; DAC; DAM DRAM, MST, NOV; DFS 5; DLB 72, 296, 321, 332; EW 12; EWL 3; GFL 1789 to the Present; LMFS 2; MTCW 1, 2; MTFW 2005; NFS 21; RGHL; RGSF 2; RGWL 2, 3; SSFS 9; TWA

Sassoon, Siegfried (Lorraine) 1886-1967 .... **CLC 36, 130; PC 12**
See also BRW 6; CA 104; 25-28R; CANR 36; DAB; DAM MST, NOV, POET; DLB 20, 191; DLBD 18; EWL 3; MTCW 1, 2; MTFW 2005; PAB; PFS 28; RGEL 2; TEA

Satterfield, Charles
See Pohl, Frederik

Satyremont
See Peret, Benjamin

Saul, John III
See Saul, John

Saul, John 1942- .... **CLC 46**
See also AAYA 10, 62; BEST 90:4; CA 81-84; CANR 16, 40, 81, 176; CPW; DAM NOV, POP; HGG; SATA 98

Saul, John W.
See Saul, John

Saul, John W. III
See Saul, John

Saul, John Woodruff III
See Saul, John

Saunders, Caleb
See Heinlein, Robert A.

Saura (Atares), Carlos 1932-1998 .... **CLC 20**
See also CA 114; 131; CANR 79; HW 1

Sauser, Frederic Louis
See Sauser-Hall, Frederic

Sauser-Hall, Frederic 1887-1961 ...... **CLC 18**
See Cendrars, Blaise
See also CA 102; 93-96; CANR 36, 62; MTCW 1

Saussure, Ferdinand de 1857-1913 .... **TCLC 49**
See also DLB 242

Savage, Catharine
See Brosman, Catharine Savage

Savage, Richard 1697(?)-1743 .... **LC 96**
See also DLB 95; RGEL 2

Savage, Thomas 1915-2003 .... **CLC 40**
See also CA 126; 132; 218; CAAS 15; CN 6, 7; INT CA-132; SATA-Obit 147; TCWW 2

Savan, Glenn 1953-2003 .... **CLC 50**
See also CA 225

Savonarola, Girolamo 1452-1498 ...... **LC 152**
See also LMFS 1

Sax, Robert
See Johnson, Robert

Saxo Grammaticus c. 1150-c. 1222 .... **CMLC 58**

Saxton, Robert
See Johnson, Robert

Sayers, Dorothy L(eigh) 1893-1957 . **SSC 71; TCLC 2, 15**
See also BPFB 3; BRWS 3; CA 104; 119; CANR 60; CDBLB 1914-1945; CMW 4; DAM POP; DLB 10, 36, 77, 100; MSW; MTCW 1, 2; MTFW 2005; RGEL 2; SSFS 12; TEA

Sayers, Valerie 1952- .... **CLC 50, 122**
See also CA 134; CANR 61; CSW

Sayles, John (Thomas) 1950- .... **CLC 7, 10, 14, 198**
See also CA 57-60; CANR 41, 84; DLB 44

Scamander, Newt
See Rowling, J.K.

Scammell, Michael 1935- .... **CLC 34**
See also CA 156

Scannel, John Vernon
See Scannell, Vernon

Scannell, Vernon 1922-2007 .... **CLC 49**
See also CA 5-8R; 266; CANR 8, 24, 57, 143; CN 1, 2; CP 1, 2, 3, 4, 5, 6, 7; CWRI 5; DLB 27; SATA 59; SATA-Obit 188

Scarlett, Susan
See Streatfeild, Noel

Scarron 1847-1910
See Mikszath, Kalman

Scarron, Paul 1610-1660 .... **LC 116**
See also GFL Beginnings to 1789; RGWL 2, 3

Schaeffer, Susan Fromberg 1941- ..... **CLC 6, 11, 22**
See also CA 49-52; CANR 18, 65, 160; CN 4, 5, 6, 7; DLB 28, 299; MTCW 1, 2; MTFW 2005; SATA 22

Schama, Simon 1945- .... **CLC 150**
See also BEST 89:4; CA 105; CANR 39, 91, 168

Schama, Simon Michael
See Schama, Simon

Schary, Jill
See Robinson, Jill

Schell, Jonathan 1943- .... **CLC 35**
See also CA 73-76; CANR 12, 117

Schelling, Friedrich Wilhelm Joseph von 1775-1854 .... **NCLC 30**
See also DLB 90

Scherer, Jean-Marie Maurice 1920-
See Rohmer, Eric
See also CA 110

Schevill, James (Erwin) 1920- .... **CLC 7**
See also CA 5-8R; CAAS 12; CAD; CD 5, 6; CP 1, 2, 3, 4, 5

Schiller, Friedrich von 1759-1805 ...... **DC 12; NCLC 39, 69, 166**
See also CDWLB 2; DAM DRAM; DLB 94; EW 5; RGWL 2, 3; TWA

Schisgal, Murray (Joseph) 1926- .... **CLC 6**
See also CA 21-24R; CAD; CANR 48, 86; CD 5, 6; MAL 5

Schlee, Ann 1934- .... **CLC 35**
See also CA 101; CANR 29, 88; SATA 44; SATA-Brief 36

Schlegel, August Wilhelm von 1767-1845 .... **NCLC 15, 142**
See also DLB 94; RGWL 2, 3

Schlegel, Friedrich 1772-1829 .... **NCLC 45**
See also DLB 90; EW 5; RGWL 2, 3; TWA

Schlegel, Johann Elias (von) 1719(?)-1749 .... **LC 5**

Schleiermacher, Friedrich 1768-1834 .... **NCLC 107**
See also DLB 90

Schlesinger, Arthur M., Jr. 1917-2007 .... **CLC 84**
See Schlesinger, Arthur Meier
See also AITN 1; CA 1-4R; 257; CANR 1, 28, 58, 105; DLB 17; INT CANR-28; MTCW 1, 2; SATA 61; SATA-Obit 181

Schlink, Bernhard 1944- .... **CLC 174**
See also CA 163; CANR 116, 175; RGHL

Schmidt, Arno (Otto) 1914-1979 ...... **CLC 56**
See also CA 128; 109; DLB 69; EWL 3

Schmitz, Aron Hector 1861-1928
See Svevo, Italo
See also CA 104; 122; MTCW 1

Schnackenberg, Gjertrud 1953- ...... **CLC 40; PC 45**
See also AMWS 15; CA 116; CANR 100; CP 5, 6, 7; CWP; DLB 120, 282; PFS 13, 25

Schnackenberg, Gjertrud Cecelia
See Schnackenberg, Gjertrud

Schneider, Leonard Alfred 1925-1966
See Bruce, Lenny
See also CA 89-92

Schnitzler, Arthur 1862-1931 ..... **DC 17; SSC 15, 61; TCLC 4**
See also CA 104; CDWLB 2; DLB 81, 118; EW 8; EWL 3; RGSF 2; RGWL 2, 3

Schoenberg, Arnold Franz Walter 1874-1951 .... **TCLC 75**
See also CA 109; 188

Schonberg, Arnold
See Schoenberg, Arnold Franz Walter

Schopenhauer, Arthur 1788-1860 . **NCLC 51, 157**
See also DLB 90; EW 5

Schor, Sandra (M.) 1932(?)-1990 ..... **CLC 65**
See also CA 132

Schorer, Mark 1908-1977 .... **CLC 9**
See also CA 5-8R; 73-76; CANR 7; CN 1, 2; DLB 103

Schrader, Paul (Joseph) 1946- . **CLC 26, 212**
See also CA 37-40R; CANR 41; DLB 44

Schreber, Daniel 1842-1911 .... **TCLC 123**

Schreiner, Olive (Emilie Albertina) 1855-1920 .... **TCLC 9**
See also AFW; BRWS 2; CA 105; 154; DLB 18, 156, 190, 225; EWL 3; FW; RGEL 2; TWA; WLIT 2; WWE 1

Schulberg, Budd 1914- .... **CLC 7, 48**
See also AMWS 18; BPFB 3; CA 25-28R; CANR 19, 87, 178; CN 1, 2, 3, 4, 5, 6, 7; DLB 6, 26, 28; DLBY 1981, 2001; MAL 5

Schulberg, Budd Wilson
See Schulberg, Budd

Schulman, Arnold
See Trumbo, Dalton

Schulz, Bruno 1892-1942 .. **SSC 13; TCLC 5, 51**
See also CA 115; 123; CANR 86; CDWLB 4; DLB 215; EWL 3; MTCW 2; MTFW 2005; RGSF 2; RGWL 2, 3

Schulz, Charles M. 1922-2000 .... **CLC 12**
See also AAYA 39; CA 9-12R; 187; CANR 6, 132; INT CANR-6; MTFW 2005; SATA 10; SATA-Obit 118

Schulz, Charles Monroe
See Schulz, Charles M.

Schumacher, E(rnst) F(riedrich) 1911-1977 .... **CLC 80**
See also CA 81-84; 73-76; CANR 34, 85

Schumann, Robert 1810-1856 ...... **NCLC 143**

Schuyler, George Samuel 1895-1977 . **HR 1:3**
See also BW 2; CA 81-84; 73-76; CANR 42; DLB 29, 51

Schuyler, James Marcus 1923-1991 .. **CLC 5, 23; PC 88**
See also CA 101; 134; CP 1, 2, 3, 4, 5; DAM POET; DLB 5, 169; EWL 3; INT CA-101; MAL 5; WP

Schwartz, Delmore (David) 1913-1966 . **CLC 2, 4, 10, 45, 87; PC 8; SSC 105**
See also AMWS 2; CA 17-18; 25-28R; CANR 35; CAP 2; DLB 28, 48; EWL 3; MAL 5; MTCW 1, 2; MTFW 2005; PAB; RGAL 4; TUS

Schwartz, Ernst
See Ozu, Yasujiro

Schwartz, John Burnham 1965- .... **CLC 59**
See also CA 132; CANR 116

Schwartz, Lynne Sharon 1939- .... **CLC 31**
See also CA 103; CANR 44, 89, 160; DLB 218; MTCW 2; MTFW 2005

Schwartz, Muriel A.
See Eliot, T(homas) S(tearns)

Schwarz-Bart, Andre 1928-2006 .... **CLC 2, 4**
See also CA 89-92; 253; CANR 109; DLB 299; RGHL

Sexton, Anne (Harvey) 1928-1974 ..... **CLC 2,**
  4, 6, 8, 10, 15, 53, 123; PC 2, 79; WLC
  5
    See also AMWS 2; CA 1-4R; 53-56; CABS
    2; CANR 3, 36; CDALB 1941-1968; CP
    1, 2; DA; DA3; DAB; DAC; DAM MST;
    POET; DLB 5, 169; EWL 3; EXPP; FL
    1:6; FW; MAL 5; MBL; MTCW 1, 2;
    MTFW 2005; PAB; PFS 4, 14; RGAL 4;
    RGHL; SATA 10; TUS
Shaara, Jeff 1952- .... **CLC 119**
    See also AAYA 70; CA 163; CANR 109,
    172; CN 7; MTFW 2005
Shaara, Michael 1929-1988 .... **CLC 15**
    See also AAYA 71; AITN 1; BPFB 3; CA
    102; 125; CANR 52, 85; DAM POP;
    DLBY 1983; MTFW 2005; NFS 26
Shackleton, C.C.
    See Aldiss, Brian W.
Shacochis, Bob .... **CLC 39**
    See Shacochis, Robert G.
Shacochis, Robert G. 1951-
    See Shacochis, Bob
    See also CA 119; 124; CANR 100; INT CA-
    124
Shadwell, Thomas 1641(?)-1692 .... **LC 114**
    See also DLB 80; IDTP; RGEL 2
Shaffer, Anthony 1926-2001 .... **CLC 19**
    See also CA 110; 116; 200; CBD; CD 5, 6;
    DAM DRAM; DFS 13; DLB 13
Shaffer, Anthony Joshua
    See Shaffer, Anthony
Shaffer, Peter 1926- ... **CLC 5, 14, 18, 37, 60;**
  DC 7
    See also BRWS 1; CA 25-28R; CANR 25,
    47, 74, 118; CBD; CD 5, 6; CDBLB 1960
    to Present; DA3; DAB; DAM DRAM,
    MST; DFS 5, 13; DLB 13, 233; EWL 3;
    MTCW 1, 2; MTFW 2005; RGEL 2; TEA
Shakespeare, William 1564-1616 . **PC 84, 89;**
  WLC 5
    See also AAYA 35; BRW 1; CDBLB Be-
    fore 1660; DA; DA3; DAB; DAC; DAM
    DRAM, MST, POET; DFS 20, 21; DLB
    62, 172, 263; EXPP; LAIT 1; LATS 1:1;
    LMFS 1; PAB; PFS 1, 2, 3, 4, 5, 8, 9;
    RGEL 2; TEA; WLIT 3; WP; WS; WYA
Shakey, Bernard
    See Young, Neil
Shalamov, Varlam (Tikhonovich)
    1907-1982 .... **CLC 18**
    See also CA 129; 105; DLB 302; RGSF 2
Shamloo, Ahmad
    See Shamlu, Ahmad
Shamlou, Ahmad
    See Shamlu, Ahmad
Shamlu, Ahmad 1925-2000 .... **CLC 10**
    See also CA 216; CWW 2
Shammas, Anton 1951- .... **CLC 55**
    See also CA 199; DLB 346
Shandling, Arline
    See Berriault, Gina
Shange, Ntozake 1948- .. **BLC 1:3, 2:3; CLC**
  8, 25, 38, 74, 126; DC 3
    See also AAYA 9, 66; AFAW 1, 2; BW 2;
    CA 85-88; CABS 3; CAD; CANR 27, 48,
    74, 131; CD 5, 6; CP 5, 6, 7; CWD; CWP;
    DA3; DAM DRAM, MULT; DFS 2, 11;
    DLB 38, 249; FW; LAIT 4, 5; MAL 5;
    MTCW 1, 2; MTFW 2005; NFS 11;
    RGAL 4; SATA 157; YAW
Shanley, John Patrick 1950- .... **CLC 75**
    See also AAYA 74; AMWS 14; CA 128;
    133; CAD; CANR 83, 154; CD 5, 6; DFS
    23
Shapcott, Thomas W(illiam) 1935- .. **CLC 38**
    See also CA 69-72; CANR 49, 83, 103; CP
    1, 2, 3, 4, 5, 6, 7; DLB 289

Shapiro, Jane 1942- .... **CLC 76**
    See also CA 196
Shapiro, Karl 1913-2000 ... **CLC 4, 8, 15, 53;**
  PC 25
    See also AMWS 2; CA 1-4R; 188; CAAS
    6; CANR 1, 36, 66; CP 1, 2, 3, 4, 5, 6;
    DLB 48; EWL 3; EXPP; MAL 5; MTCW
    1, 2; MTFW 2005; PFS 3; RGAL 4
Sharp, William 1855-1905 .... **TCLC 39**
    See Macleod, Fiona
    See also CA 160; DLB 156; RGEL 2
Sharpe, Thomas Ridley 1928-
    See Sharpe, Tom
    See also CA 114; 122; CANR 85; INT CA-
    122
Sharpe, Tom .... **CLC 36**
    See Sharpe, Thomas Ridley
    See also CN 4, 5, 6, 7; DLB 14, 231
Shatrov, Mikhail .... **CLC 59**
Shaw, Bernard
    See Shaw, George Bernard
    See also DLB 10, 57, 190
Shaw, G. Bernard
    See Shaw, George Bernard
Shaw, George Bernard 1856-1950 ..... **DC 23;**
  TCLC 3, 9, 21, 45, 205; WLC 5
    See Shaw, Bernard
    See also AAYA 61; BRW 6; BRWC 1;
    BRWR 2; CA 104; 128; CDBLB 1914-
    1945; DA; DA3; DAB; DAC; DAM
    DRAM, MST; DFS 1, 3, 6, 11, 19, 22;
    DLB 332; EWL 3; LAIT 3; LATS 1:1;
    MTCW 1, 2; MTFW 2005; RGEL 2;
    TEA; WLIT 4
Shaw, Henry Wheeler 1818-1885 .. **NCLC 15**
    See also DLB 11; RGAL 4
Shaw, Irwin 1913-1984 .... **CLC 7, 23, 34**
    See also AITN 1; BPFB 3; CA 13-16R; 112;
    CANR 21; CDALB 1941-1968; CN 1, 2,
    3; CPW; DAM DRAM, POP; DLB 6,
    102; DLBY 1984; MAL 5; MTCW 1, 21;
    MTFW 2005
Shaw, Robert (Archibald)
    1927-1978 .... **CLC 5**
    See also AITN 1; CA 1-4R; 81-84; CANR
    4; CN 1, 2; DLB 13, 14
Shaw, T. E.
    See Lawrence, T(homas) E(dward)
Shawn, Wallace 1943- .... **CLC 41**
    See also CA 112; CAD; CD 5, 6; DLB 266
Shaykh, al- Hanan
    See al-Shaykh, Hanan
Shchedrin, N.
    See Saltykov, Mikhail Evgrafovich
Shea, Lisa 1953- .... **CLC 86**
    See also CA 147
Sheed, Wilfrid 1930- .... **CLC 2, 4, 10, 53**
    See also CA 65-68; CANR 30, 66, 181; CN
    1, 2, 3, 4, 5, 6, 7; DLB 6; MAL 5; MTCW
    1, 2; MTFW 2005
Sheed, Wilfrid John Joseph
    See Sheed, Wilfrid
Sheehy, Gail 1937- .... **CLC 171**
    See also CA 49-52; CANR 1, 33, 55, 92;
    CPW; MTCW 1
Sheldon, Alice Hastings Bradley
    1915(?)-1987
    See Tiptree, James, Jr.
    See also CA 108; 122; CANR 34; INT CA-
    108; MTCW 1
Sheldon, John
    See Bloch, Robert (Albert)
Sheldon, Walter J(ames) 1917-1996
    See Queen, Ellery
    See also AITN 1; CA 25-28R; CANR 10

Shelley, Mary Wollstonecraft (Godwin)
    1797-1851 .... **NCLC 14, 59, 103, 170;**
  SSC 92; WLC 5
    See also AAYA 20; BPFB 3; BRW 3;
    BRWC 2; BRWS 3; BYA 5; CDBLB
    1789-1832; CLR 133; DA; DA3; DAB;
    DAC; DAM MST, NOV; DLB 110, 116,
    159, 178; EXPN; FL 1:3; GL 3; HGG;
    LAIT 1; LMFS 1, 2; NFS 1; RGEL 2;
    SATA 29; SCFW 1, 2; SFW 4; TEA;
    WLIT 3
Shelley, Percy Bysshe 1792-1822 .. **NCLC 18,**
  93, 143, 175; PC 14, 67; WLC 5
    See also AAYA 61; BRW 4; BRWR 1; CD-
    BLB 1789-1832; DA; DA3; DAB; DAC;
    DAM MST, POET; DLB 96, 110, 158;
    EXPP; LMFS 1; PAB; PFS 2, 27; RGEL
    2; TEA; WLIT 3; WP
Shepard, James R.
    See Shepard, Jim
Shepard, Jim 1956- .... **CLC 36**
    See also AAYA 73; CA 137; CANR 59, 104,
    160; SATA 90, 164
Shepard, Lucius 1947- .... **CLC 34**
    See also CA 128; 141; CANR 81, 124, 178;
    HGG; SCFW 2; SFW 4; SUFW 2
Shepard, Sam 1943- .... **CLC 4, 6, 17, 34, 41,**
  44, 169; DC 5
    See also AAYA 1, 58; AMWS 3; CA 69-72;
    CABS 3; CAD; CANR 22, 120, 140; CD
    5, 6; DA3; DAM DRAM; DFS 3, 6, 7,
    14; DLB 7, 212, 341; EWL 3; IDFW 3, 4;
    MAL 5; MTCW 1, 2; MTFW 2005;
    RGAL 4
Shepherd, Jean (Parker)
    1921-1999 .... **TCLC 177**
    See also AAYA 69; AITN 2; CA 77-80; 187
Shepherd, Michael
    See Ludlum, Robert
Sherburne, Zoa (Lillian Morin)
    1912-1995 .... **CLC 30**
    See also AAYA 13; CA 1-4R; 176; CANR
    3, 37; MAICYA 1, 2; SAAS 18; SATA 3;
    YAW
Sheridan, Frances 1724-1766 .... **LC 7**
    See also DLB 39, 84
Sheridan, Richard Brinsley
    1751-1816 . **DC 1; NCLC 5, 91; WLC 5**
    See also BRW 3; CDBLB 1660-1789; DA;
    DAB; DAC; DAM DRAM, MST; DFS
    15; DLB 89; WLIT 3
Sherman, Jonathan Marc 1968- .... **CLC 55**
    See also CA 230
Sherman, Martin 1941(?)- .... **CLC 19**
    See also CA 116; 123; CAD; CANR 86;
    CD 5, 6; DFS 20; DLB 228; GLL 1;
    IDTP; RGHL
Sherwin, Judith Johnson
    See Johnson, Judith (Emlyn)
    See also CANR 85; CP 2, 3, 4, 5; CWP
Sherwood, Frances 1940- .... **CLC 81**
    See also CA 146; 220; CAAE 220; CANR
    158
Sherwood, Robert E(mmet)
    1896-1955 .... **TCLC 3**
    See also CA 104; 153; CANR 86; DAM
    DRAM; DFS 11, 15, 17; DLB 7, 26, 249;
    IDFW 3, 4; MAL 5; RGAL 4
Shestov, Lev 1866-1938 .... **TCLC 56**
Shevchenko, Taras 1814-1861 .... **NCLC 54**
Shiel, M(atthew) P(hipps)
    1865-1947 .... **TCLC 8**
    See Holmes, Gordon
    See also CA 106; 160; DLB 153; HGG;
    MTCW 2; MTFW 2005; SCFW 1, 2;
    SFW 4; SUFW

Smith, Martin Cruz 1942- .. **CLC 25; NNAL**
See Smith, Martin Cruz
See also BEST 89:4; BPFB 3; CA 85-88;
CANR 6, 23, 43, 65, 119, 184; CMW 4;
CPW; DAM MULT, POP; HGG; INT
CANR-23; MTCW 2; MTFW 2005;
RGAL 4

Smith, Patti 1946- .... **CLC 12**
See also CA 93-96; CANR 63, 168

Smith, Pauline (Urmson)
1882-1959 .... **TCLC 25**
See also DLB 225; EWL 3

Smith, Rosamond
See Oates, Joyce Carol

Smith, Seba 1792-1868 .... **NCLC 187**
See also DLB 1, 11, 243

Smith, Sheila Kaye
See Kaye-Smith, Sheila

Smith, Stevie 1902-1971 .... **CLC 3, 8, 25, 44;
PC 12**
See also BRWS 2; CA 17-18; 29-32R;
CANR 35; CAP 2; CP 1; DAM POET;
DLB 20; EWL 3; MTCW 1, 2; PAB; PFS
3; RGEL 2; TEA

Smith, Wilbur 1933- .... **CLC 33**
See also CA 13-16R; CANR 7, 46, 66, 134,
180; CPW; MTCW 1, 2; MTFW 2005

Smith, Wilbur Addison
See Smith, Wilbur

Smith, William Jay 1918- .... **CLC 6**
See also AMWS 13; CA 5-8R; CANR 44,
106; CP 1, 2, 3, 4, 5, 6, 7; CSW; CWRI
5; DLB 5; MAICYA 1, 2; SAAS 22;
SATA 2, 68, 154; SATA-Essay 154; TCLE
1:2

Smith, Woodrow Wilson
See Kuttner, Henry

Smith, Zadie 1975- .... **CLC 158**
See also AAYA 50; CA 193; MTFW 2005

Smolenskin, Peretz 1842-1885 .... **NCLC 30**

Smollett, Tobias (George) 1721-1771 ... **LC 2,
46**
See also BRW 3; CDBLB 1660-1789; DLB
39, 104; RGEL 2; TEA

Snodgrass, W.D. 1926- .... **CLC 2, 6, 10, 18,
68; PC 74**
See also AMWS 6; CA 1-4R; CANR 6, 36,
65, 85, 185; CP 1, 2, 3, 4, 5, 6, 7; DAM
POET; DLB 5; MAL 5; MTCW 1, 2;
MTFW 2005; PFS 29; RGAL 4; TCLE
1:2

Snodgrass, William De Witt
See Snodgrass, W.D.

Snorri Sturluson 1179-1241 .... **CMLC 56**
See also RGWL 2, 3

Snow, C(harles) P(ercy) 1905-1980 ... **CLC 1,
4, 6, 9, 13, 19**
See also BRW 7; CA 5-8R; 101; CANR 28;
CDBLB 1945-1960; CN 1, 2; DAM NOV;
DLB 15, 77; DLBD 17; EWL 3; MTCW
1, 2; MTFW 2005; RGEL 2; TEA

Snow, Frances Compton
See Adams, Henry (Brooks)

Snyder, Gary 1930- . **CLC 1, 2, 5, 9, 32, 120;
PC 21**
See also AAYA 72; AMWS 8; ANW; BG
1:3; CA 17-20R; CANR 30, 60, 125; CP
1, 2, 3, 4, 5, 6, 7; DA3; DAM POET; DLB
5, 16, 165, 212, 237, 275, 342; EWL 3;
MAL 5; MTCW 2; MTFW 2005; PFS 9,
19; RGAL 4; WP

Snyder, Zilpha Keatley 1927- .... **CLC 17**
See also AAYA 15; BYA 1; CA 9-12R, 252;
CAAE 252; CANR 38; CLR 31, 121;
JRDA; MAICYA 1, 2; SAAS 2; SATA 1,
28, 75, 110, 163; SATA-Essay 112, 163;
YAW

Soares, Bernardo
See Pessoa, Fernando

Sobh, A.
See Shamlu, Ahmad

Sobh, Alef
See Shamlu, Ahmad

Sobol, Joshua 1939- .... **CLC 60**
See Sobol, Yehoshua
See also CA 200; RGHL

Sobol, Yehoshua 1939-
See Sobol, Joshua
See also CWW 2

Socrates 470B.C.-399B.C. .... **CMLC 27**

Soderberg, Hjalmar 1869-1941 ...... **TCLC 39**
See also DLB 259; EWL 3; RGSF 2

Soderbergh, Steven 1963- .... **CLC 154**
See also AAYA 43; CA 243

Soderbergh, Steven Andrew
See Soderbergh, Steven

Sodergran, Edith (Irene) 1892-1923
See Soedergran, Edith (Irene)
See also CA 202; DLB 259; EW 11; EWL
3; RGWL 2, 3

Soedergran, Edith (Irene)
1892-1923 .... **TCLC 31**
See Sodergran, Edith (Irene)

Softly, Edgar
See Lovecraft, H. P.

Softly, Edward
See Lovecraft, H. P.

Sokolov, Alexander V(sevolodovich) 1943-
See Sokolov, Sasha
See also CA 73-76

Sokolov, Raymond 1941- .... **CLC 7**
See also CA 85-88

Sokolov, Sasha .... **CLC 59**
See Sokolov, Alexander V(sevolodovich)
See also CWW 2; DLB 285; EWL 3; RGWL
2, 3

Solo, Jay
See Ellison, Harlan

Sologub, Fyodor .... **TCLC 9**
See Teternikov, Fyodor Kuzmich
See also EWL 3

Solomons, Ikey Esquir
See Thackeray, William Makepeace

Solomos, Dionysios 1798-1857 .... **NCLC 15**

Solwoska, Mara
See French, Marilyn

Solzhenitsyn, Aleksandr 1918-2008 ... **CLC 1,
2, 4, 7, 9, 10, 18, 26, 34, 78, 134, 235;
SSC 32, 105; WLC 5**
See Solzhenitsyn, Aleksandr Isayevich
See also AAYA 49; AITN 1; BPFB 3; CA
69-72; CANR 40, 65, 116; DA; DA3;
DAB; DAC; DAM MST, NOV; DLB 302,
332; EW 13; EXPS; LAIT 4; MTCW 1,
2; MTFW 2005; NFS 6; RGSF 2; RGWL
2, 3; SSFS 9; TWA

Solzhenitsyn, Aleksandr I.
See Solzhenitsyn, Aleksandr

Solzhenitsyn, Aleksandr Isayevich
See Solzhenitsyn, Aleksandr
See also CWW 2; EWL 3

Somers, Jane
See Lessing, Doris

Somerville, Edith Oenone
1858-1949 .... **SSC 56; TCLC 51**
See also CA 196; DLB 135; RGEL 2; RGSF
2

Somerville & Ross
See Martin, Violet Florence; Somerville,
Edith Oenone

Sommer, Scott 1951- .... **CLC 25**
See also CA 106

Sommers, Christina Hoff 1950- ...... **CLC 197**
See also CA 153; CANR 95

Sondheim, Stephen 1930- .. **CLC 30, 39, 147;
DC 22**
See also AAYA 11, 66; CA 103; CANR 47,
67, 125; DAM DRAM; DFS 25; LAIT 4

Sondheim, Stephen Joshua
See Sondheim, Stephen

Sone, Monica 1919- .... **AAL**
See also DLB 312

Song, Cathy 1955- .... **AAL; PC 21**
See also CA 154; CANR 118; CWP; DLB
169, 312; EXPP; FW; PFS 5

Sontag, Susan 1933-2004 ... **CLC 1, 2, 10, 13,
31, 105, 195**
See also AMWS 3; CA 17-20R; 234; CANR
25, 51, 74, 97, 184; CN 1, 2, 3, 4, 5, 6, 7;
CPW; DA3; DAM POP; DLB 2, 67; EWL
3; MAL 5; MBL; MTCW 1, 2; MTFW
2005; RGAL 4; RHW; SSFS 10

Sophocles 496(?)B.C.-406(?)B.C. .... **CMLC 2,
47, 51, 86; DC 1; WLCS**
See also AW 1; CDWLB 1; DA; DA3;
DAB; DAC; DAM DRAM, MST; DFS 1,
4, 8, 24; DLB 176; LAIT 1; LATS 1:1;
LMFS 1; RGWL 2, 3; TWA; WLIT 8

Sordello 1189-1269 .... **CMLC 15**

Sorel, Georges 1847-1922 .... **TCLC 91**
See also CA 118; 188

Sorel, Julia
See Drexler, Rosalyn

Sorokin, Vladimir .... **CLC 59**
See Sorokin, Vladimir Georgievich
See also CA 258

Sorokin, Vladimir Georgievich
See Sorokin, Vladimir
See also DLB 285

Sorrentino, Gilbert 1929-2006 .... **CLC 3, 7,
14, 22, 40, 247**
See also CA 77-80; 250; CANR 14, 33, 115,
157; CN 3, 4, 5, 6, 7; CP 1, 2, 3, 4, 5, 6,
7; DLB 5, 173; DLBY 1980; INT
CANR-14

Soseki
See Natsume, Soseki
See also MJW

Soto, Gary 1952- ... **CLC 32, 80; HLC 2; PC
28**
See also AAYA 10, 37; BYA 11; CA 119;
125; CANR 50, 74, 107, 157; CLR 38;
CP 4, 5, 6, 7; DAM MULT; DLB 82;
EWL 3; EXPP; HW 1, 2; INT CA-125;
JRDA; LLW; MAICYA 2; MAICYAS 1;
MAL 5; MTCW 2; MTFW 2005; PFS 7;
RGAL 4; SATA 80, 120, 174; WYA; YAW

Soupault, Philippe 1897-1990 .... **CLC 68**
See also CA 116; 147; 131; EWL 3; GFL
1789 to the Present; LMFS 2

Souster, (Holmes) Raymond 1921- .... **CLC 5,
14**
See also CA 13-16R; CAAS 14; CANR 13,
29, 53; CP 1, 2, 3, 4, 5, 6, 7; DA3; DAC;
DAM POET; DLB 88; RGEL 2; SATA 63

Southern, Terry 1924(?)-1995 .... **CLC 7**
See also AMWS 11; BPFB 3; CA 1-4R;
150; CANR 1, 55, 107; CN 1, 2, 3, 4, 5,
6; DLB 2; IDFW 3, 4

Southerne, Thomas 1660-1746 .... **LC 99**
See also DLB 80; RGEL 2

Southey, Robert 1774-1843 .... **NCLC 8, 97**
See also BRW 4; DLB 93, 107, 142; RGEL
2; SATA 54

Southwell, Robert 1561(?)-1595 .... **LC 108**
See also DLB 167; RGEL 2; TEA

Southworth, Emma Dorothy Eliza Nevitte
1819-1899 .... **NCLC 26**
See also DLB 239

Souza, Ernest
See Scott, Evelyn

Soyinka, Wole 1934- .. **BLC 1:3, 2:3; CLC 3,
5, 14, 36, 44, 179; DC 2; WLC 5**
See also AFW; BW 2, 3; CA 13-16R;
CANR 27, 39, 82, 136; CD 5, 6; CDWLB
3; CN 6, 7; CP 1, 2, 3, 4, 5, 6 ,7; DA;
DA3; DAB; DAC; DAM DRAM, MST,

MULT; DFS 10; DLB 125, 332; EWL 3; MTCW 1, 2; MTFW 2005; PFS 27; RGEL 2; TWA; WLIT 2; WWE 1

Spackman, W(illiam) M(ode)
1905-1990 .... **CLC 46**
See also CA 81-84; 132

Spacks, Barry (Bernard) 1931- .... **CLC 14**
See also CA 154; CANR 33, 109; CP 3, 4, 5, 6, 7; DLB 105

Spanidou, Irini 1946- .... **CLC 44**
See also CA 185; CANR 179

Spark, Muriel 1918-2006 .... **CLC 2, 3, 5, 8, 13, 18, 40, 94, 242; PC 72; SSC 10, 115**
See also BRWS 1; CA 5-8R; 251; CANR 12, 36, 76, 89, 131; CDBLB 1945-1960; CN 1, 2, 3, 4, 5, 6, 7; CP 1, 2, 3, 4, 5, 6, 7; DA3; DAB; DAC; DAM MST, NOV; DLB 15, 139; EWL 3; FW; INT CANR-12; LAIT 4; MTCW 1, 2; MTFW 2005; NFS 22; RGEL 2; TEA; WLIT 4; YAW

Spark, Muriel Sarah
See Spark, Muriel

Spaulding, Douglas
See Bradbury, Ray

Spaulding, Leonard
See Bradbury, Ray

Speght, Rachel 1597-c. 1630 .... **LC 97**
See also DLB 126

Spence, J. A. D.
See Eliot, T(homas) S(tearns)

Spencer, Anne 1882-1975 ...... **HR 1:3; PC 77**
See also BW 2; CA 161; DLB 51, 54

Spencer, Elizabeth 1921- .... **CLC 22; SSC 57**
See also CA 13-16R; CANR 32, 65, 87; CN 1, 2, 3, 4, 5, 6, 7; CSW; DLB 6, 218; EWL 3; MTCW 1; RGAL 4; SATA 14

Spencer, Leonard G.
See Silverberg, Robert

Spencer, Scott 1945- .... **CLC 30**
See also CA 113; CANR 51, 148; DLBY 1986

Spender, Stephen 1909-1995 ..... **CLC 1, 2, 5, 10, 41, 91; PC 71**
See also BRWS 2; CA 9-12R; 149; CANR 31, 54; CDBLB 1945-1960; CP 1, 2, 3, 4, 5, 6; DA3; DAM POET; DLB 20; EWL 3; MTCW 1, 2; MTFW 2005; PAB; PFS 23; RGEL 2; TEA

Spengler, Oswald (Arnold Gottfried)
1880-1936 .... **TCLC 25**
See also CA 118; 189

Spenser, Edmund 1552(?)-1599 ...... **LC 5, 39, 117; PC 8, 42; WLC 5**
See also AAYA 60; BRW 1; CDBLB Before 1660; DA; DA3; DAB; DAC; DAM MST, POET; DLB 167; EFS 2; EXPP; PAB; RGEL 2; TEA; WLIT 3; WP

Spicer, Jack 1925-1965 .... **CLC 8, 18, 72**
See also BG 1:3; CA 85-88; DAM POET; DLB 5, 16, 193; GLL 1; WP

Spiegelman, Art 1948- .... **CLC 76, 178**
See also AAYA 10, 46; CA 125; CANR 41, 55, 74, 124; DLB 299; MTCW 2; MTFW 2005; RGHL; SATA 109, 158; YAW

Spielberg, Peter 1929- .... **CLC 6**
See also CA 5-8R; CANR 4, 48; DLBY 1981

Spielberg, Steven 1947- .... **CLC 20, 188**
See also AAYA 8, 24; CA 77-80; CANR 32; SATA 32

Spillane, Frank Morrison
See Spillane, Mickey
See also BPFB 3; CMW 4; DLB 226; MSW

Spillane, Mickey 1918-2006 .. **CLC 3, 13, 241**
See Spillane, Frank Morrison
See also CA 25-28R; 252; CANR 28, 63, 125; DA3; MTCW 1, 2; MTFW 2005; SATA 66; SATA-Obit 176

Spinoza, Benedictus de 1632-1677 .. **LC 9, 58**

Spinrad, Norman (Richard) 1940- ... **CLC 46**
See also BPFB 3; CA 37-40R, 233; CAAE 233; CAAS 19; CANR 20, 91; DLB 8; INT CANR-20; SFW 4

Spitteler, Carl 1845-1924 .... **TCLC 12**
See also CA 109; DLB 129, 332; EWL 3

Spitteler, Karl Friedrich Georg
See Spitteler, Carl

Spivack, Kathleen (Romola Drucker)
1938- .... **CLC 6**
See also CA 49-52

Spivak, Gayatri Chakravorty
1942- .... **CLC 233**
See also CA 110; 154; CANR 91; FW; LMFS 2

Spofford, Harriet (Elizabeth) Prescott
1835-1921 .... **SSC 87**
See also CA 201; DLB 74, 221

Spoto, Donald 1941- .... **CLC 39**
See also CA 65-68; CANR 11, 57, 93, 173

Springsteen, Bruce 1949- .... **CLC 17**
See also CA 111

Springsteen, Bruce F.
See Springsteen, Bruce

Spurling, Hilary 1940- .... **CLC 34**
See also CA 104; CANR 25, 52, 94, 157

Spurling, Susan Hilary
See Spurling, Hilary

Spyker, John Howland
See Elman, Richard (Martin)

Squared, A.
See Abbott, Edwin A.

Squires, (James) Radcliffe
1917-1993 .... **CLC 51**
See also CA 1-4R; 140; CANR 6, 21; CP 1, 2, 3, 4, 5

Srivastava, Dhanpat Rai 1880(?)-1936
See Premchand
See also CA 118; 197

Ssu-ma Ch'ien c. 145B.C.-c.
86B.C. .... **CMLC 96**

Ssu-ma T'an (?)-c. 110B.C. .... **CMLC 96**

Stacy, Donald
See Pohl, Frederik

Stael
See Stael-Holstein, Anne Louise Germaine Necker
See also EW 5; RGWL 2, 3

Stael, Germaine de
See Stael-Holstein, Anne Louise Germaine Necker
See also DLB 119, 192; FL 1:3; FW; GFL 1789 to the Present; TWA

Stael-Holstein, Anne Louise Germaine
Necker 1766-1817 .... **NCLC 3, 91**
See Stael; Stael, Germaine de

Stafford, Jean 1915-1979 .. **CLC 4, 7, 19, 68; SSC 26, 86**
See also CA 1-4R; 85-88; CANR 3, 65; CN 1, 2; DLB 2, 173; MAL 5; MTCW 1, 2; MTFW 2005; RGAL 4; RGSF 2; SATA-Obit 22; SSFS 21; TCWW 1, 2; TUS

Stafford, William (Edgar)
1914-1993 .... **CLC 4, 7, 29; PC 71**
See also AMWS 11; CA 5-8R; 142; CAAS 3; CANR 5, 22; CP 1, 2, 3, 4, 5; DAM POET; DLB 5, 206; EXPP; INT CANR-22; MAL 5; PFS 2, 8, 16; RGAL 4; WP

Stagnelius, Eric Johan 1793-1823 . **NCLC 61**

Staines, Trevor
See Brunner, John (Kilian Houston)

Stairs, Gordon
See Austin, Mary (Hunter)

Stalin, Joseph 1879-1953 .... **TCLC 92**

Stampa, Gaspara c. 1524-1554 .. **LC 114; PC 43**
See also RGWL 2, 3; WLIT 7

Stampflinger, K.A.
See Benjamin, Walter

Stancykowna
See Szymborska, Wislawa

Standing Bear, Luther
1868(?)-1939(?) .... **NNAL**
See also CA 113; 144; DAM MULT

Stanislavsky, Constantin
1863(?)-1938 .... **TCLC 167**
See also CA 118

Stanislavsky, Konstantin
See Stanislavsky, Constantin

Stanislavsky, Konstantin Sergeievich
See Stanislavsky, Constantin

Stanislavsky, Konstantin Sergeivich
See Stanislavsky, Constantin

Stanislavsky, Konstantin Sergeyevich
See Stanislavsky, Constantin

Stannard, Martin 1947- .... **CLC 44**
See also CA 142; DLB 155

Stanton, Elizabeth Cady
1815-1902 .... **TCLC 73**
See also CA 171; DLB 79; FL 1:3; FW

Stanton, Maura 1946- .... **CLC 9**
See also CA 89-92; CANR 15, 123; DLB 120

Stanton, Schuyler
See Baum, L(yman) Frank

Stapledon, (William) Olaf
1886-1950 .... **TCLC 22**
See also CA 111; 162; DLB 15, 255; SCFW 1, 2; SFW 4

Starbuck, George (Edwin)
1931-1996 .... **CLC 53**
See also CA 21-24R; 153; CANR 23; CP 1, 2, 3, 4, 5, 6; DAM POET

Stark, Richard
See Westlake, Donald E.

Statius c. 45-c. 96 .... **CMLC 91**
See also AW 2; DLB 211

Staunton, Schuyler
See Baum, L(yman) Frank

Stead, Christina (Ellen) 1902-1983 ... **CLC 2, 5, 8, 32, 80**
See also BRWS 4; CA 13-16R; 109; CANR 33, 40; CN 1, 2, 3; DLB 260; EWL 3; FW; MTCW 1, 2; MTFW 2005; NFS 27; RGEL 2; RGSF 2; WWE 1

Stead, William Thomas
1849-1912 .... **TCLC 48**
See also BRWS 13; CA 167

Stebnitsky, M.
See Leskov, Nikolai (Semyonovich)

Steele, Richard 1672-1729 ... **LC 18, 156, 159**
See also BRW 3; CDBLB 1660-1789; DLB 84, 101; RGEL 2; WLIT 3

Steele, Timothy (Reid) 1948- .... **CLC 45**
See also CA 93-96; CANR 16, 50, 92; CP 5, 6, 7; DLB 120, 282

Steffens, (Joseph) Lincoln
1866-1936 .... **TCLC 20**
See also CA 117; 198; DLB 303; MAL 5

Stegner, Wallace (Earle) 1909-1993 .. **CLC 9, 49, 81; SSC 27**
See also AITN 1; AMWS 4; ANW; BEST 90:3; BPFB 3; CA 1-4R; 141; CAAS 9; CANR 1, 21, 46; CN 1, 2, 3, 4, 5; DAM NOV; DLB 9, 206, 275; DLBY 1993; EWL 3; MAL 5; MTCW 1, 2; MTFW 2005; RGAL 4; TCWW 1, 2; TUS

Stein, Gertrude 1874-1946 .... **DC 19; PC 18; SSC 42, 105; TCLC 1, 6, 28, 48; WLC 5**
See also AAYA 64; AMW; AMWC 2; CA 104; 132; CANR 108; CDALB 1917-1929; DA; DA3; DAB; DAC; DAM MST, NOV, POET; DLB 4, 54, 86, 228; DLBD 15; EWL 3; EXPS; FL 1:6; GLL 1; MAL 5; MBL; MTCW 1, 2; MTFW 2005; NCFS 4; NFS 27; RGAL 4; RGSF 2; SSFS 5; TUS; WP

Steinbeck, John (Ernst) 1902-1968 ... **CLC 1, 5, 9, 13, 21, 34, 45, 75, 124; SSC 11, 37, 77; TCLC 135; WLC 5**
See also AAYA 12; AMW; BPFB 3; BYA 2, 3, 13; CA 1-4R; 25-28R; CANR 1, 35; CDALB 1929-1941; DA; DA3; DAB; DAC; DAM DRAM, MST, NOV; DLB 7, 9, 212, 275, 309, 332; DLBD 2; EWL 3; EXPS; LAIT 3; MAL 5; MTCW 1, 2; MTFW 2005; NFS 1, 5, 7, 17, 19, 28; RGAL 4; RGSF 2; RHW; SATA 9; SSFS 3, 6, 22; TCWW 1, 2; TUS; WYA; YAW

Steinem, Gloria 1934- .... **CLC 63**
See also CA 53-56; CANR 28, 51, 139; DLB 246; FL 1:1; FW; MTCW 1, 2; MTFW 2005

Steiner, George 1929- .... **CLC 24, 221**
See also CA 73-76; CANR 31, 67, 108; DAM NOV; DLB 67, 299; EWL 3; MTCW 1, 2; MTFW 2005; RGHL; SATA 62

Steiner, K. Leslie
See Delany, Samuel R., Jr.

Steiner, Rudolf 1861-1925 .... **TCLC 13**
See also CA 107

Stendhal 1783-1842 .... **NCLC 23, 46, 178; SSC 27; WLC 5**
See also DA; DA3; DAB; DAC; DAM MST, NOV; DLB 119; EW 5; GFL 1789 to the Present; RGWL 2, 3; TWA

Stephen, Adeline Virginia
See Woolf, (Adeline) Virginia

Stephen, Sir Leslie 1832-1904 .... **TCLC 23**
See also BRW 5; CA 123; DLB 57, 144, 190

Stephen, Sir Leslie
See Stephen, Sir Leslie

Stephen, Virginia
See Woolf, (Adeline) Virginia

Stephens, James 1882(?)-1950 .... **SSC 50; TCLC 4**
See also CA 104; 192; DLB 19, 153, 162; EWL 3; FANT; RGEL 2; SUFW

Stephens, Reed
See Donaldson, Stephen R.

Stephenson, Neal 1959- .... **CLC 220**
See also AAYA 38; CA 122; CANR 88, 138; CN 7; MTFW 2005; SFW 4

Steptoe, Lydia
See Barnes, Djuna
See also GLL 1

Sterchi, Beat 1949- .... **CLC 65**
See also CA 203

Sterling, Brett
See Bradbury, Ray; Hamilton, Edmond

Sterling, Bruce 1954- .... **CLC 72**
See also AAYA 78; CA 119; CANR 44, 135, 184; CN 7; MTFW 2005; SCFW 2; SFW 4

Sterling, George 1869-1926 .... **TCLC 20**
See also CA 117; 165; DLB 54

Stern, Gerald 1925- .... **CLC 40, 100**
See also AMWS 9; CA 81-84; CANR 28, 94; CP 3, 4, 5, 6, 7; DLB 105; PFS 26; RGAL 4

Stern, Richard (Gustave) 1928- ... **CLC 4, 39**
See also CA 1-4R; CANR 1, 25, 52, 120; CN 1, 2, 3, 4, 5, 6, 7; DLB 218; DLBY 1987; INT CANR-25

Sternberg, Josef von 1894-1969 .... **CLC 20**
See also CA 81-84

Sterne, Laurence 1713-1768 .. **LC 2, 48, 156; WLC 5**
See also BRW 3; BRWC 1; CDBLB 1660-1789; DA; DAB; DAC; DAM MST, NOV; DLB 39; RGEL 2; TEA

Sternheim, (William Adolf) Carl 1878-1942 .... **TCLC 8**
See also CA 105; 193; DLB 56, 118; EWL 3; IDTP; RGWL 2, 3

Stevens, Margaret Dean
See Aldrich, Bess Streeter

Stevens, Mark 1951- .... **CLC 34**
See also CA 122

Stevens, R. L.
See Hoch, Edward D.

Stevens, Wallace 1879-1955 . **PC 6; TCLC 3, 12, 45; WLC 5**
See also AMW; AMWR 1; CA 104; 124; CANR 181; CDALB 1929-1941; DA; DA3; DAB; DAC; DAM MST, POET; DLB 54, 342; EWL 3; EXPP; MAL 5; MTCW 1, 2; PAB; PFS 13, 16; RGAL 4; TUS; WP

Stevenson, Anne (Katharine) 1933- .. **CLC 7, 33**
See also BRWS 6; CA 17-20R; CAAS 9; CANR 9, 33, 123; CP 3, 4, 5, 6, 7; CWP; DLB 40; MTCW 1; RHW

Stevenson, Robert Louis (Balfour) 1850-1894 ...... **NCLC 5, 14, 63, 193; PC 84; SSC 11, 51; WLC 5**
See also AAYA 24; BPFB 3; BRW 5; BRWC 1; BRWR 1; BYA 1, 2, 4, 13; CD-BLB 1890-1914; CLR 10, 11, 107; DA; DA3; DAB; DAC; DAM MST, NOV; DLB 18, 57, 141, 156, 174; DLBD 13; GL 3; HGG; JRDA; LAIT 1, 3; MAICYA 1, 2; NFS 11, 20; RGEL 2; RGSF 2; SATA 100; SUFW; TEA; WCH; WLIT 4; WYA; YABC 2; YAW

Stewart, J(ohn) I(nnes) M(ackintosh) 1906-1994 .... **CLC 7, 14, 32**
See Innes, Michael
See also CA 85-88; 147; CAAS 3; CANR 47; CMW 4; CN 1, 2, 3, 4, 5; MTCW 1, 2

Stewart, Mary (Florence Elinor) 1916- .... **CLC 7, 35, 117**
See also AAYA 29, 73; BPFB 3; CA 1-4R; CANR 1, 59, 130; CMW 4; CPW; DAB; FANT; RHW; SATA 12; YAW

Stewart, Mary Rainbow
See Stewart, Mary (Florence Elinor)

Stifle, June
See Campbell, Maria

Stifter, Adalbert 1805-1868 ... **NCLC 41, 198; SSC 28**
See also CDWLB 2; DLB 133; RGSF 2; RGWL 2, 3

Still, James 1906-2001 .... **CLC 49**
See also CA 65-68; 195; CAAS 17; CANR 10, 26; CSW; DLB 9; DLBY 01; SATA 29; SATA-Obit 127

Sting 1951-
See Sumner, Gordon Matthew
See also CA 167

Stirling, Arthur
See Sinclair, Upton

Stitt, Milan 1941- .... **CLC 29**
See also CA 69-72

Stockton, Francis Richard 1834-1902
See Stockton, Frank R.
See also AAYA 68; CA 108; 137; MAICYA 1, 2; SATA 44; SFW 4

Stockton, Frank R. .... **TCLC 47**
See Stockton, Francis Richard
See also BYA 4, 13; DLB 42, 74; DLBD 13; EXPS; SATA-Brief 32; SSFS 3; SUFW; WCH

Stoddard, Charles
See Kuttner, Henry

Stoker, Abraham 1847-1912
See Stoker, Bram
See also CA 105; 150; DA; DA3; DAC; DAM MST, NOV; HGG; MTFW 2005; SATA 29

Stoker, Bram . **SSC 62; TCLC 8, 144; WLC 6**
See Stoker, Abraham
See also AAYA 23; BPFB 3; BRWS 3; BYA 5; CDBLB 1890-1914; DAB; DLB 304; GL 3; LATS 1:1; NFS 18; RGEL 2; SUFW; TEA; WLIT 4

Stolz, Mary 1920-2006 .... **CLC 12**
See also AAYA 8, 73; AITN 1; CA 5-8R; 255; CANR 13, 41, 112; JRDA; MAICYA 1, 2; SAAS 3; SATA 10, 71, 133; SATA-Obit 180; YAW

Stolz, Mary Slattery
See Stolz, Mary

Stone, Irving 1903-1989 .... **CLC 7**
See also AITN 1; BPFB 3; CA 1-4R; 129; CAAS 3; CANR 1, 23; CN 1, 2, 3, 4; CPW; DA3; DAM POP; INT CANR-23; MTCW 1, 2; MTFW 2005; RHW; SATA 3; SATA-Obit 64

Stone, Oliver 1946- .... **CLC 73**
See also AAYA 15, 64; CA 110; CANR 55, 125

Stone, Oliver William
See Stone, Oliver

Stone, Robert 1937- .... **CLC 5, 23, 42, 175**
See also AMWS 5; BPFB 3; CA 85-88; CANR 23, 66, 95, 173; CN 4, 5, 6, 7; DLB 152; EWL 3; INT CANR-23; MAL 5; MTCW 1; MTFW 2005

Stone, Robert Anthony
See Stone, Robert

Stone, Ruth 1915- .... **PC 53**
See also CA 45-48; CANR 2, 91; CP 5, 6, 7; CSW; DLB 105; PFS 19

Stone, Zachary
See Follett, Ken

Stoppard, Tom 1937- ... **CLC 1, 3, 4, 5, 8, 15, 29, 34, 63, 91; DC 6, 30; WLC 6**
See also AAYA 63; BRWC 1; BRWR 2; BRWS 1; CA 81-84; CANR 39, 67, 125; CBD; CD 5, 6; CDBLB 1960 to Present; DA; DA3; DAB; DAC; DAM DRAM, MST; DFS 2, 5, 8, 11, 13, 16; DLB 13, 233; DLBY 1985; EWL 3; LATS 1:2; MTCW 1, 2; MTFW 2005; RGEL 2; TEA; WLIT 4

Storey, David (Malcolm) 1933- . **CLC 2, 4, 5, 8**
See also BRWS 1; CA 81-84; CANR 36; CBD; CD 5, 6; CN 1, 2, 3, 4, 5, 6; DAM DRAM; DLB 13, 14, 207, 245, 326; EWL 3; MTCW 1; RGEL 2

Storm, Hyemeyohsts 1935- ... **CLC 3; NNAL**
See also CA 81-84; CANR 45; DAM MULT

Storm, (Hans) Theodor (Woldsen) 1817-1888 ... **NCLC 1, 195; SSC 27, 106**
See also CDWLB 2; DLB 129; EW; RGSF 2; RGWL 2, 3

Storni, Alfonsina 1892-1938 . **HLC 2; PC 33; TCLC 5**
See also CA 104; 131; DAM MULT; DLB 283; HW 1; LAW

Stoughton, William 1631-1701 .... **LC 38**
See also DLB 24

Stout, Rex (Todhunter) 1886-1975 ..... **CLC 3**
See also AITN 2; BPFB 3; CA 61-64; CANR 71; CMW 4; CN 2; DLB 306; MSW; RGAL 4

Stow, (Julian) Randolph 1935- ... **CLC 23, 48**
See also CA 13-16R; CANR 33; CN 1, 2, 3, 4, 5, 6, 7; CP 1, 2, 3, 4; DLB 260; MTCW 1; RGEL 2

Stowe, Harriet (Elizabeth) Beecher
1811-1896 .... **NCLC 3, 50, 133, 195;**
WLC 6
See also AAYA 53; AMWS 1; CDALB
1865-1917; CLR 131; DA; DA3; DAB;
DAC; DAM MST, NOV; DLB 1, 12, 42,
74, 189, 239, 243; EXPN; FL 1:3; JRDA;
LAIT 2; MAICYA 1, 2; NFS 6; RGAL 4;
TUS; YABC 1

Strabo c. 64B.C.-c. 25 .... **CMLC 37**
See also DLB 176

Strachey, (Giles) Lytton
1880-1932 .... **TCLC 12**
See also BRWS 2; CA 110; 178; DLB 149;
DLBD 10; EWL 3; MTCW 2; NCFS 4

Stramm, August 1874-1915 .... **PC 50**
See also CA 195; EWL 3

Strand, Mark 1934- .. **CLC 6, 18, 41, 71; PC**
63
See also AMWS 4; CA 21-24R; CANR 40,
65, 100; CP 1, 2, 3, 4, 5, 6, 7; DAM
POET; DLB 5; EWL 3; MAL 5; PAB;
PFS 9, 18; RGAL 4; SATA 41; TCLE 1:2

Stratton-Porter, Gene(va Grace) 1863-1924
See Porter, Gene(va Grace) Stratton
See also ANW; CA 137; CLR 87; DLB 221;
DLBD 14; MAICYA 1, 2; SATA 15

Straub, Peter 1943- .... **CLC 28, 107**
See also BEST 89:1; BPFB 3; CA 85-88;
CANR 28, 65, 109; CPW; DAM POP;
DLBY 1984; HGG; MTCW 1, 2; MTFW
2005; SUFW 2

Straub, Peter Francis
See Straub, Peter

Strauss, Botho 1944- .... **CLC 22**
See also CA 157; CWW 2; DLB 124

Strauss, Leo 1899-1973 .... **TCLC 141**
See also CA 101; 45-48; CANR 122

Streatfeild, Mary Noel
See Streatfeild, Noel

Streatfeild, Noel 1897(?)-1986 .... **CLC 21**
See also CA 81-84; 120; CANR 31; CLR
17, 83; CWRI 5; DLB 160; MAICYA 1,
2; SATA 20; SATA-Obit 48

Stribling, T(homas) S(igismund)
1881-1965 .... **CLC 23**
See also CA 189; 107; CMW 4; DLB 9;
RGAL 4

Strindberg, (Johan) August
1849-1912 ... **DC 18; TCLC 1, 8, 21, 47;**
WLC 6
See also CA 104; 135; DA; DA3; DAB;
DAC; DAM DRAM, MST; DFS 4, 9;
DLB 259; EW 7; EWL 3; IDTP; LMFS
2; MTCW 2; MTFW 2005; RGWL 2, 3;
TWA

Stringer, Arthur 1874-1950 .... **TCLC 37**
See also CA 161; DLB 92

Stringer, David
See Roberts, Keith (John Kingston)

Stroheim, Erich von 1885-1957 ..... **TCLC 71**

Strugatskii, Arkadii (Natanovich)
1925-1991 .... **CLC 27**
See Strugatsky, Arkadii Natanovich
See also CA 106; 135; SFW 4

Strugatskii, Boris (Natanovich)
1933- .... **CLC 27**
See Strugatsky, Boris (Natanovich)
See also CA 106; SFW 4

Strugatsky, Arkadii Natanovich
See Strugatskii, Arkadii (Natanovich)
See also DLB 302

Strugatsky, Boris (Natanovich)
See Strugatskii, Boris (Natanovich)
See also DLB 302

Strummer, Joe 1952-2002 .... **CLC 30**

Strunk, William, Jr. 1869-1946 ...... **TCLC 92**
See also CA 118; 164; NCFS 5

Stryk, Lucien 1924- .... **PC 27**
See also CA 13-16R; CANR 10, 28, 55,
110; CP 1, 2, 3, 4, 5, 6, 7

Stuart, Don A.
See Campbell, John W(ood, Jr.)

Stuart, Ian
See MacLean, Alistair (Stuart)

Stuart, Jesse (Hilton) 1906-1984 ... **CLC 1, 8,**
11, 14, 34; SSC 31
See also CA 5-8R; 112; CANR 31; CN 1,
2, 3; DLB 9, 48, 102; DLBY 1984; SATA
2; SATA-Obit 36

Stubblefield, Sally
See Trumbo, Dalton

Sturgeon, Theodore (Hamilton)
1918-1985 .... **CLC 22, 39**
See Queen, Ellery
See also AAYA 51; BPFB 3; BYA 9, 10;
CA 81-84; 116; CANR 32, 103; DLB 8;
DLBY 1985; HGG; MTCW 1, 2; MTFW
2005; SCFW; SFW 4; SUFW

Sturges, Preston 1898-1959 .... **TCLC 48**
See also CA 114; 149; DLB 26

Styron, William 1925-2006 .. **CLC 1, 3, 5, 11,**
15, 60, 232, 244; SSC 25
See also AMW; AMWC 2; BEST 90:4;
BPFB 3; CA 5-8R; 255; CANR 6, 33, 74,
126; CDALB 1968-1988; CN 1, 2, 3, 4,
5, 6, 7; CPW; CSW; DA3; DAM NOV,
POP; DLB 2, 143, 299; DLBY 1980;
EWL 3; INT CANR-6; LAIT 2; MAL 5;
MTCW 1, 2; MTFW 2005; NCFS 1; NFS
22; RGAL 4; RGHL; RHW; TUS

Styron, William Clark
See Styron, William

Su, Chien 1884-1918
See Su Man-shu
See also CA 123

Suarez Lynch, B.
See Bioy Casares, Adolfo; Borges, Jorge
Luis

Suassuna, Ariano Vilar 1927- .... **HLCS 1**
See also CA 178; DLB 307; HW 2; LAW

Suckert, Kurt Erich
See Malaparte, Curzio

Suckling, Sir John 1609-1642 . **LC 75; PC 30**
See also BRW 2; DAM POET; DLB 58,
126; EXPP; PAB; RGEL 2

Suckow, Ruth 1892-1960 .... **SSC 18**
See also CA 193; 113; DLB 9, 102; RGAL
4; TCWW 2

Sudermann, Hermann 1857-1928 .. **TCLC 15**
See also CA 107; 201; DLB 118

Sue, Eugene 1804-1857 .... **NCLC 1**
See also DLB 119

Sueskind, Patrick 1949- .... **CLC 44, 182**
See Suskind, Patrick

Suetonius c. 70-c. 130 .... **CMLC 60**
See also AW 2; DLB 211; RGWL 2, 3;
WLIT 8

Sukenick, Ronald 1932-2004 ..... **CLC 3, 4, 6,**
48
See also CA 25-28R; 209; 229; CAAE 209;
CAAS 8; CANR 32, 89; CN 3, 4, 5, 6, 7;
DLB 173; DLBY 1981

Suknaski, Andrew 1942- .... **CLC 19**
See also CA 101; CP 3, 4, 5, 6, 7; DLB 53

Sullivan, Vernon
See Vian, Boris

Sully Prudhomme, Rene-Francois-Armand
1839-1907 .... **TCLC 31**
See Prudhomme, Rene Francois Armand
See also DLB 332; GFL 1789 to the Present

Su Man-shu .... **TCLC 24**
See Su, Chien
See also EWL 3

Sumarokov, Aleksandr Petrovich
1717-1777 .... **LC 104**
See also DLB 150

Summerforest, Ivy B.
See Kirkup, James

Summers, Andrew James
See Summers, Andy

Summers, Andy 1942- .... **CLC 26**
See also CA 255

Summers, Hollis (Spurgeon, Jr.)
1916- .... **CLC 10**
See also CA 5-8R; CANR 3; CN 1, 2, 3;
CP 1, 2, 3, 4; DLB 6; TCLE 1:2

Summers, (Alphonsus Joseph-Mary
Augustus) Montague
1880-1948 .... **TCLC 16**
See also CA 118; 163

Sumner, Gordon Matthew .... **CLC 26**
See Police, The; Sting

Sun Tzu c. 400B.C.-c. 320B.C. ...... **CMLC 56**

Surrey, Henry Howard 1517-1574 ... **LC 121;**
PC 59
See also BRW 1; RGEL 2

Surtees, Robert Smith 1805-1864 .. **NCLC 14**
See also DLB 21; RGEL 2

Susann, Jacqueline 1921-1974 .... **CLC 3**
See also AITN 1; BPFB 3; CA 65-68; 53-
56; MTCW 1, 2

Su Shi
See Su Shih
See also RGWL 2, 3

Su Shih 1036-1101 .... **CMLC 15**
See Su Shi

Suskind, Patrick .... **CLC 182**
See Sueskind, Patrick
See also BPFB 3; CA 145; CWW 2

Suso, Heinrich c. 1295-1366 .... **CMLC 87**

Sutcliff, Rosemary 1920-1992 .... **CLC 26**
See also AAYA 10; BYA 1, 4; CA 5-8R;
139; CANR 37; CLR 1, 37, 138; CPW;
DAB; DAC; DAM MST, POP; JRDA;
LATS 1:1; MAICYA 1, 2; MAICYAS 1;
RHW; SATA 6, 44, 78; SATA-Obit 73;
WYA; YAW

Sutherland, Efua (Theodora Morgue)
1924-1996 .... **BLC 2:3**
See also AFW; BW 1; CA 105; CWD; DLB
117; EWL 3; IDTP; SATA 25

Sutro, Alfred 1863-1933 .... **TCLC 6**
See also CA 105; 185; DLB 10; RGEL 2

Sutton, Henry
See Slavitt, David R.

Suzuki, D. T.
See Suzuki, Daisetz Teitaro

Suzuki, Daisetz T.
See Suzuki, Daisetz Teitaro

Suzuki, Daisetz Teitaro
1870-1966 .... **TCLC 109**
See also CA 121; 111; MTCW 1, 2; MTFW
2005

Suzuki, Teitaro
See Suzuki, Daisetz Teitaro

Svevo, Italo .... **SSC 25; TCLC 2, 35**
See Schmitz, Aron Hector
See also DLB 264; EW 8; EWL 3; RGWL
2, 3; WLIT 7

Swados, Elizabeth 1951- .... **CLC 12**
See also CA 97-100; CANR 49, 163; INT
CA-97-100

Swados, Elizabeth A.
See Swados, Elizabeth

Swados, Harvey 1920-1972 .... **CLC 5**
See also CA 5-8R; 37-40R; CANR 6; CN
1; DLB 2, 335; MAL 5

Swados, Liz
See Swados, Elizabeth

Swan, Gladys 1934- .... **CLC 69**
See also CA 101; CANR 17, 39; TCLE 1:2

Swanson, Logan
See Matheson, Richard

Taylor, Peter (Hillsman) 1917-1994 .. **CLC 1,
4, 18, 37, 44, 50, 71; SSC 10, 84**
See also AMWS 5; BPFB 3; CA 13-16R;
147; CANR 9, 50; CN 1, 2, 3, 4, 5; CSW;
DLB 218, 278; DLBY 1981, 1994; EWL
3; EXPS; INT CANR-9; MAL 5; MTCW
1, 2; MTFW 2005; RGSF 2; SSFS 9; TUS

Taylor, Robert Lewis 1912-1998 .... **CLC 14**
See also CA 1-4R; 170; CANR 3, 64; CN
1, 2; SATA 10; TCWW 1, 2

Tchekhov, Anton
See Chekhov, Anton (Pavlovich)

Tchicaya, Gerald Felix 1931-1988 .. **CLC 101**
See Tchicaya U Tam'si
See also CA 129; 125; CANR 81

Tchicaya U Tam'si
See Tchicaya, Gerald Felix
See also EWL 3

Teasdale, Sara 1884-1933 .... **PC 31; TCLC 4**
See also CA 104; 163; DLB 45; GLL 1;
PFS 14; RGAL 4; SATA 32; TUS

Tecumseh 1768-1813 .... **NNAL**
See also DAM MULT

Tegner, Esaias 1782-1846 .... **NCLC 2**

Teilhard de Chardin, (Marie Joseph) Pierre
1881-1955 .... **TCLC 9**
See also CA 105; 210; GFL 1789 to the
Present

Temple, Ann
See Mortimer, Penelope (Ruth)

Tennant, Emma 1937- .... **CLC 13, 52**
See also BRWS 9; CA 65-68; CAAS 9;
CANR 10, 38, 59, 88, 177; CN 3, 4, 5, 6,
7; DLB 14; EWL 3; SFW 4

Tenneshaw, S.M.
See Silverberg, Robert

Tenney, Tabitha Gilman
1762-1837 .... **NCLC 122**
See also DLB 37, 200

Tennyson, Alfred 1809-1892 ... **NCLC 30, 65,
115, 202; PC 6; WLC 6**
See also AAYA 50; BRW 4; CDBLB 1832-
1890; DA; DA3; DAB; DAC; DAM MST,
POET; DLB 32; EXPP; PAB; PFS 1, 2, 4,
11, 15, 19; RGEL 2; TEA; WLIT 4; WP

Teran, Lisa St. Aubin de .... **CLC 36**
See St. Aubin de Teran, Lisa

Terence c. 184B.C.-c. 159B.C. ...... **CMLC 14;
DC 7**
See also AW 1; CDWLB 1; DLB 211;
RGWL 2, 3; TWA; WLIT 8

Teresa de Jesus, St. 1515-1582 .... **LC 18, 149**

Teresa of Avila, St.
See Teresa de Jesus, St.

Terkel, Louis .... **CLC 38**
See Terkel, Studs
See also AAYA 32; AITN 1; MTCW 2; TUS

Terkel, Studs 1912-2008
See Terkel, Louis
See also CA 57-60; 278; CANR 18, 45, 67,
132; DA3; MTCW 1, 2; MTFW 2005

Terry, C. V.
See Slaughter, Frank G(ill)

Terry, Megan 1932- .... **CLC 19; DC 13**
See also CA 77-80; CABS 3; CAD; CANR
43; CD 5, 6; CWD; DFS 18; DLB 7, 249;
GLL 2

Tertullian c. 155-c. 245 .... **CMLC 29**

Tertz, Abram
See Sinyavsky, Andrei (Donatevich)
See also RGSF 2

Tesich, Steve 1943(?)-1996 .... **CLC 40, 69**
See also CA 105; 152; CAD; DLBY 1983

Tesla, Nikola 1856-1943 .... **TCLC 88**

Teternikov, Fyodor Kuzmich 1863-1927
See Sologub, Fyodor
See also CA 104

Tevis, Walter 1928-1984 .... **CLC 42**
See also CA 113; SFW 4

Tey, Josephine .... **TCLC 14**
See Mackintosh, Elizabeth
See also DLB 77; MSW

Thackeray, William Makepeace
1811-1863 ...... **NCLC 5, 14, 22, 43, 169;
WLC 6**
See also BRW 5; BRWC 2; CDBLB 1832-
1890; DA; DA3; DAB; DAC; DAM MST,
NOV; DLB 21, 55, 159, 163; NFS 13;
RGEL 2; SATA 23; TEA; WLIT 3

Thakura, Ravindranatha
See Tagore, Rabindranath

Thames, C. H.
See Marlowe, Stephen

Tharoor, Shashi 1956- .... **CLC 70**
See also CA 141; CANR 91; CN 6, 7

Thelwall, John 1764-1834 .... **NCLC 162**
See also DLB 93, 158

Thelwell, Michael Miles 1939- .... **CLC 22**
See also BW 2; CA 101

Theobald, Lewis, Jr.
See Lovecraft, H. P.

Theocritus c. 310B.C.- .... **CMLC 45**
See also AW 1; DLB 176; RGWL 2, 3

Theodorescu, Ion N. 1880-1967
See Arghezi, Tudor
See also CA 116

Theriault, Yves 1915-1983 .... **CLC 79**
See also CA 102; CANR 150; CCA 1;
DAC; DAM MST; DLB 88; EWL 3

Theroux, Alexander 1939- .... **CLC 2, 25**
See also CA 85-88; CANR 20, 63; CN 4, 5,
6, 7

Theroux, Alexander Louis
See Theroux, Alexander

Theroux, Paul 1941- .... **CLC 5, 8, 11, 15, 28,
46, 159**
See also AAYA 28; AMWS 8; BEST 89:4;
BPFB 3; CA 33-36R; CANR 20, 45, 74,
133, 179; CDALBS; CN 1, 2, 3, 4, 5, 6,
7; CP 1; CPW 1; DA3; DAM POP; DLB
218, 218; EWL 3; HGG; MAL 5; MTCW 1,
2; MTFW 2005; RGAL 4; SATA 44, 109;
TUS

Theroux, Paul Edward
See Theroux, Paul

Thesen, Sharon 1946- .... **CLC 56**
See also CA 163; CANR 125; CP 5, 6, 7;
CWP

Thespis fl. 6th cent. B.C.- .... **CMLC 51**
See also LMFS 1

Thevenin, Denis
See Duhamel, Georges

Thibault, Jacques Anatole Francois
1844-1924
See France, Anatole
See also CA 106; 127; DA3; DAM NOV;
MTCW 1, 2; TWA

Thiele, Colin 1920-2006 .... **CLC 17**
See also CA 29-32R; CANR 12, 28, 53,
105; CLR 27; CP 1, 2; DLB 289; MAI-
CYA 1, 2; SAAS 2; SATA 14, 72, 125;
YAW

Thiong'o, Ngugi Wa
See Ngugi wa Thiong'o

Thistlethwaite, Bel
See Wetherald, Agnes Ethelwyn

Thomas, Audrey (Callahan) 1935- .... **CLC 7,
13, 37, 107; SSC 20**
See also AITN 2; CA 21-24R, 237; CAAE
237; CAAS 19; CANR 36, 58; CN 2, 3,
4, 5, 6, 7; DLB 60; MTCW 1; RGSF 2

Thomas, Augustus 1857-1934 .... **TCLC 97**
See also MAL 5

Thomas, D.M. 1935- ..... **CLC 13, 22, 31, 132**
See also BPFB 3; BRWS 4; CA 61-64;
CAAS 11; CANR 17, 45, 75; CDBLB
1960 to Present; CN 4, 5, 6, 7; CP 1, 2, 3,

4, 5, 6, 7; DA3; DLB 40, 207, 299; HGG;
INT CANR-17; MTCW 1, 2; MTFW
2005; RGHL; SFW 4

Thomas, Dylan (Marlais) 1914-1953 .... **PC 2,
52; SSC 3, 44; TCLC 1, 8, 45, 105;
WLC 6**
See also AAYA 45; BRWS 1; CA 104; 120;
CANR 65; CDBLB 1945-1960; DA; DA3;
DAB; DAC; DAM DRAM, MST, POET;
DLB 13, 20, 139; EWL 3; EXPP; LAIT
3; MTCW 1, 2; MTFW 2005; PAB; PFS
1, 3, 8; RGEL 2; RGSF 2; SATA 60; TEA;
WLIT 4; WP

Thomas, (Philip) Edward 1878-1917 . **PC 53;
TCLC 10**
See also BRW 6; BRWS 3; CA 106; 153;
DAM POET; DLB 19, 98, 156, 216; EWL
3; PAB; RGEL 2

Thomas, J.F.
See Fleming, Thomas

Thomas, Joyce Carol 1938- .... **CLC 35**
See also AAYA 12, 54; BW 2, 3; CA 113;
116; CANR 48, 114, 135; CLR 19; DLB
33; INT CA-116; JRDA; MAICYA 1, 2;
MTCW 1, 2; MTFW 2005; SAAS 7;
SATA 40, 78, 123, 137; SATA-Essay 137;
WYA; YAW

Thomas, Lewis 1913-1993 .... **CLC 35**
See also ANW; CA 85-88; 143; CANR 38,
60; DLB 275; MTCW 1, 2

Thomas, M. Carey 1857-1935 .... **TCLC 89**
See also FW

Thomas, Paul
See Mann, (Paul) Thomas

Thomas, Piri 1928- .... **CLC 17; HLCS 2**
See also CA 73-76; HW 1; LLW

Thomas, R(onald) S(tuart)
1913-2000 .... **CLC 6, 13, 48**
See also BRWS 12; CA 89-92; 189; CAAS
4; CANR 30; CDBLB 1960 to Present;
CP 1, 2, 3, 4, 5, 6, 7; DAB; DAM POET;
DLB 27; EWL 3; MTCW 1; RGEL 2

Thomas, Ross (Elmore) 1926-1995 .. **CLC 39**
See also CA 33-36R; 150; CANR 22, 63;
CMW 4

Thompson, Francis (Joseph)
1859-1907 .... **TCLC 4**
See also BRW 5; CA 104; 189; CDBLB
1890-1914; DLB 19; RGEL 2; TEA

Thompson, Francis Clegg
See Mencken, H(enry) L(ouis)

Thompson, Hunter S. 1937(?)-2005 .. **CLC 9,
17, 40, 104, 229**
See also AAYA 45; BEST 89:1; BPFB 3;
CA 17-20R; 236; CANR 23, 46, 74, 77,
111, 133; CPW; CSW; DA3; DAM POP;
DLB 185; MTCW 1, 2; MTFW 2005;
TUS

Thompson, James Myers
See Thompson, Jim

Thompson, Jim 1906-1977 .... **CLC 69**
See also BPFB 3; CA 140; CMW 4; CPW;
DLB 226; MSW

Thompson, Judith (Clare Francesca)
1954- .... **CLC 39**
See also CA 143; CD 5, 6; CWD; DFS 22;
DLB 334

Thomson, James 1700-1748 .... **LC 16, 29, 40**
See also BRWS 3; DAM POET; DLB 95;
RGEL 2

Thomson, James 1834-1882 .... **NCLC 18**
See also DAM POET; DLB 35; RGEL 2

Thoreau, Henry David 1817-1862 .. **NCLC 7,
21, 61, 138, 207; PC 30; WLC 6**
See also AAYA 42; AMW; ANW; BYA 3;
CDALB 1640-1865; DA; DA3; DAB;
DAC; DAM MST; DLB 1, 183, 223, 270,
298; LAIT 2; LMFS 1; NCFS 3; RGAL
4; TUS

Townsend, Sue .... **CLC 61**
See Townsend, Susan Lilian
See also AAYA 28; CA 119; 127; CANR
65, 107; CBD; CD 5, 6; CPW; CWD;
DAB; DAC; DAM MST; DLB 271; INT
CA-127; SATA 55, 93; SATA-Brief 48;
YAW

Townsend, Susan Lilian 1946-
See Townsend, Sue

Townshend, Pete
See Townshend, Peter

Townshend, Peter 1945- .... **CLC 17, 42**
See also CA 107

Townshend, Peter Dennis Blandford
See Townshend, Peter

Tozzi, Federigo 1883-1920 .... **TCLC 31**
See also CA 160; CANR 110; DLB 264;
EWL 3; WLIT 7

Tracy, Don(ald Fiske) 1905-1970(?)
See Queen, Ellery
See also CA 1-4R; 176; CANR 2

Trafford, F. G.
See Riddell, Charlotte

Traherne, Thomas 1637(?)-1674 .. **LC 99; PC 70**
See also BRW 2; BRWS 11; DLB 131;
PAB; RGEL 2

Traill, Catharine Parr 1802-1899 .. **NCLC 31**
See also DLB 99

Trakl, Georg 1887-1914 .... **PC 20; TCLC 5**
See also CA 104; 165; EW 10; EWL 3;
LMFS 2; MTCW 2; RGWL 2, 3

Trambley, Estela Portillo .... **TCLC 163**
See Portillo Trambley, Estela
See also CA 77-80; RGAL 4

Tranquilli, Secondino
See Silone, Ignazio

Transtroemer, Tomas Gosta
See Transtromer, Tomas

Transtromer, Tomas (Gosta)
See Transtromer, Tomas
See also CWW 2

Transtromer, Tomas 1931- .... **CLC 52, 65**
See also CA 117; 129; CAAS 17; CANR
115, 172; DAM POET; DLB 257; EWL
3; PFS 21

Transtromer, Tomas Goesta
See Transtromer, Tomas

Transtromer, Tomas Gosta
See Transtromer, Tomas

Transtromer, Tomas Gosta
See Transtromer, Tomas

Traven, B. 1882(?)-1969 .... **CLC 8, 11**
See also CA 19-20; 25-28R; CAP 2; DLB
9, 56; EWL 3; MTCW 1; RGAL 4

Trediakovsky, Vasilii Kirillovich
1703-1769 .... **LC 68**
See also DLB 150

Treitel, Jonathan 1959- .... **CLC 70**
See also CA 210; DLB 267

Trelawny, Edward John
1792-1881 .... **NCLC 85**
See also DLB 110, 116, 144

Tremain, Rose 1943- .... **CLC 42**
See also CA 97-100; CANR 44, 95; CN 4,
5, 6, 7; DLB 14, 271; RGSF 2; RHW

Tremblay, Michel 1942- .... **CLC 29, 102, 225**
See also CA 116; 128; CCA 1; CWW 2;
DAC; DAM MST; DLB 60; EWL 3; GLL
1; MTCW 1, 2; MTFW 2005

Trevanian .... **CLC 29**
See Whitaker, Rod

Trevisa, John c. 1342-c. 1402 .... **LC 139**
See also BRWS 9; DLB 146

Trevor, Glen
See Hilton, James

Trevor, William 1928- ... **CLC 1, 2, 3, 4, 5, 6, 7; SSC 21, 58**
See also BRWS 4; CA 9-12R; CANR 4, 37,
55, 76, 102, 139; CBD; CD 5, 6; DAM
NOV; DLB 14, 139; EWL 3; INT CANR-
37; LATS 1:2; MTCW 1, 2; MTFW 2005;
RGEL 2; RGSF 2; SSFS 10; TCLE 1:2;
TEA

Trifonov, Iurii (Valentinovich)
See Trifonov, Yuri (Valentinovich)
See also DLB 302; RGWL 2, 3

Trifonov, Yuri (Valentinovich)
1925-1981 .... **CLC 45**
See Trifonov, Iurii (Valentinovich); Tri-
fonov, Yury Valentinovich
See also CA 126; 103; MTCW 1

Trifonov, Yury Valentinovich
See Trifonov, Yuri (Valentinovich)
See also EWL 3

Trilling, Diana (Rubin) 1905-1996 . **CLC 129**
See also CA 5-8R; 154; CANR 10, 46; INT
CANR-10; MTCW 1, 2

Trilling, Lionel 1905-1975 ..... **CLC 9, 11, 24; SSC 75**
See also AMWS 3; CA 9-12R; 61-64;
CANR 10, 105; CN 1, 2; DLB 28, 63;
EWL 3; INT CANR-10; MAL 5; MTCW
1, 2; RGAL 4; TUS

Trimball, W. H.
See Mencken, H(enry) L(ouis)

Tristan
See Gomez de la Serna, Ramon

Tristram
See Housman, A(lfred) E(dward)

Trogdon, William (Lewis) 1939-
See Heat-Moon, William Least
See also AAYA 66; CA 115; 119; CANR
47, 89; CPW; INT CA-119

Trollope, Anthony 1815-1882 .... **NCLC 6, 33, 101; SSC 28; WLC 6**
See also BRW 5; CDBLB 1832-1890; DA;
DA3; DAB; DAC; DAM MST, NOV;
DLB 21, 57, 159; RGEL 2; RGSF 2;
SATA 22

Trollope, Frances 1779-1863 .... **NCLC 30**
See also DLB 21, 166

Trollope, Joanna 1943- .... **CLC 186**
See also CA 101; CANR 58, 95, 149; CN
7; CPW; DLB 207; RHW

Trotsky, Leon 1879-1940 .... **TCLC 22**
See also CA 118; 167

Trotter (Cockburn), Catharine
1679-1749 .... **LC 8**
See also DLB 84, 252

Trotter, Wilfred 1872-1939 .... **TCLC 97**

Troupe, Quincy 1943- .... **BLC 2:3**
See also BW 2; CA 113; 124; CANR 43,
90, 126; DLB 41

Trout, Kilgore
See Farmer, Philip Jose

Trow, George William Swift
See Trow, George W.S.

Trow, George W.S. 1943-2006 .... **CLC 52**
See also CA 126; 255; CANR 91

Troyat, Henri 1911-2007 .... **CLC 23**
See also CA 45-48; 258; CANR 2, 33, 67,
117; GFL 1789 to the Present; MTCW 1

Trudeau, Garry B. .... **CLC 12**
See Trudeau, G.B.
See also AAYA 10; AITN 2

Trudeau, G.B. 1948-
See Trudeau, Garry B.
See also AAYA 60; CA 81-84; CANR 31;
SATA 35, 168

Truffaut, Francois 1932-1984 ... **CLC 20, 101**
See also CA 81-84; 113; CANR 34

Trumbo, Dalton 1905-1976 .... **CLC 19**
See also CA 21-24R; 69-72; CANR 10; CN
1, 2; DLB 26; IDFW 3, 4; YAW

Trumbull, John 1750-1831 .... **NCLC 30**
See also DLB 31; RGAL 4

Trundlett, Helen B.
See Eliot, T(homas) S(tearns)

Truth, Sojourner 1797(?)-1883 ...... **NCLC 94**
See also DLB 239; FW; LAIT 2

Tryon, Thomas 1926-1991 .... **CLC 3, 11**
See also AITN 1; BPFB 3; CA 29-32R; 135;
CANR 32, 77; CPW; DA3; DAM POP;
HGG; MTCW 1

Tryon, Tom
See Tryon, Thomas

Ts'ao Hsueh-ch'in 1715(?)-1763 .... **LC 1**

Tsurayuki Ed. fl. 10th cent. - .... **PC 73**

Tsushima, Shuji 1909-1948
See Dazai Osamu
See also CA 107

Tsvetaeva (Efron), Marina (Ivanovna)
1892-1941 .... **PC 14; TCLC 7, 35**
See also CA 104; 128; CANR 73; DLB 295;
EW 11; MTCW 1, 2; PFS 29; RGWL 2, 3

Tuck, Lily 1938- .... **CLC 70**
See also AAYA 74; CA 139; CANR 90

Tuckerman, Frederick Goddard
1821-1873 .... **PC 85**
See also DLB 243; RGAL 4

Tu Fu 712-770 .... **PC 9**
See Du Fu
See also DAM MULT; TWA; WP

Tulsidas, Gosvami 1532(?)-1623 .... **LC 158**
See also RGWL 2, 3

Tunis, John R(oberts) 1889-1975 ..... **CLC 12**
See also BYA 1; CA 61-64; CANR 62; DLB
22, 171; JRDA; MAICYA 1, 2; SATA 37;
SATA-Brief 30; YAW

Tuohy, Frank .... **CLC 37**
See Tuohy, John Francis
See also CN 1, 2, 3, 4, 5, 6, 7; DLB 14,
139

Tuohy, John Francis 1925-
See Tuohy, Frank
See also CA 5-8R; 178; CANR 3, 47

Turco, Lewis 1934- .... **CLC 11, 63**
See also CA 13-16R; CAAS 22; CANR 24,
51, 185; CP 1, 2, 3, 4, 5, 6, 7; DLBY
1984; TCLE 1:2

Turco, Lewis Putnam
See Turco, Lewis

Turgenev, Ivan (Sergeevich)
1818-1883 ..... **DC 7; NCLC 21, 37, 122; SSC 7, 57; WLC 6**
See also AAYA 58; DA; DAB; DAC; DAM
MST, NOV; DFS 6; DLB 238, 284; EW
6; LATS 1:1; NFS 16; RGSF 2; RGWL 2,
3; TWA

Turgot, Anne-Robert-Jacques
1727-1781 .... **LC 26**
See also DLB 314

Turner, Frederick 1943- .... **CLC 48**
See also CA 73-76, 227; CAAE 227; CAAS
10; CANR 12, 30, 56; DLB 40, 282

Turton, James
See Crace, Jim

Tutu, Desmond M(pilo) 1931- .... **BLC 1:3; CLC 80**
See also BW 1, 3; CA 125; CANR 67, 81;
DAM MULT

Tutuola, Amos 1920-1997 .... **BLC 1:3, 2:3; CLC 5, 14, 29; TCLC 188**
See also AAYA 76; AFW; BW 2, 3; CA
9-12R; 159; CANR 27, 66; CDWLB 3;
CN 1, 2, 3, 4, 5, 6; DA3; DAM MULT;
DLB 125; DNFS 2; EWL 3; MTCW 1, 2;
MTFW 2005; RGEL 2; WLIT 2

Visconti, Luchino 1906-1976 .... **CLC 16**
See also CA 81-84; 65-68; CANR 39

Vitry, Jacques de
See Jacques de Vitry

Vittorini, Elio 1908-1966 .... **CLC 6, 9, 14**
See also CA 133; 25-28R; DLB 264; EW
12; EWL 3; RGWL 2, 3

Vivekananda, Swami 1863-1902 .... **TCLC 88**

Vizenor, Gerald Robert 1934- .... **CLC 103, 263; NNAL**
See also CA 13-16R, 205; CAAE 205;
CAAS 22; CANR 5, 21, 44, 67; DAM
MULT; DLB 175, 227; MTCW 2; MTFW
2005; TCWW 2

Vizinczey, Stephen 1933- .... **CLC 40**
See also CA 128; CCA 1; INT CA-128

Vliet, R(ussell) G(ordon)
1929-1984 .... **CLC 22**
See also CA 37-40R; 112; CANR 18; CP 2,
3

Vogau, Boris Andreyevich 1894-1938
See Pilnyak, Boris
See also CA 123; 218

Vogel, Paula A. 1951- .... **CLC 76; DC 19**
See also CA 108; CAD; CANR 119, 140;
CD 5, 6; CWD; DFS 14; DLB 341;
MTFW 2005; RGAL 4

Voigt, Cynthia 1942- .... **CLC 30**
See also AAYA 3, 30; BYA 1, 3, 6, 7, 8;
CA 106; CANR 18, 37, 40, 94, 145; CLR
13, 48; INT CANR-18; JRDA; LAIT 5;
MAICYA 1, 2; MAICYAS 1; MTFW
2005; SATA 48, 79, 116, 160; SATA-Brief
33; WYA; YAW

Voigt, Ellen Bryant 1943- .... **CLC 54**
See also CA 69-72; CANR 11, 29, 55, 115,
171; CP 5, 6, 7; CSW; CWP; DLB 120;
PFS 23

Voinovich, Vladimir 1932- .. **CLC 10, 49, 147**
See also CA 81-84; CAAS 12; CANR 33,
67, 150; CWW 2; DLB 302; MTCW 1

Voinovich, Vladimir Nikolaevich
See Voinovich, Vladimir

Vollmann, William T. 1959- ...... **CLC 89, 227**
See also AMWS 17; CA 134; CANR 67,
116, 185; CN 7; CPW; DA3; DAM NOV,
POP; MTCW 2; MTFW 2005

Voloshinov, V. N.
See Bakhtin, Mikhail Mikhailovich

Voltaire 1694-1778 .. **LC 14, 79, 110; SSC 12, 112; WLC 6**
See also BYA 13; DA; DA3; DAB; DAC;
DAM DRAM, MST; DLB 314; EW 4;
GFL Beginnings to 1789; LATS 1:1;
LMFS 1; NFS 7; RGWL 2, 3; TWA

von Aschendrof, Baron Ignatz
See Ford, Ford Madox

von Chamisso, Adelbert
See Chamisso, Adelbert von

von Daeniken, Erich 1935- .... **CLC 30**
See also AITN 1; CA 37-40R; CANR 17,
44

von Daniken, Erich
See von Daeniken, Erich

von Eschenbach, Wolfram c. 1170-c.
1220 .... **CMLC 5**
See Eschenbach, Wolfram von
See also CDWLB 2; DLB 138; EW 1;
RGWL 2

von Hartmann, Eduard
1842-1906 .... **TCLC 96**

von Hayek, Friedrich August
See Hayek, F(riedrich) A(ugust von)

von Heidenstam, (Carl Gustaf) Verner
See Heidenstam, (Carl Gustaf) Verner von

von Heyse, Paul (Johann Ludwig)
See Heyse, Paul (Johann Ludwig von)

von Hofmannsthal, Hugo
See Hofmannsthal, Hugo von

von Horvath, Odon
See von Horvath, Odon

von Horvath, Odon
See von Horvath, Odon

von Horvath, Odon 1901-1938 .... **TCLC 45**
See von Horvath, Oedoen
See also CA 118; 194; DLB 85, 124; RGWL
2, 3

von Horvath, Oedoen
See von Horvath, Odon
See also CA 184

von Kleist, Heinrich
See Kleist, Heinrich von

Vonnegut, Kurt, Jr.
See Vonnegut, Kurt

Vonnegut, Kurt 1922-2007 .... **CLC 1, 2, 3, 4, 5, 8, 12, 22, 40, 60, 111, 212, 254; SSC 8; WLC 6**
See also AAYA 6, 44; AITN 1; AMWS 2;
BEST 90:4; BPFB 3; BYA 3, 14; CA
1-4R; 259; CANR 1, 25, 49, 75, 92;
CDALB 1968-1988; CN 1, 2, 3, 4, 5, 6,
7; CPW 1; DA; DA3; DAB; DAC; DAM
MST, NOV, POP; DLB 2, 8, 152; DLBD
3; DLBY 1980; EWL 3; EXPN; EXPS;
LAIT 4; LMFS 2; MAL 5; MTCW 1, 2;
MTFW 2005; NFS 3, 28; RGAL 4;
SCFW; SFW 4; SSFS 5; TUS; YAW

Von Rachen, Kurt
See Hubbard, L. Ron

von Sternberg, Josef
See Sternberg, Josef von

Vorster, Gordon 1924- .... **CLC 34**
See also CA 133

Vosce, Trudie
See Ozick, Cynthia

Voznesensky, Andrei (Andreievich)
1933- .... **CLC 1, 15, 57**
See Voznesensky, Andrey
See also CA 89-92; CANR 37; CWW 2;
DAM POET; MTCW 1

Voznesensky, Andrey
See Voznesensky, Andrei (Andreievich)
See also EWL 3

Wace, Robert c. 1100-c. 1175 .... **CMLC 55**
See also DLB 146

Waddington, Miriam 1917-2004 .... **CLC 28**
See also CA 21-24R; 225; CANR 12, 30;
CCA 1; CP 1, 2, 3, 4, 5, 6, 7; DLB 68

Wagman, Fredrica 1937- .... **CLC 7**
See also CA 97-100; CANR 166; INT CA-
97-100

Wagner, Linda W.
See Wagner-Martin, Linda (C.)

Wagner, Linda Welshimer
See Wagner-Martin, Linda (C.)

Wagner, Richard 1813-1883 ..... **NCLC 9, 119**
See also DLB 129; EW 6

Wagner-Martin, Linda (C.) 1936- .... **CLC 50**
See also CA 159; CANR 135

Wagoner, David (Russell) 1926- .... **CLC 3, 5, 15; PC 33**
See also AMWS 9; CA 1-4R; CAAS 3;
CANR 2, 71; CN 1, 2, 3, 4, 5, 6, 7; CP 1,
2, 3, 4, 5, 6, 7; DLB 5, 256; SATA 14;
TCWW 1, 2

Wah, Fred(erick James) 1939- .... **CLC 44**
See also CA 107; 141; CP 1, 6, 7; DLB 60

Wahloo, Per 1926-1975 .... **CLC 7**
See also BPFB 3; CA 61-64; CANR 73;
CMW 4; MSW

Wahloo, Peter
See Wahloo, Per

Wain, John (Barrington) 1925-1994 . **CLC 2, 11, 15, 46**
See also CA 5-8R; 145; CAAS 4; CANR
23, 54; CDBLB 1960 to Present; CN 1, 2,
3, 4, 5; CP 1, 2, 3, 4, 5; DLB 15, 27, 139,
155; EWL 3; MTCW 1, 2; MTFW 2005

Wajda, Andrzej 1926- .... **CLC 16, 219**
See also CA 102

Wakefield, Dan 1932- .... **CLC 7**
See also CA 21-24R, 211; CAAE 211;
CAAS 7; CN 4, 5, 6, 7

Wakefield, Herbert Russell
1888-1965 .... **TCLC 120**
See also CA 5-8R; CANR 77; HGG; SUFW

Wakoski, Diane 1937- ...... **CLC 2, 4, 7, 9, 11, 40; PC 15**
See also CA 13-16R, 216; CAAE 216;
CAAS 1; CANR 9, 60, 106; CP 1, 2, 3, 4,
5, 6, 7; CWP; DAM POET; DLB 5; INT
CANR-9; MAL 5; MTCW 2; MTFW
2005

Wakoski-Sherbell, Diane
See Wakoski, Diane

Walcott, Derek 1930- . **BLC 1:3, 2:3; CLC 2, 4, 9, 14, 25, 42, 67, 76, 160; DC 7; PC 46**
See also BW 2; CA 89-92; CANR 26, 47,
75, 80, 130; CBD; CD 5, 6; CDWLB 3;
CP 1, 2, 3, 4, 5, 6, 7; DA3; DAB; DAC;
DAM MST, MULT, POET; DLB 117,
332; DLBY 1981; DNFS 1; EFS 1; EWL
3; LMFS 2; MTCW 1, 2; MTFW 2005;
PFS 6; RGEL 2; TWA; WWE 1

Waldman, Anne (Lesley) 1945- .... **CLC 7**
See also BG 1:3; CA 37-40R; CAAS 17;
CANR 34, 69, 116; CP 1, 2, 3, 4, 5, 6, 7;
CWP; DLB 16

Waldo, E. Hunter
See Sturgeon, Theodore (Hamilton)

Waldo, Edward Hamilton
See Sturgeon, Theodore (Hamilton)

Walker, Alice 1944- .... **BLC 1:3, 2:3; CLC 5, 6, 9, 19, 27, 46, 58, 103, 167; PC 30; SSC 5; WLCS**
See also AAYA 3, 33; AFAW 1, 2; AMWS
3; BEST 89:4; BPFB 3; BW 2, 3; CA 37-
40R; CANR 9, 27, 49, 66, 82, 131;
CDALB 1968-1988; CN 4, 5, 6, 7; CPW;
CSW; DA; DA3; DAB; DAC; DAM MST,
MULT, NOV, POET, POP; DLB 6, 33,
143; EWL 3; EXPN; EXPS; FL 1:6; FW;
INT CANR-27; LAIT 3; MAL 5; MBL;
MTCW 1, 2; MTFW 2005; NFS 5; RGAL
4; RGSF 2; SATA 31; SSFS 2, 11; TUS;
YAW

Walker, Alice Malsenior
See Walker, Alice

Walker, David Harry 1911-1992 ...... **CLC 14**
See also CA 1-4R; 137; CANR 1; CN 1, 2;
CWRI 5; SATA 8; SATA-Obit 71

Walker, Edward Joseph 1934-2004
See Walker, Ted
See also CA 21-24R; 226; CANR 12, 28,
53

Walker, George F(rederick) 1947- .. **CLC 44, 61**
See also CA 103; CANR 21, 43, 59; CD 5,
6; DAB; DAC; DAM MST; DLB 60

Walker, Joseph A. 1935-2003 .... **CLC 19**
See also BW 1, 3; CA 89-92; CAD; CANR
26, 143; CD 5, 6; DAM DRAM, MST;
DFS 12; DLB 38

Walker, Margaret 1915-1998 .... **BLC 1:3; CLC 1, 6; PC 20; TCLC 129**
See also AFAW 1, 2; BW 2, 3; CA 73-76;
172; CANR 26, 54, 76, 136; CN 1, 2, 3,
4, 5, 6; CP 1, 2, 3, 4, 5, 6; CSW; DAM
MULT; DLB 76, 152; EXPP; FW; MAL
5; MTCW 1, 2; MTFW 2005; RGAL 4;
RHW

Walker, Ted .... **CLC 13**
See Walker, Edward Joseph
See also CP 1, 2, 3, 4, 5, 6, 7; DLB 40

Wallace, David Foster 1962-2008 .... **CLC 50, 114; SSC 68**
See also AAYA 50; AMWS 10; CA 132; 277; CANR 59, 133; CN 7; DA3; MTCW 2; MTFW 2005

Wallace, Dexter
See Masters, Edgar Lee

Wallace, (Richard Horatio) Edgar 1875-1932 .... **TCLC 57**
See also CA 115; 218; CMW 4; DLB 70; MSW; RGEL 2

Wallace, Irving 1916-1990 .... **CLC 7, 13**
See also AITN 1; BPFB 3; CA 1-4R; 132; CAAS 1; CANR 1, 27; CPW; DAM NOV, POP; INT CANR-27; MTCW 1, 2

Wallant, Edward Lewis 1926-1962 ... **CLC 5, 10**
See also CA 1-4R; CANR 22; DLB 2, 28, 143, 299; EWL 3; MAL 5; MTCW 1, 2; RGAL 4; RGHL

Wallas, Graham 1858-1932 .... **TCLC 91**

Waller, Edmund 1606-1687 .... **LC 86; PC 72**
See also BRW 2; DAM POET; DLB 126; PAB; RGEL 2

Walley, Byron
See Card, Orson Scott

Walpole, Horace 1717-1797 ..... **LC 2, 49, 152**
See also BRW 3; DLB 39, 104, 213; GL 3; HGG; LMFS 1; RGEL 2; SUFW 1; TEA

Walpole, Hugh (Seymour) 1884-1941 .... **TCLC 5**
See also CA 104; 165; DLB 34; HGG; MTCW 2; RGEL 2; RHW

Walrond, Eric (Derwent) 1898-1966 . **HR 1:3**
See also BW 1; CA 125; DLB 51

Walser, Martin 1927- .... **CLC 27, 183**
See also CA 57-60; CANR 8, 46, 145; CWW 2; DLB 75, 124; EWL 3

Walser, Robert 1878-1956 ..... **SSC 20; TCLC 18**
See also CA 118; 165; CANR 100; DLB 66; EWL 3

Walsh, Gillian Paton
See Paton Walsh, Jill

Walsh, Jill Paton .... **CLC 35**
See Paton Walsh, Jill
See also CLR 2, 65, 128; WYA

Walter, William Christian
See Andersen, Hans Christian

Walters, Anna L(ee) 1946- .... **NNAL**
See also CA 73-76

Walther von der Vogelweide c. 1170-1228 .... **CMLC 56**

Walton, Izaak 1593-1683 .... **LC 72**
See also BRW 2; CDBLB Before 1660; DLB 151, 213; RGEL 2

Walzer, Michael (Laban) 1935- ...... **CLC 238**
See also CA 37-40R; CANR 15, 48, 127

Wambaugh, Joseph, Jr. 1937- ...... **CLC 3, 18**
See also AITN 1; BEST 89:3; BPFB 3; CA 33-36R; CANR 42, 65, 115, 167; CMW 4; CPW 1; DA3; DAM NOV, POP; DLB 6; DLBY 1983; MSW; MTCW 1, 2

Wambaugh, Joseph Aloysius
See Wambaugh, Joseph, Jr.

Wang Wei 699(?)-761(?) . **CMLC 100; PC 18**
See also TWA

Warburton, William 1698-1779 .... **LC 97**
See also DLB 104

Ward, Arthur Henry Sarsfield 1883-1959
See Rohmer, Sax
See also CA 108; 173; CMW 4; HGG

Ward, Douglas Turner 1930- .... **CLC 19**
See also BW 1; CA 81-84; CAD; CANR 27; CD 5, 6; DLB 7, 38

Ward, E. D.
See Lucas, E(dward) V(errall)

Ward, Mrs. Humphry 1851-1920
See Ward, Mary Augusta
See also RGEL 2

Ward, Mary Augusta 1851-1920 ... **TCLC 55**
See Ward, Mrs. Humphry
See also DLB 18

Ward, Nathaniel 1578(?)-1652 .... **LC 114**
See also DLB 24

Ward, Peter
See Faust, Frederick (Schiller)

Warhol, Andy 1928(?)-1987 .... **CLC 20**
See also AAYA 12; BEST 89:4; CA 89-92; 121; CANR 34

Warner, Francis (Robert Le Plastrier) 1937- .... **CLC 14**
See also CA 53-56; CANR 11; CP 1, 2, 3, 4

Warner, Marina 1946- .... **CLC 59, 231**
See also CA 65-68; CANR 21, 55, 118; CN 5, 6, 7; DLB 194; MTFW 2005

Warner, Rex (Ernest) 1905-1986 ...... **CLC 45**
See also CA 89-92; 119; CN 1, 2, 3, 4; CP 1, 2, 3, 4; DLB 15; RGEL 2; RHW

Warner, Susan (Bogert) 1819-1885 .... **NCLC 31, 146**
See also AMWS 18; DLB 3, 42, 239, 250, 254

Warner, Sylvia (Constance) Ashton
See Ashton-Warner, Sylvia (Constance)

Warner, Sylvia Townsend 1893-1978 .. **CLC 7, 19; SSC 23; TCLC 131**
See also BRWS 7; CA 61-64; 77-80; CANR 16, 60, 104; CN 1, 2; DLB 34, 139; EWL 3; FANT; FW; MTCW 1, 2; RGEL 2; RGSF 2; RHW

Warren, Mercy Otis 1728-1814 ..... **NCLC 13**
See also DLB 31, 200; RGAL 4; TUS

Warren, Robert Penn 1905-1989 .. **CLC 1, 4, 6, 8, 10, 13, 18, 39, 53, 59; PC 37; SSC 4, 58; WLC 6**
See also AITN 1; AMW; AMWC 2; BPFB 3; BYA 1; CA 13-16R; 129; CANR 10, 47; CDALB 1968-1988; CN 1, 2, 3, 4; CP 1, 2, 3, 4; DA; DA3; DAB; DAC; DAM MST, NOV, POET; DLB 2, 48, 152, 320; DLBY 1980, 1989; EWL 3; INT CANR-10; MAL 5; MTCW 1, 2; MTFW 2005; NFS 13; RGAL 4; RGSF 2; RHW; SATA 46; SATA-Obit 63; SSFS 8; TUS

Warrigal, Jack
See Furphy, Joseph

Warshofsky, Isaac
See Singer, Isaac Bashevis

Warton, Joseph 1722-1800 ... **LC 128; NCLC 118**
See also DLB 104, 109; RGEL 2

Warton, Thomas 1728-1790 .... **LC 15, 82**
See also DAM POET; DLB 104, 109, 336; RGEL 2

Waruk, Kona
See Harris, (Theodore) Wilson

Warung, Price .... **TCLC 45**
See Astley, William
See also DLB 230; RGEL 2

Warwick, Jarvis
See Garner, Hugh
See also CCA 1

Washington, Alex
See Harris, Mark

Washington, Booker T(aliaferro) 1856-1915 .... **BLC 1:3; TCLC 10**
See also BW 1; CA 114; 125; DA3; DAM MULT; DLB 345; LAIT 2; RGAL 4; SATA 28

Washington, George 1732-1799 .... **LC 25**
See also DLB 31

Wassermann, (Karl) Jakob 1873-1934 .... **TCLC 6**
See also CA 104; 163; DLB 66; EWL 3

Wasserstein, Wendy 1950-2006 . **CLC 32, 59, 90, 183; DC 4**
See also AAYA 73; AMWS 15; CA 121; 129; 247; CABS 3; CAD; CANR 53, 75, 128; CD 5, 6; CWD; DA3; DAM DRAM; DFS 5, 17; DLB 228; EWL 3; FW; INT CA-129; MAL 5; MTCW 2; MTFW 2005; SATA 94; SATA-Obit 174

Waterhouse, Keith (Spencer) 1929- . **CLC 47**
See also BRWS 13; CA 5-8R; CANR 38, 67, 109; CBD; CD 6; CN 1, 2, 3, 4, 5, 6, 7; DLB 13, 15; MTCW 1, 2; MTFW 2005

Waters, Frank (Joseph) 1902-1995 .. **CLC 88**
See also CA 5-8R; 149; CAAS 13; CANR 3, 18, 63, 121; DLB 212; DLBY 1986; RGAL 4; TCWW 1, 2

Waters, Mary C. .... **CLC 70**

Waters, Roger 1944- .... **CLC 35**

Watkins, Frances Ellen
See Harper, Frances Ellen Watkins

Watkins, Gerrold
See Malzberg, Barry N(athaniel)

Watkins, Gloria Jean
See hooks, bell

Watkins, Paul 1964- .... **CLC 55**
See also CA 132; CANR 62, 98

Watkins, Vernon Phillips 1906-1967 .... **CLC 43**
See also CA 9-10; 25-28R; CAP 1; DLB 20; EWL 3; RGEL 2

Watson, Irving S.
See Mencken, H(enry) L(ouis)

Watson, John H.
See Farmer, Philip Jose

Watson, Richard F.
See Silverberg, Robert

Watts, Ephraim
See Horne, Richard Henry Hengist

Watts, Isaac 1674-1748 .... **LC 98**
See also DLB 95; RGEL 2; SATA 52

Waugh, Auberon (Alexander) 1939-2001 .... **CLC 7**
See also CA 45-48; 192; CANR 6, 22, 92; CN 1, 2, 3; DLB 14, 194

Waugh, Evelyn 1903-1966 .. **CLC 1, 3, 8, 13, 19, 27, 44, 107; SSC 41; WLC 6**
See also AAYA 78; BPFB 3; BRW 7; CA 85-88; 25-28R; CANR 22; CDBLB 1914-1945; DA; DA3; DAB; DAC; DAM MST, NOV, POP; DLB 15, 162, 195; EWL 3; MTCW 1, 2; MTFW 2005; NFS 13, 17; RGEL 2; RGSF 2; TEA; WLIT 4

Waugh, Evelyn Arthur St. John
See Waugh, Evelyn

Waugh, Harriet 1944- .... **CLC 6**
See also CA 85-88; CANR 22

Ways, C.R.
See Blount, Roy, Jr.

Waystaff, Simon
See Swift, Jonathan

Webb, Beatrice (Martha Potter) 1858-1943 .... **TCLC 22**
See also CA 117; 162; DLB 190; FW

Webb, Charles (Richard) 1939- .... **CLC 7**
See also CA 25-28R; CANR 114

Webb, Frank J. .... **NCLC 143**
See also DLB 50

Webb, James, Jr.
See Webb, James

Webb, James 1946- .... **CLC 22**
See also CA 81-84; CANR 156

Webb, James H.
See Webb, James

Webb, James Henry
See Webb, James

Webb, Mary Gladys (Meredith) 1881-1927 .... **TCLC 24**
See also CA 182; 123; DLB 34; FW; RGEL 2

Westlake, Donald Edwin
  See Westlake, Donald E.
Westmacott, Mary
  See Christie, Agatha (Mary Clarissa)
Weston, Allen
  See Norton, Andre
Wetcheek, J. L.
  See Feuchtwanger, Lion
Wetering, Janwillem van de
  See van de Wetering, Janwillem
Wetherald, Agnes Ethelwyn
    1857-1940 .... **TCLC 81**
    See also CA 202; DLB 99
Wetherell, Elizabeth
  See Warner, Susan (Bogert)
Whale, James 1889-1957 .... **TCLC 63**
    See also AAYA 75
Whalen, Philip (Glenn) 1923-2002 .... **CLC 6, 29**
    See also BG 1:3; CA 9-12R; 209; CANR 5, 39; CP 1, 2, 3, 4, 5, 6, 7; DLB 16; WP
Wharton, Edith (Newbold Jones)
    1862-1937 ... **SSC 6, 84; TCLC 3, 9, 27, 53, 129, 149; WLC 6**
    See also AAYA 25; AMW; AMWC 2; AMWR 1; BPFB 3; CA 104; 132; CDALB 1865-1917; CLR 136; DA; DA3; DAB; DAC; DAM MST, NOV; DLB 4, 9, 12, 78, 189; DLBD 13; EWL 3; EXPS; FL 1:6; GL 3; HGG; LAIT 2, 3; LATS 1:1; MAL 5; MBL; MTCW 1, 2; MTFW 2005; NFS 5, 11, 15, 20; RGAL 4; RGSF 2; RHW; SSFS 6, 7; SUFW; TUS
Wharton, James
  See Mencken, H(enry) L(ouis)
Wharton, William 1925-2008 ..... **CLC 18, 37**
    See also CA 93-96; 278; CN 4, 5, 6, 7; DLBY 1980; INT CA-93-96
Wheatley (Peters), Phillis
    1753(?)-1784 .... **BLC 1:3; LC 3, 50; PC 3; WLC 6**
    See also AFAW 1, 2; CDALB 1640-1865; DA; DA3; DAC; DAM MST, MULT, POET; DLB 31, 50; EXPP; FL 1:1; PFS 13, 29; RGAL 4
Wheelock, John Hall 1886-1978 .... **CLC 14**
    See also CA 13-16R; 77-80; CANR 14; CP 1, 2; DLB 45; MAL 5
Whim-Wham
  See Curnow, (Thomas) Allen (Monro)
Whisp, Kennilworthy
  See Rowling, J.K.
Whitaker, Rod 1931-2005
    See Trevanian
    See also CA 29-32R; 246; CANR 45, 153; CMW 4
White, Babington
  See Braddon, Mary Elizabeth
White, E. B. 1899-1985 .... **CLC 10, 34, 39**
    See also AAYA 62; AITN 2; AMWS 1; CA 13-16R; 116; CANR 16, 37; CDALBS; CLR 1, 21, 107; CPW; DAM POP; DLB 11, 22; EWL 3; FANT; MAICYA 1, 2; MAL 5; MTCW 1, 2; MTFW 2005; NCFS 5; RGAL 4; SATA 2, 29, 100; SATA-Obit 44; TUS
White, Edmund 1940- .... **CLC 27, 110**
    See also AAYA 7; CA 45-48; CANR 3, 19, 36, 62, 107, 133, 172; CN 5, 6, 7; DA3; DAM POP; DLB 227; MTCW 1, 2; MTFW 2005
White, Edmund Valentine III
  See White, Edmund
White, Elwyn Brooks
  See White, E. B.
White, Hayden V. 1928- .... **CLC 148**
    See also CA 128; CANR 135; DLB 246

White, Patrick (Victor Martindale)
    1912-1990 ...... **CLC 3, 4, 5, 7, 9, 18, 65, 69; SSC 39; TCLC 176**
    See also BRWS 1; CA 81-84; 132; CANR 43; CN 1, 2, 3, 4; DLB 260, 332; EWL 3; MTCW 1; RGEL 2; RGSF 2; RHW; TWA; WWE 1
White, Phyllis Dorothy James 1920-
    See James, P. D.
    See also CA 21-24R; CANR 17, 43, 65, 112; CMW 4; CN 7; CPW; DA3; DAM POP; MTCW 1, 2; MTFW 2005; TEA
White, T(erence) H(anbury)
    1906-1964 .... **CLC 30**
    See also AAYA 22; BPFB 3; BYA 4, 5; CA 73-76; CANR 37; CLR 139; DLB 160; FANT; JRDA; LAIT 1; MAICYA 1, 2; RGEL 2; SATA 12; SUFW 1; YAW
White, Terence de Vere 1912-1994 ... **CLC 49**
    See also CA 49-52; 145; CANR 3
White, Walter
  See White, Walter F(rancis)
White, Walter F(rancis)
    1893-1955 ..... **BLC 1:3; HR 1:3; TCLC 15**
    See also BW 1; CA 115; 124; DAM MULT; DLB 51
White, William Hale 1831-1913
    See Rutherford, Mark
    See also CA 121; 189
Whitehead, Alfred North
    1861-1947 .... **TCLC 97**
    See also CA 117; 165; DLB 100, 262
Whitehead, Colson 1969- ...... **BLC 2:3; CLC 232**
    See also CA 202; CANR 162
Whitehead, E(dward) A(nthony)
    1933- .... **CLC 5**
    See Whitehead, Ted
    See also CA 65-68; CANR 58, 118; CBD; CD 5; DLB 310
Whitehead, Ted
  See Whitehead, E(dward) A(nthony)
    See also CD 6
Whiteman, Roberta J. Hill 1947- ...... **NNAL**
    See also CA 146
Whitemore, Hugh (John) 1936- .... **CLC 37**
    See also CA 132; CANR 77; CBD; CD 5, 6; INT CA-132
Whitman, Sarah Helen (Power)
    1803-1878 .... **NCLC 19**
    See also DLB 1, 243
Whitman, Walt(er) 1819-1892 .. **NCLC 4, 31, 81, 205; PC 3, 91; WLC 6**
    See also AAYA 42; AMW; AMWR 1; CDALB 1640-1865; DA; DA3; DAB; DAC; DAM MST, POET; DLB 3, 64, 224, 250; EXPP; LAIT 2; LMFS 1; PAB; PFS 2, 3, 13, 22; RGAL 4; SATA 20; TUS; WP; WYAS 1
Whitney, Isabella fl. 1565-fl. 1575 ..... **LC 130**
    See also DLB 136
Whitney, Phyllis A. 1903-2008 .... **CLC 42**
    See also AAYA 36; AITN 2; BEST 90:3; CA 1-4R; 269; CANR 3, 25, 38, 60; CLR 59; CMW 4; CPW; DAM POP; JRDA; MAICYA 1, 2; MTCW 2; RHW; SATA 1, 30; SATA-Obit 189; YAW
Whitney, Phyllis Ayame
  See Whitney, Phyllis A.
Whitney, Phyllis Ayame
  See Whitney, Phyllis A.
Whittemore, (Edward) Reed, Jr.
    1919- .... **CLC 4**
    See also CA 9-12R, 219; CAAE 219; CAAS 8; CANR 4, 119; CP 1, 2, 3, 4, 5, 6, 7; DLB 5; MAL 5
Whittier, John Greenleaf
    1807-1892 .... **NCLC 8, 59; PC 93**
    See also AMWS 1; DLB 1, 243; RGAL 4

Whittlebot, Hernia
  See Coward, Noel (Peirce)
Wicker, Thomas Grey
  See Wicker, Tom
Wicker, Tom 1926- .... **CLC 7**
    See also CA 65-68; CANR 21, 46, 141, 179
Wicomb, Zoe 1948- .... **BLC 2:3**
    See also CA 127; CANR 106, 167; DLB 225
Wideman, John Edgar 1941- .. **BLC 1:3, 2:3; CLC 5, 34, 36, 67, 122; SSC 62**
    See also AFAW 1, 2; AMWS 10; BPFB 4; BW 2, 3; CA 85-88; CANR 14, 42, 67, 109, 140; CN 4, 5, 6, 7; DAM MULT; DLB 33, 143; MAL 5; MTCW 2; MTFW 2005; RGAL 4; RGSF 2; SSFS 6, 12, 24; TCLE 1:2
Wiebe, Rudy 1934- . **CLC 6, 11, 14, 138, 263**
    See also CA 37-40R; CANR 42, 67, 123; CN 1, 2, 3, 4, 5, 6, 7; DAC; DAM MST; DLB 60; RHW; SATA 156
Wiebe, Rudy Henry
  See Wiebe, Rudy
Wieland, Christoph Martin
    1733-1813 .... **NCLC 17, 177**
    See also DLB 97; EW 4; LMFS 1; RGWL 2, 3
Wiene, Robert 1881-1938 .... **TCLC 56**
Wieners, John 1934- .... **CLC 7**
    See also BG 1:3; CA 13-16R; CP 1, 2, 3, 4, 5, 6, 7; DLB 16; WP
Wiesel, Elie 1928- ...... **CLC 3, 5, 11, 37, 165; WLCS**
    See also AAYA 7, 54; AITN 1; CA 5-8R; CAAS 4; CANR 8, 40, 65, 125; CDALBS; CWW 2; DA; DA3; DAB; DAC; DAM MST, NOV; DLB 83, 299; DLBY 1987; EWL 3; INT CANR-8; LAIT 4; MTCW 1, 2; MTFW 2005; NCFS 4; NFS 4; RGHL; RGWL 3; SATA 56; YAW
Wiesel, Eliezer
  See Wiesel, Elie
Wiggins, Marianne 1947- .... **CLC 57**
    See also AAYA 70; BEST 89:3; CA 130; CANR 60, 139, 180; CN 7; DLB 335
Wigglesworth, Michael 1631-1705 .... **LC 106**
    See also DLB 24; RGAL 4
Wiggs, Susan .... **CLC 70**
    See also CA 201; CANR 173
Wight, James Alfred 1916-1995
    See Herriot, James
    See also CA 77-80; SATA 55; SATA-Brief 44
Wilbur, Richard 1921- .. **CLC 3, 6, 9, 14, 53, 110; PC 51**
    See also AAYA 72; AMWS 3; CA 1-4R; CABS 2; CANR 2, 29, 76, 93, 139; CDALBS; CP 1, 2, 3, 4, 5, 6, 7; DA; DAB; DAC; DAM MST, POET; DLB 5, 169; EWL 3; EXPP; INT CANR-29; MAL 5; MTCW 1, 2; MTFW 2005; PAB; PFS 11, 12, 16, 29; RGAL 4; SATA 9, 108; WP
Wilbur, Richard Purdy
  See Wilbur, Richard
Wild, Peter 1940- .... **CLC 14**
    See also CA 37-40R; CP 1, 2, 3, 4, 5, 6, 7; DLB 5
Wilde, Oscar 1854(?)-1900 ... **DC 17; SSC 11, 77; TCLC 1, 8, 23, 41, 175; WLC 6**
    See also AAYA 49; BRW 5; BRWC 1, 2; BRWR 2; BYA 15; CA 104; 119; CANR 112; CDBLB 1890-1914; CLR 114; DA; DA3; DAB; DAC; DAM DRAM, MST, NOV; DFS 4, 8, 9, 21; DLB 10, 19, 34, 57, 141, 156, 190, 344; EXPS; FANT; GL 3; LATS 1:1; NFS 20; RGEL 2; RGSF 2; SATA 24; SSFS 7; SUFW; TEA; WCH; WLIT 4

Wilson, William S(mith) 1932- .... **CLC 49**
See also CA 81-84

Wilson, (Thomas) Woodrow
1856-1924 .... **TCLC 79**
See also CA 166; DLB 47

Winchester, Simon 1944- .... **CLC 257**
See also AAYA 66; CA 107; CANR 90, 130

Winchilsea, Anne (Kingsmill) Finch
1661-1720
See Finch, Anne
See also RGEL 2

Winckelmann, Johann Joachim
1717-1768 .... **LC 129**
See also DLB 97

Windham, Basil
See Wodehouse, P(elham) G(renville)

Wingrove, David 1954- .... **CLC 68**
See also CA 133; SFW 4

Winnemucca, Sarah 1844-1891 .... **NCLC 79;**
NNAL
See also DAM MULT; DLB 175; RGAL 4

Winstanley, Gerrard 1609-1676 .... **LC 52**

Wintergreen, Jane
See Duncan, Sara Jeannette

Winters, Arthur Yvor
See Winters, Yvor

Winters, Janet Lewis .... **CLC 41**
See Lewis, Janet
See also DLBY 1987

Winters, Yvor 1900-1968 .. **CLC 4, 8, 32; PC**
82
See also AMWS 2; CA 11-12; 25-28R; CAP
1; DLB 48; EWL 3; MAL 5; MTCW 1;
RGAL 4

Winterson, Jeanette 1959- .... **CLC 64, 158**
See also BRWS 4; CA 136; CANR 58, 116,
181; CN 5, 6, 7; CPW; DA3; DAM POP;
DLB 207, 261; FANT; FW; GLL 1;
MTCW 2; MTFW 2005; RHW; SATA 190

Winthrop, John 1588-1649 .... **LC 31, 107**
See also DLB 24, 30

Winton, Tim 1960- .... **CLC 251; SSC 119**
See also AAYA 34; CA 152; CANR 118;
CN 6, 7; DLB 325; SATA 98

Wirth, Louis 1897-1952 .... **TCLC 92**
See also CA 210

Wiseman, Frederick 1930- .... **CLC 20**
See also CA 159

Wister, Owen 1860-1938 ..... **SSC 100; TCLC**
21
See also BPFB 3; CA 108; 162; DLB 9, 78,
186; RGAL 4; SATA 62; TCWW 1, 2

Wither, George 1588-1667 .... **LC 96**
See also DLB 121; RGEL 2

Witkacy
See Witkiewicz, Stanislaw Ignacy

Witkiewicz, Stanislaw Ignacy
1885-1939 .... **TCLC 8**
See also CA 105; 162; CDWLB 4; DLB
215; EW 10; EWL 3; RGWL 2, 3; SFW 4

Wittgenstein, Ludwig (Josef Johann)
1889-1951 .... **TCLC 59**
See also CA 113; 164; DLB 262; MTCW 2

Wittig, Monique 1935-2003 .... **CLC 22**
See also CA 116; 135; 212; CANR 143;
CWW 2; DLB 83; EWL 3; FW; GLL 1

Wittlin, Jozef 1896-1976 .... **CLC 25**
See also CA 49-52; 65-68; CANR 3; EWL
3

Wodehouse, P(elham) G(renville)
1881-1975 .. **CLC 1, 2, 5, 10, 22; SSC 2,**
115; TCLC 108
See also AAYA 65; AITN 2; BRWS 3; CA
45-48; 57-60; CANR 3, 33; CDBLB
1914-1945; CN 1, 2; CPW 1; DA3; DAB;
DAC; DAM NOV; DLB 34, 162; EWL 3;
MTCW 1, 2; MTFW 2005; RGEL 2;
RGSF 2; SATA 22; SSFS 10

Woiwode, L.
See Woiwode, Larry (Alfred)

Woiwode, Larry (Alfred) 1941- ... **CLC 6, 10**
See also CA 73-76; CANR 16, 94; CN 3, 4,
5, 6, 7; DLB 6; INT CANR-16

Wojciechowska, Maia (Teresa)
1927-2002 .... **CLC 26**
See also AAYA 8, 46; BYA 3; CA 9-12R,
183; 209; CAAE 183; CANR 4, 41; CLR
1; JRDA; MAICYA 1, 2; SAAS 1; SATA
1, 28, 83; SATA-Essay 104; SATA-Obit
134; YAW

Wojtyla, Karol (Josef)
See John Paul II, Pope

Wojtyla, Karol (Jozef)
See John Paul II, Pope

Wolf, Christa 1929- ...... **CLC 14, 29, 58, 150,**
261
See also CA 85-88; CANR 45, 123; CD-
WLB 2; CWW 2; DLB 75; EWL 3; FW;
MTCW 1; RGWL 2, 3; SSFS 14

Wolf, Naomi 1962- .... **CLC 157**
See also CA 141; CANR 110; FW; MTFW
2005

Wolfe, Gene 1931- .... **CLC 25**
See also AAYA 35; CA 57-60; CAAS 9;
CANR 6, 32, 60, 152; CPW; DAM POP;
DLB 8; FANT; MTCW 2; MTFW 2005;
SATA 118, 165; SCFW 2; SFW 4; SUFW
2

Wolfe, Gene Rodman
See Wolfe, Gene

Wolfe, George C. 1954- .... **BLCS; CLC 49**
See also CA 149; CAD; CD 5, 6

Wolfe, Thomas (Clayton)
1900-1938 .... **SSC 33, 113; TCLC 4, 13,**
29, 61; WLC 6
See also AMW; BPFB 3; CA 104; 132;
CANR 102; CDALB 1929-1941; DA;
DA3; DAB; DAC; DAM MST, NOV;
DLB 9, 102, 229; DLBD 2, 16; DLBY
1985, 1997; EWL 3; MAL 5; MTCW 1,
2; NFS 18; RGAL 4; SSFS 18; TUS

Wolfe, Thomas Kennerly, Jr.
1931- .... **CLC 147**
See Wolfe, Tom
See also CA 13-16R; CANR 9, 33, 70, 104;
DA3; DAM POP; DLB 185; EWL 3; INT
CANR-9; MTCW 1, 2; MTFW 2005; TUS

Wolfe, Tom .... **CLC 1, 2, 9, 15, 35, 51**
See Wolfe, Thomas Kennerly, Jr.
See also AAYA 8, 67; AITN 2; AMWS 3;
BEST 89:1; BPFB 3; CN 5, 6, 7; CPW;
CSW; DLB 152; LAIT 5; RGAL 4

Wolff, Geoffrey 1937- .... **CLC 41**
See also CA 29-32R; CANR 29, 43, 78, 154

Wolff, Geoffrey Ansell
See Wolff, Geoffrey

Wolff, Sonia
See Levitin, Sonia

Wolff, Tobias 1945- .... **CLC 39, 64, 172; SSC**
63
See also AAYA 16; AMWS 7; BEST 90:2;
BYA 12; CA 114; 117; CAAS 22; CANR
54, 76, 96; CN 5, 6, 7; CSW; DA3; DLB
130; EWL 3; INT CA-117; MTCW 2;
MTFW 2005; RGAL 4; RGSF 2; SSFS 4,
11

Wolitzer, Hilma 1930- .... **CLC 17**
See also CA 65-68; CANR 18, 40, 172; INT
CANR-18; SATA 31; YAW

Wollstonecraft, Mary 1759-1797 .... **LC 5, 50,**
90, 147
See also BRWS 3; CDBLB 1789-1832;
DLB 39, 104, 158, 252; FL 1:1; FW;
LAIT 1; RGEL 2; TEA; WLIT 3

Wonder, Stevie 1950- .... **CLC 12**
See also CA 111

Wong, Jade Snow 1922-2006 .... **CLC 17**
See also CA 109; 249; CANR 91; SATA
112; SATA-Obit 175

Wood, Ellen Price
See Wood, Mrs. Henry

Wood, Mrs. Henry 1814-1887 ...... **NCLC 178**
See also CMW 4; DLB 18; SUFW

Wood, James 1965- .... **CLC 238**
See also CA 235

Woodberry, George Edward
1855-1930 .... **TCLC 73**
See also CA 165; DLB 71, 103

Woodcott, Keith
See Brunner, John (Kilian Houston)

Woodruff, Robert W.
See Mencken, H(enry) L(ouis)

Woodward, Bob 1943- .... **CLC 240**
See also CA 69-72; CANR 31, 67, 107, 176;
MTCW 1

Woodward, Robert Upshur
See Woodward, Bob

Woolf, (Adeline) Virginia 1882-1941 .. **SSC 7,**
79; TCLC 1, 5, 20, 43, 56, 101, 123,
128; WLC 6
See also AAYA 44; BPFB 3; BRW 7;
BRWC 2; BRWR 1; CA 104; 130; CANR
64, 132; CDBLB 1914-1945; DA; DA3;
DAB; DAC; DAM MST, NOV; DLB 36,
100, 162; DLBD 10; EWL 3; EXPS; FL
1:6; FW; LAIT 3; LATS 1:1; LMFS 2;
MTCW 1, 2; MTFW 2005; NCFS 2; NFS
8, 12, 28; RGEL 2; RGSF 2; SSFS 4, 12;
TEA; WLIT 4

Woollcott, Alexander (Humphreys)
1887-1943 .... **TCLC 5**
See also CA 105; 161; DLB 29

Woolman, John 1720-1772 .... **LC 155**
See also DLB 31

Woolrich, Cornell .... **CLC 77**
See Hopley-Woolrich, Cornell George
See also MSW

Woolson, Constance Fenimore
1840-1894 .... **NCLC 82; SSC 90**
See also DLB 12, 74, 189, 221; RGAL 4

Wordsworth, Dorothy 1771-1855 . **NCLC 25,**
138
See also DLB 107

Wordsworth, William 1770-1850 .. **NCLC 12,**
38, 111, 166, 206; PC 4, 67; WLC 6
See also AAYA 70; BRW 4; BRWC 1; CD-
BLB 1789-1832; DA; DA3; DAB; DAC;
DAM MST, POET; DLB 93, 107; EXPP;
LATS 1:1; LMFS 1; PAB; PFS 2; RGEL
2; TEA; WLIT 3; WP

Wotton, Sir Henry 1568-1639 .... **LC 68**
See also DLB 121; RGEL 2

Wouk, Herman 1915- .... **CLC 1, 9, 38**
See also BPFB 2, 3; CA 5-8R; CANR 6,
33, 67, 146; CDALBS; CN 1, 2, 3, 4, 5,
6; CPW; DA3; DAM NOV, POP; DLBY
1982; INT CANR-6; LAIT 4; MAL 5;
MTCW 1, 2; MTFW 2005; NFS 7; TUS

Wright, Charles 1935- ... **CLC 6, 13, 28, 119,**
146
See also AMWS 5; CA 29-32R; CAAS 7;
CANR 23, 36, 62, 88, 135, 180; CP 3, 4,
5, 6, 7; DLB 165; DLBY 1982; EWL 3;
MTCW 1, 2; MTFW 2005; PFS 10

Wright, Charles Penzel, Jr.
See Wright, Charles

Wright, Charles Stevenson
1932-2008 .... **BLC 1:3; CLC 49**
See also BW 1; CA 9-12R; CANR 26; CN
1, 2, 3, 4, 5, 6, 7; DAM MULT, POET;
DLB 33

Wright, Frances 1795-1852 .... **NCLC 74**
See also DLB 73

Wright, Frank Lloyd 1867-1959 .... **TCLC 95**
See also AAYA 33; CA 174

Literary Criticism Series
Cumulative Topic Index

This index lists all topic entries in Gale's *Children's Literature Review* (CLR), *Classical and Medieval Literature Criticism* (CMLC), *Contemporary Literary Criticism* (CLC), *Drama Criticism* (DC), *Literature Criticism from 1400 to 1800* (LC), *Nineteenth-Century Literature Criticism* (NCLC), *Short Story Criticism* (SSC), and *Twentieth-Century Literary Criticism* (TCLC). The index also lists topic entries in the Gale Critical Companion Collection, which includes the following publications: *The Beat Generation* (BG), *Feminism in Literature* (FL), *Gothic Literature* (GL), and *Harlem Renaissance* (HR).

Topic Index

NCLC Cumulative Nationality Index

AMERICAN

Adams, John **106**
Adams, John Quincy **175**
Alcott, Amos Bronson **1, 167**
Alcott, Louisa May **6, 58, 83**
Alger, Horatio Jr. **8, 83**
Allston, Washington **2**
Apess, William **73**
Audubon, John James **47**
Barlow, Joel **23**
Bartram, William **145**
Beecher, Catharine Esther **30**
Bellamy, Edward **4, 86, 147**
Bird, Robert Montgomery **1, 197**
Boker, George Henry **125**
Boyesen, Hjalmar Hjorth **135**
Brackenridge, Hugh Henry **7**
Brentano, Clemens (Maria) **1, 191**
Brown, Charles Brockden **22, 74, 122**
Brown, William Wells **2, 89**
Brownson, Orestes Augustus **50**
Bryant, William Cullen **6, 46**
Calhoun, John Caldwell **15**
Channing, William Ellery **17**
Child, Francis James **173**
Child, Lydia Maria **6, 73**
Chivers, Thomas Holley **49**
Cooke, John Esten **5**
Cooke, Rose Terry **110**
Cooper, James Fenimore **1, 27, 54, 203**
Cooper, Susan Fenimore **129**
Cranch, Christopher Pearse **115**
Crèvecoeur, Michel Guillaume Jean de **105**
Crockett, David **8**
Cummins, Maria Susanna **139**
Dana, Richard Henry Sr. **53**
Delany, Martin Robinson **93**
Dickinson, Emily (Elizabeth) **21, 77, 171**
Douglass, Frederick **7, 55, 141**
Dunlap, William **2**
Dwight, Timothy **13**
Emerson, Mary Moody **66**
Emerson, Ralph Waldo **1, 38, 98**
Field, Eugene **3**
Foster, Hannah Webster **99**
Foster, Stephen Collins **26**
Frederic, Harold **10, 175**
Freneau, Philip Morin **1, 111**
Garrison, William Lloyd **149**
Hale, Sarah Josepha (Buell) **75**
Halleck, Fitz-Greene **47**
Hamilton, Alexander **49**
Hammon, Jupiter **5**
Harris, George Washington **23, 165**
Hawthorne, Nathaniel **2, 10, 17, 23, 39, 79, 95, 158, 171, 191**
Hawthorne, Sophia Peabody **150**
Hayne, Paul Hamilton **94**
Holmes, Oliver Wendell **14, 81**
Hooper, Johnson Jones **177**
Horton, George Moses **87**
Irving, Washington **2, 19, 95**

Jackson, Helen Hunt **90**
Jacobs, Harriet A(nn) **67, 162**
James, Alice **206**
James, Henry Sr. **53**
Jefferson, Thomas **11, 103**
Kennedy, John Pendleton **2**
Kirkland, Caroline M. **85**
Lanier, Sidney **6, 118**
Larcom, Lucy **179**
Lazarus, Emma **8, 109**
Lincoln, Abraham **18, 201**
Lippard, George **198**
Longfellow, Henry Wadsworth **2, 45, 101, 103**
Longstreet, Augustus Baldwin **159**
Lowell, James Russell **2, 90**
Madison, James **126**
Melville, Herman **3, 12, 29, 45, 49, 91, 93, 123, 157, 181, 193**
Mowatt, Anna Cora **74**
Murray, Judith Sargent **63**
Neal, John **161**
Osgood, Frances Sargent **141**
Parker, Theodore **186**
Parkman, Francis Jr. **12**
Parton, Sara Payson Willis **86**
Paulding, James Kirke **2**
Peabody, Elizabeth Palmer **169**
Pinkney, Edward **31**
Poe, Edgar Allan **1, 16, 55, 78, 94, 97, 117**
Prescott, William Hickling **163**
Rowson, Susanna Haswell **5, 69, 182**
Sedgwick, Catharine Maria **19, 98**
Shaw, Henry Wheeler **15**
Sigourney, Lydia Howard (Huntley) **21, 87**
Simms, William Gilmore **3**
Smith, Joseph Jr. **53**
Smith, Seba **187**
Solomon, Northup **105**
Southworth, Emma Dorothy Eliza Nevitte **26**
Stowe, Harriet (Elizabeth) Beecher **3, 50, 133, 195**
Taylor, Bayard **89**
Tenney, Tabitha Gilman **122**
Thoreau, Henry David **7, 21, 61, 138, 207**
Thorpe, Thomas Bangs **183**
Timrod, Henry **25**
Trumbull, John **30**
Truth, Sojourner **94**
Tyler, Royall **3**
Very, Jones **9**
Warner, Susan (Bogert) **31, 146**
Warren, Mercy Otis **13**
Webster, Noah **30**
Webb, Frank J. **143**
Whitman, Sarah Helen (Power) **19**
Whitman, Walt(er) **4, 31, 81, 205**
Whittier, John Greenleaf **8, 59**
Willis, Nathaniel Parker **194**
Wilson, Harriet E. Adams **78**
Winnemucca, Sarah **79**

ARGENTINIAN

Echeverria, (Jose) Esteban (Antonino) **18**
Hernández, José **17**
Sarmiento, Domingo Faustino **123**

AUSTRALIAN

Adams, Francis **33**
Clarke, Marcus (Andrew Hislop) **19**
Gordon, Adam Lindsay **21**
Harpur, Charles **114**
Kendall, Henry **12**

AUSTRIAN

Grillparzer, Franz **1, 102**
Lenau, Nikolaus **16**
Nestroy, Johann **42**
Raimund, Ferdinand Jakob **69**
Sacher-Masoch, Leopold von **31**
Stifter, Adalbert **41, 198**

BRAZILIAN

Alencar, Jose de **157**
Alves, Antônio de Castro **205**

CANADIAN

Crawford, Isabella Valancy **12, 127**
De Mille, James **123**
Haliburton, Thomas Chandler **15, 149**
Lampman, Archibald **25, 194**
Moodie, Susanna (Strickland) **14, 113**
Richardson, John **55**
Traill, Catharine Parr **31**

CHINESE

Li Ju-chen **137**

COLOMBIAN

Isaacs, Jorge Ricardo **70**
Silva, José Asunción **114**

CUBAN

Avellaneda, Gertrudis Gómez de **111**
Casal, Julián del **131**
Manzano, Juan Francisco **155**
Martí (y Pérez), José (Julian) **63**
Villaverde, Cirilo **121**

CZECH

Macha, Karel Hynek **46**

DANISH

Andersen, Hans Christian **7, 79**
Grundtvig, Nicolai Frederik Severin **1, 158**
Jacobsen, Jens Peter **34**
Kierkegaard, Søren **34, 78, 125**

DUTCH

Multatuli (Eduard Douwes Dekker) **165**

NCLC-207 Title Index

ISBN-13: 978-1-4144-2139-1
ISBN-10: 1-4144-2139-7

90000

9 781414 421391